Aviation Law

Aviation Law
Cases and Materials

Robert M. Jarvis
Professor of Law
Nova Southeastern University

James T. Crouse
Senior Lecturing Fellow
Duke University

James R. Fox
Professor of Law
Pennsylvania State University

Gregory S. Walden
Adjunct Professor of Law
George Mason University

Carolina Academic Press
Durham, North Carolina

ISBN 1-59460-030-9
LCCN 2006921462

Carolina Academic Press
700 Kent Street
Durham, NC 27701
Telephone (919) 489-7486
Fax (919) 493-5668
www.cap-press.com

Printed in the United States of America

To Walter E. Rutherford, Esq.,
who gave me my first job
in the aviation industry
—R.M.J.

To Edna,
with all my love
—J.T.C.

To my son,
Henry Maxwell Fox
—J.R.F.

To my wife Glenda,
for her love, patience,
and understanding
—G.S.W.

Contents

Table of Cases

Preface

Because of its perceived specialized nature and a lack of demand from both sides of the lectern, aviation law has tended to rank low in the curriculum priorities of most law schools. The absence of a suitable casebook—indeed, of any casebook until just recently—has only added to the challenges faced by those who have sought to take or teach the course. Accordingly, it is our hope that this text—which examines contemporary issues through intriguing cases, detailed notes, challenging problems, and frequent references to popular culture—will spur more professors and students to embrace the subject.

In addition to wanting a fun, interesting, and up-to-date book, we had a second goal in mind when we undertook this project. Unlike other casebook authors, who have approached the subject as both esoteric and self-contained, we see aviation law as a microcosm of the law school experience, touching as it does on (among others) administrative law, antitrust, bankruptcy, conflicts, constitutional law, contracts, environmental law, international law, labor law, local government law, professional responsibility, property, sales, taxation, and torts. Accordingly, we have eschewed the narrow and the technical and instead focused on broad themes and questions. In this way, we hope to make clear just how much of everyday life is touched by flying and dispel the myth that an aviation law course is useful only for those few students who either hold a pilot's license or already have decided to enter the field upon graduation.

Several procedural matters should be noted. First, the research for this book closed in October 2005 (although a few last-minute additions did find their way into the text). Second, we have been liberal in our editing and normally have not indicated where language has been deleted, repositioned, or, in the event of errors in the original, corrected. Third, the principal air law treaties referred to in the readings can be found in the book's appendices. Lastly, for those who want to become better acquainted with the industry, Chapter 1 contains numerous suggestions for doing so.

In closing, we hope you will enjoy using this book as much as we have enjoyed writing it, and to that end we invite your comments and suggestions for future editions. All such thoughts should be sent to Professor Robert M. Jarvis, Nova Southeastern University Law Center, 3305 College Avenue, Fort Lauderdale, FL 33314-7721, telephone (954) 262-6172, telefax (954) 262-3835, e-mail jarvisb@nsu.law.nova.edu.

Acknowledgments

In preparing this work, we have received help from countless individuals and institutions as well as from the Publisher's staff. We are particularly grateful, however, to Linda Heller, Zane J. Kelleher, and Michael E. Meyer.

We also wish to express our appreciation to the following authors and their publishers for permission to reprint their works:

Paul Stephen Dempsey, *Transportation: A Legal History*, 30 Transportation Law Journal 235 (2003)

Martin Fackler & Don Phillips, *Japan Has Designs on a New Concorde*, N.Y. Times, Oct. 11, 2005, at C1

Federal Aviation Administration, *Pilot's Handbook of Aeronautical Knowledge* (2003)

Richard H. Jack, *Ultralight Aircraft: A Need for Better Regulation Than 14 C.F.R. § 103*, 51 Journal of Air Law and Commerce 415 (1986)

E. Rebecca Kreis, *A Comparative Analysis of the Aviation Network Within the European Community and the Ad-Hoc Network Between the United States and Central America*, 24 Transportation Law Journal 303 (1997)

Leslie Miller, *Civilian-Jet Antimissle System Starts to Take Shape, Firms Say*, Phil. Inquirer, Nov. 11, 2005, at A12 (from the Associated Press wire service)

Thomas E. Reinert, Jr., *Airline Labor Disruptions: Is the RLA Still Adequate?*, 15 Air & Space Lawyer 4 (Winter 2001)

Wendell K. Smith, *The General Aviation Case*, 12 Utah Bar Journal 17 (Feb. 1999)

Jim Toomey, *Sherman's Lagoon* (2005) (distributed by King Features Syndicate)

Matthew L. Wald, *Safety Board Blames Pilot Error in Crash of Kennedy Plane*, N.Y. Times, July 7, 2000, at B5

Craig Whitlock, *Europeans Probe Secret CIA Flights*, Wash. Post, Nov. 17, 2005, at A22

Jeffrey S. Wieand, *Jet Way: How to Buy and Keep That Corporate Plane*, 6 Business Law Today 58 (Mar./Apr. 1997)

Wikipedia, *Aviation History* (2005)

Carl Wilkinson, *What Happened Next?*, London Observer, Oct. 27, 2002, at 102

About the Authors

Robert M. Jarvis is a professor of law at the Shepard Broad Law Center of Nova Southeastern University (www.nsulaw.nova.edu) in Fort Lauderdale, Florida. Prior to joining NSU, he practiced international transportation law with the New York City law firms of Haight, Gardner, Poor & Havens (now Holland & Knight LLP) and Baker & McKenzie LLP, where he represented Compañía Dominicana de Aviación, the national airline of the Dominican Republic. A past transportation editor of *Preview of United States Supreme Court Cases*, his interest in aviation comes from his father, one of the first American executives of El Al Israel Airlines.

James T. Crouse is a senior lecturing fellow at the Duke University School of Law in Durham, North Carolina, and the founder of Crouse Law Offices (www.crouselaw.com) in Raleigh, North Carolina. A four-time presenter at the Southern Methodist University Air Law Symposium, he has participated in numerous aviation crash cases, including Atlantic Southeast Airways Flight 7527, Comair Flight 3272, and USAir Flight 427. He also was lead liability counsel in the world's largest civilian helicopter disaster. A retired lieutenant colonel and army aviator, he has served as a maintenance, medical evacuation, and research and development test pilot.

James R. Fox is a professor of law and the past director of the law library at the Dickinson School of Law of The Pennsylvania State University (www.dsl.psu.edu) in Carlisle, Pennsylvania. In addition to co-authoring the multi-volume encyclopedia *The Regulation of International Commercial Aviation: The International Regulatory Structure*, contributing to the leading treatise *Aviation Accident Law*, and having his work published in the *Annals of Air and Space Law*, he has served as a visiting fellow at the Institute of Air and Space Law at McGill University and taught European Aviation Law at the University of Vienna.

Gregory S. Walden is an adjunct professor of law at the George Mason University School of Law in Arlington, Virginia, and of counsel to the Washington, D.C. law firm of Patton Boggs LLP (www.pattonboggs.com), where he represents air carriers, airports, and fixed-base operators. Prior to entering private practice, he served as Chief Counsel to the Federal Aviation Administration, Associate White House Counsel for President George H.W. Bush, and transition ethics counsel for President-Elect George W. Bush. Earlier in his career, he clerked for Judge Robert H. Bork of the United States Court of Appeals for the District of Columbia.

To invent an airplane is nothing. To build one is something. But to fly is everything.

—*Otto Lilienthal (1848–96),*
German aviation pioneer

[As] the patent in suit is a valid one, the patentees may fairly be considered pioneers in the practical art of flying with heavier-than-air machines.

—*Wright Co. v. Herring-Curtiss Co.,*
211 F. 654, 655 (2d Cir. 1914)
(upholding the Wright Brothers' patent)

Come fly with me!
Let's fly, let's fly away!

—*Frank Sinatra (1957)*

Gimme a ticket for an aeroplane,
Ain't got time to take a fast train.

—*Joe Cocker (1970)*

Let's roll!

—*Final words of Todd Beamer before he*
and the other passengers on United Airlines
Flight 93 stormed the cockpit on 9/11

It is a new world for this industry.

—*Jane F. Garvey, FAA Administrator, in*
a speech to the National Press Club
shortly after 9/11

Aviation Law

Chapter 1

Introduction

A. OVERVIEW

In the upcoming chapters of this book, we will examine the rights and responsibilities of the various parties who collectively make up the aviation industry. Here, however, our focus is more general. After a brief review of the principles of flight, we will identify the various sources of aviation law (also known as "aeronautics law," "air law," and "air and space law") and then discuss the field's ethical challenges.

B. THE CHALLENGE OF FLIGHT

PILOT'S HANDBOOK OF AERONAUTICAL KNOWLEDGE

Federal Aviation Administration Chs. 2–3 (2003)

In the 17th century, [the English] philosopher and mathematician Sir Isaac Newton propounded three basic laws of motion. It is certain that he did not have the airplane in mind when he did so, but almost everything known about motion goes back to his three simple laws.

Newton's first law states, in part, that a body at rest tends to remain at rest, and a body in motion tends to remain moving at the same speed and in the same direction. This simply means that, in nature, nothing starts or stops moving until some outside force causes it to do so. An airplane at rest on the ramp will remain at rest unless a force strong enough to overcome its inertia is applied. Once it is moving, however, its inertia keeps it moving, subject to the various other forces acting on it. These forces may add to its motion, slow it down, or change its direction.

Newton's second law implies that when a body is acted upon by a constant force, its resulting acceleration is inversely proportional to the mass of the body and is directly proportional to the applied force.

What is being dealt with here are the factors involved in overcoming Newton's First Law of Inertia. It covers both changes in direction and speed, including starting up from rest (positive acceleration) and coming to a stop (negative acceleration, or deceleration).

Newton's third law states that whenever one body exerts a force on another, the second body always exerts on the first a force that is equal in magnitude but opposite in direction. In an airplane, the propeller moves and pushes back the air; consequently, the air pushes the propeller (and thus the airplane) in the opposite direction—forward. In a jet airplane, the engine pushes a blast of hot gases backward; the force of equal and opposite reaction pushes against the engine and forces the airplane forward.

A half century after Sir Newton presented his laws, Daniel Bernoulli, a Swiss mathematician, explained how the pressure of a moving fluid (liquid or gas) varies with its speed of motion. Specifically, he stated that an increase in the speed of movement or flow would cause a decrease in the fluid's pressure. This is exactly what happens to air passing over the curved top of the airplane wing.

An appropriate analogy can be made with water flowing through a garden hose. Water moving through a hose of constant diameter exerts a uniform pressure on the hose; but if the diameter of a section of the hose is increased or decreased, it is certain to change the pressure of the water at that point. Suppose the hose was pinched, thereby constricting the area through which the water flows. Assuming that the same volume of water flows through the constricted portion of the hose in the same period of time as before the hose was pinched, it follows that the speed of flow must increase at that point. Therefore, if a portion of the hose is constricted, it not only increases the speed of the flow, but also decreases the pressure at that point. Like results could be achieved if streamlined solids (airfoils) were introduced at the same point in the hose. This same principle is the basis for the measurement of airspeed (fluid flow) and for analyzing the airfoil's ability to produce lift.

Newton's and Bernoulli's discoveries [provide the basis for] how an airplane wing can sustain flight when the airplane is heavier than air. Perhaps the explanation can best be reduced to its most elementary concept by stating that lift (flight) is simply the result of fluid flow (air) about an airfoil—or in everyday language, the result of moving an airfoil (wing), by whatever means, through the air.

Since it is the airfoil which harnesses the force developed by its movement through the air, [an] explanation of [its] structure [is necessary]. An airfoil is a structure designed to obtain reaction upon its surface from the air through which it moves or that moves past such a structure. By looking at a typical airfoil profile, such as the cross section of a wing, one [will] see [that] there is a difference in the curvatures of the upper and lower surfaces of the airfoil ([this] curvature is called camber). The camber of the upper surface is more pronounced than that of the lower surface, which is somewhat flat in most instances. [In addition], the two extremities of the airfoil profile also differ in appearance. The end which faces forward in flight is called the leading edge, and is rounded; while the other end, the trailing edge, is quite narrow and tapered.

The construction of the wing, so as to provide actions greater than its weight, is done by shaping the wing so that advantage can be taken of the air's response to certain physical laws, and thus develop two actions from the air mass; a positive pressure lifting action from the air mass below the wing, and a negative pressure lifting action from lowered pressure above the wing. As the airstream strikes the relatively flat lower surface of the wing when inclined at a small angle to its direction of motion, the air is forced to rebound downward and therefore causes an upward reaction in positive lift, while at the same time airstream striking the upper curved section of the "leading edge" of the wing is deflected upward. In other words, a wing shaped to cause an action on the air, and forcing it downward, will provide an equal reaction from the air, forcing the wing upward. If a wing is constructed in such form that it will cause a lift force greater than the weight of the airplane, the airplane will fly.

AVIATION HISTORY

en.wikipedia.org/wiki/Aviation_history (2005)

Humanity's desire to fly probably dates back to the first time prehistoric man observed birds. Through all of recorded history, aspects of this desire have surfaced from time to time. The most well known is the legendary story of Daedalus and Icarus. Daedalus was trapped on the island of Minos, and so built wings out of feathers and wax for himself and his son. His son Icarus flew too close to the sun and the wax melted, destroying the wings and causing Icarus to fall into the sea, killing him. The legend was designed to be a cautionary tale about attempting to reach heaven, similar to the Tower of Babel story in The Bible. Nevertheless, it exemplifies man's desire to fly.

The modern history of aviation has had several broad trends. Aircraft designers have struggled to make their planes go faster, fly higher, and be controlled more easily. To that [end], engine designs have moved towards more compact, more powerful designs, beginning with steam engines and ending with jet and rocket engines. Planes have become more streamlined and made of stronger and lighter materials. Initially airplanes were made of canvas and wood. Today, airplanes are made of aluminum and, increasingly, carbon fiber, which is prized for its lightness and strength. The methods used to control planes have advanced significantly as well. Initially, planes were controlled by moving your entire body (gliders) or warping the planes' wings (Wright Brothers). Modern planes are controlled by computers, which can make planes that were otherwise unflyable able to fly, such as the F-117.

Before the 20th Century

There were many early attempts to fly, covering the full range of legend to fact. Leonardo da Vinci was the first person to seriously design an aircraft, designing a glider in the 15th century. While this glider was never built by Leonardo, its plans were preserved and it was constructed in the late 20th century from materials that would have been available to da Vinci. The design was deemed flight worthy and the prototype actually flew. However, a considerable amount of interpretation of his design, with modern knowledge of aerodynamic principles in mind, was made. Leonardo also sketched designs for a helicopter, but this design would not have flown.

The first published paper on aviation was "Sketch of a Machine for Flying in the Air" by Emanuel Swedenborg published in 1716. This flying machine consisted of a light frame covered with strong canvas and provided with two large oars or wings moving on a horizontal axis, and so arranged that the upstroke met with no resistance while the downstroke provided the lifting power. Swedenborg knew that the machine would not fly, but suggested it as a start and was confident that the problem would be solved. He said:

> It seems easier to talk of such a machine than to put it into actuality, for it requires greater force and less weight than exists in a human body. The science of mechanics might perhaps suggest a means, namely, a strong spiral spring. If these advantages and requisites are observed, perhaps in time to come someone might know how better to utilize our sketch and cause some addition to be made so as to accomplish that which we can only suggest. Yet there are sufficient proofs and examples from nature that such flights can take place without danger, although when the first trials are made you may have to pay for the experience, and not mind an arm or leg.

Swedenborg was prescient in his observation that powering the aircraft through the air was the crux of flying. Sufficiently light and powerful engines[, however,] would not be available for powered flight until the gasoline engine designed by the Wright Brothers.

The first known human flight ever took place in Paris in 1783. Francois Pilatre de Rozier and Francois d'Arlandes went 5 miles (8 km) in a hot air balloon invented by the Montgolfier Brothers. The balloon was powered by a wood fire, and was uncontrolled, that is, it flew wherever the wind took it. For the first flight, the balloon was tethered, and ultimately reached a height of 26 m. Ballooning became a major "rage" in Europe in the late 18th century, providing the first detailed understanding of the relationship between altitude and the atmosphere.

The first powered, controlled, sustained lighter-than-air flight took place in 1852. Henri Giffard flew 15 miles (24 km) in France, with a steam engine mounted on a dirigible. Throughout the latter half of the 19th century and the first half of the 20th century, the airship was considered to be a serious option for air transport.

During the last years of the 18th century, Sir George Cayley became interested in aircraft and started the first rigorous study of the physics involved in flight. In 1799, he exhibited a plan for a glider, which was [quite] modern in having a separate tail for control and having the pilot suspended below the center of gravity to provide stability, and flew it as a model in 1804. Over the next five decades Cayley worked on and off on the problem, during which he invented most of basic aerodynamics and introduced such terms as lift and drag. Later he turned his research to building a full-scale version of his design, first flying it unmanned in 1849. [In] 1853, his coachman made a short flight at Brompton, near Scarborough in Yorkshire.

Another person who continually but slowly advanced the state of the art was Frank Wenham, who unsuccessfully attempted to build a series of unmanned gliders. During his work he found that the majority of the lift from a bird-like wing appeared to be generated at the front, and concluded that long, thin wings would be better than the bat-like ones suggested by many, because they would have more leading edge for their weight. Today this measure is known as aspect ratio. He presented a paper on his work to the newly formed Royal Aeronautical Society of Great Britain in 1866, and decided to prove it by building the world's first wind tunnel in 1871. Members of the Society used the tunnel and were surprised, and delighted, to learn that cambered wings generated considerably more lift than expected by Cayley's Newtonian reasoning, with lift-to-drag ratios of about 5:1 at 15 degrees. This clearly demonstrated the ability to build practical heavier-than-air flying machines—what remained was the problem of powering them and controlling the flight.

The 1880s became a period of intense study, characterized by the "gentlemen scientists" who represented most research efforts until the 20th century. Starting in the 1880s a number of advancements were made in construction that led to the first truly practical gliders. Three names in particular remain well known [from this period] in the aviation world: Otto Lilienthal, Percy Pilcher and Octave Chanute. One of the first truly modern gliders appears to have been built by John J. Montgomery; it flew in a controlled manner outside of San Diego on August 28, 1883. It was not until many years later that his efforts became well known. Another delta hang-glider had been constructed by Wilhelm Kress as early [as] 1877 near Vienna.

Otto Lilienthal of Germany duplicated Wenham's work and greatly expanded on it in 1874, publishing all of his research in 1889. He also produced a series of ever-better gliders, and in 1891 was able to make flights of 25 meters or more "routinely." He rigorously documented his work, including photographs, and for this reason is one of the best known of the early pioneers. He also promoted the idea of "jumping before you fly," suggesting that researchers should start with gliders and work their way up, instead of simply designing a powered machine on paper and hoping it would work.

By the time of his death in 1896 he had made 2,500 flights on a number of designs. [A] gust of wind broke the wing of his latest design, causing him to fall from a height of roughly 56 ft (17 m), fracturing his spine. He died the next day, with his last words being "sacrifices must be made." Lilienthal had been working on small engines suitable for powering his designs at the time of his death, but no one took up his work on the engine and gliders until the Wright Brothers.

Picking up where Lilienthal left off, Octave Chanute took up aircraft design after an early retirement and funded the development of several gliders. In the summer of 1896 his troop flew several of their designs many times at Miller Beach, Indiana, eventually deciding that the best was a biplane design that looks surprisingly modern. Like Lilienthal, he heavily documented his work [by] photographing it, and was busy corresponding with like-minded hobbyists around the world. Chanute was particularly interested in solving the problem of natural stability of the aircraft in flight, one which birds corrected for by instinct, but that humans would have to do manually. The most disconcerting problem was longitudinal stability, because as the angle of attack of a wing increased, the center of pressure moved forward and made the angle increase more. Without immediate correction, the craft would pitch up and stall.

Throughout this period, a number of attempts were made to produce a true powered airplane. However, the majority of these were of somewhat laughable quality, built by interested hobbyists who did not have a full understanding of the problems being discussed by Lilienthal and Chanute. In France, Clément Ader successfully launched his steam-powered Eole for a short hop near Paris in 1890. After this test he immediately turned to a larger design, which took five years to build. However, this design, the Avion III, was too heavy and was never able to leave the ground.

Sir Hiram Maxim studied a series of designs in England, eventually building a monstrous 7,000 lb (3,175 kg) design with a wingspan of 105 feet (32 m), powered by two advanced low-weight steam engines which delivered 180 hp (134 kW) each. Maxim built it to study the basic problems of construction and power and it remained without controls. [R]ealizing that it would be unsafe to fly at any altitude, he instead had an 1,800 foot track constructed for test runs. After a number of test runs working out bugs, on July 31, 1894 [he and his assistants] started a series of runs at increasing power settings. The first two were successful, with the craft "flying" on the rails. In the afternoon, the crew of three fired the boilers to full power, and after reaching over 42 mph (68 km/h) about 600 ft (183 m) down the track the machine produced so much lift it pulled itself free of the track and crashed after flying at low altitudes for about 200 feet (61 m). Declining fortunes left him unable to continue his work until the 1900s, when he was able to test a number of smaller designs powered by gasoline.

Another successful early experimenter was Samuel Pierpont Langley. After a distinguished career in astronomy and a [stint at] at the Smithsonian Institution, Langley started a serious investigation into aerodynamics at what is today the University of Pittsburgh. In 1891, he published Experiments in Aerodynamics, [which] detail[ed] his research, and then turned to building his designs. On May 6, 1896, his Aerodrome No. 5 made the first fully successful flight of a powered heavier-than-air craft of substantial size, flying twice with one flight of 3,300 ft (1,000 m) and a second of 2,300 ft (700 m), at about 25 mph (40 km/h). On November 28, another successful flight was made with a similar model, the Aerodrome No. 6. It flew a distance of approximately 1,460 m (4,790 ft).

In the United Kingdom [an] attempt at heavier-than-air flight was made by the aviation pioneer Percy Pilcher. Pilcher had built several working gliders—The Bat, The Beetle, The Gull and The Hawk—which he flew successfully during the mid to late 1890s. In 1899, he constructed a prototype powered aircraft which, recent research has shown, would have been capable of flight. However, he died in a glider accident before he was able to test it, and his plans were forgotten for many years.

1900–1914

With the success of the Aerodrome No. 5 and its follow-on No. 6, Langley started looking for funding to build a full-scale man-carrying version of his designs. He succeeded in winning $50,000 in funding from the government, perhaps spurred on by the recent opening of the Spanish-American War. Langley planned on building a scaled-up version known as the Aerodrome A, and started with the smaller quarter-scale Aerodrome, which flew twice on June 18, 1901, and then again with a newer and more powerful engine in 1903.

With the basic design apparently successfully tested, he then turned to the problem of a suitable engine. He contracted Stephen Balzer to build him one, but was disappointed when it delivered only 8 horsepower (6 kW) instead of 12 hp (9 kW) as he expected. Langley's assistant, Charles Manly, then reworked the design into a five-cylinder water-cooled radial that delivered 52 horsepower (39 kW) at 950 rpm, a feat that took years to duplicate. Now with both power and a design, Langley put the two together with great hopes.

To his dismay, the resulting aircraft proved to be too fragile. He had apparently overlooked the effects of minimum gauge, and simply scaling up the original small models resulted in a design that was too heavy to hold itself up. Two launches in late 1903 both ended with the Aerodrome crashing into the water almost immediately after launch. His attempts to gain further funding failed, and his efforts ended.

Only weeks later the Wright Brothers successfully flew their aptly-named Flyer. Following Lilienthal's principles of jumping before flying, the brothers built and tested a series of improving glider designs from 1900 to 1902, before attempting to build a powered design. The Wrights appear to be the first design team to make serious studied attempts to solve both the power and control problems at the same time. Both proved difficult, but they never lost interest and eventually delivered an engine of their own design with the needed performance, as well as solving the control problem through a system known as "wing warping." Although this method was used only briefly during the history of aviation, it worked at the low airspeeds their designs would fly at, and proved to be a key advance.

The Wrights made the first controlled powered heavier-than-air flight at Kitty Hawk, North Carolina on December 17, 1903. The first flight by Orville Wright, of 120 feet (37 m) in 12 seconds, was recorded in a famous photograph. In the fourth flight of the same day, Wilbur Wright flew 852 feet (260 m) in 59 seconds. The flights were witnessed by 4 lifesavers and a boy from the village, making them arguably the first public flight and certainly the first well documented one.

Although his attempts failed, the Smithsonian Institution continued to boast that Langley's Aerodrome was the first machine "capable of flight," due to Glenn Curtiss making several modifications to the Aerodrome and successfully flying it in 1914.

At the time, a number of other inventors had made (or claimed to [have made]) short flights. Gustave Whitehead claimed to have flown a powered aircraft on August 14, 1901. He failed to document the flight, but a later replica of his Number 21 was flown successfully. Lyman Gilmore also claimed to have achieved success on May 15, 1902. In New Zealand, South Canterbury farmer and inventor Richard Pearse constructed a monoplane aircraft that he reputedly flew on March 31, 1903. However, even Pearse himself admitted the flight was uncontrolled and ended in a crash-landing on a hedge without having gained any altitude. Karl Jatho conducted a short motorized flight in August 1903, just a few months after Pearse. Jatho's wing design and airspeed did not allow his control surfaces to act properly to allow him to control the design very well.

Also some time in the summer of 1903, eyewitnesses claimed to have seen Preston Watson make his initial flights at Errol, near Dundee, in the east of Scotland. However, once again lack of photographic or documentary evidence makes the claim difficult to verify. Many claims of flight are complicated by the fact that many early flights were done at such low altitude that they did not clear the ground effect and the complexities involved in the differences between unpowered and powered aircraft.

The Wright Brothers conducted numerous additional public flights (over 80) in 1904 and 1905 from Huffman Prairie in Dayton, Ohio and invited friends, neighbors and newspaper reporters to them although few came.

Alberto Santos-Dumont made a public flight in Europe on September 13, 1906 in Paris. His design, like the Wright Brothers', used a canard elevator and wing-warping, and covered a distance of 221 m (725 ft). Since the plane did not need headwinds or catapults to take off, this flight is considered by some as the first true powered flight. Also, since the earlier attempts of Pearse, Jatho, Watson, and the Wright Brothers received less attention from the popular press then Santos-Dumont's flight, its importance to society, especially in Europe, is often considered to be greater despite occurring some years later.

Two English inventors—Henry Farman and John William Dunne—were also working separately on powered flying machines. In January 1908, Farman won the Grand Prix d'Aviation with a machine which flew for 1 km, though by this time many longer flights had already been done. For example, the Wright Brothers had made flights over 39 km long by 1905. Dunne's early work was sponsored by the British military and tested in great secrecy in Glen Tilt in the Scottish Highlands. His best early design, the D4, flew in December 1908 near Blair Atholl in Perthshire. Dunne's main contribution to early aviation was stability, which was a key problem with the planes designed by the Wright Brothers and Samuel Cody.

On May 14, 1908 the Wright Brothers made what is accepted to be the first two-person aircraft flight with Charlie Furnas as a passenger.

Thomas Selfridge became the first person killed in a powered airplane on September 17, 1908 when Wilbur crashed his two-passenger plane during military tests at Fort Myer in Virginia.

In late 1908, Madame Hart O. Berg became the first woman to fly when she flew with Wilbur Wright in Le Mans, France.

Controversy in the credit for invention of the airplane has been fueled by Pearse's and Jatho's essentially non-existent efforts to inform the popular press, by the Wrights' secrecy while their patent was prepared, by the pride of nations, and by the number of firsts made possible by the basic invention. For example, the Romanian engineer Traian Vuia (1872–1950) also claimed to have [built the] first self-propelled, heavier-than-air aircraft able to take off autonomously, without a headwind, and entirely driven by its on-board installations. Vuia piloted the airplane he designed and built on March 18, 1906, at Montesson, near Paris. None of his flights were longer than 100 feet (30 m) in length. In comparison, by the end of 1904 the Wright Brothers had sustained flights up to 39 minutes and 24.5 miles (39 km) in 1905, circling over Huffman Prairie.

At the same time that fixed wing aircraft were advancing, rigid body dirigibles were also becoming more advanced. Indeed, rigid body dirigibles would be far more capable than fixed wing aircraft in terms of pure cargo carrying capacity for decades. Dirigible design and advancement was brought about by the German count, Ferdinand von Zeppelin.

Construction of the first Zeppelin airship began in 1899 in a floating assembly hall on Lake Constance in the Bay of Manzell, Friedrichshafen. This was intended to facilitate the difficult starting procedure, as the hall could easily be aligned with the wind. The prototype airship LZ 1 (LZ for "Luftschiff Zeppelin") had a length of 128 m, was driven by two 14.2 ps (10.6 kW) Daimler engines and balanced by moving a weight between its two nacelles.

The first Zeppelin flight occurred on July 2, 1900. It lasted for only 18 minutes, as LZ 1 was forced to land on the lake after the winding mechanism for the balancing weight broke. Upon repair, the technology proved its potential in subsequent flights, beating the 6 m/s velocity record of French airship La France by 3 m/s, but could not yet convince possible investors. It would be several years before the Count was able to raise enough funds for another try.

The first helicopter known to have risen off the ground took place in 1907 (Cornu, France), [al]though the first practical helicopter was the Focke FA-61 (Germany, 1936).

1914–1918: World War I

Almost as soon as they were invented, planes were drafted for military service. The first country to use planes for military purposes was Bulgaria, whose planes attacked and reconnoitered the Ottoman positions during the First Balkan War 1912–13. The first war to see major use of planes in offensive, defensive and reconnaissance capabilities was World War I.

The Allies and Central Powers both used planes extensively. The most famous plane of the war is the Sopwith Camel; it was credited with more aerial victories than any other Allied plane, but was also notorious for its awkward handling resulting in the death of many rookie pilots. Aviators were styled as modern day knights, doing individual combat with their enemies. Several pilots became famous for their air to air combats. The most well-known today is Manfred von Richthofen, better known as the Red Baron, who shot down 80 planes in air to air combat with several different planes, the most celebrated of which was the Fokker Dr.I. His record of air to air kills still stands today. On the allied side, René Paul Fonck is credited with the most victories.

While the concept of using the aeroplane as a weapon of war was generally laughed at before World War I, the idea of using it for photography was one that was not lost on any of the major forces. All of the major forces in Europe had light aircraft, typically derived from pre-war sporting designs, attached to their reconnaissance departments. While early efforts were hampered by the light loads carried, improved two-seat designs soon appeared that were entirely practical.

And with the arrival of practical reconnaissance aircraft came the problem of the enemy's practical reconnaissance aircraft. It was not long before aircraft were shooting at each other, but the lack of any sort of steady point to aim from made such efforts comical. The French made a more serious effort to solve this problem, and in late 1914 Roland Garros had attached a fixed machine gun to the front of his plane, allowing him to aim and fly with the same actions. Although he was shot down and captured, he became the first "ace," and succeeded in starting the air war.

1918–1939

The years between World War I and World War II saw a large advancement in aircraft technology.

Airplanes went from being constructed of mostly wood and canvas to being constructed almost entirely of aluminum. Engine development proceeded apace, with engines moving from in-line water cooled gasoline engines to rotary air cooled engines, with a commensurate increase in propulsive power. Pushing all of this forward were a series of prizes for various distance and speed records. For example, Charles Lindbergh took the Orteig Prize of $25,000 for his solo non-stop crossing of the Atlantic, the first person to achieve this, although not the first to carry out a non-stop crossing. That was achieved eight years earlier when Captain John Alcock and Lieutenant Arthur Brown co-piloted a Vickers Vimy non-stop from St. John's, Newfoundland to Clifden, Ireland on June 14, 1919, winning the £10,000 ($50,000) Northcliffe prize in the process.

After WWI there were many experienced fighter pilots who were eager to show off their new skills. Many American pilots became barnstormers, flying into small towns across the country and showing off their flying skills, as well as taking paying passengers for rides. Eventually the barnstormers grouped into more organized displays of their prowess. A series of air shows sprang up around the country, with air races, acrobatic stunts, and feats of air superiority being the main attraction. The air races drove engine and airframe development—the Schneider Trophy, for example, led to a series of ever faster and sleeker monoplane designs culminating in the Supermarine S.6B, a direct forerunner of the Spitfire. With pilots competing for cash prizes, there was more incentive to go faster than just personal prestige. Amelia Earhart was perhaps the most famous of those on the barnstorming/air show circuit. She was also the first female pilot to achieve many records such as crossing the Atlantic [Ocean and the] English channel.

On the lighter-than-air front, the first crossings of the Atlantic were made by airship in July 1919 by His Majesty's Airship R34 and crew when they flew from East Lothian,

Scotland to Long Island, New York and then back to Pulham, England. By 1929, airship technology had advanced to the point that the first round-the-world flight was completed by the Graf Zeppelin in September; in October, the same aircraft inaugurated the first commercial transatlantic service. However, the age of the dirigible ended in 1937 with [a] terrible fire aboard the Zeppelin Hindenburg. After the now famous footage of the Hindenburg burning and crashing on the Lakehurst, New Jersey, landing field, people stopped using airships, despite the fact that most people on board survived. Perhaps the Hindenburg, combined with the Winged Foot Express disaster that occurred on July 21, 1919, in Chicago, Illinois, in which 12 civilians died, turned people off on the whole concept of riding around in a giant vessel of highly flammable gas. Flammable gas dirigibles didn't burn and crash often, but when they did crash they caused a disproportionate amount of destruction to the crash zone compared with the aeroplanes of the time. It wasn't so much body count as it was shock value that caused the retirement of the world's airships.

In the 1930s development of the jet engine began in Germany and in England. In England, Frank Whittle patented a design for a jet engine in 1930 and began developing a workable engine towards the end of the decade. In Germany, Hans von Ohain patented his version of a jet engine in 1936 and began developing a similar engine. The two men were unaware of each others work, and both Germany and Britain had developed jet aircraft by the end of World War II.

1939–1945: World War II

All countries involved in the war stepped up production and development of aircraft and flight-based weapon delivery systems, such as the German V-2 missile. World War II [also] saw the development of the first long range bomber and the first jet fighter. The first functional jet plane was the Heinkel He 178 (Germany), flown by Erich Warsitz in 1939. An earlier prototype was the Coanda-1910 that did a short flight on December 16, 1910. The first cruise missile (V-1) and the first ballistic missile (V-2) were also developed by Germany. Long range bombers made the bigger difference in the war of those technologies. Jet fighters did not have [a] significant impact, nor [did] cruise and ballistic missiles, in part because the V-1 was not very effective and the V-2 was never produced in useful numbers. The P-51 Mustang was critical to the success of the heavy bomber, allowing much lower losses than otherwise.

1945–1991: The Cold War

Commercial aviation really took hold after World War II using mostly ex-military aircraft in the business of transporting people and goods. Within a few years, many companies existed with routes that criss-crossed North America, Europe and other parts of the world. This was accelerated due to the glut of heavy and super-heavy bomber airframes like the B-29 and Lancaster that could easily be converted into commercial aircraft. The DC-3 also made for easier and longer commercial flights. By 1952, the British state[-run] airline BOAC introduced into service the first jet airliner, the De Havilland Comet. While a technical achievement, the plane suffered a series of highly public failures, as the shape of the windows led to cracks due to metal fatigue. The fatigue was caused by cycles of pressurization and depressurization of the cabin, and eventually led to catastrophic failure of the plane's fuselage. By the time the problems were overcome, other jet airliner designs had already taken to the skies, including the Boeing 707, which established new levels of comfort, safety and passenger expectations. The 707 ushered in the age of mass commercial air travel as we enjoy it today.

Even with the end of World War II, there was still a need for advancement in airplane and rocket technology. Not long after the war ended, in October of 1947, Chuck Yeager took the rocket powered Bell X-1 past the speed of sound. Although anecdotal evidence exists that some fighter pilots may have done so while dive-bombing ground targets during the war, this [was] the first controlled, level flight to cross the sound barrier. Further barriers of distance were eliminated in 1948 and 1952 as the first jet crossing of the Atlantic occurred and the first non-stop flight to Australia occurred.

In 1961, ths sky was literally no longer the limit for manned flight as Yuri Gagarin orbited once around the planet within 108 minutes. This action further heated up the space race that had started in 1957 with the launch of Sputnik 1 by the Soviet Union. The United States responded by launching Alan Shepard into space on a suborbital flight in a Mercury space capsule. The space race would ultimately lead to the current pinnacle of human flight, the landing of men on the moon in 1969.

This historic achievement in space was not the only progress made in aviation at this time however. In 1967, the X-15 set the air speed record for an airplane at 4,534 mph or Mach 6.1 (7,297 km/h). Aside from vehicles designed to fly in outer space, this record still stands as the air speed record for powered flight.

The same year that Neil Armstrong and Buzz Aldrin set foot on the moon, 1969, Boeing came out with its vision for the future of air travel, unveiling the Boeing 747 for the first time. This plane is still one of the largest aircraft ever to fly, and it carries millions of passengers each year. Commercial aviation progressed even further in 1976 as British Airways inaugurated supersonic service across the Atlantic, courtesy of the Concorde. A few years earlier the SR-71 Blackbird had set the record for crossing the Atlantic in under 2 hours, and Concorde followed in its footsteps with passengers in tow.

The last quarter of the 20th century saw a slowing of the pace of advancement seen in the first three quarters of the century. No longer was revolutionary progress made in flight speeds, distances and technology. This part of the century saw the steady improvement of flight avionics [as well as] a few minor milestones in flight progress.

For example, in 1979 the Gossamer Albatross became the first human powered airplane to cross the English channel. This achievement finally saw the realization of centuries of dreams of human flight, but it ultimately did not have an impact on either commercial or military aviation. In 1986, Dick Rutan and Jeana Yeager flew an airplane around the world unrefueled and without landing. In 1999, Bertrand Piccard became the first person to circle the earth in a balloon. By the end of the 20th Century there were no major or minor accomplishments left to be made in subsonic aviation. Focus was turning to the ultimate conquest of space and flight at faster than the speed of sound. The Ansari X prize inspired entrepreneurs and space enthusiasts to build their own rocket ships to fly faster than sound and climb into the lowest reaches of space.

1991–Future

In April 2001, the unmanned aircraft Global Hawk flew from Edwards Air Force Base in the United States to Australia non-stop and unrefueled. This is the longest point-to-point flight ever undertaken by an unmanned aircraft, and took 23 hours and 23 minutes. In October 2003 the first totally autonomous flight across the Atlantic by a computer-controlled model aircraft occurred.

In commercial aviation, the early 21st century saw the end of an era with the retirement of the Concorde. Supersonic flight was not very [cost-effective], as the planes were required to fly over the oceans if they wanted to break the sound barrier. The Concorde also was fuel hungry and could carry a limited amount of passengers due to its highly streamlined design.

Despite this setback, and the general slowing of progress, it is generally agreed that the 21st century will be a bright one for aviation. Planes and rockets offer unique capabilities in terms of speed and carrying capacity that should not be underestimated. As long as there is a need for people to get to places quickly, there will be a need for aviation.

JAPAN HAS DESIGNS ON A NEW CONCORDE

Martin Fackler & Don Phillips
N.Y. Times, Oct. 11, 2005, at C1

Deep in the Australian outback, a Japanese team took a small step forward on Monday in its plan to build a supersonic commercial jet.

The engineers, backed by the Japanese government and several companies, flew a small, unmanned model of a supersonic jetliner in Woomera, South Australia.

A model of the jet, 11.5 meters long, or about 38 feet, and resembling an arrow with its swept-back wings and long, sleek body, took off attached to a solid-fuel rocket. The model reached an altitude of 19 kilometers, or 12 miles, before floating back by parachute, according to the Japan Aerospace Exploration Agency, which heads development of the supersonic jet. The engineless model reached a speed of Mach 2, or about 1,500 miles per hour.

Kenichi Saito, a spokesman for the agency, said the unmanned test flight went as planned, The Associated Press reported from Sydney.

"Everything was very good and the aircraft landed also normally," Mr. Saito said. "We are going to conduct the analysis, but currently we think this flight was a success."

The project has had little support from the aerospace industry and none from airlines or major aircraft manufacturers. Its budget is tiny compared with most other aerospace projects, and any hope for a full-size plane is far in the future. But the Japanese persist in hoping that the project someday will propel their nation to the front ranks of the global aircraft industry.

Takaaki Akuto, another spokesman for the Japan Aerospace Exploration Agency, said the agency hoped to have an actual jet flying by 2025, although it was unclear where the money or the orders would come from. The plan calls for the jet to carry 300 passengers at speeds of up to Mach 2.4, fast enough to cut the current flight time from Tokyo to New York to 6 hours from 12.

The agency says it hopes that the jet will become the successor to the French and British-built Concorde, the first supersonic commercial jet, which ceased flying two years ago after a fatal crash and losses of billions of dollars.

"The purpose is to show the world that Japan can take a leading role" in developing new aircraft, Mr. Akuto said. "Until now, Japan has been a secondary player behind companies like Boeing and Airbus."

Three years ago, a similar test ended in failure when the unmanned aircraft detached prematurely from the rocket and slammed into the desert.

The agency leads a consortium of government research labs and private companies, including the biggest aerospace companies in Japan: Mitsubishi Heavy Industries, Kawasaki Heavy Industries and Ishikawajima-Harima Heavy Industries.

In June, Japanese and French industry groups signed a three-year agreement to conduct joint research into new technologies for supersonic flight, looking, for instance, at ways to reduce engine noise and to develop light composite materials capable of resisting extreme pressures. The French were not involved in the flight on Monday, according to the agency.

To succeed, the jet would have to overcome a host of problems that plagued the Concorde and that persuaded more established players like Boeing to give up plans to build a supersonic successor. These include noise, pollution and the high cost of flying beyond the sound barrier, which consumes far more fuel than normal commercial flight.

Japan's space agency says that more advanced engines will produce a quarter the amount of nitrogen oxide, a pollutant, and be no louder than conventional jumbo jets.

The Concorde was taken out of service in 2003 after the crash in the Paris area in 2000 that killed 113 people. The jet failed to earn back the billions of dollars that the British and French governments had invested in it.

HOUSE RESOLUTION 500

Introduced October 18, 2005 by Representative E. Clay Shaw, Jr. (R-Fla.)
Referred October 18, 2005 to the Committee on Armed Services
Referred November 10, 2005 to the Subcommittee on Military Personnel
Approved (420 to 2) November 17, 2005 by the full House

Whereas on December 5, 1945, the 5 Avenger torpedo bombers of Flight 19, originating at the Naval Air Station of Fort Lauderdale, Florida, and its crew of 14 Navy airmen, disappeared;

Whereas the Mariner rescue aircraft sent to search for Flight 19, originating at the Naval Air Station of Banan River, Florida, and its crew of 13 Navy airmen, also disappeared on that date;

Whereas December 5, 2005, marks the 60th anniversary of the disappearance of Flight 19;

Whereas the loss of Flight 19 occurred during peacetime;

Whereas the disappearance of Flight 19 sparked one of the largest air and sea rescue searches in history covering over 250,000 square miles;

Whereas all investigations of the disappearance of Flight 19 have failed to recover any aircraft, debris, or remains;

Whereas there remain unanswered questions concerning the disappearance of Flight 19; and

Whereas there are continuing efforts with the latest technology to determine the location of the lost aircraft and crews: Now, therefore be it

Resolved, That the House of Representatives—

(1) recognizes the 60th anniversary of the disappearance of the 5 naval Avenger torpedo bombers of Flight 19 and the naval Mariner rescue aircraft sent to search for Flight 19;

(2) honors the memory of the 27 Navy airmen lost in these disappearances;

(3) recognizes the historical significance of Flight 19;

(4) acknowledges continuing efforts to determine what caused these disappearances; and

(5) commends the Naval Historical Center for preserving the history of Flight 19.

Notes

1. For a further look at the science and history of flight (the subjects examined in the *FAA* and *Wikipedia* readings), *see, e.g.*, Bill Gunston, *Aviation: The First 100 Years* (2002); John Metcalf, *Flight: 100 Years of Aviation* (2002); Riccardo Niccoli, *History of Flight: From the Flying Machine of Leonardo da Vinci to the Conquest of Space* (2002); T.A. Heppenheimer, *Flight: A History of Aviation Photographs* (2004). *See also* Herbert A. Johnson, *The Wright Patent Wars and Early American Aviation*, 69 J. Air L. & Com. 21 (2004) (describing the long and costly battle of the Wright Brothers to be recognized as the inventors of the airplane); Matthew Healey, *A Famous Error Is One for the Record Books*, N.Y. Times, Oct. 20, 2005, at A19 (reporting on the sale, for $2.97 million, of a block of four "Inverted Jennies," a blue-and-red 1918 postage stamp with a face value of 24 cents that depicts the Curtiss JN-4 biplane, the mainstay of the United States in World War I—due to a printing error, 100 show the aircraft flying upside-down, or inverted); www.aviation-central.com (color illustrations of numerous famous planes, including Air Force One, Howard Hughes's "Spruce Goose," and Charles Lindbergh's "The Spirit of St. Louis").

Decidedly more fanciful explanations of flight can be found in popular culture, beginning with such figures as Santa Claus and Superman. In a 1977 episode of the long-running sitcom *Happy Days* (ABC, 1974–84) entitled "Fonz-How, Inc.," for example, Howard and Richard Cunningham (played by Tom Bosley and Ron Howard) put a humorous spin on the origins of the airplane:

> Howard: You know, the Wright Brothers, they invented the airplane in their bicycle shop.
>
> Richard: Yeah, but they were just trying to build a very wide bicycle and it took off.

Likewise, in the television comedy *The Flying Nun* (ABC, 1967–70), Sister Bertrille (Sally Field) discovered that when the wind was just right, she could fly due to the shape of her cornette—a talent she temporarily lost when she was given a new, wingless habit in the episode "The New Habit" (1969). For other such fare, *see, e.g.*, *Around the World in 80 Days* (2004, starring Steve Coogan—balloon and airplane), *Chitty Chitty Bang Bang* (1968, Dick Van Dyke—flying car), and *The Rocketeer* (1991, Bill Campbell—jet pack).

Although Sister Bertrille is fictional, she brings to mind the Franciscan priest Joseph of Cupertino (1603–63). Known as the Flying Friar because his followers claimed he could float through the air, he was canonized by Pope Clement XIII in 1767 and today is revered as the patron saint of aviators and air travelers. Such persons also receive special protection from St. Thérèse of Lisieux (1873–97; canonized 1925) and from Our Lady of Loreto, the house in which the Virgin Mary was born (because tradition says that a group of angels lifted up the building in the 13th century and flew it from the Holy Land to Italy). *See further* www.catholic-forum.com/saints/pst00012.htm.

For additional discussions of flight and popular culture, *see, e.g.*, Judy Rumerman, *Social History of Aviation and Spaceflight—An Overview*, at www.centennialofflight.gov/essay/Social/SH-OV1.htm, and Dominick Pisano, *The Social and Cultural History of Aviation and Spaceflight*, at www.centennialofflight.gov/essay/Social/SH-OV2.htm. *See also* www.flighthumor.com (a web site devoted to aviation jokes).

2. There are more than 350 aviation museums in the United States. Although the best-known one is the Smithsonian's National Air and Space Museum in Washington, D.C. (www.nasm.si.edu), such collections are located throughout the country. *See further Aviation Museum Locator*, at aeroweb.brooklyn.cuny.edu/museums/museums.htm. *See also* Harriet Baskas, *History in Plane Sight*, at www.usatoday.com/travel/columnist/baskas/2005-11-15-baskas_x.htm (noting that some airports, such as those in Las Vegas, Milwaukee, and San Francisco, operate their own museums).

Like other educational institutions, aviation museums occasionally find themselves involved in litigation. For a sampling of such cases, *see Miles v. Naval Aviation Museum Foundation, Inc.*, 289 F.3d 715 (11th Cir. 2002) (liable for patron's injuries); *Wisdom v. Intrepid Sea-Air Space Museum*, 993 F.2d 5 (2d Cir. 1993) (subject to federal civil rights laws); *Museum of Flight Foundation v. United States*, 63 F. Supp. 2d 1257 (W.D. Wash. 1999) (did not owe income tax on lease of historic airplane); *Florida Dep't of Revenue v. Naval Aviation Museum Foundation, Inc.*, 907 So. 2d 586 (Fla. Dist. Ct. App. 2005) (required to pay taxes on gift shop sales); *Kalamazoo Aviation History Museum v. City of Kalamazoo*, 346 N.W.2d 862 (Mich. Ct. App. 1984) (entitled to tax-exempt status). *See also International Aircraft Recovery, L.L.C. v. Unidentified, Wrecked, and Abandoned Aircraft*, 218 F.3d 1255 (11th Cir. 2000), *cert. denied*, 531 U.S. 1144 (2001) (dispute over right to salve sunken World War II torpedo bomber).

3. As the *Concorde* article reflects, humans are constantly pressing forward in their effort to conquer flight. Yet as *Resolution 500* (which commemorates the incident that gave rise to the legend of the Bermuda Triangle) reminds us, there is still much about flying that we do not know. Indeed, one of the world's most enduring unanswered questions centers around the fate of Amelia Earhart, who disappeared in 1937 while at the controls of her twin-engine Lockheed Electra. For other unexplained air mysteries, *see* Lexi Krock, *Mysterious Plane Crashes*, at www.pbs.org/wgbh/nova/vanished/crashes.html.

Problem 1

As senior counsel to the president, one of your responsibilities is to help put together the federal budget. At a recent meeting, some White House staffers felt the country should be devoting more money to aviation research (akin to the "Japanese Concorde" project), while others thought the first priority should be on making existing airplanes safer. Which approach do you favor? *See* Michael Cabbage, *NASA Cuts Aviation Research for Space*, Orlando Sentinel, Feb. 27, 2005, at A1.

C. SOURCES OF AVIATION LAW

1. LEGISLATION

A COMPARATIVE ANALYSIS OF THE AVIATION NETWORK WITHIN THE EUROPEAN COMMUNITY AND THE AD-HOC NETWORK BETWEEN THE UNITED STATES AND CENTRAL AMERICA

E. Rebecca Kreis
24 Transp. L.J. 303 (1997)

International air law includes both public and private branches of law, which arise from aircraft navigation rules, aeronautical rules, and international principles. The International Aeronautical Congress of 1889, held in Paris, was the birthplace of international air law. The first international aeronautical organization, the International Aeronautical Federation, was established sixteen years later, and was one of the first forums where these laws were discussed. In 1901, the first scientific work on international air law was announced in Paris, written by a Frenchman, P.A.J. Fauchille (1858–1926), in the Revue Générale de Droit International Public, and titled Le Domaine Aérien et le Régime Juridique des Aérostates. This publication was followed shortly by the 1902 conference in Brussels on International Law. One of the main topics of this conference was the legal status of free balloons. In 1906, the Convention International Aérienne was drafted by the French, stating that airspace, like the high seas, is open to trade and travel. However, this draft was never approved by any country.

The first bilateral air agreement in history took place with the exchange of notes between the government of France and the German Reich in Berlin on July 26, 1913. This agreement stated that until a multilateral air convention could be established, both parties would allow, under special conditions, each other's aircraft into their airspace. Due to the air bombardments of World War I, the principle of cuius solum, that "each state has full and exclusive sovereignty over its territory's air space," was adopted immediately after the conclusion of the war. This principle was later included in the Paris Aeronautical Convention of October 13, 1919. As this was the first time that international aeronautical norms and principles were formulated, this convention may be seen as the "cradle of international air law." These norms included general principles for the regulation of air navigation, the nationality of airplanes, certification of airplanes as airworthy, certificates of competence for pilots, rights of passage over the territories of the signatories and restrictions on military airplanes, rules which must be observed in flight, restrictions on air routes, promotion of civil aviation for the contracting states, and mechanisms for the settlement and resolution of disputes between parties. At the same time, the International Commission for Air Navigation (CINA) was formed, which served as the governing international air organization until 1943.

Due to a few clauses contained in the convention which indirectly discriminated against neutral countries and the losers of the first World War, the convention was not ratified by Russia or by the United States of America. This created difficulties for negotiating developments in international air law. The first air agreement to concern Central America was the Ibero-American Convention on Air Navigation (Convención Ibero-

Americana sobre Navigación Aerea) written in Madrid, and signed on November 1, 1926 by Spain, Costa Rica, Mexico, Paraguay, and the Dominican Republic. This agreement was virtually identical to the Paris convention, with the exception of the elimination of the controversial articles.

The next convention concerning international air law also concerned Central America. The Convention on Trade Navigation (Convención sobre Aviación Internaciónal) [better known as the Havana Convention] was signed on February 20, 1928 by eleven Latin American states. This convention was prepared specifically to regulate private commercial aviation in the Americas, thereby defending the Latin American states against the unrestricted expansion of United States airline routes within the western hemisphere.

On October 12, 1929, the Warsaw Aeronautical Convention on international aircraft transport, prepared by CINA, was signed. This convention established multilateral regulations with respect to the limits of responsibility for airlines and the standardization of transportation documents. Next, the conference in the Hague produced the "Hague Aeronautical Convention on Sanitary Conditions of Air Navigation" on April 12, 1933. This convention was replaced by the Washington Convention of December 15, 1944. On May 29, 1933, the Rome Aeronautical Conventions on the Protection of Aircraft and on the Unification of Some of the Provisions on Damages Caused by Aircraft to Third Persons on the Ground were signed. The latter of these was replaced by the Brussels Protocol of November 30, 1938. The Brussels convention of November 29, 1938 was the last agreement signed before World War II, and concerned assistance and salvage of aircraft at sea; however, this agreement was never enacted as it was not ratified by a sufficient number of signatories.

Of these pre-war conventions, a few are still in force. These are the Warsaw Convention, which was modified three times, May 27, 1947, June 7, 1954, and May 21, 1961; the Hague Convention; and the Rome Convention, both modified November 28, 1955.

WWII and Post WWII

From 1926 to 1946, the International Technical Committee of Experts in Aeronautical Legislation, under the auspices of the League of Nations, acted as promoter for, and governing body over, international air law. Its duties were taken over in 1947 by the creation of the International Civil Aviation Organization (ICAO).

The ICAO was created during World War II when England and the United States started negotiations for the creation of a new aeronautical convention to replace the Paris Convention of 1919. The United States wanted the internationalization of air routes, due to the potentials for air transportation created by the war. The United States, with the hope of using its military aircraft for civilian purposes after WWII, hosted the International Civil Aviation Conference in Chicago from Nov. 1 to Dec. 7, 1944. Fifty-four States attended, with the noticeable absence of the USSR, which did not participate due to the presence of Portugal and Spain.

The negotiating states came with different expectations. Consequently, the [results were] both extraordinarily flexible and lacking in clout. The United States wanted to pass a clause giving "the privilege of friendly passage accorded to nations." This would have opened the airspace of the world to those powers with the ability to establish a global network of air routes. France opposed this clause. The treaties which came out of the [meeting] strove to provide a compromise for all nations[.] [Thus, in addition to creating] the Provisional [International] Civil Aviation Organization on August 15, 1945, two years before the ICAO was established, [the delegates prepared]:

- the Convention on International Civil Aviation, also known as the Chicago Aeronautical Convention of 1944, which served to replace the Paris Convention of 1919 and the Havana Convention of 1928;
- the Treaty on the Transit of Air Services; and,
- the Treaty on International Air Transportation.

[Pursuant to the treaties], the ICAO plays a role as a governing body over all of the member states. Individual bilateral and multilateral agreements as well as contracts concluded by member states or airlines operating in those states must be registered with the ICAO. The ICAO also keeps copies of all national aviation laws.

There are two weaknesses in the ICAO. First, the ICAO cannot mandate or enforce any regulations or agreements. Its job is mainly to develop and to recommend the implementation of international technical standards. The signatories of the convention are then required to impose the standards on their airlines. This does not always happen. Second, the ICAO has little impact on international airline economic regulation, due to a schism between delegates. This task has fallen to individual governments, in part due to a 1946 meeting in Bermuda [between the United States and Great Britain, generally referred to as "Bermuda One"].

After the ICAO convention, there were many more international agreements signed, including the Geneva Convention of 1948 in the International Recognition of Rights Aboard Aircraft, signed on June 19, 1948; the 1952 Convention on Damages Caused [by Foreign Aircraft to Third Parties on the Surface], which replaced the Rome Convention of 1933; the Hague Protocol of 1955, along with recommendations to settle issues arising from chartering, renting and exploiting of aircraft, and to examine the possibility of unifying private international air law and regulating international air disputes; the Convention on Crimes and Other Offenses Committed on Board an Aircraft, adopted in Tokyo on October 14, 1963; the Hague Convention on Combating Unlawful Seizure of Aircraft, signed on December 16, 1970, which supplanted the Tokyo agreement; the Guatemala Air Protocol of March 8, 1978; a revision of the Warsaw Convention of 1929; and the revised Hague Protocol of 1955. In addition, there have been many regional aeronautical agreements[.]

ULTRALIGHT AIRCRAFT: A NEED FOR BETTER REGULATION THAN 14 C.F.R. § 103

Richard H. Jack
51 J. Air L. & Com. 415 (1986)

[In the United States, the first efforts to develop a body of aviation law were undertaken by the states.] In developing aviation common law, the various state legislatures acted in a piecemeal fashion until 1922, when the National Conference of Commissioners of Uniform State Laws approved the Uniform State Law for Aeronautics. In the fourteen years following approval of the Act, twenty-one states adopted it. Additional uniform laws were promulgated by the Commission, however, the state acceptance rate declined. Additionally, some states enacted their own aviation statutes.

The federal government exercised no control over aviation until the outbreak of World War I in 1914, when its potential use as a weapon became apparent. On March 3,

1915, the Naval Appropriations Act became law with a rider which established the Advisory Committee for Aeronautics (NACA). This committee was charged with the "scientific study of problems of flight with a view to their practical solutions." The committee's primary function was the development of American military air power.

By the end of the World War I, NACA recommended the enactment of legislation controlling civil aviation, but Congress passed no legislation. In 1918, however, NACA persuaded the Post Office Department to set up an airmail service. The limitations on civil aviation became apparent through the problems encountered by this new service and by the financial problems encountered by entrepreneurs of new commercial airline companies. In 1919, NACA drafted a bill which would have authorized the Department of Commerce to license pilots, inspect aircraft, and supervise airfield usage. Although President Wilson submitted the bill to Congress, no action was taken. In Europe, however, governments regulated and generously subsidized civil aviation. In 1919, the International Convention on Air Navigation met in Paris to set forth a body of rules, "recognizing the progress of aerial navigation ... appreciating the necessity of an early agreement upon ... rules ... to encourage ... peaceful intercourse." These rules were signed by each major power except the United States.

The first federal safety legislation proposed in the rapidly expanding field of post-World War I civil aviation was the Wadsworth Bill. By the time the House was ready to act, the Senate substituted the Bingham-Parker Bill for the Wadsworth Bill. The House and Senate ironed out their differences, and the resulting legislation became the Air Commerce Act of 1926. The legislative history of the Air Commerce Act demonstrates that the Senate emphasized the business of flying while the House emphasized safety.

Reflectively, although Bingham and his followers believed they saw the future of aviation (and they probably did if compared to their colleagues who kept forestalling passage of regulation), in fact they had no realistic vision of its future growth. For example, in outlining which of the existing offices would be responsible for the various tasks necessary to implement the new Act, the Senate Report notes: "The Department of Commerce has offices in all our seaports where its Bureau of Navigation and its Steamboat Service carry on their work. These offices can readily be used without additional expense for necessary aviation inspectors who must provide for the examination of pilots and airplanes...," and calls the new act a plan of "comparative simplicity."

The legal development instituted by the Air Commerce Act was not capable of coping with the developing technology and business of aviation. The Europeans, as in 1919, continued to lead the way in international legal development. The Aeronautics Branch of the Department of Commerce became snowed under with new responsibilities. In 1934 it became the Bureau of Air Commerce under the supervision of the Department of Commerce. At the same time Senator McCarran guided the Airmail Act of 1934 through Congress. Senator McCarran had pressed for, and in this act achieved, Presidential authority to appoint a commission of five members for the purpose of forming a unified aviation policy for the country. This commission was the Federal Aviation Commission. The commission's efforts resulted in the Civil Aeronautics Act of 1938 which had roughly the same purpose as the Air Commerce Act of 1926: development of commercial aviation with a high standard of safety. The Air Commerce Act made the commission independent of the commerce department. In June, 1940, the agency created by the Civil Aeronautics Act of 1938 was split into two agencies. Commerce and safety would be handled by the new Civil Aeronautics Board (CAB). The reorganization also created the Civil Aviation Administration (CAA), to which in 1948 the CAB delegated a number of rule-making powers, notably the power to investigate accidents involving aircraft under 12,500 lbs. gross weight—the size of a small cargo plane (such as the famous Douglas DC-3/C-47). The CAA was transferred to the Department of Commerce in 1950.

Despite the tinkering, aviation regulation was not keeping up with the technological developments in aviation. One of the prime areas of safety concern continued to be airspace allocation and a perceived need for improvements in radio navigation and air control system. Congress knew the airways were simply too crowded for the available controls to insure air safety. The Bureau of the Budget knew it [too], and on May 4, 1955, appointed a committee to study the matter (The Harding Committee, or Aviation Facilities Study Group). The President knew it [too], and in February 1956 appointed a Special Assistant for Aviation Facilities Planning to study the matter. But it took a disaster to spark real action in the federal government.

In [June] 1956, the Grand Canyon midair collision [killed 128 persons]. Out of th[is] disaster came the [successor to the CAA, the] Federal Aviation Agency, [whose purpose was to] "provide for the safe and efficient use of the navigable airspace by both civil and military operations."

TRANSPORTATION: A LEGAL HISTORY

Paul Stephen Dempsey
30 Transp. L.J. 235 (2003)

[Following the passage of] the Federal Aviation Act of 1958 [came] the creation of the U.S. Department of Transportation [DOT] in 1966. [In addition to transferring the Federal Aviation Agency to this new department, where it was renamed the Federal Aviation Administration [FAA]], Congress established [within DOT the] independent National Transportation Safety Board [NTSB], giving it power to conduct investigations and hold hearings to determine "the cause or probable cause of transportation accidents and reporting the facts, conditions, and circumstances relating to such accidents." The NTSB became truly independent and effectively autonomous from DOT with the Independent Safety Board Act of 1974.

With the [election] of Jimmy Carter as President in 1976, [further changes took place]. Convinced by his staff that he could make a "quick hit" politically, Carter embraced the deregulation movement [begun under] his predecessor, champion[ing] and then sign[ing] into law the Air Cargo Deregulation Act of 1977 [and] the Airline Deregulation Act of 1978.

In 1977, Carter tapped economist Alfred Kahn to serve as Chairman of the Civil Aeronautics Board [CAB]. As Chairman of the New York Public Utilities Commission, Kahn had advocated deregulation before the Kennedy Subcommittee. Kahn criticized traditional CAB regulation as having "(a) caused air fares to be considerably higher than they otherwise would be; (b) resulted in a serious misallocation of resources; (c) encouraged carrier inefficiency; (d) denied consumers the range of price/service options they would prefer, and; (e) created a chronic tendency toward excess capacity in the industry."

As CAB Chairman, Kahn implemented a number of revolutionary deregulatory initiatives that liberalized entry and pricing. Soon carriers were authorized to enter new markets and offer consumers significant discounts over previous levels. The immediate results appeared overwhelmingly successful, with carriers in the late 1970s stimulating new demand by offering low fares, filling capacity, and enjoying robust profits.

The Airline Deregulation Act of 1978 called for a gradual transition from regulation to competition, eliminating most entry controls, except "fitness," on December 31, 1981, and domestic rate regulation on December 31, 1982. The Act also included an unprecedented provision mandating the extermination (a/k/a "sunset") of the CAB on December 31, 1984—the first major federal agency to be obliterated in the nation's history. [Pursuant to the Act, the CAB's] remaining responsibilities were transferred to DOT. Those primarily involved the regulation of international routes and rates, small community subsidies, and mergers. The latter was transferred from DOT to the U.S. Department of Justice in 1989, following serious public criticism of DOT's approval of each of the 21 merger proposals that had been submitted to it during its brief reign over the matter.

Despite [initial] euphoria, the first several decades of deregulation have been the darkest financial period in history for the airline industr[y]. Concentration became an epidemic—[t]he eight largest airlines, which in 1978 accounted for 81% of the domestic passenger market, dominated 94% by 1989. United Airlines acquired many of the international routes of Pan American World Airways, which was liquidated. American Airlines acquired Air Cal, Reno, and TWA as well as many of the international routes of Eastern Airlines, which was liquidated. Delta Air Lines acquired Western Airlines. Northwest Airlines acquired Republic Airlines, itself the product of the merger of North Central, Republic, and Hughes Airwest. Continental was the product of the merger of Continental, Texas International, New York Air, People Express, and Frontier Airlines, as well as several regional carriers. USAirways (formerly Allegheny Airlines) acquired Piedmont and PSA. Southwest Airlines acquired Muse and Morris Air.

Not only were national concentration levels at unprecedented levels, [but] regionally carriers had established hub-and-spoke systems, in which airlines maintained market power. Nearly all hubs were virtual monopolies, with megacarriers dominating more than 60% of gates, flights, and passengers. The General Accounting Office found that rates were 27% higher in monopoly hubs than in nonhubs. Pricing reflected the level of competition in any market, rather than marginal costs. The domination by giant airlines of hubs, landing and takeoff slots, computer reservations systems, [and] frequent flyer programs made it exceedingly difficult for new entrants to challenge the established megacarriers. But overall, pricing was set at unsustainable levels, causing the industry to lose all the profit it had earned in its history.

By 1992, the airline industry had suffered more than 150 bankruptcies and 50 mergers. Alfred Kahn admitted, "There is no denying that the profit record of the industry since 1978 has been dismal, that deregulation bears substantial responsibility, and that the proponents of deregulation did not anticipate such financial distress—either so intense or so long-continued." But the $18 billion of economic losses of the early 1990s were modest in contrast to the $30 billion the airline industry lost in the early 21st Century.

Notes

1. Writing at the time of the 1919 Paris Convention (the text of which is reproduced in Appendix 1 of this casebook), one commentator observed: "The most difficult category of questions of all those to which human flight has given rise is the complex of problems

relating to judicial competence and the law to be applied in the air." J.M. Spaight, *Aircraft in Peace and the Law* 106 (1919). Part of the difficulty, of course, has to do with definition: just what does aviation law encompass? According to one source, the answer is as follows:

> Air law and space law are separate and distinct branches of law, although they are occasionally treated as one ("Aerospace Law"). Air law, the older of the 2, is the body of public and private law, both national and international, that regulates aeronautical activities and other uses of airspace. Space law, on the other hand, regulates activities of states and private entities in outer space, primarily the use of satellites. The essential difference between air law and space law stems from the legal status of airspace and of outer space. Whereas airspace, except over the high seas and Antarctica, is under the sovereignty of subjacent states, outer space is governed by the regime of freedom. The question of boundaries between outer space and airspace is awaiting international agreement; it is virtually certain, however, that the boundary will not be placed higher than 100 km above sea level.
>
> The origin of space law can be traced to the launching on 4 October 1957 of Sputnik I, the first artificial Earth satellite. Since that time the legal regulation of outer-space activities has been largely centered in the UN Committee on the Peaceful Uses of Outer Space. The bulk of space law consists of norms incorporated in 5 multilateral treaties. The most important is the 1967 Treaty on Principles Governing the Activities of States in the Exploration and Use of Outer Space, including the Moon and Other Celestial Bodies (also known as the Outer Space Treaty). The major principles of the treaty are freedom of access to, and use of, outer space; prohibition against national claims to sovereignty in any part of outer space; and a ban on the placing of weapons of mass destruction anywhere in outer space.

The Canadian Encyclopedia, *Air and Space Law*, at tceplus.com. *See also* P.P.C. Haanappel, *The Law and Policy of Air Space and Outer Space: A Comparative Approach* (2003).

2. As Ms. Kreis explains, the 1944 Chicago Conference marked a major milestone in aviation history (ironically, however, the meeting was viewed by contemporary observers as a failure because of its inability to reach agreement on various economic issues affecting international air transport). Its accomplishments have been summarized thusly:

> The Chicago Conference adopted three major agreements of significant importance to the multilateral regulation of international air transports.
>
> [1] [The] Convention on International Civil Aviation, also known as the Chicago Convention, provides the fundamental legal framework for the regulation of world civil aviation. The Chicago Convention [also] is the constitution of the International Civil Aviation Organization. Two amendments to the Chicago Convention that are important to the air transport regulatory side are Article 83 bis, which allows the transfer of certain functions and duties from a State of registry of an aircraft to the State of the operator in case of lease, charter, or interchange, [and] Article 3 bis, which reconfirms the prohibition against the use of weapons against civil aircraft in flight and sovereignty over airspace.
>
> [2] [The] International Air Services Transit Agreement, also known as [the] Two Freedoms Agreement, provides [for] the multilateral exchange of rights of overflight and non-traffic stop for scheduled air services among its Contracting States.

> [3] [The] International Air Transport Agreement, also known as the Five Freedoms Agreement, establishes five freedoms of the air for scheduled international air services, but does not contain any provisions on fair competition or for the regulation of capacity or fares and rates.

Chicago Convention Acts, at www.caa.md/?id=2879. The text of these agreements can be found in Appendices 3–5.

Although the United States is a party to both the Chicago Convention and the Two Freedoms Agreement, it is not a party to the Five Freedoms Agreement (the same is true for most countries). Thus, to obtain these rights, nations must negotiate bilateral or multilateral agreements (an example of the former is the 1977 U.S.-U.K. accord, known as "Bermuda II," which appears in Appendix 16—so-called because it replaced a 1946 agreement that also was negotiated in Bermuda; an example of the latter is the 2001 MALIAT pact, which can be found in Appendix 27). To facilitate such negotiations, the United States has promulgated a model bilateral agreement (*see* Appendix 30).

As it happens, there actually are nine air freedoms, as follows:

> 1) The right to fly over another country without landing (conditioned on the giving of appropriate notice).
>
> 2) The right to land in another country for technical reasons (such as refueling or emergency repairs), called a non-traffic stop. ("Traffic" in commercial aviation refers to the transportation of persons, property, or mail for compensation.)
>
> 3) The right to transport traffic from one's home country to another country.
>
> 4) The right to transport traffic from another country to one's home country.
>
> 5) The right to transport traffic from another country to a third country, so long as the flight starts or ends in one's home country (known as "beyond rights").
>
> 6) The right to transport traffic originating in another country through one's home country to a third country (known as "behind homeland rights"). In other words, the right to carry traffic between two foreign countries via one's home country.
>
> 7) The right to transport traffic originating in another country to a third country on a journey that does not start or end in one's home country (known as "turn-around rights").
>
> 8) The right to take on traffic at one place in another country and transport it to another place in the same country (known as "cabotage").
>
> 9) The right to engage in cabotage that is not part of transportation to or from one's home country (known as "pure cabotage").

For a further discussion, *see* Brian F. Havel, *In Search of Open Skies: Law and Policy for a New Era in International Aviation* (1997; second edition forthcoming 2006).

Although the United States generally favors free competition when it comes to aviation, its devotion to this principle is not absolute. Thus, for example, Congress (for both national security and economic reasons) generally has prohibited cabotage, placed limits on the foreign ownership and control of airlines, required government employees and property to fly aboard American carriers whenever possible, and sharply restricted so-called "wet leases" from foreign carriers (in contrast to a "dry lease," in which only an aircraft is leased, a wet lease includes both the aircraft and at least one crew member).

See further Barry Humphreys, *Guarded Optimism: A View From Europe*, 18 Air & Space Law. 1 (Fall 2003); Thomas Lehrich & Jennifer Thibodeau, *Citizenship Requirements and Why Branson Can't Save United*, 18 Air & Space Law. 8 (Summer 2003); Conor McAuliffe, *The Proposed U.S.-EC Agreement: A Glass Half Full*, 19 Air & Space Law. 1 (Fall 2004); Allan I. Mendelsohn, *Myths of International Aviation*, 68 J. Air L. & Com. 519 (2003); Ved P. Nanda, *Substantial Ownership and Control of International Airlines in the United States*, 50 Am. J. Comp. L. 357 (2002). Given the woeful state of the domestic airline industry, however, some of these restrictions may be eased in the future. *See* Jeff Bailey, *Proposal Would Expand Foreign Role in Airlines*, N.Y. Times, Nov. 3, 2005, at C11 (describing the Bush administration's interest in helping beleaguered carriers tap overseas capital).

3. As noted above, the Chicago Convention does more than simply set out the guiding principles of international air law; it also acts as the constitution of the International Civil Aviation Organization (ICAO) (pronounced "i-kay-oh"), a specialized organ of the United Nations with headquarters in Montreal and a membership (as of October 2005) of 189 countries. The ICAO's web site (www.icao.org) contains a wealth of information about its history, structure, purposes, and programs, as well as links to numerous national aviation bodies.

The decision to locate the ICAO in Montreal came about in two stages. Two days before the close of the Chicago Conference, the Executive Committee recommended that the organization be headquartered in Canada (where most of the preparatory work for the conference had taken place) but did not designate a specific city. *See* Duane W. Freer, *Chicago Conference (1944)—Despite Uncertainty, the Spirit of Internationalism Soars*, 41 ICAO Bull. 42, 44 (Sept. 1986). After the delegates accepted this suggestion, the Canadian government quickly picked Montreal because it was "the country's leading metropolis, its most cosmopolitan and international city ... [and] the country's hub of international civil air transport." Duane W. Freer, *The PICAO Years—1945 to 1947*, 41 ICAO Bull. 36, 36 (Oct. 1986).

The choice of Montreal was confirmed at the Provisional ICAO Assembly in 1946, but the city's relatively harsh climate soon led to calls for a different location. In accordance with Article 45 of the Chicago Convention, serious efforts to move the headquarters arose in 1950, 1952, and 1954 (with Brussels, Lisbon, and Mexico City suggested as alternatives), but nothing came of these initiatives and the matter now is considered settled. *See further* Duane W. Freer, *Gear Up! 1947 to 1957*, 41 Bull. 52, 52–53 (Nov. 1986).

One particularly knotty problem that the delegates to the Chicago Conference faced was the fact that while everyone knew that an international organization would soon be set up to take the place of the failed League of Nations, no one knew what shape or form it would take (the meeting creating the United Nations would not convene until April 1945). Thus, Article 64 of the Chicago Convention simply provided that the ICAO was authorized to join "any general organization set up by the nations of the world to preserve peace."

Once the United Nations did come into existence, the ICAO found its entry barred by the fact that one of its members (Spain) was a fascist state. The ICAO therefore added a provision to the Chicago Convention (Article 93 bis) that allowed it to change its membership to meet the UN's admission standards. Although a crisis could have ensued, it was averted when Spain agreed to withdraw from the ICAO (it later rejoined after it was admitted to the UN in 1955).

4. The pieces by Mr. Jack and Professor Dempsey collectively trace the development of the Federal Aviation Administration (FAA) (www.faa.gov), National Transportation

Safety Board (NTSB) (www.ntsb.gov), and Department of Transportation (www.dot.gov). In a nutshell, the FAA is in charge of aviation safety and grants to airports; the NTSB is in charge of accident investigations, aviation safety recommendations, and appeals from certain FAA enforcement actions; and the DOT is in charge of international economic regulation and domestic consumer protection. For a further discussion of these roles and the conflicts they sometimes engender (particularly for the FAA, whose statutory duties require it to both assist and police aviation—commonly referred to the "dual mandate" problem), *see, e.g.*, Mark C. Niles, *On the Hijacking of Agencies (and Airplanes): The Federal Aviation Administration, "Agency Capture," and Airline Security*, 10 Am. U.J. Gender Soc. Pol'y & L. 381 (2002), and Lea Ann Carlisle, Comment, *The FAA v. the NTSB: Now That Congress Has Addressed the Federal Aviation Administration's "Dual Mandate," Has the FAA Begun Living Up to Its Amended Purpose of Making Air Travel Safer, Or Is the National Transportation Safety Board Still Doing Its Job Alone?*, 66 J. Air L. & Com. 741 (2001).

The DOT, FAA, and NTSB are not the only relevant federal actors. Depending on the issue at stake, the Department of Justice, Environmental Protection Agency, or Occupational Safety and Health Administration, among many others, also play a role in shaping the country's aviation policies. In addition, as a result of 9/11, two new entities have come on the scene: the Department of Homeland Security (www.dhs.gov) and its Transportation Security Administration (TSA) (www.tsa.gov). In another part of his article, Professor Dempsey explains their roles as follows:

> Until 1961, there were no domestic United States laws specifically addressing the 20th Century crime of aircraft hijacking. After defining the crime in that year, the United States discovered that the solution to this new type of terrorism was not to be realized by the imposition of penalties.
>
> The Antihijacking Act of 1974 imposed a penalty of 20 years imprisonment or death if a passenger [was] killed during a hijacking and authorized the President to suspend the landing rights of any nation that harbor[ed] hijackers. The Aircraft Sabotage Act of 1984 imposed penalties of up to $100,000 or twenty years imprisonment, or both, for hijacking, damage, destruction, or disabling an aircraft or air navigation facility. The Security and Development Act of 1985 authorized expenditures for enhancing security at foreign airports. The Act required the DOT Secretary to assess security at foreign airports and notify the public if a foreign airport fail[ed] to correct a security breach.
>
> The Aviation Security Improvement Act of 1990 established a Director of Intelligence and Security in the Office of the DOT Secretary, and an Assistant FAA Administrator for Civil Aviation Security, and gave the FAA responsibility to oversee security at major airports. FAA security managers were directed to supervise security arrangements. The FAA carried out periodic threat and vulnerability assessments and published guidelines on such topics as airport design and construction, screening of passengers and property, public notification of threats, security personnel investigation and training, cargo and mail screening, research and development activities, security standards at foreign airports, and international security negotiations.
>
> On the morning of September 11, 2001, 19 suicide terrorists hijacked four aircraft in flight. American Airlines flight 11 and United Airlines flight 175 crashed into New York's World Trade Center. American Airlines flight 77

crashed into the Pentagon. And United Airlines flight 93 crashed in rural Pennsylvania, a suicide mission apparently aborted by vigilante passengers.

The tragic events of September 11, 2001, revealed that the airport and airway security umbrella was far more porous than theretofore widely recognized. Within weeks of that catastrophe, Congress passed two pieces of legislation—the Air Transportation Safety and System Stabilization Act and the Aviation and Transportation Security Act [ATSA].

Recognizing that a competitive airline industry is essential to national commerce and that the three-day shut down of the industry had caused it significant economic harm, Congress promulgated the Air Transportation Safety and System Stabilization Act. That legislation provided the U.S. airline industry with $15 billion in relief ($5 billion immediately, and up to $10 billion in loans). It capped the liability of the two airlines involved—United Airlines and American Airlines—at their insurance limits and eliminated punitive damages. To deal with the human tragedy, it established a no-fault September 11th Victims' Compensation Fund directed by a Special Master who would determine compensation, as reduced by payments from collateral sources. Injured parties or estates that chose to forego the Compensation Fund could bring suit in the federal district court for the southern district of New York. If they decide[d] to litigate they [would] have to establish traditional common law negligence and proximate cause, both of which [could] be formidable barriers to recovery.

In order to restore the public's confidence in flying, three days before Thanksgiving, 2001, Congress passed the Aviation and Transportation Security Act, which included ninety-one new measures, fifty-five of which had designated implementation deadlines. The most significant of ATSA's mandates included federalizing the airport security function (which had theretofore been performed by the airlines, under FAA regulations), imposing minimum job qualifications upon security employees, imposing background checks on airport employees, [and] requiring impregnable cockpit doors. Having concluded that the FAA had been historically slow to implement its wishes, Congress created a new multimodal Transportation Security Administration [TSA] within the U.S. Department of Transportation.

Fourteen months after the terrorist attacks on the World Trade Center and Pentagon, Congress passed the Homeland Security Act of 2002 [HSA], which established a new cabinet-level executive branch agency, the Department of Homeland Security [DHS], headed by a Secretary of Homeland Security. It was the most sweeping overhaul of federal agencies since President Harry Truman asked Congress to create the Central Intelligence Agency and unify the military branches under the Department of Defense in 1947.

In creating DHS, Congress consolidated twenty-two existing agencies that had combined budgets of approximately $40 billion and employed some 170,000 workers. Several of the agencies historically ha[d] been involved in airport and airline passenger and cargo review, including the Customs Service, Immigration and Naturalization Service, Animal and Plant Inspection Service of the Department of Agriculture, and the nascent Transportation Security Administration.

30 Transp. L.J. at 322–25. Even before the creation of the DHS and the TSA, however, various treaties had been promulgated to combat aviation terrorism. *See* Appendices 10, 14, and 20–21.

5. Domestic aviation law is contained principally in Title 49 ("Transportation") of the United States Code and in Title 14 ("Aeronautics and Space") of the Code of Federal Regulations. Citations in court decisions, however, may be to the underlying legislation (e.g., the Federal Aviation Act of 1958) or to a previous codification of Title 49, such as 49 U.S.C. App. (short for "Appendix"). In 1994, Congress recodified the aviation laws; as a result, they now appear at 49 U.S.C. §§40101–50105. Despite minor changes in wording, this effort was not intended to affect the substantive meaning of any statute. *See* Act of July 5, 1994, Pub. L. No. 103-272, 108 Stat. 745. As will become clear, the "federalization" of aviation law is pervasive and the preemption of state law runs throughout the field. *See further* J. Scott Hamilton, *Allocation of Airspace as a Scarce National Resource*, 22 Transp. L.J. 251 (1994).

One also should be aware of 18 U.S.C. §7(5), which extends federal criminal jurisdiction to:

> Any aircraft belonging in whole or in part to the United States, or any citizen thereof, or to any corporation created by or under the laws of the United States, or any State, Territory, District, or possession thereof, while such aircraft is in flight over the high seas, or over any other waters within the admiralty and maritime jurisdiction of the United States and out of the jurisdiction of any particular State.

See generally Kate B. Enroth, Comment, *United States v. Georgescu: Special Aircraft Jurisdiction in the United States*, 18 Brook. J. Int'l L. 225 (1992) (discussing *United States v. Georgescu*, 723 F. Supp. 912 (E.D.N.Y. 1989)).

6. Since the publication of Professor Dempsey's article in 2003, the economic fortunes of the airline industry have continued to decline. In September 2005, for example, Delta Air Lines (the nation's No. 3 carrier) and Northwest Airlines (its No. 4 carrier) both filed for bankruptcy within hours of each other. *See* Micheline Maynard, *Bankruptcy for 2: Storm Broke the Camel's Back*, N.Y. Times, Sept. 15, 2005, at C1. The net result was that 47% of the country's airline seats were under the supervision of bankruptcy judges.

Both Delta and Northwest blamed rising fuel prices, which had increased 50% during the year and were poised to rise higher in the wake of Hurricane Katrina, which devastated New Orleans and the Gulf Coast. In a larger sense, however, their filings reflected an overall weakness among operators, brought on by a combination of factors (including 9/11, cut-throat competition from low-cost start-ups, and mounting labor and pension obligations). Although no one seriously believes that the end of commercial aviation is in sight, the make-up of the industry is likely to change greatly during the next decade as a result of mergers, takeovers, and liquidations. In addition, the cost of air travel is likely to climb significantly even if fuel prices stabilize. For a further discussion, *see, e.g.*, Simon Calder, *No Frills: The Truth Behind the Low-Cost Revolution in the Skies* (2002); Rigas Doganis, *Flying Off Course: The Economics of International Airlines* (3d ed. 2002); Barbara S. Peterson, *Blue Streak: Inside JetBlue, The Upstart That Rocked An Industry* (2004); Stephen Shaw, *Airline Marketing and Management* (5th ed. 2004); Donald J. Carty et al., *The Future of Air Travel: Three to Five Years Ahead*, 68 J. Air L. & Com. 765 (2003); Micheline Maynard, *Get Out the Glue for a New Business Model: The Reinvention of Airlines, Part 2*, N.Y. Times, July 11, 2004, §3, at 1. *See also* Jonathan Lewinsohn, Note, *Bailing Out Congress: An Assessment and Defense of the Air Transportation Safety and System Stabilization Act of 2001*, 115 Yale L.J. 438 (2005).

7. Whatever else happens to the airline industry in the next few years, one thing that is not likely to change is its penchant for branding professional sports venues. During

2005, fans attended games in such places as the Air Canada Centre (home of the NBA's Toronto Raptors and the NHL's Toronto Maple Leafs), America West Arena (scheduled, because of the carriers' recent merger, to become US Airways Center in January 2006) (NBA Phoenix Suns/NHL Phoenix Coyotes), American Airlines Arena (NBA Miami Heat), American Airlines Center (NBA Dallas Mavericks/NHL Dallas Stars), Continental Airlines Arena (NBA New Jersey Nets/NHL New Jersey Devils), Delta Center (NBA Utah Jazz), FedEx Field (NFL Washington Redskins), FedEx Forum (NBA Memphis Grizzlies), and United Center (NBA Chicago Bulls/NHL Chicago Blackhawks). Previously, fans also had cheered at the Canadian Airlines Saddledome (1995–2000) (NHL Calgary Flames) (the name was changed to the Pengrowth Saddledome after Canadian Airlines was acquired by Air Canada), Trans World Dome (1995–2001) (NFL St. Louis Rams) (now known as the Edward Jones Dome because of TWA's demise), and USAir Arena (1993–97) (NBA Washington Bullets/NHL Washington Capitals) (after the teams moved to the new MCI Center, the arena was torn down to make room for a shopping center).

Since 2000, Broadway patrons also have gotten in on the action by attending shows at the American Airlines Theatre (formerly the Selwyn Theatre). In 2004, for example, the theater hosted a very successful revival of *Twelve Angry Men*, Reginald Rose's penetrating examination of the jury system.

Could the idea be taken a step farther and result in airports selling their names to the highest bidder? Currently, airports are named (when they are named at all) for aviation pioneers (e.g., Charles Lindbergh in San Diego, William Mitchell in Milwaukee, and Chuck Yeager in Charleston, West Virginia), celebrities (e.g., Louis Armstrong in New Orleans, Bob Hope in Burbank, and John Wayne in Orange County, California), politicans (e.g., George Bush in Houston, John F. Kennedy in New York, and Ronald Reagan in Washington, D.C.), or prominent local citizens (e.g., Albert Lambert in St. Louis, Edward Logan in Boston, and Butch O'Hare in Chicago)—although following 9/11 Newark International Airport was renamed Newark Liberty International Aiport to honor the victims of United Airlines Flight 93, which had taken off from the airport and was en route to San Francisco when it was seized by the terrorists. In November 2005, however, Allegheny County councilman Ed Kress proposed auctioning off the name of Pittsburgh International Airport, although the idea immediately drew criticism. *See What's in a Name? Selling the Airport's Moniker Shouldn't Fly*, Pitt. Post-Gazette, Nov. 16, 2005, at B6 (shuddering at the prospect of travelers flying from Big Mac and Fries International to Viagra Field via Alka-Seltzer Airport). Another potential stumbling block is that most sponsors would want to have their name incorporated in the airport's three-letter location identifier (e.g., "LAX" stands for Los Angeles International Airport while "MIA" represents Miami International Airport), which would require FAA approval.

Problem 2

Aware that commercial space travel is rapidly moving from far-fetched notion to serious possibility, a congressional committee is holding hearings on the subject. While some members believe that aviation law can be used to resolve any disputes that arise during such trips, others believe that an entirely new body of law will be needed. As majority counsel, what advice would you give to the committee? *See* R. Thomas Rankin, Note, *Space Tourism: Fanny Packs, Ugly T-Shirts, and the Law in Outer Space*, 36 Suffolk U. L. Rev. 695 (2003).

2. CASE LAW

GUILLE v. SWAN

19 Johns. 381 (N.Y. Sup. Ct. 1822)

SPENCER, Chief Justice.

[Swan sued Guille in the Justices' Court, in an action of trespass, for entering his close, and treading down his roots and vegetables, &c. in a garden in the city of New-York. The facts were, that Guille ascended in a balloon in the vicinity of Swan's garden, and descended into his garden. When he descended, his body was hanging out of the car of the balloon in a very perilous situation, and he called to a person at work in Swan's field, to help him, in a voice audible to the pursuing crowd. After the balloon descended, it dragged along over potatoes and radishes, about thirty feet, when Guille was taken out. The balloon was carried to a barn at the farther end of the premises. When the balloon descended, more than two hundred persons broke into Swan's garden through the fences, and came on his premises, beating down his vegetables and flowers. The damage done by Guille, with his balloon, was about 15 dollars, but the crowd did much more. The plaintiff's damages, in all, amounted to 90 dollars. It was contended before the Justice, that Guille was answerable only for the damage done by himself, and not for the damage done by the crowd. The Justice was of the opinion, and so instructed the jury, that the defendant was answerable for all the damages done to the plaintiff. The jury, accordingly, found a verdict for him, for 90 dollars, on which the judgment was given, and for costs.]

The counsel for the plaintiff in error supposes, that the injury committed by his client was involuntary, and that done by the crowd was voluntary, and that, therefore, there was no union of intent; and that upon the same principle which would render Guille answerable for the acts of the crowd, in treading down and destroying the vegetables and flowers of S., he would be responsible for a battery, or a murder committed on the owner of the premises.

The intent with which an act is done is by no means the test of the liability of a party to an action of trespass. If the act cause the immediate injury, whether it was intentional, or unintentional, trespass is the proper action to redress the wrong. It was so decided, upon a review of all the cases, in Percival v. Hickey, 18 Johns. Rep. 257. Where an immediate act is done by the co-operation, or the joint act of several persons, they are all trespassers, and may be sued jointly or severally; and any one of them is liable for the injury done by all. To render one man liable in trespass for the acts of others, it must appear, either that they acted in concert, or that the act of the individual sought to be charged, ordinarily and naturally, produced the acts of the others.

The case of Scott v. Shepard, 2 Black. Rep. 892, is a strong instance of the responsibility of an individual who was the first, though not the immediate, agent in producing an injury. Shepard threw a lighted squib, composed of gunpowder, into a market house, where a large concourse of people were assembled; it fell on the standing of Y., and to prevent injury, it was thrown off his standing, across the market, when it fell on another standing; from thence, to save the goods of the owner, it was thrown to another part of the market house, and in so throwing it, it struck the plaintiff in the face, and, bursting, put out one of his eyes. It was decided, by the opinions of three Judges against one, that Shepard was answerable in an action of trespass, and assault and battery. De Grey, Ch. J., held that throwing the squib was an unlawful act, and that whatever mischief followed, the person throwing it was the author of the mischief. All that was done subsequent to the original throwing was a continuation of the first force and first act. Any innocent person removing the danger from himself was justifiable; the blame lights upon the first thrower; the new direction and new force flow out of the first force. He laid it down as a principle that every one who does an unlawful act, is considered as the doer of all that follows.

A person breaking a horse in Lincolns-Inn-Fields hurt a man and it was held that trespass would lie. In Leame v. Bray, 3 East Rep. 595, Lord Ellenborough said, if I put in motion a dangerous thing, as if I let loose a dangerous animal, and leave to hazard what may happen, and mischief ensue, I am answerable in trespass; and if one (he says) put an animal or carriage in motion, which causes an immediate injury to another, he is the actor, the causa causans.

I will not say that ascending in a balloon is an unlawful act, for it is not so; but, it is certain, that the aeronaut has no control over its motion horizontally; he is at the sport of the winds, and is to descend when and how he can; his reaching the earth is a matter of hazard. He did descend on the premises of the plaintiff below, at a short distance from the place where he ascended. Now, if his descent, under such circumstances, would, ordinarily and naturally, draw a crowd of people about him, either from curiosity, or for the purpose of rescuing him from a perilous situation; all this he ought to have foreseen, and must be responsible for. Whether the crowd heard him call for help or not is immaterial; he had put himself in a situation to invite help, and they rushed forward, impelled, perhaps, by the double motive of rendering aid and gratifying a curiosity which he had excited. Can it be doubted, that if the plaintiff in error had beckoned to the crowd to come to his assistance, that he would be liable for their trespass in entering the enclosure? I think not. In that case, they would have been co-trespassers, and we must consider the situation in which he placed himself, voluntarily and designedly, as equivalent to a direct request to the crowd to follow him. In the present case, he did call for help, and may have been heard by the crowd; he is, therefore, undoubtedly, liable for all the injury sustained.

Judgment affirmed.

CROSBY v. COX AIRCRAFT COMPANY OF WASHINGTON

746 P.2d 1198 (Wash. 1987) (en banc)

CALLOW, Justice.

Should owners and operators of flying aircraft be held strictly liable for ground damage caused by operation of the aircraft, or should their liability depend on a finding of negligence?

The trial court determined that strict liability was applicable and awarded judgment in favor of the plaintiff landowners. We find that the general principles of negligence should control. We reverse and remand for trial.

I

The case involves a claim for property damage caused when a plane owned by Cox Aircraft Co. and piloted by Hal Joines (the pilot) crash-landed onto Douglas Crosby's property. The plane was a DeHavilland DHC-3 Otter aircraft. Its engine had recently been converted from piston-driven to turbine and the conversion had been undertaken in strict conformity with Federal Aviation Administration (FAA) requirements. FAA certification of the plane's fuel system was still pending at the time of the accident.

On December 19, 1984, the pilot flew the airplane over the Olympic Peninsula and then turned back to Seattle, intending to land at Boeing Field. However, the engine ran out of fuel in mid-flight and the pilot was forced to crash land the plane at Alki Point in West Seattle. The plane landed on the roof of Crosby's garage, causing $3,199.89 in damages.

Crosby sued both the pilot and Cox Aircraft. His complaint raised the following alternative allegations: (1) that the pilot was negligent in his operation of the plane; (2) that Cox Aircraft was negligent in its maintenance of the plane; (3) that Cox Aircraft, the alleged employer of the pilot, should be held vicariously liable for all negligence of the pilot under the doctrine of respondeat superior; and (4) that both the pilot and Cox Aircraft should be held strictly liable for all damages caused by the crash landing. The pilot and Cox Aircraft denied liability and filed a third-party complaint against Parker Hannifin Corporation alleging that Parker had equipped the plane with a defective fuel system control valve which failed to operate properly, thus causing the plane's engine to run out of fuel and forcing the pilot to make the crash landing.

The trial court granted partial summary judgment for Crosby, holding that both the pilot and Cox Aircraft were strictly liable for all damage done to Crosby's property. The court did not address Crosby's negligence claims, nor the third-party complaint against Parker. The pilot and Cox Aircraft appealed. We accepted certification.

The Boeing Company and the Washington State Trial Lawyer's Association (WSTLA) have both filed amicus curiae briefs regarding the appropriate standard of liability to be imposed. Boeing argues that the liability of aircraft owners and operators for ground damage should be governed by a negligence standard. WSTLA contends (as does plaintiff Crosby), on the other hand, that strict liability should be applied. The defendants argue for yet a third standard—a "rebuttable presumption" of negligence on the part of the aircraft owner and operator. We hold that the general principles of negligence control.

II

This is the first case in this State to directly deal with the standard of liability governing ground damage caused by aircraft. Mills v. Orcas Power & Light Co., 56 Wash.2d 807, 821 n. 6, 355 P.2d 781 (1960), alluded to this issue, but only in dicta. No subsequent cases have considered the question, and the Legislature has enacted no statute on the matter.

Plaintiff Crosby and amicus party WSTLA urge us to adopt Restatement (Second) of Torts § 520A (1977):

> § 520A. Ground Damage From Aircraft
>
> If physical harm to land or to persons or chattels on the ground is caused by the ascent, descent or flight of aircraft, or by the dropping or falling of an object from the aircraft,
>
> (a) the operator of the aircraft is subject to liability for the harm, even though he has exercised the utmost care to prevent it, and
>
> (b) the owner of the aircraft is subject to similar liability if he has authorized or permitted the operation.

This provision establishing strict liability is said to be a "special application" of §§ 519–20, the Restatement sections governing liability for "abnormally dangerous" activities. (See § 520A, Comment (a)). Sections 519–20 provide:

§ 519. General Principle

(1) One who carries on an abnormally dangerous activity is subject to liability for harm to the person, land or chattels of another resulting from the activity, although he has exercised the utmost care to prevent the harm.

(2) This strict liability is limited to the kind of harm, the possibility of which makes the activity abnormally dangerous.

§ 520. Abnormally Dangerous Activities

In determining whether an activity is abnormally dangerous, the following factors are to be considered:

(a) existence of a high degree of risk of some harm to the person, land or chattels of others;

(b) likelihood that the harm that results from it will be great;

(c) inability to eliminate the risk by the exercise of reasonable care;

(d) extent to which the activity is not a matter of common usage;

(e) inappropriateness of the activity to the place where it is carried on; and

(f) extent to which its value to the community is outweighed by its dangerous attributes.

The defendants urge us to reject Restatement § 520A. They contend that aviation can no longer be designated an "abnormally dangerous activity" requiring special rules of liability. We agree.

In the early days of aviation, the cases and treatises were replete with references to the hazards of "aeroplanes." The following assessment is typical:

> [E]ven the best constructed and maintained aeroplane is so incapable of complete control that flying creates a risk that the plane even though carefully constructed, maintained and operated, may crash to the injury of persons, structures and chattels on the land over which the flight is made.

Restatement (First) of Torts, § 520, Comment b (1938). As colorfully stated in Prosser & Keeton on Torts § 78, at 556 (5th ed. 1984):

> Flying was of course regarded at first as a questionable and highly dangerous enterprise, the province exclusively of venturesome fools....

In 1922 the Commission on Uniform State Laws proposed a new Uniform Aeronautics Act which, inter alia, made owners of aircraft strictly liable for all ground damage caused by the "ascent, descent or flight of the aircraft." Twenty-three states originally adopted this act by statute. By 1943, however, the Commissioners recognized that the act had become "obsolete," and it was removed from the list of uniform laws. 1 L. Kreindler, Aviation Accident Law § 6.01[1] at 6-1 to 6-2 (1986).

The number of states imposing strict liability has diminished significantly. At present, only six states retain the rule, and even these states apply it only to the owner of the aircraft. The aircraft operator remains liable only for damages caused by his own negligence. See Del.Code Ann., title 2, § 305 (1985); Hawaii Rev.Stat. § 263-5 (1985); Minn.Stat. § 360.012, subd. 4 (1986); N.J.Stat.Ann. § 6:2-7 (West 1973); S.C.Code § 55-3-60 (1977); Vt.Stat.Ann., title 5, §§ 224–225 (1972).

The modern trend followed by a majority of states is to impose liability only upon a showing of negligence by either the aircraft owner or operator. 1 L. Kreindler,

§ 6.01[5] at 6-9. Several states have legislated this rule by providing that ordinary tort law (or the law applicable to torts on land) applies to aviation accidents. Moreover, a number of courts have expressly disavowed the notion that aviation is an "ultrahazardous activity" requiring special rules of liability. Boyd v. White, 128 Cal.App.2d 641, 655, 276 P.2d 92 (1954); Wood v. United Air Lines, 32 Misc.2d 955, 960, 223 N.Y.S.2d 692 (1961), aff'd, 16 A.D.2d 659, 226 N.Y.S.2d 1022, appeal dismissed, 11 N.Y.2d 1053, 230 N.Y.S.2d 207, 184 N.E.2d 180 (1962); Little v. McGraw, 250 Ark. 766, 769, 467 S.W.2d 163 (1971). As observed in Boyd, 128 Cal.App.2d at 651, 276 P.2d 92:

> The courts and the law formerly looked upon aviation with the viewpoint still expressed in the American Law Institute, Restatement, Torts, Vol. 3, § 520, holding that aviation is an ultra-hazardous activity, similar to the operation of automobiles in the early days of the horseless carriage, and requiring those who take part in it to observe the highest degree of care. The Uniform Aeronautic Act, adopted in time by twenty-three states, imposed absolute liability on the owner, as well as the operator or lessee, of every aircraft for any damage to person or property caused by its operation provided there was no contributory negligence on the part of him who was thus harmed. With the passage of time, however, this view came to be modified, and the trend of decisions established it to be the general rule that, properly handled by a competent pilot exercising reasonable care, an airplane is not an inherently dangerous instrument, so that in the absence of statute the ordinary rules of negligence control, and the owner (or operator) of an airship is only liable for injury inflicted upon another when such damage is caused by a defect in the plane or its negligent operation. By 1945, coincident with the opening of the postwar civilian aviation period, the number of states retaining the portions of the Uniform Aeronautic Act dealing with an owner's liability had dropped to eighteen. (See also 6 Am.Jur.(Rev.), § 60, p. 36.)

We have discovered no cases relying on Restatement (Second) of Torts § 520A. That section is said to be a "special application" of § 519 and § 520(a–f), which impose strict liability on persons engaging in abnormally dangerous activities. An analysis of the individual factors listed in § 520 further persuades us that strict liability is inappropriate here.

Factor (a) of § 520 requires that the activity in question contain a "high degree of risk of some harm to the person, land or chattels of others." No such showing has been made. Indeed, statistics indicate that air transportation is far safer than automobile transportation. See, e.g., 3 Harper, James & Gray, The Law of Torts § 14.13 at 309–10 n.64 (1986); Comment, Aviation Law: Owner-Lessor Liability—The Need for Uniformity, 36 Maine L.Rev. 93, 98–99 (1984). Factor (b) speaks to the gravity of the harm—that is, in the unlikely event that an airplane accident occurs, whether there is a "likelihood that the [resulting harm] will be great." It is apparent that this possibility is present. However, this must be further evaluated in light of factor (c), which speaks of the "inability to eliminate the risk by the exercise of reasonable care." Given the extensive governmental regulation of aviation, see generally 14 CFR Ch. I (1978) (Federal Aviation Administration regulations), and the continuing technological improvements in aircraft manufacture, maintenance and operation, we conclude that the overall risk of serious injury from ground damage can be sufficiently reduced by the exercise of due care. Finally, factors (d), (e), and (f) do not favor the imposition of strict liability. Aviation is an activity of "common usage," it is appropriately conducted over populated areas, and its value to the community outweighs its dangerous attributes. Indeed, aviation is an integral part of modern society.

The causes of aircraft accidents are legion and can come from a myriad of sources. Every aircraft that flies is at risk from every bird, projectile and other aircraft. Accidents may be caused by improper placement of wires or buildings or from failure to properly mark and light such obstructions. The injury to the ground dweller may have been caused by faulty engineering, construction, repair, maintenance, metal fatigue, operation or ground control. Lightning, wind shear and other acts of God may have brought about a crash. Any listing of the causes of such accidents undoubtedly would fall short of the possibilities. In such circumstances the imposition of liability should be upon the blameworthy party who can be shown to be at fault. In King v. United States, 178 F.2d 320 (5th Cir.1949), a United States Army Air Force student pilot got drunk and took off in a training plane at midnight. Shortly thereafter he crashed into the plaintiff's home causing damages. The plaintiff brought suit under the Federal Tort Claims Act against the United States. The court found that the act of the student pilot was without the knowledge or consent of the Air Force, was unauthorized and that the pilot was acting outside of the scope of his duties. The court held that there should be no recovery against the government, stating succinctly:

> In a case of this nature, the United States cannot escape liability if a private person under similar circumstances should be held liable.
>
> There are no special statutory provisions that regulate or govern the responsibility of persons owning and operating airplanes. In the absence of such statutes, the rules of law applicable generally to torts govern. The ordinary rules of negligence and due care are invoked.

King at 321. See also Dahlstrom v. United States, 228 F.2d 819 (8th Cir.1956); Maitland v. Twin City Aviation Corp., 254 Wis. 541, 37 N.W.2d 74 (1949).

We are not persuaded that we should create a special rule of liability governing only ground damage caused by aircraft accidents. We note, for example, that passengers of airplanes involved in accidents must prove negligence to recover damages. Rathvon v. Columbia P. Airlines, 30 Wash.App. 193, 202–05, 633 P.2d 122 (1981); Baker v. United States, 417 F.Supp. 471, 486–88 (W.D.Wash.1975); 1 L. Kreindler, §6.01[1] at 6-3. As stated in Rathvon, 30 Wash.App. at 210–211, 633 P.2d 122:

> A carrier's failure to discover a latent defect is not negligence if it exercised the highest degree of care reasonably consistent with the practical operation of its business, and used the best precautions that were in common, practical use in the same business and had proved to be effective in discovering defects. Heggen v. Seattle, 47 Wn.2d 576, 288 P.2d 830 (1955).

We conclude that whether or not [the defendants] failed to exercise the highest degree of care according to the standards expressed above remains a genuine issue of material fact. This is true even though the likelihood of serious injury to a passenger is at least as great as is the case with persons or property on the ground.

We also emphasize that, although the plaintiff's recovery will depend on a showing of negligence, the plaintiff may of course employ the doctrine of res ipsa loquitur, if appropriate, to establish his negligence claim. Res ipsa is now frequently used in aviation crash cases and is widely recognized as an acceptable means of proving negligence. 1 L. Kreindler, §3.09[2] at 3-31. See generally Annot., Res Ipsa Loquitur in Aviation Accidents, 25 A.L.R.4th 1237 (1983).

Finally, the plaintiff raises an alternative argument that we apply the rule of strict liability to ground damages arising out of "test flights" of aircraft. We decline to do so. Plaintiff has cited no authority to support his claim that test flights of aircraft qualify as "abnormally dangerous" under Restatement (Second) of Torts §§ 519–20. The question is not whether test flights are more dangerous than routine aviation flights, but rather, whether they are so inherently dangerous that a "high degree of risk of harm" cannot be eliminated by the exercise of reasonable care. § 520(a), (c). In light of the extensive government regulation regarding the design, development, and testing of new and modified aircraft, see generally 14 CFR Ch. I, Subchapter C (1978) (Federal Aviation Administration certification procedures and airworthiness standards), we conclude that test flights are not abnormally dangerous.

We hold that owners and operators of flying aircraft are liable for ground damage caused by such aircraft only upon a showing of negligence. The partial summary judgment entered in favor of the plaintiff is reversed and the cause is remanded for trial.

BRACHTENBACH, Justice, dissenting.

What a peculiar, aberrant twist of tort law is created by the majority. Almost a decade ago we held that when a wine glass shatters in the hands of a wine drinker, the seller of the wine, who merely supplied the glass, is strictly liable. The law demanded and gave compensation without proof of fault. Shaffer v. Victoria Station, Inc., 91 Wash.2d 295, 588 P.2d 233 (1978). Today the majority tells the wholly innocent, inactive homeowner into whose home an airplane suddenly crashes "you must prove by a preponderance of the evidence that someone was at fault; never mind that you had no part in this damage, go forth and prove negligence and if you cannot, the loss is all yours." How can that be? The majority's answer is that it cannot fit these facts into a magic phrase—abnormally dangerous—which started in an 1868 case from England, Rylands v. Fletcher, 3 L.R.-E. & I. App. 330 (1868).

In fact and theory, it is a policy question whether to impose liability upon the pilot and owner of an airplane which crashes into the person or property of a wholly innocent person on the ground. Compelling, persuasive policy reasons exist to impose such strict liability. Those reasons should be explored and evaluated rather than simply accepting the pigeonhole conclusion that aviation is not abnormally dangerous as defined by the black letter rule of the Restatement (Second) of Torts, therefore, ipso facto, strict liability cannot be imposed. If the Restatement (Second) of Torts is to be followed, as the majority proposes, strict liability should result as discussed hereafter.

Unfortunately, the majority totally fulfills the prophecy of one text writer:

> It is predictable that some courts will be less likely to impose strict liability as a matter of common law development if the case cannot be fitted into some familiar mold such as trespass or abnormally dangerous activity. While this fact must be recognized, it should be regretted. Surely the step so clearly called for here is a small one as compared with many that courts have taken without aid of statute.

3 F. Harper, F. James & O. Gray, Torts § 14.13, at 311 n.68 (2d ed. 1986). My position is summarized by the same text:

> As the science of aviation has advanced, there seems to have been increasing reluctance to characterize it as an abnormally dangerous activity. But unwillingness to call aviation abnormally dangerous would not by any means prove that strict liability is inappropriate here. Ample justification for imposing it may be found in frequent difficulties of proof and the fact that these risks are properly allocated to aviation, especially where the victim is no participant in the enterprise.

3 F. Harper, F. James & O. Gray, Torts § 14.13, at 311 (2d ed. 1986) (footnote omitted).

If we assume that the aircraft operator is without legal fault, i.e., is not negligent, the policy issue is then clear. Which of two persons should bear the loss? In this case we have a totally innocent, nonacting homeowner whose property is suddenly invaded and damaged by an airplane—operated by the person who voluntarily chose to fly that airplane, for his own purpose and benefit. The result of the majority is that the wholly innocent, nonactive, nonbenefited, but damaged person must shoulder the burden of proving that the person who set in motion the forces which caused the damage was negligent.

It is apparent that fairness and common sense suggest that the loss should not be allocated to the innocent bystander. Much of the rationale for adopting strict product liability is applicable here and will be discussed hereafter.

The underlying policy which dictates strict liability is put thusly by the late Dean Prosser:

> There is "a strong and growing tendency, where there is blame on neither side, to ask, in view of the exigencies of social justice, who can best bear the loss and hence to shift the loss by creating liability where there has been no fault."

W. Prosser, Torts §75, at 494 (4th ed. 1971) (footnote and citation omitted).

The majority ignores this underlying policy question by noting that (1) air transportation is far safer than automobile transportation; (2) extensive governmental regulation and technological improvements reduce the overall risk of serious injury on the ground; (3) aviation is an integral part of society; and (4) the causes of aircraft accidents are legion. Those reasons are rather like consoling the widow by telling her that statistically her husband should have lived another 20 years.

One writer employs an appealing analysis which dictates strict liability. Professor Vold examines the benefits and creation of risks from a particular activity. If there is mutuality in the receipt of benefits and the creation of risks to others, the standard of liability is negligence. Thus where each user of a highway receives the direct benefit of such use but whose presence and conduct increases the risk of harm to the other, the law of negligence applies. But one-sidedness in the receipt of benefits and creation of risks should lead to strict liability. Vold, Strict Liability for Aircraft Crashes and Forced Landings on Ground Victims Outside of Established Landing Areas, 5 Hastings L.J. 1 (1953). This analysis is logical and satisfies the demands of justice. Its application here leads to strict liability.

Another factor favoring strict liability is the reality that the plaintiff in an aviation accident case faces difficult and potentially expensive burdens of proof. "Running through aviation cases, and frequently explaining their unusual results, is the frequently overwhelming difficulty and expense of investigation and preparation, and inherent problems and limitations of proof." 1 L. Kreindler, Aviation Accident Law §1.03[1], at 1-12 (1986).

It is widely recognized that difficulties of proof may justify imposition of strict liability. Indeed, such fact is described as a common feature of strict liability cases. Peck, Negligence and Liability Without Fault in Tort Law, 46 Wash.L.Rev. 225, 240 (1971).

The majority's holding is an extreme example of the unfairness of its conclusion and the denial of the realities of litigation. The plaintiff's only claim is for property damage of $3,199.89. The defendant aircraft owner denies negligence in maintenance or operation of the airplane. The defendant joined the manufacturer/distributor of a part used in the fuel system, alleging defective design or manufacture. The defendant joined six other property owners who may have been damaged. The hapless plaintiff, seeking a maximum of $3,199.89, is now, under the majority's holding, faced with the formidable task of proving negligence and is in the midst of a third-party fight over the very cause of the crash, plus an anticipated battle of experts over design and manufacture of an integral part of a fuel system in a plane being test flown for FAA certification. It takes no great insight to recognize that the expense of litigation amounts to a denial of plaintiff's right to damages.

The majority emphasizes that "although the plaintiff's recovery will depend on a showing of negligence, the plaintiff may of course employ the doctrine of res ipsa loquitur, if appropriate, to establish his negligence claim." The majority cites 1 L. Kreindler, Aviation Accident Law § 3.09[2], at 3-31 (1986), to support its assertion that res ipsa is now frequently used in aviation cases and is widely recognized as an acceptable means of proving negligence. That same author, in the same volume, states: "Suffice it to say that the use of res ipsa loquitur has been notoriously unsuccessful in airline crash cases." 1 L. Kreindler, § 1.03 [2], at 1-14. Nor does the majority cite the same author, same volume, § 3.09 [3] [f], at 3-41: "Thus where the specified purpose of the given flight is to test new or unproven aircraft, and an accident happens, a passenger may not have the benefit of res ipsa loquitur even though the defendant is an airline."

Another policy reason favoring strict liability is the ability of the offending activity to spread the financial risk through its enterprise or through liability insurance. Again, this is a judicially accepted rationale. Restatement (Second) of Torts § 402A, comment c (1965); Ulmer v. Ford Motor Co., 75 Wash.2d 522, 452 P.2d 729 (1969); Peck, 46 Wash.L.Rev. at 241.

Turning to the Restatement (Second) of Torts, the majority's result is exactly contrary to § 520A:

> If physical harm to land or to persons or chattels on the ground is caused by the ascent, descent or flight of aircraft, or by the dropping or falling of an object from the aircraft,
>
> (a) the operator of the aircraft is subject to liability for the harm, even though he has exercised the utmost care to prevent it, and
>
> (b) the owner of the aircraft is subject to similar liability if he has authorized or permitted the operation.

Restatement (Second) of Torts § 520A (1976).

To justify its rejection of the clear rule of § 520A, the majority holds that § 520A can have validity only if aviation can be denominated an abnormally dangerous activity. The majority then analyzes the factors set forth in § 520 to conclude that this particular activity did not meet the criteria of § 520, therefore § 520A does not apply. It relies upon comment a to § 520A: "This Section is a special application of the rule stated in § 519, together with that stated in § 520."

This result ignores the very scheme of these interrelated sections. Section 519 declares the general principle of liability; § 520 lists the factors to be considered in determining whether an activity is abnormally dangerous. Section 520A declares a special rule to ground damage. What the majority overlooks is that the authors of the Restatement (Second) of Torts in 1977 expressly intended that § 520A stand on its own, i.e., that it in fact was a special rule, quite distinct from § 520 requirements.

The majority, instead, rejects the very judgment and conclusion which led to the insertion of § 520A. This is proved by comment a to § 519 which states that it must be read together with various sections, including § 520A. This is highlighted by the comment to clause (c) under § 520 which clearly indicates that § 520A was a separate rule, quite apart from the factors of § 520, i.e., § 520A was in fact a separate and distinct rule of liability. It states: "As to strict liability for ground damage resulting from aviation, see § 520A." Restatement (Second) of Torts § 520, at 39 (1977).

It is crystal clear that § 520A was not intended to be dependent upon a separate analysis under § 520 as the majority holds. When § 520A was introduced into the Restatement of Torts, the Advisers and the Council of The American Law Institute all agreed that there should be a separate section on ground damage from aircraft. The proposed section would have imposed no liability unless the harm was intentional or caused by negligence except for abnormally dangerous operation. Nine of the thirteen advisers rejected the proposal, wishing to retain strict liability. Those advisers included such illuminaries as Fleming, Keeton, Seavey, Traynor and Wade. The Council accepted the new section as written. The Reporter, William L. Prosser, was not free from doubt. Restatement (Second) of Torts (Tent. Draft No. 10, 1964) and Reporter's Notes to Institute, at 69. Eventually the Institute disapproved the distinction between "normal" and "abnormal" flight and adopted the present strict liability contained in § 520A. Restatement (Second) of Torts, at 1 (Tent. Draft No. 12, 1966). It was published in volume 3 in 1977. Section 520A remains in existence today, but the majority does not adopt it, preferring to reach a result contrary to that of eminent scholars and practitioners who fought out the very battle which the majority now resurrects.

The majority attempts to buttress its result by an analysis of each factor listed in § 520, finding most to be lacking. Such analysis is irrelevant in light of the language in the comments and of the history of § 520A. Nonetheless I will review the majority's conclusions. First, it is not necessary that each of the factors in § 520 be present to meet the test. Comment f states that ordinarily several of the six elements will be required for strict liability, but that it is not necessary that each of them be present, especially if others weigh heavily.

The heart of § 520 is contained in this language: "The essential question is whether the risk created is so unusual, either because of its magnitude or because of the circumstances surrounding it, as to justify the imposition of strict liability for the harm that results from it, even though it is carried on with all reasonable care." Restatement (Second) of Torts § 520, comment f, at 37–38 (1977).

The first factor in § 520(a) is a high degree of risk of harm. The majority asserts that no such showing has been made, relying on statistics cited in several footnotes. This conclusion misses the point. The question is not whether it is statistically more safe to fly in an airplane than ride in a car, which is all the majority states. The question rather is whether there is a high degree of risk of some harm when an airplane lands on someone's house. Comment g makes it perfectly clear that if the potential harm is sufficiently great, the likelihood that it will take place may be comparatively slight and yet the activity be regarded as abnormally dangerous.

This comment is perfectly logical. The actor cannot hide behind relative statistics; if serious potential harm exists, that is enough. The harm need not occur in 51 percent of the activities. Any other interpretation, such as the majority's, would allow the defendant to escape by proving "while our dynamite leveled 3 square city blocks, it doesn't happen very often."

The majority acknowledges that the likelihood of great harm exists, factor (b). Factor (c) speaks of the inability to eliminate the risk by the exercise of reasonable care.

The majority concludes that because of extensive governmental regulation and continuing technological improvements in aircraft manufacture, maintenance, and operation the overall risk of serious injury from ground damage can be "sufficiently reduced by the exercise of due care." Where the majority gets its technical information escapes me, although I know for certain that it is not from the record.

The comment makes clear that what is referred to is the unavoidable risk remaining even though the actor has taken reasonable care. It is interesting to note that after asserting that due care "sufficiently" (whatever that means) reduces the risk of serious injuries, the majority immediately states that the causes of aircraft accidents are legion, and can come from a myriad of sources including lightning, wind shear and acts of God. Indeed the majority speculates that any listing of accident causes undoubtedly would fall short of the possibilities.

Thus the majority's reasoning is that regulation and technology prove that aircraft can be operated with minimal risk, but the causes of accidents, including acts of God, are so legion that the possibilities cannot be listed.

The majority manipulates its own statistics about aviation safety by including statistics for regularly scheduled commercial airlines. To the extent that it is relevant, it is significant to note that the accident rate for general aviation is more than 6.5 times greater than for scheduled commercial airlines. National Transportation Safety Board, Annual Report app. A (1985). Further casting doubt upon the validity of the majority's conclusory statements that regulation and improved technology has "sufficiently reduced" the risk of harm are the actual statistics. The accident rate per 100,000 hours for general aviation in 1980 was 9.86 whereas in 1984 it had only reduced to 9.56. National Transportation Safety Board, Annual Report app. G, (1985). In any event, such statistics are of little consolation to this losing plaintiff.

The majority in five lines concludes that factors (d), (e), and (f) do not favor imposition of strict liability. Factor (d) is the extent to which the activity is not a matter of common usage. The majority simply says it is a matter of common usage. Once again the majority ignores the expressed thrust of the Restatement. Comment i indicates that an activity is a matter of common usage if it is customarily carried on by the great mass of mankind or by many people in the community. The majority likewise ignores the reasoning of our holding in Langan v. Valicopters, Inc., 88 Wash.2d 855, 864, 567 P.2d 218 (1977) where we recognized that crop dusting is prevalent and done in large portions of the Yakima Valley, but was not of common usage when carried on by 287 aircraft. An analogy makes clear the faulty premise in the majority's reasoning. Elevators are in common usage and are used by many. That does not make the operation of elevators a matter of common usage.

While there are relatively significant numbers of private pilots, such flying is hardly customarily carried on by the great mass of mankind or by many people in the community. "Many people in the community" is necessarily a relative term. How many people in the community carry on the activity in relation to the size of the community? Using the very statistics cited by the majority (Comment, Aviation Law: Owner-Lessor Liability—The Need for Uniformity, 36 Me.L.Rev. 93 (1984)) the percentage of private pilots in the United States is .0003 percent of the population. When three people out of 10,000 are private pilots it is readily apparent that flying of private aircraft is not carried on by "many people in the community." To a certainty, private flying of a plane to test a noncertified fuel system is not of common usage, the majority's contrary bald assertion notwithstanding.

I agree, as a general proposition, that flying over populated areas is not an inappropriate activity, factor (e). However, attempting to land in a populated area where there is no airport is not appropriate. The locale of the particular incident is what is important, e.g., oil drilling in a residential area is not an appropriate activity. Green v. General Petroleum Corp., 205 Cal. 328, 270 P. 952 (1928).

The last factor, (f), value to the community is marginally relevant and does not outweigh those factors which favor strict liability.

The drafters of the Restatement (Second) of Torts rejected the very points relied upon by the majority. They recognized the great improvement in safety, but found that the risk of harm to anyone on the ground is obvious, that it cannot be said that danger of ground damage has been so eliminated or reduced that ordinary rules of negligence would apply, and that the gravity of the harm is still a factor even though there may be relatively few cases where it occurs. Further, there was the obvious fact that those on the ground are quite helpless to select any locality in which they will not be exposed to the risk, however minimized it may be. Finally they note that while thousands participate in aviation, those who actually carry on the activity itself are relatively few. Restatement (Second) of Torts, at 1 (Tent. Draft No. 12, 1966).

In summary, I would affirm the trial court which held that strict liability applies.

VIRGILIO EX REL. VIRGILIO v. CITY OF NEW YORK

407 F.3d 105 (2d Cir. 2005),
cert. denied, 2006 WL 89113 (2006)

WESLEY, Circuit Judge.

In a series of tragic and terrifying attacks on September 11, 2001, terrorists killed thousands in Pennsylvania, Virginia, and New York, caused extensive damage to the Pentagon, and brought about the collapse of the North and South Towers of the World Trade Center ("WTC"). As with other catastrophes, true heros responded, not the least among them the brave firefighters, police, and first-response units of the City of New York. Plaintiffs are the personal representatives of firefighters who lost their lives in responding to the WTC following the attacks. Plaintiffs' complaint focuses on the failure of radio-transmission equipment in the North and South Towers that prevented firefighters from receiving evacuation orders before the Towers' collapse. Plaintiffs commenced this action for wrongful death against New York City (the "City") on December 22, 2003, and filed an amended complaint as of right on January 20, 2004, that added Motorola, Inc. ("Motorola") as a defendant.

Plaintiffs claim that Motorola negligently and intentionally provided the City with radio-transmission communication equipment for firefighters that Motorola knew to be ineffective in high-rise structures like the Towers of the WTC, that Motorola made fraudulent material misrepresentations to secure contracts with the City, and that those acts and representations caused decedents' deaths. Plaintiffs also press a series of wrongful death claims against the City based upon its alleged failure to meet duties imposed on the City under New York law to provide adequate and safe radio-transmission equipment. Finally, in Count 8 of the Amended Complaint, plaintiffs allege that the City and Motorola engaged in concerted action in an attempt to deprive firefighters of adequate protection and to "engage in fraudulent misrepresentations and deceitful conduct."

Shortly after the disaster, Congress passed the Air Transportation Safety and System Stabilization Act (the "Air Stabilization Act" or the "Act"). Pub.L. No. 107-42, 115 Stat. 230 (2001). The statute limited liability for the air carriers involved in the tragedy to their insurance coverage, see Air Stabilization Act § 408(a); created the Victim Compensation Fund (the "Fund") to provide no-fault compensation to victims who were injured in the attacks and to personal representatives of victims killed in the attacks, see id. §§ 402(3), 405(a)(1), (b), (c); and provided an election of remedies—all claimants who filed with the Fund waived the right to sue for injuries resulting from the attacks except for collateral benefits, see id. § 405(c)(3)(B)(I). On November 19, 2001, the Act was amended by the Aviation and Transportation Security Act (the "Aviation Security Act"). Pub.L. No. 107-71, 115 Stat. 597 (2001). Significantly, the amendments extended liability limits to aircraft manufacturers, those with a proprietary interest in the WTC, and the City of New York, see id. § 201(b), while allowing Fund claimants to sue individuals responsible for the attacks notwithstanding the waiver, see id. § 201(a).

Under the Act, the final date by which claimants could submit claims to the Fund was December 22, 2003. See Air Stabilization Act §§ 405(a)(3), 407; 28 C.F.R. 104.62. The Special Master appointed to oversee the Fund, Kenneth R. Feinberg, extended the filing date to January 22, 2004, for those claimants who previously submitted incomplete claims. The Special Master promulgated an application form that notified claimants of the waiver provision and required claimants to sign an acknowledgment of waiver. The acknowledgment of waiver tracked the language of the statutory waiver provision.

A number of September 11-related cases were consolidated before Judge Hellerstein. On December 19, 2003, Judge Hellerstein issued an order addressing when the waiver via assertion of Fund claims would become effective. See In re September 11 Litig., 21 MC 97, 2003 WL 23145579 (S.D.N.Y. Dec.19, 2003). Judge Hellerstein held that "submission" of Fund claims—triggering the waiver provision—occurs on the earlier of when a Fund filing is substantially complete as determined by the Special Master or January 22, 2004. Id. at *2.

A day after filing their amended complaint, plaintiffs moved by Order to Show Cause on January 21, 2004, asking that the court permit them to continue their lawsuit against defendants despite having filed claims with the Fund. Alternatively, plaintiffs asked the court to stay Judge Hellerstein's earlier orders—which required that cases brought by 9/11 victims with Fund awards pending as of January 22, 2004, be dismissed—or to place their case on the suspense docket of the consolidated In re September 11 Litigation docket until a general consolidated conference previously set by Judge Hellerstein for February 6, 2004, took place. Because of the January 22nd deadline for completing previously filed but incomplete Fund claims, Judge Haight held a hearing on the 22nd on the motion and issued a ruling from the bench finding that the statute's waiver provision barred the suit against the City or Motorola: "'the plaintiffs' claims against both the City and Motorola are subject to the limitation on civil actions provided for in Section 405(c)(3)(B)(i) of the statute.'" Virgilio v. Motorola, Inc., 307 F.Supp.2d 504, 514 (S.D.N.Y.2004) (Haight, J.) (quoting transcript).

On January 29, 2004, Judge Haight issued a detailed decision that set forth his reasons for finding that plaintiffs' claims were barred as a result of their decision to file with the Fund. See id. at 514–20. Although the court denied the relief requested in the Order to Show Cause on a finding that the waiver provision barred plaintiffs' claims, it did not dismiss the amended complaint as defendants had yet to file answers and had little time to oppose the Order to Show Cause other than through argument of counsel before Judge Haight. Because plaintiffs' case raised 9/11 claims similar to those in [the] In re September 11 Litigation, Judge Haight transferred the case to Judge Hellerstein's "suspense docket" of the consolidated In re September 11 Litigation docket. Id. at 521.

On January 30, 2004, the next day, the City moved to dismiss the amended complaint pursuant to Fed.R.Civ.P. 12(b)(6) or for summary judgment on several grounds, including the Act's waiver provision; the expiration of the statute of limitations for wrongful death actions against municipalities; and plaintiffs' failure to serve timely notices of claim against the City. Motorola moved to dismiss the amended complaint on the ground of waiver.

Judge Hellerstein dismissed the complaint in an unpublished decision. See Virgilio v. Motorola, Inc., No. 03 Civ. 10156(AKH), 2004 WL 433789 (S.D.N.Y. Mar.10, 2004). The district court adopted Judge Haight's decision noting that "the waiver provision applies to all of the claims against Motorola and the City of New York.... As plaintiffs have elected their remedy, they have also waived the right to bring a civil action 'for damages sustained as a result of the terrorist-related aircraft crashes of September 11, 2001.'" Id. at *2 (quoting Air Stabilization Act § 405(c)(3)(B)(i)).

Plaintiffs appealed, and we now affirm.

Discussion

When confronted with an appeal from the dismissal of a complaint, we review the matter anew, see, e.g., Conopco, Inc. v. Roll Int'l, 231 F.3d 82, 86 (2d Cir.2000), and take as true the complaint's allegations. A complaint may be dismissed for failure to state a claim only if there are no legal grounds upon which relief may be granted. See Jacobs v. Ramirez, 400 F.3d 105, 106 (2d Cir.2005); Fed.R.Civ.P. 12(b)(6). The task at hand reduces itself to examining the statute and assessing its impact on this case.

A. Statutory Scheme

The Air Stabilization Act establishes the Fund and delegates to the Attorney General the authority to appoint a Special Master to oversee victim compensation. See Air Stabilization Act §§ 401–09. As Congress noted, one purpose of the Fund is "to provide compensation to any individual (or relatives of a deceased individual) who was physically injured or killed as a result of the terrorist-related aircraft crashes of September 11, 2001." Id. § 403. However, eligibility for Fund payment "is conditioned upon a waiver by claimants of 'the right to file any civil action' in state or federal court" except for civil actions against those responsible for the attack or to recover collateral source obligations. Schneider v. Feinberg, 345 F.3d 135, 139 (2d Cir.2003) (quoting Air Stabilization Act § 405(c)(3)(B)). Because the Act seeks to provide quick no-fault compensation decisions for victims while capping the litigation exposure of front-line defendants, it is quite clear that the Act's "general purpose is to protect the airline industry and other potentially liable entities from financially fatal liabilities while ensuring that those injured or killed in the terrorist attacks receive adequate compensation." Canada Life Assurance Co. v. Converium Rückversicherung (Deutschland) AG, 335 F.3d 52, 55 (2d Cir.2003) (citing 147 Cong. Rec. S9594 (daily ed. Sept. 21, 2001) (statement of Sen. McCain)).

Sections 405 and 408(b) set forth general guidelines and requirements for Fund claims and create a federal cause of action for claims relating to 9/11. See id. §§ 405, 408(b). Section 405(c)(3)(B)(i) contains the waiver provision central to this case:

> (B) LIMITATION ON CIVIL ACTION.—
>
> (i) IN GENERAL. Upon the submission of a claim under this title, the claimant waives the right to file a civil action (or to be a party to an action) in any Federal or State court for damages sustained as a result of the terrorist-related aircraft crashes of September 11, 2001. The preceding sentence does not

> apply to a civil action to recover collateral source obligations, or to a civil action against any person who is a knowing participant in any conspiracy to hijack any aircraft or commit any terrorist act.

As amended by the Aviation Security Act, § 201(a).

While section 405 creates a system for determining Fund eligibility outside of the litigation context, section 408 funnels all civil litigation for actions "resulting from or relating to the terrorist-related aircraft crashes of September 11, 2001" into the Southern District of New York by granting that court "original and exclusive jurisdiction" over such actions, id. § 408(b)(3), and provides that the "substantive law for decision in any such suit shall be derived from the law ... of the State in which the crash occurred unless such law is inconsistent with or preempted by Federal law," id. § 408(b)(2). As noted above, section 408 caps the liability of air carriers, aircraft manufacturers, holders of proprietary interests in the WTC, and the City. See id. § 408(a), 408(a)(1), 408(a)(3); Aviation Security Act § 201(b).

B. Statutory Waiver Provision: Air Stabilization Act § 405(c)(3)(B)(i)

We agree with the district court that under the plain language of the statute, claimants who have filed claims with the Fund have waived "the right to file a civil action ... for damages sustained as a result of the terrorist-related aircraft crashes of September 11, 2001" and that the waiver bars claims for "damages sustained" against non-airline defendants. We affirm the district court's determination and find plaintiffs' claim barred by their election of remedies.

Plaintiffs assert that the waiver provision does not apply to claims against the defendants because the correct interpretation of that section bars suits against only the airplane-transportation industry. Plaintiffs present three arguments to support their contention: they assert that the district court misinterpreted Congress's purpose in enacting the Air Stabilization Act; that the waiver provision should be examined in the context of its relationship to the statute and subsequent amendments to the Air Stabilization Act; and that the legislative history of the waiver provision supports a narrower interpretation of that provision than that employed by the district court. The City and Motorola counter that the plain language unambiguously bars the current suit and that the legislative history of the Act further supports their view.

When interpreting a statute, the "first step ... is to determine whether the language at issue has a plain and unambiguous meaning with regard to the particular dispute in the case. Our inquiry must cease if the statutory language is unambiguous and 'the statutory scheme is coherent and consistent.'" Robinson v. Shell Oil Co., 519 U.S. 337, 340, 117 S.Ct. 843, 136 L.Ed.2d 808 (1997) (quoting United States v. Ron Pair Enters., Inc., 489 U.S. 235, 240, 109 S.Ct. 1026, 103 L.Ed.2d 290 (1989)). Further, "[t]he plainness or ambiguity of statutory language is determined by reference to the language itself, the specific context in which that language is used, and the broader context of the statute as a whole." Id. at 341 (citing Estate of Cowart v. Nicklos Drilling Co., 505 U.S. 469, 477, 112 S.Ct. 2589, 120 L.Ed.2d 379 (1992) and McCarthy v. Bronson, 500 U.S. 136, 139, 111 S.Ct. 1737, 114 L.Ed.2d 194 (1991)). Thus, we begin with the language of the statute itself.

In our view, the waiver provision is unambiguous. The language of the waiver provision clearly states that Fund claimants waive their right to bring civil actions resulting from any harm caused by the 9/11 attacks: "[u]pon the submission of a claim..., the claimant waives the right to file a civil action ... in any Federal or State court for damages sustained as a result of the terrorist-related aircraft crashes of September 11, 2001." Air Stabilization Act § 405(c)(3)(B)(i). The waiver provision plainly requires litigants to choose between risk-free compensation and civil litigation. If this waiver provision is ambiguous as plaintiffs suggest, few if any statutory provisions could be viewed as clear.

The overall structure of the Act highlights two predominate concerns: to insulate the airline industry from massive—virtually limitless—liability arising from the sudden and devastating acts of wanton cruelty on 9/11 and to provide an adequate no-fault system of compensation to victims. See Canada Life Assurance Co., 335 F.3d at 55. The statute balanced the certainty of a no-fault recovery against the relinquishment of one's right to bring a federal action—created by the statute—for injuries arising from the disaster. See Schneider, 345 F.3d at 139; Canada Life Assurance Co., 335 F.3d at 55 (noting Fund compensation "in exchange for a waiver of their rights to file a civil action"); cf. § 408(b) (creating a federal cause of action for "damages arising out of the hijacking"). Without the Act, victims and their families could seek compensation only through litigation in state or federal courts. The terrorists carried out four separate attacks in three locations—two of which involved the damage or destruction of government and office buildings and a concomitant loss of lives within those structures and the areas adjacent to them. Thus, the number of plaintiffs, possible defendants, and theories of recovery were as diverse as the confluence of misfortunes that befell each victim. Moreover, the litigation scatter pattern presented the possibility of lawsuits in state and federal courts nationwide.

While the potential liability to the air carriers and airplane manufacturers involved was monumental, the prospect for recovery by the victims and their families was not certain. A verdict against the air carriers or other potential defendants, such as the City or Motorola, was not guaranteed. In addition, the scope of liability was so substantial that the prospect of Bankruptcy Court for the air carriers was real. In order to provide the certainty of recovery for victims and their families, Congress created the Fund, which provides loss-based awards without an assessment of fault or responsibility for the loss. All the victims or their representatives need establish is presence at the site of a 9/11 attack and physical injury or death as a result of the attacks. See Air Stabilization Act § 405(c)(2).

The Act centralizes the victims' litigation claims in one federal court while applying the substantive state law of the locus of the injury. It recognizes that the airline industry might not be able to withstand the litigation tidal wave the attacks would create. It also recognizes that such an onslaught would likely leave many victims and their families waiting years, while blame for the attacks and the resulting injuries is parsed out among hundreds of defendants leaving plaintiffs to recover only a small pro rata share of a fair award in Bankruptcy Court. Thus, the statute carries out a careful balancing of a number of important interests. It gives claimants a reasonable choice between an administrative claim or litigation centralized in one court in which the primary defendants would have limits to their exposure. In our view, there is no inconsistency in compensating victims and their families at a price of complete litigation peace.

It is clear to us that plaintiffs' claims are within the scope of the waiver provision. Here, plaintiffs damages arose "as a result" of the terrorist-related attacks. Plaintiffs assert that the waiver should not reach defendants' alleged tortious conduct. In plaintiffs' view, defendants' acts independently caused plaintiffs' injuries. But, in fact, the injuries to plaintiffs and their loved ones resulted from a series of interrelated events that began with the terrorist attack. Even assuming independent, successive tortious acts by both the terrorists and defendants, as we must on this motion to dismiss, we are hard pressed to find plaintiffs' damages did not result—at least in part—from the terrorist attacks.

Indeed, plaintiffs overlook the very language of the statute that defines their eligibility for compensation for the Fund. The Act provides that anyone, or their relative, who was present at and injured or killed as a result of the terrorist-related aircraft crashes of September 11, 2001, may file a claim with the Fund. See Air Stabilization Act § 405(c)(2). In our view, plaintiffs cannot embrace the statute's broad view that many people, in widely differing circumstances, died "as a result" of the attacks while simultaneously constricting the same language in the waiver to include only the airlines. Compare id. § 405(c)(2) with id. § 405(c)(3)(B)(i).

Plaintiffs also contend that amendments to the Air Stabilization Act reveal the limited scope of the waiver provision. This argument continues to ignore the plain language of the waiver and confuses the effect of the amendments. On November 19, 2001, Congress amended the Air Stabilization Act in two significant respects. Section 201(a) of the Aviation Security Act altered the exception in the waiver provision to allow "civil action[s] against any person who is a knowing participant in any conspiracy to hijack any aircraft or commit any terrorist act." Thus, Fund claimants have not waived their right to sue those responsible for the attacks. Certainly, had Congress chosen to constrict the scope of the waiver further, as plaintiffs would have us do, it could have done so—it did not.

The amendment also altered section 408. As originally enacted, this section capped the airlines' liability for compensatory and punitive damages at the level of insurance carried by the airlines. See Air Stabilization Act § 408(a). Thus, even if a plaintiff chose to pursue civil litigation over filing a Fund claim, the airlines' exposure in federal court would not exceed their coverage. The amendment brought the City (and others) within the protection of the liability cap:

> Liability for all claims, whether for compensatory or punitive damages or for contribution or indemnity arising from the terrorist-related aircraft crashes of September 11, 2001, against the City of New York shall not exceed the greater of the city's insurance coverage or $350,000,000. If a claimant ... submits a claim under section 405, the claimant waives the right to file a civil action (or to be a party to an action) in any Federal or State court for damages sustained as a result of the terrorist-related aircraft crashes of September 11, 2001, including any such action against the City of New York.

Aviation Security Act § 201(b)(2) (amending Air Stabilization Act § 408(a) and adding § 408(a)(1), (3)).

Plaintiffs contend that the amendment's repetition of the waiver language in the liability-limiting section indicates that the protection of section 405's waiver provision is limited to actions against airline industry-related defendants. They argue that had the waiver included the City before the amendment, there would be no need to mention the waiver when limiting the City's exposure in federal court. In essence, plaintiffs would define the sweep of the waiver by the scope of the limitation of liability sections of the statute. That ignores the fact that the language of the waiver is broad and unlimited while the limitation of liability provision is specific. It also ignores the purpose and effect of each provision.

Limitations on liability are just that. They are caps on recoveries in litigation against defendants facing primary, stunning exposure by nonclaim-filing plaintiffs. The waiver provision on the other hand seeks to force a choice between a risk-free claim with the Fund or a lawsuit in federal court. Thus, a plaintiff who elects litigation still faces the prospect that the primary defendants will exhaust their coverage—and their liability—

before plaintiff achieves a verdict, while a plaintiff choosing the certainty of the Fund does so at the cost of releasing all his claims with only limited exceptions.

Contrary to plaintiffs' argument, neither the extension of limited liability to the City nor the inclusion of waiver language in that extension support the assertion that the waiver provision of section 405 protects only the airlines or the air-transportation industry. The restatement of the waiver did not pronounce a new extension of the waiver to the City, nor did it introduce an ambiguity into the clear and concise waiver provision. The clause notes that the filing of a claim waives one's right to bring an action in federal court for injuries resulting—in part—from the terrorist attacks against anyone, including the City, other than collateral-source obligors or those responsible for the attacks. See Air Stabilization Act § 408(b)(3) (as amended by Aviation Security Act § 201(b)). In our view, the amendments reinforce the view that the plain and broad language of section 405(c)(3)(B)(i) already encompassed any claim for damages sustained as a result of the terrorist-related aircraft crashes.

C. Scope of Waiver for "Damages Sustained" and Viability of Any Remaining Claim to Punitive Damages Under New York Law

Plaintiffs assert that even if the waiver provision applies to the City and Motorola, the waiver refers only to compensatory damages. They contend that under New York law they may maintain an action solely for punitive damages against the City and Motorola. Defendants counter that this argument, not offered below, is waived; that the plain meaning of "damages sustained" bars any civil recovery; and that New York law bars plaintiffs from suing solely for punitive damages without a concomitant claim for compensatory damages....

In our view the statutorily imposed waiver—set out in the acknowledgment each plaintiff signed when they filed their Fund claim—is the functional equivalent of [a] satisfaction and release. Under the language of the statute, plaintiffs have waived their right to file "a civil action" for damages sustained. Plaintiffs had a right to seek damages to redress the wrongs they and their loved ones suffered through a civil action against defendants. That right encompassed compensatory damages and, if appropriate, punitive damages for egregious conduct. But once the compensatory claim was satisfied, the parasitic claim for punitive damages was also extinguished. Adopting plaintiffs' position would require us to ignore well-established New York law and to abrogate the clear language of Congress that once a Fund claim is made, the universe of potential defendants is constricted to only terrorists responsible for the carnage and collateral-source providers.

D. Plaintiffs' Due Process Arguments

Lastly, the plaintiffs contend the district court erred in failing to conduct a factual inquiry into whether each plaintiff made a knowing and voluntary waiver of their right to bring a civil action before filing Fund claims. Plaintiffs never raised this argument below. We decline to exercise our discretion to entertain it. Unlike the interpretation of the scope of the waiver provision or the viability of claims for punitive damages under New York law, plaintiffs' argument for why the district court should have conducted a factual inquiry into the "knowing and voluntary" nature of the waiver conflicts with the positions of the parties presented to Judge Haight or Judge Hellerstein; we will not entertain it. We have considered plaintiffs' remaining contentions and find them without merit for substantially the same reasons stated in the opinions issued by Judge Haight and Judge Hellerstein.

* * *

We close with a general observation. The events of September 11, 2001, changed this nation in ways that will not be fully understood for generations to come. However, the pain and sense of loss that the victims and their families feel need not wait the judgment of history—their anguish, we are sure, is a daily companion. As judges, we are not unmindful of the great sacrifice that many of New York's bravest men and women made on behalf of those who were trapped in the burning towers at Church and Vesey Streets. If Article III of the Constitution somehow gave us the power to turn back time and undo the disaster we would set to the task without reservation. Unfortunately, we have only the power to assess the law as it is given to us by Congress. Such is the nature of judging.

Notes

1. *Guille* generally is recognized as the world's first reported aviation case. Notice, however, that the issue it raises (liability for damage done to persons and property on the ground by a falling aircraft) is the same one that, nearly 200 years later, confronts the courts in *Crosby* and *Virgilio*. How is this possible?

As it happens, the risks to ground interests posed by aircraft was an early concern of aviation law experts. As a result, in 1933 an international treaty on the subject was concluded in Rome; in 1938, a protocol was added at Brussels. In 1952, a successor instrument was promulgated, again in Rome (*see* Appendix 7); in 1978, a protocol was added at Montreal (*see* Appendix 17). The Rome Convention (as it is commonly called) imposes absolute liability for surface injuries but caps damages according to the weight of the aircraft. Although it participated in its drafting, the United States has declined to join the treaty because it continues to favor higher damage limits and liability based on a rebuttal presumption of fault. *See further* Harold Caplan, *Post 9/11-Air Carrier Liability Towards Third Parties on Land or Water as a Consequence of War or Terrorism*, 30 Air & Space L. 5 (2005).

2. While the court in *Guille* opts for strict liability, the court in *Crosby* finds comparative negligence to be the correct standard. In *Virgilio*, however, the court defers to a non-adjudicatory system of governmental compensation (the September 11th victims' fund). Of these three models, which one do you prefer (and why)? *See further* Erin G. Holt, *The September 11 Victim Compensation Fund: Legislative Justice Sui Generis*, 59 N.Y.U. Ann. Surv. Am. L. 513 (2004). *See also* Speedy Rice & Shana Fitzpatrick, *Terrorism and the Aviation Industry: Insights From the 1929 Warsaw Convention*, 78 N.D. L. Rev. 713 (2002).

3. As *Crosby* explains, § 520 of the *Restatement of Torts* and § 520A of the *Restatement (Second) of Torts* both deemed flying to be an "abnormally dangerous" activity. However, in Proposed Final Draft No. 1 (2005) of the *Restatement (Third) of Torts: Liability for Physical Harm*, these provisions have been replaced with a new catch-all (designated § 20) that covers all abnormally dangerous activities. In a lengthy aside to comment k, the reporters include "a special note on aviation ground damage" that extensively reviews the history of §§ 520 and 520A. It then concludes as follows:

> Given all of the above, the majority opinion in Crosby v. Cox Aircraft Co., 746 P.2d 1198 (Wash.1987), is undoubtedly correct in concluding that aviation does not fit the formal Restatement criteria for an abnormally dangerous activity. The risk of serious ground damage when all reasonable care is exercised is

> very small; and given both the number of flights and the percentage of the population that travels by air, commercial aviation is in common usage. Nevertheless, as Comment f has emphasized, one rationale for strict liability relates to the defendant's exclusive control over the instrumentality of harm, and this rationale is impressively applicable in aviation ground-damage cases. As the dissent in Crosby states, the plaintiff in a ground-damage case may well be a "wholly innocent, inactive homeowner into whose home an airplane suddenly crashes." Id. at 1202, 1203.
>
> In light of all of this, the issue of strict liability for aviation ground damage can be regarded as difficult. Even so, the doctrinal argument against strict liability—that almost all airline crashes are due to negligence—confirms that the strict-liability issue is no longer one that has major practical significance (and similarly explains why there are so few modern cases considering the issue). In these circumstances, the issue is left open in this Restatement.

In your opinion, is flying abnormally dangerous? In answering this question, be sure to keep in mind the difference between commercial and general aviation (this distinction was downplayed by the *Crosby* majority but was rightly deemed important by Justice Brachtenbach in his dissent). In 2004, commercial aviation recorded 17 million hours of flight and suffered 21 accidents, of which one was fatal (13 people died), a casualty rate of 0.124 per 100,000 flight hours. In contrast, general aviation logged 25.9 million hours of flight and suffered 1,614 accidents, of which 312 were fatal (killing 556 people), a casualty rate of 6.22 per 100,000 flight hours. *See Aviation Accident Statistics*, at www.ntsb.gov/aviation/stats.htm. (These figures, it should be pointed out, reflect only United States aviation and exclude experimental, military, and ultralight aircraft). *See also* Evan P. Singer, Comment, *Recent Developments in Aviation Safety: Proposals to Reduce the Fatal Accident Rate and the Debate Over Data Protection*, 67 J. Air L. & Com. 499 (2002), and Brian Knowlton & Don Phillips, *August Ranks as the Deadliest Month for Air Crashes in 3 Years*, N.Y. Times, Aug. 25, 2005, at A6 (discussing the unusually large number of commercial flights, all outside the United States, that crashed in August 2005).

The greater risks posed by non-commercial aviation become particularly apparent when one considers the numerous celebrities who have died in these sorts of flights. Such persons include: Representative (and House Majority Leader) Hale Boggs Sr. (D-La.) (1972), Governor Mel Carnahan (D-Mo.) (2000), singer Patsy Cline (1963), baseball player Roberto Clemente (1972), singer Jim Croce (1973), singer John Denver (1997), United Nations Secretary-General Dag Hammarskjöld (1961), singer Aaliyah Haughton (2001), Senator John Heinz (R-Pa.) (1991), singer Buddy Holly (1959), publisher John F. Kennedy, Jr. (1999), boxer Rocky Marciano (1969), baseball player Thurman Munson (1979), TV star Ricky Nelson (1985), singer Otis Redding (1967), humorist Will Rogers (1935), golfer Payne Stewart (1999), and Senator Paul Wellstone (D-Minn.) (2002). It should be pointed out, however, that general aviation gets safer every year as new technology and better training becomes available. *See further* www.gaservingamerica.com.

Problem 3

A group of legal experts has proposed the creation of an "International Court of Air Transportation" to hear air law disputes. In addition to governments, private parties would be amenable to suit. According to its proponents, the transnational nature of the aviation industry makes the creation of such a tribunal imperative. From a constitutional standpoint, what obstacles would such a plan face in the United States? *See* Brian F. Havel, *The Constitution in an Era of Supranational Adjudication*, 78 N.C. L. Rev. 257 (2000).

3. STATECRAFT

WHAT HAPPENED NEXT?

Carl Wilkinson
London Observer, Oct. 27, 2002, at 102

[On May 27, 1987, Mathias Rust, a German teenager,] made headlines when he landed a Cessna light aircraft in [Moscow's] Red Square. He was sentenced to four years in a Soviet labour camp and served 432 days. He returned to Hamburg in 1988, where he now lives with his second wife, Athena. [What follows is his explanation for why he did what he did.]

I got my private pilot's license in autumn 1986.

I was 19 and very political. I was interested in relations between East and West, particularly the Reykjavik meeting between [Soviet President Mikhail] Gorbachev and [President Ronald] Reagan. I realised that the aircraft was the key to peace. I could use it to build an imaginary bridge between East and West. I didn't tell anybody about my plan because I was convinced my family or friends would stop me. I didn't think much about what would happen afterwards. My main focus was on my mission to get there and land. I believed that something would work out.

I hired a Cessna in Hamburg and flew to Moscow via Helsinki in May 1987. My plan was to land in Red Square, but there were too many people and I thought I'd cause casualties. I had thought about landing in the Kremlin, but there wasn't enough space. I wanted to choose somewhere public, because I was scared of the KGB. I approached Red Square three times, trying to find somewhere to land, before discovering a wide bridge nearby. I landed there and taxied into Red Square. As it turned out, the day I chose—28 May—was the holiday of the border patrol. I suspect that's how I got away with it.

My landing caused plenty of confusion. People came up and surrounded the plane and soon the police arrived to take me away. The defence and air defence ministers were both replaced and more than 2,000 officers lost their jobs. I was sentenced to four years in a labour camp, but spent my time in the interrogation prison because the KGB couldn't guarantee my safety.

I was locked up for 22 hours a day in a 10 sq-metre cell, but at least nobody could harm me.

My parents came to visit every two months and brought plenty of books. I had one companion. He was a teacher from the Ukraine who spoke English so we could communicate a bit. I learn[ed] a few Russian words, but it was hard to concentrate. Imprisonment hit me so hard—much harder than I had thought.

After my trial, my flying club got permission to bring the plane back to Germany. It was originally worth about 75,000DM [£ 24,000], and I think they sold it for 160,000DM [£ 51,000]. It's owned by a Japanese businessman who's stored it, waiting for the value to go up. He compared it to Charles Lindbergh's [The Spirit of St. Louis]!

Arriving home in Germany was difficult, as I faced a lot of negative media attention. It affected me badly: I lost 10Kg and had stomach problems. It took the legs out from under me. I couldn't go out for weeks because there was always someone shouting at me in the street, and I received many death threats. My parents were angry, but they were relieved that I was in good condition. They had been afraid the Russians would torture me. They told me not to do it again! You have to be young to be able to do things like that. Now I'm more cautious. I'm proud that I was able to do what I did—psychologically it was a great wall to climb—but sometimes I regret it.

ALEJANDRE v. REPUBLIC OF CUBA

996 F. Supp. 1239 (S.D. Fla. 1997)

KING, District Judge.

I. Introduction

The government of Cuba, on February 24, 1996, in outrageous contempt for international law and basic human rights, murdered four human beings in international airspace over the Florida Straits. The victims were Brothers to the Rescue pilots, flying two civilian, unarmed planes on a routine humanitarian mission, searching for rafters in the waters between Cuba and the Florida Keys.

As the civilian planes flew over international waters, a Russian built MiG-29 of the Cuban Air Force, without warning, reason, or provocation, blasted the defenseless planes out of the sky with sophisticated air-to-air missiles in two separate attacks. The pilots and their aircraft disintegrated in the mid-air explosions following the impact of the missiles. The destruction was so complete that the four bodies were never recovered.

The personal representatives of three of the deceased instituted this action against the Republic of Cuba ("Cuba") and the Cuban Air Force to recover monetary damages for the killings. One of the victims was not a U.S. citizen and his family therefore could not join in the suit. This is the first lawsuit to rely on recent legislative enactments that strip foreign states of immunity for certain acts of terrorism. Neither Cuba nor the Cuban Air Force has defended this suit, asserting through a diplomatic note that this Court has no jurisdiction over Cuba or its political subdivisions. A default was thus entered against both Defendants on April 23, 1997 pursuant to Rule 55(a) of the Federal Rules of Civil Procedure. Because this is a lawsuit against a foreign state, however, the Court may not enter judgment by default. Rather, the claimants must establish their "claim or right to relief by evidence that is satisfactory to the Court." 28 U.S.C. § 1608(e) (1994); see Compania Interamericana Export-Import, S.A. v. Compania Dominicana de Aviacion, 88 F.3d 948, 951 (11th Cir.1996). These three consolidated cases proceeded to trial on November 13, 14, and 20, 1997, on the issues of liability and damages. Because the Court finds that neither Cuba nor the Cuban Air Force is immune from suit for the killings, and because the facts amply prove both Defendants' liability and Plaintiffs' damages, the Court will enter judgment against Defendants.

II. Findings of Fact

At trial, Plaintiffs presented extensive testimonial and documentary evidence in support of their claims. Because Cuba has presented no defense, the Court will accept as true Plaintiffs' uncontroverted factual allegations. See Thomson v. Wooster, 114 U.S. 104, 5 S.Ct. 788, 29 L.Ed. 105 (1885); Nishimatsu Const. Co. v. Houston Nat'l Bank, 515 F.2d 1200, 1206 (5th Cir.1975). The pertinent facts are as follows.

A. The Victims

Armando Alejandre was forty-five years old at the time of his death. Although born in Cuba, Alejandre made Miami, Florida his home at an early age and became a naturalized U.S. citizen. Alejandre served an active tour of duty for eight months in Vietnam, completed his college education at Florida International University, and worked as a consultant to the Metro-Dade Transit Authority at the time of his death. He is survived by his wife of twenty-one years, Marlene Alejandre, who serves as the Personal Representative of his estate, and his daughter Marlene, a college student. Both are Plaintiffs in this lawsuit.

Carlos Alberto Costa was born in the United States in 1966 and resided in Miami. He was only twenty-nine years old when the Cuban government ended his life. Always interested in aviation and hoping to someday oversee the operations of a major airport, Costa earned his bachelor's degree at Embry-Riddle Aeronautical University and worked as a Training Specialist for the Dade County Aviation Department. He is survived by his parents, Mirta Costa and Osvaldo Costa, and by his sister, Mirta Mendez, all of whom sue on his behalf.

Mario Mañuel De la Peña was also born in the United States and was a mere twenty-four years old at the time of his death. Working toward his goal of being an airline pilot, De la Peña was in his last semester at Embry-Riddle when he was killed. During that semester he had obtained a coveted and highly competitive internship with American Airlines. Embry-Riddle granted De la Peña a bachelor's degree in Professional Aeronautics posthumously. He is survived by a younger brother, Michael De la Peña, and his parents, Mario T. De la Peña and Miriam De la Peña, both of whom are Plaintiffs in this case.

B. The Shootdown

Alejandre, Costa, and De la Peña were all members of a Miami-based humanitarian organization known as Hermanos al Rescate, or Brothers to the Rescue. The organization's principal mission was to search the Florida Straits for rafters, Cuban refugees who had fled the island nation on precarious inner tubes or makeshift rafts, often perishing at sea. Brothers to the Rescue would locate the rafters and provide them with life-saving assistance by informing the U.S. Coast Guard of their location and condition.

On the morning of February 24, 1996, two of Brothers to the Rescue's civilian Cessna 337 aircraft departed from Opa Locka Airport in South Florida. (A third Brothers to the Rescue Cessna 337 aircraft also departed on the mission. That plane returned safely to the United States.) Costa piloted one plane, accompanied by Pablo Morales, a Cuban national who had once been a rafter himself. De la Peña piloted the second plane, with Alejandre as his passenger. Before departing, the planes notified both Miami and Havana traffic controllers of their flight plans, which were to take them south of the 24th parallel. The 24th parallel, well north of Cuba's twelve-mile territorial sea, is the northernmost boundary of the Havana Flight Information Region. Commercial and civilian aircraft routinely fly in this area, and aviation practice requires that they notify Havana's traffic controllers when crossing south through the 24th parallel. Both Brothers to the Rescue planes complied with this custom by contacting Havana, identifying themselves, and stating their position and altitude.

While the two planes were still north of the 24th parallel, the Cuban Air Force launched two military aircraft, a MiG-29 and a MiG-23, operating under the control of Cuba's military ground station. The MiGs carried guns, close range missiles, bombs, and rockets and were piloted by members of the Cuban Air Force experienced in combat. Excerpts from radio communications between the MiG-29 and Havana Military Control detail what transpired next:

MiG-29: OK, the target is in sight; the target is in sight. It's a small aircraft. Copied, small aircraft in sight.

MiG-29: OK, we have it in sight, we have it in sight.

MiG-29: The target is in sight.

Military Control: Go ahead.

MiG-29: The target is in sight.

Military Control: Aircraft in sight.

MiG-29: Come again?

MiG-29: It's a small aircraft, a small aircraft.

MiG-29: It's white, white.

Military Control: Color and registration of the aircraft?

Military Control: Buddy.

MiG-29: Listen, the registration also?

Military Control: What kind and color?

MiG-29: It is white and blue.

MiG-29: White and blue, at a low altitude, a small aircraft. Give me instructions.

MiG-29: Instructions!

MiG-29: Listen, authorize me....

MiG-29: If we give it a pass, it will complicate things. We are going to give it a pass. Because some vessels are approaching there, I am going to give it a pass.

MiG-29: Talk, talk.

MiG-29: I have it in lock-on, I have it in lock-on.

MiG-29: We have it in lock-on. Give us authorization.

MiG-29: It is a Cessna 337. That one. Give us authorization, damn it!

Military Control: Fire.

MiG-29: Give us authorization, damn it, we have it.

Military Control: Authorized to destroy.

MiG-29: I'm going to pass it.

Military Control: Authorized to destroy.

MiG-29: We already copied. We already copied.

Military Control: Authorized to destroy.

MiG-29: Understood, already received. Already received. Leave us alone for now.

Military Control: Don't lose it.

MiG-29: First launch.

MiG-29: We hit him! Damn! We hit him! We hit him! We retired him!

MiG-29: Wait to see where it fell.

MiG-29: Come on in, come on in! Damn, we hit. Fuckers!

MiG-29: Mark the place where we took it out.

MiG-29: We are over it. This one won't mess around anymore.

Military Control: Congratulations to the two of you.

MiG-29: Mark the spot.

....

MiG-29: We're climbing and returning home.

Military Control: Stand by there circling above.

MiG-29: Over the target?

Military Control: Correct.

MiG-29: Shit, we did tell you, Buddy.

Military Control: Correct, the target is marked.

MiG-29: Go ahead.

Military Control: OK, climb to 3200, 4000 meters above the destroyed target and maintain economical speed.

MiG-29: Go ahead.

Military Control: I need you to stand by ... there. What heading did the launch have?

MiG-29: I have another aircraft in sight.

MiG-29: We have another aircraft.

Military Control: Follow it. Don't lose the other small aircraft.

MiG-29: We have another aircraft in sight. It's in the area where (the first aircraft) fell. It's in the area where it fell.

MiG-29: We have the aircraft in sight.

Military Control: Stand by.

MiG-29: Comrade, it's in the area of the event.

MiG-29: Did you copy?

MiG-29: OK, this aircraft is headed 90 degrees now.

MiG-29: It's in the area of the event, where the target fell. They're going to have to authorize us.

MiG-29: Hey, the SAR isn't needed. Nothing remains, nothing.

Military Control: Correct, keep following the aircraft. You're going to stay above it.

MiG-29: We're above it.

Military Control: Correct....

MiG-29: For what?

MiG-29: Is the other authorized?

Military Control: Correct.

MiG-29: Great. Let's go Alberto.

MiG-29: Understood; we are now going to destroy it.

Military Control: Do you still have it in sight?

MiG-29: We have it, we have it, we're working. Let us work.

MiG-29: The other is destroyed; the other is destroyed. Fatherland or death, shit! The other is down also.

The missiles disintegrated the Brothers to the Rescue planes, killing their occupants instantly and leaving almost no recoverable debris. Only a large oil slick marked the spot where the planes went down. The Cuban Air Force never notified or warned the civilian planes, never attempted other methods of interception, and never gave them the opportunity to land. The MiGs' first and only response was the intentional and malicious destruction of the Brothers to the Rescue planes and their four innocent occupants. Such behavior violated clearly established international norms requiring the exhaustion of all measures before resort to aggression against any aircraft and banning the use of force against civilian aircraft altogether. (These norms have been codified in various international instruments. See, e.g., Convention on International Civil Aviation, Dec. 7, 1944, 61 Stat. 1180, 15 U.N.T.S. 295 (both the United States and Cuba are parties to the Convention). The proscription on using force against civilian planes attaches even if they penetrate foreign airspace. See, e.g., Kay Hailbronner, Freedom of the Air and the Convention on the Law of the Sea, 77 Am. J. Int'l L. 490, 514 (1983) ("Even if an order to land is deliberately disregarded, a civil unarmed aircraft that intrudes into foreign airspace may not be fired upon."). Common sense dictates that the negligible threat civilian planes may pose does not justify the possible loss of life.)

C. The International Reaction

The international community moved quickly and in unison to condemn the murders. The United Nations Security Council, the European Union, and the International Civil Aviation Organization ("ICAO") were among the many to issue statements deploring Cuba's excessive use of force. The French Ministry of Foreign Affairs stated that "France regrets the use of such brutal methods which nothing can justify, regardless of the circumstances, toward aircraft presenting no threat to the safety of the population." Statement of the Spokesperson of the French Ministry of Foreign Affairs (Feb. 26, 1996) (Pls.' Ex. 26(b)). Following an extensive investigation, the ICAO issued a report in June 1996 concluding that the planes were shot down over international waters. The ICAO also adopted a resolution reaffirming the prohibition of the use of weapons against civilian aircraft in flight and declaring such practices incompatible with elementary considerations of humanity and the dictates of customary international law.

The shootdown elicited a similar reaction from the United States and even precipitated the enactment of the Cuban Liberty and Democratic Solidarity (LIBERTAD) Act of 1996, 22 U.S.C.A. §§6021–6091 (West.Supp.1997), which includes an entire section devoted to a condemnation of the Cuban attack, see id. §6046. Among other findings, Congress characterized the shootdown as wholly disproportionate: "The response chosen by Fidel Castro, the use of lethal force, was completely inappropriate to the situation presented to the Cuban Government, making such actions a blatant and barbaric violation of international law and tantamount to cold-blooded murder." Id. §6046(a)(10). Finally, Congress concluded: "The Congress strongly condemns the act of terrorism by the Castro regime in shooting down the Brothers to the Rescue aircraft on February 24, 1996." Id. §6046(b)(1).

III. Conclusions of Law

A. Jurisdiction and Liability

District courts have original jurisdiction to hear suits, not barred by foreign sovereign immunity, that are brought against foreign states. See 28 U.S.C. § 1330 (1994). Under the Foreign Sovereign Immunities Act of 1976 ("FSIA"), 28 U.S.C.A. §§ 1602–1611 (West 1994 & Supp.1997), a federal court lacks subject matter jurisdiction to hear a claim against a foreign state unless the claim falls within one of the FSIA's enumerated exceptions, id. § 1605; see Saudi Arabia v. Nelson, 507 U.S. 349, 355, 113 S.Ct. 1471, 123 L.Ed.2d 47 (1993). For example, if a foreign state commits a tortious act or engages in commercial activities in the United States, it may fall into one of the FSIA's exceptions and be stripped of immunity from suit in U.S. courts. 28 U.S.C.A. § 1605(2),(5). Most recently, Congress crafted an additional, narrow exception to foreign sovereign immunity through the Anti-Terrorism and Effective Death Penalty Act of 1996 ("AEDPA"), Pub.L. No. 104-132, § 221, 110 Stat. 1214. AEDPA amended the FSIA to allow suits in U.S. courts against a foreign state that engages in acts of terrorism under certain specified circumstances. As a result,

> the FSIA now provides that a foreign state shall not be immune from the jurisdiction of U.S. courts in any case in which money damages are sought against a foreign state for personal injury or death that was caused by an act of torture, extrajudicial killing, aircraft sabotage, hostage taking, or the provision of material support or resources ... for such an act if such act or provision of material support is engaged in by an official, employee, or agent of such foreign state while acting within the scope of his or her office, employment, or agency.

28 U.S.C.A. § 1605(a)(7). In addition, section 1605(a)(7) imposes the following requirements: (1) the U.S. must have designated the foreign state as a state sponsor of terrorism pursuant to section 6(j) of the Export Administration Act of 1979; (2) the act must have occurred outside the foreign state; and (3) the claimants and victims must have been U.S. nationals at the time the acts occurred. Id. § 1605(a)(7)(A)–(B). The record of this trial clearly establishes that all of these requirements have been met.

Having established an exception to foreign sovereign immunity, Plaintiffs base their substantive cause of action on a different statute, also enacted in 1996, entitled Civil Liability for Acts of State Sponsored Terrorism, Pub.L. 104-208, § 589, 110 Stat. 3009 (codified at 28 U.S.C.A. § 1605 note (West.Supp.1997)) ("Civil Liability Act"). The Civil Liability Act creates a cause of action against agents of a foreign state that act under the conditions specified in FSIA section 1605(a)(7). It thus serves as an enforcement provision for acts described in section 1605(a)(7). If Plaintiffs prove an agent's liability under this Act, the foreign state employing the agent would also incur liability under the theory of respondeat superior. Because, as detailed above, Plaintiffs have presented compelling evidence that all of the relevant statutory requirements have been met, the Court finds that both the Cuban Air Force and Cuba are liable for the murders of Alejandre, Costa, and De la Peña.

B. Damages

The amount of damages that Plaintiffs may recover in this case is specified in the Civil Liability Act. It provides that an agent of a foreign state who commits an extrajudicial killing as described in FSIA section 1605(a)(7) shall be liable for "money damages which may include economic damages, solatium, pain and suffering, and punitive damages." 28 U.S.C.A. § 1605 note. Thus, the Cuban Air Force is liable for both compensatory and punitive damages. Under the theory of respondeat superior, Cuba is liable for the same amount of damages as its agent, with the exception of punitive damages, which the FSIA prohibits against foreign states. 28 U.S.C. § 1606.

1. Compensatory Damages

To support their claim for compensatory damages, Plaintiffs presented the testimony of Dr. David Williams, an expert economist. Using widely-accepted methodology, Dr. Williams calculated the present value of De la Peña's and Costa's lost wages and benefits. He also calculated the present value of Alejandre's lost wages, benefits, and services to his family. The Court finds Dr. Williams's calculations to be reasonable and therefore adopts his figures for lost wages, benefits, and services.

In addition, Plaintiffs request damages for pain and suffering. The record is replete with testimony from Plaintiffs and other family members of the deceased, which attests in painful detail to the grief they have suffered as a result of the killings. The Court finds this evidence more than sufficient to justify the awards for pain and suffering that Plaintiffs request. Thus, total compensatory damages for each Plaintiff shall be awarded as follows:

[1] To the Estate of ARMANDO ALEJANDRE:

for loss of future income earning potential: $1,326,525

for loss of household services: $206,388

Estate of ARMANDO ALEJANDRE:

Marlene Alejandre (Wife)

for mental pain and suffering: $7,500,000

for loss of companionship and protection: $500,000

Marlene Victoria Alejandre (Daughter)

for mental pain and suffering: $7,500,000

for loss of parental companionship and guidance: $500,000

Total: $17,532,913

[2] To the Estate of CARLOS ALBERTO COSTA:

for loss of future income earning potential: $5,130,704

Estate of CARLOS ALBERTO COSTA:

Osvaldo Costa (Father)

for mental pain and suffering: $5,000,000

for loss of society and companionship: $500,000

Mirta Costa (Mother)

for mental pain and suffering: $5,000,000

for loss of society and companionship: $500,000

Total: $16,130,704

[3] To the Estate of MARIO M. DE LA PEÑA:

for loss of future income earning potential: $5,264,294

Estate of MARIO M. DE LA PEÑA:

Mario De la Peña (Father)

for mental pain and suffering: $5,000,000

for loss of society and companionship: $500,000

Miriam De la Peña (Mother)

for mental pain and suffering: $5,000,000

for loss of society and companionship: $500,000

Total: $16,264,294

2. Punitive Damages

In addition to compensatory damages, punitive damages are explicitly permitted by the Civil Liability Act. Because this is the first case to proceed to trial under this Act, however, there is no precedent to guide the Court in determining whether punitive damages are appropriate in this particular case, and if so, in what amount. Thus, the Court will look both to the traditional purpose behind awarding punitive damages and to analogous federal court cases addressing the role of punitive damages in cases of egregious international human rights violations.

The purpose of punitive, or exemplary, damages has traditionally been twofold. First, they may serve as a tool to punish truly reprehensible conduct. See Paul v. Avril, 901 F.Supp. 330, 336 (S.D.Fla.1994) (observing that exemplary damages are appropriate when defendant's actions are "malicious, wanton, and oppressive"); Michael L. Rustad, How the Common Good Is Served by the Remedy of Punitive Damages, 64 Tenn. L.Rev. 793, 799 (1997) (noting that punitive damages combat "willful and gross disregard of public safety"). In this way, the aggrieved plaintiff is given a socially acceptable avenue of retaliation, and, perhaps more importantly, the "punitive nature of exemplary awards also affords society a means of retribution for wrongs against the community interest." Judith Camile Glasscock, Emptying the Deep Pocket in Mass Tort Litigation, 18 St. Mary's L.J. 977, 982 (1987). Punitive damages are also an appropriate remedy in international law. As the Supreme Court has observed, "[A]n attack from revenge and malignity, from gross abuse of power, and a settled purpose of mischief ... may be punished by all the penalties which the law of nations can properly administer." The Marianna Flora, 24 U.S. (11 Wheat.) 1, 41, 6 L.Ed. 405 (1825).

The law also provides for awards of punitive damages upon the sound reasoning that they will deter others from committing similar acts. Courts reason that if a sizeable monetary sum over and above compensatory damages is assessed against the wrongdoer, he and others may be prevented from engaging in similar behavior in the future. As acknowledged in the Restatement (Second) of Torts, punitive damages are meant both "to punish [a defendant] for his outrageous conduct and to deter him and others like him from similar conduct in the future." Restatement (Second) of Torts §908(1) (1977); see Pacific Mut. Life Ins. Co. v. Haslip, 499 U.S. 1, 15, 111 S.Ct. 1032, 113 L.Ed.2d 1 (1991) (jury is "instructed to consider the gravity of the wrong and the need to deter similar wrongful conduct" in deciding whether to award punitive damages).

Most courts faced with gross violations of international human rights have employed the tool of punitive damages to achieve these dual purposes. By granting large exemplary awards, courts have both expressed their condemnation of human rights abuses and attempted to deter other international actors from engaging in similar practices. Most of these cases have been brought pursuant to the authority of the Alien Tort Claims Act ("ATCA"), 28 U.S.C. § 1350, which allows aliens to sue in U.S. federal court for torts that violate "the law of nations or a treaty of the United States."

An early example is the seminal case of Filartiga v. Pena-Irala, 577 F.Supp. 860 (E.D.N.Y.1984), which addressed the propriety of punitive damages under the ATCA. In Filartiga, two Paraguayan citizens brought suit against a Paraguayan general, alleging that he tortured and murdered Joelito Filartiga in retaliation for his father's political beliefs. Id. at 861. The court found that an international norm prohibiting torture was so strong and widespread as to have crystallized into a precept of international law. The court reasoned that the violation of such a norm against torture could only be vindicated by imposing punitive damages. In determining a specific amount, the court considered both the assets of the defendant and the nature of the acts at issue. The court explained:

> Chief among the considerations the court must weigh is the fact that this case concerns not a local tort but a wrong as to which the world has seen fit to speak. Punitive damages are designed not merely to teach a defendant not to repeat his conduct but to deter others from following his example. To accomplish that purpose this court must make clear the depth of the international revulsion against torture and measure the award in accordance with the enormity of the offense. Thereby the judgment may perhaps have some deterrent effect.

Id. at 866 (internal citation omitted). These considerations led the court to assess $5 million in punitive damages against the individual general for each plaintiff.

Cuba's extrajudicial killings of Mario T. De la Peña, Carlos Alberto Costa, and Armando Alejandre violated clearly established principles of international law. More importantly, they were inhumane acts against innocent civilians. The fact that the killings were premeditated and intentional, outside of Cuban territory, wholly disproportionate, and executed without warning or process makes this act unique in its brazen flouting of international norms. There appears to be no precedent for a military aircraft intentionally shooting down an unarmed, civilian plane.

[Indeed, the] only conceivable parallel may be the shootdown of KAL Flight 007 by the former Soviet Union in 1983. That incident can be distinguished, however, by two keys facts: First, the Soviets were arguably under the impression that the KAL plane was a military aircraft, and, second, the plane had strayed into Soviet airspace. Neither of these facts is true in this case.

The Court must therefore fashion a remedy consistent with the unprecedented nature of this act. See Filartiga, 577 F.Supp. at 865 ("The nature of the acts is plainly important."). The Court finds that Plaintiffs have proven their clear entitlement to punitive damages. Based upon this record, the Court would be shirking its duty were it to refrain from entering a substantial punitive damage award for the dual purpose of (1) expressing the strongest possible condemnation of the Cuban government for its responsibility for commission of this monstrous act, and (2) deterring Defendants from ever again committing other crimes of terrorism.

In addition to considerations of the heinousness of Cuba's act, the Court will follow the traditional approach of considering the Cuban Air Force's assets in its assessment of punitive damages. See Restatement (Second) of Torts §908(2) (1977) ("In assessing punitive damages, the trier of fact can properly consider the character of the defendant's act, the nature and extent of the harm to the plaintiff that the defendant caused or intended to cause and the wealth of the defendant.").

Of course, it would be impossible for the Court to calculate precisely the assets of the Cuban Air Force. The record contains, however, testimony as to the value and number of the MiG fighter jets in the Cuban Air Force. Because this testimony is both uncontroverted and credible, the Court will accept it as true. The record reflects that each MiG is worth approximately $45 million, and that the Cuban Air Force owns approximately 102 MiGs. The total value of this fleet, which is undoubtedly only a fraction of the Cuban Air Force's total assets, is therefore approximately $4.59 billion. The Court finds that 1% of this total, or $45.9 million, should be assessed against the Cuban Air Force for each of the killings. This figure is dictated by the unparalleled nature of Cuba's actions and comports with similar judgments against individual, non-governmental defendants. See Haslip, 499 U.S. at 19 (upholding punitive damages award that was more than four times amount of compensatory damages). Monetary damages, in whatever amount, can never adequately express the revulsion of this Court, and every civilized society, over these callous murders. Perhaps, however, this decision may serve in some small way as a deterrent to others in the future.

Accordingly, after a careful review of the record, and the Court being otherwise fully advised, it is

ORDERED and ADJUDGED that judgment is hereby entered on behalf of Plaintiffs and against Defendants the Republic of Cuba and the Cuban Air Force for total compensatory damages of $49,927,911. Further, judgment is hereby entered for Plaintiffs and against the Defendant the Cuban Air Force (only) as punitive damages, the sum of One Hundred Thirty Seven Million, Seven Hundred Thousand Dollars ($137,700,000).

The total compensatory and punitive damages herewith awarded to Plaintiffs are $187,627,911, for which sum execution may issue forthwith against the Defendants Cuba and the Cuban Air Force and against any of their assets wherever situated.

SOLICITATION, OFFER AND AWARD

United States Agency for International Development
Solication Number TRN-03-011 (Feb. 12, 2003)
www.usaid.gov/iraq/pdf/web_airports.pdf

PURPOSE

International and domestic airports constitute an important set of links both within Iraq and between Iraq and the rest of the world. Whether receiving humanitarian supplies, freight, or personnel, it will be important for both operational and symbolic reasons that airports within Iraq be quickly restored to some level of adequate service. The contractor shall provide airport assessments and operation management expertise to ensure that materials, supplies and people flow efficiently and safely through airports in Iraq assigned by the Government.

CONTRACT TYPE AND CONTRACT SERVICES

This is a Cost Reimbursement (CPFF Level of Effort) term contract. For the consideration set forth below, the Contractor shall provide the deliverables or outputs described [herein] in accordance with the performance standards specified [herein].

STATEMENT OF WORK

I. Objective and Summary

The objective of this [contract] is to provide assessment and operation management technical expertise capabilities for specified airports in Iraq—two international and three domestic airports (to be determined). The purpose is to ensure that personnel, U.S. technical assistance materials and supplies, and other relief and rehabilitation cargoes, including food assistance and materials for reconstruction, enter the country smoothly. The Contractor shall provide all personnel, supervision, vehicles, equipment, tools, materials, and other items and services necessary to perform assessments and undertake operational management of specified airports. The activity supports USAID mission and other relief programs and will be carried out through a cost reimbursement, level of effort completion contract of up to eighteen months duration with an option for two extensions of up to one year each.

II. Background

Annually, significant amounts of USAID-funded and other relief and development supplies and materials as well as technical expertise, are flown throughout the world. The logistics of transportation are complex, and many factors determine the extent to which such supplies and materials reach destinations in a timely manner. The costs of inadequacies and constraints in the airport system are many, and include increased costs due to delay and deterioration of materials and supplies.

Frequently, airports operate inadequately, often due to poor logistical management, inadequate equipment and equipment maintenance, slow customs clearance, and poor coordination with land transport. Additional constraints may arise, such as inadequate fuel bunkering and supply capacities, and poor security. Airport management may be the responsibility of the national government, of a local government, of a civil authority, or of the military.

Overall, many of the airports utilized for transport of U.S. technical assistance and USAID-funded goods operate at levels far below the standards of the International Civil Aviation Organization (ICAO). Inadequacies of operation may be due to a legacy of neglected maintenance, poor site planning and development, lack of trained management, inadequate supporting infrastructure, such as electricity, or inappropriate and overly-restrictive local regulations and procedures. In instances of local or regional conflict, airport operations may be greatly constricted or simply halt, greatly impeding the flow of incoming materials and supplies.

The purpose of this activity is to provide USAID with a capability to improve airport management and operations so that the flow of USAID-funded and other goods and technical assistance is adequate and as unimpeded as feasible. This capability requires assessment of specified airports, development of plans to overcome airport-imposed constraints, and the provision of technical and other assistance needed to ensure that the specified airports can manage an adequate flow of cargo. Since in the instance of local or regional conflict, airports may fail to be operational, the capability to be provided under this statement of work includes the direct provision of personnel to manage all aspects of the specified airports. The overall activity will be undertaken in support of and in cooperation with national or local authorities. Where operations have been directly under the management of the Contractor, the activity will include plans and assistance for a transition from Contractor management back to national or local management.

Additional sensitive information will be provided during the pre-proposal conference.

Special Security Conditions:

U.S. Citizenship is required of KEY persons selected to perform under classified portions of this Contract. At a minimum an "Interim Secret" personnel security clearance issued by the Department of Defense will be required before the issuance of a USAID/RRB Badge or permission to proceed to Post is granted. USAID/SEC will be responsible for validating security clearances of all proposed/selected contractors and will work with the Facility Security Officer of the selected company to transmit security clearance data to U.S. Officials abroad where access to restricted sites and/or facilities is necessary to accomplish the task(s) outlined [herein]. No classified information will be provided to the contractor for the purpose of review, work, or storage at the contractor's facility. All access will occur at the Government's facility either within the U.S. or overseas.

No duplication or retransmission of Classification National Security Information is permitted by the contractor without written authorization from the CTO. Any public release of information regarding this award must be approved in advance of release by the CTO (refer to Section H.10 of this contract for specific security guidance).

Implementation in Iraq shall not take place until a permissive environment exists and USAID instructs the contractor to proceed. Currently there are several statutory restrictions on assistance to Iraq. No assistance under this contract shall be provided to Iraq until USAID has determined that it is consistent with U.S. foreign policy and permitted by law. In particular, the contractor shall not proceed with any payments to local consultants until instructed by USAID. In addition, the contractor is subject to the requirements of the Office of Foreign Assets Control (OFAC), certain other U.S. Government rules and regulations, as well as compliance with all applicable UN sanctions against Iraq.

III. Statement of Work

The Contractor shall provide services and management in the following areas:

A. Technical assistance to make management assessments of two international and three domestic Iraqi airports to be specified by USAID. Such assessments will address all airport resources, systems, utilities and facilities in place for the control, safety, service and security of aircraft in the air and on the ground at the specified airport locations as well as all airport resources, systems, utilities and facilities necessary or required for the control, safety, service and security of aircraft in the air and on the ground at specified airport locations.

B. Technical and other assistance to plan implementation of airport improvements, including site improvements, freight unloading and storage, labor management, transport improvement, customs clearance, security, and many other aspects of airport operation.

C. Technical and other assistance to directly manage and operate part or all of the two international and three domestic Iraqi airports, to be specified by USAID. Such direct operation will ensure the adequate throughput of USAID-funded and other freight, emergency supplies, developmental materials and other technical assistance.

The Contractor will work closely with the USAID Contractor undertaking infrastructure reconstruction and construction (i.e. runway repairs). The assistance to be provided is further described in the tasks below....

BLOCKING PROPERTY OF CERTAIN PERSONS AND PROHIBITING THE EXPORT OF CERTAIN GOODS TO SYRIA

69 Fed. Reg. 26751, Exec. Order No. 13338 (May 11, 2004)

By the authority vested in me as President by the Constitution and the laws of the United States of America, including the International Emergency Economic Powers Act (50 U.S.C. §§ 1701 et seq.) (IEEPA), the National Emergencies Act (50 U.S.C. §§ 1601 et seq.) (NEA), the Syria Accountability and Lebanese Sovereignty Restoration Act of 2003, Public Law 108-175 (SAA), and section 301 of title 3, United States Code,

I, GEORGE W. BUSH, President of the United States of America, hereby determine that the actions of the Government of Syria in supporting terrorism, continuing its occupation of Lebanon, pursuing weapons of mass destruction and missile programs, and undermining United States and international efforts with respect to the stabilization and reconstruction of Iraq constitute an unusual and extraordinary threat to the national security, foreign policy, and economy of the United States and hereby declare a national emergency to deal with that threat. To address that threat, and to implement the SAA, I hereby order the following:

....

Sec. 2. The Secretary of Transportation shall not permit any air carrier owned or controlled by Syria to provide foreign air transportation as defined in 49 U.S.C. § 40102(a)(23), except that he may, to the extent consistent with Department of Transportation regulations, permit such carriers to charter aircraft to the Government of Syria for the transport of Syrian government officials to and from the United States on official Syrian government business. In addition, the Secretary of Transportation shall prohibit all takeoffs and landings in the United States, other than those associated with an emergency, by any such air carrier when engaged in scheduled international air services.

....

Sec. 8. With respect to the prohibitions contained in section 2 of this order, consistent with subsection 5(b) of the SAA, I hereby determine that it is in the national security interest of the United States to waive, and hereby waive, application of subsection 5(a)(2)(D) of the SAA insofar as it pertains to: aircraft of any air carrier owned or controlled by Syria chartered by the Syrian government for the transport of Syrian government officials to and from the United States on official Syrian government business, to the extent consistent with Department of Transportation regulations; takeoffs or landings for non-traffic stops of aircraft of any such air carrier that is not engaged in scheduled international air services; takeoffs and landings associated with an emergency; and overflights of United States territory.

Sec. 9. [I] direct the Secretary of Transportation, in consultation with the Secretary of State, to take such actions, including the promulgation of rules and regulations, as may be necessary to carry out section 2 of this order....

Sec. 13. (a) This order is effective at 12:01 eastern daylight time on May 12, 2004. (b) This order shall be transmitted to the Congress and published in the Federal Register.

CIVILIAN-JET ANTIMISSLE SYSTEM STARTS TO TAKE SHAPE, FIRMS SAY

Leslie Miller

Phil. Inquirer, Nov. 11, 2005, at A12

Two companies working for the government say they have successfully flight-tested systems to defend passenger airplanes against shoulder-fired missiles.

BAE Systems PLC and Northrop Grumman Corp. both say they will meet the government's deadline of producing a workable system by January.

It is unclear whether Congress or the White House will require airlines to use the technology and, if they do, who will pay the multibillion-dollar tab for deployment and maintenance.

Rep. John L. Mica (R.-Fla.), chairman of the House Transportation and Infrastructure subcommittee on aviation, is leading the push in Congress to equip U.S. planes with the technology. A bill by Mica would require the systems on the largest airliner, the Airbus superjumbo A380, which is supposed to go into service late next year. The legislation, if enacted, would affect any A380 that flies in the United States.

Mica also plans to introduce a bill to require systems on some planes that may pose a particular risk, such as international flights. He said the government may pay for part of the systems.

"I don't believe terrorists will be successful in taking down a domestic aircraft," Mica said, "but I think we're overdue for international aircraft to be hit."

Congress has agreed to pay for developing technology to counter lightweight rocket launchers but balked at proposals to spend the billions needed to protect all 6,800 commercial U.S. airliners.

No passenger plane has been downed by a shoulder-fired missile outside a combat zone. But terrorists linked with al-Qaeda are believed to have fired two SA-7 missiles that narrowly missed an Israeli passenger jet in Kenya in November 2002.

Under pressure from Congress, the Homeland Security Department last year gave Northrop and BAE $45 million each to adapt military missile-defense systems for use by airlines. Military systems require too much maintenance—and fire by mistake too often—to be used on a passenger jet.

BAE and Northrop Grumman conducted flight tests Wednesday and yesterday to demonstrate that their prototypes were aeronautically sound and would not impair the planes' ability to fly.

An American Airlines Boeing 767 with BAE's Jeteye system successfully flew figure eights over Alliance Field in Fort Worth, Texas. Northrop Grumman's Guardian system was tested Wednesday on an MD-11 jet that flew around after taking off from California's Mojave Airport.

The Guardian system jammed 177 simulated missiles in a separate test, Northrop spokeswoman Katie Lamb said.

Both Northrop and BAE systems use lasers to jam the guidance systems of incoming missiles, which lock on the heat of an aircraft's engine. Northrop and BAE are required to come up with systems that will cost less than $1 million each to install.

Airlines caution that the systems will consume a large chunk of the limited funds that can be spent to defend airplanes from terrorists.

"It's a huge expenditure of resources to deal with one type of threat," said John Meanen, executive vice president for the Air Transport Association, which represents major airlines. "We have to ask, 'Are there better ways of doing this?'"

EUROPEANS PROBE SECRET CIA FLIGHTS

Craig Whitlock
Wash. Post, Nov. 17, 2005, at A22

Several European governments have opened investigations into a fleet of CIA-operated airplanes that have crisscrossed the continent hundreds of times in recent years. The aim is to determine whether U.S. officials secretly used local airports and military bases to transfer terrorism suspects under conditions that violate local and international treaties.

This week, officials in Spain, Sweden, Norway and in the European Parliament said they had either opened formal inquiries or demanded answers from U.S. officials about CIA flights, in response to growing public opposition in Europe to U.S. anti-terrorism tactics.

In other countries, criminal probes have deepened into the alleged kidnapping of terrorism suspects by the CIA. In Italy, prosecutors last week filed a formal extradition request for 22 U.S. citizens alleged to be CIA operatives who are charged with kidnapping a radical Muslim cleric in Milan in 2003 and flying him to his native Egypt, where he said he was tortured.

A German prosecutor said Wednesday that he had opened a separate criminal investigation involving the same abduction to examine whether the CIA broke German laws by first bringing the cleric to Ramstein Air Base and forcibly detaining him there before putting him on a CIA-chartered plane to Egypt.

Another German prosecutor is conducting a third criminal probe into the disappearance of a German citizen who said he was taken into custody last year while on vacation in Macedonia and secretly imprisoned in Afghanistan by U.S. operatives who accused him of being a terrorist. The man has said he was released three months later, after his captors realized they had seized the wrong man.

In recent weeks, Ireland and Denmark have also protested the presence of CIA-operated aircraft in their countries, in response to concerns that the planes could have been transferring prisoners, either to the U.S. naval base in Guantanamo Bay or to secret CIA-run prisons elsewhere in the world.

The Danish Foreign Ministry has asked the CIA to avoid Danish airspace altogether when transporting secretly held prisoners or flying for other "purposes that are incompatible with international conventions." The request came after Danish officials disclosed that a plane that had been chartered by the spy agency stopped for unknown reasons for 23 hours last March at Copenhagen airport.

The inquiries and investigations are coming partly in response to a flurry of European media reports retracing the flight plans of the airplanes, as well as a Nov. 2 Washington Post report that the CIA set up a secret prison system for terrorism suspects in eight countries, including several in Eastern Europe, since the Sept. 11, 2001, hijackings in the United States.

Since 2001, many European intelligence and law enforcement agencies have worked closely and quietly with the CIA to help track down members of al-Qaida and other terrorism suspects around the world. But in public, European governments are now increasingly distancing themselves from their transatlantic ally as allegations mount that the United States has employed and abetted torture and violated international law with the secret detentions.

In Spain, judicial authorities are investigating whether CIA airplanes that made more than a dozen stops on the island of Majorca and the Canary Islands in the past two years were transferring terrorism suspects. A previous inquiry by Majorcan investigators found no evidence of prisoners, but prosecutors recently decided to reopen the case.

"If it is confirmed that this is true, we would be facing very serious acts that would break the rules concerning the treatment of people in any democratic system," Interior Minister Jose Antonio Alonso said Tuesday. "They would be very serious and intolerable acts."

European prosecutors and other officials said it was unlikely their probes would shed much light on CIA operations, much less convict U.S. operatives of criminal acts. But they said they had a duty to investigate serious allegations of wrongdoing.

Eberhard Bayer, a German prosecutor in the city of Zweibruecken, said he had opened a criminal investigation into whether CIA operatives were guilty of kidnapping, illegal restraint or coercion in the case of Hassan Mustafa Osama Nasr, the cleric who was secretly brought to nearby Ramstein Air Base from Milan in February 2003 en route to Egypt.

Bayer said he had few leads to go on and did not know the identities of any of the Americans who allegedly had custody of Nasr while he was in Germany. He said he had queried U.S. military authorities at Ramstein.

"Now we must wait for a response, which we may not receive," he acknowledged in a telephone interview Wednesday. "If it is true that these are CIA people, I can hardly imagine that the CIA would allow its people to be extradited."

The CIA declined to comment for this report. CIA and other U.S. officials have said they carry out such operations only in countries that are political allies and whose intelligence officials grant permission.

Daniel Fried, the State Department's assistant secretary for European affairs, said Monday during a visit to Berlin that he had not heard many complaints from European officials about the CIA's anti-terrorism operations in Europe.

"It is true that these issues are debated in Europe; they are debated in the United States as well," Fried said in response to a question about the reported CIA secret jails and prisoner transfers. "The U.S. has acted and will act consistent with the law and with international norms."

Notes

1. As Mathias Rust recounted to the *Observer*, his landing in Red Square caused a massive shake-up of the Soviet government. It is now recognized that this helped speed up the ultimate collapse of the U.S.S.R.:

> Mikhail Gorbachev took advantage of [Rust's appearance], replacing the defense and air defense ministers (both of whom were opposed to glasnost and

> perestroika) with men who supported his policies. More than 2,000 officers (again, most of whom were opposed to Gorbachev's reforms) lost their jobs. This move was critical in winning over the previously fiercely conservative and anti-reform military.

Mathias Rust, at en.wikipedia.org/wiki/Mathias_Rust. For a further look at Rust's role in ending the Cold War, *see, e.g.*, William E. Odom, *The Collapse of the Soviet Military* (1998).

2. After the plaintiffs in *Alejandre* won their case, they were forced to embark on a long effort to collect on the judgment. *See* 42 F. Supp. 2d 1317 (S.D. Fla.), *vacated*, 183 F.3d 1277 (11th Cir.), *rehearing denied*, 205 F.3d 1357 (11th Cir. 1999), and 64 F. Supp. 2d 1245 (S.D. Fla. 1999). Eventually, however, they were able to garnish $96.7 million in U.S.-blocked Cuban funds. *See* Victims of Trafficking and Violence Protection Act of 2000, § 2002, Pub. L. No. 106-386, 114 Stat. 1541 (2000). The parents of Carlos A. Costa subsequently donated $500,000 to the Immigration and Human Rights Clinic at Florida International University's College of Law, which was then renamed in their son's honor. *See further* Robert L. Steinback, *Cuban Funds to Assist FIU With Law Clinic*, Miami Herald, Oct. 26, 2004, at 4B.

In addition to the *Alejandre* case, Cuba and the United States have clashed over the periodic theft of airplanes by political dissidents fleeing the Castro regime. Although Cuban officials insist that such planes must be returned under the 1970 Hague Convention for the Suppression of Unlawful Seizure of Aircraft (*see* Appendix 12), the United States disagrees. *See further* Diane Lourdes Dick, Note, *The Case of the Little Yellow Cuban Biplane: Can Interest Analysis Reconcile Conflicting Provisions in Federal Statutes and International Treaties?*, 57 Fla. L. Rev. 91 (2005).

3. In the course of his opinion in *Alejandre*, Judge King makes reference to the 1983 shoot-down of Korean Air Lines Flight 007 by the U.S.S.R. after the plane, which was en route from New York to Seoul, mistakenly drifted into Soviet airspace. The tragedy, which claimed 269 lives, quickly led the ICAO to prepare a protocol to the Chicago Convention (*see* Appendix 19) that adds a provision (Article 3 bis) establishing how civilian airplanes are to be intercepted. The United States is the only major power that has not adopted the protocol. Nevertheless, it invoked Article 3 bis in its protests regarding the shoot-down of the Brothers to the Rescue planes. Earlier, however, when the Navy cruiser U.S.S. Vincennes accidentally shot down Iran Air Flight 655 over international waters in July 1988, causing 290 deaths, the United States refused to accept responsibility (it did, however, eventually agree to pay the Iranian victims $61.8 million in compensation on an ex gratia basis).

For a further discussion, *see, e.g.*, *Zicherman v. Korean Air Lines Co.*, 516 U.S. 217 (1996) (summarizing the KAL 007 litigation); Darren C. Huskisson, *The Air Bridge Denial Program and the Shootdown of Civil Aircraft Under International Law*, 56 A.F. L. Rev. 109 (2005) (describing the United States's reliance on shoot-downs to combat drug smugglers); Michael Milde, *Aeronautical Incidents and International Law*, 16 Air & Space Law. 1 (Fall 2001) (arguing that Article 3 bis does not prevent states from shooting down civilian aircraft if they represent a genuine threat, as in 9/11).

4. The rehabilitation of Iraq's airports, outlined in the USAID's 2003 solicitation circular, and the 2004 Executive Order suspending flights between Syria and the United States, are just two examples of the intersection of aircraft and statecraft. In your opinion, what are the consequences of turning commercial aviation into a political tool or bargaining chip? *See further* Paul Stephen Dempsey, *Flights of Fancy and Fights of Fury:*

Arbitration and Adjudication of Commercial and Political Disputes in International Aviation, 32 Ga. J. Int'l & Comp. L. 231 (2004).

5. Should airliners be equipped with defensive weapons, such as an anti-missile system? If so, what about offensive weapons? *See further* Keith Sealing, *Thirty Years Later: Still Playing Catch-Up With the Terrorists*, 30 Syracuse J. Int'l L. & Com. 339 (2003) (arguing that the United States knew for years that missile attacks on airliners posed a serious threat yet did nothing).

6. The CIA's secret air network, discussed in the *Washington Post* article, is but the latest example of one country using another country's airspace for a clandestine purpose. Of the many such incidents that have taken place, the most notorious one remains the 1960 U-2 spy plane crisis:

> On May 1, 1960 (fifteen days before the scheduled opening of an East-West summit conference in Paris), a U.S. Lockheed U-2 spy plane, piloted by Gary Powers, left Peshawar, Pakistan intending to overfly the Soviet Union and land at Bodø, Norway. The goal of the mission was to photograph ICBM development sites in and around Sverdlovsk and Plesetsk in the Soviet Union. Attempts to intercept the plane by Soviet fighters failed due to the U-2's extreme altitude, but eventually one of the 14 SA-2 Guideline surface-to-air missiles launched at the plane managed to get close enough. According to Soviet defector Viktor Belenko, a Soviet fighter pursuing Powers was caught and destroyed in the missile salvo. Powers' aircraft was badly damaged, and crashed near Sverdlovsk, deep inside Soviet territory. Powers was captured after making a parachute landing.
>
> Four days after Powers disappeared, NASA issued a very detailed press release noting that an aircraft had "gone missing" north of Turkey. The press release speculated that the pilot might have fallen unconscious while the autopilot was still engaged, even claiming that "the pilot reported over the emergency frequency that he was experiencing oxygen difficulties." To bolster this, a U-2 plane was quickly painted in NASA colors and shown to the media.
>
> After hearing this, Soviet premier Nikita Khrushchev announced to the Supreme Soviet (and hence the world) that a "spyplane" had been shot down, whereupon the U.S. issued a statement claiming that it was a "weather research aircraft" which strayed into Soviet airspace after the pilot had "difficulties with his oxygen equipment" while flying over Turkey. The White House, presuming Powers was dead, gracefully acknowledged that this might be the same plane, but still proclaimed "there was absolutely no deliberate attempt to violate Soviet airspace and never has been," and attempted to continue the facade by grounding all U-2 aircraft to check for "oxygen problems."
>
> On May 7, Khrushchev dropped the bombshell:
>
> "I must tell you a secret. When I made my first report I deliberately did not say that the pilot was alive and well ... and now just look how many silly things [the Americans] have said."
>
> Not only was Powers still alive, but his plane was essentially intact. The Soviets managed to recover the surveillance camera and even developed the photographs. Powers' survival pack, including 7500 roubles and jewelry for women, was also recovered.
>
> [As a result of the incident, the previously scheduled] Paris Summit between Dwight Eisenhower and Nikita Khrushchev collapsed, in large part be-

> cause Eisenhower refused to apolog[ize for] the incident, [as] demanded by Khrushchev. Khrushchev left the talks on May 16.
>
> [A short time later,] Powers was convicted of espionage and sentenced to 3 years' imprisonment and 7 years of hard labor. But he only served one and three-quarter years before being exchanged for Colonel Ivanovich Abel [in February 1962 in a hand-off that famously took place] on the Glienicke Bridge in Potsdam, Germany.

U-2 Crisis of 1960, at en.wikipedia.org/wiki/U-2_Crisis_of_1960.

Forty years later, the United States found itself embroiled in an almost identical crisis with China, although this time the matter was resolved much more quickly and peacefully:

> On April 1, 2001, a United States Navy EP-3E was intercepted by People's Liberation Army Air Force J-8 fighter jets about 70 miles off the Chinese island of Hainan. The People's Republic of China later claimed that [the] plane was spying on Chinese military facilities. One of the Chinese jets bumped the wing of the EP-3E, which was forced to make an emergency landing on Hainan. The Chinese pilot, Wang Wei, was missing and presumed dead following the incident.
>
> The crew of 24 was detained and released April 11 after the U.S. issued the "letter of the two sorries" [which apologized for the entry into Chinese airspace and the death of the fighter pilot]. The plane was airlifted to Dobbins Air Force Base in Georgia on July 3, 2001.
>
> The EP-3E was carrying sensitive listening equipment. Navy protocol calls for [the] destruction of this equipment in the event the plane is captured or if there is a chance it will be boarded by non-U.S. personnel. Chinese military [officials] did board the plane after it landed in Hainan but it is not known if any sensitive information was retrieved.
>
> [The] incident [is] often compared to the U-2 spy plane crisis of 1960.

U.S.-China Spy Plane Incident, at en.wikipedia.org/wiki/U.S.-China_spy_plane incident. For a further discussion, *see, e.g.*, Eric Donnelly, *The United States-China EP-3 Incident: Legality and Realpolitik*, 9 J. Conflict & Security L. 25 (2004); W. Allan Edmiston, III, Comment, *Showdown in the South China Sea: An International Incidents Analysis of the So-Called Spy Plane Crisis*, 16 Emory Int'l L. Rev. 639 (2002); Margaret K. Lewis, Note, *An Analysis of State Responsibility for the Chinese-American Airplane Collision Incident*, 77 N.Y.U. L. Rev. 1404 (2002).

7. The United States, of course, is not alone when it comes to conducting covert activity in foreign airspace. On July 4, 1976, for example, Israeli commandos carried out Operation Thunderbolt, a daring raid on Entebbe International Airport that resulted in the freeing of a group of mostly Jewish hostages from Air France Flight 139 (which had been hijacked the previous week while en route from Athens to Paris). Subsequently, the Ugandan government asked the United Nations Security Council to sanction Israel for having violated its sovereignty. In defending his country's actions, Ambassador Chaim Herzog commented:

> We come with a simple message to the Council: we are proud of what we have done because we have demonstrated to the world that the dignity of man, human life and human freedom constitute the highest values. We are proud not only because we have saved the lives of over a hundred innocent people—men, women and children—but because of the significance of our act for the cause of human freedom.

Chaim Herzog, *Heroes of Israel: Profiles of Jewish Courage* 284 (1989). Moved by these words, the Council rejected Uganda's motion. Two movies later were made about the incident: *Victory at Entebbe* (1976, with Anthony Hopkins), and *Raid on Entebbe* (1977, with Peter Finch).

8. After years in development, the world is about to witness the launching of the Airbus A380, a truly extraordinary aircraft:

> The 555-seat, double-deck Airbus A380 is the most ambitious civil aircraft program yet. When it enters service [sometime in 2007], the A380 will be the world's largest airliner, easily eclipsing Boeing's 747.
>
> Airbus first began studies on a very large 500-seat airliner in the early 1990s. The European manufacturer saw developing a competitor and successor to the Boeing 747 as a strategic play to end Boeing's dominance of the very large airliner market and round out Airbus' product line-up.
>
> Airbus began engineering development work on such an aircraft, then designated the A3XX, in June 1994. Airbus studied numerous design configurations for the A3XX and gave serious consideration to a single deck aircraft which would have seated 12 abreast and twin vertical tails. However, Airbus settled upon a twin deck configuration, largely because of the significantly lighter structure required.
>
> Key design aims include the ability to use existing airport infrastructure with little modifications to the airports, and direct operating costs per seat 15–20% less than those for the 747-400. With 49% more floor space and only 35% more seating than the previous largest aircraft, Airbus is ensuring wider seats and aisles for more passenger comfort. Using the most advanced technologies, the A380 is also designed to have 10–15% more range, lower fuel burn and emissions, and less noise.
>
> The A380 features an advanced version of the Airbus common two crew cockpit, with pull-out keyboards for the pilots, extensive use of composite materials such as GLARE (an aluminum/glass fibre composite), and four 302 to 374kN (68,000 to 84,000lb) class Rolls-Royce Trent 900 or Engine Alliance (General Electric/Pratt & Whitney) GP7200 turbofans now under development.
>
> Several A380 models are planned: the basic aircraft is the 555-seat A380-800 (launch customer Emirates). The 590-ton MTOW 10,410km (5620nm) A380-800F freighter will be able to carry a 150-ton payload and is due to enter service in 2008 (launch customer FedEx). Potential future models will include the shortened, 480-seat A380-700, and the stretched, 656-seat A380-900.
>
> On receipt of the required 50th launch order commitment, the Airbus A3XX was renamed A380 and officially launched on December 19, 2000. In early 2001 the general configuration design was frozen, and metal cutting for the first A380 component occurred on January 23, 2002, at Nantes in France. In 2002 more than 6,000 people were working on A380 development.
>
> On January 18, 2005, the first Airbus A380 was officially revealed in a lavish ceremony, attended by 5,000 invited guests including the French, German, British and Spanish president and prime ministers, representing the countries that invested heavily in the 10-year, $13 billion+ aircraft program, and the CEOs of the 14 A380 customers, who had placed firm orders for 149 aircraft by then.

The Airbus A380, at www.airliners.net/info/stats.main?id=29.

Since the A380's plans were first announced, the plane has caused considerable friction between the United States and the European Union due to the financial subsidies (variously estimated at $15 billion) provided by the latter to EADS, the Airbus's manufacturer. In turn, the European Union has accused the United States of unfairly aiding the Boeing Company. The charges and counter-charges currently are being reviewed by the World Trade Organization. *See New Step in Resolving Aircraft Subsidy Dispute*, N.Y. Times, Sept. 24, 2005, at B2. For a further discussion, *see, e.g.*, Daniel I. Fisher, Note, *"Super Jumbo" Problem: Boeing, Airbus, and the Battle for the Geopolitical Future*, 35 Vand. J. Transnat'l L. 865 (2002).

Problem 4

Two American airplane manufacturers wish to merge. Although the United States Department of Justice has no objection to the pairing, European antitrust officials have decided to look into the matter. Assuming neither company has any production facilities in the E.U., can it block the merger? *See Commission Decision 97/816/EC of 30 July 1997 Declaring a Concentration (Merger) Between Boeing Co. and McDonnell Douglas Corp. Compatible with the Common Market and the Functioning of the European Economic Area (EEA) Agreement*, 1997 O.J. (L 336) 16.

C. PROFESSIONAL RESPONSIBILITY

THE GENERAL AVIATION CASE

Wendell K. Smith
12 Utah B.J. 17 (Feb. 1999)

The elements of tort law applicable to claims and litigation arising from aircraft accidents are the same as in any other negligence or product liability case. However, without a substantial knowledge of aviation it can be difficult to assess what duty was owed by which persons and to whom, whether that duty was breached, and whether the breach was the proximate cause of the damages. Likewise, without a substantial knowledge of aircraft structures, flight controls, engines, aircraft systems, and instruments, it is difficult to assess whether an aircraft or aircraft component was defective and whether it was unreasonably dangerous.

Does this mean an attorney without a background in aviation should not take an aviation case? Not necessarily. It means that you are going to have to spend a lot of time learning about aircraft and aviation terminology. It means you are going to need a firm grasp of the facts and you are going to have to rely heavily on experts. One note of caution. Before taking an aviation case read Rule 1.1 of the Rules of Professional Conduct. This Rule states that a lawyer shall provide competent representation to a client and shall possess the legal knowledge and skill reasonably necessary to provide that representation. This does not mean you cannot take an aviation case without a substantial knowledge of aviation. It does mean that you can accept an aviation case provided the requisite level of competence can be achieved by reasonable preparation.

So, what is the first step? It is imperative that you know all the facts and that you learn them as soon as possible. How do you get the facts? Don't wait for the National Transportation Safety Board (NTSB) report. It can take over a year for this report to become available. By then, a lot of evidence will be destroyed, altered, or lost, and the key witness may be dead or have disappeared. You need to conduct your own investigation and you need to do it as soon as you can gain access to the wreckage and the witnesses. How do you conduct an investigation? Hire an expert. Let the expert conduct the investigation. Personal participation in the investigation is essential if you are going to gain a complete understanding of the facts. You will learn more by one visit to the accident site, or by viewing the wreckage, than you can learn in man hours of reading reports and statements and viewing photos.

The investigation of general aviation aircraft accidents falls under the jurisdiction of the NTSB. Most fatal general aviation accidents are investigated by the NTSB. However, the NTSB may delegate the investigation of these accidents to the FAA. Less serious, non mid-air accidents are generally delegated to the FAA for investigation. [As a] side note, if you have a client who was involved in an aviation accident, remember the FAA wears two hats. They may be conducting a safety investigation, [but] they also have jurisdiction to take certification action against airmen who violate a Federal Aviation Regulation (FAR). The unwary pilot may help the FAA in the safety investigation only to find himself or herself a respondent in an adverse action by the FAA.

The NTSB will not permit attorneys or their representatives to participate in an investigation. However, the NTSB will provide you with the names of the witnesses the investigator has interviewed. The NTSB will also grant access to the wreckage when it has been released by the investigator. Access to the wreckage is generally obtained by coordination with the insurance carrier.

It is important that you take the statements of witnesses as soon as possible. Witness testimony is perishable evidence. It is not necessary to obtain permission of the NTSB to interview witnesses. The best place to interview a witness is at the spot where the witness saw the accident. This will permit the witness to describe the events in relation to the surrounding terrain, buildings, etc. The decision as to whether to take witness statements in the presence of your expert depends upon whether you want to protect the statement from discovery. The advantage of having your expert present is that the expert can guide you in what questions to ask. The questioning of the witness in this manner will probably give you more information than if the expert is not present. The disadvantage is that the presence of the expert may constitute a waiver of attorney work product privilege if your expert is designated to testify at the trial as an expert witness. If you elect to have your interview notes protected as attorney work product, you should conduct the interview alone based upon guidance from your expert as to the questions to be asked and the information to be obtained from the witness.

Your expert should then conduct an investigation to determine the cause of the crash. The expert should also determine whether any Federal Aviation Regulations (FAR's) may have been violated by the manufacturer, aircrew, maintenance provider, owner, or air traffic controller.

The NTSB does not always have all the answers. Therefore, if you wait for the NTSB report you may be disappointed. I recently investigated the crash of a DC-3 with my expert. Our investigation identified the cause of the fire that caused the crash. The NTSB report indicated the cause of the fire was unknown.

Another reason not to rely on the NTSB report is that the probable cause determination is inadmissable into evidence at trial by statute. Additionally, NTSB investigators may not be called as witnesses at trial and they may not render opinions as to the cause of the crash. The NTSB permits the deposition to be taken of their investigators. However, the testimony of these investigators is limited strictly to the facts. What did they see, hear, touch, taste, smell, and who did they interview? These depositions may be used at trial.

What is the next step? Once you have all the facts, the next step is to identify the possible defendants and formulate a theory of liability. I once worked on a case stemming from the crash of a Saber Liner in Pennsylvania. The aircraft was landing at an airport that was located atop a mesa with a drop off of about 300 feet on each end of the runway. After touching down, the aircraft failed to stop and went off the end of the runway. Everyone aboard was killed by the post-crash fire. It was determined that the aircraft failed to stop because the crew had turned off the electric hydraulic pump in flight and had failed to turn it on prior to landing. Consequently, when the hydraulic pressure in the accumulator was depleted they had no brakes. The aircraft was not equipped with an engine-driven hydraulic pump.

Who would be the defendants in this crash and what theories of liability would you use? The parties that were obviously negligent were the cockpit crew. The pre-landing check list requires that the hydraulic pump be turned on prior to landing. In fact, company policy stated that the pump was not to be turned off in flight. The aircrew was negligent in disregarding company policy and failing to follow the pre-landing check list. What about the pilots? Is there any theory of liability that could be used to recover for their wrongful deaths? What about product liability? Was the design of this aircraft defective by not having an engine-driven hydraulic pump? If so, did this design defect render the aircraft unreasonably dangerous? Was pilot error induced by the design of the aircraft's hydraulic system? These issues were not litigated; however, in my opinion, the families of the crew could have recovered under this theory of liability.

Another theory of liability that can be used in a large number of aircraft crashes is Negligence Per Se. This is because an FAR is generally violated in connection with an aircraft accident. It can generally be shown that there was a causal connection between the violation of the FAR and the accident. In other words, if it can be shown that the harm that resulted from the violation of the FAR was the kind of harm the FAR was designed to prevent, you have a case of Negligence Per Se.

Due to the total destruction that sometimes accompanies aircraft accidents, it is not always possible to determine the exact cause. In situations of this nature Res Ipsa Loquitur can be used as a theory or liability. An example of where this was used successfully was the crash of an Air Force C-135 that had been extensively modified by a government contractor. Shortly after the modification the aircraft disappeared in the South Pacific. The court allowed recovery under the theory of Res Ipsa Loquitur.

Sometimes liability can rest with the FAA. This might be the case if the pilot of the aircraft was given incorrect weather information by the FAA prior to the flight or if an air traffic controller provided inaccurate information to the pilot. For example, I once litigated a case where the air traffic controller became confused as to which aircraft he was talking to and provided traffic advisories to the pilot that caused the pilot to look in the direction opposite to the conflicting traffic. A mid-air collision resulted.

In summary, an aviation case requires a high degree of specialized knowledge. However, with proper preparation and a good expert you can learn what you need to know to handle an aviation case. Investigate, know the facts, and develop a theory of liability based on those facts.

MATTER OF ANIS

599 A.2d 1265 (N.J.),
cert. denied, 504 U.S. 956 (1992)

PER CURIAM.

The familiar spectacle of lawyers and their agents preying on the victims of disaster has occasioned revulsion and prompted calls for reform. In the aftermath of the tragic release of poison gas at the Union Carbide plant in Bhopal, India, "American lawyers rushed to India in an attempt to retain clients and in their zeal brought shame and discredit to the American Bar." Eric S. Roth, Confronting Solicitation of Mass Disaster Victims, 2 Geo. J. Legal Ethics 967, 972 (1989) (Roth). The examples of abuse are chilling. Shortly after the crash of a Northwest airliner in Detroit on August 16, 1987, a man posing as a Catholic priest appeared on the scene to console the families of the victims. He "'hugged crying mothers and talked with grieving fathers of God's rewards in the hereafter. He even sobbed along with dazed families * * *. Then he would pass out the business card of a Florida attorney * * * and repeatedly urge them to call the lawyer.'" Roth, supra, 2 Geo. J. Legal Ethics at 972 n.19 (quoting Matt Beer, 'Priest' at Crash Site Recommends Lawyer, Nat'l L.J., Oct. 5, 1987, at 3). After the crash of Pan Am Flight 103 in Scotland, one victim's widow reported solicitation "by no less than 30 attorneys within 24 hours of the crash." Ibid. (citing Andrew Blum, Lawyers Start Mapping Pan Am Crash Tactics, Nat'l L.J., Jan. 9, 1989, at 3, 20).

Other examples abound. "How much money would you like to get out of this case?" a letter asked the mother of a child who had recently suffered brain damage in an automobile accident. It was one of three letters she had received from attorneys within two weeks of her son's accident. In the same envelope was a police report with the lawyer's card stapled to it. In the view of an Oregon Bar Association commentator, "[s]uch a letter clearly offends common decency." Richard Sanders, Lawyer Advertising and Solicitation: the Good, the Bad, the Unethical, 50 Or. St. B. Bull. 5 (June 1990); see generally Linda S. Althoff, Solicitation After an Air Disaster: The Status of Professional Rules and Constitutional Limits, 54 J. Air. L. & Com. 501 (1988) (Althoff) (discussing ethical and constitutional dimensions of solicitation).

The question in this case is whether the commercial speech guarantees of the First Amendment confer on lawyers the right to engage in such conduct—conduct that clearly offends common decency. We think not and therefore disapprove the ruling of our Committee on Attorney Advertising, which held that such a solicitation letter cannot constitute unethical conduct because it is a protected form of commercial speech. We conclude that a public reprimand is the appropriate measure of discipline under the circumstances of this case.

I

This case arises from the tragic disaster on December 21, 1988, involving Pan American Flight 103 over Lockerbie, Scotland. On that homeward-bound holiday flight, American passengers, many of them college students, were the victims of international terrorism. One of the victims was Alexander Lowenstein, a student at Syracuse University and resident of Morristown, New Jersey. His remains were identified on January 3, 1989. The following day, respondent and his brother, Fady F. Anis, sent the following solicitation letter to Peter Lowenstein, Alexander's father:

> Dear Mr. Lowenstein:
>
> Initially, we would like to extend our deepest sympathy for the loss of your son, Mr. Alexander Lowenstein. We know that this must be a very traumatic experience for you, and we hope that you, along with your relatives and friends, can overcome this catastrophe which has not only affected your family but has disturbed the world.
>
> As you may already realize, you have a legal cause of action against Pan American, among others, for wrongful death due to possible negligent security maintenance. If you intend to take any legal recourse, we urge you to consider to retain our firm to prosecute your case.
>
> Both my partner [Fady] and myself are experienced practitioners in the personal injury field, and feel that we can obtain a favorable outcome for you against the airline, among other possible defendants.
>
> We would also like to inform you that if you do decide to retain our services, you will not be charged for any attorneys fees unless we collect a settlement or verdict award for you.
>
> Before retaining any other attorney, it would be worth your while to contact us, since we will substantially reduce the customary one-third fee that most other attorneys routinely charge. Please call us to schedule an appointment at your earliest convenience. If you are unable to come to our office, please so advise us and we will have an attorney meet you at a location suitable to your needs.
>
> Very truly yours,
>
> (Mr.) Magdy F. Anis
> MFA/seb
>
> P.S. There is no consultation fee.

The hollow sentiments of the letter's opening line could only have deepened the family's suffering. On January 12, 1989, Peter Lowenstein filed a complaint with the Office of Attorney Ethics (OAE). The OAE referred the letter to the Committee on Attorney Advertising (Committee). A formal complaint alleged that respondent and his brother had improperly engaged in a written communication with a prospective client when they knew or should have known that the person's physical, emotional, or mental state was such that the prospective client could not exercise reasonable judgment in employing a lawyer. That conduct violates RPC 7.3(b)(1). An amended complaint charged the two attorneys with engaging in false and misleading advertising by sending a letter that was misleading and contained material misrepresentations in violation of RPC 7.1(a)(1). Respondent and his brother have raised a due process challenge to the amended charge, seeking dismissal on the grounds of "unfairness." We have considered their procedural arguments and have concluded that under In re Logan, 70 N.J. 222, 231, 358 A.2d 787 (1976), they have been afforded "sufficient opportunity to meet the charge."

The attorneys also asserted that their conduct was constitutionally protected, citing Shapero v. Kentucky Bar Ass'n, 486 U.S. 466, 108 S.Ct. 1916, 100 L.Ed.2d 475 (1988), and referring to an unanswered inquiry that they had sent to the Committee. Consideration of the full record convinced the Committee that clear and convincing evidence demonstrated that the attorneys had engaged in false and misleading advertising in violation of RPC 7.1(a)(1). The Committee reasoned that although the letter stated that respondent and his brother Fady would substantially reduce the customary one-third fee, it did not state the amount of the fee and failed to indicate any range of fees for the legal services to be rendered. Indeed, it suggested that other attorneys would charge a one-third fee on a recovery, despite the rule that in the event of a recovery in excess of $250,000 no attorney may charge that amount absent a court order. See R. 1:21-7.

The Committee also found that the letter misrepresented the professional backgrounds of both brothers for the purpose of retaining employment in potentially sophisticated litigation, a violation of RPC 7.1(a)(1). Respondent had been admitted to the bar in 1987 and his brother, Fady, in 1984. Neither brother was a certified civil or criminal trial attorney, and neither of them had ever tried a case to a judge or jury or handled a personal injury matter involving the negligence of an airline. The Committee concluded that

> [t]here is absolutely no basis in the record to suggest to the public that they were experienced practitioners in the personal injury field in general and, implicitly, international aircraft litigation in particular. Their perception of themselves, if such was the case, was clearly erroneous. Their representation as to their experience constituted a false and misleading communication.

The Committee determined that without the misleading statement, the targeted direct mail solicitation, notwithstanding the shocking circumstances in which it arose, was constitutionally protected. It reasoned that Shapero, supra, 486 U.S. 466, 108 S.Ct. 1916, 100 L.Ed.2d 475, which had disapproved blanket bans on all targeted mail solicitation, required that result.

The Committee recommended that both attorneys be publicly reprimanded. The Disciplinary Review Board (DRB), which pursuant to our Rules of Procedure reviews such disciplinary recommendations, determined that clear and convincing evidence fully supported the Committee's conclusion that respondent, Magdy F. Anis, had engaged in unethical conduct. It did not agree, however, that the facts merited discipline in the case of his brother, Fady F. Anis. Fady had been out of the State when Magdy had mailed the letter and had not participated in its mailing. The DRB also dismissed a related charge against both Fady and Magdy of violating RPC 5.1(a) (failure to make reasonable efforts to ensure that all members of a law firm conform to the Rules of Professional Conduct). Because the solicitation letter was dated two weeks after the Lockerbie crash, the DRB concluded that it was debatable whether the attorneys would have known that the families would be unable to exercise reasonable judgment with respect to retaining counsel. Accordingly, it found no violation of RPC 7.3(b)(1), albeit not on the constitutional basis of protected speech that the Committee had found. The DRB recommended a private reprimand for Magdy Anis. The Court issued an order to show cause why he should not be otherwise disciplined.

II

The time has long since passed when we can view the practice of law as a matter of public trust in which a barrister's fee was but a gratuity for the performance of a public service. Barristers wore their purses at their backs to allow the payment of fees "without any face-to-face exchange or acknowledgment of the commercial transactions." Althoff, supra, 54 J. Air L. & Com. at 519 n.117. The time has not yet come, however, when we must view the practice of law as akin to the sale of aluminum siding. It is not that we think any the less of those engaged in such a calling; we expect the truth of them too. See N.J.A.C. 13:45A-16.1 to -16.2. It is simply that we expect much more from attorneys. We have adopted a model of professionalism commensurate with the duties of our calling:

> [T]hrough all the [years] * * * the legal profession has played a role all its own. The bar has not enjoyed prerogatives; it has been entrusted with anxious responsibilities. One does not have to inhale the self-adulatory bombast of after-dinner speeches to affirm that all the interests of man that are comprised under the constitutional guarantees given to "life, liberty and property" are in the professional keeping of lawyers.

In re Vincenti, 92 N.J. 591, 603, 458 A.2d 1268 (1983) (quoting Schware v. Board of Examiners, 353 U.S. 232, 247, 77 S.Ct. 752, 760, 1 L.Ed.2d 796, 806 (1957) (Frankfurter, J., concurring)).

From a profession charged with such responsibilities, there must always be exacted "a high sense of honor." Ibid. That standard surely translates into conduct that does not fall below the meager level of common decency that should attend the usual affairs of humankind.

Respondent's conduct falls within a window left open in Shapero, supra, 486 U.S. 466, 108 S.Ct. 1916, 100 L.Ed.2d 475. In a long series of cases the Supreme Court has etched out a pattern for decision in such matters. We reviewed most of the early cases in In re Felmeister & Isaacs, 104 N.J. 515, 537, 518 A.2d 188 (1986), our seminal decision on attorney advertising.

The Supreme Court has devised a standardized legal test for commercial speech cases. Such speech is entitled to constitutional protection only if it concerns lawful activities and is not misleading. Government may regulate even protected speech with laws that directly advance a substantial governmental interest and are appropriately tailored to that purpose. Peel v. Attorney Disciplinary Comm., 496 U.S. 91, —, 110 S.Ct. 2281, 2287, 110 L.Ed.2d 83, 94 (1990). A blanket ban on a targeted direct mail solicitation of parties facing a foreclosure suit could be regarded as a violation of commercial speech rights, Shapero, supra, 486 U.S. 466, 108 S.Ct. 1916, 100 L.Ed.2d 475, but such a solicitation presents none of the factors that concern us here.

The non-intrusive nature of the communication in Shapero is what commended the solicitation to commercial speech protection. See Shapero, supra, 486 U.S. at 475–78, 108 S.Ct. at 1922–24, 100 L.Ed.2d at 485–87. In contrast, the form of solicitation at issue here is so universally condemned that its intrusiveness can hardly be disputed. An editorial cartoon in a Miami newspaper portrayed lawyers after the Delta 911 air crash disaster as "'vultures, members of the law firm of Pickem, Pickem, Scavage & Bone.... Don't Call Us—We'll Call You!'" Howard R. Messing, The Latest Word on Solicitation, Fla. Bar J., May 1986, at 17 n.3 (quoting The Miami Herald, Aug. 16, 1985, at 20A). Those are not the reactions of competitors, nor of establishment lawyers, nor even of airline industry officials. Those are the reactions of the very public that lawyers serve.

We have always emphasized that one of the central goals of attorney discipline is to maintain public confidence in the bar and in the professionalism of its members. We have not enacted a blanket ban on targeted direct mail solicitation. We believe, however, that the proscription of RPC 7.3(b)(1) against such direct solicitation of clients who are vulnerable and probably not able to make a reasoned judgment on their behalf surely embraces the hours and days after such a tragic disaster occurs or, as here, after the loss becomes known. Members of the plaintiffs' bar candidly admit that people are particularly vulnerable at such times. They criticize the controversial "Alpert letter" that survivors often receive from airlines on the basis that "the letter takes advantage of families when they are emotionally weak and vulnerable and attempts to get them to settle for less money than they might recover after filing a lawsuit." Roth, supra, 2 Geo. J. Legal Ethics at 976–77. (The "Alpert letter" is an inverse form of solicitation used by an airline's insurer that is designed to dissuade survivors and the families of victims of mass disaster from filing lawsuits or hiring an attorney on a contingent-fee basis. Id. at 975–76.)

The DRB reasoned that respondent could not be held to have violated RPC 7.3(b)(1) because no proof existed that the respondent actually knew that the Lowenstein family would be unable to make a reasoned judgment about retaining counsel. We disagree. The standard that we attach to this Rule of Professional Conduct is an objective one. We believe that an ordinarily prudent attorney would recognize that within the hours and days following a tragic disaster, families would be particularly weak and vulnerable. Indeed, experience confirms such objective expectations. A mother, faced with attorney solicitation shortly after her daughter's death in a car crash, reacted: "give me some time—I am still grieving." Alessandra Stanley, Bronx Crash, Then Contest of Lawyers, N.Y. Times, June 17, 1991, at B1. That some recipients might not be offended by such a letter does not rebut the generality of experience that the intrusive nature of such solicitation compounds the suffering of victims or their families. Similarly, an objective standard relieves lawyers of the burden of ascertaining whether prospective clients might be unduly sensitive. Whatever doubts may exist about the outer limits embraced by RPC 7.3(b)(1), any reasonable lawyer would conclude that an obsequious letter of solicitation delivered the day after a death notice would reach people when they "could not exercise reasonable judgment in employing a lawyer * * *." RPC 7.3(b)(1). Although respondent proffered that he delayed mailing his letter so that "it wouldn't be tasteless," he admitted that he did not know at the time that he mailed the letter whether Alexander's body had yet been identified.

Respondent's contention that the limitations placed on attorney advertising by RPC 7.3(b)(1) are unconstitutionally overbroad is without merit. The United States Supreme Court has stated that the overbreadth doctrine does not normally apply to commercial speech. See Board of Trustees v. Fox, 492 U.S. 469, 481, 109 S.Ct. 3028, 3035, 106 L.Ed.2d 388, 404 (1989).

We have no doubt, then, that the commercial speech guarantees of the First Amendment do not protect attorney conduct that is universally regarded as deplorable and beneath common decency because of its intrusion upon the special vulnerability and private grief of victims or their families. Even in the limited context of the bland, targeted direct mail solicitation of mortgagors in a foreclosure proceeding, the dissenting members in Shapero emphasized the substantial public interest concomitant with the special role of attorneys. 486 U.S. at 488–91, 108 S.Ct. at 1929–31, 100 L.Ed.2d at 494–96 (O'Connor, J., dissenting). In her dissenting opinion, Justice O'Connor pointed out the reason that we regulate lawyers at all, indeed, to a greater extent than most other professions are regulated:

> Operating a legal system that is both reasonably efficient and tolerably fair cannot be accomplished * * * under modern conditions, without a trained and specialized body of [attorneys]. This training is one element of what we

> mean when we refer to the law as a "learned profession." * * * One distinguishing feature of any profession, unlike other occupations that may be equally respectable, is that membership entails an ethical obligation to temper one's selfish pursuit of economic success by adhering to standards of conduct that could not be enforced either by legal fiat or through the discipline of the market * * *.
>
> Imbuing the legal profession with the necessary [legal and] ethical standards is a task that involves a constant struggle with the relentless natural force of economic self-interest. * * * Restrictions on advertising and solicitation by lawyers * * * act as a concrete day-to-day reminder to the practicing attorney of why it is improper for any member of this profession to regard it as a trade or occupation like any other.

Id. at 488–90, 108 S.Ct. at 1929–30, 100 L.Ed.2d at 494–96.

We have recognized the attorneys' right to distribute truthful, non-deceptive advertising of their services. See RPC 7.1. Indeed, lawyer advertising may provide alternative avenues of relief to members of the public who are unaware of the legal options available to them. Even in cases of mass disaster, general public notices in affected regions might serve that end without the offensive intrusiveness of a targeted solicitation. See Althoff, supra, 54 J. Air L. & Com. at 520–21 n.119.

Nothing in the Constitution, however, requires us to countenance solicitation that intrudes upon victims or their families in the initial throes of their grief. In imposing discipline for such conduct, we wish to make it clear that we do not seek to convert into constitutional doctrine some sort of an effete etiquette for lawyers nor even a disguised version of the previously-disapproved standard of dignity for attorney advertising. See In re Felmeister & Isaacs, supra, 104 N.J. at 547, 518 A.2d 188. What we are talking about here, as is our concurring member, is conduct that is patently offensive to the common sensibilities of the community because it intrudes upon the private grief of victims or their families, serves only to compound their sorrow, and solicits representation of them at a moment of their extreme vulnerability.

On the basis of our independent review of the record, see R. 1:20-5(a), we find clear and convincing evidence that respondent solicited legal representation at a time when he knew or should have known that the prospective clients could not exercise reasonable judgment in employing an attorney, in violation of RPC 7.3(b)(1). We realize that there may be other cases in which it will be more difficult to draw the line of ethical propriety. Would a truthful solicitation letter sent fifteen or thirty days after a tragic loss reach people when they are no longer emotionally weak or vulnerable? We cannot say with certainty, since our assumptions in such cases are largely untested. It may be that there are degrees of loss or suffering. Common sense tells us that the mildly-injured survivors of an overturned-bus incident might be less vulnerable than were the Lockerbie families. Hence, we attempt no permanent bright-line rule in this opinion. We hereby refer the issue to our Committee on Attorney Advertising to conduct the type of informational hearing that might best inform us how we might draw a clearer line of vulnerability. In such a hearing process, the Committee might invite comments from the public or public organizations concerned with the delivery of legal services.

We are mindful that whatever lines we draw may economically disadvantage New Jersey lawyers in relation to unscrupulous lawyers from unregulated jurisdictions. We cannot, however, establish our attorney discipline at the lowest common denominator of ethics. Even those attorneys from other jurisdictions must abide by our Rules of Professional Conduct when they perform services in New Jersey. See R. 1:20-1(a). Pending the suggested hearing process, and in order to give New Jersey attorneys reasonable interim guidance, absent some case-specific indications to the lawyer that the family could not exercise reasonable judgment in the matter, we shall not impose discipline for truthful letters of solicitation sent more than two weeks after such a disaster occurs and loss becomes known.

III

Based on our independent review of the record, we also find clear and convincing evidence that the respondent engaged in misleading advertising in the two respects cited.

His letter incorrectly implied that a normal attorney's fee would be one-third, despite the "graduated fee" provisions of Rule 1:21-7. His argument that the Warsaw Convention invariably limits damages to $75,000 only illustrates his inexperience in this type of potentially complex litigation. When damage is caused by an airline's "willful misconduct," it may be subject to unlimited compensatory liability. See In re Air Disaster at Lockerbie, Scotland, 928 F.2d 1267, 1285–86 (2d Cir.1991); In re Korean Air Lines Disaster of September 1, 1983, 932 F.2d 1475, 1488–89 (D.C.Cir.1991) ("It is settled that willful misconduct negates the due care exclusion from liability contained in Article 20 and the monetary limitations contained in Article 22."). In addition, others might have been made parties defendant.

His letter also falsely implied that he was experienced in litigating aircraft accidents. Nothing could be further from the truth. Even were we to credit fully his proffer of proof about the general negligence practice of his firm, there is simply no correlation between such an office practice and the degree of expertise in aircraft accident trials that his letter implied.

We recognize respondent's youth and inexperience, but we cannot agree that the private reprimand recommended by the DRB will sufficiently measure the discipline to be imposed. The entire record of the proceedings below is before us in this review. Rule 1:20-5(a) requires the Court to review all presentments to the DRB that recommend public discipline. The Committee on Attorney Advertising had recommended that the DRB impose a public reprimand. We conclude that the written solicitation of understandably vulnerable clients and the false and misleading nature of the letter warrant a public reprimand.

Respondent is to reimburse the Ethics Financial Committee for appropriate administrative costs.

[The concurring opinion of Justice Handler is omitted.]

DEMPSEY v. ASSOCIATED AVIATION UNDERWRITERS

141 F.R.D. 248 (E.D. Pa.),
aff'd mem., 977 F.2d 567 (3d Cir. 1992)

DALZELL, District Judge.

Plaintiffs Chester and Helen Jane Dempsey filed this diversity action after settling a state court action in Montgomery County, Pennsylvania. In the state court litigation, the Dempseys sued various parties including Cessna Aircraft Company, which manufactured an airplane in which Chester Dempsey was severely injured. The Dempseys and Cessna ultimately agreed to a $300,000.00 settlement on a joint tortfeasor basis, and the Dempseys executed a release in Cessna's favor.

Plaintiffs now bring this action, alleging that during discovery prior to settlement Cessna withheld a crucial document it should have produced pursuant to a document request in the federal court action. Plaintiffs claim that if this document—a draft Cessna service bulletin regarding the problem of undrainable water in fuel tanks of Cessna aircraft—had been produced, they never would have agreed to the settlement. Cessna's counsel disclosed the existence of the document after Cessna had settled the state court case.

Plaintiffs have not tendered the $300,000.00 back to Cessna in order to challenge the settlement. Rather, plaintiffs now bring this new federal suit, charging that Cessna and its insurer, Associated Aviation Underwriters ("AAU"), committed fraud in negotiating the settlement. Plaintiffs have also named Lonnie Williams, the Claims Manager of AAU's Overland Park, Kansas, office, as a defendant. The Dempseys seek "a minimum" of $1.7 million in compensatory damages and punitive damages "in excess of" $25 million.

This case raises, among other issues, the question of whether a defendant's allegedly improper failure to produce documents in pre-trial discovery permits a settling plaintiff, upon learning of the non-disclosure after the settlement, to keep the money paid in settlement yet sue for additional damages arising from the alleged non-disclosure. Cessna has moved to dismiss the Dempseys' complaint for failure to state a claim pursuant to Fed.R.Civ.P. 12(b)(6), or, in the alternative, for summary judgment pursuant to Fed.R.Civ.P. 56. Defendants AAU and Williams have moved to dismiss pursuant to Fed.R.Civ.P. 12(b)(6), and Williams also moved to dismiss for lack of personal jurisdiction pursuant to Rule 12(b)(2).

We have considered some materials in addition to the pleadings, and have heard extensive oral argument and received supplementary submissions. To the extent that matters outside the complaint have been taken into account these motions will be treated as motions for summary judgment pursuant to Fed.R.Civ.P. 56. As will be seen, however, we largely take the Dempseys' allegations as true, even as amplified in the eloquent argument of their counsel, as we test their legal sufficiency. Ransom v. Marrazzo, 848 F.2d 398, 401 (3d Cir.1988).

Without in any way condoning evasions of duties under the liberal federal discovery rules, we predict that the Pennsylvania Supreme Court would hold that the powerful public interest settlements serve, which is reinforced by maintaining their finality, requires that the settlement and associated release should remain intact as the complete resolution of the parties' dispute. This is an especially confident prediction where, as here, plaintiffs retain the consideration for their release and such settlement is entered into by plaintiffs counselled by sophisticated counsel of their choice.

Cessna's Motion to Dismiss, or for Summary Judgment

Although Cessna is a Kansas corporation with its principal place of business in Wichita, Kansas, there is no dispute between the Dempseys and Cessna that Pennsylvania law governs the dispute between them.

Referring to the leading Pennsylvania Supreme Court authority, Cessna correctly cites Pennsylvania law's high value of promoting and maintaining the finality of civil settlements. The Pennsylvania Supreme Court, in Nocito v. Lanuitti, 402 Pa. 288, 167 A.2d 262 (1961), held that a party who executes a release allegedly procured by fraud, may, upon discovering the fraud, either disaffirm the release and offer to return the consideration, or affirm the voidable contract and waive the fraud. Id., 402 Pa. at 289, 167 A.2d at 263. More recently, the Pennsylvania Superior Court, in Hess v. Evans, 288

Pa.Super. 180, 431 A.2d 347 (1981), held that plaintiffs could not "proceed by alleging that the release was obtained as the result of fraud and misrepresentation and at the same time retain the consideration that was paid to them," id., 288 Pa.Super. at 182, 431 A.2d at 348, citing and discussing Nocito at 431 A.2d 349.

Under Erie Railroad Co. v. Tompkins, this Court is of course bound to apply Pennsylvania law as the Pennsylvania Supreme Court has delineated it. Doubtless in recognition of this fundament of our federalism, plaintiffs cite a recent Pennsylvania Superior Court case, Briggs v. Erie Ins. Group, 406 Pa.Super. 560, 594 A.2d 761 (Pa.Super.1991), which they aver undermines the authority of Nocito. Absent suggestions from the Justices of the Pennsylvania Supreme Court, however, a federal court sitting in its diversity jurisdiction cannot lightly assume that the views of an intermediate appellate court, however recent, are a more reliable indicator of how the Supreme Court of Pennsylvania would decide the present controversy than existing Supreme Court authority, whatever its vintage. This is particularly so given the fact that Nocito can hardly be described as articulating ancient doctrine that serves some arguably outdated policy. See, e.g., Rothman v. Fillette, 503 Pa. 259, 266, 469 A.2d 543, 546 (1983) ("There is a strong judicial policy in favor of parties voluntarily settling lawsuits."); Gray v. Nationwide Mutual Ins. Co., 422 Pa. 500, 223 A.2d 8, 13 (1966) ("it is fundamental that the law favors settlements").

There is no authority suggesting that the Pennsylvania Supreme Court's policy favoring settlements, and securing the finality of amicable resolutions of disputes, is not as strong as it ever was. We therefore decline plaintiffs' invitation to overrule Nocito based upon Briggs.

The terms of the settlement bargained between plaintiffs and Cessna leave no doubt that they intended to settle all claims the Dempseys had against Cessna, even those unknown to them. As is common in Pennsylvania releases, the Joint Tortfeasor Release plaintiffs gave Cessna provided, in relevant part:

> We, Chester Dempsey and Helen Jane Dempsey (hereinafter referred to as Releasor) for and in consideration of the sum of Three Hundred Thousand Dollars ($300,000.00) to be paid to us by The Cessna Aircraft Company only (hereinafter referred to as Releasee) do hereby remise, release and forever discharge the said Releasee ... from all causes of action or claims, known or unknown, for damages arising out of the [state court action].... It is the intention of Releasor that this Release shall be complete and shall cover all such damages, injuries and claims against Releasee, it shall not be subject to any claim of mistake of fact and that it expresses full and complete settlement of a liability claimed and denied, and is intended to avoid litigation between the parties to this Release and is to be final and complete as between them.

Plaintiffs signed this Joint Tortfeasor Release represented at all times by one of the most experienced aviation lawyers in America. After twenty-three years' practice in aviation cases plaintiffs' counsel [Arthur Alan Wolk] has, according to the reported decisions in the GENFED and STATES LEXIS libraries, been involved in no less than forty-four reported decisions, the bulk of them having to do with aviation liability claims. Indeed, as will be seen below in the analysis of the Rule 11 motions, Cessna and plaintiffs' counsel are hardly strangers to one another.

The particular circumstances of this case, therefore, would seem to present the least likely setting in which to depart from the Nocito rule.

Settlements before trial are by definition entered into on incomplete records. Pretrial disputes about compliance with the discovery rules (regrettably) abound. To allow parties to pretrial settlements to keep the benefits of their bargains and still get more would destroy the finality and certitude the parties receive in settlements in exchange for surrendering the contingencies of their claims and defenses against each other. Unsurprisingly, Pennsylvania law calls for no such extraordinary result.

Plaintiffs will therefore keep the bargain they made in October of 1991, but will not be allowed to bite at the same apple again. Cessna's motion to dismiss will, therefore, be GRANTED.

AAU's Motion to Dismiss

Plaintiffs also seek to assert a direct claim against Cessna's insurer, American Aviation Underwriters, as well as AAU's Claims Manager, Lonnie Williams. The gist of the Dempseys' claim against the insurer is that, working with its insured, AAU withheld the document that plaintiffs now say would have radically increased the value of their claim against Cessna.

In order for plaintiffs to maintain any claim against AAU, there must be some legal duty AAU owed plaintiffs. If, as plaintiffs seem to suggest, the insurer was at one with its insured in this enterprise, plaintiffs' claim against the insurer must necessarily fall, as its claim against the insured did, pursuant to the analysis set forth at length supra. If plaintiffs have any claim against the insurer greater than, or independent of, their claim against Cessna, it must exist because of a separate legal duty AAU owed plaintiffs.

Because of the importance of this latter point, and because we were not satisfied with the parties' initial canvassing of this issue, we ordered supplemental briefing. We benefitted from extensive oral argument on December 27, 1991, and supplemental submissions received later.

Besides ordering briefing on the existence of a duty, we also asked counsel to advise us of their views as to whether New York or Pennsylvania law applied to the claim against AAU because it appeared that AAU was, as alleged, a New York insurer. We ultimately learned that AAU is an unincorporated association of twelve insurers, having its principal place of business in New Jersey. See Transcript at 71. Nothing has been brought to our attention to suggest that any conflict exists among the states cited, and indeed it would appear that Pennsylvania's laws, which the parties agree apply, conform with the precepts cited herein.

It is useful to begin with a brief review of Cessna's insurance coverage with AAU. AAU's coverage of Cessna would not include payment of any settlement or judgment in either the settled state court action or the present litigation, had either gone to verdict. It is undisputed that Cessna's insurance arrangement with AAU has a nine-figure retention for both losses and defense costs applicable to the Dempseys' claim. As of the oral argument, Cessna's incurred judgments, settlements and defense costs were under twenty-five percent of this applicable retention. Thus, in the resolution of the state court action Cessna was only using its own money.

Doubtless in recognition of the fact that no one from AAU directly negotiated with either the Dempseys or their counsel, the Dempseys now claim that AAU was, in fact, dealing directly with them in the person of Cessna's counsel. At oral argument, the Dempseys' counsel flatfootedly stated that Mr. Wellington, who throughout the state court and federal court litigation was Cessna's counsel, was also AAU's "agent." On the undisputed reality of Cessna's insurance arrangement with AAU, however, Mr. Wellington was both legally and factually representing only Cessna. Cessna's money paid Mr. Wellington. Cessna's money, and only Cessna's, was at risk. Even if a more traditional insurance arrangement existed here, however, Mr. Wellington's ethical duty was exclusively to the insured, Cessna, and not AAU. See ABA Comm. on Ethics and Professional Responsibility, Informal Op. 1476 (1981), reprinted in P. Allen, L. Occhino, R. Robins & R. Wells, ABA/BNA Lawyers' Manual on Professional Responsibility 801:326 (1986); Point Pleasant Canoe Rental, Inc. v. Tinicum Township, 110 F.R.D. 166, 170 (E.D.Pa.1986) and cases cited therein; Rule of Professional Conduct 1.7, Comment "Interest of Person Paying for Lawyer's Service," reprinted in Pennsylvania Rules of Court, 834–835 (1991). Plaintiffs' "agency" theory is, therefore, without merit, and they are therefore left to find a naked legal duty existing between a distant AAU and themselves.

No Pennsylvania case has been brought to our attention that questions the absence of a legal duty an insurer of a commercial insured owes claimants against its insured. As the Fourth Circuit noted about a contention similar to what the Dempseys make here:

> Such an argument assumes that an insurance carrier which, in reviewing with its insured a claim against the latter learns that its insured was at fault in some particular, owes a duty to advise the claimant of such dereliction on the part of its insured. Obviously, the carrier has no such duty and no court, so far as we know, has ever so held.

In re A.H. Robins Co., Inc., 880 F.2d 709, 751 (4th Cir.1989), cert. denied, 493 U.S. 959, 110 S.Ct. 377, 107 L.Ed.2d 362 (1989). Although one could hypothesize more difficult cases—where, for example, representatives of the insurer directly conducted settlement negotiations that defraud the claimant—that scenario simply did not occur here. Nowhere in plaintiffs' new complaint is there an allegation that AAU in effect took over the negotiations; to the contrary, the settlement was the result of the efforts of Cessna's counsel, [the] well-known and respected major Philadelphia law firm [of Schnader, Harrison, Segal & Lewis]. Indeed, the alleged villain within AAU, Mr. Williams, never left his office in Overland Park, Kansas, or spoke directly with plaintiffs' counsel prior to the consummation of the settlement.

To accept the existence of an independent duty of an insurer to claimants of commercial insureds would necessarily mean that any settlement with an insured defendant would also have to include its insurance carrier. It is difficult to see how such an added complication would promote the strong Pennsylvania policy, noted above, favoring settlement of civil litigation.

Under these circumstances, because AAU owed no duty of any kind to plaintiffs, AAU's motion to dismiss must be GRANTED.

Lonnie Williams's Motion to Dismiss

Defendant Lonnie Williams has filed a motion to dismiss under Fed.R.Civ.P. 12(b)(2) in addition to his motion under Fed.R.Civ.P. 12(b)(6). Although under the analysis of Worldwide Volkswagen Corp. v. Woodson, 444 U.S. 286, 100 S.Ct. 559, 62 L.Ed.2d 490 (1980), it would appear more likely than not that personal jurisdiction does not exist as to Mr. Williams, we need not walk those difficult paths because of our disposition of the Rule 12(b)(6) motion of Mr. Williams' employer, AAU. There is certainly no basis in the complaint to conclude that plaintiffs' claims against Mr. Williams rise any higher than those against his employer, and therefore the action will be dismissed for failure to state a claim against Mr. Williams as well.

Rule 11 Motion(s)

Reflecting the apparent blood feud at least between the insurer and plaintiffs' counsel, defendants AAU and Lonnie Williams have filed a motion for sanctions against plaintiffs' counsel pursuant to Fed.R.Civ.P. 11. Plaintiffs' counsel has, unsurprisingly, vigorously defended himself and has informally filed a cross-motion for such sanctions against AAU's counsel.

As is well known, Rule 11 provides, in relevant part:

> The signature of an attorney ... constitutes a certificate by the signer that ... to the best of the signer's knowledge, information, and belief formed after reasonable inquiry [the complaint] is well grounded in fact and is warranted by existing law or a good faith argument for the extension, modification, or reversal of existing law, and that it is not interposed for any improper purpose such as to harass or to cause unnecessary delay or needless increase in the cost of litigation.

At a minimum, plaintiffs' counsel had the benefit of the Pennsylvania Superior Court's decision in Briggs that gave him, in our view, a good faith belief that the reasoning behind the Briggs holding might be extended to his clients' claims against Cessna, AAU and Mr. Williams. In the materials filed under seal in response to the motions against him, plaintiffs' counsel has also appended an affidavit of a former AAU Claims Adjuster that strongly suggests that AAU's admiration for plaintiffs' counsel is, like Colonel Qaddafi's for the United States, under firm control. This affidavit at a minimum gave plaintiffs' counsel a good faith basis for his averment that the defendants improperly hid the ball to the detriment of his clients.

Rule 11 represents an admonition to federal litigants and their counsel that they must observe limits to their advocacy. It also condemns an "anything goes" style of practice in federal court. It seems fair to say that the gist of plaintiffs' claims here is that they are the victims of an "anything goes" approach to the federal discovery rules. As noted at the outset of this Memorandum, this Court in no way condones such behavior, and thus we can understand and sympathize with the motivations that prompted the instant action. We therefore reject the contention that plaintiffs' counsel has filed this action in bad faith, and in contravention of Rule 11.

In view of our disposition of AAU's motion, to the extent plaintiffs have made a Rule 11 motion against defendants or their counsel, it, too, is denied.

KRIEGER v. ADLER, KAPLAN & BEGY

1997 WL 323827 (N.D. Ill.),
later proceedings at 1997 WL 349988 (N.D. Ill. 1997)

LEINENWEBER, District Judge.

Plaintiff Roy Krieger ("Krieger") sues defendant Adler, Kaplan & Begy ("AKB"), a Chicago law firm that terminated his employment as an associate. Although Krieger filed a fifteen-count complaint, ten of those counts were dismissed by this court on January 5, 1996. Krieger v. Adler, Kaplan & Begy, No. 94 C 7809, 1996 WL 6540 (N.D.Ill. Jan. 5, 1996). Remaining are claims of fraud, breach of contract, violations of the Illinois Wage Payment and Collection Act, 820 ILCS 115/1 et seq. (West 1993 & Supp. 1997), and unfair competition, as well as a claim for an accounting under Illinois law. Defendant now moves for summary judgment. For the following reasons, defendant's motion is granted in part and denied in part.

BACKGROUND

The facts of this case are spelled out in the court's opinion on defendant's motion to dismiss. Krieger, 1996 WL 6540. Therefore, the court will confine itself to a short statement of facts.

As of early 1991, Krieger, who worked [in Washington, D.C.] as a "resident partner" for the law firm of Kroll & Tract ("Kroll"), and AKB were competitors in the field of aviation law. However, in August, 1991, plaintiff's employment with Kroll was terminated, apparently because Krieger refused to relocate to New York. Krieger contacted Fred C. Begy, III ("Begy"), one of the name partners at AKB, to discuss the possibility of joining AKB and opening a Washington, D.C. office. Krieger mentioned that he had just received a $60,000 retainer from Executive Credit Corporation ("ECC") in connection with a fraud case that he could bring to the firm. Begy rejected the notion of opening a Washington, D.C. office, but offered to discuss the possibility of Krieger joining the Chicago office of AKB.

Plaintiff discussed this possibility with Begy in a series of conversations in August, 1991. According to plaintiff, during these negotiations, Begy told him that AKB was a well-managed, stable law firm that would provide plaintiff with client introductions and assist him in developing new business and his professional reputation. Plaintiff asserts that Begy also told him that, while he could not immediately make plaintiff a partner, the firm had an established partnership track and plaintiff would become a partner a short time after joining AKB. Until then, the firm would create a separate category of "Senior Trial Attorney" in order to show the professional world that Krieger held a status higher than "associate." Begy stated that AKB planned to promote four additional associates to this title in order to preserve its partnership track. Plaintiff also contends that Begy promised to pay him $85,000 per year plus a bonus of 10% on all fees collected from business brought to the firm by plaintiff. Begy also agreed to accept the ECC case and transfer of the $60,000 retainer.

At the time, plaintiff, who lived and was licensed to practice law in Washington, D.C., had an offer to join the D.C.-based Pension Benefit Guarantee Corporation ("PBGC"), contingent upon approval from the Office of Management and Budget ("OMB"). However, based upon the negotiations with Begy, plaintiff declined to pursue this offer, moving instead to Chicago to join AKB. In doing so, Krieger canceled his Criminal Justice Act eligibility status in the District of Columbia.

Prior to plaintiff's August 27, 1991 start date, James Bragg, AKB's Business Manager, sent plaintiff a letter outlining the terms of the employment agreement. Krieger contends that the letter changed certain material terms and omitted others. The letter states that plaintiff will be joining AKB's "associate staff" in the position of "senior trial attorney," at a salary of $85,000. Additionally, a "discretionary" bonus, not less than 10% of the fees received from new clients plaintiff brought to the firm, would be paid at the end of 1991. Furthermore, AKB agreed to consider Krieger for "non-equity partner" within two years. Because plaintiff was on vacation, however, he did not receive this letter until several weeks after joining AKB. Though the letter conflicted with plaintiff's understanding of the agreement in numerous material ways, according to plaintiff, he did not formally object to the contents of the letter so as to not "disaffect Defendant." Pl.'s Resp. at 14.

The year-and-a-half relationship was rocky from the beginning. Rather than holding plaintiff out as a "Senior Trial Attorney," Krieger's name continued to be listed on firm letterhead under the heading of "associate"; the firm also listed him as an associate in the Martindale-Hubbell Law Directory. In late 1991 and early 1992, Krieger traveled to London in connection with an aviation case and to deliver a keynote address at an aviation insurance convention. On the first trip, AKB told Krieger to concentrate on existing firm business and not use the trip to call on his contacts. After the second trip, Krieger told the firm about a possible client with whom he had met and who had potential business for the firm, but the firm decided not to follow-up on the lead. According to plaintiff, by not allowing Krieger to cultivate his contacts, his opportunities for generating business and increasing his value professionally were stymied.

Over the following year, plaintiff and defendant disagreed over travel reimbursements and the handling of cases. In November, 1992, Krieger was invited to deliver another presentation in London, but AKB refused to pay for the trip. Krieger, therefore, traveled to London at his own expense, though he did entertain some firm clients while in London.

On February 2, 1993, Krieger was informed that AKB planned to discharge him. Several checks were offered to Krieger representing a $250.00 bonus for 1992 and reimbursement for various expenses. Plaintiff declined to accept most of these checks for fear of waiving his right to contest the amounts owed to him. For instance, Krieger believes he was entitled to a much larger bonus in 1992 from fees generated in the ECC litigation.

On March 3, 1993, Begy informed Krieger that he would be terminated at noon the next day, although he would be paid through March 5, 1993. Though ECC decided to continue having their case handled by AKB, they demanded that Krieger take two depositions scheduled to be held in California the week of March 8, 1993. Krieger agreed to take these depositions despite the fact that AKB agreed to pay only his plane fare and not his salary for the week.

FRAUDULENT INDUCEMENT

Under Count I, Krieger argues that defendant made material, factual misrepresentations aimed at luring him into accepting employment with AKB. There are two categories of statements to which plaintiff refers. The first category includes statements related to defendant's stability and existing structure. The second category includes express promises made to Krieger as to the conditions of his employment.

Turning to the first category of statements, Krieger accuses Begy of having falsely represented, during negotiations, that "Defendant had excellent established relations with aviation insurers worldwide, including AIG Aviation and other of Plaintiff's client contacts, [and] that Defendant was a reputable, well managed, stable law firm, providing ethical practice of law, and proper staffing, management and supervision of matters in litigation." Pl.'s 12(N) ¶ 81; see also Krieger Dep. at 321. Plaintiff alleges that defendant made these statements knowing that they were false in order to induce plaintiff into accepting employment with AKB. Pl.'s Resp. Mem. at 23.

"Under Illinois law, to succeed in an action for fraud a plaintiff must prove: (1) that the defendant made false statements of material fact, (2) knowing that they were false, and (3) intending that the plaintiff would rely on them; (4) that plaintiff did rely, (5) that this reliance was justified, and that (6) plaintiff suffered damage as a result." General Motors Acceptance Corp. v. Central Nat'l Bank of Mattoon, 773 F.2d 771, 778 (7th Cir.1985). Plaintiff, however, cannot prove the first or the fifth elements.

A statement that merely expresses an opinion is generally not actionable misrepresentation. Peterson Indus. v. Lake View Trust & Sav. Bank, 584 F.2d 166, 169 (7th Cir.1978). "[A] representation is one of opinion rather than fact if it only expresses the speaker's belief, without certainty, as to the existence of a fact." Lagen v. Balcor Co., 210 Ill.Dec. 773, 778, 653 N.E.2d 968, 973 (Ill.App.Ct.1995) (quoting Marino v. United Bank of Ill., 92 Ill.Dec. 204, 484 N.E.2d 935)). For instance, financial projections are usually considered to be statements of opinion. Id. Similarly, statements that recommend a seller's product are considered to be statements of opinion by the seller and do not constitute fraud. Sandy Creek Condominium Assoc. v. Stolt and Egner, Inc., 204 Ill.Dec. 709, 715, 642 N.E.2d 171, 177 (Ill.App.Ct.1994). In determining whether a statement is one of fact or opinion, the court looks to the surrounding facts and circumstances. LaScola v. U.S. Sprint Communications, 946 F.2d 559, 568 (7th Cir.1991). Specifically, the court must:

> focus on the circumstances surrounding the representation[s] to determine whether the plaintiff may have justifiably relied on the opinion as though it were a statement of fact. Among the relevant factors in such a case are the access of the parties to outside information and the relative sophistication of the parties.

Id. (quoting West v. Western Cas. and Sur. Co., 846 F.2d 387, 393 (7th Cir.1988)).

In the present case, even if defendant did make statements that touted the quality and reputation of AKB, such statements were made in the process of recruiting Krieger. As the Seventh Circuit noted in LaScola, such puffery is common between a prospective employer and employee and are "merely statements of opinion [that] 'cannot qualify as fraudulent misrepresentations.'" 946 F.2d at 56 (quoting Spiegel v. Sharp Elecs. Corp., 81 Ill.Dec. 238, 242, 466 N.E.2d 1040, 1044 (Ill.App.Ct.1984)). Plaintiff could not have justifiably relied on such obvious self-touting. This is especially true in the present case, where Krieger was an experienced aviation lawyer who could have called his contacts, as well as former employees of AKB, to inquire as to whether AKB was, in fact, a stable, well-respected firm. See Peterson, 584 F.2d at 169. Although it might, for example, be argued that had Begy specifically stated that relations with AIG, a large and important underwriter, were good, that would have been a statement of fact rather than opinion, plaintiff admits that Begy never specifically mentioned relations with AIG. Krieger Dep. at 322.

Plaintiff also contends that defendant concealed facts indicating its internal instability, such as its excessive turnover in attorneys, its discharge of an attorney for her refusal to conceal evidence, its poor administration, its lack of an established partnership track, and its poor rate of promoting associates to partner, having promoted only one associate to partner in its four year existence. As to these claims, the court similarly finds that no reasonable jury could find that such omissions constituted fraud. For the same reasons that Krieger could not have justifiably relied on affirmative representations of defendant's quality and reputation, Krieger could not reasonably have expected AKB to point to all the negative aspects of the firm when in the process of recruiting him. While it is true that Illinois does not create a general duty of reasonable care by victims of deliberate frauds, a victim that ignores a known or obvious risk cannot recover. AMPAT/ Midwest, Inc. v. Illinois Tool Works Inc., 896 F.2d 1035, 1041–42 (7th Cir.1990). It is obvious that, during negotiations, a potential employer will stress only the positive aspects of its firm. Krieger was an experienced attorney who should have recognized this danger and who could have easily done a background check on AKB. Looking at the past few years of the Martindale-Hubbell Law Directory, for instance, would have shown the high turnaround at AKB, as well as the fact that only one associate had made partner in four years. The rest of the alleged concealed facts could easily have been discovered with a few phone calls to colleagues and past employees at AKB. It is not unreasonable to expect plaintiff to make some small effort to investigate the firm he is considering joining.

Additionally, in order to prove fraud through concealment of material facts, plaintiff must show that defendant had a duty to disclose. In re Marriage of Broday, 195 Ill. Dec. 326, 331, 628 N.E.2d 790, 795 (Ill.App.Ct.1994). During negotiations there was no fiduciary relationship between plaintiff and defendant and, therefore, no such duty existed. Thus, under the facts of this case, the alleged concealment cannot constitute fraud.

Finally, as to whether defendant fraudulently misrepresented that AKB had an established partnership track, it is unclear to the court whether plaintiff is alleging that defendant lied by stating that such a set structure existed, or that defendant fraudulently concealed the fact that there was no partnership track, or both. In arguing these claims, plaintiff mainly points to the fact that only one AKB associate was promoted to partner in four years. Such evidence does not lead to the conclusion that a partnership track did not exist. Defendant may very well have had a partnership track, of which only one person met the requirements. In fact, plaintiff points to a statement made by Begy at his deposition in which Begy asserts that the firm did have a partnership track at the time he talked with plaintiff in August, 1991. Begy Dep. at 100. However, plaintiff does offer the testimony of James E. Beckley, apparently a former partner at AKB who left the firm just prior to plaintiff's arrival. Beckley states in his deposition that he did not know of a written policy on the promotion of non-partners to partners. Beckley Dep. at 17. When asked if he was aware of an established partnership track, Beckley responded, "Hell if I know." Id. Beckley's ignorance of any established partnership track is suspicious. Thus, the court finds that there is a genuine issue of material fact as to whether such a track did exist and, if it did, whether Krieger was justified in relying on Begy's assertion that there was such a policy.

The court next turns to the alleged promises made to plaintiff regarding the plaintiff's conditions of employment. Plaintiff asserts that Begy represented to him that defendant would: (1) pay him an annual bonus of not less than 10% of fees collected from new clients plaintiff brought to the firm; (2) make plaintiff a partner soon after Krieger joined the firm; (3) provide client introductions; (4) assist plaintiff in developing his professional reputation and support plaintiff's efforts to develop business from which he would receive the bonus; and (5) provide plaintiff with the title of "Senior Trial Attorney," hold him out as such, and create a separate class of attorneys so designated. Pl.'s 12(N) ¶81. Plaintiff argues that these promises were not kept and that he was defrauded into rejecting another job offer in reliance on the promises. Defendant claims that summary judgment is warranted as the alleged representations were only statements of future intent and plaintiff has not produced evidence that defendant did not intend to keep its alleged promises at the time they were made. Def.'s Reply Mem. at 4.

Promissory fraud is not actionable in Illinois unless the false promise or representation of intended future conduct is part of a "scheme" to defraud. J.H. Desnick, M.D. v. American Broadcasting Cos., Inc., 44 F.3d 1345, 1354 (7th Cir.1995) (citing Illinois law). The "scheme" exception applies whenever "a party makes a promise of performance, not intending to keep the promise but intending for another party to rely on it, and where the other party relies on it to his detriment." Bower v. Jones, 978 F.2d 1004, 1011 (7th Cir.1992) (quoting Concord Indus., Inc. v. Marvel Indus. Corp., 78 Ill.Dec. 898, 901, 462 N.E.2d 1252, 1255 (Ill.App.Ct.1984)). However, "[p]romissory fraud is a disfavored cause of action in Illinois because fraud is easy to allege and difficult to prove or disprove." Bower, 978 F.2d at 1012 (citing Hollymatic Corp. v. Holly Systems, Inc., 620 F.Supp. 1366, 1369 (N.D.Ill.1985)). The limitation on such actions reflects an interest in preventing every breach of contract claim from becoming a suit for fraud. J.H. Desnick, 44 F.3d at 1354. Therefore, the plaintiff has a high burden:

> In order to survive the pleading stage, a claimant must be able to point to specific, objective manifestations of fraudulent intent—a scheme or device. If he cannot, it is in effect presumed that he cannot prove facts at trial entitling him to relief. If the rule were otherwise, anyone with a breach of contract claim could open the door to tort damages by alleging that the promises broken were never intended to be performed. Presumably, it is this result that the Illinois rule seeks to avoid.

Bower, 978 F.2d at 1012 (quoting Hollymatic, 620 F.Supp. at 1369).

Turning first to the alleged promise to pay Krieger not less than 10% of the fees collected from new clients plaintiff brought to the firm, the court finds summary judgment warranted. While plaintiff may or may not have a valid claim against AKB for breach of contract, there is no evidence in the record that AKB did not intend to pay Krieger this bonus at the time the representation was made. In fact, plaintiff admits that defendant did pay him the proper bonus in 1991. Pl.'s Resp. Mem. at 28. Without any evidence of a fraudulent intent, there is no genuine issue of material fact.

Turning next to the alleged promise that plaintiff would be made a partner soon after joining the firm, the court finds no credible evidence leading to the conclusion that such a promise was fraudulently made. While defendant may or may not have told Krieger that the firm had a partnership track, the direct evidence plaintiff points to in order to prove the promise of imminent partnership is quite weak. Plaintiff asserts that Begy told him during negotiations that the firm could not make Krieger "a deal on the front end," but could make him "a deal on the back end." Krieger Dep. at 376. According to Krieger, these words conveyed that partnership would be imminent. "He told me that I would be a partner within a short period of time. I don't know if he specifically said two years at that point in time during that conversation." Id. at 366.

As for the statement that a deal could only be made "on the back end," such a statement is too vague to be considered a false statement of material fact. Such a statement could have a host of different interpretations and plaintiff certainly could not have justifiably relied on such a statement as a promise of future partnership. Furthermore, even if Begy had told plaintiff that he would be made a partner within "a short time," plaintiff cannot point to any specific time frame in which Begy promised partnership. Id. Such a promise is, therefore, too indefinite to be relied upon. Additionally, there is no evidence in the record that at the time such a statement was made, Begy did not intend to make Krieger a partner within a few years. Obviously, the relationship deteriorated quickly; it is quite possible that Begy changed his mind. Thus, there is no genuine issue of material fact that this statement was fraudulently made.

As to the alleged promises that defendant would provide client introductions, assist plaintiff in developing his professional reputation, and support plaintiff's efforts to develop business from which he would receive the bonus, the court finds that there are no genuine issues of material fact. Plaintiff argues that defendant promised to support his "efforts to develop business through providing trips to London," Pl.'s 12(M) ¶41, but that, while sending him to London twice, defendant prevented plaintiff from taking advantage of such contacts. Plaintiff points first to the December, 1991 trip, in which plaintiff was sent to London on firm business, but was instructed by Begy to focus only on the specific case the firm was in London to work on and not to meet with contacts. Begy Dep. at 156. Next, Krieger points to the second London trip in February, 1992, in which plaintiff traveled to London to give a speech. According to plaintiff, an adjuster in the Lloyd's claims office, Bob Chapman, contacted plaintiff after the speech to discuss whether AKB would be interested in assisting him in the litigation of the Nation Air crash in Saudi Arabia. Begy Dep. at 187. However, after Krieger told Begy of this conversation, Begy did not make any effort to contact Chapman. Id. at 189. According to Begy, defendant had previously had conversations with Belmont & Sons, the London firm litigating the case for Chapman, about assisting in the case, and Begy felt there was no opportunity for AKB to get involved in the case. Id.

Even if the court assumes that the above facts are true, with all inferences given to plaintiff, Krieger has not provided any evidence of fraudulent intent. At the time Begy represented to defendant that AKB would support plaintiff's development of business with trips to London, he may very well have intended to provide these trips. Plaintiff admits that on his second trip to London he was allowed to contact clients. More importantly, however, by providing plaintiff with two trips to London, defendant did expose Krieger to the London market. By allowing Krieger to interact with London clients and by paying for him to travel to London to give a speech, defendant assisted plaintiff in fostering contacts. The assistance may not have been to the extent plaintiff wished or even to the extent required by the alleged oral agreement, however, no reasonable jury could find that when Begy offered such assistance, he did so with the intention of fraudulently inducing plaintiff into accepting employment.

Finally, turning to the alleged promises that defendant would provide plaintiff with the title of "Senior Trial Attorney," would hold him out as such, and would create a separate class of attorneys so designated, the court finds that genuine issues of material fact do exist, making summary judgment inappropriate. Plaintiff asserts that during negotiations, without any intention of following through, Begy made these promises in order to lure plaintiff into employment. Begy argues that he told Krieger only that plaintiff could hold himself out as a "Senior Trial Attorney," not that a separate category of attorneys would be created or that the firm would hold him out as such. Begy Dep. at 101–02. Giving plaintiff the benefit of the doubt, the court cannot say at this time that defendant did not make the alleged representations. In fact, the August 19, 1991 letter sent to Krieger by AKB business manager James R. Bragg, specifically states that AKB is "pleased that [Krieger] has accepted the position of senior trial attorney" with AKB, Krieger Dep. Ex. 8, although it also states the Krieger will be joining AKB's "associate staff." Id. Given the fact that the letter was sent soon after Begy made the alleged promise, and the fact that within a matter of months it became apparent that AKB had no intention of holding Krieger out as anything but an "associate," a reasonable jury could find that Begy made an express promise that he never had an intention of keeping. Additionally, a reasonable jury could find that plaintiff relied on this promise in moving to Chicago and in rejecting another job offer.

BREACH OF CONTRACT

In Count III of plaintiff's Amended Complaint, Krieger asserts that the two parties entered into an oral contract that included the following terms: (1) AKB would employ plaintiff as a "Senior Trial Attorney," and hold him out as such; (2) AKB would grant plaintiff partnership imminently; (3) AKB would permanently employ plaintiff; (4) AKB would pay plaintiff $85,000/year plus an annual bonus of not less than 10% of the fees collected from new clients brought in by plaintiff; (5) AKB would promote plaintiff; and (6) AKB would support plaintiff's efforts to develop business and would introduce plaintiff to new clients. Defendant moves for summary judgment arguing that the oral contract is barred by the statute of frauds and that the alleged terms are not clear and definite.

The Illinois Statute of Frauds reads as follows:

> No action shall be brought ... upon any agreement that is not to be performed within the space of one year from the making thereof, unless the promise or agreement upon which such action shall be brought, or some memorandum or note thereof, shall be in writing, and signed by the party to be charged therewith, or some other person thereunto by him lawfully authorized.

740 ILCS 80/1 (West 1993). The Illinois courts have interpreted this statute to mean that a contract must be put in writing if it is not capable of being performed within a year. Lamaster v. Chicago & N.E. Ill. Dist. Council of Carpenters Apprentice and Trainee Program, 766 F.Supp. 1497, 1507 (N.D.Ill.1991). The question the court faces, therefore, is whether the oral contract, as alleged by Krieger, is capable of being performed within a year.

Krieger's amended complaint states that Begy required plaintiff to agree never to leave the employment of AKB. Am Compl. ¶ 18. In its January 5, 1996 ruling, the court ruled that such a requirement did not create an implied promise of permanent employment. Therefore, plaintiff was an at-will employee with no claim to permanent employment. Krieger, 1996 WL 6540, at *6. Although there is a striking absence of recent case law on this subject, the court finds that an oral contract for at-will employment is outside the scope of the Statute of Frauds. See Balstad v. Solem Machine Co., 168 N.E.2d 732, 734 (Ill.App.Ct.1960) (concluding that an at-will employment contract is outside the scope of the Statute of Frauds); see also Lamaster, 766 F.Supp. at 1506–09 (discussing history of Illinois Statute of Frauds extensively). Since neither party was required to continue performance of the contract for any specific length of time, plaintiff's resignation or defendant's termination of the contract within a year would have caused the contract to be performed within one year of contracting. Therefore, the alleged oral contract is outside the scope of the statute of frauds.

Additionally, defendant asks the court to find the alleged contract term for a 1992 bonus barred by the Statute of Frauds since, under the terms of the alleged contract, the 1992 bonus would not be paid until well beyond a year from the date of contracting. To so hold, the court would have to find that the 1992 bonus term is an agreement separate from the 1991 bonus term. Defendant has cited no case law supporting the concept of breaking a contract into individual terms for Statute of Frauds purposes and the court declines to do so here. The entire contract could have been performed within a year of contracting and, therefore, the annual bonus term is not barred by the Statute of Frauds.

Defendant argues in the alternative that the alleged terms were not clear and definite and are, therefore, barred under Illinois law. Under Illinois law, the terms of an employment contract must be clear and definite. Duldulao v. Saint Mary of Nazareth Hosp. Ctr., 106 Ill.Dec. 8, 12, 505 N.E.2d 314, 318 (Ill.1987). The question of whether the alleged promises in the oral contract are clear and definite is a question of law to be determined by the court. Mansourou v. John Crane, Inc., 188 Ill.Dec. 119, 122, 618 N.E.2d 689, 692 (Ill.App.Ct.1993).

The court has already found that defendant did not offer permanent employment and, therefore, will not discuss this alleged term. It is evident that the promise to employ plaintiff as a "Senior Trial Attorney" and to hold him out as such is clear and definite, as are the salary terms, including the bonus. Additionally, the court finds that the alleged promise to promote defendant and to support plaintiff's development of business, while open to different interpretations, could be considered to be an offer. However, as to the alleged promise to make Krieger a partner within "a short period of time," such a term is too vague to be considered an offer. Plaintiff asserts that Begy told him that, while he could not make him a partner immediately, he could make him "a deal on the back end." Such a statement is also too vague to be considered a definite term. Therefore, the court finds that defendant's alleged promise to make plaintiff a partner is too indefinite to be considered a term of the contract and grants summary judgment as to this issue. In addition, since the court has already ruled that the contract did not contain a promise of permanent employment, summary judgment is appropriate as to this alleged contract term as well. The remainder of the terms are all that can be considered to be part of the alleged oral contract.

[The remainder of the court's opinion is omitted.]

IN THE MATTER OF EDDLEMAN

389 P.2d 296 (Wash. 1964) (en banc),
cert. denied, 379 U.S. 990 (1965)

HALE, Judge.

When Anton R. Johansen of Fairbanks, Alaska, consulted William R. Eddleman, a Seattle attorney, in June of 1951, neither could foretell the strange series of events soon to follow, much less that their transactions engendered disciplinary proceedings of the gravest nature.

Johansen, a certified aviation mechanic, owned a two-motored commercial airplane, designated either as a C-47 or a DC-3, which was parked at Boeing Field, Seattle. Hard pressed by numerous creditors, some of whom held liens against his plane, he had talked with Mr. Richard H. Keatinge, a Los Angeles attorney. Since the plane and most of the creditors were in the Seattle area, Mr. Keatinge referred Johansen to respondent Eddleman.

At the time of the first meeting between Johansen and Eddleman, the airplane had not flown for some 22 months, needed mechanical overhaul and maintenance, and repairs to the aileron to cure the damage caused when the wing had been struck by a fork lift operated by Pan American Airlines. This last damage Pan American had agreed to mend.

Following their first meeting, a number of conversations between Johansen and Eddleman occurred, at some of which John Sweet, a young attorney in respondent's office, was present. These conversations culminated in a definitive plan. Johansen agreed to deliver title of the plane to respondent, who, in turn, undertook to raise some money, using both the plane and his personal bank accounts as collateral. Eddleman said he would place the plane in operating condition, pay off all of Johansen's personal creditors, discharge the liens against the plane and obtain repayment of his own funds by chartering the plane out. The plan was explicit [except] for one salient point: How were Johansen's rights in the plane to be preserved so that, when the time came that both he and it were free of debts and Eddleman had been paid for his services, the airplane would revert to him?

Johansen assented to the plan in general but demurred to its details when he learned that he was to transfer title to Eddleman and receive nothing in writing for it. John Sweet likewise informed both of them that the agreement ought to be put in writing. Respondent said that, since he would be advancing money on his personal credit, he had to be free from the claims of Johansen's creditors. He would not place himself in the position where he could be forced to show a document establishing Johansen's ownership of or claims in the airplane. He insisted that Johansen's ownership be extinguished of record. Mr. Eddleman's refusal to reduce the agreement to writing makes the first item of complaint with which respondent was charged.

Johansen remained unconvinced and reluctant to part with title to the airplane until John Sweet, in a private interview with him, assured him that he would, if the situation so required, testify that Johansen was entitled to a return of the airplane upon repayment of all sums advanced by Eddleman together with a reasonable fee for Eddleman's services. Thus assured by Mr. Sweet, Johansen gave Eddleman title to the airplane.

Respondent, Mr. Johansen and Mr. Sweet compiled a list of Johansen's creditors and lien claimants and the amounts of their claims. Respondent borrowed $24,000 from the National Bank of Commerce on both the strength of his title to the airplane and two $5,000 personal bank accounts as collateral. Since he was about to leave Seattle for several weeks, he assigned Mr. Sweet the job of negotiating with the creditors and their attorneys to compromise the claims and reach a final settlement with each of them. Mr. Sweet says that Mr. Eddleman gave him categorical authority to settle each claim for a prescribed amount, and upon this basis he gave the creditors and their attorneys his personal assurances that the money would be paid on the agreed amounts. Upon his return from the trip, Mr. Eddleman repudiated the settlements, disclaiming authority in Mr. Sweet to reach final compromise. Thereupon, Mr. Sweet resigned from Mr. Eddleman's office.

Through Mr. Keatinge, respondent formed a California corporation named 'Kearn, Inc.' and purchased all of the stock in it. Mr. Keatinge's office associates were carried on the company books as the incorporators, directors and officers, but their functions were purely nominal as Mr. Eddleman was, in fact, the corporation. He transferred title to the airplane to Kearn, Inc., receiving no consideration therefor, and the plane, now free from all liens and rehabilitated mechanically through respondent's efforts and funds, was flown to California where its base of operations remained during respondent's period of control.

In this fashion, any physical evidence of Johansen's claims to or ownership in the plane were extinguished by the transfer to Kearn, Inc., and the removal of the airplane from Boeing Field to California. In California, the plane was leased out through respondent's efforts under three separate successive agreements to different lessees. In September or October, 1951, the first revenue derived from these leases, [and] the sum of $5,000 was repaid to the National Bank of Commerce on its loan to Eddleman.

Out of respondent's refusal to give written evidence of Johansen's rights in the plane comes the next incident for which respondent is held to answer in this disciplinary proceeding. It took place in June, 1952.

Eddleman assumed that he had discharged all of Johansen's debts from the funds advanced to him by the National Bank of Commerce, but discovered otherwise when served with a writ of garnishment in the case of Blattman v. Johansen, issued out of the Superior Court of King County, cause No. 446298, demanding answer under oath as to 'what amount, if any, you are indebted to * * * and what effects, if any, * * * you have in your possession or under your control' of A. R. Johansen and wife. To this writ, respondent made formal answer in writing saying that he was 'not indebted to defendants, A. R. Johansen and D. V. Johansen * * * and * * * did not have * * * any effects belonging to said A. R. Johansen and D. V. Johansen.' The answer prayed for dismissal of the writ and for a reasonable attorney's fee.

This answer, deliberately made under oath, was false and intentionally misleading. At that time, the plane was in the possession of a corporation created and owned by respondent for the express purpose of managing the airplane. Kearn, Inc., his dummy corporation, did have possession and control of property in which Johansen had a marketable interest.

In May, preceding answer to the writ, attorneys Paul and Morgan, who had brought the Blattman case against the Johansens (Doris Blattman then being a secretary to the law firm of Paul and Morgan and assignee of the claims), submitted to respondent in that action nine separate interrogatories to be answered seriatim under oath. The first question read as follows:

> 1. Did [you] directly or indirectly, as principal or agent, have a contract with the above named defendants during 1951, relating to a DC-3 Aircraft?

Eight other questions followed, asking for information as to the capacity in which the witness acted, whether as principal or agent, whether the contract was oral or in writing, to state its terms in detail, and whether it had been assigned, and, if in writing, who was the custodian of it, and other inquiries of a similar nature. On June 18th, only a few days after he had answered the writ of garnishment in writing, respondent made written answer to the interrogatories as follows:

> ANSWER TO QUESTION NO. 1: NO
>
> In view of the answer to Question No. 1, questions No. 2 through No. 9 inclusive cannot be answered by this witness.

At the disciplinary hearing on this phase of the complaint, Eddleman sought to justify his answer, claiming that the airplane which he had received from Johansen was a C-47 and not properly labeled as a DC-3, and that, thus, he was technical but truthful in saying that he had no contract with Johansen concerning a DC-3 plane.

All witnesses having knowledge of airplanes are agreed that the designations C-47 and DC-3 are and were interchangeable. C-47 is the name for the military version of the DC-3, and R-4D is its designation by the naval service. In all of the negotiations leading to the transfer of the title and the subsequent chartering of the plane, the two designations were interchangeable. Eleven separate exhibits filed in the hearing show that the plane was referred to and designated as a DC-3, including a lease negotiated by respondent to a Currey Air Transport Company; a mortgage by Kearn, Inc., respondent's wholly owned corporation, to the bank; four insurance riders; several memoranda as to the leases; a repair order; and a letter written by Mr. Eddleman.

Altogether, respondent gave three explanations to the hearing panel for his denial of a contract concerning a DC-3 airplane: (1) He said that he had no contract at all with Mr. Johansen in 1951; (2) that as a part of the original understanding with Mr. Johansen, he thought he was to be engaged as Mr. Johansen's lawyer, but, on learning that Mr. Johansen intended to retain Mr. Robert Beresford as his attorney, there was no meeting of the minds and he had in fact no agreement, and, thus, no contract; and (3) the airplane was a C-47 and not a DC-3.

Through a welter of conflicting and irreconcilable testimony, we can find no basis on which to sustain respondent's answer. Accordingly, the answer to interrogatory

No. 1 must be deemed false and misleading and given with a design and purpose to deceive.

Any claim to candor in its making evaporates in the next event when attorney Frederick Paul, counsel for plaintiff Doris Blattman, the next day, on January 6, 1953, took respondent's oral deposition before a court reporter.

[The court here provides a lengthy excerpt from the deposition.]

We agree with the panel that these answers involved moral turpitude, dishonesty and corruption and constituted fraud and chicanery in violation of Canons of Professional Ethics 15, 22, 29, 32, RCW Vol. O.

That respondent intended to exclude Johansen from any claim of ownership in the plane is seen from his letter to Johansen written January 7, 1953, the day following the oral deposition. On January 5th, Johansen had written respondent pointing out that a year and one half had passed since he had turned the plane over to respondent; he wished an accounting of the plane's earnings and expenditures, and requested that no further arrangements be made for operation of the plane. He advised respondent that he (Johansen) could make payment in full to him as soon as they arrived at a reasonable figure. Respondent's letter of January 7, 1953, to Johansen, stated in part:

> Your letter of January 5, appears to have been written by someone not familiar with the sale of NC74663 to myself nor my sale to a corporation. As you know, I have never lent you any money nor do I have any legal obligation to return same. Neither is there any obligation to make an accounting, however if you are interested in the purchase or operation of this plane I am advised the corporation is very interested and will be glad to make available full records of operation and expense as well as any other information you require to make an immediate offer concerning which I called you * * *.

With this letter respondent burned his bridges behind him, for in it he not only claimed ownership of the plane but dealt at arm's length with his client by negotiating with him for a sale of the plane as though he were a stranger.

Shortly thereafter, apparently upon being reminded that both Mr. [Wayne] Booth [a Seattle attorney] and Mr. Beresford were prepared to testify that Johansen had made neither a gift nor a sale of the airplane to Eddleman, but, on the contrary, that he (Eddleman) had admitted to them his obligation to return the plane to Johansen, Eddleman shifted his ground, and, in a letter on January 28, 1953, indicated that he would return the airplane upon receiving reimbursement for all moneys advanced by him together with a reasonable attorney's fee. This evidence establishes almost conclusively that respondent never had rights to the ultimate ownership of the plane nor did he honestly believe in the existence of such rights.

Negotiations between Johansen and respondent for the return of the plane to Johansen, upon his repeated and persistent demands, culminated in [a] meeting in November, 1954. Mr. Johansen's attorney, Mr. Beresford, accompanied him to the meeting. Mr. Eddleman had prepared and brought to the meeting several copies of a release for signature. In accordance with [an] agreement earlier reached, Mr. Johansen paid respondent a fee of $9,000 for services in managing the plane, rehabilitating his credit, and kindred professional services. Respondent then turned the plane over to Johansen by transferring to him all of the stock in Kearn, Inc. This gave Johansen his airplane and mastery of the corporation. The parties signed mutual releases exonerating each from further liability arising from the airplane transaction. Mr. Eddleman had paid $1,020 for the stock in Kearn, Inc., so his actual fee on the receipt of the $9,000 came to $7,980.

This exchange of releases did not terminate the relationship of the parties, for some time later Mr. Johansen learned of [a leasing] fee paid to Eddleman by Skycoach Air Lines Agency. He asked Mr. Beresford to bring suit against Eddleman for an accounting.

Mr. Beresford, remembering the execution of the mutual releases at the bank, advised against such an action as he assumed that insufficient evidence would be available to abrogate the releases. Thereupon, Mr. Johansen employed Mr. Frederick Paul—the same attorney who had confronted respondent in the garnishment proceeding, the written interrogatories and the depositions—to bring suit against respondent for an accounting of the use of the airplane and income derived therefrom during its operation by Kearn, Inc. Mr. Paul seems to have accepted this employment with more than customary eagerness, and his zeal in prosecuting the claim can in no way be said to have been diminished by his prior professional relationships with respondent.

The trial of this cause, Johansen v. Eddleman (King County, No. 515126), produced another item of the disciplinary complaint; it comes from the testimony given by respondent at the trial. He testified in superior court in this case that, in the summer of 1951, when he took over the plane, he believed its value to be $43,000—that indirectly he had received an offer in this amount from a party in Wyoming.

He admitted that, except for his paying about $27,000 of Johansen's debts, Johansen received nothing from respondent for his giving up to respondent title to the aircraft. He said again he felt no legal obligation to return the airplane but only a moral one upon payment of a reasonable fee and reimbursement for all debts discharged by him. But counsel could not pin him down in his examination as to what, in respondent's estimation, a reasonable fee might have been. He said that his claim to ownership was subject to only a moral obligation to return the airplane—and this on compliance with conditions to be laid down by respondent. It was this moral obligation, coupled with Johansen's violent disagreement with respondent's claim of ownership, that [according to] respondent [caused him] to accept the offer contained in a letter from Beresford in January, 1953, of a fee of $9,000 for return of the plane.

Respondent insisted in his testimony that, notwithstanding his acceptance of the Beresford offer, Johansen never had an option to repurchase the plane, that respondent's granting such an option to repurchase was in fact a mere matter of grace to resolve a dispute with a client. He admitted that, despite Johansen's problems with creditors, Johansen was not without resources as he held a high certificate under Federal regulations as an aviation mechanic authorizing him to certify to the most intricate and important repairs that could be done to an airplane and that Johansen also was a member of the nonscheduled aircraft industry owning a transport operational certificate having a market value of possibly $100,000.

Concerning the previous conflicting statements given by him concerning his arrangements with Johansen, he stuck by his earlier position that Johansen had only respondent's moral undertaking as a lawyer and a gentleman to accept full reimbursement plus a fee to be fixed by respondent in exchange for the airplane.

At the conclusion of the evidence, the trial court found as a fact that the fees received by respondent from Skycoach Air Lines Agency were not excessive for the services and, in addition, was the best bargain to be made under the circumstances. Hence, it was found that respondent received no secret profit and that plaintiff suffered no loss. The case was accordingly dismissed. We affirmed on appeal. Johansen v. Eddleman, 54 Wash.2d 871, 343 P.2d 737.

* * *

This disciplinary proceeding, initiated by formal complaint filed at the direction of the Board of Governors, came on regularly for hearing before a hearing panel consisting of a member of the Board of Governors and two other lawyers. At the conclusion of the hearings, the panel made findings of fact, conclusions of law and recommendations. It drew seven distinct and separate conclusions, based on distinct and separate events, that respondent's conduct, over a protracted period, had been markedly unethical. It made five separate and distinct recommendations that respondent be suspended for a period of three years, and on two other claims that respondent be reprimanded. Thereupon, the findings of fact, conclusions and recommendations of the hearing panel were referred to the Board of Governors.

The Board approved and adopted the findings of fact; it approved the conclusions and the general conclusions of the hearing panel. The Board declined to concur in the recommendations of the hearing panel in all items except two. It modified one recommendation, a three-year suspension, by recommending a reprimand; two items of the recommendations that respondent be reprimanded, the Board approved; four items, on which the hearing panel recommended three-year suspensions, were modified by the Board by a recommendation of suspension for one year. In the light of all of these findings, conclusions and recommendations, ours is the duty to make a final judgment.

Respondent concedes his departure from the ethical standards of the profession in some degree, but asserts that a reprimand is sufficient punishment to both protect the public and vindicate the profession. He points out that his lapses in judgment and professional behavior are in part counterbalanced by the good results obtained by him for a difficult client. He claims that no one was harmed or cheated by him or suffered any pecuniary loss. Many of his client's debts were discharged, including some attorney's fees that perhaps would never have been paid.

And, when it was all over, he returned to his client a fine, serviceable airplane free from all debts and liens, thus yielding to the client, through respondent's professional services, a benefit computed by respondent at about $65,000 in value. He points to the long period of time during which he is held accountable, commencing with events in 1951, and asks the benefit of the doubts normally thought to inhere in proof based on conversations only partially, or inaccurately, remembered, or obscured by both time and passing events.

He asks that these events be reviewed in the softened light of time and distance, and that we consider that Mr. Paul—who pursued him so relentlessly after the deceptive answer to the writ of garnishment had been given—harbored toward respondent a feeling of enmity and ill will.

Time has neither dimmed nor softened the effects of respondent's misconduct as a lawyer, but, on the contrary, sharply etches his actions against a continuing daily practice of his profession over several years. Nothing he did or said can thus be held to be the product of sudden anger, or yielding to an overwhelming temptation. Rather, his actions demonstrate a determined will to prevail, whatever the costs or consequences. Time after time, he had the chance to alter his conduct, to make amends and withdraw from the course he pursued with such ardor.

Mr. Eddleman's course of conduct over a period of years brings him squarely within the letter and spirit of Rule for the Discipline of Attorneys 1, RCW Vol. O; 57 Wash.2d xlvi; 4 Orland's Wash.Prac.Supp. 107. Both the hearing panel and the Board of Governors fittingly described this course of conduct in a formal general conclusion, as follows:

> The evidence submitted to the Hearing Panel shows that respondent was guilty of acts involving moral turpitude, dishonesty or corruption; that he violated his oath and duties as an attorney, violated various canons of ethics of the profession adopted by the Supreme Court of the State of Washington, and was guilty of a course of conduct demonstrating unfitness to practice law.

We start with his sly refusal to give his client a written proof of the client's rights in the airplane against respondent's duty to return the same to his client. By this device he assumed control of his client's property at virtually no risk to himself, for, by his own evidence, he advanced some $27,000 on a plane for which he had been offered $41,000. The Korean conflict had been on for nearly a year. By expending the $27,000, respondent, who had knowledge of the air transport business, knew that not only would all liens be lifted but that the plane would be restored to flying status.

From that point on, including his deceitful answers to the writ of garnishment, his false and misleading answers to the written interrogatories under oath, he showed his continuing unfitness to continue in the profession; and in his false, deceitful and misleading answers under oath on oral deposition, he continued a course of action demonstrably characterized by deceit, pettifoggery and dishonor. His evasions under oath, both in the trial of the accounting action in the superior court, and in the trial of this disciplinary proceeding before the hearing panel, showed that time and travail had taught respondent little concerning the ethics of the profession or his responsibilities to it, the court and the public.

We do not think the long period over which these violations took place makes the respondent less culpable, but, on the contrary, emphasizes his continuing unfitness to practice law. He was, and is, unfit to continue in the profession, and he is, therefore, disbarred. His name shall be stricken from the roll of attorneys.

FINLEY, Judge, dissenting.

I do not concur in the majority opinion. It is my view that the court, in disposing of this matter, should adopt the recommendations of the Washington State Bar Association Board of Governors, nothing more, nothing less.

HUNTER, Judge, dissenting.

I dissent. I feel disbarment is too severe a penalty in view of the circumstances out of which the unethical conduct of the respondent arose; the failure of evidence to establish that the respondent profited at his client's expense; and which, to the contrary, shows a substantial financial advantage gained by the client by reason of the respondent's services.

I believe the Board of Governors of the State Bar Association had this over-all picture in mind when it recommended four one-year suspensions from the law practice and three reprimands as punishment for the respondent. I deem this sufficient and would follow the Board's recommendation.

POYHONEN, Judge pro tem, dissenting.

I would adopt the recommendations of the Board of Governors of the Washington State Bar Association. I believe that the board must have taken into consideration the fact that respondent's misconduct, serious as it was, arose in most part in connection with events six to thirteen years ago. Time and distance alone would not excuse him, but in recommending the punishment to be imposed in 1964 the board may very well have taken into consideration the respondent's conduct as a lawyer during the past six years.

Notes

1. As Mr. Smith's article advises, having a basic working knowledge of aeronautical principles is beneficial. Accordingly, you may wish to review one or more of the following sources: David F. Anderson & Scott Eberhardt, *Understanding Flight* (2001); Chris Carpenter, *Flightwise: Principles of Aircraft Flight* (2002); Albert Helfrick, *Principles of Avionics* (3d ed. 2004); Bill Lane & Azriela Jaffe, *The Complete Idiot's Guide to Flying and Gliding* (2000). You also may want to dip into the airplane thrillers of John J. Nance, the well-known pilot and aviation lawyer. Among his many best sellers are *Medusa's Child* (1997), *Pandora's Clock* (1995), and *The Last Hostage* (1998). *See further* www.johnjnance.com.

Many students also find it helpful to obtain a copy of an aviation dictionary, such as: Dale Crane, *Dictionary of Aeronautical Terms* (3d ed. 1997); David Crocker, *Dictionary of Aviation* (2d ed. 2005); Bharat Kumar, *An Illustrated Dictionary of Aviation* (2002). Other dictionaries can be found on-line. *See, e.g., ABCs of Aviation—Aviation Glossary,* at www.gaservingamerica.com/library_pdfs/AVIATI_2.PDF; *AvGlossary,* at www.speednews.com/glossary/index.shtml; *AvSpeak: A Glossary of Aviation Terms and Abbreviations,* at www.aerofiles.com/glossary.html.

2. In the course of his article, Mr. Smith points out that "NTSB investigators may not be called as witnesses at trial and they may not render opinions as to the cause of the crash. The NTSB permits the deposition to be taken of their investigators. However, the testimony of these investigators is limited strictly to the facts." 12 Utah B.J. at 18. What do you think accounts for these restrictions? Are they reasonable, or should they be repealed? *See further* Christopher R. Christensen, *Changing Tides in the Law Regarding Admissibility of NTSB Final Accident Reports,* 19 Air & Space Law. 4 (Spring 2005); John F. Easton & Walter Mayer, *The Rights of Parties and Civil Litigants in an NTSB Investigation,* 68 J. Air L. & Com. 205 (2003); John D. Goetz & Dana Baiocco, *Excluding NTSB Final Aircraft Accident Reports and FAA Airworthiness Directives at Trial,* 17 Air & Space Law. 8 (Spring 2003); Jack London, *Issues of Trustworthiness and Reliability of Evidence From NTSB Investigations in Third Party Liability Proceedings,* 68 J. Air L. & Com. 39 (2003); Lorri E. Badolato, Note, *Opinion, Probable Cause, Factual Investigation: The Admissibility of NTSB Reports and Investigator's Opinions in Aviation Accident Litigation,* 4 Suffolk J. Trial & App. Advoc. 25 (1999). For a more general discussion, *see* Barnes W. McCormick & Myron P. Papadakis, *Aircraft Accident Reconstruction and Litigation* (3d ed. 2003).

3. As matters turned out, the Lockerbie bombing that got Magdy Anis into so much trouble took 15 years of international efforts to resolve:

> [Following] the 1988 bombing of Pan Am flight 103 over Lockerbie, Scotland, killing all of the 259 passengers aboard and 11 people on the ground, Libya invoked sovereign immunity to shield it from accountability and liability.
>
> A decade later, a three-judge tribunal of Scottish judges sitting in the Netherlands convicted Abdel Basset Ali al-Megrahi, a Libyan national security official, of having planted the sophisticated sixteen-ounce Semtex plastic explosive which took down the 200-ton jumbo jet. No one with knowledge of the region believed that Libya's leader, Colonel Muammar Qaddafi, could have

> been unaware of what al-Megrahi was plotting against the flagship airline of the United States. But foreign leaders, except for the hapless Manuel Noriega (captured by U.S. forces in Panama in 1992 after his fall from office), are not hauled into U.S. courts to answer for past crimes. As to Qaddafi, he had merely to "accept responsibility" without admitting culpability and all would be forgotten, if not forgiven.
>
> In 2003, Libya entered into a $2.7 billion settlement ($10 million per family) accompanied with the proviso that it did not constitute an admission of culpability. The United Nations, and then the United States (for the most part), lifted economic sanctions. Trade relations were quickly resumed. [And v]isiting heads of state made their way to Tripoli.

Allan Gerson, *Terrorism and Genocide: Determining Accountability and Liability*, 28 T. Jefferson L. Rev. 79, 81–82 (2005).

4. Because of cases like *Anis*, Congress passed the Aviation Disaster Family Assistance Act of 1996 (ADFAA), thereby prohibiting lawyers from soliciting during the first 30 days following an air casualty. It took this step shortly after the United States Supreme Court upheld a state ethics rule that banned the soliciting of all accident victims for 30 days. *See The Florida Bar v. Went For It, Inc.*, 515 U.S. 618 (1995). In 2000, Congress lengthened the ADFAA's "black out" period to 45 days. *See* 49 U.S.C. § 1136(g)(2). For a detailed look at the soliciting of aviation accident cases, *see* Lester Brickman, *The Market for Contingent-Fee Financed Tort Litigation: Is It Price Competitive?*, 25 Cardozo L. Rev. 65 (2003). As Professor Brickman observes:

> Very few aviation accident cases are brought annually, on the order of approximately 200. The cases are very lucrative and often involve little or no liability risk because airline companies or their insurers often concede liability and agree to settle the claims. Lawyers compete for these lucrative cases by openly soliciting claimants. For these reasons a handful of law firms have come to dominate aviation accident litigation. Many aviation accident claims, however, are solicited by lawyers who do not specialize in that field of litigation but who intend to sell the claims to one of the dominant firms in exchange for a referral fee.

Id. at 107–08.

Besides advertising limits, some states now certify lawyers as having special expertise in aviation law in an attempt to steer the public to qualified practitioners. Florida, for example, has been doing so since 1995. *See* Robert L. Feldman, *Aviation Law*, 77 Fla. B.J. 44 (Apr. 2003) (explaining that to be so recognized Florida lawyers must pass a written test on aviation law and have a specified amount of relevant experience). Additionally, two publishers have begun compiling annual lists of the "best" attorneys in the field. *See Euromoney's Guide to the World's Leading Aviation Lawyers* and *The International Who's Who of Aviation Lawyers*.

5. Do you agree with how Judge Dalzell handled the issues in *Dempsey*? What, if anything, would you have done differently? Interestingly, studies have found that aviation tort claims are resolved in favor of plaintiffs at a much higher rate than other types of claims. *See further* R. Daniel Truitt, *Hints of an Uneven Playing Field in Aviation Torts: Is There Proof?*, 61 J. Air L. & Com. 577 (1996).

6. As the *Krieger* case points out, the aviation bar is both small and highly specialized, with members having great awareness of each other's reputations and clients (how

then did Krieger miss the red flags swirling around AKB? Although the court says that AKB had no legal duty to reveal its problems to Krieger, did it have an ethical duty to do so?). It is estimated that there are no more than about 5,000 aviation lawyers in the entire country (including those who work for the government), and many aviation law firms are boutique shops with niche practices.

Despite its lack of size, the field is rich in opportunities for professional development and comradery. Many aviation lawyers are members of one or both of the national aviation bar associations—the Lawyer Pilots Bar Association (www.lpba.org) and the National Transportation Safety Board Bar Association (www.ntsbbar.org). (Both of these organizations permit law students to join as junior members; the LPBA also sponsors an annual national law student writing competition.) In addition, a number of generalist bar associations have their own aviation law entities. Among the more prominent ones are the American Bar Association's Forum on Air and Space Law (www.abanet.org/forums/airspace/home.html), the Association of Trial Lawyers of America's Aviation Law Section (www.atla.org/groups/Aviation.pdf), and the International Bar Association's Aviation Law Committee (www.ibanet.org/legalpractice/Aviation_Law.cfm).

Aviation lawyers also benefit from having their own case reporters and law journals, such as *Air and Space Law*, *Air & Space Lawyer*, *Annals of Air Law*, *Aviation Law Reports*, *Aviation Litigation Reporter*, and *Journal of Air Law and Commerce*. Moreover, a number of handy reference works on aviation law exist, including: Jerry A. Eichenberger, *General Aviation Law* (2d ed. 1997); J. Scott Hamilton, *Practical Aviation Law* (4th ed. 2004); Charles F. Krause & Kent C. Krause, *Aviation Tort and Regulatory Law* (2d ed. 2002); Lee S. Kreindler et al., *Aviation Accident Law* (2002); J. David McClean et al., *Shawcross and Beaumont on Air Law* (4th ed. rev. 2004); V. Foster Rollo, *Aviation Law: An Introduction* (5th ed. 2000); I. H. Ph. Diederiks-Verschoor, *An Introduction to Air Law* (7th rev. ed. 2001).

Each year also sees the holding of numerous aviation law meetings, with the most important ones for American lawyers being Embry-Riddle Aeronuatical University's Aviation Law and Insurance Symposium in Orlando in January (www.erau.edu/ec/pd/symposium.html); Southern Methodist University's Air Law Symposium in Dallas in February (www.smu.edu/lra/Symposia/ALS/Overview.asp); and the ABA Tort Trial and Insurance Practice (TIPS)'s Aviation and Space Law Conference in Washington, D.C. in November (www.abanet.org/tips/cle/aviation/pdf.). Lawyers interested in a more extensive study of the subject normally spend time at McGill University's famed Institute of Air and Space Law in Montreal (www.mcgill.ca/iasl/), which offers both a graduate certificate and an LL.M. in Air and Space Law. In 2004, DePaul University's College of Law in Chicago announced the establishment of the International Aviation Law Institute (www.law.depaul.edu/institutes%5Fcenters/aviation%5Flaw/) to provide a similar course of instruction in the United States.

Lastly, there are many aviation trade magazines, newsletters, and web sites—for a comprehensive directory, *see* www.thirtythousandfeet.com. The industry also receives extensive coverage from the mainstream press, particularly in the pages of the *Journal of Commerce*, *New York Times*, *USA Today*, *Wall Street Journal*, and *Washington Post*.

7. Most students who take an aviation law class, of course, do not plan to enter the field after graduation. However, if you are interested in such a job, the following advice should be helpful:

> I frequently receive these questions [about how to have a career in aviation law] and will offer you my observations based on 20 years of experience in this

field. Aviation Law usually involves aviation accident law, FAA enforcement law or FAA regulatory law. The transactional work associated with the formation of aviation businesses and the acquisition of aircraft is really just business law.

Most aviation lawyers handle crashes and defend pilots in enforcement actions. As a result, most aviation legal work is litigation. To be good at aviation litigation, one must be a good trial lawyer. To be a good trial lawyer, one must gain trial experience. Lead counsel, big case, trial experience is very hard to get outside of the Government. Accordingly, I would strongly recommend anyone who wants a career in aviation law to get a job with the FAA or the Justice Department Aviation Unit so that they can gain experience trying substantial aviation cases. Alternatively, you can start as an associate in a plaintiff or defense aviation law firm, but plan on carrying bags and working in the library for a number of years.

By definition, an aviation lawyer should have a thorough understanding of the aviation industry. This usually means more than having a private pilot's license. The typical private pilot does not have a comprehensive grasp of the air traffic control system, in that he or she does not have an IFR rating or commercial experience. Furthermore, most private pilots have limited or no experience with aviation manufacturing, air carrier operations or other commercial activities of the aviation industry. Lawyers who practice aviation law full time work regularly on the commercial side of aviation involving operations under Part 135 and Part 121. Thus, private pilot training is of some, but little, relevance to these matters. Indeed, there are many successful aviation lawyers who have no flight training whatsoever. Through experience, they have learned the specialty and know the industry well. (A private pilot's license, coupled with a law degree can be very relevant for handling the defense of general aviation pilots and FAA license revocation suspension proceedings.)

Some aviation lawyers have a technical background in engineering, which is certainly helpful in product liability matters. But an aviation lawyer usually has to hire an aviation accident reconstruction expert with an engineering background to testify in complex cases. Also, many aircrashes involve operational errors where engineering design is not a genuine issue.

As a generalization, an aviation lawyer should not only have good litigation skills (succinct analysis, writing and advocacy), but should also have a talent for learning technical things. (In their spare time, they can be found tinkering with boats, clicking on computers or building and repairing mechanical things, that is when not travelling to depositions as passengers on the airlines).

One advantage aviation lawyers have is that they work with interesting people in the aviation industry. In my experience, most people who have responsible positions in the aviation industry got those positions not simply to make money or to have a job, but because they are fascinated with aviation. Any time you share a fascination with your clients, your practice will be more rewarding.

Phillip J. Kolczynski, *Hangar Talk*, at www.landings.com/_landings/Forums/al/al-gen-issues.html.

For a further look at lawyers and flying, *see, e.g.*, Linda Campillo, *Peer of Flying*, 60 Or. St. B. Bull. 19 (May 2000); W. Marcus W. (Mark) Nye, *Flying is a Kick*, 40 Advocate (Idaho) 11 (July 1997); Ruth E. Piller, *Res Ipsa: Lockheed Attorney Flies to Nearby Venues*, 40 Hous. Law. 52 (July/Aug. 2002); Beth Warrington, *Soaring to the Clouds to Earn a Law Degree*, 74 J. Kan. B.A. 5 (Jan. 2005); *Legal Eagle: New HBA President Scott*

Rozzell is Committed to His Profession, Community, Family ... and His Vintage Plane, 34 Hous. Law. 8 (July/Aug. 1996).

8. The *Eddleman* case obviously is not typical (one hopes!), although it does point out that aviation lawyers often find themselves in a position to do great harm to their clients, many of whom appear on their doorsteps in extremis. After reading both the majority and dissenting opinions, do you think Eddleman got what he deserved? If you had been on the court, would you have voted for disbarment, suspension, or some other form of punishment? What about John Sweet—should he have been sanctioned for his role in the case? And what about Richard Keatinge—should he have been reprimanded by the California Supreme Court for his help in setting up Kearn, Inc.?

Problem 5

An aviation lawyer agreed to represent an accident victim on a contingent fee basis. After three years of work, the lawyer was able to negotiate what she felt was an excellent settlement for the client. The amount also would provide the lawyer with a handsome payday. The client, however, balked at the figure, insisting that the case was worth at least 20% more than what was being offered. Given this turn of events, what options are available to the lawyer? *See State ex rel. Counsel for Discipline v. Sipple*, 660 N.W.2d 502 (Neb.), *cert. denied*, 540 U.S. 985 (2003).

Chapter 2

Aircraft

A. OVERVIEW

If an aircraft malfunctions, lawsuits may be brought against the entities that designed it, built it, sold it, or, as happens frequently, modified or repaired it.

Actions against manufacturers and similarly-situated parties can be based on a number of different theories, including contract, breach of warranty, and fraud, although negligence and products liability are the two most common grounds. To be successful, a plaintiff must overcome both the standard sorts of defenses as well as certain more specialized ones. In addition, difficult venue and choice of law questions frequently arise in such cases.

Before an airplane can legally fly, however, it must be properly certificated. In most instances, the documentation will include a mortgage (over time, other liens also may accrue and be recorded). And, of course, to keep flying, it must pay its taxes. We will examine these subjects first and then turn to the liability issues.

B. DOCUMENTATION

JET WAY: HOW TO BUY AND KEEP THAT CORPORATE PLANE

Jeffrey S. Wieand

6 Bus. L. Today 58 (Mar./Apr. 1997)

Buying an airplane is similar in some ways to buying a house. For example, there is likely to be a short "offer to purchase" document reminiscent of similar documents widely used to create a skeletal contract to purchase residential real estate. The seller will probably insist on a "deposit," in the form of earnest money to be held in escrow. The deposit is frequently held by an aircraft title company, which will charge a relatively modest fee based on the size of the deposit. These firms have offices in Oklahoma City, Okla., where the FAA aircraft registry is located.

The offer to purchase should set forth the principal terms of the transaction, including the manufacturer, model number, serial number and FAA registration number of the aircraft and its engines, the price and the proposed closing date. The offer to purchase should be contingent on the parties' entry into a mutually acceptable aircraft purchase agreement and should give the buyer the opportunity to conduct a detailed pre-purchase inspection of the aircraft, including a flight check, usually at the buyer's expense. A number of aviation companies will perform this service for a fee. The pre-purchase inspection will usually result in a "punch list" of items to be remedied. In many cases, the company conducting the inspection can remedy the defects itself relatively quickly. The seller [sh]ould typically expect the deposit to become non-refundable when these discrepancies are cured.

To purchase the plane, you will need a written aircraft purchase agreement. Like the offer to purchase, the agreement should be very specific about the description of the aircraft and all of the equipment and personal property that is included in the price.

In addition to standard representations concerning matters such as legal existence, approvals, authority, conflicts and validity, the purchase agreement should contain representations and warranties about the aircraft. The agreement should state that the aircraft is in compliance with all mandatory service bulletins and airworthiness directives and that maintenance under the manufacturer's recommended program is current. The seller should also represent that the logs and records provided with the aircraft are complete and up to date. If the plane is reputed to have no damage history, the agreement should make this clear.

Given the staggering potential liability associated with an aircraft (imagine crashing into a school or a nuclear power plant), the seller will want to include language disclaiming any implied or unspecified warranties. Although this is customary and standard, state law may to some extent invalidate such disclaimers. The purchaser should at least make certain that any warranties running to the seller from the manufacturers of the aircraft, engines and parts will be transferred to the purchaser. The seller should also warrant title to the aircraft free of liens and encumbrances. This warranty is generally given effect through a separately provided warranty bill of sale. The seller will want the purchaser to indemnify it for damages and expenses resulting from the purchaser's ownership or operation of the aircraft, and the purchaser should endeavor to obtain a corresponding indemnity from the seller.

Like any good purchase contract, an aircraft purchase agreement will contain conditions precedent to the obligations of the parties, provisions governing termination of the contract, and covenants regarding the payment of expenses and brokers', consultants' and finders' fees.

In addition to any state registration, the corporate jet must be registered with the FAA aircraft registry in Oklahoma City, Okla. 49 U.S.C. Section 1403. Registration is accomplished by filing an Aircraft Registration Application on AC Form 8050-1 and a bill of sale on AC Form 8050-2. Liens on registered aircraft are also recorded at the registry. The recording of a lien on the aircraft on the FAA registry is sufficient to perfect the lien, although other forms of perfection under state law may be possible. See Danning v. World Airways Inc., 647 F.2d 977 ([9th Cir.] 1981), cert. den., 454 U.S. 1146 (1982). A secured lender may request additional state UCC filings to perfect a lien on personal property on the aircraft.

You should check to see that any aircraft to be purchased is free of recorded liens by retaining an Oklahoma City title company to conduct a lien search on the FAA registry. As part of your closing (ideally by a conference call in which a lawyer or a representative of a title company participates from the FAA registry) you will want to confirm the filing of your registration application, bill of sale and any lien releases.

ICKES v. FEDERAL AVIATION ADMINISTRATION

299 F.3d 260 (3d Cir. 2002)

PER CURIAM.

The petitioner, Don R. Ickes ("Ickes"), seeks review of an Emergency Cease and Desist Order (the "Emergency Order") issued by the respondent, the Federal Aviation Administration (the "FAA"). The FAA issued the Emergency Order to bring Ickes and his aircraft into compliance with federal regulations and to prevent the flight of aircraft during a weekend of fly-by demonstrations that Ickes planned to conduct on his property in Osterburg, Pennsylvania. Ickes claims that the FAA abused its authority in issuing the Emergency Order because he flies only ultralight vehicles, which, unlike aircraft, are not subject to federal certification and registration requirements. He also contends that the circumstances surrounding his air show did not give rise to an emergency so as to justify the issuance of a cease and desist order with immediate effect. We hold that the FAA did not err in subjecting Ickes and his aircraft to regulation or in determining that his air show posed an exigent danger warranting an immediate response. We will, therefore, affirm the Emergency Order.

I.

Ickes resides in Osterburg, where he owns a thirty-eight acre tract of land that he refers to as both "Ickes Airport" and "Ickes Recreational Park." Ickes claims to be an experienced aviator, and he has operated an airfield on the Osterburg property since at least 1987. According to Ickes, he uses the airfield solely for the recreational purpose of flying ultralight vehicles. An "ultralight vehicle" is defined in relevant part as one that

> (a) Is used or intended to be used for manned operation in the air by a single occupant; ... and
>
> (e) If powered:
>
> (1) Weighs less than 254 pounds empty weight ... ;
>
> (2) Has a fuel capacity not exceeding 5 U.S. gallons; [and]
>
> (3) Is not capable of more than 55 knots calibrated airspeed at full power in level flight....

14 C.F.R. § 103.1 (2002). Unlike "aircraft," which can be operated only if registered under 49 U.S.C. § 44103 (1997), see 49 U.S.C. § 44101; 14 C.F.R. § 47.3, vehicles that meet the definition of an ultralight presently are not required to be registered or to bear markings of any type, are not required to meet airworthiness certification standards, and their operators are not required to meet any aeronautical knowledge, age, or experience requirements or to have airman or medical certificates. 14 C.F.R. § 103.7. Ultra-

lights are, nevertheless, subject to various operating restrictions. E.g., 14 C.F.R. § 103.9(a) ("No person may operate any ultralight vehicle in a manner that creates a hazard to other persons or property"); 14 C.F.R. § 103.15 ("No person may operate an ultralight vehicle over any congested area of a city, town, or settlement, or over any open air assembly of persons.").

The FAA has repeatedly cited Ickes for his failure to register the Challenger II as an aircraft and for other regulatory infractions. Specifically, on February 25, 1992, the FAA's Eastern Regional Counsel assessed Ickes a civil penalty of $3,000 after finding that he piloted the Challenger II to and from Altoona-Blair County Airport (a short distance from Ickes' property) without an airworthiness certificate, registration, or pilot certificate. The FAA expressly found that the Challenger II must be registered as an aircraft. Notably, Ickes did not seek agency or judicial review of this order.

On May 6, 1999, the FAA's Eastern Regional Counsel then issued an emergency order to revoke Ickes' Student Pilot Certificate. Among other things, the FAA found that Ickes operated the Challenger II on numerous occasions in the latter half of 1998 in a manner that endangered life and property on the ground, including flying too low and without proper training for solo flight. The FAA concluded that Ickes lacked the "degree of care, judgment, and responsibility required of the holder of a Student Pilot Certificate." Ickes again did not seek review of the FAA order.

On January 25, 2001, the FAA's Eastern Regional Counsel assessed Ickes another civil penalty, this time for $28,000, after finding that he operated the Challenger II from October through November, 1998, without a registration, proper markings, or an airworthiness certificate. Once again, the FAA determined that Ickes' Challenger II—which it found was capable of more than 50 knots calibrated airspeed at full power in level flight, had an empty weight of 300 pounds, a 42-horsepower engine, and a fuel capacity in excess of 5 gallons—was an aircraft. Ickes did not seek further review.

Finally, between February and May, 2001, the FAA received reports, mainly from Ickes' neighbors, that Ickes continued to fly the Challenger II. The FAA then learned that Ickes posted an advertisement on an Internet website in which he invited the public to attend a gathering on his property from June 29, 2001 through July 1, 2001. Ickes billed the event as an "EAA Ultralight Chapter Gathering at the Ickes Recreational Park." He promised fly-by demonstrations as well as a "candy drop for children," "horseback riding," and "dirtbike trails and demonstrations."

Upon learning of Ickes' proposed air show, and noting Ickes' history of unlawful use of the Challenger II, the FAA issued the Emergency Order on June 28, 2001, to preempt Ickes' use of aircraft during the event. In particular, the FAA required in the Emergency Order that Ickes immediately cease and desist from operating the Challenger II or any other aircraft until such time as he obtains airman, airworthiness, medical, and registration certificates; affixes appropriate identification markings to his aircraft; and submits the aircraft to an authorized person for appropriate maintenance inspection and approval for service prior to operation.

Ickes timely filed a petition for review of the Emergency Order in this Court. We have jurisdiction pursuant to 49 U.S.C. § 46110(a).

II.

Ickes presents three main arguments for our review. First, he maintains that the Commerce Clause does not give Congress the power to regulate his Challenger II because it never flies across state lines. Second, he asserts that his Challenger II is an ultralight vehicle and that the FAA has improperly treated it as an aircraft. Third, he claims that no exigent circumstances existed to justify the FAA's issuance of a preemptive cease and desist order. We review his constitutional claim first.

A.

Ickes argues that Congress lacked Commerce Clause authority to regulate his operation of the Challenger II, as he contends that his flights are purely an intrastate recreational activity and do not affect interstate air commerce or endanger air safety. The Supreme Court has identified three broad areas of activity subject to regulation under the Commerce Clause: (1) the use of the channels of interstate commerce; (2) protection of the instrumentalities of interstate commerce, or persons or things in interstate commerce, even though the threat may come only from intrastate activities; and (3) activities having a substantial relation to interstate commerce. United States v. Lopez, 514 U.S. 549, 558–59, 115 S.Ct. 1624, 131 L.Ed.2d 626 (1995); see also United States v. Morrison, 529 U.S. 598, 608–09, 120 S.Ct. 1740, 146 L.Ed.2d 658 (2000). It is beyond dispute that Congress's power over interstate commerce includes the power to regulate use of the nation's navigable airspace, which is a channel of interstate commerce. In addition, because airplanes constitute instrumentalities of interstate commerce, United States v. Bishop, 66 F.3d 569, 588 (3d Cir.1995), any threat to them, such as the one posed by Ickes' flights of his Challenger II, is properly subjected to regulation even if the threat comes from a purely intrastate activity. See id.; see also United States v. McHenry, 97 F.3d 125, 127 (6th Cir.1996). Ickes' constitutional challenge, therefore, is without merit.

Ickes next asserts that his Challenger II is an ultralight vehicle and that the FAA has improperly treated it as an aircraft. He also claims that no exigent circumstances existed to justify the FAA's issuance of a preemptive cease and desist order. We will address each of these arguments in turn.

B.

Ickes insists that his Challenger II is an ultralight vehicle notwithstanding the FAA's repeated findings that it is eligible for registration as an aircraft. He claims that the vehicle qualifies as an "ultralight trainer" and that he is authorized to use it for instructional purposes. He contends that the plane was properly registered with Aero Sports Connection ("ASC"), a nonprofit organization that supports ultralight flying activities. The FAA granted ASC an exemption from regulation in 1995 so that it could train and then authorize individuals to give basic flight instruction using two-seat aircraft (like the Challenger II) that would otherwise exceed the weight and speed specifications for ultralights. Ickes received instructor certification under the ASC program, and the ASC issued him an exemption to operate a two-seat aircraft for instructional purposes. Thus, Ickes contends, the FAA improperly determined that his Challenger II is an aircraft.

Our review of this purely factual question is limited. We must accept the FAA's finding as conclusive "if it is supported by substantial evidence." 49 U.S.C. § 46110(c). "Substantial evidence is such relevant evidence as a reasonable mind might accept as adequate to support a conclusion ... taking into account whatever in the record fairly detracts from its weight." Van Dyke v. NTSB, 286 F.3d 594, 597 (D.C.Cir.2002) (quotation marks and citations omitted); see also Penobscot Air Services v. FAA, 164 F.3d 713, 717–18 (1st Cir.1999) (discussing the substantial evidence standard).

It is undisputed that the Challenger II has two seats, and that fact alone removes it from the ultralight category because it is not "used or intended to be used for manned operation in the air by a single occupant." 14 C.F.R. § 103.1(a). Furthermore, Ickes does not dispute the FAA's finding (nor did he ever appeal or petition for review of the findings in the earlier FAA proceedings) that his plane has an empty weight of 300 pounds, a fuel capacity in excess of 5 gallons, and a potential cruise speed of approximately 56–69 knots. See 14 C.F.R. § 103.1(e). Thus, based on its physical characteristics, Ickes' Challenger II is not an ultralight.

As to the ASC exemption, the record reflects that Ickes' authorization to conduct ultralight training using his Challenger II expired on June 30, 2000, almost one year before the FAA issued the Emergency Order. Ickes has failed to show that he can claim a valid exemption extending through the time when the Emergency Order was issued. (In fact, Ickes' ASC exemption may have expired or been withdrawn as early as October 5, 1998. Supplemental Appendix at 5. We will assume June 30, 2000, was the expiration date for purposes of our analysis here.)

The only evidence Ickes cites from the relevant period in 2001 are two letters, dated January 14, 2001 and April 16, 2001, from Bob Enos, a basic flight instructor certified by the United States Ultralight Association. The Enos letters reflect that Ickes completed a written examination demonstrating aeronautical knowledge for flight in a "Challenger II Trainer." Enos also offered an endorsement of Ickes' ability to make safe solo flights in a Challenger II for a period of 90 days from issuance of the letters. Ickes seems to suggest that, because Enos authorized him to make solo flights in a "Challenger II Trainer," the vehicle qualified as an ultralight. Reply Br. at 14.

We find nothing in the Enos letters, however, that even arguably exempts the Challenger II from regulation as an aircraft. Although the letters referred to Ickes' plane as a "Challenger II Trainer," it is undisputed that the plane's physical and operational characteristics placed it outside the ultralight category. Moreover, Ickes has produced no evidence to show that he could claim the benefit of the ASC exemption, or any other exemption from regulation, during 2001. As such, the record fails to support his assertion that the Challenger II qualified as an ultralight trainer during that time.

In sum, while Ickes has shown that his Challenger II might have been properly deemed an ultralight trainer when his ASC exemption was in effect, we find substantial evidence to support the FAA's determination that the vehicle qualified as an aircraft when the FAA issued the Emergency Order on June 28, 2001.

C.

Ickes next contends that his air show presented no exigent circumstances, that the FAA's treatment of the situation as an emergency was an error in judgment, and that the FAA abused its authority by issuing a cease and desist order without providing him with notice and an opportunity to be heard. Ickes thus contends that the FAA's treatment of the situation as an emergency was an error in judgment. We reject this contention.

Contrary to Ickes' suggestion that "[t]he grievances feeding this controversy have been primarily non-safety in nature," Appellant's Br. at 7, the FAA's concerns were almost exclusively safety-related. Ickes' decision to conduct a public air show at which he intended to fly his Challenger II—an aircraft that had not been properly registered or inspected in compliance with federal law—raised an indisputable safety concern for the people who would attend the show, for anyone or anything on the ground within the potential flight range of that aircraft, and for any aircraft that might pass through the airspace surrounding Ickes' property. The record reveals that a low-level federal airway, identified as V469, passes immediately north of Osterburg, and a number of additional airways are within several miles of Osterburg, as are Altoona-Blair County Airport and Johnstown-Cambria County Airport, both of which receive commercial air traffic.

Moreover, Ickes had a history of endangering life and property on the ground, as evidenced by the FAA's finding in 1999 that he operated the Challenger II in a reckless manner on numerous occasions. Ickes never sought review of that agency finding, and in fact he never formally challenged any of the numerous infractions cited in the FAA's prior orders against him. Given this record, safety was undoubtedly the FAA's predominant concern in treating the situation here as an emergency.

As to the FAA's authority to respond to an emergency, Congress has conferred broad power upon the FAA Administrator to conduct investigations and to issue orders that the Administrator "considers necessary" to carry out the FAA's mandate. 49 U.S.C. § 40113(a).

In view of this broad discretion, our standard of review when assessing an FAA response to a perceived emergency is appropriately deferential: we ask only whether the finding of an emergency "'was a "clear error of judgment" lacking any rational basis in fact.'" Id. (quoting Nevada Airlines, Inc. v. Bond, 622 F.2d 1017, 1021 (9th Cir.1980)). The present record reveals no clear error of judgment. The FAA duly noted the inherent public danger posed by those who operate aircraft unlawfully in this country. Ickes, moreover, had a verified history of unlawful operation of the Challenger II, the FAA had received reports in early 2001 that he continued making such flights, and Ickes' advertisement over the Internet invited the public to gather on his property for a weekend of fly-by demonstrations. It is undisputed that the demonstrations were to include the Challenger II, an aircraft that Ickes failed to have certified as airworthy or inspected by an authorized mechanic.

Ickes also did not hold a valid pilot certificate or airman medical certificate. The FAA thus had concrete information as to specific dates on which Ickes planned to conduct unlawful flights of an aircraft, and it had a limited time in which to stop those flights so as to protect the safety of the people and property that could be harmed by Ickes' malfeasance. We conclude that Ickes' air show posed an undeniable exigent danger. We see no clear error of judgment in the FAA's invocation of its broad powers under § 46105(c) in an attempt to stop his unlawful flights. Given that the FAA committed no error in deeming Ickes' air show an emergency that required an immediate response, the agency certainly did not err in foregoing prior notice pursuant to 14 C.F.R. § 13.20(b).

Order affirmed.

AIR ONE HELICOPTERS, INC. v. FEDERAL AVIATION ADMINISTRATION

86 F.3d 880 (9th Cir. 1996)

THOMPSON, Circuit Judge.

Air One Helicopters, Inc. (Air One), the undisputed owner of a helicopter, has been ensnared in webs of bureaucratic regulation spun by two countries, Spain and the

United States. The effect has been to preclude Air One from registering its helicopter with the Federal Aviation Administration (FAA) even though it is crystal clear Air One owns the aircraft, has discharged the lien which once attached to it, and the aircraft's current registration in Spain is no longer valid.

We grant review and end the bureaucratic gridlock. We reverse the FAA's denial of Air One's application, and direct the FAA to register the helicopter showing Air One as its owner.

I
FACTS

Air One bought the helicopter, a Sikorski S-58T, serial number 58-1626, in 1990 from a Spanish company, Helisca Helicopters, S.A. (Helisca), and attempted to register the aircraft with the FAA pursuant to federal law and FAA implementing regulations. See 49 U.S.C.App. §1401 et seq.; 14 C.F.R. §47.37. (Title 49 has been revised since the incidents giving rise to this petition. The revisions do not make any substantive changes in the law relevant to this case. We will refer to the old citations in the text because they governed the actions of the parties. 49 U.S.C.App. §1401 is now codified at 49 U.S.C. §44101, et seq.)

In 1992, the FAA issued an opinion letter which stated that Air One's helicopter was not eligible for registration because the aircraft was still registered in Spain. An aircraft cannot have dual registration under the Chicago Convention on International Civil Aviation (Chicago Convention). See 61 Stat. 1180, T.I.A.S. 1591 (December 7, 1944). The FAA instructed Air One to obtain from the Direccion General de Aviacion Civil (DGAC), Spain's national aircraft registry, a statement that the helicopter's Spanish registration was no longer valid. Without such a statement, the FAA deemed Air One's helicopter ineligible for registration in the United States.

Air One unsuccessfully petitioned the DGAC in Spain for a statement of de-registration. The DGAC refused to provide such a statement because the registry showed a lien on the helicopter in the name of a Norwegian corporation, Sameiet Heli Invest I (Sameiet). The DGAC insists Air One must obtain an official corporate document from Sameiet declaring the corporation has been paid in full for the helicopter before the DGAC will de-register the aircraft.

Sameiet, however, was never a corporate entity registered under Norwegian law or elsewhere, and it no longer exists in any form. Therefore, there is no possibility that Air One will ever be able to obtain the official corporate document from Sameiet which the DGAC in Spain demands.

Air One has diligently attempted to get the DGAC to de-register the aircraft without such a statement, but the DGAC has steadfastly resisted these efforts. Air One provided the DGAC with a sworn affidavit from Asmud Simonson, the President of the parent company of Sameiet, stating that Helisca had paid Sameiet in full for the helicopter. The record indicates that Simonson "formed" Sameiet for the sole purpose of buying and selling this particular helicopter. Although he used the Sameiet name in its corporate form for the transaction, he did not incorporate Sameiet under Norwegian law, or anywhere else. As a result, there never were any officers or directors of Sameiet, and it never had a corporate seal. There is absolutely no way it can provide the official corporate document the DGAC demands.

Simonson's affidavit explaining the circumstances was deemed insufficient by the DGAC, which again demanded a corporate document. Air One has since enlisted the assistance of the United States Embassy in Madrid, but it was unable to persuade the

DGAC to de-register the helicopter. Air One, with the cooperation of Simonson and Helisca, retained legal counsel in Spain. The attorneys advised Air One that bringing a court challenge there will be unsuccessful because of the Spanish judiciary's deference to the DGAC's administrative decisions and that a court challenge might take up to ten years.

Air One filed two registration applications with the FAA explaining these circumstances and including all of the relevant correspondence. Each time, the FAA has responded with letters stating Air One's helicopter is ineligible for registration in the United States unless Air One obtains a de-registration statement from Spain.

II
DISCUSSION

The first question we consider is whether we have jurisdiction to entertain Air One's petition for review. The FAA argues the position it has taken in its opinion letter and in its two additional letters is not reviewable because these letters do not constitute "final agency action" within the meaning of section 1006(a) of the Federal Aviation Act, 49 U.S.C.App. § 1486(a) (now codified at 49 U.S.C. § 46110).

The FAA contends the letters do not amount to a definitive statement of the agency's position, nor do they impose any obligation, deny any right, or fix any legal relationship as required by our decision in Air California v. U.S. Dep't of Transportation, 654 F.2d 616, 620–21 (9th Cir.1981).

Whether or not the letters amount to final agency action, we are not precluded from reviewing the FAA's failure to register the helicopter. The FAA has admitted that any further attempts by Air One to obtain a different decision will be futile. It is a common rule of judicial economy that we will not require a party to exhaust administrative procedures when exhaustion would be futile. SAIF Corp./Oregon Ship v. Johnson, 908 F.2d 1434, 1440–41 (9th Cir.1990). Here, there is no question it would be futile for Air One to attempt to persuade the FAA to change the position it clearly sets forth in the letters. Accordingly, we will treat the letters as final agency action and consider the merits of Air One's petition for review.

Agency decisions may be set aside only if "arbitrary, capricious, an abuse of discretion, or otherwise not in accordance with the law." 5 U.S.C. § 706(2)(A); Henderson v. FAA, 7 F.3d 875, 877 (9th Cir.1993).

The FAA contends that its decision cannot be an abuse of discretion because it lacks any discretion to register Air One's helicopter so long as the helicopter is registered in Spain. The FAA argues that this is a basic requirement imposed upon it by the Chicago Convention. 61 Stat. at 1185. The FAA is correct that the Convention prohibits dual registration, but we can determine when and if a registration in a foreign country remains valid.

Chapter III, Article 18 of the Chicago Convention provides: "An aircraft cannot be validly registered in more than one State, but its registration may be changed from one State to another." Id. The FAA has adopted regulations to determine the validity of a foreign registration. See 14 C.F.R. § 47.37(b)(1) ("satisfactory evidence of termination" includes a statement by a foreign official or decree of a court applying foreign law that the registration has ended or become invalid). It is the FAA, not the Chicago Convention, that declares what will suffice as satisfactory evidence of an invalid foreign registration.

We hold the FAA's decision refusing to register Air One's helicopter is contrary to law, because the Spanish registration is no longer valid.

The FAA based its decision on 14 C.F.R. §47.37, which sets forth the evidentiary burden an applicant for registration must bear. Section 47.37(b)(1) requires an applicant to provide "a statement by the official having jurisdiction over the national aircraft registry of the foreign country, that the registration has ended or is invalid...."

Air One cannot meet this evidentiary burden. But the reason it can't is not because the lien is valid, but because the appropriate Spanish bureaucrat won't say the lien is no longer valid—even though everyone concerned knows that it is no longer valid. The appropriate Spanish official refuses to say whether the lien is no longer valid unless he receives a document from the abortive Norwegian "corporation." That document, however, is not only impossible to provide, it would add nothing of substance to what is already before the DGAC. On the basis of the record, there can be no doubt the lien has been discharged, is no longer valid, and the helicopter's registration in Spain is at an end.

Further delay would serve only to diminish even more the value of Air One's ownership interest in the helicopter. While Air One has not presented the statement by the foreign official referred to in 14 C.F.R. §47.37(b)(1), it has indisputably proved that getting the statement is impossible and the helicopter's registration in Spain has ended. In the circumstances of this case, this is sufficient.

III
CONCLUSION

Air One's petition for review is granted. The FAA is ordered to register the Sikorski S-58T helicopter, serial number 58-1626, showing Air One Helicopters, Inc. as the owner.

O'SCANNLAIN, Circuit Judge, dissenting.

I respectfully dissent. While I empathize with Air One's plight, I conclude that (1) this court lacks jurisdiction to entertain Air One's petition for review, (2) the court lacks authority to rule that the Spanish registration is invalid (and has erred by doing so without applying Spanish law), and (3) the majority's opinion ordering the FAA to register Air One's helicopter in the United States directly conflicts with both a statute and a treaty.

I

The appropriate jurisdictional test is that outlined in Air California v. U.S. Dept. of Transportation, 654 F.2d 616 (9th Cir.1981). In that case, this court stated that under 49 U.S.C.App. §1486(a), [now] 49 U.S.C. §46110, FAA "[a]dministrative orders are not final and reviewable 'unless and until they impose an obligation, deny a right, or fix some legal relationship as a consummation of the administrative process.'" Id. at 621 (citations omitted).

Air One argues that the FAA letters in this case are final orders because they effectively deny Air One its right to register its helicopter. I disagree. None of the letters denied Air One's registration application; to the contrary, the letters merely told Air One what it needed to provide in order to get the application approved, namely a certificate from a Spanish authority (either the Spanish National Aircraft Registry or a Spanish court) that the Spanish registration was invalid. Accordingly, the letters do not impose any obligation, deny any right or fix any legal relationship as the consummation of the administrative process.

The majority states that "[w]hether or not the [FAA] letters amount to final agency action," this court has jurisdiction to review the FAA's alleged "failure to register the helicopter" because exhaustion of administrative remedies would be futile. In support of its conclusion on this point, it states that "[t]he FAA has admitted that any further attempts by Air One to obtain a different decision will be futile."

I cannot agree with this latter statement. The FAA has not conceded that exhaustion of administrative remedies would be futile; to the contrary, the FAA has said that it would accept a final judgment or decree from a court of competent jurisdiction in Spain that the registration is invalid. See Appellee's Brief at 26–27; Jan. 3, 1996 memorandum from Kenneth G. Caplan, Special Attorney to the U.S. Attorney General. The relevant federal regulations state that such a judgment would constitute "satisfactory evidence of termination of the foreign registration." 14 C.F.R. § 47.37(b)(2). Air One cannot argue that any efforts to obtain a different decision from the FAA would be "futile" when it refuses to pursue the very remedy which the FAA has suggested and which is mandated by the relevant federal regulations. In addition, in light of Air One's decision not to pursue such a judgment in the Spanish courts, I respectfully submit that the majority's statement that "bringing a court challenge will be unsuccessful" is nothing more than pure speculation.

Accordingly, Air One has a remedy available to it, and the FAA's letters do not "impose an obligation, deny a right, or fix some legal relationship as a consummation of the administrative process." Air California, 654 F.2d at 621. For that reason, they "are not final and reviewable," id., and this court lacks jurisdiction to hear Air One's appeal.

II

Even if this court has jurisdiction to consider Air One's appeal, I do not believe that we have authority to hold that the Spanish registration is invalid.

The majority states that "we can determine when and if a registration in a foreign country remains valid." Op. at 883. In doing so, the majority apparently relies on 14 C.F.R. § 47.37(b)(2). However, it has misapplied the provision. That regulation states that

> satisfactory evidence of termination of the foreign registration may be—
>
> ....
>
> (2) A final judgment or decree of a court of competent jurisdiction that determines, under the law of the country concerned, that the registration has become invalid.

14 C.F.R. § 47.37(b)(2). I strongly doubt that this court is one of "competent jurisdiction" to determine that the Spanish registration is invalid; I suspect that only a Spanish court so qualifies.

More important, however, is the fact that the majority does not even purport to apply Spanish law in holding the Spanish registration invalid, as is clearly required by the regulation. Even assuming that we are a "court of competent jurisdiction" to decide the issue, the parties have not provided any briefing on Spanish law, and we should not decide such an issue in a vacuum.

III

Finally, the majority's opinion also forces the FAA to register Air One's helicopter even though the FAA can do so only by violating both a statute and a treaty. First, under federal law, "[a]n aircraft [owned by a citizen of the United States] may be registered [in the United States] only when the aircraft is—(1) not registered under the laws of a foreign country...." 49 U.S.C. § 44102(a). As Air One concedes, its helicopter is in fact "registered under the laws of a foreign country." The majority's opinion ordering the FAA to register Air One's helicopter in the United States clearly contravenes this statute.

Second, as the majority notes, Chapter III, Article 18 of the Chicago Convention states that "[a]n aircraft cannot be validly registered in more than one State...." The only Spanish authority yet to rule on the subject has stated that the aircraft is in fact "validly registered" in Spain. Accordingly, the majority's opinion clearly places the United States in violation of this treaty. In addition, the majority's decision to invalidate the Spanish registration, before the Spanish courts have even been given an opportunity to rule on the subject, contravenes basic principles of international comity. Finally, the majority's opinion provides a dangerous precedent which may encourage foreign courts to rule, in subsequent cases, that aircraft registered by the FAA in the United States are not in fact "validly" registered here. The practical effect of the majority's ruling is thus to render the treaty a virtual nullity.

IV

There is no question that Air One has been the victim of a protracted, intercontinental bureaucratic nightmare, and I empathize completely with Air One's plight and with the majority's strong desire to remedy it. However, federal courts are courts of limited jurisdiction. Because of that fact, we sometimes confront cases, such as the one at bar, where we simply lack authority to act. And even if we do act, we must always do so in a manner consistent with federal laws and regulations. Because I fear that the majority's opinion may be inconsistent with these principles, I respectfully dissent.

LEWISTOWN PROPANE COMPANY v. FORD

42 P.3d 229 (Mont. 2002)

REGNIER, Justice.

Lewistown Propane Company ("Lewistown Propane") brought an action against Tom Ford to collect on an unpaid account. After Ford executed a Confession of Judgment, Lewistown Propane obtained a writ of execution and levied execution on an aircraft. Raymond Becky sought to intervene, claiming that Ford had transferred the plane to him before Lewistown Propane levied on the aircraft. The Tenth Judicial District Court, Fergus County, issued an order permanently restraining Lewistown Propane from executing on the aircraft. Lewistown Propane appeals and we reverse.

The following issue is dispositive of this appeal: Did the District Court err in ruling that no lienable interest remains with a judgment creditor when a judgment debtor conveys an airplane to a third party prior to an entry of judgment without registering the conveyance with the Federal Aviation Administration?

PROCEDURAL AND FACTUAL BACKGROUND

The facts surrounding this matter are largely undisputed. Lewistown Propane is a Montana corporation that sells and provides propane, fertilizer and other similar products to the public. Ford, or his family members, purchased products from Lewistown Propane for which they have never paid. On September 8, 1999, Ford, as an individual and on behalf of the Ford Cattle Company, executed a Promissory Note and Agreement (the "Promissory Note"). Under the terms of the Promissory Note, Ford agreed to pay

Lewistown Propane $28,503.62 within six months of the date of the note, along with interest of 10% per annum.

On December 14, 1999, Lewistown Propane filed a complaint against Ford and his family members for collection of the Promissory Note and payment of its account receivable. Ford subsequently filed a Confession of Judgment (the "Confession") with the District Court. The Confession was dated March 7, 2000, one day before the due date of the Promissory Note, and was for $28,503.62 plus interest.

During this time, Raymond Becky had allegedly been helping Ford to refinance his debt. On February 11, 2000, Ford sold three pieces of farm machinery and a 1974 Super Piper Cub Aircraft PA18-150 (the "Piper aircraft") to Becky. Neither Ford nor Raymond Becky notified the State of Montana or the Federal Aviation Administration (the "FAA") that Ford had transferred the airplane to Becky.

As consideration for the transfer of assets, Ford was to receive an interest in a business venture in British Columbia, Canada, known as the Gold River Power Corporation. To this end, Becky pledged the assets from the sale as collateral for a loan from Western Security Bank of Butte, Montana. The funds from the sale were then wired to Canada for use in purchasing the Gold River pulp facility. During this time, Ford retained possession of the aircraft and farm machinery in Fergus County.

In an attempt to collect on its judgment, Lewistown Propane inquired about the ownership of the Piper aircraft with the Montana Department of Transportation Aeronautics Division and the FAA. Through these records, Lewistown Propane determined that the Piper aircraft was registered in Ford's name, no liens or encumbrances existed against the plane and Ford had paid the annual registration fees to the FAA. On July 7, 2000, Lewistown Propane obtained a Writ of Execution and, about a week later, seized the Piper aircraft. Lewistown Propane has had the plane in its possession since that time. On July 17, 2000, Lewistown Propane filed a Notice of Execution Levy addressed to Ford, advising him that it had executed on the Piper aircraft and intended to sell the plane in order to satisfy its judgment against Ford. Upon learning of Lewistown Propane's seizure of the aircraft, Becky moved for permission to intervene in the case, which the District Court granted on July 24, 2000. As part of the same motion, Becky sought a stay of execution of judgment, which the District Court also granted.

The District Court entered an Order Permanently Granting Ex Parte Motion to Stay Execution of Judgment as it Relates to a 1974 Super Piper Cub Aircraft PA18-150 on October 23, 2000. In that order, the District Court directed Lewistown Propane to return the aircraft to Becky. Lewistown Propane now appeals.

DISCUSSION

Did the District Court err in ruling that no lienable interest remains with a judgment creditor when a judgment debtor conveys an airplane to a third party prior to an entry of judgment without registering the conveyance with the Federal Aviation Administration?

Section 503(c) of the Federal Aviation Act of 1958 requires that "every aircraft transfer must be evidenced by an instrument, and every such instrument must be recorded, before the rights of innocent third parties can be affected." Philko Aviation, Inc. v. Shacket (1983), 462 U.S. 406, 409–10, 103 S.Ct. 2476, 2478, 76 L.Ed.2d 678, 682. Congress' purpose in creating this registration scheme was to establish a central clearing house of recorded titles so that a person can readily find any legal interest against an aircraft. See Philko, 462 U.S. at 411, 103 S.Ct. at 2479, 76 L.Ed.2d at 683 (citing Hearings on HR 9738 Before the House Comm. on Interstate and Foreign Commerce, 75th

Cong., 3d Sess., p. 407 (1938)) (testimony of F. Fagg, Director of Air Commerce, Dept. of Commerce). Under this scheme, state law determines the priorities between competing claims, but "all interests must be federally recorded before they can obtain whatever priority to which they are entitled under state law." Philko, 462 U.S. at 413, 103 S.Ct. at 2480, 76 L.Ed.2d at 684. This case thus requires us to determine the priority between a judgment creditor and a third party purchaser under Montana law where the parties to the sale did not federally register the conveyance.

While we have not yet addressed this question, several other jurisdictions have decided this issue. A Hawaii Court of Appeals, for instance, determined that a third party purchaser's ownership interest in an aircraft derived through an unrecorded conveyance did not cut off a judgment creditor's right to levy on the aircraft. See Bank of Honolulu v. Davids (1985), 6 Haw.App. 25, 709 P.2d 613, 619. Other courts, however, have come to an opposite conclusion on the grounds that a judgment creditor does not have the same claim as would an innocent purchaser for value because a judgment creditor derives his rights from the debtor. In these cases, the courts have reasoned that because a debtor does not have a claim for the aircraft against the party to whom he sold it, the creditor, in turn, no longer has a claim for the aircraft. See, e.g., Compass Ins. Co. v. Moore (8th Cir.1986), 806 F.2d 796; General Dynamics Corp. v. Zantop Int'l Airlines (Ct.App.1985), 147 Ariz. 92, 708 P.2d 773.

Turning to Montana law, Ford and Becky urge us to follow our decisions involving the conveyance of real property. Under this line of cases, judgment liens on real property only attach to the actual interest of the judgment debtor. See, e.g., Hannah v. Martinson (1988), 232 Mont. 469, 472, 758 P.2d 276, 278–79 (holding that a sale of real property cut off a judgment creditor's lien because a judgment lien can only attach to the actual interest of the judgment debtor); Vaughn v. Schmalsle (1890), 10 Mont. 186, 195, 25 P. 102, 103 (noting that an unrecorded mortgage supersedes a subsequently acquired judgment lien because a judgment creditor does not acquire superior rights to the debtor's assets than the debtor had when the judgment was rendered). Therefore, Ford and Becky argue that because the sale was valid between them, Lewistown Propane no longer has an interest in the Piper aircraft.

The Piper aircraft, however, is personal property. We thus conclude that a more analogous precedent is a previous decision of ours regarding the conveyance of personal property. In Kovacich v. Norgaard (1986), 221 Mont. 26, 716 P.2d 633, a judgment creditor attempted to levy on a truck owned by a judgment debtor. Before the creditor could levy on the truck, the debtor conveyed the truck to a third party. As with the case now before us, the parties to the conveyance failed to properly register the change in ownership. The creditor eventually levied on the truck, but the debtor obtained a writ of prohibition to stop the sale. The district court set aside the writ of prohibition and we affirmed the court's ruling. In reaching our conclusion, we noted that the parties' failure to follow the proper procedure for transferring title in relation to third parties was particularly significant. See Kovacich, 221 Mont. at 28, 716 P.2d at 634. We reasoned that "[c]reditors and subsequent purchasers must be protected from failure of a secured party to file proof of a security interest. Likewise, judgment creditors are entitled to rely on ownership as reflected in the division's records." Kovacich, 221 Mont. at 28, 716 P.2d at 635.

Here, it is uncontested that Becky and Ford failed to follow the proper procedure under Federal law for conveying an aircraft. Therefore, applying Kovacich by analogy, we conclude that Lewistown Propane, as a judgment creditor, was entitled to rely on the records of the FAA. Because Becky's ownership interest was unrecorded at the time of

Lewistown Propane's execution of the levy, Becky's interest is thus invalid as to Lewistown Propane and could not cut off its right to levy on the aircraft.

Ford and Becky argue that, because they have since recorded the transfer with the FAA and Lewistown Propane has not yet recorded its interest in the Piper aircraft, their interest in the plane is now superior. This argument is without merit because a failure to record affects the rights of innocent third parties. See Philko, 462 U.S. at 409–10, 103 S.Ct. at 2478, 76 L.Ed.2d at 682. Ford and Becky, however, were both clearly aware that Lewistown Propane had levied on the aircraft when they registered the transfer with the FAA. Therefore, they are not innocent third parties and may not rely on the federal recording statute to defeat Lewistown Propane's claim.

Reversed.

CRESTON AVIATION, INC. v. TEXTRON FINANCIAL CORPORATION

900 So. 2d 727 (Fla. Dist. Ct. App. 2005)

STEVENSON, Judge.

This is an appeal from an order of final summary judgment, which determined that a mechanic's lien on an airplane was invalid. Because the lien was not properly filed according to Florida law, we affirm. Likewise, we affirm the related order granting attorney's fees.

The primary question in this case is whether the requirement in section 329.51, Florida Statutes (2004), that a lienor must file a verified notice of lien for repairs to an airplane in the county where the airplane was located at the time the services were last furnished is preempted by federal law, which requires that notice of mechanic's liens on aircraft located in the United States be filed with the FAA. We agree with the trial court that there is no preemption.

In the instant case, the aircraft in question was owned by Tack I, Inc., with appellee Textron Financial Corporation holding a security interest. After Tack I defaulted under the security agreement, it released the aircraft back to Textron. At the time of the release, the aircraft was in the physical possession of appellant, Creston Aviation, Inc., which claimed a lien on the aircraft for services under Florida Statutes sections 329.01 and 329.51. Textron then filed a petition for writ of replevin pursuant to Florida Statutes section 78.068 and sought attorney's fees against Creston under section 713.76(2), maintaining that Creston's lien had been wrongfully filed. Creston released the aircraft to Textron after Textron posted a pre-judgment replevin bond in accordance with section 78.068(3). Creston then responded with a counterclaim and third party complaint in which it sued Tack I for the unpaid balance for fuel and maintenance services provided to the aircraft and sought to foreclose against Tack I and Textron a claim of lien, which it filed with the Federal Aviation Administration pursuant to Florida Statutes sections 329.01 and 329.51. Along with the complaint, Creston filed a Notice of Lis Pendens.

By way of summary judgment, the trial court found that Creston's lien was not enforceable because Creston did not comply with section 329.51, which provides that notice of any lien claimed on an aircraft under section 713.58 must be filed in the county where the aircraft was located at the time the labor, services, fuel or materials was last furnished. In this case, the repairs were done in Broward County. Creston argues that the trial court erred in finding the lien invalid because Creston had filed a notice of lien with the Federal Aviation Administration's aircraft registry in Oklahoma City and that compliance with this federal regulation preempted any state law requirements. We disagree that there was federal preemption here.

Pursuant to the Federal Aviation Act of 1958, the FAA maintains an office in Oklahoma City for the registration of all ownership documents pertaining to any civil aircraft bought or sold within the United States and for the recording of any security interests, or other liens which purport to affect the title to any such aircraft. See 49 U.S.C. §44107(a)–(b) (2000). Creston argues that it is this set of requirements which preempt Florida law on the subject of the validity and enforceability of any notice of mechanics liens in regard to an aircraft. The federal authorities indicate that the preemption engendered by these rules is not as expansive as Creston suggests.

Until a lien or other interest affecting title in a civil aircraft is recorded in the federal registry, it is valid only against those with actual notice and that person's heirs and devisees. See 49 U.S.C. §44108(a) (2000). After the lien is filed with the federal registry, it is valid against all persons. See 49 U.S.C. §44108(b) (2000). The purpose of the recording provisions was to create a central clearing house for recordation of title and liens affecting civil aircraft in the United States so that a person would know where to find ready access to this type of information. See Aircraft Trading & Servs., Inc. v. Braniff, Inc., 819 F.2d 1227 (2d Cir.1987).

In In re Holiday Airlines Corp., 620 F.2d 731 (9th Cir.1980), the court determined that artisans liens are within the ambit of the Federal Aviation Act recording statute. In Holiday, the court stated quite explicitly that:

> The provisions of the Federal Aviation Act preempt State law insofar as they relate to the priority of liens. State Securities Co. v. Aviation Enterprises, Inc., 355 F.2d 225 (10th Cir.1966); Pope v. National Aero Finance Co., Inc., 236 Cal.App.2d 722, 46 Cal.Rptr. 233 (1965). But matters touching on the validity of liens are determined by underlying State law. See 49 U.S.C. [§] 1406; State Securities Co. v. Aviation Enterprises, Inc., supra; Texas National Bank of Houston v. Aufderheide, 235 F.Supp. 599 (E.D.Ark.1964); Aircraft Investment Corp. v. Pezzani & Reid Equipment Co., 205 F.Supp. 80 (E.D.Mich.1962).

Id. at 733.

The Supreme Court of the United States has held that the federal recording statute preempts any state law which would give priority to a claim against an aircraft where that claim was not recorded with the FAA in Oklahoma City, and where the competing claim was recorded with the FAA. See Philko Aviation, Inc. v. Shacket, 462 U.S. 406, 103 S.Ct. 2476, 76 L.Ed.2d 678 (1983). In Philko, a corporation, operated by Roger Smith, sold a new airplane to the Shackets at an airport in Illinois. The Shackets paid the full price, took possession of the aircraft, and expected Smith to take care of all of the paperwork, including the recordation of the original bill of sale with the FAA. Instead of taking care of the paperwork to properly transfer title to the Shackets, Smith purported to sell the same airplane to Philko Aviation, Inc. Smith told Philko that the airplane was in Michigan having some electronic equipment installed. After Smith gave Philko the title documents, Philko's bank recorded them with the FAA.

After Smith's fraud came to light, the Shackets filed an action to determine title to the plane. Philko argued that it had title because the Shackets had never recorded their interest in the airplane with the FAA. The Shackets maintained that, under Illinois state law regarding transfers, they were the rightful owners. Ultimately, the United States Supreme Court held that the requirement that the interest in the aircraft be recorded with the FAA preempted any state law which would allow the Shackets' interests to be superior to that of Philko, which had made the required filing with the FAA:

> Any other construction would defeat the primary congressional purpose for enactment of § 503(c) [of the Federal Aviation Act of 1958, now codified at 49 U.S.C. § 44108 (2000)], which was to create "a central clearing house for recordation of titles so that a person, wherever he may be, will know where he can find ready access to the claims against, or liens, or other legal interests in an aircraft." [See] Hearings before the House Comm. on Interstate and Foreign Commerce, 75 Cong., 3d Sess., p. 407 (April 1, 1938) (testimony of F. Fagg, Director of Air Commerce, Dept. of Commerce). Here, state law does not require any documentation whatsoever for a valid transfer of an aircraft to be effected. An oral sale is fully valid against third parties once the buyer takes possession of the plane. If the state law allowing this result were not preempted by § 503(c), then any buyer in possession would have absolutely no need or incentive to record his title with the FAA, and he could refuse to do so with impunity, and thereby prevent the "central clearing house" from providing "ready access" to information about his claim.

462 U.S. at 411, 103 S.Ct. 2476.

A similar interpretation of the scope of preemption of the federal provisions at issue was made in Aircraft Investment Corp. v. Pezzani & Reid Equipment Co., 205 F.Supp. 80 (E.D.Mich.1962). In this diversity action, Aircraft Investment Corporation, a Texas company, sought to foreclose on a chattel mortgage interest it held in an airplane located in Michigan. Initially, Pezzani & Reid Equipment Company ("Pezzani"), a Michigan corporation, contracted to purchase the airplane from Air-O-Fleet, a Michigan retailer of airplanes. Air-O-Fleet ordered the new airplane from the manufacturer and obtained financing from Aircraft Investment Corporation. Air-O-Fleet executed a chattel mortgage on the plane in favor of Aircraft Investment Corporation and was to remit the proceeds of the retail sale of the airplane in payment of the note. One day after Pezzani paid Air-O-Fleet and took possession of the plane, Aircraft Investment Corporation filed its chattel mortgage with the FAA. Air-O-Fleet went bankrupt shortly thereafter and had not paid the note and mortgage. Aircraft Investment Corporation then filed suit to recover the amount due under the mortgage or to recover the airplane from Pezzani, the retail purchaser.

In federal district court, Aircraft Investment Corporation maintained that it was entitled to relief on its mortgage because it recorded its interest with the FAA prior to any recording by Pezzani. In turn, Pezzani argued that it took possession of the airplane prior to Aircraft Investment Corporation recording its interest with the FAA and without having notice of the mortgage. Additionally, Pezzani argued that the purported chattel mortgage was invalid under both Michigan and Texas law for various reasons. In denying Aircraft Investment Corporation's motion for summary judgment on its chattel mortgage foreclosure action, the district court stated:

> [Aircraft Investment Corporation] suggests that Congress has pre-empted the entire field of conveyancing of interests in aircraft. This view is erroneous.... Congress has said only that until an instrument purporting to convey an interest

> in an aircraft is recorded, in accordance with the Act, it is void as to third parties without notice. Upon federal recordation, it is valid without further recording. In providing for the recordation of various instruments pertaining to transactions affecting title or interest in aircraft, Congress has not impaired the existence and effectiveness of state laws creating and defining such instruments. Excepting the recording section of the Federal Aviation Act, the validity of the chattel mortgage here in question must be measured by the appropriate state law.

205 F.Supp. at 82.

It is apparent that the supremacy of the federal regulation requiring recordation of interests in aircraft with the FAA is operative to the extent that if the title or lien interest is not recorded in the FAA Aircraft Registry, then it will not be valid as against third parties without notice, regardless of any state law to the contrary. See Philko, 462 U.S. at 406, 103 S.Ct. 2476; Aero Support Sys., Inc. v. F.D.I.C., 726 F.Supp. 651 (N.D.Tex.1989). Neither the federal statute itself, nor the holding of the United States Supreme Court in Philko, supports Creston's argument that the federal requirement that notice of mechanic's liens on aircraft be filed with the FAA precludes the State of Florida from imposing requirements which affect the "enforceability" of those liens in Florida. We have considered the other procedural and substantive arguments advanced by Creston, but find no error. Accordingly, we affirm the order of the trial court finding the lien invalid for failure to comply with state law. In addition, we find no error in the trial court's order granting Textron attorney's fees for its efforts to clear the aircraft of Creston's invalid claim of lien.

KOPPIE v. UNITED STATES

1 F.3d 651 (7th Cir. 1993)

CUMMINGS, Circuit Judge.

Plaintiff Chad M. Koppie sued Ligon Air, an Indiana partnership, and the Federal Aviation Administration ("FAA"), over the ownership of a plane. Koppie claims that Ligon Air is in control of the aircraft, a Convair 880, which he rightly owns, and that the FAA took the wrong side in the dispute by issuing a Certificate of Registration to Ligon Air rather than to him. Plaintiff claims that these misdeeds by Ligon Air and the federal government cost him $667,000, but the district judge was not convinced and neither are we. Koppie's case against Ligon Air is based on diversity jurisdiction and his claim against the government is a federal question stemming from the Federal Tort Claims Act, 28 U.S.C. §§ 2671–2680.

Koppie purchased, or thought he purchased, the Convair from Hudson General Corporation in 1987 for a mere $5,000, a strikingly good deal for an aircraft that originally cost $10 million. Hudson had obtained title through satisfaction of a garnishment lien against Ligon Air, which owed it money for storing and maintaining the plane. But unbeknownst to Koppie, the aircraft had made its way back into the hands of Ligon Air through a circuitous route. Koppie took ownership subject to the recorded interest of Cromwell State Bank, the original lienholder, and Cromwell assigned its interest to something called the "880 Partnership," which then resold the plane to Ligon Air. Both the 880 Partnership and Ligon Air are owned by the same two people, Susan and Cliff Pettit. Koppie knew something was amiss when in June or July of 1987 he went to the airport to look after his plane and discovered Michael Potter, whom he thought was an agent for Ligon Air, working on the aircraft.

In the meantime, Koppie had applied for a Certificate of Aircraft Registration from the FAA. On June 23, 1987, he received a letter denying his request because of the conflicting claims over ownership. The letter said in part:

> Review of the aircraft file indicates it was repossessed May 23, 1987, premised upon a security agreement, which was recorded by the FAA on July 9, 1982, and subsequently sold to Ligon Air, 105 West 2nd St., Ligonier, IN 46767. In view of the repossession and subsequent sale, we are unable to issue a certificate of aircraft registration in your name at this time.

Having learned that his ownership of the plane was in serious dispute, Koppie signed two documents releasing whatever interests he might have had in the Convair in return for consideration of $36,000 from Michael Potter. Koppie eventually received and accepted the money, and the plane was flown to South Africa, where it remains.

The district court granted Ligon Air's motion for summary judgment in December 1991, but judgment was not officially rendered until August of 1992 (plaintiff's app. at 29). At that time the district judge also handed down an order and judgment granting the FAA's motion for summary judgment. Koppie now claims that the release of his interests in the Convair was nullified by a subsequent document between him and Michael Potter and Western Continental Holdings, Ltd. But in that document Potter and Western Continental Holdings acknowledged that they have no interest of any kind in the plane. The document is thus meaningless. Clearly, it is impossible for a person who owns no interest in a piece of property to execute an agreement for consideration transferring ownership of the property to another. This is akin to the proverbial selling of the Brooklyn Bridge. Since the subsequent document has no validity, Koppie's earlier decision to accept $36,000 for the relinquishment of all claims to the Convair prevents him from now complaining that he, not Ligon Air, owns the aircraft.

As for the FAA, Koppie alleged in his first amended complaint under the Federal Tort Claims Act that the agency wrongfully denied him a Certificate of Aircraft Registration and tortiously converted Koppie's property. The major flaw in this argument is that merely registering an aircraft with the FAA does not determine ownership and has no legal effect. Under 49 U.S.C. § 1401(f), the purpose of registering a plane is to define its nationality for international travel, and the statute states explicitly: "Such certificate shall be conclusive evidence of nationality for international purposes, but not in any proceeding under the laws of the United States. Registration shall not be evidence of ownership of aircraft in any proceeding [such as here] in which ownership by a particular person is, or may be an issue." See Northwestern Flyers, Inc. v. Olson Bros. Mfg. Co., Inc., 679 F.2d 1264, 1270 n.13 (8th Cir.1982) (registration does not control questions of title). Since the registration does not even have effect in American courts, and the statute expressly forbids the kind of ownership claim made here based on certification, Koppie is clearly stretching credulity in arguing that the FAA harmed him with regard to ownership by failing to grant him, rather than Ligon Air, a certificate. In essence, such a certificate is worthless as far as proving ownership, and thus Koppie could not by definition have lost anything by its denial.

The district court also held that Koppie's claims against the FAA were barred by the Federal Tort Claims Act's exception for government officials performing discretionary functions, 28 U.S.C. § 2680, and by the doctrine of collateral estoppel because a summary judgment order had already been issued against Koppie in favor of Ligon Air. Having decided that the federal government is simply not liable in these circumstances for rendering an opinion about ownership, we need not reach these two issues. The judgments for both defendants are affirmed, but Ligon Air's motion for sanctions is denied because, although unsuccessful, plaintiff's appeal was not frivolous within the meaning of Rule 38 of the Federal Rules of Appellate Procedure.

Notes

1. One item not mentioned by Mr. Wieand is the need to arrange for adequate insurance when buying an airplane. For descriptions of such policies, *see* John D. Perovich, Annotation, *Property Insurance on Aircraft; Risks and Losses Covered*, 48 A.L.R.3d 1120 (1973 & 2004 Supp.), and Rod D. Margo, *Aspects of Insurance in Aviation Finance*, 62 J. Air L. & Com. 423 (1996).

2. Since the publication of Mr. Wieand's article, the corporate jet industry has witnessed a boom in "fractional ownership," a concept often likened to vacation time-share rentals:

> Part of the growth is a result of dissatisfaction with commercial airlines. A greater portion, however, stems from the heightened awareness of the value of business aviation as an economic tool. Following the tragic events of September 11, 2001, business aircraft and fractional ownership programs are also viewed by many companies as a way in which to increase security for their employees.
>
> [F]ractional ownership programs allow a party to acquire less than a whole aircraft. In general terms, fractional ownership programs are multi-year programs covering a pool of aircraft, most of which are owned by more than one party and all of which are placed in a dry lease exchange pool and available to any program participant when the aircraft in which such participant owns an interest is not available. As an integral part of these multi-year programs, a single management company provides the management services to support the operation of the aircraft by the owners and administers the aircraft exchange program on behalf of all of the participants. By purchasing an interest in an aircraft that is part of the program, an owner gains round-the-clock access to a private aircraft at a fraction of the cost. Because fractional ownership programs allow parties to purchase the percentage of an aircraft reflecting their actual needs, the programs appeal to a wide range of users including newcomers to business aviation as well as companies seeking to supplement their own fleet of business aircraft without the expense of having to purchase or lease additional aircraft.
>
> Due to their flexibility and broad market appeal, existing fractional ownership programs continue to grow and a wide variety of new programs, both foreign and domestic, have come on line. Some of the newer and smaller "fractional ownership programs" have solicited potential new customers interested in sharing specific aircraft, while other sales of fractional shares have been advertised in classifieds on the internet.

Eileen M. Gleimer, *The Regulation of Fractional Ownership: Have the Wings of the Future Been Clipped?*, 67 J. Air L. & Com. 321, 322–28 (2002).

As Ms. Gleimer points out, "fractional ownership was introduced in 1986 by Executive Jet Aviation through its NetJets program." *Id.* at 328. In January 2004, NetJets (www.netjets.com) gained added fame when it was featured on the second episode (entitled "Sex, Lies and Altitude") of Donald Trump's hit reality show *The Apprentice*. For more staid looks at the subject, *see* Philip E. Crowther, *Taxation of Fractional Programs: "Flying Over Uncharted Waters,"* 67 J. Air L. & Com. 241 (2002), and Kristen A. Bell, Comment, *Where Do They Fit? Fractional Ownership Programs Wedged Into Current Air*

Law Decisions and Guidelines, 69 J. Air L. & Com. 427 (2004) (summarizing recent changes made by the FAA to enhance the safe operation of such aircraft).

3. Airshows like the one in *Ickes* have a long and colorful history:

> Before the second world war, airshows were associated with long distance air races, often lasting many days and covering thousands of miles. While the Reno Air Races keep this tradition alive, most airshows today primarily feature a series of aerial demos of relatively short duration (10–40 minutes).
>
> [W]ith a handful of exceptions (such as the mid-winter airshow at MCAS Yuma, AZ), the airshow "season" starts in early spring and ends around mid-fall. Magazines aimed at aircraft enthusiasts will normally include a list of forthcoming airshows in their February, March or April editions.
>
> The annual Oshkosh Airshow [in] Wisconsin, organized by the Experimental Aircraft Association, is attended by more people and by more aircraft than any other airshow. The week-long event focuses on experimental aircraft, such as homebuilts and warbirds, but also feature[s] aerobatics acts, military aircraft, and airliners.
>
> The two largest air and aerospace trade shows are [England's] Farnborough Air Show [begun in 1920], held [in] even years, and the Paris Air Show, [founded in 1909 and] held [in] odd years. In addition to displays for the general public, these two shows have important showcases and display halls for professionals. They are traditionally one of the main occasions when major aerospace players announce deals.
>
> At airshows held [at] US airfields, crowds are restricted from being within 500 feet of the runway, faster jets may be required to keep a 1500 feet distance, [and] [a]ll aerobatic maneuvers must be performed inside the "airshow box" (a rectangular volume of space with the runway at one edge, extending behind the runway and up to a certain altitude over this area.) There are many other rules and restrictions on what airshow performers can do. These safety restrictions make US airshows very safe. Mechanical malfunctions and pilot error (most often a combination of both) are responsible for a handful of airshow accidents every year, but even then, most pilots manage to eject safely or to survive their crashes.

Airshow, at en.wikipedia.org/wiki/Airshow. For a further look at airshows, *see, e.g.*, *Cleveland National Air Show, Inc. v. U.S. Department of Transportation*, 430 F.3d 757 (6th Cir. 2005) (air show not permitted to fly near Jacobs Field during Cleveland Indians baseball game because of security concerns).

4. In addition to shining a spotlight on airshows, the *Ickes* case is an example of the FAA's far-ranging jurisdiction. For a further discussion of its powers, *see, e.g.*, Walter W. Jones, Jr., Annotation, *What Constitutes "Order" of Civil Aeronautics Board or of Administrator of Federal Aviation Agency Subject to Judicial Review, Or What Orders Are Subject to Such Review, Under §1006(A) of Federal Aviation Act (49 U.S.C.A. §1486(A))*, 14 A.L.R. Fed. 725 (1973 & 2005 Supp.); Olga Barreto, *Safety Oversight: Federal Aviation Administration, International Civil Aviation Organization, and Central American Aviation Safety*, 67 J. Air L. & Com. 651 (2002); Suzanne E. Thompson, Comment, *Why, After All This Time, Is the FAA Just Now Taking Steps to Mandate Child Restraint Systems on Aircraft?*, 37 Gonz. L. Rev. 533 (2001/2002).

5. After reading *Air One*, with whom do you find yourself agreeing more: Judge Thompson or Judge O'Scannlain? How worried are you by the possibility that other

countries will refuse to recognize American aircraft registrations (or de-registrations) as a result of the decision? If the majority had upheld the FAA's position, what do you think Air One would have done next? If you had been Air One's counsel, what advice would you have given it?

6. Are *Lewiston* and *Creston* in conflict? Can they be reconciled? Even if they can, does it make any sense to allow states to enact their own filing requirements? What purpose is served by them? *See further* P.G. Guthrie, Annotation, *Construction and Effect of 49 US Code § 1403, Governing Recordation of Ownership, Conveyances, and Encumbrances on Aircraft*, 22 A.L.R.3d 1270 (1968 & 2005 Supp.); John I. Karesh, *Repossession and Foreclosure of Aircraft From the Perspective of the Federal Aviation Act and the Uniform Commercial Code*, 65 J. Air L. & Com. 695 (2000); William C. Boston, *Registration of Aircraft and Recording of Security Instruments Under Federal Law*, 48 Consumer Fin. L.Q. Rep. 466 (1994).

7. *Koppie* raises an interesting question: when, if ever, should the FAA be held liable for mistakes in its registry? What if, for example, one of its employees fails to record a document, or records it improperly, or is slow to record it, or provides (either intentionally or innocently) misinformation to a user of the registry? Would liability attach in any of these circumstances? Should it? *Cf. Zephyr Aviation, L.L.C. v. Dailey*, 247 F.3d 565 (5th Cir. 2001).

8. In March 2006, the FAA's registry in Oklahoma City will be joined by a new international registry (based in Shannon, Ireland) that will provide further protection for aircraft creditors:

> From 1996 to 2001, states participated in negotiations under the auspices of the UN International Institute for the Unification of Private Law to draft a convention that would establish an international legal regime for the creation, perfection, and priority of security, title-retention, and leasing interests in [mobile] equipment. In November 2001, the convention was adopted by fifty-three states, including the United States, at Cape Town, South Africa (and thus is commonly referred to as the "Cape Town Convention"). The convention is designed to address three types of equipment: aircraft, railway rolling stock, and outer space assets. While the convention contains provisions that apply generally to such equipment, more specific provisions concerning each of the three types of equipment are to be included in protocols to the convention. The first protocol, on aircraft equipment (including airframes, aircraft engines, and helicopters above certain thresholds), was completed at the same time as the Cape Town Convention, while the other two protocols remain under negotiation.
>
> On May 9, 2003, the United States signed the convention. In November, President Bush transmitted the convention to the Senate for advice and consent, subject to seven declarations (three for the convention and four for the protocol). In testimony before the Senate Foreign Relations Committee, the U.S. Department of Transportation's general counsel explained the benefits of the convention and its first protocol as follows: "As a general matter, the Convention adopts the asset-based financing practices already widely used in the United States and weaves them into an international agreement. Specifically, the Convention establishes an 'international interest' which is a secured credit or leasing interest with defined rights in a piece of equipment. These rights consist primarily of 1) the ability to repossess or sell or lease the equipment in case of default; and 2) the holding of a transparent finance priority in the equipment. Priority

will be established when a creditor files, on a first-in-time basis, a notice of its security interest, in a new high-technology international registry. Once an international interest has been filed by a creditor and becomes searchable at the international registry, that creditor's interest will have priority over all subsequent registered interests and all unregistered interests, with a few exceptions. The Federal Aviation Administration (FAA), which currently operates an aircraft registry, will serve as the authorized entry point into the International Registry."

Sean D. Murphy, *Cape Town Convention on Financing of High-Value, Mobile Equipment*, 98 Am. J. Int'l L. 852, 852–53 (2004). For a further look at the treaty and its protocol (which are reprinted in Appendices 28 and 29), as well as its predecessor, the 1948 Geneva Convention (Appendix 6), *see, e.g.*, Lorne S. Clark, *The 2001 Cape Town Convention on International Interests in Mobile Equipment and Aircraft Equipment Protocol: Internationalising Asset-Based Financing Principles for the Acquisition of Aircraft and Engines*, 69 J. Air L. & Com. 3 (2004); Sandeep Gopalan, *Securing Mobile Assets: The Cape Town Convention and Its Aircraft Protocol*, 29 N.C. J. Int'l L. & Com. Reg. 59 (2003); B. Patrick Honnebier, *The Fully-Computerized International Registry for Security Interests in Aircraft and Aircraft Protocol That Will Become Effective Toward the Beginning of 2006*, 70 J. Air L. & Com. 63 (2005); David G. Mayer & Frank L. Polk, *Cape Town Convention: Complex Questions and Significant Opportunities*, 24 LJN's Equip. Leasing Newsl. 1 (Oct. 2005).

9. In completing an aircraft financing deal, lawyers often must get creative if they are to meet their clients' objectives. For an interesting example, *see* Angelo Luigi Rosa, *Harmonizing Risk and Religion: The Utility of Shari'a-Compliant Transaction Structuring in Commercial Aircraft Finance*, 13 Minn. J. Global Trade 34 (2004) (describing how an Airbus A330 was financed for $88.6 million in accordance with Koranic law, which prohibits the charging of interest).

Problem 6

An airplane mechanic agreed to overhaul a customer's engine. When he was not paid for the job, he held on to the engine and asserted a common law, non-consensual, possessory lien. Subsequently, the customer went bankrupt and the trustee sought to recover the engine, claiming that the mechanic's lien was invalid because it had not been either federally- or state-recorded. Is the mechanic out of luck? *See In re Tower Air*, 319 B.R. 88 (Bankr. D. Del. 2004).

C. TAXES

WARDAIR CANADA, INC. v. FLORIDA DEPARTMENT OF REVENUE

477 U.S. 1 (1986)

Justice BRENNAN delivered the opinion of the Court.

Appellant Wardair Canada Inc., a Canadian airline that operates charter flights to and from the United States, maintains in this action that the Commerce Clause of the

Constitution precludes Florida from applying to it a tax on aviation fuel purchased in that State. Wardair also asserts that the Florida tax "must fall because it violates a clear unequivocal directive of Congress," allegedly implicit in the Federal Aviation Act, 49 U.S.C.App. § 1301 et seq. (1982 ed. and Supp. II), that the Federal Government has exclusive regulatory power over foreign air commerce. Brief for Appellant v, 15.

We disagree with appellant's view and analysis of the operation of the Commerce Clause, and find that Congress has not acted to pre-empt state taxes such as that imposed by Florida. Accordingly, we affirm the judgment of the Supreme Court of Florida upholding the tax.

I

Florida has for many years taxed the sale of fuel to common carriers, including airlines, within the State. Prior to April 1, 1983, the tax was prorated on a mileage basis, so that a carrier was liable for only the portion of the otherwise payable tax that was equal to the ratio of its Florida mileage to its worldwide mileage for the previous fiscal year. Fla.Stat. § 212.08(4) (1975). Effective April 1, 1983, the Florida law was amended to repeal the mileage proration formula for airlines, and the fuel tax was established at a rate of 5% on a deemed price of $1.148 per gallon. Fla.Stat. § 212.08(4)(a)(2) (1985). Under the amended law, an airline was liable for the full amount of the fuel tax whether that fuel was used to fly within or without the State, and regardless of whether the airline engaged in a substantial or a nominal amount of business within the State. The effect of this amendment was, of course, to increase substantially the tax liability of airlines, such as foreign airlines, who fly largely outside of Florida, and who had, under the old scheme, paid little Florida tax on fuel.

Shortly after the new law was enacted, appellant filed suit in state court attacking its validity insofar as it authorized the assessment and collection of a tax on fuel used by foreign airlines exclusively in foreign commerce. Wardair argued, among other things, that the law was unconstitutional under the Commerce Clause and that it was inconsistent with the Nonscheduled Air Services Agreement, May 8, 1974, United States-Canada, Art. XII, 25 U.S.T. 787, T.I.A.S. No. 7826 (U.S.-Canadian Agreement or Agreement), a bilateral agreement between the Governments of Canada and the United States regulating air charter service between the two countries. Wardair's case was consolidated for trial with a similar suit brought by a number of other foreign airlines.

In a separate order addressing only Wardair's claims, the trial court rejected the Commerce Clause arguments but found that the U.S.-Canadian Agreement expressed a "federal policy" to exempt foreign airlines from fuel taxes. The court further found that this "policy" precluded the individual States from acting in this area and thus preventing the United States from "speaking with one voice" with respect to foreign commerce. In reaching this conclusion, the court relied largely on our decision in Japan Line, Ltd. v. County of Los Angeles, 441 U.S. 434, 99 S.Ct. 1813, 60 L.Ed.2d 336 (1979). The court granted appellant a permanent injunction against the Florida Department of Revenue from assessing and collecting the fuel tax from Wardair.

The case was certified to the Supreme Court of Florida, which reversed, in part, the trial court. 455 So.2d 326 (1984). The Supreme Court first noted that the U.S.-Canadian Agreement by its terms exempted carriers only from national, as opposed to state or local (or, in the case of Canada, provincial) excise taxes, inspection fees, and other charges, and thus held that the Agreement did not pre-empt state sales taxes. Nor was the court persuaded that the Florida tax was invalid under the Foreign Commerce

Clause. The court again referred to the fact that the Agreement exempted only national taxes, and "presume[d] this has been done intentionally." Id., at 329. Having determined that the Federal Government had, in effect, itself elected not to prohibit the States from taxing aviation fuel, the court rejected the contention that the state tax "prevents our federal government from speaking with one voice," ibid., and thus distinguished Japan Line. We noted probable jurisdiction, 474 U.S. 943, 106 S.Ct. 307, 88 L.Ed.2d 284 (1984), and now affirm.

II

Wardair suggests that by enacting the Federal Aviation Act (Act), Congress "left no room for local government participation" with respect to foreign air travel. Brief for Appellant 39. Appellant does not expressly label this a preemption argument; rather, it relies on metaphor and tells us that "in the field of foreign air commerce it is the Federal Government that calls the tune. It is the Federal Government that is the conductor of the music, deciding how it is to be played and who are the players." Id., at 44. We assume that appellant intends, by this metaphor, to persuade us that Congress has determined to "occupy the field" of international aviation, and thus to pre-empt all state regulation. The argument is without merit.

It is of course true, as appellant notes, that Congress has, through the Act, regulated aviation extensively. The agencies charged by Congress with regulatory responsibility over foreign air travel exercise power, as appellant observes, over licensing, route services, rates and fares, tariffs, safety, and other aspects of air travel. However, state law is not preempted whenever there is any federal regulation of an activity or industry or area of law. The Supremacy Clause, among other things, confirms that when Congress legislates within the scope of its constitutionally granted powers, that legislation may displace state law, and this Court has throughout the years employed various verbal formulations in identifying numerous varieties of pre-emption. See, e.g., Louisiana Public Service Comm'n v. FCC, 476 U.S. 355, 368–369, 106 S.Ct. 1890, ——, 90 L.Ed.2d 369 (1986). But we have consistently emphasized that the first and fundamental inquiry in any pre-emption analysis is whether Congress intended to displace state law, and where a congressional statute does not expressly declare that state law is to be preempted, and where there is no actual conflict between what federal law and state law prescribe, we have required that there be evidence of a congressional intent to pre-empt the specific field covered by the state law. Pacific Gas & Electric Co. v. State Energy Resources Conservation and Development Comm'n, 461 U.S. 190, 103 S.Ct. 1713, 75 L.Ed.2d 752 (1983); Silkwood v. Kerr-McGee Corp., 464 U.S. 238, 104 S.Ct. 615, 78 L.Ed.2d 443 (1984). In the present case, not only is there no indication that Congress wished to preclude state sales taxation of airline fuel, but, to the contrary, the Act expressly permits States to impose such taxes. Section 1113 of the Act, as added, 87 Stat. 90, and as amended, 49 U.S.C.App. § 1513, addresses the issue of "State taxation of air commerce," detailing in § 1113(a) the kinds of taxes which are prohibited and in § 1113(b) those which are permissible. Among the permissible taxes are "sales or use taxes on the sale of goods or services." It is, of course, plausible that Congress never considered whether States should be permitted to impose sales taxes on foreign, as opposed to domestic, carriers, and therefore we do not rely on the existence of this section to answer the Commerce Clause issue raised here by appellant and considered by us infra. However, this section of the Act does provide the complete response to appellant's pre-emption argument. For what § 1113(b) shows is that, to the degree that Congress considered the power of the States to tax air travel, it expressly and unequivocally permitted the States to exercise that authority. In other words, rather than prohibit state regulation in the area, Congress invited it. This is not the stuff of pre-emption.

III

In cases involving the so-called dormant Commerce Clause, both interstate and foreign, the Federal Government has not affirmatively acted, and it is the responsibility of the judiciary to determine whether action taken by state or local authorities unduly threatens the values the Commerce Clause was intended to serve. See Southern Pacific Co. v. Arizona, 325 U.S. 761, 65 S.Ct. 1515, 89 L.Ed. 1915 (1945). In recognition of the importance of this conviction, we have acknowledged the self-executing nature of the Commerce Clause and held on countless occasions that, even in the absence of specific action taken by the Federal Government to disapprove of state regulation implicating interstate or foreign commerce, state regulation that is contrary to the constitutional principle of ensuring that the conduct of individual States does not work to the detriment of the Nation as a whole, and thus ultimately to all of the States, may be invalid under the unexercised Commerce Clause. See H.P. Hood & Sons, Inc. v. DuMond, 336 U.S. 525, 69 S.Ct. 657, 93 L.Ed. 865 (1949); Southern Pacific Co. v. Arizona, supra.

When a state tax is challenged as violative of the dormant Interstate Commerce Clause, we have asked four questions: is the tax applied to an activity with a substantial nexus with the taxing State; is the tax fairly apportioned; does the tax discriminate against interstate commerce; and is the tax fairly related to the services provided by the State. Complete Auto Transit, Inc. v. Brady, 430 U.S. 274, 279, 97 S.Ct. 1076, 1079, 51 L.Ed.2d 326 (1977). In Japan Line, supra, we noted that when the state tax allegedly interferes with the Federal Government's authority to regulate foreign commerce, two additional questions must be asked: "first, whether the tax, notwithstanding apportionment, creates a substantial risk of international multiple taxation, and, second, whether the tax prevents the Federal Government from speaking with one voice when regulating commercial relations with foreign governments." Id., at 451, 99 S.Ct., at 1823.

In the present case, appellant concedes that Florida's tax satisfies the four-part test set out in Complete Auto. In other words, it is not disputed that if this case did not involve foreign commerce, the Florida tax on the sale of aviation fuel would not contravene the Commerce Clause. Appellant also recognizes that there is no threat of multiple international taxation in this case, since the tax is imposed only upon the sale of fuel, a discrete transaction which occurs within one national jurisdiction only. Appellant and the United States as amicus curiae thus rely entirely on the final factor identified in Japan Line, and argue that the Florida tax violates the Foreign Commerce Clause because it threatens the ability of the Federal Government to "speak with one voice." Specifically, they urge that there exists a federal policy of reciprocal tax exemptions for aircraft, equipment, and supplies, including aviation fuel, that constitute the instrumentalities of international air traffic, and that this "policy" represents the statement that the "one voice" of the Federal Government wishes to make and which is threatened by the state law. We disagree. In our view, the evidence relied upon by appellant and the United States not only fails to reveal any such federal policy, but, even more fundamentally, shows also that in the context of this case we do not confront federal governmental silence of the sort that triggers dormant Commerce Clause analysis. On the contrary, the international agreements cited demonstrate that the Federal Government has affirmatively acted, rather than remained silent, with respect to the power of the States to tax aviation fuel, and thus that the case does not call for dormant Commerce Clause analysis at all. Moreover, in our view the actions taken by the Federal Government accept the authority of States to tax as Florida has here, and lend further support to the position and views advanced by appellee and relied on by the Florida Supreme Court in rejecting Wardair's arguments.

Appellant and the United States maintain that the policy of tax exemption for the instrumentalities of international air traffic is manifested by, among other things, (1) the Chicago Convention on International Civil Aviation, opened for signature, Dec. 7, 1944, 61 Stat. 1180 (Chicago Convention), an international convention to which the United States and 156 other nations, including Canada, are parties; (2) a Resolution (Resolution) adopted November 14, 1966, by the International Civil Aviation Organization (ICAO), an organization of which the United States is a member by virtue of being a party to the Chicago Convention; (3) more than 70 bilateral agreements, including the U.S.-Canadian Agreement, into which the United States has entered with various foreign countries dealing with international aviation. But what these documents show is that while there appears to be an international aspiration on the one hand to eliminate all impediments to foreign air travel—including taxation of fuel—the law as it presently stands acquiesces in taxation of the sale of that fuel by political subdivisions of countries. Thus, Article 24(a) of the Chicago Convention by its terms precludes the imposition of local taxes on fuel only when the fuel is "on board an aircraft ... on arrival ... and retained on board on leaving" a contracting party; it does not prohibit taxation of fuel purchased in that country. 61 Stat. 1186. We agree with amici National Governors' Association et al. that the negative implications of this provision support recognizing Florida's power to tax; certainly, the provision demonstrates the international community's awareness of the problem of state and local taxation of international air travel, specifically aviation fuel, and represents a decision by the parties to that Convention to address the problem by curtailing and limiting only some of the localities' power to tax, while implicitly preserving other aspects of that authority.

Nor does the Resolution provide support for appellant's contention that there is a clear national policy of exempting aviation fuel from state sales taxes. While the Resolution undeniably does endorse an international scheme whereby fuel would be exempt "'from all customs and other duties,'" which it defines as including "'import, export, excise, sales, consumption and internal duties and taxes of all kinds levied by any taxing authority within a State,'" Brief for United States as Amicus Curiae 12 (Sept. 17, 1985), quoting Resolution pp. 3, 4, the Resolution is formally merely the work product of an international organization of which the United States is a member; it is has not been specifically endorsed, let alone signed, entered into, agreed upon, approved, or passed by either the Executive or Legislative branch of the Federal Government. In other words, no action has been taken to give the Resolution the force of law. While it is not argued by either appellant or by the United States as amicus that this Resolution in and of itself should operate to pre-empt state law, we also think it untenable to assert, as they do, that this Resolution represents a policy of the United States, as opposed to a policy of an organization of which the United States is one of many members.

Our reluctance in this regard is bolstered by the fact that the United States has, since the time that the Convention came into force, become a party to more than 70 bilateral aviation agreements, and in not one of these agreements has the United States agreed to deny the States the power asserted by Florida in this case. Most of these agreements explicitly commit the United States to refrain from imposing national taxes on aviation fuel used by airlines of the other contracting party, see Brief for United States as Amicus Curiae 14–17, 19, but as the United States concedes, "none of our bilateral aviation agreements explicitly interdicts state or local taxes on aviation fuel used by foreign airlines in international traffic." Id., at 17. Most strikingly as it relates to the case before us, the U.S.-

Canadian Agreement itself limits the tax exemption to be afforded to foreign air carriers to "national duties and charges." App. A-58. Taxation by political subdivisions of either the United States or Canada are not mentioned, an omission which must be understood as representing a policy choice by the contracting parties, especially in light of the fact that the Resolution addressed this concern eight years before the United States and Canada entered into the Agreement. We note that throughout the time that the U.S.-Canadian Agreement has been in force, some American States, as well as some Canadian Provinces, have imposed taxes within their jurisdictions on aviation fuel used by Canadian and American carriers respectively in international travel. Furthermore, there was not, until recently, any challenge to the localities' legal authority to do so. Although not dispositive, this course of conduct suggests that the parties to the Agreement and those most immediately affected by it understood it to permit this sort of taxation.

What all of this makes abundantly clear is that the Federal Government has not remained silent with regard to the question whether States should have the power to impose taxes on aviation fuel used by foreign carriers in international travel. By negative implication arising out of more than 70 agreements entered into since the Chicago Convention, the United States has at least acquiesced in state taxation of fuel used by foreign carriers in international travel. Again, in the U.S.-Canadian Agreement only "national" charges are barred, and we presume that drafters from two federalist nations understood this as representing a choice not to preclude local taxation. It would turn dormant Commerce Clause analysis entirely upside down to apply it where the Federal Government has acted, and to apply it in such a way as to reverse the policy that the Federal Government has elected to follow. For the dormant Commerce Clause, in both its interstate and foreign incarnations, only operates where the Federal Government has not spoken to ensure that the essential attributes of nationhood will not be jeopardized by States acting as independent economic actors. However, the Federal Government is entitled in its wisdom to act to permit the States varying degrees of regulatory authority. In our view, the facts presented by this case show that the Federal Government has affirmatively decided to permit the States to impose these sales taxes on aviation fuel. Accordingly, there is no need for us to consider, and nothing in this opinion should be understood to address, whether, in the absence of these international agreements, the Foreign Commerce Clause would invalidate Florida's tax.

In Japan Line, 441 U.S., at 451, 99 S.Ct., at 1823, we explained that Foreign Commerce Clause analysis requires that a court ask whether a state tax "prevents the Federal Government from 'speaking with one voice when regulating commercial relations with foreign governments.'" But we never suggested in that case or any other that the Foreign Commerce Clause insists that the Federal Government speak with any particular voice.

In light of the above, the judgment of the Supreme Court of Florida is affirmed.

[The concurring opinion of Chief Justice Burger is omitted.]

Justice BLACKMUN, dissenting.

In Japan Line, Ltd. v. County of Los Angeles, 441 U.S. 434, 99 S.Ct. 1813, 60 L.Ed.2d 336 (1979), this Court recognized that the Commerce Clause commits to the exclusive authority of the Federal Government the regulation of those aspects of foreign commerce that by their very nature "necessitate a uniform national rule." Id., at 449, 99 S.Ct., at 1822. In regulating commercial relations with foreign governments, "'the Federal Government must speak with one voice.'" Ibid., quoting Michelin Tire Corp. v. Wages, 423 U.S. 276, 285, 96 S.Ct. 535, 540, 46 L.Ed.2d 495 (1976). As a result, the Court in Japan Line held that the imposition of California's ad valorem property tax on foreign-owned containers used exclusively in foreign commerce was unconstitutional. The tax imposed in this case by Florida on fuel is indistinguishable, for Commerce Clause purposes, from the tax imposed by California on containers in Japan Line. Because a State's taxation on fuel used in foreign commerce will prohibit the Federal Government from speaking with "one voice," I believe that this application of Florida's tax violates the Constitution.

The decision today leaves Florida and other States free to tax foreign aviation, and will hinder the United States in its efforts to attain reciprocal tax immunity with foreign governments. Florida's action may well undermine reciprocity agreements since other countries may react to Florida's tax with various retaliatory measures against United States carriers abroad, retaliation that "of necessity would be felt by the Nation as a whole." Japan Line, 441 U.S., at 453, 99 S.Ct., at 1824. Florida's actions may also hamper the United States' position in negotiations designed to achieve the federal policy of reciprocity because the Nation cannot speak with "one voice." In Japan Line, this Court made clear that a State, "by its unilateral act, cannot be permitted to place ... impediments before this Nation's conduct of its foreign relations and its foreign trade." Ibid. Because the Court's decision today permits just that, I respectfully dissent.

CITGO PETROLEUM CORPORATION v. UNITED STATES

104 F. Supp. 2d 106 (C.I.T. 2000)

RESTANI, Judge.

This matter challenging the imposition of the Harbor Maintenance Tax ("HMT") upon aircraft fuel withdrawn from a bonded warehouse for use in international flight is before the court on Cross Motions for Summary Judgment, pursuant to USCIT Rule 56. The court finds that the fuel cargo at issue is exempt from the tax.

FACTS

Plaintiff, Citgo Petroleum Corporation, is a domestic corporation that imports jet turbine fuel for sale to foreign and domestic airlines engaged in international traffic from, to and through airports in the United States. Pl.'s Statement of Undisputed Material Facts ¶ 1 (hereinafter "Pl.'s Statement"). Plaintiff imported jet turbine fuel into Port Everglades, Florida. Id. at ¶ 3. During the course of 1991, plaintiff discharged five cargoes of jet turbine fuel into a United States Customs Service bonded storage tank at that port. Id. at ¶¶ 2–3. At the time of unloading, plaintiff filed warehouse entries and paid the HMT upon those cargoes. Id. at ¶ 3.

Plaintiff subsequently withdrew the fuel and transported it to receiving aircraft. Pl.'s Statement ¶¶ 4 & 6. When technical requirements for duty-free treatment were met, plaintiff claimed entitlement to duty-free and tax-free treatment pursuant to 19 U.S.C. § 1309 (1994) for fuel for some receiving aircraft. Id. at ¶ 6. For aircraft that Customs determined were not entitled to such exemption, plaintiff tendered duties and taxes to Customs. Id. at ¶ 9. There appears to be no dispute as to the entitlement to § 1309 exemptions for the entries at issue. The only issue presented to the court is whether the HMT is within the exemption.

Customs subsequently liquidated the entries. Pl.'s Statement ¶ 11. After liquidation, plaintiff protested and requested refunds of the HMT, alleging that the fuel was exempt from the HMT pursuant to 19 U.S.C. § 1309. Pl.'s Mot. for Summ. J., Tab A, at 1. Customs denied the protest. Id. Plaintiff brings this action challenging the denial of its protest. Jurisdiction lies under 28 U.S.C. § 1581(a) (1994). Amoco Oil Co. v. United States, 63 F.Supp.2d 1332, 1334 (C.I.T. 1999); Thomson Consumer Electronics, Inc. v. United States, 62 F.Supp.2d 1182, 1184 (C.I.T. 1999).

The issue before the court is whether the HMT paid by a domestic corporation upon cargoes of jet fuel imported into bonded warehouses and later withdrawn as supplies for aircraft engaged in foreign trade are "internal revenue taxes" within the meaning of 19 U.S.C. § 1309(a). Section 1309 provides that supplies for "aircraft registered in the United States and actually engaged in foreign trade" may "be withdrawn ... from any customs bonded warehouse ... free of duty and internal-revenue tax." 19 U.S.C. § 1309(a)(1)(c).

DISCUSSION

First, it is clear that the HMT is a tax. Because the HMT is a tax, it was declared unconstitutional as to exports. United States v. U.S. Shoe Corp., 523 U.S. 360, 362–63, 118 S.Ct. 1290, 140 L.Ed.2d 453 (1998). The HMT is set forth in the Internal Revenue Code. Id. at 367, 118 S.Ct. 1290. The court also found the HMT to be an internal revenue tax in U.S. Shoe Corp. v. United States, 20 CIT 206, 208 (1996). The court incorporated the U.S. Shoe opinion in IBM Corp. v. United States, No. 94-10-00625, 1998 WL 325156 (C.I.T. 1998), rev'd on other grounds, 201 F.3d 1367 (Fed.Cir.2000). In IBM, the appellate court accepted, at least for the purpose of argument, that the tax was an internal revenue tax. IBM, 201 F.3d at 1371. It stated a bit more, however.

> Because Congress codified the HMT as part of Title 26 of the United States Code, entitled "Internal Revenue Code," we may reasonably conclude that Congress considered the HMT to be an internal revenue tax. Furthermore, while it may be true that the constitutionality of the HMT was challenged because the HMT taxed goods exported out of the United States, the HMT is clearly derived from internal sources—the U.S. exporter—rather than external sources—the foreign recipient; HMT revenues were collected in the United States from domestic companies based on their use of ports and harbors in this country. Thus, both the structure and the content of the HMT point toward it being an internal revenue tax, and thus entitled on refund to the interest award provided under § 2411.

IBM, 201 F.3d at 1371–72. This is also consistent with the court's decision in BMW Mfg. Corp. v. United States, in which the court found that the HMT was not a customs duty. 69 F.Supp.2d 1355, 1358 (C.I.T. 1999). BMW also recognized that the HMT is a generalized charge for port use. Id.; see also Texport Oil Co. v. United States, 185 F.3d 1291, 1297 (Fed.Cir.1999) ("The HMT is a generalized Federal charge for the use of certain harbors.") There is nothing inconsistent, however, between the general purpose of the charge and its status as an internal revenue tax. As the court recognized in BMW, Congress wanted the HMT charge applied as widely as possible. BMW, 69 F.Supp.2d at 1358–59.

Against this background, the court addresses whether Congress created an exemption to the HMT tax applicable in this case in order to serve some other purpose. Congress has provided some exemptions in the HMT act itself for various reasons, including commercial competitiveness. See, e.g., 26 U.S.C. § 4462(d)(1) (1994) (relating to bonded commercial cargo); see also BMW, 69 F.Supp.2d at 1359 n.5. Plaintiff claims no exemption in the HMT statute itself. Plaintiff argues, however, that on its face 19 U.S.C. § 1309, which is not in the Act establishing the HMT, would appear to provide an applicable exemption. The court in BMW recognized that other general exemptions found outside the HMT might apply. BMW, 69 F.Supp.2d at 1358.

Both parties agree that the key term "internal revenue tax" found in § 1309 does not have an invariable meaning and that statutory purpose is the key. United States v. Leeb, 20 F.2d 355, 356 (2d Cir.1927). As indicated, the purpose of the HMT is clear: to maintain harbors by charging for nearly every port use. 26 U.S.C. § 4461 (1994). Section 1309 has an equally evident purpose of promoting equal footing between U.S. vessels and aircraft with foreign vessels and aircraft. S.Rep. No. 86-1491 (1960), reprinted in 1960 U.S.C.C.A.N. 2780, 2785 (quoting with approval from the Bureau of the Budget report that "the original and main purpose for the exemption from duty and taxes of ships' supplies was to place U.S. vessels engaged in foreign trade on an equal footing with foreign vessels. Such exemption extends back to the 19th century tariff acts and was eventually extended to aircraft.") Section 1309's long history will be recounted in brief.

Section 22 of the Act of July 14, 1862, granted the privilege of duty free withdrawal of articles from bonded warehouses to be used as vessels-of-war supplies, if the United States was granted reciprocal privileges. Act of July 14, 1862, § 22, 12 Stat. 543, 560. Section 16 of the Act of June 26, 1884, extended the privilege to any vessel engaged in foreign trade. Act of June 26, 1884, § 16, 1 Rev. Stat. Supp. 440, 443. Section 16 of the Tariff Act of 1897 extended the privilege further to duties and internal revenue taxes on vessel supplies of either foreign or domestic production. Tariff Act of 1897, § 16, 30 Stat. 151, 207 (July 24, 1897). Now, of course, the privilege applies to aircraft as well as vessels. See 19 U.S.C. § 1309. The privilege is also reflected in international agreements to which the United States is a party, as befits the reciprocal privilege history of the provision.

Article 24(a) of the Convention on International Civil Aviation (the "Chicago Convention"), exempted fuel and other supplies aboard aircraft in international flight status from taxation. Convention on International Civil Aviation, opened for signature Dec. 7, 1944, art. 24(a), 61 Stat. 1180, 1186, 15 U.N.T.S. 295, 310 (entered into force Apr. 4, 1947). The International Civil Aviation Organization ("ICAO"), established by the Convention, extended the exemption to fuel and other consumable technical supplies taken abroad. Policies on Taxation in the Field of International Air Transport, Section I(1), ICAO Doc. 8632 (3d ed.2000) [hereinafter "Policies on Taxation"]. This principle has remained consistent since 1966, when the ICAO first adopted this policy. See Policies on Taxation in the Field of International Air Transport, Section I, ICAO Doc. 8632-C/968 (2d ed.1994 and 1st ed.1966).

Defendant argues that the international agreements do not apply or inform the interpretation of 19 U.S.C. § 1309 because the payor of the tax is a domestic corporation. That does not appear to be a limitation within the agreements. (This argument [also] seems somewhat nonsensical. Taxes are usually paid by domestic parties and customs duties by United States' importers.) The focus of the agreements, as with § 1309, seems to be reciprocal benefits for aircraft in international flight. The ultimate purchaser, no doubt, would have higher fuel prices passed on to it.

Also, the government argues that, because pursuant to 26 U.S.C. § 4461(c)(2)(B) liability for the HMT attaches at the time of unloading of the imported fuel, the exemption found in the international agreements does not apply. The ICAO policies at issue, however, clearly specify refunds of duties or taxes previously paid. See Policies on Taxation, Section I(1), [which] reads in relevant part:

> The Council resolves that:

1. With respect to taxes on fuel, lubricants or other consumable technical supplies:

a) when an aircraft registered in one Contracting State, or leased or chartered by an operator of that State, is engaged in international air transport to, from or through a customs territory of another Contracting State its fuel, lubricants and other consumable technical supplies shall be exempt from customs or other duties on a reciprocal basis, or alternatively, in the cases of fuel, lubricants and other consumable technical supplies taken on board as per subparagraphs ii) or iii) such duties shall be refunded, when …

ii) the fuel, etc., is taken on board for consumption during the flight when the aircraft departs from an international airport of that other State either for another customs territory of that State or for the territory of any other State, provided that the aircraft has complied, before its departure from the customs territory concerned, with all customs and other clearance regulations in force in that territory;

b) the foregoing exemption being based upon reciprocity, no Contracting State complying with this Resolution is obliged to grant to aircraft registered in another Contracting State or aircraft leased or chartered by an operator of that State any treatment more favourable than its own aircraft are entitled to receive in the territory of that other State;

c) notwithstanding the underlying principle of reciprocity, Contracting States are encouraged to apply the exemption, to the maximum extent possible, to all aircraft on their arrival from and departure for other States;

d) the expression "customs and other duties" shall include import, export, excise, sales, consumption and internal duties and taxes of all kinds levied upon the fuel, lubricants and other consumable technical supplies; and

e) the duties and taxes described in d) above shall include those levied by any taxing authority within a Contracting State, whether national or local. These duties and taxes shall not be or continue to be imposed on the acquisition of fuel, lubricants or consumable technical supplies used by aircraft in connection with the international air services except to the extent that they are based on the actual costs of providing airports or air navigation facilities and services and used to finance the costs of providing them[.]

Policies on Taxation, Section I(1), ICAO Doc. 8632.

Th[is] resolution specifically covers "import, export, excise, sales, consumption, and internal duties and taxes of all kinds levied upon the fuel, lubricants and other consumable technical supplies." Id. at Section I(1)(d). There appears to be no limit to the exemption based on whether it is the airline or the supplier that must pay the tax or when it attaches.

Moreover, 19 U.S.C. § 1309 is not limited by the drawback statute at issue in Texport, 185 F.3d at 1296–97. 19 U.S.C. § 1313 (1994), which was at issue there, only allowed drawback of duties paid upon importation. There is nothing in either the HMT statute or 19 U.S.C. § 1309 which indicates an intention to narrow § 1309 so that it would only allow refund of duties or taxes paid on importation. Nor is there any sign that Congress wished to disregard specific international commitments on aircraft fuel supplies. Rather, it seems that 19 U.S.C. § 1309 is broadly worded to be consistent with the international agreements discussed herein. The court would be remiss in adopting a narrow reading. Both the plain words of § 1309 and its purpose indicate a refund of the taxes paid should be made.

Accordingly, in each instance at issue herein in which plaintiff qualified for the 19 U.S.C. § 1309 exemption, a refund of the HMT shall be made.

AMERICAN AIRLINES, INC. v. JOHNSON

56 S.W.3d 502 (Tenn. Ct. App. 2000)

FARMER, Judge.

American Airlines, Inc., appeals the trial court's final judgment denying its request for a refund of use taxes paid on aviation fuel purchased out of state during the years 1992 through 1995. We affirm the trial court's judgment.

The material facts in this case are not in dispute. American Airlines is a Delaware corporation which has its principal place of business in Texas. American Airlines is qualified to do business in the state of Tennessee, and it conducts operations at a location in the Nashville International Airport. During the period from January 1, 1992, to December 31, 1995, American Airlines paid over $7 million in use taxes on aviation fuel that it used in its operations at the Nashville airport. American Airlines purchased the aviation fuel outside the state of Tennessee, transported the fuel via pipeline into the state, placed the fuel in storage for an average of fourteen days, and then pumped the fuel into its aircraft at the Nashville airport. Using this fuel, American Airlines' aircraft transported passengers and freight to out-of-state destinations.

In July 1996, American Airlines filed a complaint against the Commissioner of Revenue seeking a refund of the use taxes it paid on aviation fuel from 1992 to 1995. In support of its claim, American Airlines contended that the fuel was exempt from Tennessee sales and use tax based on the import-for-export exemption contained in Tennessee Code Annotated section 67-6-313(a) (1994). Alternatively, American Airlines contended that it should have been required to pay a use tax only on that portion of the fuel actually used by its aircraft in flight over the state of Tennessee.

Both parties subsequently filed motions for summary judgment on the issue of whether the aviation fuel was subject to the Tennessee use tax. The trial court ruled in favor of the Commissioner, holding that the aviation fuel was subject to the Tennessee use tax and, further, that the fuel was not exempt from taxation under the import-for-export provision contained in section 67-6-313(a).

On appeal, American Airlines contends that the trial court erred in ruling that all of the aviation fuel that it purchased outside the state and loaded into the fuel tanks of its aircraft in Nashville was subject to the Tennessee use tax. Specifically, American Airlines contends that it should not have to pay a use tax on the percentage of the fuel that was "burned off" after its aircraft left the state. Alternatively, American Airlines contends that the fuel "burned off" outside the state was exempt from the use tax under the import-for-export provision of section 67-6-313(a).

We begin our analysis of these issues with the well-established rule that courts must construe tax statutes liberally in favor of the taxpayer and, conversely, strictly against the taxing authority. See White v. Roden Elec. Supply Co., 536 S.W.2d 346, 348 (Tenn.1976); Memphis St. Ry. v. Crenshaw, 165 Tenn. 536, 55 S.W.2d 758, 759 (Tenn.1933). Where any doubt exists as to the meaning of a taxing statute, courts must resolve this doubt in favor of the taxpayer. See Memphis Peabody Corp. v. MacFarland, 211 Tenn. 384, 365 S.W.2d 40, 42 (1963); accord Carl Clear Coal Corp. v. Huddleston, 850 S.W.2d 140, 147 (Tenn.Ct.App.1992). Courts may not extend by implication the right to collect a tax "beyond the clear import of the statute by which it is levied." Boggs v. Crenshaw, 157 Tenn. 261, 7 S.W.2d 994, 995 (1928). By the same token, courts must give effect to the "plain import of the language of the act" and must not use the strict construction rule to thwart "the legislative intent to tax." International Harvester Co. v. Carr, 225 Tenn. 244, 466 S.W.2d 207, 214 (1971); see also Bergeda v. State, 179 Tenn. 460, 167 S.W.2d 338, 340 (1943) (indicating that courts "must give full scope to the legislative intent and apply a rule of construction that will not defeat the plain purposes of the act").

In enacting the Tennessee Retailers' Sales Tax Act, the legislature intended "to tax every retail sale of tangible personal property and every use of personal property in this state," unless the legislature expressly excerpted the sale or use from taxation. We believe that this definition of the term "use" was broad enough to cover American Airlines' acts of storing the aviation fuel in Tennessee, pumping the fuel into the tanks of its aircraft at the Nashville airport, and then using the fuel in the operation of its aircraft. Accordingly, we reject American Airlines' contention that the term "actually used" should be narrowly defined to include only the fuel that was "burned off" in Tennessee. See, e.g., Beecham Lab. v. Woods, 569 S.W.2d 456, 457 (Tenn.1978) (holding that warehousing and distribution of pharmaceutical samples clearly fell within Act's definition of "use").

On appeal, American Airlines argues that this interpretation of the statute is inconsistent with the remainder of the Retailers' Sales Tax Act, which purports to tax only personal property that "is used, consumed, distributed, or stored for use or consumption in this state." Tenn.Code Ann. §67-6-203(a) (1994). In light of the legislature's broad definition of the term "use," we do not perceive any inconsistency between the result reached here and other provisions of the Act. In accordance with this definition, American Airlines "used" the aviation fuel when it pumped the fuel into its aircraft for use in the aircraft's operation. We further note that, in making this argument, American Airlines does not describe any specific applications of the use tax that would be inconsistent with our holding today.

American Airlines focuses on the phrase "actually used in the operation of airplane or aircraft motors" to support its contention that it should only have been taxed for that portion of aviation fuel used to power its aircraft while still in the state of Tennessee. Tenn.Code Ann. §67-6-217 (1994). Again, we decline to adopt such a restrictive interpretation of the statute. We recognize that a portion of the aviation fuel continued to power American Airlines' aircraft after it left the state of Tennessee. Given the legislature's expansive definition of the term "use," however, we conclude that the aviation fuel was "used" in the operation of American Airlines' aircraft while still in Tennessee and that such use was taxable.

In urging this court to reverse the trial court's ruling, American Airlines cites an article on the subject of state taxation of jet fuel for the proposition that "[t]he burn-off rule has been adopted by the legislatures of several states, including ... Tennessee." Robert L. Mandel, How States Tax Jet Fuel, 4 St. Tax Notes Mag. 185, 186 (1993). We note, however, that the article's author neither cites any authority for this proposition nor discusses the statutory language upon which he bases this conclusion. Moreover, we find no support for such an apportionment in the Act itself or in case law interpreting the Act. To the contrary, our supreme court has consistently rejected the argument that the Tennessee use tax should be apportioned on the basis of an aircraft's intrastate use to interstate use, reasoning that the Act makes no provision for such apportionment and that the court has no authority to apportion on any basis. See Service Merchandise Co. v. Jackson, 735 S.W.2d 443, 445 (Tenn.1987); Vector Co. v. Benson, 491 S.W.2d 612, 615 (Tenn.1973).

We also reject American Airlines' alternative argument that it was entitled to an exemption for the portion of the aviation fuel that was "burned off" outside the state of Tennessee. In enacting the Retailers' Sales Tax Act, the legislature indicated that it did not intend "to levy a tax upon articles of tangible personal property imported into this state or produced or manufactured in this state for export." Tenn.Code Ann. § 67-6-313(a) (1994). Citing this provision, American Airlines contends that the aviation fuel that remained in its aircraft after the aircraft left the state of Tennessee was being exported and, thus, was exempt from taxation under the import-for-export provision.

We conclude that this argument lacks merit. Although the rule is well-established that taxing legislation should be liberally construed in favor of the taxpayer and strictly construed against the taxing authority, it is an equally important principle of Tennessee tax law that "exemptions from taxation are construed against the taxpayer who must shoulder the heavy and exacting burden of proving the exemption." Rogers Group, Inc. v. Huddleston, 900 S.W.2d 34, 36 (Tenn.Ct.App.1995). The exemption "must be expressed in clear language which includes the taxpayer," and it "must not be broadened beyond the command of the provision." Sears, Roebuck & Co. v. Woods, 708 S.W.2d 374, 378 (Tenn.1986). The exemption "must positively appear and will not be implied." LeTourneau Sales & Serv., Inc. v. Olsen, 691 S.W.2d 531, 534 (Tenn.1985). "Every presumption is against the exemption and a well-founded doubt is fatal to the claim." Tibbals Flooring Co. v. Huddleston, 891 S.W.2d 196, 198 (Tenn.1994); United Canners, Inc. v. King, 696 S.W.2d 525, 527 (Tenn.1985).

Applying these rules of construction, we conclude that American Airlines has failed to demonstrate that its use of aviation fuel was entitled to the import-for-export exemption contained in section 67-6-313(a). In construing this provision, our supreme court has indicated that "no one incurs tax liability with respect to goods by virtue of their transportation through this State in the channels of interstate commerce;" however, "any stoppage or bringing to rest [of] these goods within the State for sale at retail, use, consumption, distribution or storage for subsequent use, does subject such goods to the taxing power of the State." Texas Gas Transmission Corp. v. Benson, 223 Tenn. 279, 444 S.W.2d 137, 139 (1969). In the present case, American Airlines brought the aviation fuel into the state of Tennessee, stored the fuel in Tennessee, and subsequently used the fuel in the operation of its aircraft in Tennessee. Under these facts, American Airlines could not claim the import-for-export exemption contained in the Act.

Our denial of the claimed exemption is supported by our supreme court's decision in Serodino, Inc. v. Woods, 568 S.W.2d 610 (Tenn.1978). In that case, the taxpayer ordered parts from out of state, brought the parts into Tennessee, and installed the parts on barges that it was repairing or renewing. See Serodino, 568 S.W.2d at 613. Thereafter, the barges were placed back into interstate commerce and used by their respective owners outside of Tennessee. See id. Among its other claims, the taxpayer argued that the parts ordered for renewal work were exempt from taxation under the Act's import-for-export provision. See id. The supreme court rejected this argument, reasoning that

> the evidence does not sustain the taxpayer's claim that parts ordered for renewal work are imported into Tennessee or are produced and manufactured in this state for export, so as to be exempt under T.C.A. §67-3007 [now section 67-7-313(a)]. Those parts are received and installed by the taxpayer's employees at its Tennessee facilities.

Id. at 613–14.

We similarly conclude that the aviation fuel purchased by American Airlines was not entitled to the import-for-export exemption. Just as the barge parts were received and installed by the taxpayer at its Tennessee facility, the aviation fuel was received by American Airlines and pumped into its aircraft at the Nashville airport. The fact that the barge parts and aviation fuel were subsequently used in states other than Tennessee did not bring them within the Act's import-for-export exemption.

In so holding, we distinguish the cases cited by American Airlines because, in those cases, no portion of the goods for which the exemption was claimed was distributed or used in the state of Tennessee. See Beecham Lab. v. Woods, 569 S.W.2d 456 (Tenn.1978) (taxpayer withdrew pharmaceutical samples from its Bristol warehouse and distributed samples outside Tennessee); Young Sales Corp. v. Benson, 224 Tenn. 88, 450 S.W.2d 574 (1970) (taxpayer withdrew insulation from its Memphis warehouse and shipped materials to job sites outside Tennessee). Here, American Airlines distributed and began using the aviation fuel within the state of Tennessee.

We also decline to follow the Georgia supreme court's decision in Undercofler v. Eastern Air Lines, Inc., 221 Ga. 824, 147 S.E.2d 436 (1966). We recognize that the Georgia exemption contained virtually the same language as the Tennessee exemption. Contrary to Tennessee's rules of construction, however, the Georgia court indicated that it was construing the exemption in favor of the taxpayer. See Undercofler, 147 S.E.2d at 441.

The trial court's judgment is affirmed, and this cause is remanded for further proceedings consistent with this opinion. Costs of this appeal are taxed to the appellant, American Airlines, Inc., and its surety, for which execution may issue if necessary.

EXECUTIVE AIRCRAFT CONSULTING, INC. v. CITY OF NEWTON

845 P.2d 57 (Kan. 1993)

ABBOTT, Justice.

Executive Aircraft Consulting, Inc. (Executive Aircraft) filed a declaratory judgment action, challenging the legality of a "fuel flowage fee," which the City of Newton and Harvey County (defendants) had adopted by ordinance. The trial court found that this fee on all aviation fuel transported onto the premises of the Newton City-County Airport (Airport) was an illegal tax, in violation of K.S.A. 79-3424 (prohibiting any political subdivision except the State of Kansas from imposing a motor vehicle fuel tax) and K.S.A. 12-194 (prohibiting a city or county from imposing an excise tax upon the sale or transfer of personal or real property, other than a retailers' sales tax and a compensating use tax). The defendants appeal.

The defendants had and have a retail sales facility at the Airport that, among other things, sells aviation fuel to the general public. It is the only sales facility for aviation fuel at the Airport. Executive Aircraft is in the business of refurbishing aircraft and buys and sells aircraft. It operates its business at the Airport on property leased from defendants. It uses a large quantity of aviation fuel.

Executive Aircraft purchased a tanker truck and would purchase aviation fuel whenever it could buy it at the lowest price and then refuel its planes out of the tanker truck. It would also buy fuel from suppliers who would deliver fuel to the Airport and pump it into Executive Aircraft's tanker truck.

The defendants became concerned about the loss of revenue from Executive Aircraft and the possibility that other tenants might do the same thing. The defendants countered by adopting a city/county ordinance that establishes a license requirement to transport aviation fuel to and upon the Airport's premises and assesses a fuel flowage fee of five cents per gallon on all aviation fuel so transported. The ordinance establishes criminal penalties for violations. The ordinance provides for the proceeds from the fuel flowage fees to be deposited into an airport improvement fund to finance public improvements at the Airport.

Executive Aircraft filed a declaratory judgment action, asking the trial court to invalidate that part of the ordinance imposing the fuel flowage fee. Executive Aircraft argued the fuel flowage fee is a locally levied tax on the distribution or delivery of motor vehicle fuel, in violation of K.S.A. 79-3424; is a locally levied excise tax on the sale or transfer of personal property, in violation of K.S.A. 12-194; and did not operate impartially, in violation of K.S.A. 3-116.

Executive Aircraft subsequently filed a motion for judgment on the pleadings on the tax issues—whether the fuel flowage fee violated K.S.A. 79-3424 and K.S.A. 12-194. Executive Aircraft maintained that judgment on the pleadings was not appropriate with respect to its claims concerning K.S.A. 3-116 because of the possibility of disputed facts concerning whether the ordinance discriminated against Executive Aircraft. In response, the defendants claimed that all three issues were susceptible to judgment on the pleadings.

On January 3, 1992, the trial court heard arguments and then entered judgment in favor of Executive Aircraft. With regard to the tax issues, the court ruled that the defendants did not have the authority to impose the fuel flowage fee and that the portion of the ordinance imposing the fuel flowage fee was illegal. The court did not address the K.S.A. 3-116 claim.

The defendants timely appealed to the Court of Appeals. The case was transferred to this court, pursuant to K.S.A. 20-3018(c). The defendants claim the trial court erred in finding that the fuel flowage fee was a locally levied tax on motor vehicle fuel in violation of K.S.A. 79-3424 and a locally levied excise tax in violation of K.S.A. 12-194. The defendants argue that the fuel flowage fee does not violate the statutes because a fee, by definition, is outside the scope of the tax statutes and because this fee was issued in furtherance of its proprietary functions. The defendants conceded at trial and on appeal that but for the defendants' exercising their proprietary functions, the fuel flowage fee would be a tax.

The defendants base their authority to impose the fuel flowage fee upon the home rule provision of the Kansas Constitution. "[T]he home rule powers granted to cities by constitutional amendment and to counties by legislative act appear to be similar and parallel each other in many particulars." Missouri Pacific Railroad v. Board of Greeley County Comm'rs, 231 Kan. 225, 226, 643 P.2d 188 (1982). There also are differences between city and county home rule. See Heim, Kansas Local Government Law § 3.64 (1991) (comparison of city and county home rule powers). These differences, however, are immaterial to resolving this issue. Thus, for the sake of brevity, references to constitutional home rule will be deemed to apply to both defendants.

Home rule empowers the defendants to levy any type of exaction unless the legislature preempts the field by uniform enactment. Kan.Const. art. 12, § 5(b). The defendants acknowledge that K.S.A. 79-3424 and K.S.A. 12-194 are uniform enactments.

K.S.A. 79-3424 provides:

> The business of using, manufacturing or selling of motor-vehicle fuels shall not be subject to any excise, license, privilege or occupation tax other than the one herein imposed, whether such tax be imposed by the state of Kansas or by any municipal corporation or other political subdivision of this state; and no municipal corporation, or other political subdivision of this state, shall levy or collect any tax upon, or measured by, the sale, receipt, distribution or use of motor-vehicle fuel, or any excise, license, privilege or occupational tax upon the business of manufacturing, using, selling or delivering motor-vehicle fuels.

Motor vehicle fuels encompass aviation fuel. K.S.A.1991 Supp. 79-3408(d)(4).

K.S.A. 12-194 provides:

> No city or county shall levy or impose an excise tax or a tax in the nature of an excise, other than a retailers' sales tax and a compensating use tax, upon the sale or transfer of personal or real property, or the use thereof, or the rendering of a service, but the provisions of this section shall not be construed as prohibiting any city from (a) contracting with a utility for a fixed charge based upon a percentage of gross receipts derived from the service permitted by grant, right, privilege or franchise to such utility; (b) imposing an occupation tax or license fee for the privilege of engaging in any business, trade, occupation or profession, or rendering or furnishing any service, but the determination of any such license fee shall not be based upon any amount the licensee has received from the sale or transfer of personal or real property, or for the rendering or furnishing of a service, or on the income of the licensee; or (c) levying any occupation tax or license fee imposed by such city prior to the effective date of this act. No license fee described in subsection (b) of this section shall be imposed upon any utility contracting with and subject to a charge, described in subsection (a) of this section, by such city.

The defendants correctly assert that the ordinance is entitled to a presumption of validity and should not be stricken unless its infringement upon a statute is clear beyond substantial doubt. See City of Wichita v. Wallace, 246 Kan. 253, 257, 788 P.2d 270 (1990); see also Blevins v. Hiebert, 247 Kan. 1, 16, 795 P.2d 325 (1990) ("A city or county ordinance should be permitted to stand unless an actual conflict exists between the ordinance and a statute, or unless the legislature has clearly preempted the field so as to preclude local governmental action."); cf. Kan.Const. art. 12, § 5(d) ("Powers and authority granted cities pursuant to this section shall be liberally construed for the purpose of giving to cities the largest measure of self-government."); Claflin v. Walsh, 212 Kan. 1, 7, 509 P.2d 1130 (1973) ("Section 5(d) of Article 12 [of the Kansas Constitution] requires a liberal construction of the powers and authority granted cities for the purpose of giving to cities the largest measure of self-government. This provision simply means that the home rule power of cities is favored and should be upheld unless there is a sound reason to deny it.... Unless there is [an] actual conflict between a municipal ordinance and a statute, the city ordinance should be permitted to stand.").

The defendants also contend tax statutes must be construed strictly and their prohibitions restricted to the express, specific language of the statutes. This court has established the following principles in construing tax statutes: "Tax laws are statutory and do not exist apart from the statute. As such, they must be strictly construed." In re Order of Board of Tax Appeals, 236 Kan. 406, Syl. ¶ 5, 691 P.2d 394 (1984), overruled on other grounds In re Application of U.S.D. No. 437 for Tax Relief, 243 Kan. 555, 757 P.2d 314 (1988).

"Tax statutes will not be extended by implication beyond the clear import of language employed therein, and their operation will not be enlarged so as to include matters not specifically embraced. Where there is reasonable doubt as to the meaning of a taxing act, it will be construed most favorably to the taxpayer." Fleming Company v. McDonald, 212 Kan. 11, Syl. ¶ 1, 509 P.2d 1162 (1973); Equitable Life Assurance Society v. Hobbs, 154 Kan. 1, Syl. ¶ 1, 114 P.2d 871 (1941). Any reasonable doubt concerning the meaning of these tax statutes must be construed in favor of the taxpayer, not the municipality.

According to the defendants, because constitutional home rule expressly recognizes forms of exactions not expressly prohibited in the two tax statutes, the legislature did not intend to preempt this field for all forms of exactions. Specifically, the defendants argue that because the fuel flowage fee is a proprietary fee, it is outside the scope of K.S.A. 79-3424 and K.S.A. 12-194, which prohibit a locally levied tax or excise, not a locally levied proprietary fee. In essence, the defendants' argument is based upon the Latin maxim expressio unius est exclusio alterius—"the expression of one excludes the other." See Board of Johnson County Comm'rs v. Greenhaw, 241 Kan. 119, 129, 734 P.2d 1125 (1987).

The fact that the fuel flowage fee has been entitled a fee is not the decisive factor in ascertaining whether the fee violates either tax statute. We must determine what the legislature intended to prohibit. In order to do that, we must examine the nature and purpose of a fee and of a tax.

Other jurisdictions have addressed the distinctions between a tax and a fee. The United States Supreme Court has stated that "an 'enforced contribution to provide for the support of government,' [is] the standard definition of a tax. [Citation omitted.]" United States v. Mississippi Tax Comm'n, 421 U.S. 599, 606, 95 S.Ct. 1872, 1877, 44 L.Ed.2d 404 (1975). "A fee ... is incident to a voluntary act ... which, presumably, bestows a benefit on the applicant, not shared by other members of society." National Cable Television Assn. v. U.S., 415 U.S. 336, 340–41, 94 S.Ct. 1146, 1149, 39 L.Ed.2d 370 (1974). The District of Columbia Court of Appeals has noted: "A 'fee' is a payment for a special privilege or service rendered, and not a revenue measure. If the 'fee' unreasonably exceeds the value of the specific services for which it is charged it will be held invalid." National Cable Television Ass'n, Inc. v. F.C.C., 554 F.2d 1094, 1106 (D.C.Cir.1976). Massachusetts has declared:

> Fees imposed by a governmental entity tend to fall into one of two principal categories: user fees, based on the rights of the entity as proprietor of the instrumentalities used, [citation omitted], or regulatory fees (including licensing and inspection fees), founded on the police power to regulate particular businesses or activities. [Citations omitted.] Such fees share common traits that distinguish them from taxes: they are charged in exchange for a particular governmental service which benefits the party paying the fee in a manner "not shared by other members of society," [citation omitted]; they are paid by

> choice, in that the party paying the fee has the option of not utilizing the governmental service and thereby avoiding the charge, [citation omitted], and the charges are collected not to raise revenues but to compensate the governmental entity providing the services for its expenses.

Emerson College v. Boston, 391 Mass. 415, 424–25, 462 N.E.2d 1098 (1984).

In New York, "taxes are burdens of a pecuniary nature imposed generally upon individuals or property for defraying the cost of governmental functions, while, on the other hand, charges are sustainable as fees where they are imposed upon a person to defray or help defray the cost of particular services rendered for his account." Matter of Hanson v. Griffiths, 204 Misc. 736, 738, 124 N.Y.S.2d 473 (1953), aff'd, 283 App.Div. 662, 127 N.Y.S.2d 819 (1954). See Mtr. of Joslin v. Regan, 63 App.Div.2d 466, 470, 406 N.Y.S.2d 938 (1978) ("fees have been characterized as 'a visitation of the costs of special services upon the one who derives a benefit from them.'"), aff'd, 48 N.Y.2d 746, 422 N.Y.S.2d 662, 397 N.E.2d 1329 (1979).

Kentucky has determined: "'The distinction between a fee and a tax is one that is not always observed with nicety in judicial decisions, but any payment exacted by the state or its municipal subdivisions as a contribution toward the cost of maintaining governmental functions, where the special benefits derived from their performance is merged in the general benefit, is a tax.' On the other hand, a fee is generally regarded as a charge for some particular service." Dickson, Sheriff v. Jeff. Co. Bd. of Education, 311 Ky. 781, 786, 225 S.W.2d 672 (1949).

In South Dakota, "[t]he distinction between fees and taxes is that taxes are imposed for the purpose of general revenue while license or other fees are ordinarily imposed to cover the cost and expense of supervision or regulation. [Citation omitted.]" Valandra v. Viedt, 259 N.W.2d 510, 512 (S.D.1977).

Thus, a tax is a forced contribution to raise revenue for the maintenance of governmental services offered to the general public. In contrast, a fee is paid in exchange for a special service, benefit, or privilege not automatically conferred upon the general public. A fee is not a revenue measure, but a means of compensating the government for the cost of offering and regulating the special service, benefit, or privilege. Payment of a fee is voluntary—an individual can avoid the charge by choosing not to take advantage of the service, benefit, or privilege offered.

Executive Aircraft argues that the fuel flowage fee is a tax because the fuel flowage fee is not related to any special service being provided to the fuel transporters. Executive Aircraft suggests the fuel transporters may live too far away to benefit from using the Airport in any other capacity. Executive Aircraft also claims the purpose of the fuel flowage fee is to raise revenue to support the Airport, which would eliminate the need to raise the mill levy.

Counsel for the defendants admitted at oral argument in the trial court that the fuel flowage fee was a "revenue raising measure." Defense counsel argued:

> [I]f we look at [it] from the point of view of the subject which would be a fuel distributor coming in here, they don't have any right or privilege to conduct their business on the airport facility, and if they want to, of course, our concern is to the extent they can do that they're in competition with the—with our own revenue producing activities, so if you're gonna do that and be in competition then you should contribute, too, to the cost.... If we say that we can't require the—these fuel distributors to contribute and help make up for

> what we're losing in revenue on the other when we aren't the ones selling the fuel....
>
> [The fuel distributors are] having the privilege of coming on [the Airport's premises] and doing this business. Circumventing, not illegally, but doing so in a way that competes with other revenue sources of the airport. We have the right to protect that.

The trial court found that the operation of the Airport is a proprietary function. For support, the court cited 3 McQuillin, Municipal Corporations § 11.03.05 (3d ed. 1990), in which it is stated: "The operation of an airport by a municipality ... is generally held to be a proprietary rather than a governmental function." The defendants jointly operate the Airport.

Kansas law also supports the proposition that a municipality's operation of an airport is a proprietary function. In Wendler v. City of Great Bend, 181 Kan. 753, Syl. ¶ 5, 316 P.2d 265 (1957), in the context of governmental immunity from tort liability, this court held: "A municipal airport is essentially a part of a city's system of transportation facilities and as such assumes its proper place in the general field of transportation and commerce. The various commercial transactions by a municipality in the operation of an airport from which it seeks to derive revenue are only in part indicative of its commercial character, the full significance of its commercial nature being exemplified by the desired opportunities of a municipality for increased prosperity to be secured through air commerce. This classifies the airport with such public utilities as electric light, gas, water and transportation systems—universally classed as proprietary." See Hillhouse v. City of Kansas City, 221 Kan. 369, 373, 559 P.2d 1148 (1977) (airport as proprietary function mentioned in the context of discussing why foreign municipal corporations should be treated the same as foreign private corporations; jurisdiction question raised in tort liability suit); Parker v. City of Hutchinson, 196 Kan. 148, 150–51, 410 P.2d 347 (1966) (airport as proprietary function discussed in context of governmental immunity from tort liability).

In its journal entry on motion for judgment on the pleadings, after acknowledging that the operation of the Airport was a proprietary function, the trial court found that "imposition of the fuel flowage fee was the exercise of legislative power." The trial court noted: "In its governmental power, the City and County may command; in its private character, it sometimes must bargain and barter." In its memorandum decision on the defendants' motion for reconsideration, the trial court indicated imposition of the fee was a governmental or legislative activity because it was non-commercial in nature and because a private individual or company could not accomplish the same. For example, failure to pay the fee results in criminal sanctions—imprisonment not exceeding 30 days and/or a fine not exceeding $500. Additionally, by imposing the fuel flowage fee, the defendants unilaterally altered its lease agreement with Executive Aircraft and accomplished an "ex parte facto rent increase" without providing a comparable increase of service.

We have acknowledged the difficulty in classifying an activity as either governmental or proprietary.

> The cases attempting to resolve this problem are legion and are replete with conflicts and inconsistencies. Moreover, when an activity partakes of both governmental and proprietary characteristics, the problem of categorizing that activity becomes even more uncertain. The end result of such conflicts and uncertainties is that "shadowy distinctions between government functions and

> proprietary affairs ... have been used to decide cases, all without much rhyme or reason...." (Wendler v. City of Great Bend, 181 Kan. 753, 758, 316 P.2d 265.)

Brown v. Wichita State University, 217 Kan. 279, 305, 540 P.2d 66 (1975), aff'd in part, vacated in part, 219 Kan. 2, 547 P.2d 1015 (1976). See Krantz v. City of Hutchinson, et al., 165 Kan. 449, 455, 196 P.2d 227 (1948). Each case must be decided on its own facts. Carroll v. Kittle, 203 Kan. 841, 849, 457 P.2d 21 (1969).

Both parties cite a 1989 Attorney General Opinion to support their arguments. The Attorney General was asked if a flowage fee on the per gallon sale of motor fuels, which had been imposed by municipal airport authorities as part of the rent in a lease agreement, was a local excise tax in violation of the same statutes involved in the instant case. The Attorney General concluded that the flowage fee was part of the rent, "a charge for a service rendered," and not a tax. Att'y Gen. Op. No. 89-57, p. 4.

The defendants claim the Attorney General Opinion examines the relationship between proprietary fees and taxes. According to the defendants, the opinion supports their position for the following reasons: The Attorney General noted that an airport authority is authorized statutorily to enter into contracts that lease part or all of the airport for aviation purposes; that all types of public revenue are not taxes; and that if "a city is authorized to provide a service for compensation, the charge imposed is not a tax." Att'y Gen. Op. No. 89-57, p. 3. The Attorney General concluded "the airport authority is exacting the charge in its capacity as lessor rather than by virtue of its sovereignty" and "the fact that the rent is in part determined by the gross receipt of sales of gasoline does not render the rent charged a tax on the gasoline, or the selling of the same." Att'y Gen. Op. No. 89-57, pp. 3–4.

Executive Aircraft maintains the opinion is distinguishable factually. Most importantly, in the circumstances addressed in the opinion, the fee was part of the negotiated lease agreement between the airport authority and the lessee.

The defendants contend the fact that flowage fees were incorporated into the rental agreement is a distinction without a difference. According to the defendants, the fuel flowage fee in this case serves the same function as the negotiated charge in the lease agreement addressed in the Attorney General Opinion because in both instances those assessed the fees are on the premises for business purposes. In both circumstances, without the municipality providing and maintaining the premises, there would be no opportunity to take advantage of the business opportunities. The defendants argue that the mechanism by which the fee is exacted is not important: "A rental charge is simply another of the several types of exactions that cities have the authority and power to employ, being also separate and distinct from a 'tax.'"

The defendants' arguments are not persuasive. The factual differences are significant. The Attorney General Opinion recognized that the rental arrangements were an important factor by mentioning such when setting forth the issue: "Our question is whether the flowage fee on the sale of gasoline charged as part of the rent imposes an excise tax on the sale of gasoline in violation of K.S.A. 12-194 ... and K.S.A. 79-3424." Att'y Gen. Op. No. 89-57, p. 2.

We are cited many cases concerning airports charging fees that have been held both permissible and impermissible. Many are distinguishable because of statutory authority or statutory prohibition.

The distinction between a fee and a tax does not depend upon its label, but rather on the nature and function of the charge. Any applicable statutes must be considered in determining the validity of such a charge. The adoption of a charge for the privilege of non-aeronautical parties doing business at a publicly owned airport generally is governed by the same rules and regulations that apply to a private landowner. Thus, there must be some aspect of contract or consent; otherwise, the charge is a tax.

Here, there is a strong legislative intent to preempt local units of government from collecting revenue on the sale of motor vehicle fuel. Although a proprietor could enter into a lease to compute rent based on gallonage of fuel sold, the unilateral imposition of a fee based on gallonage transported onto the airport amounts to a tax and is thus prohibited by K.S.A. 79-3424. We are satisfied the infringement is clear beyond a substantial doubt, and the trial court was correct in so holding.

Having decided the "fuel flowage fee" is a tax prohibited by K.S.A. 79-3424, the remaining issues are moot.

Affirmed.

Notes

1. Although each of the foregoing cases involves jet fuel, aircraft and their operators also pay numerous other taxes (both state and federal). *See, e.g.*, Annotation, *Situs of Aircraft, Rolling Stock, and Vessels for Purposes of Property Taxation*, 3 A.L.R.4th 837 (1981 & 2004 Supp.); Pablo M.J. Mendes de Leon & Steven A. Mirmina, *Protecting the Environment by Use of Fiscal Measures: Legality and Propriety*, 62 J. Air L. & Com. 791 (1997); Troy A. Rolf, *Taxing the CEO's Jet: Federal Taxation of Corporate and Private Aircraft Ownership and Operations*, 66 J. Air L. & Com. 1605 (2001). *See also* Celestino Pena, *Latin American Aviation: Past, Present, Future*, 17 Air & Space Law 13 (Spring 2003) (claiming that Latin America is the most expensive aviation region in the world in terms of direct and indirect taxes).

2. As between Justice Brennan and Justice Blackmun, who do you think has the better argument in *Wardair*? What do you think of Judge Restani's reasoning in *CITGO*? What about Judge Farmer's conclusion in *American Airlines* and Justice Abbott's in *Executive Aircraft*? Given these decisions, is there a need for a single uniform national, or perhaps even international, aviation tax (or fee)? If so, how would it be calculated, collected, and distributed?

Problem 7

A state statute imposes an excise tax on aviation fuel at a rate of 6.9 cents per gallon. The same statute defines "aviation fuel" in a manner that includes kerosene. Must the tax be paid when kerosene is sold to non-aviation users? *See United Specialties of America v. Department of Revenue*, 786 So. 2d 1210 (Fla. Dist. Ct. App. 2001).

D. LIABILITY

ALASKAN OIL, INC. v. CENTRAL FLYING SERVICE, INC.

975 F.2d 553 (8th Cir. 1992)

ARNOLD, Chief Judge.

This case arises from the sale of a Beechcraft airplane owned by G.W. Davis Construction Company (Davis) to Alaskan Oil, Inc. Approximately one year after this sale,

Alaskan Oil sold the plane for salvage after finding that it had deteriorated so much as to be "economically unfeasible" to repair. On December 19, 1989, Alaskan Oil sued Davis and Central Flying Service, Inc., the company which acted as the selling agent, seeking to recover the losses it sustained as a result of the plane's failing to perform as expected. The jury returned a verdict for Central Flying and Davis on breach of warranty and fraud claims, but found for Alaskan Oil on its strict liability claim, awarding it $54,500.00. The District Court upheld these findings, and Central Flying Service now appeals. We affirm.

I.

In early 1987, Alaskan Oil hired Corporate Airways to help it find a used aircraft suitable for purchase. Corporate Airways' president, Dan Steinman, was assigned the task of finding this plane. Pursuant to his authority, Steinman entered into a contract for the purchase of a 1970 Beechcraft airplane which was owned by Davis. Central Flying Service, the company which had possession of the aircraft and to which Davis owed a substantial amount of money for repair work and storage, brokered the deal. The contract was completed on March 3, 1987.

In the year after the sale, Alaskan Oil experienced many problems with the plane. During this time, both engines were replaced, the fuel cell and de-icing boots were replaced, and large amounts of corrosion were discovered. In March of 1988, the plane was flown to Wichita, Kansas, for inspection. The inspection found that the plane was so corroded as to be "economically unfeasible" to repair. Alaskan Oil sold the aircraft for salvage and initiated this action against Davis and Central Flying Service.

At trial, both sides presented evidence relating to the condition of the aircraft before and after its sale. The jury found that Davis and Central Flying had not broken any warranties given to Alaskan Oil, nor committed any acts of fraud. The jury did find Davis and Central Flying liable to Alaskan Oil on a theory of strict liability and awarded it $54,500.00, apportioning 80 per cent of the liability to Central Flying.

On this appeal, Central Flying argues that a verdict for strict liability is improper when the only damages suffered were economic losses to the product sold. In addition, it argues that there was insufficient evidence to support the conclusion that the plane was in a defective condition and unreasonably dangerous when it was sold to Alaskan Oil. Finally, Central Flying argues that it was not a "supplier" as defined in §§4-86-102 and 16-116-102 of the Arkansas Code. Finding these arguments to be without merit, we affirm.

II.

The majority of courts in the United States hold that a strict liability action cannot be successful if the only damages that occur are to the product itself. See, e.g., East River Steamship Corp. v. Transamerica Delaval, Inc., 476 U.S. 858, 866–71, 90 L. Ed. 2d 865, 106 S. Ct. 2295 (1986). The appellants, relying upon this theory, argue that Alaskan Oil may not recover in strict liability because, as Alaskan Oil concedes, the only damages that occurred were to the plane itself. They further argue that Arkansas law supports this position. We disagree.

We believe Arkansas law has endorsed the minority view allowing recovery in instances where the only damages are to the product itself. In Blagg v. Fred Hunt Co., Inc., 272 Ark. 185, 189–190, 612 S.W.2d 321, 323–324 (1981), the Arkansas Supreme Court quoted extensively from the New Jersey Supreme Court's opinion in Santor v. A

& M Karagheusian, Inc., 44 N.J. 52, 207 A.2d 305 (1965), the case which is widely acknowledged as the "progenitor" of the minority view. East River Steamship Corp., 476 U.S. at 868–69. In a later opinion, the Arkansas Supreme Court acknowledged that the Blagg opinion indicated that Arkansas followed the minority view established in Santor. See Berkeley Pump Co. v. Reed-Joseph Land Co., 279 Ark. 384, 391, 653 S.W.2d 128, 131 (1983). Given these two pronouncements, we hold that Arkansas law permits recovery under strict liability even when the only damages sustained are to the defective product itself.

In order to recover strict liability damages, Alaskan Oil must show that the plane was unreasonably dangerous. The appellants argue that there was insufficient evidence to support the jury's conclusion that the plane was in a defective condition and unreasonably dangerous when purchased. In support of this claim, they point to the fact that, among other things, the plane never crashed and that no one was injured as a result of its use. There is evidence, however, which supports the jury's finding that the plane was in a defective condition and unreasonably dangerous. Both sides presented evidence on the plane's history of corrosion problems, with the jury finding Alaskan Oil's more persuasive. This is a decision that the jury was entitled to make, and we will not disturb it.

Finally, Central Flying argues that it cannot be held responsible under Arkansas's strict liability laws because it is not a "supplier" of the product as defined in the statute. Arkansas products liability law states that "a supplier of a product" is liable for damages if:

> (1) The supplier is engaged in the business of manufacturing, assembling, selling, leasing or otherwise distributing the product;
>
> (2) The product was supplied by him in a defective condition which rendered it unreasonably dangerous; and
>
> (3) The defective condition was a proximate cause of the harm to person or to property.

Ark. Code. Ann. § 4-86-102(a) (1987). A "supplier" is defined as:

> Any ... entity engaged in the business of selling a product, whether the sale is for resale, or for use or consumption. "Supplier" includes a retailer, wholesaler, or distributor and also includes a lessor or bailor engaged in the business of leasing or bailment of a product....

Ark. Code. Ann. § 16-116-102(3) (1987). Central Flying argues that it merely brokered the sale of this plane, which was owned by Davis, and that as such, it was not a supplier.

In ruling upon the appellants' motion for judgment notwithstanding the verdict, the District Court held that Central Flying was more than a mere agent in this transaction and that it could be found to be a supplier under the statute. We agree. The relationship between Davis and Central Flying was more than that of seller and agent. Indeed, Central Flying had a substantial interest in the sale of the plane because Davis had fallen substantially behind in its payments for maintenance and storage. The plane was sold for $65,000, of which Central received $53,000 to pay off the balance that Davis owed it. Central had an interest of its own. It acted not only for Davis, but also for its own account.

The judgment of the District Court is affirmed.

TURBINES, INC. v. DARDIS

1 S.W.3d 726 (Tex. Ct. App. 1999)

BOYD, Chief Justice.

After considering appellees' motion for rehearing, we withdraw our opinion of May 25, 1999, and substitute the following opinion.

In this appeal appellant, Turbines, Inc., presents five issues challenging a judgment against it for claims arising out of an airplane crash. In response to a jury verdict, the trial court awarded Van Dardis (Dardis), the pilot of the plane, and his wife Danna Renee Dardis, $435,455 in actual damages and $500,000 in exemplary damages for their claims of negligence, gross negligence, and strict products liability.

In its first two issues, Turbines questions the submission of jury questions on strict products liability and an instruction on res ipsa loquitur; in issues three and four, it challenges the sufficiency of the evidence of negligence and gross negligence; and in issue five, it assigns error to the admission of evidence that Turbines had temporarily surrendered its repair station certificate. For the reasons stated herein, we reverse the judgment of the trial court and render judgment that appellees take nothing.

The nature of Turbines' challenges require a rather detailed recitation of the evidence presented in the trial court. Turbines is in the business of performing maintenance and repair on turbine aircraft engines. They have a repair station certificate from the Federal Aviation Administration (FAA) to perform work on engines manufactured by Pratt & Whitney. The certificate excluded authority to perform certain procedures, such as overhauls. G & G AeroServ, Inc. performs mechanical work on aircraft engines and airframes.

Working together, Turbines and G & G developed a procedure for modifying a model of aircraft used for crop dusting, the Piper Brave, from its original piston engine to a turbine engine. The purpose of the modification was to provide the airplane with increased power and reliability. Although the Piper Brave airframe was only rated for 375 horsepower, the PT6 turbine engine could produce 550 horsepower. Part of the modification included instrument markings to indicate the maximum power setting for the engine so the pilot would not exceed the 375 horsepower limit. G & G obtained approval from the FAA in the form of a Supplemental Type Certificate (STC) to perform this modification commercially. Dardis was an aviation mechanic certified by the FAA and a co-owner of G & G. Dardis worked primarily on turbine engines and helped obtain the STC.

Glen Carlson, a resident of Montana, owned a Piper Brave and asked G & G to convert it to a turbine engine in accordance with the STC. The model of engine selected for the conversion was a Pratt & Whitney PT6A-6. Turbines assembled and tested a used PT6A-6 turbine engine in the summer of 1993 and subsequently shipped it to G & G. Dardis personally installed the new engine and tested it before flight. The aircraft was certified as airworthy by G & G on March 22, 1994.

The following day, Dardis departed from Lubbock International Airport to return the plane to Carlson. Shortly after takeoff, Dardis noticed sparks from the exhaust and an elevated engine temperature. He returned to the Lubbock airport to investigate the problems. When these conditions were reported to Turbines, Jim Mills, President of Turbines, asked Dardis to return half of the engine, the power section, for inspection. Turbines was unable to find any defects in the power section but replaced a bearing and returned the power section to G & G. After Dardis reinstalled the power section, he continued to express concern over an elevated engine temperature.

The Crash

On April 1, 1994, Dardis again attempted to return the modified plane to Carlson in Montana. After an uneventful flight from Lubbock, Dardis landed in Beloit, Kansas, to show the plane to agricultural pilots and potential customers. After showing the plane to these pilots, Dardis taxied onto the runway for departure.

According to Dardis, he performed a normal takeoff and the plane performed properly during takeoff. He climbed to about "a couple hundred feet" at the "best angle of climb," leveled out, then made a 180 degree right turn with a 30 to 45 degree bank angle. After he leveled the plane from making the turn, the airplane "just lost power." It immediately lost airspeed and the right wing stalled and dropped. Dardis attempted to apply full power but the engine did not respond and the plane continued to "fall." Dardis crashed through a hangar and came to rest on the building's concrete floor.

The eyewitness accounts presented by Turbines consisted of the testimony of three pilots who witnessed the takeoff and ensuing crash: Robert Kadel, an agricultural pilot with 8,000 hours of flight experience, 6,000 hours of which were in agricultural aircraft; Jim Rome, an agricultural pilot with 14,000 hours of flight experience; and Steve Thompson, an airline transport pilot and flight instructor with 10,000 hours of flight experience. Each testified that when Dardis departed from the Beloit airport, he only taxied about 1,000 feet down the 3,600 foot runway before turning around to depart to the south. Each testified Dardis's ground roll was very short and the airplane climbed at a very steep angle. They also testified that when Dardis made a 180 degree turn, it was a very sharp turn in which he banked the plane approximately 60 degrees. According to Rome, the bank angle further increased to almost 90 degrees, which would place the wings in an almost vertical position. Kadel explained that a high bank angle significantly increases the airspeed required to avoid a stall. Kadel and Rome testified that the airplane stalled and rolled or went into a spin and rapidly lost altitude until it crashed into the hangar. Thompson said the plane "fell" into the hangar. Each of the pilots testified that there was no change in the engine sound during the flight.

As is apparent from these differing accounts, Dardis's theory was that the crash was caused by a sudden engine failure, while Turbines took the position that Dardis did not maintain sufficient airspeed, caused the plane to stall at a low altitude, and was unable to recover control. The remaining evidence presented at trial consisted of expert testimony from post-accident investigations. We will examine the evidence of each party in turn.

Evidence on Engine Failure

In support of his theory of engine failure, Dardis presented expert testimony that the engine was not producing power at the time it struck the ground and that the cause of the engine failure was the failure of a bleed valve in the compressor section of the engine. The first expert called by Dardis was David Hall. Hall's expert testimony was that the engine was producing little or no power at the time it struck the ground. This opinion was based on examinations of the propeller and engine. Factors leading to this conclusion were that the propeller was bent off of the supporting shaft rather than being twisted off and that the exhaust case, which provides the structural connection between the front and rear of the engine, was "bent and kinked" but not severely twisted, as he would expect if the engine had been producing high power on impact. Hall declined to give an opinion on why the engine was not producing power at impact.

Dardis also presented the testimony of Don Hamill. Hamill was a former employee of Pratt & Whitney where his duties focused on investigation of external components of Pratt & Whitney engines. In his investigation, Hamill ruled out other systems, such as the fuel system, as the source of any failure. When he went to examine a component called the compressor bleed valve, he found that it was missing. Because he was not able to examine the valve and had ruled out malfunction in other systems, Hamill concluded that a failure in the bleed valve caused a loss of power and resulting crash.

Hamill supported his conclusion by explaining the operation and construction of the valve, together with the known history of the valve installed on this engine. The testimony of Hamill and others explained that turbine engines consist of two sections, a compressor section and a power section. The compressor section supplies compressed air to the power section where it is mixed with fuel and burned. At low engine speeds, the compressor supplies more air than is needed by the power section and the bleed valve allows the excess pressure to be vented. The valve remains open (venting pressure) until the engine reaches about 80 percent of its maximum power, at which point it begins to close. The valve is designed to close by the time the engine reaches full power.

The valve operates by using the pressure with the differential between two points acting on a rubber diaphragm. It was Hamill's opinion that a pinhole in the diaphragm would result in an increase in engine temperature. He further stated that the maintenance manual directed a mechanic to check the bleed valve when the engine experienced a high temperature. On cross-examination, Turbines showed that the temperatures experienced by Dardis were within normal limits and the manual did not require any action. Hamill continued to assert that a 200 degree increase in temperature should have caused Turbines to investigate the valve, even though that was not a diagnostic criteria in the engine manual. He also stated that a tear in the diaphragm would result in a loss of power of the type described by Dardis.

With regard to the particular bleed valve installed on this engine, Hamill used the serial number from the engine records to determine that the same valve was on the engine from at least 1968, and possibly as early as 1964, when the engine was built. The engine was used in an aviation mechanics school in France for several years, during which it was not used in an aircraft. It was used in one or more aircraft in the 1980s. In 1992, the engine was returned to Pratt & Whitney for inspection and repair after it was shut down in flight while being used on a King Air. After disassembly, but before inspection or repair, the engine was sold to Turbines, where it was reassembled and tested before being shipped to G & G. Hamill opined that the alternate periods of storage and use, together with age, embrittled the rubber diaphragm, making it susceptible to failure.

Through Hamill's testimony, Turbines introduced four engine service bulletins addressing the compressor bleed valve on the PT6A engine. They were bulletin numbers 1413, 1414, 1415, and 1417, issued in 1985. Each contained a number of sections, including the reason for the bulletin, a description, whether compliance was optional, recommended or required. Each also contained specific steps for complying with the bulletin. Bulletin 1413 was listed as optional, the other three were "recommended - desirable." Pratt & Whitney recommended performing the work "when disassembly of [the] engine is sufficient to afford access to the affected part." According to the engine records, none of these service bulletins had been implemented. Hamill did not give an opinion that the failure to implement these bulletins fell below the standard of care for an aviation mechanic.

In controversion of Dardis's engine failure theory, Turbines called Roy Haight, chief inspector for Turbines. Haight described the process Turbines uses when assembling an engine. He explained that although Turbines does not perform engine overhauls, it assembles engines using the overhaul manual because it imposes stricter criteria. With regard to the compressor bleed valve, Haight stated that the fact the valve had been on the engine since 1968 was not significant because the records showed it only had 900 hours of flight time which, he stated, was a very low number of hours. After Turbines assembles an engine, it performs several tests, one of which involves running the engine with several instruments attached. During this test, one end of a hose is attached to the outlet of the bleed valve and the other end is placed in a container of water. The operator watches the bubbles produced while increasing engine power to ensure that the valve closes at the proper rate. Haight stated that the bleed valve on the engine sold to G & G operated properly in the test.

Haight also sought to explain the effect of a failure of the bleed valve. He stated that because the valve did not begin to close until the engine reached 80 percent of its total power, even if the valve failed, the engine would produce approximately 400 horsepower. The valve was designed to fail in the open position so the engine would continue to operate even if it could not produce full power. His opinion was based on personal experience in testing engines where the bleed valve had failed.

Evidence on Pilot Error

In addition to the eyewitness testimony set out above, Turbines presented the testimony of Warren Wandel in support of its position that the crash was the result of pilot error. Wandel cited the Pilot's Operating Handbook for the modified Piper Brave to show that the stall speed in straight and level flight was 70 miles per hour. When given a set of hypothetical facts concerning the same aircraft flying at an airspeed of 70 to 80 miles per hour, as Dardis admitted in deposition testimony, then banking 30 to 45 degrees to turn, it was Wandel's opinion that the aircraft would experience a stall.

In an attempt to rebut this testimony, Dardis presented the testimony of Dennis Way, a pilot and flight instructor. Way also cited the Pilot's Operating Handbook to determine the stall speed in straight and level flight. However, because the aircraft was lightly loaded, he concluded that the stall speed was 63 miles per hour. Citing a chart in the handbook which does not appear in this record, Way testified that the stall speed would have increased to 77 miles per hour in a 45 degree bank and 90 miles per hour for a 60 degree bank. He suggested that Dardis's deposition testimony as to his speed was incorrect because had he been flying between 70 and 80 miles per hour, he would have stalled at the beginning of the turn rather than at the end, where the witnesses agreed the stall occurred.

Turbines identified Dardis's limited experience as a pilot as evidence supporting its theory of pilot error. The record showed that Dardis had a private pilot's license with 300 hours of flight time. As a point of reference, the regulations governing eligibility for pilots' licenses require a minimum of 40 hours of flight experience before being eligible to obtain a private pilot's license. The flight experience requirement for a commercial pilot's license in single or multi-engine airplanes is 250 hours. Gary Bradley stated he was against Dardis flying the plane back to the owner and that there were more experienced pilots available to return the plane. Turbines [also] presented evidence concerning medications Dardis was taking at the time of the crash.

* * *

Turbines' first point presents two distinct challenges—the first assigns error to jury question one asking whether the engine was defective when Turbines sold it to G & G.

The second point challenges the sufficiency of the evidence supporting the jury's finding that the engine was defective. In support of its first challenge, Turbines argues submission of the product defect question was error because 1) the evidence conclusively showed no defect existed, and 2) the trial court had already granted a directed verdict in favor of G & G on the same issue.

To determine whether there was some evidence of a product defect supporting Dardis's strict products liability claim, we must first review the factors which may render a product defective. Our supreme court has adopted the strict products liability standard set forth in section 402A of the Restatement (Second) of Torts. Uniroyal Goodrich Tire Co. v. Martinez, 977 S.W.2d 328 (1998); McKisson v. Sales Affiliates, Inc., 416 S.W.2d 787, 788–89 (1967). That section provides:

> (1) One who sells any product in a defective condition unreasonably dangerous to the user or consumer or to his property is subject to liability for physical harm thereby caused to the ultimate user or consumer, or to his property, if
>
> (a) the seller is engaged in the business of selling such a product, and
>
> (b) it is expected to and does reach the user or consumer without substantial change in the condition in which it is sold.
>
> (2) The rule stated in Subsection (1) applies although
>
> (a) the seller has exercised all possible care in the preparation and sale of his product, and
>
> (b) the user or consumer has not bought the product from or entered into any contractual relation with the seller.

Restatement (Second) of Torts, §402A (1965). A product may be unreasonably dangerous because of a defect in design, manufacturing, or marketing. Uniroyal, 977 S.W.2d at 335; Thiele v. Chick, 631 S.W.2d 526, 530 (Tex.App.—Houston [1st Dist.] 1982, writ ref'd n.r.e.).

The trial court's question did not limit the jury to finding a single type of defect. Consequently, Turbines challenges the evidence supporting each category of product defect. It argued that 1) it did not design or manufacture the engine or its components, 2) Dardis's own expert, Hamill, testified there was no design, manufacturing, or marketing defect in the compressor bleed valve, and 3) there was no other evidence of a defect.

Dardis argues that he was not required to establish what the defect was and that "evidence of a product's malfunction will sustain a jury finding." He cites General Motors Corp. v. Hopkins, 548 S.W.2d 344 (Tex. 1977) (overruled in part, Turner v. General Motors Corp., 584 S.W.2d 844, 847 (Tex. 1979)), as support. Dardis appears to characterize Hopkins as holding that the circumstantial evidence of a defect which arises from the malfunction can be any defect and does not have to be a defect in design, manufacture, or marketing. We find no support for that contention in Hopkins or elsewhere. In Hopkins, the plaintiff's entire case was tried on the theory of a design defect.

The portion of the opinion cited by Dardis was in the court's discussion of General Motors' claim of misuse. The relevant paragraph stated:

> There is a related question of the proof of the condition of a product as of the time when the product left the hands of the defendant supplier. If the plaintiff has no evidence of a specific defect in the design or manufacture of

> the product, he may offer evidence of its malfunction as circumstantial proof of the product's defect. See Williams v. Ford Motor Co., 411 S.W.2d 443 (Mo.App. 1966); Greco v. Bucciconi Engineering Co., 407 F.2d 87 (3rd Cir. 1969). The age and use of that product during the time intervening between the purchase and malfunction will tend to support or defeat the circumstantial weight of the malfunction as proof of the original defect.

This statement in Hopkins must be reconciled with cases such as Hernandez v. Nissan Motor Corp. U.S.A., 740 S.W.2d 894 (Tex.App.—El Paso 1987, writ denied), which held that "the mere fact that an accident occurred is not sufficient proof that the automobile was defective." Id. at 895. Similarly, in Carroll v. Ford Motor Co., 462 S.W.2d 57 (Tex.Civ.App.—Houston [14th Dist.] 1970, no writ), the court wrote, "strict liability eliminates both privity and negligence, but it does not prove the plaintiff's case. The plaintiff must prove that he has been injured or damaged by a defective product, and the mere possibility that this may have occurred is not enough." Id. at 61. See also Bass v. General Motors Corp, 447 S.W.2d 443 (Tex.Civ.App.—Fort Worth 1968, writ ref'd n.r.e.).

Unlike the undisputed fact in Hopkins that the vehicle air bag did not activate, whether the aircraft engine failed here was a heavily disputed issue at trial. The argument advanced by Dardis starts with the assumption that the engine failed. The only evidence of failure of the bleed valve is the inference made by Hamill that the bleed valve must have failed because he excluded the possibility of malfunction in the other engine systems. Dardis then uses this circumstantial evidence that the bleed valve failed to function properly as the circumstantial evidence that there was a defect of an unknown type. The same expert who opined that the valve failed stated that the failure was due to age and there was no defect in the design, manufacture, or marketing of the component.

In his motion for rehearing, Dardis contends that this analysis disapproves of circumstantial evidence to establish product defects. We disagree. Circumstantial evidence permits a factfinder to infer the fact to be proven by the circumstances shown by the proponent of the fact. Our rejection of the conclusion asserted by Dardis stems not from the circumstantial nature of the evidence, but the fact that in his argument, the conclusion of one inference was itself used as circumstantial evidence, requiring another inference to establish the ultimate fact. It is well established that facts may not be found based on chains of inferences. See Hunsucker v. Omega Industries, 659 S.W.2d 692, 697 (Tex.App.—Dallas 1983, no writ).

The only theory under which we could find that the age of the valve could be a manufacturing defect is if Turbines were treated as the manufacturer of the engine. Dardis does not cite, and we have not found, any controlling authority holding that one who reassembles an engine may be treated as a manufacturer. On rehearing he cites three cases which, he contends, support the imposition of strict liability in this circumstance. Two of the three additional cases cited by Dardis concerned the liability of defendants who modified a product rather than simply performing mechanical work on it. Green v. Los Angeles, 40 Cal. App. 3d 819, 115 Cal. Rptr. 685 (1974) (crane); Court v. Grzelinski, 72 Ill. 2d 141, 379 N.E.2d 281, 19 Ill. Dec. 617 (Ill. 1978) (automobile gas tank). Because Turbines did not modify the engine, those cases are inapplicable. The third case, Crandell v. Larkin & Jones Appliance Co., 334 N.W.2d 31 (S.D. 1983), appears to offer some support for Dardis's position. In Crandell, suit was filed against the appliance company that refurbished and sold a used clothes dryer. Due to the malfunction of its thermostats, which were pitted and worn, the dryer caused a fire. The court found the seller liable, noting "the application of strict liability to sellers of used products, who rebuild or recondition those products, helps to protect the reasonable expectations of consumers." Id. at 34. See also Markle v. Mulholland, 265 Ore. 259, 509 P.2d 529 (Or. 1973) (retreaded tire).

However, the most nearly analogous cases we have found, also from other jurisdictions, support a contrary conclusion. In Winans v. Rockwell International, 705 F.2d 1449 (5th Cir. 1983), applying Louisiana law, the court held that strict liability would not apply to an engine manufacturer for defects resulting from its rebuilding of an engine it originally manufactured, but would only apply for defects in the original manufacture. 705 F.2d at 1452. On rehearing, Dardis seeks to distinguish Winans by noting that under [the] Louisiana law of products liability, liability was limited to manufacturers and had not been applied to sellers of new or used products. However, Winans is representative of a series of cases declining to apply strict products liability to those whose relationship to a product is primarily performing service on, rather than creating, the product. Our review of these cases, and the additional cases cited by Dardis, convinces us that our disposition of this issue is correct.

Dardis concedes that Turbines' conduct in assembling the engine "does not precisely fit a category of 'manufacturing' defect" because it did not manufacture the bleed valve. He argues, however, that when Turbines "rebuilt the engine, [it] failed to follow the manufacturer's recommendation as to replacement of an old valve with a new or fresh valve." While this argument might be relevant to a negligence claim, it is not relevant to Turbines' liability in a strict products liability cause of action. See Winans, supra. Moreover, the argument is not supported by the evidence.

Each of the service bulletins relied on by Dardis appears in the record. As we noted in the factual statement, each sets out the specific steps required to implement the bulletin. An examination of the steps required to implement each bulletin reveals that none of them required replacement of the valve or the rubber diaphragm. In each case, the instructions required the valve assembly to be modified rather than replaced with a new part. This is made clear from the step in each set of instructions directing the mechanic to, for example, "reidentify by striking out old compressor bleed valve assembly part number and marking new P/N 3010143 in an adjacent position." Therefore, even if each service bulletin had been followed exactly, the compressor bleed valve would have a new part number, but not a new rubber diaphragm.

On this record, we are convinced that the evidence of a defect in the design, manufacture, or marketing of the engine was no more than a surmise or suspicion of a fact and amounted to no evidence, and that, as a matter of law, Turbines could not be liable for a manufacturing defect resulting from its performance of mechanical work on the engine. Therefore, we hold that submission of question one was error and sustain Turbines' first issue.

We reject [however] Turbines' argument that the trial court erred in submitting question one because it had directed a verdict in favor of G & G on all claims, including one for strict products liability. Turbines has presented no authority in support of its argument that dismissal of a strict products liability claim against one defendant requires dismissal of that cause of action against another defendant, or estops the plaintiff asserting those claims.

We next address Turbines' third issue which assigns error to the submission of jury question two on negligence. The elements of a negligence cause of action are 1) a legal duty, 2) breach of that duty, and 3) damages proximately caused by that breach. Greater Houston Transp. Co. v. Phillips, 801 S.W.2d 523, 525 (Tex. 1990). Turbines does not challenge the existence of a duty. Its challenges are to the legal sufficiency of the evidence on breach and proximate cause.

Expert testimony is necessary when the alleged negligence is of such a nature as not to be within the experience of the layman. Roark v. Allen, 633 S.W.2d 804, 809 (Tex. 1982) (diagnosing a skull fracture); Hager v. Romines, 913 S.W.2d 733, 734–35 (Tex.App.—Fort Worth 1995, no writ) (flying an airplane and aerially applying herbicide). The expert testimony must establish both the standard of care and the violation of that standard. 913 S.W.2d at 734–35. The performance of mechanical work on turbine aircraft engines is not within the experience of a layman. Therefore, Dardis was obligated to present expert testimony on the standard of care and that Turbines' conduct did not meet that standard.

In a reply brief, Dardis argues that Turbines' failure to object to the definition of ordinary care as "that degree of care that would be used by a person of ordinary prudence under the same or similar circumstances" waives any complaint as to the standard of care. He does not cite any authority for that proposition. We disagree. The circumstances at issue were those of an aircraft turbine engine mechanic. Because a lay jury could not know the degree of care of an ordinary person in those circumstances without expert testimony, Dardis was obligated to present evidence on that issue.

Dardis lists seven acts of alleged negligence with references to the record in support of the submission of question two. In our review of Turbines' third issue, we must examine the evidence of each alleged act to determine if it provides legally sufficient evidence for a jury to find Turbines breached its duty. We address each alleged act in turn.

A. Turbines performed work for which they were not qualified to perform according to the manufacturer's recommendations.

It is not clear from the use of the word "qualified" whether Dardis contends that Turbines did not possess the necessary skills to perform the work or they were not authorized to perform the work. The testimony cited in support of this contention is that of Don Hamill, who opined that Turbines' repair station certificate prohibited it from performing work from the overhaul manual. He did not testify that Turbines lacked the skill to perform the work.

Hamill, who was not a licensed mechanic and had no training in the Federal Aviation Regulations, offered no reference to any regulation in support of his testimony that Turbines was not permitted to work from the overhaul manual. Even if his statement concerning use of the overhaul manual was accepted as true by the jury, he did not testify that a reasonably prudent mechanic working under that repair station certificate would not have done the work Turbines did. The only other theory on which Hamill's testimony could support a finding of breach is that by violating this unidentified regulation, Turbines' conduct was negligence per se. However, Dardis did not plead negligence per se or submit or obtain a jury issue on that question. There is no evidence that Turbines breached its duty by undertaking to perform the work it did on the engine.

B. Failing to obtain and review the engine history file before Turbines "rebuilt" the engine to determine the cause of the previous engine failures.

The evidence cited in support of this allegation shows that Turbines did not determine the cause of the "loud noise" leading to the in-flight shutdown of the engine before it was sent to Pratt & Whitney. There was no evidence of the standard of care for an aviation mechanic or that the failure to make this determination fell below that standard of care. The closest evidence Dardis presented was his cross-examination of

Haight, when he asked if it would be "a prudent thing" to get the full history of an engine that had suffered damage. Haight's response that "it's always beneficial" cannot be taken as evidence of either the standard of care or that the failure to obtain that information was a breach of that standard.

C. Failing to replace the compressor bleed valve when rebuilding the engine as recommended by the manufacturer's service bulletin.

The evidence in support of this contention fails in two independent respects. First, as discussed above, although they contained the word "replace," none of the manufacturer's service bulletins required replacement of the compressor bleed valve. As discussed above, each provided specific directions for modifying some portion of the valve and altering the part number to reflect the modified status of the valve. They did not direct replacement of the valve with a new part, although that was a permissible method to implement the service bulletins. Second, and most importantly, there was no evidence of the standard of care of an aircraft powerplant mechanic with regard to service bulletins or that the failure to implement bulletins was below that standard of care. Hamill explained the purpose and function of service bulletins and quoted from the bulletin that it was "recommended - desirable." He did not state that a reasonable and prudent aviation mechanic would have implemented the bulletin or that the failure to do so fell below the standard of care of such a mechanic. Consequently, there is no evidence to support a finding that the failure to implement the service bulletins was a breach of Turbines' duty.

D. Failing to fully inspect or test the compressor bleed valve.

The record is directly contrary to this contention. Haight testified on direct that the bleed valve was inspected as part of the hot section inspection and tested. He also described the specific steps performed in a functional test of the valve. Dardis appears to argue that the valve was not tested because the engine records do not contain a specific entry for that component. Haight explained that the engine build records certify performance of the steps in the engine manual and that the records do not list each component individually. The evidence shows that the valve was inspected and tested.

E. Failing to adequately inspect and repair the power section of the engine following Dardis's first flight.

The only evidence cited in support of this contention is the testimony of Jim Mills of Turbines and the warranty repair invoice from Turbines. Mills testified that Dardis complained of sparks and elevated temperature in the engine. Turbines inspected the engine and found no problems, but replaced a bearing. Mills explained to Dardis that the -6 engine model operated approximately 100 degrees hotter than the -20 engine model. There was no evidence of Turbines' standard of care with regard to inspection and repair after such a complaint or that its conduct fell below that standard of care.

F. Failing to investigate the elevated engine temperature reported by Dardis.

As evidence of Turbines' negligence, Dardis cites the testimony of Hamill that "if you get a shift of two hundred degrees, it's telling you something," and "the increase in temperature seen by Mr. Van Dardis prior to his crash is indicative, in my opinion, that the bleed valve was saying I have got a little hole in it. The trouble shooting in the manual tells you to check the bleed valve. That was not done." However, Hamill admitted on cross-examination that the engine manual did not require any action if the temperature was below 995 degrees. The temperature reported by Dardis was 810 degrees. He also agreed that none of the engine manuals or service bulletins directed a mechanic to determine the cause of a temperature increase that was below 995 degrees. Hamill did not testify that an ordinary and prudent aviation mechanic would have disregarded the service manual and attempted to determine the cause of a temperature increase or that the failure to do so fell below the standard of care for an aviation mechanic.

G. Certified that the engine and power section were inspected, repaired and airworthy when they were not.

The only evidence cited in support of this argument is an invoice containing a certification of inspection and airworthiness. The term airworthy is defined in section 603(c) of the Federal Aviation Act (49 U.S.C.App. § 1423), and with regard to aircraft has been held to mean that the aircraft is 1) in conformity with the aircraft type certificate, and 2) in a condition for safe flight. We have found no authority that a different standard would apply to the airworthiness of aircraft components. Whether the engine was airworthy is a matter which required expert testimony. Dardis failed to provide expert testimony that the engine was not airworthy. Without such testimony, we may not simply infer lack of airworthiness from evidence of a failure. Moreover, there is no evidence of the standard of care for performing such an inspection or that Turbines' inspection or certification were below that standard of care.

* * *

Because the conduct of Turbines was such that expert testimony was necessary to establish the standard of care and breach of that standard, after our examination of each of the acts alleged to have been a breach of its duty and the supporting evidence, we find that there was no legal evidence of breach. On rehearing, Dardis does not challenge our holding that there was failure of proof on the standard of care or breach, but rather, that those elements could be inferred under the doctrine of res ipsa loquitur based on the jury's general knowledge. Although not cited by Dardis, a similar argument was accepted by our supreme court in Harmon v. Sohio Pipeline Co., 623 S.W.2d 314, 315 (Tex. 1981). This holding makes our disposition of Turbines' second issue challenging the submission of an instruction on res ipsa loquitur particularly significant, and ultimately dispositive of Dardis's final argument on the third issue.

The instruction challenged by Turbines stating the doctrine of res ipsa loquitur provided:

> In answering this question [on negligence] you may infer negligence by a person but are not compelled to do so, if you find that (1) the character of the occurrence is such that it would ordinarily not happen in the absence of negligence and (2) the instrumentality causing the occurrence was under the [sole] (sic) management and control of such person at the time that the negligence, if any, probably happened.

Turbines argues that the instruction was improper because "Dardis did not negate the possibility of pilot error as a cause of the accident" and that he did not establish that the instrumentality causing the accident was in Turbines' control.

When applicable, the doctrine of res ipsa loquitur creates a permissible inference of negligence on the part of the defendant. The purpose of res ipsa loquitur is to relieve the plaintiff of the burden of proving a specific act of negligence by the defendant when it is impossible for the plaintiff to determine the sequence of events, or when the defendant has superior knowledge or means of information to determine the cause of the accident. Jones v. Tarrant Utility Co., 638 S.W.2d 862, 865 (Tex. 1982). As correctly stated in the trial court's instruction, this doctrine is applicable only when the following two factors are present: (1) the character of the injury is such that it would not have occurred in the absence of negligence; and (2) the instrumentality which caused the injury is shown to have been under the sole management and control of the defendant. Gaulding v. Celotex Corp., 772 S.W.2d 66, 68 (Tex. 1989). The first factor is necessary to support the inference of negligence and the second to support the inference that the defendant was the negligent party. Mobil Chemical Co. v. Bell, 517 S.W.2d 245, 251 (Tex. 1974). Many jurisdictions recognize a requirement that the plaintiff establish the accident was not the result of any voluntary action or contribution by the plaintiff. See, e.g., Newing v. Cheatham, 15 Cal. 3d 351, 540 P.2d 33, 124 Cal. Rptr. 193 (Cal. 1975). Although this requirement, derived from § 328D(1)(b) of the Restatement (Second) of Torts (1965), is not stated as an element by Texas courts, they do require that the plaintiff "so reduce" the likelihood of other causes that the jury can reasonably find by a preponderance of the evidence that the negligence, if any, lies at the defendant's door. Mobil, 517 S.W.2d at 251.

Turbines challenges both factors of the doctrine. It initially argues that the first factor was not met because "expert testimony is required unless the alleged negligent act is plainly within the common knowledge of laypersons" and cites the medical malpractice case of Haddock v. Arnspiger, 793 S.W.2d 948, 951 (Tex. 1990) as support. It then cites McKinney v. Air Venture Corp., 578 S.W.2d 849, 851 (Tex.Civ.App.—Fort Worth 1979, writ ref'd n.r.e.), for the proposition that flying an aircraft is not within the knowledge of the average person. These arguments fail to address the first element of res ipsa loquitur.

We initially note the doctrine of res ipsa loquitur was not involved in McKinney. Next, the application of the doctrine to medical malpractice cases is subject to different standards than other types of negligence cases. Haddock, 793 S.W.2d at 951. Finally, because application of the doctrine does not require evidence of a specific act of negligence, the focus is not on "the alleged negligent act" but on the nature of the accident or injury. General knowledge of aviation has progressed sufficiently that the average person can form an opinion as to whether it is unlikely that aircraft would crash in the absence of negligence. Prosser and Keeton on Torts, 5th ed. § 39 (West 1984).

In challenge of the second factor of res ipsa loquitur, Turbines argues that it did not have the requisite control over the engine and that Dardis failed to negate his own negligence as a cause of the accident. In support of its argument that it did not have sufficient control to justify an inference of negligence on its part, Turbines points to evidence that it did not exercise any control over the compressor section of the engine, which included the bleed valve, since June 1993, almost a year before the accident. Dardis responds by citing a passage in Mobil that it "is sufficient if the defendant was in control at the time that the negligence inferable from the first factor probably occurred, so reasonable probabilities point to the defendant and support a reasonable inference that he was the negligent party." 517 S.W.2d at 251. The difficulty in applying this holding to the facts of this case is that the negligence inferable from the first factor could be either negligence in assembling the engine or negligent operation of the aircraft by Dardis. This uncertainty weighs against application of the doctrine on these facts.

Although there are no Texas cases addressing the control factor of res ipsa loquitur in similar situations, the available authority suggests that the second element was not satisfied. In Marathon Oil Co. v. Sterner, 632 S.W.2d 571 (Tex. 1982), the plaintiff was the employee of a contractor hired to perform work on a tank at a plant owned and operated by Marathon. He asserted the applicability of res ipsa loquitur when he was injured by exposure to gas in the tank. The court found the doctrine inapplicable on the issue of control because the contractor had been performing work on the tank for a week before the injury and it was "equally probable" that the negligence was attributable to the contractor. Id. at 574.

Opinions from other states support the view that, when res ipsa loquitur is applied to aircraft collision cases, it is the pilot who is in exclusive control. Tompkins v. Northwestern Union Trust Co., 198 Mont. 170, 645 P.2d 402 (Montana 1982), is factually similar in that, as here, the parties presented two equally plausible theories of the crash, mechanical failure and pilot error. The court held that it was the pilot who was in control of the instrumentality even though another party was responsible for maintenance of the aircraft. 645 P.2d at 406. The fact that the pilot in Tompkins died and the only testimony on the crash was by conflicting expert opinions does not alter the analysis because here, Dardis's testimony of mechanical failure was controverted by three pilot-witnesses, leaving two equally plausible theories. See also Winans, 705 F.2d at 1455; Webb v. Zurich Ins. Co., 194 So. 2d 436 (La. App. 1966) (res ipsa could not be applied to manufacturer after delivery because of lack of control); Shemwell v. Ailshire, 384 S.W.2d 104 (Mo.App. 1964) (owner who rented aircraft not liable under res ipsa when engine failed on landing because pilot had control); LeJeune v. Collard, 44 So. 2d 504, 506 (La.App. 1950) (where there was evidence of either mechanical failure or negligence by student pilot, for res ipsa purposes, pilot was in control of plane, not flight school owner).

Turbines also argues that Dardis failed to show the applicability of res ipsa loquitur because he "failed to show that pilot error did not contribute to the accident." It cites Winans, supra, and Curry v. Chevron, USA, 779 F.2d 272 (5th Cir. 1985), for the proposition that in aviation cases, the plaintiff must establish that pilot error did not contribute to the accident. Dardis seeks to distinguish those cases on the basis that each involved a challenge to the denial of a res ipsa loquitur instruction rather than a challenge to the granting of an instruction, and that they were based on Louisiana law which, unlike Texas law, requires a plaintiff asserting res ipsa loquitur to totally negate other potential causes.

Although we agree with Dardis that the nature of the challenge to the trial court's action is relevant, we do not agree with his characterization of Louisiana law. The Fifth Circuit did not require the plaintiffs to totally negate other potential causes, only to establish that the defendant's negligence was the "most plausible" explanation for the accident. Winans, 705 F.2d at 1454. We do not agree that this standard differs in any meaningful way from the application of res ipsa loquitur in Texas law. The portion of Mobil relied on by Turbines provides: "The possibility of other causes does not have to be completely eliminated, but their likelihood must be so reduced that the jury can reasonably find by a preponderance of the evidence that the negligence, if any, lies at the defendant's door." 517 S.W.2d at 251. This statement provides limited guidance for determining when the likelihood of other causes has been sufficiently reduced. However, our supreme court explicated this statement in Marathon Oil Co. v. Sterner, 632 S.W.2d 571 (Tex. 1982). There the court wrote: "When the plaintiff's evidence only shows it is equally probable that the negligence was that of another, the court must direct the jury that [the] plaintiff has not proven his case." Id. at 574. See also Le Blanc, Inc. v. Gulf Bitulithic Co., 412 S.W.2d 86, 96 (Tex.Civ.App.—Tyler 1967, writ ref'd n.r.e.); City of Houston v. Church, 554 S.W.2d 242, 243–44 (Tex.Civ.App.—Houston [1st Dist.] 1977, writ ref'd n.r.e.). This formulation appears in the opinions of other jurisdictions to consider the issue. See e.g., Knowlton v. Sandaker, 150 Mont. 438, 436 P.2d 98 (Mont. 1968) (res ipsa submission improper when evidence showed two equally plausible explanations).

Here, there was facially credible evidence supporting both Turbines' theory of pilot error and Dardis's theory of engine failure. Viewing the evidence as a whole, the theories are equally probable and we cannot say that Dardis established that the negligence of Turbines was the most probable cause of the crash.

In summary of Turbines' second issue, our review of the factors relevant to the doctrine of res ipsa loquitur, we find the trial court erred in submitting an instruction on that doctrine. First, there was no evidence that application of the doctrine was necessary to fulfill its purpose of relieving the burden on the plaintiff when he cannot determine the sequence of events, or when the defendant has superior knowledge or means of information to determine the cause of the accident. Second, Dardis did not establish Turbines' exclusive control over the instrumentality causing the injury, and third, Dardis failed to show that negligence by Turbines, as opposed to his own negligence, was the most probable explanation of the crash. We therefore sustain Turbines' second issue.

Our sustention of Turbines' second issue also provides the resolution of its third issue on negligence. Because we hold that Dardis failed, as a matter of law, to establish the applicability of res ipsa loquitur, and presented no evidence that Turbines breached its duty to him, we sustain Turbines' second and third issues and reverse the judgment in favor of Dardis on his negligence claim.

Turbines' fourth issue challenges the sufficiency of the evidence supporting the jury's finding of gross negligence. We need not address this issue because such issues are necessarily conditioned on a proper finding of negligence. Ballesteros v. Jones, 985 S.W.2d 485, 500 (Tex.App.—San Antonio 1998, no pet. h.).

Because of our disposition of Turbines' first three issues, we need not address its fifth issue challenging the admission of certain evidence. For the reasons we have expressed, we overrule the motion for rehearing and continue our rendition of judgment that appellees take nothing against Turbines.

PROMPT AIR, INC. v. FIREWALL FORWARD, INC.

707 N.E.2d 235 (Ill. App. Ct. 1999)

HOFFMAN, Justice.

The plaintiff, Prompt Air, Inc., appeals from an order of the circuit court dismissing its strict product liability claim against the defendant, Firewall Forward, Inc. In determining the propriety of the circuit court's dismissal order, we are required to address the circumstances under which the installer of defective component parts can be held strictly liable in tort for resulting damages.

The plaintiff filed the instant action against the defendant and Kelpak Industries, Inc. (Kelpak), seeking recovery for damages sustained when an airplane the plaintiff owned was required to make a forced landing due to engine failure. The complaint, pled in three counts, sought recovery against the defendant on a strict liability theory and against Kelpak for both strict liability and fraud. In its complaint, the plaintiff alleged that, in November 1988, Porsche-Galesburg Aircraft Sales (Porsche) contracted with the defendant for the overhaul of the subject airplane's engine. In that same month, the defendant delivered the engine's turbocharger to Kelpak to be overhauled and repaired. After Kelpak completed its work, it delivered the turbocharger back to the defendant. Thereafter, the defendant completed its overhaul of the engine, reassembled it, and returned the aircraft to Porsche. The plaintiff purchased the airplane in August

1995. On December 20, 1995, while one of the plaintiff's employees was operating the aircraft, the engine lost all power, necessitating a forced landing. According to the plaintiff, the engine failed because the turbocharger was defective. Specifically, the plaintiff alleged that "the turbocharger was defective, unsafe, and not reasonably safe for its intended use in that it contained automotive parts rather than airplane parts."

Kelpak filed a special appearance and was dismissed from this action in response to its motion contesting the court's power to exercise in personam jurisdiction over it. The plaintiff has not contested Kelpak's dismissal, and Kelpak is not a party to this appeal.

The defendant moved for involuntary dismissal of the plaintiff's claim against it, contending that, as a mere installer of the turbocharger, it is not subject to strict tort liability for the plaintiff's damages. The circuit court, relying on the holding in Hinojasa v. Automatic Elevator Co., 92 Ill.App.3d 351, 48 Ill.Dec. 150, 416 N.E.2d 45 (1980), found that the plaintiff had no "cognizable cause of action as pleaded" and granted the defendant's motion. For the reasons which follow, we reverse the order dismissing its strict tort liability claim against the defendant, and remand the cause to the circuit court for further proceedings.

Based upon the well-pled allegations in the plaintiff's complaint and reasonable inferences drawn therefrom, we assume for the purposes of our review that the defendant overhauled the plane's engine and reassembled it using a defective turbocharger. From the uncontradicted affidavit submitted in support of the defendant's motion, we will also assume that the defendant did not overhaul the turbocharger and did not incorporate automotive parts therein. However, the affidavit of the defendant's president admits both that the turbocharger is a component part of the engine and that it was the defendant who sent the turbocharger to Kelpak to be overhauled. That affidavit goes on to state: "Firewall bills its customers a flat rate, with some cost contingencies, for overhauling an engine. In the instant matter, as is company practice, the bill for services contained no specific cost or profit for Kelpak's overhaul of the turbocharger."

The defendant argues that, as an installer of a component part supplied by Kelpak, it was not involved in the sale of a product, received no profit from placing the defective turbocharger in the stream of commerce, and is, therefore, not subject to liability under the doctrine of strict tort liability. See Hinojasa, 92 Ill. App. 3d at 354. We believe that this argument, although viscerally appealing, fails to survive close scrutiny.

In Suvada v. White Motor Co., 32 Ill. 2d 612, 210 N.E.2d 182 (1965), our supreme court adopted the concept of strict tort liability as expressed in section 402A of the Restatement (Second) of Torts. Under this section, strict liability is imposed upon "one who sells any product in a defective condition unreasonably dangerous to the user or consumer." Restatement (Second) of Torts § 402A (1965). Read literally, section 402A refers only to the strict liability of one who "sells" a product. However, since the adoption of strict liability in Suvada, the courts of this state have refused to be confined to a narrow definition of the term "seller" in determining those who are subject to strict tort liability. See Bainter v. Lamoine LP Gas Co., 24 Ill. App. 3d 913, 915–16, 321 N.E.2d 744 (1974). The doctrine has been expanded to include "all persons in the distributive chain" of a defective product. Hammond v. North American Asbestos Corp., 97 Ill. 2d 195, 206, 454 N.E.2d 210, 73 Ill. Dec. 350 (1983). This expansive application is grounded in the very public policy reasons underlying the adoption of strict tort liability, and the determination of whether a particular transaction falls within its ambit can be made only by reference to those same policy justifications. Lowrie v. City of Evanston, 50 Ill. App. 3d 376, 381–83, 365 N.E.2d 923, 8 Ill. Dec. 537 (1977).

When an entity is within the original chain of distribution and reaps a profit by placing a product in the stream of commerce, imposition of strict tort liability is justified as a means of shifting the burden of loss from the injured user for two primary reasons. First, at the point in time when the product passes through its hands, such an entity is capable of preventing the product from proceeding through the stream of commerce. Crowe v. Public Building Comm'n, 74 Ill. 2d 10, 15, 383 N.E.2d 951, 23 Ill. Dec. 80 (1978). Second, its position in the marketing process enables it to exert pressure on the manufacturer to enhance the product's safety. Hammond, 97 Ill. 2d at 206.

The defendant bases its argument for affirmance on the holding in Hinojasa which stands for the proposition that the installer of a defective product who neither supplies the product nor creates the defect by improper installation is not subject to strict tort liability. The Hinojasa court rested its decision on an analysis of the policy justifications underlying strict tort liability, and its conclusion that a mere installer reaps no profit from placing the product in the stream of commerce and lacks the ability to exert pressure upon the product's manufacturer to enhance safety. Hinojasa, 92 Ill. App. 3d at 354. We have no quarrel with the general proposition of law articulated in Hinojasa or the court's supporting reasoning. However, we take issue with the defendant's contention that Hinojasa "is factually on 'all fours' with the instant matter."

In Hinojasa the manufacturer of the defective product engaged the defendant to install it, and the defendant was required to follow the manufacturer's plans and specifications. See Hinojasa, 92 Ill. App. 3d at 352–53. Had Porsche or some agent of Porsche engaged Kelpak to overhaul the turbocharger and independently hired the defendant to install it, we would have no difficulty in applying Hinojasa and finding that, as a mere installer, the defendant is not subject to strict tort liability. In this case, however, it was the defendant who engaged the services of Kelpak. Further, from the affidavit of the defendant's own president, it can be reasonably inferred that the defendant paid Kelpak for overhauling the turbocharger and passed along the cost of that service as part of the "flat rate" it charged Porsche for overhauling the plane's engine.

One who sells, supplies, or distributes a defective product in the regular course of business incident to the rendition of a service may be held strictly liable in tort. Cunningham v. MacNeal Memorial Hospital, 47 Ill. 2d 443, 450–52, 266 N.E.2d 897 (1970); Niffenegger v. Lakeland Construction Co., 95 Ill. App. 3d 420, 422–24, 420 N.E.2d 262, 50 Ill. Dec. 945 (1981). The critical question is not whether the defendant's principal function was to render a service. Rather, the question is whether the defendant played an integral role in the distribution of a defective product. The defendant's characterization of itself as a mere installer of the defective turbocharger is belied by the allegations contained in the plaintiff's complaint and the admissions contained in the affidavit filed by the defendant's president. The record in this case supports the inference that the defendant procured and paid for the reconditioning of the turbocharger by Kelpak and, thereafter, installed the defective turbocharger when it reassembled the plane's engine. Unlike the installer in Hinojasa, this defendant participated in placing a defective product in the stream of commerce, derived an economic benefit therefrom, and was in a position to exert pressure to ensure the product's safety.

In view of the foregoing, we are of a belief that the policy considerations underlying the doctrine of strict tort liability justify its application to one who, in the course of rendering a service, procures and installs a defective component part. Consequently, we find that the trial court erred in dismissing the plaintiff's strict liability claim against the defendant.

Reversed and remanded.

Notes

1. In addition to the very detailed web sites of such groups as the American Institute of Aeronautics and Astronautics (www.aiaa.org) and the General Aviation Manufacturers Association (www.gama.aero), as well as such companies as Airbus (www.airbus.com), Boeing (www.boeing.com), Bombardier (www.bombardier.com), and Cessna (www.cessna.com), a vast literature exists on the design, manufacture, and overhauling of aircraft. *See, e.g.*, Thomas C. Corke, *Design of Aircraft* (2002); Bill Gunston, *World Encyclopedia of Aircraft Manufacturers: From the Pioneers to the Present Day* (1994); Brian H. Rowe & Martin Ducheny, *The Power to Fly: An Engineer's Life* (2004).

Popular culture also has examined these subjects. Examples include Neville Shute's novel *No Highway* (1948) (the 1951 screen version, entitled *No Highway in the Sky*, starred James Stewart), Michael Crichton's best seller *Airframe* (1996), the movie *Flight of the Phoenix* (2004) (with Dennis Quaid), and the television characters Steve Douglas (played by Fred MacMurray), an aeronautical engineer on *My Three Sons* (ABC and CBS, 1960–72), and Chester A. Riley (Jackie Gleason, then William Bendix), an airplane riveter on *The Life of Riley* (DuMont, 1949–50; NBC, 1953–58). In addition, the names of two of Seattle's professional sports teams—the Seattle Pilots (MLB, 1969) and the Seattle SuperSonics (NBA, since 1967)—pay homage to the Boeing Company, which was founded in Seattle in 1916 and headquartered there until 2001 (when it moved to Chicago).

2. In *Alaskan Oil*, Chief Judge Arnold outlines the majority and minority positions regarding defective products that damage themselves. In your view, which represents the sounder approach to the problem of economic-only losses? Regardless of your answer, would a uniform rule be preferable? *See further* Brian G. Gilpin & John Scott Hoff, *The Economic Loss Doctrine: The Death of Subrogation*, 10 Air & Space Law. 1 (Spring 1996), and J. Denny Shupe & Todd R. Steggerda, *Toward a More Uniform and "Reasonable" Approach to Products Liability Litigation: Current Trends in the Adoption of the Restatement (Third) and Its Potential Impact on Aviation Litigation*, 66 J. Air L. & Com. 129 (2000).

3. Early in its opinion, the *Turbines* court mentions that G & G had obtained a Supplemental Type Certificate that allowed it to modify Piper Brave planes. In *G.S. Rasmussen & Associates, Inc. v. Kalitta Flying Service, Inc.*, 958 F.2d 896, 898–99 (9th Cir. 1992), *cert. denied*, 508 U.S. 959 (1993), the Ninth Circuit provided the following description of such certificates:

> The FAA is charged by Congress with promoting air safety, see 49 U.S.C.App. § 1421(a), and pursues this mission vigorously and effectively in cooperation with the private aviation industry. One of the FAA's most important functions is to prescribe standards and to measure compliance with a multistep certification process for airplane design and production. See generally United States v. Varig Airlines, 467 U.S. 797, 804–07, 104 S.Ct. 2755, 2759–61, 81 L.Ed.2d 660 (1984).
>
> Because the certification procedure is complex and expensive, the FAA certifies airplane types rather than individual planes. Aircraft manufacturers are required to test and analyze new airplane designs themselves; the FAA then determines the airworthiness of the design based on the manufacturer-generated engineering data and test results. Once a manufacturer has demonstrated the safety of its design, the FAA issues it a Type Certificate. See 49 U.S.C.App.

> § 1423(a)(2); 14 CFR § 21.21(b). The manufacturer can then obtain a production certificate by proving to the FAA that each duplicate airplane will comply with the Type Certificate. See 49 U.S.C.App. § 1423(b); 14 CFR §§ 21.133–21.143. Finally, the manufacturer can obtain airworthiness certification for subsequent aircraft, without undergoing independent testing, by demonstrating that they conform to the Type Certificate. See 49 U.S.C.App. § 1423(c); 14 CFR § 21.183.
>
> This case involves a closely related FAA certification scheme: Supplemental Type Certificates (STCs)—which, as the name implies, certify changes to planes already type-certificated. Anyone who wishes to make a major alteration to an airplane must obtain an STC. 14 CFR § 21.113. The STC serves the same function for alterations as the Type Certificate does for initial manufacture: It allows the FAA inspector to shortcut the airworthiness certification process by incorporating an approved design. STCs are obtained through the same arduous process as Type Certificates: The applicant must present engineering and test data sufficient to prove to the FAA the airworthiness of the proposed modification. See 14 CFR §§ 21.115–21.117.

For additional information about the FAA's certification process, *see* www.faa.gov/certification/aircraft.

4. Can the holdings in *Turbines* and *Prompt Air* be reconciled? If not, what accounts for the different results? One possibility, of course, is that in *Turbines* the defendant effectively challenged Dardis's flying ability, while in *Prompt Air* no questions were raised about the pilot. As one might expect, whenever possible defendants try to shift blame from the aircraft to the pilot. *See further* John A. Glenn, Annotation, *Pilot's Contributory Negligence or Assumption of Risk as Defense in Action for His Injuries or Death Resulting From Airplane Accident*, 35 A.L.R.3d 614 (1971 & 2004 Supp.).

5. As the court in *Prompt Air* explains, someone tampered with Porsche's turbocharger by replacing its parts with those from an automobile. While this is a rather rare occurrence, it is not uncommon for counterfeit (also known as "unapproved" or "bogus") parts to find their way into airplanes. Although aviation officials have known about this problem since at least 1957 (when the Flight Safety Foundation issued a landmark report on the subject), the high cost of bona fide parts has made the trade in fake ones extremely difficult to combat. For a further discussion, *see, e.g.*, James L. Burt, III, *'Bogus' Aircraft: Offenses and Defenses*, 61 J. Air L. & Com. 859 (1996); Robert W. Luedeman, *Flying Underground: The Trade in Bootleg Aircraft Parts*, 62 J. Air. L. & Com. 93 (1996); Beverly Jane Sharkey, *The Federal Aviation Administration Suspected Unapproved Parts Program: The Need to Eliminate Safety Risks Posed By Unapproved Aircraft Parts*, 65 J. Air L. & Com. 795 (2000).

6. For a further look at the types of claims that can be raised in an aviation design or manufacturing case, *see, e.g.*, Theresa Ludwig Kruk, Annotation, *Res Ipsa Loquitur in Aviation Accidents*, 25 A.L.R.4th 1237 (1983 & 2004 Supp.); Sonja A. Soehnel, Annotation, *Products Liability: Personal Injury or Death Allegedly Caused by Defect in Aircraft or Its Parts, Supplies, or Equipment*, 97 A.L.R.3d 627 (1980 & 2005 Supp.); Jay M. Zitter, Annotation, *Products Liability: Helicopters*, 72 A.L.R.5th 299 (1999 & 2005 Supp.). *See also Grier v. Cochran Western Corp.*, 705 A.2d 1262 (N.J. Super. Ct. App. Div. 1998) (rejecting plaintiff's claim that manufacturer failed to provide adequate warnings regarding the dangers posed by improper operation of a belt conveyor truck used to load and unload airplanes).

7. Lastly, it should be pointed out that airplane accidents often lead to safer planes. *See further* Ken Kaye, *The High Price of Safer Skies: Accidents Led to Innovations That Im-*

proved Air Travel, S. Fla. Sun-Sentinel, July 31, 2005, at 1H. Among the many examples cited by Mr. Kaye are: Air Florida Flight 90 (crashed due to inexperienced crew/led to stiffer standards for de-icing); Delta Flight 191 (wind shear/Doppler radar); Eastern Flight 401 (distracted crew/improved warning systems); Northwest Orient Flight 705 (thunderstorm/better cockpit instruments); USAir Flight 427 (faulty tail rudder/all Boeing 737s fitted with new rudders). *See also* Van Stewart, Comment, *"Privileged Communications?": The Bright Line Rule in the Use of Cockpit Voice Recorder Tapes*, 11 CommLaw Conspectus 389 (2003) (discussing the increasing role cockpit tapes are playing in improving air safety).

As a result of the foregoing, some aviation plaintiffs' lawyers are critical of confidential or quick settlements, believing they block improvements. *See further Litigation With a Foreign Flavor: A Comparison of the Warsaw Convention and the Hamburg Rules*, 59 J. Air L. & Com. 907, 911–14 (1994) (remarks of Lee S. Kreindler, Esq.). Is this concern legitimate? If so, should such settlements be prohibited?

Problem 8

While considering a particular airplane, a buyer learned that the FAA had issued an Emergency Airworthiness Directive for the model that required all "flap tracks" to be inspected sometime during the next 15 flights. The directive also referred readers to a service bulletin issued by the company that, in conjunction with the original manufacturer, had modified the tracks a few months earlier. After reviewing the directive (but not the bulletin), the buyer went ahead with the purchase. A short time later, the FAA grounded all of the planes when further testing revealed that the modification had compromised the airframe's integrity, resulting in the need for extensive (and expensive) repairs. Given these facts, what recourse (if any) does the buyer have? *See Washington Jet, Inc. v. Rockwell International Corporation*, 524 F. Supp. 442 (N.D. Ill. 1981).

E. DEFENSES

CLEVELAND v. PIPER AIRCRAFT CORPORATION

985 F.2d 1438 (10th Cir.),
cert. denied, 510 U.S. 908 (1993)

LAY, Senior Circuit Judge.

Piper Aircraft Corporation brings this interlocutory appeal under 28 U.S.C. § 1292(b), challenging pre-trial rulings by the district court. Edward Cleveland brought suit against Piper for injuries he received in 1983 while piloting a Super Cub airplane, which crashed during takeoff. He alleged he suffered severe injuries due to the negligent design of the plane. In May 1986, a jury returned a $2.5 million verdict in favor of Cleveland. On appeal this court determined the special verdict form improperly restricted jurors from allocating fault to all potentially responsible parties. See Cleveland v. Piper Aircraft Corp., 890 F.2d 1540, 1546–51 (10th Cir.1989), reh'g denied, 898 F.2d 778 (10th Cir.1990). A new trial was awarded Piper. On remand, the district court permitted Piper to amend its answer and assert a defense that state common law was preempted by the Federal Aviation Act of 1958 and its corresponding regulations. The district court, among other rulings, denied Piper's motion for summary judgment on this defense. Additionally, the trial court granted plaintiff's motion to limit the second trial to the issue of liability and ruled that only the witnesses and exhibits presented in the first trial could be introduced in the second trial. Piper sought permission to appeal these rulings under 28 U.S.C. § 1292(b); the trial court certified the appeal and this court granted permission.

I. FACTS

Cleveland was injured July 8, 1983 while attempting to take off from the Mid-Valley Airport in Los Lunas, New Mexico, in a Piper Super Cub Model PA-18-150. The plane was towing a glider that was attached by rope to the aircraft's tail. Cleveland and a cinematographer were planning to film the glider's flight for a television commercial. With assistance from a Federal Aviation Administration (FAA) certified mechanic, Cleveland had removed the front pilot's seat from the plane and installed a camera. At the time of the accident, Cleveland was piloting the plane from the rear pilot seat.

A few days before Cleveland planned to shoot the commercial, the owner of the Mid-Valley airport became concerned about the safety of the operation and about compliance with FAA regulations. The owner closed the airport to prevent Cleveland from taking off. On the morning of the accident, the owner noticed activity at the airport and parked his van in the runway to prevent takeoffs and landings. Shortly thereafter, Cleveland attempted to fly the reconfigured Piper airplane. During takeoff, the aircraft struck the owner's parked van. Cleveland's head struck the camera, resulting in serious head and brain injuries.

Cleveland's wife, the conservator of his estate, brought this diversity action against Piper, which manufactured and sold the Super Cub in 1970. At the conclusion of the trial, a jury determined that Piper negligently designed the aircraft without adequate forward vision from the rear seat and negligently failed to provide a rear shoulder harness. However, the jury was not asked to compare the negligence of the parties responsible for the initial collision—the plane striking the van—with the negligence of those responsible for the second injury—Cleveland's head striking the camera. On this basis, we reversed and ordered a new trial. Id. at 1546.

II. FEDERAL PREEMPTION

Piper claims that the district court erred in denying its motion for summary judgment on preemption grounds. The basic principles of law in this area are well settled. Piper argues that the Federal Aviation Act of 1958, 49 U.S.C. app. §§ 1301 et seq., and the regulations it has spawned impliedly preempt state tort actions by occupying the field of airplane safety. It asserts that the web of federal laws and regulations govern the field in a comprehensive manner, leaving no room for state regulation.

Preemption questions turn on congressional intent. Schneidewind v. ANR Pipeline Co., 485 U.S. 293, 299, 99 L. Ed. 2d 316, 108 S. Ct. 1145 (1988). The mere fact that Congress has enacted detailed legislation addressing a matter of dominant federal interest does not indicate an intent to displace state law entirely. English v. General Elec. Co., 496 U.S. 72, 87, 110 L. Ed. 2d 65, 110 S. Ct. 2270 (1990); Hillsborough County v. Automated Medical Lab., Inc., 471 U.S. 707, 716–20, 85 L. Ed. 2d 714, 105 S. Ct. 2371 (1985). Congress may reserve for the federal government the exclusive right to regulate safety in a given field, yet permit the states to maintain tort remedies covering much the same territory. Silkwood v. Kerr-McGee Corp., 464 U.S. 238, 253, 78 L. Ed. 2d 443, 104 S. Ct. 615 (1984). This is so even though an award of damages may have the same effect as direct state regulation. See San Diego Bldg. Trades Council v. Garmon, 359 U.S. 236, 247, 3 L. Ed. 2d 775, 79 S. Ct. 773 (1959).

The district court determined the plain language of the Federal Aviation Act suggests that Congress intended that the Act have no general preemptive effect. We agree.

Congress enacted the Federal Aviation Act of 1958, Pub. L. No. 85-726, 72 Stat. 731, "to establish a new Federal agency with powers adequate to enable it to provide for the safe and efficient use of the navigable airspace by both civil and military operations." H.R. Rep. No. 2360, 85th Cong., 2d Sess. 1, reprinted in 1958 U.S.C.C.A.N. 3741, 3741. The Act directed the Federal Aviation Agency to regulate "air commerce in such manner as to best promote its development and safety and fulfill the requirements of national defense." Pub. L. No. 85-726, § 103, 72 Stat. 740 (1958) (codified at 49 U.S.C. app. § 1303 (1988)). Although the legislative history states the Act provides the Federal Aviation Agency with "full responsibility and authority" over safety, H.R. Rep. No. 2360, reprinted in 1958 U.S.C.C.A.N. at 3741, the Act also assigned the Civil Aeronautics Board responsibility for safety, "emphasized ... that air carriers themselves retained certain responsibilities," and did not address what, if any, responsibility remained for the states.

The Act contains a savings clause that states:

> Nothing contained in this Act shall in any way abridge or alter the remedies now existing at common law or by statute, but the provisions of this Act are in addition to such remedies.

49 U.S.C. app. § 1506. As other courts have held, this section shows that Congress did not intend to occupy the field of airplane safety to the exclusion of the state common law. See In re Air Crash Disaster, 635 F.2d 67, 74–75 (2d Cir. 1980); In re Mexico City Aircrash, 708 F.2d 400, 407 (9th Cir. 1983) (dictum); Sunbird Air Servs., Inc. v. Beech Aircraft Corp., 789 F. Supp. 360, 362 (D. Kan. 1992); Holliday v. Bell Helicopters Textron, Inc., 747 F. Supp. 1396, 1398–99 (D. Haw. 1990); In Re Air Crash Disaster, 721 F. Supp. 1185, 1187 (D. Colo. 1988); Brunwasser v. Trans World Airlines, Inc., 541 F. Supp. 1338, 1345–46 (W.D. Pa. 1982); Alaska Airlines, Inc. v. Sweat, 568 P.2d 916, 927 (Ala. 1977); Elsworth v. Beech Aircraft Corp., 37 Cal. 3d 540, 691 P.2d 630, 635, 208 Cal. Rptr. 874 (Cal. 1984), cert. denied, 471 U.S. 1110, 85 L. Ed. 2d 861, 105 S. Ct. 2345 (1985). We arrived at the same conclusion in dicta in McCord v. Dixie Aviation Corp., 450 F.2d 1129, 1131 (10th Cir. 1971).

By its very words, the statute leaves in place remedies then existing at common law or by statute. Tort liability for design defects was established in the law of many states by the late 1950s and had been extended to airplane crash cases. See, e.g., DeVito v. United Airlines, 98 F. Supp. 88, 96–97 (E.D.N.Y. 1951) (failure to warn); Dix W. Noel, Manufacturer's Negligence of Design or Directions for Use of a Product, 71 Yale L.J. 816, 816, 821 (1962); see also Restatement of Torts § 398 (1938) (establishing liability for "chattle made under a plan or design which makes it dangerous for the uses for which it is manufactured"). There is nothing inconsistent with Congress's goal of maximum safety and common law claims.

Last term, the Supreme Court analyzed the Act's savings clause in the context of a challenge to state laws prohibiting deceptive advertising of air fares. In Morales v. Trans World Airlines, Inc., 119 L. Ed. 2d 157, 112 S. Ct. 2031, 2034 (1992), the Court stated the presence of the savings clause and, prior to 1978, the absence of an express preemption clause, resulted in the states retaining their traditional regulatory powers in this area. Since Congress has not enacted an express preemption clause governing airplane safety, Morales supports our conclusion that the savings clause demonstrates the Federal Aviation Act does not preempt state common law.

A tool of statutory interpretation, expressio unius est exclusio alterius, also bolsters this conclusion. In Cipollone v. Liggett Group, Inc., 120 L. Ed. 2d 407, 112 S. Ct. 2608, 2618 (1992), the Court used this doctrine to hold that implied preemption is generally inapplicable to a federal statute that contains an express preemption provision. The Court stated that "enactment of a provision defining the pre-emptive reach of a statute implies that matters beyond that reach are not preempted." Id.

In the present case, Piper asserts that Cleveland's claims are impliedly preempted by the Federal Aviation Act of 1958, 49 U.S.C. app. §§1301 et seq., and corresponding federal regulations. Piper does not maintain that Cleveland's claims are expressly preempted.

The Act governs two broad areas of congressional concern and contains an express preemption provision governing one of them—rates and routes. 49 U.S.C. app. §1305(a). Under Cipollone, this implies that the other broad area of congressional concern—air safety—is not preempted because it is "beyond [the] reach" of the express preemption provision. Cipollone, 112 S. Ct. at 2618. Although §1305(a) was not part of the original Act, its inclusion in 1978 shows that Congress, like the states and the Civil Aeronautics Board, which at that time enforced portions of the statute, believed the Act lacked general preemptive reach.

The United States, which has filed an amicus brief urging preemption, points us to 49 U.S.C. app. §1508(a), which it suggests evinces Congress's intent to occupy the field of air safety. That section of the original Act, see Pub. L. No. 85-726, 72 Stat. 798, states that the United States has "complete and exclusive national sovereignty in the air space above the United States." The Government suggests that in this section Congress "made clear" that "air commerce is an exclusively federal function." However, §1508(a) addresses Congress's intent to keep the United States free from military planes from foreign nations, and not domestic safety concerns. Thus, it is inapplicable.

We conclude that Congress has not indicated a "clear and manifest" intent to occupy the field of airplane safety to the exclusion of state common law. To the contrary, it appears through the savings clause that Congress has intended to allow state common law to stand side by side with the system of federal regulations it has developed.

Piper also suggests that the Federal Aviation Act impliedly preempts state tort claims because the federal regulatory framework actually conflicts with state common law duties. Such a conflict will be found if it is "a physical impossibility" to comply with both state and federal law, Florida Lime & Avocado Growers, Inc. v. Paul, 373 U.S. 132, 142–43, 10 L. Ed. 2d 248, 83 S. Ct. 1210 (1963), or when the state law is an obstacle to accomplishing Congress's full purposes and objectives, California Coastal Comm'n v. Granite Rock Co., 480 U.S. 572, 581, 94 L. Ed. 2d 577, 107 S. Ct. 1419 (1987) (quoting Hines v. Davidowitz, 312 U.S. 52, 67, 85 L. Ed. 581, 61 S. Ct. 399 (1941)). In particular, Piper focuses on Cleveland's claims that the plane's design was defective because it leaves a rear-seat pilot with poor forward visibility and because the rear seats lack shoulder harnesses. We find that [it] is not impossible to meet both state common law standards and the federal regulations.

Piper maintains that Cleveland's claims are an attack on the tailwheel design, which is approved by the FAA. See 14 C.F.R. pt. 25 app. A. However, the federal regulations Piper has cited require only that the plane be designed "so that ... the pilot's view is sufficiently extensive, clear, and undistorted, for safe operation." 14 C.F.R. §23.773(a)(1).

The regulations do not require the precise design that Piper has utilized. As the district court noted, Cleveland has presented evidence that Piper could have improved visibility without altering the tailwheel design simply by raising the rear pilot seat. Thus, there is no irreconcilable conflict.

Piper also asserts that it fully complied with the seat belt requirements because the regulations in place when the FAA approved its design of the plane did not require shoulder harnesses. It asserts that the FAA did not make later requirements retroactive. This, however, is not an argument for preemption since it would have been possible to install a shoulder harness on the rear pilot's seat without conflicting with the federal regulations.

Furthermore, as noted previously, the Federal Aviation Act authorizes promulgation of "minimum standards." 49 U.S.C. app. § 1421. By themselves, minimum standards such as these are not conclusive of Congress's preemptive intent. Ray v. Atlantic Richfield Co., 435 U.S. 151, 168, 55 L. Ed. 2d 179, 98 S. Ct. 988 (1978). However, minimum standards may be evidence of such intent. Florida Lime & Avocado Growers, Inc. v. Paul, 373 U.S. 132, 147–48, 10 L. Ed. 2d 248, 83 S. Ct. 1210 (1963). The district court determined that by designating the standards as minimum, Congress indicated that it did not want to bar states from adopting additional or more stringent standards. See also Holliday v. Bell Helicopters Textron, Inc., 747 F. Supp. 1396, 1400–01 (D. Haw. 1990); Perry v. Mercedes Benz of North America, Inc., 957 F.2d 1257, 1264–65 (5th Cir. 1992) ("minimum standard" requirement for automobiles). This is consistent with the Act's purpose of promoting safety. 49 U.S.C. app. §§ 1302, 1303; H.R. Rep. No. 2360, 85th Cong., 2d Sess. 1, reprinted in 1958 U.S.C.C.A.N. 3741, 3741.

The United States, however, suggests an alternative interpretation. It urges that rather than giving states the option to heighten standards, the "minimum standards" limitation allows manufacturers to improve safety beyond that which the federal government requires. This, too, would be consistent with the Act's purposes. While we are skeptical that Congress was concerned that administrative agencies and manufacturers would otherwise feel constrained to improve the safety of products, we need not resolve this ambiguity. In determining congressional intent on preemption questions, we look for "clear and manifest" indicators. English v. General Elec. Co., 496 U.S. 72, 79, 110 L. Ed. 2d 65, 110 S. Ct. 2270 (1990). We find none here.

Piper also suggests that Cleveland's claims are preempted because the FAA and its predecessor agencies approved the airplane's design. However, FAA approval is not intended to be the last word on safety. The FAA has given manufacturers broad responsibilities for assuring their own compliance by appointing aircraft company employees to "act as surrogates of the FAA in examining, inspecting, and testing aircraft for purposes of certification." United States v. Varig Airlines, 467 U.S. 797, 807, 81 L. Ed. 2d 660, 104 S. Ct. 2755 (1984). The Varig Court said:

> The FAA certification process is founded upon a relatively simple notion: the duty to ensure that an aircraft conforms to FAA safety regulations lies with the manufacturer and operator, while the FAA retains the responsibility for policing compliance. Thus, the manufacturer is required to develop the plans and specifications and perform the inspections and tests necessary to establish that an aircraft design comports with the applicable regulations; the FAA then reviews the data for conformity purposes by conducting a "spot check" of the manufacturer's work.

Id. at 816–17. Thus, FAA certification is, by its very nature, a minimum check on safety.

Furthermore, when the Court recently applied the doctrine of expressio unius est exclusio alterius to preemption cases, it excluded consideration of all forms of implied preemption, including conflict preemption. Cipollone, 112 S.Ct. at 2618. Justice Blackmun's concurring opinion made this explicit. Id. at 2625 ("We resort to principles of implied pre-emption—that is, inquiring whether Congress has occupied a particular field with the intent to supplant state law or whether state law actually conflicts with federal law—only when Congress has been silent with respect to pre-emption.") (citation omitted); see also id. at 2633 (Scalia, J., dissenting) (asserting that this aspect of the decision "works mischief"). Congress's inclusion of § 1305(a) preempting state regulation of air rates and routes suggests that it intended the Federal Aviation Act not to preempt common law claims such as those set forth in this suit. See Holliday, 747 F. Supp. at 1400 n.3 (pre-Cipollone analysis).

Thus, we agree with the district court that Cleveland's claims are not preempted by federal law.

[The remainder of the court's opinion is omitted.]

GODWIN AIRCRAFT, INC. v. HOUSTON

851 S.W.2d 816 (Tenn. Ct. App. 1992)

CRAWFORD, Judge.

This case involves the purchase of an airplane by plaintiff-appellee, Godwin Aircraft, Inc. (hereinafter Godwin), from a Georgia resident, Ray R. Houston, d/b/a Washington County Air Service (hereinafter Houston).

Godwin filed a complaint against Houston in the Chancery Court of Shelby County, Tennessee. The complaint seeks damages allegedly caused by defendant's fraud, misrepresentation and breach of contract in the purchase of an aircraft. Defendant first filed a motion to dismiss for lack of personal jurisdiction, which was denied. Defendant's answer, in addition to relying on lack of jurisdiction, joined issue in the material allegations of the complaint.

The plane was sold at a national auction held in Oklahoma City, Oklahoma on June 19, 20, and 21, 1991, under the terms of a contract between Oklahoma Aircraft Dealers Association and the defendant-appellant, Ray Houston.

The auction catalog set out the terms of the auction which includes the following:

> The aircraft listed in this catalog have been submitted by the owner. In no way is the Oklahoma Aircraft Dealers Association responsible for their accuracy. Understand you buy "as is" "where is." Inspect aircraft and log books prior to bidding. If you are high bidder and bid is accepted by the owner, aircraft is considered sold!

The procedure used at the auction was for the individual planes to be rolled out for potential bidders to inspect and then the bidding begins. The potential bidder has the opportunity to inspect the log book for each particular aircraft. In the instant case, Houston not only was the owner of the subject aircraft, but was also an authorized inspector for the Federal Aviation Administration (FAA). On December 22, 1989, Houston, as the authorized inspector, made the following certification in the aircraft log book. "I CERTIFY THAT THIS AIRCRAFT HAS BEEN INSPECTED IN ACCORDANCE WITH THE ANNUAL INSPECTION AND FOUND TO BE IN AN AIRWOR-

THY CONDITION. I.A. 255921619 R. Ray Houston." The certification on December 22, 1989, was made when the aircraft had 2,601 hours, and the aircraft at the time of the sale had 2,728.8 hours. Godwin became the successful bidder and Houston provided clear title to the aircraft and the bill of sale to Godwin.

Houston testified that an electronic transfer of funds from Godwin's bank to Houston's account in Georgia was arranged at the time the bill of sale was passed in Oklahoma City. Godwin testified that no funds were wired at that time, but were ultimately wired from Boatman's Bank in Memphis to Houston's bank in Georgia. Houston flew the plane from Oklahoma City to the General Dewitt Spain Airport on Second Street in Memphis. Houston testified that he offered to fly the plane to Memphis as a convenience to himself in order to save air fare on his return flight to Georgia. Godwin and several witnesses in his behalf testified that Houston insisted upon flying the aircraft to Memphis himself. The plane was left on Godwin's ramp at the airport.

A few days after the plane arrived at the Spain airport, the plane was flown to Jonesboro, Arkansas, for an examination by a prospective purchaser, a company owned by Mark Haggenmacher. Haggenmacher had the plane inspected by Dale Sharp, an A & P mechanic with 22 years experience. After a preliminary inspection by Sharp, the plane was returned to Godwin at the Spain airport. After the plane was returned, Godwin learned that Sharp's preliminary inspection indicated that several airworthiness directives (AD) issued by the FAA had not been complied with, such as inspection of turbo charges, inspection of [the] exhaust system, inspection of fuel cells, inspection of hoses in the engine compartment, and inspection of the heater. In addition, the preliminary report also noted inoperable flaps.

After the plane was returned to Memphis, a more detailed inspection was made by two A & P mechanics, Steve Wallace and Glen Mitchell. Wallace testified that the inoperable flaps were caused because there was no flap motor and transmission in the airplane. There was also evidence of a disregard of an AD concerning cracks in the engine casing where repairs were attempted instead of required replacement. Wallace further testified that parts of the turbo charger and exhaust system were cracked and missing and exhaust gasses had scarred the left engine support beam which could cause the engine to fail. In his opinion, this scarring of the beam was a result of at least 200 hours of operation and that this condition would have been evident on inspection at the time of the Houston inspection 127 hours earlier as noted in the aircraft log. Wallace further testified about a bent elevator push rod and evidence that an attempt had been made to repair the push rod, both of which should have been evident upon an annual inspection. Wallace opined that at the time the aircraft was sold at auction it was not airworthy.

Glen Mitchell, an aircraft inspector and pilot, testified that the bent elevator push rod could have caused loss of control of the aircraft. He likewise found the cause of the inoperable flaps to be the absence of a flap motor. Mitchell also testified concerning the disregard of the engine casing AD. He testified that the majority of all the parts on the exhaust and turbo were cracked and deteriorated beyond repair, and that the engine support beam was corroded and severely damaged which could cause a crash. He opined that damage to the support beam occurred over a 150 to 200 hour period and that this damage had to have been evident in an inspection 127 hours previous to the time he inspected it.

Alan Godwin, President of Godwin Aircraft, testified that he had 19 years experience in the aircraft business. He stated that although the auction was "as is—where is," this aircraft was represented as being in an airworthy condition by virtue of the annual inspection signed off by Houston himself. The only time Godwin saw the aircraft before the auction was when it was run through the auction block. He had time to inspect the log book and read the certification that the plane was airworthy. He testified that Houston insisted on flying the aircraft to Memphis, although Godwin had five extra pilots available who could have flown the plane. This testimony was corroborated by Mark Haggenmacher.

An expert for the United States Testing Company also testified concerning physical testing done to the engine support beam to determine the extent of the damage done and the period of time over which it had occurred. He reached the conclusion that the damage occurred over a long period of time and that his company could not replicate the corrosion by test in twelve cycles of 180 hours.

Houston's testimony did not specifically contradict the existence of the defects in the aircraft. He testified that mistakes do happen in aircraft logs, but he did not deny that the aircraft was defective and unairworthy. He is a pilot and aircraft inspector licensed by the FAA and was the owner and operator of the subject aircraft. During the time that he owned the aircraft, he maintained the plane and fulfilled federal regulations regarding required inspections. As a licensed aircraft inspector, he conducted the required inspections and signed the plane's log indicating that the inspections had been completed. He flew the plane to Oklahoma City for the auction and listed it for sale. He further testified that the catalog made no express representation as to the condition of the aircraft, except that it contained language by which it was noted that the plane's auto pilot was inoperable, which fact was known to the buyer prior to the auction. He testified that he made no warranties, express or implied, to anyone, and he had no contact with the plaintiff until after the auction. Houston further testified that the plane was located at the airport in Oklahoma City for approximately three days prior to the auction and available for buyer inspection at any time. He stated that after the bid was made and accepted, the completion of the sales transfer took place while the parties were in Oklahoma. Houston noted in his testimony that Godwin's mechanics discovered the defects through visual inspection, which visual inspection could have been made by Godwin prior to making a bid on the aircraft. He further testified that with regard to his inspection prior to the auction which is recorded in the log book, he was the owner and sole operator of the plane and that he had not contemplated plans to sell the plane at that time. He indicated that the defects subsequently discovered could have occurred during the time period between his last inspection and the purchase at the auction.

After a bench trial, the chancellor awarded plaintiff compensatory damages in the amount of $41,171.88 and punitive damages in the amount of $10,375.00. Defendant has appealed.

[Following a lengthy discussion, the court rejected Houston's assertions that personal jurisdiction was lacking and the log book notations did not constitute actionable misrepresentations.]

The next issue for review is whether the "as is, where is" disclaimer, and Godwin's opportunity to inspect the aircraft prior to the sale, should relieve the seller of liability for the misrepresentation that the aircraft was airworthy.

In the case at bar, the log book certified by Houston declared the aircraft to be in airworthy condition. The evidence supports the trial court's findings that the certification was untrue, and that Houston intended to keep this information from Godwin until after delivery of the aircraft in Memphis. The record also contains proof that Godwin specifically inspected the log book to determine whether the aircraft was airworthy and that he relied upon the certification made to that effect. There is also proof that several of the more serious defects would not have been revealed unless the aircraft had been partially dismantled.

Houston further argues that the "as is, where is" disclaimer absolves him from liability. We must respectfully disagree. In the case at bar, the trial court found, and we have agreed, that the evidence does not preponderate against the finding that specific misrepresentations were made which were relied upon by the purchaser. In Morris v. Mack's Used Cars, 824 S.W.2d 538 (Tenn.1992), our Supreme Court held that disclaimers permitted by the Uniform Commercial Code do not constitute a defense under the Tennessee Consumer Protection Act. The court noted that the Act created a separate and distinct cause of action for unfair or deceptive acts or practices. While we do not have a Consumer Protection Act case here, we do have a tortious misrepresentation case, which likewise is a distinct and separate cause of action from breach of warranty cases under the Uniform Commercial Code. In the case at bar, the action for tortious misrepresentation is analogous to an action for deceptive trade practices under the Consumer Protection Act.

The trial court found that defendant Houston made material misrepresentation and that he willfully continued these representations until delivery of the aircraft in Memphis. The evidence does not preponderate against the trial court's findings in this regard.

The judgment of the trial court is affirmed and this case is remanded to the trial court for such further proceedings as may be necessary. Costs of the appeal are assessed against the appellant.

BURROUGHS v. PRECISION AIRMOTIVE CORP.

93 Cal. Rptr. 2d 124 (Ct. App. 2000)

BAMATTRE-MANOUKIAN, Acting Presiding Justice.

Plaintiffs suffered injuries in the crash of a light aircraft, allegedly due to a malfunction in the engine's carburetor. Defendant is an aircraft parts manufacturer who did not manufacture or sell this particular model of carburetor but acquired the product line from a predecessor who had acquired it from the original manufacturer. The carburetor was manufactured and sold in 1968, over 25 years prior to the accident. A recent federal statute of repose (The General Aviation Revitalization Act of 1994 (GARA), Pub.L. No. 103-298, 108 Stat. 155, 49 U.S.C. §40101 note) bars claims arising from accidents involving light aircraft brought against "the manufacturer of any new component ... or other part of the aircraft, in its capacity as a manufacturer" (Pub.L. No. 103-298, §2(a), 108 Stat. 1552) more than 18 years after the product is first sold. The trial court in this case granted summary judgment against plaintiffs, finding that the federal statute barred their claims against defendant in its capacity as successor to the original manufacturer.

Two questions are presented in this appeal. Is defendant a "manufacturer" within the meaning of the federal statute? If the statute applies to bar plaintiffs' claims against defendant acting in its capacity as a manufacturer, can plaintiffs nonetheless proceed against defendant on a theory that defendant breached an independent duty to warn about the defective product? We find that defendant, as the successor manufacturer, stands in the shoes of the manufacturer and is entitled to the protection of GARA. We further find that defendant, in engaging in the conduct complained of by plaintiffs, was acting in its capacity as a manufacturer pursuant to the duties and obligations imposed by federal law on manufacturers of general aviation aircraft and aircraft parts. Plaintiffs' theory of independent liability is not viable under these circumstances. We therefore affirm the judgment.

BACKGROUND

On February 26, 1995, a two-seater aircraft piloted by plaintiff James Burroughs took off from Reed-Hillview Airport in San Jose. The passenger was plaintiff Jared Burroughs, James Burroughs's nephew. Shortly after takeoff, the aircraft lost power and crashed. Both James and Jared Burroughs suffered serious personal injuries. Plaintiff Joseph Burroughs, father of Jared, witnessed the crash from the ground.

Plaintiffs' expert stated that the source of the plane's losing power was a defective carburetor containing a float made from composite materials. Over time and with changes in the chemistry of gasoline, the composite float absorbed fuel and became heavy. The float's loss of buoyancy caused a change in the fuel-air mixture, resulting in interruption of power. The carburetor, known as the Marvel-Schebler Aviation carburetor, or MSA carburetor, model MA-3A, was manufactured in 1968 by the Marvel-Schebler Division of Borg-Warner Corporation (now known as Borg-Warner Security Corp., hereafter Borg-Warner). Borg-Warner sold its Marvel-Schebler carburetor line to Facet Aerospace Products Co. in 1983 (a subsidiary of Facet Enterprises, Inc., hereafter Facet). Facet sold the Marvel-Schebler product line to Zenith Fuel Systems, Inc., in 1990, and shortly thereafter defendant Precision Airmotive Corp. (Precision) acquired the product line. Although Precision began manufacturing aircraft carburetors in 1991, it did not manufacture, design or sell the model of carburetor involved in the accident in this case.

Problems with composite carburetor floats absorbing fuel and sinking were well documented. Facet issued a service bulletin in May of 1984 to "All Outlets," recommending the replacement of composite floats with metal floats in all Marvel-Schebler carburetors "at next overhaul or immediately." Later that year, in August of 1984, Facet requested that the Federal Aviation Administration (FAA) issue an airworthiness directive relating to the replacement of composite floats in Marvel-Schebler carburetors. An airworthiness directive (AD) is a finding by the FAA of an unsafe condition in a product and it orders corrective action with which aircraft owners must comply. A notice of proposed rulemaking appeared in the Federal Register proposing the composite floats to be replaced with metal floats by 1988. The notice further stated that Facet, which had purchased the Marvel-Schebler carburetor line, had obtained a design change which would reintroduce a metal float compatible with the chemistry of current blends of aviation gasoline. Facet had available a replacement kit for approximately $57, which would require approximately four hours to install.

Shortly thereafter, in July of 1990, Precision acquired the Marvel-Schebler product line. In October of 1990, Precision issued a "Mandatory Service Bulletin" (No. MSA-1) "to clarify time of compliance for replacement of the carburetor float and to reflect acquisition of the Facet Aerospace product line (Marvel Schebler Aviation Carburetors) by Precision Airmotive Corporation." The bulletin noted that reports from the field indicated that composite floats "may be absorbing fluid and sinking." It stated that Precision considered it was "mandatory" to replace the composite floats with metal floats "within the next 90 days or 25 hours of engine operation" if the aircraft was experiencing a flooding carburetor, rough engine or inconsistent engine shutdown. The bulletin provided information about metal float replacement kits which were available from local distributors.

In September of 1991, the AD had not been issued and Precision wrote again to the FAA requesting the issuance of an AD requiring replacement of composite floats with metal floats in all Facet/Marvel-Schebler carburetors. The letter stated: "As the new manufacturer of the Facet/Marvel Schebler carburetor, Precision Airmotive feels very strongly that the composite floats constitute a significant safety of flight problem and must be removed from service." Randy Jenson, manager of engineering and product support for Precision, met with a representative of the FAA regarding the AD requested for replacement of the composite float and two other AD's requested by Precision.

In November of 1991, Precision sent out a new service bulletin package, with a revised Mandatory Service Bulletin No. MSA-1, to all repair stations and maintenance personnel. This package included a cover letter informing the recipient that Precision was now the original equipment manufacturer (OEM) of the Marvel-Schebler carburetor, having purchased the product line from Facet. Revised No. MSA-1 required that the Marvel-Schebler composite float be removed "immediately" and replaced with a metal float as per the instructions in the replacement kit.

Vern Miller, the mechanic for the aircraft in question in this case, stated that he was aware of reports of composite floats absorbing fuel and sinking and that he had received the Mandatory Service Bulletins issued by Precision. However, when he conducted the annual inspection of the aircraft in September of 1994, just months before the accident, he did not inspect the carburetor to see if it had a metal or a composite float. He did not feel it was necessary to comply with the Mandatory Service Bulletins because he did not believe the bulletins constituted an "airworthiness requirement." He performed the annual inspection and certified the aircraft as airworthy.

The owner of the aircraft, David Gray, stated that he did not receive a copy of Service Bulletin MSA-1 from Precision. In September of 1993, he did receive a notice sent by Textron-Lycoming informing him of the active service publications which could pertain to the model of engine in his airplane. This notice suggested that he have his maintenance facility review the list of service bulletins for their relevance to his specific model of engine. The notice further explained that Service Bulletins "describe mandatory procedures that must be observed for safety reasons...." It advised him to "please make sure you have complied with each of [the Service Bulletins.]" The notice then listed 20 active Service Bulletins, including the MSA-1 issued by Precision. However, copies of these service bulletins were not attached to the notice. Gray stated that he expected his mechanic, Vern Miller, to be familiar with the mandatory service bulletins and to comply with them during his annual inspection.

Plaintiffs sued Gray, Miller (doing business as Vern Miller Aviation), Precision, and Textron-Lycoming, Inc. The complaint was amended to add defendant Borg-Warner. Plaintiffs alleged theories of negligence, strict liability and breach of warranty relating to the design, manufacture and maintenance of the aircraft's engine and carburetor. Motions for summary adjudication by Borg-Warner and Textron-Lycoming were granted as to all three causes of action of plaintiffs James and Jared Burroughs on the ground that their claims were time-barred under the provisions of the federal GARA (Pub.L. No. 103-298, 108 Stat. 1552, 49 U.S.C. §40101 note). That statute provides for an 18-year limitations period for lawsuits against manufacturers of general aviation aircraft or component parts of such aircraft. The court likewise granted Precision's motion for summary adjudication under GARA as to the theories of strict liability and breach of warranty on the ground that Precision was a successor to the manufacturer of the carburetor, but the court denied Precision's motion as to the negligence cause of action, finding that, "liberally construed," the complaint stated a cause of action for negligence on a theory of product support.

Thereafter, Precision filed a second motion for summary adjudication as to the remaining cause of action for negligence of plaintiffs James and Jared Burroughs on grounds that 1) this was a product liability claim which was barred and preempted by GARA, 2) Precision owed no independent duty with regard to the product, and 3) even if it had a duty, Precision satisfied that duty by issuing the service bulletins. The court granted the motion for summary adjudication, finding that Precision, as a successor to the original manufacturer of the product, was entitled to the protection of GARA and that any duty to warn was the same duty owed by the original manufacturer and not an independent duty. Judgment was entered in favor Precision.

ANALYSIS

The General Aviation Revitalization Act of 1994

Defendant and two amici curiae, the General Aviation Manufacturers Association and the Product Liability Advisory Council, Inc., argue that the federal act, GARA, bars any claim against Precision by virtue of its assumption of the duties imposed by federal law on the manufacturer of an aircraft or component part.

In pertinent part, GARA provides that "no civil action for damages or death or injury to persons or damage to property arising out of an accident involving a general aviation aircraft may be brought against the manufacturer of the aircraft or the manufacturer of any new component, system, subassembly, or other part of the aircraft, in its capacity as a manufacturer if the accident occurred ... [more than 18 years after the date of delivery of the aircraft and/or component to the first purchaser or lessee]." (GARA, Pub.L. No. 103-298, § 2(a), 108 Stat. 1552.)

GARA established a "'statute of repose to protect general aviation manufacturers from long-term liability in those instances where a particular aircraft has been in operation for a considerable number of years. A statute of repose is a legal recognition that, after an extended period of time, a product has demonstrated its safety and quality, and that it is not reasonable to hold a manufacturer legally responsible for an accident or injury occurring after that much time has elapsed.'" (Altseimer v. Bell Helicopter Textron, Inc. (E.D.Cal. 1996) 919 F. Supp. 340, 342, quoting 140 Cong. Rec. H4998, H4999 (Daily ed. July 27, 1994).) A statute of repose differs from a statute of limitations in that statutes of limitation bar suits filed more than a specified period of time after an injury occurs or is discovered, whereas a statute of repose is a bar on all suits brought more than a specified period after the date of manufacture of a product and delivery to the purchaser. Because the date of injury is not a factor used in computing the running of the time period and because statutes of repose typically do not have tolling provisions, they "acquire a substantive nature, barring rights of action even before injury has occurred if the injury occurs subsequent to the prescribed time period." (Wayne v. Tennessee Valley Authority (5th Cir. 1984) 730 F.2d 392, 402; Alexander v. Beech Aircraft Corp. (10th Cir. 1991) 952 F.2d 1215, 1223.) GARA expressly preempts state law. Section 2(d) provides that "This section supersedes any State law to the extent that such law permits a civil action described in subsection (a) to be brought after the applicable limitation period for such civil action established by subsection (a)." (GARA, Pub.L. No. 103-298, § 2(d), 108 Stat. 1552.)

The statute does not apply if manufacturers fail to fulfill their obligations to report known defects or other safety information to the FAA. (GARA, Pub.L. No. 103-298, § 2(b)(1), 108 Stat. 1552.) It also does not provide protection for a manufacturer acting in any other capacity than "as a manufacturer." (GARA, § 2(a).) For example, if the manufacturer committed a negligent act repairing or servicing an aircraft or as a pilot, and such act was the proximate cause of an accident, the victims would not be barred from bringing suit against the manufacturer acting in a capacity other than as a manufacturer. There are also exceptions in the statute for passengers being transported for medical emergencies and persons injured on the ground or in other aircraft. (GARA, §2(b)(2), (3).)

Another perceived element of fairness in the legislation is that GARA is a "rolling" statute of repose. When any part or sub-assembly in an aircraft is replaced with a new part, a new 18-year period begins for that part from the date it is installed. (GARA, Pub.L. No. 103-298, §2(a)(2), 108 Stat. 1552; GARA, H.R. No. 103-525(II), 103d Cong., 2d Sess., supra, p. 1647.) Since almost every major component of the aircraft will be replaced over its lifetime, the "rolling" aspect of the statute of repose was intended to provide that victims and their families would have recourse against the manufacturer of the new component part in the event of a defect in the new part causing an accident.

Given all of these considerations, "[t]he legislation attempts to strike a fair balance by providing some certainty to manufacturers, which will spur the development of new jobs, while preserving victims' rights to bring suit for compensation in certain particularly compelling circumstances. In essence, the bill acknowledges that, for those general aviation aircraft and component parts in service beyond the statute of repose, any design or manufacturing defect not prevented or identified by the Federal regulatory process by then should, in most instances, have manifested itself." (GARA, H.R. No. 103-525(II), 103 Cong., 2d Sess., supra, p. 1648.)

Applying GARA to the facts before us, its provisions clearly shield the manufacturer of the carburetor, Borg-Warner, and the engine, Textron-Lycoming, Inc., from liability for claims based on any defect in the Marvel-Schebler carburetor. Plaintiffs do not argue otherwise. The particular model of carburetor was manufactured and sold in 1968, over 25 years prior to the accident.

Plaintiffs claim that GARA does not apply to Precision, however, because Precision is not the "manufacturer" of the carburetor. The term "manufacturer" is nowhere defined in GARA, and GARA does not specifically include successor manufacturers within the protection of the statute. Although Precision did not actually manufacture the particular carburetor in this case, it is a manufacturer of general aviation aircraft parts, including carburetors, and it took over the manufacturer's responsibilities for the Marvel-Schebler product line. Precision is part of the general aviation industry which GARA was specifically enacted to "revitalize," as the title of the act indicates, and Precision is thus precisely the type of entity GARA was designed to protect from the long tail of liability. The central objective of GARA would be materially undermined if its protection did not apply to a successor to the manufacturer who, as part of its ongoing business, acquired a product line long after the particular product had been discontinued and years after the statute of repose had run as to the original manufacturer. To construe GARA to allow liability claims against the successor manufacturer in these circumstances while barring the same claims against the actual manufacturer would defeat its purpose. We conclude, as we explain further below, that if GARA applies to shield the original manufacturer of a defective product from product liability claims such as the failure to warn alleged here, a successor manufacturer who has taken over the duties and obligations of the original manufacturer as to that product is also protected from liability for such claims.

We believe GARA contains an implicit recognition that as a matter of federal law, by virtue of the extensive rules and regulations governing the aviation industry, a successor manufacturer steps into the shoes of the predecessor with regard to the duties of reporting defects. The drafters of GARA recognized that the aircraft industry is unique because of the extensive "cradle to grave" federal regulatory oversight of the industry. (GARA, H.R. No. 103-525(II), 103d Cong., 2d Sess., supra, p. 1647.) For instance, a holder of a parts manufacturer approval (PMA), such as Precision, must report to the FAA "any failure, malfunction, or defect in any product, part, process or article manufactured by it" that has resulted or could result in an incident such as engine failure. (14 C.F.R. § 21.3 (1999).) Precision, as the holder of the PMA on the Marvel-Schebler line of carburetors, was obliged to comply with these reporting requirements even though technically the particular model of carburetor in question here was not "manufactured by it." Applicable regulations regarding maintenance, preventive maintenance, and alterations of aircraft provide that the manufacturer's instructions for continued airworthiness are to be followed as contained in the maintenance manuals, service bulletins, service letters and service instructions. (14 C.F.R. § 91.403(c) (1999).) Again, after Precision took over the Marvel-Schebler carburetor line in 1990, it became the entity responsible for issuing these manuals and bulletins and fulfilling the manufacturer's obligations for continued airworthiness. In the eyes of the FAA, Precision was the "new manufacturer" of the Marvel-Schebler carburetor.

As plaintiffs' expert explained, when Precision purchased the Marvel-Schebler carburetor product line in 1990, "it became the Original Equipment Manufacturer ('OEM'). In the aviation field, this means that it [Precision] now stands in the same shoes as the two prior companies with respect to providing service information and replacement parts for existing carburetors.... It was the only source of FAA-approved service bulletins and instructions, maintenance manuals, parts catalogs and replacement parts." Thus Precision took over the manufacturer's obligations "with respect to continuing airworthiness" of the Marvel-Schebler product line. (See GARA, Pub.L. No. 103-298, § 2(b)(1), 108 Stat. 1552.) It obtained and became the holder of a PMA issued by the FAA, and it identified itself in its service bulletins and to the FAA as the new OEM for the Marvel-Schebler float carburetor.

Independent Liability

Plaintiffs contend that even if Precision cannot be held derivatively liable for breaching a duty to warn assumed from its predecessors, Precision can nonetheless be liable for a failure to warn independent of its status as a successor manufacturer, in which case it would be outside the reach of GARA. Plaintiffs argue that this theory of independent liability applies here because Precision established an ongoing relationship with purchasers of the Marvel-Schebler carburetor, from which it derived an economic benefit, and because it was aware of known defects in the carburetor. Thus, it had a duty to warn those customers of the defects. Precision breached this duty, they contend, by failing to send its Mandatory Service Bulletins directly to owners of aircraft with engines containing the Marvel-Schebler carburetor, a list of whom is readily available from the FAA.

We reject plaintiffs' theory of independent liability for a number of reasons. First, California has not adopted an independent duty to warn theory of liability. Even if we were inclined to do so here, however, it is not warranted in the circumstances of this case. Precision does not contend that it had no duty to warn of the problems associated with the Marvel-Schebler carburetor. Precision's duties and obligations concerning this product, including a continuing duty to warn, were imposed on it by federal law. Imposing a separate and independent duty based on general principles of tort law would not only be superfluous in light of the federal statutory scheme regulating and overseeing the duties of manufacturers in the general aviation industry, but would also directly conflict with that statutory scheme. None of the cases plaintiffs rely on from other jurisdictions finding a duty to warn involve products in the general aviation aircraft industry, an industry which is regulated "to a degree not comparable to any other." (GARA, H.R. No. 103-525(II), 103d Cong., 2d Sess., supra, p. 1647.)

Furthermore, plaintiffs' cases discussing general tort principles do not consider the effect of products liability statutes of repose. Cases that do involve statutes of repose have routinely applied such statutes to bar claims against successor manufacturers when the claim against the manufacturer is barred. (See Allison v. ITE Imperial Corp. (S.D. Miss. 1990) 729 F. Supp. 45, 46; Henry v. Raynor Mfg. Co. (D.Minn. 1990) 753 F. Supp. 278, 279–280; Gardner v. Navistar Intern. Transp. Corp. (1991) 213 Ill.App.3d 242 [157 Ill.Dec. 88, 571 N.E.2d 1107, 1108, 1114]; Frankenmuth Mut. Ins. Co. v. Marlette Homes (1998) 456 Mich. 511, n.1 [573 N.W.2d 611, 612]; Jackson v. Coldspring Terrace Property (Tex.App. 1997) 939 S.W.2d 762, 764, 768–769 [successor to franchisor entitled to benefit of statute of repose although not involved in actual construction of product].) This is a logical application of statutes of repose, which are product based and represent a legislative determination that once a product crosses the specified age threshold, claims arising from manufacturing defects are simply no longer viable.

As discussed in the previous section, when Precision became the OEM, it stepped into the shoes of the manufacturer and took on the duties and obligations with respect to this product which are imposed by federal law. Those duties, including a duty to warn, are coextensive with the duties of a manufacturer acting in its capacity as a manufacturer. Congress has clearly occupied the field in this area and GARA bars claims based on a breach of a manufacturer's duty to warn, as those duties are described and defined by federal law and regulated by the FAA. Furthermore, GARA would expressly preempt any claim based on state tort law establishing a manufacturer's independent duty to warn. (GARA, Pub.L. No. 103-298, § 2(d), 108 Stat. 1552.) Thus, in order to survive summary judgment, plaintiffs must raise a triable factual issue that there was negligent conduct by Precision outside the scope of the duties imposed on it by federal law as the successor manufacturer of the product. In other words, plaintiffs must show that Precision was not acting "in its capacity as a manufacturer" when it committed the acts complained of here. Nothing in plaintiffs' factual showing indicates that Precision was acting outside the scope of its duties as the successor manufacturer.

The judgment is affirmed.

GRAY v. LOCKHEED AERONAUTICAL SYSTEMS COMPANY

125 F.3d 1371 (11th Cir. 1997),
vacated on other grounds, 524 U.S. 924 (1998)

HATCHETT, Chief Judge.

BACKGROUND

On October 7, 1989, appellees' decedents, Lt. Douglas G. Gray, Lt. John T. Hartman and Lt. (j.g.) David S. Jennings, were killed and Air Warfare Technician Second Class (AW2) Tracy Mann was injured when they ejected from a S-3 "Viking" jet aircraft (S-3) shortly before the aircraft crashed into the sea. Lockheed manufactured and sold the S-3 to the United States Navy in 1975.

In the 1960s, the Navy sought proposed designs for a new anti-submarine warfare aircraft (ASW) to neutralize the threat that submarines posed. Lockheed submitted its request for proposal, the Navy accepted, and the S-3 became the Navy's new ASW aircraft. Navy engineers and Lockheed employees worked closely together on many aspects of the S-3's development, and the Navy held a series of preliminary design reviews and critical design reviews. Upon completion of its manufacture, the S-3 passed all of the Navy's acceptance tests, and Lockheed delivered the S-3 to the Navy.

On the day of the crash, the decedents boarded a S-3 on the U.S.S. John F. Kennedy, which was located 125 miles off the coast of Virginia, as part of naval flight operations. Gray, the pilot of the S-3, sat in the left-front seat, and Hartman, the mission commander, sat in the right-front seat. Mann, the sensor operator and the only crash survivor, sat in the left-rear seat, and Jennings, the tactical coordinator, sat in the right-rear seat.

Prior to flying the S-3, Gray and other crewmembers properly conducted the required preflight checks. Gray verified that the S-3's control surfaces (i.e., the ailerons, spoilers, and elevators) worked properly. Gray executed a "control wipeout," which means he moved the pilot's control stick laterally and longitudinally through its range of motion. That maneuver allowed the aircrew and sailors on the JFK's deck to observe the movement of the control surfaces. After Gray properly configured the control surfaces for takeoff, the S-3 was catapulted from the deck of the carrier in order to give it sufficient speed to achieve flight.

With both engines at full power and sounding normal, the S-3's launch appeared normal; the S-3's wings were leveled and it began a shallow climb. After approximately two seconds, Gray initiated a slow right roll by moving the control stick to the left. Gray attempted to halt the roll when the S-3 reached 20 degrees of bank angle, the normal bank angle for clearing a turn. The S-3 failed to respond to Gray's movement of the control stick and continued the right roll. When the S-3 reached 45 degrees of bank angle, Mann heard Gray exclaim "Oh my God! Eject! Eject! Eject!" Hartman immediately initiated the sequence that would eject all four occupants from the S-3. Mann and Jennings, the two rear occupants, ejected first when the S-3 reached 90 degrees of right bank angle; and Gray and Hartman ejected when the S-3 was at or beyond 120 degrees of right bank angle. Their parachutes having scarce time to open, all three decedents struck the water with great force and suffered fatal bodily injuries upon impact with the water.

Appellees blame the S-3's crash in part on design defects in the S-3's aileron servo (the servo). Part of the S-3's flight control system, the servo is contained in the S-3's fuselage and it links the pilot with the ailerons. An aileron is "a movable part of an airplane wing or a movable airfoil external to the wing at the trailing edge for imparting a rolling motion and thus providing lateral control." Webster's New Collegiate Dictionary 24 (1979). On the S-3, a cable connects the pilot's control stick to the servo's input arm, and a rod from a ram mounted inside the servo passes through the S-3's wings and attaches to the ailerons.

The S-3 has two jet engines that drive separate hydraulic pumps. The two hydraulic pumps each power a hydraulic system, creating 3000 pounds per square inch (psi) of hydraulic pressure in each system. Ordinarily, the servo functions in the "powered" mode using hydraulic power. In this mode, the pilot has no mechanical link with the ailerons. Instead, the pilot's movement of the control stick triggers a sequence of functions causing hydraulic pressure in the servo to raise or lower the ailerons. If a hydraulic failure occurs, the servo should automatically switch to "manual" mode, a process known as the Emergency Flight Control System (EFCS). A latch and pin located inside the servo are key to the operation of the EFCS:

> When the hydraulic pressure in both systems drops below 800 psi, a shutoff valve at the bottom of the servo should "trip," cutting off all hydraulic pressure in the

> servo. The absence of hydraulic pressure in the servo allows the springs to expand; this expansion should move the pin into the latch, an event called "latch-up."

Gray v. Lockheed Aeronautical Systems Co., 880 F. Supp. 1559, at 1563 (N.D. Ga. 1995). Once EFCS latch-up occurs, the pilot has a direct mechanical link to the ailerons but has to use more effort to move the control stick.

Although Lockheed designed, manufactured, and sold the S-3 to the Navy, Lockheed sub-contracted the manufacturing of the S-3's servo to the Bertea Corporation (Bertea), which is now a subsidiary of the Parker-Hannifin Corporation. Bertea also developed the acceptance test procedure (ATP) for the servo. An ATP tests whether a product performs in accordance with its design specifications. The district court found that the ATP Bertea developed for the servo had several shortcomings. Although very important, the ATP did not measure the speed of the EFCS latch-up; nor did the ATP test the servo's operation while subjected to simulated flight demands.

In the spring of 1990, the Navy recovered the crashed S-3. Post-crash testing of the servo revealed some malfunctions and deviations from design specifications. First, Douglas Crawford, a Lockheed engineer, found when he "deviated from the ATP and moved the servo's input arm to stimulate commands from the control stick, the servo's shutoff valve tripped at 1400 psi, not the specified 800 psi." Gray, 880 F. Supp. at 1564. "The servo's shutoff valve 'sensed' 800 psi, even though the actual pressure was 1400 psi." Gray, 880 F. Supp. at 1564. Second, Crawford observed a chip on the pin involved in the EFCS latch-up process, and concluded "the chip showed the pin had been fluctuating in and out of the latch due to hydraulic pressure fluctuation in the servo." Gray, 880 F. Supp. at 1564. Third, although the specifications for the pin and latch both required a measurement of .3750, plus or minus .0001, the components here failed to meet that measurement; the pin measured .3749 but the latch measured .3740. Jesse Dooman, one of the appellees' expert witnesses, testified, and the district court found, "that the out-of-tolerance latch would adversely affect the speed of latch-up." Gray, 880 F. Supp. at 1564.

CONTENTIONS

Lockheed contends that the "military contractor defense" barred appellees' claim for the servo's alleged defective design. According to Lockheed, the district court misapplied the standards for application of the defense; acted unreasonably in requiring Lockheed to produce evidence that the Navy reviewed and approved specific engineering drawings of the servo; and incorrectly rejected as insufficient the narrative descriptions that Lockheed introduced of the servo. Lockheed maintains that the Navy exercised final responsibility for the S-3's entire design; closely reviewed and approved the design specifications of the servo; and found that the servo complied with its relevant specifications. Lockheed further contends that the district court erred in finding Lockheed strictly liable for a defectively designed servo. In Lockheed's estimation, the district court adopted a theory of causation that Navy experts specifically rejected; made insufficient findings; and failed to require appellees to prove a reasonable alternative design for the servo that would have prevented the accident. Lockheed argues that it cannot be held liable in negligence because it neither manufactured nor installed the replacement servo in the crashed S-3. The Navy, Lockheed also adds, approved the ATP for the servo.

The appellees contend that Lockheed did not satisfy the conditions for the military contractor defense. According to the appellees, Lockheed's bid to win the S-3 contract from the Navy had no detailed design specifications for the servo; Lockheed produced no detailed specifications of the servo; and the narrative specifications Lockheed did introduce were inadequate. The appellees also argue that Lockheed had final approval over the servo's design, and the Navy's post-contract review did not constitute approval of that design. Moreover, appellees contend that the Navy's continuing purchase of the servo provides no proof that the servo met reasonably precise specifications, and further contend that the servo did not conform to the Navy's general specifications.

Appellees additionally contend that the district court applied the correct theory of causation and found Lockheed strictly liable. Requiring a plaintiff to produce evidence of an alternative design, appellees argue, places an undue burden on a plaintiff, where the original product fails to function because of a design defect. Appellees assert the record contains abundant evidence of alternative designs for the servo. Appellees also contend that Lockheed's failure to ensure an adequate ATP for the servo constituted negligence. Appellees note that Lockheed produced no evidence that the Navy approved or controlled the ATP, and further observe that the only competent evidence showed that Lockheed and Bertea controlled the ATP.

The Military Contractor Defense

Appellees argue that a design defect in the servo, a part of the S-3's flight control system, caused the aircraft to crash. Although Lockheed denied liability, Lockheed invoked the military contractor defense for immunity. In Boyle v. United Technologies Corp., 487 U.S. 500, 108 S. Ct. 2510, 101 L. Ed. 2d 442 (1988), the Supreme Court held that, under certain circumstances, government contractors are shielded from state tort liability for equipment manufactured for our nation's military. This "defense derives from the principle that where a contractor acts under the authority and direction of the United States, it shares the sovereign immunity" that the government enjoys. Harduvel v. General Dynamics Corp., 878 F.2d 1311, 1316 (11th Cir.1989) (citation omitted), cert. denied, 494 U.S. 1030, 110 S. Ct. 1479, 108 L. Ed. 2d 615 (1990). The displacement of liability occurs "only where ... a 'significant conflict' exists between an identifiable 'federal policy or interest and the [operation] of state law'... or the application of state law would 'frustrate specific objectives' of federal legislation." Boyle, 487 U.S. at 507, 108 S. Ct. at 2516 (citation omitted). Stripped to its essentials, the military contractor defense is available only when the defendant demonstrates with respect to its design and manufacturing decisions that "the government made me do it." In re Joint Eastern and Southern District New York Asbestos Litigation, 897 F.2d 626, 632 (2d Cir.1990).

1. First Boyle condition

To establish the first Boyle condition, the contractor must prove that the military approved "reasonably precise specifications" for the equipment. This condition requires the existence of two factors: reasonably precise specifications and government approval of them. The Fifth Circuit in Trevino v. General Dynamics Corp., 865 F.2d 1474 (5th Cir.), cert. denied, 493 U.S. 935, 110 S. Ct. 327, 107 L. Ed. 2d 317 (1989), defined "reasonably precise specifications" as

> the requirement that the specification be precise means that the discretion over significant details and all critical design choices will be exercised by the government. If the government approved imprecise or general guidelines, then discretion over important design choices would be left to the government contractor.

865 F.2d at 1481. The contractor must show that the Navy "actually participated in discretionary design decisions, either by designing [the servo] itself or approving specifications" that the contractor prepared. Harduvel, 878 F.2d at 1316.

In reviewing the record, several considerations inform our analysis. Where the government merely approves imprecise or general guidelines, the contractor retains the discretion over the important design decision and enjoys no immunity against liability based on the Boyle defense. Trevino, 865 F.2d at 1481. A finding that the military approved the specifications requires more than a tacit approval: the approval must be meaningful, not a mere formality. Oliver v. Oshkosh Truck Corp., 96 F.3d 992 (7th Cir.1996), cert. denied, — U.S. —, 117 S. Ct. 1246, 137 L. Ed. 2d 328 (1997); Trevino, 865 F.2d at 1481 (approval involves more than a "rubber stamp"). In Harduvel, this court explained that a contractor may satisfy the first condition where the design of the product resulted from a "'continuous back and forth'" between the military and the contractor. Harduvel, 878 F.2d at 1320 (citation omitted).

After careful review of the record, we conclude that the district court did not err in ruling that Lockheed failed to satisfy the first Boyle condition. Lockheed presented no evidence that the Navy approved reasonably precise specifications for the servo. The district court requested a copy of the servo's engineering drawings, and Lockheed only produced a general narrative description of the servo's specifications entitled "Equipment Specifications—Power Servos, Primary Flight Controls." Lockheed had prepared this narrative before the Navy's procurement process for S-3 and incorporated it into its bid to the Navy for the S-3's contract. The document simply sets forth the general requirements for the aileron servo, i.e., automatic reversion if both hydraulic systems fail, and servos with manual reversion on ailerons. The Fourth Circuit explained in Kleemann v. McDonnell Douglas Corp., 890 F.2d 698 (4th Cir.1989), cert. denied, 495 U.S. 953, 110 S. Ct. 2219, 109 L. Ed. 2d 545 (1990), that military hardware does not suddenly spring into being from initial design and procurement specifications, but evolves through drawings, blueprints and mockups agreed upon by the parties. See Harduvel, 878 F.2d at 1320–21; Ramey, 874 F.2d 946 at 948 n.4–5. The ultimate design of the product is determined not only by the original procurement and contract specifications, but also by specific, quantitative engineering analysis developed during the actual production process. Kleemann, 890 F.2d at 702. We conclude that although the narrative may embody some aspects of the servo's specifications, it does not comprise the precise design specifications that the Boyle test requires. We also conclude that even though Lockheed sub-contracted the responsibility for manufacturing the servo to Bertea, Lockheed retained ultimate discretion over design and testing procedures for the servo.

2. Second Boyle condition

To demonstrate the second Boyle condition, a contractor must show that the equipment at issue conformed to precise, government-approved specifications. While the record lacks evidence of any reasonably precise specifications of the servo's design, this court assumes nonetheless that the Navy approved the narrative description that Lockheed alleges as the servo's specifications. In Harduvel, this court explained: "To say that a product failed to conform to specifications is just another way of saying that it was defectively manufactured." 878 F.2d at 1321. Non-conformance, however, means more than that the ultimate design feature does not achieve its intended goal. The alleged defect must exist independently of the design itself; it must result from a deviation from the required military specifications. See Kleemann, 890 F.2d at 703.

A contractor may show conformity through evidence that the military was "present and actively involved throughout the design, review, development and testing of the [equipment at issue]." In re Air Disaster at Ramstein Air Base, Germany on 8/29/90, 81 F.3d 570, 575 (5th Cir.), amended on denial of reh'g, 88 F.3d 340 (5th Cir.), cert. denied, — U.S. —, 117 S. Ct. 583, 136 L. Ed. 2d 513 (1996). In Kleemann, the Fourth Circuit expounded "where the procurement process involves this kind of continuous exchange between the contractor and the government, the process itself becomes persuasive evidence of the product conformity to precise specifications." 890 F.2d at 702. Additionally, such evidence tends to show that the government retained discretion and the contractor had no freedom to deviate from the government's specifications. Trevino, 865 F.2d at 1481.

Even if this court relies on the narrative description as a specification, the record does not support Lockheed's contention that it satisfied the second Boyle condition. The basic design of the servo called for an automatic manual reversion system or EFCS that operated without a hazardous lag. In the event of a hydraulic failure, the EFCS causes the flight controls to instantly revert to a manual operation mode enabling the pilot to control and safely land the aircraft. The servo at issue did not meet those specifications. The district court found that chattering in the servo demonstrated that it suffered from a hazardous lag and that the pilot's control stick had to be within 60 percent of its centered position in order for the EFCS latch-up mechanism to occur. Gray, 880 F. Supp. at 1567. Those defective and unspecified conditions affected the operation of the automatic manual reversion system.

Additional evidence showed defects in two key components that the servo uses when it goes into the manual reversion mode. The pin and latch which link the pilot's control stick with the ailerons did not meet their specified dimensions of .3750, plus or minus .0001; the pin measured .3749 but the latch measured .3740. The district court found that the out-of-tolerance latch could adversely affect the speed of the latch-up; and that "friction in the EFCS mechanism and a mis-sized latch impeded the servo's ability to transition swiftly into EFCS." Gray, 880 F. Supp. at 1566. Moreover, the shutoff valve in the servo operated at a higher-than-specified pressure; the servo attempted transition into the EFCS at 1400 psi, instead of the specified 800 psi.

3. Third Boyle condition

A contractor may satisfy the third Boyle condition through evidence that it warned the government of all the dangers known to it, but not to the government. Having denied the Boyle defense on the first two conditions, the district court did not address the third condition. We nonetheless consider this element and conclude that Lockheed failed to warn the Navy and to ascertain the nature of the flight control problems.

The operations manual that Lockheed prepared for the S-3 does not warn pilots about how critical the positioning of the control stick is to effect an emergency latch-up. Without that information, Gray did not realize that the control stick had to be within 60 degrees of the centered position for the EFCS mechanism to occur. Lockheed should have explained that under certain circumstances, the pilot must act affirmatively [by] moving the control stick within 60 degrees of its centered position to engage the automatic manual reversion system. Furthermore, the Navy's involvement in the development of the S-3 does not satisfy the threshold showing of adequate warning for that aircraft's servo. See Kleemann, 890 F.2d at 701.

[The remainder of the court's opinion is omitted.]

BAHSOON v. PEZETEL, LTD.

768 F. Supp. 507 (E.D.N.C. 1991)

DUPREE, District Judge.

Plaintiffs filed this products liability action against defendants seeking damages for the alleged wrongful deaths of Khadige Bahsoon and Helene M. Houayek, who died following a helicopter accident which occurred in Sierra Leone, West Africa. Plaintiff Hisham Bahsoon also sues as the natural guardian of Ghina Bahsoon, a passenger on the same helicopter flight who survived, but was allegedly injured as a result of the accident. The action is now before the court upon defendants' motions to dismiss pursuant to: (1) F.R.Civ.P. 12(b)(1) for lack of subject matter jurisdiction; (2) F.R.Civ.P. 12(b)(2) for lack of personal jurisdiction; and (3) the common law doctrine of forum non conveniens. Defendants have also moved for summary judgment on jurisdictional grounds.

I. FACTS

On or around September 18, 1988, a Kania-SP-SAC helicopter departed from the Freetown Airport in Sierra Leone, West Africa carrying the pilot and seven passengers. Shortly after its take-off, the helicopter crashed into the Sierra Leone River where two of the passengers, Khadige Bahsoon and Helene Houayek, died before rescuers arrived. The others on board survived, although one, Ghina Bahsoon, was seriously injured.

All plaintiffs, as well as those persons whose interests they represent, are citizens of Sierra Leone. The named plaintiffs were appointed as executors of the estates of the two decedents by the High Court of Sierra Leone. The defendants are Pezetel, Ltd. (Pezetel), PZL-Swidnik (PZL), and Melex USA, Inc. (Melex). Pezetel and PZL are agencies of the Polish government and are corporations organized under the laws of Poland. Melex is a corporation organized under the laws of the state of Delaware and whose offices are located in Raleigh, North Carolina. Melex is owned in part by defendant Pezetel. Plaintiffs seek recovery based upon theories of negligence, strict liability and breach of warranty.

Pezetel and PZL are engaged in the manufacture and trade of helicopters, including the Kania-SP-SAC which was involved in the accident in Sierra Leone. Melex, although partially owned by Pezetel, is a separate corporate entity. Melex is listed in the 1990 World Aviation Directory as a marketing agent for the PZL-M1-2 helicopter as well as other products of PZL.

Both Pezetel and PZL are wholly owned by the Polish government. The Kania helicopter involved in the accident here was manufactured in 1979. Sometime thereafter, it was leased by the Polish government to Provincial Air Services, Ltd. in Sierra Leone. The only evidence now before the court of connections between these two defendants and the United States is as follows: (1) Pezetel and PZL at one time sold golf carts in the United States; (2) Pezetel and PZL are listed in the 1990 World Aviation Directory as companies which sell and lease helicopters; (3) the engine in the helicopter that crashed was manufactured by Allison Gas Turbine Operations, a General Motors Corporation subsidiary, which is situated in Indianapolis, Indiana; (4) Pezetel owns stock in Melex and Melex markets some models of the Kania helicopter; and (5) the Canadian Aviation Safety Board has stated in an unauthenticated accident report that the helicopter involved in the accident was required to conform to United States Federal Aviation Regulations.

All parties appear to agree that the helicopter which crashed in Sierra Leone in 1988 was manufactured by Pezetel and/or PZL. Plaintiffs contend that as a distributor, Melex is liable in products liability the same as a manufacturer. In support of their current motions to dismiss, defendants have submitted the affidavit of Sylwester Pieckowski, the secretary of Melex USA, Inc. He states that Melex is a corporate entity distinct from both Pezetel and PZL. He further testifies that Melex had no contact with the Kania helicopter that was involved in the Sierra Leone crash and did not do business with the Sierra Leone entity that leased the helicopter from the Polish government. Pieckowski also states that the type of helicopter that was involved in the accident is not sold or distributed by Melex in the United States and that Melex has never had any connection with the pilot or passengers.

II. ANALYSIS

Defendants claim that they are entitled to immunity under the Foreign Sovereign Immunities Act (FSIA), 28 U.S.C. §§1602–1611, and therefore the court lacks subject matter jurisdiction to hear the claim. See, e.g., Canadian Overseas Ores Limited v. Compania de Acero del Pacifico S.A., 727 F.2d 274 (2d Cir. 1984) (foreign sovereign immunity is a question of subject matter jurisdiction). Because the court must have subject matter jurisdiction in order to rule on the other pending motions, that question will be addressed first.

The FSIA "establishes comprehensive and exclusive standards to be used in resolving questions of sovereign immunity raised by foreign states in either federal or state court in the United States." Williams v. Shipping Corporation of India, 653 F.2d 875, 878 (4th Cir. 1981). 28 U.S.C. §1604 states:

> Subject to existing international agreements to which the United States is a party at the time of enactment of this Act a foreign state shall be immune from jurisdiction of the courts of the United States and of the States except as provided in sections 1605 to 1607 of this chapter.

Immunity is thus the general rule and must be adhered to by the court unless it is clearly shown that an exception applies. Gibbons v. Republic of Ireland, 532 F. Supp. 668 (D.D.C. 1982).

The exceptions to the FSIA are set forth in 28 U.S.C. §1605. Subsection (a)(2) of that provision states that immunity will not be available in cases:

> in which the action is based upon a commercial activity carried on in the United States by the foreign state; or upon an act performed in the United States in connection with a commercial activity of the foreign state elsewhere; or upon an act outside the territory of the United States in connection with a commercial activity of the foreign state elsewhere and that act causes a direct effect in the United States.

28 U.S.C. §1605 (a)(2).

The term "commercial activity" is defined as "either a regular course of commercial conduct or a particular commercial transaction or act." Id. at §1603(d). Immunity extends to both foreign states and their instrumentalities. See, e.g., Carey v. National Oil Corporation, 592 F.2d 673 (2d Cir. 1979) (corporation wholly owned by the Libyan government held to be a foreign state within the [meaning of the] FSIA). However, a corporation which is a citizen of a state of the United States cannot be a foreign instrumentality entitled to immunity. 28 U.S.C. § 1603(b)(3).

The terms of 28 U.S.C. § 1605(a)(2) set forth three distinct circumstances under which a foreign sovereign's commercial activities can result in a forfeiture of immunity. First, the action can be related to commercial activity actually carried on in the United States by the foreign sovereign. Second, the suit may relate to an act performed in the United States by the foreign sovereign which is related to commercial activity carried on elsewhere. Third, the action may be based upon a commercial activity performed elsewhere, but which has an effect in the United States. Here, plaintiffs claim that the action is based upon commercial activity carried on by the foreign sovereign in the United States and therefore the first clause applies. Plaintiffs' position is that Pezetel and PZL have continuously carried on various business activities in the United States, particularly through Melex, which activates the application of this exception and precludes them from invoking the immunity defense in the current action.

"The [FSIA] clearly contemplates a direct connection between the injury suffered and the contacts with the United States." Tigchon v. Island of Jamaica, 591 F. Supp. 765, 768 (W.D. Mich. 1984). Under the exception set forth in the first clause of Section 1605(a)(2), the foreign sovereign must engage in some type of commercial activity in the United States and there must be some nexus between that activity and the lawsuit which the plaintiff asks the United States court to entertain. See also Compania Mexicana de Aviacion, S.A. v. United States District Court for the Central District of California, 859 F.2d 1354 (9th Cir. 1988); Vencedora Oceanica Navigacion, S.A. v. Compagnie Nationale Algerienne de Navigation, 730 F.2d 195 (5th Cir. 1984); Sugarman v. Aeromexico, Inc., 626 F.2d 270 (3d Cir. 1980). An examination of cases involving the application of this provision to similar facts proves instructive.

In Compania Mexicana de Aviacion, S.A. v. United States District Court for the Central District of California, supra, all of the passengers on board an airplane owned by the Mexican government were killed in a crash which occurred in Mexico. An action was filed in the United States against the airline on behalf of sixty-nine Mexican decedents. Plaintiffs argued, inter alia, that the first clause of the commercial activity exception precluded immunity because the airplane had been serviced in Chicago on the day before the crash during a stopover on its way to Los Angeles. Plaintiffs contended that this constituted commercial activity in the United States which was sufficient to preclude immunity.

The Ninth Circuit disagreed and held that the "FSIA requires that there be a significant 'nexus' between the cause of action and the 'commercial activity' carried on in the United States." Id. at 1360. The fact that the airplane had been serviced in Chicago on the day before the crash was not enough. The court stated that to subject all government-owned carriers who make stops in the United States to the jurisdiction of our courts on that basis alone would be incompatible with both the FSIA and the Warsaw Convention. The defendant had performed no act in the United States in connection with the action before the court and therefore was entitled to sovereign immunity.

In Vencedora Oceanica Navigacion v. Compagnie Nationale Algerienne de Navigation, supra, the plaintiff, a Panamanian company, sued the defendant, an instrumentality of the Algerian government, in the Southern District of Texas seeking to recover for the loss of its vessel which occurred somewhere between Egypt and Spain. Plaintiff alleged that jurisdiction existed because defendant did continuing business in the United

States. The court held that simply doing business in the United States was insufficient to bring a defendant within the parameters of 28 U.S.C. § 1605(a)(2) in situations where the cause of action before the court has no connection with that business. To hold otherwise would "open the floodgates to any controversy around the world, against any foreign entity 'doing business' in the United States." Id. at 202. An "unprecedented assertion of jurisdiction" such as this could not have been the intent of Congress in passing the Foreign Sovereign Immunities Act. Id. The purpose of the Act is to allow the assertion of jurisdiction only over litigation which has some connection with the United States.

Melex is a company based in Raleigh, North Carolina and incorporated under the laws of Delaware. As such, it is a citizen of both North Carolina and Delaware and therefore not entitled to immunity under the FSIA. See 28 U.S.C. § 1332(c)(1) ("a corporation shall be deemed to be a citizen of any State by which it has been incorporated and of the State where it has its principal place of business").

Pezetel and PZL are, however, corporations owned entirely by the Polish government and organized under the laws of Poland. Consequently, they are both presumptively immune from suit in this court. Plaintiffs argue that because Pezetel and PZL do business in the United States and operate in this country through Melex, this action falls within the exception set forth in the first clause of 28 U.S.C. § 1605(a)(2). For the reasons set forth below, the court disagrees and holds that Pezetel and PZL, as instrumentalities of the government of Poland, are entitled to sovereign immunity.

First, Melex has presented sworn testimony stating that it had no connection whatever with the helicopter involved in this accident. Although it does market products for Pezetel and PZL in the United States, it states that those marketing efforts do not include the product involved in the accident in Sierra Leone. The only contrary evidence that plaintiffs have presented is that Melex was listed in a 1990 trade journal as a marketing agent for the "M1-2 helicopter." See Exhibit 1 to Affidavit of Paul Edelman. This alone does not suffice to supply the required nexus.

Second, merely doing business in the United States is insufficient to trigger the provisions of Section 1605(a)(2). The cause of action must be related to that business. Therefore, even assuming that Melex did market the same product that was involved in the accident at the same time that the accident occurred, that would also be insufficient to subject Pezetel and PZL to the jurisdiction of the United States courts absent some evidence that Melex had some connection with the helicopter involved in the accident in Sierra Leone. That particular helicopter was rented by the Polish government to a company in Sierra Leone and there is no evidence connecting Melex with its manufacture, sale or distribution.

Third, the fact that Pezetel and PZL advertise in international trade magazines is inconsequential absent some evidence that this activity is in some way related to the current cause of action. The court fails to see any connection between this 1990 trade journal advertisement and the 1988 helicopter crash of a 1979 model helicopter in Sierra Leone.

Fourth, simply using an American component in a product does not automatically subject a foreign manufacturer to the jurisdiction of the American courts. Therefore, plaintiffs' argument that the requisite jurisdictional connection is established by the fact that the helicopter engine was manufactured in the United States is likewise flawed. It is also difficult to see how Allison Gas Turbine Operations, the alleged engine manufacturer, could have such a close nexus to this action as to preclude immunity for Pezetel and PZL when it has not even been named as a defendant.

The named plaintiffs, as well as the real parties in interest to this lawsuit, are all residents of Sierra Leone. The two passengers who allegedly died as a result of the accident were also from that country. Pezetel and PZL are instrumentalities of the Polish government. There is simply no aspect of this case involving the United States of America in any way. There is consequently no nexus between the commercial activities carried on by Pezetel and PZL in the United States and plaintiffs' claims. As stated above, the commercial activity which plaintiffs rely upon to assert jurisdiction must be the same commercial activity upon which the lawsuit is based. Here, it is not, and all claims against Pezetel and PZL are dismissed for lack of subject matter jurisdiction.

Melex is thus the only named defendant that remains a party to this lawsuit. As a United States citizen, it is not entitled to immunity as a foreign sovereign under the FSIA. Additionally, 28 U.S.C. § 1332 provides that the United States federal courts "shall have original jurisdiction of all civil actions where the matter in controversy exceeds ... $50,000 ... and is between ... (2) citizens of a State and citizens or subjects of a foreign state...." Because there is diversity of citizenship and the amount in controversy exceeds the jurisdictional minimum, this court has subject matter jurisdiction over plaintiffs' claims against defendant Melex. [T]he court expresses no opinion on the issue of the liability, if any, of Melex at this time.

Notes

1. As the *Cleveland* case makes clear, deciding whether a particular claim or cause of action is preempted by federal law is a difficult and time-consuming task. Yet as has been pointed out elsewhere, courts are increasingly being called upon to make such determinations:

> No issue in modern products liability law is more important, or more inscrutable, than the doctrine of federal preemption. The doctrine is important because the defense of federal preemption in recent years has grown from little more than a blip on the radar screen to one of the most powerful defenses in all of products liability law. The doctrine is inscrutable because it is a formless and elusive creature, based on ephemeral notions of federalism and the oft-obscure intent of Congress, that vacillate according to shifting political sentiments—on federal versus states rights, on Congress versus the courts, and on regulatory versus products liability law. Despite the best efforts of courts and commentators to bring order to the chaos, the law on federal preemption has obstinately refused to set anchor in enduring principles. Instead, it continues to wallow in a state of utter chaos.
>
> In general, federal courts are more willing than state courts to find preemption. State courts normally are more focused on protecting the right to compensation of their citizens harmed by the unlawful behavior of others (a right often protected by state constitutions), whereas federal courts of limited jurisdiction generally are more concerned about the doctrine of federal supremacy.

David G. Owen, *Federal Preemption of Products Liability Claims*, 55 S.C. L. Rev. 411, 412–14 (2003).

2. Despite its status as the leading aviation case rejecting the defense of federal preemption, *Cleveland* remains controversial and commentators continue to be divided over the issue. For a useful canvassing of the pros and cons, *see* Sean S. Kelly, Comment, *Federalism in Flight: Preemption Doctrine and Air Crash Litigation*, 28 Transp. L.J. 107

(2000). As the writer explains, "The Supreme Court must grant certiorari if the issue is to resolve. Until the Supreme Court rules, preemption itself will remain a patchwork of state authority. The preemption issue will not fly away on its own, and only Supreme Court action can bring the Circuit Courts back into formation." *Id.* at 146.

3. Should Ray Houston's "as is, where is" defense have prevailed in the *Godwin* case? Given that it did not, what protection, if any, does a seller get from such language? *See further* E.T. Tsai, Annotation, *Construction and Effect of Affirmative Provision in Contract of Sale By Which Purchaser Agrees to Take Article "As Is," in the Condition in Which It Is, or Equivalent Term*, 24 A.L.R.3d 465 (1969 & 2005 Supp.); Jeffrey A. Grebe, *What Is "As Is" in Florida?*, 30 Stetson L. Rev. 875 (2001); Janet L. Richards, *"As Is" Provisions—What Do They Really Mean?*, 41 Ala. L. Rev. 435 (1990).

It should be pointed out that auctions have long been used to buy and sell airplanes, although nowadays many purchasers head straight to such internet sites as www.airplanemart.com, www.avbuyer.com, www.findaircraft.com, and www.globalplanesearch.com.

4. GARA's statute of repose, although seemingly straightforward, has led to a spate of litigation. Several years after deciding *Burroughs*, for example, the California Court of Appeal returned to the issue in *Hiser v. Bell Helicopter Textron Inc.*, 4 Cal. Rptr. 3d 249 (Ct. App. 2003), a case involving a fatal helicopter crash. After extended consideration, the court held that the 18-year period of repose must be applied separately to each individual part:

> At issue is the interpretation and application of the "rolling" statute of repose found in section 2(a)(2). Defendant contends a new 18-year limitation period begins to run only with respect to the specific new part shown to be a cause of the accident. Thus, according to defendant, "[p]laintiff had to prove that the cause of the crash was a defect in one of the pieces in the [1982] retrofit kit."
>
> Plaintiff, on the other hand, contends the installation of the 1982 retrofit kit created an entirely new fuel transfer system, thereby commencing a new 18-year limitation period with respect to defects in any element or component of the reconfigured system. Plaintiff's argument is not without some appeal. After all, plaintiff's principal legal theory was strict products liability based on a design defect, and she argued, in part, the fuel transfer system as a whole was defectively designed when the 1982 retrofit kit was installed.
>
> [W]e conclude there is no room to argue that replacement of a few parts of a larger system starts the rolling limitation period anew for all parts in the larger system. Under this circumstance, the larger system has not been replaced in its entirety as a unit, and for those parts, components, or sub-assemblies that have not been replaced, a new limitation period does not commence.
>
> Had Congress wished to draft GARA to cover the circumstances urged by plaintiff, it could easily have written the rolling statute of repose to commence anew whenever a component, system, sub-assembly, or other part is replaced or modified, provided that the replaced or modified component, system, sub-assembly, or other part caused the alleged damage. [W]e reject plaintiff's suggested interpretation of GARA in favor of the interpretation that we conclude flows more naturally from the actual language chosen by Congress.

Id. at 256–57. For similar cases, *see Estate of Kennedy v. Bell Helicopter Textron, Inc.*, 283 F.3d 1107 (9th Cir. 2002) (statute of repose began running when helicopter was initially delivered to the Navy, not several years later when it was sold as military surplus and certified as a general aviation aircraft); *Caldwell v. Enstron Helicopter Corp.*, 230 F.3d 1155 (9th Cir. 2000) (revised flight manual constituted new helicopter "part" for GARA purposes); Kristine Cordier Karnezis, Annotation, *Construction and Application of General Aviation Revitalization Act*, 189 A.L.R. Fed. 257 (2003 & 2004 Supp.).

5. As *Burroughs* explains, § 2(b) of GARA provides an exception to the period of repose where

> [t]he claimant pleads with specificity the facts necessary to prove, and proves, that the manufacturer with respect to a type certificate for, or obligations with respect to continuing airworthiness of, an aircraft or a component, system, subassembly, or other part of an aircraft[,] knowingly misrepresented to the Federal Aviation Administration, or concealed or withheld from the Federal Aviation Administration, required information that is material and relevant to the performance or the maintenance or operation of such aircraft, or the component, system, subassembly, or other part, that is causally related to the harm which the claimant allegedly suffered[.]

49 U.S.C. § 40101 note § 2(b)(1). For a case in which the plaintiff was able to offer detailed proof that the manufacturer had withheld important design information for decades, *see Robinson v. Hartzell Propeller Inc.*, 326 F. Supp. 2d 631 (E.D. Pa. 2004).

6. While GARA has helped to revitalize the general aviation industry, many observers have criticized its statute of repose as overly generous:

> There are several arguments against GARA. For example, if a manufacturer of an aircraft is only liable for its product for eighteen years, why is it acceptable to hold businesses that manufactured and used asbestos products liable for fifty-plus years after the contact with the substance actually occurred? Many individuals feel that this is a real double standard—one that was engineered by lobbyists for the general aviation industry. Others ask whether there is a real difference between the latency of a disease caused by inhaling asbestos and the latency of an improperly engineered component in an aircraft that malfunctions after twenty years of operation. Despite the positive effects GARA has spurred, these effects may come at the expense of bad policy. The Act even arguably violates individual constitutional rights. [And] why was eighteen years chosen as the period of limitations? Why not ten, fifteen, or even twenty years? This choice seems arbitrary to many observers.

Chad Key, Comment, *General Aviation in the New Millennium: Promising Rebirth—or Imminent Extinction?*, 66 J. Air L. & Com. 789, 812 (2001). *See also* James F. Rodriguez, Note, *Tort Reform & GARA: Is Repose Incompatible With Safety?*, 47 Ariz. L. Rev. 577 (2005).

7. Where GARA is unavailable, aircraft manufacturers sometimes are able to use a state statute of repose. *See, e.g.*, *Butchkosky v. Enstrom Helicopter Corp.*, 855 F. Supp. 1251 (S.D. Fla. 1993) (dismissing case based on Florida's 12-year statute of repose). For a further discussion, *see* Jay M. Zitter, Annotation, *Validity and Construction of Statute Terminating Right of Action for Product-Caused Injury at Fixed Period After Manufacture, Sale, or Delivery of Product*, 30 A.L.R.5th 1 (1995 & 2005 Supp.). For an interesting case in which a state statute of repose was struck down as being an unconstitutional restriction on the plaintiff's access to the court system, *see Berry v. Beech Aircraft Corp.*, 717 P.2d 670 (Utah 1985).

8. In addition to GARA's statute of repose, the court in *Burroughs* also considered, and rejected, the plaintiffs' claim that the defendant had an independent duty to warn, in part because it could find no previous aviation cases that had imposed such a duty. Was this a sound decision? *See further* David J. Marchitelli, Annotation, *Liability of Successor Corporation for Injury or Damage Caused by Product Issued by Predecessor, Based on Successor's Independent Duty to Warn Third Party of Danger or Defect*, 92 A.L.R.5th 227 (2001 & 2004 Supp.).

9. Although the court in *Gray* turned away Lockheed's government contractor defense, the *Boyle* defense (as it also is called) has been successfully used by scores of aircraft manufacturers:

> [The defense] has become a versatile shield against liability employed by government contractors defending a wide range of tort lawsuits. Federal courts, otherwise faced with increasingly crowded dockets, have readily applied the Boyle defense in dismissing large numbers of tort-based lawsuits at the summary judgment stage. The Boyle defense has become a major impediment to the plaintiff's bar in the field of aviation litigation, and lawyers have expended serious efforts attempting to punch a hole through this legal shield recently brandished with impunity by manufacturing defendants.
>
> Although the Boyle defense may seem harsh in operation to those unfamiliar with the government procurement system, the rationale articulated by Justice Scalia is sound, correct, and pragmatic. As Justice Powell, who was then sitting on the Eleventh Circuit, stated so elegantly [in Harduvel v. General Dynamics Corp., 878 F.2d 1311, 1322 (11th Cir. 1989)]: "With respect to consumer goods, state tort law may hold manufacturers liable where [the] balance [between safety concerns and cost and performance] is found unreasonable. In the sensitive area of federal military procurement, however, the balance is not one for state tort law to strike. Although the defense may sometimes seem harsh in its operation, it is a necessary consequence of the incompatibility of modern products liability law and the exigencies of national defense."

Colin P. Cahoon, *Boyle Under Siege*, 59 J. Air L. & Com. 815, 816, 866 (1994). Do you agree with Justice Powell's conclusion? For a further discussion, *see* Brian Sheppard, Annotation, *The Government-Contractor Defense to State Products-Liability Claims*, 53 A.L.R.5th 535 (1997 & 2004 Supp.).

10. In addition to the government contractor defense, plaintiffs who seek to sue for injuries sustained on military aircraft face a second problem. In *Machin v. Zuckert*, 316 F.2d 336 (D.C. Cir.), *cert. denied*, 375 U.S. 896 (1963), it was held that accident reports prepared by the armed forces for the purpose of preventing future mishaps are privileged. In *United States v. Weber Aircraft Corp.*, 465 U.S. 792 (1984), the Supreme Court approved this rule despite the intervening passage of the Freedom of Information Act. *See further* Nicole Wolfe Stout, *Privileges and Immunities Available for Self-Critical Analysis and Reporting: Legal, Practical and Ethical Considerations*, 69 J. Air L. & Com. 561, 598–601 (2004) (explaining that following an accident, the responsible service branch prepares two reports—dubbed "collateral" and "safety"—of which only the former is available to the public).

The *Machin* privilege has been the subject of much criticism. As one set of commentators has complained:

> Servicemen and women whose flight safety the military seeks to protect would undoubtedly be dismayed to learn that the so-called safety program al-

> lows contractors to sell defective products with impunity. While professing to have the future flight safety of military personnel at heart, the military services would do well to remember that product liability litigation has itself been integral to the development of safer products. Concealing the sole reliable account of a disaster under a shroud of executive privilege does not further, but vitiates, the government's professed interest, while assigning liability for the design and manufacture of defective products would further flight safety.

James T. Crouse & Roberta J. Sharpe, *The Fourth Horseman Rears Its Ugly Head: The Machin Privilege Threatens Doom to Service Members' Product Liability Claims* (unpublished paper presented at the 27th Annual SMU Air Law Symposium) (Feb. 1993).

11. Because of its inartful drafting, the FSIA can prove tricky (as *Bahsoon* illustrates). At its heart, however, the statute is really quite simple: foreign governments and their instrumentalities cannot be sued in either federal or state court unless they expressly waive their immunity or engage in commercial activity in the United States that injures the plaintiff. Foreign commercial activity also qualifies if it produces a "direct effect" in the United States.

In *Dole Food Company v. Patrickson*, 538 U.S. 468 (2003), a non-aviation case, the Supreme Court made it significantly more difficult for foreign companies to invoke the FSIA by requiring that they be directly owned by their governments. Because many foreign aviation entities are only indirectly owned by their governments (using so-called "tiered" or "pooled" corporate structures), it is probable that the number of aviation cases dismissed on FSIA grounds will decrease in the future:

> Following the Dole decision, a number of significant aviation entities that are indirectly owned by foreign states will no longer be protected by foreign sovereign status when they are sued in United States courts. Case law indicates that South African Airways and Aerolineas Argentinas, for example, are, or have been, indirectly owned by their respective governments through a tiered ownership structure. Foreign state owned manufacturers such as Avions de Transport Regional, G.I.E., Airbus, and Augusta S.P.A., also have, or have had, tiered ownership structures. In addition, since much FSIA case law has, until now, simply stated that an entity is an agency or instrumentality without giving information about that entity's ownership structure, it is quite possible that many foreign government controlled aviation entities also have tiered ownership structures which are not apparent in the case law.

Allan H. Collier, *The Foreign Sovereign Immunities Act and Its Impact on Aviation Litigation*, 69 J. Air L. & Com. 519, 539 (2004). For a further discussion, *see Wong ex rel. Leung Yuen Man v. Boeing Co.*, 2003 WL 22078379 (N.D. Ill. 2003) (dismissing, due to *Dole*, the FSIA claim of China Airlines because it was only indirectly owned by the Chinese government).

Problem 9

Following the conclusion of certain military expeditions, the federal government found itself with a surplus of aviation equipment. To rectify the situation, officials arranged for bulk sales to private companies, who then resold individual parts to the general public. Many years later, a group of citizens sued the government, claiming that some of the items had been fashioned from hazardous materials and had caused them to develop cancer. If the government moves to have the case dismissed based on the "discretionary function exception" of the Federal Tort Claims Act, 28 U.S.C. §2680(a), how should the court rule? *See Johnston v. United States*, 597 F. Supp. 374 (D. Kan. 1984).

F. VENUE AND CHOICE OF LAW

LACEY v. CESSNA AIRCRAFT COMPANY

932 F.2d 170 (3d Cir. 1991)

BECKER, Circuit Judge.

This appeal requires us to revisit the doctrine of forum non conveniens and to explore again the impact of Piper Aircraft Co. v. Reyno, 454 U.S. 235, 70 L. Ed. 2d 419, 102 S. Ct. 252 (1981), on that doctrine. The setting is the marathon struggle of Graeme MacArthur Lacey, an Australian citizen who suffered severe burns as a result of a plane crash in British Columbia, to litigate his products liability action in the Western District of Pennsylvania. Lacey's antagonists are Cessna Aircraft Company ("Cessna"), the manufacturer of the aircraft; Teledyne, Inc. ("Teledyne"), the manufacturer of the aircraft's engines; and Hanlon & Wilson Company ("Hanlon & Wilson"), the manufacturer of the aircraft's exhaust system. These defendants insist that Lacey's action cannot proceed fairly in the Western District of Pennsylvania, and that instead it should be litigated in British Columbia.

The district court, accepting defendants' arguments, dismissed Lacey's suit on forum non conveniens grounds. We reversed, holding, inter alia, that the defendants had not submitted sufficient evidence to facilitate proper forum non conveniens analysis, and that the district court had not adequately considered the relevant private and public interest factors outlined in Gulf Oil Corp. v. Gilbert, 330 U.S. 501, 91 L. Ed. 1055, 67 S. Ct. 839 (1947), and in Piper. [See] Lacey v. Cessna Aircraft Co., 862 F.2d 38, 49 (3d Cir. 1988).

On remand, the district court again dismissed Lacey's suit, conditioning its dismissal on the fulfillment of several requirements, most notably on the defendants' agreement to "make available to plaintiff in British Columbia, for discovery and trial, all relevant witnesses and documents within defendants' control." Lacey v. Cessna Aircraft Co., 736 F. Supp. 662, 669 (W.D. Pa. 1990). The district court, in response to our earlier reversal, accorded specific deference to Lacey's forum choice and analyzed seriatim the private and public interest factors. In so doing, the court concluded that the relevant factors preponderate strongly in favor of proceeding in British Columbia. This appeal followed.

Lacey challenges the court's second forum non conveniens dismissal on numerous grounds. Positing that there is a special obligation on defendants to proceed expeditiously with forum non conveniens motions, Lacey attacks as an abuse of discretion the court's decision to admit certain untimely materials, particularly Hanlon & Wilson's "statement of position." Absent this submission, Lacey claims, defendants' forum non conveniens motions would have failed as a matter of law. Additionally, Lacey insists that the district court's forum non conveniens analysis is flawed because the court failed: (1) to indicate with the requisite precision the amount of deference due plaintiff's forum choice; (2) to "entangle" itself sufficiently in the facts of the case; and (3) to analyze adequately and correctly the relevant private and public interest factors.

With respect to this latter point, Lacey places particular emphasis on the court's assessment of three factors, namely, relative ease of access to sources of proof, application of foreign law, and relative advantages and obstacles to a fair trial. He argues that the district court's treatment of these factors was in error because it incorrectly: (1) assumed that the evidence essential to plaintiff's products liability claim is in defendants' control; (2) concluded that plaintiff would be able to discover in British Columbia evidence in the possession of non-parties in the United States; (3) determined that British Columbia law would apply if this case were to proceed in the Western District of Pennsylvania; and (4) assigned dispositive weight to the possibility of joining all potentially culpable parties in British Columbia.

Many of Lacey's challenges fall well short of the mark. In particular, we think that the district court: (1) acted within its discretion in accepting Hanlon & Wilson's untimely submission; (2) accorded adequate weight to plaintiff's forum choice; and (3) immersed itself sufficiently in the facts of the case. Furthermore, we are mindful that the district court's forum non conveniens determination may be reversed only if there has been a clear abuse of discretion. If the district court has considered and balanced reasonably all of the relevant private and public interest factors, we must affirm. Piper, 454 U.S. at 257. Despite our deferential standard of review, we believe, regretfully, that Lacey has identified a serious shortcoming in the district court's analysis that requires yet another remand.

At this stage of the litigation, the crux of Lacey's complaint is that a defect in the aircraft's exhaust system, which allegedly was manufactured by Hanlon & Wilson in Pennsylvania, caused the crash. That theory is supported by the final report of the Canadian Aviation Safety Board ("CASB"). In May of 1985, however, Hanlon & Wilson sold its aircraft exhaust system business to an Oklahoma corporation and transferred to that company all of the documents pertaining thereto. As a result, and contrary to the assumption on which the district court's order overtly depends, Hanlon & Wilson now represents that no documents relating to or personnel familiar with the company's prior aircraft exhaust business are under its control. Lacey therefore contends that the court's order requiring defendants to produce in British Columbia all relevant witnesses and documents in their custody is inadequate to ensure his access to sources of proof. We agree. Lacey also submits that this problem is exacerbated by his inability to discover in British Columbia, or, still more important, ultimately obtain, evidence within the control of non-parties in the United States. We think that this submission has force as well.

In dismissing Lacey's action, the district court did not consider the impediments that Lacey might face in gaining access to sources of proof in British Columbia, impediments that potentially rob British Columbia of its practical value as a forum. In view of this error, as well as other subsidiary points discussed below, we are unable to defer to the district court's conclusion "that the public and private interests both preponderate strongly in favor of dismissal." 736 F. Supp. at 669. Rather, we think that an order which dismisses a suit on forum non conveniens grounds without taking into account a critical limitation on the plaintiff's ability to prosecute his or her action in the alternative forum constitutes an abuse of discretion. We therefore will reverse the district court's dismissal of Lacey's suit and remand the case with instructions to determine whether Lacey would have access in British Columbia to witnesses and documents essential to his products liability action. If Lacey would not have access to essential evidence at trial in British Columbia, we believe that the court must deny defendants' motions to dismiss. In the course of our extended discussion, we will explain why this holding fully comports with the Supreme Court's decision in Piper.

FACTS AND PROCEDURAL HISTORY

Because the instant undertaking represents the fifth published opinion this case has spawned, we will abbreviate our recitation of the facts. Lacey is an Australian citizen who, in 1985, was working temporarily in British Columbia for that province's forest service. Lacey boarded a Cessna 421A aircraft for a non-scheduled passenger flight from Invermere Airport to Kamloops, both of which are in British Columbia. Five people, in addition to Lacey, were on board—the pilot, Chris Pederson, and four other passengers, all of whom were residents of British Columbia. Almost immediately after takeoff, the aircraft's right engine lost power, and the plane crashed in a clearing not far from the runway. Lacey, the other passengers, and the pilot were able to exit the aircraft, but they sustained serious burn injuries. Lacey was treated for three months at Foothills Hospital in Calgary, and then transferred to a hospital in Melbourne, Australia. After the crash, certain parts of the aircraft were sent to the CASB for examination. The CASB's final report attributed the crash to the plane's exhaust system, stating that "the right engine lost power when metal pieces from the deteriorating internal sliding sleeves in the exhaust stack entered the turbocharger and prevented the turbine from turning."

The Cessna 421A in which Lacey was a passenger was manufactured by Cessna, a Kansas corporation with its principal place of business in Kansas. The aircraft's engines were manufactured by Teledyne, a Delaware corporation with its principal place of business in California, and the aircraft's exhaust system was manufactured by Hanlon & Wilson, a Pennsylvania corporation with its principal place of business in Pennsylvania. The actions of the following non-party British Columbia corporations were also implicated by the crash: Sunrise Aviation Ltd., which operated the aircraft; Shaffer Aero Ltd., which maintained the aircraft; and Warner Aviation Ltd. or Capital Glass Ltd., which owned or leased the aircraft.

On July 17, 1987, Lacey instituted the instant diversity action in the district court for the Western District of Pennsylvania seeking compensatory and punitive damages. Two months later, defendants Cessna, Hanlon & Wilson, and Teledyne moved separately to dismiss Lacey's suit on forum non conveniens grounds. Claiming that the crash was caused either in whole or in part by pilot error or by negligent maintenance, and noting that both the pilot and the corporations responsible for maintaining the aircraft are citizens of British Columbia and not subject to the district court's personal jurisdiction, the defendants asserted that this case cannot proceed fairly in the Western District of Pennsylvania.

On November 9, 1987, the district court granted defendants' motions, concluding that the forum non conveniens issue is "resolved quite simply by reference to Piper." 674 F. Supp. at 11. The court condensed its entire analysis into three paragraphs:

> The case at bar closely mirrors Reyno, and all the factors suggest a more appropriate forum is British Columbia, Canada. None of the potential witnesses, on either liability or damages, are located here. All are clearly beyond the reach of compulsory process. Even those persons plaintiff identifies as witnesses on the issue of product defect are located in such places as Witchita [sic], Kansas, Oklahoma City, Oklahoma, and Burbank, California, all inconvenienced by this forum as much as by British Columbia. The plane itself and all other physical evidence is located in Canada. Plaintiff's physicians and all medical records and damages evidence are located in either Canada or Australia. Such perti-

> nent information as plane maintenance reports, weather information, and crash investigations is located in Canada.
>
> In short, Pennsylvania's only connection with the litigation is the fact that defendant Hanlon & Wilson is a Pennsylvania corporation. Consequently, Pennsylvania has at best a negligible interest in this matter, in contrast to that of British Columbia. In stark counterpoint to this forum's lack of interest in the matter is the burden imposed. The length and complexity of the case would appear to be considerable, and the choice of law principles may require us to divine and apply Canadian or Australian law.
>
> This forum having only a tangential interest in the subject matter of the case at hand, and this forum imposing serious inconvenience on the witnesses and parties alike, the action will be dismissed on the basis of forum non conveniens. An alternative forum, convenient to more of the witnesses and the situs of important physical evidence, is British Columbia, Canada.

Id.

Although the legal profession generally extols conciseness as a virtue, in this particular instance, we held that the court's brevity was a vice:

> [A] district court abuses its discretion when it summarily grants or denies a motion to dismiss on forum non conveniens grounds. Rather, the district court is required to develop adequate facts to support its decision and to articulate specific reasons for its conclusion.

862 F.2d at 39. Concluding that the district court had not fulfilled this responsibility, we remanded for further consideration. Lacey's suit thereafter lay dormant for almost four months, until the district court ordered the defendants to submit supplemental briefs and supporting evidentiary material. Cessna and Teledyne filed their material before the court's March 31st deadline, but Hanlon & Wilson did not, prompting Lacey to object "loudly." Although the district court "shared plaintiff's distaste for defendant's delay," 717 F. Supp. at 365–66, it allowed Hanlon & Wilson to state its position with respect to Cessna's and Teledyne's forum non conveniens arguments by filing its own papers, which Hanlon & Wilson ultimately did on August 25th.

Upon review of the affidavits and supplemental briefs submitted by the parties on remand, the court again dismissed Lacey's complaint. Heeding our instructions, the court acknowledged that although Lacey is a foreign citizen, his forum choice is entitled to "at least some weight." The district court accordingly stated that it would "not lightly disturb plaintiff's choice of forum" and that it would "hold defendants to establishing a strong preponderance in favor of dismissal." 736 F. Supp. at 664.

The district court then analyzed each of the relevant private and public interest factors. It determined that certain factors favor dismissal (relative ease of access to sources of proof, relative advantages and obstacles to a fair trial, imposition of jury duty on people of an unrelated forum, local interest in local controversies, application of foreign law, and the ability of a forum to deal with the litigation as a whole); that other factors are neutral; and that no factors favor keeping the case in Pennsylvania. Overall, the court concluded that "the public and private interests both preponderate strongly in favor of dismissal." Id. at 669. This dismissal, however, was "conditioned on several items designed to protect plaintiff and to ameliorate to the extent possible any inconvenience imposed on plaintiff by discovery and trial in British Columbia." Id.

Lacey advances several contentions on appeal. He argues, first, that the district court abused its discretion in allowing Hanlon & Wilson to submit out of time its "statement of position." He asserts, second, that the court failed adequately to assess the deference due his forum choice. Finally, Lacey contends that the district court's examination of the various relevant factors involved both abuses of discretion and errors of law. We will examine each of these arguments in turn.

THE METHODOLOGY FOR RESOLVING FORUM NON CONVENIENS MOTIONS

A. Scope of Review

Our scope of review of the district court's forum non conveniens determination is quite constrained. As the Supreme Court stated in Piper:

> The forum non conveniens determination is committed to the sound discretion of the trial court. It may be reversed only when there has been a clear abuse of discretion; where the court has considered all relevant public and private interest factors, and where its balancing of these factors is reasonable, its decision deserves substantial deference.

454 U.S. at 257. In light of this admonition, we have held that "our review is limited to consideration of whether the district court abused its discretion, and we do not perform a de novo resolution of forum non conveniens issues." Lacey, 862 F.2d at 43. We have also held, however, that a district court abuses its discretion: (1) "when it fails to consider adequately and to determine the amount of deference due the foreign plaintiff's choice of forum," or (2) "when it clearly errs in weighing the factors to be considered." Lony v. E.I. Du Pont de Nemours & Co., 886 F.2d 628, 632 (3d Cir. 1989).

B. Deference Due a Foreign Plaintiff's Forum Choice

In Piper, the Supreme Court remarked that although "there is ordinarily a strong presumption in favor of the plaintiff's choice of forum, ... that ... presumption applies with less force when the plaintiff or real parties in interest are foreign." 454 U.S. at 255. Proceeding from this language, the district court, in its first dismissal, simply stated that Piper accorded "little weight" to a foreign plaintiff's forum choice. 674 F. Supp. at 11. On appeal, we held that this treatment was inadequate, noting that the district court had "not articulated whether it accorded any deference to plaintiff's forum choice." 862 F.2d at 45. Concluding that Lacey's choice "should have been accorded at least some weight," we remanded the case to the district court with instructions to consider that neither British Columbia nor Pennsylvania is convenient to Lacey and to indicate how much deference it accords Lacey's choice. Id. at 46.

Before the district court reopened this case on remand, we decided another forum non conveniens case, Lony, in which we again commented on the deference due a foreign plaintiff's forum choice. Parsing the language of Piper, we stated that "the reason for giving a foreign plaintiff's choice less deference is not xenophobia, but merely a reluctance to assume that the choice is a convenient one." Lony, 886 F.2d at 634. We noted, however, that this reluctance "can readily be overcome by a strong showing of convenience." Id.

With Piper, Lony, and our first Lacey opinion as authority, the district court proceeded to discuss the deference due Lacey's forum choice:

> We recognize that a certain presumption attaches to plaintiff's choice of forum, and that choice is not to be lightly disturbed. However, the degree of

> deference to be accorded plaintiff's choice of forum in this case is problematic. Because plaintiff is a foreign national with no connection to the forum, his choice is not entitled to the same degree of deference accorded a resident or citizen who chooses his own forum. On the other hand, the Court of Appeals in remanding this case has indicated that, because plaintiff is forced to choose between two inconvenient fora, his choice is due "at least some weight." Of course, this provides little direction and is impossible to quantify. But suffice it to say we will not lightly disturb plaintiff's choice of forum and will hold defendants to establishing a strong preponderance in favor of dismissal.

736 F. Supp. at 663–64 (citations omitted). Lacey argues that this analysis is inadequate because the court did not indicate the "amount of deference" it accorded his forum choice. We disagree.

Lony requires a district court to indicate the amount of deference it gives a foreign plaintiff's forum choice. Unlike Lacey, we do not read this language as requiring a court somehow to mark on a continuum the precise degree of deference it accords a plaintiff's choice. Indeed, the district court in this case expressly eschewed such an illusory exercise, stating frankly that it was "impossible to quantify" the applicable level of deference. 736 F. Supp. at 663. The court instead indicated the amount of deference it accorded Lacey's forum choice by expressly imposing on defendants a more stringent burden. Specifically, the court stated that defendants must establish "a strong preponderance in favor of dismissal." This treatment, we think, satisfies both our remand instructions and the requirements set forth in Lony. Although other formulas may be equally sound, the one used here demonstrates that the court accorded not insignificant weight to the plaintiff's forum choice and indicates roughly how much weight was accorded.

C. The Defendants' Burden

"It is settled that the defendant bears the burden of persuasion as to all elements of the forum non conveniens analysis." Lacey, 862 F.2d at 43–44. This burden comprises two basic elements. The defendant must establish, initially, that an adequate alternative forum exists as to all defendants. Id. at 44. If the defendant satisfies this burden, it must then show that the private and public interest factors weigh heavily in favor of dismissal. Id.

The requirement of an adequate alternative forum is generally satisfied "when the defendant is 'amenable to process' in the other jurisdiction." Piper, 454 U.S. at 254 n.22 (citation omitted). Occasionally, however, if the alternative forum offers a clearly unsatisfactory remedy, it will nonetheless be inadequate. The latter situation arises, for instance, when the subject matter of the suit is not cognizable in the alternative forum. Id. at 254 n.22.

Once a defendant establishes that another forum is adequate (and available) to hear the case, the focus then shifts to the private and public interest factors catalogued in Gulf Oil and Piper. The private interest factors include:

> relative ease of access to sources of proof; availability of compulsory process for attendance of unwilling, and the cost of obtaining attendance of willing, witnesses; possibility of view of premises, if view would be appropriate to the action; and all other practical problems that make a trial of a case easy, expeditious and inexpensive.

Gulf Oil, 330 U.S. at 508. The public interest factors include:

> the administrative difficulties flowing from court congestion; the "local interest in having localized controversies decided at home"; the interest in having the trial of a diversity case in a forum that is at home with the law that must govern the action; the avoidance of unnecessary problems in conflict of laws, or in application of foreign laws; and the unfairness of burdening citizens in an unrelated forum with jury duty.

Piper, 454 U.S. at 241 n.6. To prevail on a forum non conveniens motion, the movant must show that the balance of these factors tips decidedly in favor of trial in the foreign forum. See In re Air Crash, 821 F.2d at 1164 ("The moving defendant must ... establish that the private and public interests weigh heavily on the side of trial in the foreign forum."). If, when added together, the relevant private and public interest factors are in equipoise, or even if they lean only slightly toward dismissal, the motion to dismiss must be denied.

D. The Degree to Which the District Court Must "Entangle" Itself in the Facts of the Case

The linchpin of Lacey's argument before the district court was that this case is likely to be a products liability action centering on an alleged defect in the airplane's exhaust system. Because that exhaust system was purportedly manufactured by Hanlon & Wilson in Pennsylvania, and because all evidence relating to its design and manufacture is presumably located in the United States and hence amenable to discovery under the Federal Rules of Civil Procedure, Lacey argued that trial in his chosen forum "will best serve the convenience of the parties and the ends of justice," Koster v. American Lumbermens Mutual Casualty Co., 330 U.S. 518, 527, 91 L. Ed. 1067, 67 S. Ct. 828 (1947). On appeal, Lacey reiterates that the products liability aspect of this case will predominate. He suggests that the district court did not recognize this because it neglected to scrutinize closely the evidence before it.

Lacey relies on the CASB's final report to establish that product defect, not pilot error or negligent maintenance, will be the focus of this case. The CASB attributed the crash to the aircraft's exhaust system and exonerated the pilot and the maintenance firms. Several factors, Lacey submits, confirm the overarching importance of the CASB's report. He notes that our earlier opinion suggested that the court had short shrifted the CASB's findings. See, e.g., 862 F.2d at 44. Lacey maintains, further, that Piper is similarly instructive in this regard. See 454 U.S. at 239 (mentioning a similar report by the British Department of Trade which suggested the possibility of pilot error, but found no evidence of product defect). Finally, Lacey emphasizes that Teledyne, in related litigation, expressly relied on the CASB's report when it stated that Hanlon & Wilson's "negligent design and/or manufacture of the exhaust system are believed to be a direct and proximate cause of the aircrash." In view of the foregoing, Lacey concludes, the district court accorded insufficient weight to the CASB's findings, and thus failed to appreciate the true focus of this case. Lacey claims that this fundamental error tainted the court's entire analysis.

Faced with Lacey's emphasis on the products liability aspect of this case, the defendants rejoin in kind, arguing that the central issue instead will be pilot error and negligent maintenance. Defendants assert, first, that a competent pilot could have kept the Cessna 421A airborne, despite the failure of its right engine. Second, they contend that the firms responsible for maintaining the aircraft were negligent for failing to replace and to inspect regularly an exhaust system declared "obsolete" by Cessna in 1977. Defendants argue, third, that the CASB's findings are unsupported by the FAA's file concerning prior problems with the Cessna 421A's exhaust system. The defendants thus conclude that the "accident was caused by the negligence of a Canadian pilot and ... the negligence of Canadian corporations maintaining the aircraft," and urge that trial in British Columbia is therefore preferable.

In order to balance the relevant private and public interest factors, the district court must immerse itself to a certain degree in the facts of the case. We think, nonetheless, that Lacey has misapprehended the extent of the court's inquiry at this nascent stage of the litigation. The record here consists entirely of affidavits. No discovery has taken place; in fact, the defendants have not even answered Lacey's complaint. The district court, as a result, cannot now determine what the ultimate focus of the trial will be, yet the parties urge the court to do just that. We think, instead, that in resolving a forum non conveniens motion, the district court must do no more than delineate the likely contours of the case by ascertaining, among other things, the nature of the plaintiff's action, the existence of any potential defenses, and the necessary sources of proof.

We think that the district court in this case entangled itself sufficiently in the facts. On remand, the defendants submitted extensive affidavits and supplemental briefs in support of their contention "that faulty maintenance and pilot error were the proximate causes of the aircrash, rather than any defective component." 736 F. Supp. at 666. After reviewing these submissions, the district court concluded that "there is evidence to support defendants' position concerning the proximate cause and the liability of the potential third party defendants." Id. at 667. In short, the court immersed itself in the record, found support for both Lacey's products liability claim and defendants' assertions of pilot error and negligent maintenance, and then proceeded to examine the necessary sources of proof. At this stage of the case, such analysis is sufficient.

E. Is the Piper/Gulf Oil Balancing Exercise a Quantitative Or Qualitative Exercise?

The final consideration in the methodology for resolving forum non conveniens motions is the determination of the nature of the balancing exercise. Although the Gulf Oil Court presented its eleven private and public interest factors as rough equals, the Supreme Court surely did not promulgate a mechanical jurisprudence. We believe instead that, depending on the case, some factors are "more equal" than others. If, for example, the barriers to obtaining access to essential sources of proof in the foreign forum are so severe as to render that forum (practically speaking) an inadequate alternative, that consideration (i.e., "ease of access to sources of proof") cannot be viewed as a run-of-the-mill criterion easily trumped by a countervailing numerical count. As will be seen, that is the case here.

THE RELEVANT PRIVATE AND PUBLIC INTEREST FACTORS

Because the district court determined that several private and public interest factors are "neutral" in this case, and because Lacey does not challenge the court's assessment of every factor, we will only discuss in detail those factors that continue to have relevance to the resolution of defendants' forum non conveniens motions.

A. Access to Sources of Proof in British Columbia

The main impetus for the district court's dismissal was its belief that British Columbia "would be capable of dealing with this litigation as a unified whole." 736 F. Supp. at 667. In particular, the court thought that British Columbia was a forum in which Lacey could prosecute his products liability action and the defendants could institute actions for contribution or indemnity against several potential third-party defendants. This analysis unravels, however, if Lacey would not have access in British Columbia to the necessary sources of proof. Appreciating the significance of ensuring Lacey's access to proof in British Columbia, the court conditioned its dismissal "on defendants making all relevant witnesses and documents in their control available to plaintiff in the alternative forum for discovery and trial." Id. at 664. Because the district court thought that "the primary evidence on product liability would come from defendants' witnesses and records," it believed that this condition would remedy all access to proof problems. Id. at 665. The court referred to this condition throughout its opinion, evincing its centrality to the court's dismissal. See, e.g., id. at 664, 666, 669.

Lacey argues that the district court's condition will not afford him access to sources of proof in British Columbia because evidence essential to his products liability claim is no longer in defendants' control. First, he points out that Hanlon & Wilson sold its aircraft exhaust system business in May of 1985 to Wall Colmonoy Corporation ("Colmonoy"), an Oklahoma corporation. Pursuant to the terms of this sale, all related documents were transferred to Colmonoy. Robert Bolte, the president of Hanlon & Wilson, thus has stated that Hanlon & Wilson "no longer has in its possession any documentation" with respect to the exhaust system in question. He also has averred that "other than [himself], Hanlon & Wilson does not have any employees who have knowledge of the exhaust system," and that his knowledge "would not be of material value unless [he] were given [the] opportunity to review" documents now in Colmonoy's possession.

Second, Lacey maintains that the passage of time has removed from Cessna's and Teledyne's control evidence which may prove critical to Lacey's lawsuit. The relevant exhaust system was designed by Hanlon & Wilson and Cessna in approximately 1966. This exhaust system, however, began to experience difficulties in the early 1970's, and was thus redesigned in the mid-1970's by Cessna and another company. In light of this long history and the transience of the contemporary corporate world, many potentially relevant witnesses may no longer be employed by Cessna. Similarly, because the aircraft's engines were manufactured by Teledyne more than nine years ago, the same problem exists with respect to that company—i.e., personnel with relevant knowledge may no longer be subject to its control.

The defendants were unable to rebut Lacey's access to proof argument. At oral argument, Cessna sought to assuage our concerns by assuring us that it possessed sufficient documents and witnesses to satisfy Lacey's needs. This strikes us as something the district court should examine. The district court assumed that the evidence essential to Lacey's products liability action is still in defendants' custody. This assumption, as noted above, was central to the court's entire calculus, but unfortunately, it appears to have arisen from a misapprehension. It now appears that Hanlon & Wilson has no evidence in its control concerning the aircraft's exhaust system, and that some vital witnesses may now be former employees of Cessna and Teledyne. We therefore agree with Lacey's contention that the district court did not adequately consider this private interest factor. The district court should ascertain (on the remand which follows) whether Lacey would have access to essential sources of proof in British Columbia. Of particular interest is whether Cessna has in its control sufficient evidence pertaining to the exhaust system at issue here.

B. Means Available in British Columbia to Discover Non-Party Witnesses and Documents Located in the United States: Are They Adequate to Afford Lacey Access to Essential Sources of Proof at Trial in British Columbia?

If the witnesses and documents essential to Lacey's products liability action are no longer in defendants' control, the critical issue becomes whether Lacey can discover in British Columbia evidence in the possession of non-parties in the United States, such as

Colmonoy and Cessna's and Teledyne's former employees. Based on the affidavit of J. J. Camp, Q.L., a British Columbia lawyer, Lacey contends that "no discovery is possible under British Columbia's practice as to non-party witnesses in the United States." Camp also reports that a British Columbia court will not order a non-party outside of that province to produce documents, because the court could not compel compliance with such an order. Although this passage of the Camp affidavit deals specifically with documents in other Canadian provinces, it would apply a fortiori to documents in the possession of non-parties in the United States.

Teledyne rejoins that "the Affidavit submitted to the District Court [by George Nathason, Q.L., also a British Columbia lawyer] establishes that letters rogatory and other procedures can be used in Canada to obtain discovery in the United States."

We do not read the Nathason affidavit as necessarily conflicting with the Camp affidavit. First of all, Nathason appears to agree with Camp's assertion that foreign witnesses' testimony can be obtained only for use at trial, and not for discovery. In addition, the procedure whereby a litigant in British Columbia applies for a letter of request to obtain such trial testimony appears cumbersome regardless of which expert's account is credited. More importantly, nothing in either affidavit indicates that a British Columbia court would compel a non-party in the United States to produce documents in its possession. We therefore suspect that defendants' former employees in the United States could not be deposed in British Columbia for discovery purposes, and that documents which are no longer in defendants' custody, especially those which were transferred by Hanlon & Wilson to Colmonoy, also would be unavailable in British Columbia.

Ordinarily, this factor, by itself, would not militate against dismissal, for all that is necessary is access to proof at trial. Here, however, it appears that critical evidence is outside of defendants' control, that the procedure necessary to obtain the trial testimony of non-party witnesses in the United States is exceedingly rigorous, and that British Columbia courts will not compel non-parties in the United States to produce documents at trial. When viewed in conjunction with these other factors, the unavailability of civil discovery in British Columbia highlights and provides cumulative evidence of the serious impediments that Lacey would face in gaining access to essential sources of proof at trial in that forum.

Moreover, the questions of availability of discovery to identify relevant non-party witnesses residing outside of British Columbia and of putative access to the testimony of those witnesses at trial in British Columbia are inextricably intertwined. To obtain a letter of request, a litigant must identify in advance both the names of the non-party witnesses whose testimony is needed at trial and the likely content of that testimony. Therefore, absent at least some means to discover this essential information, Lacey may be unable to avail himself of letters of request to obtain the trial testimony of non-party witnesses residing in the United States.

Despite the clear import of these affidavits, the district court, after "having reviewed the pertinent rules for foreign discovery," concluded that British Columbia "affords plaintiff ample opportunity to obtain relevant information." 736 F. Supp. at 665. This conclusion, however, was premised on the assumption that "the primary evidence on product liability would come from defendants' witnesses and records," which would be available in British Columbia under defendants' agreement to produce all documents and witnesses in their possession. Id. As noted in this opinion, that assumption now appears to be unfounded. According to Lacey (and the president of Hanlon & Wilson, Robert Bolte), the primary evidence on products liability will not come from defendants' witnesses and records, because the lion's share of that evidence—perhaps all of it—is now in the possession of a third party, Colmonoy. If on remand this representation proves true, then the premise on which the district court depended in analyzing the means available in British Columbia to discover evidence has been undermined. The district court on remand therefore should reconsider whether British Columbia's discovery rules will afford Lacey access to essential sources of proof at trial with the understanding that much of the evidence necessary to Lacey's action might be outside of defendants' control.

C. Application of Foreign Law

The Supreme Court observed in Piper that "the need to apply foreign law pointed towards dismissal." 454 U.S. at 260. Here, the district court, believing that "British Columbia has a decidedly greater interest in this litigation," determined that British Columbia law would apply if Lacey's action were to proceed before it, and hence counted this factor as favoring dismissal. 736 F. Supp. at 668. Lacey contends that the court's choice of law analysis was flawed. We agree.

We are guided here by our decision in Reyno v. Piper Aircraft Co., 630 F.2d 149 (3d Cir. 1980). Piper involved a suit against two American manufacturers brought by the personal representatives of several Scottish citizens who were killed in a plane crash in Scotland. In deciding whether to apply Pennsylvania's strict liability law or Scotland's negligence law, we inferred from our understanding of basic tort law the general policies that underlie these competing standards of care. We hypothesized, first, that Scotland eschewed strict liability in favor of a negligence standard in order to encourage industry within its borders. We similarly opined that Pennsylvania adopted strict liability in order to shift some of the burden of injuries from consumers onto producers and to induce manufacturers to be more careful. Based on our estimate of the two jurisdictions' interests, we concluded that there was a false conflict:

> Applying Pennsylvania's strict liability standard to its resident manufacturer would serve that state's interest in the regulation of manufacturing. Scotland's interest in encouraging industry within its borders would not be impaired, however, by applying a stricter standard of care on a foreign corporation which has no industrial operation in Scotland. Furthermore, Scotland would have no interest in denying compensation to its residents for the purpose of benefiting a foreign corporation. Finally, imposition of strict liability on Piper cannot be said to be unfair to it. Inasmuch as Pennsylvania, the state in which Piper makes its product, and the vast majority of American jurisdictions in which most of Piper's aircraft are sold and fly, have strict liability, that is the legal standard under which it plans its operations.

630 F.2d at 168 (footnote omitted). Because Pennsylvania's interest could be served without interfering with any significant interest of Scotland, we determined that Pennsylvania law should apply.

We think that this reasoning applies with equal force to the case sub judice. The conflict here appears to result primarily from the fact that Pennsylvania has adopted strict liability, whereas British Columbia has not. Reasoning by analogy from Piper, however, we believe that this is a false conflict. Applying Pennsylvania's law of strict liability would further Pennsylvania's interest in deterring the manufacture of defective products and in shifting the costs of injuries onto producers, but would not impair British Columbia's interest in fostering industry within its borders. Conversely, applying British Columbia's negligence standard would not serve British Columbia's interest, but would harm Pennsylvania's interest. In view of this analysis, it appears that this case, like Piper, presents a false conflict, and that the district court probably should apply the law of Pennsylvania—the jurisdiction whose interests would be damaged if its law were not applied.

Absent detailed research into the policies undergirding Pennsylvania and British Columbia law, however, and at this stage of the litigation with the record still relatively undeveloped, we are reluctant to declare with finality that Pennsylvania law applies in this case. We think, nonetheless, that Piper raises real doubts regarding the district court's conclusion that British Columbia law would apply. We thus think that the court incorrectly held that the need to apply foreign law "weighs strongly in favor of dismissal." Instead, we believe that this factor is neutral.

D. Summary: Balancing the Relevant Factors

[W]e have attempted, in an effort to expedite the progress of this case, to offer the district court guidance in approaching its tasks on remand. For almost four years, Lacey and his antagonists doggedly have litigated the full spectrum of forum non conveniens issues. In remanding this case (for the second time), we do not wish to send the parties back to square one. We therefore have tried to focus the district court's inquiry on remand to a single factor [i.e., whether Lacey would have access in British Columbia to sufficient evidence in support of his products liability action], which it is free to determine on the facts and the law. By articulating a formula into which the district court can plug its access to proof answer, we hope to obviate the need for a third or fourth appeal. We do not think that the Piper Court intended its decision to allow such ping-pong between trial and appellate courts to continue unabated, producing delay that inevitably harms injured plaintiffs.

The district court's order of dismissal on forum non conveniens grounds therefore will be reversed and the case remanded for further proceedings consistent with this opinion.

[The concurring opinion of District Judge Pollak and the dissenting opinion of Circuit Judge Nygaard are omitted.]

IN RE AIR CRASH DISASTER AT SIOUX CITY, IOWA, ON JULY 19, 1989

734 F. Supp. 1425 (N.D. Ill. 1990)

CONLON, District Judge.

I. Background

On July 19, 1989, United Airlines Flight 232 from Denver to Chicago crashed during an attempted emergency landing at Sioux City, Iowa, after the aircraft lost hydraulic power. Of the 296 people on board, 112 were killed in the tragic crash. The aircraft, owned and operated by United Airlines, was a DC-10 manufactured by McDonnell Douglas. General Electric manufactured the CF6-6 engines utilized on the aircraft.

Flight 232's passengers were from thirty states and two foreign countries. Ninety-three passengers were from Colorado. Eighteen cases were transferred to the Northern District of Illinois for pre-trial purposes by order of the Judicial Panel on Multidistrict Litigation. The cases were transferred from district courts located in ten states.

United Airlines is a Delaware corporation with its principal place of business in Illinois. United maintained the aircraft in California. United's flight crew training center is located in Colorado. The aircraft's builder, McDonnell Douglas, is a Maryland corporation with its principal place of business in Missouri. McDonnell Douglas designed and manufactured the aircraft in California. The third defendant, General Electric, is a New York corporation with its principal place of business in New York. General Electric designed and manufactured the engines on Flight 232 in Ohio.

Defendants argue that plaintiffs may not bring claims for punitive damages in this action. They maintain that punitive damage claims should be dismissed because they violate the due process clause of the Fourteenth Amendment. In addition, defendants argue that the Federal Aviation Act preempts punitive damage claims in air crash incidents. In the alternative, defendants request the court to determine the state law governing punitive damages as to each claim....

IV. Determination Of State Law Applicable In Each Case

A federal court ordinarily must apply the choice of law principles of the state in which it sits. Klaxon Co. v. Stentor Electric Mfg. Co., 313 U.S. 487, 85 L. Ed. 1477, 61 S. Ct. 1020 (1941). When a case is transferred, the transferee court must apply the choice of law rules of the state where the transferor court sits. Van Dusen v. Barrack, 376 U.S. 612, 11 L. Ed. 2d 945, 84 S. Ct. 805 (1964); Air Crash Disaster Near Chicago, 644 F.2d 594, 610 (7th Cir.), cert. denied sub nom. Lin v. Am. Airlines, 454 U.S. 878, 70 L. Ed. 2d 187, 102 S. Ct. 358 (1981) ("Air Crash"). In this litigation, at least twelve cases originating in eight different states assert claims for punitive damages.

In Air Crash, the Seventh Circuit resolved the choice of law issues in consolidated multidistrict litigation regarding an air crash in Illinois. The court expressly adopted the concept of depecage, "the process of applying rules of different states on the basis of the precise issue involved." Id. at 611. Accordingly, this opinion resolves the choice of law question regarding only the issue of punitive damages.

A. Cases Transferred From California

Three cases were filed in federal courts located in California. California employs a "comparative impairment" analysis. Under this analysis, when a true conflict exists, a court should apply the law of the state whose interests would be more impaired if its law were not applied. Bernhard v. Harrah's Club, 16 Cal. 3d 313, 320, 128 Cal. Rptr. 215, 219, 546 P.2d 719, 723 (1976).

Initially, the court must determine which states' interests to consider. In Air Crash, the court applied California's comparative impairment test. Air Crash, 644 F.2d at 621–628. The court restricted the analysis to three states representing the principal place of business, the place of the alleged misconduct and the state in which the injury occurred. The court noted that the domiciliary states of the plaintiffs or their representatives are not relevant to the question of punitive damages. Id. at 622.

After narrowing the analysis to the relevant states, the court must determine whether an apparent conflict exists between the punitive damages laws of those states. Id. at 621, citing Offshore Rental Co. v. Continental Oil Co., 22 Cal. 3d 157, 148 Cal. Rptr. 867, 870, 583 P.2d 721, 724 (1978). If an apparent conflict exists, the court examines the applicable law to see if a "moderate and restrained interpretation" of the law reveals that only one state has a legitimate interest in the application of its policy. Air Crash, 644 F.2d at 621, citing Bernhard, 16 Cal. 3d at 320, 128 Cal. Rptr. at 219, 546 P.2d at 723. When a restrained or moderate interpretation of state law fails to resolve the conflict, a "true" conflict exists.

True conflicts are resolved by applying the law of the state whose interest would be the more impaired if its law were not applied. Id.; Clothesrigger, Inc. v. GTE Corp., 191 Cal. App. 3d 605, 614, 236 Cal. Rptr. 605, 614 (1987). The process is "'essentially a process of allocating respective spheres of lawmaking influence.'" Air Crash, 644 F.2d at 622, quoting Offshore Rental, 22 Cal. 3d at 165, 148 Cal. Rptr. at 872, 583 P.2d at 726 (citations omitted). The court must consider (1) whether one state's punitive damages provision is more strongly held than that of other interested states, and (2) the "fit" between the purpose of each potentially applicable punitive damages provision and the circumstances of the case. Air Crash, 644 F.2d at 622 (citations omitted).

In this case, the injury occurred in Iowa. However, Iowa was not the place of departure or scheduled destination. Under any theory of liability, the fact that the accident occurred in Iowa was a mere fortuity. Consequently, Iowa's interest in the action does not merit further consideration under California choice of law principles. The analysis is limited to the principal place of business of each defendant and the place of the conduct at issue.

1. United Airlines

[This portion of the court's opinion is omitted.]

2. McDonnell Douglas

McDonnell Douglas designed and built the aircraft in California. Its principal place of business is Missouri. In Air Crash, McDonnell Douglas was a defendant. Under analogous circumstances, the Seventh Circuit wrestled with the question whether Missouri or California punitive damages policies would be more impaired if they were not applied. The court concluded that both states' policies would be equally impaired. The court decided that a California court would escape the quandary by applying Illinois law. Air Crash, 644 F.2d at 622–626.

Subsequent decisions by California state courts indicate that in the event California shares an equal interest in application of its law with another state, a California court would apply California law. See Am. Nat'l Bank of Commerce v. Corondoni, 169 Cal. App. 3d 368, 215 Cal. Rptr. 331 (1985) (California's general preference is to apply its own law). California courts have "repeatedly asserted that California has an important interest in regulating products manufactured in California." Corrigan v. Bjork Shiley Corp., 182 Cal. App. 3d 166, 180, 227 Cal. Rptr. 247, cert. denied sub nom. Shiley Inc. v. Corrigan, 479 U.S. 1049, 93 L. Ed. 2d 973, 107 S. Ct. 921 (1987). Since Missouri and California law would be equally impaired if not applied, California law governs claims for punitive damages against McDonnell Douglas.

3. General Electric

General Electric manufactured the engines on Flight 232 in Ohio. Its principal place of business is New York. As discussed above, Iowa was the fortuitous site of the crash, and Iowa has no real interest in imposing punitive damages against General Electric. Colorado has some interest in having its punitive damages law applied in this case because Denver has a busy airport from which Flight 232 departed. However, Ohio and New York have stronger interests than either Colorado or Iowa. Consequently, the comparative impairment analysis is limited to Ohio and New York.

A brief summary of the punitive damage laws of Ohio and New York reveals that a true conflict exists. Ohio prohibits punitive damage awards in wrongful death actions. Rubeck v. Huffman, 54 Ohio St. 2d 20, 374 N.E.2d 411, 413, 8 Ohio Op. 3d 11 (1978). In order to award punitive damages in other actions, a jury must find clear and convincing evidence that a manufacturer "manifested a flagrant disregard of the safety of persons who might be harmed by the product in question." Ohio Rev. Code § 2307.80(A).

New York permits awards of punitive damages in wrongful death actions, N.Y. Est. Powers & Trusts Law § 5-4.3(b), survival actions, N.Y. Est. Powers & Trusts Law § 11-3.2(b), and ordinary personal injury actions. New York allows imposition of punitive damages for conduct that is "morally culpable, or is actuated by evil and reprehensible motives." Walker v. Sheldon, 10 N.Y.2d 401, 404, 179 N.E.2d 497, 498, 223 N.Y.S.2d 488, 490 (1961).

General Electric argues that Ohio has expressed a stronger, more recent interest in the imposition of its punitive damages law. General Electric points out that Ohio law is codified and offers greater protection to a corporation than New York law. However, the fact that New York's punitive damage provision was not codified may imply that the state legislature agrees with the judicial resolution of the punitive damages standard. The fact that Ohio law affords greater protection to defendants than New York law indicates only that Ohio has struck a different balance between deterrence and protection than New York.

Ohio's interests would be more impaired if its punitive damages policy were not applied. General Electric manufactures aircraft engines in Ohio and not in New York. General Electric's principal place of business is in New York because other holdings, including the National Broadcasting Company, Kidder, Peabody Group, Inc. and GE Turbine Operations, are located in New York. Since the alleged wrongful acts occurred in Ohio, and Ohio is the principal place of business of General Electric's aircraft engine manufacturing division, Ohio has a greater opportunity to balance interests of deterrence against protection of General Electric regarding airplane engine manufacturing. Ohio law governs the punitive damage claims against General Electric.

B. Cases Transferred From Colorado, Iowa, New York, and Georgia and Cases Filed in Illinois

Six cases stating claims for punitive damages were filed in Colorado, Iowa, Illinois, New York and Georgia. Colorado, Iowa, Illinois and New York all apply the "most significant relationship" test described in § 145 et seq. of the Restatement (Second) of the Conflict of Laws ("the Restatement"). The Supreme Court of Georgia has never decided whether the Restatement should be applied in air crash cases, but [I predict] Georgia would adopt the Restatement if the question were raised.

The Seventh Circuit delineated the Restatement test in Air Crash, 644 F.2d at 611–612:

> The Restatement (Second) provides two sets of criteria for the measurement of the "most significant relationship." The first set of criteria includes general factors such as the needs of the interstate system; relevant policies of the forum and other interested states; protection of justified expectations; the basic policies underlying the particular field of law; certainty, predictability and uniformity of result; and ease in the determination and application of the law to be applied. The second set of criteria includes the contacts to be taken into account in applying these principles. These contacts are: (1) the place of the in-

> jury; (2) the place of misconduct; (3) the domicile, residence, nationality, place of incorporation and place of business of the parties; and (4) the place where the relationship between the parties is centered. These contacts are to [be] evaluated according to their relative importance to the issue involved and according to the purposes sought to be achieved by the relevant rules of the interested states.

The most significant relationship test must be applied independently to each defendant.

1. United Airlines

[This portion of the court's opinion is omitted.]

2. McDonnell Douglas

The Restatement analysis regarding McDonnell Douglas is limited to California, site of the alleged wrongful conduct, Missouri, McDonnell Douglas' principal place of business, Maryland, its place of incorporation, and Iowa, the site of the injury. For the reasons stated above, Iowa law will not be applied. As between California and Missouri, in Air Crash the Seventh Circuit determined that these states had an equal interest in the application of their punitive damage laws and resolved the conflict by application of Illinois law, the site of the crash. Since no acceptable alternative to California or Missouri law exists in this case, a resolution to the conflict must be reached.

The Restatement § 145, comment c, provides: "if the primary purpose of the tort rule involved is to deter or punish misconduct, ... the state where the conduct took place may be the state of dominant interest and thus that of most significant relationship...." See Houston North Hosp. Prop. v. Telco Leasing, Inc., 688 F.2d 408, 409, n.3b (5th Cir. 1982). See also Restatement § 145 comment e. At this early stage of the litigation, some doubt exists about the site of allegedly wrongful conduct. Conceivably, wrongful conduct resulting in the accident could have occurred in either state. However, the design and manufacture of the aircraft occurred in California. Since faulty design and manufacture are the basis for the punitive damage claims against McDonnell Douglas, California law appropriately governs these actions. California does not permit punitive damages in wrongful death actions but does permit punitive damages in survival actions.

3. General Electric

General Electric manufactured and designed the aircraft's engine in Ohio. New York is General Electric's principal place of business. General Electric's aircraft engine business takes place predominantly in Ohio. As discussed above, New York's relationship to General Electric's aircraft engine manufacturing business is objectively less than Ohio's interest. Accordingly, Ohio law governs punitive damage claims against General Electric. Ohio law permits punitive damages in survival actions but not in wrongful death actions.

C. Cases Transferred From Pennsylvania and the District of Columbia

Two cases asserting punitive damage claims were originally brought in Pennsylvania and the District of Columbia. Pennsylvania and the District of Columbia apply a combination of the governmental interest analysis and the most significant relationship test. In Air Crash, the Seventh Circuit observed that "the tests to be used, although containing significant differences, mandate an analytical inquiry which is basically the same." Air Crash, 644 F.2d at 610. Since California's governmental interest analysis and the Restatement test produced the same result for each defendant, it is unnecessary to repeat the analysis with regard to the combined tests employed by Pennsylvania and the District of Columbia.

The choice of law rules of Pennsylvania and the District of Columbia would result in application of ... California law to claims against McDonnell Douglas and Ohio law to claims against General Electric.

[The remainder of the court's opinion is omitted.]

Notes

1. After the close of discovery, the *Lacey* defendants renewed their motion to have the case dismissed on forum non conveniens grounds. In the interim, however, the Third Circuit had decided *Lony v. E.I. Du Pont de Nemours & Co.*, 935 F.2d 604 (3d Cir. 1991) (*Lony II*), holding that "whenever discovery in a case has proceeded substantially so that the parties already have invested much of the time and resources they will expend before trial, the presumption against dismissal on the grounds of forum non conveniens greatly increases." *Id.* at 614. Relying on *Lony II* and the fact that much of the discovery conducted by the *Lacey* parties would be unusable in British Columbia, Judge Cohill denied the defendants' motion to dismiss. *See Lacey v. Cessna Aircraft Company*, 849 F. Supp. 394 (W.D. Pa. 1994).

In the course of his opinion, Judge Cohill chided the Third Circuit for placing defendants who attempt to argue forum non conveniens in a no-win position: "We recognize that defendants might be chagrined by the apparent catch-22 borne of Lony II, for defendants were ordered to undertake substantial discovery to determine whether dismissal was appropriate, only to be told that that discovery renders dismissal inappropriate." *Id.* at 398. While the Third Circuit has to date shown no concern about this issue, some circuits have sought to avoid the problem by requiring less detailed findings from their district courts. *See further Gschwind v. Cessna Aircraft Co.*, 161 F.3d 602 (10th Cir. 1998), *cert. denied*, 526 U.S. 1112 (1999); *Empresa Lineas Maritimas Argentinas, S.A. v. Schichau-Unterweser, A.G.*, 955 F.2d 368 (5th Cir. 1992); Gary Knapp, Annotation, *Forum Non Conveniens in Products Liability Cases*, 76 A.L.R.4th 22 (1989 & 2004 Supp.).

2. Were you impressed by Judge Conlon's handling of the various choice of law issues in the *Sioux City* case? Professor Stanley Cox was not:

> In re Air Crash Disaster at Sioux City, Iowa involved consolidated claims originally filed in at least ten jurisdictions arising from a single airline crash. The court, after first grouping the jurisdictions into common choice-of-law theories, very meticulously and independently applied each choice-of-law theory to the facts of the case. However, if the smoke is cleared away—surprise! surprise!—the same substantive law was applied to the same defendant under each of the different choice-of-law theories. The meticulousness of the court's choice-of-law applications, which, for any single application if considered in isolation, seemed legitimate, masked the reality that the court applied a single law to each defendant for the whole case.

Stanley E. Cox, *Applying the Best Law*, 52 Ark. L. Rev. 9, 26 (1999). Is Professor Cox's criticism accurate? Is it fair? If so, what should the court have done instead?

3. There is a famous airplane joke that nearly everyone has told (or heard), without realizing that it actually implicates the issues just discussed. It also is a good reminder that attorneys must pay attention to even the smallest details if they are to be successful. Do you remember it? If not, read on:

> A plane is flying from Canada to the United States. Half the passengers are Canadians and half Americans. The plane goes into a tailspin. It crashes precisely on the border between Canada and America. Where are the survivors buried?
>
> Despite the obvious answer (survivors are not buried), many people wrestle with and ruminate over [this] riddle before discovering the solution, especially when the riddle [is] spoken and not written. [This] childhood joke points out how we fail to pay attention to the plain meaning of words because of a confusing context.
>
> The very same sort of ingrained attitudes, mental habits and adherence to the wrong notions [that make the survivors question hard to answer right away] can prevent attorneys from seeing obvious facts in an array of legal settings that are right in front of our noses. An antidote for this mental torpor can be found in the practice of carefully and thoroughly observing and paying attention to the most basic matters that we are addressing in a case or transaction.

Lee Applebaum, *Simple Observations Can Provide Creative Litigation Solutions*, at finemanbach.com/publications/simple.cfm.

Problem 10

A foreign country airplane manufacturer agreed to sell one of its new jets to a buyer located in a different foreign country. As part of the negotiations, the parties agreed that if a dispute arose, it would be submitted "for resolution to the courts of the State of New York." Other than this contract provision, neither the transaction nor the parties have any connection to New York. Is the clause enforceable as written? *See Bank of America Nat. Trust and Sav. Ass'n v. Envases Venezolanos, S.A.*, 740 F. Supp. 260 (S.D.N.Y.), *aff'd mem.*, 923 F.2d 843 (2d Cir. 1990).

Chapter 3

Airmen

SHERMAN'S LAGOON

A. OVERVIEW

Pilots, mechanics, and flight attendants, collectively known as "airmen" (a sexist term that nevertheless continues to be used by both the government and the industry) are the backbone of any flying enterprise. Accordingly, this chapter examines some of the more common legal issues that arise in connection with them. It also looks at the Railway Labor Act of 1926, 45 U.S.C. §§ 151–188, a statute that, despite its name and vintage, governs labor relations in the airline industry.

B. PILOTS

ABDULLAH v. AMERICAN AIRLINES, INC.

181 F.3d 363 (3d Cir. 1999)

ROTH, Circuit Judge.

After a jury had awarded plaintiffs-appellants Khaled Abdullah, Audrey James, Eardley James, and Velma George damages for injuries sustained during an American Airlines flight, the District Court of the Virgin Islands, Division of Saint Croix, ordered a new trial. The court's action was based on its conclusion that it had improperly relied upon territorial common law to establish the standards of care that were used by the jury to determine that negligence on the part of American Airlines' employees had caused appellants' injuries. Abdullah v. American Airlines, Inc., 969 F.Supp. 337, 340–41 (D.V.I.1997).

The court found that the 1958 Federal Aviation Act (FAA), Pub.L. No. 85-726, 72 Stat. 731 (codified as amended at 49 U.S.C. §§40101–49105), implicitly preempts territorial standards for aviation safety, and that the jury should not have been instructed on a territorial law standard of care. Abdullah, 969 F.Supp. at 341. Concluding that the error regarding federal preemption resulted in the admission of evidence on standards of care that was not limited to federally established standards of care and that this evidence was prejudicial, the court ordered a new trial. Id. at 340. At plaintiffs' request, the District Court then certified the following issue for appeal: "Does federal law preempt the standards for air safety, but preserve State and Territorial damage remedies?"

We answer both parts of this certified question with a "yes." As to the first part of the question, contrary to courts that have found that federal law does not preempt state and territorial air safety standards, or that federal law only preempts discrete aspects thereof, we find implied federal preemption of the entire field of aviation safety. As to the second part, we conclude that, despite federal preemption of the standards of care, state and territorial damage remedies still exist for violation of those standards.

Our finding on preemption is based on our determination that the FAA and relevant federal regulations establish complete and thorough safety standards for interstate and international air transportation and that these standards are not subject to supplementation by, or variation among, jurisdictions. Thus, we agree with the District Court that it was error to rely upon territorial safety standards in determining American Airlines' liability in this case.

In coming to our conclusion on preemption, we do not, however, agree with the narrow nature of the federal standard set out by the District Court. We conclude instead that there is an overarching general standard of care under the FAA and its regulations. This standard arises in particular from 14 C.F.R. §91.13(a): "No person may operate an aircraft in a careless or reckless manner so as to endanger the life or property of another." Thus, we do not agree with the District Court's determination that evidence on "reasonable standard of care" should necessarily have been excluded—as long as a "reasonable standard of care" is compatible with an avoidance of carelessness or recklessness in the operation of the aircraft. We will remand this case to the District Court to review both the testimony and the jury instructions on standards of care in order to determine if they are consistent with the standards we set out here. If they are, the jury verdict should be reinstated. If they are not, the District Court should proceed with a new trial, and in that trial the court should follow the federal standards as we establish them here.

I. Background

Plaintiffs Khaled Abdullah, Audrey James, Eardley James, and Velma George were passengers on American Airlines Flight 1473 from New York to San Juan, Puerto Rico, on August 28, 1991. En route, the aircraft encountered severe turbulence which caused serious injuries to a number of passengers, including the plaintiffs. The First Officer had noticed a weather system developing in the flight path and had illuminated the seatbelt sign. He had also gone to the back of the aircraft to warn the flight attendants that the ride could get choppy in ten minutes. None of the crew, however, alerted the passengers of the expected turbulence. Nor did the pilot change course in order to avoid the storm. Some of the injured passengers were wearing their seatbelts; some were not.

Plaintiffs filed two separate lawsuits against defendant American Airlines, Inc., alleging negligence on the part of the pilot and flight crew in failing to take reasonable precautions to avoid the turbulent conditions known to them and in failing to give warnings reasonably calculated to permit plaintiffs to take steps to protect themselves.

A jury trial commenced on August 7, 1995, in the District Court of the Virgin Islands, Division of Saint Croix. The plaintiffs' cases were consolidated for trial. On August 25, 1995, the jury found American liable, found plaintiffs to be without any contributory fault, and awarded monetary damages aggregating more than two million dollars.

American filed a post-trial motion which requested dismissal and/or a new trial plus attorney's fees and costs. Among the grounds asserted was that the District Court had improperly used territorial common law to establish the standards of care for the pilots, flight attendants, and passengers. American argued that the FAA implicitly preempts the standards for airline safety.

The District Court issued an opinion on June 5, 1997, holding that the FAA impliedly preempts state and territorial regulation of aviation safety and standards of care for pilots, flight attendants, and passengers, but that plaintiffs may recover under state and territorial law for violation of federal standards. Abdullah, 969 F.Supp. at 341. The District Court held that its error of law regarding preemption, which resulted in admission of evidence regarding standards other than the federal standards, warranted a new trial.

Upon motion of the plaintiffs, the District Court certified this issue for interlocutory review. We granted interlocutory review.

II. Jurisdiction and Standard of Review

Subject matter jurisdiction in the District Court rested on diversity of citizenship. 28 U.S.C. § 1332. We accepted jurisdiction over this matter pursuant to 28 U.S.C. § 1292(b), which permits us to accept an interlocutory appeal where there is "substantial ground for a difference of opinion" on an issue and "an immediate appeal ... may materially advance the ultimate termination of the litigation."

The appeal involves a question of law, so that the standard of review is plenary. Epright v. Environmental Resources Management, Inc. Health & Welfare Plan, 81 F.3d 335, 339 (3d Cir.1996). The scope of review is not limited to the issues articulated in the section 1292(b) certification motion. "As the text of § 1292(b) indicates, appellate jurisdiction applies to the order certified to the court of appeals, and is not tied to the particular question formulated by the district court." Yamaha Motor Corp. v. Calhoun, 516 U.S. 199, 205, 116 S.Ct. 619, 133 L.Ed.2d 578 (1996). "[T]he appellate court may address any issue fairly included within the certified order because 'it is the order that is appealable, and not the controlling question identified by the district court.'" Id. (quoting 9 J. Moore & B. Ward, Moore's Federal Practice ¶ 110.25[1], p. 300 (2d ed.1995)).

III. Discussion

The power of Congress to preempt state law derives from the Supremacy Clause of Article VI of the Constitution, which provides that the laws of the United States "shall be the supreme Law of the Land; ... any Thing in the Constitution or Laws of any state to the Contrary notwithstanding." U.S. Const. Art. VI, cl. 2. "Consideration of issues arising under the Supremacy Clause 'start[s] with the assumption that the historic police powers of the States [are] not to be superseded by ... Federal Act unless that [is] the clear and manifest purpose of Congress.'" Cipollone v. Liggett Group, Inc., 505 U.S. 504, 516, 112 S.Ct. 2608, 120 L.Ed.2d 407 (1992) (quoting Rice v. Santa Fe Elevator Corp., 331

U.S. 218, 230, 67 S.Ct. 1146, 91 L.Ed. 1447 (1947)). "Accordingly, '[t]he purpose of Congress is the ultimate touchstone' of pre-emption analysis." Id. (citation omitted). The Supreme Court has cautioned that "despite the variety of these opportunities for federal preeminence, we have never assumed lightly that Congress has derogated state regulation, but instead have addressed claims of preemption with the starting presumption that Congress does not intend to supplant state law." New York State Conf. of Blue Cross & Blue Shield Plans v. Travelers Ins. Co., 514 U.S. 645, 654, 115 S.Ct. 1671, 131 L.Ed.2d 695 (1995). The Court in Cipollone stated the test for preemption:

> Congress' intent may be "explicitly stated in the statute's language or implicitly contained in its structure and purpose." Jones v. Rath Packing Co., 430 U.S. 519, 525, 97 S.Ct. 1305, 51 L.Ed.2d 604 (1977). In the absence of an express congressional command, state law is pre-empted if that law actually conflicts with federal law, see Pacific Gas & Elec. Co. v. State Energy Resources Conservation and Dev. Comm'n, 461 U.S. 190, 204, 103 S.Ct. 1713, 75 L.Ed.2d 752 (1983), or if federal law so thoroughly occupies a legislative field "'as to make reasonable the inference that Congress left no room for the States to supplement it.'" Fidelity Fed. Sav. & Loan Assn. v. de la Cuesta, 458 U.S. 141, 153, 102 S.Ct. 3014, 73 L.Ed.2d 664 (1982) (quoting Rice v. Santa Fe Elevator Corp., 331 U.S. at 230, 67 S.Ct. 1146).

505 U.S. at 516, 112 S.Ct. 2608.

The instant case concerns the species of preemption known as field preemption. Field preemption occurs if federal law "thoroughly occupies" the "legislative field" in question, i.e., the field of aviation safety. The Supreme Court has characterized field preemption in this way:

> Congress implicitly may indicate an intent to occupy a given field to the exclusion of state law. Such a purpose properly may be inferred where the pervasiveness of the federal regulation precludes supplementation by the States, where the federal interest in the field is sufficiently dominant, or where "the object sought to be obtained by the federal law and the character of obligations imposed by it ... reveal the same purpose."

Schneidewind v. ANR Pipeline Co., 485 U.S. 293, 300, 108 S.Ct. 1145, 99 L.Ed.2d 316 (1988) (quoting Rice, 331 U.S. at 230, 67 S.Ct. 1146). Thus, implied federal preemption may be found where federal regulation of a field is pervasive, Rice, 331 U.S. at 230, 67 S.Ct. 1146, or where state regulation of the field would interfere with Congressional objectives. See Silkwood v. Kerr-McGee Corp., 464 U.S. 238, 248, 104 S.Ct. 615, 78 L.Ed.2d 443 (1984).

Our finding of implied field preemption here is based on our conclusion that the FAA and relevant federal regulations establish complete and thorough safety standards for interstate and international air transportation that are not subject to supplementation by, or variation among, jurisdictions. While some courts have found federal law to preempt discrete aspects of air safety, e.g. French v. Pan Am Express, Inc., 869 F.2d 1 (1st Cir.1989); World Airways, Inc. v. International Bhd. of Teamsters, 578 F.2d 800 (9th Cir.1978); Kohr v. Allegheny Airlines, Inc., 504 F.2d 400 (7th Cir.1974), we hold that federal law establishes the applicable standards of care in the field of air safety, generally, thus preempting the entire field from state and territorial regulation.

In regard, however, to the second part of the certified question, although the term "field preemption" suggests a broad scope, the scope of a field deemed preempted by federal law may be narrowly defined. For instance, in In re TMI Litigation Cases Consolidated II, 940 F.2d 832, 859 (3d Cir.1991) (TMI II), and In re TMI, 67 F.3d

1103, 1106–07 (3d Cir.1995) (TMI III), we held that federal regulation of nuclear safety preempted state tort law on the standard of care. Still, even though federal law controlled the standard of care, we held that the question whether causation and damages were federally preempted was a separate consideration. See TMI III, 67 F.3d at 1107.

Similarly, in the instant case, we find that Congress, in enacting the FAA and relevant regulations, intended generally to preempt state and territorial regulation of aviation safety. Nevertheless, we find that plaintiffs may recover damages under state and territorial remedial schemes.

In coming to our answers to the certified question, we depart from the precedent established by a number of cases which hold that federal law does not preempt any aspect of air safety. See In re Air Crash Disaster at John F. Kennedy Int'l Airport, 635 F.2d 67, 74–75 (2d Cir.1980); Trinidad v. American Airlines, 932 F.Supp. 521 (S.D.N.Y.1996); In re Air Crash Disaster at Stapleton Int'l Airport, 721 F.Supp. 1185, 1187 (D.Colo.1988). As explained below, we find these cases to be unpersuasive, either because these courts presumed, without deciding through in-depth analysis, that the FAA did not preempt state or territorial air safety standards, or because these courts followed the preemption language of the Airline Deregulation Act (ADA), 49 U.S.C. § 41713(b)(1) (formerly § 1305(a)(1)), an economic deregulation statute that we find inapposite to resolving preemption questions relating to the safety of air operations. Cf. Taj Mahal Travel, Inc. v. Delta Airlines, Inc., 164 F.3d 186, 190–95 (3d Cir.1998) (finding that defamation action was not preempted by the ADA because it did not involve a regulatory or public utility function). We conclude that Congress's intent to preempt state and territorial regulations of air safety is not affected by the language of the ADA.

Federal Preemption of Air Safety Standards

As the District Court set out in its thorough examination of the legislative history, the FAA was enacted in response to a series of "fatal air crashes between civil and military aircraft operating under separate flight rules." United States v. Christensen, 419 F.2d 1401, 1404 (9th Cir.1969) (quoting 1958 U.S.C.C.A.N. 3741, 3742). Congress's purpose in enacting the FAA was "to promote safety in aviation and thereby protect the lives of persons who travel on board aircraft." In re Mexico City Aircrash of October 31, 1979, 708 F.2d 400, 406 (9th Cir.1983); accord Rauch v. United Instruments, Inc., 548 F.2d 452, 457 (3d Cir.1976).

Congress found the creation of a single, uniform system of regulation vital to increasing air safety. City of Burbank v. Lockheed Air Terminal, Inc., 411 U.S. 624, 639, 93 S.Ct. 1854, 36 L.Ed.2d 547 (1973) (noting that "a uniform and exclusive system of federal regulation" is required "if the congressional objectives underlying the [FAA] are to be fulfilled"); Christensen, 419 F.2d at 1404 (remarking that "the whole tenor of the [FAA] and its principal purpose is to create and enforce one unified system of flight rules"). By enacting the FAA, Congress intended to rest sole responsibility for supervising the aviation industry with the federal government:

> [A]viation is unique among transportation industries in its relation to the federal government—it is the only one whose operations are conducted almost wholly within federal jurisdiction, and are subject to little or no regulation by States or local authorities. Thus, the federal government bears virtually complete responsibility for the promotion and supervision of this industry in the public interest.

S.Rep. No. 1811, 85th Cong., 2d Sess. 5 (1958).

Similarly, the House Report accompanying the FAA indicates that one of the purposes of the Act is to give "[t]he Administrator of the new Federal Aviation Agency ... full responsibility and authority for the advancement and promulgation of civil aeronautics generally, including promulgation and enforcement of safety regulations." H.R.Rep. No. 2360, reprinted in 1958 U.S.C.C.A.N. 3741, 3741. In addition, in a letter included as part of the House Report, the Airways Modernization Board Chairman wrote: "It is essential that one agency of government, and one agency alone, be responsible for issuing safety regulations if we are to have timely and effective guidelines for safety in aviation." Id. at 3761.

Thus, legislative history reveals that Congress intended the Administrator, on behalf of the Federal Aviation Administration, to exercise sole discretion in regulating air safety. And this is exactly what Congress accomplished through the FAA. Congress enacted Chapter 447, Safety Regulation, and directed the Administrator to "carry out this chapter in a way that best tends to reduce or eliminate the possibility or recurrence of accidents in air transportation." 49 U.S.C. §44701(c). See City of Burbank, 411 U.S. at 627, 93 S.Ct. 1854 (noting that Congress gave the Administrator of the Federal Aviation Administration "broad authority" with respect to air safety standards).

To effectuate this broad authority to regulate air safety, the Administrator of the FAA has implemented a comprehensive system of rules and regulations, which promotes flight safety by regulating pilot certification, pilot pre-flight duties, pilot flight responsibilities, and flight rules.

In Kohr v. Allegheny Airlines, Inc., 504 F.2d 400 (7th Cir.1974), a mid-air collision case, the Seventh Circuit found the rights and liabilities of the parties to be federally preempted. The court wrote of Congress's objective in enacting the FAA: "[T]he principal purpose of the [FAA] is to create one unified system of flight rules and to centralize in the Administrator of the Federal Aviation Administration the power to promulgate rules for the safe and efficient use of the country's airspace." Id. at 404. The court found a "predominant, indeed almost exclusive, interest of the federal government in regulating the affairs of the nation's airways." Id. at 403.

Similarly, the Second Circuit recognized the broad scope of the FAA and its implied federal preemption of state air safety standards in British Airways Bd. v. Port Authority of New York, 558 F.2d 75 (2d Cir.1977), and held that, by enacting the 1968 noise control amendments to the FAA, Congress "intended to strengthen the FAA's regulatory role within the area already totally preempted—control of flights through navigable airspace." Id. at 84; see also id. at 83 (stating that without federal preemption, "[t]he likelihood of multiple, inconsistent rules would be a dagger pointed at the heart of commerce—and the rule applied might come literally to depend on which way the wind was blowing.").

The understanding of the courts in these early cases, that the FAA's broad scope implied federal preemption of aviation safety standards, has been affirmed over time. In recent decades, courts of appeals have found implied federal preemption of various aspects of air safety that states have attempted to regulate. For example, the First Circuit in French v. Pan Am Express, Inc., 869 F.2d 1 (1st Cir.1989), found pilot regulation, which related to air safety, to be federally preempted. Id. at 6. The court held that "such an intent is implicit in the pervasiveness of relevant federal regulation, the dominance of the federal interest, and the legislative goal of establishing a single, uniform system of control over air safety." Id. at 6–7. The court explained:

> The intricate web of statutory provisions affords no room for the imposition of state law criteria vis-a-vis pilot suitability. We therefore conclude, without

> serious question, that preemption is implied by the comprehensive legal scheme which imposes on the [Administrator] the duty of qualifying pilots for air service.

Id. at 4.

Because the legislative history of the FAA and its judicial interpretation indicate that Congress's intent was to federally regulate aviation safety, we find that any state or territorial standards of care relating to aviation safety are federally preempted. Our analysis is sustained by reference to the broad scope of the FAA, described above. It also is supported by decisions in which courts found federal preemption of discrete, safety-related matters, such as airspace management, flight operations, and aviation noise, because of the promulgation of specific federal regulations over those aspects of air safety. See, e.g., City of Burbank, 411 U.S. at 633, 93 S.Ct. 1854; San Diego Unified Port Dist. v. Gianturco, 651 F.2d 1306, 1316 (9th Cir.1981); Price v. Charter Township, 909 F.Supp. 498 (E.D.Mich.1995); see also [Gianturco, supra] at 1351 n.22 (citing numerous cases in which the courts held flight control regulation to reduce noise federally preempted); Gustafson v. City of Lake Angelus, 76 F.3d 778, 786 (6th Cir.1996) (stating in dictum that "[federal] regulations preempt local law in regard to aircraft safety, the navigable airspace, and noise control"); id. at 792 (Jones, J., concurring) (agreeing with the majority that local land and water use are not preempted, but that aviation safety, navigable airspace and noise control are preempted).

It follows from the evident intent of Congress that there be federal supervision of air safety and from the decisions in which courts have found federal preemption of discrete, safety-related matters, that federal law preempts the general field of aviation safety. Indeed, it would be illogical to conclude that, while federal law preempts state and territorial regulation of matters such as pilot licensing, it does not preempt regulations relating to the exercise of the specific skill for which licensing is necessary—pilots' operation of aircraft.

Moreover, our move from specific to general regulation is not without support in [the] FAA regulations themselves. For example, 14 C.F.R. §91.13(a), which governs "Careless or Reckless Operation," supplies a comprehensive standard of care to be exercised by pilots and flight crew. It provides, "No person may operate an aircraft in a careless or reckless manner so as to endanger the life or property of another." In a case then where there is no specific provision or regulation governing air safety, §91.13(a) provides a general description of the standard required for the safe operation of aircraft.

Thus, in determining the standards of care in an aviation negligence action, a court must refer not only to specific regulations but also to the overall concept that aircraft may not be operated in a careless or reckless manner. The applicable standard of care is not limited to a particular regulation of a specific area; it expands to encompass the issue of whether the overall operation or conduct in question was careless or reckless. Moreover, when a jury is determining what constitutes careless or reckless operation of an aircraft, expert testimony on various aspects of aircraft safety may be helpful to the jury. In the present case, for example, the regulations on the use of seat belts and on the illumination of the "fasten seat belt" sign set the standard for determining both whether American operated the aircraft carelessly or recklessly and whether the passengers, who had not fastened their seatbelts, were contributorily negligent. In addition, expert testimony may help the jury to understand whether the way in which warnings of turbulence and/or illumination of seatbelt signs were conveyed to the passengers constituted careless or reckless operation.

We conclude, therefore, that because of the need for one, consistent means of regulating aviation safety, the standard applied in determining if there has been careless or reckless operation of an aircraft, should be federal; state or territorial regulation is preempted.

[The remainder of the court's opinion is omitted.]

LINDSAY v. NATIONAL TRANSPORTATION SAFETY BOARD

47 F.3d 1209 (D.C. Cir. 1995)

RANDOLPH, Circuit Judge.

The most remarkable thing about this case is that petitioner thinks he is fit to hold a pilot's certificate. The Administrator of the Federal Aviation Administration revoked his certificate, a decision the National Transportation Safety Board sustained. To reconstruct the events precipitating this agency action, and to understand this petition for review of the Board's decision, we must go to central Florida and the pre-dawn hours of Sunday, October 17, 1993.

Two men and two women are at the Shamrock Lounge in Leesburg, drinking heavily. Their common interest is skydiving. Both men are also pilots. Neither woman is. One of the men, Phillip Smith, owns an aging Cessna Model 182, a single engine four-seater aircraft. He keeps his plane at the Leesburg Municipal Airport. Smith is with his girlfriend, Debra Hall, a bartender at the Shamrock. The other man, petitioner Paul Lindsay, holds an FAA airline transportation pilot certificate and has logged 4500 hours of flying time. Lindsay is with his girlfriend, Sandra Sprincis, a nurse who resides in a trailer in the nearby town of Umatilla. Lindsay lives with his mother some 10 miles away, but sometimes stays with Sprincis. They have driven to the bar together in Sprincis' car.

It is 1:30 a.m., and the Shamrock Lounge is about to close for the evening. "It's a nice night for a flight," the men observe. With that, their reckless, irresponsible plan is hatched. Lindsay wants to pilot Smith's plane. He has flown it before. Smith decides to fly it himself. That detail settled, the four men and women leave the bar and drive in Debra Hall's car to Leesburg Airport, 3 miles away. On the way, they stop to buy some beer.

Later, reports reach the Leesburg sheriff's office about a plane flying erratically over the town, a plane perhaps in trouble. Officers arriving at Leesburg Airport at 2:39 a.m. discover Hall's car and piles of clothing on the ground. No one is around. The runway is dark. While the officers wait, a Cessna 182 lands. Philip Smith is in the pilot's seat and very drunk. Hall is next to him. In the back are Lindsay and Sprincis, both naked.

The officers ask Smith to step out. He complies, promptly fails a sobriety test and is arrested for violating Florida law. A deputy sheriff escorts Smith to his cruiser and drives him to the county jail. Other officers stay behind interviewing Hall, Lindsay and Sprincis. Hall gets out of the plane. Lindsay refuses to budge. He is loud, obnoxious and, like Smith, very drunk. He brags about his flying skills. He refuses to tell the officers his address. His girlfriend Sprincis gives them her address in Umatilla and gives the same address for Lindsay.

Sprincis tries to persuade Lindsay to leave with her and Debra Hall. He refuses. He tells Sprincis to "go ahead with" Hall. Lindsay promises to "beat her home anyway." The officers radio the lieutenant to report Lindsay's recalcitrance. By this time, it is 4:00 a.m. The lieutenant radios back that Smith has given Lindsay permission to stay in his plane. Sprincis decides to remain with him. Hall departs in her car, apparently sufficiently recovered from the effects of alcohol. At 4:12 a.m., the officers drive out of the airport, leaving Lindsay and Sprincis there alone. Two of the officers park close by, hidden in the darkness, watching the airport entrance and runway, concerned that Lindsay might try to take off in Smith's plane. The officers maintain their lookout until 4:41 a.m. All is quiet, and they leave to respond to another call.

About 5:00 a.m., a lieutenant and his deputy, having left Smith in jail, return to the Leesburg Airport. It is not yet light. The Cessna is gone. So are Lindsay and Sprincis. Remembering the address Sprincis had given them, they drive 12 miles to Umatilla. There on the runway of the Umatilla Airport they find Smith's plane. Sprincis' trailer is a few hundred yards away, across the street. The door is locked, and when the lieutenant knocks, no one answers. Later that day the police impound the plane.

These largely undisputed facts were adduced during a two-day hearing before an administrative law judge on Lindsay's challenge to the FAA Administrator's emergency order revoking his pilot's certificate. FAA regulations prohibited Lindsay from recklessly operating an aircraft, 14 C.F.R. § 91.13, and from acting as a crewmember of a civil aircraft "[w]ithin 8 hours after the consumption of any alcoholic beverage," 14 C.F.R. § 91.17(a)(1).

Attorneys for both sides stipulated that the only issue at the hearing would be whether Lindsay piloted Smith's plane on its October 17 flight from Leesburg to Umatilla. The ALJ, for reasons we will describe, found that the FAA Administrator had not proven his case. The National Transportation Safety Board reinstated the revocation on appeal.

We have three issues. The first is whether the Board erred in reversing the ALJ's decision. The second is whether the Board's decision upholding the order of revocation is supported by substantial evidence. The third is whether, by presenting an affirmative defense, Lindsay waived any objection to the ALJ's refusal to rule in his favor at the close of the Administrator's case-in-chief.

The Board overturned the ALJ's decision because the ALJ had failed to apply the preponderance of evidence standard in assessing the Administrator's proof. In order to put the Board's reversal in perspective, we need to recount some of the additional evidence produced during the hearing.

The FAA's investigation revealed that when Debra Hall left Leesburg Airport shortly after 4:00 a.m. on October 17 she took Smith's keys with her. Unknown to Hall, however, Smith's plane could be operated without those keys. The pilot-side door did not lock and any sort of key inserted into the ignition switch would turn on the engine. An FAA investigator called Hall on October 18, the day after the flights, and asked her whether she knew who flew the plane to Umatilla. Hall said Lindsay flew it. Asked about the source of her knowledge, Hall stated—in language the investigator recorded in his notes—that because she could not figure out how the plane could have been flown to Umatilla without the keys, "I confronted [Lindsay] at the jail when I bailed Phillip out [about noon on October 17] and he told me he flew it to Umatillo [sic]."

At the hearing, Hall admitted having told the investigator that Lindsay piloted the plane to Umatilla. But she then denied having any knowledge to back up her assertion and said that when she had asked Lindsay at the jail, he told her he had not flown the plane. The investigator's contemporaneous notes show otherwise, of course, as does the investigator's testimony at the hearing. It is true, as Lindsay stresses, that at one point the transcript reports the investigator saying Hall told him Lindsay flew the plane to

"Leesburg." But this appears to be either a slip of the tongue or a mistranscription. There is no other indication of any flight from Umatilla to Leesburg, and the ALJ understood the investigator to have been testifying about the flight from Leesburg to Umatilla.

When the Administrator rested, Lindsay moved for a judgment vacating the emergency revocation order on the ground that the FAA had failed to make out a prima facie case against him. The ALJ denied the motion, and Lindsay proceeded to put on his defense. There is no need to recite the defense in great detail. The ALJ found Lindsay's witnesses, including Lindsay himself, not credible. Lindsay testified that after the police left the airport, he and Sprincis got out of the plane, walked over to a phone booth and called Keith Jordan, a skydiver friend who lived in Leesburg. Jordan said he received the call about 4:00 a.m. With him in his apartment was Edward Carter, an aerial photographer who videotaped skydivers. Carter said he had travelled with Lindsay and Sprincis to Leesburg the evening before, and had been waiting for them to pick him up so that he could spend the night in Sprincis' trailer in Umatilla. After Lindsay's call awakened him, Jordan dressed and he and Carter drove in Jordan's car to the Leesburg Airport, about 10 minutes away. When they arrived, Carter got out of the car, spoke with Lindsay, walked over to the plane with him, and together they unsuccessfully tried to secure the pilot-side door. Lindsay came back to the car and told Jordan and Sprincis that Carter was going to fly the plane to Umatilla. Jordan, Lindsay and Sprincis then drove out of the airport and back to Jordan's apartment, where they spent the night. Carter testified that he flew Smith's plane to Umatilla, about a 10-minute flight. He talked briefly with the security guard, Raymond Cruitt, and then walked over to Sprincis' trailer and fell asleep. He heard the officers knocking on the door of the trailer later in the morning, but decided not to answer.

The holes in this story are large, and the ALJ did not believe it. We will put aside the fact that if Jordan and Carter had arrived at the Leesburg Airport when they said, the officers maintaining surveillance would have seen them, but did not. The most glaring defect in Lindsay's defense is elsewhere—in the utter implausibility of Carter's having flown Smith's plane to Umatilla.

Carter was a pilot, but he was not much of one. Since 1969 he had logged only 100 hours. When the FAA Administrator started inquiring about whether he still had a valid license to fly, Carter invoked his Fifth Amendment privilege against self-incrimination. Carter had never flown Smith's plane, and he did not have Smith's permission to fly it on October 17. He was unfamiliar with the Leesburg Airport. Yet according to him he decided to take off in the dead of night, without lights, on an unfamiliar runway that dropped off into a lake, in a plane he had never flown, without checking the oil level in the plane, and without even knowing how much, if any, fuel it had remaining.

What was the urgency that caused Carter to decide to risk his life to get to Umatilla, a mere 15-minute drive away? When the FAA investigator asked him this rather obvious question before the hearing, Carter said he had no particular reason. At the hearing he changed his story. He explained that he had to get back to open up "Skyworld," a skydiving school at the Umatilla Airport, at 7:30 a.m., and when he met Lindsay and Sprincis at the Leesburg Airport he did not know where Sprincis had left her car. This is, to put it mildly, lame. Sprincis surely knew where she had left her car—at the Shamrock Lounge, only 3 miles from the Leesburg Airport. All Carter had to do was ask her. Besides, Jordan was supposedly there with his car. There is no reasonable explanation why, if he were telling the truth, Carter did not even ask Jordan to give him a lift to Umatilla. Carter still had hours to go before he supposedly had to open up at Skyworld. And yet he says he borrowed—that is, stole—Smith's plane to make the 12-mile trip.

What of Raymond Cruitt, the self-described person responsible for keeping "things clean and neat and security" at the Umatilla Airport, the person to whom Carter allegedly spoke as he was walking from Smith's plane to the trailer? In rambling and disjointed testimony, Cruitt said that Carter had committed "perjury," that Carter had not flown Smith's plane because the actual pilot was one "Lawrence Eugene Kavel," a member of a group dealing in "hypnosis, mind control, disguises," a person Cruitt met some twenty years ago in Washington, D.C., but still recognized through the darkness despite his older appearance, a person Cruitt thought might be a government agent. Cruitt "yelled out to him, I said, well who are you screwing over tonight?" and "he says, you better go back and get in bed because the police are on their way." And so Cruitt went back to bed. Needless to say, the ALJ found Cruitt to be "unreliable" and attached no weight to his "bizarre" testimony.

As to the Administrator's witnesses, the ALJ viewed them as "entirely credible." The ALJ also found that Debra Hall had made the statements the FAA investigator attributed to her; her contrary testimony at the hearing was not "credible." As to Jordan and Sprincis, they had an obvious "bias," and there was "considerable doubt" about their version of the events at the Leesburg Airport. Carter was simply not "a credible witness."

Despite these findings, the ALJ thought Lindsay had introduced "an element of doubt" sufficient to preclude a finding that the Administrator had satisfied his burden of proof. Nonetheless, the ALJ said that he was unconvinced Lindsay "did not commit the alleged violations."

We sustain the Board's ruling that the ALJ misapplied the preponderance of evidence standard. The ALJ had two versions of the events before him. For the Administrator to prevail, the ALJ had to find only that it was, in the familiar formulation, "more likely true than not true" that Lindsay flew the plane to Umatilla. 3 EDWARD J. DEVITT ET AL., FEDERAL JURY PRACTICE AND INSTRUCTIONS § 72.04 (4th ed. 1987); see Concrete Pipe & Products of California, Inc. v. Construction Laborers Pension Trust, 508 U.S. 602,—, 113 S.Ct. 2264, 2279, 124 L.Ed.2d 539 (1993). This standard called for the ALJ to make a comparative judgment about the evidence, rather than a statement about what actually occurred. Certainty was not necessary, nor was the absence of any reasonable doubt. As the Board correctly put it, the ALJ's own findings reveal his belief that it was more probable than not that Lindsay made the flight.

As to the Board's ruling that Lindsay violated the regulations, there is substantial evidence to support it. Someone flew Smith's plane to Umatilla. All the credible evidence points to that someone being Lindsay. He had already demonstrated no hesitation about flying while intoxicated. At the bar he offered to fly the plane on its first outing of the night. Drunk or not, he was the only one among the cast of possible pilots who had the experience and ability to fly out of Leesburg in the dark and land safely in Umatilla. He had flown Smith's plane before. It is fair to assume that while he was sitting in the plane waiting for the police to leave, he knew that he could start the engine without Smith's keys. He was the one who defiantly remained in the plane. He is the one who bragged that without any means of transportation other than the plane, he would beat

Sprincis back to Umatilla if she drove there with Hall. And he is the one Hall identified as having admitted to being the pilot on that flight. Substantial evidence is "such relevant evidence as a reasonable mind might accept as adequate to support a conclusion" (Consolidated Edison Co. v. NLRB, 305 U.S. 197, 229, 59 S.Ct. 206, 217, 83 L.Ed. 126 (1938)), taking "into account whatever in the record fairly detracts from its weight" (Universal Camera Corp. v. NLRB, 340 U.S. 474, 488, 71 S.Ct. 456, 464, 95 L.Ed. 456 (1951)). That standard has been satisfied.

All that remains is Lindsay's claim that the Board erred in making the following ruling:

> At the close of the Administrator's case the respondent moved to dismiss, arguing that the Administrator had not established a prima facie case. The law judge disagreed and denied that motion. On appeal here the respondent challenges that determination. However, since respondent put on evidence in defense of the charges after the rejection of his motion to dismiss, we think he effectively waived his right to object to the law judge's ruling, for once the case is appealed to us, the issue becomes not the correctness of the law judge's view that the burden of going forward with evidence had shifted to the respondent, but, rather, the sufficiency of the evidence in the record, viewed as a whole.

The Board's decision strikes us as entirely correct. The rule it embodies has long governed appeals in the federal courts. A defendant waives an appeal of the denial of a directed verdict motion by putting on evidence. The Supreme Court so held in Bogk v. Gassert, 149 U.S. 17, 23, 13 S.Ct. 738, 739–40, 37 L.Ed. 631 (1893): "A defendant has an undoubted right to stand upon his motion for a nonsuit, and have his writ of error if it be refused; but he has no right to insist upon his exception, after having subsequently put in his testimony and made his case upon the merits, since the court and jury have the right to consider the whole case as made by the testimony." See, e.g., Alston v. Bowins, 733 F.2d 161, 163–64 (D.C.Cir.1984). We have not considered whether all of the Board's previous decisions are consistent with this approach. Even if some are not, the Board's failure to follow or to explain those decisions is harmless. 5 U.S.C. §706. The Administrator's evidence in his case-in-chief surely was, for the reasons already given, enough to withstand Lindsay's motion.

The petition for review is denied.

DEL BALZO v. COLLIER

1993 WL 657778 (N.T.S.B. 1993)

POPE, Administrative Law Judge.

This has been a proceeding under the provisions of Section 609 of the Federal Aviation Act and the provisions of the rules of practice in air safety proceedings of the National Transportation Safety Board. Larry J. Collier, the Respondent, has appealed an Order of Suspension dated March 22, 1993, in which the Administrator suspends any and all Airman Certificates held by the Respondent, including his Commercial Pilot Certificate Number 302388019, for a period of 180 days because of alleged violations of the Federal Aviation Regulations.

The Administrator's Order of Suspension, which pursuant to Section 821.31(a) of the Board's Rules serves as the Complaint, alleges that:

> One. At all times material herein you were and are now the holder of Commercial Pilot Certificate 302388019.

Two. On or about May 7, 1992, you operated N8321B, a Cessna 172, as Pilot-in-Command on a flight in the vicinity of the National Aeronautics and Space Administration's Space Shuttle Launch Facility, Port Canaveral, Florida.

Three. During the aforementioned flight you operated your aircraft within Restricted Area R-2934 without permission of the using or controlling agency once at approximately 2130 hours local time and again at approximately 2200 hours local time, notwithstanding that the R-2934 area was being used for the launch of the Space Shuttle and that a NOTAM [Notice to Airmen] had been issued for said launch.

As a result, you violated the following sections of the Federal Aviation Regulations:

(a) Section 91.103(a) in that you as Pilot-in-Command began a flight without familiarizing yourself with the boundaries and confines of Restricted Area R-2934.

(b) Section 91.133(a) in that you operated an aircraft within a restricted area contrary to the restrictions imposed when you did not have permission of the using or controlling agency.

(c) Section 91.13 in that you operated an aircraft in a reckless or careless manner so as to endanger the lives or property of another.

To prove his case the Administrator called three witnesses. His first witness was Air Safety Inspector Dawn Veatch who testified to her observations and actions on May 7, 1992, when she was aboard an FAA aircraft providing aerial security in the vicinity of the Space Center for a Shuttle launch where there are areas of restricted airspace above and in the vicinity of the Space Center.

The inner zone, designated as R-2934, which goes from the ground to infinity is prohibited to air traffic 24 hours a day, seven days a week. The outer zone from 11,000 feet to infinity is in effect during the times of launches and is announced by NOTAMs. She stated that a NOTAM was in effect when she observed Respondent's aircraft on May 7th, 1992.

Inspector Veatch and her partner, Inspector Hunt, were operating an unmarked FAA aircraft at 12,000 feet when they received notice of a possible intruder from Air Traffic Control at Patrick Air Force Base. Shortly after that, Air Traffic Control notified them that there was an intruder at 12,000 feet and vectored them to an interception. The interception took place at 12,000 feet in the outer restricted zone and Inspector Veatch travelled with the intruder into the inner restricted zone to a point about one mile west of the Shuttle landing strip. She said that she circled the intruding aircraft, the Cessna 172, waggled her wings, lowered her gear, tried to establish radio contact, and otherwise tried to get the attention of the pilot, but was unsuccessful. The intruder turned and headed out of the inner zone and Inspector Veatch discontinued surveillance and resumed patrol. She said that the Shuttle launch was delayed because of the intruder and the countdown resumed after the intruder left the inner zone.

After the launch, Inspector Veatch was notified that the intruder was back and she observed him again penetrate the inner zone. This time she followed the intruder out of the restricted zones to the Melbourne Airport where the intruder landed and at her request was detained by Airport Security.

When she and her partner interviewed the pilot he identified himself as the Respondent but did not have a Pilot or Medical Certificate in his possession or on his aircraft.

She saw that instead of a door handle on one of his aircraft's doors he was using a pair of vise-grip pliers, which is not provided for in the aircraft's Type certification.

She also discovered in his log book that he had made a number of repairs to his aircraft himself, as described in Paragraphs 6(1), (2) and (3) of the Complaint.

She advised him that he would be in violation if he operated the aircraft without a Pilot and Medical Certificate in his possession and while the plane was unairworthy because of unapproved repairs. She did not ground the aircraft.

After she and her partner departed she learned from the Airport Authorities that the Respondent also took off in his aircraft.

She conceded that while the original intercept was at 12,000 feet she may have descended to 11,000 feet while circling and following the Respondent, and as he exited the inner control zone Air Traffic Control told her that he was at 11,000 feet.

Inspector Veatch's testimony was corroborated in important details by the testimony of her partner, Inspector Hunt, and as to radar observation and tracking of the intruder by the deposition containing the testimony of Dina M. Tomczak, the Patrick Air Force Base Air Traffic Controller. Ms. Tomczak is out of the country pursuant to military orders and was unavailable as a witness. Her observation of her radar showed the Respondent at 12,000 feet in the inner restricted zone and at 11,000 feet in the outer restricted zone, in violation of both restricted zones.

Respondent testified that his violation of the restricted zone was inadvertent. He stated that instead of setting his VOR [VHF omnidirectional range navigation system] for a 340 degree radial he mistakenly entered a 350 degree radial and that took him into the inner restricted zone without his knowledge. He was very rattled by being buzzed and circled by the unmarked aircraft and turned and left the inner zone at 10,500 feet, which was under the outer restrictive zone. He showed a videotape which he took showing the FAA plane above his aircraft.

He said that he subsequently discovered that he needed bifocal glasses and that vision problems had caused him to mis-set his VOR radial. He said that he did not violate the restricted airspace a second time, although he admitted that he turned back to videotape the launch when he heard the countdown reach nine minutes.

He admitted that he made the repairs noted in the log book and said that he did not know that was improper. There is no evidence here that the Respondent holds any kind of certificate authorizing him to make aircraft repairs. He said the vise-grips did not make the plane unairworthy, which he equated to being unsafe.

He admitted that he did not have his License or Medical Certificate with him and that he took off again that night from the Melbourne Airport even though Inspector Veatch had told him it would be a violation. He explained that it would have been too inconvenient to return to his home any other way.

Upon consideration of the entire record and having had the opportunity to observe the demeanor of the witnesses I make the following findings of fact in law. I conclude that Respondent is a credible witness; however, I also find that although he may not have intended to violate the restricted airspace zones around the Space Center on May 7, 1992, there is overwhelming evidence that he did so as described by the two Aviation

Safety Inspectors who observed him visually and the Air Traffic Controller who observed the violations on radar.

Respondent admitted that on the first occasion he inadvertently strayed into the restricted zone through a mis-setting of instruments, but he said that he was flying at 10,500 feet when he turned back to videotape the launch, so that he did not enter the outer restricted zone whose bottom is at 11,000 feet.

In this regard, however, whatever the Respondent may generally think he had done the visual observations of the two Safety Inspectors and by the radar operator confirm the two separate violations, both of which penetrated both the outer and inner zones, the first of which disrupted the Space Shuttle countdown and both of which would have endangered the Shuttle astronauts and the Shuttle had it had to attempt an emergency landing on the Shuttle landing strip.

Inadvertence is no defense to violation of restricted airspace. Respondent should not have been flying an aircraft if his vision did not allow him to accurately read and set his instruments. And as a pilot he is charged with the responsibility to familiarize himself with applicable charts and navigate his aircraft accurately. Clearly he did neither.

In his testimony, Respondent virtually admitted all other of the alleged violations by admitting the underlying facts. That he may have thought that they were trivial or stale or inconvenient to observe is no defense.

Upon consideration of all the substantial, reliable and probative evidence of record I find that the Administrator has proven by a preponderance of the evidence that Respondent on or about May 7, 1992, violated Sections 91.103(a), 91.133(a), [and] 91.13 of the Federal Aviation Regulations.

UNITED STATES AVIATION UNDERWRITERS, INC. v. NATIONAL INSURANCE UNDERWRITERS

344 N.W.2d 532 (Wis. Ct. App. 1984)

SCOTT, Chief Judge.

United States Aviation Underwriters, Inc. and Whitman Aviation, Inc. appeal from a judgment dismissing their action for monetary damages against National Insurance Underwriters, Inc. and the denial of their post-conviction motions. The primary issue before us is whether a pilot's failure to yield the right-of-way while landing as prescribed by 14 C.F.R. §91.67(f) (1983) constitutes negligence per se. We hold that 14 C.F.R. §91.67, as promulgated under the authority of 49 U.S.C. §1348 (1976), is a safety statute. Because the evidence establishes that the respondents' pilot violated §91.67(f), we conclude that his operation of the respondents' aircraft constituted negligence as a matter of law. Therefore, we reverse and remand with directions that judgment be directed in favor of the appellants and damages awarded accordingly.

The facts of the case legally significant to this appeal are not in dispute. The case arises out of a collision between two aircraft—a Piper Lance and a Piper Arrow—on June 6, 1979 at the Burlington, Wisconsin airport. The appellants, United States Aviation, Inc. and Whitman Aviation, Inc., are the insurer and owner of the Piper Arrow which was operated at the time of the accident by Robert Lawn and William Curler. The respondents, National Insurance Underwriters, Inc. and Dale Baugh, are the insurer and operator of the Piper Lance.

The two aircraft collided while both were attempting to land at the Burlington airport. Apparently neither pilot saw the other aircraft. Both planes were destroyed in the accident. The appellants sought to recover the damages resulting from the destruction of the Piper Arrow, and the action was tried before a jury on January 31, 1983.

The evidence presented at trial established that the respondents' Piper Lance landed on top of the appellants' aircraft. Both Baugh and a defense expert witness testified to this fact.

At trial, neither party disputed the applicability of the Federal Aviation Regulations, specifically 14 C.F.R. §91.67(f), concerning the right-of-way rules for landing of aircraft. The trial court included this provision as part of the instructions submitted to the jury. The appellants argued that Baugh was negligent as a matter of law for failing to yield the right-of-way to the Piper Arrow during landing and asked the trial court to enter a finding accordingly. The trial court declined to do so and left it up to the jury to determine whether Baugh had violated 14 C.F.R. §91.67(f) and was negligent in operating the Piper Lance. The trial court did determine as a matter of law that the pilot of the Piper Arrow was not negligent in the operation of that aircraft. The jury returned a verdict finding Baugh not negligent in the operation of the Piper Lance.

On post-conviction motions, the appellants argued that Baugh was negligent as a matter of law for violating 14 C.F.R. §91.67(f) and that the evidence did not support the jury's finding that Baugh was not negligent as to lookout. The appellants requested the trial court to change the special verdict answers to reflect affirmative responses to the questions concerning whether Baugh was causally negligent in the operation of the Piper Lance. The trial court denied these motions and entered judgment dismissing the action.

On appeal, the appellants renew their arguments made during the post-conviction stage. We hold 14 C.F.R. §91.67(f) is a safety regulation, the evidence established Baugh violated this provision, and that this violation constitutes negligence per se.

A safety statute is a legislative enactment designed to protect a specified class of persons from a particular type of harm. Walker v. Bignell, 100 Wis.2d 256, 268, 301 N.W.2d 447, 454 (1981). 14 C.F.R. §91.67(f) provides:

> Aircraft, while on final approach to land, or while landing, have the right-of-way over other aircraft in flight or operating on the surface. When two or more aircraft are approaching an airport for the purpose of landing, the aircraft at the lower altitude has the right-of-way, but it shall not take advantage of this rule to cut in front of another which is on final approach to land, or to overtake that aircraft.

This regulation was promulgated under the authority of the Federal Aviation Program, 49 U.S.C. §1348(c) (1976), which provides that:

> The Administrator is further authorized and directed to prescribe air traffic rules and regulations governing the flight of aircraft, for the navigation, protection, and identification of aircraft, for the protection of persons and property on the ground, and for the efficient utilization of the navigable airspace, including rules as to safe altitudes of flight and rules for the prevention of collision between aircraft, between aircraft and land or water vehicles, and between aircraft and airborne objects.

The language of this section dictates the purpose and nature of the rules and regulations promulgated thereunder—in part, to protect persons and property by preventing collisions between aircraft. 14 C.F.R. §91.67(f) facilitates this purpose by prescribing specific right-of-way procedures required for the safe landing of two or more aircraft. We conclude that §91.67(f) is a safety provision because it was promulgated and designed to protect persons from injury and property from damage resulting from collisions between aircraft occurring during landing.

There is no question 14 C.F.R. §91.67(f) applied to the aircraft in this case. See Sheboygan Airways, Inc. v. Industrial Commission, 209 Wis. 352, 360–61, 245 N.W. 178, 181–82 (1932). Neither party objected to its substantive inclusion as a jury instruction.

There is no dispute that the planes collided while both were attempting to land and that Baugh's Piper Lance landed on top of the Piper Arrow. Both Baugh and Mr. Harris, the defense's expert witness, testified that the Piper Lance landed on top of the Piper Arrow. The applicability of 14 C.F.R. §91.67(f) and this testimony require the conclusion that Baugh failed to yield the right-of-way. We conclude there is no evidence to support a finding that Baugh did not violate §91.67(f).

The violation of a safety statute constitutes negligence per se if "the harm inflicted was the type the statute was designed to prevent and ... the person injured was within the class of persons sought to be protected." Walker, 100 Wis.2d at 268, 301 N.W.2d at 454. The collision which occurred between the Piper Arrow and the Piper Lance is precisely the type of accident which observance of 14 C.F.R. §91.67(f) was designed to prevent. The occupants in the Piper Arrow and the Piper Lance are within the class of persons the regulation was promulgated to protect. We hold, therefore, that Baugh's violation of §91.67(f) constituted negligence per se. The trial court erred in not so finding and in not answering question # 1 of the special verdict accordingly.

The respondents contend that the verdict finding that Baugh was not negligent in the operation of the Piper Lance is supported by the jury's belief in the credible expert testimony that Baugh was not negligent in failing to maintain a proper lookout for the Piper Arrow. The respondents seem to be arguing that the duty to yield the right-of-way is interrelated and, in fact, dependent upon a pilot's additional duty of lookout—in effect, that if Baugh was not negligent in failing to see the Piper Arrow, then there could also be no finding of negligence as to the duty to yield the right-of-way set out under 14 C.F.R. §91.67(f). This position is erroneous for it fails to recognize that these duties are separate and distinct.

The right-of-way regulation, 14 C.F.R. §91.67(f), imposes the duty of yielding right-of-way regardless of lookout. Cf. Zartner v. Scopp, 28 Wis.2d 205, 216, 137 N.W.2d 107, 113 (1965). We recognize that automobile rules of the road do not apply directly to aviation cases. Air Wisconsin, Inc. v. North Central Airlines, Inc., 98 Wis.2d 301, 326–27, 296 N.W.2d 749, 760–61 (1980). However, we find the determination in Zartner, that lookout and yielding the right-of-way constitute separate duties, analogous and adopt it for purposes of aviation cases. We hold the duty to yield right-of-way under §91.67(f) is separate from and independent of a pilot's duty of lookout. A finding that a pilot failed to yield right-of-way constitutes negligence regardless of an opposite determination as to lookout. The duty to yield the right-of-way is an absolute duty, the violation of which is negligence as a matter of law. In this case, the undisputed evidence establishing that Baugh violated §91.67(f) requires a finding that he was negligent in operating the Piper Lance regardless of a finding that he was not negligent as to lookout.

Because the trial court found as a matter of law that Robert Lawn was not negligent in the operation of his aircraft, the court should also have answered question # 2 of the special verdict in the affirmative. Given that Baugh was negligent in operating his aircraft and Lawn was not negligent, Baugh's negligence as a matter of law caused the damages awarded to the plaintiffs.

Finally, because the question of liability involved in its entirety a legal determination, the trial court should have directed verdict in favor of the appellants. We, therefore, reverse and remand to the trial court for a judgment on the verdict as modified by this opinion.

JETCRAFT CORPORATION v. FLIGHTSAFETY INTERNATIONAL, INC.

781 F. Supp. 687 (D. Kan. 1991)

KELLY, District Judge.

On December 10, 1988, a Cessna 650 owned by plaintiff Jetcraft made its final approach toward Runway 31 of the Hutchinson Municipal Airport. Johnny De Los Santos, a commercial pilot licensed by the FAA and employed by Transporte Aero, S.A., sat in the left-hand front seat of the aircraft and conducted the final approach. Beside him, in the right-hand front seat, sat Wesley D. Kimball, a flight instructor for defendant FlightSafety International, which had agreed to provide flight training for De Los Santos and the other passengers in the plane: Javier Vargas, Jose Gomez, and Jose Aruro Jiminez. At the time of the final approach, Vargas was also in the cockpit, sitting in the jump seat immediately behind Kimball and De Los Santos.

De Los Santos approached the field to conduct a "touch and go" landing under the supervision of Kimball. In a "touch and go" landing, the airplane is landed but not brought to a full stop. Instead, full power is applied to allow the aircraft to take off again.

As De Los Santos maneuvered the plane for its final approach, Kimball, as the pilot in the right-hand co-pilot seat, was the person responsible for the extension of the flaps and landing gear. De Los Santos called for Kimball to extend full flaps. Kimball complied, extending the flaps.

De Los Santos then called for Kimball to lower the landing gear. Kimball moved the landing gear handle to the down position. The red "gear unlocked" light on the instrument panel illuminated. A few seconds later, the landing gear extended and three green landing gear annunciator lights illuminated while the red "gear unlocked" light extinguished. The three green lights indicated to the pilots that the left, right, and nose landing gear were extended and locked in place. Kimball told De Los Santos, "Down and three green lights." De Los Santos replied: "Check."

De Los Santos noticed that his final approach, as indicated by the visual approach slope indicator, was a little high. He then descended to an appropriate position. Intending to reduce power on the airplane to idle when the plane descended to 50 feet, De Los Santos told Kimball to make an altitude call when the airplane reached that altitude. As the plane descended, Kimball confirmed on two separate occasions that the three landing gear lights continued to glow.

A slight crosswind of five to seven knots blew from the right side of the runway. De Los Santos gave the plane a slight amount of right rudder to correct for the wind. As the plane touched down, the left landing gear collapsed. Inside the cockpit, the landing gear unsafe horn sounded. The green landing light for the left landing gear no longer glowed green.

De Los Santos tried to advance the throttle to add power to the plane, which at this time was traveling at almost 90 knots. Vargas, seeing De Los Santos try to add power, warned, "We are crashing, pull the power back." But, immediately after the landing gear unsafe horn sounded, the left wing touched the runway. The aircraft veered off the runway and came to a stop after hitting the frangible light stanchions lining the runway.

Jetcraft has now brought the present action, in which it seeks recovery for the damage to the Cessna 650. In the present motion [for summary judgment], Jetcraft seeks a determination that defendant FlightSafety, and its agent Kimball, owed it a duty of due care, that the defendants breached this duty, and that the breach was the proximate cause of the damages to the Jetcraft airplane. In support of its motion, Jetcraft argues that the doctrines of collateral estoppel, negligence per se, and res ipsa loquitur support each of the determinations of duty, breach, and proximate cause.

The parties disagree as to the cause of the accident. Jetcraft suggests that it was the fault of Kimball, who somehow retracted the landing gear after initially placing the gear into the down and locked position. In support of this suggestion, Jetcraft points out that the landing gear extended and retracted a number of times before the accident without any abnormality. It further points to the results of a National Transportation Safety Board Factual Report of the accident, which stated: "Extensive testing over a three month period failed to produce any evidence of any malfunction of the landing gear system or related components which could have resulted in a [sic] unlocked condition of the main landing gear."

FlightSafety denies the suggestion that the failure of the landing gear was caused by Kimball, and the suggestion that there was nothing defective in the gear. Kimball expressly denies moving the landing gear handle after the gear was first down and locked. Jetcraft has provided no direct evidence contradicting this denial. Indeed, during a post-accident discussion with Jetcraft officers, De Los Santos stated that he did not see any movement of Kimball's arm during the accident sequence, nor did he see Kimball move the landing gear handle during the accident sequence.

The Cessna 650 which is the focus of the present case had made 464 takeoff and landing cycles prior to the December 10, 1988 accident. Both parties dispute the status of discovery with regard to prior landing gear failures during the prior flight history of the Cessna 650. The defendants aver in their response that no formal discovery has been conducted on the issue. Plaintiff Jetcraft denies this. Neither side supports its position with reference to evidence in the record. On the other hand, the record does establish that, just four days prior to the accident, a maintenance report for the aircraft indicated "landing gear light inoperative." Jetcraft notes that maintenance workers replaced a landing gear light, and that as a result, "the system was fully operational four days later." (Pltf's Reply, at 15). Jetcraft, however, does not bother to provide any evidentiary support in its reply for the conclusion that the system was "fully operational." The coincidence of a problem with the landing lights, so shortly before the accident, when coupled with an absence of any direct evidence of negligence by Kimball, helps to create a clear issue of material fact as to the cause of the accident.

Finally, in connection with the National Transportation Safety Board test results, FlightSafety points out that the tests do not establish that there was nothing mechanically defective in the landing gear assembly, only that the NTSB was unable to find evidence of a malfunction. Moreover, certain test results indicate problems with the landing gear assembly. In attempting to extend the landing gear actuator to the point which would cause the green down and locked indicator lights to glow, engineers were unable to achieve positive results on the first two occasions. On the third attempt, engineers were able to obtain a down and locked indication—by the application of a tensile load of 4,700 pounds, over 100 times the force load normally necessary to get the gear down and locked.

Kimball, De Los Santos, and Vargas each had prior flight experience. Both De Los Santos and Vargas were commercial pilots licensed by the FAA and employed by the plaintiff Transporte Aero, S.A. De Los Santos had some 2,600 to 2,700 total flying hours as a pilot, including 450 to 500 hours as a pilot in command of jet aircraft. Vargas had some 3,150 total flying hours as a pilot, including 1,600 to 1,700 hours as a pilot in command of jet aircraft.

Kimball has been a flight instructor since 1946. He began work for FlightSafety as a simulation instructor in April, 1986, and as a flight instructor in January, 1987. Kimball has some 9,000 hours of pilot in command experience.

1. Collateral Estoppel

Jetcraft argues that Kimball and FlightSafety are collaterally estopped to argue the issues of duty, breach, and causation owing to the results of FAA proceedings after the December 10, 1988 crash. Jetcraft argues that prior proceedings before the FAA preclude the relitigation of the issues relating to the defendant's alleged violation of FAA regulations.

On May 19, 1989, the FAA sent Kimball a notice of proposed certificate action, in which Kimball was alleged to have violated 14 C.F.R. §§61.57(c) and 91.9. Section 61.57(c) provides in part:

> No person may act as a pilot in command of an aircraft carrying passengers, nor of an aircraft certificated for more than one required pilot flight crewmember, unless within the preceding 90 days, he has made three takeoffs and three landings as the sole manipulator of the flight controls in an aircraft of the same category and class and, if a type rating is required, of the same type.

On the other hand, 14 C.F.R. §91.13(a) [the precursor of §91.9] provides that "[n]o person may operate an aircraft in a careless or reckless manner so as to endanger the life or property of another."

On May 23, 1989, Kimball requested an informal conference to consider the allegations. The informal conference was held between Kimball and FAA personnel on June 22, 1989. As a result of this conference, the FAA found that Kimball had violated §61.57(c) and suspended Kimball's certificate for 60 days. The allegation of a violation of §91.9 was dropped.

On May 26, 1989, the FAA sent a notice of proposed civil penalty to FlightSafety, alleging the violation of §91.9 on the basis of Kimball's supposed failure to have the level of prior flight experience required by §61.57(c). On June 14, 1989, FlightSafety paid the proposed civil penalty by sending a check in the amount of $1,000.00 to the FAA.

Jetcraft's attempt to establish collateral estoppel with regard to the FAA proceedings should be rejected. Jetcraft was not a party to those proceedings, nor was it in privity with a party. Accordingly, due to this lack of mutuality, Jetcraft is not entitled to claim preclusive effect for any issues determined during the course of the proceedings.

In its reply, Jetcraft attempts to argue that FlightSafety is collaterally estopped from disputing the findings of a violation of §61.57(c), even though Jetcraft was neither itself a party nor in privity with a party to the earlier FAA proceedings against Kimball and

FlightSafety. On the basis of an isolated comment in Goetz v. Board of Trustees, 203 Kan. 340, 349, 454 P.2d 481 (1969), Jetcraft argues that mutuality of parties is not required for the use of collateral estoppel under Kansas law.

In describing the distinctions between res judicata and collateral estoppel, the court in Goetz stated in passing:

> Another distinction between the two doctrines, res judicata and collateral estoppel, is that collateral estoppel does not require mutuality of parties.

203 Kan. at 349–50, 454 P.2d 481 (citation omitted). This comment by the court was clearly dicta. The court also held directly that collateral estoppel "prevents a second litigation of the same issues between the same parties or their privies." Id., at 349, 454 P.2d 481. The court found that, for purposes of resolving a widow plaintiff's rights to the pension of her deceased husband, the wife should be considered as in privity with the husband, and hence collaterally estopped from relitigating issues initially raised by the husband in earlier proceedings.

The suggestion in Goetz that collateral estoppel does not require mutuality of parties has found no further support in the rulings of Kansas courts. Rather, the Kansas Supreme Court has consistently required, as a prerequisite to the use of collateral estoppel, that the parties of the subsequent litigation be identical to or in privity with parties in the earlier action. Jones v. Bordman, 243 Kan. 444, 460, 759 P.2d 953 (1988); Jackson Trak Group, Inc. v. Mid States Port Auth., 242 Kan. 683, 690, 751 P.2d 122 (1988); Patrons Mut. Ins. Ass'n v. Harmon, 240 Kan. 707, 732 P.2d 741 (1987); McDermott v. Kansas Public Serv. Co., 238 Kan. 462, 712 P.2d 1199 (1986); Wells v. Davis, 226 Kan. 586, 603 P.2d 180 (1979); Neville v. Hennigh, 214 Kan. 681, 522 P.2d 443 (1974); Bud Jennings Carpets & Draperies v. Greenhouse, 210 Kan. 92, 499 P.2d 1096 (1972). The supreme court in McDermott explicitly concluded that "abandonment of the mutuality rule, it seems to us, would be unfair." 238 Kan. at 473, 712 P.2d 1199. In Jones, the court reached the same conclusion, stating that, under Kansas law, "collateral estoppel, or issue preclusion, require[s] mutuality, i.e., the issue subject to preclusion must have arisen in a prior case in which both of the current parties were adequately represented." 243 Kan. at 460, 759 P.2d 953.

Faced with such consistent and explicit adherence to the rule of mutuality, for the plaintiffs to suggest herein—on the basis of an isolated comment in dicta in an early case—that mutuality is not required is quite remarkable.

In addition to the lack of mutuality, Jetcraft's collateral estoppel argument fails since the prior adjudication did not provide a sufficient level of formal protections and procedures to warrant giving its findings preclusive effect. Although adjudicative determinations of an administrative agency may be given preclusive effect where the "agency conducts a trial-type hearing, makes findings, and applies the law," no preclusion will occur where the formality of the proceedings before the agency is sufficiently diminished. Neunzig v. Seaman U.S.D. No. 345, 239 Kan. 654, 659, 722 P.2d 569 (1986) (quoting 4 Davis, Administrative Law § 21:3 (2d ed.1983)). In Neunzig, the court held that collateral estoppel was justified where the prior determination was made by an administrative "hearing committee possess[ing] many of the functions associated with court proceedings" and "the type of procedural protection a court provides." Id., at 660, 722 P.2d 569.

In the present case, Kimball was not accompanied at the informal hearing held on June 22, 1988 by an attorney. Nor was any hearing officer or administrative law judge present. The only persons attending the meeting were Kimball, an FAA attorney, and two FAA investigators. The FAA memorandum reflecting this hearing itself reflects the informal nature of the proceedings, which it refers to as an "INFORMAL CONFERENCE."

Jetcraft notes that under 14 C.F.R. § 13.19(c)(5), a pilot subjected to possible certificate action is not limited to an informal conference on the matter but may request a formal hearing. A formal hearing allows for the taking of depositions, subpoena of witnesses, examination of witnesses under oath, cross-examination by the respondent, [and] "adequate opportunity to present arguments." See 14 C.F.R. §§ 13.37–63.

But the issue for which Jetcraft seeks preclusion here was not resolved by means of a formal § 13.19(c)(5) proceeding, with all the protections accorded therein. Rather, the issue was resolved by an informal conference, a proceeding which simply does not rise to a sufficient level of formality to support collateral estoppel. Kimball may have had the right to request a different type of tribunal, but that is not relevant. The purpose of collateral estoppel or issue preclusion is to prevent the relitigation of issues of fact or law which were actually considered by a former judgment. Restatement (Second) of Judgments § 38 (1982). Accordingly, in determining whether the formality accorded in the prior proceeding was sufficient to justify preclusion, the focus should be on the protections and procedures of the tribunal which actually resolved the issue, and not the protections accorded under other types of proceedings which could have—but were not—used to resolve the issue. Jetcraft has failed to provide any evidence or argument that the informal conference conducted on June 22, 1988 was of sufficient formality to justify the imposition of collateral estoppel.

In addition to the lack of mutuality, and the informal nature of the FAA proceedings, Jetcraft's arguments of collateral estoppel must fail for a final and independent reason. As noted above, collateral estoppel bars claims which were actually litigated between the parties. Jetcraft seeks a determination that Kimball violated 14 C.F.R. § 61.57(c) (by conducting the December 10th training flight without sufficient flight experience), while FlightSafety violated 14 C.F.R. § 91.9 (by operating an aircraft in a careless or reckless manner).

Yet in the earlier proceedings before the FAA, that agency made no findings of a violation as claimed by Jetcraft. The citation against FlightSafety was derivative only, premised on the allegedly wrongful actions of Kimball. As to Kimball, the FAA dropped the allegations of careless or reckless flight operation in violation of § 91.9. The only direct findings in the case relate to § 61.57(c). As to that provision, the FAA found Kimball had the necessary flight experience, and premised its temporary suspension of Kimball's certificate on the mere fact that the paperwork reflecting the experience was insufficient:

> Mr. Kimball had made the appropriate number of simulator takeoffs and landings required by [Exemption] 4058 and met all other requirements. However, training records were not completed to show such and there was no certification by another instructor that simulator training was completed.... [T]he takeoffs and landings were satisfactorily completed but were performed without other FlightSafety personnel present to witness or conduct a proper review for certification.... As such, it was agreed that the FAA should proceed with a violation of 61.57(c) but drop the 91.9 violation, in that, on this occasion, noncompliance with the certification and record-keeping functions of the exemption alone did not endanger the lives or property of others.

FAA Memorandum of Informal Conference, June 22, 1989.

The FAA's finding of a violation of § 61.57(c) related solely to record-keeping requirements, and explicitly that Kimball had the requisite flight experience. It also explicitly found that the violation of record-keeping requirements did not affect the safety of the lives or property of others. Jetcraft's attempt to establish the FAA adjudication as a finding of fault which is in any way relevant to the issues in the present action is clearly unwarranted.

Jetcraft, in attempting to salvage its claim of collateral estoppel, argues in its Reply that § 61.57(c) contains no independent paperwork requirements. Apparently Jetcraft is attempting to argue what the FAA should have found. In so doing, Jetcraft seeks to have its cake (the preclusive effect of a finding of a violation of FAA requirements) while eating it too (by wholly ignoring the explicitly stated reasons for the FAA's findings).

The FAA finding that Kimball violated § 61.57(c) establishes nothing that has any relevance in the present action. Nor does FlightSafety's payment of the $1,000.00 civil penalty establish issue preclusion as to any relevant matter. The claims against FlightSafety were limited to derivative claims arising from the actions of Kimball.

FlightSafety paid the civil penalty prior to the resolution of the charges against Kimball. The May 26 notice of proposed civil penalty merely alleges that FlightSafety violated § 91.9 by Kimball's alleged failure to have the flight experience required by § 61.57(c). Other than the mere fact of the proposed finding and the subsequent payment, there is no other evidence before the court. Faced with this absence of any direct admission by FlightSafety, collateral estoppel is not justified. And, in any event, the absence of mutuality again prevents the application of collateral estoppel on the basis of the payment of the civil penalty.

2. Negligence Per Se

Jetcraft next argues that even if Kimball and FlightSafety are not collaterally estopped from contending that they complied with FAA regulations, the undisputed material facts nonetheless demonstrate a violation of the regulations, and hence constitute negligence per se. Jetcraft argues that Kimball, as the pilot in charge of the aircraft, was ultimately responsible for the safety of the flight. 14 C.F.R. § 91.3 (1988). Under 14 C.F.R. § 91.3(a) (1990), "the pilot in command of an aircraft is directly responsible for, and is the final authority as to, the operation of that aircraft."

As the cases cited by Jetcraft, Hayes v. United States, 899 F.2d 438 (5th Cir.1990); AAR Corp. v. United States, Case No. 6-2781-W (W.D.Okla. Nov. 30, 1987), clearly establish, the pilot in command assumes a duty for proper control of the plane, but is not made thereby a guarantor of the safety of the flight. Independent evidence is required to demonstrate breach of the duty and that that breach was the proximate cause of the plaintiff's injuries.

Here, the record does not establish beyond a reasonable doubt that the crash of the Jetcraft Cessna 650 was caused by a failure of Kimball to properly assume the duties of pilot in command. As noted earlier, the parties present different theories as to the cause of the crash. According to FlightSafety, the crash was caused by some malfunction of the plane's landing gear. According to Jetcraft, the crash was caused by Kimball's failure to operate the landing gear properly. Jetcraft's theory is an inference, based upon an alleged lack of defect in the landing gear assembly.

That inference is not sufficient to justify the imposition of summary judgment. The true, and potentially defective, state of the landing gear assembly remains disputed by the parties and unresolved in the evidentiary record. Moreover, Kimball has directly and affirmatively denied any error with regard to the operation of the landing gear. Accordingly, summary judgment should not issue. With regard to the supposed violations of FAA regulations §§ 61.57(c) and 91.9, as noted earlier, the present state of the record supports at best the conclusion that the defendants, while failing to comply with certain documentary or certificatory requirements of the regulations, adhered to the substance of the regulations requiring minimum prior flight experience.

3. Res Ipsa Loquitur

Finally, Jetcraft suggests that Kimball and FlightSafety may be found to have breached their duty of due care under the doctrine of res ipsa loquitur. That doctrine, however, is not implicated in the present action since it requires that the instrumentality causing damage to the plaintiff be in the exclusive control of the defendant. Although Kimball, as pilot in command of the aircraft, had the authority to control the flight operations of the aircraft, he did not have exclusive control over the aircraft as that term is used for purposes of establishing res ipsa loquitur.

There is no evidence that, merely because Kimball was the pilot in command of the aircraft during the December 10, 1988 training flight, he also had sole control over the design, construction, and maintenance of the landing gear assembly. As a prerequisite to the use of the doctrine of res ipsa loquitur, the proximate cause of the plaintiff's damages must be determined. John T. Arnold Assoc. v. City of Wichita, 5 Kan.App.2d 301, 615 P.2d 814 (1980). In this case, however, the proximate cause of the crash of the aircraft is not known at the present time, and must await determination at the trial of the present matter.

4. Motion to Supplement

As a final matter, Jetcraft has moved to supplement its motion for summary judgment on the basis of a June 9, 1989 letter from the FAA. The letter bears upon the existence of Exemption 4058, which allows FlightSafety to count pilot simulator time toward the amount of flying time required by instructors under §61.57(c). Jetcraft apparently seeks to advance the position that the exemption does not exist.

In response to a Freedom of Information Act request by counsel, an FAA manager writes in the June 9 letter: "In reviewing our files, we do not show any documents or correspondence written to FlightSafety or to Mr. Wesley Kimbell [sic], relating to waivers from Section 61.57(c)."

The motion to supplement will be denied. The letter does not establish that the exemption does not exist (as Jetcraft purports). It merely states that the FAA was not able to locate the documentation on the exemption. FlightSafety, on the other hand, attaches to its memorandum in opposition a copy of the exemption. The exemption is repeatedly referenced in other FAA correspondence. The suggestion that, despite all this, the exemption is imaginary is not warranted given the unsworn, ambiguous, and limited nature of the June 9 letter. Consequently, the motion to supplement will be denied.

COLEMAN v. WINDHAM AVIATION INC.

2005 WL 1793907 (R.I. Super. Ct. 2005)

THOMPSON, Associate Justice.

Pursuant to Rule 56 of the Superior Court Rules of Civil Procedure, this matter comes before the Court on a motion for partial summary judgment filed by Plaintiff Christine Coleman ("Plaintiff"). The Plaintiff's motion requires the Court to determine whether the applicable statutory law imposes vicarious liability on the owner of an aircraft for any negligence attributed to an authorized lessee of said aircraft. Specifically, the Plaintiff asks the Court to declare that—in the event a jury finds Brooks Kay negligent—Windham Aviation ("Defendant" or "Defendant Windham") is vicariously liable for said negligence. Invoking the doctrine of federal preemption, Defendant Windham has filed a timely objection advancing the argument that 49 U.S.C. §44112 negates the imposition of vicarious liability solely on the basis of ownership. Although there are numerous defendants, the current motion deals only with Defendant Windham. On June 13, 2005, the parties presented oral arguments to the Court on this motion. For the reasons set forth below, the Plaintiff's motion for partial summary judgment is granted.

Facts

Given that the issue before the Court is strictly a matter of law, the Court will confine the recitation of facts to only those relevant to the resolution of the Plaintiff's motion for partial summary judgment. For purposes of this motion, the Court will adopt the narrative set forth in the National Transport Safety Board's Factual Report ("NTSB Report") concerning the events of November 16, 2003.

On November 16, 2003, Stephen Coleman ("Coleman") and Hardy Lebel ("Lebel") were operating a Cessna 180, FAA Registration N34AG, Aircraft Serial Number N32561 ("Cessna"). Coleman and Lebel were practicing take-off and landing procedures at Westerly State Airport. Both Coleman and Lebel had decades of flying experience including time spent in the employment of New England Aviation, Inc. as commercial pilots.

On even date, Co-Defendant Brooks Kay ("Kay") who held a single-engine land airplane rating, rented a Piper PA-28-181, FAA Registration N2885D ("Piper") from Defendant Windham. Kay obtained $50,000 in liability insurance coverage through Defendant Windham. Additionally, Defendant Windham had liability insurance coverage for the corporation in the amount of $1,000,000. Defendant Windham is a corporation located in Windham, Connecticut and authorized to do business under the laws of the State of Connecticut.

Kay took off from Windham Airport in Connecticut with the intent to land at Westerly State Airport in Rhode Island. After he reached Westerly State Airport, Kay made his first attempt to land on Runway 32; however, he determined he was high on final approach. Consequently, he was forced to abort the landing. Upon the second final approach to land the Piper on Runway 32, Kay observed the Cessna "about to get on Runway 32." NTSB Report at 1. According to Kay, he thought the Cessna would remain on the displaced threshold portion of the runway until after he landed the Piper. For this reason, Kay continued his approach and attempted to land on Runway 32. Tragically, the Cessna did not remain on the displaced threshold, and the Piper and Cessna collided as the Cessna attempted to take off from Runway 32. The force of the collision caused the Cessna to turn perpendicular to the runway and impact the ground. Both Coleman and Lebel suffered fatal injuries. Despite the severity of the collision, Kay managed to ground the Piper. Neither Kay nor his two passengers sustained injuries.

As a result of the fatal collision between the Cessna and the Piper, the Plaintiff filed the underlying wrongful death action to recover losses allegedly caused by the collective negligence of the various defendants. In filing the instant motion, the Plaintiff has requested the Court to declare that—in the event a jury finds that the negligence of Brooks Kay proximately caused the fatal collision—Defendant Windham Aviation is vicariously liable for said negligence by virtue of its ownership of the leased Piper.

Standard of Review

"Summary judgment is appropriate if, viewing the evidence in the light most favorable to the nonmoving party, no material questions of fact exist and the moving party is entitled to judgment as a matter of law." Konar v. PFL Life Ins. Co., 840 A.2d 1115, 1117 (R.I.2004). Pursuant to Rule 56(c), "summary judgment, interlocutory in character, may be rendered on the issue of liability alone although there is a genuine issue as to the amount of damages."

For purposes of the Plaintiff's motion for partial summary judgment, it is critical to note that Defendant Windham does not dispute its ownership of the Piper at the time of the accident nor does it dispute that it authorized Kay to operate the Piper. Because no facts material to the issue of vicariously liability exist, the Court's analysis proceeds directly to whether the Plaintiff is entitled to judgment as a matter of law.

In support of her motion for partial summary judgment, the Plaintiff argues that the underlying action is governed by state law—either Rhode Island or Connecticut. The Plaintiff contends that application of either state's law will lead to the same result. Without providing a counter-argument to the imposition of vicarious liability under either Rhode Island or Connecticut state law, the Defendant objects to the instant motion suggesting the Court refer to a different statutory scheme. The Defendant argues that federal law—specifically 49 U.S.C. §44112—preempts state law by exempting aircraft owners not in actual possession or control from the imposition of vicarious liability for the negligence of lessees.

To determine whether judgment as a matter of law is warranted, the Court must determine whether §44112 insulates Defendant Windham from vicarious liability thereby preempting conflicting state laws. If the Court finds that federal law does not apply, the Court must then ascertain whether Rhode Island or Connecticut state law controls the action.

Vicarious Liability

The Defendant's invocation of federal preemption altered the relative simplicity of a choice of law between two neighboring states by adding a different dimension to the analysis. Defendant Windham argues that the language of 49 U.S.C. §44112 clearly exempts aircraft owners from the imposition of vicarious liability. Accordingly, Defendant Windham contends that §44112 preempts any provision of state law which purports to impose vicarious liability on the basis of aircraft ownership. Captioned Limitation of liability, section 44112 reads as follows:

> (a) Definitions.—In this section—
>
> (1) "lessor" means a person leasing for at least 30 days a civil aircraft, aircraft engine, or propeller.
>
> (2) "owner" means a person that owns a civil aircraft, aircraft engine, or propeller.
>
> (3) "secured party" means a person having a security interest in, or security title to, a civil aircraft, aircraft engine, or propeller under a conditional sales contract, equipment trust contract, chattel or corporate mortgage, or similar instrument.

(b) Liability.—A lessor, owner, or secured party is liable for personal injury, death, or property loss or damage on land or water only when a civil aircraft, aircraft engine, or propeller is in the actual possession or control of the lessor, owner, or secured party, and the personal injury, death, or property loss or damage occurs because of—

(1) the aircraft, engine, or propeller; or

(2) the flight of, or an object falling from, the aircraft, engine, or propeller.

Although a cursory review of §44112 seems to not only support the Defendant's argument but also present a conflict with applicable state tort law liability, a deeper examination of the statute reveals a contrary result. Both an identification of the nature of the statute and a review of its legislative history have propelled the Court's analysis through a labyrinth of congressional reports, statutory provisions, and case law to reach the proper conclusion.

The proper starting point for this venture is the recognition that §44112 is a recodification of former Title 49 of the United States Code governing Transportation. In discussing the effect of recodification, the often cited Sutherland treatise on statutory construction states:

> Inasmuch as the function of a code is principally to reorganize the law and to state it in simpler form, the presumption is that change in language is for purposes of clarity rather than for a change in meaning....
>
> The disclosure of a changed intention must be clear for it is presumed that if the language used in the code fairly admits of a construction consistent with the old law it was not the legislature's intent to change the meaning of the law through a revision of the language.

1A Norman J. Singer, Sutherland on Statutes and Statutory Construction §28.11 at 657–60 (6th ed.2003).

With respect to the federal statute at issue, the purpose of the recodification was to "revise, codify, and enact without substantive change certain general and permanent laws, related to transportation, as subtitles II, III, and V–X of title 49, United States Code, 'Transportation,' and to make other technical improvements in the Code." Pub.L.No. 103-272 (1994). A brief review of the corresponding Congressional committee reports evinces Congress's strong presumption against affecting any substantive change of the predecessor statute. The statement of purpose contained in House Report 103-180 confirms the presumption against substantive change:

> The purpose of H.R. 1758 is to restate in comprehensive form, without substantive change, certain general and permanent laws related to transportation and to enact those laws as subtitles II, III, and V–X of title 49, United States Code, and to make other technical improvements in the Code. In the restatement, simple language has been substituted for awkward and obsolete terms, and superseded, executed, and obsolete laws have been eliminated....
>
> Since the purpose of H.R. 1758 is to codify changes in the law without making any substantive change in the law, no oversight findings or recommendations have been made with respect to the bill.

H.R. Rpt. 103-180, at 1-6 (Jul. 15, 1993).

The United States Supreme Court addressed the effect of recodification on the substance of a predecessor law in Cass v. United States, 417 U.S. 72 (1974). In Cass, the Court interpreted the rounding provision in 10 U.S.C. §687(a) which provided readjustment pay to armed forces reservists who were involuntarily released from active duty. Section 687(a)—passed in 1956—mandated that reservists have served at least five years to obtain readjustment pay.

In 1962, § 687(a) was part of a Congressional recodification of certain military laws. The committee reports regarding the 1962 recodification explicitly stated that Congress intended no substantive change to the original statute; however, the arrangement of the recodification raised the issue of whether the rounding provision applied not only to the computation of readjustment pay but also to the five-year eligibility requirement.

After reviewing the legislative history of the predecessor statute, the Court held that the rounding provision applied only to computation of the amount of pay not to the determination of eligibility.

> [C]ongressional comments, combined with the fact that no consideration of any change in eligibility standards appears in either the cited committee reports or in the proceedings leading to adoption of the codification bill ... conclusively demonstrate that Congress did not reduce the minimum period of qualifying service for entitlement to readjustment benefits from five to four and one-half years when it substituted the words in the codified version of § 687(a) for the unambiguous language of the prior substantive enactments. We are unpersuaded by petitioners' claim that the codified version is nevertheless to be accepted as correctly expressing the will of Congress and as a mere unexplained version of the language of prior law. Here the meaning of the predecessor statute is clear and quite different from the meaning petitioners would ascribe to the codified law; and the revisers expressly stated that changes in language resulting from the codification were to have no substantive effect....
>
> In resolving ambiguity, we must allow ourselves some recognition of the existence of sheer inadvertence in the legislative process.

Id. at 82–84 (internal citations omitted).

Similar to the congressional comments referenced by the Supreme Court in Cass, both the committee reports and the corresponding public laws regarding the recodification of Title 49 explicitly state Congress did not intend to substantively change the law. Additionally, there was no consideration by either the House or the Senate of proposed substantive changes to Title 49. Following the Supreme Court's holding in Cass, this Court must effectively disregard any substantive change affected by the recodification of Title 49. Because the Plaintiff suggests that the recodification has, in fact, impermissibly expanded the scope of the predecessor statute and run afoul of the legislature's expressed intent, the Court must look to the language and attendant legislative history of the predecessor statute of § 44112—former 49 U.S.C. § 1404.

Predecessor Statute

The predecessor statute of § 44112, 49 U.S.C. § 1404—captioned "Limitation of security owners' liability"—reads as follows:

> No person having a security interest in, or security title to, any civil aircraft, aircraft engine, or propeller under a contract of conditional sale, equipment trust, chattel or corporate mortgage, or other instrument of similar nature, and no lessor of any such aircraft, aircraft engine, or propeller under a bona fide lease of thirty days or more, shall be liable by reason of such interest or title, or by reason of his interest as lessor or owner of the aircraft, aircraft engine, or propeller so leased, for any injury to or death of persons, or damage to

> or loss of property, on the surface of the earth (whether on land or water) caused by such aircraft, aircraft engine, or propeller, or by the ascent, descent, or flight of such aircraft, aircraft engine, or propeller or by the dropping or falling of an object therefrom, unless such aircraft, aircraft engine, or propeller is in the actual possession or control of such person at the time of such injury, death, damage, or loss.

A review of the legislative history supports the Plaintiff's argument that the recodification substantively alters § 1404 by extending the exemption accorded to owners/lessors for only security purposes to include all owners and lessors. Such an extension not only reflects a change in language but a fundamental contradiction of the predecessor statute's stated purpose—to encourage the financing of private airplanes:

> Provisions of present Federal and State law might be construed to impose upon persons who are owners of aircraft for security purposes only, or who are lessors of aircraft, liability for damages caused by the operation of such aircraft even though they have no control over the operation of the aircraft. This bill would remove this doubt by providing clearly that such persons have no liability under such circumstances.
>
> The relief thus provided from potential unjust and discriminatory liability is necessary to encourage such persons to participate in the financing of aircraft purchases....
>
> An owner in possession or control of aircraft, either personally or through an agent, should be liable for damages caused. A security owner not in possession or control of the aircraft, however, should not be liable for such damages. This bill would make it clear that this generally accepted rule applies and assures the security owner or lessee, that he would not be liable when he is not in possession or control of the aircraft.
>
> The limitation with respect to leases of 30 days or more, in case of lessors of aircraft, was included for the purpose of confining the section to leases executed as a part of some arrangement for financing purchases of aircraft....
>
> It is the conviction of the committee that the bill should be passed to remove one of the obstacles to the financing of purchases of new aircraft.

H.R. Rpt. 80-2091, at 1-2 (June 1, 1948).

After reviewing the committee reports, the Court has no difficulty concluding that Congress passed § 1404 to facilitate the financing of private airplanes by exempting owners or lessors holding only a security interest in an aircraft from liability for negligent operation of that aircraft. In addition, the report also explicitly states the intent of Congress to hold owners in possession of an aircraft, either personally or through an agent, liable for damages caused by negligent operation. Therefore, the recodification impermissibly extends the scope of the exemption well beyond the confines of the predecessor statute. Because the Court is bound by the intent of the predecessor statute, the Court finds that § 44112 does not provide an exemption for Defendant Windham as they outright owned the Piper involved in the fatal collision. Consequently, the Court must decide whether Defendant Windham will be liable under applicable state law.

Choice of Law

When deciding choice of law questions, Rhode Island adheres to the doctrine of depecage which requires the Court to resolve choice of law questions on an issue-by-issue basis. LaPlante v. American Honda Motor Co., Inc., 27 F.3d 731, 741 (1st Cir.1994). "Under the doctrine of depecage, different substantive issues in a tort case may be resolved under the laws of different states where the choices influencing decisions differ." Id. Accordingly, the Court must determine the applicable law for resolution of the narrow issue of vicarious liability.

In the instant case, the parties agree that both Rhode Island and Connecticut impose vicarious liability on aircraft owners for negligent operation of authorized operators. Under Rhode Island law, the applicable provision—G.L. (1956) § 1-4-3—reads:

> Whenever any aircraft is used, operated, or caused to be operated in this state and an action is begun to recover damages for injuries arising to the person or to the property or for the death of a person, arising out of an accident or collision in which that aircraft was involved, or arising out of an accident caused by the dropping or falling of any object from that aircraft, evidence that at the time of the accident or collision it was registered in the name of the defendant as owner is prima facie evidence that it was then being operated by and under the control of a person for whose conduct the defendant was wholly responsible, and absence of that responsibility is an affirmative defense to be set up in the answer and proved by the defendant; and for the purposes of this chapter, the term 'owner' includes the legal title holder and any person, firm, copartnership, association or corporation having the lawful possession or control of an aircraft under a written sale agreement.

The applicable provisions of Connecticut law lead to the same conclusion. First, § 15-34(20) defines operation of aircraft as follows:

> The use of aircraft for the purpose of air navigation includes the navigation or piloting of aircraft. Any person who causes or authorizes the operation of aircraft, whether with or without the right of legal control thereof, shall be deemed to be engaged in the operation of aircraft within the meaning of the statutes of this state.

Next, § 15-72 states:

> No person shall operate any aircraft carelessly, negligently or recklessly, or in such a manner as to endanger the property, life or limb of any person, having regard to the proximity of other aircraft, weather conditions, field conditions and, while in flight, the territory flown over.

Given that § 15-34(20) deems an owner who authorizes another to operate his or her aircraft to be engaged in the operation of aircraft, said owner would be liable for negligent operation of that aircraft under § 15-72.

After reviewing the applicable statutory provisions, the Court agrees with the parties that the application of either Rhode Island or Connecticut law will lead to the same result on the issue of vicarious liability. Consequently, the situation presents a false conflict. A false conflict exists when "(1) there is no true conflict of laws because only one state is interested in the application of its law or (2) the laws of the two states are found to be compatible." Engine Specialties, Inc. v. Bombardier, Ltd., 605 F.2d 1, 19 (1st Cir.1979). "It is a well-established—and prudential—principle that when the result in a case will not be affected by the choice of law, an inquiring court, in its discretion, may simply bypass the choice. See, e.g., Fashion House, Inc. v. K Mart Corp., 892 F.2d 1076, 1092 (1st Cir.1989). That course is especially attractive where, as here, the parties have taken the position that either state's law will lead to the same result."

Lexington Ins. Co. v. Gen. Accident Ins. Co. of Am., 338 F.3d 42, 46–47 (1st Cir. 2003).

In the case at bar, Rhode Island and Connecticut have compatible laws on the issue of vicarious liability for owners of aircraft. Consequently, the Court will invoke its discretion to bypass the choice of law question because the parties have conceded that the application of either state's law will lead to the same result—the imposition of vicarious liability on Defendant Windham. Therefore, the Court holds that if a jury finds Kay negligently operated the Piper thereby causing the fatal accident on November 16, 2003, Defendant Windham is vicariously liable for that negligence.

Conclusion

After consideration of the parties' oral arguments and respective thorough memoranda, the Court finds that the material facts are not in dispute and that the Plaintiff is entitled to judgment as a matter of law. Accordingly, the Court hereby grants the Plaintiff's motion for partial summary judgment on the issue of vicarious liability. Counsel shall prepare an order to reflect the Court's decision.

GOODLETT v. KALISHEK

223 F.3d 32 (2d Cir. 2000)

CABRANES, Circuit Judge.

The question presented in this diversity action is whether the New York doctrine of primary assumption of the risk bars plaintiff's claim for the wrongful death of her husband, Richard Lee Goodlett ("Goodlett"). Goodlett died as a result of a midair collision immediately following the finish of an airplane race in which he and defendant Christopher Kalishek ("Kalishek") had participated. Kalishek appeals from a judgment of the United States District Court for the Eastern District of New York (Arthur D. Spatt, Judge), entered September 30, 1999, after a jury trial, finding him partially liable for Goodlett's death. We agree with Kalishek that plaintiff's action is barred under New York law by the doctrine of primary assumption of the risk, and therefore we reverse the judgment of the District Court. In a cross-appeal, plaintiff seeks a new trial with respect to the issue of damages. In light of our conclusion that plaintiff's action is barred altogether, her cross-appeal is moot.

I.

The facts relevant to this appeal may be stated briefly and, unless noted otherwise, are undisputed. The action arises out of a midair collision on June 22, 1997 between an airplane flown by Goodlett and an airplane flown by Kalishek at Gabreski Airport in Westhampton Beach, New York. Goodlett and Kalishek were participants in an air race involving four single-seat home-built airplanes powered by car engines that had been modified by each pilot for use in air racing. The race was conducted around a two-mile oval race-course, marked by six inflatable pylons, with a race lane 250 feet wide. During the race, the pilots flew their airplanes at altitudes of 30 to 150 feet and at speeds between 100 and 200 miles per hour.

The air race that resulted in Goodlett's death was organized by the Formula V Air Racing Association (the "Association"), an organization—of which Goodlett was President—composed at the time of six active race pilots and approximately 20 non-pilot members. The Association established race pilot qualifications, technical specifications for airplanes, and competition rules for the sport of "Formula V air racing." In several ways, the Association emphasized to prospective pilots the risks inherent in the sport of air racing. In a section of the Association's "Guide for the New Air Race Pilot" titled "RISKS," for example, the Association warned participating pilots:

> Air racing ... contains an element of danger. Pilots have been killed in air racing accidents ... [ellipsis in original] you must be aware that the potential for injury or death is present.... The race pilot's greatest fear is a mid-air collision between two race-planes during a race. Several mid-air collisions have occurred during the history of air racing; usually both pilots are killed.

In addition, pilots were cautioned about the "dangers inherent in participation" and the "history of air racing accidents" both when they applied for certification as race pilots and before the start of each race.

The accident that gave rise to this action occurred approximately 14 seconds after Goodlett and Kalishek crossed the finish line in the June 22, 1997 race. Goodlett finished the race in second place, well behind the first-place finisher but not far ahead of Kalishek (who was, in turn, not far ahead of the fourth-place finisher). After crossing the finish line, both Goodlett and Kalishek initially proceeded straight ahead at full power, and race speed, approximately 30 to 50 feet above the ground. The parties dispute what happened next—whether Goodlett made a sharp left turn around one of the racecourse pylons as if he were continuing to race or whether Goodlett initiated the proscribed landing procedures—but, in any event, Kalishek followed Goodlett into a left-hand turn. As Goodlett and Kalishek were turning, their airplanes collided. The collision caused both airplanes to crash to the ground, resulting in Goodlett's death and serious injuries to Kalishek.

Plaintiff, Goodlett's surviving wife, filed the present complaint in October 1997, alleging that Kalishek's negligence caused Goodlett's death. The complaint did not allege intentional or reckless misconduct on the part of Kalishek. Notwithstanding a pending motion for summary judgment by Kalishek, a jury trial was commenced on August 24, 1999. At the close of plaintiff's evidence and again at the close of all the evidence, Kalishek moved for judgment as a matter of law on the ground that plaintiff's action was barred by New York's doctrine of primary assumption of the risk. In a decision from the bench, the District Court found that the doctrine would have barred plaintiff's action had the collision between Goodlett and Kalishek occurred during the race itself. However, because the collision occurred after the finish of the race, the District Court concluded that the doctrine was inapplicable and that Goodlett's assumption of the risk, if any, went to the issue of comparative fault, which was a question for the jury under N.Y. C.P.L.R. § 1411 (McKinney 1997). Accordingly, the District Court denied Kalishek's motions and submitted the case to the jury.

On September 9, 1999, the jury returned a verdict finding that Goodlett was 60% at fault and Kalishek was 40% at fault for the accident. The jury awarded plaintiff damages for past loss of support, future loss of support, and conscious pain and suffering. After reducing the award for future loss of support to present value and decreasing the total damages in proportion to Goodlett's share of the fault, the District Court entered judgment against Kalishek in the sum of $390,213. This appeal followed.

II.

The parties agree that New York law applies to this wrongful death action. Under New York law, assumption of the risk is generally not an absolute defense to a negligence action, let alone an issue of law for the court to decide. See N.Y. C.P.L.R. § 1411 (establishing that, in a personal injury or wrongful death action, "the culpable conduct attributable to the claimant..., including... assumption of risk, shall not bar recovery," but will "diminish[ ]" the damages "otherwise recoverable" by the claimant in proportion to his culpable conduct). See generally Arbegast v. Board of Educ. of S. New Berlin Cent. Sch., 65 N.Y.2d 161, 165–70, 490 N.Y.S.2d 751, 480 N.E.2d 365 (1985) (discussing New York law before and after enactment of C.P.L.R. § 1411 in 1975). In Turcotte v. Fell, 68 N.Y.2d 432, 510 N.Y.S.2d 49, 502 N.E.2d 964 (1986), however, the New York Court of Appeals effectively established an exception to this rule for injuries sustained as a result of participation in a sport or recreational activity. By electing to participate in such an activity, the Court of Appeals reasoned, an individual "consent[s] ... to those injury-causing events which are known, apparent, or reasonably foreseeable consequences of the participation." Id. at 439, 510 N.Y.S.2d 49, 502 N.E.2d 964. This consent operates to relieve other participants in the activity of a duty to use reasonable care, see id. at 437–38, 510 N.Y.S.2d 49, 502 N.E.2d 964, and, absent evidence of "reckless or intentionally harmful conduct," an action for personal injury or wrongful death will therefore be barred as a matter of law, id. at 437, 510 N.Y.S.2d 49, 502 N.E.2d 964; see id. at 439–40, 510 N.Y.S.2d 49, 502 N.E.2d 964.

Although similar in nature and effect, the so-called "primary assumption of the risk" doctrine differs analytically from the traditional assumption of the risk doctrine that was abolished as an absolute defense to liability by C.P.L.R. § 1411. As explained by one New York court, the traditional assumption of the risk doctrine

> is akin to comparative negligence; it does not bar recovery, but diminishes recovery in the proportion to which it contributed to the injuries.... [In contrast,] the doctrine of primary assumption of risk is not a measure of plaintiff's comparative fault, but a measure of the defendant's duty of care. Primary assumption of risk eliminates ... the tort-feasor's duty of care to the plaintiff and ... constitutes a complete bar to recovery, notwithstanding [C.P.L.R. § 1411].

Lamey v. Foley, 188 A.D.2d 157, 594 N.Y.S.2d 490, 494 (4th Dep't 1993); see also Turcotte, 68 N.Y.2d at 437–39, 510 N.Y.S.2d 49, 502 N.E.2d 964 (explaining why the common law doctrine of primary assumption of the risk was unaffected by the enactment of C.P.L.R. § 1411). Commentators have nevertheless criticized the continuing vitality of the doctrine of primary assumption of the risk as inconsistent with the comparative negligence regime established by § 1411. See, e.g., Lee S. Michaels & Paul C. Campbell, 1993–94 Survey of New York Law: Tort Law, 45 SYRACUSE L.REV. 693, 723 (1995). Notwithstanding this criticism, our obligation in this diversity case is to apply New York law as the New York Court of Appeals would apply it. See, e.g., Rounds v. Rush Trucking Corp., 211 F.3d 185, 188 (2d Cir.2000). Therefore, unless and until the Court of Appeals disavows the doctrine of primary assumption of the risk, we are bound to apply it when appropriate.

According to the New York Court of Appeals, the inquiry into whether an individual has assumed the risks inherent in a sport or recreational activity "includes consideration of the participant's knowledge and experience in the activity generally." Turcotte, 68 N.Y.2d at 440, 510 N.Y.S.2d 49, 502 N.E.2d 964; see also Rutnik v. Colonie Ctr. Court Club Inc., 249 A.D.2d 873, 672 N.Y.S.2d 451, 452 (3d Dep't 1998) ("[W]here the injured party had previously participated in the sports activity on numerous occasions it is not unreasonable to conclude that he or she assumed the obvious risk of injury in participating in that activity." (internal quotation marks and ellipsis omitted)). However, for purposes of determining whether the doctrine of primary assumption of the risk negates a defendant's duty of care—thereby barring a plaintiff's action—"knowledge plays a role but inherency is the sine qua non." Morgan v. State, 90 N.Y.2d 471, 484, 662 N.Y.S.2d 421, 685 N.E.2d 202 (1997). Thus, for example, the risks of being bumped or kicked by a horse during a race or exhibition, see Turcotte, 68 N.Y.2d at 440–41, 510 N.Y.S.2d 49, 502 N.E.2d 964; Norkus v. Scolaro, 267 A.D.2d 666, 699 N.Y.S.2d 550, 551 (3d Dep't 1999); Lewis v. Erie County Agricultural Soc'y, 256 A.D.2d 1114, 684 N.Y.S.2d 733, 734 (4th Dep't 1998); Rubenstein v. Woodstock Riding Club Inc., 208 A.D.2d 1160, 617 N.Y.S.2d 603, 604–05 (3d Dep't 1994), of crashing at the end of a bobsled run or after sledding down a hill, see Morgan, 90 N.Y.2d at 479–81, 662 N.Y.S.2d 421, 685 N.E.2d 202; Hernandez v. City of New York, 267 A.D.2d 280, 699 N.Y.S.2d 901, 901 (2d Dep't 1999), of failing to execute properly a martial arts technique, see Morgan, 90 N.Y.2d at 481–82, 662 N.Y.S.2d 421, 685 N.E.2d 202, of paralysis caused by a block in a high school football game, see Benitez v. New York City Bd. of Educ., 73 N.Y.2d 650, 655, 543 N.Y.S.2d 29, 541 N.E.2d 29 (1989), of slipping or falling during various sports played outdoors, see Flores v. City of New York, 266 A.D.2d 148, 699 N.Y.S.2d 345, 346 (1st Dep't 1999) (outdoor basketball); Sheridan v. City of New York, 261 A.D.2d 528, 690 N.Y.S.2d 620, 620 (2d Dep't 1999) (same); Collins v. City of New York, 251 A.D.2d 443, 674 N.Y.S.2d 399, 399 (2d Dep't 1998) (same); Rubin v. Hicksville Union Free Sch. Dist., 247 A.D.2d 601, 669 N.Y.S.2d 359, 360 (2d Dep't 1998) (lacrosse); Morales v. New York City Hous. Auth., 187 A.D.2d 295, 589 N.Y.S.2d 456, 457 (1st Dep't 1992) (football), and of being struck by a ball or bat during a game of baseball or stickball, see Steegmuller v. Siegel, 202 A.D.2d 855, 609 N.Y.S.2d 359, 359 (3d Dep't 1994); Checchi v. Socorro, 169 A.D.2d 807, 565 N.Y.S.2d 175, 176 (2d Dep't 1991); Cuesta v. Immaculate Conception Roman Catholic Church, 168 A.D.2d 411, 562 N.Y.S.2d 537, 537 (2d Dep't 1990), "are risks which various participants are legally deemed to have accepted personal responsibility for because they commonly inhere in the nature of those activities," Morgan, 90 N.Y.2d at 484, 662 N.Y.S.2d 421, 685 N.E.2d 202.

With these principles and examples of New York law in mind, we are confident that the New York Court of Appeals would hold that the present action is barred by the doctrine of primary assumption of the risk. The sport of Formula V air racing involves flying small home-built airplanes using converted car engines in tight formation, at speeds of 100 to 200 miles per hour, and at altitudes of 30 to 150 feet. The risk of a fatal crash, whether as a result of a midair collision or some other cause, plainly inheres in one's participation in this sport, as is evidenced by the fact that there had been several accidents in previous air races that resulted in death or serious injury to pilots and the fact that the sponsoring Association explicitly warns pilots that there is a risk of midair collisions (and that such collisions "usually" result in the deaths of both pilots).

Further, Goodlett was obviously aware of the risks involved: He had been flying airplanes for over 23 years, and had worked as both a commercial pilot and a flight instructor; he had participated in a number of previous Formula V air races (and, on several occasions, was forced to make emergency landings due to engine failure); and, at the time of his death, he served as President of the Association, the organization that sponsors the air races and cautions pilots about "the potential for injury or death." In short, "[t]he accident in this case was solely the result of dangers and calculations inherent in a highly dangerous sport," id. at 486, 662 N.Y.S.2d 421, 685 N.E.2d 202, and these dangers were both "fully comprehended" by Goodlett and "perfectly obvious," Turcotte, 68 N.Y.2d at 439, 510 N.Y.S.2d 49, 502 N.E.2d 964. Accordingly, the doctrine of primary assumption of the risk applies, and Kalishek may not be held liable for Goodlett's death.

Plaintiff's arguments against application of the doctrine—that Goodlett did not expressly consent to assume the risk of death, that the rules and regulations governing air races imposed on Kalishek a duty of reasonable care, and that the collision occurred after the finish of the race—are without merit. First, under the doctrine of primary assumption of the risk, express consent is immaterial because consent is "implied from the act of the electing to participate in the activity." Turcotte, 68 N.Y.2d at 439, 510 N.Y.S.2d 49, 502 N.E.2d 964. Second, whether or not race pilots are governed by rules and regulations when flying, the doctrine of primary assumption of the risk operates to "relieve" a defendant of his legal duty to use reasonable care. Turcotte, 68 N.Y.2d at 441, 510 N.Y.S.2d 49, 502 N.E.2d 964; accord Morgan, 90 N.Y.2d at 484, 662 N.Y.S.2d 421, 685 N.E.2d 202; see also N.Y. C.P.L.R. §1411 Practice Commentary C1411:2, at 566 ("'[P]rimary' assumption of risk eliminates the defendant's duty of care to the plaintiff...."). Lacking a legal duty to use reasonable care, Kalishek may not be held liable for otherwise negligent conduct. See Turcotte, 68 N.Y.2d at 438, 510 N.Y.S.2d 49, 502 N.E.2d 964 ("[T]he defendant is relieved of legal duty to the plaintiff; and being under no duty, he cannot be charged with negligence." (internal quotation marks omitted)); cf. id. at 441, 510 N.Y.S.2d 49, 502 N.E.2d 964 (applying the doctrine of primary assumption of the risk to horse racing despite a municipal regulation prohibiting "foul riding").

Finally, contrary to the District Court (and the suggestion of the dissent), we conclude that it is legally irrelevant that the collision between Goodlett and Kalishek occurred 14 seconds after the nine-minute race finished rather than during the race proper. Under Turcotte and Morgan, a participant in an inherently risky activity consents to any risks that "flow from such participation." Id. at 484, 662 N.Y.S.2d 421, 685 N.E.2d 202. Thus, in Morgan, in which the bobsledding accident occurred after the plaintiff had crossed the finish line, see 90 N.Y.2d at 480, 662 N.Y.S.2d421, 685 N.E.2d 202, the New York Court of Appeals held that the plaintiff had assumed the relevant risk, see id. at 486, 662 N.Y.S.2d 421, 685 N.E.2d 202. Here, common sense dictates that the risk of an accident occurring immediately after an air race finishes, when the race pilots continue to fly their airplanes at race speed—that is, 100 to 200 miles per hour—and in tight formation, is a risk that "flow[s]" from participation.

III.

In sum, we conclude that the doctrine of primary assumption of the risk applies to this action and, thus, that Kalishek owed Goodlett "no more than a duty to avoid reckless or intentionally harmful conduct." Turcotte, 68 N.Y.2d at 437, 510 N.Y.S.2d 49, 502 N.E.2d 964. Because there is no allegation, let alone proof, that Kalishek's conduct was reckless or intentionally harmful, plaintiff's wrongful death claim is barred as a matter of law. Accordingly, the judgment of the District Court is reversed and the complaint is dismissed.

FEINBERG, Circuit Judge, dissenting.

The majority believes that two decisions of the New York Court of Appeals, Turcotte v. Fell, 68 N.Y.2d 432, 510 N.Y.S.2d 49, 502 N.E.2d 964 (1986), and Morgan v. State, 90 N.Y.2d 471, 662 N.Y.S.2d 421, 685 N.E.2d 202 (1997), govern the outcome of this appeal. The majority is "confident" that the New York Court of Appeals would hold that the present action is barred by the doctrine of primary assumption of the risk. I do not share that confidence. Indeed, it is not at all clear to me that the [district] judge erred in concluding that the case should go to the jury.

It is certainly true, as the majority notes, that all pilots were aware of the risks of participation in air races. However, the evidence suggests that a different set of expectations applied to post-race flight: (1) according to the National Transportation Safety Board, there have been no airplane accidents after the end of a race; (2) defendant Kalishek admitted that he was never aware of any risk of a post-race collision; and (3) Kalishek's expert testified that he was not aware of any post-race collisions either. After all, the Association's guide for new pilots warns that, "The race pilot's greatest fear is a mid-air collision between two race-planes during a race." I [therefore] would certify to the New York Court of Appeals the question whether, on the facts before us, Goodlett assumed the risk of collision after the race was over, thereby completely barring this action by his executrix.

Notes

1. As Judge Roth observes in the *Abdullah* case, "the FAA has implemented a comprehensive system of rules and regulations, which promotes flight safety by regulating pilot certification, pilot pre-flight duties, pilot flight responsibilities, and flight rules." 181 F.3d at 369. *See also* John D. Perovich, Annotation, *Construction of Provision of Aviation Liability Policy Which Requires Pilot of Insured Aircraft to Have Appropriate License or Certification*, 72 A.L.R.3d 525 (1976 & 2004 Supp.). *But see Skidmore v. Delta Air Lines, Inc.*, 2000 WL 1844675 (N.D. Tex. 2000) (criticizing *Abdullah's* "novel suggestion that the federal standard of care should be applied in state personal injury actions brought by airline passengers" and holding that § 91.13 "does not establish a standard of civil liability because it does not clearly define the required conduct.").

Besides demonstrating aeronautical knowledge and ability, the FAA also requires pilots to take and pass various medical exams. An aviator who fails such a test will be grounded unless he or she is able to obtain a waiver from the FAA. (During the second season (1990–91) of the NBC comedy *Wings*, for example, Joe Hackett (played by Timothy Daly) lost his license for a time because of high blood pressure.) *See further* Richard P. Shafer, Annotation, *Validity of Federal Aviation Administration Regulations (14 CFR §§ 67.13, 67.15, 67.17) Prescribing Standards for Issuance of Medical Certificates to Airmen*, 59 A.L.R. Fed. 682 (1982 & 2004 Supp.). *See also* Carolyn Marshall, *U.S. Says 46 Pilots Lied to Obtain Their Licenses*, N.Y. Times, July 20, 2005, at A13 (reporting on an 18-month joint investigation by the Department of Transportation and the Social Security Administration that resulted in grand jury indictments in the Eastern and Northern Districts of California; the defendants were discovered to be holding or renewing pilot licenses at the same time they were seeking or receiving federal disability payments).

One of the FAA's most controversial medical rules is its requirement that commercial airline pilots stop flying at age 60. Although regularly challenged, the rule has been repeatedly upheld. *See further Yetman v. Garvey*, 261 F.3d 664 (7th Cir. 2001) (rejecting broad-based attack on rule); *Professional Pilots Federation v. Federal Aviation Administration*, 118 F.3d 758 (D.C. Cir. 1997), *cert. denied*, 523 U.S. 1117, *rehearing denied*, 524 U.S. 968 (1998) (tracing rule's history); Harry A. Rissetto, *Age Discrimination Act and Americans With Disabilities Act Issues Affecting Airline Employees*, SK007 ALI-ABA 879 (Oct. 21–23, 2004) (discussing failed congressional attempts to change the rule). Recently, however, many such individuals, their pensions decimated by the airline industry's numerous bankruptcies, have asked that the prohibition be lifted so that they can go back to work and rebuild their savings. *See* John Hughes, *Airline Pilots Want Age-60 Ceiling Pushed Back*, S. Fla. Sun-Sentinel, May 26, 2005, at 1D. Should their request be granted?

In November 2005, the United States Senate's Commerce, Science, and Transportation Committee, rejecting the position of the FAA and instead siding with the European Joint Aviation Authority and the ICAO, endorsed a bill that would allow pilots to fly until 65 so long as the plane's co-pilot is under 60. *See Commerce Committee Approves Legislation to Amend the Age Restriction for Pilots*, at commerce.senate.gov/news room/printable.cfm?id=249035. While the action was applauded by Southwest Airlines' pilots, those from American Airlines criticized it. If you were in Congress, how would you cast your vote?

2. When a pilot is found to have violated an air regulation, the FAA can, depending on the nature and severity of the violation: 1) issue an administrative disposition (such as a warning notice or letter of correction); 2) suspend or revoke the pilot's certificate; or, 3) seek a monetary fine through a civil penalty action. If a pilot believes the proposed punishment is unwarranted (or too harsh), he or she can request a hearing before an NTSB administrative law judge. Either the FAA or the pilot (or both) can challenge the resulting decision in a federal appeals court. *See further Darst v. Federal Aviation Administration*, 57 Fed. Appx. 530 (3d Cir. 2003); W.J. Dunn, Annotation, *Revocation or Suspension of Airman's License or Certificate*, 78 A.L.R. 1150 (1961 & 2004 Supp.); Hilary B. Miller, *Hoover Revisited—Appellate Review of FAA Emergency Certificate Actions*, 67 J. Air L. & Com. 841 (2002); Tom M. Dees, III, Comment, *They Are Trying to Take My License Away—What Do I Do Now? A Practitioner's Guide to Certificate Revocation & Suspension Defense Litigation*, 66 J. Air L. & Com. 261 (2000).

Another arrow in the FAA's quiver is its authority, pursuant to 49 U.S.C. §44709(a), to require certificate holders (including airmen) to undergo re-inspection or re-examination when the facts suggest a lack of competency or qualifications. Should a similar rule apply to lawyers?

3. On first glance, the *Lindsay* case, which involved drunk flying, would seem to be exceptional. Yet in June 2005, a state jury found two America West pilots guilty of attempting to fly their Airbus A319 after an all-night drinking binge at a Miami sports bar. The pair were stopped just as they were about to embark on a flight to Phoenix with 124 passengers and three flight attendants. For their acts, Captain Thomas P. Cloyd Jr. was given five years in prison while co-captain Christopher S. Hughes received two-and-a-half years. *See Drunken Pilots Sentenced to Prison*, N.Y. Times, July 22, 2005, at A16. Although the men initially convinced a federal court that the state had no authority to try them, this decision was overturned on appeal. *See Hughes v. Eleventh Judicial Circuit of Florida*, 274 F. Supp. 2d 1334 (S.D. Fla. 2003), *rev'd*, 377 F.3d 1258 (11th Cir. 2004), *cert. denied*, 125 S. Ct. 881 (2005).

For a general look at the problem of drunken flying, *see* Denise Urzendowski Scofield, Comment, *Knowing When to Say When: Federal Regulation of Alcohol Consumption by Air Pilots*, 57 J. Air L. & Com. 937 (1992). *See also* Gary Trichter & Christian Samuelson, *Pilots, DWI, Suspensions & Legal Malpractice*, 23 Champion 18 (June 1999) (discussing the impact of a drunk driving charge on a pilot's ability to keep flying).

4. The *Del Balzo* case also might seem exceptional, but it, too, is not—flights into restricted airspace happen all the time. *See, e.g.*, Mark Hosenball, *Entering D.C. Airspace—As Usual*, Newsweek, May 23, 2005, at 9 (reporting that during the period between 9/11 and May 2005, there were 2,211 intrusions just in the areas around Camp David, the Capitol building, and the White House). As a result, Representative John Mica (R-Fla.) has proposed increasing the maximum fine for such incidents from $1,100 to $100,000.

See Leslie Miller, *Stiffer Fines Sought for Pilots*, S. Fla. Sun-Sentinel, July 22, 2005, at 13A (noting that the bill faces strong opposition from aircraft owners and pilots).

5. Being intoxicated and flying into restricted airspace are just two of the many ways to err while piloting a plane. In addition to failing to yield (the violation at issue in *Aviation Underwriters*), other examples include flying between buildings in a densely populated city and performing aerobatic maneuvers in an aircraft not certified for such stunts. *See also* Matthew L. Wald, *Just Before Dying, A Thrill at 41,000 Feet*, N.Y. Times, June 14, 2005, at A15 (describing the deaths of two pilots who decided to try to join the mythical "410 Club" by taking their Bombardier CR J200 jet to its limit of 41,000 feet).

Section 91.13 of the Federal Aviation Regulations attempts to address such situations by prohibiting a person (whether an individual or a company) from operating an aircraft in a "careless or reckless manner so as to endanger the life or property of another." The terms "careless" and "reckless" are not defined and often are used interchangeably. They are, however, distinct concepts and the FAA need only prove one of them. "Careless" connotes inadvertence, indifference, or lack of due care. "Reckless," on the other hand, denotes deliberate or heedless conduct, although neither term requires an intent to endanger life or property.

Actual endangerment also is not required—the potential to endanger will suffice. *See Administrator v. Preston*, 3 N.T.S.B. 3730 (1981) (pilot mistakenly flew into active restricted airspace where air-to-air missile testing had just occurred; the Board rejected his argument that because he flew into the area one minute after the testing was completed he had not endangered the life of his passenger).

A particularly good example of improper conduct can be found in *Administrator v. Miller*, 1999 WL 13327 (N.T.S.B. 1999). A pilot landed his airplane, parked it in front of the terminal, and left both engines running and the tires unchocked while he went inside for a cup of coffee. When the FAA sought a 60-day suspension, the pilot argued that his actions were proper and, in fact, authorized by his employer as a means of extending the life of the plane's starter. The Board easily upheld the suspension, observing that "[w]e are hard pressed to envision a situation where the respondent's actions could ever be reasonable." *Id.* at *1.

6. Throughout its opinion, the *Jetcraft* court treats Kimball as the "pilot in command" (PIC). Although none of the parties challenged this determination, in other situations the identity of the PIC has been hotly contested, with one pilot trying to shift the blame to another pilot. *See, e.g.*, *Cooper v. Hinson*, 109 F.3d 997 (4th Cir. 1997); *Friesen-Hall v. Colle*, 17 P.3d 349 (Kan. 2001); *Administrator v. Basco*, 1999 WL 721997 (N.T.S.B. 1999).

7. As the public now knows, flight schools like the one in *Jetcraft* played an unwitting role in the 9/11 attacks:

> In the early summer of 2000, [several of the 9/11 pilots] arrived in the United States to begin flight training. Mohamed Atta and Marwan al Shehhi had not settled on where they would obtain their flight training. In contrast, Ziad Jarrah had already arranged to attend the Florida Flight Training Center (FFTC) in Venice, Florida. Jarrah arrived in Newark on June 27 and then flew to Venice. He immediately began the private pilot program at FFTC, intending to get a multi-engine license.
>
> While Jarrah quickly settled into training in Florida, Atta and Shehhi kept searching for a flight school. After visiting the Airman Flight School in Nor-

man, Oklahoma (where Zacarias Moussaoui would enroll several months later and where another al Qaeda operative, Ihab Ali, had taken lessons in the mid-1990s), Atta started flight instruction at Huffman Aviation in Venice, Florida, and both Atta and Shehhi subsequently enrolled in the Accelerated Pilot Program at that school. By the end of July, both of them took solo flights, and by mid-August they passed the private pilot airman test. They trained through the summer at Huffman, while Jarrah continued his training at FFTC.

In mid-September, Atta and Shehhi applied to change their immigration status from tourist to student, stating their intention to study at Huffman until September 1, 2001. In late September, they decided to enroll at Jones Aviation in Sarasota, Florida, about 20 miles north of Venice. According to the instructor at Jones, the two were aggressive, rude, and sometimes even fought with him to take over the controls during their training flights. In early October, they took the Stage I exam for instruments rating at Jones Aviation and failed. Very upset, they said they were in a hurry because jobs awaited them at home. Atta and Shehhi then returned to Huffman. In the meantime, Jarrah obtained a single-engine private pilot certificate in early August.

Jarrah was supposed to be joined at FFTC by Ramzi Binalshibh, who even sent the school a deposit. But Binalshibh could not obtain a U.S. visa. His first applications in May and June 2000 were denied because he lacked established ties in Germany ensuring his return from a trip to the United States. In September, he went home to Yemen to apply for a visa from there, but was denied on grounds that he also lacked sufficient ties to Yemen. In October, he tried one last time, in Berlin, applying for a student visa to attend "aviation language school," but the prior denials were noted and this application was denied as well.

The three pilots in Florida continued with their training. Atta and Shehhi finished up at Huffman and earned their instrument certificates from the FAA in November. In mid-December 2000, they passed their commercial pilot tests and received their licenses. They then began training to fly large jets on a flight simulator. At about the same time, Jarrah began simulator training, also in Florida but at a different center. By the end of 2000, less than six months after their arrival, the three pilots on the East Coast were simulating flights on large jets.

National Commission on Terrorist Attacks Upon the United States, *The 9/11 Commission Report* 223–27 (2004).

Because of the foregoing events, flight schools now are required to extensively check the backgrounds of their students and take other steps to help the government identify potential terrorists. *See further* 8 U.S.C. § 1372 and 49 U.S.C. § 44939. *See also* Abby Goodnough, *Hard Times are Plaguing Flight Schools in Florida*, N.Y. Times, Sept. 14, 2003, § 1, at 20 (reporting that many foreign applicants are enrolling in flight schools in countries with less demanding background checks, such as Australia and South Africa).

Besides clamping down on flight schools, Congress has mandated more secure cockpit doors and the installation of surveillance equipment on commercial aircraft. More controversially, it has authorized pilots to carry handguns to thwart would-be hijackers. Is this a good idea? At least some observers believe the answer is "no," arguing that turning pilots into cops jeopardizes rather than enhances air safety. *See further* Monica G. Renna, Comment, *Fire in the Sky: A Critical Look at Arming Pilots With Handguns*, 68 J. Air L. & Com. 859 (2003) (proposing various alternatives, including hiring more sky marshals).

8. Did the court in *Coleman* reach the correct conclusion? Or was the defendant entitled, under 49 U.S.C. §44112, to be relieved of liability? How do you think the issue will be resolved by other courts? For a further discussion, *see* K.J. Roberts, Annotation, *Tort Liability of One Renting or Loaning Airplane to Another*, 4 A.L.R.2d 1306 (1949 & 2004 Supp.). *See also* Robert A. Brazener, Annotation, *Liability of Bailee of Airplane for Damage Thereto*, 44 A.L.R.3d 862 (1972 & 2004 Supp.).

9. Are you at all troubled by the outcome in *Goodlett*? Should airplanes ever be used to race? Despite his previous experience and position as association president, did the decedent really know what he was getting himself into? Even if he did, do you find yourself agreeing with Judge Feinberg that because the race had ended, the primary assumption defense was no longer available (or do you accept Judge Cabranes's conclusion that there must be some amount of time after a race is finished when it is still in force, so as to give pilots a chance to land?). *See further* W.R. Habeeb, Annotation, *Liability for Injury to or Death of Participant in Game or Contest*, 7 A.L.R.2d 704 (1949 & 2004 Supp.), and Paul A. Lange, *Tort Liability Surrounding Homebuilt, Amateur-Built, and Experimental Aircraft*, 60 J. Air L. & Com. 575 (1994–95). *See also* Dan Ramsey & Earl Downs, *The Complete Idiot's Guide to Sport Flying* (2005), and www.airrace.org.

10. In April 1996, Jessica Dubroff died while trying to fly cross-country. What made her effort so remarkable was that she was only seven years old. In the wake of her death, legislation was passed to prevent similar tragedies:

> Jessica Dubroff (May 5, 1988–April 11, 1996) was a 7-year-old uncertificated student pilot who was attempting to become the youngest person to fly a plane across the United States when, 24 hours into her flight, her small plane crashed after takeoff from Cheyenne, Wyoming.
>
> During her flight, which included several stopovers, Dubroff became an instant media celebrity. Her flight was vigorously followed by supporters and media outlets such as CNN, ABC, FOX and others who monitored her flight every day for the duration of her trip, reporting each time she landed or took off, until the tragic ending of her "Sea to Shining Sea Flight."
>
> Dubroff took off from Cheyenne in heavy rain and a sudden storm. These weather conditions contributed to the plane's crash within a few minutes of takeoff. Jessica Dubroff, her father Lloyd Dubroff, and her flight instructor Joe Reid were killed in the crash. She spoke to her mother on the telephone moments before the crash with the last words, "Mom, do you hear the rain? Do you hear the rain? I just want to take off in the plane."
>
> The National Transportation Safety Board investigation concluded that pilot Joe Reid had made an "improper decision to take off into deteriorating weather conditions when the airplane was overweight and when the density altitude was higher than he was accustomed to, resulting in a stall caused by failure to maintain airspeed. Contributing to the pilot in command's decision to take off was a desire to adhere to an overly ambitious itinerary, in part, because of media commitments."
>
> A [2004] book about Jessica Dubroff's life [entitled "Will You All Rise"] has been published by her mother, Lisa Blair Hathaway.
>
> The accident, and its associated publicity, led to Federal legislation [see 49 U.S.C. §44724] that prohibits anyone who does not hold at least a private pilot certificate and a current medical certificate from being allowed to manipulate

the controls of an aircraft during any record attempt, aeronautical competition, or aeronautical feat.

Jessica Dubroff, at en.wikipedia.org/wiki/Jessica_Dubroff.

11. More information about pilots is available from a number of sources, including the web sites of the Air Line Pilots Association (www.alpa.org), Aircraft Owners and Pilots Association (www.aopa.org), Experimental Aircraft Association (www.eaa.org), Helicopter Association International (www.rotor.com), International Aerobatic Club (www.iac.org), National Business Aviation Association, Inc. (www.nbaa.org), and National Broadcast Pilots Association (www.nbpa.rotor.org).

In addition, there have been numerous movies made about pilots, including: *Air America* (1990) (starring Mel Gibson as a CIA pilot), *Amelia Earhart: The Final Flight* (1994) (Diane Keaton as aviatrix Amelia Earhart), *Blue Thunder* (1983) (Roy Scheider as a police helicopter pilot), *Catch Me If You Can* (2002) (Leonardo DiCaprio as airline pilot imposter Frank Abagnale Jr.), *God is My Co-Pilot* (1945) (Dennis Morgan as Flying Tiger Robert Scott), *Memphis Belle* (1990) (Matthew Modine as B-17 bomber captain Dennis Dearborn), *The Aviator* (2004) (Leonardo DiCaprio as aviation pioneer Howard Hughes), *The Blue Max* (1966) (George Peppard as a World War I ace), *The Court-Martial of Billy Mitchell* (1955) (Gary Cooper as Air Corps General Billy Mitchell), *The Flying Irishman* (1939) (Douglas "Wrong Way" Corrigan portraying himself), *The Great Waldo Pepper* (1975) (Robert Redford as a 1920s barnstormer), *The Right Stuff* (1983) (Sam Shepard as test pilot Chuck Yeager), *The Spirit of St. Louis* (1957) (James Stewart as flying legend Charles Lindbergh), *Thirty Seconds Over Tokyo* (1944) (Spencer Tracy as General James Doolittle), *Those Magnificent Men in Their Flying Machines* (1965) (air race across Europe), and *Top Gun* (1986) (Tom Cruise as an elite fighter pilot).

Likewise, a number of television shows have starred or featured pilots as characters, including *Black Sheep Squadron* (NBC, 1976–78) (World War II flying outfit), *Hogan's Heroes* (CBS, 1965–71) (air force POW camp), *Northern Exposure* (CBS, 1990–95) (Janine Turner as bush pilot Maggie O'Connell), *Petticoat Junction* (CBS, 1963–70) (Mike Minor as crop duster Steve Elliott), *Sky King* (NBC, 1952, 1956–59) (Kirby Grant as rancher Sky King, who uses his Cessna T-50 to patrol his land), *Tales of the Gold Monkey* (ABC, 1982–83) (Stephen Collins as seaplane pilot Jake Cutter), *The Bob Newhart Show* (CBS, 1972–78) (Bill Daily as airline navigator Howard Borden), *The Hogan Family* (NBC, 1986–91) (Josh Taylor as airline pilot Michael Hogan), and *Wings* (NBC, 1990–97) (rival commuter airline pilots).

Lastly, one would be remiss if he or she failed to mention the most famous pilot of all time: Snoopy. His aerial battles with the real-life Manfred von Richthofen, during which he flew a Sopwith Camel (cleverly disguised as a dog house) and repeatedly shouted "Curse you, Red Baron!," helped make him the star of Charles M. Schulz's beloved comic strip *Peanuts* (www.snoopy.com).

Problem 11

A woman pilot, possessing all of the necessary FAA certificates, training, and experience, was turned down for the position of global captain. In rejecting her, the airline explained that it required applicants to have 20/100 eyesight. Although the woman has 20/200 eyesight, with glasses her vision is 20/20. If she sues, claiming a violation of the Americans with Disabilities Act, 42 U.S.C. §§ 12101–12213, how should the court rule? *See Sutton v. United Air Lines, Inc.*, 527 U.S. 471 (1999).

C. MECHANICS

BORREGARD v. NATIONAL TRANSPORTATION SAFETY BOARD

46 F.3d 944 (9th Cir. 1995)

GOODWIN, Circuit Judge.

Robert Borregard appeals an NTSB decision affirming an FAA Emergency Order revoking his aircraft mechanic certificate and inspection authority on the charge that Borregard altered an aircraft's maintenance logs for a fraudulent purpose in violation of 14 C.F.R. §43.12(a)(3). Borregard contends that the Board's finding that he breached §43.12(a)(3) is not supported by substantial evidence and that the revocation of his certificates was an inappropriate and unconstitutional response to the charged violation. Because the Board's decision is not arbitrary and capricious and is supported by substantial evidence, we affirm. The penalty, too, was appropriate in light of the gravity of Borregard's infraction and established Board precedent.

The Legal Standard

The Board's interpretation of §43.12(a)(3) is arguably contrary to the plain meaning of the regulation. Correctly understanding §43.12(a)(3) as an attempted fraud provision, the Board enunciated the elements of a §43.12(a)(3) violation: 1) a false representation; 2) in regard to a material fact; 3) made with knowledge of its falsity; and 4) with the intent to deceive.

The language and purpose of §43.12(a)(3), however, may call for a less exacting standard. The regulation prohibits "[a]ny alteration, for fraudulent purpose." By requiring that the alteration be actually false and made with knowledge of that falsity, the Board has effectively read the word "any" out of the regulation and replaced it with an implicit "knowingly false." The elements of attempted fraud would seem to be met so long as the actor subjectively believes the alteration is false, whether or not the information is actually false.

Although we note this lurking question, we do not need to make such subtle interpretive distinctions today as Borregard clearly violated §43.12(a)(3) even under the more stringent standard applied by the Board.

Each Element of a §43.12(a)(3) Violation is Supported

Each element of a §43.12(a)(3) violation is supported by substantial evidence. The basic facts of the case are not in dispute. Borregard initially entered October 24 as the date of inspection in the engine log of the plane at issue and October 28 as the inspection date in the air frame log. In fact, the inspection had not been completed by October 24 or 28. Keith Mason, the director of maintenance of Squadron Two Flying Club, Borregard's employer, asked Borregard to backdate the annual inspection to September in an apparent attempt to shield a club member from any liability arising from his flying an uncertified plane. Borregard covered the entries of the October dates with a sticker and entered September 1 as the date he completed the annual inspection. Once Borregard learned that the FAA had received the false records, he attempted to cover up his misstatement. He again placed stickers over the entries, rewriting October 24 in the logs and submitting the new copies to the FAA. Later, he wrote "void" over the new October 24 entry. He finally recorded November 1 as the completion date, despite the fact that as of November 1, the annual inspection still had not been completed.

Borregard concedes that he made all the above date changes and that he knew that the inspection had not been completed even by November 1, the latest date entered. Accordingly, there is no question that the four entries were false and that Borregard knew of their falsity. Entry of the exact completion date only satisfies the air safety regulations. Administrator v. Olsen, NTSB Order No. 3582 at 10.

Borregard argues that he had no intent to deceive the FAA. In a nutshell, he argues that he intended to defraud only those who would rely on the records of Squadron Two, not the FAA. However, the fact that Borregard intended to defraud certain people and not others does not negate his bad intent. The pilots, mechanics, insurers, and anyone else who might rely on Squadron Two's safety records, even the public at large, are within the ambit of those protected by the air safety regulations requiring that maintenance records for aircraft be trustworthy. Cf. Administrator v. Berglin, NTSB Order No. EA-3846 at 5. Furthermore, there is substantial evidence suggesting that Borregard intended to defraud the FAA. Borregard knowingly presented false information to the FAA, sending the FAA copies of re-doctored records showing an October 24 inspection date. Later, Borregard showed up at the hearing with records bearing a November 1 completion date, when, by Borregard's own testimony, the inspection was completed after November 1.

As a matter of law, Borregard's false entries in the logs are material. The test of materiality is whether the false statements had the natural tendency to influence, or were capable of influencing, the decision of the FAA inspector to whom the logbook was submitted. Janka v. NTSB, 925 F.2d 1147, 1150 (9th Cir.1991). As one would expect, materiality in the context of regulations requiring logbooks has been interpreted broadly to include any logbook entry which in any way illustrates compliance with the referenced regulations. Administrator v. Olsen, NTSB Order No. EA-3582 at 10. Clearly, certifying that maintenance on a plane had been completed when in fact it had not is material.

The Propriety of Revocation of Licenses as a Penalty

Borregard contends that revocation of his mechanic and inspection certificates is not an appropriate sanction for the violation charged in that 1) it violates his substantive due process rights and 2) his actions do not show a lack of qualification. Both arguments are contrary to the great weight of authority.

The "liberty" that the Constitution protects does include choice of occupation. Board of Regents v. Roth, 408 U.S. 564, 573, 92 S.Ct. 2701, 2707, 33 L.Ed.2d 548 (1972). However, the state has broad discretion to regulate professions through the police power, subject only to rational basis review. Schware v. Board of Examiners, 353 U.S. 232, 239, 77 S.Ct. 752, 756, 1 L.Ed.2d 796 (1957). Because the qualification standards requiring accurate entries in maintenance logs are rationally connected to the public interest in safe air travel, there is no constitutional violation here.

Numerous cases have upheld the revocation of licenses not only for fraudulent entries, but the lesser included offense of intentionally false entries. The law is well-settled that "[a]n Inspection Authorization holder who knowingly misrepresents a logbook entry bearing on the condition of an aircraft ... clearly lacks the judgment a qualified certificate holder is expected and required to possess." Administrator v. Rice, 5 NTSB

2285 (1987). "[O]ne intentionally false log entry would be sufficient, in and of itself, to warrant revocation." Administrator v. Olsen, NTSB Order No. EA-3582 (1992), aff'd Olsen v. NTSB, 14 F.3d 471, 476 (9th Cir.1994). See also Administrator v. Berglin, NTSB Order No. EA-03846 (1993) and Administrator v. Coomber, NTSB Order No. EA-4283. Thus, revocation of Borregard's inspection authority was the appropriate and expected response to the fraudulent log entries.

Likewise, Board precedents have implicitly held that integrity is a prerequisite to holding a pilot or mechanic certificate. See Administrator v. Barron, 5 NTSB 256 (1985); Administrator v. Coomber, NTSB Order No. EA-4283; and Olsen v. NTSB, 14 F.3d at 476. Considering that this Court in Olsen affirmed revocation of a mechanic certificate for an intentionally false log entry in violation of §43.12(a)(1), there can be no argument that an attempted fraud, a more serious violation, cannot warrant such a sanction. Hart v. McLucas, 535 F.2d 516, 520 (9th Cir.1976) (fraudulent entries carry a greater degree of culpability than intentionally false ones and, therefore, warrant more severe sanctions). Thus, revocation of Borregard's mechanic certificate was also an appropriate and predictable sanction.

Conclusion

Reflecting on his own error of acquiescing to his employer, Borregard confessed, "I'm stupid. I really, really am stupid." While Borregard, who is arguably a simple naif manipulated by others, may be entitled to pity, he is not entitled to a mechanic certificate with inspection authority. Lack of judgment is just as serious a shortcoming for an airplane mechanic entrusted with certifying the airworthiness of planes as is a lack of mechanical skills. Borregard was correctly found in violation of §43.12(a)(3), even under the stringent legal standard applied. Ninth Circuit and NTSB precedent, as well as common sense, support revocation of the certificates as an appropriate penalty.

FANT v. CHAMPION AVIATION, INC.

689 So. 2d 32 (Ala. 1997)

KENNEDY, Justice.

Anthony J. Fant sued Champion Aviation, Inc. ("Champion"), and others, seeking damages based on claims of negligence, wantonness, fraud, and breach of contract. The fraud claims included claims alleging innocent misrepresentation, reckless misrepresentation, intentional misrepresentation, suppression, and deceit. All claims were submitted to the jury, which awarded Fant a general verdict of $51,011.79 in compensatory damages and $100,000 in punitive damages.

Champion filed a motion for JNOV, or in the alternative, remittitur or a new trial. The trial court granted the motion for a new trial, stating that it had "erred in charging the jury on all of the requested charges of fraud." Fant appeals from the grant of the new trial. Champion cross-appeals from the denial of the JNOV.

Fant's Appeal

Whether to grant a motion for a new trial is within the trial court's discretion, and the court's ruling on that question will not be reversed absent an abuse of that discretion. Colbert County-Northwest Alabama Healthcare Authority v. Nix, 678 So.2d 719 (Ala.1995).

Fant's claims arise out of Champion's mechanical work on Fant's airplane. Champion sought out Fant's business. Fant hired Champion to remove his airplane engine, rebuild it, and replace it. When placing the propeller back on the airplane after installing the engine, the mechanic failed to properly adjust the torque on the propeller bolts. While the airplane was in flight, all but one of the bolts were sheared off and Fant had to make an emergency landing. Fant had substantial damage to his airplane.

Fant presented evidence that Champion was having financial difficulty when it sought out Fant's business. Fant also presented evidence that Champion mechanic Kevin Smith was to perform the installation. Smith, besides being an airframe and power plant mechanic, was an authorized inspector; he was to remove and replace the engine and conduct the annual inspection of the airplane. Before the engine was replaced, Smith had a disagreement with Champion over his salary and he subsequently resigned. However, Smith offered to complete the work on Fant's airplane. Champion's vice-president recommended to Champion's other officers that they allow Smith to complete the job, but they rejected this recommendation, apparently for financial reasons.

Champion hired Dan Boman, who was an airframe and plant mechanic. Boman had never been in charge of installing an engine, nor had he ever worked on the type of airplane Fant had. Boman so informed Champion's vice-president. Because Boman was not an authorized inspector, Champion hired Harold Cordle to handle the inspection.

When he tried to reattach the propeller to the airplane, Boman could not get the propeller to "line up." Boman used the instruction manual for the airplane, but did not telephone the manufacturer for assistance. Cordle happened to be at Champion's hangar while Boman was trying to reattach the propeller. Cordle placed the parts of the propeller in the proper order for reattachment and then Boman put the propeller back on the airplane.

Fant presented evidence that Boman did not know whether the propeller had been properly attached, that he did not know whether the slip ring used to connect the propeller was in the proper location, and that he did not have the proper tools to tighten the nuts that attached the propeller to the airplane and did not know how tight to fasten the nuts. Boman testified that he improperly reused fiber locking nuts on the plane. Fant presented expert evidence that reusing the nuts was a dangerous practice in the airplane industry.

After Boman attached the propeller, he performed a 100-hour service on the airplane. He certified that the airplane complied with all of the service bulletins from the manufacturer. However, there was evidence at trial that Boman falsified several entries in the service logbook. For example, Boman certified that he had installed a new circuit board during this service, as required by the manufacturer; in fact, however, he did not touch any circuit boards or electrical equipment on the airplane when he performed the service.

On July 27, 1994, while Fant and his pilot were returning to Birmingham from Minnesota, the airplane engine began to race wildly and the propeller system malfunctioned. The airplane lost altitude, shook violently, and spewed oil onto the windshield, blocking the pilot's view. When the plane landed, Fant discovered that the propeller was loose. A Federal Aviation Agency [sic] inspector and an authorized inspector for the manufacturer examined the airplane. They found that the propeller system had been improperly installed and that the improper installation had caused the accident.

The FAA inspector interviewed Boman after the accident. Boman told the investigator that he did not have the proper tools to tighten the bolts that attached the propeller to the airplane and that he had had to guess what the proper degree of tightness should be. The FAA inspector also testified that the slip ring was not in the right place. The FAA suspended Boman for four months.

The trial judge's order granting the new trial did not set out which fraud charges he believed were erroneously given, and the verdict was a general one; therefore, we do not know which of the alleged types of fraud the jury found. However, it appears [from the record] that the trial judge granted the new trial because he believed that there was no suppression and, therefore, that the jury instructions on suppression were given in error.

Section 6-5-102, Ala.Code 1975, states: "Suppression of a material fact which the party is under an obligation to communicate constitutes fraud. The obligation to communicate may arise from the confidential relations of the parties or from the particular circumstances of the case." A duty to disclose arises either from a confidential relationship between the parties or from the particular facts in the case. Baker v. Bennett, 603 So.2d 928 (Ala.1992), cert. denied, 507 U.S. 912, 113 S.Ct. 1260, 122 L.Ed.2d 658 (1993). Whether there was a duty to communicate is a question for the jury, which should consider the relationship of the parties, the value of the particular facts suppressed, and the relative knowledge of each party. Baker, supra.

Viewing the facts most favorable to Fant, as we are required to do, we conclude that there was evidence from which the jury could find a duty to disclose, and we conclude that the suppression charge was therefore proper. When Fant contracted with Champion, Smith was its mechanic and Fant believed that Smith was to work on his airplane. Champion hired Boman, who Champion knew had never been in charge of an engine installation on a propeller-type airplane. Champion knew that Boman had difficulty in reattaching the propeller to the plane. Champion allowed Boman to do much of his work unsupervised. The evidence indicated that, based on Champion's expertise and the knowledge of its mechanics, Fant relied on Champion to properly do the technical work on his airplane. There are obvious safety implications in allowing an airplane to be placed back in service as airworthy when Champion knew of the problems Boman had in mounting the propeller of the airplane.

Accordingly, we reverse the order granting the new trial.

Champion's cross-appeal

As to the breach of contract claim, Champion argues that there was a lack of consideration on Fant's part, because, it says, Fant had not paid for the repairs when the accident occurred. Thus, it says, it was entitled to a JNOV on the contract claim.

The basic elements of a contract are an offer and an acceptance, consideration, and mutual assent to the essential terms of the agreement. Pinyan v. Community Bank, 644 So.2d 919 (Ala.1994). Consideration must be present when the contract is made. The requirement of consideration means that a gratuitous promise is not enforceable. Here, we have a promise to repair, given in exchange for a promise to pay, with both parties benefitting from the exchange of promises. The fact that the money had not been paid does not mean consideration was lacking. We note that it was shortly after the repairs were made that the accident occurred, and we find no merit to the argument that there was a lack of consideration. We conclude that the trial court properly denied a JNOV as to the contract claim.

As to the wantonness and fraud claims also, the trial court properly denied a JNOV. As discussed above, there was substantial evidence that Champion knew that Boman had never worked on a propeller-type airplane before and that he had difficulty in installing the propeller on Fant's airplane. There was substantial evidence that the accident was caused by a loose propeller. Also, Boman failed to disclose that he had reused fiber locking nuts to attach the propeller; reusing fiber locking nuts is a dangerous practice in the airplane industry. Further, Boman falsified records in completing the service on the plane.

Accordingly, the order granting a new trial is reversed; the order denying Champion's JNOV motion is affirmed; and the case is remanded.

[The partial dissent of Justice Maddox is omitted.]

HAIMBERG v. R & M AVIATION, INC.

5 Fed. Appx. 543 (7th Cir. 2001)

PER CURIAM.

Yossi Haimberg sued R & M Aviation, Inc. and its owner, Michael Carey, stating five separate causes of action based on an allegedly deficient airplane inspection. One count was dismissed before trial, and after a three-day jury trial, the district court directed a verdict for the defendants on two counts. On a fourth count, the jury awarded Haimberg $50,000 in compensatory damages, and on the fifth count, the court awarded Haimberg $670.00. Both sides subsequently filed post-trial motions, all of which the district court denied. Both the plaintiff and the defendants appeal. We affirm.

I. Background

Yossi Haimberg is a resident of Florida with his own medical services business. Haimberg is also a licensed pilot and, in September 1996, he began searching for a used aircraft that would accommodate his business and personal needs. On the Internet, Haimberg came across an advertisement by Aircraft Sales Corporation ("ASC") of Wheeling, Illinois, for a Piper Navajo, the type of airplane he wanted.

Before completing the purchase, Haimberg wanted an inspection to determine whether the airplane was in compliance with Federal Aviation Administration directives and to determine its true condition. Because he lived in Florida, Haimberg asked ASC to recommend a local mechanic knowledgeable about Piper airplanes. On ASC's recommendation, Haimberg contacted R & M Aviation, Inc. ("R & M"), an FAA-approved aircraft repair station located in DeKalb, Illinois. Haimberg testified that he phoned R & M's owner/operator, Michael Carey, and asked whether he had any business contacts with ASC. Although Carey denied any such relationship, it turned out that he had conducted extensive business with ASC. At trial, Carey admitted that he had worked on over 50 aircraft for ASC and in August 1996 had even performed repair work on the Piper Navajo in question.

Because he was not aware of this information at the time, Haimberg hired R & M to perform the pre-purchase inspection. Haimberg and Carey agreed that the inspection would require about fourteen to sixteen hours of billable labor. However, Haimberg testified that he instructed Carey, if the time frame was insufficient, to call him to discuss how to proceed. Carey testified that the inspection consisted of a physical inspection of the aircraft, review of the aircraft logs and research into applicable FAA Airworthiness Directives. After the inspection, Carey provided a summary of the inspection results to

Haimberg by telephone, as well as a written report. The written report included an indication that "no damage history was detected in the logs or visible on the aircraft," that "our overall impression of the aircraft was good," that "in August of this year [1996], R & M Aviation, Inc. installed a fresh overhauled heater, and we serviced the air conditioning system at that time and it worked very well," and that "the Airworthiness Directives list is included, but only shows the major components due to the time restrictions."

However, R & M's inspection is more noteworthy for the information it did not contain. Although the report referred to R & M's earlier heating and air conditioning work, it made no mention that, two weeks prior to R & M's inspection, AMR Combs, an FAA-approved repair station in Grand Rapids, Michigan, had performed a pre-purchase inspection on the Piper airplane and refused to return the plane to service because it was not airworthy. AMR Combs found that the airplane was not in compliance with at least one FAA directive. Also, AMR Combs' inspection report listed approximately forty-two discrepancies or problems with the aircraft, while R & M listed only a few of those discrepancies on its own report.

There is some discrepancy as to when Carey and R & M knew of AMR Combs' inspection. Carey testified that he was not aware of the AMR Combs inspection until he had completed his own inspection. However, in response to written interrogatories, Carey stated that R & M was made aware of the inspection about the same time as it began its own inspection for Haimberg. Additionally, an AMR Combs mechanic testified that he had most likely inserted a maintenance sticker into the flight logbooks indicating that he had performed an inspection and grounded the airplane. Those logbooks accompanied the airplane when R & M received it to do its pre-purchase inspection for Haimberg. In any case, Carey admitted that he had AMR Combs' discrepancy list while he still had the aircraft and that he did not call AMR Combs about it, that he did not make a follow-up call to Haimberg regarding the discrepancies, and that he did not request more time to reconsider the completeness of his own inspection.

After receiving R & M's inspection report, Haimberg negotiated with ASC to repair the problems found by R & M. That repair work was performed by R & M, and Haimberg then purchased the airplane from ASC for $168,400. Upon delivery of the plane to him in Florida, Haimberg discovered a number of significant problems beyond those listed on R & M's pre-inspection report, including leaking fuel tanks, bad rings and cylinders, a faulty fuel delivery system, water leakage in the avionics bays, and worn landing gear. In addition, the airplane was not in compliance with certain FAA directives, and an FAA inspector grounded the airplane pending repairs. In the ensuing months, Haimberg spent over $75,000 repairing the airplane.

Haimberg sued R & M and Carey based on five theories, although Count III, a negligence claim, was dismissed on the plaintiff's motion before trial. Count I alleged violations of the Illinois Consumer Fraud and Deceptive Practices Act, 815 ILCS 505/1 et seq. (the "Act"). This Count was tried to the court. See Martin v. Heinold Commodities, Inc., 163 Ill.2d 33, 205 Ill.Dec. 443, 643 N.E.2d 734, 755 (Ill.1994) (no right to jury for claim under the Act). The court concluded that, by failing to inform Haimberg of their relationship with ASC, the defendants had fraudulently induced Haimberg to hire them to inspect the airplane and consequently awarded Haimberg $670.00, the cost of the inspection. Counts II and V alleged common law fraud and breach of contract, respectively. At the close of evidence, the court directed a verdict for both defendants on both counts. Count IV alleged that the defendants had negligently misrepresented the condition of the airplane. The jury agreed and awarded Haimberg $50,000 in compensatory damages. Both sides filed post-trial motions, which the district court denied. Both sides now appeal.

II. DISCUSSION

A. Illinois' Moorman Economic Loss Doctrine

The defendants initially ask us to consider whether the district court erred in permitting Haimberg to recover $50,000 based on the defendants' negligent misrepresentation in light of Illinois' economic loss doctrine, which restricts recovery of economic damages in tort cases. See Moorman Mfg. Co. v. Nat'l Tank Co., 91 Ill.2d 69, 61 Ill.Dec. 746, 435 N.E.2d 443 (1992). Because this is a question of law, we review the district court's conclusion de novo. See Harrell v. Cook, 169 F.3d 428, 431 (7th Cir.1999).

Specifically, the Moorman doctrine prohibits recovery in tort for purely economic losses, which include "costs of repair," Moorman, 61 Ill.Dec. 746, 435 N.E.2d at 449, such as the $50,000 award in the present case. The Illinois Supreme Court based the economic loss doctrine on the conclusion that when the "defect is of a qualitative nature and the harm relates to the consumer's expectation that a product is of a particular quality so that it is fit for ordinary use, contract, rather than tort, law provides the appropriate set of rules for recovery." Id., 61 Ill.Dec. 746, 435 N.E.2d at 451. However, the Illinois Supreme Court has also recognized certain exceptions to its Moorman doctrine. See id., 61 Ill.Dec. 746, 435 N.E.2d at 452; Fireman's Fund Ins. Co. v. SEC Donohue, Inc., 176 Ill.2d 160, 223 Ill.Dec. 424, 679 N.E.2d 1197, 1199 (1997). One exception applies "where one who is in the business of supplying information for the guidance of others in their business transactions makes negligent representations." Moorman, 61 Ill.Dec. 746, 435 N.E.2d at 452. A "precise, case-specific inquiry is required to determine whether a particular enterprise is 'in the business of supplying information for the guidance of others in their business transactions.'" Rankow v. First Chicago Corp., 870 F.2d 356, 361 (7th Cir.1989). The district court concluded that the defendants were in the business of supplying information and therefore the Moorman doctrine did not preclude Haimberg's recovery based on their negligent misrepresentation.

The Illinois Supreme Court has stated that the appropriate focus of this exception is whether the defendant is truly in the business of supplying information or whether the information is instead provided "ancillary to the sale or in connection with the sale of merchandise or other matter." Fireman's Fund, 223 Ill.Dec. 424, 679 N.E.2d at 1201. If it is the former, the information provider exception applies and the Moorman doctrine does not preclude recovery of economic damages; if it is the latter, the exception does not apply and the Moorman doctrine precludes the recovery of economic damages. In deciding whether information is incidental to a tangible product, a court should look to the ultimate result of the work. See id. (information provided was incidental to the end product—the water system that engineer had designed—and therefore Moorman doctrine applied); 2314 Lincoln Park West Condo. Ass'n v. Mann, Gin, Ebel & Frazier, Ltd., 136 Ill.2d 302, 144 Ill.Dec. 227, 555 N.E.2d 346 (1990) (information provided was incidental to condominiums that architects had designed and therefore Moorman doctrine applied).

The defendants argue that the pre-purchase inspection was incidental to a tangible product, the airplane, and therefore recovery of economic damages is prohibited. However, the district court found that the pre-purchase inspection report was not likely to "manifest itself physically." In other words, the information would never become an airplane, as would an architect's design for a building. Rather, its ultimate purpose was to assist the plaintiff in his decision to either purchase or reject the airplane. See Tribune Co. v. Geraghty & Miller, Inc., No. 97 C 1889, 1997 WL 438836 (N.D.Ill. July 25, 1997) (company hired to evaluate whether property, which plaintiff was considering purchasing, contained any environmental concerns could be held liable for its negligent misrepresentation, and Moorman doctrine did not preclude recovery of economic damages).

The district court relied on, and we find instructive, a recent Illinois appellate court decision addressing whether the Moorman doctrine barred recovery against an architect or engineer hired solely to provide information, rather than to design a building. See Tolan and Son, Inc. v. KLLM Architects, Inc., 308 Ill.App.3d 18, 241 Ill.Dec. 427, 719 N.E.2d 288 (1999). The Tolan court acknowledged that there was a continuum of business providers, ranging from pure information providers, such as lawyers, accountants and inspectors, to middle ground cases, such as insurance agents and financial advisors, to tangible product providers, such as manufacturers. Id., 241 Ill.Dec. 427, 719 N.E.2d at 296–97. The first category "includes businesses that provide a product that consists solely of information. The supplying of information need not encompass the enterprise's entire undertaking but must be central to the business transaction between the parties.... This category involves those situations where the value of the services lies in the analytical work." Id. at 297 (citations omitted). The court then concluded that where an architect or engineer was engaged solely to provide information, "it could be considered to be in the business of supplying information for the guidance of others." Id. at 298.

In the present case, the information provided, the pre-purchase inspection report, constituted the entire transaction between Haimberg and the defendants. The district court appropriately likened the defendants' dealings with Haimberg to a client's dealings with an accountant or lawyer. In such cases, the client relies upon the professional's knowledge and expertise, which cannot be memorialized in a contract. The "value of the services rendered lies in the ideas behind the documents, not in the documents themselves.... Application of the Moorman doctrine limiting recovery of purely economic losses to contract, therefore, is inappropriate where a relationship results in something intangible." Congregation of the Passion, Holy Cross Province v. Touche Ross & Co., 159 Ill.2d 137, 201 Ill.Dec. 71, 636 N.E.2d 503, 515 (1994). While Haimberg may have later decided to hire R & M to provide other more tangible services, such as repair work, here it was hired by Haimberg solely to provide information upon which he would rely in deciding whether or not to buy the airplane. The value of these services lay entirely in the defendants' analytical work, their inspection of the condition of the airplane. Accordingly, we find that the district court did not err in permitting Haimberg to recover economic damages in tort.

B. Judgment as a Matter of Law

Next, the defendants contend that the district court erred in denying their motion for judgment as a matter of law on Haimberg's negligent misrepresentation claim. The standard of review for the denial of a motion for judgment as a matter of law is de novo. See Tincher v. Wal-Mart Stores, Inc., 118 F.3d 1125, 1129 (7th Cir.1997). This court limits its inquiry to whether the evidence presented, combined with all reasonable inferences permissibly drawn therefrom, is sufficient to support the verdict when viewed in the light most favorable to the non-moving party. Id.

Under Illinois law, to prevail on a claim for negligent misrepresentation, the plaintiff must establish (1) a false statement of material fact, (2) negligence in ascertaining the truth of the defendant's statement, (3) an intention to induce the other party to act, (4) action by the other party in reliance on the truth of the statements, (5) damage to the other party resulting from such reliance, and (6) duty owed by the defendant to plaintiff to communicate accurate information. See Weisblatt v. Chicago Bar Ass'n, 292

Ill.App.3d 48, 225 Ill.Dec. 993, 684 N.E.2d 984, 990 (1997). The defendants argue that the record contains no evidence to establish that they made a false statement of material fact. In ruling on the defendant's post-trial motion, the district court concluded that the jury had sufficient evidence from which it could find that the defendant made a false statement of material fact. We agree. First, the jury learned that Carey failed to supplement the pre-purchase inspection report with the additional report from AMR Combs. Next, an AMR Combs mechanic testified that he had most likely inserted a maintenance sticker into the flight logs which accompanied the airplane, indicating that R & M had that information available to it when it did its own inspection. In addition, Carey testified that once he learned of AMR Combs' inspection, he did nothing to reconcile his own inspection to at least determine whether or not he thought AMR Combs' negative findings were valid. Together this evidence was more than sufficient to establish that the defendants failed to disclose to Haimberg the true condition of the airplane.

The failure to disclose a material fact is no less a misrepresentation than an affirmative assertion of a falsehood. See Stewart v. Thrasher, 242 Ill.App.3d 10, 182 Ill.Dec. 930, 610 N.E.2d 799, 803 (1993). At the very least, Haimberg needed this information to make an accurate determination of whether to purchase the airplane and to ascertain its value. More importantly, Haimberg needed this information for his own safety so as not to risk his life by flying a defective airplane. Therefore, viewing all of this evidence in the light most favorable to Haimberg, we believe that there was sufficient evidence for the jury to find that the defendants made a false statement. See, e.g., Perschall v. Raney, 137 Ill.App.3d 978, 92 Ill.Dec. 431, 484 N.E.2d 1286 (Ill.App.Ct.1985) (judgment against termite inspector for negligent misrepresentation was not against manifest weight of the evidence).

The defendants contend that the plaintiff knew the inspection was not an exhaustive one and therefore they should not be held liable for the inspection report's missing information. The defendants overlook the fact, however, that R & M not only failed to note significant defects with the Piper airplane, but also failed to acknowledge the existence or conclusions of another inspection performed only weeks before their own that disclosed many defects. Thus, based on the facts known to them at the time of their inspection, the defendants did not provide an accurate report, even for the limited purpose for which they were hired. Haimberg testified that he had told the defendants he was willing to pay more for the inspection if it was necessary to expand its scope. The AMR Combs inspection report clearly required a more thorough examination, yet the defendants did not even give Haimberg the chance to consider whether he wished a more exhaustive inspection. They instead declined to tell him about the AMR Combs inspection. Even if Haimberg did not request R & M to perform an exhaustive inspection, the jury had evidence from which it could conclude the defendants had negligently made false statements in the limited pre-inspection report which it was paid to provide.

C. Attorney's Fees

Lastly, we turn to plaintiff's request that we reverse the district court's order denying him attorney fees under the Illinois Consumer Fraud and Deceptive Practices Act, 815 ILCS 505/10a(c) (the "Act"). We review the district court's decision concerning attorney fees under the Act for an abuse of discretion. Casey v. Jerry Yusim Nissan, Inc., 296 Ill.App.3d 102, 230 Ill.Dec. 575, 694 N.E.2d 206, 209 (Ill.App.Ct.1998).

Section 10a(c) of the Act provides that the court "may award, in addition to the relief provided in this Section, reasonable attorney's fees and costs to the prevailing party." 815 ILCS 505/10a(c). The purpose and intent of the Act is to eradicate "all forms of deceptive and unfair business practices and to grant appropriate remedies to defrauded consumers." American Buyers Club of Mt. Vernon, Illinois, Inc. v. Honecker, 46 Ill.App.3d 252, 5 Ill.Dec. 666, 361 N.E.2d 1370, 1374 (1977). The provisions of the Act are to be liberally construed to effect its purpose. 815 ILCS 505/11a.

The district court denied Haimberg's request for attorney fees after applying the following factors [R28, at 9–10]: (1) the degree of bad faith, if any, by the defendants; (2) the defendants' ability to pay a fee award; (3) the deterrent effect of an award; (4) the relative merits of the parties' cases; and (5) whether the plaintiff's action vindicated a significant public interest instead of, or in addition to, plaintiff's own private interest. See Graunke v. Elmhurst Chrysler Plymouth Volvo, Inc., 247 Ill.App.3d 1015, 187 Ill.Dec. 401, 617 N.E.2d 858, 863–64 (1993). Applying these factors, the district court determined that this was not a case infected by bad faith, that an award of fees would have a limited deterrent effect in the future because of the limited number of pre-purchase inspections performed by R & M, that the defendants' case had merit and the case turned closely upon credibility determinations and that the plaintiff's case was overwhelmingly private in nature.

Haimberg argues that the district court's determination did not correctly measure the degree of culpability of the defendants and that it ignored significant and substantial evidence that R & M intended for Haimberg to purchase the airplane based on the false inspection report. However, the district court concluded that the defendants had not specifically intended to induce Haimberg to purchase the plane; rather, the defendants had violated the Act by failing to disclose their prior dealings with ASC and thus inducing Haimberg into hiring them to perform the inspection. Haimberg was effectively deprived of the independent pre-purchase inspection he sought, and the district court believed it was sufficient to award Haimberg the cost of the inspection, rather than the full costs of repair or attorney's fees.

Haimberg contends that the defendants knew he was considering whether to purchase the airplane, and that they provided a "good" inspection report to persuade Haimberg to do so. He claims that the defendants should have known that, by providing a positive recommendation of the airplane, they would induce him to purchase it. Haimberg relies on Warren v. LeMay to support his contention that the defendants are considered to intend the necessary consequences of their actions. See 142 Ill.App.3d 550, 96 Ill.Dec. 418, 491 N.E.2d 464, 474 (Ill.App.Ct 1986) (where termite inspector rendered faulty inspection report, he was held liable for his misrepresentation to buyers of home). However, the district court found that there was insufficient evidence at trial that the defendants knew Haimberg wanted to buy a "good" airplane. Indeed, Haimberg's mechanic testified that there are a number of reasons to purchase an airplane and that a person could be "looking for a bad airplane that they can put investment money in to make a good airplane to resell at a later time."

Haimberg also argues that the district court improperly considered the absence of bad faith by the defendant. Haimberg argues that bad faith, or the lack thereof, is an improper consideration in deciding whether to award attorneys fees to prevailing plaintiffs, rather than to prevailing defendants. See Haskell v. Blumthal, 204 Ill.App.3d 596, 149 Ill.Dec. 619, 561 N.E.2d 1315, 1319 (1990) (award of attorney's fees to a prevailing defendant is only appropriate upon a finding of bad faith by the plaintiff; no such requirement for prevailing plaintiffs); Casey, 230 Ill.Dec. 575, 694 N.E.2d at 210 (same). But see Graunke, 187 Ill.Dec. 401, 617 N.E.2d at 862 (attorney's fees may be awarded to either prevailing plaintiffs or prevailing defendants at the discretion of the trial court, and Section 10a(c) does not require a showing of bad faith by either party). Haimberg essentially argues the district court's determination that the defendants did not act in bad faith was improperly dispositive in its decision to deny attorney's fees.

In its post-trial ruling, the district court acknowledged that Illinois appellate decisions contained differing language regarding the appropriate standard to apply and determined that, even if it disregarded bad faith altogether, the remaining factors still weighed against awarding attorney's fees in this case. We note that the clear and unambiguous language of Section 10a(c) does not mention bad faith. Indeed, it does not mention any factors at all, but rather leaves the entire decision regarding an award of attorney's fees to the discretion of the trial court. In addition, the language makes no distinction between prevailing plaintiffs and prevailing defendants. However, we need not resolve this dispute and leave its resolution to the Illinois courts. Because the district court considered Haimberg's arguments in its post-trial ruling, and still denied an award of attorney's fees, there is no danger that the district court relied on an improper standard in its decision. See Graunke, 187 Ill.Dec. 401, 617 N.E.2d at 862–63 (case remanded because of possibility that trial court may have improperly considered a finding of bad faith to be a prerequisite to its exercise of discretion to award fees). Under these circumstances, we do not believe that the district court abused its discretion in denying attorney's fees to Haimberg.

III. Conclusion

For the reasons stated herein, we conclude that Illinois' Moorman doctrine of economic loss does not preclude the plaintiff's recovery of economic damages in tort because the defendants were in the business of supplying information for the guidance of others. We also find that the district court did not err in denying the defendants' motion for judgment as a matter of law, and that the jury had sufficient evidence from which it could conclude that the defendants had negligently made false statements in their inspection report. Lastly, we find that the district court did not abuse its discretion in denying the plaintiff an award of attorney's fees under the Illinois Consumer Fraud and Deceptive Practices Act. Accordingly, we affirm the decision of the district court.

LOCK v. PACKARD FLYING SERVICE, INC.

173 N.W.2d 516 (Neb. 1970)

NEWTON, Justice.

Plaintiff seeks to recover for personal injuries received in an airplane accident. Defendant operated a repair service at the city of Imperial, Nebraska, municipal airport. Plaintiff's husband, with three other persons, constituted the Chase County Flying Club which owned the airplane involved in the accident. One member of the club damaged the rudder of the plane and arranged for defendant to repair the rudder. Defendant's employees removed the rudder for the purpose of repairing it. The plane was left in its hangar with the ignition key left in the plane and no warning given of the removal of the rudder. Plaintiff's husband failed to note the absence of the rudder, took off with plaintiff as a guest passenger, crashed, and plaintiff was injured. The case was submitted to a jury which found for defendant and judgment was entered accordingly. We affirm the judgment of the trial court.

The rudder is essential as a vertical stabilizer and a plane without a rudder is not airworthy. The rudder, together with the elevator, the flaps, and the ailerons, constituted the control surfaces on the airplane. All are connected by cables to controls in the pilot's compartment and are fastened to the plane by means of hinges, bolts, nuts, and cotter pins. In the present instance, the rudder varied in width from 1 foot 8 inches to 2 feet and was 4½ feet high. The control cables were loosely hooked together when disconnected from the rudder and were open to inspection. The rudder controls were also attached to the front wheel to facilitate turning when taxiing on the ground and the fact the plane could be turned while taxiing did not indicate the rudder was present or functioning.

Applicable Federal Aviation Regulations forbid the operation of aircraft not in an airworthy condition and hold the pilot responsible for determining if a plane was safe to fly. The regulations also make the pilot primarily responsible for maintaining the aircraft in an airworthy condition. In complying with these regulations, it is necessary and customary for a pilot to make a preflight inspection of the plane. This includes checking the engine oil, draining accumulated moisture from the gas tanks, and checking all control surfaces together with their connecting cables, hinges, and fastenings to ascertain that they are in safe operating condition.

Plaintiff has assigned several grounds of alleged error. We find it unnecessary to consider these assignments. Her right to recover is dependent upon two fundamental propositions. First, was the defendant guilty of negligence in failing to give warning of the removal of the rudder? Second, was the removal of the rudder and the failure to give warning of its removal a proximate cause of the accident and of plaintiff's injury? We resolve both questions in favor of the defendant. Under such circumstances, any error assigned by plaintiff is necessarily harmless and not prejudicial.

The aircraft in which the plaintiff was injured was the property of her husband and three other persons. Under existing regulations, no one except a licensed pilot is authorized to fly a plane. Licensed pilots, such as plaintiff's husband, are charged with making preflight inspections and ascertaining that the plane is airworthy before they take off. All experienced airmen, including mechanics and repairmen, are familiar with these requirements. Defendant could not reasonably be expected to anticipate that the plane would be flown by other than experienced and licensed pilots. Neither could defendant, or any prudent person under similar circumstances, be reasonably expected to anticipate that a duly qualified pilot would neglect to make a reasonable preflight inspection or fail to notice such an open and obvious defect as a missing rudder. If there was no reasonable apprehension of danger, there was no duty to warn of the removal of the rudder. In Kolar v. Divis, 179 Neb. 756, 140 N.W.2d 658, it is stated: "Foresight, not retrospect, is the standard of diligence. It is nearly always easy, after an accident has happened, to see how it could have been avoided. But negligence is not a matter to be judged after the occurrence. It is always a question of what reasonably prudent men under the same circumstances would or should, in the exercise of reasonable care, have anticipated." In Schild v. Schild, 176 Neb. 282, 125 N.W.2d 900, it is stated: "There is negligence only where no care is exercised to avert a risk to others which reasonably should be apprehended." See also Shupe v. County of Antelope, 157 Neb. 374, 59 N.W.2d 710; Anderson v. Moser, 169 Neb. 134, 98 N.W.2d 703, 81 A.L.R.2d 956; Clouse v. County of Dawson, 161 Neb. 544, 74 N.W.2d 67, 55 A.L.R.2d 991.

The evidence discloses that the pilot of the plane was clearly negligent in failing to ascertain that it was airworthy and in flying a craft that was obviously disabled. This is not a case of a concealed or hidden defect or of one which the pilot might reasonably have been expected not to discover. The negligence of the pilot occurred subsequent to the removal of the rudder by defendant. Defendant's removal of the rudder and failure to give warning of the consequent disabling of the aircraft was not the proximate cause of the accident. "Two acts of independent source are not concurrent in causing an injury if one of them merely furnishes a condition by which such injury is made possible, and later such injury occurs through the efficient, self-acting, and independent operation of the other." Johnson v. Metropolitan Utilities Dist., 176 Neb. 276, 125 N.W.2d 708. "Ordinarily, where the negligence of one party is merely passive and potential causing only a condition while that of the other is the moving and effective cause of the accident, the latter is the proximate cause." Jarosh v. Van Meter, 171 Neb. 61, 105 N.W.2d 531, 82 A.L.R.2d 714. "Where a second actor has or should have become aware of the existence of a potential danger created by the negligence of an original tort-feasor, and thereafter, by an independent act of negligence, brings about an accident, the first tort-feasor is relieved of liability, because the condition created by him was merely a circumstance of the accident and not its proximate cause." 65 C.J.S. Negligence § 111(2), p. 1210. See also Jarosh v. Van Meter, supra. "The causal connection is broken if between the defendant's negligent act and the plaintiff's injury 'there has intervened the negligence of a third person who had full control of the situation and whose negligence was such as the defendant was not bound to anticipate and could not be said to have contemplated, which later negligence resulted directly in the injury to the plaintiff.'" Shupe v. County of Antelope, supra. "An injury that could not have been foreseen or reasonably anticipated as the probable result of the negligence is not actionable, nor is an injury that is not the natural consequence of the negligence complained of, and would not have resulted from it, but for the interposition of some new, independent cause that could not have been anticipated." Kroeger v. Safranek, 161 Neb. 182, 72 N.W.2d 831.

Defendant did nothing that in and by itself could have resulted in plaintiff's injuries. The plane could only be used by licensed, experienced pilots familiar with the plane and the dangers of flying a plane that was not airworthy. Such a pilot is aware of the necessity of a rudder on the aircraft and that without it, it would not be airworthy or manageable. He is charged at all times with making a preflight inspection of the aircraft with a view to determining its safety and airworthiness. The absence of the rudder was an obvious, not a concealed, defect which any reasonable examination by the pilot would have disclosed. Under such circumstances, defendant could not be required to anticipate injury from the absence of the rudder. It had no reason to anticipate the grossly negligent acts of the pilot. In accordance with the foregoing rules, it is apparent that the intervening acts of negligence on the part of the pilot were of such nature as to relieve defendant of any possible liability and constituted the sole proximate cause of the accident.

The judgment of the district court is affirmed.

JARMUTH v. ALDRIDGE

747 N.E.2d 1014 (Ill. App. Ct. 2001)

O'BRIEN, Justice.

Plaintiff, Jeffrey Jarmuth, appeals the entry of summary judgment in favor of defendants Kenneth W. Aldridge, doing business as KWA Leasing, who was also sued as Utility Leasing (collectively, the Aldridge defendants), on plaintiff's negligence claim arising out of an airplane crash, which resulted in the death of the pilot, Michael Garofalo (decedent), and his passenger, Vito Garofalo.

Summary judgment is appropriate where the pleadings, depositions, and admissions on file, together with the affidavits, if any, demonstrate that there is no issue as to any material fact and that the moving party is entitled to judgment as a matter of law. 735 ILCS 5/2-1005(c) (West 1998). A reviewing court applies a de novo standard of review. Outboard Marine Corp. v. Liberty Mutual Insurance Co., 154 Ill.2d 90, 102, 180 Ill.Dec. 691, 607 N.E.2d 1204 (1992).

The relevant facts are undisputed. Decedent and Vito Garofalo were killed in an airplane accident on July 28, 1994, in Racine, Wisconsin. The plane was a restored World War II vintage Vultee BT 13-A training aircraft owned by the Aldridge defendants and piloted by decedent.

Several years prior to the accident, decedent and James Skinner, employees of Waukegan Aero, Ltd. (WAL), found the Vultee in pieces in a barn in South Carolina. WAL purchased the salvaged parts and transported them to WAL's facilities where WAL's employees began the restoration process. KWA Leasing, Inc., purchased the Vultee from WAL in 1990. Thereafter WAL sent the Vultee's engine to Covington Aircraft Engines, Inc. (Covington), in pieces for an overhaul. Covington completed the engine overhaul and it was installed. WAL then performed a final restoration inspection and certified the Vultee as airworthy on May 11, 1992. Following an annual inspection, WAL again certified the Vultee as airworthy on June 4, 1993.

In June 1994, Kenneth Aldridge discovered a fuel leak from the Vultee's engine compartment and contacted Howard Siedlecki, a licensed mechanic working for Sunshine Aircraft Repair, to determine the cause of the leak and to repair it. Siedlecki examined the Vultee and discovered the fuel leak was the result of a cracked fitting that goes into the carburetor. Kenneth Aldridge told Siedlecki to repair the leak. Siedlecki removed the carburetor from the Vultee and attempted to effect the necessary repair but encountered difficulties when the carburetor threads came out of the carburetor along with the cracked fitting. Siedlecki, who did not feel competent to repair the carburetor threads, contacted Covington about the problem and was instructed to send the carburetor to Maynard & Maynard for repair work.

Maynard overhauled the carburetor, performed a water leak test on the carburetor float, certified the carburetor float as airworthy, affixed the appropriate maintenance release tag to the carburetor, and shipped the part back to Sunshine Aircraft Repair. Siedlecki then reinstalled the part, performed the Vultee's annual inspection as required by Federal Aviation Association (FAA) regulations, and certified the aircraft as airworthy on July 25, 1994. Three days later, the plane crashed while decedent was flying it to Oshkosh, Wisconsin, where it was to be sold.

Plaintiff's complaint alleged, inter alia, that the Aldridge defendants had a nondelegable duty to ensure the Vultee was airworthy, that the Aldridge defendants breached this duty when they failed to personally inspect the Vultee after it had already been inspected by a FAA-certified mechanic, and that this failure caused the death of decedent because a defect in the carburetor float allowed fuel to enter the mechanism causing the Vultee to crash. The issue is whether the facts and the law, when construed strictly against the Aldridge defendants and liberally in favor of plaintiff, create a duty to ensure the Vultee was airworthy, which could not be delegated to another.

Section 424 of the Restatement (Second) of Torts (1965) provides:

> One who by statute or by administrative regulation is under a duty to provide specified safeguards or precautions for the safety of others is subject to liability

> * * * for harm caused by the failure of a contractor employed by him to provide such safeguards or precautions.

FAA regulations impose certain duties upon owners of aircraft to ensure the safety of others. Section 121.363 provides:

> (a) Each certificate holder is primarily responsible for—
>
> (1) The airworthiness of its aircraft, including airframes, aircraft engines, propellers, appliances, and parts thereof; and
>
> (2) The performance of maintenance, preventative maintenance, and alteration of its aircraft, including airframes, aircraft engines, propellers, appliances, emergency equipment, and parts thereof, in accordance with its manual and the regulations of this chapter.
>
> (b) A certificate holder may make arrangements with another person for the performance of any maintenance, preventative maintenance, or alterations. However, this does not relieve the certificate holder of the responsibilities specified in paragraph (a) of this section.

14 C.F.R. § 121.363 (1999).

This section clearly states that the duty imposed is non-delegable; the certificate holder is not absolved of responsibility for non-compliance even though the work to be performed thereunder may have been contracted out. However, section 121.363 applies to "Air Carrier Certificate or Operating Certificate" holders, such as major airlines (14 C.F.R. § 121.1(a) (1999); see also 14 C.F.R. § 119.1 et seq. (1999) (Certification: Air Carriers and Commercial Operators)), not to private owners.

In contrast, section 91.403 provides, in pertinent part:

> (a) The owner or operator of an aircraft is primarily responsible for maintaining that aircraft in an airworthy condition, including compliance with part 39 [Airworthiness Directives] of this chapter.

14 C.F.R. § 91.403 (1999).

And section 91.405 provides, in pertinent part:

> Each owner or operator of an aircraft—
>
> (a) Shall have that aircraft inspected as prescribed in subpart E of this part and shall between required inspections * * * have discrepancies repaired * * *.;
>
> (b) Shall ensure that maintenance personnel make appropriate entries in the aircraft maintenance records indicating that the aircraft has been approved for return to service;
>
> (c) Shall have any inoperative instrument or item of equipment * * * repaired, replaced, removed, or inspected at the next required inspection; and
>
> (d) When listed discrepancies include inoperative instruments or equipment, shall ensure that a placard has been in stalled as required by Section 43.11 of this chapter.

14 C.F.R. § 91.405 (1999).

Sections 91.403 and 91.405 apply to non-commercial aircraft owners. 14 C.F.R. §§ 91.401(a), (b) (1999). The use in section 91.403 of the term "primary" responsibility clearly contemplates "secondary" responsibility, thus negating an implication that the duty to ensure the safety of a privately owned aircraft is non-delegable. Moreover, section 91.403 contains no specific language on par with that in section 121.363 regarding an owner's retention of legal responsibility. The absence of such language indicates the FAA intended no such restriction on the owner's delegation of a section 91.403 duty. Because the Vultee owned by the Aldridge defendants did not fall within the class of aircraft governed by section 121.363, but rather into the class of aircraft governed by sections 91.403 and 91.405, the Aldridge defendants were entitled to delegate the duty to ensure the Vultee was airworthy to FAA-qualified mechanics and inspectors. Because the Aldridge defendants' duty under sections 91.403 and 91.405 was delegable, the Aldridge defendants are not liable pursuant to section 424 of the Restatement (Second) of Torts.

Although there are no Illinois cases directly on point, this conclusion is supported by Cosgrove v. McDonnell Douglas Helicopter Co., 847 F.Supp. 719 (D.Minn.1994), and White v. Orr Leasing, Inc., 210 Ga.App. 599, 436 S.E.2d 693 (1993).

In Cosgrove, a helicopter pilot was forced to land when fatigue failure caused the helicopter's drive shaft to be severed. The pilot, Cosgrove, the owners, and the lessee of the helicopter sued McDonnell Douglas, successor in interest to the manufacturer of the helicopter. The jury allocated fault in varying amounts to McDonnell Douglas, the owners, the lessee, and the inspector. In a posttrial motion, McDonnell Douglas requested reapportionment of damages by allocating the inspector's share of fault to the helicopter owners. McDonnell Douglas contended that section 91.403 and 91.405 duties were non-delegable and, as a consequence, the owners were liable pursuant to section 424 of the Restatement (Second) of Torts. The court rejected this argument, finding that the express language of section 91.403 imposes upon an aircraft owner a "non-exclusive" duty. Other portions of the regulations "impose a plethora of requirements, largely expressed in obligatory 'shalls,'" (Cosgrove, 847 F.Supp. at 722) upon operators and mechanics as well as others. That the section rests "primary" responsibility for "maintenance of aircraft is not so singularly a duty of the owner or operator that public policy dictates that it may not be delegated to others." Cosgrove, 847 F.Supp. at 723.

In White, the plaintiffs asserted that section 91.403 "creates a nondelegable duty to passengers and would make [defendant owner] absolutely liable for any negligent inspection." White, 210 Ga.App. at 602, 436 S.E.2d at 696. The court, without comment on the regulation, stated, "no authority is cited by plaintiffs for the proposition that allowing a mechanic licensed by the FAA to conduct the inspection makes the owner of the plane liable for any failure of inspection as a matter of negligence per se." White, 210 Ga.App. at 602, 436 S.E.2d at 696. Summary judgment for the aircraft owners was affirmed.

Moreover the Illinois case Van Steemburg v. General Aviation, Inc., 243 Ill.App.3d 299, 183 Ill.Dec. 496, 611 N.E.2d 1144 (1993), appeal denied, 151 Ill.2d 578, 186 Ill.Dec. 395, 616 N.E.2d 348 (1993), suggests that an aircraft owner discharges his FAA-mandated maintenance duty by having such maintenance performed by licensed professionals. The case further suggests that if an owner has so delegated the duty in compliance with federal regulations, he cannot be held liable unless he knew or should have known of a defect or deficiency left unrepaired.

Here, the undisputed facts indicate that the Aldridge defendants delegated all responsibility for investigation and repair of the fuel leak, the subsequent repair of the carburetor, and the annual inspection of Vultee, to professionals licensed to perform such work. The undisputed facts also indicate that the repairs were documented in accord with FAA regulations. Plaintiff does not dispute the qualifications of Siedlecki, the aircraft mechanic who certified the plane as airworthy following the carburetor work.

Neither does plaintiff point to any failure of the Aldridge defendants to act to remedy defects or deficiencies of which they had actual or constructive notice following such certification. Indeed, there is no indication that the Aldridge defendants even saw the aircraft in the three days between completion of the Vultee's final inspection and decedent's take-off for Oshkosh, Wisconsin.

Plaintiff's reliance on Maloney v. Rath, 69 Cal.2d 442, 445 P.2d 513, 71 Cal.Rptr. 897 (1968), in support of its argument is misplaced. Maloney is a California case arising out of an automobile accident and addressing a provision of that state's vehicle code. The ruling in that case is irrelevant to the facts of the instant case involving an airplane crash, which addresses different and significantly more stringent federal regulation of aircraft.

Because there is no evidence that the Aldridge defendants were negligent in relying on properly certified FAA mechanics to perform the repair work, and there is no evidence the Aldridge defendants had actual or constructive knowledge of any defect in the Vultee subsequent to the FAA-mandated annual inspection, the Aldridge defendants cannot be held liable for the negligence, if any, of the mechanics.

Section 434 of the Restatement (Second) of Torts is an exception to the general rule that an employer is not liable for the negligent acts of an independent contractor except where the employer orders or directs the acts causing the harm or retains control over the operative details of the contractor's work (Milz v. M.J. Meadows, Inc., 234 Ill.App.3d 281, 175 Ill.Dec. 276, 599 N.E.2d 1290 (1992)), and the exception does not apply under the undisputed facts of this case (see, e.g., Ingle v. Swish Manufacturing Southeast, 164 Ga.App. 469, 471, 297 S.E.2d 506, 508 (Ga.App.1982) (directed verdict for aircraft owner proper where aircraft was delivered to independent contractor for maintenance and repair and thus any negligence by independent contractor could not be imputed to owner)).

Accordingly, the order of the circuit court granting summary judgment in favor of defendants Kenneth W. Aldridge, KWA Leasing, and Utility Leasing is affirmed.

Notes

1. Cases like *Borregard*, *Fant*, and *Haimberg* make it clear that mechanics and their facilities are expected to observe high standards. Yet as *Lock* points out, they are not automatically responsible for every mishap that occurs. As a result, cases involving aircraft repairs tend to be fact-intensive, require substantial investigation, and rely heavily on expert testimony. *See further* Robert A. Brazener, Annotation, *Liability for Alleged Negligence of Independent Servicer or Repairer of Aircraft*, 41 A.L.R.3d 1320 (1972 & 2005 Supp.); L. Ronald Jorgensen, *The Defense of Aviation Mechanics and Repair Facilities from Enforcement Actions of the Federal Aviation Administration*, 54 J. Air L. & Com. 349 (1988); Rachel A. Campbell, Comment, *Liability of Independent Servicers and Repairers of Aircraft*, 54 J. Air L. & Com. 181 (1988).

2. As Justice O'Brien explains in *Jarmuth*, private owners can delegate their maintenance responsibilities to FAA-qualified mechanics but commercial ones cannot. What is the policy rationale at work here? *See further Shay v. Flight C Helicopter Services, Inc.*, 822 A.2d 1 (Pa. Super. Ct. 2003).

3. In April 1996, the FBI arrested Theodore Kaczynski in a remote cabin outside Lincoln, Montana, thereby bringing to an end the 18-year reign of terror of the UNABOMBER. Although Kaczynski turned out to be a Harvard graduate and former UC-Berkeley professor, investigators initially thought the UNABOMBER, whose moniker

came from his early targets (universities and airlines) was a disgruntled airplane mechanic:

> The first mail bomb was sent in late May 1978 to Prof. Buckley Crist at Northwestern University. [It] was followed by bombs to airline officials and [then in November] 1979 there was a bomb placed in the cargo hold of a commercial airplane [American Airlines Flight 444, flying from Chicago to Washington, D.C.]. The bomb began smoking and the pilot was forced to make an emergency landing. Many of the passengers were treated for smoke inhalation. Only a faulty timing mechanism prevented the bomb from exploding. Authorities said it had enough firepower to obliterate the plane. The FBI became involved after this incident and came up with the code name UNABOM.
>
> The FBI at first thought the culprit was a disgruntled airline mechanic. FBI Agent John Douglas, the father of "profiling" criminals, disagreed with this. He claimed the bombs were much too sophisticated and that the bomber was most likely an academic. Profiling was a new investigative tool at the time and Douglas's theory was largely ignored. After Kaczynski's arrest, the FBI came under much criticism. It was pointed out that if they had only checked into the disgruntled academic theory, they could have easily caught this man many years earlier.

Theodore Kaczynski, at en.wikipedia.org/wiki/Theodore_Kaczynski.

4. For additional descriptions of aviation mechanics and repair facilities, see the web sites of such organizations as the Aircraft Electronics Association (www.aea.net), Aircraft Mechanics Fraternal Association (www.amfanatl.org), International Association of Machinists and Aerospace Workers (www.iamaw.org), and Professional Aviation Maintenance Association (www.pama.org). *See also* Dale Crane, *Aviation Mechanic Handbook* (4th ed. 2004), and Larry Reithmaier, *Standard Aircraft Handbook for Mechanics and Technicians* (6th ed. 1999).

Problem 12

A mechanic was killed while repairing an airplane. When his widow sought workers' compensation benefits, the employer refused to pay. It contends the mechanic caused his own death by knowingly violating a shop safety rule. If the widow sues, arguing that her husband's death (from whatever cause) obligates the employer to pay, how should the court rule? *See Boatright v. Dothan Aviation Corp.*, 176 So. 2d 500 (Ala. 1965).

D. FLIGHT ATTENDANTS

FRANK v. UNITED AIRLINES, INC.

216 F.3d 845 (9th Cir. 2000),
cert. denied, 514 U.S. 932 (2001)

FLETCHER, Circuit Judge.

From 1980 to 1994, defendant United Airlines, Inc. ("United") required flight attendants to comply with maximum weight requirements based on sex, height and age.

Failure to maintain weight below the applicable maximum subjected a flight attendant to various forms of discipline, including suspension without pay and termination. In 1992, plaintiffs filed this action on behalf of a class of female flight attendants to challenge these weight requirements.

Plaintiffs contend that by adopting a discriminatory weight policy and enforcing that policy in a discriminatory manner, United discriminated against women and older flight attendants in violation of Title VII of the Civil Rights Act of 1964 ("Title VII"), 42 U.S.C. § 2000e; the Age Discrimination in Employment Act ("ADEA"), 29 U.S.C. §§ 621–634; the Americans with Disabilities Act ("ADA"), 42 U.S.C. §§ 12101–12213; and the California Fair Employment and Housing Act ("FEHA"), Cal. Gov't Code §§ 12900–12996. The district court granted summary judgment for defendant on all of plaintiffs' class and individual claims. We have jurisdiction under 28 U.S.C. § 1291. We reverse in part and affirm in part.

I

During the 1960s and early 1970s, the standard practice among large commercial airlines was to hire only women as flight attendants. The airlines required their flight attendants to remain unmarried, to refrain from having children, to meet weight and appearance criteria, and to retire by the age of 35. See Gerdom v. Continental Airlines, Inc., 692 F.2d 602, 605–06 (9th Cir.1982) (en banc) (collecting cases). Like other airlines, defendant United had a longstanding practice of requiring female flight attendants to maintain their weight below certain levels.

After it began hiring male flight attendants in the wake of Diaz v. Pan Am. World Airways, Inc., 442 F.2d 385 (5th Cir.1971), United applied maximum weight requirements to both male and female flight attendants. Flight attendants—a group comprised of approximately 85% women during the time period relevant to this suit—are the only employees United has ever subjected to maximum weight requirements. United abandoned its weight requirements for flight attendants in 1994.

Although United historically had male flight attendants of Hawaiian descent on flights to Hawaii, those positions were treated as a separate category from other flight attendant positions, and United did not require the "Hawaiian stewards" to meet weight restrictions. Even after United began hiring men as flight attendants on non-Hawaiian flights and established maximum weight requirements for male flight attendants, the Hawaiian stewards remained exempt from weight requirements.

Between 1980 and 1994, United required female flight attendants to weigh between 14 and 25 pounds less than their male colleagues of the same height and age. For example, the maximum weight for a 5'7", 30-year-old woman was 142 pounds, while a man of the same height and age could weigh up to 161 pounds. A 5'11", 50-year-old woman could weigh up to 162 pounds, while the limit for a man of the same height and age was 185 pounds. United's weight table for men during this period was based on a table of desirable weights and heights published by the Metropolitan Life Insurance Company ("MetLife"). The comparable weight table for women was based on a table of maximum weights established by Continental Air Lines ("Continental"). A comparison of United's MetLife-derived limits for men to the Continental-derived weight limits for women reveals that United generally limited men to maximum weights that corresponded to large body frames for men on the MetLife charts but generally limited women to maximum weights that corresponded to medium body frames for women on MetLife charts.

The thirteen named plaintiffs worked for United as flight attendants while United's 1980–1994 weight policy was in effect. The named plaintiffs attempted to lose weight by various means, including severely restricting their caloric intake, using diuretics, and purging. Ultimately, however, plaintiffs were each disciplined and/or terminated for failing to comply with United's maximum weight requirements. In 1992, plaintiffs filed this employment discrimination action. They sought to represent plaintiff classes of female flight attendants for claims of sex and age discrimination, and they asserted various claims of individual discrimination.

On March 15, 1994, the parties stipulated to certify a plaintiff class for the Title VII sex discrimination claim and a plaintiff subclass of members over 40 years old for the ADEA age discrimination claim. On April 12, 1994, the district court certified a Title VII class comprised of all female flight attendants employed by United, currently or in the future, and all female flight attendants who were terminated, retired or resigned on or after January 5, 1989, as a result of their failure to comply with United's weight requirements[;] and an ADEA sub-class comprised of all female flight attendants, age 40 or above, employed by United currently, or who were terminated, retired or resigned after January 5, 1989 as a result of their failure to comply with United's weight requirements. Neither party challenges the 1989 cutoff date for certification of the class.

The parties stipulated in the class certification order that individual notice would be sent to all members of the Title VII class and all potential members of the ADEA subclass. Although the order stated that the class was certified under Federal Rule of Civil Procedure 23(b)(2), as a so-called "injunction" class action, the notice actually sent satisfied the heightened notice required for a Rule 23(b)(3) "damages" class action, set forth in Rule 23(c)(2). The parties agree that the suit subsequently became a Rule 23(b)(3) class action after United abolished its weight program in 1994, thereby eliminating the need for injunctive relief. A form of notice, attached to the stipulation, provided that class members could "opt out" of the class certified for the Title VII claim. A second form of notice, also attached to the stipulation, provided that potential class members could "opt in" to the sub-class certified for the ADEA claim.

Shortly after the class and sub-class were certified, United suspended its weight policy "until further notice" and returned to service all attendants then held out of service under its weight policy. On August 16, 1994, United eliminated the weight policy entirely. In 1995, United offered to reinstate many class and sub-class members who had been terminated under the weight policy. United did not require individuals accepting reinstatement to waive any potential claims against it arising from earlier discipline or termination.

The parties filed cross-motions for summary judgment on plaintiffs' class claim that United's weight policy discriminated against female flight attendants in violation of Title VII. On August 16, 1995, the district court denied plaintiffs' motion and granted summary judgment for United. The court held that any facial attack on the weight policy was foreclosed by claim preclusion resulting from Air Line Pilots Ass'n Int'l v. United Air Lines, Inc. ("ALPA"), 26 F.E.P. Cases 607, 1979 WL 34 (E.D.N.Y.1979), a decision resolving a facial challenge to an earlier United weight policy. The district court permitted plaintiffs to go forward under Title VII only on claims that United discriminated in the administration of its weight policy.

On February 26, 1997, the district court granted summary judgment for United on plaintiffs' remaining class claims of sex and age discrimination. The court held that plaintiffs had failed to present evidence of a pattern or practice of sex or age discrimination in the administration of the weight policy. The court further held that plaintiffs could not assert a disparate impact claim for sex discrimination based on United's administration of medical exceptions to the weight policy. Finally, applying the Tenth Circuit's decision in Ellis v. United Airlines, 73 F.3d 999 (10th Cir.1996), the court held that a disparate impact theory was not available under the ADEA.

On March 11, 1998, the district court entered an order granting summary judgment for United on all of plaintiffs' individual claims. The court decertified the age and sex discrimination classes and denied plaintiffs' application for costs.

The district court did not, in most instances, separately address plaintiffs' FEHA claims, but the parties acknowledge that those claims rise or fall with plaintiffs' federal claims.

II

We review de novo decisions granting summary judgment. See Robi v. Reed, 173 F.3d 736, 739 (9th Cir.1999). Viewing the evidence in the light most favorable to plaintiffs, we must determine whether genuine issues of material fact preclude summary judgment and whether the district court correctly applied the relevant substantive law. See Godwin v. Hunt Wesson, Inc., 150 F.3d 1217, 1220 (9th Cir.1998). Questions of claim and issue preclusion are also reviewed de novo. See C.D. Anderson & Co., Inc. v. Lemos, 832 F.2d 1097, 1100 (9th Cir.1987).

III

The district court concluded that plaintiffs' facial Title VII claim is precluded by the 1979 district court decision in ALPA v. United Air Lines, Inc., cited above. Plaintiffs in ALPA, the Air Line Pilots Association and individual named plaintiffs, claimed on behalf of a class of United flight attendants that United's 1977 weight policy discriminated against female flight attendants in violation of Title VII. Plaintiffs and United stipulated to class certification, and the district court certified a Rule 23(b)(2) class defined as "all female flight attendants who are employed by United or who may become so employed in the future, and all former female flight attendants who were employed by United on or after October 14, 1971 and were suspended, removed from service, or terminated by United for failure to meet United's flight attendant weight standards." Id. at 609.

The district court in ALPA found that United's weight standards were not facially discriminatory, see 26 F.E.P. Cases at 615, 618, but that United had discriminated in applying those standards. See id. at 621–22. The court enjoined United from discriminating on the basis of sex in enforcing its weight standards, and it ordered reinstatement, back pay, and seniority credit for female flight attendants who had suffered discrimination. See id. at 626. The court wrote:

> United is free to continue using the flight attendant weight standards promulgated by United in May 1977. Nothing in the court's decision or order is intended to pass upon the validity of any other weight standard for male or female flight attendants that United might adopt in the future.... United's current weight standards for male and female flight attendants are valid, [and] United is not prohibited from adopting other standards, and ... the validity of any other standard has not been determined.

Id. at 626.

After entry of judgment and while cross-appeals were still available, the parties settled the litigation. For their part, plaintiffs agreed not to appeal the district court's holding that the 1977 weight policy was not facially discriminatory. For its part, United agreed to alter its weight charts by slightly increasing the weight limits and agreed not to appeal the district court's decision that United had discriminated in administering the weight policy. The terms of the settlement were described in a letter to the district court, but the court was never asked to approve the settlement, as it would have been required to do under Rule 23(e) if the parties had entered into the same settlement prior to entry of judgment.

For several reasons, the district court in this case erred in giving claim preclusive effect to the ALPA judgment. First, the plaintiffs in this suit assert claims based on alleged Title VII violations arising after 1980. A claim arising after the date of an earlier judgment is not barred, even if it arises out of a continuing course of conduct that provided the basis for the earlier claim. See Lawlor v. National Screen Serv. Corp., 349 U.S. 322, 328, 75 S.Ct. 865, 99 L.Ed. 1122 (1955). Because the judgment in ALPA was entered in 1979, under Lawlor it cannot preclude claims based on events occurring after that date. See id.; see also International Techs. Consultants, Inc. v. Pilkington, PLC, 137 F.3d 1382, 1388 (9th Cir.1998) ("By winning the first action, the defendants 'did not acquire immunity in perpetuity from the antitrust laws.'").

Second, plaintiffs' Title VII claim is based on a different weight policy from that challenged in ALPA. The central criterion in determining whether there is an identity of claims between the first and second adjudications is "whether the two suits arise out of the same transactional nucleus of facts." Costantini v. Trans World Airlines, 681 F.2d 1199, 1201–02 (9th Cir.1982) (setting forth test for identity of claims); see also Hawaiian Tel. Co. v. Public Utils. Comm'n, 827 F.2d 1264 (9th Cir.1987). Recognizing the possibility of litigation over a new weight policy, the district court in ALPA explicitly stated that it was not passing on the validity of any weight standards United might adopt in the future. Because United changed its weight tables and weight policy in 1980 as part of the post-judgment settlement, we hold that plaintiffs' claims in this case do not arise from the "same transactional nucleus of facts" underlying the claims in ALPA.

Third, notice in ALPA was not sufficient under Rule 23 to preclude monetary claims in later suits, for the class in ALPA was certified and given notice as a Rule 23(b)(2) "injunction" class action. The present suit, by contrast, is a Rule 23(b)(3) "damages" class action. Rule 23(c)(2) requires a higher standard of notice for a Rule 23(b)(3) class action, under which individual notice must be provided to "all members who can be identified through reasonable effort." See Eisen v. Carlisle & Jacquelin, 417 U.S. 156, 173, 94 S.Ct. 2140, 40 L.Ed.2d 732 (1974). Further, all potential members in a Rule 23(b)(3) class must be allowed to opt out of the class. In a Rule 23(b)(2) class action, by contrast, there is no requirement for individualized notice beyond that required by due process, and class members are not allowed to opt out. We are unable to determine on the record before us whether the notice given in ALPA was distributed to all class members who would have been entitled to notice of a Rule 23(b)(3) class action. However, we do know that class members in ALPA could not opt out of the class. Under Eisen, class members in a Rule 23(b)(3) class may be bound to the result of that action only if the notice and opt-out requirements applicable to Rule 23(b)(3) actions are satisfied. Because ALPA did not satisfy the requirements applicable to a Rule 23(b)(3) class action, ALPA cannot preclude the Rule 23(b)(3) class action in this case.

Fourth, to the degree that United seeks to rely on the post-judgment settlement in ALPA, we need only point out that the settlement is not incorporated into a judgment and therefore cannot have preclusive effect. See Hydranautics v. FilmTec Corp., 204 F.3d 880, 885 (9th Cir.2000). But even if it were a judgment, we cannot know whether it sufficiently protected the interests of the unnamed class members as that class then existed. A class action settlement can be approved and entered as a judgment only after a proceeding under Rule 23(e) at which unnamed class members are invited to express their opinions of the proposed settlement. Such a proceeding, often called a "fairness hearing," is designed to protect the unnamed members of the class against the misjudgment (and, occasionally, the self-interest) of the named plaintiffs and class attorneys. We are simply not allowed to give preclusive effect to a post-judgment settlement that was never subjected to the scrutiny contemplated by Rule 23(e) and never entered as a judgment.

Finally, we note that the terms of the settlement in ALPA appear not to protect the interests of flight attendants, such as plaintiffs in this case, who might later have been subjected to discipline for failing to comply with United's post-settlement weight restrictions. The class representatives in ALPA failed to appeal the district court's decision that United's weight policy did not facially discriminate on the basis of sex. They elected, instead, to accept reinstatement and back pay for the members of the class who had been subjected to discriminatory application of the 1977 weight policy. Female flight attendants who were then employed and had not previously been adversely affected by the weight limits, but who might have been so affected in the future, had an interest in appealing the district court's order on the legality of United's policy. Those flight attendants had no interest in obtaining reinstatement and back pay. Similarly, women not then employed (but later hired) as flight attendants by United had no interest in back pay or reinstatement. Consequently, when the class representatives chose not to appeal the adverse ruling on the facial validity of the weight policy, they abandoned any representation of the interests of those present and potential future class members in order to protect present class members seeking back pay and reinstatement. See Tice v. American Airlines, 162 F.3d 966, 969 (7th Cir.1999), cert. denied, 527 U.S. 1036, 119 S.Ct. 2395, 144 L.Ed.2d 795 (1999) (refusing to give preclusive effect to prior class action because plaintiffs had been too young to join in earlier litigation and their interests had diverged from those of the earlier class representatives insofar as younger pilots would benefit from age discrimination against older pilots); Rutherford v. City of Cleveland, 137 F.3d 905, 910 (6th Cir.1998) (holding decision to abandon opposition to consent decree governing hiring in exchange for amendment to consent decree governing promotion demonstrated failure to adequately represent interests of applicants); Gonzales v. Cassidy, 474 F.2d 67 (5th Cir.1973) (holding failure to appeal denial of retroactive relief constituted inadequate representation). Because the interests of the plaintiff class in this suit were not adequately represented by the plaintiffs in ALPA, we cannot give preclusive effect in this suit to the post-judgment settlement in ALPA.

We therefore proceed to the merits of plaintiffs' claims.

IV

Title VII makes it unlawful "to discriminate against any individual with respect to ... compensation, terms, conditions, or privileges of employment, because of such individual's ... sex...." 42 U.S.C. §2000e-2(a)(1). Courts have recognized two bases on which plaintiffs may proceed: disparate treatment and disparate impact. See International Bhd. of Teamsters v. United States, 431 U.S. 324, 335 n.15, 97 S.Ct. 1843, 52 L.Ed.2d 396 (1977). Disparate treatment arises when an employer "treats some people less favorably than others because of their ... sex." Id. Disparate impact arises when an employer's practice is "facially neutral ... but ... in fact fall[s] more harshly on one group than another." Id. Disparate treatment is permissible under Title VII only if justified as a bona fide occupational qualification ("BFOQ"). A BFOQ is a qualification that is reasonably necessary to the normal operation or essence of an employer's business. See 42 U.S.C. § 2000e-2.

An employer's policy amounts to disparate treatment if it treats men and women differently on its face. For example, in UAW v. Johnson Controls, 499 U.S. 187, 111 S.Ct. 1196, 113 L.Ed.2d 158 (1991), defendant Johnson Controls barred fertile women, but not fertile men, from jobs entailing high levels of lead exposure. The Court concluded this was disparate treatment: "Johnson Controls' policy is not neutral because it does not apply to the reproductive capacity of the company's male employees in the same way as it applies to that of the females." Id. at 199–200, 111 S.Ct. 1196. The Court has made it clear that such an "explicit gender-based policy is sex discrimination under § 703(a) [of Title VII of the Civil Rights Act of 1964, 42 U.S.C. § 2000e-2(a)] and thus may be defended only as a BFOQ." Id. at 200, 111 S.Ct. 1196.

Similarly, in Healey v. Southwood Psychiatric Hosp., 78 F.3d 128 (3d Cir.1996), defendant Southwood Psychiatric Hospital explicitly treated men and women differently in scheduling its employees' shifts. The court held that "Southwood's gender-based policy is not a pretext for discrimination—it is per se intentional discrimination." Id. at 131. "When open and explicit use of gender is employed ... the systematic discrimination is in effect 'admitted' by the employer, and the case will turn on whether such overt disparate treatment is for some reason justified under Title VII. A justification for overt discrimination may exist if the disparate treatment is ... based on a BFOQ." Id. at 132. The court in Healey held that facial discrimination was permissible as a BFOQ because staffing both males and females on all shifts was necessary to provide the therapeutic care that was the "essence" of the hospital's business. See id. at 132–33.

We view plaintiffs' case as analytically indistinguishable from Johnson Controls and Healey. The uncontroverted evidence shows that United chose weight maximums for women that generally corresponded to the medium frame category of MetLife's Height and Weight Tables. By contrast, the maximums for men generally corresponded to MetLife's large frame category. The bias against female flight attendants infected United's weight maximums for all age groups. Because of this consistent difference in treatment of women and men, we conclude that United's weight policy between 1980 and 1994 was facially discriminatory.

On its face, United's weight policy "applie[d] less favorably to one gender." Gerdom v. Continental Airlines, 692 F.2d 602, 608 (9th Cir.1982) (en banc). Under United's policy, men could generally weigh as much as large-framed men whether they were large-framed or not, while women could generally not weigh more than medium-framed women. As we held in Gerdom, "[w]here a claim of discriminatory treatment is based upon a policy which on its face applies less favorably to one gender ... a plaintiff need not otherwise establish the presence of discriminatory intent." Id.

United defends its weight tables as permissible "grooming" or appearance standards. It is true that not all sex-differentiated appearance standards constitute disparate treatment that must be justified under Title VII as BFOQs. An appearance standard that imposes different but essentially equal burdens on men and women is not disparate treatment. For example, in Fountain v. Safeway Stores, Inc., 555 F.2d 753 (9th Cir.1977), we held that a store may impose different hair length requirements on men and women, and may require men but not women to wear neckties. As we wrote in that case, "regulations promulgated by employers which require male employees to conform to different grooming and dress standards than female employees is not sex discrimination within the meaning of Title VII." Id. at 754.

We need not decide whether a rule or regulation that compels individuals to change or modify their physical structure or composition, as opposed to simply presenting themselves in a neat or acceptable manner, qualifies as an appearance standard. Even if United's weight rules constituted an appearance standard, they would still be invalid. A sex-differentiated appearance standard that imposes unequal burdens on men and women is disparate treatment that must be justified as a BFOQ. Thus, an employer can require all employees to wear sex-differentiated uniforms, but it cannot require only female employees to wear uniforms. See Carroll v. Talman Fed. Sav. & Loan Ass'n of Chicago, 604 F.2d 1028 (7th Cir.1979). An airline can require all flight attendants to wear contacts instead of glasses, but it cannot require only its female flight attendants to do so. See Laffey v. Northwest Airlines, Inc., 366 F.Supp. 763 (D.D.C.1973); see also Nadine Taub, Keeping Women in Their Place: Stereotyping Per Se as a Form of Employment Discrimination, 21 B.C. L.Rev. 345, 387 (1980).

We also need not consider whether separate weight standards for men and women in themselves constitute discriminatory treatment under Johnson Controls. Even assuming that United may impose different weight standards on female and male flight attendants, United may not impose different and more burdensome weight standards without justifying those standards as BFOQs.

United is thus entitled to use facially discriminatory weight charts only if it can show that the difference in treatment between female and male flight attendants is justified as a BFOQ. See Johnson Controls, 499 U.S. at 200, 111 S.Ct. 1196; Healey, 78 F.3d at 131. The burden is on United to show that its weight policy fits in this "extremely narrow exception to the general prohibition of discrimination on the basis of sex." Dothard v. Rawlinson, 433 U.S. 321, 334, 97 S.Ct. 2720, 53 L.Ed.2d 786 (1977). To escape summary judgment, United must raise a genuine issue as to whether its discriminatory weight maximums are "reasonably necessary" to the "normal operation" of its "particular business," and that they concern job-related skills and aptitudes. Johnson Controls, 499 U.S. at 187, 111 S.Ct. 1196; 42 U.S.C. § 2000e-2(e)(1).

United provided no evidence that its facially discriminatory weight standard is a BFOQ. United made no showing that having disproportionately thinner female than male flight attendants bears a relation to flight attendants' ability to greet passengers, push carts, move luggage, and, perhaps most important, provide physical assistance in emergencies. The only evidence in the record is to the contrary. Far from being "reasonably necessary" to the "normal operation" of United's business, the evidence suggests that, if anything, United's discriminatory weight requirements may have inhibited the job performance of female flight attendants. We therefore reverse the decision of the district court and hold that because United's policy of applying medium-frame weight maximums to female flight attendants and large-frame weight maximums to male flight attendants is facially discriminatory and not justified as a BFOQ, plaintiffs are entitled to summary judgment on their disparate treatment class claim. We also reverse the district court's implicit denial of summary judgment on plaintiffs' corresponding discrimination claim under FEHA.

V

The ADEA prohibits employers from discriminating against "any individual with respect to his compensation, terms, conditions, or privileges of employment because of such individual's age." 29 U.S.C. § 623(a)(1). The district court correctly concluded that a disparate treatment class claim is not available to plaintiffs because United's weight policy discriminated on the basis of sex and weight, not on the basis of age. An employer does not violate the ADEA by discriminating based on a factor that is merely empirically correlated with age. See Hazen Paper Co. v. Biggins, 507 U.S. 604, 609–11, 113 S.Ct. 1701, 123 L.Ed.2d 338 (1993); Ellis v. United Airlines, Inc., 73 F.3d 999 (10th Cir.1996) (concluding that United's weight requirement did not violate ADEA).

Plaintiffs should, however, be permitted to go forward with their age discrimination class claim under a disparate impact theory. In its order of February 26, 1997, the district court noted that it had previously found, on August 16, 1995, that plaintiffs' age-based disparate impact claim presented triable issues of fact. But the district court concluded that the Supreme Court's decision in Hazen, as interpreted by the Tenth Circuit in Ellis in 1996, foreclosed a disparate impact claim in an ADEA case. We have since squarely decided that a disparate impact claim is cognizable in an ADEA case. See Arnett v. California Pub. Employees Retirement Sys., 179 F.3d 690, 696 (9th Cir.1999), vacated and remanded on other grounds, 528 U.S. 1111, 120 S.Ct. 930, 145 L.Ed.2d 807 (2000). The Supreme Court vacated our decision in Arnett and remanded for further consideration in light of Kimel v. Florida Bd. of Regents, 528 U.S. 62, 120 S.Ct. 631, 145 L.Ed.2d 522 (2000), in which the Court held that the ADEA does not abrogate the Eleventh Amendment. The Eleventh Amendment issue is irrelevant to a case, such as this one, in which a private rather than state entity is a defendant, and the Court's vacation of our decision has no bearing on the correctness of our conclusion that a disparate impact claim is cognizable under the ADEA. We see no reason to depart from our conclusion in Arnett and we again hold that a disparate impact claim is cognizable under the ADEA. See also EEOC v. Local 350, Plumbers and Pipefitters, 998 F.2d 641, 648 n.2 (9th Cir.1992). We therefore conclude that plaintiffs should be allowed to proceed with their disparate impact class claim. We also reverse the district court's implicit dismissal of plaintiffs' corresponding age discrimination claim under FEHA.

VI

The district court concluded that none of the named plaintiffs presented viable individual claims of discrimination under Title VII, the ADEA, the ADA, and FEHA. In light of our holding on the class claim under Title VII, we reverse summary judgment for defendant on named plaintiffs' individual claims of sex discrimination. Similarly, in light of our holding on the class claim under the ADEA, we reverse summary judgment on named plaintiffs' individual claims of age discrimination. On remand, the district court should reassess their individual claims under Title VII and the ADEA and their corresponding individual claims under FEHA in light of this opinion.

We affirm the district court's decision granting summary judgment for United on named plaintiffs' individual claims under the ADA and their corresponding claims under FEHA. The district court correctly concluded that none of the named plaintiffs presented evidence to make a prima facie case that their eating disorders "substantially limited" a major life activity and were therefore disabilities within the meaning of the ADA. See Albertson's, Inc. v. Kirkingburg, 527 U.S. 555, 119 S.Ct. 2162, 2169, 144 L.Ed.2d 518 (1999). A major life activity is a function such as "caring for oneself, performing manual tasks, walking, seeing, hearing, speaking, breathing, learning, and working." 29 C.F.R. § 1630.2. While eating disorders can substantially limit major life activities, plaintiffs have not presented evidence that their eating disorders have that effect.

With respect to the named plaintiffs' other asserted disabilities, the district court correctly concluded that none of the named plaintiffs had exhausted their administrative remedies by filing charges with the EEOC or with California's Department of Fair Employment and Housing. Named plaintiffs did file charges claiming disability discrimination based on obesity, but obesity is not like or reasonably related to other conditions, such as cancer, from which plaintiffs allegedly suffer and on which they base their other individual charges of discrimination. Named plaintiffs have therefore not exhausted their administrative remedies with respect to these conditions. See Yamaguchi v. United States Dep't of the Air Force, 109 F.3d 1475, 1480 (9th Cir.1997).

VII

Because the district court should have granted summary judgment to plaintiffs on their Title VII disparate treatment class claim and should have denied United's motion for summary judgment on plaintiffs' disparate impact ADEA class claim, we reverse the district court's decertification of the class and denial of plaintiffs' application for an award of costs.

CONCLUSION

For the foregoing reasons, we REVERSE in part, AFFIRM in part, and REMAND for further proceedings consistent with this opinion. Each party shall bear its own costs on appeal.

O'SCANNLAIN, Circuit Judge, concurring in part and dissenting in part.

I fully concur in the court's affirmance of the district court's summary judgment for United on the plaintiffs' "disparate treatment" claims under the Age Discrimination in Employment Act and individual claims under the Americans with Disabilities Act. I must respectfully dissent, however, from the reversal of the district court's grant of summary judgment for United on the plaintiffs' remaining claims under Title VII and the Age Discrimination in Employment Act. I shall not separately address the plaintiffs' claims under the California Fair Employment and Housing Act ("FEHA"), Cal. Gov't Code §§ 12900–12996, but would affirm the district court's judgment thereon for the reasons that follow....

It may seem inappropriate in this day and age to have seemingly arbitrary weight limitations for employees (a proposition with which United seems no longer to disagree), but our anti-discrimination statutes and law of civil procedure rest on policies more diverse than the eradication of business practices that strike us as distasteful or unfair. Those policies include protecting to the extent practicable the flexibility of private enterprise to respond to the demands of the market and protecting individuals from endlessly rehearsing (at potentially crippling expense) their defenses to allegations of unlawful conduct. In order to vindicate these other policies, the courts and Congress have drawn lines limiting what conduct is actionable and under what circumstances an employer may be called upon to defend his conduct. Because the majority ignores those lines, many of them well established, I concur in the court's opinion only in part and dissent as to the remainder.

GORDON v. UNITED AIRLINES, INC.

246 F.3d 878 (7th Cir. 2001)

RIPPLE, Circuit Judge.

Leroy Gordon, a probationary flight attendant for United Airlines, Inc. ("United"), was released from his employment by the company on the ground that he had deviated without authority from his flight schedule when he did not fly a scheduled flight from

Los Angeles to Seattle. The company decided that this violation of its policy, when considered in light of Mr. Gordon's overall work performance, warranted no lesser sanction. Mr. Gordon then filed this action in the district court; he alleged that United discriminated against him because of his race, in violation of Title VII of the Civil Rights Act of 1964, 42 U.S.C. § 2000e et seq., and in violation of 42 U.S.C. § 1981, and because of his age, in violation of the Age Discrimination in Employment Act, 29 U.S.C. § 623. The district court granted summary judgment for United, and Mr. Gordon now appeals. For the reasons set forth in the following opinion, we reverse the judgment of the district court and remand the case for proceedings consistent with this opinion.

Mr. Gordon also alleged that United discriminated against him because of his sex, in violation of Title VII of the Civil Rights Act of 1964, 42 U.S.C. § 2000e et seq. The district court explained, however, that Mr. Gordon had waived his sex discrimination claim because he had failed to present it to the Equal Employment Opportunity Commission ("EEOC"). According to the court, in failing to present his claim to the EEOC, he failed to exhaust his administrative remedies and, thus, waived his sex discrimination claim. Mr. Gordon does not raise this issue in his brief; therefore, he has waived this argument on appeal. See Winter v. Minnesota Mut. Life Ins. Co., 199 F.3d 399, 411 n.17 (7th Cir.1999).

I
BACKGROUND

A. Facts

Leroy Gordon, an African-American male over 40 years of age, claims that United discriminated against him because of his race and his age when it terminated his employment as a probationary flight attendant. United, however, asserts that Mr. Gordon committed a violation of company policy. According to United, that violation, when coupled with his work history, justified its decision to release Mr. Gordon from his position as a probationary flight attendant.

1.

Mr. Gordon began working at United as a Baggage Systems Operator in 1995. While working in this position, he received a Notice of Concern because he had 21 incidents of tardiness and 2 absences. Mr. Gordon questioned the validity of the allegations in this notice, but he was told that the notice would not be placed in his personnel file.

Mr. Gordon then applied for and received a transfer to United's flight attendant ("FA") program in 1996. While in training, he was 20 minutes late for a training exercise, which resulted in an incident report for failing to meet minimum dependability requirements. Mr. Gordon claims that, at that time, he was told the incident would not be made a part of his personnel record as long as there were no reoccurrences. He graduated from his training class in February 1997 and then started as a probationary flight attendant ("PFA") at Chicago O'Hare International Airport ("O'Hare"). Mr. Gordon states that his supervisor, Gina Siemieniec, told him that she would not consider his training records when evaluating him as a PFA.

In May 1997, United confronted Mr. Gordon with a check it had received from him that had been returned due to insufficient funds. Mr. Gordon had written the check in July 1996, while he was still a Baggage Systems Operator, and he claims that he thought his bank already had taken care of the matter. United informed Mr. Gordon that, if he did not pay immediately, he would be subject to disciplinary action. Mr. Gordon promptly paid. Siemieniec, who brought the matter to Mr. Gordon's attention, stated that the situation was not serious and was not relevant to his performance as an FA.

Mr. Gordon's next problem at United occurred in June 1997 when a United passenger reported that no pre-landing safety announcement had been made on his flight. The First FA is the person responsible for making the announcement, and, on this particular flight, Mr. Gordon was the First FA. In response to the passenger's complaint, Siemieniec asked Mr. Gordon for a written report. In that report, Mr. Gordon wrote, "I believe the pre-arrival announcement was made by [the Second FA], just before I was about to make it." R.21, Ex.27. Mr. Gordon claims that he was assisting a wheelchair passenger and was about to make the announcement when the Second FA made it. Indeed, he asserts that the Second FA made the announcement early. According to Siemieniec, she did not issue Mr. Gordon a warning because she decided to overlook the matter.

Finally, United claims that Mr. Gordon was unresponsive to Siemieniec's requests for Mr. Gordon to meet with her. Mr. Gordon asserts that he had attempted to visit her, but that both he and Siemieniec had unusual schedules. Siemieniec responded that the PFAs bore the responsibility for making an appointment to meet with her if they were unable to find her in her office.

We note several other relevant factors about Mr. Gordon's record at United. First, while a PFA, Mr. Gordon never received an "Interim Evaluation." An Interim Evaluation typically is given to an employee for substandard performance. After the employee receives the first Interim Evaluation, the second incident of unacceptable conduct by the employee will result in termination. Moreover, in Mr. Gordon's five-week reviews, no problems were ever documented. Finally, Mr. Gordon received awards as a PFA, including PRIDE awards for perfect attendance and Service in Every Sense awards for above-average customer service.

2.

The incident that led to Mr. Gordon's termination occurred on August 5–6, 1997. On August 5, Mr. Gordon was assigned to work a flight from O'Hare to Portland, Oregon, and then to fly deadhead (fly but not work) to Los Angeles International Airport ("LAX"). Once in Los Angeles, he was to be reassigned. When he arrived at LAX, he received his next assignment—a flight from Los Angeles to Seattle—that was to begin 21 hours later. He then was transported to a Days Inn where United had assigned him to stay the night so that he could rest before his next scheduled flight. In a report Mr. Gordon later wrote about the incident, he explained that he had experienced problems with his motel room at the Days Inn:

> I was [given] a ground level unit. This is a drive up style motel, there was a car backed up 3 to 5 feet from my door with the engine running, so when I entered the room there were exhaust fumes present. (The car moved a short time later, but the smell remained). It was a very hot night in L.A. ([around] 90°). The room had one window style air conditioning unit in the living room, but none in the bedroom. The carpet was dirty, there were holes in the walls, and insects [were] flying around the room. There were what appeared to be an unsecured window in the bathroom and kitchen sections, and there was one TV set in the living room (with no remote control). I did not feel this room was safe, sanitary or acceptable. I also was under the impression the flight attendant union agreement would not allow FA to be housed on first floor units for security reasons.

R.21, Ex. 30 at 1–2. Another PFA—a white female under 40—was also assigned to stay at the Days Inn on August 5, 1997, and she avers that she spent that night on the first floor of the Days Inn.

[Mr. Gordon] attempted to move to another room, but the Days Inn did not have one available. He called the United Crew Desk at LAX for help finding a room in a different hotel, but he was told that none were available at that time. Mr. Gordon also spoke with United's National Crew Desk which was unable to help him.

Mr. Gordon then returned to LAX. Upon arriving at the airport, he discovered that the United Crew Desk had closed. At this point, Mr. Gordon decided to take a redeye flight from Los Angeles back to Chicago. As he explained in his report, "I thought this would give me an opportunity to shower, change clothes, and still return to LAX" in time to work his next scheduled flight. Id. at 2. He arrived at O'Hare at 6 a.m. on August 6, 14 hours before his scheduled flight from Los Angeles to Seattle.

In this litigation, United concedes that, at this point, Mr. Gordon had done nothing to warrant sanctions. If he had returned to Los Angeles and made his scheduled assignment, he would not have been terminated. As United states: "It is true that if Plaintiff had returned to Los Angeles and flown his scheduled flight, he would not have been subject to discipline." Appellee's Br. at 16. However, Mr. Gordon did not return to Los Angeles to work his scheduled flight.

Once Mr. Gordon returned to O'Hare, he checked in with the United Crew Desk and spoke to the Crew Desk Supervisor, Henry Velasco. According to Mr. Gordon's report, he explained the hotel problems to Velasco and "asked if [he] should return to work the trip [from Los Angeles to Seattle], or if [he] could be excused from the [trip] because [he] had not had a legal rest." R.21, Gordon's Report to Siemieniec, Ex.30 at 4. According to both parties, a "legal rest" means the amount of time necessary before a flight attendant is eligible to begin another duty period. The minimum length is between 8–11 hours, and Mr. Gordon states that his length was 10 hours.

Mr. Gordon informed Velasco that, if his request presented a problem, he would return to Los Angeles to make his assigned flight. Velasco told him that it would not be safe for him to return to Los Angeles that day and that it was not a problem to take him off the assignment, Mr. Gordon wrote, but that he should discuss the situation with his supervisor. Mr. Gordon also explained in his report that he was not sure that the Crew Desk understood his request, that is, that he would be commuting to Los Angeles and not that he would be working a flight to Los Angeles. Finally, as Mr. Gordon concluded in his written report, "my improper deviation was unintentional.... This mistake was caused by my lack of understanding of the regulations, but my intent was not malicious in any manner." Id. at 3.

Velasco also wrote a report for Siemieniec that discussed the incident. In that report, he explained that Mr. Gordon had been unhappy with his hotel and had been unable to contact the LAX Crew Desk. Velasco then wrote that Mr. Gordon had "decided to DV8 from LAX back to ORD [O'Hare] without authorization from any crew desk." R.21, Ex.32. Once at Chicago, the report continued, Mr. Gordon advised the O'Hare Crew Desk "that he was illegal to continue flying, as he had not had a legal rest at his original layover point at LAX." Id. Velasco stated that he explained the complications of this action and told Mr. Gordon that he needed to speak with his supervisor. The report also mentioned that Mr. Gordon offered to return to LAX to pick up the balance of his assignment. As the report noted, "I explained that I could not have him flying knowing that he had not had a rest, and would not jeopardize the safety of his flying partner, the safety of the customer, and the company." Id. Thus, Velasco wrote, he removed Mr. Gordon from the remainder of his scheduled assignment and told him to contact his supervisor.

The deposition testimony of Velasco, although confusing, states that his role as supervisor of the Crew Desk merely consisted of documenting the actions of the PFAs and providing their supervisors with information about what had happened during their assignment. Yet, at his deposition, Velasco testified that he had told Mr. Gordon that the idea of Mr. Gordon's returning to Los Angeles was a safety issue because Mr. Gordon could jeopardize the safety of his flying partners, the customers on the flight, and United. Moreover, Velasco stated that he placed a Did Not Fly ("DNF") notation on Mr. Gordon's flight calendar. A DNF notation, according to Velasco, could mean any number of things, including a violation of United's rules. His role, he said, was merely to advise his immediate supervisor of the occurrence of the DNF.

Before Siemieniec discharged Mr. Gordon, she consulted United's acting department manager, James Younglove, for advice on handling Mr. Gordon's situation. Although Younglove stated Mr. Gordon's conduct "in and of itself [was] disciplinary in nature," Younglove advised Siemieniec to look at his entire record to ascertain whether any factors suggested that he was an exceptional employee that should be retained or that he had a history of problems that indicated they should not retain him. R.21, Ex.15 at 21. As Younglove explained, he would ask:

> Is this someone that has made several mistakes and I shouldn't spend a lot of time on, truthfully? Or is this somebody that is an exceptional employee; that I'm looking to find out if there's anything available to us that's out of the norm with this individual? Is there any problems dealing with family that we're aware of that the employee has brought to our attention that would have placed him in this position.

Id. at 19–20.

Siemieniec considered the incident of Mr. Gordon's missed flight and reviewed Mr. Gordon's entire work history with United when making her decision to release Mr. Gordon. After reviewing Mr. Gordon's record, she released him from his position as a probationary flight attendant. Mr. Gordon thereafter filed this action for discrimination.

B. Proceedings in the District Court

The district court granted summary judgment to United after determining that Mr. Gordon had failed to establish a prima facie case of discrimination. First, the court discussed the elements required for a plaintiff to survive summary judgment when he is attempting to prove discrimination indirectly. Under the burden-shifting standard applied to discrimination cases, the court explained, a plaintiff first must make out a prima facie case of discrimination by the employer. To make out a prima facie case, the court stated, Mr. Gordon must show "(1) he is a member of a protected class, (2) his job performance was sufficient to meet his employer's legitimate expectations, (3) his employer took an adverse employment action against him and (4) he was treated less favorably than similarly-situated, non-protected employees." R.33 at 8. Once the plaintiff has established a prima facie case, the burden then shifts to the employer to proffer a legitimate, non-discriminatory reason for its adverse employment action. Finally, the court explained, the burden shifts back to the plaintiff, who must show that the stated reason given by the employer is a pretext for discrimination.

Next, after noting that the parties agreed that Mr. Gordon falls within a protected class for both his race discrimination and age discrimination claims, the court turned to the second factor for establishing a prima facie case: "[W]hether Gordon has raised a genuine issue of material fact such that a reasonable jury could find that Gordon's job performance was sufficient to meet United's legitimate expectations." R.33 at 9. According to the court, to establish a prima facie case, "the plaintiff cannot generally aver that he was meeting the employer's legitimate expectations; rather, the plaintiff must 'specifically refute the facts which allegedly support the employer's claim of deficient performance.'" Id. (quoting Sirvidas v. Commonwealth Edison Co., 60 F.3d 375, 378 (7th Cir.1995)).

The court stated that Mr. Gordon was unable to show that he was fulfilling United's legitimate expectations at the time it released him from its employment. The court noted that Mr. Gordon received a Notice of Concern while a baggage handler, that he arrived late once while in training, that he wrote a check for insufficient funds, that he did not issue a pre-landing safety announcement, and that, in his terminating event, he deviated from his schedule without authorization. Although Mr. Gordon argued that he should have received only a "missed flight" warning for the terminating event, the court stated that United had explained that a missed flight designation was only for an incident that was accidental or was outside the FA's control. The court pointed out that, in Foster v. Arthur Andersen, LLP, 168 F.3d 1029, 1035 (7th Cir.1999), we had warned that discrimination laws do not prevent employers from making adverse employment decisions although the employee may think the infraction is de minimis. As the court concluded, "Gordon admitted to not following United procedure on several occasions; consequently, as a matter of law, Gordon has not shown that he satisfied United's legitimate expectations." R.33 at 10. The court then granted summary judgment for United.

II
DISCUSSION

A. Standard of Review

We review de novo the district court's grant of summary judgment for United and, viewing the facts in the light most favorable to Mr. Gordon, draw our own conclusions of law and fact from the record before us. See Downs v. World Color Press, 214 F.3d 802, 805 (7th Cir.2000); Sarsha v. Sears, Roebuck & Co., 3 F.3d 1035, 1038 (7th Cir.1993). A grant of summary judgment is proper only when there is no genuine issue of material fact and the moving party is entitled to judgment as a matter of law. See Fed.R.Civ.P. 56(c); Sarsha, 3 F.3d at 1038.

B. McDonnell Douglas Indirect Method of Proof

1.

A plaintiff may show that his employer discriminated against him because of his race or his age by using the burden-shifting method set forth by the Supreme Court in McDonnell Douglas Corp. v. Green, 411 U.S. 792, 93 S.Ct. 1817, 36 L.Ed.2d 668 (1973).

Although some, including our colleague in dissent, are anxious to sound the death knell for the McDonnell Douglas construct, such an action clearly is, at best, premature. As recently as last term, the Supreme Court in Reeves v. Sanderson Plumbing Products, Inc., 530 U.S. 133, 120 S.Ct. 2097, 147 L.Ed.2d 105 (2000), employed the McDonnell Douglas analysis to assess a claim under the ADEA.

Under McDonnell Douglas, a plaintiff first must establish a prima facie case of discrimination. A plaintiff establishes a prima facie case of discrimination by demonstrating that: (1) he belongs to a protected class, (2) he performed his job according to his employer's legitimate expectations, (3) he suffered an adverse employment action, and (4) similarly situated employees outside the protected class were treated more favorably by the defendant.

Once the plaintiff has established his prima facie case, a presumption of discrimination arises, and the burden shifts to the defendant to come forward with evidence of a legitimate, non-discriminatory reason for discharging the plaintiff. If the defendant meets its burden, the burden shifts back to the plaintiff to show that the defendant's stated reason for the adverse action was a pretext for discrimination. If the plaintiff meets his respective burdens under McDonnell Douglas, summary judgment is inappropriate; a plaintiff need not come forward with direct evidence of discrimination in order to survive summary judgment. See Vanasco v. National-Louis Univ., 137 F.3d 962, 965 (7th Cir.1998).

2.

At the outset, we note that not all elements of the McDonnell Douglas analysis are at issue. The parties do not dispute that Mr. Gordon belongs to a protected class or that he suffered an adverse employment action. Therefore, in determining whether Mr. Gordon has established a prima facie case, we need to consider only (1) whether Mr. Gordon was meeting the legitimate expectations of United at the time of his discharge and (2) whether similarly situated employees outside the protected class were treated more favorably.

a.

We first turn to whether Mr. Gordon was meeting the legitimate expectations of United.

First, to put it mildly, United has not spoken with one voice in defining what sort of activity by a flight attendant constitutes an unauthorized deviation. The record discloses a distinct inability on the part of United's management to provide any consistent definition. Different individuals in management positions articulated very different views on what sort of activity on the part of an employee constituted this violation of United's Code of Conduct. Indeed, it is no wonder that United had difficulty in articulating a definition because, apparently, it had charged an employee with this offense only once before (and, in the prior situation, determined that discharge of the employee was not appropriate).

We ordinarily would defer to the definition of the decision-maker in such a situation. However, the material before us on summary judgment is clearly susceptible to the interpretation that the individual who made the decision to terminate Mr. Gordon actually came to no independent conclusion on the matter but simply accepted the conclusion of lower ranking administrative personnel on this important, indeed key, definitional matter. Even if we were to assume that the decision-maker applied her own definition of unauthorized deviation, it is not at all clear that Mr. Gordon committed such an infraction. His account of his conversation with Velasco certainly would permit the trier of fact to conclude that he believed in good faith that he had sought and had been granted permission not to fly the LAX to Seattle leg that he had been assigned previously.

In short, the invocation of an offense that, to this day, United has difficulty defining, the lack of any clear management decision that Mr. Gordon's conduct violated clearly established norms, and Mr. Gordon's detailed account that he acted only with the permission of those responsible for the coordination of flight attendant assignments raise a genuine issue of material fact as to whether he had deviated at all from permissible patterns of behavior for flight attendants.

Finally, United points to incidents in Mr. Gordon's work history at United to support its contention that Mr. Gordon was not performing satisfactorily. When combining his work record with his unauthorized deviation, United asserts, it is clear that Mr. Gordon fails to meet this aspect of his prima facie case. Here too, however, there is a dispute as to whether United deviated from its established policy in considering past incidents after it had assured Mr. Gordon that these incidents would not be a matter of record. Mr. Gordon claims that his work record was not supposed to contain a notation of these incidents, and indeed, that United affirmatively had assured him that these matters would not be used in evaluations of his performance as a PFA. Moreover, Mr. Gordon asserts that all but one of these incidents were not relevant to his performance as a PFA. The remaining incident, his failure to provide the safety announcement when he was the First FA was not, according to Mr. Gordon, an infraction. Not only did Siemieniec tell Mr. Gordon that she would not include a report on the incident in his record, but the reports from the other FAs on the flight also indicate that Mr. Gordon did nothing wrong. Furthermore, United's rules of procedure state that both the First FA and the Second FA are responsible for giving the announcement. Here, the Second FA explained that she had given the announcement and admitted that she had given it early. Therefore, viewing the record in the light most favorable to Mr. Gordon, his personnel file should not have contained a record of any infractions. His personnel file did show, however, many commendations. Consequently, a trier of fact could conclude on this record that Mr. Gordon was performing up to United's expectations.

b.

The fourth prong of the McDonnell Douglas analysis requires that Mr. Gordon establish that similarly situated employees outside the protected class were treated differently. We conclude that there is a genuine issue of triable fact on this matter as well. Mr. Gordon points to two different groups of similarly situated, non-protected employees who were treated more favorably than he. First, he and only one other PFA in United's history have been charged with "unauthorized deviation." The other PFA to receive such a designation was a white female, and United did not discharge her after her unauthorized deviation. Instead, it issued her a warning and allowed her to remain with United. Despite the absence of any warnings in his record, Mr. Gordon was terminated for the same conduct that resulted in only a warning for a white female employee. Although United suggests that the other PFA's conduct was far less intentional, that conclusion is dependent upon the trier of fact's interpretation of Mr. Gordon's encounter with Velasco. As we already have noted, this encounter is open to different interpretations.

Indeed, several other employees may well have been similarly situated to Mr. Gordon. These flight attendants all had missed flights unintentionally. If a trier of fact were to determine that Mr. Gordon had missed his assigned flight unintentionally—a conclusion supportable by the record—he is similarly situated to these employees but was treated less favorably than they. Indeed, unlike Mr. Gordon, several of these PFAs already had warnings in their records at the time of their missed flights; United nevertheless characterized their actions as "missed flights" instead of "unauthorized deviations." A trier of fact reasonably could determine that Mr. Gordon, like the other flight attendants, simply missed a flight but was treated differently from the other flight attendants. Drawing all reasonable inferences in Mr. Gordon's favor, we must conclude that Mr. Gordon has demonstrated that there is a genuine issue of triable fact as to whether similarly situated employees outside the protected class were treated differently.

3.

Assuming that United has offered a facially legitimate reason for Mr. Gordon's discharge, his unauthorized deviation, we now turn to whether Mr. Gordon has demonstrated that United's stated reason is a pretext for discrimination. See McDonnell Douglas, 411 U.S. at 804, 93 S.Ct. 1817.

a.

To show pretext, Mr. Gordon bears the burden of demonstrating that United's ostensible justification for its decision is unworthy of credence. If United honestly believed its reason for discharging Mr. Gordon, Mr. Gordon cannot meet his burden. See Roberts v. Separators, Inc., 172 F.3d 448, 453 (7th Cir.1999). This is true even if United's reason for Mr. Gordon's discharge was "foolish or trivial or even baseless"; as long as United honestly believed its reason, then summary judgment for United is appropriate. Brill v. Lante Corp., 119 F.3d 1266, 1270 (7th Cir.1997); see also Crim v. Board of Educ. of Cairo Sch. Dist. No. 1, 147 F.3d 535, 541 (7th Cir.1998) (explaining that it is not enough for the plaintiff to prove that the employer's reason was doubtful or mistaken). Title VII sanctions employers who discriminate, not those who are simply inept or incompetent.

Our cases have warned, repeatedly, that we do not sit as a superpersonnel department that will second guess an employer's business decision. However, we need not abandon good reason and common sense in assessing an employer's actions. Indeed, we have stated that a "determination of whether a belief is honest is often conflated with analysis of reasonableness," Flores v. Preferred Technical Group, 182 F.3d 512, 516 (7th Cir.1999); "the more objectively reasonable a belief is, the more likely it will seem that the belief was honestly held," id. Our cases therefore have acknowledged that we need not take an employer at its word.

b.

In the present case, United's proffered justification for firing Mr. Gordon is his "unauthorized deviation." Our review of the record reveals inconsistencies in definition and disparities in application that call into question United's proffered justification and make summary judgment inappropriate.

1.

The guidelines provided to PFAs at their training establish the rules for their discipline and outline several categories under which a PFA could be disciplined for substandard performance. The applicable category here is titled "Violation of Company rules and [p]olicies." R.23, Ex.9 at 6. Under that heading, the PFA guidelines read: "Violation of the Articles of Conduct will, in most instances, result in immediate separation." Id. One of the violations of the Articles of Conduct is "Unauthorized deviation from a scheduled trip assignment." R.23, Ex.15 at 3.

The Articles of Conduct further warn that an unauthorized deviation by an employee is one of the violations of company policy that "will result in disciplinary action up to and including discharge." Id. It then notes that, for violations such as an unauthorized deviation, "[d]iscipline will normally commence with a suspension unless the particular situation or the employee's record warrants more severe action." Id.

The record makes starkly clear that, at the time of the incident, United did not have a clear definition of what constitutes an "unauthorized deviation." Apparently, the term is not defined in any United manual. Furthermore, the individuals involved in Mr. Gordon's discharge employed different definitions of the term.

Velasco offered a conflicting definition of unauthorized deviation from that of Siemieniec, the person who discharged Mr. Gordon. Velasco stated that a person commits an unauthorized deviation when he is on a layover and without authorization flies to another city, even if he returns to the city of his layover and makes his scheduled flight. Siemieniec explained in her deposition, however, that a flight attendant could fly to a different city while on a layover and return to his departure city without committing an unauthorized deviation. Siemieniec supported her definition by stating that "[p]rovided he is back in position for his scheduled flight, he has not deviated." R.23, Siemieniec dep. I, at 81.

James Younglove, the department's acting manager, echoed Siemieniec's deposition position that, if Mr. Gordon had flown home and returned in time to make his next scheduled flight, he would not have violated any United rule "[a]s long as he [was] back in their [sic] position to fly his trip." R.21, Ex.15 at 46. Similarly, Glen Scoggins, a senior staff representative for labor relations, was presented with the following hypothetical: "If a flight attendant is on layover and is scheduled to fly out of my hypothetical city at 8:00 at night ... that flight attendant took a plane to Pittsburgh, had lunch, got back to the city in which she was scheduled to fly out of in time to make her flight, has that flight attendant violated United's articles of conduct?" R.23, Scoggins dep., at 19–20. Scoggins replied: "I do not believe they violated the articles of conduct." Id. at 20. Indeed, United in its appellate brief flatly admits that the conduct that Velasco describes as an unauthorized deviation does not constitute such an infraction.

The inconsistent definition of unauthorized deviation becomes even more troubling in light of several other events. First, Siemieniec relied upon Velasco's definition of unauthorized deviation as a justification for firing Mr. Gordon, even though, according to her own deposition, she did not believe that his definition or the facts he alleged constituted an unauthorized deviation. Siemieniec's application of a different definition than the one she articulated in her deposition raises a significant question about the truthfulness of United's proffered reason for the discharge.

Second, the unauthorized deviation infraction has been invoked rarely. United's decision to characterize Mr. Gordon's conduct as an "unauthorized deviation" was an almost unprecedented occurrence. Other employees, who engaged in facially similar conduct, received only interim warnings because their conduct was deemed a "missed flight." It is not the province of this court to question an employer's decision to punish some conduct more harshly than other conduct. Nevertheless, we are not bound by the labels that an employer uses and must scrutinize the conduct behind those labels to determine if they are applied to similar conduct. Cf. Johnson v. Zema Sys. Corp., 170 F.3d 734, 743 (7th Cir.1999) (stating that "[a]n employer cannot insulate itself from claims of racial discrimination simply by providing different job titles to each of its employees" and then deny the existence of similarly situated employees). Here, an employer applied a rarely used label to sanction conduct that does not clearly fall within the chosen category. Although this alone may not cast doubt on United's sincerity, when considered together with the inconsistency noted above, it is sufficient evidence of pretext and, therefore, precludes summary judgment. See Perdomo v. Browner, 67 F.3d 140, 145 (7th Cir.1995) ("Because a fact-finder may infer intentional discrimination from an employer's untruthfulness, evidence that calls truthfulness into question precludes a summary judgment.").

2.

[A]lthough our analysis could stop here, there is additional evidence of pretext. United's proffered reason for discharge is further placed in question because no one claims responsibility for making the determination that an unauthorized deviation actually took place. Velasco stated that, in his role as Supervisor of the Crew Desk, he had no authority to make decisions; instead, he merely acted as a conduit to Mr. Gordon's supervisors. Velasco wrote in his report to Siemieniec that Mr. Gordon "decided to DV8 from LAX back to ORD [O'Hare] without authorization from any crew desk," R.21, Ex.32; yet, as Mr. Velasco repeatedly stated in his deposition, he had no decision-making authority and his role was only to provide "information as to what happen[ed] during their assignment and that is it." R.23, Velasco dep. I, at 68.

United's other supervisors, however, all claim that they did not make the decision that Mr. Gordon committed an unauthorized deviation. When Siemieniec was asked what factors she considered in making the determination that Mr. Gordon deviated without authorization, she replied: "That was already complete by the time I got involved. That was something he was dealing with at the moment at the crew desk. That determination was between him and Henry [Velasco] at the crew desk." R.28, Ex.49 at 40. She then stated that "Mr. Gordon unauthorized his own deviation." Id. These protestations, when considered together with the lack of a coherent definition of unauthorized deviation, cast significant and substantial doubt on United's assertion that it honestly believed Mr. Gordon committed an unauthorized deviation. As a result, these circumstances demonstrate triable issues of fact.

We also note that Mr. Gordon and Velasco offer different accounts of the events leading to Mr. Gordon's unauthorized deviation, a disparity which is relevant to the issue of whether United's proffered reason for discharge is a credible one. Mr. Gordon states that, after a bad experience at his hotel, he presented himself to the Crew Desk to ask permission to be released from his next assignment. Velasco acknowledges that Mr. Gordon's hotel experience was troubling but states that Mr. Gordon presented himself as illegal to fly. Mr. Gordon admits that he said he did not have a legal rest. He also states that he clearly would have had a legal rest by the time of his next flight and that Velasco had to have known that because Velasco had Mr. Gordon's schedule in front of him on his computer screen. It is undisputed that Mr. Gordon offered to return to Los Angeles to complete his scheduled assignment.

Therefore, the two individuals present at the time Mr. Gordon committed his alleged unauthorized deviation do not agree on the material facts of the occurrence. Mr. Gordon claims that he could have flown, and offered to fly, his next assigned flight. He states that he thought he received permission from Velasco to be removed. Velasco, conversely, states that Mr. Gordon presented himself as unable to fly his next assignment. United therefore claims that Mr. Gordon's removal was not authorized. There is, therefore, a genuine issue of triable fact because, when a PFA deviates from his assignment with authorization, it is not an infraction. As Siemieniec states, when flight attendants "get permission to take a different flight or do other than what they're scheduled to do then it is not unauthorized." R.23, Siemieniec dep. I, at 82. According to Mr. Gordon, he asked for authority from Velasco to miss his next flight and Velasco seemingly provided that authorization.

3.

Finally, the weakness of the proffered justification for the termination is further emphasized by the fact that the only other time that United has categorized an action as an unauthorized deviation, the involved employee, a white female, was not terminated. "A showing that similarly situated employees belonging to a different racial group received more favorable treatment can also serve as evidence that the employer's proffered legitimate, non-discriminatory reason for the adverse job action was a pretext for racial discrimination." Graham v. Long Island R.R., 230 F.3d 34, 43 (2d Cir.2000).

4.

We note that in Reeves v. Sanderson Plumbing Products, Inc., 530 U.S. 133, 142–46, 120 S.Ct. 2097, 147 L.Ed.2d 105 (2000), the Supreme Court, reinstating a jury verdict in favor of the employee, engaged in a similar factual analysis to ours in the present action to determine that a company's explanation for its employment decision was suggestive of intentional discrimination. In Reeves, the employer contended that its discharge of the employee was due to a non-discriminatory reason: the employee's failure to maintain accurate attendance records of those under his supervision. See id. at 138, 120 S.Ct. 2097. Reviewing in detail the record before it, the Court determined that, contrary to the employer's assertion, the evidence permitted the jury to conclude that the employee did maintain proper records and was not responsible for any failure to discipline late or absent employees. See id. at 144–47, 120 S.Ct. 2097. As a result, the Court determined that sufficient evidence existed to sustain a jury's determination that the employer's asserted justification was not true. See id. at 154–55, 120 S.Ct. 2097.

As in Reeves, Mr. Gordon has raised a factual issue as to whether "the employer's explanation is credible or merely a pretext for discrimination." Dey v. Colt Constr. & Dev. Co., 28 F.3d 1446, 1461 (7th Cir.1994). Mr. Gordon's argument that his discharge for unauthorized deviation was pretextual is not based on a contention that United simply misapplied its policy or that its decision-makers were confused. To so argue would be to misstate the record before us. Although United certainly ought to be permitted to argue such managerial ineptness to the jury, on summary judgment we must remember that Mr. Gordon suggests another, and equally plausible, characterization of the record. Our faithful adherence to the Supreme Court's holding in Reeves will tolerate no other conclusion. A reasonable jury could conclude, given United's inconsistent definition of unauthorized deviation, the rarity with which the unauthorized deviation provision was invoked, the disparate ways it was applied when it was invoked in Mr. Gordon's case, and United's inability to identify the management employee responsible for characterizing Mr. Gordon's conduct, that United's stated reason was a pretext for discrimination. Summary judgment is therefore inappropriate.

Conclusion

For the foregoing reasons, we reverse the judgment of the district court and remand for proceedings consistent with this opinion.

EASTERBROOK, Circuit Judge, dissenting.

This case illustrates how McDonnell Douglas Corp. v. Green, 411 U.S. 792, 93 S.Ct. 1817, 36 L.Ed.2d 668 (1973), has become so encrusted with the barnacles of multi-factor tests and inquiries that it misdirects attention. Could a reasonable trier of fact conclude that Gordon is the victim of age or race discrimination? If yes, then summary judgment must be denied; if no, then the grant of summary judgment for the employer must be affirmed. Instead of addressing this question straightforwardly, however, my colleagues follow a tortuous path to the conclusion that Gordon is entitled to a trial because United Airlines, the employer, does not have a written policy defining "unauthorized deviation," so that people may in good faith debate whether Gordon committed that infraction. I grant that United is not petrified with bureaucracy and does not cover every topic with reams of paper, as my colleagues believe that an employer must to prevail in an employment-discrimination case. United can only gaze toward the heights occupied by the Postal Service, the Social Security Administration, and the Immigration and Naturalization Service. But what has the state of its manuals and handbooks to do with race or age discrimination?

The majority's long discussion of legal criteria and prima facie cases diverts attention from the question whether a sensible trier of fact could infer that age, race, or some other forbidden characteristic made a difference. The Supreme Court set out in McDonnell Douglas to identify circumstances that would support an inference of discrimination, throwing a burden of explanation on the employer. Today's case shows how that program has failed.

In every large firm it is possible for almost every employee to make out a prima facie case. United employs thousands of flight attendants, of all ages, races, religions, sexes, and so on; some were retained while others were fired. Gordon met the airline's minimum standards, or he would not have been hired; he had received good reviews as a probationary flight attendant until the incident that precipitated his discharge; and from this it follows (he says) that all elements of McDonnell Douglas have been satisfied and it is more likely than not that his discharge was caused by his age or race. Only a lawyer trapped in a warren of "tests" and "factors" could make such a connection. Everything true about Gordon is true about United's other employees; can all of them be victims of discrimination?

Appellate judges must apply McDonnell Douglas while the Justices support it, and I therefore do not quarrel with my colleagues' conclusion that Gordon has established a prima facie case of discrimination. United provided an explanation for discharging him—that instead of appearing in Los Angeles for a flight to Seattle, Gordon flew to Chicago and told the crew desk that he had legally insufficient rest and therefore could not serve as a flight attendant that day. United understandably wants to discourage such conduct by its probationary employees, because weaseling out of flight assignments does not bode well for future performance. Unless this non-discriminatory explanation is a fraud on the court—not just an overreaction, but a lie—United must prevail.

What evidence could justify a reasonable trier of fact in concluding that United is trying to pull the wool over judicial eyes? In a word, none. My colleagues emphasize that United lacks formal policies defining "unauthorized deviation" and that its supervisors did not agree among themselves when asked what Gordon should have done. This is a fair appreciation of the record. But how does it support an inference that United (or any of its managers) is trying to bamboozle the court? "No company needs to have a set procedure for what action it will take when adjudicating every single employee problem." 6 West Limited Corp. v. NLRB, 237 F.3d 767, 778 (7th Cir.2001). Uncertainty and disagreement existed within the company, both about how employees were supposed to behave and about what supervisors should have done in response. There is additional doubt about what Gordon told the crew desk at O'Hare, as there is apt to be about every oral exchange. Gordon insists that he told United that he was unable to fly only at the moment of the conversation; United responds that this made the conversation pointless (why was Gordon at the crew desk except to get out of duty scheduled for later that day?); but no matter which inference is drawn, race and age play no role. What could anyone at United be trying to hide by taking one view of the conversation rather than another? Nothing in this record suggests that anyone is lying (let alone prevaricating to conceal reliance on Gordon's race or age). Disagreements about the characterization of ambiguous acts are part of the human condition, not proof of deceit or unlawful discrimination. A demonstration that United's practices bore more heavily on black or older workers might supply what is missing, see Bell v. EPA, 232 F.3d 546, 552–54 (7th Cir.2000), but Gordon has not adduced [such] evidence.

Gordon does not deny that United's stated reason is its actual one; the events that ended in his absence from the Los Angeles to Seattle flight led straight to his discharge. Causation is undisputed; that United was actually (and legitimately) disappointed with Gordon's conduct also is undisputed; what Gordon argues is that these events should have led to a reproof rather than a discharge. To say that such an argument can be the core of a federal employment-discrimination claim is to confuse the lack of "just cause" with "discrimination."

ROSE v. MIDWEST EXPRESS AIRLINES, INC.

2002 WL 31095361 (D. Neb. 2002)

BATAILLON, District Judge.

I. Introduction

Before me is the defendant's motion for summary judgment, Filing No. 26, which is supported by briefs and indices of evidence, Filing Nos. 27, 28, and 38. The plaintiff submitted a responsive brief and filed an index of evidence, Filing No. 35. Having carefully reviewed the record, the parties' submissions, and the applicable law, I now find that the defendant's motion for summary judgment should be granted.

II. Legal Standard

On a motion for summary judgment, the question before the court is whether the record, when viewed in the light most favorable to the non-moving party, shows that there is no genuine issue of material fact and that the moving party is entitled to judgment as a matter of law. Fed.R.Civ.P. 56(c); Mansker v. TMG Life Ins. Co., 54 F.3d 1322, 1326 (8th Cir.1995). Where unresolved issues are primarily legal rather than factual, summary judgment is particularly appropriate. Id.

In cases alleging employment discrimination, summary judgment is often an inappropriate remedy since discrimination is difficult to prove by direct evidence. "Summary judgment should be sparingly used and then only in those rare instances where there is no dispute of fact and where there exists only one conclusion. All evidence must point one way and be susceptible of no reasonable inferences sustaining the position of the non-moving party." Johnson v. Minnesota Historical Soc'y, 931 F.2d 1239, 1244 (8th Cir.1991). Since in this case only one conclusion is possible as a matter of law, summary judgment is appropriate.

III. Facts

In June 1994, the defendant, Midwest Express Airlines (Midwest Express), hired the plaintiff, Susan Rose (Rose), as a flight attendant. Midwest Express terminated Rose's employment in September 1996 for violations of company policies, but rehired her on a provisional basis in January 1997. In returning to work, Rose acknowledged that her past performance record was not erased, and that any further disciplinary action could result in termination.

Rose had several disciplinary problems after her rehiring, but Midwest Express did not finally decide to terminate her until April 2000 when a co-worker reported having observed Rose twice sleeping while on duty during flights. The "Rules of Conduct" in the Midwest Express Flight Attendant Manual make "sleeping or giving the appearance of sleeping while on duty" an infraction, the punishment for which could include termination. Midwest Express also cited Rose's poor work performance and her intimidation of and retaliation against the co-worker who had reported Rose for sleeping or appearing to sleep as additional reasons for her termination.

Rose admits that she cannot recall what she was doing during the April 7 flight when, instead of helping with a seatbelt check during turbulence, she was allegedly sleeping in a passenger seat in the rear of the plane's cabin; she acknowledges, however, that she was not praying. As to the April 14 flight, Rose told her supervisors during an investigative meeting on April 21 that she had not been sleeping during the thirty-minute taxi prior to takeoff, her head bobbing up and down, but perhaps had been instead in the "brace" position (in which the person's head faces downward and is tucked against the upper chest) or looking at her shoes. In a written statement submitted to her supervisors on April 24, Rose offered other possible explanations for what her co-worker had observed on the April 14 flight: she might have been stretching her back or she might have been praying—the first time Rose offered this latter explanation. Midwest Express terminated Rose on April 26, 2000.

The Nebraska Equal Opportunity Commission issued its determination of no reasonable cause on June 15, 2001.

Her complaint in this court alleges that her termination was unlawful religious discrimination under Title VII of the Civil Rights Act of 1964, 42 U.S.C. § 2000e et seq., and under the Nebraska Fair Employment Practices Act (NFEPA), Neb.Rev.Stat. Ann. § 48-1101 et seq. (Michie 1995). "In construing the NFEPA, the Nebraska courts have looked to federal decisions, because the NFEPA is patterned after Title VII." Orr v. Wal-Mart Stores, Inc., 297 F.3d 720, 723 (8th Cir.2002). The analysis of Rose's employment discrimination claim is thus the same for both Title VII and the NFEPA.

IV. Discussion

Title VII.

Despite the voluminous evidentiary record submitted in connection with this motion, only one factual issue appears to exist in this case: whether Rose was sleeping or gave the appearance of sleeping during a flight on April 14, 2000, or whether she was, as she claims in this suit, praying. If Rose was indeed praying rather than sleeping or appearing to sleep, the legal question becomes whether her termination was illegal. Under Title VII, an employer may not discharge an employee because of the employee's "religion." 42 U.S.C. § 2000e-2(a)(1). Religion encompasses "all aspects of religious observance and practice, as well as belief." 42 U.S.C. § 2000(e)(j). An employer is expected to accommodate an employee's religion unless the employer "demonstrates that [it] is unable to reasonably accommodate to an employee's or prospective employee's religious observance or practice without undue hardship on the conduct of the employer's business." Id.

If the complaint is to be read as alleging that Midwest Express subjected Rose to disparate treatment because of her religion, I find that Rose has not established that Midwest Express held a bias against her religion that resulted in her being treated differently than any other Midwest Express employee. In a disparate treatment case, a plaintiff must show she is a member of a protected class and then compare her treatment to that of a similarly situated member of a non-protected class, thereby establishing that she was treated less favorably than others because of her religious beliefs. See Mann v. Franklin, 7 F.3d 1365, 1370 (8th Cir.1993).

Rose is a Christian, but so are most Midwest Express employees. Rose acknowledges that the Midwest Express supervisors who made the decision to terminate her were also "praying" Christians; one even attended a church that Rose herself occasionally attends. Rose also admits that Midwest Express demonstrated no anti-Christian bias or practices and that Midwest Express had never told her or other employees that they could not pray. She claims that Midwest Express was aware that she prayed while on duty during flights, but acknowledges that Midwest Express had never prohibited the practice. Finally, another Midwest Express employee was fired the same day as Rose and for the same offense, sleeping or appearing to sleep during a flight—an offense that had nothing to do with the other employee's religion. Given these facts, Rose cannot make out a prima facie discrimination case based on disparate treatment imposed because of her religion or her religious practice of praying while on duty.

The only other way Rose could show that her termination was based on religious discrimination is to allege that Midwest Express refused to accommodate her religious beliefs or practices. To prove that an employer failed to accommodate an employee's religious beliefs or practices, the employee must present evidence that "(1) [s]he has a bona fide belief that compliance with an employment requirement is contrary to [her] religious faith; (2) [s]he has informed [her] employer about the conflict; and (3) [s]he was discharged because of [her] refusal to comply with the employment requirement." Johnson v. Angelica Uniform Group, Inc., 762 F.2d 671, 673 (8th Cir.1985). An employer is never required, however, to "accommodate a 'purely personal preference.'" Vetter v. Farmland Indus., Inc., 120 F.3d 749, 751 (8th Cir.1997) (quoting Brown v. General Motors Corp., 601 F.2d 956, 960 (8th Cir.1979)).

Midwest Express contends that Rose cannot demonstrate the first prong of this test, a bona fide religious belief that conflicts with the company rule forbidding employees from sleeping or appearing to sleep during flights. Rose offered no evidence that her religion required her to pray in a specific manner, at specific times, at specific places, or in specific circumstances. Indeed, Rose admitted that the manner, timing, and place of her prayers were entirely within her discretion: she could pray with her eyes open, standing up, moving about, doing her other duties. While the sincerity of Rose's religious beliefs with regard to prayer is not in question, I nevertheless find that those beliefs do not conflict with Midwest Express's rule on sleeping or appearing to sleep during flights.

Midwest Express also argues that Rose cannot establish the second prong of the Vetter test because she did not inform Midwest Express of her beliefs nor ask Midwest Express to accommodate her praying or manner of praying. Further, even granting Rose a strong religious belief in prayer, Midwest Express argues that it cannot accommodate a single manner of prayer that violates the no sleeping rule—a rule Rose admits to knowing about before she sought to explain away her appearance of sleeping as prayer. In response, Rose appears to argue that since other Midwest Express employees, including her supervisor, knew that she prayed during takeoffs, landings, and in-flight, Midwest

Express implicitly consented to and therefore had to accommodate her praying at whatever time and in whatever manner she chose.

Rose's argument strains the notion of both notice and accommodation. First, Rose has not proved that she told Midwest Express of her need to pray—in any manner—before she was reported for sleeping or appearing to sleep. See Johnson v. Angelica Uniform Group, Inc., 762 F.2d at 673 (no prima facie case where the plaintiff did not mention to employer need for accommodation to attend religious services before her termination for absenteeism). Midwest Express acknowledges that Rose at one point had asked for Sundays off, but that request is not the same as a request to be allowed to engage in eyes-closed, head-bowed prayer during flights.

Second, even if Rose had notified Midwest Express of her religious beliefs, Midwest Express could hardly have accommodated Rose on the no-sleeping rule. Midwest Express imposed the no-sleeping rule to comply with federal aviation regulations and for the safety of passengers and flight crew. Thus, forcing Midwest Express to accommodate Rose's chosen manner of praying could not only violate federal law but also jeopardize the safety of everyone aboard a flight to which Rose was assigned if she were "praying" with bowed head and closed eyes when an emergency arose during flight. The no-sleep rule plainly did not prevent Rose from praying. Indeed, as Midwest Express points out, the rule is facially neutral and has nothing whatever to do with praying or with religion. Rose was free to pray at any time during a flight—so long as she did not do so in a manner that gave an appearance of sleeping or that violated some other company rule or policy.

Finally, Midwest Express argues that Rose cannot meet the third prong of the Vetter test because she cannot establish that her termination was a result of her religious beliefs or practices. I agree. When Midwest Express rehired Rose in 1997, it placed her on notice that her past poor performance record was not erased and that further disciplinary infractions could result in termination. Midwest Express chose to not fire Rose for several disciplinary matters that arose after her rehiring. But when a co-worker reported Rose for sleeping or appearing to sleep in April 2000 and Rose then intimidated and retaliated against that co-worker, Midwest Express was free to accept the co-worker's version of events over Rose's version and to fire Rose.

This court's inquiry must stop at Midwest Express's decision to fire Rose, since Title VII employment discrimination laws "have not vested in the federal courts the authority to sit as super-personnel departments reviewing the wisdom or fairness of the business judgments made by employers, except to the extent that those judgments involve intentional discrimination." Hutson v. McDonnell Douglas Corp., 63 F.3d 771, 781 (8th Cir.1995). Rose's termination had nothing to do with Midwest Express discriminating against her religion or her religious practices. Her termination was based on her violation of a facially neutral no-sleeping rule, her retaliation against a co-worker, and her poor work performance.

State Law Claims.

The NFEPA specifically requires employment discrimination claims to be brought "within three hundred days after the occurrence of the alleged unlawful employment practice." Neb.Rev.Stat. Ann. 48-1118(2) (Michie 1995). Here, the alleged discrimination—Rose's termination—occurred in April 2000, but Rose did not file this suit until September 12, 2001, well past the 300 days allowed by section 48-1118(2).

Further, the NEOC issued its determination of no reasonable cause on June 15, 2001, three months before Rose filed this suit. An employee with a claim before the

NEOC may "at any stage of the proceedings prior to dismissal" file a court action. Neb.Rev.Stat. Ann. §48-1119(4) (Michie 1995). A determination of no reasonable cause constitutes a dismissal in accordance with section 48-1119(4). See Metz v. ACI Worldwide, Inc., 2002 WL 2005719, *2 (D.Neb.2002). Although Rose requests some sort of equitable tolling, I find that Rose's failure to bring her NFEPA suit before the NEOC's determination of no reasonable cause dooms her NFEPA claims.

IT IS THEREFORE ORDERED:

1. The defendant's motion for summary judgment, Filing No. 26, is granted; and,

2. Judgment for the defendant will be entered by separate order.

FERRIS v. DELTA AIR LINES, INC.

277 F.3d 128 (2d Cir. 2001),
cert. denied, 537 U.S. 824 (2002)

LEVAL, Circuit Judge.

Plaintiff Penny Ferris, a flight attendant employed by defendant Delta Air Lines ("Delta"), appeals from a grant of summary judgment by the United States District Court for the Eastern District of New York (Weinstein, J.), dismissing her claims for (1) sexual harassment under Title VII of the 1964 Civil Rights Act, 42 U.S.C. §2000e, et seq., the New York State Human Rights Law, N.Y. Exec. L. §290 et seq., and the New York City Human Rights Law, N.Y.C. Admin. Code §8-107, and (2) numerous other torts under the law of New York, including negligent hiring, retention, and supervision of an employee; assault, battery, false imprisonment, and intentional infliction of emotional distress. The suit arises from a male flight attendant's rape of Ferris during the crew's brief layover between flights in Rome. We vacate the grant of summary judgment as to the federal sexual harassment claims because a reasonable factfinder could find that Delta was responsible for a sexually hostile work environment that caused injury to Ferris. We affirm the grant of summary judgment as to the claims under New York State and New York City law.

BACKGROUND

A. Events giving rise to this lawsuit.

In reviewing a grant of summary judgment in favor of the defendant, we are obligated to consider all facts in the light most favorable to the plaintiff. They are as follows:

1. Young's rape of Ferris

In March 1998, Penny Ferris and Michael Young, both Delta flight attendants, were employed together on the crew of a Delta flight from New York City to Rome, Italy. When the flight arrived in Rome on March 17, the crew (including Ferris and Young) boarded a Delta bus to be driven to the Savoy Hotel, where Delta had reserved and paid for a block of rooms to be used by the crew until their return flight to New York on March 18. That afternoon, Ferris and Young had shopped together for wine for Ferris to bring home as a present. Young told her he had brought a bottle of a vintage Ferris was considering and offered to let her taste it in his room when they returned to the hotel. Upon their return, Ferris went to Young's room, where he had a glass of wine ready for her. After drinking about half a glass, Ferris felt faint. She tried to return to her room, but could not make her legs move. She blacked out. While she was unconscious, Young took off her clothes and raped her vaginally, orally, and anally. She partially regained consciousness intermittently during the multiple rapes, at one point telling Young to stop before blacking out again.

That night, at dinner with the other flight attendants, Ferris was in shock and confusion. During the dinner, she began to feel nauseous, and went to the bathroom and vomited. The following day, she flew back to New York, serving as crew together with Young.

On March 30, 1998—about two weeks after the rape—Ferris recounted what had happened to Vanessa Bray, who had been the "On Board Leader" (the lead flight attendant) on the March 16–18 flights. She told Bray that she thought that she might have been drugged because she was unable to do anything about what was happening to her. Ferris then asked Bray not to repeat what she had said, and Bray did not.

On April 11, 1998—about three weeks after the rape—Ferris reported the rape to Anne Estall, the Delta Duty Supervisor. In the course of a one-hour meeting, Ferris informed her that she had been raped by a flight attendant who was an Italian speaker on a March 1998 flight to Rome. Ferris refused to give Young's name. Using the Delta computer system, Estall narrowed the suspects down to two male, Italian-speaking flight attendants who had been on the March 16–18 flights. She then set up a meeting between Ferris and Maritza Biscaino, the Delta Base Manager at John F. Kennedy International Airport (JFK) for six days later.

At the meeting on April 17, 1998, Ferris told Biscaino about the rape in an interview that lasted approximately two hours. Biscaino requested a written report and the rapist's name, both of which Ferris refused to give her. In follow-up conversations with Ferris around May 4, 1998, Biscaino eventually persuaded Ferris to disclose her assailant's name.

On May 5, 1998, Biscaino and her co-base manager, Kevin Grimes, interviewed Michael Young for approximately two hours. He said that, upon arriving in Rome, he had gone to the gym, returned to his room for a nap, and spent the night with another flight attendant, Jaycee Kantz. The same day, he provided a written statement to this effect. Biscaino interviewed Kantz shortly after, and Kantz confirmed that Young had spent the night with her. Sometime in early June 1998, flight attendant Carolyn Gordon overheard a conversation between Young and another flight attendant in which Young said that he had been accused of drugging and raping a Delta flight attendant. This prompted Gordon to handwrite a memo to Delta on June 22, 1998, which recounted an experience that Gordon had had with Young in December, 1997. Gordon had accepted Young's invitation to come to his room during a layover in Rome for a glass of wine. When she got there, two glasses of wine were already poured on the nightstand. Gordon's memo implied that the wine Young gave her may have been drugged and that he took advantage of her drugged state to have sex with her, although she acknowledged that she may have suffered an adverse reaction between the wine and anti-depressant medications she had been taking.

On June 25, 1998, Ferris gave Biscaino her first written report of the incident. Ferris's written report repeated the events as previously recounted to Vanessa Bray, Estall, and Biscaino. On June 29, 1998, Biscaino and Grimes again met with Young, confronting him with the information in Ferris's written report. At the conclusion of the meeting, Biscaino and Grimes suspended Young and removed his Delta workplace identification. Delta continued to investigate Ferris's claims over the next several months, while Young was on suspension. Young refused to cooperate with the investigation, and was recommended for termination on November 5, 1998. At some point, Young submitted a handwritten resignation to Delta.

2. Delta's prior notice of Young's sexually abusive conduct with co-workers

a. Kathleen Ballweg

At Christmas time, 1993, Kathleen Ballweg and Young were flight attendants together on a Delta flight from New York to Milan. During the flight, Young invited several flight attendants to accompany him to see the Christmas Eve service in Florence. Several agreed, but changed their minds by the time the plane arrived in Florence, leaving Ballweg as the only flight attendant accompanying Young to Florence. Young raped Ballweg in her hotel room in Florence.

Upon returning to the United States, Ballweg reported the incident to a Delta supervisor at JFK. She said the supervisor should know about somebody who is potentially dangerous, and she identified Young by name. Although she believed she did not use the word "rape," she told the supervisor that she had been attacked, and clearly communicated that the attack was sexual in nature. She told the supervisor that she wanted to be anonymous, and the supervisor replied that Delta could do nothing about it unless Ballweg made a written, formal complaint, which Ballweg did not want to do. Ballweg told the supervisor that she would spread the word about Young's dangerousness, and later warned many flight attendants about Young.

Ballweg later encountered Young during a Delta layover in Frankfurt. Young called Ballweg several times in her hotel room that night, saying she should spend the night with him, and berating her with comments about sex. Ballweg again reported her experiences with Young to a Delta supervisor. She told the supervisor about the attack in Florence, noted that she had already told a supervisor about it, and told the supervisor that she thought that Young was still dangerous.

Ballweg flew with Young only one more time after the phone calls in Frankfurt. Whenever she was flying to Rome or Milan, she would check the flight attendant list to see if Young was on the flight, and tried to avoid assignment to a flight if she saw that Young would be working on it.

Delta took no action in response to Ballweg's reports.

b. Aileen Feingold

In March 1995, Delta flight attendant Aileen Feingold visited Young in Dallas for sightseeing. Young had invited her to stay at his house, telling her she would have a separate bedroom. On the night that Feingold spent at Young's house, Young entered the bedroom where she was sleeping and raped her while she was asleep.

Feingold was so distraught after the rape that she failed a training test that she took the next day. Delta subsequently cancelled one of Feingold's scheduled trips so that she could re-take the test.

Feingold later warned several Delta flight attendants that Young was a rapist. About four months after the rape, Feingold contacted Young about a suitcase that she had left at his house. Young e-mailed her, telling her that it was her problem to take care of her things, that he had heard that she was talking negatively about him, and that she had better stop because Young had friends that could get her in a lot of trouble, specifically mentioning Delta supervisor Nancy Ruhl, who was manager of in-flight service for JFK. Young also left messages at her home, telling her to shut her mouth, or he would take care of her.

Feingold then contacted Ruhl, the Delta supervisor that Young had mentioned. Feingold told Ruhl about the rape. Feingold also read Ruhl the e-mails that she had received, and offered to bring her file of Young's e-mails by Ruhl's office. Ruhl said that that would not be necessary. Feingold said that she believed she was not the first person that Young had raped, as it seemed to her that Young had a method of operation that was down pat. Feingold offered to write up a report to put in Young's file to document her allegations. She told Ruhl that she wanted to do something so that Young would not rape anyone else. Ruhl told Feingold that she would talk to Young and that she would take care of the situation, and that it was not necessary for Feingold to provide a written report.

The next day, Ruhl called Feingold and told her that she had talked to Young, that he would not bother her again, and that she had taken care of everything. She instructed Feingold never to talk to Young, and not to talk to anyone about what had happened.

Delta took no action in response to Feingold's report.

3. Michelle Zachry

Michelle Zachry, another Delta flight attendant, had also reported to Delta that Young had behaved hostilely and aggressively toward her during their work on a flight after she refused to go out to dinner with him.

Zachry flew with Young to Rome in July 1997. During the flight, Young made sexual comments to her, told her about his illegal steroid use, told her that he was involved in a sexual affair with another flight attendant, and invited Zachry to go to dinner. Later, Young called Zachry in her hotel room to ask her to go to dinner, and after she turned him down, called her back and became belligerent.

After landing from the return flight from Rome, Young came up to Zachry and began cursing and screaming at her. Passengers turned around to look at him, and another flight attendant eventually interposed himself between Young and Zachry and told Young that he needed to "chill out."

Zachry reported this incident to a supervisor. She did not give Young's name, but told the supervisor that a flight attendant had gone crazy because she would not go out to dinner with him. The supervisor did not ask any questions of her, and did not make a formal report.

In the meantime, Zachry had spoken with the flight attendant that Young had said he was having an affair with. About one week later, Zachry encountered Young on a Delta tram in the Dallas airport. Young called Zachry obscene names, and threatened to kill her. Zachry feared that Young might physically attack her.

After the incident on the tram, Zachry told Cheryl Merit, a Delta supervisor, that she was going to report an incident. Merit then accompanied Zachry to the office of Kathy Goldberger, a Delta supervisor. This time, Zachry identified Michael Young by name, and told Goldberger what had happened on the plane, on the tram, and how Young had boasted of his illegal steroid use. Goldberger asked Zachry to make a written report, telling her that they could not do anything unless Zachry made a written report, and Goldberger told Zachry that Delta "[did not] have anything on [Young]." Zachry was not willing to make a written report. Afterwards, Zachry would not fly to Rome because of her fear of encountering Michael Young.

Delta took no action in response to Zachry's report.

B. The district court's decision

In July 1999, Ferris brought this action against Young and Delta. Judge Weinstein ordered a separate initial trial on the question whether the rape had occurred. This resulted in a mistrial when the jury was unable to agree on a verdict. Delta then moved for summary judgment. The court rejected plaintiff's sexual harassment claims. See P. v. Delta Air Lines, Inc., 102 F.Supp.2d 132 (E.D.N.Y.2000) (hereinafter "P."). With respect to the rape itself, the court ruled that Ferris could not prevail because Young's hotel room in Rome was not a "work environment" within the ambit of Title VII. See id. at 141. As to the claim based on Ferris's anxiety and distress at the prospect of thereafter encountering Young at Delta, the court concluded that plaintiff's claimed injury was too hypothetical and speculative to support a claim of hostile work environment harassment. See id. at 142–43.

The court also rejected plaintiff's state tort claims. Plaintiff has not sought review of most of these rulings. On the claims for negligent retention and supervision, which plaintiff has pursued on appeal, the district court concluded that Delta could not be held liable for Young's actions because Young was not on Delta's premises or using Delta's chattels when he raped plaintiff. See id. at 144.

Judgment was entered on July 20, 2000. On this appeal, Ferris argues the district court erred in granting summary judgment to Delta on her sexual harassment claim and on her claims for negligent supervision and retention of Young.

DISCUSSION

A. Sexual harassment claims

1. Young's rape of Ferris during the layover in Rome

The district court granted summary judgment to Delta on Ferris's claim based on the rape in Rome. Because Young had no supervisory authority over Ferris and she associated voluntarily with him, and there was no evidence that Delta had affirmatively encouraged flight attendants to visit each other's rooms, the court concluded that the attack in Young's hotel room could not, as a matter of law, be found to have occurred in a "work environment." See P., 102 F.Supp.2d at 141.

Although we think the question is close, we respectfully disagree with the district court's conclusion. In our view, the rape could be found to have occurred in a work environment within the meaning of Title VII. The circumstances that surround the lodging of an airline's flight crew during a brief layover in a foreign country in a block of hotel rooms booked and paid for by the employer are very different from those that arise when stationary employees go home at the close of their normal workday. The flight crew members repeatedly spend brief layovers in a foreign country with little opportunity to develop private lives in that place. Most likely they do not speak the local language. In all likelihood, they do not have family, friends, or their own residences there. Although it is not mandatory for them to do so, they generally stay in a block of hotel rooms that the airline reserves for them and pays for. The airline in addition provides them as a group with ground transportation by van from the airport to the hotel on arrival, and back at the time for departure. It is likely furthermore in those circumstances that the crew members will have no other acquaintances in this foreign place and will band together for society and socialize as a matter of course in one another's hotel rooms. Even though the employer does not direct its employees as to how to spend their off-duty hours, the circumstances of the employment tend to compel these results. In view of the special set of circumstances that surround such a foreign layover, we disagree with the district court's conclusion. A jury could properly find on these facts that Young's hotel room was a part of Ferris's work environment within the terms of Title VII.

The Supreme Court has stated that "whether an environment is 'hostile' or 'abusive' can be determined only by looking at all the circumstances. These may include the frequency of the discriminatory conduct; its severity; whether it is physically threatening or humiliating, or a mere offensive utterance; and whether it unreasonably interferes with an employee's work performance." Harris v. Forklift Sys., Inc., 510 U.S. 17, 23, 114 S.Ct. 367, 126 L.Ed.2d 295 (1993). A plaintiff establishes a claim for hostile environment sexual harassment if she demonstrates (1) harassment that was sufficiently severe or pervasive to alter the conditions of her employment, creating an abusive working environment, and (2) a sufficient basis for imputing the conduct that created the hostile environment to her employer. See Perry v. Ethan Allen, Inc., 115 F.3d 143, 149 (2d Cir.1997).

Although a continuing pattern of hostile or abusive behavior is ordinarily required to establish a hostile environment, a single instance can suffice when it is sufficiently egregious. We have no doubt a single incident of rape can satisfy the first prong of employer liability under a hostile work environment theory. See Tomka v. Seiler Corp., 66 F.3d 1295, 1305 (2d Cir.1995) ("[E]ven a single incident of sexual assault sufficiently alters the conditions of the victim's employment and clearly creates an abusive work environment for purposes of Title VII liability."), abrogated on other grounds by Burlington Indus., Inc. v. Ellerth, 524 U.S. 742, 118 S.Ct. 2257, 141 L.Ed.2d 633 (1998).

Ferris's evidence must also satisfy the second prong by showing a sufficient basis for imputing responsibility to Delta for Young's conduct. Where the harassment was done by a co-employee without supervisory authority over the plaintiff, liability will be imputed to the employer "only if it is negligent, that is, if it either provided no reasonable avenue for complaint or knew of the harassment but did nothing about it." Richardson v. New York State Dep't of Corr. Serv., 180 F.3d 426, 441 (2d Cir.1999) (internal quotation marks omitted); see Faragher v. City of Boca Raton, 524 U.S. 775, 799, 118 S.Ct. 2275, 141 L.Ed.2d 662 (1998) (noting agreement among the circuits that liability should be imputed to employers in cases of co-worker harassment only if the employer was negligent).

A reasonable factfinder might conclude that Delta's negligence made it responsible for Ferris's rape. Delta had notice of Young's proclivity to rape co-workers. The fact that Young's prior rapes were not of Ferris but of other co-workers is not preclusive. If an employer is on notice of a likelihood that a particular employee's proclivities place other employees at unreasonable risk of rape, the employer does not escape responsibility to warn or protect likely future victims merely because the abusive employee has not previously abused those particular employees.

Supervisory personnel at Delta had been notified that Young had twice raped female co-workers and had engaged in other abusive, sexually hostile conduct toward the rape victims and a third co-worker. Not only did Delta do nothing about it, but a Delta supervisor (Ruhl) took affirmative steps to prevent the filing of a formal complaint that might have resulted in protective steps and even to prevent a prior victim (Feingold) from informally spreading cautionary words among the flight attendants about Young. Given all the circumstances, a reasonable factfinder could find that Delta was negligent in failing to take steps that might have protected Ferris from Young's proclivity to rape female co-workers.

The district court rejected the proposition that the Ballweg and Feingold rapes could constitute notice to Delta as to the harassment Ferris suffered. It reasoned that the "[e]arlier complaints of sexual improprieties involved non-work-related, off-duty encounters, substantially curtailing both the practical ability and the legal authority of Delta to investigate." P., 102 F.Supp.2d at 142. We disagree. Had the earlier non-work related incidents consisted of less grave conduct, such as off-duty flirtation, sexual innuendo, or crude talk, we might agree that such off-premises, off-duty conduct does not reasonably give notice of a likelihood that the person will represent a danger to co-employees or import his harassment into a work environment and therefore does not give rise to an employer's duty to protect co-workers. But rape is obviously a far more serious matter. The more egregious the abuse and the more serious the threat of which the employer has notice, the more the employer will be required under a standard of reasonable care to take steps for the protection of likely future victims. The district court may have been correct that Delta's ability to investigate was curtailed by the fact that the Feingold and Ballweg rapes occurred off-duty. It does not follow, however, that the off-duty nature of the rapes absolved Delta of all responsibility to take reasonable care to protect co-workers, much less justified a supervisor's affirmative steps to prevent a victim from filing a written complaint and warning co-workers.

2. Ferris's subsequent distress at the prospect of encountering Young at Delta once she was back in New York.

Because Ferris did not work with Young again after their return to New York, the district court granted summary judgment to Delta with respect to Ferris's fear of further encounters with Young on the ground that "such trepidation, standing alone, is too hypothetical and speculative to support a contention that there was an 'objectively hostile or abusive work environment.'" P., 102 F.Supp.2d at 142. We think the evidence, viewed in the light most favorable to Ferris, showed that she suffered real emotional trauma from her fear of seeing Young again while both were working as flight attendants. Ferris endeavored to keep abreast of Young's work schedule in efforts to ensure that she would not ever work on a flight he was on. But she suffered anxiety attacks at work due to her fear that she might again encounter Young, sought psychiatric help and took anti-depressants. Under the circumstances, we do not think that Ferris's fear of encountering her rapist at her workplace is too hypothetical and speculative to sustain an award of damages. We do not rule out, however, that Ferris may be chargeable with partial, or even full, responsibility for this later injury or its duration by reason of her failure to mitigate her damages when she delayed reporting the event to Delta and naming her assailant.

B. New York negligent retention and supervision claims

Ferris originally brought claims against Delta for various intentional torts under the doctrine of respondeat superior, as well as claims for negligent hiring, retention, and supervision. The district court granted summary judgment for Delta on all of Ferris's state tort claims. See P., 102 F.Supp.2d at 143–44. On appeal, Ferris pursues only her negligent retention and supervision claims.

The district court granted summary judgment for Delta on Ferris's negligent retention and supervision claims on the grounds that employers are only liable for the torts of negligent retention and supervision when the torts are committed on the employer's premises or with the employer's chattels, and that the hotel room in Rome was neither Delta's premises nor its equipment. P., 102 F.Supp.2d at 143–44.

We affirm the grant of judgment by reason of New York's Workers' Compensation statute. It provides that: "The right to compensation or benefits under this chapter, shall be the exclusive remedy to an employee ... when such employee is injured ... by the negligence or wrong of another in the same employ...." N.Y. Workers' Comp. Law § 29(6) (McKinney 1993 & Supp.2001); see also N.Y. Workers' Comp. Law § 11 (McKinney 1993 & Supp.2001). We held in Torres v. Pisano, 116 F.3d 625 (2d Cir.1997), that the New York Workers' Compensation Law barred a common law negligence claim that was asserted on the basis of an alleged hostile work environment because of co-worker harassment. Id. at 640. Ferris's state common law negligence claims are therefore precluded by the exclusive remedy provisions of New York's Workers' Compensation statute. See id.; see also Ross v. Mitsui Fudosan, Inc., 2 F.Supp.2d 522, 533 (S.D.N.Y.1998) (dismissing New York common law negligence claims arising out of sexual harassment lawsuit as barred by exclusive remedy provisions of New York Workers' Compensation Law), Burlew v. Am. Mut. Ins. Co., 63 N.Y.2d 412, 482 N.Y.S.2d 720, 472 N.E.2d 682 (1984). We therefore affirm the district court's grant of summary judgment on Ferris's negligent retention and supervision claims.

CONCLUSION

The district court's grant of summary judgment in Delta's favor as to Ferris's federal sexual harassment claims is vacated and the case remanded for further proceedings. The district court's grant of summary judgment in Delta's favor as to Ferris's state law claims for negligent retention and supervision is affirmed. The award of costs and disbursements to Delta is vacated. The costs of the appeal are awarded to Ferris.

STRAKA v. FRANCIS

867 F. Supp. 767 (N.D. Ill. 1994)

MAROVICH, District Judge.

Plaintiffs Gerrie Straka ("Straka"), Bonita Lumbrazo ("Lumbrazo"), and Mary Kay McSheffery ("McSheffery") filed this cause of action pursuant to Title VII of the Civil Rights Act of 1964 ("Title VII"), 42 U.S.C. Sec. 2000e et seq., the Civil Rights Act of 1991, and the Age Discrimination in Employment Act of 1967, as amended, 29 U.S.C. § 621, et seq. ("ADEA"). Defendants in the case are Executive Flight Management/Trans American Charter, Ltd. ("Executive Flight"), and Lincoln and Bruce Francis (collectively, "the Individual Defendants"), who are pilots employed by and shareholders of Flight Management. Lincoln Francis is the President of the company and son of Bruce Francis. Plaintiffs allege that Defendants' acts of sexual harassment and age discrimination created a hostile and intolerable work environment causing Plaintiffs' resignation and constructive discharge on April 11, 1993. Defendants counter-claim that Plaintiffs' resignation caused Flight Management to lose business and they therefore seek damages in the amount of $350,000 and such other relief as this Court deems just and proper.

Defendants filed a partial motion to dismiss the Individual Defendants, claiming that individual employees of an employer may not be held personally liable under Title VII or the ADEA. Defendants also filed counterclaims including: tortious interference with a contract between Executive Flight and a client, David D. Linnemeier ("Linnemeier"), Director of Aviation for Huizenga Holdings, Inc. (Count I); breach of an employment contract alleged to exist between Executive Flight and Plaintiffs (Count II); promissory estoppel (Count III); and equitable estoppel (Count IV). Plaintiffs filed a motion to dismiss Defendants' counterclaims.

For the reasons stated below, the Court grants Defendants' partial motion to dismiss, and Plaintiffs' motion to dismiss Counts I, II, III, and IV of Defendants' counterclaims.

BACKGROUND

Executive Flight is an Illinois corporation that provides charter airline passenger service throughout the United States. Plaintiffs are female residents of Illinois who were hired as flight attendants in September 1992 by Executive Flight. Plaintiffs were hired to provide flight attendant services for sports teams and were assigned to work pursuant to a 1992 contract negotiated in Florida between Executive Flight and Linnemeier for the Florida Marlins ("Marlins"). The contract was to provide charter jet service for the team during the 1993 professional baseball season. According to Defendants, Plaintiffs knew the contract with Linnemeier was the company's largest, that the Marlins were their most publicly recognized client, and that they were being hired and agreed to work on flights for sports teams.

Flight attendants for the Marlins' flights required training for a specially equipped DC-9 aircraft. Accordingly, Plaintiffs were trained between September 1992 and April of 1993. Their first flight with the Marlins occurred on April 1, 1993; it originated in Jacksonville, Florida and ended in Fort Lauderdale, Florida. On April 11, 1993, Plaintiffs were scheduled to work as attendants on a Marlins flight which was to depart Fort Lauderdale at 5:30 p.m. en route to San Francisco, California. Federal Aviation Administration ("FAA") regulations require two certified flight attendants on all flights, and the contract between Executive Flight and the Marlins included provision of three certified attendants on each flight. According to Defendants, Plaintiffs were aware of such regulations.

Executive Flight flew Plaintiff attendants from Chicago to Florida on April 9, 1993, two days prior to the scheduled departure. On April 10, Plaintiffs performed various routine duties in preparation for the April 11th flight, including catering arrangements and cabin preparation. According to Defendants, an unarranged congregation of Executive Flight employees and officers occurred during the evening of April 10 at a restaurant in Ft. Lauderdale. At this impromptu gathering were: Plaintiffs; Lincoln Francis, the scheduled captain for the April 11 Marlins flight; Bruce Francis; Steve Gaines, the scheduled co-pilot for the flight; Andy Townsend, a maintenance mechanic; and Linnemeier and his wife. Defendants allege that throughout the evening and beyond 9:30 p.m. Plaintiffs gave no indication of an intention to not work the Marlins flight the following day.

At about 2:00 p.m. on April 11, 1993, Plaintiffs telephoned Executive Flight's Chicago, Illinois office to provide notice that they were resigning. At some point during that same day, Plaintiffs also telephoned the caterer scheduled to provide meal service on the Marlins flight in an attempt to cancel the order. According to Defendants, Plaintiffs were aware of a provision in the Executive Flight-Marlins contract that required meal service, and that their resignation and cancellation of the catering order would prevent or substantially impede Executive Flight in discharging its contractual responsibilities.

Plaintiffs allege their continued employment was conditioned upon being subjected to repeated incidents of sexual harassment and age discrimination either participated in directly or condoned by the Defendant company through its officers, managers, and employees. Such incidents include alleged comments regarding Plaintiffs' physical appearance and attire, a lewd and lascivious gift from Defendant Bruce Francis to Plaintiff Lumbrazo, comments of a sexual nature regarding Lumbrazo's physical appearance and that Plaintiffs were too old to be flight attendants, suggestions that Plaintiffs should be "more friendly" with the players during flights and "not act like the players' mothers," and lewd and lascivious comments regarding sexual activity with Plaintiff Lumbrazo.

Plaintiffs further claim the repeated acts of sexual harassment and age discrimination caused their constructive discharge from work as of April 11, 1993; and that they, therefore, at that time telephoned their notice of resignation to Flight Management in Chicago.

DISCUSSION

I. DEFENDANTS' PARTIAL MOTION TO DISMISS

The Court will first address Defendants' motion to dismiss Individual Defendants Bruce and Lincoln Francis as defendants in this case. A complaint should not be dismissed unless the court concludes beyond a doubt that plaintiffs can prove no set of facts to support their claim which would entitle them to relief. Gorski v. Troy, 929 F.2d 1183, 1186 (7th Cir.1991); Conley v. Gibson, 355 U.S. 41, 45–46, 78 S.Ct. 99, 101–02, 2 L.Ed.2d 80 (1957). When ruling on a motion to dismiss, the court assumes the truth of all well-pled allegations and makes all possible inferences in favor of the non-movant. Falk v. U.H.H. Home Servs. Corp., 835 F.Supp. 1078, 1079 (N.D.Ill.1993).

Individual Liability under Title VII and the ADEA

The question before the Court is a narrow one: whether individual employees of an employer may be held personally liable under the ADEA or Title VII for conduct or omissions constituting sexual harassment or fostering a hostile work environment. As a general rule, this Court, a majority of the courts in this district, the Seventh Circuit, and the Supreme Court have held that individual employees, regardless of their rank or authority within the employment entity, are not personally liable for conduct or omissions constituting sexual harassment or age discrimination under Title VII or the ADEA. See, e.g., Hamilton v. City of Chicago, 93 C 3342, 1993 WL 535351, 1993 U.S.Dist. LEXIS 17889 (N.D.Ill. Dec. 13, 1993); Pelech v. Klaff-Joss, LP, 828 F.Supp. 525, 529 (N.D.Ill.1993); Pommier v. James L. Edelstein Enters, 816 F.Supp. 476, 480–81 (N.D.Ill.1993); Weiss v. Coca-Cola Bottling Co., 772 F.Supp. 407, 410 (N.D.Ill.1991); Shager v. Upjohn, 913 F.2d 398, 404 (7th Cir.1990); Kentucky v. Graham, 473 U.S. 159, 165–67, 105 S.Ct. 3099, 3104–06, 87 L.Ed.2d 114 (1985). The Court therefore grants Defendants' partial Motion to Dismiss Plaintiffs' Title VII and ADEA claims against Individual Defendants Bruce and Lincoln Francis.

II. PLAINTIFFS' MOTION TO DISMISS COUNTERCLAIMS

In order to address Defendants' counterclaims, this Court must first address the issue of choice of law. Executive Flight proposes that the Court should apply Florida law to the counterclaims because the company's contract with the Marlins was negotiated in Florida, the first flight of each Marlins trip was to originate in Florida, and the alleged wrongful conduct (i.e. Plaintiffs' resignation and related acts) occurred in that State. Plaintiffs argue that Illinois law should govern the case.

The Court's analysis, under the principles first announced in Erie Railroad Co. v. Tompkins, 304 U.S. 64, 58 S.Ct. 817, 82 L.Ed. 1188 (1938), must be based on relevant State law. Loucks v. Star City Glass Co., 551 F.2d 745, 746 (7th Cir.1977). Federal courts apply the choice-of-law test applicable to the State in which the Court sits. Kafka v. Bellevue Corp., 999 F.2d 1117, 1121 (7th Cir.1993) (citing Klaxon Co. v. Stentor Electric Mfg. Co., 313 U.S. 487, 496, 61 S.Ct. 1020, 1021–22, 85 L.Ed. 1477 (1941)); H.B. Fuller Co. v. Kinetic Systems, Inc., 932 F.2d 681, 685 (7th Cir.1991). Under Illinois choice-of-law principles, the court applies the law the parties understood would govern a case. In the absence of an expression of the parties' understanding, which is the situation in this case, courts apply a most-significant-relationship test to determine which State law should govern. Kafka at 1121; Diamond State Ins. Co. v. Chester-Jensen Co., 243 Ill.App.3d 471, 183 Ill.Dec. 435, 445–46, 611 N.E.2d 1083, 1093–94 (1993); Laport v. Lake Michigan Mgmt. Co., 252 Ill.App.3d 221, 192 Ill.Dec. 41, 46, 625 N.E.2d 1, 6 (1991); Ingersoll v. Klein, 46 Ill.2d 42, 262 N.E.2d 593 (1970).

Executive Flight's emphasis on the impromptu gathering at the Ft. Lauderdale restaurant, the scheduled departure and flight preparations conducted by the attendants in Florida, and Plaintiffs' resignation and attempt to cancel the catering order is misguided. This case involves an employment agreement and relationship formed and based in Illinois. Even if the place of performance was to occur predominantly in Florida, which is not clear from the facts presented, the acts in formation of the employment contract, if one exists, occurred by all parties in Illinois, the parties are domiciled in Illinois and must fly from Chicago to Florida prior to scheduled trips, and Plaintiffs' resignation was tendered to the Illinois office. These facts support a conclusion that Illinois is the State with the most significant relationship with the "occurrence and with the parties," as well as with the employment contract from which this litigation arises. See, e.g., Laport, 192 Ill.Dec. at 46, 625 N.E.2d at 6.

Executive Flight's focus on the negotiations regarding the contract between the company and the Marlins is similarly misguided. Beyond showing the existence of that contract for the purpose of satisfying the elements of the tort of contractual interference, the Marlins contract has only a tangential significance to the claims presented by the parties to this case and the employment relationship at issue. In addition, invoking Illinois substantive law in this case is supported by the fact that the underlying litigation, i.e., Plaintiffs' federal claim, is filed in Illinois, and that application of Illinois law to Defendant's cross-claims does not appear contrary to the public policies of Florida. See e.g., Diamond State, 243 Ill.App.3d 471, 183 Ill.Dec. 435, 611 N.E.2d 1083 (1993).

This Court concludes that given that Illinois has more significant contacts with the hiring, training, and agreements made pursuant to the employment relationship at issue in this case, Illinois law should apply in interpreting the substance of any agreements made or breached between the parties and related claims.

A. Tortious Interference of Contract—Count I

To sustain a claim for tortious interference of a contract or business relationship, the plaintiff, or, in this case, Defendant-counterclaimant Executive Flight, must show: 1) the existence of a valid and enforceable contract between the plaintiff and another, 2) the defendant's awareness of this contractual relationship, 3) defendant's intentional and unjustified inducement of a breach of the contract which causes a subsequent breach by the other, and 4) damages. HPI Health Care v. Mt. Vernon Hospital, Inc., 131 Ill.2d 145, 137 Ill.Dec. 19, 23, 545 N.E.2d 672, 676 (1989). Both parties agree that elements one, two and four of the above test have been satisfied. Both parties also focus their arguments on whether to satisfy the claim Executive Flight must show that it fully breached its contract with the Marlins because of Plaintiffs' conduct. However, case law suggests the pivotal question is whether Executive Flight has sufficiently pled that the Plaintiff flight attendants intentionally and unjustifiably induced their breach of contract, regardless of severity. See Worrick v. Flora, 133 Ill.App.2d 755, 272 N.E.2d 708,

711 (1971); HPI, 131 Ill.Dec. at 24, 545 N.E.2d at 677; and Mannion v. Stallings & Co., 204 Ill.App.3d 179, 149 Ill.Dec. 438, 443–44, 561 N.E.2d 1134, 1139–40 (1990).

The Restatement provides that one who, "without a privilege to do so, induces or otherwise purposefully causes a third person not to perform a contract with another ... is liable to the other for resulting harm." Worrick, 272 N.E.2d at 711 (citing 4 Restatement of Torts, chap. 37 §766). In intentional interference with contracts cases, courts will recognize a privilege when the defendant was acting to protect an interest which the law deems to be of equal or greater value than plaintiff's contractual rights. HPI, 131 Ill.Dec. at 24, 545 N.E.2d at 677; Mannion, 149 Ill.Dec. at 444, 561 N.E.2d at 1140. Plaintiff has the burden to plead and prove defendant's interference with a contract was intentional and unjustified and must do more than present mere assertions. The claimant must set forth factual allegations from which it can be inferred that defendant's conduct was unjustified. Id.

In this case, Executive Flight has not set forth specific facts alleging Plaintiffs resigned with the intent to interfere with Defendant's contract with the Marlins. Executive Flight also has not alleged any facts to show Plaintiffs were unjustified in tendering their resignation, particularly in light of the employment-at-will presumption. Given that Plaintiffs' interests were not merely proprietary and economic, that it is not alleged they acted for the exclusive purpose to harm or antagonize Executive Flight, and that the telephone call to the catering service caused no damage, this Court finds that the Defendant-counterclaimant has failed to sufficiently allege the necessary elements of the tort of interference with a contract or business expectancy. Thus, Plaintiffs' motion to dismiss Count I is granted.

B. Breach of Contract—Count II

Defendant's second counterclaim is for breach of contract, which turns on the threshold question of whether the employment relationship between Executive Flight and its former employee flight attendants was of such a nature as to overcome a presumption of employment at will. The question of the existence of a contact is a matter of law for determination by the court. Bennett v. Evanston Hospital, 184 Ill.App.3d 1030, 133 Ill.Dec. 113, 540 N.E.2d 979 (1989).

Absent a violation of clearly mandated public policy or a clear understanding to the contrary, employment contracts for indefinite periods are presumed to be terminable at will by either party for any reason or no reason, without cause and without liability. Id. at 1031, 133 Ill.Dec. 113, 540 N.E.2d 979 (citing Barr v. Kelso-Burnett Co., 106 Ill.2d 520, 88 Ill.Dec. 628, 478 N.E.2d 1354 (1985)). However, this presumption can be rebutted by the terms of an explicit contract. To overcome the presumption, a party must demonstrate that a promise of permanent or fixed-duration employment was clear, definite, and supported by valid consideration. Id. citing Lee v. County of Cook, 862 F.2d 139, 142 (7th Cir.1988); Lamaster v. Chicago & N.E. Ill. D.C. of Carpenters, 766 F.Supp. 1497, 1499 (N.D.Ill.1991). Illinois courts have exhibited a certain degree of strictness when applying the "clear and definite" standard. Lamaster at 1504. Expressions of "hopes and intentions," and assertions that must be inferred from circumstances and indirect evidence are insufficient to withstand a motion to dismiss.

Executive Flight contends that an oral promise by Plaintiffs to provide services for a specific duration on April 11th in exchange for compensation in the form of salary and benefits overcomes the presumption of employment at will and that failure to perform such services constitutes a breach of oral contract. Defendant [relies] on Johnson v. George J. Ball, 248 Ill.App.3d 859, 187 Ill.Dec. 634, 638, 617 N.E.2d 1355, 1359 (1993), in which the court held that a plaintiff's allegations were sufficient to state a cause of action for breach of an oral contract to employ plaintiff "through 1991." However, the allegations set forth in that case were more specific and compelling than those presented here. The party alleging existence of a specific-duration contract in Johnson alleged not only that both parties contemplated the project in question to last "through 1991," but also that in reliance on that promise, he left a higher paying position, his wife quit her job, they sold their Michigan home, moved to Illinois, signed a contract to purchase a new home and, therefore, provided adequate consideration for the specific-term employment contract. Id. at 637, 617 N.E.2d at 1358. See also Buian v. J.L. Jacobs and Co., 428 F.2d 531 (7th Cir.1970); Payne v. AHFI/Netherlands, B.V., 522 F.Supp. 18 (N.D.Ill.1980).

In contrast to Johnson, Executive Flight fails to allege specific facts evidencing a clear and definite promise or a bargained-for exchange regarding a fixed-term employment contract. The facts as presented by Executive Flight do not support a conclusion that these parties contemplated or specified a contractual duration of one day, April 11. Conclusory statements that Plaintiffs made an oral promise to provide services on a particular day, or were hired at a monthly or annual salary, if no duration is specified, are insufficient to overcome the at-will presumption. Johnson, 187 Ill.Dec. at 638, 617 N.E.2d at 1359.

At most, the flight from Chicago to Florida on April 9, the catering and cabin preparations, and the absence of any indication on the evening of April 10 at a restaurant gathering that Plaintiff flight attendants planned to not work April 11 provided Executive Flight with an expectation that the employment relationship would continue. However, absent some facts alleging a mutual, clear and explicit agreement supported by adequate consideration to maintain an employment relationship for a fixed duration, this Court cannot find that the Defendant-counterclaimant in this case has overcome the employment-at-will presumption. In the absence of such a contract for employment, the Court grants Plaintiffs' motion to dismiss Defendant's breach of contract counterclaim.

C. Promissory and Equitable Estoppel—Counts III & IV

In Count III Defendants allege that Executive Flight relied to its detriment on Plaintiffs' unambiguous promise to work the April 11, 1993 flight and that Plaintiffs should be held liable for Executive Flight's reliance expenses. In Count IV Defendants allege that Plaintiffs intentionally misled them to believe the flight attendants intended to work on the April 11 flight. The claims are substantially similar and will be combined for the purposes of this discussion.

Illinois at one time maintained a distinction between promissory estoppel and equitable estoppel, but those doctrines today overlap significantly. See, e.g., Geva v. Leo Burnett Co., 931 F.2d 1220, 1223 n.3 (7th Cir.1991). To withstand a motion to dismiss a claim for promissory estoppel, one must sufficiently allege: 1) an unambiguous promise by promisor, 2) upon which the promisee would reasonably and foreseeably rely, 3) and upon which the promisee actually relied, 4) with such reliance resulting in damages. Restatement (Second) Contracts § 90(1) (1981). See also Geva at 1223; Falk v. U.H.H. Home Services Corp., 835 F.Supp. 1078 (N.D.Ill.1993); Quake Cons., Inc. v. American Airlines, Inc., 141 Ill.2d 281, 152 Ill.Dec. 308, 322, 565 N.E.2d 990, 1004 (1990). Promissory estoppel can be invoked in contract and non-contract settings, the promise may be inferred from words and conduct, and in employment situations the alleged promise need not be for any fixed-duration. Falk at 1079–81; Geva at 1223. However, Illinois courts have resisted the use of an overly permissive use of promissory estoppel in employment settings as a means to undermine the presumption of employment at will. Falk at 1080.

Defendants rely on Falk to support their argument and, like the plaintiffs in Falk, the only element Plaintiff flight attendants challenge in this case is whether Defendants sufficiently allege an unambiguous promise given their employment-at-will status. In Falk, the court held that an employee had sufficiently stated a claim for promissory estoppel where she alleged she was informed that a new position in Chicago would increase her responsibilities and rank in the company, require extensive travel and expand her presence in the entire metropolitan area. She met with the Vice President of the company to discuss her potential new job responsibilities, and attached notes from that encounter to her complaint. The plaintiff in Falk had moved from Boston, given up a lucrative position and home in order to adopt new responsibilities in Chicago.

The court found that the plaintiff did not sufficiently allege a promise for fixed-term employment sufficient to overcome the employment-at-will presumption. However, it held that the plaintiff did state a claim regarding a promise for a certain type of employment upon which she relied to her detriment. However, where ambiguity exists such that it becomes uncertain whether a contract exists, the claim will fail. See, e.g., Camosy Inc. v. River Steel Inc., 253 Ill.App.3d 670, 191 Ill.Dec. 706, 709–10, 624 N.E.2d 894, 897–98 (1993); LaBolle v. Metropolitan Sanitary Dist., 253 Ill.App.3d 269, 195 Ill.Dec. 748, 752, 629 N.E.2d 56, 60 (1992).

The Plaintiff flight attendants in this case make the same error as the Defendant employer in Falk; they argue broadly that the "promise" for a promissory estoppel claim must allege "the existence of a promise to [be] employ[ed] for a certain duration." Id. at 1081. While this is not the case, Defendant Executive Flight fails to present a claim that an unambiguous promise was made for anything other than employment for a fixed duration—services on April 11. Given that shortfall and that Defendants have not alleged more than a vague promise or intention to perform particular services on that day, the Court cannot find that Executive Flight has pled an unambiguous promise sufficient to support a promissory or equitable estoppel claim. Therefore, Plaintiffs' motion to dismiss Counts III and IV of Defendant's counterclaims is granted.

CONCLUSION

Based on the reasoning stated above, the Court grants Defendants' partial motion to dismiss the Individual Defendants as parties to Plaintiffs' Title VII and ADEA claims, and grants Plaintiffs' motion to dismiss Defendants' counterclaims Counts I through IV.

The Court has engaged in a lengthy legal discussion of the various claims involved in this matter and is still left with this query: Having established to this Court's satisfaction that they were at-will employees and that their tenure involved such a short period of time, what relief do the plaintiffs see that they are entitled to? The Court wishes to see the parties in chambers to explore this question.

DUNCAN v. NORTHWEST AIRLINES, INC.

208 F.3d 1112 (9th Cir.),
cert. denied, 531 U.S. 1058 (2000)

REINHARDT, Circuit Judge.

In this case, we must determine whether a class-action tort suit brought against Northwest Airlines by some of its flight attendants is preempted by the Airline Deregulation Act. We hold that it is not.

I. BACKGROUND

Julie Duncan, as the named plaintiff, filed a class-action, personal-injury lawsuit against Northwest Airlines in Washington state court. Brought on behalf of non-smoking flight attendants who served as crew members on Northwest's smoking flights to and from Asia, the suit raises a claim based on Northwest's smoking policy. At the time the action was filed, Northwest prohibited smoking on all domestic and most international flights, but permitted smoking on most flights to and from Asia. In her complaint, Duncan argued that, by permitting smoking on most trans-Pacific flights, Northwest breached its duty under state law to provide a safe and healthy work environment for its employees. She further alleged that Northwest's decision to allow smoking on these flights injured the flight attendants by exposing them to secondhand smoke. The complaint sought damages, an injunction, and medical monitoring.

Prior to 1988, nearly every airline permitted smoking on both domestic and international flights. Smoking policies began to change in 1988, when a federal statute banned smoking on some domestic flights. Since then, a combination of statutory prohibitions, international agreements, and voluntary efforts by airlines have made non-smoking domestic and international flights the rule rather than the exception.

Northwest removed the suit to federal court and filed a motion to dismiss, asserting that Duncan's action was preempted by §1305(a)(1) of the Airline Deregulation Act (ADA). The district court granted Northwest's motion and dismissed the case. Duncan appealed. After the appeal was filed, Northwest banned smoking on all trans-Pacific flights.

II. DISCUSSION

On appeal, we must determine whether Duncan's tort suit is preempted by §1305(a)(1) of the ADA. Section 1305(a)(1) provides:

> [N]o state or political subdivision thereof and no interstate agency or other political agency of two or more states shall enact or enforce any law, rule, regulation, standard, or other provision having the force and effect of law relating to the rates, routes or service of any air carrier....

In 1994, section 1305(a)(1) of the ADA was amended and incorporated into the Federal Aviation Administration Authorization Act of 1994. See 49 U.S.C. §41713(b)(1). As amended, the provision reads in relevant part: "[A] State, political subdivision of a State, or political authority of at least 2 States may not enact or enforce a law, regulation, or other provision having the force and effect of law related to a price, route, or service of an air carrier that may provide air transportation under this subpart." Because the minor amendments are non-substantive, for convenience we will continue to refer to the provision as §1305(a)(1) of the ADA.

The scope of preemption under this provision depends on the interpretation of the phrase "relating to the rates, routes or service." When the district court dismissed Duncan's suit, the meaning of this phrase—and hence the scope of preemption under section 1305(a)(1)—was uncertain both in this circuit and others.

While Duncan's appeal was pending, we substantially clarified the scope of §1305(a)(1) preemption in Charas v. Trans World Airlines, Inc., 160 F.3d 1259 (9th Cir.1998) (en banc). In that case, we provided a definitive interpretation of the term "service": we concluded that "Congress used the word 'service' in the phrase 'rates, routes, or service' in the ADA's preemption clause to refer to the prices, schedules, origins and destinations of the point-to-point transportation of passengers, cargo, or mail." Id. at 1261. Accordingly, we interpreted the term "service" narrowly in order to prevent the "preemption of virtually everything an airline does." Id. at 1266.

Given our holding in Charas, it is clear that allowing smoking on Northwest's trans-Pacific flights does not constitute a "service." An airline's decision to permit (or not to permit) smoking on a flight is not a decision dealing with "the frequency and scheduling of transportation, [or] the selection of markets to or from which transportation is provided." Charas, 160 F.3d at 1265–66. Rather, like the decision to offer in-flight beverages, a rule permitting or prohibiting smoking deals with what we termed, for want of a better word, "amenities."

Northwest contends that, even if permitting smoking does not itself constitute a service, Duncan's action is still preempted by § 1305(a)(1) because it "relates to" a "service." The airline's argument proceeds in two parts. First, it contends that the result of permitting Duncan's lawsuit to proceed might be to force Northwest to prohibit smoking on any trans-Pacific flights that originate in Washington State. It argues that this forced prohibition, in turn, might compel Northwest, for economic reasons, to drop its trans-Pacific departures from Washington and reroute its other trans-Pacific flights around the state. The airline argues that this causal relationship between Duncan's tort suit and its provision of "services" renders her claim "related to" a "service."

Northwest's argument about the causal connection between its smoking policy and its ability to profit on the trans-Pacific routes is unpersuasive. As noted above, Northwest stopped allowing smoking on its trans-Pacific flights while Duncan's appeal was pending. In spite of its smoking prohibition, Northwest has not canceled its trans-Pacific flights. Thus, the airline's own business decision demonstrates conclusively that, even if Duncan's suit had forced it to prohibit smoking on flights originating in Washington (and perhaps it did), the airline would not have had to cancel its Washington-based trans-Pacific departures and reroute its other flights.

Moreover, the type of causal relationship to a "service" alleged by Northwest is not sufficient to invoke preemption under § 1305(a)(1). If it were, then, contrary to Charas, almost all personal injury claims would be preempted. This is because all successful tort suits—and certainly all successful class action tort suits—invariably carry with them an economic cost for the defendant airline. Such cases may even, in some instances, cause the airline to decide to make changes in its operations. Charas makes clear, however, that the imposition of liability as a result of a personal injury action does not sufficiently interfere with the objectives of airline deregulation to warrant preemption of the action—in other words, the connection between an award in a tort case and an airline's "services" is simply too tenuous. See 160 F.3d at 1261, 1266; see also Newman v. American Airlines, 176 F.3d 1128, 1131 (9th Cir.1999).

Finally, Northwest argues that Read-Rite Corp. v. Burlington Air Express, 186 F.3d 1190 (9th Cir.1999), somehow compels a different result. Read-Rite, however, provides no support for Northwest's position. Read-Rite concerned the law governing the loss of or damage to goods transported by interstate common carriers. In that case, we held that "state law regulating the scope of air carrier liability for loss or damage to cargo is preempted by the ADA." Id. at 1197. The crux of our holding was that claims arising from damage by common carriers had been governed by a purely federal regime for nearly the entire century. We described that regime as follows: "federal regulation by statute, federal preemption of state regulation, and regulation by federal common law of matters not covered by federal statute." Id. at 1196. Unlike personal injury claims, which state tort law has traditionally governed, federal law governed the claims at issue in Read-Rite prior to the enactment of the ADA. Consequently, Read-Rite's finding of preemption after the ADA's enactment simply maintained the regulatory status quo ante. Because it did not address the question of when preemption within a field that the states have traditionally occupied is appropriate—the question at issue in both Charas and the present case—Read-Rite is of no relevance here.

REVERSED and REMANDED.

Notes

1. In 1930, a nurse named Ellen Church (1904–65) singlehandedly invented the profession of flight attendant:

> Humanitarian, war heroine, and aviation pioneer, Ellen Church dedicated her indomitable spirit to the service of mankind. As the world's first airline stewardess, she created a new and exciting profession for young girls of the twentieth century. Employed in 1930 by United Airlines, she organized the pioneer group, "Sky Girls."
>
> As a young nurse in San Francisco, Miss Church approached officials of Boeing Air Transport, a parent company of United, and proposed that stewardesses be added to flight crews. Her idea was accepted, [and she] and seven other nurses began flying between Chicago and San Francisco on May 15, 1930. Miss Church flew for 18 months. Grounded by injury in an auto accident, she enrolled at the University of Minnesota and earned a bachelor's degree in nursing education.
>
> In December 1942, she took to the air again—this time as a captain in the Army Nurse Corps, Air Evacuation Service. For distinguished work in North Africa, Sicily, England and France, she was presented with the Air Medal. [She also] was nationally honored by United and the air transport industry.

Ellen (Marshall) Church, at www.crescoia.com/ellenchurch.html.

Following the end of World War II, commercial aviation entered a golden age. As a result, during the next two decades many women were drawn to the job of "air hostess," later renamed "stewardess," and its promises of adventure, excitement, and global sightseeing. *See further* Aimée Bratt, *Glamour and Turbulence: I Remember Pan Am, 1966–91* (1996), and Johanna Omelia & Michael Waldcock, *Come Fly With Us: A Global History of the Airline Hostess* (2003). As *Frank* explains, however, the airlines imposed strict age, grooming, marital status, and weight requirements, and becoming pregnant meant automatic dismissal.

In the 1960s, with the sexual revolution sweeping the country, airlines increasingly viewed stewardesses as a way to woo customers from competitors. A provocatively titled best seller further helped to convince the public that "stews" were "easy," *see* Trudy Baker & Rachel Jones, *Coffee, Tea or Me? The Uninhibited Memoirs of Two Airline Stewardesses* (1967), as did the X-rated film *The Stewardesses* (1969), which cost $100,000 to make and grossed $25 million, a particularly remarkable feat given that the film was banned wherever theaters tried to show it. *See further* www.thestewardesses.com.

The industry's sexist attitudes finally began to change in the 1970s as stewardesses took their employers to court, men entered the profession, and the job was restyled "flight attendant." *See further* Stacey S. Baron, Note, *(Un)Lawfully Beautiful: The Legal*

(De)Construction of Female Beauty, 46 B.C. L. Rev. 359 (2005) (discussing, inter alia, *Diaz v. Pan American World Airways, Inc.*, 442 F.2d 385 (5th Cir.), *cert. denied*, 404 U.S. 950 (1971), and *Wilson v. Southwest Airlines Co.*, 517 F. Supp. 292 (N.D. Tex. 1981)). Just as these battles were beginning to bear fruit, however, the May 1980 issue of *Playboy* temporarily set the struggle back by featuring a skimpily dressed flight attendant on its cover with the headline "Stewardesses!—A Glorious Pictorial." (In what later would be recognized as one of history's odd coincidences, the next headline was for an article entitled "America's Islam Connection.")

Today, discrimination suits are more likely to be brought for race (as in *Gordon*) or religion (as in *Rose*) than for gender. But as *Ferris* and *Straka* make all too clear, flight attendants still face sexual hazards in the workplace.

In addition, run-of-the-mill sexism has not totally disappeared. Indeed, it even may be making a comeback. In March 2003, for example, Hooters Air (www.hootersair.com) was founded in Myrtle Beach, South Carolina. Like the famous restaurant of the same name, the airline's ads feature buxom young women dressed in orange shorts and tight white t-shirts and promise to "put the fun back in flying" by providing customers with "two Hooter Girls on every flight."

Similarly, in October 2004, Delta Air Lines fired Ellen Simonetti, an eight-year employee, after she put pictures of herself on her blog "Diary of a Flight Attendant." The photos showed Simonetti wearing her uniform, standing inside a plane, and posing in slightly suggestive poses (some observers, however, felt that Delta actually was trying to send a message that it did not approve of employees having blogs). Simonetti responded by renaming her site "Diary of a Fired Flight Attendant," *see* queenofsky.journalspace.com, and looking for a book deal.

2. As the *Duncan* case points out, secondhand smoke became such a problem for flight attendants forced to work long flights that it eventually led to an international treaty on the subject (*see* Appendix 22). It also prompted flight attendants to file a class-action lawsuit against the tobacco companies that resulted in a historic agreement shifting the burden of proof on causation to the defendants. *See Philip Morris Inc. v. French*, 897 So. 2d 480 (Fla. Dist. Ct. App. 2004).

But even without secondhand smoke, the job of flight attendant is infinitely harder today than in the 1950s and 1960s. Because of larger planes, shorter turnaround times, wage and benefit cuts, surly, drunk, and aggressive passengers (a topic explored more fully in Chapter 4), and workforce reductions (to save money, many airlines now require flight attendants to perform, in addition to their regular duties, such pre- and post-flight chores as collecting tickets and cleaning cabins), flight attendants are working harder, earning less, and receiving fewer thank yous than ever before. *See further* Joann Kuzma Deveny, *99 Ways to Make a Flight Attendant Fly—Off the Handle: A Guide for the Novice or Oblivious Air Traveler* (2003); Rene Foss, *Around the World in a Bad Mood!: Confessions of a Flight Attendant* (2002); Elliott Hester, *Plane Insanity: A Flight Attendant's Tales of Sex, Rage and Queasiness at 30,000 Feet* (2002). *See also* Bill Haltom, *Flying the No-Longer-Friendly Skies*, 41 Tenn B.J. 38 (June 2005) (fondly recalling the service flight attendants used to give), and Joe Sharkey, *Fliers Already Peg 2005 as the Year of Gritted Teeth*, N.Y. Times, Nov. 8, 2005, at C11 (sympathizing with flight attendants but arguing that their workplace hardships are no excuse for the poor service now endured by most passengers).

3. For a further look at flight attendants, see the web sites of the Association of Flight Attendants (www.afanet.org) and the Association of Professional Flight Attendants

(www.apfa.org). For Hollywood's take on them, *see, e.g.*, *Airport 1975* (1974, with Karen Black as a flight attendant who must pilot a 747 after the rest of the crew is killed or incapacitated), *Stewardess School* (1986, with Judy Landers as a flight attendant in training), *Turbulence* (1997, with Lauren Holly as a flight attendant who must play a game of cat-and-mouse with a convicted killer while trying to land a 747), *View From the Top* (2003, with Gwyneth Paltrow as a rookie flight attendant), the 1986–93 ABC sitcom *Perfect Strangers* (which co-starred Rebecca Arthus and Melanie Wilson as flight attendants Mary Anne Spencer and Jennifer Lyons), the 1990–97 NBC sitcom *Wings* (which featured Rebecca Schull as retired flight attendant Fay Cochran), the BBC drama *Mile High* (which premiered in February 2003 and revolves around six flight attendants working for a London budget airline named Fresh!), and the Travel Channel show *Flight Attendant School* (which debuted in January 2006 and follows real-life candidates at Frontier Airlines' training center). *See also* Ron Hogan, *The Stewardess is Flying the Plane! American Films of the 1970s* (2005), and www.theaviarymovie.com (web site of *The Aviary*, a 2005 independent film by real-life flight attendant Silver Tree that seeks to "present[ ] an honest, accurate and entertaining portrayal of our lives in the sky and on the ground.").

Problem 13

Because of her religion, a flight attendant wore a head scarf while on duty. Her boss never asked her to remove it and none of the airline's customers complained. After 9/11, however, she was informed that she could no longer wear it because it was not part of the company's "standard-issue" uniform. Despite explaining to her superiors why she could not comply with their order, they transferred her to a "back office" position where she has no contact with the public. Her salary has not been affected, but she misses dealing with customers and views the transfer as a demotion (the company insists it is merely a lateral move). Given these facts, has she suffered any compensable injury? *See Ali v. Alamo Rent-A-Car, Inc.*, 8 Fed. Appx. 156 (4th Cir.), *cert. denied*, 534 U.S. 944 (2001).

E. COLLECTIVE BARGAINING

AIRLINE LABOR DISRUPTIONS: IS THE RLA STILL ADEQUATE?

Thomas E. Reinert, Jr.
15 Air & Space Law. 4 (Winter 2001)

The legal context for labor relations in the airline industry is provided by the Railway Labor Act (RLA), 45 U.S.C. § 151 et seq. Airlines are subject to the RLA, instead of the National Labor Relations Act (NLRA), 29 U.S.C. § 151 et seq., the federal labor law covering, effectively, all other private employers in the United States. Airlines are under a "railway" labor law as a result of both historical accident and transportation policy. In 1936, when the airline pilot union petitioned Congress for an airline collective bargaining statute, they chose the more established RLA (which was enacted in 1926 and was based on experience under earlier federal railway labor legislation), rather than the newly enacted 1935 NLRA. The RLA was a transportation industry-specific statute that provided a procedural framework for collective bargaining and grievance processing between employers and their unionized employees. In contrast, the NLRA focused more on protecting employees' rights to unionize, and was crafted more for an industrial plant context.

Because it covers essential transportation industries, the RLA is fundamentally less receptive to strikes and other job actions than is the NLRA. The RLA's first general purpose is "to avoid any interruption to commerce or to the operation of any carrier engaged therein...." In contrast, the NLRA's stated aims are protecting the employees' right of self-organization and restoring equality of bargaining power between employers and employees. Under the NLRA, the strike weapon is an acceptable and legally protected aspect of the collective bargaining process.

The basic strategy of the RLA for avoiding strikes and other job actions is deferral. The RLA mandates a collective bargaining process of direct negotiations between the carrier and the union certified to represent a "craft or class" of employees (e.g., pilots, flight attendants, mechanics, etc.). If direct negotiations do not result in an agreement, then the parties must pursue mediation under the auspices of a federal agency, the National Mediation Board (NMB).

The RLA gives the NMB discretion to determine how long the parties remain in mediation, which can be months or even years. When the NMB determines that mediation no longer is likely to prove productive, it issues a "release." The parties are then subject to a 30-day cooling-off period, during which the union cannot strike and the carrier cannot engage in self-help, such as implementing its collective bargaining proposals or locking out its employees. At the end of the cooling-off period, the parties are free to use self-help, unless the president intervenes. The president can establish a presidential emergency board (PEB), which results in an additional cooling-off period, following an investigation and report by the PEB making recommendations for the resolution of the collective bargaining dispute.

The Supreme Court aptly has termed these collective bargaining processes of the RLA as "almost interminable." Detroit & Toledo Shore Line R.R. Co. v. United Transportation Union, 396 U.S. 142, 149, 72 L.R.R.M. (BNA) 2838 (1969). For this reason, full-blown strikes in the airline industry have been relatively rare occurrences in recent history. But, also as a result, airline labor relations often are characterized by extended periods of union and employee dissatisfaction, during which unlawful job actions occur.

Union Strategy

From the union perspective, the deferral of job actions under the RLA creates both leverage and constituent problems. In bargaining, the union is unable to apply immediate economic pressure to the employer to make it acquiesce to bargaining demands. The union must depend, instead, on the threat of a powerful but deferred strike weapon. The slow pace of negotiations can frustrate the union membership and lead to allegations by these constituents that the union is not sufficiently aggressive in its bargaining position. In times of increasing economic expectations by the membership, pressure on the union leadership exists to develop alternative strategies for pressuring the employer to be more receptive to union bargaining demands.

In response, airline unions have adopted a number of tactics for concerted actions by employee members that disrupt airline operations but make it difficult to place blame (and injunctive relief) on the unions. Traditional union tactics used in circumstances where the strike weapon is illegal, such as the public sector, have included sickouts, slowdowns, and work-to-the-rule. During deregulation, airline unions have refined these techniques. Some examples are: WOE (withdrawal of enthusiasm), the campaign of delayed flights used by Texas International pilots; and CHAOS (create havoc about our system), the tactic of intermittently walking off flights used by Alaska Airlines flight attendants.

Such tactics occur during the collective bargaining process, often in an escalating fashion, to pressure the employer to agree to union bargaining demands. However, this strategy also typically involves a disavowal of union responsibility and statements by the union leadership that these "grass roots" employee actions illustrate the strength of the membership's commitment to the bargaining issue.

Carrier Response

A strong perception exists among carriers, substantiated by the recent litigation record, that these union tactics have become pandemic during the last several years. A few examples illustrate the frequency and severity of the impact of these tactics:

> 1) United Airlines' mechanics, represented by the IAM, have undertaken a variety of actions to disrupt and slow down airline operations. United obtained a TRO on November 17, 2000, which led to improved operations. United v. International Ass'n of Machinists, No. 00-CV-7265 (N.D. Ill. 2000). The court later denied a preliminary injunction, a decision on appeal to the Seventh Circuit.
>
> 2) Northwest Airlines obtained a TRO in November enjoining illegal self-help by its mechanics, represented by the Aircraft Mechanics Fraternal Association (AMFA). AMFA v. Northwest Airlines, No. CV 00-2446 (D. Minn. 2000).
>
> 3) ComAir moved for contempt sanctions against its pilots, represented by ALPA, who were enjoined last winter from concerted refusal to bid open time and from making excessive maintenance write-ups. ComAir v. ALPA, No. 99-250 (E.D. Ky. 1999).
>
> 4) Alaska Airlines filed for a TRO on May 5, 1999, when its mechanics, represented by AMFA, undertook an illegal work slowdown. Alaska Airlines, Inc. v. AMFA, No. C99-0713 (W.D. Wash. 1999). The case settled with the termination of the slowdown.
>
> 5) ABX Air obtained a TRO, and then a preliminary injunction, against its Teamsters-represented pilots' concerted refusal to bid open flying time, first to strengthen the union's position during bargaining and then to protest the termination of a pilot. ABX Air, Inc. v. Airline Prof. Ass'n, Int'l Bhd. of Teamsters, No. C-1-97-812 (W.D. Ohio 1999).
>
> 6) TWA obtained TROs against its mechanics, who staged an illegal two-hour strike during peak travel times in April 1998, and its flight attendants, who staged an illegal sick-out over the Christmas holiday in 1998. The IAM represented both groups of employees. TWA v. International Ass'n of Machinists, No. 98-CV-3369 (E.D.N.Y. 1998).

Among the factors that likely account, in part, for this trend are: increased employee bargaining expectations during the long economic expansion; the rise in dissident groups challenging union leadership; the availability of the Internet and electronic communications to foment political opposition and to spread news of disruptive tactics; and the consolidation of the airline industry.

Airlines faced with these tactics have a strategic choice. An airline can adapt its operations to minimize the impact of the employees' actions while pursuing a labor relations resolution. Alternatively, pursuing a legal action against the union can disrupt or delay such a labor relations resolution if it is available. If, however, a prompt labor relations resolution is not available, and there is substantial impact on an airline's operations, then the carrier ultimately must pursue a federal court action to enjoin the disruption.

KAUFMAN v. ALLIED PILOTS ASSOCIATION

274 F.3d 197 (5th Cir. 2001),
cert. denied, 535 U.S. 1034 (2002)

HIGGINBOTHAM, Circuit Judge.

A union of airline pilots violated the order of a federal court by continuing its work slowdown. The union has since paid substantial fines for violating the order and now faces suits seeking money damages under state law for the stoppage damages caused by the slowdown activity that violated the court order. These claimants attempt to run their state claims around "Garmon preemption" under an argument that state law would not here interfere with the federal labor machinery and its distinct remedial schemes for labor peace because the conflict complained of violates a federal court order. At the same time the state law claimants argue that they are not seeking to supplement the federal order by their suits. [District Judge Jorge A. Solis] accepted these arguments. We do not and reverse. We are persuaded that the claims are preempted under the Garmon doctrine and do not reach the question of preemption under the Airline Deregulation Act.

I

The Allied Pilots Association is the exclusive bargaining agent for the pilots of American Airlines, Inc. From February 6 through February 9, 1999 the APA staged a "sick-out"—an organized false reporting of illness to effect a work stoppage. On February 10, American sought and received a temporary restraining order from the United States District Court for the Northern District of Texas against the APA. The TRO, among other things, required the APA to make "all reasonable efforts" to end the sick-out. The APA manifestly did not do so, and on February 12, the trial judge heard American's motion to hold the APA in contempt. Ultimately, the district court awarded American $45 million in compensatory damages, a ruling which was upheld by this Court. [See] Am. Airlines, Inc. v. Allied Pilots Ass'n, 53 F.Supp.2d 909, 913 (N.D.Tex.1999), aff'd, 228 F.3d 574, 586–87 (5th Cir.2000), cert. denied, 531 U.S. 1191, 121 S.Ct. 1190, 149 L.Ed.2d 106 (2001).

This is a class action brought against the APA to recover economic damages claimed by over 300,000 displaced passengers as a result of the sick-out. The plaintiffs originally asserted claims under (1) the Railway Labor Act; (2) the Racketeer Influenced and Corrupt Organizations Act; (3) state common law claims of civil conspiracy, negligence per se, and tortious interference with contract. [T]he district court dismissed all claims with prejudice except a state claim of tortious interference with contract arising from post-TRO conduct of the APA. Finding that this claim was not preempted by federal law, the district court dismissed the claim without prejudice to its being refiled in state court. The APA now appeals that decision.

II

A

We review questions of federal preemption de novo, including Garmon preemption, which gets its name from the Supreme Court's ruling in San Diego Building Trades Council v. Garmon, 359 U.S. 236, 79 S.Ct. 773, 3 L.Ed.2d 775 (1959). Garmon preemption, first applied in the context of the National Labor Relations Act, 29 U.S.C. § 151 et seq., has been extended to the RLA. Brotherhood of R.R. Trainmen v. Jacksonville Terminal Co., 394 U.S. 369, 383, 89 S.Ct. 1109, 22 L.Ed.2d 344 (1969).

In Garmon, an employer sued a union in state court to recover damages from picketing that allegedly violated the National Labor Relations Act. The Court held that this state remedy was preempted by federal law because the state courts must yield to the exclusive jurisdiction of the NLRB—even when the NLRB has declined to take jurisdiction. Garmon, 359 U.S. at 238, 79 S.Ct. 773. Preemption is necessary because "the exercise of state power over a particular area of activity threaten[s] interference with the clearly indicated policy of industrial relations...." Id. at 243, 79 S.Ct. 773. Concerned with "conflict in its broadest sense" the Court eschewed a focus on the type of state regulation or claim, and adopted an approach that looks to the "nature of the activities which the States have sought to regulate." Id. Garmon has broad scope, and requires federal preemption of state causes of action "if they attach liability to conduct that is arguably protected ... or arguably prohibited" by federal labor relations law. Mobile Mechanical Contractors Ass'n, Inc. v. Carlough, 664 F.2d 481, 487 (5th Cir.1981).

Garmon itself recognized two exceptions to preemption. First, some conduct will "touch[ ] interests so deeply rooted in local feeling and responsibility that ... [the Court] could not infer Congress had deprived the States of the power to act." Garmon, 359 U.S. at 244, 79 S.Ct. 773. The classic example of this exception, provided by the Court in Garmon itself, is that of union activities involving violence. The second exception is for matters only of "peripheral concern" to federal labor relations law. Garmon, 359 U.S. at 243, 79 S.Ct. 773. Neither of these exceptions apply here. The sick-out was non-violent and certainly, irrespective of the TRO issue, cannot be characterized as "peripheral" to labor relations law, since it is itself a work stoppage, one which a district court found to be prohibited by the RLA.

The [Supreme] Court has explicitly rejected a formalistic implementation of Garmon, and invited a balancing of state interests and federal regulatory interests in analyzing the preemption question. Farmer v. United Brotherhood of Carpenters and Joiners of Am., 430 U.S. 290, 297, 97 S.Ct. 1056, 51 L.Ed.2d 338 (1977). The Court has thus refused to apply Garmon preemption where "it is safe to presume that judicial supervision [by the states] will not disserve the interests promoted by the federal labor statutes." Motor Coach Employees v. Lockridge, 403 U.S. 274, 297–98, 91 S.Ct. 1909, 29 L.Ed.2d 473 (1971); see also Windfield v. Groen Div. Dover Corp., 890 F.2d 764, 766 (5th Cir.1989).

At the same time, Garmon preemption is not confined to state claims made by parties to the labor relationship—third-party claims may also be preempted, because they similarly threaten the balance of labor-management relations. United Mine Workers v. Gibbs, 383 U.S. 715, 718–20, 86 S.Ct. 1130, 16 L.Ed.2d 218 (1966).

In Wisconsin Department of Industry, Labor & Human Relations v. Gould, Inc., 475 U.S. 282, 106 S.Ct. 1057, 89 L.Ed.2d 223 (1986), the Court reaffirmed the Garmon preemption principle as "prevent[ing] states not only from setting forth standards of conduct inconsistent with the substantive requirements of the NLRA, but also from providing their own regulatory or judicial remedies for conduct prohibited or arguably prohibited by the Act." Id. at 286, 106 S.Ct. 1057. In Gould the Court struck down a Wisconsin statute that prevented the state from doing business with companies that had been judicially determined to have committed three separate violations of the NLRA within a five year period. "That Wisconsin has chosen to use its spending power rather than its police power in enacting the debarment statute does not significantly lessen the inherent potential for conflict when two separate remedies are brought to bear on the same activity." Id. at 289, 106 S.Ct. 1057. Garmon preemption must extend to all types of state regulation that conflicts with federal labor relations law, whether that is by state statute, or state judicial supervision, whether in litigation between parties to the labor relationship or between downstream injured persons and parties to the labor relationship.

B

We have previously stated that Garmon preemption is required when a state cause of action poses "a serious risk of conflict with national labor policy." Carlough, 664 F.2d at 487. The [Supreme] Court has directed that we look not to the effect on labor-management relations of allowing a particular claim to proceed, but rather to conflict in the "broadest sense." Garmon, 359 U.S. at 242, 79 S.Ct. 773. Gould reminds us that adding state remedies or penalties to the mix would be a "conflict" necessitating preemption. Gould, 475 U.S. at 286, 106 S.Ct. 1057 (quoting Garmon, 359 U.S. at 247, 79 S.Ct. 773).

The plaintiffs take a narrow view of what constitutes such a conflict and argue that the federal and state legal regimes cannot be in conflict in this case, since a violation of the TRO is, of course, a violation of federal law. If the two regimes are not contradictory, they reason, there can be no preemption. This argument cannot stand in light of Gould. In Gould the plaintiff was being punished by the state remedial scheme for its violations of federal labor law. There was no contradiction between the two regimes, only a supplementation of the federal remedial scheme by the state. Therefore, the plaintiffs' niggardly view of "conflict" itself conflicts with the Supreme Court's decision in Gould and must be rejected.

Garmon preemption does not depend on the merits of an adjudication of the conduct's legality under federal labor law—both prohibited and protected conduct are shielded from liability under state law. Plaintiffs argue, however, and the district court agreed, that the TRO put the APA on notice that its conduct was illegal, and therefore Garmon preemption is not needed to vindicate the goals of federal labor law. We must disagree—if conduct is clearly protected or prohibited by federal labor law, to our eyes the case for preemption is stronger. Gould, 475 U.S. at 283–84, 106 S.Ct. 1057. Consequentially, the issuance of the TRO, indicating that the sick-out was likely to be found illegal under the RLA, only enhances the case for preemption of the state claim here. The concern of Garmon is not so much with the righting of labor wrongs, the concern of the labor relations laws themselves, as with the uniformity and singularity of remedy provided by federal law. It is a national labor policy—as this case makes vivid.

The district court also found that attaching liability to post-TRO conduct that violates state law will not meaningfully disrupt labor-management relations—that is, that it will not seriously harm the federal regulatory scheme for labor relations. Garmon preemption requires the balancing of state interests with federal regulatory interests. However, irrespective of the state interest in protecting private parties from interference with their freedom of contract, the activities here are so fundamental that Garmon preemption must immunize them from state tort liability if the RLA structure is to be preserved. While courts have refused to apply Garmon preemption to state tort claims that served substantial state interests and did not threaten interference with the federal regulatory scheme, this is not our case. Slicing the claim into before and after the TRO does not change the reality that the state law is being asked to take hold of the same controversy as the federal labor laws.

Finally, we are not persuaded by the plaintiffs' effort to distinguish the pre-TRO conduct of the APA from its post-TRO conduct. The plaintiffs argued in the district court that their claims based upon pre-TRO conduct were not Garmon preempted, but the district court held that those claims were preempted, and the plaintiffs do not appeal that determination.

"It is the conduct being regulated, not the formal description of governing legal standards, that is the proper focus of concern." Lockridge, 403 U.S. at 292, 91 S.Ct. 1909. The existence of a TRO does not transform conduct constituting a work-stoppage, and therefore central to federal labor relations law, into conduct falling outside of the ambit of Garmon. We note also that any effort to characterize this suit as arising out of a violation of the TRO encounters an additional blockade—the plaintiffs are not entitled to any remedy for violation of a TRO to which they are not a party. Northside Realty Associates, Inc. v. United States, 605 F.2d 1348, 1356–57 (5th Cir.1979) (holding that compensatory damages for nonparties could not be granted as part of Government's remedy in civil contempt proceeding against real estate corporation).

III

The APA also argues that the plaintiffs' claims are preempted by the Airline Deregulation Act. Since we have concluded that those claims are Garmon preempted, we need not reach the question of ADA preemption.

IV

Because the plaintiffs' state law claims of tortious interference with contract are Garmon preempted, we REMAND this case to the district court and instruct that the claims be DISMISSED with prejudice.

HAWAIIAN AIRLINES, INC. v. NORRIS

512 U.S. 246 (1994)

Justice BLACKMUN delivered the opinion of the Court.

This action involves the scope of federal pre-emption under the Railway Labor Act (RLA), 45 U.S.C. § 151 et seq. The RLA, which was extended in 1936 to cover the airline industry, see Act of Apr. 10, 1936, ch. 166, 49 Stat. 1189; 45 U.S.C. §§ 181–188, sets up a mandatory arbitral mechanism to handle disputes "growing out of grievances or out of the interpretation or application of agreements concerning rates of pay, rules, or working conditions," 45 U.S.C. § 153 First (I). The question in this case is whether an aircraft mechanic who claims that he was discharged for refusing to certify the safety of a plane that he considered unsafe and for reporting his safety concerns to the Federal Aviation Administration may pursue available state-law remedies for wrongful discharge, or whether he may seek redress only through the RLA's arbitral mechanism. We hold that the RLA does not pre-empt his state-law causes of action.

I

Respondent Grant Norris is an aircraft mechanic licensed by the Federal Aviation Administration (FAA). His aircraft mechanic's license authorizes him to approve an airplane and return it to service after he has made, supervised, or inspected certain repairs performed on that plane. See Certification: Airmen Other Than Flight Crewmembers, 14 CFR §§65.85 and 65.87 (1987). If he were to approve any aircraft on which the repairs did not conform to FAA safety regulations, the FAA could suspend or revoke his license. See Maintenance, Preventive Maintenance, Rebuilding and Alteration, 14 CFR §43.12 (1992).

On February 2, 1987, respondent was hired by petitioner Hawaiian Airlines, Inc. (HAL). Many of the terms of his employment were governed by a collective-bargaining agreement (CBA) negotiated between the carrier and the International Association of Machinists and Aerospace Workers. Under the CBA, respondent's duties included inspecting and repairing all parts of a plane and its engine. On July 15, 1987, during a routine preflight inspection of a DC-9 plane, he noticed that one of the tires was worn. When he removed the wheel, respondent discovered that the axle sleeve, which should have been mirror smooth, was scarred and grooved. This damaged sleeve could cause the landing gear to fail. Respondent recommended that the sleeve be replaced, but his supervisor ordered that it be sanded and returned to the plane. This was done, and the plane flew as scheduled. At the end of the shift, respondent refused to sign the maintenance record to certify that the repair had been performed satisfactorily and that the airplane was fit to fly. See 14 CFR §43.9(a) (1992). The supervisor immediately suspended him pending a termination hearing. Respondent immediately went home and called the FAA to report the problem with the sleeve. In response, the FAA initiated a comprehensive investigation, proposed a civil penalty of $964,000 against HAL, proposed the revocation of the license of the supervisor who terminated respondent, and ultimately settled all charges for a substantial fine.

Respondent then invoked the grievance procedure outlined in the CBA, and a "Step 1" grievance hearing was held on July 31, 1987. Petitioner HAL accused respondent of insubordination, claiming that his refusal to sign the record violated the CBA's provision that an aircraft mechanic "may be required to sign work records in connection with the work he performs." Respondent relied on the CBA's guarantees that an employee may not be discharged without just cause and may not be disciplined for refusing to perform work that is in violation of health or safety laws. The hearing officer terminated respondent for insubordination.

Still conforming to the CBA procedures, respondent appealed his termination, seeking a "Step 3" grievance hearing. Before this hearing took place, HAL offered to reduce respondent's punishment to suspension without pay, but warned him that "any further instance of failure to perform [his] duties in a responsible manner" could result in discharge. Respondent did not respond to this offer, nor, apparently, did he take further steps to pursue his grievance through the CBA procedures.

On December 18, 1987, respondent filed suit against HAL in Hawaii Circuit Court. His complaint included two wrongful-discharge torts—discharge in violation of the public policy expressed in the Federal Aviation Act of 1958 and implementing regulations, and discharge in violation of Hawaii's Whistleblower Protection Act, Haw.Rev.Stat. §§378-61 to 378-69 (1988). He also alleged that HAL had breached the CBA agreement. HAL removed the action to the United States District Court for the District of Hawaii, which dismissed the breach-of-contract claim as pre-empted by the RLA, and remanded the other claims to the state trial court. The trial court then dismissed respondent's claim of discharge in violation of public policy, holding that it, too, was pre-empted by the RLA's provision of exclusive arbitral procedures. The state court certified its order as final to permit respondent to take an immediate appeal.

In the meantime, respondent had filed a second lawsuit in state court, naming as defendants three of HAL's officers who allegedly directed, confirmed, or ratified the claimed retaliatory discharge. He again sought relief for, among other things, discharge in violation of public policy and of the Hawaii Whistleblower Protection Act. The Hawaii trial court dismissed these two counts as pre-empted by the RLA and certified the case for immediate appeal.

The Supreme Court of Hawaii reversed in both cases, concluding that the RLA did not pre-empt respondent's state tort actions. Norris v. Hawaiian Airlines, Inc., 74 Haw. 235, 842 P.2d 634 (1992); 74 Haw. 648, 847 P.2d 263 (1993). That court concluded that the plain language of § 153 First (I) does not support pre-emption of disputes independent of a labor agreement, 74 Haw., at 251, 842 P.2d, at 642, and interpreted the opinion in Consolidated Rail Corporation (Conrail) v. Railway Labor Executives' Assn., 491 U.S. 299, 109 S.Ct. 2477, 105 L.Ed.2d 250 (1989), to limit RLA pre-emption to "disputes involving contractually defined rights." 74 Haw., at 250, 842 P.2d, at 642. The court rejected petitioners' argument that the retaliatory discharge claims were pre-empted because determining whether HAL discharged respondent for insubordination, and thus for just cause, required construing the CBA. The court pointed to Lingle v. Norge Div. of Magic Chef, Inc., 486 U.S. 399, 108 S.Ct. 1877, 100 L.Ed.2d 410 (1988), a case involving § 301 of the Labor-Management Relations Act, 1947 (LMRA), 29 U.S.C. § 185, in which the Court held that a claim of wrongful termination in retaliation for filing a state worker's compensation claim did not require interpretation of a CBA, but depended upon purely factual questions concerning the employee's conduct and the employer's motive. Because the same was true in this action, said the Supreme Court of Hawaii, respondent's state tort claims were not pre-empted.

We granted certiorari in these consolidated cases, 510 U.S. 1083, 114 S.Ct. 908, 127 L.Ed.2d 97 (1994).

II

A

Whether federal law pre-empts a state law establishing a cause of action is a question of congressional intent. See Allis-Chalmers Corp. v. Lueck, 471 U.S. 202, 208, 105 S.Ct. 1904, 1909, 85 L.Ed.2d 206 (1985). Pre-emption of employment standards "within the traditional police power of the State" "should not be lightly inferred." Fort Halifax Packing Co. v. Coyne, 482 U.S. 1, 21, 107 S.Ct. 2211, 2222, 96 L.Ed.2d 1 (1987); see also Hillsborough County v. Automated Medical Laboratories, Inc., 471 U.S. 707, 715, 105 S.Ct. 2371, 2376, 85 L.Ed.2d 714 (1985) (a federal statute will be read to supersede a State's historic powers only if this is " 'the clear and manifest purpose of Congress' ").

Congress' purpose in passing the RLA was to promote stability in labor-management relations by providing a comprehensive framework for resolving labor disputes. Atchison, T. & S.F.R. Co. v. Buell, 480 U.S. 557, 562, 107 S.Ct. 1410, 1414, 94 L.Ed.2d 563 (1987); see also 45 U.S.C. § 151a. To realize this goal, the RLA establishes a mandatory arbitral mechanism for "the prompt and orderly settlement" of two classes of disputes. 45 U.S.C. § 151a. The first class, those concerning "rates of pay, rules or working conditions," ibid., are deemed "major" disputes. Major disputes relate to " 'the formation of collective [bargaining] agreements or efforts to secure them.' " Conrail, 491 U.S., at 302,

109 S.Ct., at 2480, quoting Elgin, J. & E.R. Co. v. Burley, 325 U.S. 711, 723, 65 S.Ct. 1282, 1290, 89 L.Ed. 1886 (1945). The second class of disputes, known as "minor" disputes, "gro[w] out of grievances or out of the interpretation or application of agreements covering rates of pay, rules, or working conditions." 45 U.S.C. § 151a. Minor disputes involve "controversies over the meaning of an existing collective bargaining agreement in a particular fact situation." Trainmen v. Chicago R. & I.R. Co., 353 U.S. 30, 33, 77 S.Ct. 635, 637, 1 L.Ed.2d 622 (1957). Thus, "major disputes seek to create contractual rights, minor disputes to enforce them." Conrail, 491 U.S., at 302, 109 S.Ct., at 2480, citing Burley, 325 U.S., at 723, 65 S.Ct., at 1289.

Petitioners contend that the conflict over respondent's firing is a minor dispute. If so, it must be resolved only through the RLA mechanisms, including the carrier's internal dispute-resolution processes and an adjustment board established by the employer and the unions. See 45 U.S.C. § 184; Buell, 480 U.S., at 563, 107 S.Ct., at 1414; Conrail, 491 U.S., at 302, 109 S.Ct., at 2480. Thus, a determination that respondent's complaints constitute a minor dispute would pre-empt his state-law actions.

B

The Court's inquiry into the scope of minor disputes begins, of course, with the text of the statute. Petitioners point out that the statute defines minor disputes to include "disputes ... growing out of grievances, or out of the interpretation or application of [CBA's]." Petitioners argue that this disjunctive language must indicate that "grievances" means something other than labor-contract disputes, else the term "grievances" would be superfluous. Accordingly, petitioners suggest that "grievances" should be read to mean all employment-related disputes, including those based on statutory or common law. Even if we were persuaded that the word "or" carried this weight, but cf., United States v. Olano, 507 U.S. 725, 732, 113 S.Ct. 1770, 1777, 123 L.Ed.2d 508 (1993) (reading "error or defect" to create one category of "error"), citing United States v. Young, 470 U.S. 1, 15, n.12, 105 S.Ct. 1038, 1046, n.12, 84 L.Ed.2d 1 (1985); McNally v. United States, 483 U.S. 350, 358–359, 107 S.Ct. 2875, 2880–2881, 97 L.Ed.2d 292 (1987) (second phrase in disjunctive added simply to make the meaning of the first phrase "unmistakable"), petitioners' interpretation produces an overlap not unlike the one it purports to avoid. Their expansive definition of "grievances" necessarily encompasses disputes growing out of "the interpretation or application" of CBA's. Thus, in attempting to save the term "grievances" from superfluity, petitioners would make the phrase after the "or" mere surplusage.

We think it more likely that "grievances," like disputes over "the interpretation or application" of CBA's, refers to disagreements over how to give effect to the bargained-for agreement. The use of "grievance" to refer to a claim arising out of a CBA is common in the labor-law context in general, see, e.g., Paperworkers v. Misco, Inc., 484 U.S. 29, 36, 108 S.Ct. 364, 370, 98 L.Ed.2d 286 (1987), and it has been understood in this way in the RLA context. See H.R.Rep. No. 1944, 73d Cong., 2d Sess., 2–3 (1934) (referring to RLA settlement of "minor disputes known as 'grievances,' which develop from the interpretation and/or application of the contracts between the labor unions and the carriers"). Significantly, the adjustment boards charged with administration of the minor-dispute provisions have understood these provisions as pertaining only to disputes invoking contract-based rights. See, e.g., NRAB Fourth Div.Award No. 4548 (1987) (function of the National Rail Adjustment Board (Board) is to decide disputes in accordance with the controlling CBA); NRAB Third Div. Award No. 24348 (1983) (issues not related to the interpretation or application of contracts are outside the Board's authority); NRAB

Third Div. Award No. 19790 (1973) ("[T]his Board lacks jurisdiction to enforce rights created by State or Federal Statutes and is limited to questions arising out of interpretations and application of Railway Labor Agreements"); Northwest Airlines/Airline Pilots Assn., Int'l System Bd. of Adjustment, Decision of June 28, 1972, p. 13 ("[B]oth the traditional role of the arbitrator and admonitions of the courts require the Board to refrain from attempting to construe any of the provisions of the [RLA]"); United Airlines, Inc., 48 LA 727, 733 (BNA) (1967) ("The jurisdiction of this System Board does not extend to interpreting and applying the Civil Rights Act").

Accordingly, we believe that the most natural reading of the term "grievances" in this context is as a synonym for disputes involving the application or interpretation of a CBA. See Webster's Third New International Dictionary 1585 (1986) (the word "or" may be used to indicate "the synonymous, equivalent, or substitutive character of two words or phrases"). Nothing in the legislative history of the RLA or other sections of the statute undermines this conclusion. But even accepting that § 151a is susceptible of more than one interpretation, no proposed interpretation demonstrates a clear and manifest congressional purpose to create a regime that broadly pre-empts substantive protections extended by the States, independent of any negotiated labor agreement.

C

Our case law confirms that the category of minor disputes contemplated by § 151a are those that are grounded in the CBA. We have defined minor disputes as those involving the interpretation or application of existing labor agreements. See, e.g., Conrail, 491 U.S., at 305, 109 S.Ct., at 2482 ("The distinguishing feature of [a minor dispute] is that the dispute may be conclusively resolved by interpreting the existing [CBA]"); Pittsburgh & Lake Erie R. Co. v. Railway Labor Executives Assn., 491 U.S. 490, 501, n.4, 109 S.Ct. 2584, 2592, n.4, 105 L.Ed.2d 415 (1989) ("Minor disputes are those involving the interpretation or application of existing contracts"); Trainmen, 353 U.S., at 33, 77 S.Ct., at 637 (minor disputes are "controversies over the meaning of an existing collective bargaining agreement"); Slocum v. Delaware, L. & W.R. Co., 339 U.S. 239, 243, 70 S.Ct. 577, 579, 94 L.Ed. 795 (1950) (RLA arbitral mechanism is meant to provide remedies for "adjustment of railroad-employee disputes growing out of the interpretation of existing agreements").

Moreover, we have held that the RLA's mechanism for resolving minor disputes does not pre-empt causes of action to enforce rights that are independent of the CBA. More than 60 years ago, the Court rejected a railroad's argument that the existence of the RLA arbitration scheme pre-empted a state statute regulating the number of workers required to operate certain equipment. Missouri Pacific R. Co. v. Norwood, 283 U.S. 249, 258, 51 S.Ct. 458, 462, 75 L.Ed. 1010 (1931) ("No analysis or discussion of the provisions of the Railway Labor Act of 1926 is necessary to show that it does not conflict with the Arkansas statutes under consideration"). Not long thereafter, the Court rejected a claim that the RLA pre-empted an order by the Illinois Commerce Commission requiring cabooses on all trains; the operative CBA required cabooses only on some of the trains. Terminal Railroad Assn. of St. Louis v. Trainmen, 318 U.S. 1, 63 S.Ct. 420, 87 L.Ed. 571 (1943). Although the Court assumed that a railroad adjustment board would have jurisdiction under the RLA over this dispute, id., at 6, 63 S.Ct., at 423, it concluded that the state law was enforceable nonetheless[.] Thus, under Norwood, substantive protections provided by state law, independent of whatever labor agreement might govern, are not pre-empted under the RLA.

Although Norwood and Terminal Railroad involved state workplace safety laws, the Court has taken a consistent approach in the context of state actions for wrongful discharge. In Andrews v. Louisville & Nashville R. Co., 406 U.S. 320, 92 S.Ct. 1562, 32 L.Ed.2d 95 (1972), the Court held that a state-law claim of wrongful termination was pre-empted, not because the RLA broadly pre-empts state-law claims based on discharge or discipline, but because the employee's claim was firmly rooted in a breach of the CBA itself. He asserted no right independent of that agreement[.] Here, in contrast, the CBA is not the "only source" of respondent's right not to be discharged wrongfully. In fact, the "only source" of the right respondent asserts in this action is state tort law. Wholly apart from any provision of the CBA, petitioners had a state-law obligation not to fire respondent in violation of public policy or in retaliation for whistle-blowing. The parties' obligation under the RLA to arbitrate disputes arising out of the application or interpretation of the CBA did not relieve petitioners of this duty.

III

Accordingly, we agree with the Supreme Court of Hawaii that respondent's claims for discharge in violation of public policy and in violation of the Hawaii Whistleblower Protection Act are not pre-empted by the RLA, and we affirm that court's judgment.

AIRLINE PILOTS ASSOCIATION, INTERNATIONAL, AFL-CIO v. TACA INTERNATIONAL AIRLINES, S.A.

748 F.2d 965 (5th Cir. 1984),
cert. denied, 471 U.S. 1100 (1985)

POLITZ, Circuit Judge.

When TACA International Airlines, S.A. (TACA), in the midst of collective bargaining negotiations, noticed its intent to relocate its pilot base from New Orleans to El Salvador and to impose unilaterally a new labor contract on its employees, the Airline Pilots Association (ALPA) invoked the Railway Labor Act, 45 U.S.C. §§151–188, and petitioned for injunctive relief. Finding TACA in violation of sections 2, 5 and 6 of the Railway Labor Act, 45 U.S.C. §§152, 155 and 156, the district court entered a temporary restraining order followed, after hearing, by a preliminary and permanent injunction prohibiting TACA from relocating the pilot base, unilaterally changing terms of employment, recruiting replacement pilots and interfering with the pilots' choice of ALPA as their bargaining agent.

TACA appeals, joined by the nation [of] El Salvador as amicus curiae, contending that its actions are authorized by the 1982 Air Transportation Agreement between the United States and El Salvador. TACA further maintains that the act of state doctrine precludes judicial intervention in the controversy and, in any event, its violations of United States law, specifically the Railway Labor Act, are excused by the foreign compulsion defense. Finding no merit in any contention advanced and concluding that the injunction was properly granted, we affirm.

Facts

TACA is incorporated under the laws of El Salvador and four-fifths of its stock is controlled by Salvadorans. The airline flies from El Salvador to Mexico, various nations in Central America, Miami, New Orleans, Houston and Los Angeles. Approximately

62% of the pilots are Salvadoran nationals, many are American citizens and more than one-half live in the United States. All TACA pilots are members of ALPA and regardless of nationality, residence or seniority, all have been based in New Orleans since 1949 when TACA first instituted service between El Salvador and New Orleans. Since 1968, TACA and ALPA have executed successive collective bargaining agreements under the Railway Labor Act.

In 1969, shortly after the first agreement was reached, TACA and ALPA were involved in litigation very similar to that now before the court. At that time the government of El Salvador requested TACA to relocate the pilot base from New Orleans to El Salvador. When TACA began relocation efforts, ALPA sought injunctive relief, maintaining that if the relocation came to fruition the collective bargaining agreement would be abrogated by Salvadoran law which would bar ALPA's representation of the pilots. The district court agreed and an appropriate injunction issued. On appeal we affirmed, holding in the process that the pilot base dispute was a "major" dispute subject to the court's jurisdiction and not a "minor" dispute resolvable by the Railway Labor Act's adjustment mechanism. Ruby v. TACA International Airlines, S.A., 439 F.2d 1359 (5th Cir.1971).

Since our decision in Ruby v. TACA, notable events have occurred which make the present factual situation different from that earlier presented. We must determine whether those changes mandate a result different from that reached in 1971.

In October 1979, TACA and ALPA entered into the most recent collective bargaining agreement, amendable as of December 31, 1983. On April 19, 1982, the governments of the United States and El Salvador executed a civil aviation agreement designed to regulate and promote air transportation between the two countries. In October of 1983, TACA and ALPA, in accordance with the terms of the collective bargaining agreement, began negotiations looking to the amendment and continuation of the current agreement.

Events continued. On December 20, 1983, El Salvador adopted a new constitution. Article 110, ¶ 4 of that constitution provides in pertinent part:

> Salvadoran public service companies will have their work center and base of operation in El Salvador.

The following day, officials from the Salvadoran Ministry of Labor ordered TACA to move its pilot base to El Salvador. TACA immediately notified its pilots that the pilot base would be moved to El Salvador, that new, individual contracts including substantial changes were to be executed and that ALPA would no longer be recognized as the pilots' bargaining agent. The pilots were given until December 30, 1983 to accept the new terms or lose their employment with TACA. Meanwhile, TACA began advertising for new pilots, preferably Salvadoran, to fly the airline's equipment. ALPA reacted to TACA's actions by seeking the injunctive relief described above.

Analysis

We note at the threshold that the parties do not dispute that TACA is in violation of section 2 First, Second, Third, Fourth and Seventh, and sections 5 and 6 of the Railway Labor Act, 45 U.S.C. §§ 152, 155, 156. TACA's refusal to recognize and bargain with ALPA, and its unilateral attempt to impose a new labor agreement on its pilot employees, violate the Railway Labor Act. These same actions were noted as violations in Ruby v. TACA, 439 F.2d at 1363.

Although subject to the charge of unnecessary iteration, we perhaps should remind that collective bargaining agreements are central to American labor law and are the essential threads of its fabric. In an Oliver Wendell Holmes lecture at Harvard Law School, entitled Reason, Contract, and Law in Labor Relations, published in 68 Harv.L.Rev. 999, 1002 (1955), Dean Harry Schulman observed:

> Collective bargaining is today, as Brandeis pointed out, the means of establishing industrial democracy as the essential condition of political democracy, the means of providing for the workers' lives in industry the sense of worth, of freedom, and of participation that democratic government promises them as citizens.

A few years later Justice Douglas reiterated in United Steelworkers v. Warrior & Gulf Navigation Co., 363 U.S. 574, 580, 80 S.Ct. 1347, 1351–52, 4 L.Ed.2d 1409 (1960) (with citations and footnotes omitted):

> A collective bargaining agreement is an effort to erect a system of industrial self-government. When most parties enter into contractual relationship they do so voluntarily, in the sense that there is no real compulsion to deal with one another, as opposed to dealing with other parties. This is not true of the labor agreement. The choice is generally not between entering or refusing to enter into a relationship, for that in all probability pre-exists the negotiations. Rather it is between having that relationship governed by an agreed-upon rule of law or leaving each and every matter subject to a temporary resolution dependent solely upon the relative strength, at any given moment, of the contending forces.

The Air Transportation Agreement

It is TACA's position that the relocation of its pilot base is authorized by the Air Transportation Agreement, an executive agreement, which should be applied to supersede and contravene inconsistent domestic laws, notably including the Railway Labor Act. TACA also contends that Article 14 of the Air Transportation Agreement requires that the pending dispute be resolved by the arbitration mechanism set forth in the agreement.

It is axiomatic that statutes and treaties are to be interpreted, to the maximum extent possible, so as to be consistent and harmonious. United States v. Lee Yen Tai, 185 U.S. 213, 22 S.Ct. 629, 46 L.Ed. 878 (1902). But the language of an international agreement, like any agreement, is to be interpreted according to its plain and obvious meaning, absent a clear indication that the parties intend otherwise. Maximov v. United States, 373 U.S. 49, 83 S.Ct. 1054, 10 L.Ed.2d 184 (1963).

The express language of the Air Transportation Agreement reflects that the parties did not intend the agreement to replace relevant domestic labor law. To the contrary. Section 1 of Article 8 of the intergovernmental agreement permits each nation to establish offices within the territory of the other nation "for the promotion and sale of air transportation." Immediately thereafter, in section 2 of Article 8, the parties prescribed:

> The designated airlines of one Party may, in accordance with the laws and regulations of the other Party relating to entry, residence and employment, bring in and maintain in the territory of the other Party managerial, sales, technical, operational and other specialist staff required for the provision of air transportation....

This agreement was reached 11 years after our decision in Ruby v. TACA. It is apparent that the representatives of the United States and El Salvador did not intend a suspension of the application of the Railway Labor Act or an abrogation of the holding of Ruby v. TACA. Nor are we persuaded that the parties to the Air Transportation Agreement intended that a dispute between private parties, here TACA and ALPA, was to be arbitrable under the agreement's provisions. We find no merit in this assignment of error.

Because we find that the Air Transportation Agreement is not inconsistent with the Railway Labor Act, we do not reach the issue of whether the Air Transportation Agreement, an executive agreement, is a "treaty" which can supersede prior acts of Congress. See Restatement (Second) of the Foreign Relations Law of the United States § 144. See e.g., Weinberger v. Rossi, 456 U.S. 25, 102 S.Ct. 1510, 71 L.Ed.2d 715 (1982).

Act of State Doctrine

TACA next argues that the act of state doctrine precludes the injunction against TACA's relocation to El Salvador, lifting as a shield the provision of the Salvadoran Constitution requiring all public service companies to have their work center and base of operations in El Salvador. TACA insists that the Salvadoran government's relocation directive is sufficient to invoke the act of state doctrine. We do not agree.

Under the act of state doctrine our courts will not question the validity of the actions of foreign governments within their own borders. The doctrine was elucidated in Underhill v. Hernandez, 168 U.S. 250, 252, 18 S.Ct. 83, 84, 42 L.Ed. 456 (1897):

> Every sovereign state is bound to respect the independence of every other sovereign state, and the courts of one country will not sit in judgment on the acts of the government of another done within its own territory. Redress of grievances by reason of such acts must be obtained through the means open to be availed of by sovereign powers as between themselves.

The act of state doctrine is not mandated by international law or the Constitution. The doctrine does, however, rest on "'constitutional' underpinnings." Banco Nacional de Cuba v. Sabbatino, 376 U.S. 398, 423, 84 S.Ct. 923, 938, 11 L.Ed.2d 804 (1964). The purpose of the doctrine is to avoid judicial interference with the role of the executive branch in international affairs. As we noted in Arango v. Guzman Travel Advisors Corp., 621 F.2d 1371, 1380 (5th Cir.1980):

> Relegating grievances from acts of this sort to executive channels of international diplomacy, the rule is an embodiment of the deference to be accorded the sovereignty of other nations; it averts potential diplomatic embarrassment from the courts of one sovereign sitting in judgment over the public acts of another.

The act of state doctrine does not preclude our review of each and every case which touches upon international relations, however minimal. In determining whether to apply the doctrine, we must weigh a number of factors. One of these is the degree of involvement of the foreign state. Industrial Investment Development Corp. v. Mitsui & Co., Ltd., 594 F.2d 48 (5th Cir.1979), cert. denied, 445 U.S. 903, 100 S.Ct. 1078, 63 L.Ed.2d 318 (1980). A second factor is the effect a judicial decision in a given case will have on our foreign relations. As the Court noted in Sabbatino, "the less important the implications of an issue are for our foreign relations, the weaker the justification for exclusivity in the political branches." 376 U.S. at 428, 84 S.Ct. at 940. A third and related factor is whether a decision in a given case will involve the adjudication of the laws, conduct or motivation of a foreign government. This principle has been decisive in two cases before this court in which parties have unsuccessfully invoked the act of state doctrine. Maltina Corp. v. Cawy Bottling Co., 462 F.2d 1021 (5th Cir.), cert. denied, 409

U.S. 1060, 93 S.Ct. 555, 34 L.Ed.2d 512 (1972); Tabacalera Severiano Jorge, S.A. v. Standard Cigar Co., 392 F.2d 706 (5th Cir.), cert. denied, 393 U.S. 924, 89 S.Ct. 255, 21 L.Ed.2d 260 (1968).

In Tabacalera, the sole shareholder of a Cuban corporation whose assets had been confiscated by the Cuban government sued to recover the purchase price of tobacco sold prior to the takeover to the defendant, an American corporation. We found that the res in the case was the debt owed to the plaintiff by an American company in Tampa, Florida. In locating the res, Judge Tuttle noted that "the situs of intangible property is about as intangible a concept as is known to the law," and added:

> The situs may be in one place for ad valorem tax purposes; it may be in another place for venue purposes; it may be in more than one place for tax purposes in certain circumstances; it may be in still a different place when the need for establishing its true situs is to determine whether an overriding national concern, like the application of the Act of State Doctrine, is involved.

392 F.2d at 714–15 (citations omitted). We then rejected the defendant's contention that, under the act of state doctrine, the confiscation by the Cuban government extinguished the debt. We held that if the res is outside the control or territory of the foreign state, the doctrine need not apply:

> when a foreign government performs an act of state which is an accomplished fact, that is when it has the parties and the res before it and acts in such a manner as to change the relationship between the parties touching the res, it would be an affront to such foreign government for courts of the United States to hold that such act was a nullity.... [But] these acts are to be recognized under the Act of State Doctrine only insofar as they were able to come to complete fruition within the dominion of the [foreign] government.

392 F.2d at 715–16.

In Maltina, Judge Wisdom emphasized that "Tabacalera and its predecessors teach that the federal courts are to take a pragmatic view of what constitutes an extraterritorial action by a foreign state." 462 F.2d at 1027. The plaintiff in that case, a successor to a Cuban corporation whose assets had been confiscated by the Cuban government, sought to preserve its right to use the United States trademark the corporation had registered before the confiscatory decree. We found, as a matter of trademark law, that the res in the case, the registered trademark of the Cuban corporation, was located in the United States. We then held that we would recognize a foreign sovereign's actions governing property located within the United States only if it was consistent with our policy and laws. Because a taking of property without compensation violates fundamental constitutional principles, we declined to apply the act of state doctrine.

Evaluating these factors in the case at bar we are persuaded that the doctrine presents no bar to the injunction entered by the district court. The factors militate against TACA's position. In so concluding, we do not denigrate the interest of El Salvador or minimize its participation in this dispute. El Salvador has ordered a corporate national to act consistent with its constitution. In its amicus, El Salvador explains its interest in securing the ultimate relocation of the pilot station of what it views as its national air carrier. However, we must remain cognizant of the fact that El Salvador is not a party to this controversy and that TACA is a private party who voluntarily chose to engage in business within the territorial confines of the United States, thereby becoming subject to all relevant domestic laws. We do not adjudicate the validity of Article 110, ¶4 of the

Salvadoran Constitution, nor do we comment on El Salvador's regulatory practices and policies involving public service companies. That is not our prerogative. We do adjudicate, however, the legality of TACA's response to the governmental directive it received. Insofar as the relationship between TACA and ALPA, that response must be made in a manner consistent with controlling provisions of United States law, specifically and primarily the Railway Labor Act.

The present controversy does not involve sensitive areas of international relations that require our deference to the initiatives of the executive branch. We are persuaded that the principles announced in Tabacalera and Maltina are dispositive here. Although Judge Tuttle's observation about the difficulty of determining the situs of intangible property remains true today, the res or interest in this case, whether we deem it the pilot base or the collective bargaining agreement, is clearly located in the United States. Since 1949, TACA has maintained its pilot base in New Orleans, availing itself of the benefits of American labor and facilities. Continuously since 1968, TACA has been a party to collective bargaining agreements with ALPA for its pilots. In 1979, the parties entered into a collective bargaining agreement which is presently amendable. Consistent with the holdings in Tabacalera, Maltina, and Ruby v. TACA, we cannot give effect to El Salvador's directive to TACA to extinguish ex parte the collective bargaining agreement and relocate the pilot base. Those acts directly affect interests located within the United States and contravene fundamental principles of American labor policy. The act of state doctrine will not be given application in this instance.

Foreign Compulsion Defense

TACA claims that its violations of the Railway Labor Act should be excused because they were done under the compulsion of Salvadoran law. In evaluating the foreign compulsion defense, we balance the following factors:

(a) vital national interests of each of the states,

(b) the extent and the nature of the hardship that inconsistent enforcement actions would impose upon the person,

(c) the extent to which the required conduct is to take place in the territory of the other state,

(d) the nationality of the person, and

(e) the extent to which enforcement by action of either state can reasonably be expected to achieve compliance with the rule prescribed by that state.

Restatement (Second), Foreign Relations Law of the United States §40. [See] In re Grand Jury Proceedings v. Field, 532 F.2d 404 (5th Cir.), cert. denied, 429 U.S. 940, 97 S.Ct. 354, 50 L.Ed.2d 309 (1976); United States v. First National City Bank, 396 F.2d 897 (2d Cir.1968).

For reasons previously discussed, we also find this defense without merit. As we have noted, collective bargaining agreements are a cornerstone of our national labor policy. We neither hold nor suggest that TACA may not relocate its pilot base. We hold only that TACA must relocate its pilot base, and effect the other intended steps, in accordance with the substantive law and procedures set forth in the Railway Labor Act and other relevant domestic laws.

The judgment of the district court is AFFIRMED.

RAMEY v. DISTRICT 141, INTERNATIONAL ASSOCIATION OF MACHINISTS AND AEROSPACE WORKERS

378 F.3d 269 (2d Cir. 2004)

MESKILL, Circuit Judge.

A group of plaintiffs sued their labor union in the United States District Court for the Eastern District of New York, Korman, J., alleging that the union breached its duty of fair representation. A jury found for the plaintiffs, and the union's motions for judgment as a matter of law and for a new trial were denied. The union appealed, and we affirm.

BACKGROUND

Plaintiffs are airline mechanics currently employed by U.S. Airways, Inc. (USAir). They were formerly employed by Eastern Airlines (Eastern). Plaintiffs have sued their labor union, the International Association of Machinists and Aerospace Workers, their local, District 141, and various union officials. For the sake of simplicity, we refer to defendants collectively as IAM.

In early 1988, while plaintiffs were employed by Eastern and represented by IAM, Eastern and the Trump Organization (Trump) announced plans for a sale of the Eastern Shuttle operation, a regional airline service, to Trump. Under the terms of the proposed sale, Trump would acquire the entire Eastern Shuttle operation, including planes, routes, landing slots and equipment. Additionally, various Eastern employees would be offered the opportunity to become employees of Trump and operate the new airline, Trump Shuttle. The sale was completed, and plaintiffs accepted the offer to work for Trump Shuttle. In March 1989, shortly after the sale went through, Eastern declared bankruptcy. During the course of the bankruptcy proceedings, IAM took the position that plaintiffs should be viewed as having "transitioned" from Eastern to Trump Shuttle, rather than having resigned from Eastern and subsequently hired by Trump Shuttle.

While employed by Trump Shuttle, plaintiffs grew frustrated with IAM's representation. Consequently, in 1990 they voted out IAM as their labor union and voted instead to be represented by the Aircraft Mechanics Fraternal Association (AMFA). In 1992, as a result of Trump Shuttle's financial difficulties, a consortium of banks took control of the airline and renamed it Shuttle, Inc. (Shuttle). Almost immediately thereafter, Shuttle entered into an agreement with USAir by which USAir would manage Shuttle's operations. This agreement also provided USAir with an option to purchase Shuttle within five years.

In August 1992, the National Mediation Board (NMB) granted USAir "single carrier status" for the purposes of collective bargaining. As a result, AMFA ceased to represent plaintiffs, and IAM, which represented the USAir mechanics, resumed its position as plaintiffs' collective bargaining representative.

Shortly afterward, so-called "mainline" USAir mechanics—those employed by USAir rather than Shuttle—went on strike. Plaintiffs were unsure whether they should join the strike. On the one hand, their previous collective bargaining agreement, which appeared to remain in effect despite USAir's assumption of control of Shuttle, included a no-strike clause that could cause them to lose their jobs if they joined in a strike. On the other hand, they were now a part of the same local as their co-workers at USAir, and there was some suggestion that their previous collective bargaining agreement was extinguished, which would free them to join the mainline strike. In the end, they opted not to join in the strike.

In late 1992 or early 1993, IAM and USAir commenced negotiations concerning the integration of plaintiffs into the mainline workforce. The effect of integration would be to include plaintiffs under the same collective bargaining agreement as the mainline employees. This was attractive to plaintiffs because it offered the prospect of higher pay and better benefits.

The integration, or "mainlining," process required USAir and IAM to come to an agreement as to how plaintiffs' seniority status would be calculated with respect to their peers in the mainline workforce. IAM has a longstanding policy of "dovetailing" seniority lists, which involves blending the two employee groups based on their pre-merger employment dates at each of the merging airlines. In applying this policy to plaintiffs, IAM had to decide what it would consider to be plaintiffs' start dates at Shuttle. Plaintiffs felt that IAM should apply their Eastern start dates because they viewed their move from Eastern to Trump Shuttle as a "transfer." IAM, however, argued that plaintiffs resigned from Eastern prior to accepting employment at Trump Shuttle and, therefore, they should only be accorded seniority classification from their start-dates at Trump Shuttle.

Plaintiffs vigorously opposed IAM's preferred position and retained Attorney Lee Seham to advocate on their behalf to IAM. Plaintiffs believed that IAM had taken this position to punish them for voting for AMFA during their brief period at Trump Shuttle and for refusing to join the mainline strike when Shuttle was taken over by USAir. Seham was unsuccessful in persuading IAM to reconsider its position. IAM subsequently presented its position to USAir. Before an agreement could be reached, however, USAir decided not to proceed with the mainlining and announced that it would not integrate the two employee groups unless and until it decided to exercise its five-year option to purchase Shuttle. Therefore, the seniority issue receded into the background and plaintiffs continued to work for USAir under a separate collective bargaining agreement.

In late 1997, USAir decided to exercise its option and, in March 1998, it announced its intention to integrate the two workforces. However, in July 1998, IAM announced that, based on preliminary discussions, it appeared that USAir would not proceed with integration "in the immediate future." Subsequently, in December 1998, plaintiffs received a memo from IAM explaining that IAM would once again take the position during negotiations that plaintiffs' Eastern seniority should not be applied. It is not clear from the record precisely when negotiations between USAir and IAM formally commenced or when plaintiffs learned of their commencement. In May 1999, USAir agreed to IAM's terms.

In late July 1999, plaintiffs instituted this action in the United States District Court for the Eastern District of New York, Korman, J., and alleged that IAM breached the duty of fair representation it owed them under the Railway Labor Act, 45 U.S.C. § 151 et seq., by failing to accord them their Eastern seniority. They maintained that IAM punished them for having chosen AMFA over IAM and for opting not to participate in the mainline mechanics' strike in 1992. IAM moved for summary judgment on various grounds, including that (1) it did not breach its duty because its position was objectively reasonable, (2) the statute of limitations had lapsed before plaintiffs instituted the action, and (3) plaintiffs had insufficient evidence to prove that IAM was motivated by hostility or animus toward plaintiffs. Judge Korman denied the motion, Ramey v. District 141, 2002 WL 32152292, 2002 U.S. Dist. LEXIS 26670 (E.D.N.Y. Nov. 4, 2002), and the case proceeded to trial.

IAM argued to the jury that its seniority decision was reasonable because plaintiffs had resigned from Eastern before they were hired by Trump Shuttle and, therefore, they were not entitled to their Eastern seniority. However, plaintiffs showed that IAM had taken the position during the Eastern bankruptcy proceeding that plaintiffs were to be viewed not as having resigned from Eastern, but rather as having "transitioned" from Eastern to Trump. Plaintiffs also elicited testimony to the effect that IAM officials were hostile toward AMFA and those associated with it.

The jury found in favor of plaintiffs, concluding that IAM breached its duty because it had stripped plaintiffs of their seniority out of animus. In particular, the jury found that, had IAM not been hostile toward plaintiffs as a result of their decision to be represented by AMFA, IAM would have sided with them on the seniority issue.

IAM moved for judgment as a matter of law and for a new trial, essentially renewing the arguments it had made in the summary judgment motion. Judge Korman denied the motion and entered judgment against IAM. The judgment included an injunction requiring IAM to negotiate with USAir to amend the seniority roster and provide plaintiffs with their Eastern start dates. In addition, because some plaintiffs had been furloughed by USAir as a result of their relatively lower start dates, the injunction requires IAM to request that USAir restore these plaintiffs to work.

This appeal followed.

DISCUSSION

IAM asserts various grounds for its appeal. First, it argues that its conduct was objectively reasonable and, thus, it did not violate its duty of fair representation. Second, it maintains that the applicable statute of limitations period had expired before plaintiffs brought this case. Third, IAM contends that Judge Korman made two erroneous evidentiary rulings during the course of the trial that merit reversal. Fourth, it challenges the jury's verdict on the ground that the verdict was not supported by sufficient evidence. Finally, IAM argues that it is entitled to judgment against any plaintiff who did not personally testify to establish damages. We reject each of these arguments in turn.

I. IAM's Challenge to the Jury's Verdict

IAM maintains, as it did below, that the judgment should be overturned because, despite the jury's finding that IAM's seniority decision was motivated by animus, there was an independent rational basis supporting its decision; namely, that they had resigned from Eastern. In other words, IAM contends that because an objective union, albeit one with different policies, could have reasonably denied plaintiffs their Eastern seniority, IAM should be immune from suit here even though it had been motivated by animus toward plaintiffs as a result of their having favored AMFA. We do not agree.

"The statutory duty of fair representation was developed [decades] ago." Vaca v. Sipes, 386 U.S. 171, 177, 87 S.Ct. 903, 17 L.Ed.2d 842 (1967). "[A] union breaches [this] duty ... when its conduct toward a member of the bargaining unit is arbitrary, discriminatory, or in bad faith." Marquez v. Screen Actors Guild, Inc., 525 U.S. 33, 44, 119 S.Ct. 292, 142 L.Ed.2d 242 (1998). Put differently, a breach occurs when a union fails to "serve the interests of all members without hostility or discrimination toward any, [ ] exercise its discretion with complete good faith and honesty, [or] avoid arbitrary conduct." Vaca, 386 U.S. at 177, 87 S.Ct. 903. "[A] union may not, without a legitimate purpose, take action favoring some of its members at the expense of others." Teamsters Local Union No. 42 v. NLRB, 825 F.2d 608, 611 (1st Cir.1987) (citing Laborers and Hod Carriers Local No. 341 v. NLRB, 564 F.2d 834, 840 (9th Cir.1977); Barton Brands, Ltd. v. NLRB, 529 F.2d 793, 800 (7th Cir.1976)). Additionally, "a union violates [its duty] when it causes an employer to discriminate against employees on arbitrary, hostile, or bad faith grounds." Barton Brands, 529 F.2d at 799.

Although our review of a union's collective bargaining "must be highly deferential [and must] recogniz[e] the wide latitude that [unions] need for the effective performance of their bargaining responsibilities," Air Line Pilots Association v. O'Neill, 499 U.S. 65, 78, 111 S.Ct. 1127, 113 L.Ed.2d 51 (1991), "a union may not juggle the seniority roster for no reason other than to advance one group of employees over another" or to punish a disfavored group, Rakestraw v. United Airlines, 981 F.2d 1524, 1535 (7th Cir.1992); see also Teamsters Local Union No. 42, 825 F.2d at 612 ("[W]hen a union attempts to prefer [one group of] workers based solely on [their loyalty to their guild]," it has breached its duty.). Finally, a union is not permitted to ignore its own policies to punish a minority group within the union. Nellis v. Air Line Pilots Association, 815 F.Supp. 1522, 1533 (E.D.Va.1993) ("A union is bound to follow its [own] policies."), aff'd, 15 F.3d 50 (4th Cir.1994).

The jury found that IAM violated these principles. Rather than treating plaintiffs as having transitioned from Eastern—a policy IAM announced in the Eastern bankruptcy proceeding—IAM instead opted to treat them as having resigned in order to strip them of their seniority status for no reason other than animus.

IAM seeks support for its position in the Seventh Circuit's Rakestraw decision. In Rakestraw, the court held that union members could not sue their union for dovetailing merger lists even though the union's decision to dovetail contradicted its own policy of arbitrating such disputes. 981 F.2d at 1527, 1533. Judge Easterbrook, writing for the court, held that because "[a] rational person could conclude that dovetailing seniority lists in a merger ... serves the interests of [the union membership] as a whole," id. at 1533, doing so could not constitute a breach of the duty of fair representation.

Even assuming we were to adopt this rule, we cannot see how it supports IAM's position. Unlike in Rakestraw, plaintiffs here do not suggest that IAM acted improperly merely by dovetailing the seniority lists. Rather, they argue that IAM was motivated by retaliatory animus in choosing which seniority dates to apply. The jury held, in effect, that IAM revoked plaintiffs' seniority because it was hostile toward them as a result of their association with AMFA. This, of course, is not objectively reasonable. In ignoring its own position regarding plaintiffs' status simply to punish them, IAM breached its duty of fair representation.

[The remainder of the court's opinion is omitted.]

Notes

1. In a portion of his article that is not reproduced above, Mr. Reinert argues that despite its vintage, the RLA is still functional. Many other commentators, however, have suggested that the time is long past due for a major overhaul of the statute. In particular, they believe Congress should make it clear that work slowdowns are illegal and provide courts with more powerful tools to prevent and punish such job actions. For a further discussion, *see, e.g.*, Samuel Estreicher & Robert Siegel, *Partial Strikes Under the Railway Labor Act: The Need for a Doctrine of Unprotected Concerted Activity*, 18 Lab. Law. 15 (2002), and Lisa Catherine Tulk, Comment, *The 1926 Railway Labor Act and the Modern American Airline Industry: Changes and "Chaos" Outline the Need for Revised Legislation*, 69 J. Air L. & Com. 615 (2004). *See also* Ronald C. Henson & John M. Gilman, *Grievance Procedures: The Carrier's Perspective*, SK007 ALI-ABA 343 (Oct. 21–23, 2004).

2. Do you agree with the Fifth Circuit's decision in *Kaufman*? Interestingly, in *Wolfson v. American Airlines, Inc.*, 170 F. Supp. 2d 87 (D. Mass. 2001), a case arising out of the same work stoppage as *Kaufman*, Judge Saris held (just prior to the Fifth Circuit's ruling) that *Garmon* did not preempt the passengers' claims (thereby agreeing with Judge Solis). In March 2002, shortly before the Supreme Court declined to grant certiorari in the *Kaufman* case, the *Wolfson* parties reached a settlement (the terms were not disclosed).

3. Disputes under the RLA are classified as either "major" or "minor." To prevent industrial gridlock, only major disputes can be brought to court; minor disputes must be submitted to binding arbitration. *See further Professional Flight Attendants Ass'n v. Northwest Airlines Corp.*, 2005 WL 1869123 (D. Minn. 2005). The Supreme Court's decision in *Norris* upset this delicate balance by permitting workers to avoid arbitration by claiming their grievance fell outside the statute's scope. Airlines responded to this change by insisting on "mandatory arbitration" clauses in their employment agreements. *See* M. Scott Barnard, Comment, *Losing Ground: The Recharacterization of the Railway Labor Act's "Minor Dispute" and Solutions to Recapture Lost Claims*, 62 J. Air L. & Com. 1117 (1992). Whether such clauses are enforceable remains an open question due to an exception contained in the Federal Arbitration Act that exempts the employment contracts of transportation workers. *See further* John J. Gallagher & Margaret H. Spurlin, *Mandatory Arbitration of Statutory Employment Claims*, SF15 ALI-ABA 795 (Oct. 2000) (discussing 9 U.S.C. § 1). In the meantime, Congress has addressed the specific issue that prompted the *Norris* case—in 2000, it enacted a federal whistleblower protection statute (49 U.S.C. § 42121) for commercial airline and airport workers. *See further* Rita Murphy, Comment, *OSHA, AIR21 and Whistleblower Protection for Aviation Workers*, 56 Admin. L. Rev. 901 (2004), and *compare Branche v. Airtran Airways, Inc.*, 342 F.3d 1248 (11th Cir. 2003) (federal act does not preempt state whistleblower statutes) *with Botz v. Omni Air International*, 286 F.3d 488 (8th Cir. 2002) (federal act does preempt state whistleblower statutes).

4. Should the Fifth Circuit have given more serious consideration to the foreign policy arguments raised by TACA? What possible reprisals could American airlines operating in El Salvador face as a result of the decision? For a comprehensive discussion, *see* Stephen B. Moldof, *The Extent to Which U.S. Labor Laws Apply in an Increasingly Globalized Business/Labor Context*, SK007 ALI-ABA 585 (Oct. 21–23, 2004).

5. The *Ramey* case is a good example of the union issues that can arise in the wake of an airline's failure. Moreover, airlines now routinely use the threat of a bankruptcy filing (which makes it possible for them to reject their collective bargaining agreements and pension liabilities) to wring salary and benefit concessions from unions. This has greatly contributed to the decline in morale among airline workers while failing to solve the industry's underlying financial problems. *See further* Jody Hoffer Gittell et al., *Mutual Gains or Zero Sum? Labor Relations and Firm Performance in the Airline Industry*, 57 Indus. & Lab. Rel. Rev. 163 (2004); Daniel P. Rollman, Comment, *Flying Low: Chapter 11's Contribution to the Self-Destructive Nature of Airline Industry Economics*, 21 Emory Bankr. Dev. J. 381 (2004); Scott L. Hazan & Todd M. Goren, *Airlines on Collision Course with Labor: The Impact of Section 1113 of the Bankruptcy Code on the US Airways' Bankruptcy Case*, 873 PLI/Comm 469 (Jan. 2005); John J. Gallagher et al., *An Unhappy Crossroads: The Interplay of Bankruptcy and Airline Labor Law*, SK007 ALI-ABA 679 (Oct. 21–23, 2004); Jonathan E. Collins, Comment, *Airlines Jettison Their Pension Plans: Congress Must Act to Save the PBGC and Protect Plan Beneficiaries*, 70 J. Air L. & Com. 289 (2005).

6. The 1987 movie *Wall Street*, starring Michael Douglas as Gordon Gekko, a ruthless financier, and Charlie Sheen as Bud Fox, a naive young trader, was ahead of its

time in foreseeing the labor wars that have engulfed the aviation industry. In it, Gekko double-crosses the unions at Blue Star, the airline where Fox's father Carl (Martin Sheen) serves as maintenance chief, by promising to invest in the company when his real plan is to liquidate its pension fund. The film earned Douglas the Oscar for Best Actor, in large part because of his now oft-repeated line, "Greed is good." *See further* Sean J. Griffith, *Deal Protection Provisions in the Last Period of Play*, 71 Fordham L. Rev. 1899, 1945 (2003) (explaining Gekko's maneuver in greater detail).

A more humorous look at airline labor relations came during the fourth season (1992–93) of the NBC sitcom *Wings*, in an episode entitled "Labor Pains." After learning that his friend Dewey, who works at Boston's Logan International Airport, is being paid twice as much as he is, Nantucket airport mechanic Lowell Mather (played by Thomas Haden Church) seeks a raise from his bosses at Aeromass and Sandpiper Air, who claim they cannot afford it. Guided by taxicab driver Antonio Scarpacci (Tony Shalhoub), Lowell stands firm and threatens to take a job with Dewey, which leads to this memorable exchange:

> Antonio: So Lowell, have they broken down and given you your raise yet?
>
> Lowell: No, and my flight leaves in five minutes.
>
> Antonio: Ah, this is my favorite part. Phase 4—the final countdown. You're not worried, are you?
>
> Lowell: Ah, no, no, absolutely not. But I have one small question. Um, if I'm not going anywhere, then why did they hire a new mechanic?
>
> Antonio: Ah, simple—to scare you into staying. He's probably not even a real mechanic.
>
> Lowell: God, they're good.
>
> Antonio: Yeah, but we are better.
>
> [Antonio leaves and Lowell runs into his replacement.]
>
> Lowell: Why, you must be the new mechanic.
>
> Gil: Right, Gil Cooper.
>
> Lowell (shaking hands): Lowell Mather. So, Gil, if you're a mechanic, I suppose you know how to change a LORAN sensor on a Cessna 402. What's the matter Gil, you don't know how, do you?
>
> Gil (shrugging his shoulders): Well sure. You reach behind the altimeter and feel for the metal Y connector, unplug the left side, find the blue wire, thread it through the new sensor housing, reseal the base unit, plug in the test coordinates, and you're in business.
>
> Lowell (looking very worried): The blue wire?

Problem 14

An American airline operates both domestic and international flights. Although it accepts that the Railway Labor Act applies to the former, it insists the statute has no effect on the latter. If its position is challenged by one of its unions, how should the court rule? *See Independent Union of Flight Attendants v. Pan American World Airways, Inc.*, 810 F. Supp. 263 (N.D. Cal. 1992).

Chapter 4

Passengers

SHERMAN'S LAGOON

A. OVERVIEW

In 1946, the world's airlines transported nine million people. By 2004, this figure had climbed to 1.8 billion, with United States carriers accounting for 689 million passengers. Because of growing demand from China, global increases of six percent are expected through at least 2008; the Federal Aviation Administration similarly projects that domestic airlines will be transporting one billion passengers annually by 2015.

Obviously, with so many people in the skies, lawsuits are inevitable. When they do arise in this country, they most often require the courts to construe either the Airline Deregulation Act of 1978 (ADA) or the Warsaw Convention of 1929 (now slowly being replaced by the Montreal Convention of 1999). Depending on the nature of the action, however, other laws (occasionally federal but more often state) also can come into play.

B. DOMESTIC TRAVEL

SPIRIT AIRLINES, INC. v. NORTHWEST AIRLINES, INC.

431 F.3d 917 (6th Cir. 2005)

HAYNES, District Judge.

Plaintiff Spirit Airlines, Inc. appeals from the district court's final order granting summary judgment to the Defendant Northwest Airlines, Inc. on Plaintiff's claims of monopolization and attempted monopolization under Section 2 of the Sherman Antitrust Act, 15 U.S.C. §2. During the pendency of this appeal, Northwest filed for bankruptcy.

The automatic stay under 11 U.S.C. §362(a)(1) applies to this appeal. In re Delta Airlines, 310 F.3d 953, 956 (6th Cir.2002). Upon the parties' stipulation, the bankruptcy court entered an order lifting the automatic stay for a decision on Spirit's appeal.

Spirit alleged that Northwest engaged in predatory pricing and other predatory tactics in the leisure passenger airline markets for the Detroit-Boston and Detroit-Philadelphia routes. In sum, the district court found that Spirit's proof had not established predatory pricing by Northwest in these markets. Specifically, the district court rejected Spirit's definition of the relevant market as limited to low fare or leisure passengers, and adopted Northwest's market definition of all passengers on these routes. With this conclusion, the district court found that Northwest's total revenues exceeded its total costs for these routes. Moreover, the district court opined that even if the low fare or leisure passenger market were the appropriate market, Northwest's expert proof demonstrated that Northwest's total revenues still exceeded its relevant costs. The district court deemed Spirit's expert proof and analysis of Northwest's costs and revenue to be implausible. Given these conclusions, the district court deemed it unnecessary to decide Spirit's other predatory practices claims.

From our review of the record, when the evidence is considered in a light most favorable to Spirit, as is required in this context, we conclude that a reasonable trier of fact could find that a separate and distinct low-fare or leisure-passenger market existed. The evidence presented by Spirit in support of such a market includes Northwest's own marketing data, the testimony of its marketing officials, the findings of government regulators and Spirit's experts. Moreover, based on the evidence presented, a reasonable trier of fact could find that at the time of predation, Northwest's prices were below its relevant costs for these routes, the market in the two relevant geographic routes was highly concentrated, Northwest possessed overwhelming market share, and the barriers to entry were high. Accordingly, a reasonable trier of fact could conclude that Northwest engaged in predatory pricing in the leisure passenger markets on these two geographic routes in order to force Spirit out of the business. Finally, based on the evidence presented by Spirit's experts, a reasonable trier of fact could find that once Spirit exited the market, Northwest raised its prices to recoup the losses it incurred during the predation period. Accordingly, we reverse the grant of summary judgment in favor of Northwest and remand the case to the district court for further proceedings consistent with this opinion.

A. FACTUAL BACKGROUND

Because the district court granted Northwest's motion for summary judgment, under the applicable law we are required to view the factual record in a light most favorable to Spirit, the non-moving party.

1. The Parties

Spirit obtained its certificate for a scheduled passenger service in Michigan in 1990 as Charter One. In 1992, Charter One changed its name to Spirit, a low fare carrier with its base of operations in Detroit. In 1992, Spirit had four airplanes servicing four cities with 140,931 passengers, approximately 125 employees and annual revenues of approximately $60 million. Spirit's primary routes were point to point flights between Detroit-Atlantic City and, for a time, Detroit-Boston. By the end of 1993, Spirit had added service to cites in Florida and in 1995, Spirit expanded to other cities. Spirit targeted local leisure or price-sensitive passengers whose travel is generally discretionary, such as passengers visiting friends and relatives, and tourists or vacationers who might not otherwise fly. Spirit's pricing strategy provided a price incentive to such leisure travelers with unrestricted, but non-refundable fares. Spirit's services lacked first class service, frequent flyer benefits, and connecting service. Leisure or low price-sensitive passengers purchase tickets with restrictions on their use, e.g., an advance purchase or stay-over requirement, in exchange for low prices for a particular route.

In 1992, Spirit approached the Detroit Metropolitan airport's management about access to additional ticket counters and gates. Because "Northwest had a stranglehold on the gates at Detroit Metro," Spirit's efforts "were futile." (J.A. 1336). Northwest controlled the majority of the gates at the Detroit airport either by lease or secondary rights from other airlines. Spirit cited an internal Northwest memorandum advocating that when Detroit built its new airport, the existing Detroit concourses should be destroyed, so that other carriers would not "benefit from the vacuum which is created once [Northwest] vacates its existing gates" at the old Detroit airport. (J.A. 41).

Spirit was allowed to use gates formerly used by Trump Shuttle and Charter, but could not secure a permanent gate arrangement. Spirit was unsuccessful in its negotiations with U.S. Airways to use two gates that Northwest subsequently acquired. The district court found that Spirit did secure short term leases from United Airlines and Continental Airlines, but that Spirit expended $100,000 to add its Detroit-Philadelphia flight. Spirit also paid a 25% higher landing fee than airlines that had leases with the Detroit airport authority.

In 1995, Spirit explored expansion of its service between Detroit and other cities, including Boston and Philadelphia. Mark Kahan, Spirit's general counsel, explained that these two major cities have business and leisure travelers. With this model, Spirit expected to attract primarily the price conscious or leisure traveler. Spirit's management considered the Detroit-Philadelphia route a particularly attractive market given its other flights from the Philadelphia airport and the route's potential base of price-sensitive and leisure travelers.

On December 15, 1995, Spirit commenced a single daily non-stop roundtrip flight between Detroit-Philadelphia on an 87-seat DC-9 airplane at a $49 fare with a load factor of 74.3 percent. Spirit soon experienced a higher load factor on the Detroit-Philadelphia route in June, 1996, rising to 88.5 percent from 64.1 percent in January, 1996. On June 28, 1996, Spirit added a second non-stop roundtrip flight for the Detroit-Philadelphia route. On April 15, 1996, Spirit started its Detroit-Boston route with one daily non-stop round trip, initially at fares of $69, $89 and $109.

By 1995, Spirit operated 10 aircraft and serviced 13 travel routes carrying 583,969 passengers and employing approximately 450 people. By 1996, Spirit increased its capacity to 11 aircraft, with 15 routes. In June 1996, Spirit had 71,364,828 seat miles with annual revenues of $62.9 million and approximately 455 employees.

Northwest was founded in 1926 as an air mail carrier for the Minneapolis to Chicago route. The firm's operations at Minneapolis grew and Northwest developed a hub there. By 1986, Northwest merged with Republic Airlines, which had hubs at Detroit and Memphis. In 1995, Northwest was the fourth largest air passenger carrier in the United States with annual revenues of $9.1 billion from its domestic and international operations. At the Detroit Metro airport, Northwest "controlled" 64 of the airport's 86 gates and had 78 percent of all passenger travel from the Detroit-Metro airport.

Northwest operates a hub-and-spoke network with hubs at Detroit, Minneapolis-St. Paul and Memphis. In the hub system, the hub serves as the connecting point for flights between other cities that serve as the "spokes." (J.A. 13). In a word, in this system passengers do not begin or end their journey on a single flight. The initial flight is from a spoke airport to the hub and after deplaning, the passenger boards a second flight to the passenger's ultimate destination, another spoke airport. Northwest offers restricted and unrestricted tickets, airport clubs, frequent flyer benefits, advanced seat selection, first and other classes of service, and on-board meals. Northwest utilizes the yield management policy, which, in essence, seeks "to maximize the revenue that we earn for our domestic network ... and ... try to sell every seat at its highest possible fare." (J.A 1573).

Prior to Spirit's entry, Northwest offered non-stop service on the Detroit-Boston and Detroit-Philadelphia routes. For the Detroit-Philadelphia route, Northwest had a 72% market share. For the Detroit-Boston route, Northwest had an 89% market share. Northwest's only competitor for the service to Philadelphia was U.S. Airways. (J.A. 779 and 780). US Airways was the highest cost service provider in the market, (J.A 3479), and Spirit's expert characterized U.S. Airways as a "compliant" competitor of Northwest. (J.A. 3796). Northwest had six daily non-stop roundtrip flights on the Detroit-Philadelphia route and U.S. Airways had four.

2. Northwest Response to Spirit's Entry

Northwest [has] adopted [a] "New Competitive Equilibrium Analysis" for its response to any new competitor on its routes. (J.A. 3514). In step one of this analysis, Northwest considers the impact of the new entrant's service on Northwest's revenue. Id. In step two, Northwest studies whether to add capacity on the route. Id. Northwest executive Paul Dailey admits that this analysis is more "art" than "science." (J.A. 1649).

At the time of Spirit's entry, Northwest's lowest unrestricted fare for [a] Detroit-Philadelphia flight was $355 and its lowest restricted fare was $125 each way. US Airways' fares were comparable to Northwest's fares. Initially, neither Northwest nor U.S. Airways reduced its fares nor added capacity after Spirit's entry into the Detroit-Philadelphia route, until Spirit achieved high load factors, e.g., as high as 88% in April 1996. Before Spirit's entry into the Detroit-Boston route, Northwest provided non-stop air passenger service on the Detroit-Boston route with 8.5 daily round trips; its lowest unrestricted fare was $411, and its lowest restricted fare was $189 each way. Prior to Spirit's entry, Northwest intended to reduce its capacity for the Detroit-Boston route in the summer of 1996 by 13.7%, to 3,238 seats from 3,753 seats.

Effective April 15, 1996, Northwest dramatically reduced its fare on the Detroit-Boston route to $69, offering this lowest fare on all of its flights. Northwest also increased its daily non-stop roundtrip flights on the Detroit-Boston route to 10.5. Prior to Spirit's entry into the market, Northwest's fare had been in excess of $300. On the Detroit-Boston route, 74.5% of Northwest's passengers flew on fares at or below $69. For this route, Northwest's passengers fares were less than Spirit's lowest fare on 93.9% of the days during which Spirit flew this route. In July 1996, 74% of Northwest's passengers on the Detroit-Boston route flew on fares at or below $69, but that percentage fell in September, 1996 to 67%. Spirit's monthly average load factors on the Detroit-Boston route during Northwest's price response were 18% (April 1996), 21% (May), 24% (June), 31% (July), 29% (August), 17% (September).

By August 20, 1996, Spirit discontinued its second flight on the Detroit-Boston route. On September 30, 1996, Spirit abandoned its Detroit-Boston route. Northwest resumed its status as the only provider of non-stop service on the route. After Spirit's exit on this route, Northwest increased its fare initially to $271 and later to $461 as its lowest unrestricted fare.

On June 19, 1996, Northwest reduced its lowest fares (including unrestricted) to $49 on all Northwest flights on the Detroit-Philadelphia route. From July to September 1996, 40.5% of Northwest's passengers flew on fares at or below $49. By September 1996, 70% of Northwest's passengers flew on fares above $49 on the Detroit-Philadelphia routes and equal to or below $69. In sum, Northwest transported passengers at fares less than Spirit's lowest fare for 92.5% of the days during the predation period.

Spirit's monthly load factors on the Detroit-Philadelphia route were 43% (July 1996), 36% (Aug.), 31% (Sept.). As a result, Spirit abandoned its Detroit-Philadelphia route on September 29, 1996. On October 28, 1996, Northwest increased its lowest unrestricted fare on the Detroit-Philadelphia route to $279, and by April 20, 1998, increased that fare to $416.

B. PROCEDURAL HISTORY

Spirit filed its Section 2 claims against Northwest for anti-competitive and exclusionary practices, including, but not limited to, predatory pricing. Spirit's complaint alleged, in pertinent part:

> As part of this unlawful scheme, and as explained more fully below, Northwest targeted certain of the routes on which it and Spirit competed and substantially increased capacity and began pricing below Northwest's average variable cost or its average total cost. Further, as part of its unlawful scheme, Northwest hampered Spirit's ability to compete at Detroit by denying Spirit access to unused gates controlled by Northwest and/or charging Spirit unreasonable and discriminatory prices to use those gates, and upon information and belief, threatening to eliminate or eliminating discounts, promotions or other benefits to companies in the greater Detroit metropolitan area if those companies designated a carrier other than Northwest for service to or from Detroit....
>
> The combination of very low prices and very high capacity on the Detroit-Boston route caused Northwest's revenues on that city pair to go into a free fall....
>
> At that time, Northwest dramatically lowered its fares, matching Spirit's $49 one-way fare, and increased capacity on the city pair....
>
> Northwest's one-two punch against Spirit in the Detroit-Boston and Detroit-Philadelphia markets produced the result Northwest intended when, by that start of the fourth quarter of 1996, Spirit was forced to abandon service in both city pairs.

Joint Appendix at 19 and 20.

Upon completion of discovery, Northwest moved for summary judgment, contending, in sum, that the evidence showed: (1) that the relevant service or product market included local and connecting passengers through the Detroit airport on the Detroit-Boston and Detroit-Philadelphia routes; (2) that at all relevant times, Northwest's revenues exceeded its average variable costs on these routes; (3) that even if Spirit's proposed market of price-sensitive or leisure travelers market were appropriate, Northwest's total revenues on these routes still exceeded its relevant costs; and (4) that Northwest's low price strategy was a pro-competitive response to Spirit's entry into these geographic markets.

In its response, Spirit relied upon its experts, who opined on the definitions of the relevant geographic and service markets, the anticompetitive characteristics of this market, the determination of the appropriate measure of Northwest's costs and the likelihood of recoupment based upon the factual record. In essence, Spirit's proof was that the relevant product or service market is the low price or price-sensitive or leisure fare travelers for the Detroit-Boston and Detroit-Philadelphia routes, the undisputed geographic markets. In Spirit's experts' opinions, the appropriate measure of costs is Northwest's incremental costs for providing the additional capacity to divert these passengers from Spirit on these routes. By these standards, Spirit's experts opined that Northwest's prices on these routes were below its average variable costs. Spirit's expert proof was that within months after Spirit's exit from these markets, Northwest successfully and completely recouped its losses with substantially higher fares and reduced capacity on these routes.

In addition, Spirit cited Northwest's high market share of enplanements at the Detroit airport, Northwest's expansion of its capacity on these routes in response to Spirit's entry, and the significant barriers to entry in this market, as enabling Northwest to engage in a successful predatory campaign to drive Spirit from this market and to recoup its lost revenues from its predatory pricing on these routes. As the competitive injury from Northwest's predation, Spirit cited the significant reduction in the number of leisure travelers on these routes who lost the competitive option of low price travel from the Detroit airport to these cities and who paid substantially higher prices to travel these routes after Spirit's exit from this market.

In its ruling, the district court adopted Northwest's definition of the relevant product or services market and found that Northwest's revenues exceeded its costs on these routes. The district court rejected Spirit's definition of the relevant service market, but concluded that even in that market, Northwest's revenues exceeded its costs on these routes. As the district court summarized:

> [T]he brute market facts established that Northwest's fares did not fall below the airline's average variable costs, and [ ] Spirit has not produced sufficient facts or identified pertinent legal authority to validate its experts' opinion that below-cost pricing occurred in some alternative, legally relevant "lowest fare" or "price-sensitive" market....
>
> The law governing claims of predatory pricing ... as explicated in Brooke Group and endorsed by scholars including Spirit's own experts, deliberately eschews any qualitative judgments about the competitive desirability of one business practice verses another. The sole and objective benchmark is whether the alleged predator's prices exceed its costs, by reference to the products it actually sells and the markets in which it actually competes with the alleged victim of predation. Under this standard, the record compels the conclusion that Northwest's prices were not predatory, because the airline operated profitably on both the Detroit-Boston and Detroit-Philadelphia routes during the entire period of alleged predation. Consequently, Spirit having failed as a matter of law to establish the first prong of the Brooke Group standard, Northwest is entitled to summary judgment in its favor on Spirit's claims of predatory pricing.

(J.A. 79, 80).

As to Spirit's remaining Section 2 claims, the district court deemed consideration of them unnecessary given its conclusion about predatory pricing:

> Given this conclusion, the Court need not address Northwest's two remaining arguments in support of its motion....
>
> This leaves only the question whether anything remains of Spirit's claims in this case. As noted at the outset, Spirit alleges that Northwest engaged in other

> forms of anticompetitive conduct apart from predatory pricing, but the parties' current round of submissions addresses only the latter theory of recovery. To resolve this uncertainty, the Court invited the parties at the December 12 hearing to submit statements of the remaining issues in this case in the event that Northwest's summary judgment motion were granted. In its submission, Spirit maintains that portions of its claims for damages and injunctive relief would remain viable even in the face of such an adverse ruling. Nonetheless, Spirit then states that these "remaining portions, unaccompanied by Northwest's act of predatory pricing, do not warrant the time, money and resources necessarily involved with the prosecution of the remaining portions of the federal antitrust action." (Plaintiff's Post-Hearing Statement of What Remains at 3). Consequently, the Court's award of summary judgment to Northwest leaves nothing further to resolve in this case.

(J.A. 80, 81 at n.29).

C. THE SUMMARY JUDGMENT RECORD

1. Market Characteristics of the Passenger Airline Industry

The proof before the district court included a Department of Transportation study finding that "low-fare air carriers provide important service and competitive benefits: fare levels are much lower and traffic levels are higher, on routes served by low-fare airlines." (J.A. 1388). Spirit's expert's analysis revealed that low fare carriers significantly reduce the fares of major carriers: "[i]n markets that do involve dominated hubs, low-cost service results in average one way fare savings of $70 per passenger, or 40 percent." (J.A. 876, n.4, quoting U.S. Department of Transportation, The Low Cost Airline Service Revolution, April, 1996 at p. 9). The record also includes a study, "Predatory Pricing in the U.S. Airline Industry" by Clinton V. Oster of Indiana University and John S. Strong of the College of William and Mary. The Oster-Strong study notes that in 1590 markets "the number of passengers traveling increased dramatically in response to the large number of seats offered at low fares." (J.A. 2591).

The Oster-Strong study also reflects that there are "Multiple Competitive Tools" in this industry that provide price and non-price bases for competition among airlines:

> Multiple Competitive Tools. While the fare a passenger pays is an important element of competition, airlines don't compete solely on the basis of the price of the ticket. Instead, they compete over multiple dimensions including: the ticket price; the number of flights a day and the timing of those flights; the characteristics of the flight itinerary such as whether the flight is nonstop, continuing single-plane service, or connecting service; rebates to the traveler in the form of frequent flier programs or corporate discounts; in-flight amenities including food service and how closely the seats are spaced together; ground amenities including club lounges; and so forth. Airlines can also compete by paying travel agent commission overrides (TACOs), to encourage travel agents to book passengers on their flights rather than those of a competitor. To focus only on a single dimension may miss the full range of the ways in which airlines can compete with one another, particularly if price and cost are narrowly defined....
>
> Airlines can offer different fares on a given flight, attaching restrictions or conditions of travel to some fares and, most importantly, offering only a lim-

> ited number of seats in some fare categories.... [A]n example of the coach/economy class fares with associated types of restrictions [is] offered by United Airlines for its flights 1956 from Denver to Miami for travel in January 2001. For this travel, United offered 6 different coach fares ranging from the lowest fare of $483 to the highest fare of $1,045.
>
> These multiple fares give an airline considerable flexibility in how to price seats on its flights. The airline could, for example, offer service at low average fares by simply making a large number of seats available in the lower fare categories, as Northwest did in the third quarter of 1996 in the Detroit to Philadelphia market. Conversely, if there is sufficient demand and no meaningful competition, the airline can offer most of its service at high average fares by making few or no seats available in the lower fare categories....
>
> However, the presence of a low-fare carrier such as Southwest reduces an airline's ability to extract high fares from travelers....
>
> The entry of a low-fare carrier dramatically shifts the distribution of fares away from the higher fare classes toward the lower fare classes. The result is that the average fare fell from about $173 to about $115. Some high fares still remain after low-fare entry, but a much smaller proportion of travelers pay them. There are still tickets sold in all of the fare categories after low-fare entry, as was the case before entry, but the proportion of tickets sold in each of these categories has changed dramatically.

(J.A. 2589, 2590, 2591).

In the airline industry, access to gates is critical, but access is not determined by open competition and, for a new entrant, gate access is a substantial barrier to entry. Professor Kenneth Elzinga, one of Spirit's experts, quoted one analyst who summarized this aspect of the market:

> While route schedules and pricing for the airline industry have been largely deregulated for over 20 years, many other aspects of the industry are still highly regulated. Perhaps the most important regulation comes from local governments, which own and manage the airports in their region and therefore control key bottlenecks to airport service: access to boarding gates and runways. Most local airport commissions allocate gates without a formal market mechanism....

(J.A. 797). Professor Elzinga's report shows that the majority of airport gates are controlled by long-term exclusive-use leases with the local airport authority. In 1996, the GAO found that 76 of the 86 gates at the Detroit airport were covered by long term leases until 2008 and Northwest had 64 of such leases.

Michael Levine, one of Northwest's experts in Northwest's action against American Airlines for predatory pricing, opined that: "The Barriers to Entry in Those Relevant Hub, Hub-Network, Regional and National Markets Are Very High. The Barriers to Entry in Hub-to-Hub City Pairs Are Also Very High. Barriers to Entry in Certain City Pairs Are Also High." (J.A. 926). In that action, Levine also stated that "[n]ew entrants are facing a higher cost of entry than even existing competitors have incurred." (J.A. 928). "Existing [airlines] obtained their initial awareness and facilities base pursuant to government regulations that protected them from competition." (J.A. 928).

Professor Keith B. Leffler, another Spirit expert, is an Associate Professor of Economics at the University of Washington who teaches and researches in the areas of industrial organization, antitrust economics and the economics of contracts. Professor Leffler analyzed Northwest's experts' reports in Northwest's action against American Airlines for predatory pricing. Professor Leffler found that in those reports, Northwest's experts opined that:

a. air travel between city-pairs are relevant economic markets in the airline industry;

b. predatory pricing can be a rational economic strategy in the airline industry;

c. recoupment from predatory pricing is likely for an airline dominant in a relevant economic market in the airline industry;

d. there are substantial barriers to entry into the airline industry;

e. business travelers constitute a distinct market segement in the airline industry;

f. the measure of the average variable cost in the airline industry should include the cost of changing capacity.

(J.A. 893–94).

2. Market Power

At the time of Spirit's entry into these geographic routes in 1995, Northwest had 78% of all passengers traveling from the Detroit Metro airport and 64 of 78 gates at the Detroit airport. During 1996, Northwest's share of the air passenger traveler market at its Minneapolis hubs was 75 to 80% of all enplanements and about 65 to 70% at its Memphis hub. Northwest's share of local passengers on the Detroit-Philadelphia route was between 60–75% of flown seats. Prior to Spirit's entry into the Detroit-Philadelphia market, Northwest carried about 70% of the non-stop traffic on this route, and offered six daily flights; US Airways was a distant second with a market share of about 27%. Prior to Spirit's entry, Northwest was the prime carrier on the Detroit-Boston route and had an 89% market share for that route. After Spirit's exit, Northwest resumed its status as the only supplier of local passenger service on the Detroit-Boston route.

After his review of these markets, Professor Elzinga concluded that Northwest possessed sufficient market power on the Detroit-Boston and Detroit-Philadelphia routes "to make predatory pricing plausible." (J.A. 3796). In Professor Elzinga's view, Northwest's match of Spirit's fares for a large number of its passengers who are price sensitive reflected Northwest's ability to engage in price discrimination by charging higher fares to passengers who are unlikely to travel on Spirit, e.g., businesses travelers, even at substantially lower prices.

3. The Relevant Market

As discussed in more detail infra, the factual record reflects that Northwest's internal documents and its marketing representatives recognize the "low price or price sensitive traveler" or "leisure traveler" as a distinct and relevant market in the air passenger travel market. After a review of this market, Spirit's experts found that a leisure travel passenger or price-sensitive market exists and cited this market as the focus of the actual competition between Spirit and Northwest. Two federal regulators studied this market and also found a distinct market for low fare or price sensitive or leisure travelers.

4. Northwest's Strategy

Aside from the market issues, Spirit's proof reflects that Northwest's Chief Executive Officer deemed the Detroit Metro Airport to be Northwest's "most unique strategic asset" that must be protected "at almost all cost." (J.A. 2396 and 2399). Northwest studied low fare carriers and estimated that competing with such airlines could cost Northwest $250–$375 million in annual revenue at its hubs. This study expressly identified Spirit as one such low cost carrier. Id.

In addition, Michael Levine, Northwest's Executive Vice President, published an article in 1987 describing a two-fold strategy to respond to low fare carriers. [See] Levine, Airline Competition In Deregulated Markets, 4 Yale J. of Reg. 393, 476–78 (1987). This strategy, entitled the "new competitive equilibrium analysis," addresses the impact of a new entrant's service in this market. "The essence of the strategy is simple. Match, or better yet, beat the new entrant's lowest restricted fare to confine its attractiveness to the leisure oriented price-sensitive sector of the market.... Make sure enough seats are available on your flights in the market to accommodate increases in traffic caused by the fare war. In short, leave no traveler with either a price or a schedule incentive to fly the new entrant." (J.A. 2549). Significantly, Levine states: "The incumbent will not operate profitably under such conditions especially, if, as is usually the case, it is a higher-cost airline than its competitor." Id.

In its comprehensive study of the industry, the United States Department of Transportation concluded that "Northwest's response forced Spirit's exit from this market and was designed to do so." (J.A. 1406).

5. Recoupment

On the issue of recoupment, Professor David Mills, a Spirit expert, describes the predator's view of below cost pricing as "an investment strategy" that is the core of [the] Elzinga-Mills recoupment test for predatory pricing. Under this test "[t]he proper benchmark to use in calculating the predator's reasonably expected gains and losses is the profit the firm would earn if the target remained in the market." (J.A. 3166). To determine predation, "[t]he first task is to compare Northwest's average fares during the months when Spirit operated its flights on the [Detroit-Boston] route to the average fares that would have prevailed on the route, but for Northwest's alleged predation." (J.A. 3169). This factor "measure[s] the monthly financial sacrifice the airline shouldered by charging prices below the otherwise prevailing level." Id. "The second task ... compares the average fares Northwest would expect to charge, during the months immediately after Spirit exited the market, to the average fares that otherwise would have prevailed in the market." Id. This second factor "measure[s] the monthly financial return Northwest could achieve by driving Spirit from the market with its predatory pricing." Id. The third factor "compare[s] the anticipated monthly sacrifice during predation with the anticipated monthly return during recoupment to understand whether predatory pricing plausibly would have been a profitable option for Northwest to exercise." (J.A. 3170).

Considering the evidence on market characteristics in this industry, and applying a number of mathematical formulae to these facts, Professor Mills concluded, in sum, that Northwest had successfully recouped its lost revenue within months after Spirit's departure from these routes.

6. Northwest's Non-Price Predatory Practices

Professor Elzinga also deemed Northwest's combination of its matching Spirit's lower prices and its expansion of its flight capacity on these routes as the keys to Northwest's successful predation against Spirit. Professor Daniel Kaplan, a Spirit expert, also challenged Northwest's strategy for the Detroit-Boston route. For example, to justify the addition of [a] DC-10, Northwest's analysts arbitrarily assumed a 362% increase in passenger traffic in Detroit-Boston upon Spirit's entry that is wholly contrary to Northwest's price-out model forecast for these flights.

D. STANDARD OF REVIEW

We review the district court's order granting Northwest's motion for summary judgment de novo. American Council of Certified Podiatric Physicians and Surgeons v. American Board of Podiatric Surgery, 185 F.3d 606, 619 (6th Cir.1999). We "must also consider all facts in the light most favorable to the non-movant and must give the non-movant the benefit of every reasonable inference." Id. The moving party's burden is to show "clearly and convincingly" the absence of any genuine issues of material fact. Sims v. Memphis Processors, Inc., 926 F.2d 524, 526 (6th Cir.1991) (quoting Kochins v. Linden-Alimack, Inc., 799 F.2d 1182, 1183 (6th Cir.1986)).

As discussed in more detail infra, we conclude that when the evidence is considered in a light most favorable to Spirit, a reasonable trier of fact could find that in the relevant geographic and service markets, the markets were highly concentrated, Northwest possessed overwhelming market share, and the barriers to entry were very high. As a result, a reasonable trier of fact could conclude that by dropping its prices below its costs as well as by quickly expanding capacity, Northwest engaged in anti-competitive conduct aimed at driving Spirit out of the relevant markets. Moreover, based on the evidence presented by Spirit's experts, a reasonable trier of fact could conclude that following Spirit's exit, Northwest recouped its losses incurred during the predation period. Accordingly, we conclude that Spirit has presented sufficient evidence of predatory pricing to withstand summary judgment in this case.

E. LEGAL ANALYSIS

Section 2 of the Sherman Act, in pertinent part, makes it unlawful to "monopolize, or attempt to monopolize, ... any part of the trade or commerce among the several States...." 15 U.S.C. §2. "[Section] 2 addresses the actions of single firms that monopolize or attempt to monopolize.... The purpose of the Act is not to protect businesses from the working of the market; it is to protect the public from the failure of the market." Spectrum Sports Inc. v. McQuillan, 506 U.S. 447, 454, 458 (1993). Under this statute, the defendant must "use ... monopoly power 'to foreclose competition, to gain a competitive advantage, or to destroy a competitor.'" Eastman Kodak Co. v. Image Tech. Servs., Inc., 504 U.S. 451, 482–83 (1992) (quoting United States v. Griffith, 334 U.S. 100, 107 (1948)).

We must decide whether Spirit has presented sufficient evidence that Northwest engaged in predatory pricing to withstand summary judgment in this case. Within that general question are several issues of what a reasonable trier of fact could find, such as whether leisure travelers constitute a distinct market in this industry; whether Northwest possessed sufficient market power to engage in predatory pricing; whether Northwest's prices in response to Spirit's entry were below an appropriate measure of its costs; whether Northwest recouped its lost profits from its reduced prices; and whether the characteristics of this market would facilitate and render economically plausible Spirit's assertion of Northwest's predatory pricing. On each issue, summary judgment principles require us to view the evidence in a light most favorable to Spirit.

[After a lengthy analysis, the court found that Spirit had made out a prima facie case based on the evidence discussed above.]

Spirit's experts provided a reasonable economic explanation of the anticompetitive effects of Northwest's two-prong response to Spirit's entry on these routes. As Professor Elzinga explained:

> The goal of predation in this case is for the incumbent firm, Northwest, to drive the entrant, Spirit, from the market. The most effective way for Northwest to do this is to divert passengers that would have otherwise flown on Spirit to Northwest, thereby lowering Spirit's revenues below its costs. This is in fact what happened. Spirit's load factor plummeted after Northwest lowered prices to match Spirit's and added capacity. Spirit's per passenger costs for serving its remaining customer base rose.

This explanation is wholly consistent with the strategy described by Levine, Northwest's executive, and is corroborated by the Oster-Strong economic study.

For these collective reasons, we reverse and remand this action for further proceedings in accordance with this opinion.

[The concurring opinion of Circuit Judge Moore is omitted.]

IN RE NORTHWEST AIRLINES CORP. ANTITRUST LITIGATION

208 F.R.D. 174 (E.D. Mich.),
petition denied, 310 F.3d 953 (6th Cir. 2002),
cert. denied, 539 U.S. 904 (2003)

ROSEN, District Judge.

I. INTRODUCTION

On October 11, 1996, Plaintiff Nelson Chase brought the first of these four consolidated antitrust actions on behalf of himself and other similarly situated air travelers, alleging that Defendants Northwest Airlines Corp., Northwest Airlines, Inc., Airline Reporting Corporation ("ARC") and others have conspired among themselves to restrain trade in violation of § 1 of the Sherman Act, 15 U.S.C. § 1, and that Defendant Northwest has engaged in unlawful monopolistic practices in violation of § 2 of the Sherman Act, 15 U.S.C. § 2. The three remaining suits were filed in 1999, with Defendants Northwest and ARC again named as Defendants, but with the addition of Defendants Delta Air Lines, Inc., U.S. Airways Group, Inc., and U.S. Airways, Inc. as parties. These four actions, with their substantially similar allegations, were consolidated for all pretrial purposes through a stipulated Order dated September 16, 1999.

As detailed in a prior Opinion and Order, see Chase v. Northwest Airlines Corp., 49 F.Supp.2d 553 (E.D.Mich.1999), this case concerns the Defendant Airlines' refusal to sell so-called "hidden-city" tickets, whereby a passenger who wishes to travel to or from one of the Airlines' hub airports is able to obtain a cheaper fare by purchasing a "spoke-hub-spoke" ticket that encompasses the desired "hub-spoke" route, and then simply discarding the unused portion of the ticket. Each of the Defendant Airlines has adopted a policy prohibiting the sale of such tickets, and the Airlines also have devised various mechanisms to enforce their prohibitions. Plaintiffs allege that the Defendant Airlines, Defendant ARC, and others have conspired to enforce these prohibitions, and that each Airline's separate prohibition constitutes an unlawful exercise of monopoly power over many of the routes that originate or terminate at its hub airports.

By motion filed on November 15, 2000, Plaintiffs now request certification of several proposed classes of airline customers under Fed.R.Civ.P. 23, including: (i) a class of ticket purchasers who seek injunctive relief from Defendants' alleged Section 1 and 2 violations; (ii) a class of ticket purchasers who purportedly suffered monetary losses as a result of Defendants' alleged Section 1 conspiracy to eliminate hidden-city ticketing; and (iii) sub-classes of customers of each individual Defendant Airline who seek to recover damages for each Airline's alleged violation of Section 2. For their part, the Defendant Airlines filed a motion for summary judgment on November 15, 2000, arguing that Plaintiffs' Section 1 and 2 claims are deficient as a matter of law in a number of respects.

Both of these motions have been fully briefed by the parties. In addition, on November 14, 2001, the Court heard oral argument on these matters. Having reviewed the parties' submissions and the voluminous record, and having considered the arguments of counsel at the November 14 hearing, the Court now is prepared to rule on Plaintiffs' and the Airline Defendants' motions.

II. FACTUAL AND PROCEDURAL BACKGROUND

The parties have submitted lengthy recitations of the facts of this case, and have provided innumerable boxes of exhibits in support of their respective positions. Needless to say, a full account of all of the facts of this case would fill an entire volume of the Federal Supplement. Accordingly, what follows is necessarily a summary of the most pertinent facts and circumstances, with more details to follow as necessary to the Court's analysis of the arguments raised in the parties' motions.

A. The Parties to These Actions

The named Plaintiffs in this consolidated action are Nelson Chase, Norman Volk, Nitrogenous Industries Corp., and Keystone Business Machines, Inc. The Defendants are (i) Northwest Airlines Corp. and Northwest Airlines, Inc. (collectively "Northwest"); (ii) U.S. Airways Group, Inc. and U.S. Airways, Inc. (collectively "U.S. Airways"); (iii) Delta Air Lines, Inc. ("Delta"); and (iv) Airline Reporting Corporation ("ARC").

Defendant ARC is an airline trade association owned and controlled by its constituent member airlines. ARC provides accreditation for travel agencies and a central clearinghouse for ticket sales made by these agencies. The remaining Defendants, of course, are major passenger airlines that provide air travel service throughout the nation and the world.

Each of the named Plaintiffs purchased at least one unrestricted, full-fare ticket from one of the Defendant Airlines during the relevant time period—on or after October 10, 1992, as to the claims against Northwest; on or after May 18, 1995, as to the claims against U.S. Airways; and on or after June 11, 1995, as to the claims against Delta. These ticket purchases all involved travel that began or ended at a Defendant Airline's hub airport—either Minneapolis, Detroit, or Memphis, for Northwest; Pittsburgh or Charlotte, for U.S. Airways; and Atlanta or Cincinnati, for Delta. In all, Plaintiffs have identified 234 "Affected City-Pair Routes" that begin or end at one of these hub airports. The named Plaintiffs seek to serve as class representatives for all passengers who purchased unrestricted, full-fare tickets on or after the above-cited dates for travel on one of these "Affected City-Pair Routes."

B. The Practice of "Hidden-City" Ticketing

This case arises from the Defendant Airlines' efforts to discourage or eliminate the practice of "hidden-city" ticketing (also referred to as "point-beyond" ticketing). To use an example that has become ubiquitous in these proceedings, consider a passenger who wishes to travel from New York to Northwest's hub airport in Detroit. Upon calling Northwest or a travel agent to inquire about fares, this passenger might discover that the unrestricted, one-way full fare for travel from New York to Detroit is $394.00. However, upon further inquiry, the passenger might learn that a one-way full fare ticket for travel from New York to Columbus, Ohio costs only $238.73. Yet, because of the hub-and-spoke layout of Northwest's flight network, it happens that a trip from New York to Columbus actually involves two segments, one from New York to Detroit and one from Detroit to Columbus. Thus, a savvy—or, Defendants would say, unscrupulous—traveler might elect to purchase a New York-Columbus ticket, disembark in Detroit, and simply throw away the unneeded portion of the ticket for travel from Detroit to Columbus.

(The parties also occasionally refer to the practice of "back-to-back" ticketing, which involves the purchase of two round-trip tickets for travel in opposite directions—for example, New York/Detroit and Detroit/New York—and permits the purchaser to avoid the premium charged for travel that does not satisfy a minimum-stay requirement. For example, if a business traveler wished to make a round trip between New York and Detroit on two consecutive midweek days, thereby failing to qualify for a less expensive fare involving a Saturday stayover, he might discover that it is cheaper to purchase two discounted round-trip tickets, each including a Saturday stayover, and to use only the first legs of these two tickets to form a composite midweek round-trip ticket, rather than purchasing a single, much more expensive round-trip ticket that reflected his actual travel plans. The practice of back-to-back ticketing, though sometimes relevant to the arguments made by the parties, is not directly at issue in this case.)

The Defendant Airlines oppose [the] practice of hidden-city ticketing, and have devised various measures to prevent it. The focus of this case is to determine the reasons for this opposition, and the lawfulness of these reasons. Plaintiffs allege that Defendants have two motives for seeking to eliminate the practice of hidden-city ticketing: (i) an agreement among themselves and other airlines that they would do so; and (ii) a concern that this practice, if permitted, would undermine the Airlines' overall fare structure, including an alleged "hub premium" imposed upon passengers traveling to or from hub airports by virtue of the Airlines' alleged monopoly power at these airports. Plaintiffs further assert that the first of these motivations violates Section 1 of the Sherman Act, and that the second violates Section 2.

The Defendant Airlines, for their part, deny that they have acted in concert in adopting and enforcing their rules against hidden-city ticketing, deny that they possess monopoly power at their respective hub airports, and affirmatively contend that their fare structures are an economically rational and wholly lawful means to recover the fixed costs of their hub-spoke systems, notwithstanding that these fare structures might give rise to the occasional hidden-city fare anomaly. Defendants further assert that each Airline may lawfully protect its fare structure by prohibiting hidden-city ticketing, and that, in the face of these prohibitions, a passenger's attempt to employ the practice of hidden-city ticketing is tantamount to fraud.

III. THE DEFENDANT AIRLINES' MOTION FOR SUMMARY JUDGMENT

A. The Standards Governing Defendants' Motion

In their present motion, the Defendant Airlines seek summary judgment in their favor on Plaintiffs' antitrust claims under both Section 1 and Section 2 of the Sherman

Act. This motion, of course, is governed by the familiar standards set forth in Federal Rule of Civil Procedure 56, under which summary judgment is proper "if the pleadings, depositions, answers to interrogatories, and admissions on file, together with the affidavits, if any, show that there is no genuine issue as to any material fact and that the moving party is entitled to judgment as a matter of law." Fed.R.Civ.P. 56(c).

B. Plaintiffs' Section 1 Antitrust Conspiracy Claim

1. The Defendant Airlines Are Not Entitled to Summary Judgment Under the So-Called "Fraud Prevention" Exception to Sherman Act Liability.

The cornerstone of Defendants' present challenge to Plaintiffs' Section 1 antitrust conspiracy claim is set forth with unmistakable clarity in the Airlines' brief, where they declare that the practice of hidden-city ticketing "is fraud." (Defendants' Motion, Br. in Support at 11.) Defendants then explain:

> [Hidden-city ticketing] is an intentional effort on the part of a passenger to trick an airline through false pretenses into selling transportation services at a price that the airline would not be willing to accept if the passenger had truthfully represented his intended itinerary. In doing so, the passenger also breaches his contract of carriage with the airline. Misrepresenting one's intended itinerary to get air transportation services at a price the airline would not otherwise have charged is no different from lying to get a bereavement fare, misrepresenting one's age to get a senior citizen discount at the movies, or switching price tags on merchandise at a grocery store.

(Id.)

Having thus stated their premise, Defendants appeal to decisions in which the Supreme Court recognized that certain exchanges of information among competitors do not run afoul of § 1 of the Sherman Act, where such exchanges are necessary to prevent fraud. [See] Cement Mfrs. Protective Ass'n v. United States, 268 U.S. 588, 45 S.Ct. 586, 69 L.Ed. 1104 (1925), [and] Maple Flooring Mfrs. Ass'n v. United States, 268 U.S. 563, 45 S.Ct. 578, 69 L.Ed. 1093 (1925). It follows, in Defendants' view, that the Airlines' joint discussions of hidden-city ticketing at trade association meetings and on other occasions do not give rise to Sherman Act liability for an antitrust conspiracy. Upon reviewing the decisions in Cement Manufacturers and Maple Flooring, the Court finds that they speak to some aspects of the present case but not to others.

Plaintiffs apparently do not dispute that the practice of hidden-city ticketing requires a passenger to breach an airline's tariff rules and contract of carriage, which are incorporated by reference into the conditions of sale of each ticket purchased. In this sense, a passenger must "misrepresent" his intended itinerary, impliedly stating as he purchases the ticket that he wishes to travel the entire spoke-hub-spoke route, but knowing that he instead will discard the tickets for travel to and from the point beyond his true destination. To this extent, then, the situation here is like the one presented in Cement Manufacturers, where contractors breached their contracts with cement manufacturers by representing that several different purchases of cement all were earmarked for use in a single project.

However, there are a number of ways in which the rubric of "fraud prevention" does not precisely carry over from Cement Manufacturers to this case. First, in Cement Manufacturers, the contractual limitation upon a contractor's purchase of cement—namely, that the cement must be used on a specific job—presumably was a quid pro quo for the manufacturer's agreement to "lock in" the maximum price for that purchase, with the manufacturer bearing the full risk of any intervening price increases. When a contractor violated this contractual limitation, purchasing cement that would not be used on the job specified in the contract, the contractor received something more than the bargained-for benefit, thereby disrupting the seemingly settled expectations of both contracting parties. It can be assumed, moreover, that the contractor was aware that "padded" purchases were contrary to the business arrangement as established and agreed to by the parties. Under these circumstances, there was no question as to the unlawful nature of the contractor's conduct in representing that each of several purchases of cement was intended for use in the same project.

This case, in contrast, involves the unilateral imposition by the Airlines of an additional condition of sale—a condition of which, it seems fair to say, many passengers are not even aware. Although Defendants suggest that a passenger's knowledge of the airlines' tariff rules is irrelevant, the very case they cite confirms that fraud requires a misrepresentation that is "calculated or intended to deceive" the injured party. VanDenBroeck v. CommonPoint Mortgage Co., 210 F.3d 696, 701 (6th Cir.2000). Package discount pricing is commonplace in many industries—children's meals at fast food restaurants and automobile luxury packages are two examples that come to mind—and the average consumer presumably would not perceive that his purchase of such a package would serve as an implied "representation" that he intends to use each and every part of that package, much less that he might be accused of fraud or deception if he chooses to discard a particular portion. While the Airlines surely would prefer to know in advance whether a passenger intends to travel on each segment for which he purchased a ticket—so that, for instance, they can sell tickets for any unused seats, and can plan their operations based on a more accurate count of passengers—their business objectives do not automatically trigger a passenger's duty to disclose his true itinerary, nor do they transform his silence on the subject into an "intent to deceive." In short, the question of "fraud" here involves a fact-intensive inquiry of a sort that was not needed in Cement Manufacturers.

Of course, a duty to disclose may be imposed by contract, and this arguably is what the Airlines have done. Even so, however, the situation here is different from the one presented in Cement Manufacturers, where, as noted, the contractors received a benefit in exchange for their agreement to a limiting contractual term. Here, the tariff rules incident to a passenger ticket are not the subject of negotiations, but instead are presented to the passenger on a take-it-or-leave-it basis, almost as in a contract of adhesion. It cannot be said here, as it could in Cement Manufacturers, that a contracting party expressly and knowingly agreed to a limiting condition in exchange for a particular benefit, and then, having received the benefit, refused to adhere to the condition. In addition, even accepting the enforceability of the Airlines' hidden-city prohibitions as a matter of contract law, it is well established that the breach of a contractual obligation cannot support a claim of fraud. See, e.g., Brock v. Consolidated Biomedical Lab., 817 F.2d 24, 25–26 (6th Cir.1987).

More importantly, Defendants' appeal to "fraud prevention" begs one of the central questions in this case—namely, whether the Airlines' prohibition on hidden-city ticketing is an anticompetitive practice that violates the Sherman Act. In Cement Manufacturers, there was no claim that the underlying industry practice of using specific job contracts was itself anticompetitive, or that any manufacturer's use of this practice was the product of concerted action. Moreover, the Government did not challenge the right of each individual manufacturer to adopt measures to enforce the terms of its own specific job contracts; indeed, the Government presumably would not have challenged even a concerted enforcement effort, but for its claim that "uniformity of prices and limitation of production [we]re necessary results" of this joint endeavor. Cement Mfrs., 268 U.S. at 592, 45 S.Ct. at 587. In rejecting the Government's claim, the Court found that the only price and production effects that had resulted from the defendants' collective information-gathering effort were those that "would naturally flow from the dissemination of that information in the trade and its natural influence on individual action." 268 U.S. at 606, 45 S.Ct. at 592.

Here, by contrast, Plaintiffs' § 2 claim expressly challenges the lawfulness of each Airline's individual prohibition on hidden-city ticketing, alleging that this represents the anticompetitive exercise of each Defendant's alleged monopoly power, with an attendant impact upon the price of travel to or from Defendants' hub airports. Clearly, an individual Airline could not immunize itself from Sherman Act liability merely by characterizing the prohibited practice as "fraudulent" and enacting rules to prevent it. Just as clearly, § 1 would forbid any collective effort by Defendants to prohibit a practice that each could not lawfully proscribe on its own. Thus, while Cement Manufacturers did not address the propriety of an industry practice, but only the collective means of its enforcement, the present case implicates both questions, and the two are intertwined. The success of Defendants' appeal to "fraud prevention," then, necessarily depends to a degree upon their success in defeating Plaintiffs' § 2 claims, and factual issues as to the latter—a question addressed below—would preclude summary judgment as to the former.

More generally, Defendants' "fraud prevention" argument misconceives the nature of Plaintiffs' complaint about the Airlines' prohibition on hidden-city ticketing. Plaintiffs do not claim any "entitlement" to purchase hidden-city tickets, but presumably would be pleased to purchase tickets reflecting their actual hub-spoke itineraries, so long as the price of these tickets did not include a hub "premium" imposed as a product of an Airline's alleged monopoly power. Likewise, Plaintiffs presumably would not balk at disclosing their true hub-spoke travel plans to the Airlines, provided that they were required to pay only the discounted price that reflected any hidden-city savings opportunity. Indeed, according to Plaintiffs' experts, if Defendants are enjoined from enforcing their prohibitions on hidden-city ticketing, the Airlines' eventual response will be to lower their hub-spoke fares, thereby defeating their passengers' incentive to "misrepresent" their itineraries in order to obtain a cheaper hidden-city fare. In sum, while misrepresentation was the lynchpin of the scheme employed by the contractors in Cement Manufacturers, and the means through which they sought to avoid paying the prevailing market price in effect at the time they actually needed additional cement, the species of "fraud" practiced by airline customers in this case is not an essential prerequisite to the achievement of the fare structure sought by Plaintiffs, but is only a byproduct of these customers' "self-help" efforts to circumvent an allegedly unlawful pricing scheme imposed by the Airlines.

Finally, Plaintiffs' § 1 claim goes beyond the mere sharing of information, and charges that Defendants agreed to a concerted course of action. The Court in Cement Manufacturers was careful to point out that the manufacturers had not reached any agreement or understanding as to the use they would make of the information they had gathered, but instead remained "free to act upon [it] or not as they cho[ ]se." Cement Mfrs., 268 U.S. at 603–04, 45 S.Ct. at 591. In the present case, if the evidence shows only that Defendants collectively discussed the issue of hidden-city ticketing and shared information as to their respective prohibitions on the practice, but that they did not agree on a concerted policy or course of conduct with regard to this practice,

Plaintiffs' § 1 claim will fail under the authority of Maple Flooring. And, in fact, this is the next of Defendants' challenges to the Section 1 claim in this case—namely, that the evidentiary record does not give rise to a reasonable inference of collusive action. Accordingly, having rejected Defendants' claim that the "fraud prevention" rule of Cement Manufacturers precludes their liability as a matter of law, the Court now turns to this next challenge.

2. Plaintiffs Have Produced Sufficient Evidence of Concerted Action to Withstand Summary Judgment on Their Section 1 Claim.

[C]ourts have adopted fairly stringent standards for assessing claimed violations of § 1 of the Sherman Act. [T]he Sixth Circuit has adopted a two-step inquiry for resolving a motion for summary judgment on an antitrust conspiracy claim. See Riverview Investments, Inc. v. Ottawa Community Improvement Corp., 899 F.2d 474, 483 (6th Cir.), cert. denied, 498 U.S. 855, 111 S.Ct. 151, 112 L.Ed.2d 117 (1990). First, the Court must ask whether Plaintiffs' evidence of conspiracy is "ambiguous," meaning that it is "as consistent with the defendants' permissible independent interests as with an illegal conspiracy." 899 F.2d at 483. If so, the Court then must consider whether there is "any evidence that tends to exclude the possibility that the defendants were pursuing these independent interests." 899 F.2d at 483. "A plaintiff thus fails to demonstrate a conspiracy if, using ambiguous evidence, the inference of a conspiracy is less than or equal to an inference of independent action." 899 F.2d at 483; see also Blomkest Fertilizer, Inc. v. Potash Corp., 203 F.3d 1028, 1033 (8th Cir.2000) ("a litigant may not proceed by first assuming a conspiracy, and then explaining the evidence accordingly.").

In their present motion, Defendants argue that Plaintiffs' evidence fails this test, as it is ambiguous and is just as consistent with an inference of independent action as with an inference of conspiracy. Principally, Defendants contend (i) that each Defendant Airline has an independent business interest in prohibiting hidden-city ticketing; (ii) that the record reflects disparate adoption of hidden-city prohibitions by each Airline and disparate enforcement of these measures, thereby undermining any inference of concerted action; and (iii) that Plaintiffs' evidence of discussions among airline representatives about hidden-city ticketing is insufficient as a matter of law to establish a § 1 violation, absent further evidence of an agreed-upon course of conduct. Upon reviewing the record in light of Defendants' assertions, the Court finds that Plaintiffs' evidence of a § 1 conspiracy, while considerably short of overwhelming, would nevertheless permit a reasonable inference of collusive action.

Defendants' evidence of independent interests and actions is more equivocal than they would have the Court believe. First, Defendants sweep too broadly in their claim that each airline is indifferent to the hidden-city ticketing policies of other airlines, and is wholly free to adopt (or not) a prohibition on this practice by reference solely to its own independent business interests, and without fear of competitive losses to another airline. Even Defendants concede, in their reply brief, that this analysis does not necessarily continue to hold true for routes between two carriers' hub airports. (See Defendants' Reply Br. at 12.) Similarly, Northwest's former Chief Accounting Officer, Mark Osterberg, pointed out that hub airports shared by two carriers give rise to different competitive considerations: "Let's take Dallas. Let's suppose in Dallas, Delta elects to enforce hidden-city ticketing and American elects not to. They are both hub carriers in Dallas. If I want to do hidden-city ticketing and I'm a customer, I'm a passenger, I'm going to go on the carrier that's not going to enforce it." (Plaintiffs' Exhibits, Tab 95, Osterberg Dep. at 113.)

Thus, the relevant question, in terms of an airline's economic self-interest, would seem to be whether the financial gains from unilaterally enforcing a hidden-city prohibition on all hub-spoke routes would exceed the anticipated losses on hub-to-hub routes and at shared hubs if the airline's competitors chose not to prohibit hidden-city ticketing. Neither side's argument and evidence on this point is particularly compelling [and] questions of fact remain on the issue of each Airline's individual business interest in adopting a unilateral prohibition against hidden-city ticketing.

Next, the Court cannot concur in the dispositive weight Defendants would give to the evidence of each Airline's separate adoption and disparate enforcement of its tariff rules against hidden-city ticketing. [E]ven if an Airline already had adopted a tariff rule against hidden-city ticketing prior to the onset of the conspiracy alleged by Plaintiffs, this would not preclude the conclusion that this Airline nevertheless joined the conspiracy, and thereby agreed to retain its prior prohibition on hidden-city ticketing, or to enforce a previously dormant tariff rule. While it might well be more difficult to prove a conspiracy that involves only subtle changes in the conduct of its constituent members—and although a given member's prior adoption of the supposed object of the conspiracy is strong evidence that this member's actions were independently motivated, and not the product of collusion—Defendants' evidence of prior prohibitions does not alone establish, as a matter of law, that the Airlines could not have conspired to deter the practice of hidden-city ticketing. Nor is Plaintiffs' claim of conspiracy fatally undermined by minor variances in the particular means of enforcement chosen by each individual Airline—an agreement need not dictate every conceivable aspect of each conspirator's behavior in order to violate § 1.

Nonetheless, to survive summary judgment, Plaintiffs still must offer sufficient evidence of an agreement to act collectively against hidden-city ticketing.

In [this respect], Plaintiffs have produced some evidence that the Airlines' views on this subject evolved as a result of direct discussions among their representatives at industry meetings. The record can be read to suggest, for instance, that the airlines' international association, IATA, gradually arrived at the view that the analogous international practice of "cross-border" ticketing was counteracted most effectively by treating it as fraudulent. A 1989 IATA statement on the topic acknowledged that cross-border ticketing "is not fraud in the strict sense of criminal activity," but instead represented "a prevalent form of revenue dilution" and a "potentially substantial threat to yield maximization." (Plaintiffs' Exhibits, Tab 12, Dep. Ex. 206.) Over time, however, this practice was increasingly discussed in the context of fraud prevention, and was identified as an appropriate target for working groups and task forces that dealt with matters of fraud. Plaintiffs also point to an excerpt of the minutes of the March 17, 1993 meeting of the Joint ATA/IATA North American Fraud Prevention Task Force, whose membership included Northwest and U.S. Airways:

> Concern was expressed at a number of manipulative practices carried out by ARC agents that were treated simply as tariff matters whereas it was a Member's belief that such practices were fraudulent in nature in that they contained elements of deception and dishonesty that were prejudicial to the airlines. Practices such as hidden-city ticketing ... were, in general, not categorized as fraud. Members agreed that there were indeed problems in this area and that there was a need for an increasing awareness of these practices as being fraudulent....

(Plaintiffs' Exhibits, Tab 34, 3/17/93 Meeting Minutes at 6.) The Court finds that this evidence, among other materials in the record, could support an inference that the Airlines did not independently decide to treat hidden-city ticketing as fraud, but instead arrived at that conclusion as a "meeting of the minds" at industry gatherings.

The Court further concludes that this evidence serves as a "plus factor" which, if credited, would tend to exclude the possibility that the Airlines were acting independently. First, the labeling of hidden-city ticketing as fraud would tend to overcome any individual Airline's inclination to weigh the competitive advantages and disadvantages of allowing the practice, and would instead provide a common motive for all Airlines to take action against it. Indeed, the record is replete with statements of the need for an industry-wide effort to combat fraud; Plaintiffs quote, for example, an airline representative's statement at a 1998 IATA Revenue Protection Forum that "I see that there is absolutely NO competition among airlines as far as fraud prevention is concerned." (Plaintiffs' Exhibits, Tab 57, Dep. Ex. 130 at 3.)

Moreover, separate from these industry exhortations against hidden-city ticketing as "fraud," Plaintiffs have produced evidence which suggests that the proactive discussions of "cross-border" ticketing at IATA meetings might have spilled over into the Airlines' views of hidden-city ticketing as a practice that also should be more aggressively targeted. There seems to be little doubt that IATA, through certain working groups and task forces, affirmatively recommended steps that airlines could take to deter the practice of cross-border ticketing. Yet, it appears that IATA and its sub-groups did not always scrupulously observe the distinction between cross-border and hidden-city ticketing, so that it is not unreasonable to infer that recommendations as to the former practice might have affected the airlines' behavior with respect to the latter one.

In light of the Airlines' apparent consensus that hidden-city ticketing is a species of "fraud," and given the evidence that the Airlines discussed the practice and occasionally encouraged greater diligence at their industry gatherings, the Court finds that the present record would permit a reasonable inference that the Airlines' efforts to deter hidden-city ticketing are attributable to a common scheme or meeting of the minds, and do not simply reflect separate, legitimate business judgments as to a prudent course of action.

3. Defendants Are Not Entitled to Summary Judgment under a "Rule of Reason" Analysis of Their Alleged Conduct.

Finally, even assuming that the Airlines' prohibitions against hidden-city ticketing reflect an agreement to oppose the practice, Defendants argue that their justifications for adopting these prohibitions would pass muster under a "Rule of Reason" analysis. The Court harbors substantial doubt, however, as to whether a full-scale Rule of Reason analysis is required under the circumstances presented here. Even if so, the present record does not permit the Court to declare the outcome of such an analysis as a matter of law.

In another recent case also involving airline policy—in that case, a policy regarding the use of baggage templates at Dulles Airport, in order to limit the size of carry-on baggage—the Fourth Circuit surveyed the three different levels of analysis that have been applied to determine whether an agreement among competitors, or a "horizontal restraint," violates § 1 of the Sherman Act:

> In determining whether a plaintiff has proved that a horizontal agreement violates Section 1, the Supreme Court has authorized three methods of analysis: (1) per se analysis, for obviously anticompetitive restraints, (2) quick-look analysis, for those with some procompetitive justification, and (3) the full "rule

> of reason," for restraints whose net impact on competition is particularly difficult to determine. The boundaries between these levels of analysis are fluid; there is generally no categorical line to be drawn between restraints that give rise to an intuitively obvious inference of anticompetitive effect and those that call for more detailed treatment. Instead, the three methods are best viewed as a continuum, on which the amount and range of information needed to evaluate a restraint varies depending on how highly suspicious and how unique the restraint is. In all cases, however, the criterion to be used in judging the validity of a restraint on trade is its impact on competition.
>
> The first approach, per se analysis, permits courts to make categorical judgments that certain practices, including price fixing, horizontal output restraints, and market-allocation agreements, are illegal per se. Practices suitable for per se analysis have been found over the years to be one[s] that would always or almost always tend to restrict competition and decrease output, and that are not designed to increase economic efficiency and render markets more, rather than less, competitive. Such restrictions have such predictable and pernicious anticompetitive effect, and such limited potential for procompetitive benefit, that they are deemed unlawful per se without any need to conduct a detailed study of the markets on which the restraints operate or the actual effect of those restraints on competition.
>
> At the other end of the spectrum, if the reasonableness of a restraint cannot be determined without a thorough analysis of its net effects on competition in the relevant market, courts must apply a full rule-of-reason analysis. In such cases a plaintiff must prove what market ... was restrained and that the defendants played a significant role in the relevant market because [a]bsent this market power, any restraint on trade created by [a] defendant's action is unlikely to implicate Section 1. The required analysis varies by case and may extend to plenary market examination, covering the facts peculiar to the business, the history of the restraint, and the reasons why it was imposed, as well as the availability of reasonable, less restrictive alternatives.
>
> Sometimes, the anticompetitive impact of a restraint is clear from a quick look, as in a per se case, but procompetitive justifications for it also exist. Such intermediate cases may involve[ ] an industry in which horizontal restraints on competition are essential if the product is to be available at all, or in which a horizontal restraint otherwise plausibly increase[s] economic efficiency and renders markets more, rather than less, competitive. For these cases, abbreviated or "quick-look" analysis fills in the continuum between per se analysis and the full rule of reason.

Continental Airlines, Inc. v. United Airlines, Inc., 277 F.3d 499, 508–10 (4th Cir.2002) (internal quotations and citations omitted).

In Continental, a Dulles Airport management council, consisting of all airlines serving the airport, and defendant United, the primary carrier at Dulles, had instituted a policy of installing baggage templates at the airport's two security checkpoints, and requiring that all carry-on baggage must fit through these templates. Each airline was given a supply of "medallions" that it could provide to select passengers—typically, first-class, business-class, and full coach fare passengers—whose baggage was then exempt from the template limitation.

Plaintiff Continental dissented from this decision, alleging that it deprived the airline of its ability to compete on the basis of its more liberal carry-on baggage policy. In particular, Continental had expanded the overhead bin storage on its fleet of aircraft, and had increased its gate-checking services, so that carry-on bags could be quickly checked at the gate if the space on board had been exhausted.

The District Court applied a quick-look Rule of Reason analysis to this policy, and concluded that the defendants' procompetitive justifications were wanting as a matter of law. See Continental Airlines, Inc. v. United Air Lines, Inc., 126 F.Supp.2d 962, 974–81 (E.D.Va.2001). The lower court reasoned that a full Rule of Reason analysis was not necessary, where the baggage template policy "amount[s] to an agreement to provide a lower quality product and hence counts as an output restriction," in that it "standardizes, and thereby eliminates open competition on, an element of the bargain between carriers and passengers." 126 F.Supp.2d at 975. "In this regard, it is elementary economics that insofar as defendants' restriction standardizes an element of competition and prevents airlines like Continental from offering a better product and superior service to consumers with regard to carry-on baggage capacity and policies, the economic effect of the restriction is no different from the effect of a horizontal agreement among competitor airlines to fix the price of air carriage service for consumers." 126 F.Supp.2d at 975–76.

The District Court also found, however, that something more than per se analysis was required, because the airlines "operate out of shared airport facilities and thus must form agreements from time to time concerning the use of these facilities," and because "[s]ome agreements of this sort may further procompetitive goals." 126 F.Supp.2d at 977. The Court then rejected the defendants' three proffered procompetitive justifications—improved on-time performance, enhanced onboard safety, and improved passenger comfort and convenience—and awarded summary judgment in favor of Continental.

The Fourth Circuit reversed, and remanded the matter to the District Court for further assessment of the baggage template policy under a more fully developed record. In so ruling, the Court observed that the unique architectural configuration at Dulles—a "bottleneck" facility with two common security checkpoints, and with past experience indicating that these two checkpoints could not vary in their treatment of carry-on baggage—"force[s] all of its airlines to cooperate on a single decision as to the use of templates." Continental, 277 F.3d at 512. "When the economic implications of physical or geographical limitations require coordination among competitors, the Supreme Court has long applied Section 1 of the Sherman Act with flexibility." 277 F.3d at 512–13. The Court further reasoned:

> Moreover, beyond the general need for greater cooperation at Dulles than at other airports, United and Continental each make a more specific claim, related to Dulles's unique configuration, as to why their respective preferred outcomes benefit competition. Each argues that only a uniform policy in accordance with its preference will make possible an entire service that would not otherwise be available at Dulles: assertedly, Continental must win to offer flights with carry-on largesse, and United must win to offer flights with carry-on rigor. The district court may ultimately have to choose between two procompetitive claims; either outcome would both help and hurt competition, and which helps competition more than the other may be far from plain.

277 F.3d at 513.

Under these circumstances, the Fourth Circuit found that additional analysis was necessary "to determine the nature of the challenged restraint's net effect on competition." 277 F.3d at 513. The Court also held that the lower court had erred in determining that the defendants' procompetitive justifications were implausible as a matter of law. Accordingly, the case was remanded for further consideration of these issues under a more fully developed factual record. The Court did not decide, however, whether a modified quick-look analysis would suffice on remand, or whether a more extensive Rule of Reason analysis would be required to properly assess the lawfulness of the challenged restraint.

Continental provides valuable guidance in determining the proper level of analysis to apply in this case. In particular, by comparing that case to this one, the Court is fairly readily able to reject the extreme positions offered by the two sides here, and to conclude that the proper level of scrutiny lies somewhere in between per se and full-scale Rule of Reason analysis. It follows that Defendants are not entitled to summary judgment in their favor on Plaintiffs' § 1 claim, and that the Court must await a full evidentiary record before deciding what sort of analysis should govern this claim.

C. Plaintiffs' Section 2 Monopolization Claims

Defendants also seek summary judgment in their favor on Plaintiffs' § 2 claims against each individual Defendant Airline. Most of the grounds for Defendants' motion do not warrant extended discussion here, as they already have been addressed in the Court's prior ruling regarding the opinions of Plaintiffs' experts. These include: (i) that Plaintiffs have failed to establish that their 234 hub-spoke city-pairs are appropriate markets upon which to base § 2 monopolization claims; (ii) that Plaintiffs have not demonstrated the existence of monopoly power in each of these markets; and (iii) that Plaintiffs and their experts have drawn unwarranted inferences—both as to the existence and exercise of monopoly power, and as to the existence and extent of damages suffered by members of the Plaintiff class—from the mere existence of some hidden-city savings opportunities for each hub-spoke market. Because the opinions of Plaintiffs' experts have been deemed admissible on these points, at least at the present juncture, this proffered expert testimony raises genuine issues of fact under the present record that preclude an award of summary judgment on these grounds. The battle of the parties' experts, in other words, must await resolution at trial.

This leaves only a single remaining argument in support of Defendants' motion—namely, that each Airline's prohibition against hidden-city ticketing has purely "intrabrand" effects which cannot support a claim under § 2. As explained in the Court's initial published Opinion in this case:

> In order to state a viable monopolization claim under § 2, an anti-trust plaintiff must allege: (1) the possession of monopoly power in the relevant market; and (2) the willful acquisition, maintenance, or use of that power by anti-competitive or exclusionary means. Section 2 requires both elements because the mere possession of monopoly power is not illegal.

Chase, 49 F.Supp.2d at 565 (internal quotations and citations omitted). Then, as now, Defendants challenged the second element of this standard, asserting that Plaintiffs had not identified any actionable anticompetitive conduct. The Court rejected this contention at the outset of this litigation, and finds an insufficient basis for concluding differently at this juncture.

The Court is confident that none of the broad principles relied upon by Defendants establishes the per se lawfulness of their hidden-city prohibitions. Moreover, the Court's tentative assessment of the marketplace, fails to lead to a firm conclusion, as a matter of law, that the Airlines' prohibitions raise no anticompetitive concerns. Accordingly, Defendants are not entitled to summary judgment in their favor on Plaintiffs' §2 claims.

[The remainder of the court's opinion is omitted.]

IN RE AMERICAN AIRLINES, INC. PRIVACY LITIGATION

370 F. Supp. 2d 552 (N.D. Tex. 2005)

FITZWATER, District Judge.

Defendants' Fed.R.Civ.P. 12(b)(6) motions to dismiss require that the court decide whether plaintiffs have stated claims under the Electronic Communications Privacy Act-Stored Communications ("ECPA"), 18 U.S.C. §2701 et seq., and whether plaintiffs' state-law claims are preempted by the Airline Deregulation Act of 1978 ("ADA"), and, if not, whether plaintiffs have stated state-law claims on which relief can be granted. For the reasons that follow, the court holds that plaintiffs' ECPA actions fail to state a claim, that their state-law claims, except their breach of contract action, are expressly preempted by the ADA, and that they have failed to state a breach of contract claim on which relief can be granted. The court therefore grants defendants' motions to dismiss and allows plaintiffs to replead.

I

These are consolidated cases pending in this court for coordinated or consolidated pretrial proceedings by order of the Judicial Panel on Multidistrict Litigation. See In re Am. Airlines, Inc., Privacy Litig., 342 F.Supp.2d 1355 (J.P.M.L.2004). Plaintiffs bring putative nationwide class actions on behalf of persons allegedly injured when defendants AMR Corp. and American Airlines, Inc. (collectively, "American") authorized Airline Automation, Inc. ("AAI") to disclose highly confidential passenger information—passenger name records ("PNRs")—to the Transportation Security Administration ("TSA"), without the passengers' consent. They allege that, without the passengers' consent, and perhaps without American's permission, AAI accessed and provided the information to four private research companies: defendants Fair, Isaac and Company, Infoglide Software Corporation, Lockheed Martin Corporation (collectively, "vendor defendants"), and Ascent Technology, Inc. ("Ascent"). Plaintiffs maintain that defendants intentionally accessed, without authorization, a facility through which an electronic communication service is provided or exceeded their authority in order to obtain stored electronic communications that included plaintiffs' personally-identifiable information.

In Kimmell v. AMR Corp., et al., No. 3:04-CV-0750-D, and Baldwin v. AMR Corp., et al., No. 3:04-CV-1148-D, plaintiffs sue under 18 U.S.C. §2707 for violations of the ECPA and on state-law claims for breach of contract, trespass to property, invasion of privacy, unjust enrichment, and deceptive trade practices under the Texas Deceptive Trade Practices—Consumer Protection Act, Tex. Bus. & Com.Code Ann. §§17.41–17.826 (Vernon 2002 & Supp.2004–05), and similar statutes of 48 other states and the District of Columbia that prohibit unfair and deceptive acts and practices. In Rosenberg v. AMR Corp., et al., No. 3:04-CV-2564-D, plaintiff sues under the ECPA and for breach of contract, deceptive trade practices under N.Y. Gen. Bus. Law §349 (McKinney 2004) and similar statutes of 48 other states and the District of Columbia that prohibit unfair and deceptive acts and practices, trespass to property, invasion of privacy, and unjust enrichment.

American owns and operates an Internet website—http://www.aa.com—that enables customers to purchase tickets for air transportation and provides users the ability to send or receive wire or electronic communications. AAI plays a role in maintaining the website. American also owns or operates SABRE, a computer reservation system or server ("CRS") used in providing air transportation-related services, such as ticket reservations and sales. It, too, provides users the ability to send or receive wire or electronic communications. The website also enables users to send or receive electronic communications to the CRS. When American takes reservations or sells air transportation over the telephone or via the Internet, it collects personally-identifiable information from its passengers, including name, address, telephone numbers, AAdvantage account and flight information, credit/debit card information, emergency contacts, seating and dietary preferences, passport number, and country of residence. The information is bundled and maintained in a PNR.

American's website sets out its privacy policy, which is part of the contract of carriage with passengers. The policy states the limitations American observes in disclosing or sharing customer information and represents that information security is one of its highest priorities. In sum, the policy represents that American does not sell customer information or share a customer's email address with third parties unless required by law, and does not disclose customer information to companies affiliated with American, or unaffiliated third parties, except to fulfill products or services the customer requests, and may disclose this information to United States or other countries' tax, security, or regulatory authorities, if required by law. American represents that access to personal information about customers is limited to employees and agents who need to know the information to provide products and services, that personal information is maintained under strict physical, electronic, and procedural safeguards that comply with federal regulations, that security standards and procedures are regularly reviewed to protect against unauthorized access, and that American participates in the Council of Better Business Bureaus' online privacy program and complies with its privacy and security standards.

In or about June 2002 American, through its agent, AAI, turned over approximately 1.2 million electronically-stored PNRs. American and AAI accessed this personal information without the passengers' prior authorization and/or beyond their consent. AAI also purportedly lacked American's consent. AAI, in turn, disclosed the information to the vendor defendants and Ascent. When the news broke that JetBlue Airways Corporation had disclosed such information, American initially denied that it had released passenger personal information. In 2004, however, it admitted that it had authorized AAI to disclose highly confidential personal passenger information to TSA, although it contends that AAI exceeded its authority by accessing, transferring, or making PNRs available to the vendor defendants and Ascent. AAI maintains that American was fully aware of, and authorized, this access.

Defendants move to dismiss these actions for failure to state a claim, contending that plaintiffs cannot recover under the ECPA, their state-law actions are preempted under the ADA, and, if any causes of action are not preempted, plaintiffs have failed to state claims on which relief can be granted.

II

The court considers first whether defendants are entitled to dismissal of plaintiffs' ECPA claims. "[A] complaint should not be dismissed [under Rule 12(b)(6)] for failure to state a claim unless it appears beyond doubt that the plaintiff can prove no set of facts in support of his claim which would entitle him to relief." Ramming v. United

States, 281 F.3d 158, 161 (5th Cir.2001) (per curiam) (quoting Conley v. Gibson, 355 U.S. 41, 45–46, 78 S.Ct. 99, 2 L.Ed.2d 80 (1957)).

A

As clarified at oral argument, plaintiffs allege that AAI violated §2701 of the ECPA by intentionally accessing without authorization, and/or in excess of its authorization, plaintiffs' PNRs and, in turn, divulging their contents to the vendor defendants. Plaintiffs assert that the vendor defendants are also liable directly and as aiders and abettors and co-conspirators. AAI argues that plaintiffs' §2701-based claim fails because, inter alia, by pleading that American authorized AAI to disclose 1.2 million PNRs to TSA, they implicitly concede that American authorized AAI to access the PNRs in any American electronic communication service. AAI also maintains that plaintiffs cannot recover because, while there may be some dispute regarding whether American provided AAI the PNRs with the understanding that it would disclose them only to TSA, they have not pleaded specific facts that support the conclusion that AAI originally obtained the data without American's consent.

The court concludes that plaintiffs have failed to state a §2701-based claim against AAI. Their amended complaints each assert that American authorized AAI to disclose the PNRs to TSA. See, e.g., Kimmell Am. Compl. 38. As AAI points out, an implicit corollary to these averments is that AAI obtained the passengers' information with American's knowledge and consent, i.e., it had American's authorization to access the PNRs in the first place. Absent an explicit allegation that American authorized AAI to disclose the PNRs to TSA after AAI had obtained unauthorized access to American's facility—a premise that is so at odds with common sense that it cannot reasonably be inferred absent such specificity—the amended complaints undercut the premise that AAI lacked American's authorization to access its facility.

Plaintiffs are therefore limited to the contention that AAI violated §2701 by exceeding its authorization to access American's facility. Although plaintiffs include conclusory allegations that AAI in fact exceeded its authorization, see, e.g., Kimmell Am. Compl. ¶51, the factual basis for these assertions is that AAI lacked authorization to disclose the PNRs to any entity other than TSA, i.e., the vendor defendants and Ascent. See, e.g., id. ¶¶39, 40 ("While [American] admits that it authorized AAI to disclose highly confidential personal passenger information to the TSA, it contends that AAI exceeded its authority by accessing, transferring or making PNRs available to [the vendor defendants] and non-party Ascent. AAI, however, claims that [American] was fully aware of and authorized access by [the vendor defendants] and non-party Ascent."). The facts plaintiffs plead demonstrate that they are relying on a theory of unauthorized disclosure of information, not of access that exceeded what was authorized.

The purpose of §2701 is to prevent unauthorized access to a facility through which an electronic communication service is provided. See In re N.W. Airlines Privacy Litig., 2004 WL 1278459, at *2 (D.Minn. June 6, 2004) (dismissing §2701-based claim because "[p]laintiffs' complaint is not with how Northwest obtained the information, but with how Northwest subsequently used the information."); Sherman & Co. v. Salton Maxim Housewares, Inc., 94 F.Supp.2d 817, 821 (E.D.Mich.2000) ("Because section 2701 of the ECPA prohibits only unauthorized access and not the misappropriation or disclosure of information, there is no violation of section 2701 for a person with authorized access to the database no matter how malicious or larcenous his intended use of that access. Section 2701 outlaws illegal entry, not larceny."); Educ. Testing Serv. v. Stanley H. Kaplan Educ. Ctr., Ltd., 965 F.Supp. 731, 740 (D.Md.1997) ("[I]t appears evident that the sort of trespasses to which the [ECPA] applies are those in which the trespasser gains access to information to which he is not entitled to see, not those in which the trespasser uses the information in an unauthorized way."); State Wide Photocopy Corp. v. Tokai Fin. Servs., Inc., 909 F.Supp. 137, 145 (S.D.N.Y.1995) ("Section 2701 is aimed at parties accessing facilities without authorization."). Section 2701 does not proscribe unauthorized use or disclosure of information obtained from authorized access to a facility. See N.W. Airlines, 2004 WL 1278459, at *2; Sherman & Co., 94 F.Supp.2d at 820 (citing Wesley Coll. v. Pitts, 974 F.Supp. 375, 389 (D. Del.1997, aff'd, 172 F.3d 861 (3d Cir.1998) (unpublished table decision)). Yet this is what plaintiffs are alleging concerning AAI's disclosure of PNRs to the vendor defendants.

Other courts have described the conduct that § 2701 prohibits as computer "hacking." See, e.g., State Wide, 909 F.Supp. at 145 ("[I]t appears that the ECPA was primarily designed to provide a cause of action against computer hackers (i.e., electronic trespassers)."). Although plaintiffs allege that AAI "hacked" into American's electronic communication service or remote computing service, see, e.g., Kimmell Am. Compl. ¶ 1, this is a conclusory assertion that the court need not accept for purposes of deciding defendants' Rule 12(b)(6) motion. Accordingly, the court holds that plaintiffs have failed to state a § 2701-based claim against AAI.

Plaintiffs seek to hold the vendor defendants liable under § 2701 directly and as aiders and abettors and co-conspirators of American's violations of the ECPA. The court concludes that the vendor defendants are also entitled to dismissal. First, plaintiffs have failed to state a claim against them directly because, despite the conclusory allegations that these defendants accessed American's facility, the facts plaintiffs plead all point to their having received the PNRs from American and/or AAI. See, e.g., Kimmell Compl. ¶ 42 ("[American] and/or AAI accessed a facility ... and made [the contents of the communications] available for access by [the vendor defendants] and non-party Ascent."). Plaintiffs have failed to state a direct cause of action based on unauthorized access. Second, because plaintiffs clarified at oral argument that they are not asserting § 2701-based liability against American, the vendor defendants cannot be held liable under § 2701 as aiders and abettors or co-conspirators of American. Third, even if plaintiffs' clarification means that they intend to hold the vendor defendants liable as aiders and abettors of or co-conspirators with AAI, because the court is dismissing plaintiffs' § 2701-based claim against AAI, it follows that the vendor defendants cannot be held liable as aiders and abettors or co-conspirators. See In re Managed Care Litig., 298 F.Supp.2d 1259, 1286 (S.D.Fla.2003) (holding that civil liability for aiding and abetting requires showing that substantive offense was committed); Coppock v. Northrup Grumman Corp., 2003 WL 21730668, at *14 n.17 (N.D.Tex. July 22, 2003) (Fitzwater, J.) ("A claim for civil conspiracy is generally not viable without the commission of an underlying wrongful act[.]").

B

The court turns next to whether plaintiffs have stated a § 2702-based claim against American. With certain exceptions, § 2702 prohibits a provider of an electronic communication service or of a remote computing service to the public from knowingly divulging the contents of a communication in electronic storage or carried or maintained on the service. Plaintiffs allege that American violated § 2702 by authorizing the disclosure of passenger information.

American argues, inter alia, that, even assuming that its computer reservation system is an electronic communication service or a remote computing service, its conduct falls within the exception to liability set out in § 2702(b)(3), which permits disclosure of electronic communications "with the lawful consent of ... an ... intended recipient of such communication[.]" Plaintiffs respond that American cannot avail itself of this exception because its consent was unlawful in that it violated American's privacy policy, or because American was not the intended recipient of the electronic communications in question.

Plaintiffs have failed sufficiently to plead that American's consent was unlawful because it was given in violation of its privacy policy. Nor do they cite authority in their opposition memorandum that supports the assertion that consent under § 2702(b)(3) is not lawful if given in breach of a contract. Section 2702 is a criminal statute, and the mere breach of a contract normally is not "unlawful" in a criminal sense. See United States v. Blankenship, 382 F.3d 1110, 1133 (11th Cir.2004) ("It is not illegal for a party to breach a contract[.]"); Benderson Dev. Co. v. United States Postal Serv., 998 F.2d 959, 962 (Fed.Cir.1993) ("To breach a contract is not unlawful; the breach only begets a remedy in law or in equity."); Cram Roofing Co. v. Parker, 131 S.W.3d 84, 91 (Tex.App.2003, no pet.) (en banc) ("While a contract may indeed have the force of law, breach of a contract is not necessarily an illegal activity."). Moreover, the concept of "lawful consent" in § 2702(b)(3) is probably more akin to that found in other criminal statutes, i.e., consent given by one who has the legal capacity to consent. Cf., e.g., United States v. Chavarriya-Mejia, 367 F.3d 1249, 1251 (11th Cir.) (noting that law presumes children cannot lawfully consent to sexual contact), cert. denied, —U.S.—, 125 S.Ct. 95, 160 L.Ed.2d 182 (2004). Even if American was contractually bound by its privacy policy not to disclose passenger information and can be held liable for breach of contract, this obligation did not deprive it of the legal capacity under § 2702(b)(3) to consent to disclosure.

Plaintiffs also maintain that § 2702(b)(3) is inapplicable on the basis that the intended recipient of their electronic communications was SABRE instead of American. This contention is not supported, however, by their amended complaints. Plaintiffs allege that they conveyed personal information to American. Under § 2702(b)(3), American need only be an intended recipient, not the intended recipient. They also aver that they sent their personal information in reliance upon American's promise not to disclose it to third parties, except to provide travel services. This allegation of reliance on American's promise is inconsistent with the argument that they did not intend American to be a recipient of their personal information.

Accordingly, the court holds that plaintiffs have failed to state a § 2702-based claim against American. Plaintiffs' ECPA claim against all defendants is dismissed.

III

The court next addresses whether plaintiffs' state-law claims are expressly preempted by the ADA or are impliedly preempted by federal action in the field of aviation transportation security.

A

The court turns first to express preemption.

1

It is beyond question that, by enacting the ADA, Congress intended to preempt aspects of state law that govern air carriers. Section 41713(b)(1) provides:

> Except as provided in this subsection, a State ... may not enact or enforce a law, regulation, or other provision having the force and effect of law related to a price, route, or service of an air carrier that may provide air transportation under this subpart.

49 U.S.C. § 41713(b)(1). (Earlier cases refer to § 1305(a), which was recodified in 1994 with slight, nonsubstantive changes in language. See Lyn-Lea Travel Corp. v. Am. Airlines, Inc., 283 F.3d 282, 286 n.4 (5th Cir.2002). For example, § 1305(a) uses "relating to" rather than "related to," as does § 41713(b)(1).)

The Supreme Court reads broadly the "related to" language of this section and, in turn, the preemptive effect of the ADA. See Morales v. Trans World Airlines, Inc., 504 U.S. 374, 383, 112 S.Ct. 2031, 119 L.Ed.2d 157 (1992) ("The ordinary meaning of [relating to] is a broad one ... and the words thus express a broad pre-emptive purpose."). Laws of general applicability may be preempted by the ADA; they need not actually prescribe airline prices, routes, or services. See Hodges v. Delta Airlines, Inc., 44 F.3d 334, 336 (5th Cir.1995) (en banc). Moreover, "ADA preemption is not limited to claims brought directly against air carriers. Rather, claims are preempted if they 'relate to' the prices, routes or services of an air carrier." Lyn-Lea Travel Corp. v. Am. Airlines, Inc., 283 F.3d 282, 287 n.8 (5th Cir.2002) (citations omitted). Nor is preemption limited to state laws or regulations. See id. at 287–89 (holding, inter alia, that common law claims were preempted).

Not all claims that may have economic repercussions, however, are sufficiently related to an airline's prices, routes, or services to be preempted. "'[S]ome state actions may affect [airline fares] in too tenuous, remote, or peripheral a manner' to have pre-emptive effect." Morales, 504 U.S. at 390 (quoting Shaw v. Delta Air Lines, Inc., 463 U.S. 85, 100 n.21, 103 S.Ct. 2890, 77 L.Ed.2d 490 (1983)). Thus, for example, in Smith v. America West Airlines, Inc., 44 F.3d 344 (5th Cir.1995) (en banc), the claims of passengers who alleged that an airline was negligent in permitting a hijacker to board an aircraft were not preempted, despite the potential economic effects that could arise from a damages award. Id. at 345. The effects were too remotely related to fares to trigger ADA preemption. Id. at 347 ("If [plaintiffs] ultimately recover damages, the judgment could affect the airline's ticket selling, training or security practices, but it would not regulate the economic or contractual aspects of boarding. Any such effect would be 'too tenuous, remote or peripheral' to be preempted by [the statutory predecessor to § 41713]." (quoting Morales, 504 U.S. at 390)). Moreover, ADA preemption "does not displace state tort actions for personal physical injuries or property damage caused by the operation and maintenance of aircraft." Witty v. Delta Air Lines, Inc., 366 F.3d 380, 382 (5th Cir.2004) (quoting Hodges, 44 F.3d at 336).

2

The court initially decides whether plaintiffs' state-law claims for trespass to property, invasion of privacy, deceptive trade practices, and unjust enrichment are expressly preempted. Defendants contend, inter alia, that they are because PNRs are created when passengers make reservations for air carrier service and contain information necessary or convenient to provide the services American renders as an air carrier, and plaintiffs admit they conveyed personally-identifiable information to American when purchasing tickets for air transportation. They also cite plaintiffs' allegation that American's statements about privacy, customer information, and security are part of the contract of carriage.

Plaintiffs respond to this argument at two levels. As a general matter, they maintain that Congress enacted the ADA to ensure, following airline deregulation, that the states would not enact their own forms of economic regulation. They therefore assert that courts, including the Fifth Circuit, hold that claims are preempted only when their purpose or effect inhibits or frustrates this goal. Plaintiffs posit that their claims seeking redress for privacy rights violations have no connection to airline competition or economic deregulation of the airline industry, nor would they frustrate Congress' goal in enacting the ADA. At a more specific level, plaintiffs contend that these claims do not relate to American's rates, routes, or services. Concerning the pertinent component of airline services, they cite authority from outside this circuit to argue that the ADA definition encompasses only "the actual provision of transportation service." Ps. Consol. Mem. at 31.

The court holds that plaintiffs' actions for trespass to property, invasion of privacy, deceptive trade practices, and unjust enrichment are expressly preempted because they relate to at least one of American's services. This conclusion follows from analyzing in combination the Fifth Circuit's definition of "services," the Supreme Court's expansive construction of the term "relate to" in §41713(b)(1), and the factual bases for plaintiffs' claims. In Hodges the en banc court adopted the panel opinion's definition of "services."

"Services" generally represent a bargained-for or anticipated provision of labor from one party to another. If the element of bargain or agreement is incorporated in our understanding of services, it leads to a concern with the contractual arrangement between the airline and the user of the service. Elements of the air carrier service bargain include items such as ticketing, boarding procedures, provision of food and drink, and baggage handling, in addition to the transportation itself. These matters are all appurtenant and necessarily included with the contract of carriage between the passenger or shipper and the airline. It is these [contractual] features of air transportation that we believe Congress intended to de-regulate as "services" and broadly to protect from state regulation. Hodges, 44 F.3d at 336 (quoting Hodges v. Delta Airlines, Inc., 4 F.3d 350, 354 (5th Cir.1993)). Therefore, plaintiffs are incorrect in contending that "service" under the ADA "means the actual provision of transportation service." Ps. Consol. Mem. at 31. Plaintiffs' claims "relate to" American's services if they have a connection with or reference to them. See Hodges, 44 F.3d at 336 ("Consequently, '[s]tate enforcement actions having a connection with or reference to airline "rates, routes or services" are preempted' under [the statutory predecessor to §41713(b)(1)]."')." Morales commands that whatever state laws 'relate to ... services' are broadly preempted[.]" Id.

Plaintiffs allege that American collects personally-identifiable information from customers when taking reservations or selling air transportation. They also assert that American's privacy policy is part of the contract of carriage and prohibits American or its agents from disclosing their personal information, except in limited circumstances. See Ps. Consol. Mem. at 25 ("The privacy policy is unquestionably one of a number of terms that form the basis for the transportation agreement between passengers and American."). Their state-law claims for trespass to property, invasion of privacy, deceptive trade practices, and unjust enrichment are preempted because they have a connection at least with American's ticketing service, including the reservation component. Congress surely intended to immunize airlines from a host of potentially-varying state laws and state-law causes of action that could effectively dictate how they manage personal information collected from customers to facilitate the ticketing and reservation functions that are integral to the operation of a commercial airline.

These claims are likewise preempted to the extent asserted against AAI and the vendor defendants. See Lyn-Lea Travel, 283 F.3d at 287 n.8 (stating that ADA preemption is not limited to claims brought directly against air carriers but also preempts claims that relate to air carrier's services). The court recognizes that there will be instances in which state-law claims that would be preempted if brought against an airline will be too attenuated, remote, or peripheral to be preempted if asserted against an entity such as a vendor to an airline. The court need not decide today, however, precisely where that line should be drawn. See Hodges, 44 F.3d at 336 (noting that, in Morales, [the] Supreme Court had "[r]efus[ed] to state exactly where the line would be drawn in a close case[.]"). Although perhaps tautologically phrased, it can be said to occur on a relatedness continuum at the point where the state law's regulation of the entity's conduct is too attenuated, remote, or peripheral to be related to an airline's services. In the present case that point is not reached. Plaintiffs allege that American authorized AAI—whom plaintiffs assert plays a role in maintaining American's website—to disclose passenger information to TSA, and that it disclosed the information—perhaps without American's permission—to the vendor defendants. E.g., Kimmell Am. Compl. ¶¶27, 38–39. They assert, inter alia, that the vendor defendants aided and abetted and conspired with American to commit trespass to property, invasion of privacy, deceptive trade practices, and unjust enrichment. E.g., id. ¶47. Their claims against AAI and the vendor defendants are based on conduct that relates to American's ticketing service and its reservation component and for that reason are preempted.

3

The court next considers whether the ADA expressly preempts plaintiffs' breach of contract claim against American.

In American Airlines, Inc. v. Wolens, 513 U.S. 219, 115 S.Ct. 817, 130 L.Ed.2d 715 (1995), the Supreme Court recognized that the ADA's preemption clause does not "shelter airlines from suits alleging no violation of state-imposed obligations, but seeking recovery solely for the airline's alleged breach of its own, self-imposed undertakings." Id. at 228. "[T]erms and conditions airlines offer and passengers accept are privately ordered obligations and thus do not amount to a State's enact[ment] or enforce[ment] [of] any law, rule, regulation, standard, or other provision having the force and effect of law within the meaning of [the ADA preemption provision]." Id. (citations, footnote, and internal quotation marks omitted); see also Trujillo v. Am. Airlines, Inc., 938 F.Supp. 392, 394 (N.D.Tex.1995) (Fitzwater, J.) ("State causes of action are available to enforce bargains for services into which an airline voluntarily entered [.]"), aff'd, 98 F.3d 1338 (5th Cir.1996) (per curiam) (unpublished table decision). Plaintiffs' breach of contract action against American rests on a self-imposed undertaking concerning the handling of passengers' confidential information and therefore is not preempted under the holding in Wolens.

American maintains, however, that Wolens, Smith v. Comair, Inc., 134 F.3d 254 (4th Cir.1998), and Delta Air Lines, Inc. v. Black, 116 S.W.3d 745 (Tex.2003), cert. denied, 540 U.S. 1181, 124 S.Ct. 1418, 158 L.Ed.2d 84 (2004), support the conclusion that the breach of contract claim is preempted because it cannot be adjudicated without resort to outsides sources of law. In particular, American points out that its privacy policy informs customers that their personal information may be shared as required by law and provided to United States or foreign tax, security, and regulatory authorities, if required by law. In Wolens the Supreme Court held:

> The ADA's preemption clause..., read together with the [Federal Aviation Act's] saving clause, stops States from imposing their own substantive standards with respect to rates, routes, or services, but not from affording relief to a party who claims and proves that an airline dishonored a term the airline itself stipulated. This distinction between what the State dictates and what the airline itself undertakes confines courts, in breach-of-contract actions, to the parties' bargain, with no enlargement or enhancement based on state laws or policies external to the agreement.

Wolens, 513 U.S. at 232–33 (footnote omitted). In Comair the plaintiff's breach of contract claim was preempted because the airline raised federal defenses, and his claim could only be adjudicated by reference to law and policies external to the parties' bargain. Comair, 134 F.3d at 258–59. In Delta Air Lines the Texas Supreme Court held that a breach of contract action was preempted because, although the contract incorporated Department of Transportation regulations, the plaintiff sought to enlarge the airline's obligations and seek additional remedies not available under the contract's terms. Delta Air Lines, 116 S.W.3d at 755.

The court concludes that the principle stated in Wolens is factually inapposite to plaintiffs' breach of contract claim, and that Comair and Delta Air Lines are also distinguishable. Wolens differentiates between holding an airline to the bargain it struck and to one enlarged or enhanced by state laws or policies external to the agreement. In this case, as plaintiffs have pleaded their claim, American agreed to be bound to its privacy policy, except as required by law. In other words, the laws that American maintains are external to the contract are expressly incorporated into it. Unlike Comair, which was an appeal from a summary judgment in which the airline had raised federal-law defenses, Comair, 134 F.3d at 256, 258, plaintiffs in this case rely on a contract that incorporates the laws that American contends are external, and the court is assessing at the Rule 12(b)(6) stage whether they have a stated a claim. And as distinguished from Delta Air Lines, plaintiffs do not seek to modify the contract to press a right that is external to its terms. As pleaded, this case presents a question more like one that the Supreme Court held in Wolens was not external to the contract. As the Comair court explained in interpreting Wolens:

> American Airlines argued that whether it breached the frequent-flyer contract depended on resolution of the external policy issue of whether to recognize American's express reservation of the right to modify the rules governing its frequent-flyer contracts. The Court summarily rejected this argument, explaining that interpretation of the company's express reservation was merely another issue within the parties' contractual relationship and therefore not preempted.

Comair, 134 F.3d at 258 (citations omitted). As in Wolens, the possibility that American is permitted or required by law to share plaintiffs' personal information is within the parties' contractual relationship.

Accordingly, the court concludes that plaintiffs' breach of contract claim against American is not expressly preempted.

B

American also maintains that plaintiffs' state-law claims are impliedly preempted. The court need only address this argument in connection with plaintiffs' breach of contract claim.

American argues that plaintiffs' state-law claims are impliedly preempted because "[t]here simply is no room for the laws of the several states in the regulation of interactions between air carriers and the TSA, or cooperation between the airlines and TSA." American Sept. 23, 2004 Br. at 15. Without suggesting a view concerning whether any of plaintiffs' other claims are impliedly preempted, the court holds that the breach of contract action is not. In this respect, it is American's own contractual undertaking, enforceable under state contract law, that regulates its relationship with TSA, not the laws of the several states.

American also asserts, based on Buckman Co. v. Plaintiffs' Legal Committee, 531 U.S. 341, 121 S.Ct. 1012, 148 L.Ed.2d 854 (2001), and Brown v. Nationsbank Corp., 188 F.3d 579 (1999), that the claims are preempted because the relationship between TSA and American is inherently federal in character, and the question whether American properly authorized AAI to release PNR information to TSA is a question for federal regulatory agencies, not state common law. Whatever force these authorities may otherwise have, they do not compel the conclusion that American urges in the breach-of-contract context.

The court holds that plaintiffs' breach of contract claim is not impliedly preempted.

IV

American also moves to dismiss the breach of contract claim on the merits, contending that plaintiffs have failed to state a claim on which relief can be granted. American posits that this action fails because, inter alia, plaintiffs do not allege that they incurred damages as a result of American's breach.

The district court may dismiss a claim when it is clear that the plaintiff can prove no set of facts in support of his claim that would entitle him to relief. In analyzing the complaint,

> [the court] will accept all well-pleaded facts as true, viewing them in the light most favorable to the plaintiff. [The court] will not, however, accept as true conclusory allegations or unwarranted deductions of fact. The issue is not whether the plaintiff will ultimately prevail, but whether he is entitled to offer evidence to support his claim. Thus, the court should not dismiss the claim unless the plaintiff would not be entitled to relief under any set of facts or any possible theory that he could prove consistent with the allegations in the complaint.

Great Plains Trust Co. v. Morgan Stanley Dean Witter & Co., 313 F.3d 305, 312–13 (5th Cir.2002) (Rule 12(c) decision) (citations, original brackets, and internal quotation marks omitted).

The elements of a cause of action for breach of contract under Texas and New York law are: (1) existence of a contract, (2) performance or tendered performance by the plaintiff, (3) breach of the contract by the defendant, and (4) damages incurred by the plaintiff as a result of the breach. E.g., Lee v. Tyco Elecs. Power Sys., Inc., 2005 WL 1017821, at *4 (N.D.Tex. Apr.27, 2005) (Fitzwater, J.) (Texas law); Kasada, Inc. v. Access Capital, Inc., 2004 WL 2903776, at *21 (S.D.N.Y. Dec.14, 2004) (New York law). Plaintiffs allege that they sustained injury as a result of defendants' deceptive practice and invasion of privacy. E.g., Kimmell Am. Compl. ¶¶ 46, 67, 77. Their assertion that they were injured in these respects is insufficient to allege the inelecutable element that they incurred damages as a result of American's breach of contract.

Plaintiffs appear to complain of two separate disclosures of their personal information: one to TSA (with American's permission) and the other to the vendor defendants (with or without American's authorization). It is unclear whether the disclosure giving rise to plaintiffs' deceptive trade practices and invasion of privacy claims against American also supports their breach of contract claim or whether they allege that they incurred damages as a result of both disclosures. When the court assesses whether plaintiffs would be entitled to relief under any set of facts or any possible theory that they could prove consistent with the allegations in their complaints, it becomes clear that they have failed to plead the essential element of damages flowing from the breach. Accordingly, the court concludes that plaintiffs have failed to state a claim for breach of contract.

V

Although the court has granted defendants' motions to dismiss, plaintiffs have requested leave to amend, which the court grants. Despite the fact that plaintiffs have already filed amended complaints, this is the first time the court has addressed whether their pleadings sufficiently state a claim on which relief can be granted. They have not yet advised the court that they are unwilling or unable to amend in a manner that will avoid dismissal. And plaintiffs may have little difficulty remedying the pleading deficiency in their breach of contract claim. The court has also dismissed sua sponte a component of plaintiffs' § 2701-based ECPA claim against AAI and, in doing so, has noted that plaintiffs can attempt to cure the deficiency in their pleadings by amendment. It will therefore give them an additional opportunity to avoid dismissal.

The court grants defendants' motions to dismiss, and it grants plaintiffs leave to file amended complaints within 30 days of the date this opinion is filed.

STONE v. CONTINENTAL AIRLINES

804 N.Y.S.2d 652 (N.Y.C. Civ. Ct. 2005)

LEBEDEFF, Justice.

This matter brings up a bread-and-butter airline issue: the measure of damages governing the claims of passengers "bumped" from domestic airline flights. [This is] an issue rarely explored in detail notwithstanding that more than 30,000 passengers a year could raise similar claims, as permitted by federal statute and regulations (49 U.S.C.S. § 41713, known as the "Airline Deregulation Act" or "ADA"; 14 C.F.R. part 250).

This case has simple facts. Claimant Thatcher A. Stone, a partner in [the] New York law firm [of Akerman Senterfitt] and a lecturer in aviation and airline industry law at the University of Virginia School of Law, made arrangements for a Colorado ski trip for himself and his 13-year-old daughter for the 2004 Christmas season, to depart New York on December 25th and return from Telluride on January 1st. Their flights were booked with Continental Airlines ("Continental"). After their baggage was checked and the father and daughter were at the airline gate, they were "bumped" from the flight. The Continental representative who testified at the trial stated that Continental records reveal claimant was offered an alternate flight two or more days later, but claimant only remembers clearly an offer of a flight departing one day before their scheduled return. Because the airline would not unload their luggage and could give no firm advice regarding how long the airline would take to return the baggage, which included cold-weather sportswear for both and the father's ski equipment, the father and daughter returned home and were unable to make any firm alternate ski or "getaway" plans. Continental refunded the price of the airline tickets while claimant was in the airline terminal.

Claimant seeks recovery for out-of-pocket losses and deprivation of the use of the contents of luggage, as well as damages under New York's consumer protection statutes and punitive damages. He testified that his loss included $1,360 for unrecoverable pre-paid ski lodge accommodations, lift tickets and his daughter's equipment rental, and that the entire experience involved inconveniences and stresses upon himself and his daughter because of the "bumping" and the scheduled holiday "that never was."

"Bumping" Claims and Federal Limitations

As any airline traveler knows, "bumping" of an unlucky passenger occurs when more passengers appear to take a flight than the number of seats available on a given flight, and it arises because tickets are sold above and beyond the airplane's seating capacity. The United States Supreme Court, addressing an instance in which consumer advocate Ralph Nader was "bumped" from a flight, described overbooking as "a common industry practice, designed to ensure that each flight leaves with as few empty seats as possible" (Nader v. Allegheny Airlines, Inc., 426 U.S. 290, 293 [1976]).

The claims of "bumped" passengers are governed by federal regulation which require an airline to offer compensation to "bumped" passengers (14 C.F.R. part 250, entitled Oversales, originally published at 41 Fed.Reg. 16,478, and entitled Priority Rules, Denied-Boarding Compensation Tariffs and Reports of Unaccommodated Passengers [Apr. 19, 1976]). If a "bumped" passenger rejects an airline's offer, the passenger is entitled to "seek to recover damages in a court of law or in some other manner" under 14 C.F.R. § 250.9(b), which language is universally regarded as permitting a claim for contract damages which may exceed the amount of compensation offered by an airline.

Under 14 C.F.R. § 250.5, a "bumped" passenger is entitled to compensation of $400 per passenger or a lower amount computed "at the rate of 200% of the sum of the value of the passenger's remaining flight coupons up to the Passenger's next Stopover, or if none, to the Passenger's final destination"; an identical text appears in the Continental Contract of Carriage as paragraph (4)(a). This compensation rule applies only if a passenger is actually "bumped" from the flight because of overbooking (24 C.F.R. § 250.6; see Delta Air Lines, Inc. v. Black, 116 S.W.3d 745, 46 Tex.Sup.Ct.J. 1147 [Sup.Ct. Tex.2003], cert. denied, 540 U.S. 1181 [2004], passenger not "bumped" who declined coach seat when first class seat not available, and O'Carroll v. American Airlines, Inc., 863 F.2d 11 [5 Cir.1989], cert. denied sub nom. O'Carroll v. Chaparral Airlines, Inc., 490 U.S. 1106 [1989], intoxicated passengers removed from airplane [were] not "bumped").

All tickets for domestic flights embrace these same rights, for every airline's Contract of Carriage must be consistent with [the] federal rules (14 C.F.R. § 253.4). As described in a comprehensive law review article with an analysis of the economics of overbooking by Elliott Blanchard, Terminal 250: Federal Regulation of Airline Overbooking, 79 N.Y.U. L.Rev. 1799, 1807–1808 and fn. 3 (2004), since 1990, on average, almost 900,000 domestic passengers are "bumped" annually, and 2003 study data developed by the United States Department of Transportation indicates that 96 percent of such passengers accept the compensation offered by airlines, leaving approximately 36,000 "bumped" passengers per year who refuse such offers and are entitled to raise damages claims.

Any other claim which a passenger asserts arises from "bumping" must be parsed out and separately assessed. The bulk of other claims are barred by reasons of law, including federal preemption (49 U.S.C.A. §41713[b][1], local jurisdictions "may not enact or enforce a law ... related to a price, route, or service of an air carrier"; see Anne K. Wooster, Annotation, Construction and Application of §105 Airline Deregulation Act [49 U.S.C.A. §41713], Pertaining to Preemption of Authority Over Prices, Routes, and Services, 149 A.L.R. Fed. 299; see also Jim Leslie, Passenger Bumping, 3-AUG Nev. Law. 10 [1994], review of available claims relating to carriage and luggage, including claims of discrimination). Under federal law, an airline may not be sued for many general matters touching upon airline operation (see, e.g., Smith v. Comair, 134 F.3d 254 [4th Cir.1998], and Delta Air Lines, Inc. v. Black, supra), but an airline may be sued for some contract issues apart from "bumping" claims (see American Airlines, Inc. v. Wolens, 513 U.S. 219 [1995], frequent flyer program contractually adopted by airline). Following such a judicial review of the claims asserted in this case, the court is satisfied that New York State's consumer protection statutes cannot serve as the proper basis for claims against the airline. Additionally, a punitive damage claim against an airline is barred by federal preemption, even for a "bumped" passenger. West v. Northwest Airlines, Inc., 995 F.2d 148, 151 [9th Cir. 1993], cert. denied, 510 U.S. 1111 [1994].

Accordingly, the court severs and dismisses the consumer protection and punitive damages claims, which leaves only the contract damages claim before the court.

Contract Damages for a "Bumped" Passenger

A "bumped" passenger is entitled to contract damages upon no greater proof than facts establishing (1) ticket purchase, (2) involuntary denial of boarding within the meaning of the federal regulations, (3) non-acceptance of an airline's offer of compensation, and (4) damages. Such a claim for contract damages is measured under state law.

As the items to be embraced within contract damages for a passenger "bumped" from a domestic flight, only a handful of cases on point nationwide have granted relief on this issue (see Smith v. Piedmont Aviation, Inc., 567 F.2d 290, 292 [5th Cir.1978], reciting as a factor in damages, inconvenience and a need to make alternate arrangements, including rental of a car to reach destination, $1,051.80 awarded; Lopez v. Eastern Airlines, Inc., 677 F. Supp. 181, 183 [S.D.N.Y. 1988], "inconvenience, delay and uncertainty are worth something even in the absence of out-of-pocket costs" for passenger arriving at midnight instead of at a mid-evening hour, $450 awarded; Goranson v. Trans World Airlines, 121 Misc.2d 68, 78 and 80 [City Ct. White Plains, 1983], "courts have held that damages may consist of a wide variety of elements, including expenses for substitute or alternate transportation, meals, compensation for humiliation, outrage and inconvenience" and damages held to include cost of unused pre-paid arrangements where replacement flight delayed departure for two days, $1,500 awarded; Levy v. Eastern Airlines, 113 Misc.2d 847 [Civ.Ct. N.Y. Co.1982, Hentel, J.], accepting as prima facie measure of damages twice face value of tickets, $1,074 awarded).

There are a few additional opinions which can only be used to illustrate types of actual or potential damages which could be claimed, for they [did] not award damages. Some deny relief on independent substantive grounds (Delta Air Lines, Inc. v. Black, supra, 116 S.W.3d at 748, Dallas husband and wife requested cost of chartering "private jet to and from Las Vegas at a cost of $13,150, which included the aircrew's expenses in Las Vegas for two days"; Alam v. P.I.A., 1995 WL 17201349, *1 [S.D.N.Y 1995, Lee, Magis. J.], report adopted 1995 WL 489709 [S.D.N.Y 1995], passenger sought cost of an alternate ticket, "'lodging, travel, loss of earnings, and sundry expenses' while his family was delayed"; Sassouni v. Olympic Airways, 769 F.Supp. 537 [S.D.N.Y 1991], emotional distress claimed because alternate international passage offered involved travel on a religious holiday). Two did not set forth the legal basis of liability (Cenci v. Mall Airways, Inc., 140 Misc.2d 907 [City Ct. Albany 1988], partial refund of ticket price directed; Musso v. Tourlite Intern., Inc., 131 Misc.2d 575 [Civ. Ct. N.Y. Co. Small Claims 1986], damages awarded based upon cost of substitute airline tickets and rental car used for local transportation during delay period). Older "bumping" cases arising prior to the adoption of the current federal regulations such as Karp v. North Central Air Lines, Inc., 583 F.2d 364 (7th Cir.1978), and Wills v. Trans World Airlines, Inc., 200 F. Supp. 360 (S.D.Cal.1961) are not considered here because of differences in both the available causes of action and the rules governing cognizable damages.

In addition to case law, two sets of federal regulations give some guidance as to the dollar amount of damages which an airline should reasonably foresee in a "bumping" situation. The first regulation is the "bumping" regulation and airlines must contemplate that an impacted passenger would assert a claim exceeding the $400 per ticket lodestar compensation figure adopted in 1978 by the federal regulations, as well the fact that the $400 figure would be adjusted to its current economic value. Taking judicial notice of inflation (29 Am.Jur.2d Evidence § 68, Current financial data; interest, discount, and exchange rates, "the effect that inflation has already had on the value of money over a specific period of time is judicially noticeable"), the inflation-adjusted equivalent to the 1978 figure of $400 is equal to $1,219.63 in 2005 dollars for each passenger, according to a U.S. Bureau of Labor Statistics inflation calculator. [This] calculator appears on the Internet at http:// data.bls.gov/cgi-bin/cpicalc.pl (accessed Nov. 9, 2005), and is based upon adjustments to the Consumer Price Index ("CPI"), with the current year including CPI data for the most recent available month. The appropriateness of an inflation adjustment was noted by Elliott Blanchard, Terminal 250: Federal Regulation of Airline Overbooking, supra, 79 N.Y.U. L.Rev. at 1826.

And, still along general lines, it can be observed that the airline could also expect a somewhat increased claim where the "bumped" passenger has (1) a round trip scheduled with (2) a return flight date showing an appreciable layover period. The formula set forth in 14 C.F.R. § 250.5 ignores round-trip passengers, for it refers only to the ticket price to "the Passenger's next Stopover, or if none, to the Passenger's final destination...." It would appear that Continental does not distinguish flyers on a return or one-way ticket from passengers on the first portion of a round-trip—a distinction which an airline could add to its priority "bumping" rules, which each airline establishes independently under C.F.R. § 250.3 notwithstanding that such a distinction might reduce costs and inconvenience flowing from disruption of ground arrangements for a round-trip customer.

A second element is that a "bumped" passenger is also often exposed to the problem of lost or delayed luggage, which typically is checked before a passenger is denied boarding privileges. Under 14 C.F.R. § 254.4, an airline may be liable for "provable direct or consequential damages" for lost, destroyed, or delayed baggage up to the amount of $2,800 per passenger for domestic flights (see, discussing applicable law for claim when amount was $1,250 per passenger, Finestone v. Continental Airlines, Inc., 195 Misc.2d 795 [App. Term 2d Dept.2003]).

Accordingly, taking together both regulations regarding the loss of the flight boarding privileges and the deprivation of luggage and totaling the dollar figures, a working current economic figure of roughly $4,019 would appear to be within the expectation of an airline per "bumped" passenger, subject to proof of higher or lower damages. Plaintiff's claim of $4,000 in damages clearly is inside this recognizable ballpark.

Against this background, the court can turn to a New York definition of cognizable damages. A starting point is the basic consideration that contract damages can be "general, thus requiring only that plaintiff prove that they flowed naturally from the breach, or ... special ... which, to be compensable, must have been foreseeable and within the contemplation of the parties at the time the contract was made" (American List Corp. v. U.S. News and World Report, Inc., 75 N.Y.2d 38, 41 [1989]; accord Pakistan Arts & Entertainment Corp. v. Pakistan International Airlines Corp., 232 A.D.2d 29 [2d Dept.1997]). There are three identifiable ingredients of such damages.

First, as to out-of-pocket expenses flowing from the loss of passage, claimant testified that he was unable to recoup $1,360 of pre-paid expenses. This item falls within the class of traditionally recognized damages for "bumped" passengers. Had claimant arranged a substitute trip, other supplemental calculations might be required (Wells v. Holiday Inns, Inc., 522 F.Supp. 1023, 1025 [D.C.Mo.1981], involving "overbooking" at a hotel, offsetting savings against increased costs, as well as recognizing an allowance for typical expenses involved in a change of travel plans, such as telephone calls to family members).

Second, it is well settled that an award for inconvenience, delay and uncertainty is cognizable under New York law. Here, a father and teenage daughter were bumped on the outward leg of a week-long round trip during the holiday season to a resort location, leaving the claimant father subject to the immediate upset of being denied boarding in a public setting, and with resulting inconvenience continuing for some period of time thereafter. Inconvenience damages represent compensation for normal reactions and are clearly distinguishable from, and definitively not a disguised award for, severe emotional distress as often pleaded in tort cases.

Although the basis for inconvenience damages was not explored closely in the cases which awarded them to New York passengers, this type of award stems from a well settled exception to the "general rule [that] mental suffering resulting from a breach of contract is not a subject of compensation * * * * [which] does not obtain, however, as between a common carrier or an innkeeper and an insulted and abused passenger or guest, or the proprietor of a public resort and a patron publicly ejected" (Boyce v. Greeley Sq. Hotel Co., 228 N.Y. 106, 111 [1920], see Johnson v. Jamaica Hosp., 62 N.Y.2d 523, 528 [1984], recognizing continued viability of exception on proper facts; Lumauig v. Philippine Airlines, 624 F. Supp. 238 [S.D.N.Y. 1985], considering exception but finding emotional distress claim went beyond its scope; see also Pollock v. Holsa Corp., 98 A.D.2d 265, 266–267 [1st Dept.1984], plaintiff's hotel room given to another, resulting in long drive at night to another location, court observing, "The 'physical discomfort' experienced by plaintiff as a result of this inconvenience is an item of damage that was within the contemplation of the parties"). This principle is appropriately applied when a license to use a public accommodation is withdrawn in the presence of others (Aaron v. Ward, 203 N.Y. 351, 354 [1911], involving a bathhouse, exception applies where "[t]he action is for a breach of the defendant's contract, and not for a tortious expulsion"; Morningstar v. Lafyette Hotel Co., 211 N.Y. 465, 467 [1914], expelled customer perceived to be "a chronic faultfinder"). On the record presented and the law, inconvenience damages of $1,000 are awarded.

Third, regarding the deprivation of use of the contents of checked luggage, this factor was also present and claimant testified that, had their baggage been made available, he would have arranged for a local substitute ski trip. This portion of the claim was unopposed in that the claimant testified, without protest or objection, that the luggage should have been removed from the flight (see, both cases awarding some damages for failure to remove luggage from a flight, Cohen v. Varig Airlines [S.A. Empresa de Viacao Aerea Grandense], 62 A.D.2d 324 [1st Dept. 1978], and Kupferman v. Pakistan International Airlines, 108 Misc.2d 485 [Civ. Ct. N.Y. Co.1981]). [T]he airline did not argue that any contractual limitation of liability or principle of law limited or barred consideration of this claim. For a general reference as to this area of "baggage" law, see Stephen C. Fulton, Airline Baggage Claims: A Tour Through the Legal Minefield, 5 Fla. Int'l L.J. 349 (1990).

Further, given that the father and daughter were scheduled for a week-long trip and that their luggage had already been taken from them, the airline was on notice at the time of "bumping" that special damages could arise (17 N.Y. Jur.2d Carriers § 367, Special damages, "special damages for loss of use of a piece of equipment ... are not recoverable absent evidence that the carrier knew or should have known that the owner would likely suffer the loss of use if equipment was not delivered as scheduled" or as would have been proper).

An allowance for the deprivation of use of the contents of the luggage is warranted, bearing in mind that "[m]oney damages are substitutional relief designed in theory 'to put the injured party in as good a position as he would have been put by full performance of the contract, at the least cost to the defendant and without charging him with harms that he had no sufficient reason to foresee when he made the contract'" (Freund v. Washington Square Press, Inc., 34 N.Y.2d 379, 382 [1974], quoting 5 Corbin, Contracts, § 1002, pp. 31–32). As to valuation, as set forth in Lake v. Dye, 232 N.Y.209, 214 (1921), "the amount of the recovery ought not to be restricted to the price which could be realized by a sale in the market" but should consider the owner's "actual money loss, all the circumstances and conditions considered, resulting from his being deprived of the property, not including ... any sentimental or fanciful value he may ... place upon [the property]." The owner of the personal property may give testimony as to such value (N.Y.Jur.2d Damages § 87, Personal articles; wearing apparel [2005], "The owner of clothing or other personal item who is familiar with its quality and condition is credited with having some knowledge of its value and may give an estimate of its value without having to qualify as an expert"), and clearly may also testify regarding the anticipated use of the items checked.

Recognizing that 14 C.F.R. § 254.4 sets a limit of $2,800 per passenger on claims for lost, destroyed, or delayed baggage, the court awards $750 as rough compensation, giving consideration of a replacement rental value of the father's ski equipment and the replacement cost of purchase of winter sports wear at a non-luxurious quality for temporary use. Such an amount would have placed claimant in a position that he could have arranged a substitute local ski trip or day-trips for himself and his daughter, as he stated he would have done had he not already been subject to an out-of pocket loss [of] over $1,000 by reason of defendant's conduct. Given that no such trips were arranged, the court will not attempt to fix a figure for the cost of anything more than adequate compensation for the deprivation of use of the checked materials.

As to the damages testimony, this court had its opportunity to "view the witnesses, hear the testimony and observe demeanor" (People v. Bleakley, 69 N.Y.2d 490, 495 [1987]; see also Northern Westchester Professional Park Assocs. v. Town of Bedford, 60

N.Y.2d 492, 499 [1983], and Hoover v. Durkee, 212 A.D.2d 839, 841 [3rd Dept.1995]). To the extent that there was a dispute as to the facts, the court found claimant credible and credits his version of the facts as true or that, given the explanation he received under pressing circumstances, he was left under the impression were true. It does appear that claimant was not given an offer of compensation in writing, as required by the federal regulations (14 C.F.R. § 250.9), and that the airline also failed to post the required information regarding its "bumping" policies (14 C.F.R. § 250.11).

Based on the foregoing, judgment shall enter for the total amount of $3,110.00, comprised of the three items as to which damages have been granted above, with interest from December 25, 2004, the date of the "bumping." The court determines that such award achieves substantial justice in this Small Claims matter (N.Y.C.C.A. § 1805[a]). It is noted that plaintiff did not assert a claim on behalf of the minor daughter.

RUBIN v. UNITED AIR LINES, INC.

117 Cal. Rptr. 2d 109 (Ct. App. 2002)

JOHNSON, Acting Presiding Justice.

An airline passenger brought suit against an airline and others after Los Angeles Police Department officers removed her from a commercial flight about to depart for Hawaii. Her suit alleged causes of action for false arrest, false imprisonment, assault, battery and emotional distress. The airline claimed it was entitled to summary judgment as a matter of law because a provision of the Airline Deregulation Act of 1978 expressly preempted her state law tort claims. 49 United States Code section 41713, subdivision (b)(1). In the alternative, the airline claimed it was also entitled to judgment as a matter of law because it acted within its statutory discretion by refusing to transport a passenger it decided was, or might be, inimical to airline safety. 49 United States Code section 44902, subdivision (b). The trial court granted summary judgment in favor of the airline.

We hold a passenger whom the airline believes is, or might become, inimical to the safety of the aircraft or its passengers may be ejected from a flight without subjecting the airline to tort liability if at the time airline personnel had a reasonable basis for believing the passenger presented a safety risk. We further conclude the airline's actions in this case were reasonable as a matter of law. Accordingly, we affirm the summary judgment.

FACTS AND PROCEEDINGS BELOW

Appellant, Ms. Adrienne Rubin, decided to join her husband, Stanford Rubin, a trusts and estates attorney [with the Los Angeles law firm of Loeb & Loeb] who was then in Hawaii. She purchased an airline ticket from respondent United Airlines, Inc. (United). She paid for a coach ticket and upgraded the ticket to first class by using her husband's frequent flyer miles.

On October 28, 1998, Ms. Rubin arrived at the Los Angeles International Airport approximately an hour before the plane was scheduled to depart. She went directly to the gate with her bags.

She waited in line a long time before she could present her ticket to the agent at the gate. Ms. Rubin had a first class itinerary card with a seat designation of 2F. However, the United computer showed no first-class reservation for her. The agent explained Ms. Rubin needed to surrender an additional 3,000 frequent flyer miles to qualify for a first class upgrade because, for some reason, 3,000 miles had been recredited to her husband's account. The agent directed Ms. Rubin to the customer service counter nearby.

Approximately 30 minutes remained before the flight for Hawaii was to depart. It took nearly 15 minutes for Ms. Rubin to reach the front of the line at the customer service counter. When the United agent finally located Ms. Rubin's frequent flyer account on the computer she discovered Ms. Rubin did not have the needed 3,000 miles in her account. Ms. Rubin told the agent to take the miles from her husband's account. Only 10 or so minutes remained before the plane was due to take off. The agent told Ms. Rubin to go to the gate while she continued to try to locate Mr. Rubin's frequent flyer account number.

Ms. Rubin went to the gate and told the gate agent she had a first class seat and wanted to board. The agent responded all first class seats on the flight had already been assigned. He explained the flight was very full but two or three seats were available in the coach section. The agent offered Ms. Rubin the option of taking one of the seats in coach or flying first class on a later flight. He apparently did not indicate a specific coach seat assignment. Ms. Rubin explained she had to leave on this flight because she and her husband had an engagement later in the day she did not want to miss. Ms. Rubin was adamant about wanting a first class seat, and on this particular flight.

The gate agent notified the service director on board there was a person about to board who was insisting on leaving on this flight and insisting on a first class seat. The service director decided he would at least accommodate Ms. Rubin's wish to leave on this flight.

The service director met Ms. Rubin in the jetway. Ms. Rubin told the service director she had a first class ticket, a seat assignment of 2F, and could not understand why the airline had given her seat away. Ms. Rubin told the service director she had to fly first class because she had a special diet. The director reiterated all first class seats were now assigned and occupied. He explained if she wanted to take this fight she would have to fly coach in seat 26B.

Ms. Rubin entered the plane. She did not go to seat 26B in coach. According to Ms. Rubin, the service director did not specify any particular seat but told her she could sit anywhere in coach. Instead, Ms. Rubin entered (or attempted to enter) the first class cabin to determine for herself whether seat 2F was in fact occupied. As the service director put it, "that's when the hair came up on the back of my neck, because, ... you're violating everything that it's about, because it was clearly stated to Mrs. Rubin that the first-class seats were full."

The purser of an aircraft has primary responsibility for the safety of the passengers and has ultimate authority over the other flight attendants. When she saw Ms. Rubin enter (or attempt to enter) the first class cabin, the purser, according to Ms. Rubin, "went ballistic." Ms. Rubin got into a lengthy and loud discussion with the purser. The service director intervened and again directed Ms. Rubin to take her seat in 26B. Instead, Ms. Rubin dropped her luggage in the doorway of the aircraft and took a bulkhead emergency row seat immediately behind the first class section. The service director told Ms. Rubin to store her bag. Ms. Rubin refused and told the director he could do it himself or have someone else store the bag if he wished. The service director and another stewardess repeatedly told Ms. Rubin she could not sit in row 9 either, both because she had been assigned seat 26B and because she was not "emergency row qualified."

The service director left to consult with the purser. The purser, in the meantime, had already talked to the captain. The purser told the captain she had an irate passenger on board who refused to follow directions and who had attempted to make an unauthorized entry into the first class section. Based on the purser's representations, the captain agreed Ms. Rubin's demeanor and refusal to follow directions had the potential to create a safety problem in flight. The purser told the service director she would not fly if Ms. Rubin remained on board. The captain, purser and service director decided Ms. Rubin should be deplaned.

When the service director returned to the cabin Ms. Rubin was no longer sitting in row 9. She was instead sitting in another person's seat who had been in the lavatory. The person whose seat Ms. Rubin occupied was now sitting on the armrest of an aisle seat. The service director told Ms. Rubin she would have to deplane. In response, she instead finally took her assigned seat in 26B. By this time the flight was at least 15 minutes past schedule for takeoff. The other passengers were becoming impatient and unruly. Some yelled at United personnel suggesting they do something to regain control of the situation.

A gate agent came on board to take Ms. Rubin off the plane. Ms. Rubin was talking loudly on her cell phone. She refused to acknowledge his presence or mission. He could not get Ms. Rubin to pay attention to him or to stop talking on the telephone. He left the plane in frustration. Now the flight was some 20 to 25 minutes past departure time. United personnel decided to call the Los Angeles Airport Police.

Passengers started applauding when the police officers boarded the plane. The Los Angeles police officers asked Ms. Rubin to leave the plane. Ms. Rubin kept interrupting to explain she believed she had a first class seat assignment and could not understand why United had given her seat away. The officers told Ms. Rubin the airplane was not going to take off with her on it. Ms. Rubin refused to leave the plane voluntarily. She refused to leave her seat, refused to stand up and refused to walk. The officers had to pick Ms. Rubin up out of her seat and carry her by her shoulders off the plane. As they proceeded in this fashion through the aisles passengers applauded and whistled. They also yelled and hurled wads of paper at Ms. Rubin.

In the view of one officer, the situation on board was "a mob scene." He believed the other passengers were so frustrated and upset with Ms. Rubin because of the trouble and delay, he believed if United had permitted Ms. Rubin to stay on the flight "it could have gotten ugly."

The officers took Ms. Rubin off the plane. Her luggage was still where she had dropped it in the doorway. The service director removed her bag to the jetway.

The officers detained Ms. Rubin at the police station for several hours. The officers contacted the Federal Aviation Administration and the Federal Bureau of Investigations as is required when investigating a potential federal charge of obstructing a flight crew. A representative from the F.A.A. arrived and interviewed Ms. Rubin, as did a sergeant from the Los Angeles Police Department. Ultimately, Ms. Rubin was not charged. The officers returned Ms. Rubin to the airport and she flew first class on the next flight to Hawaii.

Ms. Rubin filed suit against United, the City of Los Angeles, and the Los Angeles police officers who removed her from the plane. Her complaint alleged causes of action for false arrest, false imprisonment, unlawful search and seizure, assault, battery, and emotional distress. United moved for summary judgment claiming Ms. Rubin's state tort law causes of action were expressly preempted by the Airline Deregulation Act. In the alternative, United claimed it was entitled to judgment as a matter of law in any event, asserting it had acted within the broad discretion accorded airlines by federal law to decide when a passenger presents a security risk sufficient to be removed from a flight. United argued there were no material factual disputes and asserted it was thus entitled to judgment as a matter of law.

The trial court granted United's motion and this appeal followed. The City of Los Angeles and the named Los Angeles Police Department officers have since settled with Ms. Rubin and are not parties to this appeal.

DISCUSSION

I. STANDARD OF REVIEW

On appeal from an order granting summary judgment we independently assess the correctness of the trial court's ruling by applying the same legal standard as the trial court in determining whether any triable issues of material fact exist, and whether the defendant is entitled to judgment as a matter of law. In doing so we construe the moving party's affidavits strictly, construe the opponent's affidavits liberally, and resolve doubts about the propriety of granting the motion in favor of the opposing party. We review the trial court's grant of summary judgment in favor of United with these standards in mind.

II. DECISIONAL LAW IS UNSETTLED, AND THUS INCONCLUSIVE, WHICH STATE LAW TORT CLAIMS ARE PREEMPTED BY FEDERAL LAW

The Airline Deregulation Act of 1978 (ADA) prohibits states from "enact[ing] or enforc[ing] a law, regulation, or other provision having the force and effect of law related to a price, route, or service of an air carrier...." 49 United States Code section 41713, subdivision (b)(1). This case concerns the scope of this preemptive provision as applied to a suit raising state tort law claims regarding, as United alleges, claims arising from its boarding procedures. United claims "boarding procedures" are classified as a "service" and state claims challenging this airline service are expressly preempted by federal law. Ms. Rubin, by contrast, claims the airline gives a too all-encompassing reading to the term "service." She argues Congress used "service" in the public utility sense to only refer to the provision of air transportation to and from various markets at various times, citing Charas v. Trans World Airlines, Inc. (9th Cir.1998) 160 F.3d 1259, 1265–66. She asserts her claims do not affect these services and thus are not preempted by the ADA.

Until 1978, the Federal Aviation Act of 1958 (FAA), 72 Statutes 731, as amended, 49 United States Code Appendix section 1301 et seq., empowered the Civil Aeronautics Board (CAB) to regulate the interstate airline industry. Before 1978 the FAA contained no clause preempting state regulation. In fact, the Act contained a savings clause stating: "Nothing contained in this chapter shall in any way abridge or alter the remedies now existing at common law or by statute, but the provisions of this chapter are in addition to such remedies." Originally title 49 United States Code Appendix section 1506, recodified at 49 United States Code section 40120, subdivision (c); see American Airlines, Inc. v. Wolens (1995) 513 U.S. 219, 222, 115 S.Ct. 817, 130 L.Ed.2d 715.

Thereafter, Congress determined relying on competitive market forces rather than pervasive federal regulation would further efficiency, low prices, variety and quality. Thus, in 1978 Congress enacted the Airline Deregulation Act (ADA), which largely deregulated domestic air transport. To prevent states from "un[doing] federal deregulation with regulation of their own," Morales v. Trans World Airlines, Inc. (1992) 504 U.S. 374, 378, 112 S.Ct. 2031, 119 L.Ed.2d 157, the ADA included a preemption clause. This clause now states in pertinent part:

> (b) Preemption. (1) Except as provided in this subsection, a State, political subdivision of a State, or political authority of at least 2 States may not enact or enforce a law, regulation, or other provision having the force and effect of law related to a price, route, or service of an air carrier that may provide air transportation under this subpart [49 United States Code Section 41101 et seq.].

Formerly 49 United States Code Appendix section 1305, subdivision (a)(1), reenacted as 49 United States Code section 41713, subdivision (b)(1) without substantive change (Pub.L.103-272, § 1(e), 108 Stat. 1143).

The United States Supreme Court has twice addressed the scope of the ADA's preemption clause. In Morales v. Trans World Airlines, Inc., supra, 504 U.S. 374, 112 S.Ct. 2031, 119 L.Ed.2d 157, the Court addressed the question whether airlines were subject to states' laws banning deceptive advertising. The Court concluded state restrictions on advertising were precisely the type of economic regulation Congress intended to preempt in deregulating the airline industry. "Restrictions on advertising serve to increase the difficulty of discovering the lowest cost seller ... and [reduce] the incentive to price competitively...." Morales v. Trans World Airlines, Inc., supra, 504 U.S. at p. 388, 112 S.Ct. 2031. The Court held states' action for deceptive advertising had the "forbidden significant effect" on "price" and were thus preempted by the ADA. Morales v. Trans World Airlines, Inc., supra, 504 U.S. at p. 388, 112 S.Ct. 2031.

Although the Court did not define the precise perimeters of the ADA's preemption clause, the Court noted not all state law claims would be preempted. "[W]e do not ... set out on a road that leads to pre-emption of state laws against gambling and prostitution as applied to airlines ... [s]ome state actions may affect [airline fares] in too tenuous, remote, or peripheral a manner to have pre-emptive effect." Morales v. Trans World Airlines, Inc., supra, 504 U.S. at p. 390, 112 S.Ct. 2031.

The Court again explored the boundaries of the ADA's preemption clause in American Airlines, Inc. v. Wolens. American Airlines, Inc. v. Wolens, supra, 513 U.S. 219, 115 S.Ct. 817, 130 L.Ed.2d 715. In reviewing the airline's unilateral decision to devalue the plaintiffs' frequent flyer miles the Court commented, "[w]e need not dwell on the question whether plaintiffs' complaints state claims 'relating to [air carrier] rates, routes, or services.'... Plaintiffs' claims relate to 'rates,' i.e., American's charges in the form of mileage credits for free tickets and upgrades, and to 'services,' i.e., access to flights and class-of-service upgrades unlimited by retrospectively applied capacity controls and blackout dates." American Airlines, Inc. v. Wolens, supra, 513 U.S. at p. 226, 115 S.Ct. 817.

The Court nevertheless concluded the plaintiffs' "routine breach-of-contract" claims were not preempted. American Airlines, Inc. v. Wolens, supra, 513 U.S. at p. 232, 115 S.Ct. 817. "We do not read the ADA's preemption clause, however, to shelter airlines from suits alleging no violation of state-imposed obligations, but seeking recovery solely for the airline's alleged breach of its own, self-imposed undertakings. As persuasively argued by the United States, terms and conditions airlines offer and passengers accept are privately ordered obligations 'and thus do not amount to a State's "enact[ment] or enforce[ment] [of] any law, rule, regulation, standard, or other provision having the force and effect of law" within the meaning of [the ADA's preemption clause.]'" American Airlines, Inc. v. Wolens, supra, 513 U.S. at pp. 228–229, 115 S.Ct. 817. Reading the ADA's preemption clause together with the Act's savings clause retaining existing statutory and common law remedies, made clear the ADA only "stops States from imposing their own substantive standards with respect to rates, routes, or services, but not from affording relief to a party who claims and proves that an airline dishonored a term the airline itself stipulated." American Airlines, Inc. v. Wolens, supra, 513 U.S. at pp. 232–233, 115 S.Ct. 817.

Although the Court touched briefly on the meaning of the term "service" in the ADA's preemption clause, American Airlines, Inc. v. Wolens, supra, 513 U.S. at p. 226, 115 S.Ct. 817 [the term "service" encompasses "access to flights and class-of-service upgrades"], it has not directly addressed the term's precise scope. Intermediate appellate courts have taken widely divergent views in their interpretation of the term "service." Some courts define the term quite narrowly. This narrower interpretation is exemplified by the Ninth Circuit Court of Appeals decision in Charas v. Trans World Airlines, Inc., supra, 160 F.3d 1259. The court's Charas decision involved a series of consolidated cases all involving claims against airlines for personal injuries. The Ninth Circuit held the term "service" encompasses "the prices, schedules, origins and destinations of the point-to-point transportation of passengers, cargo, or mail," but not the "provision of in-flight beverages, personal assistance to passengers, the handling of luggage, and similar amenities." Charas v. Trans World Airlines, Inc., supra, 160 F.3d at p. 1261. The Third Circuit has expressly agreed with the Ninth Circuit's definition. See Taj Mahal Travel, Inc. v. Delta Airlines, Inc. (3d Cir.1998) 164 F.3d 186, 194.

Other circuits, by contrast, have adopted a much more expansive definition of the term "service." This broader definition is typified by the Fifth Circuit's decision in Hodges v. Delta Airlines, Inc. (5th Cir.1995) 44 F.3d 334, 336. In Hodges a passenger filed suit against the airline for personal injuries he received when a case of rum fell from the overhead bin and injured him. The Hodges court found claims for personal injuries were not preempted because it defined "service" in terms of the contractual features of air transportation. It included within this definition of "service" items "such as ticketing, boarding procedures, provision of food and drink, and baggage handling, in addition to the transportation itself." Hodges v. Delta Airlines, Inc., supra, 44 F.3d at p. 336. According to the Hodges court, "[t]hese matters are all appurtenant and necessarily included with the contract of carriage between the passenger or shipper and the airline. It is these [contractual] features of air transportation that we believe Congress intended to de-regulate as 'services' and broadly to protect from state regulation." Hodges v. Delta Airlines, Inc., supra, 44 F.3d at p. 336. A few federal circuit courts are in accord with the broader definition of "service" adopted by the Hodges' court. See, e.g., Smith v. Comair, Inc. (4th Cir.1998) 134 F.3d 254, 259 ["Undoubtedly, boarding procedures are a service rendered by an airline"]; Travel All Over The World, Inc. v. Kingdom of Saudi Arabia (7th Cir.1996) 73 F.3d 1423, 1433 [same].

Division One of this District's Court of Appeal has essentially adopted the so-called majority view as expressed in the Hodges opinion. In Romano v. American Trans Air (1996) 48 Cal.App.4th 1637, 56 Cal.Rptr.2d 428 the court concluded the ADA does not preclude a personal injury action for damages suffered as the result of a flight attendant's failure to restrain one passenger from attacking another. In reaching its conclusion the Romano court noted the following factors: (1) the ADA does not expressly preempt personal injury actions; (2) the ADA's savings clause preserved common law and statutory remedies; (3) the ADA requires an air carrier to have insurance in an amount prescribed by the Department of Transportation to cover claims for personal injuries and property losses "'resulting from the operation or maintenance of aircraft'" which the court noted would be unnecessary if personal injury claims were preempted. Romano v. American Trans Air, supra, 48 Cal.App.4th 1637, 1643, 56 Cal.Rptr.2d 428, fn. omitted ("Since there is no provision in the ADA for personal injury or property damage lawsuits, it follows ineluctably that liability insurance would be unnecessary if an injured passenger could not sue an airline for damages—and that, therefore, Congress intended that airlines respond to common law claims for personal injury damages.") (Citing American Airlines, Inc. v. Wolens, supra, 513 U.S. at p. 231, fn. 7, 115 S.Ct. 817 and Hodges v. Delta Airlines, Inc., supra, 44 F.3d at p. 338.) Although the Romano court did not purport to classify the types of claims against an airline which would be preempted as a "service," the court noted [that] in 1979 the department charged with enforcing the ADA (formerly the CAB, now the Department of Transportation) interpreted the ADA "to preempt economic factors 'that go into the provision of the quid pro quo for passenger's fare, including flight frequency and timing, liability limits, reservation and boarding practices, insurance, smoking rules, meal service, entertainment, bonding and corporate financing...." Romano v. American Trans Air, supra, 48 Cal.App.4th at p. 1642, 56 Cal.Rptr.2d 428, citing 44 Federal Register 9948, 9951 (Feb. 15, 1979).

United urges this court to adopt the broadly preemptive definition of "service" of the Hodges lines of cases. In the alternative, United suggests we follow Division One of this court and, as mentioned in dicta in Romano, find the present case involves "boarding procedures," and thus an airline "service" preempted by section 41713, part of the ADA. Ms. Rubin, by contrast, urges the narrower interpretation of the Ninth Circuit in Charas and requests this court to find her state law tort claims not preempted by the ADA.

We need not decide which of the competing definitions of "service" most accurately reflects Congress's intent in adopting section 41713. Regardless of the types of state claims which should be preempted under the rubric of "services" in the ADA, we conclude United properly exercised the discretion given it in section 44902 of the FAA to refuse Ms. Rubin passage in the circumstances presented in this case.

III. THE UNDISPUTED FACTS ESTABLISH AS A MATTER OF LAW UNITED HAD A REASONABLE BELIEF MS. RUBIN WAS OR COULD BE INIMICAL TO THE SAFETY OF THE FLIGHT WHICH JUSTIFIED UNITED IN REFUSING HER PASSAGE

Former section 1111, now section 44902, of the FAA, was originally enacted by Congress in 1961. This provision authorizes an airline to "refuse to transport a passenger or property the carrier decides is, or might be, inimical to safety." Section 44902 now provides:

> (a) Mandatory refusal. The Administrator of the Federal Aviation Administration shall prescribe regulations requiring an air carrier, intrastate air carrier, or foreign air carrier to refuse to transport—
>
> (1) a passenger who does not consent to a search under section 44901(a) of this title establishing whether the passenger is carrying unlawfully a dangerous weapon, explosive, or other destructive substance; or
>
> (2) property of a passenger who does not consent to a search of the property establishing whether the property unlawfully contains a dangerous weapon, explosive, or other destructive substance.
>
> (b) Permissive refusal. Subject to regulations of the Administrator, an air carrier, intrastate air carrier, or foreign air carrier may refuse to transport a passenger or property the carrier decides is, or might be, inimical to safety.

(c) Agreeing to consent to search. An agreement to carry passengers or property in air transportation or intrastate air transportation by an air carrier, intrastate air carrier, or foreign air carrier is deemed to include an agreement that the passenger or property will not be carried if consent to search the passenger or property for a purpose referred to in this section is not given.

Congress originally enacted this provision to help combat an air piracy problem. See 1 United States Code Congressional and Administrative News (1961) 87th Congress, 1st Session, pp. 520–522; 2 United States Code Congressional and Administrative News (1961) 87th Congress, 1st Session, pp. 2563–2582. However, section 44902 is not, as Ms. Rubin suggests, reserved strictly for would-be terrorists and hijackers. Airlines have also invoked their discretion under this statute, as they have under common law, to exclude passengers in any number of circumstances. See, e.g., Cordero v. Cia Mexicana De Aviacion, S.A. (9th Cir.1982) 681 F.2d 669 [airline did not allow passenger to re-board because it believed he was the passenger who had offended the pilot]; Smith v. Comair, Inc., supra, 134 F.3d 254 [passenger refused permission to reboard because he did not have photo identification]; Adamsons v. American Airlines, Inc. (1982) 58 N.Y.2d 42, 457 N.Y.S.2d 771, 444 N.E.2d 21 [airline acted within its discretion in refusing transport to a paralyzed person unaccompanied by an assistant who had a catheter and Foley disposal bag attached to her body and when seated in a wheelchair constantly cried out in excruciating pain]. As the Second Circuit noted in Williams v. Trans World Airlines, an airline's duty to perform its services with the highest possible degree of safety in the public interest has both a statutory and common law basis. All commercial airlines are common carriers, and as such, owe a duty of utmost care for their safety. (Williams v. Trans World Airlines (2d Cir.1975) 509 F.2d 942, 946, fn. 8 [an airline's statutory authority to exclude a passenger is consistent with the "common law rule that 'where a carrier has reasonable cause to believe and does believe, that the safety or convenience of its passengers will be endangered by a person who presents himself for transportation, it may refuse to accept such person for transportation and is not bound to wait until events have justified its belief.'] 14 Am.Jur.2d, Carriers, § 865 at 309"; see also Cordero v. Cia Mexicana De Aviacion S.A., supra, 681 F.2d 669, 672, fn. 3.

On the other hand, although the discretion given an airline under this provision to refuse to transport a passenger for safety reasons is "decidedly expansive, [it] is not unfettered." O'Carroll v. American Airlines, Inc. (5th Cir.1989) 863 F.2d 11, 12. If an airline's refusal of transportation is arbitrary or capricious, its refusal can give rise to a claim by the offended passenger for damages. See, for example, Smith v. Comair, Inc., supra, 134 F.3d at p. 259, in which the court held: "Suits stemming from outrageous conduct on the part of an airline toward a passenger will not be preempted under the ADA if the conduct too tenuously relates or is unnecessary to an airline's service. [Citation.] If, for example, an airline held a passenger without a safety or security justification, a claim based on such actions would not relate to any legitimate service and would not be preempted." (See also Cordero v. Cia Mexicana De Aviacion, S.A., supra, 681 F.2d at pp. 671–672 [jury could have concluded airline acted unreasonably when it excluded the passenger "without even the most cursory inquiry into the complaint against him"].) Stated another way, the decision to accept or refuse transport to a passenger based on considerations of safety and security "lies exclusively with the air carrier" and if such discretion is "exercised in good faith and for a rational reason" it will be upheld. Adamsons v. American Airlines, Inc., supra, 58 N.Y.2d at p. 47, 457 N.Y.S.2d 771, 444 N.E.2d 21.

One of the leading cases interpreting this provision is the Second Circuit's decision in Williams v. Trans World Airlines, supra, 509 F.2d 942 (Williams). In Williams the F.B.I. informed the airline a passenger arriving in Detroit on its London flight had an outstanding warrant for his arrest, had previously been diagnosed as schizophrenic, and might be met at the airport with a demonstration. Williams, supra, 509 F.2d at p. 944. Although the airline found the passenger compliant and unarmed, it decided to rely on the F.B.I. report to deny Williams transport out of London. Williams brought suit claiming the airline's decision to exclude him was unreasonable and was instead motivated by racial discrimination. Williams, supra, 509 F.2d at p. 946. He argued the F.B.I. information was so inaccurate on its face it should have put the airline on inquiry to make an exhaustive investigation of the facts before acting to exclude him. The Court of Appeals affirmed a finding [that] Williams's exclusion from the aircraft was not motivated by racial or political prejudice, holding the airline had a right to accept the F.B.I. report at face value. In reaching this conclusion, the court found a carrier may exercise its discretion to exclude a passenger so long as the carrier acts on evidence which "would cause a reasonably careful and prudent air carrier of passengers to form the opinion that the presence aboard a plane of the passenger-applicant 'would or might be inimical to safety of flight.'" Williams, supra, 509 F.2d at p. 948.

The Williams court rejected the plaintiff's assertion the airline should have conducted a thorough investigation into the F.B.I. report for accuracy before refusing him transportation. Instead the court stated the airline's decision should be judged on the basis of the facts as known to the airline at the time, and without regard to hindsight. "Congress was certainly aware that decisions under § 1511 [now section 44902] would in many instances probably have to be made within minutes of the plane's scheduled take-off time, and that the carrier's formulation of opinion would have to rest on something less than absolute certainty. The statute did not contemplate that the flight would have to be held up or cancelled until certainty was achieved. The test of whether or not the airline properly exercised its power under § 1511 [now section 44902] to refuse passage to an applicant or ticket-holder rests upon the facts and circumstances of the case as known to the airline at the time it formed its opinion and made its decision and whether or not the opinion and decision were rational and reasonable and not capricious or arbitrary in the light of those facts and circumstances. They are not to be tested by other facts later disclosed by hindsight...." Williams, supra, 509 F.2d at p. 948.

Many courts have since applied the Williams standard or a variant to test the reasonableness of an airline's decision to refuse passage. Circumstances justifying an airline's decision to refuse passage follow no consistent pattern. For example, Adamsons v. American Airlines, Inc., supra, 58 N.Y.2d 42, 457 N.Y.S.2d 771, 444 N.E.2d 21, did not present what one might consider to be a typical safety risk. In Adamsons a passenger with paralyzed legs, suffering from an undiagnosed disease, yet having arranged for no special assistance on the flight, arrived at the airport in an ambulance with a catheter and a Foley disposal bag attached to her body. She repeatedly cried out in pain as airline personnel attempted to board her in a wheelchair. New York state's highest court held the airline did not abuse its discretion under what is now section 44902 in refusing to transport her. The plaintiff when purchasing her ticket had informed the airline she was paralyzed, needed a wheelchair, and was not contagious. However, the airline did not discover the extent of her illness until 45 minutes before departure time. The passenger was then traveling alone and airline personnel had no idea what assistance she might require during the several hour flight from Haiti to New York. With so little time remaining before departure it was impossible for airline personnel to thoroughly investigate the patient's condition. Adamsons v. American Airlines, Inc., supra, 58 N.Y.2d at p. 49, 457 N.Y.S.2d 771, 444 N.E.2d 21.

The court held in the circumstances the airline's decision to refuse passage was reasonable as a matter of law. Adamsons v. American Airlines, Inc., supra, 58 N.Y.2d at p.

48, 457 N.Y.S.2d 771, 444 N.E.2d 21 ["Applying this standard to the facts of this case, we hold that, as a matter of law, defendant did not abuse its discretion in refusing to transport plaintiff to New York."] The court noted an airline usually must make such decisions on the spur of the moment, shortly before takeoff, and without the benefit of complete and accurate information. Adamsons v. American Airlines, Inc., supra, 58 N.Y.2d at p. 47, 457 N.Y.S.2d 771, 444 N.E.2d 21. The court added the airline's responsibility for the safety of its passengers is so important a judge or jury should be wary of second guessing the carrier's judgment "months later in the calm of a courtroom." Adamsons v. American Airlines, Inc., supra, 58 N.Y.2d at p. 48, 457 N.Y.S.2d 771, 444 N.E.2d 21, quoting Cordero v. CIA Mexicana De Aviacion, S.A. (1981) 512 F.Supp. 205, affirmed in part, reversed in part Cordero v. Cia Mexicana De Aviacion, S.A., supra, 681 F.2d 669.

Smith v. Comair, Incorporated, supra, 134 F.3d 254, presents an entirely different factual situation. In Smith the passenger sued the airline for breach of contract, false imprisonment and emotional distress because the airline had refused to permit him to reboard his flight after a layover. At the point of his original departure the airline had failed to ask for proof of his identification. Smith v. Comair Inc., supra, 134 F.3d at p. 256. When detained during the layover the passenger admitted he could not independently confirm his identity. He had left his driver's license in the glove compartment of his car then parked at the airport and did not carry either his birth certificate or social security card on his person. The passenger was eventually permitted to return home. Smith v. Comair Inc., supra, 134 F.3d at pp. 256–257.

The appellate court concluded the passenger's claims were either preempted or not actionable and granted summary judgment in favor of the airline. In so doing the court noted, "Air travel in modern society presents formidable safety and security concerns and often passengers with criminal intentions are the source of that threat. Federal law—in conjunction with its broad preemption of state-law claims related to airlines' services—appropriately grants airlines latitude in making decisions necessary to safeguard passengers from potential security threats. Section 44902(b) recognizes airlines' boarding practices as a specific area of federal concern." Smith v. Comair Inc., supra, 134 F.3d at p. 258. Because the passenger had breached the airline's security measures, the court held the airline was justified in refusing him passage. See also Sedigh v. Delta Airlines, Inc. (E.D.N.Y.1994) 850 F.Supp. 197, 201–202 [airline acted reasonably in removing passenger personnel noticed was nervous, sweating profusely, making several long trips to the lavatory without flushing the toilet and was overheard saying something about killing Jews]; Zervigon v. Piedmont Aviation, Inc. (S.D.N.Y.1983) 558 F.Supp. 1305, 1307 [airline's actions in removing a group of eight passengers was reasonable as a matter of law because one assaulted a flight attendant and others in the group were overheard talking about sharing their experience on the flight with friends in the "capital," leading other passengers, crew and the pilot to believe the group intended to hijack the plane to Cuba].

By contrast, where an airline refused to allow a passenger to reboard the plane after a stopover on grounds he had insulted the captain and crew, the court in Cordero v. Cia Mexicana De Aviacion, S.A., supra, 681 F.2d 669, upheld the jury's finding the airline had acted unreasonably in failing to investigate the passenger's claim he had been mistaken for another disorderly passenger. Accordingly, the court found section 44902 did not shield the airline from liability. On a flight, which had already been delayed, the pilot announced an unscheduled stop and one passenger shouted insults at the pilot. Cordero v. Cia Mexicana De Aviacion, S.A., supra, 681 F.2d at p. 670. At the airport during the stop, the plaintiff circulated a petition complaining about the delay. Airline personnel then prevented the plaintiff from reboarding, claiming he was the one who had insulted the pilot. The airline refused to investigate his claim of mistaken identity and excluded him from the flight. Cordero v. Cia Mexicana De Aviacion, S.A., supra, 681 F.2d at p. 670. The Ninth Circuit reversed the judgment notwithstanding the verdict in favor of the airline, finding ample evidence in the trial record from which the jury might have concluded the airline acted unreasonably in excluding the plaintiff "without even the most cursory inquiry into the complaint against him." Cordero v. Cia Mexicana De Aviacion, S.A., supra, 681 F.2d at p. 672; see also Rombom v. United Air Lines, Inc. (S.D.N.Y.1994) 867 F.Supp. 214, 225 [airline's motion for summary judgment denied where passenger who airline accused of being boisterous and failing to follow directions claimed the airline had her arrested out of spite and maliciousness unrelated to any safety or security reason].

Schaeffer v. Cavallero (S.D.N.Y.1999) 54 F.Supp.2d 350 is another decision in which the court found an airline had failed to demonstrate a reasonable basis for refusing passage. In Schaeffer a passenger became very upset when a flight attendant told him one of his two bags had to be checked. He relented but when he did not receive a receipt for his bag he "so vociferously pursued his demand for the receipt" he was asked to deplane. Schaeffer v. Cavallero, supra, 54 F.Supp.2d at p. 351. He refused to leave the plane and had to be physically removed by the police. The passenger brought suit for battery, false imprisonment and other claims. The trial court denied the airline's motion for summary judgment finding it a triable issue of material fact whether the airline had acted reasonably. The court found a reasonable jury could conclude he was removed from the plane, not because he posed a safety risk, but in retaliation for his verbal protests, in which case the airline's action would be arbitrary and capricious. Schaeffer v. Cavallero, supra, 54 F.Supp.2d at p. 351.

After trial the court clarified its rulings. The court acknowledged airlines have broad discretion under section 44902 to refuse to transport passengers the airline believes are or might be inimical to safety. "But to say (as defendants essentially argue) that any time an impolite or unpleasant passenger debates a non-safety issue with an airline employee in a boisterous or abusive manner he automatically poses a potential threat to safety would be in effect to set no meaningful limits to the carrier's exercise of its discretion and thus to eliminate the statutory standard altogether. Where no safety issue is reasonably implicated, even grouches have a right to gripe without being grounded." Schaeffer v. Cavallero, supra, 54 F.Supp.2d at p. 352. Nevertheless, the court held the passenger could not prevail on his battery and false imprisonment claims. The court found because the passenger had refused to leave the plane on his own, "require [ing] the police to effectuate the removal was the sole proximate cause of the police-related torts of which he complains. By opting for the method of disembarkation that could result in additional injuries," the passenger had assumed and consented to the risk. Schaeffer v. Cavallero, supra, 54 F.Supp.2d at p. 352.

In the present case, by contrast, the record evidence establishes as a matter of law Ms. Rubin presented a safety risk which justified United's decision to remove her from the plane. Unlike the situation in Schaeffer v. Cavallero, Ms. Rubin was not simply loudly belligerent about a non-safety matter. Also unlike Cordero v. Cia Mexicana De Aviacion, S.A., this was not a case of misidentifying the objectionable passenger. Nor did Ms. Rubin present any evidence tending to suggest United ejected her from the flight simply to retaliate against her for arguing with the purser. Instead the evidence demonstrates Ms. Rubin committed what in the industry is considered a serious breach of security by making or attempting to make an unauthorized entry into the first class cabin. In addition, the evidence demonstrates Ms. Rubin deliberately and repeatedly refused to follow directions from any of the uniformed airline personnel regarding the safety issues of proper stowing of luggage and emergency row seating.

In his deposition testimony the service director explained airlines had developed a heightened sensitivity to safety issues after events such as the Gulf War, the Oklahoma City bombing, the bombing of the World Trade Towers, and the explosion of Pam Am flight 103 over Lockerbie, Scotland. As a result of these events airlines learned they had become potential targets, and at the direction of the Federal Aviation Administration, airlines and airports started taking safety issues much more seriously. According to the service director, it was for this reason the purser perceived Ms. Rubin's unauthorized intrusion, or attempted intrusion, into the first class area as a threatening act. All seats in first class were occupied thus all the purser knew was someone was attempting to enter the forward cabin who clearly had no business being there. The service director stated "the hair came up on the back of his neck" as he watched Ms. Rubin drop her bag and "run into" first class. Instead of leaving the area as directed Ms. Rubin argued loudly with the purser for several minutes and insisted she be permitted to fly in the fully occupied first class cabin. Even Ms. Rubin described the argument as a "confrontation."

Although the service director intervened in an attempt to accommodate Ms. Rubin she refused to follow his directions as well. She refused to stow her bag as directed, and in fact told the director if he did not want the bag in the doorway, he could stow it himself. The director told Ms. Rubin her assigned seat was 26B. Ms. Rubin refused to go to the back of the plane and instead sat in an empty seat immediately behind the first class cabin. United personnel told Ms. Rubin she could not sit in the emergency row bulkhead seat and repeatedly asked her to move. According to the service director, given her demonstrated unwillingness to follow directions, Ms. Rubin was not considered "emergency row qualified." It was only after much pleading Ms. Rubin finally moved. However, she still refused to follow orders to sit in seat 26B. She instead moved a bit further back and sat in someone's seat who was then in the lavatory. When the person returned from the lavatory, United personnel had to again request Ms. Rubin to leave the seat.

In the meantime the purser alerted the pilot who came out of the cockpit to assess the situation. The flight was already considerably delayed and many passengers were becoming upset and unruly. The pilot, purser and service director conferred and decided Ms. Rubin should be removed from the flight. As the service director described the situation, "it was unacceptable behavior, it was unsafe behavior. I had a riot going on, just about, and this is where I draw the line."

Although a pilot necessarily relies in part on the purser and operations director in making the decision to deplane a passenger, a pilot has ultimate responsibility for the overall safety of the aircraft, its crew and passengers. (See 14 C.F.R. 121.537, subd. (d) [pilot has complete control over and responsibility for all passengers and crew "without limitation"].) The Federal Aviation Administration has enacted numerous regulations granting considerable discretion to airlines and pilots to control dangerous or unruly behavior. For example, regulations grant authority (1) to the pilot and crew members to prohibit anyone from interfering, intimidating or threatening a crew member or interfering with his or her duties (14 C.F.R. §§ 91.11, 121.580); (2) jointly to the pilot and director of operations for the initiation, continuation, diversion or termination of a flight (14 C.F.R. § 121.537, subd. (b)); (3) to the pilot to ensure no flight crewmember is engaged in any activity which might distract the person from his or her duties during a critical phase of the flight. (14 C.F.R. § 121.542, subd. (b); see generally Weigand, Air Rage and Legal Pitfalls for State Based Claims Challenging Airline Regulation of Passenger Conduct During Flight (2001) 45 Jun B. B.J. 10.)

Ms. Rubin refused to comply with the gate agent's request to leave the plane voluntarily. In fact, she refused to stop talking on her cell phone long enough to even acknowledge his presence. The gate agent testified he thought Ms. Rubin could have been a danger to other passengers on the airplane because of her "aggressive behavior." The gate agent reasoned, "She wouldn't listen. She wouldn't listen to the uniform[ed] crew member[s], she wouldn't listen to the service director. She was very loud. And in her conversation on the phone, that was very loud, and completely ignoring my presence less than 20 inches from her, looking her dead in the eye...."

United personnel then summoned the assistance of the Los Angeles Airport Police Department. Given the length of the delay of 20 to 25 minutes, and the volatile situation they discovered on board, the police officers were ready to arrest Ms. Rubin and file charges against her for obstructing a flight crew. Indeed, one of the officers believed because so many of the passengers were angry at Ms. Rubin her own personal safety would have been at risk had she remained on the flight.

The FAA makes it a criminal offense for a person to assault or intimidate a member of the flight crew in any way which interferes with his or her ability to perform his or her duties. 49 United States Code section 46504 provides: "An individual on an aircraft in the special aircraft jurisdiction of the United States who, by assaulting or intimidating a flight crew member or flight attendant of the aircraft, interferes with the performance of the duties of the member or attendant or lessens the ability of the member or attendant to perform those duties, shall be fined under title 18, imprisoned for not more than 20 years, or both. However, if a dangerous weapon is used in assaulting or intimidating the member or attendant, the individual shall be imprisoned for any term of years or for life." (See also cases collected in Mann, All The (Air) Rage: Legal Implications Surrounding Airline and Government Bans on Unruly Passengers In The Sky (Fall 2000) 65 J. Air. L. & Com. 857.)

In short, the undisputed evidence establishes Ms. Rubin did, or at least attempted to, make an unauthorized entry into the first class forward cabin area, which airline personnel consider a threatening act. Moreover, the undisputed evidence establishes Ms. Rubin repeatedly and deliberately refused to comply with any of the directions from any of the airline personnel regarding safety issues. This evidence in combination, coupled with the unruly and potentially dangerous situation she helped create on board, is sufficient as a matter of law to establish United, when it made its decision, had a reasonable basis for believing Ms. Rubin, was, "or might be, inimical to safety," 49 United States Code section 44902(b) [an air carrier "may refuse to transport a passenger or property the carrier decides is, or might be, inimical to safety"], which in turn justified removing her from this particular flight.

Ms. Rubin's allegedly triable issues of fact, for example, whether the flight was already somewhat delayed, whether the outraged purser unilaterally decided to have her ejected, or whether the passengers instead applauded because they were promised a free movie, are too immaterial to alter this conclusion. Similarly, the fact or result of the parties' prior arbitration is irrelevant to this proceeding. Accordingly, we further conclude the trial court correctly granted judgment in United's favor and dismissed the action.

DISPOSITION

The judgment is affirmed. Respondent is awarded costs on appeal.

DETERRA v. AMERICA WEST AIRLINES, INC.

226 F. Supp. 2d 298 (D. Mass. 2002)

COHEN, Magistrate Judge.

Legislation aimed [at] eliminat[ing] discrimination on aircrafts or by the airlines has suffered rather bumpy travel over several paths. In or about 1982, the Civil Aeronautics Board, based on Section 504 of the Rehabilitation Act of 1973, promulgated regulations proscribing discrimination. In 1986, the Supreme Court of the United States concluded that those regulations could not be construed so as to apply to private air carriers—i.e., air carriers not receiving federal financial assistance. United States Department of Transportation v. Paralyzed Veterans of America, 477 U.S. 597, 106 S.Ct. 2705, 91 L.Ed.2d 494 (1986).

In response to the Paralyzed Veterans of America decision, Congress in 1986 enacted the Air Carrier Access Act ("ACAA"). [See] 49 U.S.C.App. § 1374(c). Th[e] statute, as enacted at that time, provided [in pertinent part]: "(1) No air carrier may discriminate against any otherwise qualified handicapped individual, by reason of such handicap, in the provision of air transportation."

In 1994, Section 41705 of Title 49 was enacted as P.L. 103-272 [replacing § 1374(c)]. Section 41705 provide[s] in [pertinent part]: "In providing air transportation, an air carrier may not discriminate against an otherwise qualified individual on the following grounds: (1) the individual has a physical or mental impairment that substantially limits one or more major life activities; (2) the individual has a record of such an impairment; (3) the individual is regarded as having such an impairment."

This is an action in which the plaintiff alleges that he was discriminated against by the defendant on account of a handicap. In Count I of the complaint, plaintiff seeks compensatory damages under the ACAA. In Count II, plaintiff seeks punitive damages under the ACAA. In Count III, plaintiff seeks compensatory damages for a common law breach of contract. Counts IV through VI are pendent state law tort claims (Count IV alleges negligence, Count V alleges intentional infliction of emotional distress, and Count VI alleges negligent infliction of emotional distress).

The above-entitled case was referred to this court for all proceedings, including trial and entry of judgment, with the consent of the parties and consistent with the provisions of 28 U.S.C. § 636(c) and Rule 4(c)(1) of the Rules for United States Magistrate Judges in the United States District Court for the District of Massachusetts.

Defendant has filed a Motion for Partial Summary Judgment Pursuant to Fed. R.Civ. P 56 (# 32). By Memorandum and Order and Procedural Order (# 41) dated March 28, 2002, this court entered a Memorandum and Order allowing that motion for summary judgment vis a vis the pendent state law claims for the reasons set forth in that Memorandum and Order and Procedural Order (# 41). By the terms of that same order, this court scheduled a hearing on that motion vis a vis the remaining counts (Counts I and II) of the complaint, to wit: plaintiff's claim for compensatory damages under the ACAA (Count I), and plaintiff's claim for punitive damages under the ACAA (Count II). That hearing was held on April 18, 2002.

I. General Undisputed Facts

For purposes of defendant's Motion for Summary Judgment, this court finds the following facts to be undisputed:

1. As of August 7, 1999, plaintiff was wheelchair-bound due to a degenerative neuromuscular disorder which rendered him a paraplegic.

2. Together with his brother Daniel Deterra and sister-in-law, Catherine Deterra, plaintiff had reservations to travel on an America West flight to Boston, Massachusetts scheduled to depart from Las Vegas, Nevada at approximately 11:30 p.m. on August 7, 1999.

3. When plaintiff entered the ticket line at the Las Vegas Airport on August 7, 1999, to check in for his flight, plaintiff waited in line in his wheelchair for over an hour. He was not advanced to the front of the ticket line by America West as had occurred in Boston.

4. Plaintiff arrived at the gate for boarding his flight at least 35 minutes before the flight's scheduled departure. At that time, the boarding of first class passengers from the terminal through the jetbridge, the tunnel-like structure leading from the terminal to the aircraft, had already begun.

5. Plaintiff attempted to communicate with the America West gate agents after they refused to stop the line to allow Plaintiff to board. He tried to tell the gate agents that he had to board first, because it would be too difficult to board him with all other passengers on the plane, but they ignored him, would not answer him and would not look directly at him. Instead of talking to him, they looked over him and talked to his brother and sister-in-law.

6. When plaintiff's brother, Daniel, asked an America West agent named Jay to allow plaintiff to go to the front of the line and board ahead of the other passengers, Jay responded that they would need to wait until after the other passengers had boarded. In particular, according to plaintiff's brother, Daniel, when he and his wife and the plaintiff went to the counter in the gate area, they were told "We've already started boarding people. It will have to be later. It will have to be done at the end."

7. Plaintiff and/or his relatives disagreed with America West's response. Catherine Deterra claims that she asked to speak to a supervisor, was told by an America West agent named Robert that there was no supervisor available, and he gave her a telephone number to contact. She claims that she was told by the woman she spoke to at that number that the woman was "dismayed" at what was happening but that there was no one available to resolve the problem due to the late hour.

8. After it appeared that the other passengers had entered the jetbridge to board, Daniel Deterra addressed the America West employee who was standing in the gate area nearby and who had told them they would have to wait, saying "Are you fucking assholes ready to board him now?" Daniel Deterra admits that he was very upset and might have been mad when he made this remark. He admits that he said it "a little louder than normal" and in a "perturbed voice."

9. Wayne DeMello, a friend traveling with the Deterras, recalls that when the group arrived at the gate to board the flight, other passengers were already boarding through the jetbridge and he heard one of the America West agents tell Daniel Deterra that they would have to wait and board last. He recalls that Daniel Deterra was loud and swore, and that DeMello told Daniel he wasn't supposed to be loud and told him, "you can't say that here." He told Daniel Deterra to calm down because there was no need for him to be screaming.

10. Plaintiff and Daniel Deterra both admit that if Daniel Deterra had not acted in the manner set forth in Paragraphs I.8 and I.9 above, plaintiff, his brother and sister-in-law could have boarded their original flight after the other passengers had boarded.

11. According to plaintiff, the America West agents indicated that Daniel Deterra's words were too forceful and that plaintiff, his relatives, and the two friends with them, would not be allowed to board the flight.

12. Plaintiff's brother immediately apologized to both gate agents, Jay and Robert, for his remarks. (See Exhibit 3, Excerpts from Daniel Deterra Deposition, pp. 70, 72, 74.) Robert stated that he understood Daniel Deterra's frustration regarding the boarding situation.

13. After general boarding had been completed, the gate agents advised plaintiff that he and his sister-in-law, Catherine, would be permitted to board the flight, but that plaintiff's brother, Daniel, would not be permitted to board that flight. Believing that he needed the assistance of his brother, Daniel, plaintiff chose not to take that flight. All three—plaintiff, Daniel Deterra, and Catherine Deterra, were rebooked for the next flight at 12:40 p.m., and they took that flight, arriving in Boston about three hours later than they would have had they been boarded on the original flight.

II. Plaintiff's Claims

Plaintiff does not contend that he was denied a reasonable accommodation under the ACAA on account of the fact that he had a long wait in the ticket line when he first arrived at the airport, or that he was denied a reasonable accommodation on account of the fact that he took the next flight out which arrived three hours later. Instead, he contends, as argued by counsel for plaintiff at the hearing on the motion for summary judgment, that he was denied a reasonable accommodation within the meaning of the ACAA only on account of the following: (1) because airline agents "talked over the plaintiff" directly to plaintiff's brother, Daniel; (2) because airline agents treated plaintiff in a humiliating and derogatory fashion by referring to him, on account of his handicap, as an "It"; and (3) because the airline did not have a "complaint resolution officer" present when the incident at the boarding area arose.

III. Summary Judgment Standard

To survive a motion for summary judgment, the opposing party must demonstrate that there is a genuine issue of material fact requiring a trial. Fed.R.Civ.P., 56(e); Matsushita Electric Industrial Co. v. Zenith Radio Corp., 475 U.S. 574, 587, 106 S.Ct. 1348, 89 L.Ed.2d 538 (1986). As the Supreme Court recently has made clear, the standard for granting summary judgment "mirrors" the standard for a directed verdict under Fed.R.Civ.P. 50(a). Anderson v. Liberty Lobby, Inc., 477 U.S. 242, 250, 106 S.Ct. 2505, 91 L.Ed.2d 202 (1986).

IV. Discussion

In the circumstances, vis a vis the three claims asserted by the plaintiff as indicated in Part II above, this court finds and concludes that plaintiff cannot, on the basis of the undisputed material facts, make out a triable claim under the ACAA (Count I).

1. The "Talking Over Plaintiff's Head" Claim

As indicated above, plaintiff contends that agents of the defendant airline denied plaintiff a reasonable accommodation by "talking over his [plaintiff's] head" and directing their remarks to plaintiff's brother, Daniel, instead of to the plaintiff.

In this court's view, this conduct, standing alone, does not constitute prohibited discrimination within the meaning of the ACAA. Beyond the plain words of the statute, there is little legislative history surrounding the enactment of the ACAA—at least in terms of defining its scope. One court, however, has appropriately interpreted the ACAA as follows (Rivera v. Delta Air Lines, Inc., 1997 WL 634500 *7 (E.D.Pa.1997)):

> The ACAA prohibits air carriers from discriminating against an individual because they have, or are regarded as having, a disability. The regulations promulgated in connection with the ACAA explain that the Act requires air carriers: (1) to provide services and benefits without discrimination on the basis of disability; and (2) to provide disabled individuals with certain services, equipment or assistance. 14 C.F.R. §§382.7, 382.39 (1996). In other words, all persons are entitled to be treated equally, but "qualified handicapped individuals" are further entitled to certain services.

In this case, plaintiff makes no argument that he was denied those certain services, equipment or assistance, beyond those provided to all travelers, specifically referred to in the implementing regulations. And nothing in the implementing regulations suggest that qualified handicapped individuals should or must be boarded before all other boarders, or, at any particular time. Indeed, to the extent that the implementing regulations refer to boardings of aircraft at all, the implementing regulations suggest to the contrary—that is, that it is discriminatory to pre-board qualified handicapped individuals as a matter of policy. [See] Section 382.7(a)(2) of Title 14 of the Code of Federal Regulations, [which] provides: "A carrier shall not ... require an individual with a disability to accept special services (including, but not limited to, preboarding) not requested by the passenger."

[In addition to prohibiting discriminating in boarding,] Section 382.7 [also prohibits discrimination] relating to, among other things, aircraft accessibility, "refusal" of transportation, requiring advance notice of travel by a handicapped person, requiring (with certain special exceptions) a handicapped person from traveling with his or her own "attendant," seating assignments, seating accommodation, provision of certain services and equipment (e.g., wheelchairs, etc.), boarding assistance on small and large aircrafts—none of which includes preboarding; assistance in stowage of personal equipment, treatment of mobility aids and assistive devices, passenger information (e.g., seating locations, lavatory information, etc.), accommodations for those with hearing impairments, security screening, providing transportation to those with communicable diseases (except where the health and safety of others would be endangered), requir[ing] that handicapped persons have medical certificates, [etc.].

While not suggesting that these specific regulations are exclusive to other species or manners of discrimination falling with the ambit of the ACAA, th[ey] are telling in one respect. All relate to the manner in which handicapped persons are provided services—e.g., seating, access to lavatories, wheelchair assistance—by the airlines. None suggest that demeanor of airline employees standing alone, uncivil as that demeanor may be, entitles the handicapped passenger to bring suit for damages under the ACAA. This court accordingly finds and concludes that, even if the airline agents "talk[ed] over his [plaintiff's] head," directing their remarks to the plaintiff's brother, that isolated occurrence, not relating to the actual services provided by the airline, no matter how distasteful or uncivil it may well have been, does not warrant an action for damages under the ACAA.

2. The "It" Reference

Plaintiff's second claim is that he is entitled to damages under the ACAA because airline agents treated plaintiff in a humiliating and derogatory fashion by referring to him, on account of his handicap, as an "It." That claim is predicated on the colloquy occurring at the airport as reported by plaintiff's sister-in-law, to wit:

> [W]hen she [plaintiff's sister-in-law] told one of the America West agents at the gate that "He (Deterra) needs to get on so that we can get him safely into the chair," the agent said, "It's going to have to wait until last." She also recalls that when she complained that she could not believe they were not going to be able to board, the agent said, "We can't handle it now" and "Look, it's going to have to wait until last."

Even assuming that one could reasonably infer from the word "it" in the context of the above-referenced colloquy the sinister meaning ascribed to it by plaintiff, that, alone, for the reasons set forth in Part IV.1 immediately above, does not warrant damage relief under the ACAA.

In any event, based on the record before this court, this court concludes that no reasonable trier of fact could reasonably conclude that the agents, in using the word "it" as referred to above, intended anything demeaning whatsoever on account of the fact that the plaintiff was handicapped. In context, given the full colloquy, the use of the word "it" was grammatically correct and expected. That colloquy cannot reasonably support an inference, an inference which could be drawn by a reasonable trier of fact, that the agents of the airline demeaned the plaintiff on account of his handicap.

3. The Want of a Complaint Resolution Officer

Plaintiff's final fallback is that he is entitled to bring suit for monetary damages on account of the fact that, at the time of the incident referred to in the complaint, the airlines did not immediately make a Complaint Resolution Officer present.

Section 382.65 [of Title 14 of the C.F.R.] provides in pertinent part:

> Each carrier providing scheduled service shall establish and implement a complaint resolution mechanism, including designating one or more complaint resolution official(s)(CRO) to be available at each airport which the carrier serves.
>
> The carrier shall make a CRO available to any person who complains of alleged violations of this part during all times the carrier is operating at the airport.
>
> The carrier may make the CRO available via telephone, at no cost to the passenger, if the CRO is not present in person at the airport at the time of the complaint. If a telephone link to the CRO is used, TDD service shall be available so that persons with hearing impairments may readily communicate with the CRO.

Plaintiff can show (see Part I.7 above):

> Plaintiff and/or his relatives disagreed with America West's response. Catherine Deterra claims that she asked to speak to a supervisor, was told by an America West agent named Robert that there was no supervisor available, and he gave her a telephone number to contact. She claims that she was told by the woman she spoke to at that number that the woman was "dismayed" at what was happening but that there was no one available to resolve the problem due to the late hour.

Based on this, plaintiff says that the defendant violated the provisions of Section 382.65 by not having a CRO available at the time of the incident, and based on this shortcoming, and this shortcoming alone, plaintiff says that he is entitled to money damages in an action brought under the ACAA.

In this court's view, plaintiff has not established that Congress intended, where an air carrier fails to have a Complaint Resolution Officer present—unintentionally, that is, not for discriminatory purposes—and where that unintentional failure did not cause any discernible discrimination within the meaning of the language of the ACAA or the promulgated regulations, to [permit a plaintiff use] of a federal court [to pursue] compensatory (not to mention punitive) damages.

For these reasons, in the circumstances presented here, even though a Complaint Resolution Officer was not available at the time of the incident, contrary to the provisions of Section 382.65 of the applicable regulations, that, standing alone, is insufficient to state a claim upon which relief may be granted in the federal courts under the ACAA.

V. Conclusion

For the reasons set forth herein, and for the reasons set forth in the Memorandum and Order and Procedural Order (# 41) of this court dated March 28, 2002, defendant's motion for summary judgment is allowed, and judgment shall enter against plaintiff for all claims set forth in the complaint, and in favor of defendant.

STAGL v. DELTA AIR LINES, INC.

117 F.3d 76 (2d Cir. 1997)

CALABRESI, Circuit Judge.

Eleanor Stagl appeals from a judgment of the United States District Court for the Eastern District of New York (Manuel L. Real, Judge), granting a motion by the defendant, Delta Air Lines, Inc. ("Delta"), for judgment as a matter of law at the close of her presentation of evidence at trial.

In June 1993, Stagl filed a personal injury action against Delta alleging that she was injured in an accident that resulted from Delta's negligent supervision and management of its baggage retrieval system. The United States District Court for the Eastern District of New York (John R. Bartels, Judge) granted summary judgment to Delta and dismissed Stagl's action on the grounds that Stagl had failed to establish that Delta had a duty to make safe the baggage retrieval area, and that, in any event, Delta had fulfilled its duty to act reasonably under the circumstances. On appeal, this court vacated the grant of summary judgment, reversed the court's denial of Stagl's cross-motion to compel additional discovery, and remanded for further proceedings. We held that Delta owed Stagl a duty to maintain its luggage retrieval area in a reasonably safe condition and that there might exist genuine issues of material fact with respect to whether Delta had discharged its duty and whether Delta's conduct was the proximate cause of Stagl's injuries. See Stagl v. Delta Airlines, Inc., 52 F.3d 463 (2d Cir.1995).

On remand, the district court conducted a jury trial. At the end of Stagl's case-in-chief, the court granted Delta's motion for judgment as a matter of law, holding that there was insufficient evidence to support a jury determination that the accident was foreseeable since no evidence had been presented that similar prior accidents had occurred. Stagl appeals this judgment. She argues that the judgment is inconsistent with this court's opinion in Stagl and with New York tort law. She further contends that the district court violated the doctrine of the law of the case and the Federal Rules of Evidence when it found that Grahme Fischer, a mechanical engineer, was unqualified to give expert testimony at trial. Finally, Stagl objects to the district court's exclusion of other evidence regarding the circumstances surrounding her accident. Because we find that the district court erred in excluding this other testimony, in ruling that Fischer was unqualified to give expert testimony, and in concluding that evidence of prior accidents was necessary to prove negligence, we vacate the district court's judgment.

I. BACKGROUND

We assume familiarity with the facts of this case set forth in our prior opinion, see Stagl, 52 F.3d at 465–66, and therefore only briefly summarize the circumstances giving rise to this action. On May 1, 1993, Stagl, an elderly woman, was injured near the baggage carousel after landing in LaGuardia Airport on a delayed Delta flight from Orlando, Florida. She brought this diversity action in the district court, alleging that the airline had negligently failed to take any measures to control the crowd at the baggage carousel or to provide a means by which elderly and disabled people could retrieve their luggage safely. She further alleges that Delta's inaction proximately caused her physical injuries.

At trial, Stagl testified that at the baggage carousel, there was a crowd of passengers, many of whom were "pushing and shoving." She stated that there were no announcements, signs, or Delta personnel near the carousel discouraging this behavior. According to her testimony, when a passenger retrieved his bag from the carousel, his bag hit another bag which in turn hit Stagl, knocking her down and breaking her hip. Two Delta employees testified with respect to the conditions near the baggage carousels. During the testimony of Stagl and the Delta personnel, the court, on the ground that such testimony was irrelevant, refused to allow answers to many questions about the conditions at the airport at the time of the accident.

In response to a motion in limine by Delta, the district court also excluded the testimony of Stagl's expert, Grahme Fischer. It held that Fischer was "not qualified to give an opinion with reference to the facts of this case or to help the jury in the determination of the facts of this case and the cause of the accident to Mrs. Stagl ... [because] [h]is expertise is not in this area." No other expert testified on behalf of Stagl.

At the end of Stagl's case-in-chief, the court granted judgment in favor of Delta as a matter of law, ruling that, since there was no evidence that prior accidents of this sort had occurred, no reasonable jury could conclude that Stagl's accident was foreseeable.

II. DISCUSSION

Our prior holding in this case was that, under New York law, Delta owed Stagl a duty of reasonable care and that the presence of an intervenor, the passenger whose bag removal from the carousel allegedly led indirectly to Stagl's injury, did not as a matter of law break the chain of causation. We therefore found that the question of proximate cause was one for the jury to decide. See Stagl, 52 F.3d at 473–74. On the prior appeal, we also assessed whether the affidavits submitted by Stagl in opposition to Delta's motion for summary judgment were enough to demonstrate the existence of genuine issues of material fact and held that they were. On remand, the issue for the district court was whether the evidence presented by Stagl at trial sufficed to get to a jury.

The district court nevertheless was mistaken in its principal holding that without evidence of prior accidents Stagl could not meet her burden of proving (a) that the accident was foreseeable, and hence (b) that Delta had breached its duty of reasonable care.

The court was perhaps misled in this respect by the fact that, in our earlier opinion, we noted that the plaintiff was seeking discovery to see whether such accidents had happened before and that the district court had erred in not letting her do so. Id. at 474. We pointed out that the existence of such accidents would be relevant to the issues of negligence and of proximate cause. Id. But our discussions of Delta's alleged breach of duty and Stagl's cross motion for additional discovery also made clear that such evidence—though relevant—was not necessary to a showing of negligence in the particular case. Id. at 470–73, 474. If there is sufficient other evidence of negligence, no evidence of prior accidents is required. The district court was therefore wrong in granting judgment to Delta as a matter of law.

The district court also erred in excluding much of Stagl's evidence. Whether there was, in this case, sufficient evidence of negligence to get to a jury, depends, among other things, on the foreseeability of an injury of this sort, on the conditions around the carousel at the time of the accident, and on what the defendant could reasonably have done, even apart from installing other systems of baggage delivery, to protect the plaintiff. In addition to attempting to introduce Fischer as an expert witness, the plaintiff tried to testify to some of these factors herself. She also sought to introduce witnesses who were present at the accident so that they could speak to the same questions. But the district court excluded almost all such testimony on the ground that it was irrelevant. This ruling is manifestly incorrect, since the testimony would have tended to prove material issues in dispute.

Nor was this error harmless, as it might have been had the district court been correct in its view that either evidence by a qualified expert or evidence of prior accidents is essential to proving negligence. Instead, neither of these is necessary if enough other evidence of negligence is presented. It follows that precluding Stagl's legitimate attempt to introduce just such other relevant evidence was not harmless.

The district court's exclusion of Stagl's expert was also erroneous. Fischer has an undergraduate degree from Manhattan College and a master of science from Columbia University, both in mechanical engineering. He has worked as a licensed engineer in New York for approximately twenty years. The focus of the defendant's voir dire examination of Fischer—the primary basis for the district court's determination that his testimony would not be allowed—concerned whether Fischer had expertise in airline terminal or baggage claim area design. Fischer admitted that he did not, but testified credibly that his field of expert knowledge is the interaction between machines and people.

In alleging that the baggage delivery system was unreasonably unsafe for older people, Stagl suggests that the interaction between the baggage claim system employed by Delta and the passengers attempting to claim their baggage caused her injury. This interaction between people and machinery is clearly of the sort that Fischer has worked with in depth. And, as we pointed out, testimony about that interaction, and the existence of methods that would make it safer, is directly relevant to Delta's possible negligence in this case. Moreover, such testimony would most likely be beyond the knowledge of an average juror. Nonetheless, the court concluded that Fischer was unqualified because his expertise was insufficiently tailored to the facts of this case.

It is hard to imagine an expert in airport terminal design or baggage claim systems who developed that expertise in any way other than by working for the airline industry. Accordingly, to require the degree of specificity the court imposed came close to letting that industry indirectly set its own standards. At times this cannot be avoided. But where, as here, well-trained people with somewhat more general qualifications are available, it is error to exclude them. For this reason, the court should have allowed Fischer, an undoubted expert in human-machine interactions, to testify.

III. CONCLUSION

Even with all the limitations the court imposed on Stagl's presentation of evidence, she has come very close to introducing enough facts to allow a reasonable jury to rule in her favor. How much more evidence, if any, would be needed to avoid a judgment as a matter of law against her, need not be decided today. It is enough for us to hold that the district court erred in requiring Stagl to introduce evidence of prior similar accidents, in finding that Fischer was unqualified to provide expert testimony regarding alternative safety measures, and in excluding, as irrelevant, testimony designed to demonstrate that Delta had breached its duty of reasonable care to Stagl. Accordingly, we vacate the district court's judgment and remand for further proceedings consistent with this opinion.

J.C. PENNEY LIFE INSURANCE COMPANY v. PILOSI

393 F.3d 356 (3d Cir. 2004)

ROSENN, Circuit Judge.

This litigation has its genesis in an optimistic gambling junket to Atlantic City and a return flight that ended tragically in death. The ill-fated flight was part of a bi-weekly shuttle operated by Executive Airlines ("EA") on behalf of Caesars Casino ("Caesars"). Elaine Pilosi, a passenger on the junket, lost her life when the EA airplane in which she was traveling crashed. Mrs. Pilosi left two sons who were the beneficiaries of an accidental death insurance policy that she had purchased from the defendant, J.C. Penney Life Insurance Company ("J.C. Penney Life" or "the Insurer"). The policy had three categories of losses, two of which are pertinent in this litigation. Part I provided benefits of $1 million for accidental death in "a public conveyance ... operated by a duly licensed common carrier for regular passenger service." Part II provided for payment of $100,000 for accidental death in a private passenger automobile. And Part III provided for the payment of $50,000 for all other injuries.

J.C. Penney Life paid $50,000 under Part III of the policy and rejected the claim of the Pilosi brothers ("Pilosis" or "Insured") for $1 million under Part I. The Insurer sued for a declaratory judgment pursuant to 28 U.S.C. § 2201 in the United States District Court for the Middle District of Pennsylvania seeking a determination that the Pilosis were not entitled to the $1 million benefit. The Pilosis responded and also raised affirmative defenses asserting, inter alia, that J.C. Penney Life's claim is barred by the doctrine of waiver and/or estoppel, by its own bad faith, and by the doctrine of frustration of the purpose of the contract. In addition, the Pilosis counterclaimed for breach of contract and bad faith denial of their claim under 42 Pa.C.S.A. § 8371. The District Court, in a carefully considered opinion of a difficult case, entered summary judgment for the Pilosis in the sum of $1 million but rejected their claim under Pennsylvania law for bad faith damages. The Pilosis timely appealed the entry of summary judgment in favor of J.C. Penney Life on the bad faith claim, and J.C. Penney Life cross-appealed the entry of summary judgment awarding $1 million coverage. We affirm in part and reverse the summary judgment against J.C. Penney Life.

I.

The District Court had subject matter jurisdiction under 28 U.S.C. § 1332(a), as the diversity and amount-in-controversy requirements were met. The matter in controversy exceeds the sum of $75,000, exclusive of interest and costs, and arises between citizens of different states. J.C. Penney Life, a corporation duly organized and existing under the laws of Vermont, and having its principal place of business in Texas, is a citizen of both Vermont and Texas. Both Pilosis are citizens of Pennsylvania. This Court has jurisdiction under 28 U.S.C. § 1291, as an appeal from a final judgment that disposed of all parties' claims.

"Disposition of an insurance action on summary judgment is appropriate, when, as here, there are no material underlying facts in dispute." McMillan v. State Mut. Life Assurance Co. of Am., 922 F.2d 1073, 1074 (3d Cir.1990). The only contested issue in the instant case involves the interpretation of the scope of coverage of the insurance contract. "The interpretation of the scope of coverage of an insurance contract is a question of law properly decided by the court, a question over which [this court] exercise[s] plenary review." Med. Protective Co. v. Watkins, 198 F.3d 100, 103 (3d Cir.1999); McMillan, 922 F.2d at 1074.

Where federal jurisdiction is based on diversity of citizenship, as it is here, we apply the choice of law rules of the state in which the District Court sat. St. Paul Fire & Marine Ins. Co. v. Lewis, 935 F.2d 1428, 1431 n.3 (3d Cir.1991) (citing Klaxon Co. v. Stentor Elec. Mfg. Co., 313 U.S. 487, 496, 61 S.Ct. 1020, 85 L.Ed. 1477 (1941)). This action was instituted in the Middle District of Pennsylvania. Under Pennsylvania choice of law rules, an insurance contract is governed by the law of the state in which the contract was made. Crawford v. Manhattan Life Ins. Co., 208 Pa.Super. 150, 221 A.2d 877, 880 (1966); McMillan, 922 F.2d at 1074. "An insurance contract is 'made' in the state in which the last act legally necessary to bring the contract into force takes place." Crawford, 221 A.2d at 880. "In most cases, this last act is delivery of the policy to the insured and the payment of the first premium by him." Ruhlin v. N.Y. Life Ins. Co., 106 F.2d 921, 923 (3d Cir.1939).

In the instant case the policy makes no mention of insurance coverage being contingent upon delivery of the policy. However, the policy provided that coverage "will become effective on the Certificate Effective Date shown on the Schedule Page provided [that J.C. Penney Life] receive[s] the initial premium within 21 days of the Certificate Effective Date and while you are alive." The Certificate Effective Date was two days after Mrs. Pilosi orally accepted J.C. Penney Life's telephone solicitation offering three months of coverage at no cost and no obligation to continue. Payment of the first three monthly premiums was made by Mrs. Pilosi's credit card company as part of a promotion that it offered in conjunction with J.C. Penney Life. Because the first three premium payments were automatically triggered upon Mrs. Pilosi's oral acceptance, the last act legally necessary to bring the contract into force was Mrs. Pilosi's telephonic acceptance of the policy. This occurred at her residence in Pennsylvania. Therefore, Pennsylvania law governs construction of the terms of the insurance policy.

A. "Public Conveyance"

The threshold issue is whether the EA airplane in which Mrs. Pilosi died qualifies as a "public conveyance." Counsel for the Pilosis strenuously argue that, much like a taxicab, the airplane was a public conveyance. Although Caesars controlled who was allowed to board this particular flight, the Pilosis assert that the airplane was available for any member of the public at-large to charter before and after the Caesars flight. On the other hand, the Insurer contends that the airplane was not a public conveyance because members of the public at-large were not free to purchase tickets for the flight.

Unfortunately, the policy does not define "public conveyance." However, the record reveals that the carrier was, indeed, a public conveyance. The airplane in which Mrs. Pilosi was traveling was owned and operated by an air carrier licensed by the Federal Aviation Administration to conduct common carriage. The airplane belonged to a company that was engaged in the business of hiring out airplanes for general public use.

More importantly, EA made its services available to the general public. According to the deposition of EA's CEO, Michael Peragine, EA was open to "anyone who had money who wanted to fly." Thus, EA could be hired by anyone with the ability to pay, either before or after the Caesars flight. Analogous to a public taxicab, which the Pennsylvania Supreme Court has held to be a "public conveyance," Primrose v. Cas. Co., 232 Pa. 210, 81 A. 212, 214 (1911), "[t]he use of no one of [EA's] machines was limited to any particular person, but anyone able to pay the price and privilege of riding in it ... could do so." Id. at 213.

J.C. Penney Life challenges the taxicab analogy. It disputes the Pilosis' reliance on the holding in Terminal Taxicab Co., Inc. v. Kutz, 241 U.S. 252, 255, 36 S.Ct. 583, 60 L.Ed. 984 (1916). The issue in Terminal Taxicab was whether a taxicab company that offered its services to hotel guests pursuant to a contract with the hotel still retained its public character. The Court held that the taxicab company retained its public character even though it served primarily hotel guests. The Court noted that "[n]o carrier serves all the public. His customers are limited by place, requirements, ability to pay and other facts...." Id.

J.C. Penney Life's efforts to distinguish Terminal Taxicab are unpersuasive. J.C. Penney Life distinguishes the Terminal Taxicab taxi from the EA airplane on the ground that anyone could access the taxis stationed in front of the hotel, while the airplane was restricted to Caesars passengers. J.C. Penney Life's insistence that a vehicle must be available for "walk-up passengers" in order to qualify as a "public conveyance" misses the point.

As both the Terminal Taxicab and Primrose Courts articulate, passenger limitations imposed by any particular customer with regard to any particular taxi ride—i.e., designating the passengers, the destination, and the schedule of the trip—do not negate the public character of the conveyance. Terminal Taxicab, 241 U.S. at 255, 36 S.Ct. 583; Primrose, 81 A. at 213–14; see also Brill v. Indianapolis Life Ins. Co., 784 F.2d 1511, 1514 (11th Cir.1986) (holding that hiring a helicopter on a particular occasion limited the helicopter's "operation; however these limitations as to time, place and passengers were no different than those imposed on the taxi service discussed in Terminal Taxicab Co. For purposes of the one flight..., the decedent and his employer had the exclusive use of the helicopter as to contents, direction and time of use. Their control was not so pervasive, however, as to negate the public character of [the helicopter's] service.").

J.C. Penney Life claims that the proper test to determine whether a conveyance is public or private is the extent to which the public has access to the conveyance. Under J.C. Penney Life's test, however, the plane qualifies as public because it can be accessed by any member of the public who has the financial means to rent it. J.C. Penney Life is insensible to the public nature of the air taxi because general members of the public may not board the flight on those occasions when Caesars charters the plane. But being temporarily restricted to a paying client does not transform a public conveyance into a private carrier. When a patron enters a public taxicab, the cab is effectively private for the duration of the fare. However, once the fare is completed, anyone may hire the taxi. The same goes for an air taxi, such as EA. When the plane is engaged by a person, that person is the very public to which the plane is available.

The final indicator that EA's plane was a "public conveyance" is that Caesars did not use exclusively the particular aircraft employed for the fateful flight—the November 16 Echo Juliet. J.C. Penney Life's assertion that the flight was private rather than public would be more persuasive if, instead of being available for public hire, the EA jet was reserved exclusively for Caesars. However, other members of the public in addition to Caesars could use the Echo Juliet plane when not otherwise committed. Caesars merely procured EA's services on a regular basis. We are therefore convinced that the plane was a public, rather than private, conveyance. However, this conclusion does not resolve the issue, for we must examine other pertinent terms of the policy contract.

B. Interpretation of the Policy Language

We turn to the proper interpretation of the clause "operated by a duly licensed common carrier for regular passenger service." A reasoned analysis reveals that "regular passenger service" modifies the adjective "licensed," so that coverage extends narrowly to those common carriers specifically licensed to conduct regular passenger service.

1. Pennsylvania Law on the Interpretation of Insurance Contracts

Where an insurance policy provision is ambiguous, it is to "be construed against the insurer and in favor of the insured...." McMillan, 922 F.2d at 1075; State Farm Fire & Cas. Co. v. MacDonald, 850 A.2d 707, 710 (2004). An ambiguity exists when the questionable term or language, viewed in the context of the entire policy, is "reasonably susceptible of different constructions and capable of being understood in more than one sense." Med. Protective, 198 F.3d at 103 (citing Reliance Ins. Co. v. Moessner, 121 F.3d 895, 900 (3d Cir.1997), in turn citing Gamble Farm Inn, Inc. v. Selective Ins. Co., 440 Pa.Super. 501, 656 A.2d 142, 143–44 (1995) (quoting Hutchison v. Sunbeam Coal Corp., 513 Pa. 192, 519 A.2d 385, 390 (1986))). Where, however, "the language of an insurance contract is clear and unambiguous, a court is required to enforce that language." Med. Protective, 198 F.3d at 103 (citing Standard Venetian Blind, 469 A.2d at 566).

In the instant case, the policy requires that the insured must have been traveling in a public conveyance "operated by a duly licensed common carrier for regular passenger service by ... air." The parties dispute which word the clause "for regular passenger service" modifies. The Pilosis argue that the phrase "for regular passenger service" modifies "operated," meaning that the common carrier must be duly licensed and must be operated for regular passenger service. On the other hand, J.C. Penney Life argues that the disputed clause modifies "licensed," so a carrier is not covered unless its license specifically authorizes regular passenger service. Although the meaning of the clause is disputed, "[a] contract is not rendered ambiguous by the mere fact that the parties do not agree upon the proper construction." MacDonald, 850 A.2d at 710. When the disputed language is read in context with the policy's definitions, only one interpretation is reasonable.

As stated above, the insurance policy requires that the conveyance be "operated by a duly licensed common carrier for regular passenger service by ... air." The policy, in turn, defines "common carrier" to mean "an air ... conveyance operated under a license for regularly scheduled passenger service." Read in context, therefore, the phrase requires the airline to possess a license for regularly scheduled passenger service to qualify as "a common carrier for regular passenger service." There is no reasonable alternative interpretation. The explicit definition of "common carrier" is adequate to put the Pilosis on notice that there would be no coverage unless the carrier was licensed for regular passenger service. Peerless Dyeing Co., Inc. v. Indus. Risk Insurers, 392 Pa.Super. 434, 573 A.2d 541, 544 (1990) ("When a word or phrase is specifically defined within the policy, that definition controls in determining the applicability of the policy.").

The Pilosis believe the policy language is ambiguous. They therefore urge application of the rule of insurance construction that interprets policy clauses providing coverage in a manner which affords the greatest possible protection to the insured. See Geisler v. Motorists Mut. Ins. Co., 382 Pa.Super. 622, 556 A.2d 391, 393 (1989). Although this rule does, indeed, represent the law in this area, application is warranted only where the language is, in fact, ambiguous. The canon does not apply where, as here, the language of the policy, viewed in context, is clear. Treasure Craft Jewelers, Inc. v. Jefferson Ins. Co. of N.Y., 431 F.Supp. 1160, 1163 (E.D.Pa.1977) ("[R]ule of strict construction against the insurance company has no application where the language is clear and unambiguous.") (citing Sidebothom v. Metro. Life Ins. Co., 339 Pa. 124, 14 A.2d 131, 132 (1940)). The plain meaning of the phrase "operated by a duly licensed common carrier for regular passenger service," when viewed in conjunction with the definition of "common carrier," is that coverage extends only to those carriers that are licensed for regular passenger service. See Loomer v. M.R.T. Flying Serv., 384 Pa.Super. 244, 558 A.2d 103, 105 (1989) ("Where the terms of the insurance contract are not ambiguous ... [the] Court must read the policy in its entirety and give the words therein their plain and proper meanings.").

To be sure, the burden of drafting with precision rests with the insurance company, the author of the policy. McMillan, 922 F.2d at 1076. However, where, as here, the scrivener has adopted precise language to accomplish its purpose of limiting coverage to those carriers licensed for regular passenger service, that intent must control. Accordingly, it was erroneous to have found the language of Part I of the policy ambiguous.

2. Rules of Statutory Interpretation

In addition to the plain language of the policy, rules of statutory interpretation demonstrate that the plane must be licensed for regularly scheduled passenger service. A general rule of statutory construction, the "doctrine of last antecedent," teaches that "qualifying words, phrases, and clauses are to be applied to the words or phrase immediately preceding, and are not to be construed as extending to and including others more remote." Resolution Trust Corp. v. Nernberg, 3 F.3d 62, 65 (3d Cir.1993); see United States v. Hodge, 321 F.3d 429, 436 (3d Cir.2003); Commonwealth of Pa., Dep't of Pub. Welfare v. United States Dep't of Health & Human Servs., 80 F.3d 796, 808 (3d Cir.1996). This rule suggests that the clause "for regular passenger service" modifies the antecedent adjective "licensed," rather than the verb "operated," which is located distally in the middle of the sentence. See also 2A Norman J. Singer, Sutherland Statutory Construction § 47.33 (6th ed. 2000) ("Referential and qualifying words and phrases, where no contrary intention appears, refer solely to the last antecedent.").

To be sure, "this rule [of the last antecedent] is not an absolute and can assuredly be overcome by other indicia of meaning...." Barnhart v. Thomas, 540 U.S. 20, 124 S.Ct. 376, 380, 157 L.Ed.2d 333 (2003) (applying the rule of last antecedent to statutes). However, in this case other indicia point overwhelmingly towards the conclusion that the clause modifies the word "licensed." Even if we were to ignore the contrary meaning provided by the definition of "common carrier," construing the phrase as the Pilosis urge would contort the language beyond its limits because such an interpretation would require a reorganization of the clause. The rewritten phrase would read: "operated by a duly licensed common carrier and operated for regular passenger service." By contrast, interpreting the phrase to mean that the airline must be licensed for regular passenger service requires no such reorganization. By rewriting the policy to read that EA was a "duly licensed carrier" and "operated for regular passenger service," the District Court created an ambiguity where one does not exist. See Fosse v. Allianz Life Ins. Co. of N. Am., 1994 WL 139413, at *3 (E.D.Pa. Apr.20, 1994) ("An ambiguity does not arise simply because an alternative interpretation of a word can be created through reasoning that renders common words meaningless.").

In light of the plain language of the policy and the contextual clarity provided by the definition of "common carrier," coupled with the absence of any reasonable alternative interpretation of the coverage language, the policy is unambiguous in requiring that the flight be licensed for regular passenger service.

C. "Regular Passenger Service"

Both the plain meaning of the policy language and rules of statutory interpretation reveal that insurance coverage extends narrowly to those common carriers specifically licensed to conduct regularly scheduled passenger service. Furthermore, EA's license includes a significant provision that "[t]he certificate holder is not authorized and shall not ... [c]onduct Scheduled Operations at Authorized Airports." But even assuming that coverage did extend to all licensed common carriers operating regularly scheduled passenger service, the Pilosis cannot overcome the reality that EA was not conducting regularly scheduled passenger service within the meaning of the policy and under the terms of its license.

The EA shuttle flew patrons from Scranton, Pennsylvania to Atlantic City, New Jersey on alternating Saturdays at 4:30 P.M., and returned the following morning at 2:00 A.M. Although the ill-fated flight was part of a regular pattern of flights engaged by the casino, EA did not dictate the schedule; rather, its client, Caesars, did. EA was operating a service for a client who hired the flight for its convenience on alternate Saturdays. There is a distinction between an airline that accommodates a client who regularly engages a flight once every two weeks and an airline that conducts regularly scheduled passenger service. We hold that when the time and destination of the service is dictated by the convenience or business of the charterer and the airline's license specifically prohibits regularly scheduled service at authorized airports, the service does not qualify as "regular passenger service" under the terms of the policy. Merely chartering a plane on a regular basis does not transform an airline operating on-demand into a regularly scheduled service provider. See Fosse, 1994 WL 139413, at *2 (holding that where an air taxi service operated upon demand, it did not operate its flights pursuant to a set schedule).

As mentioned previously, EA provided on-demand air taxi service. EA was licensed as a "charter operation providing taxi services" under 14 C.F.R. § 135. In addition, EA's FAA Air Carrier Operating Certificate designated the airline as an on-demand air taxi. Moreover, the preliminary accident report filed by the National Transportation Safety Board described the aircraft as an on-demand charter flying a "non-scheduled" flight. Finally, the airline's Operations Specifications not only provided that EA "is not authorized and shall not ... [c]onduct Scheduled Operations at Authorized Airports[,]" but defined a "scheduled operation" by an air carrier as one "for which the certificate holder or its representative offers in advance the departure location, departure time, and arrival location." 14 C.F.R. §119.3. The facts of this case demonstrate that EA does not meet the definition of "regular passenger service."

To summarize, Part I of the policy provided benefits of $1 million for accidental death in a public conveyance operated by a duly licensed common carrier for regular passenger service. The EA flight was, indeed, a public conveyance, but was not "operated by a duly licensed common carrier for regular passenger service" as required by the plain language of the policy. Because all of the elements of Part I are not satisfied, it was error as a matter of law to grant summary judgment in favor of the Pilosis on the issue of coverage.

D. Bad Faith

[This portion of the court's opinion is omitted.]

II.

The District Court's grant of summary judgment in favor of the Pilosis on the amount of coverage is reversed because the Part I policy requirements were not satisfied. For the same reason, we affirm the District Court's denial of the Pilosis' bad faith claim. Each side to bear its own costs.

McKEE, Circuit Judge, concurring.

I agree that we must reverse the order granting summary judgment in favor of the insureds because they are not entitled to coverage under Part I of the insurance policy. I therefore join Parts I.B and I.C of the majority opinion. I also agree that the insureds have not made out their bad faith claim under 42 Pa.C.S. §8371, and I therefore agree that we must affirm the district court's grant of summary judgment in favor of J.C. Penney Life on the insureds' bad faith claim. However, I write separately because I do not agree that the plane that crashed qualifies as a "public conveyance" under the terms of the insurance policy. Accordingly, I can not agree with the analysis in Part I.A. of the majority opinion.

I.

According to J.C. Penney Life, Caesars Casino controlled who could board charter flights like the one at issue here. No one could make a reservation for those flights. Rather, Caesars' Pennsylvania marketing representative was responsible for the required coordination and arrangements. In order to travel on one of these charter flights, a person had to meet Caesars' definition of a qualified player for its gambling business, or be a guest of someone Caesars deemed a "qualified player." Although it was not favored, Caesars would also allow passengers who, in Caesars' estimation, had the potential to qualify as a "qualified player" or someone who was a guest of a "qualified player." However, even some of Caesars regular customers might not qualify to travel on these charters. J.C. Penney Life says that Caesars used the flight for its own interests to increase its gambling business.

According to J.C. Penney Life, no passenger ever paid a fare for any of these flights, and Caesars never sold any seats or packages in connection with the flights. Obviously, the flights were never advertised. Rather, the flights were exclusively a "complimentary" perquisite that Caesars created and controlled, and doled out to those it defined as "high rollers" based upon its own customer ratings. Given these restrictions, and the near total exclusion of the public, the Executive Airlines ("EA") flight at issue here simply can not qualify as a "public conveyance."

II.

I believe the majority's focus on testimony that EA was "open to 'anyone who had money and wanted to fly'" misses the point. The flights that Caesars chartered were clearly not open to anyone with money who wanted to fly. The fact that Mrs. Pilosi's plane "could be hired by anyone with the ability to pay, either before or after the Caesar flight," does not establish that the particular flight that Mrs. Pilosi was on was a "public conveyance" while it was under the exclusive use and control of Caesars Resort. The fact that the plane was a public conveyance sometime does not establish that it was a public conveyance all of the time. This is particularly true when it was totally inaccessible to the general public. This is not to say that a charter loses its public nature merely because it is hired by a particular person. However, where, as here, a contract with a private party so restricts access to a charter as to arbitrarily place it beyond the reach of the general public, it can no [longer] be considered public.

It is beyond dispute that the limitations here exceed the usual limitations inherent in charters that can be hired by any member of the public with ability to pay. Indeed, exclusion here is the raison d'etre of Caesars' charter. It is the exclusion of the public that makes Caesars' charters valuable. Moreover, the charter flight benefitted Caesars and a select few high rollers that Caesars chose for its own purposes. The flight did not benefit the universe of Caesars' patronizing public. Accordingly, I conclude that availability of Caesars' charter was so limited and exclusive that it can not be deemed a "public conveyance."

Notes

1. For many years, the federal government, concerned about operator stability and wanting to ensure nationwide service, shielded the airline industry from competition. Finally, however, in 1978 Congress reversed course and passed the ADA. As a result, the major carriers (also known as "legacy carriers") suddenly found themselves beset by start-up operators (who, by cherry-picking routes and avoiding expensive union contracts, were able to offer dramatically lower fares). In response, the majors quickly resolved to beat back the challengers by playing hard ball. Although aware of what was going on, the federal government was slow to react. When it finally did bring a test case (against American Airlines for flights between its hub at Dallas-Fort Worth and four other cities), the courts held that its tests were flawed and failed to prove below-cost pricing. *See United States v. AMR Corp.*, 140 F. Supp. 2d 1141 (D. Kan. 2001), *aff'd*, 335 F.3d 1109 (10th Cir. 2003). Thus, the decision in *Spirit Airlines*—which was handed down just as this casebook was going into print—has the potential to be very significant:

> Although it has been 10 years since the price wars that led to the lawsuit, the case is particularly relevant now, airline experts say, as major carriers including Northwest regain their financial strength by slashing their costs through the bankruptcy process to better compete with low-cost carriers such as Spirit.
>
> "The big airlines are probably more dangerous for low-fare carriers today than they were before," [Spirit attorney Richard Alan] Arnold said.
>
> Airline expert Terry Trippler said Northwest is known as a fierce competitor and that Spirit is wise to pursue this case. When major carriers such as Northwest and Delta Air Lines, "get their labor cost structure down, the low-cost carriers are going to be in for the fight of their life," said Trippler of Minneapolis-based Cheapseats.com.

> The industry will be watching this case, said R. Hewitt Pate, a Washington D.C.-based attorney who leads the antitrust practice at the law firm Hunton & Williams.
>
> "There's no doubt that it's something that airlines are going to have to take seriously."
>
> While the appeals court decision is a good sign for Spirit, the carrier has a major legal battle to fight. "Winning a predatory pricing case is something that is extremely difficult and extremely rare," Pate said.

Jewel Gopwani, *NWA Case on Prices is Revived*, Det. Free Press, Nov. 10, 2005, at 1C. For earlier discussions of the subject, *see, e.g.*, Paul Stephen Dempsey, *Predation, Competition & Antitrust Law: Turbulence in the Airline Industry*, 67 J. Air L. & Com. 685 (2002); Charles E. Koob, *Whither Predatory Pricing? The Divergence Between Judicial Decisions and Economic Theory: The American Airlines and Virgin Atlantic Airways Cases*, 3 Sedona Conf. J. 9 (2002); Dennis J. Keithly, Comment, *To Trap the White Tiger and Unicorn, the Government Needs Better Traps: An Examination of the Viability of Predatory Pricing Claims in the Airline Industry*, 69 J. Air L. & Com. 837 (2004) (the title of this article refers to a famous debate between two FTC commissioners regarding which metaphor more aptly described predatory pricing).

2. While reading the *Northwest Antitrust Litigation* case, did you feel any sympathy for Nelson Chase? Of course, other than patronizing low-cost carriers (when they are available), consumers have few easy ways to avoid high ticket prices (short of not flying at all). This fact figured prominently in a number of episodes of the NBC sitcom *Seinfeld* (1989–98), including "The Implant" (1993):

> Betsy: So, when's the funeral? Well, Aunt Clarice was so ill, I guess it was really a blessing. Yeah, I'll fly home as soon as I can. Okay. You, too. Get some sleep. [Betsy looks over to George, who fakes sympathy.]
>
> [Cut to George, Jerry, and Kramer sitting in a sauna.]
>
> Jerry: So, you goin' to the funeral?
>
> George: Why, you think I should?
>
> Jerry: What, are you kidding? It's a golden opportunity to advance the relationship. She's crying, you put your arm around her and console her ... you're the consolation guy!
>
> George: I'm the consolation guy ... ?
>
> Kramer: Consolation guy is big.
>
> Jerry: Her aunt dying is the best thing that ever happened to you....
>
> George: It's in Detroit though, it's an expensive flight.
>
> Kramer: Why don't you get a "death in the family" fare?
>
> George: What?
>
> Kramer: You go to the airlines, you tell them you got a death in the family. They give you 50% off the fare.
>
> George: Really?
>
> Kramer: In fact, listen ... I'll go down there with ya. You know, we'll tell them there's a death in my family, you buy the ticket, I'll split it ... then I'll get the bonus miles and you'll get to Detroit for a quarter of the price!

[Cut to George and Kramer at the airline ticket counter. Kramer is pretending to be grief-stricken.]

George (to clerk): You see, my friend here, his aunt passed away last night.

Clerk (to Kramer): Oh, I'm very sorry.

Kramer: I saw her last week, she looked healthy and peaceful, but ... she knew....

Clerk: You poor thing!

Kramer (breaking into tears): I ... I....

George [to Kramer]: You don't think you can buy the ticket yourself ... ? No, there, there ... you sit, and I'll purchase the ticket for you.

Clerk: You're a good friend.

George: I understand you offer a 50%-off "bereavement" fare ... ?

Clerk: Yes, all you have to do is pay the full fare now, then return to any one of our counters with a copy of the death certificate, and we'll refund half your fare.

George: The death certificate?

Clerk: Yes, yes, we do need documentation or you know, people could take advantage.

George: What kind of a sick person would do a thing like that?

Clerk: I know! But it happens.

For a further look at hidden city ticketing and similar stratagems, *see* Zachary Garsek, *Giving Power Back to the Passengers: The Airline Passengers' Bill of Rights*, 66 J. Air L. & Com. 1187 (2001).

3. In addition to competitors and passengers, airlines also have had their pricing policies challenged by travel agents. *See, e.g.*, *Lyn-Lea Travel Corp. v. American Airlines, Inc.*, 283 F.3d 282 (5th Cir.), *cert. denied*, 537 U.S. 1044 (2002) (reduction of commissions); *All World Professional Travel Services, Inc. v. American Airlines, Inc.*, 282 F. Supp. 2d 1161 (C.D. Cal. 2003) (post-9/11 refund charges); *Power Travel International, Inc. v. American Airlines, Inc.*, 257 F. Supp. 2d 701 (S.D.N.Y. 2003) (elimination of commissions). Invariably, such suits are dismissed due to ADA preemption or for failure to state a claim.

4. Because the ADA uses somewhat vague language ("related to a price, route, or service"), courts must determine, on a case-by-case basis, whether a particular state cause of action has survived preemption. Given the time and cost involved, not to mention the potential for inconsistent results, is there a need for Congress to revisit the statute? If so, what type of action should it take? *See further* Timothy M. Ravich, *Re-Regulation and Airline Passengers' Rights*, 67 J. Air L. & Com. 935 (2002).

5. In its opinion in *Morales*, the Supreme Court suggested that many types of state laws are not preempted by the ADA and offered as one clear-cut example bans on gambling. *See* 504 U.S. at 390. Yet as matters currently stand, it is the federal government, rather than the states, that has stopped gambling from taking place aboard airlines:

On August 23, 1994, the United States Congress passed the Federal Aviation Administration Authorization Act. Section 41311 of the law (the Gorton

> Amendment) prohibits any air carrier from installing, transporting, operating or permitting the use of any gambling device on an aircraft. This law applies to foreign airlines as well as to airlines based in the United States. As a result, gambling is banned on all international aircraft flying into or out of the United States.
>
> The Gorton Amendment has had a significant impact on air carriers worldwide. Several foreign airlines have been planning to offer gambling to their passengers. Recent technological advances have made it possible for airlines to install entertainment video systems with gambling software. However, the Gorton Amendment prevents foreign airlines from allowing gambling on planes serving the U.S., even when foreign aircraft fly over the high seas or their own airspace. Foreign airlines around the world have united to protest this law.

Brian C. O'Donnell, Comment, *Gambling to be Competitive: The Gorton Amendment and International Law*, 16 Dick. J. Int'l L. 251, 251 (1997). Given how helpful gambling would be to airlines (because it would open up vast new streams of revenue), should Congress rethink its position? *See further* Jesse Witt, Comment, *Aces & Boats: As the Popularity of Cruise Ship Gambling Soars, Why Do the Airlines Remain Grounded?*, 28 Transp. L.J. 353 (2001).

6. Since 9/11, air carriers have been under tremendous pressure to reveal confidential information about their customers to the federal government to help thwart future attacks (as occurred in *American Airlines*). Do you think they should? The arguments for and against such disclosures have been summarized as follows:

> In the aftermath of the September 11th attacks, the Transportation Security Administration (TSA) was founded in 2001. Its mission is to protect the nation's transportation systems. The Computer Assisted Passenger Pre-Screening System II (CAPPS II) is an automated screening system authorized by Congress as part of the TSA Enabling Act. It is a threat assessment tool, with an emphasis on prevention, based on continuously changing intelligence information. The TSA claims that CAPPS II will enhance aviation security, refine the passenger secondary screening selection process, and improve airport passenger flow.
>
> How effective will CAPPS II be? Would the "shoe bomber," Richard Reid, have been caught by a profiling program? The answer is "maybe." His criminal record, perhaps combined with his conversion to Islam and his name change, would have probably triggered a yellow flag. If so, the heightened security procedures would have detected the explosives in his shoes. Instead, he nearly succeeded in bombing an American Airlines flight. Clearly, something must be done to prevent radical criminals like Reid from sauntering through security while grandmothers are frisked.
>
> The TSA and many members of the traveling public hope that the CAPPS II profiling system will offer a solution to this dilemma. After all, preventing terrorist attacks is an important national goal. If we have "nothing to hide," why should Americans be concerned about CAPPS II?
>
> [Nevertheless, m]any Americans, not just civil libertarians, are alarmed about the CAPPS II profiling system. Briefly, privacy concerns and ethical dilemmas that are likely issues include:
>
> • The principle of treating everyone as a suspect without cause is wrong. Requiring citizens to submit to background investigations to travel in their own country is un-American.

• There is too much secrecy in the program. The government has no right to spy on its citizens.

• It is immoral to collect personal data on individuals and analyze them with sophisticated algorithms to try to predict a person's future behavior. There are no "thought crimes."

• Personal information can fall into the wrong hands and be misused. Never before has so much information from so many sources been collected in a single place.

• The government may use the information gathered for unauthorized purposes. "Function creep" is inevitable as the IRS, law enforcement, and various other agencies seek access to the data. Furthermore, people will be arrested at the airport for infractions that have nothing to do with security of the flight.

• Racial, ethnic, and even gender discrimination will rear its ugly head as people are scrutinized based on these immutable characteristics.

• Some indications suggest that the data will remain on file for 50 years.

• There is the potential for identity theft, fraud, and sale of information to private interests and businesses.

• People may lose their fundamental right to travel if they have bad credit or owe fines or child support.

Furthermore, there are practical considerations:

• The error rate is unacceptable. If just one percent of the population scores a false positive, more than 6 million unjustified inquiries are performed per year.

• Once a person is erroneously targeted as a "red" or "yellow," the procedures for removing oneself from the list are onerous.

• Frequent credit checks result in lower credit ratings for travelers.

• The system will not prevent future hijackings since hijackers will figure out and undermine the system. For example, this can be accomplished via identity theft.

• The system will encourage airport employees to be complacent, as they will allow the computer to do evaluations for them.

Deborah von Rochow-Leuschner, *CAPPS II and the Fourth Amendment: Does It Fly?*, 69 J. Air L. & Com. 139, 141–49 (2004). For a further discussion of CAPPS II, which now is known as "Secure Flight" and currently is on hold, *see* Mardi Ruth Thompson & Kapila Juthani, *Providing Smarter Security and Customer Service: TSA's Secure Flight and Registered Traveler Programs*, 19 Air & Space Law. 8 (Spring 2005). *See also* Seth F. Kreimer, *Watching the Watchers: Surveillance, Transparency, and Political Freedom in the War on Terror*, 7 U. Pa. J. Const. L. 133 (2004); Arnulf S. Gubitz, Note, *The U.S. Aviation and Transportation Security Act of 2001 in Conflict with the E.U. Data Protection Laws: How Much Access Does the United States Need to Combat Terrorism?*, 39 New Eng. L. Rev. 431 (2005); Leigh A. Kite, Note, *Red Flagging Civil Liberties and Due Process Rights of Airline Passengers: Will a Redesigned CAPPS II System Meet the Constitutional Challenge?*, 61 Wash. & Lee L. Rev. 1385 (2004).

7. In his description of American's operations, Judge Fitzwater refers to its computer reservation system (known as SABRE). In 2004, the federal government ended its decades-long oversight of CRSs, a move many commentators felt was long overdue:

With the enactment of the Airline Deregulation Act of 1978, Congress deregulated important business aspects of the U.S. commercial airline industry, including rates, routes, and services. Airline deregulation in turn stimulated the use of computer reservation systems ("CRS") as newly-deregulated airlines found in CRSs a critical distribution channel through which to efficiently and effectively communicate fares and book passengers. The government did not also reform its regulation of CRSs, however, prompting deregulation proponents to make the dramatic characterization that: "[J]ust before the crypt of the Civil Aeronautics Board ["CAB"] finally slammed shut, a gnarled hand reached up and grabbed the airline reservations network. On November 14, [1984], only six weeks before its demise, the board put into effect its final regulations governing airline-owned computer reservations systems. And although the CAB gave up the ghost on regulating the airlines themselves, it has bequeathed to its institutional successor, the Department of Transportation ["DOT"], a tight grip on the airlines' main means of booking customers."

Market power and antitrust concerns prompted the DOT to interpose regulations between airlines and CRSs for the benefit of consumers in the first place. The DOT's CRS regulations continued for twenty years. As of July 31, 2004, however, the airline CRS industry, a "poster child of unintended consequences of government regulation," will be deregulated entirely.

Four circumstances prompted CRS deregulation and made clear that the "[t]ime has come to see what competition looks like." First, the competitive environment between airlines and CRSs is unprecedented, as no airline has a controlling stake in any CRS. Second, into the 1990s, travel agents booked almost all airline travel reservations, but modernly, alternative distribution channels, of which the Internet is the most impressive, have found commercial applications. Accordingly, consumers are empowered to affirmatively avoid intermediaries and transactional costs by accessing services and products directly from air carriers for free. Third, a fundamental predicate of CRS regulation has been turned inside-out. That is, in the early period of airline deregulation, government authorities, if not the airline industry players themselves, were concerned about muscular, dominant carriers using the very CRSs they owned and controlled as weapons against new entrants and/or existing carriers. In fact, today, so-called low fare point-to-point carriers such as Southwest Airlines and JetBlue Airways, whose business models stimulate direct on-line bookings, are the muscular, profitable airlines, not the so-called hub-and-spoke-based legacy carriers. Finally, arguably, the CRS rules themselves have played no role in stimulating or sustaining low-cost carriers or competition within the deregulated commercial airline marketplace, achieving instead the undesired and pernicious purpose of insulating CRSs from competition even among themselves. Consequently, the DOT has reassessed the need for regulation and opted, after a lengthy seven-year comment period, to deregulate the CRS industry.

Timothy M. Ravich, *Deregulation of the Airline Computer Reservation Systems (CRS) Industry*, 69 J. Air L. & Com. 387, 387–89 (2004). For a further discussion, *see* Cindy R. Alexander & Yoon-Ho Alex Lee, *The Economics of Regulatory Reform: Termination of Airline Computer Reservation System Rules*, 21 Yale J. on Reg. 369 (2004).

8. Thatcher Stone and his daughter Rebecca were not the only travelers to have their 2004 holiday plans ruined—between Thanksgiving and New Year's Day, the airlines ex-

perienced an unprecedented number of service meltdowns (according to a federal report, more than 500,000 passengers were affected by delays and cancellations during Christmas week alone). Indeed, things were so bad that just before the 2005 holiday season began, the industry publicly promised to do better. *See further* Amy Gunderson, *After 2004 Holiday Woes, Airlines Make Changes*, N.Y. Times, Nov. 20, 2005, § 5, at 2.

Of course, not everyone minds being bumped—indeed, some people actually try to book on congested routes to increase their chances of earning free travel and other forms of compensation. *See further Airline Bumping Guide*, at www.bestfares.com/travel/desks/story.asp?id=2348 ("People often ask which flights are best to book if you want to be bumped. It's not an exact science. Even if the flight is overbooked, a high no-show factor can mean that the plane takes off with plenty of available seats. High-demand business flights offer no guarantee since many passengers are flying on unrestricted tickets without penalty for no-shows."), and Christopher Elliott, *The Power of the Bump*, N.Y. Times, Nov. 22, 2005, at C8 (noting that after decades of being happy with vouchers for free future travel, bumped passengers are increasingly demanding cash, further straining carriers' bottom lines).

9. As Justice Johnson explains, Ms. Rubin was attempting to use frequent flyer miles for her trip to Hawaii. American Airlines created the first frequent flyer program in 1981 as a short-term promotion; it proved so popular, however, that both American and its competitors had no choice but to make such programs a permanent part of the industry's landscape. Today, it is estimated that 163 million people (of whom two-thirds are in the United States) belong to at least one such program and collectively are holding 10 trillion unused miles. While 43% of new miles are earned through flying, 57% are collected by buying products or services from third parties (such as banks and credit card companies, who purchase miles from the airlines—a fact that has proven increasingly important to cash-strapped carriers). On average, seven to nine percent of an airline's annual passenger load are frequent flyers who have used miles to obtain (or upgrade) seats. *See further* Joe Sharkey, *Have Frequent-Flier Miles? Use Them or Lose Them*, N.Y. Times, Mar. 15, 2005, at C18, and Joe Sharkey, *Tipping Point May Be Near for Frequent-Flier Loyalty*, N.Y. Times, Oct. 18, 2005, at C6.

The recent spate of bankruptcy filings in the airline industry has caused frequent flyers to worry that their miles may become worthless. While this has not happened so far, airlines have been steadily increasing the number of miles needed to qualify for free tickets, reducing the number of seats available for redemption, and requiring members to use their miles by a specific date (after which they expire for good). Because of the Supreme Court's decision in *Wolens*, it now is understood that airlines have the right to take such steps. *See further Monzingo v. Alaska Air Group, Inc.*, 112 P.3d 655 (Alaska 2005) (airline could change its plan so long as it gave members reasonable notice).

The advent of frequent flyer miles has given rise to a number of interesting questions, including: (a) do they constitute "income" subject to taxation?; (b) if earned while on business, do they belong to the employee or the employer?; (c) can members sell or barter them (or do they remain the property of the carrier)?; and, (d) should they be considered individual or marital property in divorce cases? At present, the answers are: (a) "no" (although the Internal Revenue Service has from time to time considered taxing miles, it has not been able to devise a workable method for doing so); (b) "the employee" (like the government, most companies have concluded that the bookkeeping costs are too overwhelming and therefore let employees keep business-related miles as a "perq");

(c) "no" (although selling or bartering miles initially was quite popular, airlines quickly stepped in and put a stop to the practice by amending their rules; now, a person who attempts to sell or barter his or her miles typically risks forfeiture as well as expulsion from the program); and, (d) "it depends" (courts have split over the issue, and the decisions tend to be fact-sensitive). For a further look at the legal issues spawned by frequent flyer miles, *see* Lisa Hoffman, *The Frequent Flyer Mile Frenzy*, [2003] Int'l Travel L.J. 201. For a more general look at the subject, *see* www.frequentflier.com.

10. It is estimated that several hundred "air rage" (also known as "sky rage") incidents like the one involving Ms. Rubin take place each year (actual figures are hard to come by because of severe underreporting). *See generally* www.airrage.org. In large part, this can be explained by the deteriorating quality of airline service. As their financial conditions have become more dire, carriers have cut back on flights and routes (making for more crowded planes and less convenient schedules), eliminated (or begun charging for) once-standard amenities (such as serving meals and allowing overweight baggage), and pared back on personnel (thereby undermining customer service). The result is that passengers have much shorter fuses and are more prone to violence.

Responding to the problem, Congress has stiffened the penalties for assaulting or intimidating crew members. *See further United States v. Naghani*, 361 F.3d 1255 (9th Cir.), *cert. denied*, 125 S. Ct. 341 (2004); *United States v. Gilady*, 62 Fed. Appx. 481 (4th Cir. 2003); Christian Giesecke, *Unruly Passengers: The Existing Legal System and Proposed Improvements*, 26 Annals Air & Space L. 45 (2001). *See also* Kristine Cordier Karnezis, Annotation, *Propriety of Air Carrier's Refusal for Safety Reasons to Transport Person or Property Under 49 USC §44902(B)*, 192 A.L.R. Fed. 403 (2004).

Perhaps not surprisingly, Hollywood has found a way to cash in on such incidents. In January 2004, A & E began broadcasting a television series called *Airline*, which chronicles the daily lives of Southwest Airlines employees in Baltimore, Chicago, and Los Angeles. From the beginning, a prime staple of the show (whose tag line is "We all have our baggage") has been air rage scenes. *See further* www.aetv.com/tv/shows/airline/. *See also* Virginia Heffernan, *Your Flight Is Ready for Boarding (If You Are Sober, Slim, and Smell Nice)*, N.Y. Times, Jan. 5, 2004, at E10.

11. Even when they do not explode in rage, airline passengers can annoy their fellow travelers in myriad ways: clogging the aisles, failing to control their children, putting their seats all the way back, refusing to check their oversized luggage, talking loudly to their seatmates, and, most recently, watching pornography on their DVD players. *See generally* Alina Tugend, *Air Boors: If Only the Flier in Front of You Were a Fan of Miss Manners*, N.Y. Times, Aug. 2, 2005, at C7.

In addition, there is the time-honored tradition of passengers using the lavatories (or their seats while under a blanket) to have sex to become members of the "mile high club." *See further* www.milehighclub.com. For an interesting case involving one passenger complaining about two other passengers engaging in such activities, *see Vantassell-Matin v. Nelson*, 741 F. Supp. 698 (N.D. Ill. 1990). For a more humorous look at the subject, *see* "The One After Ross Says Rachel," a 1998 episode of the NBC sitcom *Friends* (1994–2004) (Monica, played by Courteney Cox, goes to the bathroom expecting Chandler, played by Matthew Perry, to follow her, but he finds himself trapped in a long-winded conversation with Joey, played by Matt LeBlanc. After waiting 30 minutes, Monica finally returns to her seat, where an oblivious Joey is still talking to a frantic Chandler).

12. If passengers like Ms. Rubin represent one end of the flying public spectrum, then famed football analyst John Madden represents the other end. Madden has not

stepped on a plane since 1979 (he travels to games in a personal motor coach), being simply too afraid to do so. In all, it is estimated that 25–60 million Americans are fearful flyers (with many having become so as a result of 9/11), including such celebrities as Cher, Glenda Jackson, Dean Koontz, and Billy Bob Thornton (on the other hand, there are stars like John Travolta, who flies himself almost everywhere and is qualified to pilot a 747). Fear of flying is so common, in fact, that many airlines and airports regularly hold fear of flying classes.

Just what do fearful flyers experience? Although many accounts have been given, the single best description remains the one that opens Erica Jong's celebrated novel *Fear of Flying*:

> There were 117 psychoanalysts on the Pan Am flight to Vienna and I'd been treated by at least six of them. And married a seventh. God knows it was a tribute either to the shrinks' ineptitude or my own glorious unanalyzability that I was now, if anything, more scared of flying than when I began my analytic adventures some thirteen years earlier.
>
> My husband grabbed my hand therapeutically at the moment of takeoff.
>
> "Christ—it's like ice," he said. He ought to know the symptoms by now since he's held my hand on lots of other flights. My fingers (and toes) turn to ice, my stomach leaps upward into my rib cage, the temperature in the tip of my nose drops to the same level as the temperature in my fingers, my nipples stand up and salute the inside of my bra (or in this case, dress—since I'm not wearing a bra), and for one screaming minute my heart and the engines correspond as we attempt to prove again that the laws of aerodynamics are not the flimsy superstitions which, in my heart of hearts, I know they are. Never mind the diabolical INFORMATION TO PASSENGERS, I happen to be convinced that only my own concentration (and that of my mother—who always seems to expect her children to die in a plane crash) keeps this bird aloft. I congratulate myself on every successful takeoff, but not too enthusiastically because it's also part of my personal religion that the minute you grow overconfident and really relax about the flight, the plane crashes instantly. Constant vigilance, that's my motto. A mood of cautious optimism should prevail. But my mood is better described as cautious pessimism. OK, I tell myself, we seem to be off the ground and into the clouds but the danger isn't past. This is, in fact, the most perilous patch of air. Right here over Jamaica Bay when the plane banks and turns and the "No Smoking" sign goes off. This may well be where we go screaming down in thousands of flaming pieces. So I keep concentrating very hard, helping the pilot (a reassuringly midwestern voice named Donnelly) fly the 250-passenger motherfucker. Thank God for his crew cut and middle-America diction. New Yorker that I am, I would never trust a pilot with a New York accent.

Erica Jong, *Fear of Flying* 3–4 (Signet Book 2003) (1973). In addition to Jong's famous work, Hollywood has examined the subject through such films as *Turbulence 2: Fear of Flying* (2000) and such characters as Bosco "B.A." Baracus (played by Mr. T) on the NBC drama *The A-Team* (1983–87), Emily Hartley (Suzanne Pleshette) on the CBS sitcom *The Bob Newhart Show* (1972–78), and Carla Tortelli (Rhea Perlman) on the NBC sitcom *Cheers* (1982–93).

As might be expected, aerophobia (also known as aviatophobia and aviophobia) has led to several interesting legal decisions. In *In re Muto*, 739 N.Y.S.2d 67 (App.

Div. 2002), for example, an attorney was disbarred, in part, because of his fear of flying:

> [R]espondent asserts that his failures to appear for hearings in New Orleans (the venue of a number of his clients' cases) should be deemed excused due to his fear of flying. Respondent claims that each time he arranged to travel to New Orleans, he believed he would be able to board the airplane, but he ultimately was unable to do so. We agree with the Referee and the Hearing Panel that, under the circumstances of this case, the matter of respondent's fear of flying is more aggravating than it is mitigating. Respondent, in spite of his awareness that he suffered from this condition, not only took on matters involving hearings in a distant city, he failed to advise his clients of the risk that he would be unable to appear at such hearings due to his disability.

Id. at 70. Likewise, in *Elvin Associates v. Franklin*, 735 F. Supp. 1177 (S.D.N.Y. 1990), singer Aretha Franklin was held liable after she backed out of a planned show due to her fear of flying:

> In the interim, Springer had already set about making the necessary arrangements to get the production going. During discussions with several promoters he learned for the first time that Franklin had recently cancelled several performances, purportedly due to a newly acquired fear of flying. Springer spoke with Citron at William Morris regarding these incidents, and the latter stated that the cancellations resulted from commitments made by prior agents for Franklin without her approval, and reassured Springer that there was no such problem here. Springer also spoke with Franklin, who reassured him that she wanted to do the show and that she would fly as necessary. Springer offered to make alternative arrangements for transportation to the various performance sites, and to alter the performance schedule to accommodate slower forms of transportation. Franklin told Springer that she was uncomfortable traveling more than 200 miles per day by ground transportation, but strongly assured him that she would overcome her fear of flying.
>
> As planned, rehearsals began on June 4 without Franklin, and continued for several days. Franklin did not arrive in New York on June 7 and, indeed, never came to New York for the rehearsals. Kramer immediately sought an explanation from Franklin's representatives and was informed that she would not fly. Springer paid the cast through the end of that week, but then suspended the production. He ultimately abandoned [his] attempt at mounting the production [and this] lawsuit ensued, with Springer suing in the name of Elvin Associates....
>
> Franklin's expression to Springer of her fear of flying did not, as she has contended, make her promise conditional or coat it with a patina of ambiguity that should have alerted Springer to suspend his efforts to mount the production. Although Franklin rejected Springer's offer to make alternative ground transportation arrangements, her primary reason for doing so was that she was determined to overcome her fear of flying, and it was reasonable for Springer to rely on her reassurances that she would be able to fly. Moreover, it was also entirely reasonable for him to assume that if she could not overcome her fear she would travel to New York by other means, even if it meant spreading the trip over several days. In short, Franklin's fear of flying provides no basis what-

> soever for avoiding liability for failing to fulfill her promise, reiterated on several occasions, to appear. If she could not bring herself to fly, she should have traveled by way of ground transportation. It has not been established that she was otherwise unable to come to New York to meet her obligations.
>
> We conclude that under the circumstances as we have outlined them it would be unconscionable not to compensate Springer for the losses he incurred through his entirely justified reliance on Franklin's oral promises.

Id. at 1179–84. For a further discussion, *see* Duane Brown, *Flying Without Fear* (1996), and Debbie Seaman, *The Fearless Flier's Handbook* (1999).

13. Early in his opinion, Justice Johnson mentions that Ms. Rubin was deemed not to be "emergency row qualified." Experienced travelers often attempt to be assigned to such seats because they provide greater legroom (as well as placement away from children). One commentator, however, believes that these stratagems have given rise to a new cause of action:

> Most exit row passengers, however, after requesting to be seated in an exit row, "do not read the safety information provided to assist them in understanding the tasks they may need to perform in the event of an emergency evacuation."
>
> Current emergency exit row seating regulations are not sufficient to educate exit row passengers on safety information. To combat this problem as well as compensate historically undercompensated injured air travelers, exit row passengers should be held liable for injuries resulting from their inadequate attention to safety instructions. Although various complicated issues are involved, a negligence cause of action appears to be a viable way of imposing this liability. Hopefully, aviation attorneys will use this article as a guide to litigating of this new cause of action.

Wendy Gerwick, Comment, *Taking Exit Row Seating Seriously*, 68 J. Air L. & Com. 449, 449–50 (2003). Is Ms. Gerwick on to something? If she is, what, if anything, should airlines do to protect themselves?

14. Towards the end of his opinion, Justice Johnson correctly observes that airlines are "common carriers." Historically, such enterprises have been required to do three things: (a) provide their services to all on an equal basis (except unruly or dangerous persons); (b) carry out their activities with the utmost care that is practical under the circumstances; and, (c) avoid landing illegal travelers (such as stowaways and those lacking valid passports or proper identification). *See further Pittman by Pittman v. Grayson*, 149 F.3d 111 (2d Cir. 1998), *cert. denied*, 528 U.S. 818 (1999); *Allen v. American Airlines, Inc.*, 301 F. Supp. 2d 370 (E.D. Pa. 2003); *Ferguson v. Trans World Airlines, Inc.*, 135 F. Supp. 2d 1304 (N.D. Ga. 2000); *Manus v. Trans States Airlines, Inc.*, 835 N.E.2d 70 (Ill. App. Ct. 2005). Given the now widespread availability of insurance, does this heightened standard of care still make sense? *See further* Graham McBain, *Time to Abolish the Common Carrier*, [2005] J. Bus. L. 545, and Sze Ping-Fat, *The Common Carrier's Strict Liability: A Concept or a Fallacy?*, [2002] J. Bus. L. 235.

15. Although the Air Carrier Access Act, discussed in *Deterra*, has made flying easier for the 54 million Americans who are disabled, there is still much to be done. *See further* Curtis D. Edmonds, *When Pigs Fly: Litigation Under the Air Carrier Access Act*, 78 N.D. L. Rev. 687 (2002) (criticizing federal courts for interpreting the statute too narrowly); Erin M. Kinahan, *Despite the ACAA, Turbulence Is Not Just in the Sky for Dis-*

abled Travelers, 4 DePaul J. Health Care L. 397 (2001) (arguing that the Act is being undermined by inadequate training of airline personnel, passive enforcement by the Department of Transportation, and judicial hostility); Nancy J. King, *Website Access for Customers With Disabilities: Can We Get There From Here?*, 2003 UCLA J. L. & Tech. 6 (2003) (pointing out that the web sites of many airlines are difficult or impossible for disabled passengers to use); Constance O'Keefe, *Disabled Passengers and Disconcerting Rules*, 19 Air & Space Law. 1 (Spring 2005) (discussing opposition to the statute by foreign carriers); Brian Bolton, Comment, *The Battle for the Armrest Reaches New Heights: The Air Carrier Access Act and the Issues Surrounding the Airlines' Policy of Requiring Obese Passengers to Purchase Additional Tickets*, 69 J. Air L. & Com. 803 (2004) (assessing the legality of requiring heavyset passengers to buy two seats). *See also Boswell v. Skywest Airlines, Inc.*, 361 F.3d 1263 (10th Cir. 2004) (carrier had no duty to provide medical oxygen to passenger who suffered from lung disease).

16. Cases like *Stagl* occur because of the nature of airports. As has been written elsewhere:

> The airline passenger ordinarily pays little serious attention to the surroundings at the airport, merely expecting that the facilities will be adequate until the time that the passenger will board the airplane. However, the average airport, with numerous people coming and going, often at top speed and without looking, and with luggage, carts, and other obstacles strewn about, presents numerous possibilities of personal injuries.

Jay M. Zitter, Annotation, *Air Carrier's Liability for Injury From Conditions of Airport Premises*, 14 A.L.R.5th 662, 671 (1993 & 2005 Supp.). This same source further observes:

> As a matter of course, the plaintiff injured on airport premises should consider suing parties other than the airlines, such as the individual employees, the governmental entity running the airport, various concessionaires, or cleaning and maintenance services.
>
> [In addition, there] are a number of possible claims of negligence on the part of the airlines, apart from claims that the premises were defective. For example, the plaintiff may claim that the airline should have been more attentive to the special needs of the passenger. On the other hand, the airline can counter with proof that there was nothing apparent that would have caused it to determine that the passenger was in need of help. While a passenger can claim that the airline improperly allowed other persons to place luggage on the floor near the passenger, who [then] tripped, the airline can maintain that it is known to all passengers that there will be luggage all over an airport, and this is an ordinary hazard to be expected by the passenger.
>
> As in all negligence cases, the plaintiff must prove the foreseeability of the accident. For example, the defendant can show that the accident was unforeseeable based on statistical evidence that there were no accidents while using a particular type of apparatus, or that no one had been hurt at a particular location despite many people passing through there frequently. Alternatively, it could be shown that there were in fact prior accidents which the airline knew about, so that the present accident was foreseeable.
>
> The passenger can claim that, due to the nature of an airport, people will be crowded and preoccupied, so that contributory negligence in failing to see something will be more readily excused. Similarly, while an airline can claim that the passenger should have seen the obstruction, the passenger can defend

> on the ground that as to a difficult-to-see obstruction, it is much easier to see it afterwards when one knows what one is looking for, rather than to see it beforehand. Furthermore, it could be pointed out that the colors used inside a terminal were designed to blend and harmonize but not to form a striking pattern to catch the passenger's eye. The airline can also claim that the passenger was overloaded and thus unable to see where he or she was going, or was not using necessary personal aids, such as a cane.

Id. at 674–76. In your opinion, is there anything that can be done to make airports safer?

17. Given the number of people who fly and the many different types of insurance policies that pay for air-related injuries or deaths, disputes like the one in *Pilosi* are fairly common. *See further* J.A. Bryant, Jr., Annotation, *Who Is "Fare-Paying Passenger" Within Coverage Provision of Life or Accident Insurance Policy*, 60 A.L.R.3d 1273 (1974 & 2004 Supp.); C.T. Drechsler, Annotation, *Construction and Application of Provision of Life or Accident Policy Relating to Aeronautics*, 17 A.L.R.2d 1041 (1951 & 2004 Supp.); A.R. Shapiro, *Rights and Liabilities Under Airline Passengers' Trip Insurance Policy*, 29 A.L.R.3d 766 (1970 & 2004).

Conversely, there are many cases involving "aviation exclusion clauses," under which coverage is voided if the insured is injured or killed while flying. *See further* Robert A. Brazener, Annotation, *What Constitutes Operating, Riding In, or Descending From, Aircraft Within Life or Accident Policy Provisions Relating to Aeronautics*, 88 A.L.R.3d 1064 (1978 & 2004 Supp.); C.T. Drechsler, Annotation, *What Constitutes "Participation" in Aeronautics Within Provision of Life or Accident Policy Relating to Aeronautics*, 45 A.L.R.2d 462 (1956 & 2004 Supp.); Daniel E. Feld, Annotation, *Applicability of Aviation Exclusion Clause as Affected By Fact That Injury or Death Occurred After Termination of Flight*, 62 A.L.R.3d 1243 (1975 & 2004 Supp.).

For more general discussions, *see, e.g.*, Robert Eisner & Robert H. Strotz, *Flight Insurance and the Theory of Choice*, 69 J. Pol. Econ. 355 (1961); Adam F. Scales, *Man, God and the Serbonian Bog: The Evolution of Accidental Death Insurance*, 86 Iowa L. Rev. 173 (2000); Jeffrey W. Stempel, *Lachs v. Fidelity & Casualty Co. of New York: Timeless and Ahead of Its Time*, 2 Nev. L.J. 319 (2002).

18. In attempting to classify the EA flight, the Third Circuit in *Pilosi* leaned heavily on 14 C.F.R. part 135, which regulates air taxis and distinguishes them from other types of operators. Yet the FAA has recognized that its classification system needs work and has begun taking steps to bring it up-to-date:

> Th[e aviation] industry, while diverse enough to include everything from gliders and hot-air balloons, to single-engine aircraft, to the largest transport category aircraft, is divided into only four categories of operating regulations: General Aviation Part 91, On-Demand/Commuter Part 135, Transport Category Aircraft Part 125, and Domestic/Flag/Supplemental Part 121. Every type of manned aviation operation falls into at least one of these categories. The real issue is into which category or categories it falls. This is the question that may be answered very clearly or muddied even further by a joint FAA/industry endeavor that has begun already: the Part 125/135 Aviation Rulemaking Committee.
>
> From a consumer standpoint, if an individual wants to buy a ticket for one seat to travel from point A to point B, he or she contacts an airline. If an individual wants to fly from Point A to Point B, on her schedule, she contacts a charter operator. However, another type of operator exists, called a Commuter,

which provides services that can look like airline or charter service, depending on the expectation of the customer.

The Federal Aviation Administration (FAA), realizing that the public could mistake certain operators as airlines when they were not, and that questions involving the classifications of new types of aircraft and operations were beginning to be asked frequently, established a Part 135/125 Aviation Rulemaking Committee. While the title of the Committee suggests that only Parts 125 and 135 will be reviewed, the scope of its review and rewrite is broad, including Parts 91, 119, and 121. With such an extensive scope of review, one of the main issues, as pointed out by several comments to this rulemaking action, is applicability: which rules govern which types of operations?

The issue of applicability is most important as it relates to Parts 119, 121, and 135. Parts 121 and 135 govern all commercial transportation in aircraft, meaning that if passengers are going to pay for their air travel, they will be transported by either a Part 121 or Part 135 operator. To adequately draw the distinction between these two types of operators, the question of applicability must be focused on the issue of method of classification. To make a workable regulation that directs operations to the correct categories, a method of identifying the operation is a necessary first step. Once the method is chosen, 14 C.F.R. section 119.21 merely lays out the defined categories and directs operators to either Part 121 or 135. However, choosing the mode of classification may cause the greatest difficulty because each option creates a line that puts certain operators under less extensive regulation than others. Throughout the regulations, different levels of oversight and compliance exist based on a myriad of classifications including the following: scheduled/unscheduled operations, size of aircraft, complexity of aircraft, and location of operations. Considering all the aspects of classification and the interests of the operators that would be affected by a change, the method of classification used to draw the distinction between operation under Parts 121 and 135 should be whether the operation is scheduled or unscheduled, and this distinction should be clearly defined and consistent with the plain meaning of the words "scheduled" and "unscheduled."

Kent S. Jackson & Lori N. Edwards, *The Changing Face of Passenger Air Transportation: The Blurry Line Between Part 121 and 135 Operators*, 69 J. Air L. & Com. 319, 319–21 (2004). Given the foregoing, how would you have classified the EA flight? *See also* Articles 5 and 6 of the Chicago Convention (Appendix 3) (distinguishing between scheduled and unscheduled service).

19. On occasion, the death of an airplane passenger leads to particularly exotic litigation. For example, if a husband and wife are both killed in the same airplane accident, which one (for inheritance and tax purposes) should be treated as having died first? Likewise, when an airplane disappears, how long must a court wait before declaring the passengers legally dead? And if a person, believing she is about to die in an airplane crash, makes an accusatory statement, can her words be admitted into evidence?

To deal with the first scenario, most jurisdictions have adopted the Uniform Simultaneous Death Act, which creates a presumption of concurrent demise. *See further* Elizabeth T. Tsai, Annotation, *Construction, Application, and Effect of Uniform Simultaneous Death Act*, 39 A.L.R.3d 1332 (1971 & 2004 Supp.). The second problem has been similarly resolved by the use of so-called "Enoch Arden" statutes, which allow a court to declare an individual who has not been seen or heard from for a specified period of time (traditionally seven years, but now increasingly five years) to be treated as deceased. *See further* C.P. Jhong, Annotation, *Necessity and Sufficiency of Showing of Search and Inquiry By One Relying on Presumption of Death From 7 Years' Absence*, 99 A.L.R.2d 307 (1965 & 2004 Supp.). Lastly, under most evidence codes, statements made in contemplation of imminent death normally are admissible. *See further* Ferdinand S. Tinio, Annotation, *Statements of Declarant as Sufficiently Showing Consciousness of Impending Death to Justify Admission of Dying Declaration*, 53 A.L.R.3d 785 (1973 & 2005 Supp.).

20. For a further look at domestic airline passenger service, see the web sites of the Air Transport Association (www.airlines.org) (the trade group of American airlines), and the DOT's Aviation Consumer Protection Division (airconsumer.ost.dot.gov), as well as those of the country's leading carriers: American Airlines (www.aa.com), Continental Airlines (www.continental.com), Delta Air Lines (www.delta.com), JetBlue Airways (www.jetblue.com), Northwest Airlines (www.nwa.com), Southwest Air Lines (www.southwest.com), United Air Lines (www.united.com), and US Airways (www.usairways.com).

Of course, no discussion of the present subject would be complete without some mention of the elusive figure still known only as D.B. Cooper:

> Thirty-four years ago above [Vancouver,] Washington, [the legendary skyjacker known as D.B.] Cooper parachuted from a jetliner with $200,000—and into folk-hero stardom. He was never seen or heard from again.
>
> The FBI calls his crime the only unsolved skyjacking in history, and the agency continues to keep the case open.
>
> [California lawyer and former FBI agent Richard Tosaw, who has spent 24 years looking for Cooper,] surveyed more than 100 parachutists on whether they thought Cooper could have survived the jump; about three-fourths said it was possible if he had served in the military as a paratrooper. At that time, military service was the most likely way to have learned how to parachute. Cooper was believed to have been in his 40s at the time of the skyjacking, which means he could have served in the Korean War.
>
> The skyjacking happened on Thanksgiving eve 1971. A white man wearing a white shirt, narrow black tie, dark suit, raincoat, sunglasses and carrying a briefcase boarded Northwest Airlines Flight 305 in Portland. During the flight, he informed the crew that his briefcase contained a bomb and that he would detonate it if he wasn't given $200,000 in ransom money and four parachutes.
>
> The Boeing 727 landed in Seattle, where the passengers were released and authorities complied with Cooper's demands. The plane took off for Portland with only Cooper and the crew left on the plane. About 45 minutes later, Cooper offered the flight attendants $2,000 each as a tip and then opened a door in the back of the plane and bailed out—into darkness and a driving rainstorm.
>
> That was the last anybody saw of Cooper. Authorities don't even know whether that was his real last name. The name he provided when he bought his airline ticket was Dan Cooper. After the skyjacking, a newspaper reported that police had interviewed an Oregon man named D.B. Cooper, who turned out to be the wrong man, but the name stuck.
>
> Cooper made it to the FBI's 10 Most Wanted list.

> "This is a guy who tweaked Uncle Sam's nose and appears to have gotten away with it," said retired FBI agent Ralph Himmelsbach, trying to explain Cooper's folk-hero status. Himmelsbach, who once headed the investigation, said that although Cooper broke the law, he didn't hurt anyone—except probably himself.
>
> Himmelsbach said Cooper jumped from 10,000 feet into a minus 7 degree temperature—69 degrees below zero with wind chill—while wearing "a business suit and slip-on loafers.... It's a long shot he survived."
>
> In February 1980, an 8-year-old boy picnicking with his family along the Columbia River found a muddy wad of $20 bills totaling $5,800. Authorities confirmed the money had been part of Cooper's loot. The find corroborated the theory that Cooper probably was dead at the bottom of the river, but others speculated that he was clever enough to have placed the money in the river as a diversion.
>
> "People want to believe he got away with it. They want to believe he's alive somewhere," Tosaw said. "I just want to find his wallet, so the world will know who the hell D.B. Cooper really was."

Tomas Alex Tizon, *Pursuer Keeps Legend of Skyjacker 'D.B. Cooper' Alive*, S. Fla. Sun-Sentinel, Aug. 29, 2005, at 8A. In addition to a movie entitled *The Pursuit of D.B. Cooper* (1981, starring Treat Williams), Cooper's daring act has spawned a number of books. *See, e.g.*, Max Gunther, *D.B. Cooper: What Really Happened* (1985); Elwood Reid, *D.B.* (2004); Richard T. Tosaw, *D.B. Cooper: Dead or Alive?* (1984).

Problem 15

A group of very tall individuals wants the airlines to reserve for them any seats that offer extra legroom (such as those by the bulkhead). If the carriers refuse and the group sues, claiming discrimination, how should the court rule? *See Tall Club of Silicon Valley v. American Airlines*, 2000 WL 868524 (N.D. Cal. 2000).

C. INTERNATIONAL TRAVEL

ROBERTSON v. AMERICAN AIRLINES, INC.

401 F.3d 499 (D.C. Cir. 2005)

GARLAND, Circuit Judge.

Kathleen Robertson sued American Airlines for damages resulting from burns she sustained on a flight from Denver to Chicago. If that flight qualifies as "international transportation" within the meaning of the Warsaw Convention, Robertson's suit is barred by the Convention's statute of limitations. The district court concluded that the flight—which was one leg of a trip that began in London and ended in Washington the same day—did so qualify. We affirm.

I

In 1998, appellant Robertson was a "war games" strategist living in the Washington, D.C. area. On August 7, 1998, she had a travel agent, Nancy Thompson of Gateway

Travel, book her a round-trip flight between Denver and London on British Airways (BA), departing on September 2 and returning on September 8. Three days later, on August 10, Thompson also booked Robertson on a round-trip flight between Washington, D.C. and Denver, via Chicago, on American Airlines (AA). That flight was to depart on August 29 and to return on September 8. Thus, as initially scheduled, Robertson was to leave Washington on August 29; to stay in Denver for several days before continuing to London on September 2; and to depart London for home on September 8, with a three-hour layover in Denver. On August 24, Robertson used Gateway Travel to book an alternative route home: a one-way ticket on AA from London to Washington, via New York, departing and arriving on September 10.

As scheduled, Robertson flew from Washington to Denver on August 29. She remained for a few days in Denver, where she conducted a war games exercise with the city's mayor, and then flew from Denver to London on September 2. That day, Robertson had her initially scheduled return flights—London-Denver on BA, and Denver-Chicago-Washington on AA—changed from September 8 to September 10, the same date for which she held the alternative ticket from London to Washington on AA. Thus, Robertson had two available itineraries for her return home on September 10. First, she could take an 8:00 a.m. AA flight from London, connect in New York, and arrive in Washington at 2:10 p.m. Second, she could take a 10:20 a.m. BA flight from London, arrive in Denver at 1:20 p.m., switch to a 4:32 p.m. AA flight from Denver, connect in Chicago, and arrive in Washington at 11:19 p.m.

Robertson chose the latter—and later—alternative and departed from London on the morning of September 10 aboard the BA flight to Denver. After a three-hour layover in Denver, she boarded the AA flight to Washington by way of Chicago. En route, she asked a flight attendant to cool a "gel pack" she was using to treat a sore back. According to Robertson's complaint, the attendant returned with an air-sickness bag containing the gel pack and dry (rather than ordinary) ice. When Robertson put the bag on her back, she suffered third-degree burns.

Just short of three years later, on September 7, 2001, Robertson sued American Airlines in the Superior Court of the District of Columbia. American removed the action to the United States District Court for the District of Columbia. On January 15, 2003, American filed a motion for summary judgment, contending that the action was governed by the Warsaw Convention (Convention for the Unification of Certain Rules Relating to International Transportation by Air, Oct. 12, 1929, 49 Stat. 3000, T.S. No. 876 (1934), reprinted in 49 U.S.C. § 40105 note) because the claim arose out of international transportation, and that the Convention's two-year statute of limitations, see Art. 29(1), 49 Stat. 3021, barred Robertson's claim. Robertson argued that the Convention did not apply, and that the action was instead governed by the District of Columbia's three-year statute of limitations, D.C.Code § 12-301. The district court agreed with American and granted its motion for summary judgment. Robertson v. American Airlines, Inc., 277 F.Supp.2d 91, 100 (D.D.C.2003).

II

We review the district court's grant of summary judgment de novo. Lathram v. Snow, 336 F.3d 1085, 1088 (D.C.Cir.2003). Under Federal Rule of Civil Procedure 56(c), summary judgment should be awarded only if "there is no genuine issue as to any material fact and ... the moving party is entitled to a judgment as a matter of law." See Anderson v. Liberty Lobby, Inc., 477 U.S. 242, 247, 106 S.Ct. 2505, 91 L.Ed.2d 202 (1986). We conclude that the district court's grant of summary judgment to American Airlines was correct.

The Warsaw Convention governs air carrier liability for claims arising out of "international transportation" of persons and property by air. Art. 1(1), 49 Stat. 3014; see El Al Israel Airlines, Ltd. v. Tsui Yuan Tseng, 525 U.S. 155, 160, 119 S.Ct. 662, 142 L.Ed.2d 576 (1999). As we have noted before, the Convention's provisions sometimes advantage plaintiffs and sometimes defendants, depending upon the circumstances. Haldimann v. Delta Airlines, Inc., 168 F.3d 1324, 1326 (D.C.Cir.1999). In this case, the parties agree that if the flight on which Robertson was injured qualifies as international transportation, the Convention applies and its two-year statute of limitations bars her recovery. Appellant's Br. at 10; Appellee's Br. at 4.

Article 1(2) of the Convention defines "international transportation" as "any transportation in which, according to the contract made by the parties, the place of departure and the place of destination, whether or not there be a break in the transportation..., are situated ... within the territories of two High Contracting Parties." 49 Stat. 3014. Article 1(3) further provides that:

> Transportation to be performed by several successive air carriers shall be deemed, for the purposes of this convention, to be one undivided transportation, if it has been regarded by the parties as a single operation, whether it has been agreed upon under the form of a single contract or of a series of contracts, and it shall not lose its international character merely because one contract or a series of contracts is to be performed entirely within a territory subject to the sovereignty ... of the same High Contracting Party.

Id. at 3015. Thus, the Convention contemplates that an entirely domestic leg of an international itinerary will be covered by the Convention as part of "one undivided [international] transportation"—even if it is performed by a "successive" carrier and even if the various legs are agreed upon under "a series of contracts"—as long as it has been "regarded by the parties" as part of "a single operation."

But how do we decide how a particular trip was "regarded by the parties"? In Haldimann, we noted that, although the Convention's language "suggests that we must look to the intention of the parties," it "would seem rather difficult to do so, for they—especially the traveler—are unlikely ever to have remotely considered the question whether the transportation was 'a single operation,' or ever to have pondered what that phrase might mean." 168 F.3d at 1325. We further noted that, "in the rare case where there has been evidence of the traveler's subjective intent, and it contradicted the court's inference from specific documentary indicia, courts have held that the indicia trump subjective evidence." Id. Relying upon the available objective indicia in that case, we held that a Delta Airlines flight from Pensacola, Florida to Gainesville, Florida was part of a single operation when it was one leg of the following itinerary: from Geneva, Switzerland to Washington, D.C., on Swissair; from Washington to Pensacola to Gainesville and back to Washington, on Delta; and from Washington back to Geneva, on Swissair. Other circuits have similarly eschewed subjective in favor of objective evidence of intent in making this kind of determination. See Coyle v. P.T. Garuda Indon., 363 F.3d 979, 987 (9th Cir.2004); Petrire v. Spantax, S.A., 756 F.2d 263, 266 (2d Cir.1985). We—like the district court—follow that course here.

We begin by asking whether Robertson regarded her London-Denver travel and her Denver-Chicago-Washington travel as a single operation. There can be no genuine dispute over this question. First, on the morning of September 10, 1998, Robertson held alternative itineraries for her flight from London: one on AA through New York to Washington, and a later flight on BA connecting to AA in Denver and on to Washington via Chicago. This indicates that both the intermediate stops and the choice of carriers were incidental to her plan to fly from London to Washington that day.

Second, and in our view dispositive, Robertson scheduled her BA-AA connection in Denver so that her flight to Chicago (and on to Washington) would depart within about three hours of her arrival from London. It is unlikely that a layover of that length would even have given her time to leave the airport, and the record confirms that Robertson had no purpose for being in Denver on that day other than to make the plane connection. See In re Air Crash Disaster of Aviateca Flight 901, 29 F.Supp.2d 1333, 1342 (S.D.Fla.1997) ("Common sense dictates that when a traveler plans such a short layover between the parts of a journey, the traveler regards the layover as merely an intermediate stopping place and not his or her destination."). Accordingly, there can be no genuine dispute that Robertson regarded the Denver-Chicago trip as part of a unified journey from London to Washington.

Robertson points to a number of circumstances that she maintains are inconsistent with the conclusion that she regarded her travel as a single operation. She notes, for example, that on the outbound trip she stayed in Denver for four days, where she engaged in work that was different from the business she had in London. But the argument that these facts are inconsistent with her regarding the journey as a single operation is foreclosed by Haldimann, in which we found a single operation notwithstanding multiple-day stay-overs—with different purposes—between several legs of the plaintiffs' itinerary. See 168 F.3d at 1324, 1326; see also Art. 1(2), 49 Stat. 3014 (providing that transportation may constitute "'international transportation'... whether or not there be a break in the transportation"). In any event, this argument would not affect the conclusion that Robertson regarded the London-Denver-Washington return trip, which involved only a three-hour layover, as a single operation.

Robertson also points out that she purchased the two round-trip tickets (Denver-London-Denver and Washington-Denver-Washington) on two different airlines, that the tickets were issued in separate booklets, that she purchased them on different days, and that she received them in separate mailings. But the fact that the tickets were purchased on two different airlines is what frames the question, not what decides it: the point of Article 1(3) is that "[t]ransportation to be performed by several successive air carriers shall be deemed ... to be one undivided transportation" if regarded by the parties as a single operation. 49 Stat. 3015. Nor, as we held in Haldimann, does the fact that the tickets were issued in separate booklets "militat[e] even in the slightest against finding a 'single operation,'" since "Article 1(3) views transportation as 'undivided ... whether it has been agreed upon under the form of a single contract or of a series of contracts.'" 168 F.3d at 1326 (quoting Art. 1(3), 49 Stat. 3015). For the same reason, we regard as insignificant the fact that three days separated one purchase from the other (along with its corollary that the tickets were sent in separate mailings). Indeed, while the initial purchases were made three days apart, they plainly were coordinated to link the two round trips together; and when the return trip was changed to September 10, the London-Denver and the Denver-Washington legs were changed simultaneously.

The remaining question is how American Airlines regarded Robertson's travel. There is no doubt that if American knew the objective facts of Robertson's itinerary as set forth above, the airline—like Robertson—would have regarded the Denver-Chicago-Washington flight as part of a single operation with the London-Denver flight. But did American know? American did have a record of a London-New York-Washington ticket for Robertson dated September 10. However, because the AA ticket she ultimately used was only for Denver-Chicago-Washington, it is not clear that the airline would have known she was traveling internationally that day. Noting that other district "courts have held that a travel agent's knowledge of a plaintiff's travel intentions is imputed to the carrier," the district court resolved the issue by applying the same rule. Robertson, 277 F.Supp.2d at 99. Because Robertson's appellate briefs do not dispute it, we apply the imputation rule as well. (Robertson did dispute the rule during questioning at oral argument, but oral argument is too late to raise an objection for appellate consideration. See, e.g., Ark Las Vegas Rest. Corp. v. NLRB, 334 F.3d 99, 108 n.4 (D.C.Cir.2003); C.J. Krehbiel Co. v. NLRB, 844 F.2d 880, 883 n.1 (D.C.Cir.1988)).

Robertson concedes that a travel agency, Gateway Travel, made the reservations for all of the BA and AA flights up to and including those on September 8 (as well as for the London-New York-Washington AA flight scheduled for September 10). Appellant's Br. at 3. Although Robertson does not concede that she also used Gateway to change the September 8 tickets to September 10, she does not dispute that Gateway knew of the change, Oral Arg. Tape at 14:45–18:15, and does not assert that she or anyone other than Gateway made the change—a fact that presumably would be within her personal knowledge. Moreover, both BA's and AA's internal Passenger Name Records (PNRs) for Robertson's September 10 flights contain references to "Gateway Travel Nancy." J.A. 326, 328. Accordingly, because the only evidence in the record confirms that American (through Gateway) knew of the London-Denver leg of Robertson's trip, we concur in the district court's conclusion that there is no genuine dispute that the airline "was aware of [her] international flight plans." Robertson, 277 F.Supp.2d at 99.

III

We conclude that there is no genuine dispute that the flight on which Robertson sustained her burns qualifies as international transportation within the meaning of the Warsaw Convention. The Convention's two-year statute of limitations therefore applies, barring her claim. Accordingly, the judgment of the district court granting summary judgment in favor of American is affirmed.

SCHOPENHAUER v. COMPAGNIE NATIONALE AIR FRANCE

255 F. Supp. 2d 81 (E.D.N.Y. 2003)

SAND, District Judge.

Plaintiff Leonard Schopenhauer instituted this action against Defendant Compagnie Nationale Air France seeking compensation for baggage allegedly lost and damaged on a pair of Air France flights in late 1999. Air France brings the instant motion for partial summary judgment, seeking to limit its liability for the entirety of Schopenhauer's claim and to dismiss part of his claim for lack of jurisdiction. For the reasons set forth below the Court grants the motion in part and denies it in part.

I. Facts

Most of the material facts are not in dispute. In October 1999, through a travel agency named Magical Holidays, Inc., Schopenhauer purchased a round-trip ticket for travel on Air France from New York City to Cotonou, Republic of Benin. The trip included a four day stopover in Paris on the way to Benin, and a 13-hour stopover in Paris on the way back to New York. Magical Holidays issued Schopenhauer a ticket booklet which contained at least five detachable pages. The first four pages were passenger tickets for each of the four flights in Schopenhauer's itinerary: one ticket covered the New York-to-Paris flight, one ticket covered the Paris-to-Cotonou flight, one ticket covered the Cotonou-to-Paris return flight, and one ticket covered the Paris-to-New York return flight. The first ticket was used on Schopenhauer's first flight and is thus not in evidence, but copies of the second through fourth tickets are attached as exhibits to Schopenhauer's Affidavit in Opposition to Defendant's Motion for Summary Judgment ("Pl. Aff."). Each bears the heading "Passenger Ticket and Baggage Check," and lists, inter multa alia, Schopenhauer's name, the Air France flight number, the flight time, and the departure and destination airports. The tickets are printed on forms produced by a company called the Airlines Reporting Corporation, which supplies blank ticket stock to travel agencies. These ticket forms are identifiable by the logo "ARC."

On the right-hand side of each "Passenger Ticket and Baggage Check" is an apparently detachable stub with the heading "Boarding Pass." At the bottom of this section is a set of smaller headings, "Pcs," "Wt," "Unckd," and "Baggage ID Number"; there is [a] blank space underneath these headings, presumably to permit the entry of data. The fifth page of the booklet is also labeled "Passenger Ticket and Baggage Check," but indicates "Passenger Receipt" across the top; further, the "Boarding Pass" heading is blocked out with x's, and all four of Schopenhauer's flights are listed underneath. Magical Holidays also issued Schopenhauer a paper itinerary listing the four flights.

On November 20, 1999, Schopenhauer arrived at John F. Kennedy International Airport in New York City and checked five bags. He attempted to carry a sixth bag onto the aircraft, but the Air France cabin attendant told him that it was "too bulky" and insisted that he check it instead. Pl. Aff. at 2. Schopenhauer gave the bag to the attendant, and in return the attendant gave him an Air France "Limited Release" identification tag. The Limited Release tag bore the identification number 0057AF913435, and indicated that the flight was "AF 007" from "JFK" to "CDG." ("CDG" are the initials of Charles de Gaulle International Airport in Paris. The front side of the Limited Release tag is included as Pl. Aff. Ex. 2.)

Schopenhauer and Flight 007 arrived in Paris the next morning; the sixth bag did not. In fact the bag did not turn up again until Air France returned it to Schopenhauer, heavily looted, on January 2, 2000. Schopenhauer values the lost and damaged items from that bag at approximately $69,000. The bag was mostly filled with jewelry and electronics that Schopenhauer evidently intended to sell in Benin.

Unfortunately for Schopenhauer, among the items stored in the missing sixth bag was the rest of his ticket booklet, including the tickets for the remaining three flights in his itinerary. While waiting for Air France either to locate the bag or to issue a replacement ticket, Schopenhauer missed his intended Paris-to-Benin flight on November 25, 1999, and did not fly to Benin until Air France finally issued a replacement ticket on November 26. On the November 26 flight to Benin, Schopenhauer again checked six pieces of baggage, but upon his arrival two of the pieces were "completely destroyed" and thoroughly looted. Pl. Aff. at 3–4. Schopenhauer values the lost contents of those two bags at approximately $2200. Luckily, no further actionable mishaps occurred before Schopenhauer's return to New York.

II. Discussion

A. Air France's Arguments

In its motion for summary judgment Air France sets forth two arguments, each of which relies on the Warsaw Convention, a multilateral treaty governing international air travel. First, Air France invokes a provision of the Warsaw Convention which in certain circumstances limits an air carrier's liability for lost or damaged baggage to $20 per kilogram. Second, Air France seeks to dismiss that part of Schopenhauer's claim which relates to the damages allegedly incurred on the Paris-to-Benin flight on the basis that the Warsaw Convention does not provide for United States jurisdiction over that portion of the trip.

Air France did not question the subject matter jurisdiction of a federal court to hear cases arising under the Warsaw Convention, but rather the treaty jurisdiction of the United States to hear a case concerning damages incurred on a flight from Paris to Benin. Under Article 28(1) of the current version of the Warsaw Convention, treaty jurisdiction is proper:

> at the option of the plaintiff, in the territory of one of the High Contracting Parties, either [1] before the court of the domicile of the carrier or [2] of his principal place of business, or [3] where he has a place of business through which the contract has been made, or [4] before the court at the place of destination.

It is well settled in this Circuit that the place of destination of a round-trip journey is the same as the place of departure. See Klos v. Polskie Linie Lotnicze, 133 F.3d 164, 167 (2d Cir.1997) (noting that the argument "that jurisdiction could be based on an interim city appearing on a round-trip ticket" has been "consistently rejected"); In re Alleged Food Poisoning Incident, March, 1984, 770 F.2d 3, 4–5 (2d Cir.1985) ("We hold that when the parties have contemplated a single operation of undivided transportation only one 'destination' exists, and, in the case of a round trip, that destination is the same as the place of origin."); Gayda v. LOT Polish Airlines, 702 F.2d 424, 425 (2d Cir.1983) ("[F]or Article 28 purposes it is the 'ultimate' destination listed in the contract for carriage that controls."). Whether a trip is intended as a round trip is in turn a question of contract rather than of the passenger's subjective intent. See Klos, 133 F.3d at 167–68. It cannot reasonably be disputed in this case that Schopenhauer and Air France contracted for a round trip beginning and ending in New York City. Under the fourth heading of Article 28(1), then, treaty jurisdiction lies in the United States for any damages incurred on the Paris-to-Benin flight.

Air France sets forth two arguments in an attempt to avoid jurisdiction. First it fashions a novel "intent-of-the-baggage" standard to distinguish passenger destination from baggage destination. Under this theory, while jurisdiction for personal injury claims may depend on the ticketed round-trip destination, jurisdiction for baggage loss claims ought to depend on where the passenger intended the baggage to end up. This argument flatly contravenes unbroken precedent in this Circuit that has consistently, if implicitly, asserted treaty jurisdiction over baggage loss claims on the basis of passenger destination alone. See, e.g., Campbell v. Air Jam., Ltd., 863 F.2d 1, 2 (2d Cir.1988); Benjamins v. British European Airways, 572 F.2d 913, 915 (2d Cir.1978); Donkor v. British Airways Corp., 62 F.Supp.2d 963, 966 (E.D.N.Y.1999); Solanki v. Kuwait Airways, 1987 WL 13194, *2 (S.D.N.Y. June 24, 1987); Sabharwal v. Kuwait Airways Corp., 1984 WL 3639, *1 (E.D.N.Y. Nov. 5, 1984); Bornstein v. Scandinavian Airlines Sys., 1981 U.S. Dist. LEXIS 14569, *1 n.1 (S.D.N.Y. May 5, 1981). Moreover, Air France does not suggest how its intent-of-the-baggage standard could sidestep the numerous cases rejecting subjective-intent inquiries for the purposes of the Warsaw Convention's jurisdictional inquiry. See, e.g., Klos, 133 F.3d at 168 ("The secret or subjective intent of the parties is irrelevant."); Solanki, 1987 WL 13194, at *2. Finally, it bears mentioning that Air France has failed to provide the Court with sufficient evidence to enable it to determine exactly which items in which bags were intended to remain in Benin, and which were intended to return to New York.

Less creatively but more cynically, Air France suggests in a second argument that because the replacement ticket was issued in Paris, a new contract for carriage was made in France rather than in the United States, and thus treaty jurisdiction is improper under the third jurisdictional head of Article 28(1). Even putting aside the fact that Air France was presumptively responsible for losing Schopenhauer's original ticket in the first place, this "new contract" theory ignores the fact that because the jurisdictional heads of Article 28(1) are disjunctive in nature, jurisdiction lies in the United States under the destination theory alone. (Because Schopenhauer nowhere disputes that liability for any damages incurred on the Paris-to-Benin flight is limited to $20 per kilogram, at most a few hundred dollars depend on the resolution of this issue.)

B. The Warsaw System

Air France claims that under Article 22(2) of the Warsaw Convention, its liability for any lost or damaged baggage should be limited to $20 per kilogram. Whether this is in fact the case depends largely on an interpretation of Article 4 of the Convention, which governs the delivery of baggage checks. Yet before the Court turns to Article 4, confusion evidenced by the parties in their briefs and at oral argument compels the Court to address at some length which version of the Warsaw Convention is currently in force in the United States.

The original Convention for the Unification of Certain Rules Relating to International Transportation by Air was signed in 1929 and ratified by the United States in 1934. See 49 Stat. 3000, T.S. No. 876 (1934), reprinted in note following 49 U.S.C. §40105. The Convention created a presumption of air carrier liability for personal injury and baggage and cargo damage, but also contained strict limits on that liability. "At the time the Senate ratified the treaty, the United States (and the world) was in the midst of the Great Depression and the liability provisions in the treaty were thought to provide some benefit to carriers, passengers, and shippers alike." Chubb & Son, Inc. v. Asiana Airlines, 214 F.3d 301, 306 (2d Cir.2000). "With the growth of the world economy and the air industry, however, the liability limitation, and particularly the per-passenger limitation, became increasingly unpopular in this and other countries." Id. In 1955 a new conference convened at the Hague and proposed the Hague Protocol to amend and modernize the Warsaw Convention.

Despite various changes (including a wholesale revision of Article 4 relevant to this case), the United States remained unsatisfied with the low liability limits, especially for personal injury claims, and chose not to ratify the Hague Protocol. Much of the world adopted the new version of the Convention, but the original Warsaw Convention remained in force in the United States throughout most of this century.

At the time, the United States even considered denouncing the original Warsaw Convention, but its concerns were allayed by a non-treaty "Intercarrier Agreement" signed in Montreal in 1966, in which air carriers agreed to more liberal liability rules regarding personal injury claims. See Chubb & Son, 214 F.3d at 307 n.4.

A further conference held at Montreal in 1975 produced four additional protocols to the Warsaw Convention. Among these was the pithily titled Montreal Protocol No. 4 to Amend the Convention for the Unification of Certain Rules Relating to International Carriage by Air Signed at Warsaw on 12 October 1929 as amended by the Protocol done at the Hague on 28 September 1955. Although the bulk of Montreal Protocol No. 4 dealt with modernization of the cargo waybill provisions of the earlier versions of the Warsaw Convention, it also provided in Article 17(2) that ratification of Montreal Protocol No. 4 would have the effect of ratification of a single treaty consisting of the terms of the original Warsaw Convention, as amended by the Hague Protocol, as amended by Montreal Protocol No. 4. See S. Exec. Rep. No. 105-20, at 21. The United States ratified Montreal Protocol No. 4 on September 28, 1998, and it came into force in this country on March 4, 1999. See Chubb & Son, 214 F.3d at 307 n.4.

For ease of terminology, the Court generally refers to the "original Warsaw Convention," meaning the 1929 version, and the "current Warsaw Convention," meaning the version in effect as of March 4, 1999 and incorporating the terms of the Hague Protocol and Montreal Protocol No. 4. The Court also refers to the original and current versions as the "old" and "new" versions. When referring specifically to the 1955 Hague revisions of the original Warsaw Convention, the Court occasionally refers to the "Hague Protocol," even though those revisions did not take effect in this country until the ratification of Montreal Protocol No. 4 in 1999. The current Warsaw Convention is reprinted in S. Exec. Rep. No. 105-20, at 21.

In its motion for summary judgment, Air France correctly cited the current version of the Warsaw Convention and noted that this version applied because the flights in this case took place after the March 4, 1999 effective date of Montreal Protocol No. 4. Nonetheless, Plaintiff in his responsive papers relied on Article 4 of the original Warsaw Convention. Air France having once again raised the amendment in its reply brief and the Court having called his attention thereto at oral argument, Schopenhauer now concedes that the Hague Protocol applies.

That, however, does not end the confusion. Despite having itself alerted Plaintiff to the current status of the Warsaw Convention in the United States, Air France in its Supplemental Memorandum in Support of Motion for Summary Judgment ("Def.Suppl. Mem."), for reasons still unclear to the Court, cited and provided legal analysis relevant only to a different treaty, the so-called Convention for the Unification of Certain Rules for International Carriage by Air, done at Montreal (the "Montreal Convention"). See S.Rep. No. 106-45, at 28. The Montreal Convention is not a protocol to the original Warsaw Convention, nor (a fortiori) is it the same as Montreal Protocol No. 4; rather, it is a proposed unification and replacement of the entire Warsaw System. The Montreal Convention has attracted a certain amount of critical attention, see, e.g., Pablo Mendes De Leon & Werner Eyskens, The Montreal Convention: Analysis of Some Aspects of the Attempted Modernization and Consolidation of the Warsaw System, 66 J. Air. L. & Com. 1155 (2001), but not only has it not been ratified by the United States, it lacks the requisite number of ratifications even to come into force of its own terms. See International Civil Aviation Organization Treaty Collection, http://www.icao.int/icao/en/leb/mtl99.htm (noting that the Montreal Convention currently has twenty-seven of the thirty necessary ratifications, and that it has not been ratified by the United States) (last updated Mar. 3, 2003). The Court therefore wishes to make clear that its analysis of the instant motion is based upon the current Warsaw Convention, i.e. the original Warsaw Convention, as amended by the Hague Protocol, as amended by Montreal Protocol No. 4.

C. Article 22 Limited Liability and Article 4 Baggage Checks

Article 18(1) of the current Warsaw Convention establishes a presumption that "[t]he carrier is liable for damage sustained in the event of the destruction or loss of, or damage to, any registered baggage, if the occurrence which caused the damage so sustained took place during the carriage by air." Article 22(2)(a), however, provides that "[i]n the carriage of registered baggage, the liability of the carrier is limited to the sum of [twenty dollars] per kilogram, unless the passenger or consignor has made [alternative insurance arrangements]." The dispositive question is whether Article 22's liability limitation applies in this case: if it does, then Air France's liability is limited to $20 per kilogram; if it does not, then Schopenhauer is free to prove actual damages.

In seeking to prove that Article 22's liability limitation does not apply, Schopenhauer points to Article 4, the Convention's baggage check provision. Because there is no contention that the baggage check issued with respect to the baggage lost and damaged on the Paris-to-Benin flight was in any way insufficient, the Court hereby grants Air France's motion to limit its liability insofar as it relates to that flight. The only dispute that remains for resolution, then, is whether the baggage check Schopenhauer received with respect to the baggage allegedly lost and damaged on the New York-to-Paris flight—namely the sixth bag, which the flight attendant insisted Schopenhauer check after he boarded the plane—was sufficient to allow Air France to invoke Article 22.

In arguing that it was not sufficient, Schopenhauer points to the "Limited Release" identification tag which the flight attendant handed him in return for the sixth bag. Noting that the Limited Release tag listed only the departure and destination cities but not the number of the passenger ticket or the weight of the bag, Schopenhauer initially argued that it was clearly insufficient on that basis. In support of this contention, he cited a series of cases which precluded an air carrier from limiting its liability where the baggage check did not record the weight of the bags. See, e.g., Tchokponhove v. Air Afrique, 953 F.Supp. 79, 83 (S.D.N.Y.1996). The fatal flaw in this argument was that it relied on the original version of Article 4. The current version of Article 4 specifically eliminated the requirement that the baggage check include the ticket number and the number and weight of the bags in order to qualify for limited liability.

Again, however, this does not end the inquiry, for it is clear that the Limited Release tag also lacked the Warsaw Convention notice required by Article 4(1)(c) of the current Convention. Although Air France also relies on the Limited Release tag as the baggage check, it did not address Article 4(1)(c) in its initial papers or at oral argument. After the Court sua sponte brought it to the parties' attention, Air France responded in its supplemental briefs with two arguments, both of which continue to rely on the Limited Release tag as the baggage check.

First, Air France argues that the Limited Release tag was sufficient even without a Warsaw Convention notice because such a notice was already included in the passenger ticket, and Schopenhauer therefore had actual notice of the potential applicability of the Warsaw Convention. Indeed, Schopenhauer does not allege that he was actually ignorant of the provisions of the Convention, and Air France points out that an essentially identical Warsaw Convention notice was present on various other documents in Schopenhauer's possession. The Court rejects this argument because recent cases interpreting the Warsaw Convention have made clear that its provisions are to be enforced strictly and without regard to whether lack of compliance by the air carrier actually prejudiced the passenger.

Specifically, the Court focuses on a line of cases determining whether to limit an air carrier's liability in cases where the baggage check did not contain the particulars—most commonly the weight of the bags—required by the original Article 4. Even though the failure to record the weight of the bags was unlikely to prejudice a passenger whose bags were lost—especially if the air carrier agreed to compensate the passenger $20 per kilogram for the maximum allowable weight—courts tended to apply the Convention literally and hold air carriers to unlimited liability where they failed to deliver sufficiently particular baggage checks. See, e.g., Gill v. Lufthansa German Airlines, 620 F.Supp. 1453, 1455 (E.D.N.Y.1985) (citing cases); Maghsoudi v. Pan Am. World Airways, Inc., 470 F.Supp. 1275, 1280 (D.Haw.1979); Hill v. E. Airlines, Inc., 103 Misc.2d 306, 425 N.Y.S.2d 715, 716 (1980). In a pair of cases in the mid-1980s, the Second Circuit suggested that it might not apply the Convention strictly in the case of businesses or sophisticated commercial passengers. In Exim Industries, Inc. v. Pan American World Airways, Inc., 754 F.2d 106, 108 (2d Cir.1985), the court declined to hold a cargo carrier to the strict requirements of Article 8 (the analog to Article 4 for cargo waybills), because the cargo owner was a commercial enterprise and the omitted particulars were of "no practical significance." Next, in Republic National Bank of New York v. Eastern Airlines, Inc., 815 F.2d 232 (2d Cir.1987), the court extended Exim's holding to Article 4 itself and limited the liability of an air carrier which in place of a complete baggage check delivered only a "Limited Release" tag that did not contain the requisite baggage weight, ticket number, or Warsaw Convention notice. In so doing, the Republic National Bank court noted that 1) the passenger was a sophisticated bank courier transporting $2 million in cash for commercial purposes and was thus "more like a commercial shipper than the typical airline passenger"; 2) after having flown over 250 similar courier flights "it would be incredible for [the courier] not to be aware of the applicability of the Warsaw Convention"; and 3) the omitted particulars were merely "technical and insubstantial omissions that did not prejudice the shipper." Id. at 237–38 (quoting Exim, 754 F.2d at 108).

The emerging Exim and Republic National Bank approach was significantly undermined by the Supreme Court's decision in Chan v. Korean Air Lines, Ltd., 490 U.S. 122, 109 S.Ct. 1676, 104 L.Ed.2d 113 (1989). Chan dealt with Article 3 of the original Convention, which required that the passenger ticket contain a Warsaw Convention notice but did not explicitly state that failure to provide such a notice would preclude the carrier from invoking Article 22 to limit its liability. Plaintiffs argued that this was merely a drafting error and that it made no sense to predicate limited liability for baggage on the presence of a Warsaw Convention notice on the baggage check, but not to predicate limited liability for personal injury on such a notice in the ticket. But the Court refused to read policy into the Convention and held that it "must ... be governed by the text—solemnly adopted by the governments of many separate nations.... Where the text is clear, as it is here, we have no power to insert an amendment." Id. at 126–27, 109 S.Ct. 1676.

In the wake of Chan, the Second Circuit cabined Exim to its facts and heralded an era of strict interpretation of Warsaw Convention particularity requirements. See Mar. Ins. Co. v. Emery Air Freight Corp., 983 F.2d 437, 440 (2d Cir.1993) (declining to limit liability where a cargo waybill did not contain the required particulars and holding that "[b]oth precedent and reason counsel that courts refrain from altering even slightly the plain, unambiguous language of a treaty negotiated among diverse sovereign nations"); see also Victoria Sales Corp. v. Emery Air Freight, Inc., 917 F.2d 705, 707 (2d Cir.1990) ("[W]hen the text of a treaty is clear, a court shall not, through interpretation, alter or amend the treaty.") (citing Chan, 490 U.S. 122, 109 S.Ct. 1676, 104 L.Ed.2d 113). This Court therefore declines to carve out an excuse for Air France not to comply with Article 4 whether or not Schopenhauer had actual notice of the potential applicability of the Warsaw Convention.

In its second supplemental brief, Air France continues to rely on the Limited Release tag as the baggage check, but under a slightly different argument. It now argues that the presence of a Warsaw Convention notice in the passenger ticket obviates the need for a Warsaw Convention notice in the baggage check—not because the passenger is not prejudiced by its absence, but because the text of Article 4(2) foresees the incorporation of the Warsaw Convention notice in the passenger ticket. Essentially, Air France suggests that this language means that if the Warsaw Convention notice is incorporated in the passenger ticket, it may be dispensed with in the baggage check.

The Court rejects this contention. It would have been quite simple for the Article to provide for the preclusion of limited liability "if the baggage check does not include the Warsaw Convention notice (unless the notice is combined with or incorporated in the passenger ticket)." Alternatively, the Article could have provided for the preclusion of liability "if the baggage check and passenger ticket, when combined, do not include the Warsaw Convention notice." But the plain language of the Article quite clearly speaks in terms of the baggage check being "combined with or incorporated in the passenger ticket." The French text of the Hague Protocol, which controls in case of inconsistency among the official languages, is if anything even more clearly phrased.

A third argument that Air France might have made, but did not—indeed that Air France specifically argues against in its effort to transform the meaning of Article 4—is that Schopenhauer received a satisfactory baggage check when he first received his tickets from Magical Holidays. In other words, Air France might have argued that the entire baggage check, rather than just the Warsaw Convention notice, was incorporated in the passenger ticket pursuant to Article 4(2), and thus sufficient to invoke Article 22.

Each of the passenger tickets in this case is printed on a form headed "Passenger Ticket and Baggage Check," and which apparently contains a Warsaw Convention notice on its reverse. As such, once delivered each satisfies the liability limitation requirements of Article 3 (that a ticket have been delivered and that it contain a Warsaw Convention notice) and of Article 4 (that a baggage check have been delivered and that it contain a Warsaw Convention notice, or that it be incorporated in a passenger ticket containing a Warsaw Convention notice). Moreover, each "Passenger Ticket and Baggage Check" provides even those particulars listed in Articles 3 and 4 but not necessary in order to limit liability, to wit, an indication of the places of departure and destination or (for round trips) an international stopping point. Finally, the form also leaves space for certain baggage check particulars required by the old Warsaw Convention, but not by the current one: the place and date of issue and the number and weight of the bags.

The strongest argument against this proposition is that it is counterintuitive. In the words of Air France's brief, "To argue that the baggage check is combined into the passenger ticket departs from commonly accepted logic; that is, when one travels and purchases airline tickets from a travel agent; via the internet on a website; or from an air carrier directly by telephone, those entities do not know at that point whether or not the traveler will have luggage." Def. Reply Mem. to Pl. Suppl. Mem. at 2.

III. Conclusion

In view of the fact that both parties have litigated the instant motion under the theory that the Limited Release tag constituted the baggage check delivered to Schopenhauer in respect of the sixth bag, the Court does not find it appropriate to grant summary judgment on an alternative theory, especially a theory rejected by Air France. Air France remains free to prove, if it can, that it in fact issued a document pursuant to Article 4 that permits it to invoke the limited liability provision of Article 22.

For the above reasons the Court GRANTS the motion for summary judgment insofar as it seeks to limit Air France's liability to $20 per kilogram for the luggage allegedly lost or damaged on the Paris-to-Benin flight, and DENIES the motion for summary judgment insofar as it seeks to dismiss that part of Schopenhauer's claim for lack of jurisdiction, and further DENIES the motion insofar as it seeks to limit Air France's liability for the New York-to-Paris flight.

PARADIS v. GHANA AIRWAYS LIMITED

348 F. Supp. 2d 106 (S.D.N.Y. 2004)

STEIN, District Judge.

Michel Paradis, acting pro se, brings this New York common law breach of contract action to recover losses that he and his traveling companions suffered when returning to New York from Sierra Leone. Specifically, he seeks compensation from Ghana Airways Limited for damages stemming from its cancellation of his flight. The airline has moved to dismiss the complaint, contending that the Montreal Convention preempts this cause of action and that Paradis lacks standing to pursue damages on behalf of his companions. The motion to dismiss the complaint is granted because the Montreal Convention and its predecessor, the Warsaw Convention, both preempt state law claims based on delay in air transportation.

FACTUAL BACKGROUND

The facts as alleged in the complaint are as follows: Paradis coordinated a trip to Sierra Leone for his law school student organization, Universal Jurisdiction [of Fordham University], which provides volunteer legal services in developing countries. (Am.Compl.¶¶ 8, 9). On April 29, 2004, Paradis purchased round-trip tickets for himself and four other members of Universal Jurisdiction to travel on Ghana Airways between New York City and Freetown, Sierra Leone, departing from New York on May 29, 2004 and returning from Sierra Leone three weeks later, on June 18, 2004. (Am.Compl.¶ 11). The group's itinerary between New York and Freetown included a connection in Accra, Ghana during both the departing and the returning trips. (Am.Compl.¶¶ 11–12).

When in Sierra Leone, Paradis and his companions confirmed their return flight two days before their scheduled departure. (Am.Compl.¶ 18). They went to the airport on Friday, June 18, arriving at around 12:00 p.m. for their 3:00 p.m. flight to Accra. (Am.Compl.¶¶ 12, 19). At approximately 4:15 p.m.—an hour and fifteen minutes after the scheduled departure time—an announcement was made that the flight had been cancelled. (Am.Compl.¶¶ 12, 25). Ghana Airways had no ticket desks at the airport, but its staff informed Paradis there were no other flights leaving that day and that he should make arrangements with the Ghana Airways office in Freetown the next business day. (Am.Compl.¶¶ 20, 27).

The group left the airport and arrived back in Freetown at around 5:00 p.m. (Am.Compl.¶ 28). Because members of the group were anxious to return to the United States for various prior commitments, including summer employment, a bar examination review course and mandatory meetings for organizations (Am.Compl.¶¶ 48–51), Paradis made a reservation with another air carrier, Astreaus Airways, for seats on a flight that would leave Sierra Leone at 10:30 that same night, Friday June 18, and fly to Gatwick Airport in England. (Am.Compl.¶ 31). Paradis searched the internet for flights from Gatwick to New York and learned that the group would most likely be able to acquire tickets for that leg upon arrival at Gatwick. (Am.Compl.¶¶ 31–32, 56–57).

Paradis then called the Ghana Airways office in New York and inquired about later Ghana Airways flights out of Sierra Leone. (Am.Compl.¶ 30). The agent in New York claimed to be unaware of the cancellation of Paradis' flight. (Am.Compl.¶ 30). Paradis "was given no assurances of subsequent flight availability and was told to take up the matter with the GHANA AIRWAYS office in Freetown, Sierra Leone, which at [that] hour on a Friday was closed." (Am.Compl. at ¶ 30). Paradis' conversation with the agent then shifted to how much Ghana Airways would pay to compensate the group for the cost of securing transportation on other carriers. (Am.Compl.¶ 32). The agent allegedly refused to offer anything more than $559 per ticket, one-half the original ticket price and substantially less than the approximately $1,500 per person total that Paradis projected it would cost to purchase tickets for the Astreaus Airways flight to Gatwick and another flight from Gatwick to New York. (Am.Compl.¶¶ 32, 34). In the context of that discussion about reimbursement for alternative flight arrangements, the agent allegedly told Paradis that "finding a way back to New York was 'your problem.'" (Am.Compl.¶ 42).

Paradis and his companions feared being stranded if they spent their remaining cash on accommodations while waiting for Ghana Airways' next flight, scheduled for the following Friday, to leave, especially because they did not have guaranteed seats. (Am.Compl.¶ 47). Consequently, they purchased the tickets Paradis had reserved on Astreaus Airways and left Sierra Leone later that same night, June 18. (Am.Compl.¶¶ 53, 55). Upon his return to the United States, Paradis exerted extensive, albeit unsuccessful, efforts to negotiate a satisfactory settlement with Ghana Airways for the out-of-pocket losses the group suffered as a result of the cancelled flight. (Am.Compl.¶¶ 59–98).

Within six weeks of his arrival back in New York, Paradis brought suit in New York Supreme Court against Ghana Airways for breach of contract pursuant to New York law and for damages occasioned by delay pursuant to the Warsaw Convention. (See generally Notice of Removal of Def. Ghana Airways Ltd. Ex. A). Ghana Airways promptly removed the action to the United States District Court for the Southern District of New York on the grounds that the airline is an instrumentality of a foreign state. See 28 U.S.C. §§ 1441, 1603(a); (Notice of Removal of Def. Ghana Airways Ltd.). Ghana Airways also asserted that the action was removable on the basis of federal question jurisdiction, since a treaty of the United States was involved. See 28 U.S.C. § 1331; (Notice of Removal of Def. Ghana Airways Ltd.).

Paradis then filed an Amended Complaint that omitted his Warsaw Convention claim and asserted only a state law breach of contract claim. (See generally Am. Compl.). Ghana Airways has moved to dismiss the Amended Complaint for failure to state a claim upon which relief can be granted, pursuant to Fed.R.Civ.P. 12(b)(6), on the grounds that Paradis' state law claim is preempted by a treaty to which the United States is a party and that Paradis lacks standing to recover for losses suffered by his traveling companions.

DISCUSSION

Motion to Dismiss

In considering a motion to dismiss a complaint pursuant to Fed.R.Civ.P. 12(b), a court must assume that the allegations set for the complaint are true, and the motion may be granted "'only if it is clear that no relief could be granted under any set of facts that could be proved consistent with the allegations.'" Laborers Local 17 Health & Benefit Fund v. Philip Morris, Inc., 191 F.3d 229, 234 (2d Cir.1999) (quoting Hishon v. King & Spalding, 467 U.S. 69, 73, 104 S.Ct. 2229, 81 L.Ed.2d 59 (1984)). A court may rely only on the factual allegations set forth in the complaint itself and not on additional matters asserted in affidavits, exhibits, or other papers submitted in conjunction with the motion. See Friedl v. City of New York, 210 F.3d 79, 83–84 (2d Cir.2000).

The complaint need only provide "a short and plain statement of the claim showing that the pleader is entitled to relief." Swierkiewicz v. Sorema N.A., 534 U.S. 506, 512, 122 S.Ct. 992, 152 L.Ed.2d 1 (2002) (quoting Fed.R.Civ.P. 8(a)(2)). The pleadings drafted by pro se litigants are held to even "less stringent standards than formal pleadings drafted by lawyers ..." and a court "'must construe the complaint liberally' and 'interpret [it] to raise the strongest arguments that [it] suggest[s].'" Haines v. Kerner, 404 U.S. 519, 520, 92 S.Ct. 594, 30 L.Ed.2d 652 (1972); see also Soto v. Walker, 44 F.3d 169, 173 (2d Cir.1995) (quoting Burgos v. Hopkins, 14 F.3d 787, 790 (2d Cir.1994)). Paradis may not merit such forgiving treatment given the fact that he recently passed the New York bar examination. See New York State Bar Results, N.Y.L.J., Nov. 18, 2004, at 13; Padilla v. Payco Gen. American Credits, Inc., 161 F.Supp.2d 264, 271 (S.D.N.Y.2001). Nonetheless, even if the Court accords Paradis the level of deference given to ordinary pro se plaintiffs, because his claim is preempted, his complaint fails to state a cause of action upon which relief can be granted, pursuant to Fed.R.Civ.P. 12(b)(6).

Defendant's Arguments: Preemption and Standing

Ghana Airways seeks dismissal of the complaint on two grounds, namely that Paradis' state law claim is preempted by the treaty popularly known as the Montreal Convention and that he lacks standing to pursue relief for damages incurred by his traveling companions.

The Conventions

In November of 2003, before any of the events involved in this litigation, the Montreal Convention entered into force in the United States, superseding a prior air carriage treaty commonly known as the Warsaw Convention. See Ehrlich v. American Airlines, 360 F.3d 366, 371 & n.4 (2d Cir.2004). The Montreal Convention is formally known as the Convention for the Unification of Certain Rules for International Carriage by Air Done at Montreal on 28 May 1999, reprinted in S. Treaty Doc. No 106-45, 1999 WL 33292734 (2000). The Warsaw Convention is formally known as the Convention for the Unification of Certain Rules Relating to International Transportation by Air, 49 Stat. 3000, T.S. No. 876 (1934), reprinted in note following 49 U.S.C. § 40105.

The parties disagree about which treaty applies to this action. The airline urges that the Montreal Convention governs, whereas Paradis contends that the Warsaw Convention serves as the applicable law because the contract between the parties so provided. (See Am. Compl. Ex. B).

The key provision of whichever Convention applies is its statement of preemptive effect. Article 24(1) of the Warsaw Convention states that "[i]n the carriage of passengers and baggage, any action for damages, however founded, can only be brought subject to the conditions and limits set out in this convention." That version of Article 24(1) derived from an amendment to the Warsaw Convention generally referred to as the Montreal Protocol. The Montreal Convention, which later replaced the Warsaw Convention entirely, offers in its Article 29 similar language to that of the Montreal Protocol: "In the carriage of passengers, baggage and cargo, any action for damages, however founded, whether under this Convention or in contract or in tort or otherwise, can only be brought subject to the conditions and such limits of liability as are set out in this Convention...."

The Montreal Protocol is formally known as Montreal Protocol No. 4 to Amend the Convention for the Unification of Certain Rules Relating to International Carriage by Air, signed at Warsaw on October 12, 1929 as amended by the Protocol Done at the Hague on September 28, 1955, reprinted in S. Exec. Rep. No. 105-20 pp. 21–32 (1998). Before the Montreal Protocol amended Article 24(1) of the Warsaw Convention, it read, "In the cases covered by articles 18 and 19[, which includes claims for delay,] any action for damages, however founded, can only be brought subject to the conditions and limits set out in this convention." King v. American Airlines, 284 F.3d 352, 357 (2d Cir.2002) (quoting 49 U.S.C.A. §40105 note).

Defendant posits that the Montreal Convention should apply because it was already in effect at the time of the events at issue. See Ehrlich, 360 F.3d at 371. Plaintiff contends that the Warsaw Convention is the applicable treaty, because the contract on the ticket invoked the Warsaw Convention rather than the Montreal Convention. Nevertheless, the Court need not determine which convention applies, because they have substantially the same preemptive effect; Article 29 of the Montreal Convention simply clarified the language of the Montreal Protocol's amendment to Article 24(1) of the Warsaw Convention. See Article-by-Article Analysis of the Convention for the Unification of Certain Rules for International Carriage by Air Done at Montreal May 28, 1999, S. Treaty Doc. No 106-45, 1999 WL 33292734 (2000) (describing Article 29 of the Montreal Convention as having been "taken from" Montreal Protocol No. 4). Here, the preemptive effect is identical regardless of whether the Montreal Convention or the Warsaw Convention (together, "the Conventions") applies; thus, the Court need not decide which Convention controls.

Non-Performance

The Conventions preempt all state law claims within their scope. See Shah v. Pan Am. World Servs., Inc., 148 F.3d 84, 97–98 (2d Cir.1998); Fishman v. Delta Air Lines, Inc., 132 F.3d 138, 141 (2d Cir.1998); see also El Al Israel Airlines v. Tseng, 525 U.S. 155, 176 119 S.Ct. 662, 142 L.Ed.2d 576 (1999) (holding that the Warsaw Convention preempts a state law claim against an airline for injury even though the circumstances did not satisfy the Convention's conditions for imposing liability). Paradis brings a state law claim for relief, drawing a distinction between cases of mere delay in travel that the Conventions cover—see Warsaw Convention Article 19 ("The carrier shall be liable for damage occasioned by delay in the transportation by air of passengers, baggage or goods"); Montreal Convention Article 19 ("The carrier is liable for damage occasioned by delay in the carriage by air of passengers, baggage or cargo.")—and cases of contract non-performance to which state law applies.

He contends that the Conventions regulate the terms of carriage by air, but that this case is not covered by the Conventions because it involves the failure to so carry. Nevertheless, the facts, as alleged, fail to state a claim for relief that escapes the preemptive effect of the Conventions. Paradis reacted to a delay by immediately procuring substitute transportation and demanding reimbursement from the airline. A passenger cannot convert a mere delay into contractual non-performance by choosing to obtain more punctual conveyance. See Fields v. BWIA Intern. Airways Ltd., No. 99 Civ. 2493, 2000 WL 1091129, *4, 2000 U.S. Dist. LEXIS 9397, at *13 (E.D.N.Y. July 7, 2000) ("Plaintiff's attempt to make the claim sound in breach of contract terms does not change the fact that the claim, however founded, arose out of a delay in transportation.") (quoting Sassouni v. Olympic

Airways, 769 F.Supp. 537, 540–41 (S.D.N.Y.1991)). Although the group allegedly "feared being stranded" (Am. Compl. at ¶47) and had various presumably bona fide reasons for needing to return to the United States instanter, Ghana Airways had not failed to perform its contract obligations at the time the group left Sierra Leone.

The contract on the ticket did not require Ghana Airways to provide prompt transportation. Rather, the contract read, in pertinent part, as follows:

> Carrier undertakes to use its best efforts to carry the passenger and baggage with reasonable dispatch. Times shown in timetables or elsewhere are not guaranteed and form no part of this contract. Carrier may without notice substitute alternate carriers or aircraft, and may alter or omit stopping places shown on the ticket in case of necessity. Schedules are subject to change without notice. Carrier assumes no responsibility for making connections.

(Am.Compl.Ex. B).

After cancellation of the Ghana Airways flight, Paradis decided to book a flight with a different carrier that would leave within several hours. Ghana Airways did not have the opportunity to fulfill its contractual obligation; failure to provide a substitute airplane within several hours of cancellation is not a failure to exercise "best efforts to carry the passenger ... with reasonable dispatch." That is particularly true in Sierra Leone, a severely impoverished nation that has only one airport with a paved runway and that has just recently emerged from an eleven-year civil war, see CIA World Factbook 2004, Sierra Leone, available at http://www.cia.gov/cia/publications/factbook/geos/sl.html (Nov. 15, 2004), but the Court's reasoning does not depend on the challenging conditions in that nation.

Repudiation

Plaintiff contends that in addition to failing to perform its obligations pursuant to the contract, the carrier "repudiated any future performance" when its agent referred to Paradis' travel complications as "your problem." (Mem. of Law in Opp. to Def.'s Mot. to Dismiss, Dated Oct. 15, 2004 at 1). Pursuant to the common law of New York, a party may repudiate certain types of contracts prior to the time of performance, thereby entitling the non-repudiating party to damages for total breach. See Norcon Power Partners, L.P. v. Niagara Mohawk Power Corp., 92 N.Y.2d 458, 462, 705 N.E.2d 656, 682 N.Y.S.2d 664 (1998); Long Is. R.R. Co. v. Northville Indus. Corp., 41 N.Y.2d 455, 463, 393 N.Y.S.2d 925, 362 N.E.2d 558 (1977). "A repudiation can be either 'a statement by the obligor to the obligee indicating that the obligor will commit a breach that would of itself give the obligee a claim for damages for total breach' or 'a voluntary affirmative act which renders the obligor unable or apparently unable to perform without such a breach.'" Norcon Power, 92 N.Y.2d at 462, 682 N.Y.S.2d 664, 705 N.E.2d 656 (quoting Restatement (Second) of Contracts §250). Repudiation occurs "when a breaching party's words or deeds are unequivocal." Id.; see also Palazzetti Import/Export, Inc. v. Morson, No. 98 Civ. 722, 2001 WL 1568317, at *9 (S.D.N.Y. Dec. 6, 2001) ("The renunciation ... must rise to the level of a clear and unqualified refusal to perform the entire contract.").

The Ghana Airways agent made the "your problem" comment in response to Paradis' request for a form of relief that the airline was not required to provide. (See Am. Compl. ¶¶32–46). The contract made no provision for reimbursement of the cost of more punctual, alternative transportation in the event of a flight cancellation. The complaint puts the "your problem" comment in context and makes clear that there was never any repudiation of Ghana Airways' obligations pursuant to the contract.

Preemption of Plaintiff's Claim

A plaintiff cannot "circumvent [the Warsaw Convention] merely by recharacterizing her claims as sounding in state law." Fields, 2000 WL 1091129, *4, 2000 U.S. Dist. LEXIS 9397, at *13. Any other rule would undermine the U.S. Supreme Court's instruction that "[t]he cardinal purpose of the Warsaw Convention ... is to 'achiev[e] uniformity of rules governing claims arising from international air transportation.'" El Al Israel Airlines v. Tseng, 525 U.S. 155, 169 119 S.Ct. 662, 142 L.Ed.2d 576 (1999) (citation omitted).

Paradis argues that his state law claim withstands the preemptive effect of the Conventions because he sues for non-performance of contract rather than for delay. To support that position, he relies principally on Wolgel v. Mexicana Airlines, 821 F.2d 442 (7th Cir.1987), an action brought by a husband and wife because they had been "bumped" from a Mexicana Airlines flight. (Many of the cases involving an inability to fly as scheduled involve "bumping," an airline industry practice whereby passengers are denied seats as a result of intentional overselling meant to minimize the number of empty seats on planes. See Nader v. Allegheny, 426 U.S. 290, 292, 96 S.Ct. 1978, 48 L.Ed.2d 643 (1976).)

Although the Warsaw Convention provided the sole remedy for "delay," the United States Court of Appeals for the Seventh Circuit construed the word "delay," as used in the Convention, to exclude situations when passengers "never leave the airport." Id. at 444–45. Wolgel's distinction between "bumping" and "delay" has been undercut by the U.S. Supreme Court's message in Tseng "that the application of the Convention is not to be accomplished by a miserly parsing of its language." King v. American Airlines, 146 F.Supp.2d 159, 162 (N.D.N.Y.2001).

The circumstances of Wolgel are readily distinguishable from those that Paradis faced in Sierra Leone. The Wolgels were deprived of all benefit of their bargain. The airline denied them boarding on the initial leg of their round-trip itinerary and had provided no compensation even five years later when the plaintiffs brought suit. See Wolgel, 821 F.2d at 443. Paradis, who flew the initial leg of his round-trip itinerary, has offered no factual allegations that Ghana Airways failed to offer substitute transportation. Indeed, the staff at the airport and the agent in New York both instructed him to make arrangements with the Ghana Airways office in Freetown the following business day. Paradis and his companions were so keen to leave Sierra Leone that they did not give the airline a reasonable opportunity to perform.

Other courts have refused to allow recovery for breach of contract when plaintiffs responded to delays as Paradis did, by booking alternative flights. See, e.g., Minhas v. Biman Bangladesh Airlines, No 97 Civ. 4920, 1999 WL 447445 (S.D.N.Y. June 30, 1999); Ratnaswamy v. Air Afrique, No. 95 C 7670, 1998 WL 111652 (N.D.Ill. March 3, 1998); Alam v. Pakistan Int'l Airlines Corp., 92 Civ. 4356, 1995 WL 17201349, 1995 U.S. Dist. LEXIS 11919 (S.D.N.Y. July 27, 1995); Malik v. Butta, 92 Civ. 8703, 1993 WL 410168, 1993 U.S. Dist. LEXIS 1442 (S.D.N.Y. Oct. 14, 1993).

In Ratnaswamy v. Air Afrique, No. 95 C 7670, 1998 WL 111652, at *2–3 (N.D.Ill. March 3, 1998), for example, a husband and wife sued, inter alia, for breach of contract when, despite having reconfirmed their tickets, they were denied boarding on a return flight from Senegal to New York City. Id. at *1–2. The defendant airline, Air Afrique, refused to compensate plaintiffs by providing them tickets for a flight on another carrier. Id. at *2. The airline instructed the plaintiffs to wait three days for the next Air Afrique flight, seats on which were not guaranteed; instead of complying, the plaintiffs bought more expensive tickets to return on an earlier flight operated by a different airline. Id. at *2. The Ratnaswamy court held that because the plaintiffs had already flown six out of seven Air Afrique segments of their planned itinerary, the suit was actually "for damages they allegedly sustained as a result of their delay in leaving Africa." Id. at *4. Distinguishing its own Circuit's opinion in Wolgel, the Ratnaswamy court held that the plaintiffs' state law claims were "within the purview of the convention," which provided the "exclusive remedy" for delay, and were accordingly preempted. Id. (citation omitted).

Similarly, in Minhas v. Biman Bangladesh Airlines, No. 97 Civ. 4920, 1999 WL 447445, at *1 (S.D.N.Y. June 30, 1999), Judge Barbara S. Jones rejected the state law claims of Minhas, who had been bumped off of a return flight from New Delhi to New York in March of 1997. The plaintiff remained in India for 45 extra days after that, trying unsuccessfully to get a return flight from the defendant airline. Id. Eventually, when Minhas was informed in late April that no flight would be available to New York until some time in July, her spouse bought her a ticket on another airline. Id. As a result of the delay and her concomitant inability to access study materials, Minhas claimed that she was unable to sit for the California bar examination in July as she had planned. Id. Although Minhas did not specify whether she brought her claims in contract or tort, Judge Jones held broadly that "[c]laims arising from so-called 'bumping' are within the scope of Article 19 of the Convention," and granted the airline's motion for partial summary judgment. Id. at *2.

Just as the plaintiffs in Minhas and Ratnaswamy, Paradis did not afford the airline an opportunity to perform its remaining obligations pursuant to the contract. The several extra hours Paradis spent in Sierra Leone did not expose Ghana Airways to liability for contractual non-performance. Moreover, there was no indication that Ghana Airways intended to repudiate its contractual obligations. The Conventions apply and therefore preempt Paradis' state law breach of contract claim.

Standing

The Court need not address defendant's contention that Paradis does not have standing to bring this action on behalf of his traveling companions, because plaintiff's breach of contract claim is preempted by the relevant air carriage treaty.

CONCLUSION

The motion of Ghana Airways to dismiss the Complaint is granted without prejudice.

OLYMPIC AIRWAYS v. HUSAIN

540 U.S. 644 (2004)

Justice THOMAS delivered the opinion of the Court.

Article 17 of the Warsaw Convention (Convention for the Unification of Certain Rules Relating to International Transportation by Air, Oct. 12, 1929, 49 Stat. 3000, T.S. No. 876 (1934), note following 49 U.S.C. §40105) imposes liability on an air carrier for a passenger's death or bodily injury caused by an "accident" that occurred in connection with an international flight. In Air France v. Saks, 470 U.S. 392, 105 S.Ct. 1338, 84 L.Ed.2d 289 (1985), the Court explained that the term "accident" in the Convention refers to an "unexpected or unusual event or happening that is external to the passenger," and not to "the passenger's own internal reaction to the usual, normal, and expected operation of the aircraft." Id., at 405, 406, 105 S.Ct. 1338. The issue we must decide is whether the "accident" condition precedent to air carrier liability under Article 17 is satisfied when the carrier's unusual and unexpected refusal to assist a passenger is a link in a chain of causation resulting in a passenger's pre-existing medical condition being aggravated by exposure to a normal condition in the aircraft cabin. We conclude that it is.

I

The following facts are taken from the District Court's findings, which, being unchallenged by either party, we accept as true. In December 1997, Dr. Abid Hanson and his wife, Rubina Husain (hereinafter respondent), traveled with their children and another family from San Francisco to Athens and Cairo for a family vacation. During a stopover in New York, Dr. Hanson learned for the first time that petitioner allowed its passengers to smoke on international flights. Because Dr. Hanson had suffered from asthma and was sensitive to secondhand smoke, respondent requested and obtained seats away from the smoking section. Dr. Hanson experienced no problems on the flights to Cairo.

For the return flights, Dr. Hanson and respondent arrived early at the Cairo airport in order to request non-smoking seats. Respondent showed the check-in agent a physician's letter explaining that Dr. Hanson "has [a] history of recurrent anaphylactic reactions," App. 81, and asked the agent to ensure that their seats were in the non-smoking section. The flight to Athens was uneventful.

After boarding the plane for the flight to San Francisco, Dr. Hanson and respondent discovered that their seats were located only three rows in front of the economy-class smoking section. Respondent advised Maria Leptourgou, a flight attendant for petitioner, that Dr. Hanson could not sit in a smoking area, and said, "'You have to move him.'" 116 F.Supp.2d 1121, 1125 (N.D.Cal.2000). The flight attendant told her to "'have a seat.'" Ibid. After all the passengers had boarded but prior to takeoff, respondent again asked Ms. Leptourgou to move Dr. Hanson, explaining that he was "'allergic to smoke.'" Ibid. Ms. Leptourgou replied that she could not reseat Dr. Hanson because the plane was "'totally full'" and she was "too busy" to help. Ibid.

Shortly after takeoff, passengers in the smoking section began to smoke, and Dr. Hanson was soon surrounded by ambient cigarette smoke. Respondent spoke with Ms. Leptourgou a third time, stating, "'You have to move my husband from here.'" Id., at 1126. Ms. Leptourgou again refused, stating that the plane was full. Ms. Leptourgou told respondent that Dr. Hanson could switch seats with another passenger, but that respondent would have to ask other passengers herself, without the flight crew's assistance. Respondent told Ms. Leptourgou that Dr. Hanson had to move even if the only available seat was in the cockpit or in business class, but Ms. Leptourgou refused to provide any assistance.

Dr. Hanson and respondent did not know at the time that, despite Ms. Leptourgou's representations, the flight was actually not full. There were 11 unoccupied passenger seats, most of which were in economy class, and 28 "non-revenue passengers," 15 of whom were seated in economy class rows farther away from the smoking section than Dr. Hanson's seat. 116 F.Supp.2d, at 1126.

About two hours into the flight, the smoking noticeably increased in the rows behind Dr. Hanson. Dr. Hanson asked respondent for a new inhaler because the one he had been using was empty. Dr. Hanson then moved toward the front of the plane to get some fresher air. While he was leaning against a chair near the galley area, Dr. Hanson gestured to respondent to get his emergency kit. Respondent returned with it and gave him a shot of epinephrine. She then awoke Dr. Umesh Sabharwal, an allergist, with whom Dr. Hanson and respondent had been traveling. Dr. Sabharwal gave Dr. Hanson another shot of epinephrine and began to administer CPR and oxygen. Dr. Hanson died shortly thereafter. Id., at 1128. For religious reasons, no autopsy was performed to determine the cause of death.

Respondents filed a wrongful-death suit in California state court. Petitioner removed the case to federal court, and the District Court found petitioner liable for Dr. Hanson's death. The District Court held that Ms. Leptourgou's refusal to reseat Dr. Hanson constituted an "accident" within the meaning of Article 17. Applying Saks' definition of that term, the court reasoned that the flight attendant's conduct was external to Dr. Hanson and, because it was in "blatant disregard of industry standards and airline policies," was not expected or usual. 116 F.Supp.2d, at 1134.

The Ninth Circuit affirmed. Applying Saks' definition of "accident," the Ninth Circuit agreed that the flight attendant's refusal to reseat Dr. Hanson "was clearly external to Dr. Hanson, and it was unexpected and unusual in light of industry standards, Olympic policy, and the simple nature of Dr. Hanson's requested accommodation." 316 F.3d 829, 837 (C.A.9 2002). We granted certiorari, 538 U.S. 1056, 123 S.Ct. 2215, 155 L.Ed.2d 1105 (2003), and now affirm.

II

A

The Warsaw Convention's governing text is in French. We cite to the official English translation of the Convention, which was before the Senate when it consented to ratification of the Convention in 1934. See 49 Stat. 3014; Air France v. Saks, 470 U.S. 392, 397, 105 S.Ct. 1338, 84 L.Ed.2d 289 (1985).

We begin with the language of Article 17 of the Convention, which provides:

> The carrier shall be liable for damage sustained in the event of the death or wounding of a passenger or any other bodily injury suffered by a passenger, if the accident which caused the damage so sustained took place on board the aircraft or in the course of any of the operations of embarking or disembarking.

49 Stat. 3018.

After a plaintiff has established a prima facie case of liability under Article 17 by showing that the injury was caused by an "accident," the air carrier has the opportunity to prove under Article 20 that it took "all necessary measures to avoid the damage or that it was impossible for [the airline] to take such measures." 49 Stat. 3019. Thus, Article 17 creates a presumption of air carrier liability and shifts the burden to the air carrier to prove lack of negligence under Article 20. Lowenfeld & Mendelsohn, The United States and the Warsaw Convention, 80 Harv. L.Rev. 497, 521 (1967). Article 22(1) caps the amount recoverable under Article 17 in the event of death or bodily injury, and Article 25(1) removes the cap if the damage is caused by the "wilful misconduct" of the airline or its agent, acting within the scope of his employment. See 49 Stat. 3019, 3020. Additionally, Article 21 enables an air carrier to avoid or reduce its liability if it can prove the passenger's comparative negligence. See id., at 3019.

In Saks, the Court recognized that the text of the Convention does not define the term "accident" and that the context in which it is used is not "illuminating." 470 U.S., at 399, 105 S.Ct. 1338. The Court nevertheless discerned the meaning of the term "accident" from the Convention's text, structure, and history as well as from the subsequent conduct of the parties to the Convention.

Neither party here contests Saks' definition of the term "accident" under Article 17 of the Convention. Rather, the parties differ as to which event should be the focus of the "accident" inquiry. The Court's reasoning in Saks sheds light on whether the flight attendant's refusal to assist a passenger in a medical crisis is the proper focus of the "accident" inquiry.

In Saks, the Court addressed whether a passenger's "'loss of hearing proximately caused by normal operation of the aircraft's pressurization system'" was an "'accident.'" Id., at 395, 105 S.Ct. 1338. The Court concluded that it was not, because the injury was her "own internal reaction" to the normal pressurization of the aircraft's cabin. Id., at 406, 105 S.Ct. 1338.

The Court noted two textual clues to the meaning of the term "accident." First, the Convention distinguishes between liability under Article 17 for death or injuries to passengers caused by an "accident" and liability under Article 18 for destruction or loss of baggage caused by an "occurrence." Id., at 398, 105 S.Ct. 1338. The difference in these provisions implies that the meaning of the term "accident" is different from that of "occurrence." Ibid.

Second, the Court found significant the fact that Article 17 focuses on the "accident which caused" the passenger's injury and not an accident that is the passenger's injury. Ibid. The Court explained that it is the cause of the injury—rather than the occurrence of the injury that must satisfy the definition of "accident." Id., at 399, 105 S.Ct. 1338. And recognizing the Court's responsibility to read the treaty in a manner "consistent with the shared expectations of the contracting parties," ibid., the Court also looked to the French legal meaning of the term "accident," which when used to describe the cause of an injury, is usually defined as a "fortuitous, unexpected, unusual, or unintended event." Id., at 400, 105 S.Ct. 1338.

Accordingly, the Court held in Saks that an "accident" under Article 17 is "an unexpected or unusual event or happening that is external to the passenger," and not "the passenger's own internal reaction to the usual, normal, and expected operation of the aircraft." Id., at 405, 406, 105 S.Ct. 1338.

The Court emphasized that the definition of "accident" "should be flexibly applied after assessment of all the circumstances surrounding a passenger's injuries." Id., at 405, 105 S.Ct. 1338. The Court further contemplated that intentional conduct could fall within the "accident" definition under Article 17[.] The Court cited approvingly several lower court opinions where intentional acts by third parties—namely, torts committed by terrorists—were recognized as "accidents" under a "broa[d]" interpretation of Article 17. Ibid. (citing lower court cases).

[This] interpretation comports with another provision of the Convention. Specifically, Article 25 removes the cap on air carrier liability when the injury is caused by the air carrier's "wilful misconduct." 49 Stat. 3020. Because there can be no liability for passenger death or bodily injury under the Convention in the absence of an Article 17 "accident," such "wilful misconduct" is best read to be included within the realm of conduct that may constitute an "accident" under Article 17.

As such, Saks correctly characterized the term "accident" as encompassing more than unintentional conduct.

The Court focused its analysis on determining "what causes can be considered accidents," and observed that Article 17 "embraces causes of injuries" that are "unexpected or unusual." Id., at 404, 405, 105 S.Ct. 1338. The Court did not suggest that only one event could constitute the "accident," recognizing that "[a]ny injury is the product of a chain of causes." Id., at 406, 105 S.Ct. 1338. Thus, for purposes of the "accident" inquiry, the Court stated that a plaintiff need only be able to prove that "some link in the chain was an unusual or unexpected event external to the passenger." Ibid.

B

Petitioner argues that the "accident" inquiry should focus on the "injury producing event," Reply Brief for Petitioner 4, which, according to petitioner, was the presence of ambient cigarette smoke in the aircraft's cabin. Because petitioner's policies permitted smoking on international flights, petitioner contends that Dr. Hanson's death resulted from his own internal reaction—namely, an asthma attack—to the normal operation of the aircraft. Petitioner also argues that the flight attendant's failure to move Dr. Hanson was inaction, whereas Article 17 requires an action that causes the injury. We disagree.

As an initial matter, we note that petitioner did not challenge in the Court of Appeals the District Court's finding that the flight attendant's conduct in three times refusing to move Dr. Hanson was unusual or unexpected in light of the relevant industry standard or petitioner's own company policy. 116 F.Supp.2d, at 1133. Petitioner instead argued that the flight attendant's conduct was irrelevant for purposes of the "accident" inquiry and that the only relevant event was the presence of the ambient cigarette smoke in the aircraft's cabin. Consequently, we need not dispositively determine whether the flight attendant's conduct qualified as "unusual or unexpected" under Saks, but may assume that it was for purposes of this opinion.

Petitioner's focus on the ambient cigarette smoke as the injury producing event is misplaced. We do not doubt that the presence of ambient cigarette smoke in the aircraft's cabin during an international flight might have been "normal" at the time of the flight in question. But petitioner's "injury producing event" inquiry—which looks to "the precise factual 'event' that caused the injury"—neglects the reality that there are often multiple interrelated factual events that combine to cause any given injury. Brief for Petitioner 14. In Saks, the Court recognized that any one of these factual events or happenings may be a link in the chain of causes and—so long as it is unusual or unexpected—could constitute an "accident" under Article 17. 470 U.S., at 406, 105 S.Ct. 1338. Indeed, the very fact that multiple events will necessarily combine and interrelate to cause any particular injury makes it difficult to define, in any coherent or non-question-begging way, any single event as the "injury producing event."

Petitioner's only claim to the contrary here is to say: "Looking to the purely factual description of relevant events, the aggravating event was Dr. Hanson remaining in his assigned non-smoking seat and being exposed to ambient smoke, which allegedly aggravated his pre-existing asthmatic condition leading to his death," Brief for Petitioner 24, and that the "injury producing event" was "not the flight attendant's failure to act or violation of industry standards," Reply Brief for Petitioner 9–10. Petitioner ignores the fact that the flight attendant's refusal on three separate occasions to move Dr. Hanson was also a "factual 'event,'" Brief for Petitioner 14, that the District Court correctly found to be a "'link in the chain'" of causes that led to Dr. Hanson's death. 116 F.Supp.2d, at 1135. Petitioner's statement that the flight attendant's failure to reseat Dr. Hanson was not the "injury producing event" is nothing more than a bald assertion, unsupported by any law or argument.

An example illustrates why petitioner's emphasis on the ambient cigarette smoke as the "injury producing event" is misplaced. Suppose that petitioner mistakenly assigns respondent and her husband to seats in the middle of the smoking section, and that respondent and her husband do not notice that they are in the smoking section until after the flight has departed. Suppose further that, as here, the flight attendant refused to assist respondent and her husband despite repeated requests to move. In this hypothetical case, it would appear that, "[l]ooking to the purely factual description of relevant events, the aggravating event was [the passenger] remaining in his assigned ... seat and being exposed to ambient smoke, which allegedly aggravated his pre-existing asthmatic condition leading to his death." Brief for Petitioner 24. To argue otherwise, petitioner would have to suggest that the misassignment to the smoking section was the "injury producing event," but this would simply beg the question. The fact is, the exposure to smoke, the misassignment to the smoking section, and the refusal to move the passenger would all be factual events contributing to the death of the passenger. In the instant case, the same can be said: The exposure to the smoke and the refusal to assist the passenger are happenings that both contributed to the passenger's death.

And petitioner's argument that the flight attendant's failure to act cannot constitute an "accident" because only affirmative acts are "event[s] or happening[s]" under Saks is unavailing. 470 U.S., at 405, 105 S.Ct. 1338. The distinction between action and inaction, as petitioner uses these terms, would perhaps be relevant were this a tort law negligence case. But respondents do not advocate, and petitioner vigorously rejects, that a negligence regime applies under Article 17 of the Convention. The relevant "accident" inquiry under Saks is whether there is "an unexpected or unusual event or happening." Ibid. The rejection of an explicit request for assistance would be an "event" or "happening" under the ordinary and usual definitions of these terms. See American Heritage Dictionary 635 (3d ed.1992) ("event": "[s]omething that takes place; an occurrence"); Black's Law Dictionary 554–555 (6th ed.1990) ("event": "Something that happens"); Webster's New International Dictionary 885 (2d ed.1949) ("event": "The fact of taking place or occurring; occurrence" or "[t]hat which comes, arrives, or happens").

The dissent cites two cases from our sister signatories England and Australia—Deep Vein Thrombosis and Air Travel Group Litigation, [2004] Q. B. 234, and Qantas Ltd. v. Povey, [2003] VSCA 227, ¶17, 2003 WL 23000692, ¶17 (Dec. 23, 2003) (Ormiston, J.A.), respectively—and suggests that we should simply defer to their judgment on the matter. But our conclusion is not inconsistent with Deep Vein Thrombosis and Air Travel Group Litigation, where the England and Wales Court of Appeals commented on the District Court and Court of Appeals opinions in this case, and agreed that Dr. Hanson's death had resulted from an accident. The England court reasoned: "The refusal of the flight attendant to move Dr. Hanson cannot properly be considered as mere inertia, or a non-event. It was a refusal to provide an alternative seat which formed part of a more complex incident, whereby Dr. Hanson was exposed to smoke in circumstances that can properly be described as unusual and unexpected." [2004] Q. B., at 254, ¶50.

To the extent that the precise reasoning used by the courts in Deep Vein Thrombosis and Air Travel Group Litigation and Povey is inconsistent with our reasoning, we reject the analysis of those cases for the reasons stated in the body of this opinion. In such a circumstance, we are hesitant to "follo[w]" the opinions of intermediate appellate courts of our sister signatories, post, at 1231 (SCALIA, J., dissenting). This is especially true where there are substantial factual distinctions between these cases, see EWCA Civ. 1005, ¶29, 2003 WL 21353471, at *659, ¶29 (confronting allegations of a "failure to warn of the risk of [deep-vein thrombosis], or to advise on precautions which would avoid or minimize that risk"); VSCA 227, ¶3, 2003 WL 23000692, ¶3 (noting plaintiff alleged a failure to provide "any information or warning about the risk of [deep-vein thrombosis] or of any measures to reduce the risk"), and where the respective courts of last resort—the House of Lords and High Court of Australia—have yet to speak.

Moreover, the fallacy of petitioner's position that an "accident" cannot take the form of inaction is illustrated by the following example. Suppose that a passenger on a flight inexplicably collapses and stops breathing and that a medical doctor informs the flight crew that the passenger's life could be saved only if the plane lands within one hour. Suppose further that it is industry standard and airline policy to divert a flight to the nearest airport when a passenger otherwise faces imminent death. If the plane is within 30 minutes of a suitable airport, but the crew chooses to continue its cross-country flight, "[t]he notion that this is not an unusual event is staggering." McCaskey v. Continental Airlines, Inc., 159 F.Supp.2d 562, 574 (S.D.Tex.2001). (We do not suggest—as the dissent erroneously contends—that liability must lie because otherwise "harsh results," post, at 1234 (SCALIA, J., dissenting), would ensue. This hypothetical merely illustrates that the failure of an airline crew to take certain necessary vital steps could quite naturally and, in routine usage of the language, be an "event or happening.")

Confirming this interpretation, other provisions of the Convention suggest that there is often no distinction between action and inaction on the issue of ultimate liability. For example, Article 25 provides that Article 22's liability cap does not apply in the event of "wilful misconduct or ... such default on [the carrier's] part as, in accordance with the law of the court to which the case is submitted, is considered to be equivalent to wilful misconduct." 49 Stat. 3020. Because liability can be imposed for death or bodily injury only in the case of an Article 17 "accident" and Article 25 only lifts the caps once liability has been found, these provisions read together tend to show that inaction can give rise to liability. Moreover, Article 20(1) makes clear that the "due care" defense is unavailable when a carrier has failed to take "all necessary measures to avoid the damage." Id., at 3019. These provisions suggest that an air carrier's inaction can be the basis for liability.

The Montreal Protocol No. 4 to Amend the Convention for the Unification of Certain Rules relating to International Carriage by Air (1975) amends Article 25 by replacing "wilful misconduct" with the language "done with intent to cause damage or recklessly and with knowledge that damage would probably result," as long as the airline's employee or agent was acting "within the scope of his employment." S. Exec. Rep. No. 105-20, p. 29 (1998). In 1998, the United States gave its advice and consent to ratification of the protocol, and it entered into force in the United States on March 4, 1999. See El Al Israel Airlines, Ltd. v. Tsui Yuan Tseng, 525 U.S. 155, 174, n.14, 119 S.Ct. 662, 142 L.Ed.2d 576 (1999). Because the facts here took place in 1997–1998, Montreal Protocol No. 4 does not apply.

Finally, petitioner contends that the Ninth Circuit improperly created a negligence-based "accident" standard under Article 17 by focusing on the flight crew's negligence as the "accident." The Ninth Circuit stated: "The failure to act in the face of a known, serious risk satisfies the meaning of 'accident' within Article 17 so long as reasonable alternatives exist that would substantially minimize the risk and implementing these alternatives would not unreasonably interfere with the normal, expected operation of the airplane." 316 F.3d, at 837. Admittedly, this language does seem to approve of a negligence-based approach. However, no party disputes the Ninth Circuit's holding that the flight attendant's conduct was "unexpected and unusual," ibid., which is the operative language under Saks and the correct Article 17 analysis.

For the foregoing reasons, we conclude that the conduct here constitutes an "accident" under Article 17 of the Warsaw Convention. Accordingly, the judgment of the Court of Appeals is affirmed.

Justice SCALIA, with whom Justice O'CONNOR joins as to Parts I and II, dissenting.

When we interpret a treaty, we accord the judgments of our sister signatories "'considerable weight.'" Air France v. Saks, 470 U.S. 392, 404, 105 S.Ct. 1338, 84 L.Ed.2d 289 (1985). True to that canon, our previous Warsaw Convention opinions have carefully considered foreign case law. See, e.g., El Al Israel Airlines, Ltd. v. Tsui Yuan Tseng, 525 U.S. 155, 173–174, 119 S.Ct. 662, 142 L.Ed.2d 576 (1999); Eastern Airlines, Inc. v. Floyd, 499 U.S. 530, 550–551, 111 S.Ct. 1489, 113 L.Ed.2d 569 (1991); Saks, supra, at 404, 105 S.Ct. 1338. Today's decision stands out for its failure to give any serious consideration to how the courts of our treaty partners have resolved the legal issues before us.

This sudden insularity is striking, since the Court in recent years has canvassed the prevailing law in other nations (at least Western European nations) to determine the meaning of an American Constitution that those nations had no part in framing and that those nations' courts have no role in enforcing. See Atkins v. Virginia, 536 U.S. 304, 316–317, n.21, 122 S.Ct. 2242, 153 L.Ed.2d 335 (2002) (whether the Eighth Amendment prohibits execution of the mentally retarded); Lawrence v. Texas, 539 U.S. 558, 576–577, 123 S.Ct. 2472, 2483, 156 L.Ed.2d 508 (2003) (whether the Fourteenth Amendment prohibits the criminalization of homosexual conduct). One would have thought that foreign courts' interpretations of a treaty that their governments adopted jointly with ours, and that they have an actual role in applying, would be (to put it mildly) all the more relevant.

The Court's new abstemiousness with regard to foreign fare is not without consequence: Within the past year, appellate courts in both England and Australia have rendered decisions squarely at odds with today's holding. Because the Court offers no convincing explanation why these cases should not be followed, I respectfully dissent.

I

The Court holds that an airline's mere inaction can constitute an "accident" within the meaning of the Warsaw Convention. Ante, at 1228–1230. It derives this principle from our definition of "accident" in Saks as "an unexpected or unusual event or happening that is external to the passenger." 470 U.S., at 405, 105 S.Ct. 1338. The Court says this definition encompasses failures to act like the flight attendant's refusal to reseat Hanson in the face of a request for assistance.

That is far from clear. The word "accident" is used in two distinct senses. One refers to something that is unintentional, not "on purpose"—as in, "the hundred typing monkeys' verbatim reproduction of War and Peace was an accident." The other refers to an unusual and unexpected event, intentional or not: One may say he has been involved in a "train accident," for example, whether or not the derailment was intentionally caused. As the Court notes, ante, at 1226–1227, n.6, Saks adopted the latter definition rather than the former. That distinction is crucial because, while there is no doubt that inaction can be an accident in the former sense ("I accidentally left the stove on"), whether it can be so in the latter sense is questionable.

Two of our sister signatories have concluded that it cannot. In Deep Vein Thrombosis and Air Travel Group Litigation, [2003] EWCA Civ. 1005, 2003 WL 21353471 (July 3, 2003), England's Court of Appeal, in an opinion by the Master of the Rolls that relied heavily on Abramson v. Japan Airlines Co., 739 F.2d 130 (C.A.3 1984), and analyzed more than a half-dozen other non-English decisions, held as follows:

> A critical issue in this appeal is whether a failure to act, or an omission, can constitute an accident for the purposes of Article 17. Often a failure to act results in an accident, or forms part of a series of acts and omissions which together constitute an accident. In such circumstances it may not be easy to distinguish between acts and omissions. I cannot see, however, how inaction itself can ever properly be described as an accident. It is not an event; it is a non-event. Inaction is the antithesis of an accident.

[2004] Q.B., at 246, ¶ 25 (Lord Phillips, M.R.).

Six months later, the appellate division of the Supreme Court of Victoria, Australia, in an opinion that likewise gave extensive consideration to American and other foreign decisions, agreed:

> The allegations in substance do no more than state a failure to do something, and this cannot be characterised as an event or happening, whatever be the concomitant background to that failure to warn or advise. That is not to say that a failure to take a specific required step in the course of flying an aircraft, or in picking up or setting down passengers, cannot lead to an event or happening of the requisite unusual or unexpected kind and thus be an accident for the purpose of the article. A failure by a pilot to use some device in the expected and correct manner, such as a failure to let down the landing wheels or a chance omission to adjust the level of pressurisation, may lead, as has been held, to an accident contemplated by Article 17, but I would venture to suggest that it is not the failure to take the step which is properly to be characterised as an accident but rather its immediate and disastrous consequence whether that be the dangerous landing on the belly of the aircraft or an immediate unexpected and dangerous drop in pressurisation.

Qantas Ltd. v. Povey, [2003] VSCA 227, ¶ 17, 2003 WL 23000692 (Dec. 23, 2003) (Ormiston, J. A.).

We can, and should, look to decisions of other signatories when we interpret treaty provisions. Foreign constructions are evidence of the original shared understanding of the contracting parties. Moreover, it is reasonable to impute to the parties an intent that their respective courts strive to interpret the treaty consistently. (The Warsaw Convention's preamble specifically acknowledges "the advantage of regulating in a uniform manner the conditions of ... the liability of the carrier." 49 Stat. 3014.) Finally, even if we disagree, we surely owe the conclusions reached by appellate courts of other signatories the courtesy of respectful consideration.

The Court nonetheless dismisses Deep Vein Thrombosis and Povey in responding to this dissent. Ante, at 1229, n.9. As to the former, it claims (choosing its words carefully) that the "conclusion" it reaches is "not inconsistent" with that case. Ibid. The reader should not think this to be a contention that the Master of the Rolls' opinion might be read to agree with today's holding that inaction can constitute an "accident." To repeat the conclusion of that opinion: "Inaction is the antithesis of an accident." [2004] Q.B., at 247, ¶ 25. What it refers to is the fact that the Master of the Rolls distinguished the Court of Appeals' judgment below (announced in an opinion that assumed inaction was involved, but did not at all discuss the action-inaction distinction) on the ground that action was involved—namely, "insistence that [Hanson] remain seated in the area exposed to smoke." Id., ¶ 50. As I explain below, see Part II, infra, that theory does not quite work because, in fact, the flight attendant did not insist that Hanson remain seated. But we can ignore this detail for the time being. The point is that the English court thought Husain could recover, not because the action-inaction distinction was irrelevant, but because, even though action was indispensable, it had in fact occurred.

The Court charts our course in exactly the opposite direction, spending three pages explaining why the action-inaction distinction is irrelevant. See ante, at 1228–1230. If the Court agrees with the Master of the Rolls that this case involves action, why does it needlessly place us in conflict with the courts of other signatories by deciding the then-irrelevant issue of whether inaction can constitute an accident? It would suffice to hold that our case involves action and end the analysis there. Whether inaction can constitute an accident under the Warsaw Convention is a significant issue on which international consensus is important; whether Husain can recover for her husband's death in this one case is not. As they stand, however, the core holdings of this case and Deep Vein Thrombosis—their rationes decidendi—are not only not "not inconsistent"; they are completely opposite.

Equally unavailing is the reliance, ante, at 1229–1230, on Article 25 of the Warsaw Convention (which lifts liability caps for injury caused by a "default" of the airline equivalent to willful misconduct) and Article 20 (which precludes the airline's due-care defense if it fails to take "all necessary measures" to avoid the injury). The Court's analytical error in invoking these provisions is to assume that the inaction these provisions contemplate is the accident itself. The treaty imposes no such requirement. If a pilot negligently forgets to lower the landing gear, causing the plane to crash and killing all passengers on board, then recovery is presumptively available (because the crash that caused the deaths is an accident), and the due-care defense is inapplicable (because the pilot's negligent omission also caused the deaths), even though the omission is not the accident. Similarly, if a flight attendant fails to prevent the boarding of an individual whom she knows to be a terrorist, and who later shoots a passenger, the damages cap might be lifted even though the accident (the shooting) and the default (the failure to prevent boarding) do not coincide. Without the invented restriction that the Article 20 or 25 default be the accident itself, the Court's argument based on those provisions loses all force.

As for the Court's hypothetical of the crew that refuses to divert after a passenger collapses, ante, at 1229: This would be more persuasive as a reductio ad absurdum if the Eleventh Circuit had not already ruled out Article 17 liability in substantially these very circumstances. See Krys v. Lufthansa German Airlines, 119 F.3d 1515, 1517–1522, 1527–1528 (C.A.11 1997). A legal construction is not fallacious merely because it has harsh results. The Convention denies a remedy, even when outrageous conduct and grievous injury have occurred, unless there has been an "accident." Whatever that term means, it certainly does not equate to "outrageous conduct that causes grievous injury." It is a mistake to assume that the Convention must provide relief whenever traditional tort law would do so. To the contrary, a principal object of the Convention was to promote the growth of the fledgling airline industry by limiting the circumstances under which passengers could sue. See Tseng, 525 U.S., at 170–171, 119 S.Ct. 662. Unless there has been an accident, there is no liability, whether the claim is trivial, cf. Lee v. American Airlines Inc., 355 F.3d 386, 387 (C.A.5 2004) (suit for "loss of a 'refreshing, memorable vacation'"), or cries out for redress.

Were we confronting the issue in the first instance, perhaps the Court could persuade me to its view. But courts in two other countries have already rejected it, and their reasoning is no less compelling than the Court's. I would follow Deep Vein Thrombosis and Povey and hold that mere inaction cannot be an "accident" under Article 17.

II

Respondents argue that, even if the Convention distinguishes action from inaction, this case involves sufficient elements of action to support recovery. That argument is not implausible; as noted earlier, the court in Deep Vein Thrombosis suggested that "[t]he refusal of the attendant to move [Hanson] could be described as insistence that he remain seated in the area exposed to smoke." [2004] Q.B. at 254, ¶ 50. I cannot agree with this analysis, however, because it miscomprehends the facts of this case.

Preliminarily, I must note that this was not the rationale of the District Court. That court consistently referred to the relevant "accident" not as the flight attendant's insistence that Hanson remain seated, but as her "failure" or "refusal" to reseat him. See 116 F.Supp.2d 1121, 1131–1135 (N.D.Cal.2000). Its findings of fact were infected by its erroneous legal assumption that Article 17 makes no distinction between action and inaction. The only question is whether we can nonetheless affirm on the ground that, since there was action in any event, this error was harmless.

It was not. True, in response to the first request, the flight attendant insisted that Husain and her husband "'have a seat.'" Id., at 1125. This insistence might still have been implicit in her response to the second request. But these responses were both given while the plane was still on the ground, preparing to take off. The flight attendant's response to Husain's third request—made once the plane was in the air and other passengers had started smoking—was quite different. She did not insist that Husain and her husband remain seated; on the contrary, she invited them to walk around the cabin in search of someone willing to switch.

That the flight attendant explicitly refused Husain's pleas for help after the third request, rather than simply ignoring them, does not transform her inaction into action. The refusal acknowledged her inaction, but it was the inaction, not the acknowledgment, that caused Hanson's death. Unlike the previous responses, the third was a mere refusal to assist, and so cannot be the basis for liability under Article 17.

The District Court's failure to make the distinction between the flight attendant's pretakeoff responses and her in-flight response undermines its decision in two respects. First, the court's findings as to airline and industry policy did not distinguish between reseating a passenger while in flight and reseating a passenger while still on the ground preparing to take off. In fact, some of the evidence on this point specifically related only to in-flight behavior. See id., at 1132 (testimony of a chief cabin attendant that the flight attendant should have reseated Hanson immediately after Husain's third request); ibid. (testimony of a company official that its policy is to move passengers "who become ill during flights"). To establish that it is company policy to reseat an asthmatic does not establish that it is company policy to do so before takeoff, while the attendants are busy securing the plane for departure and before anyone has started smoking. In other words, there may have been nothing unusual about the initial insistence that Hanson stay seated, and for that reason no "accident." We do not know the policy in this more specific regard. The District Court made no findings because it applied an erroneous legal standard that did not require it to distinguish among the three requests.

But even if the flight attendant's insistence that Hanson remain seated before takeoff was unusual or unexpected, and hence an accident, it was not a compensable cause of Hanson's death. It was perhaps a but for cause (had the flight attendant allowed him to move before takeoff, he might have lived, just as he might have lived if he had taken a different flight); but it was not a proximate cause, which is surely a predicate for recovery. Any early insistence that Hanson remain seated became moot once the attendant later told Husain and her husband they were free to move about.

There is, however, one complication, which I think requires us to remand this case to the District Court: Although the flight attendant, once the plane was aloft, invited Husain to find another passenger willing to switch seats, she did not invite Husain to find an empty seat, but to the contrary affirmatively represented that the plane was full. If such a misrepresentation is unusual and unexpected; and (the more difficult question) if it can reasonably be said that it caused Hanson's death—i.e., that Husain would have searched for and found an empty seat, although unwilling to ask another passenger to move—then a cause of action might lie. I would remand so that the District Court could consider in the first instance whether the flight attendant's misrepresentation about the plane's being full, independent of any failure to reseat, was an accident that caused Hanson's death.

Tragic though Dr. Hanson's death may have been, it does not justify the Court's putting us in needless conflict with other signatories to the Warsaw Convention. I respectfully dissent.

EHRLICH v. AMERICAN AIRLINES, INC.

360 F.3d 366 (2d Cir. 2004)

MESKILL, Circuit Judge.

Plaintiffs-appellants Gary and Maryanne Ehrlich (the Ehrlichs) experienced an ordeal that few airline passengers have the misfortune to endure. While traveling from Baltimore, Maryland to John F. Kennedy International Airport (JFK) to catch a connecting flight to London, the Ehrlichs' plane suffered an abnormal landing. On approaching JFK, their aircraft overshot the runway and was abruptly stopped by an arrestor bed before the plane would otherwise have plunged into the waters of nearby Thurston Bay.

According to the Ehrlichs, both appellants sustained physical and mental injuries during the course of that incident. They subsequently commenced an action to recover damages for those injuries pursuant to the international treaty commonly known as the Warsaw Convention. See Convention for the Unification of Certain Rules Relating to International Transportation by Air, Oct. 12, 1929, 49 Stat. 3000, 3014, T.S. No. 876 (entered into force in the United States in 1934) (Warsaw Convention), reprinted in 49 U.S.C. §40105 note.

Defendants-appellees American Airlines, Inc. (American Airlines), American Eagle Airlines, Inc. (American Eagle), and Simmons Airlines, Inc. (Simmons Airlines) (collectively the airline defendants) moved for partial summary judgment. The United States District Court for the Eastern District of New York, Amon, J., granted their motion on the ground that they could not be held liable under the Warsaw Convention for mental injuries that were not caused by physical injuries. See Ehrlich v. American Airlines, 2002 U.S. Dist. LEXIS 21419, at *10–*11 (E.D.N.Y. June 21, 2002).

This appeal asks us to resolve whether passengers can hold carriers liable in accordance with the Warsaw Convention for mental injuries that accompany, but are not caused by, bodily injuries. For the reasons that follow, we hold that they may not and affirm the district court's grant of partial summary judgment.

BACKGROUND

On May 8, 1999, Gary and Maryanne Ehrlich boarded American Eagle Flight No. 4925 in Baltimore, Maryland. They intended to travel to JFK, where they were scheduled to connect to an American Airlines flight to London. When their flight reached JFK, the plane approached the airport at a high rate of speed, overshot its designated runway, and was abruptly stopped from potentially plunging into Thurston Bay by an arrestor bed. The passengers subsequently evacuated that aircraft by jumping approximately six to eight feet from its doorway.

The arrestor bed at JFK is an Engineered Materials Arresting System (EMAS). See The Port Authority of New York and New Jersey, Airport Information & Facts, at 4, at http://www.panynj.gov/aviation/jfk_fact_ sheet.pdf (last visited Mar. 4, 2004) (describing, inter alia, JFK's arrestor bed). These systems are designed to stop an aircraft that overruns the end of a runway "by exerting predictable deceleration forces on its landing gear as the EMAS material crushes." Federal Aviation Administration, Advisory Circular No. 150/5220-22, Engineered Materials Arresting Systems (EMAS) for Aircraft Overruns, at ¶ 6(a) (Aug. 21, 1998), available at http://www.faa.gov/arp/pdf/5220-22.pdf. In scientific shorthand, an EMAS is made of water, foam, and cement, and deforms under the weight of an aircraft tire; as the tire crushes the material, the drag forces decelerate the aircraft, bringing it to a stop.

The Ehrlichs contend that they suffered bodily injuries during the course of both the abnormal landing and the ensuing evacuation. Gary Ehrlich allegedly sustained knee injuries, while Maryanne Ehrlich purportedly sustained injuries to, inter alia, her neck, back, shoulder, hips, and right knee. Since the abnormal landing, Maryanne Ehrlich has also allegedly developed hypertension and a heart problem.

In addition to these bodily injuries, the Ehrlichs further contend that they sustained mental injuries. According to the evidence presented to the district court, both Gary and Maryanne Ehrlich suffered from a fear of flying after the accident. Moreover, Gary Ehrlich apparently experienced nightmares after which he awoke in the middle of the night recalling the abnormal landing and evacuation. Similarly, Maryanne Ehrlich reports that she periodically has trouble sleeping as a result of the accident.

On September 27, 1999, the Ehrlichs commenced the instant action against American Airlines, American Eagle, and Simmons Airlines in the United States District Court for the Eastern District of New York, pursuant to the Warsaw Convention, in an effort to recover damages for their aforementioned physical and psychological injuries. After deposing the Ehrlichs, the airline defendants moved for partial summary judgment. They asked the district court to dismiss the Ehrlichs' claims for mental injuries on two grounds. First, the airline defendants argued that the Ehrlichs had failed to prove that they had sustained such injuries. Second, the airline defendants contended that, even if the Ehrlichs had suffered those injuries, the damages in question did not flow from their bodily injuries and that carriers were liable under the Warsaw Convention only for psychological injuries that were caused by bodily injuries.

The Ehrlichs vigorously opposed that motion. They argued that they had, in fact, sustained mental injuries. They also took the position that carriers could be held liable under the Warsaw Convention as long as a mental injury accompanied a physical injury, regardless of whether the two distinct types of injuries shared a causal relationship. Finally, although they never filed a formal cross-motion for partial summary judgment with respect to the matter, the Ehrlichs asked the court to grant them partial summary judgment on the issue of carrier liability. In essence, the Ehrlichs argued that, under the International Air Transport Association Intercarrier Agreement on Passenger Liability (Intercarrier Agreement), the airline defendants were strictly liable for damages up to the equivalent of $140,000 and that the airlines bore the burden of proving that they had taken all necessary measures to avoid damages sustained in excess of that sum.

The district court heard oral argument on May 31, 2001, at which time the court granted the Ehrlichs' so-called "cross-motion" for partial summary judgment on the issue of liability under the Intercarrier Agreement. Ehrlich, 2002 U.S. Dist. LEXIS 21419, at *3. However, the court initially reserved decision on the airline defendants' motion for partial summary judgment. In June 2002, after further considering the issue, the district court granted partial summary judgment in favor of the airline defendants. See id. at *1.

On reviewing the applicable case law, the court determined that, "[u]nder the Warsaw Convention, a plaintiff may only recover for emotional damages caused by physical injuries." Id. at *10. This proved to be a critical conclusion, as the court found that the Ehrlichs had offered no evidence demonstrating a causal connection between their mental and physical injuries. Id. at *10–*11. Because the district court concluded that the Ehrlichs had "not raised a genuine issue of fact regarding a causal connection between their alleged bodily injuries and their mental suffering," the court granted the airline defendants' motion for partial summary judgment, holding that the Ehrlichs could "not recover for their emotional trauma resulting solely from the aberrant landing and evacuation." Id. at *11.

Shortly thereafter, the Ehrlichs sought to certify the issue for an interlocutory appeal pursuant to 28 U.S.C. § 1292(b). The district court denied their motion and set a trial date for the remaining Warsaw Convention issues pertaining to liability for bodily injuries. However, the parties managed to resolve those issues before trial. On October 31, 2002, the Ehrlichs stipulated to the discontinuance of their action with prejudice against American Airlines and Simmons Airlines. At the same time, American Eagle filed an Offer of Judgment in which it presented the Ehrlichs with the opportunity to take a judgment in the amount of $100,000 against that airline. Several days later, the Ehrlichs accepted American Eagle's offer on the condition that their acceptance was "without prejudice to plaintiffs' right to appeal from" the order of partial summary judgment.

The district court issued a Judgment that conformed to both American Eagle's offer and the Ehrlichs' conditional acceptance thereof. The court entered a judgment in the amount of $100,000 against American Eagle in complete satisfaction of the Ehrlichs' claims for bodily injury. The court also entered a judgment in favor of the airline defendants pursuant to its earlier order granting their motion for partial summary judgment with respect to the Ehrlichs' claims for mental injuries; the judgment entered by the district court was expressly without prejudice to the Ehrlichs' right to appeal from that partial summary judgment decision. This timely appeal followed.

DISCUSSION

The Warsaw Convention System

The Ehrlichs seek to hold American Eagle liable for their mental injuries pursuant to the Warsaw Convention. The Ehrlichs contend that under Article 17, passengers may hold carriers liable for their mental injuries whenever they sustain physical injuries regardless of whether their psychological damages were caused by bodily injuries. However, these arguments implicate not only the Warsaw Convention itself but also the most recent addition to its derivative liability regime, namely the treaty commonly referred to as the Montreal Convention, see Convention for the Unification of Certain

Rules for International Carriage by Air, May 28, 1999 (entered into force on Nov. 4, 2003) (Montreal Convention), reprinted in S. Treaty Doc. No. 106-45, 1999 WL 33292734 (2000), and, to a more significant extent, the negotiations that led to the adoption of that treaty.

The Montreal Convention is the product of an effort by the International Civil Aviation Organization, a specialized agency of the United Nations, to reform the Warsaw Convention so as to "harmonize the hodgepodge of supplementary amendments and intercarrier agreements" of which the Warsaw Convention system of liability consists. Carl E. Fumarola, Note, Stratospheric Recovery: Recent And Forthcoming Changes In International Air Disaster Law And Its Effect On Air Terrorism Recovery, 36 Suffolk U.L.Rev. 821, 835 (2003). In May 1999, the agency convened an international conference in Montreal, Canada; nations gathered at that conference to negotiate and adopt a new treaty that would replace the Warsaw Convention. See Blanca I. Rodriguez, Recent Developments In Aviation Liability Law, 66 J. Air L. & Com. 21, 25–26 (2000). More than 500 delegates, representing 121 states, attended the conference in Montreal from May 10, 1999, until May 28, 1999. See 1 Charles F. Krause & Kent C. Krause, Aviation Tort And Regulatory Law §§ 11:13, 11:14, at 11-51 to 11-52 (2d ed.2002). On the last day of the conference, the delegates approved a new Convention for the Unification of Certain Rules for International Carriage by Air, which has come to be known as the Montreal Convention. See Rodriguez, supra, at 26. Fifty-two countries, including the United States, immediately signed the treaty. See Letter of Submittal of Strobe Talbott (June 23, 2000) (Talbott Letter), reprinted in S. Treaty Doc. No. 106-45, 1999 WL 33292734.

The Montreal Convention is not an amendment to the Warsaw Convention. See Schopenhauer v. Compagnie Nationale Air France, 255 F.Supp.2d 81, 87 (E.D.N.Y. 2003); see also Rodriguez, supra, at 26. Rather, the Montreal Convention is an entirely new treaty that unifies and replaces the system of liability that derives from the Warsaw Convention. See Schopenhauer, 255 F.Supp.2d at 87; see also J.C. Batra, Modernization Of The Warsaw System—Montreal 1999, 65 J. Air. L. & Com. 429, 433 (2000) ("The [Montreal Convention] ... is a new, comprehensive international treaty of private international air law that replaces the seventy year old Warsaw Convention."); Talbott Letter, supra, at 1999 WL 33292734 ("Upon entry into force, the [Montreal] Convention will take precedence over the Warsaw Convention and any of its amendments and related instruments, and as a practical matter will supersede the private inter-carrier agreements, when the State or States relevant in a particular accident are party to the new Convention.").

Whereas the "primary aim of the contracting parties to the [Warsaw] Convention" was to limit "the liability of air carriers in order to foster the growth of the ... commercial aviation industry," the contracting parties to the Montreal Convention expressly approved that treaty because, among other reasons, they recognized "the importance of ensuring protection of the interests of consumers in international carriage by air and the need for equitable compensation based on the principle of restitution." Montreal Convention, pmbl. The Senate has similarly recognized that "[t]he new Montreal Convention represents the culmination of decades of efforts by the United States and other countries to establish a regime providing increased protection for international air travelers and shippers." S. Exec. Rep. No. 108-8, at 2 (2003). Hence, commentators have described the Montreal Convention as a treaty that favors passengers rather than airlines. See, e.g., Thomas J. Whalen, The New Warsaw Convention: The Montreal Convention, 25 Air & Space L. 12, 14 (2000) ("The Montreal Convention is no longer a Convention for airlines. It is a Convention for consumers/passengers."); Batra, supra, at 443 ("the Montreal Convention recognizes the importance of ensuring protection of the interests of consumers in international air carriage").

In the proceedings below, the Ehrlichs sought to support their interpretation of Article 17 by relying, in no small measure, on the views expressed by various delegates at the International Conference on Air Law held in Montreal, Canada (Montreal Conference) in May 1999; the delegates at the conference negotiated and signed the Montreal Convention. However, although President Clinton submitted the Montreal Convention to the Senate for ratification on September 6, 2000, see President's Message to the Senate Transmitting the Convention for the Unification of Certain Rules for International Carriage by Air with Documentation, 36 Weekly Comp. Pres. Doc.2013 (Sept. 11, 2000), the district court refused to give authoritative weight to the statements of the Montreal Conference delegates because the Senate had not ratified the Montreal Convention when the court granted partial summary judgment in favor of the airline defendants. See Ehrlich, 2002 U.S. Dist. LEXIS 21419, at *6 n.2. As the district court correctly acknowledged, "[a]n unratified treaty has no force until ratified by a two-thirds vote of the Senate." Id. (citing S.E.C. v. Int'l Swiss Inv. Corp., 895 F.2d 1272, 1275 (9th Cir.1990)). Cf. Flores v. Southern Peru Copper Corp., 343 F.3d 140, 162 (2d Cir.2003) ("A State only becomes bound by—that is, becomes a party to—a treaty when it ratifies the treaty.").

After the district court arrived at its decision, the legal landscape on which the Warsaw Convention once stood changed dramatically. Shortly before the parties in this appeal appeared for oral argument in August 2003, the Senate ratified the Montreal Convention on July 31, 2003. See 149 Cong. Rec. S10,870 (daily ed. July 31, 2003).

The Montreal Convention was designed to "enter into force on the sixtieth day following the date of deposit of the thirtieth instrument of ratification" with the International Civil Aviation Organization (ICAO). Montreal Convention, arts. 53(5), (6). On September 5, 2003, after we heard oral argument in this appeal, the United States deposited the applicable instrument of ratification. See Press Statement, United States Department of State, Ratification of the 1999 Montreal Convention (Sept. 5, 2003), available at http://www.state.gov/r/pa/prs/ps/2003/23851pf.htm; Press Release, United States Department of Transportation, United States Ratifies 1999 Montreal Convention, Putting Treaty Into Effect (Sept. 5, 2003), available at http://www.dot.gov/affairs/dot10303.htm.

As the thirtieth nation to ratify the treaty and to deposit an instrument of ratification with the ICAO, the United States triggered the conditions set by Article 53 of the Montreal Convention. See Press Release, International Civil Aviation Organization, Montreal Convention of 1999 on Compensation for Accident Victims Set to Enter Into Force (Sept. 5, 2003), available at http://www.icao.int/icao/en/nr/2003/pio200314.htm. In accordance with Article 53(6), the Montreal Convention therefore entered into force on November 4, 2003. See Media Note, United States Department of State, Entry Into Force of the 1999 Montreal Convention (Nov. 4, 2003), available at http://www.state.gov/r/pa/prs/ps/2003/25920.htm; see also International Civil Aviation Organization, Treaty Collection, at http://www.icao.int/icao/en/leb/mt199.htm (last visited Mar. 4, 2004) (explaining that the Montreal Convention entered into force on Nov. 4, 2003).

In light of these events, we must consider what role, if any, the Montreal Convention and its negotiating history should play in this appeal. Despite its ratification and entry into force, we conclude that the Montreal Convention does not govern the appeal at bar and that we need not give the views expressed by various delegates at the Montreal Conference, especially to the extent that these views relate solely to the Montreal Convention itself, dispositive weight.

Ordinarily, a particular treaty does not govern conduct that took place before the treaty entered into force. See Chubb & Son v. Asiana Airlines, 214 F.3d 301, 307 n.4 (2d Cir.2000) (where the actions giving rise to a lawsuit took place in 1995, Montreal Protocol No. 4 did not affect the case despite the Senate's subsequent ratification of the protocol on September 28, 1998); see also Vienna Convention on the Law of Treaties, May 23, 1969, art. 28, 1155 U.N.T.S. 331, 339 (Vienna Convention) ("Unless a different intention appears from the treaty or is otherwise established, its provisions do not bind a party in relation to any act or fact which took place or any situation which ceased to exist before the date of the entry into force of the treaty with respect to that party."); Restatement (Third) of the Foreign Relations Law of the United States §322(1) (1987) (same). In this instance, the accident that gave rise to the Ehrlichs' lawsuit took place on May 8, 1999, and they commenced their action against the airline defendants on September 27, 1999. These events occurred several years before the Senate ratified the Montreal Convention and before that treaty entered into force. As such, neither the Montreal Convention nor the intentions of its drafters govern this appeal.

Article 17 of The Warsaw Convention

The Ehrlichs contend that, under Article 17 of the Warsaw Convention, air carriers are liable for mental injuries that accompany, but are not caused by, bodily injuries. The district court disagreed with that proposition and held that the Ehrlichs could "only recover for emotional damages caused by physical injuries." Ehrlich, 2002 U.S. Dist. LEXIS 21419, at *10.

To determine whether the district court properly construed the reach of the Warsaw Convention, we must interpret that treaty and ascertain the meaning of Article 17. The English translation of Article 17, as employed by the Senate when it ratified the Warsaw Convention in 1934, provides that:

> The carrier shall be liable for damage sustained in the event of the death or wounding of a passenger or any other bodily injury suffered by a passenger, if the accident which caused the damage so sustained took place on board the aircraft or in the course of any of the operations of embarking or disembarking.

49 Stat. at 3018. In Eastern Airlines v. Floyd, 499 U.S. 530, 552–53, 111 S.Ct. 1489, 113 L.Ed.2d 569 (1991), the Supreme Court analyzed the meaning of this provision and held that carriers could not be held liable under Article 17 for mental injuries that did not accompany bodily injuries. However, the Court "express[ed] no view as to whether passengers [could] recover for mental injuries that [were] accompanied by physical injuries." Id. at 552, 111 S.Ct. 1489.

The "mainstream view" adhered to by courts that have addressed the scope of Article 17 and considered the issue before us "is that recovery for mental injuries is permitted only to the extent the [emotional] distress is caused by the physical injuries sustained." In re Air Crash at Little Rock, Arkansas, on June 1, 1999 (Lloyd v. American Airlines), 291 F.3d 503, 509 (8th Cir.) (Lloyd), cert. denied, 537 U.S. 974, 123 S.Ct. 435, 154 L.Ed.2d 331 (2002); see also Ligeti v. British Airways PLC, 2001 WL 1356238, at *4 (S.D.N.Y. Nov. 5, 2001); Alvarez v. American Airlines, 1999 WL 691922, at *3–*5 (S.D.N.Y. Sept. 7, 1999); Longo v. Air France, 1996 WL 866124, at *2 (S.D.N.Y. July 25, 1996); Wencelius v. Air France, 1996 WL 866122, at *1 (C.D.Cal. Feb. 29, 1996); Jack v. Trans World Airlines, 854 F.Supp. 654, 663–68 (N.D.Cal.1994); In re Inflight Explosion on Trans World Airlines Aircraft Approaching Athens, Greece on April 2, 1986, 778 F.Supp. 625, 637 (E.D.N.Y.1991) (Ospina), rev'd sub nom. on other grounds Ospina v. Trans World Airlines, 975 F.2d 35 (2d Cir.1992); Burnett v. Trans World Airlines, 368 F.Supp. 1152, 1155–58 (D.N.M.1973). Only two district courts have adopted a contrary interpretation of Article 17. See In re Air Crash at Little Rock, Arkansas on June 1, 1999, 118 F.Supp.2d 916, 918–21 (E.D.Ark.2000) (Little Rock), rev'd, Lloyd, 291 F.3d at 509–11; In re Aircrash Disaster Near Roselawn, Indiana on October 31, 1994, 954 F.Supp. 175, 179 (N.D.Ill.1997) (Roselawn).

Most of the foregoing cases, like the district court below, did not consider the text of Article 17 to any significant degree. "It seems elementary to us," however, "that the language employed in Article 17 must be the logical starting point" for any effort to interpret the Warsaw Convention. Day v. Trans World Airlines, 528 F.2d 31, 33 (2d Cir.1975).

[The court next considers the meaning of the French text of Article 17, as well as the case law of various signatory nations.]

[Where] the plain text [of a treaty] is ambiguous, we [may] look to other sources, such as the post[-]ratification understanding of the contracting parties, to elucidate the treaty's meaning. In this respect, the opinions of sister signatories at international conferences may sometimes prove to be helpful. The Ehrlichs, relying extensively on the statements expressed by various delegates at the Montreal Conference, contend that the opinions of sister Warsaw Convention signatories as well as those of our Executive Branch support their interpretation of Article 17. However, [t]he official minutes of the Montreal [Conference] tell a less conclusive story.

On May 28, 1999, representatives from over fifty countries who attended the Montreal Conference in May 1999 approved the Montreal Convention. See Blanca I. Rodriguez, Recent Developments In Aviation Liability Law, 66 J. Air L. & Com. 21, 25–26 (2000). That treaty, like its Warsaw predecessor, governs the international transportation of persons, baggage, and goods by air. See Montreal Convention, art. 1(1). Article 17(1) of the Montreal Convention is similar to Article 17 of the Warsaw Convention. It provides that a "carrier is liable for damage sustained in case of death or bodily injury of a passenger upon condition only that the accident which caused the death or injury took place on board the aircraft or in the course of any of the operations of embarking or disembarking." Montreal Convention, art. 17(1).

When the delegates at the Montreal Conference discussed the scope of that provision before they approved the new Convention, they specifically considered extending a carrier's liability to mental injuries. However, their discussions did not lead to a general consensus on that subject; rather, they evidence a discordant chorus of voices.

On the third day of the Montreal Conference, the delegates from Sweden and Norway proposed that the words "or mental" be introduced in the first sentence of the applicable liability provision in the new Convention. See 1 International Civil Aviation Organization, Minutes, The International Conference On Air Law, Montreal, 10–28 May 1999, at 67 (2001) (Montreal Conference Minutes). At that stage of the Conference, a carrier's liability for injuries to passengers was set forth in Article 16 of the draft Convention under discussion. See id. If the Swedish-Norwegian proposal had been adopted, Article 16 would have read as follows: "The carrier is liable for damage sustained in the case of death or bodily or mental injury of a passenger." Id. As Sweden's delegate explained, the proposal sought to secure for passengers "the right to compensation for mental injuries that they had suffered in case of an accident. This right [would have] appl[ied] whether or not the passenger also suffered a bodily injury." Id.

The Conference delegates responded to that proposal with a wide array of positions and counter-proposals, many of which contradicted one another. Certain nations, such as Chile, Denmark, the United Kingdom, the Dominican Republic, Panama, Namibia, Colombia, Switzerland, Finland, and Spain supported the Swedish-Norwegian proposal. See id. at 67–68, 72–74. Other nations, such as Germany, France, and New Zealand, supported the expansive principle of liability on which the Swedish-Norwegian proposal rested, but disagreed about the exact words that could best effectuate it. See id. at 68, 72.

Not all nations supported the Swedish-Norwegian proposal and its expansive reach. Certain nations, such as Saudi Arabia, Ethiopia, Austria, Mauritius, Algeria, Madagascar, and India, expressed reservations about or altogether opposed the inclusion of language in the new Convention that would have held carriers liable for "mental" injuries. See id. at 69, 70–72. Other nations, such as China, Cameroon, Egypt, Italy, Senegal, and Yemen, agreed that the liability provision in the new Convention should be extended to cover mental injuries, but sought to limit the scope of that liability; they suggested that, to balance the interests of the carrier and the passenger, the new Convention should limit carrier liability for mental injuries to situations in which they resulted directly from bodily injuries. See id. at 70–73. In contrast, Singapore's delegate proposed that Article 16 should only retain the words "bodily injury," since that would "allow [recovery] for mental injury in cases where the mental injury claim, accompanied by physical injury, manifested in physical injury." Id. at 70. The delegate from the United Arab Emirates adopted a somewhat similar position; although that delegate did not support a liability provision that included the words "mental injury," the delegate was agreeable to their inclusion as a compromise as long as they were "qualified" such that they referred solely "to a mental injury that resulted in a bodily injury that was caused by the negligence or misconduct of the carrier." Id. at 72.

The divisions among the delegates that became apparent on the third day of the Montreal Conference in response to the Swedish-Norwegian proposal led the President of those proceedings, Dr. Kenneth Rattray (Dr. Rattray), to determine that further consultations on the subject were necessary. Id. at 74. Those discussions were held among members of a working group known as the "Friends of the Chairman" (alternatively referred to as the Friends), id., which consisted of a "manageable" body of twenty-eight nations, including the United States, "who were given the task of working" on certain "central issues." 1 Charles F. Krause & Kent C. Krause, Aviation Tort And Regulatory Law § 11:14, at 11–52 (2d ed.2002). The Friends met under the direction of Dr. Rattray, who served not only as the President of the Montreal Conference but also as the Chairman of that working group. See id.; see also Montreal Conference Minutes, supra, at 74.

Although the discussions held by the Friends evidence a greater degree of consensus than existed on the third day of the Conference, we bear in mind that the views expressed by such Friends were the opinions of a select and limited group of delegates whose views did not necessarily correspond to those of many other delegates who did not sit on that working group. For example, Friends such as Chile, the United Kingdom, New Zealand, Sweden, and Switzerland sought to include language in the new Convention that would have allowed passengers to recover for mental injuries even in the absence of a physical injury. See Montreal Conference Minutes, supra, at 112–14. However, that position could not easily be reconciled with the contrary views expressed earlier by various delegates in response to the Swedish-Norwegian proposal; such delegates had either resisted including a provision in the new Convention that would have allowed passengers to recover for mental injuries or sought to limit that liability to mental injuries that directly resulted from a physical injury. Indeed, after they had been briefed about the Friends' discussions, several Asian nations that were not members of the Friends of the Chairman working group continued to press for a liability provision that limited recovery for mental injuries to those "arising from" a bodily injury. See id. at 141.

Moreover, although not all of the Friends' differences were necessarily given a voice during specific meetings of the Friends of the Chairman working group, the Friends themselves were divided on the issue of liability. The Friends did not unanimously support the aforementioned expansive language initially proposed by Chile at the first session of that group. During that meeting, Egypt and Vietnam tried to limit the scope of Article 16 of the draft Convention under discussion to liability for mental injuries "associated" with bodily injuries. See id. at 112–15. Outside of the meetings of the working group, Friends such as China and India pressed for a narrower liability provision than that proposed by Chile. See id. at 141–42. When the discussions of the Friends of the Chairman working group were first described to the other general delegates of the Conference, China associated itself with the aforementioned views expressed by certain Asian nations and proposed that passengers should be allowed to recover for mental injuries that "resulted from" bodily injuries. See id. at 141. Similarly, Egypt once again suggested that the new Convention should limit liability for mental injuries by allowing passengers to recover for such injuries where they were "associated with and resulted from ... bodily injur[ies]." See id. The Indian delegate also expressed similar sentiments. He argued that "a situation did not exist [as of yet] to introduce the new concept of mental injury independent of bodily injury, as there was no way it could be measured or quantified." Id. at 142. According to the Indian delegate, "the only injury that could be recognized at present was bodily injury, and mental injury would necessarily have to be an outcome of that bodily injury." Id. Ultimately, delegates who served on the Friends of the Chairman working group continued to differ over the proper scope of the liability provision. See id. at 175–76.

This is not an exhaustive list of the many positions advanced by various delegates over the course of the Montreal Conference as to the issue of liability for mental injuries. However, these positions represent a sampling of the diverse, and often divergent, views expressed by the many delegates who attended the Conference, whether they were Friends of the Chairman or general delegates who sat together as a Commission of the Whole to negotiate the new Convention. By the time certain delegates signed the new Convention on May 28, 1999, [e]very side of this issue [had] found a voice at the Montreal [C]onference.

In essence, despite the Ehrlichs' suggestions to the contrary, the history of the negotiations that produced the Montreal Convention demonstrate that the Montreal Conference delegates did not share a common understanding when it came to the subject of liability for mental injuries. Indeed, we note that the Montreal Conference delegates eventually accommodated the different positions on this subject by adopting a so-called "consensus package" as part of which they did little more than adhere to "the concept of death or bodily injury ... contained in the Warsaw Convention." See Montreal Conference Minutes, supra, at 201. They did so by ultimately approving a liability provision in the new Montreal Convention that provides, much like Article 17 of the Warsaw Convention, that a "carrier is liable for damage sustained in case of death or bodily injury." Montreal Convention, art. 17(1).

Summary

We have reviewed, inter alia, the text of the Warsaw Convention, French law, the opinions (judicial and otherwise) of our sister Convention signatories, and the meaning attributed to Article 17 of the Convention [during the negotiations of its successor]. Our exhaustive examination of these sources leads us to conclude that a carrier may be held liable under Article 17 for mental injuries only if they are caused by bodily injuries.

[The remainder of the court's opinion is omitted.]

IN RE AIR CRASH DISASTER NEAR PEGGY'S COVE, NOVA SCOTIA ON SEPTEMBER 2, 1998

210 F. Supp. 2d 570 (E.D. Pa. 2002)

GILES, Chief Judge.

I. INTRODUCTION

Responsible for conducting consolidated pretrial proceedings in the Multidistrict Litigation arising from the crash of Swissair Flight No. 111 near Peggy's Cove, Nova Scotia, on September 2, 1998, the court now considers the motion of defendants The Boeing Co. ("Boeing") and McDonnell Douglas Corporation ("McDonnell Douglas"), joined by all other defendants, to dismiss all claims for punitive damages as precluded by the Death on the High Seas by Wrongful Act, as amended, 46 U.S.C. app. §§761–767 ("DOHSA"). They argue that DOHSA is the exclusive avenue open to plaintiffs for any monetary recovery. This is one of two motions seeking to dismiss the claims for punitive damages. The other motion, joined by defendants Swissair, SR Technics AG, SAir-group, and Delta Airlines, Inc., seeks dismissal of all claims for punitive damages on the ground that such claims are precluded by the Warsaw Convention.

For the reasons that follow, defendants' motion is granted and judgment is entered in favor of the defendants as to all claims for punitive damages.

II. BACKGROUND

Swissair Flight No. 111, a McDonnell-Douglas MD-11 aircraft, departed from New York City's John F. Kennedy Airport en route to Geneva, Switzerland. Although the precise location of the September 2, 1998 crash is undetermined at this time, defendants stipulate for the purposes of this motion that the accident site is within the 12-mile territorial waters currently claimed by the Canadian federal government. Two-hundred fifteen passengers, primarily American, Canadian, Swiss, and French domiciliaries, and fourteen crew members were killed in the crash.

Lawsuits were filed on behalf of more than 140 decedent passengers on that flight in federal courts throughout the United States. The defendants include: Swissair, which controlled and operated the international flight; Delta, which ticketed many of the American passengers, pursuant to an operating agreement between the airlines; SAir-Group, the parent holding company for Swissair; McDonnell Douglas, which manufactured the airplane; and Boeing, which owns McDonnell Douglas and acts as its successor-in-interest. In addition, the plaintiffs allege that a primary cause of the crash was a fire sparked by a malfunction in the In-Flight Entertainment ("IFEN") System. This system provided passengers with gaming, shopping, individual movies, video programming, and other services. Plaintiffs also have sued Interactive Flight Technologies, Ltd.

("IFT"), which developed, designed, built components for, and marketed the IFEN system and entered into a contract with Swissair to equip the Swissair fleet with the system; Hollingsead International ("HI"), which performed the airplane/IFEN integration engineering and installation pursuant to a contract with IFT; Santa Barbara Aerospace ("SBA"), which, pursuant to a subcontract with HI, obtained the necessary certification from the Federal Aviation Administration ("FAA") for the installation of the IFEN system and reviewed test results for environmental testing of IFEN system components; and SR Technics, which, pursuant to a contract with Swissair, provided facilities, support, and oversight for the installation of the IFEN system, monitored the quality of the workmanship of the systems installed, and certified the aircraft as airworthy following installation of the IFEN system and prior to the return of the plane to service. Plaintiffs have also sued DuPont, the manufacturer of the metallized mylar used in the aircraft's insulation blankets, which, they theorize, permitted the rapid spread of the fire.

The federal court cases were transferred to this court for coordinated and consolidated pretrial proceedings pursuant to 28 U.S.C. § 1407(a) since the cases involve common questions of fact. Pursuant to a joint agreement, Boeing and Swissair conceded liability for purposes of compensatory damages only and agreed to pay to any plaintiff full compensatory damages available under any law, foreign or domestic, that was determined applicable to a particular decedent in a particular case, provided the claim was limited to compensatory damages.

Cross-claims for contribution and indemnification were filed by and among the various defendants. Once the plaintiffs' claims for damages have been tried or settled, the defendants will resolve those issues among themselves or through trial.

Because the Canadian authorities are still investigating the crash and have not issued a final report of their findings, and to afford all parties a fair opportunity to attempt to settle claims amicably, the court stayed liability discovery pending resolution of the question whether DOHSA is the exclusive avenue for assertion of claims against defendants in actions brought in the courts of the United States. By its terms, DOHSA precludes recovery of punitive damages.

Defendants argue that DOHSA applies because the crash occurred on the high seas more than 12 nautical miles from United States shores and that it must be applied, at least, as to all U.S. domiciliary decedents.

Plaintiffs respond that DOHSA cannot apply because the crash occurred in Canadian territorial waters which, they contend, are not included in the internationally accepted scope of the term "high seas." They offer that for accidents occurring in foreign territorial waters general maritime law, in conjunction with state law, provides sufficient guidance as to appropriate legal remedies.

III. DISCUSSION

As amended in 2000, DOHSA provides, in pertinent part:

> In the case of a commercial aviation accident, whenever the death of a person shall be caused by wrongful act, neglect, or default occurring on the high seas 12 nautical miles or closer to the shore of any State, or the District of Columbia, or the Territories or dependencies of the United States, this chapter shall not apply and the rules applicable under Federal, State, and other appropriate law shall apply.

46 U.S.C. app. § 761(b).

The Amendment created a new cause of action for nonpecuniary damages:

> If the death resulted from a commercial aviation accident occurring on the high seas beyond 12 nautical miles from the shore of any State, or the District of Columbia, or the Territories or dependencies of the United States, additional compensation for nonpecuniary damages for wrongful death of a decedent is recoverable. Punitive damages are not recoverable.

46 U.S.C. app. §762(b)(1).

Nonpecuniary damages are defined as damages for loss of care, comfort, and companionship. 46 U.S.C. app. §762(b)(2).

The Amendment's application was retroactive and applicable to any death occurring after July 16, 1996 (the day before the [crash of] TWA Flight 800, see In re: Air Crash Off Long Island, New York, on July 17, 1996, 209 F.3d 200 (2d Cir.2000)), Pub.L. 106-181, Title IV, §404(c) (Apr. 5, 2000). All parties agree that if DOHSA is applicable, then it applies as amended.

On its face, Amended DOHSA seems capable of supporting both plaintiffs' and defendants' arguments. If the term "high seas" is seen as waters to which no sovereign could lay a claim, then the plaintiffs' interpretation would indeed hold water. On the other hand, if the term "high seas" is viewed as encompassing all navigable sea waters "beyond 12 nautical miles from the shore" of the United States, then defendants' interpretation would be correct. This court concludes that, given the guidelines established for resolution of a nautical statute's meaning when its language is subject to differing readings, the latter reading, defendants', is the only plausible one.

DOSHA, 46 U.S.C. app. §761, was enacted by Congress in 1920 to resolve the anomaly created by the Supreme Court's decision in The Harrisburg, 119 U.S. 199, 7 S.Ct. 140, 30 L.Ed. 358 (1886). In The Harrisburg, a steamer collided with a schooner in waters between the coast of Massachusetts and the islands of Martha's Vineyard and Nantucket, killing the first officer of the schooner. See id. at 199–200, 7 S.Ct. 140. Because the decedent's widow and child did not bring suit within the applicable state statutes of limitations, they sought to recover under general maritime law. The Court held that, in absence of an applicable state statute, general federal maritime law did not provide a remedy in cases of wrongful death. The Court reasoned that since there was no common law remedy for wrongful death on land, there could be none at sea. See id. at 212–13, 7 S.Ct. 140. It was not until 1970 that The Harrisburg was overruled. In Moragne v. States Marine Lines, Inc., 398 U.S. 375, 388, 90 S.Ct. 1772, 26 L.Ed.2d 339 (1970), a unanimous Court recognized that a remedy existed for wrongful death under general maritime law, based upon the "wholesale abandonment" of the prohibition on wrongful death actions on land in England and in the United States.

[Before Moragne,] Supreme Court decisions mitigated the harshness of [The Harrisburg] by giving more expansive interpretations to state statutes that provided recovery for deaths occurring upon navigable waters, even on the high seas, beyond a state's territorial waters. In The Hamilton, 207 U.S. 398, 403, 28 S.Ct. 133, 52 L.Ed. 264 (1907), the Court held that a citizen of Delaware could bring suit in admiralty against another under Delaware's wrongful death statute, even though the death had occurred on the high seas, seven miles off the coast of Virginia. The Court reasoned that Delaware law defined the obligations of the parties, "even when personally on the high seas." Id. The tension between the holdings in The Harrisburg and The Hamilton "created jurisdictional fictions and serious problems in choice of law that sometimes denied recovery altogether." Offshore Logistics, Inc. v. Tallentire, 477 U.S.

207, 235, 106 S.Ct. 2485, 91 L.Ed.2d 174 (1986) (Powell, J., concurring in part and dissenting in part). In response to the conflicting body of law stemming from these cases, the Maritime Law Association [of the United States] proposed to Congress a number of drafts of bills, one of which eventually became the Death on the High Seas Act.

The statute that Congress passed in 1920 created a remedy for wrongful death "occurring on the high seas beyond a marine league from the shore of any State, or the District of Columbia, or the Territories or dependencies of the United States." 46 U.S.C. app. §761. That the Congressional record is spotty and appears contradictory as to whether Congress intended the term "high seas" to include foreign territorial waters is explained by the simple fact that the question of the extent of coverage beyond a marine league from the shores of the United States was, at most, of tangential concern. Congress' concern, second only to creating a uniform remedy for maritime disasters, was one of federalism, that is, preserving then existing state law remedies to the fullest reach of state territorial waters. H.R.Rep. No. 66-674, at 4 (1920); S.Rep. No. 66-216, at 4 (1919).

In its final form, Section 1 of DOHSA provided:

> Whenever the death of a person shall be caused by wrongful act, neglect, or default occurring on the high seas beyond a marine league from the shore of any State, or the District of Columbia, or the Territories or dependencies of the United States, the personal representative of the decedent may maintain a suit for damages in the district courts of the United States, in admiralty, for the exclusive benefit of the decedent's wife, husband, parent, child, or dependent relative against the vessel, person, or corporation which would have been liable if death had not ensued.

46 U.S.C. §761 (1920). A marine league is equivalent to three nautical miles (nm).

In April 2000, Section 1 was amended to resolve a discrepancy between Proclamation No. 5928, issued by President Ronald Reagan in 1988, which extended the United States territorial waters from three to twelve nautical miles beyond the shore of any state. The scope of DOHSA had until that point been commensurate with the then-three-mile boundary of the United States' territorial sea.

The litigation flowing from the 1996 tragedy of TWA Flight 800 brought to light that it was not clear in view of the Proclamation whether the three-mile boundary ("beyond a marine league") specified in DOHSA was (1) the geographical expression of the political boundary of "high seas," that is, the extent of the federal territorial sea as it had been in 1920, subject to change according to the change in the federal definition of the territorial sea, or (2) a geographical boundary set by Congress primarily to preserve state actions in state territorial waters, and thus impervious to Executive Branch proclamations that pertain to the federal territorial seas. The TWA Flight 800 crash occurred eight nautical miles off the coast of Long Island, a point outside the explicit scope stated in DOHSA, but within the Proclamation's twelve-nautical mile boundary of the territorial sea. The Second Circuit held that, for purposes of DOHSA, the term "high seas" meant those waters beyond the territorial waters of the United States, applying the Proclamation's 12-mile limit as a new implied geographical limit upon DOHSA's reach. Thus, DOHSA was ruled not to be applicable to Flight 800, since it crashed in United States territorial waters eight miles from the U.S. coast. 209 F.3d at 215. However, that decision purposely did not opine on the applicability or inapplicability of DOHSA to crashes occurring within foreign territorial waters. See id. at 212.

Defendants argue that DOHSA's new language, "on the high seas 12 nautical miles or closer to the shore," §761(b), demonstrates that the term "high seas" in DOHSA is not used in the international sense, but is to be given a geographical meaning, since it contemplates waters 12 nms or closer to the shore as being high seas, despite President Reagan's proclaiming them to be territorial seas. (Ds' Repl. Br. at 4.)

Plaintiffs assert that the amended DOHSA paralleled the TWA Flight 800 holding, and, in so doing, Congress intended to adopt the definition of "high seas" adopted by the majority in that opinion, which, they argue, includes only international, nonsovereign waters. See TWA Flight 800, 209 F.3d at 205–07.

Without regard to whether the TWA Flight 800 majority's pre-DOHSA view is correct as to the possible meaning of "high seas" when DOHSA was enacted in 1920, this court has to look at the case law that developed after DOHSA was enacted through the time of the 2000 amendment. That case law has interpreted DOHSA consistently as applying to deaths occurring within foreign territorial waters. A court must assume that, when faced with the task of amending DOHSA, Congress was well aware of the large body of federal case law that had applied the Act to aviation accidents occurring on foreign territorial waters.

As is evidenced by its legislative history, Congress was chiefly concerned in the amendment process with the Supreme Court decision, Zicherman v. Korean Air Lines, 516 U.S. 217, 230, 116 S.Ct. 629, 133 L.Ed.2d 596 (1996), which held that plaintiffs could not recover loss of society damages under DOHSA, whereas plaintiffs, whose decedents died in an aviation accident over land, could:

> The effect of this decision is to treat families differently depending on whether their relative died in an aircraft that crashed into the ocean or one that crashed into land. If the plane crashes into the ocean, DOHSA applies and the family is entitled only to pecuniary damages. However if a plane crashes into the land or close to land, the applicable tort law would apply. These generally permit the award of non-pecuniary damages such as loss of companionship....
>
> The Supreme Court recognized the inequity of this result and stated [in Zicherman, 516 U.S. at 229, 116 S.Ct. 629,] that "Congress may choose to enact special provisions applicable to Warsaw convention cases, as some countries have done." The reported bill (H.R.603) would do this and in such a way as to ensure that all families would be treated the same regardless of where a plane happened to crash.

H.R. Rep. 106-32 (Shuster Report on H.R. 603, February 24, 1999).

It is clear from the language above, as well as the amended statute itself, that Congress was concerned with extending the nautical miles beyond the United States coastline to which DOHSA would not apply, to permit state law recoveries to the fullest extent of the Proclamation, and that it did not address DOHSA's application to foreign territorial waters.

While the legislative history as to DOHSA's application in foreign territorial waters may be muddy, one thing is clear—Congress strove to provide a sure, uniform remedy in U.S. courts for survivors of decedents killed tortiously at sea, where none existed or where one might not exist. This has recently been reiterated. In determining that an action under DOHSA precludes a wrongful death action under domestic state law, the Supreme Court, in Offshore Logistics v. Tallentire, 477 U.S. 207, 227–32, 106 S.Ct. 2485, 91 L.Ed.2d 174 (1986), explored the importance of uniformity in fashioning a remedy, both in terms of observing Congressional intent as well as preserving judicial time and resources.

This court recognizes that the Swissair cases differ from Tallentire. There, it was beyond dispute that DOHSA was applicable law. The issue had been whether the DOHSA action could be supplemented by state law. However, the overriding principles of DOHSA uniformity and exclusivity recognized in Tallentire apply here as well.

As pointed out in Jennings v. Boeing Co., 660 F.Supp. 796 (E.D.Pa.1987), aff'd without op., 838 F.2d 1206 (3d Cir.1988), because Congress only has the power to determine the boundaries of the territorial seas of the United States, and not the extent of the territorial seas of other nations, it may indeed have been Congress' understanding that DOHSA would have to apply in foreign territorial waters to protect the interests of its citizens to have a predictable remedy for their loss. "Because it was generally understood that the wrongful death statutes of the coastal states were not meant to apply to the high seas, including the territorial waters of foreign states, there was no need to limit further the scope of DOHSA's application." Jennings, 660 F.Supp. at 803 (citing Moragne, 398 U.S. at 393 n. 10, 90 S.Ct. 1772); see also Roberts v. United States, 498 F.2d 520, 524 n.7 (9th Cir.1974) (declining to decide the issue, but noting, "Because Congress only has power to fix the extent of territorial waters measured from the shores of its own country it may well have considered all waters beyond one marine league from those shores to be 'high seas' for purposes of DOHSA so long as navigable, even though within the territorial waters of a foreign state.").

IV. CONCLUSION

For the foregoing reasons, this court finds that DOHSA, as amended, applies to aviation incidents in foreign territorial waters. Because Amended DOHSA does not allow recovery for punitive damages, 46 U.S.C. app. §762(b)(1), defendants' motion to dismiss all claims for punitive damages under United States law is granted.

IN RE AIR CRASH AT TAIPEI, TAIWAN, ON OCTOBER 31, 2000

2002 WL 32155476 (C.D. Cal. 2002)

FEES, District Judge.

I. INTRODUCTION AND SUMMARY

On October 31, 2000, Singapore Airlines ("SIA") Flight SQ006 was scheduled to fly from Singapore to Los Angeles through Taipei, Taiwan. Disaster struck at the Taipei airport where Flight SQ006 attempted to take off from a runway that was under construction. Before the aircraft could become airborne, it collided with construction equipment which resulted in the death of many passengers and injury to many others. The heirs of the deceased and the injured survivors have filed numerous lawsuits that have been consolidated in the present MDL proceeding.

In all cases, Plaintiffs have named Singapore Airlines, Inc. ("SIA") as a defendant, since the accident involved an SIA aircraft piloted by SIA employees. However, a subset of Plaintiffs, those whose claims could not otherwise be pursued in the United States under Warsaw Convention jurisdiction, have named United Airlines, Inc., UAL Corporation (collectively "United") and the "Star Alliance" as defendants because they are domiciled in the United States and can therefore be sued here under the treaty. The United defendants have moved, under Rule 12(b)(1) of the Federal Rules of Civil Procedure, to dismiss the claims against them on the ground that the Warsaw Convention permits a suit against only one carrier, the airline that was transporting Plaintiffs at the time of the accident. Since only one carrier can be sued, and since SIA was that carrier, United argues that the Court lacks subject matter jurisdiction over the purported lawsuit against them.

Plaintiffs ask the Court to delay hearing Defendants' motion to dismiss and to permit a period of "jurisdictional discovery" so that Plaintiffs may obtain evidence they hope will support their contention that, with respect to the accident at the center of this case, United or the Star Alliance is a "carrier" within the meaning of the Warsaw Convention. Plaintiffs contend that United too narrowly construes the term "carrier," which is an undefined term under the treaty, and that determining the identity of the "carrier" is a fact question which must be determined on a case-by-case basis. For that reason, Plaintiffs assert that the Court cannot decide the Rule 12(b)(1) motions without first permitting discovery regarding the nature and operation of the Star Alliance.

Having reviewed controlling case law on the subject, the Court concludes that the "carrier" must include the airline that operates the aircraft involved in the accident at issue in the case. The real question is who, beyond the operator of the aircraft, may properly be included within the meaning of the term "carrier" for purposes of Warsaw Convention jurisdiction. In the Court's view, only two conditions would support a finding that United should be included within the scope of that term: (1) Flight SQ006 was undertaken by a general partnership, which included SIA and United as general partners; or (2) United acted as the agent of SIA in connection with Flight SQ006 and performed some act, within the scope of that agency, which bears some causal connection to the Taipei disaster. Neither condition is present in this case. The Star Alliance agreement executed by SIA, which is now before this Court and which Plaintiffs argue created a partnership that acted as the "carrier" in this case, expressly states the intention of the parties not to create a general partnership between and among its members. Thus, SIA, as the operator of the downed aircraft, is the "carrier" in connection with Flight SQ006—not the Star Alliance or some other unidentified partnership. Moreover, neither United nor the Star Alliance engaged in any conduct that would make them an "agent" of SIA within the meaning of Warsaw Convention jurisprudence. For these reasons, the Court concludes, for the second time, that Plaintiffs' motion for jurisdictional discovery should be DENIED.

II. STATEMENT OF FACTS

A. PLAINTIFFS' TRAVEL ON SINGAPORE AIRLINES

Plaintiffs Helen Broadfoot and Jay Spack purchased tickets outside the United States with an itinerary that had, as its ultimate destination, Australia. Their flight itinerary included transportation on October 31, 2000 from Taiwan to Los Angeles on Singapore Airlines Flight SQ006, and it is undisputed that they were on board that flight at the time of the accident that is the subject of this suit. Plaintiff David Broadfoot was not a passenger on Flight SQ006; rather, he brings a loss of consortium claim against Defendants in connection with his wife's injuries.

B. SIA's DOMICILE AND PRINCIPAL PLACE OF BUSINESS

SIA is neither domiciled in the United States nor has its principal place of business here. Plaintiffs concede that SIA is incorporated and is domiciled in Singapore, where it has its principal place of business.

C. UNITED ALR LINES, INC, AND THE STAR ALLIANCE

If SIA is held to be the "carrier" whose accident caused Plaintiffs' injuries, then this Court cannot have treaty jurisdiction over Plaintiffs' claims because the Warsaw Convention provides that such cases may be brought only where the carrier is domiciled, where it has established its principal place of business, where the passenger purchased the ticket, or the passenger's ultimate destination. In an attempt to circumvent these jurisdictional limitations, Plaintiffs assert that United, or more particularly the Star Alliance, both of whom are allegedly domiciled in the United States, was the "earner" for Warsaw Convention purposes. The Court therefore examines the nature of the Star Alliance before proceeding to consider the controlling legal principles.

United participates in "alliances" with other airlines that allow it indirect access to markets that it cannot serve either because of economics or governmental restrictions. In its 1997 10-K filed with the Securities and Exchange Commission, United explained that "[a]n alliance is a collaborative marketing arrangement between carriers which can include joint frequent flyer participation, coordination of reservations, baggage handling, and flight schedules, and code-sharing of operations." As part of its discussion of "alliances," United disclosed the formation of the Star Alliance, which it described as "an integrated worldwide transportation network which provides customers with global recognition and a wide range of other benefits." Other public records disclose that the "Star Alliance" is a federally registered trademark or trade name owned by United Air Lines, Inc.

Described in marketing materials as a "partnership of 15 independent airlines," the Star Alliance includes: Air Canada, Air New Zealand, All Nippon Airways, Ansett Australia, The Austrian Group (three airlines), British Midland, Lufthansa, Mexicana, Scandinavian Airlines, Singapore Airlines, Thai International, Varig, and United. The Alliance also includes numerous "regional" partners, such as Aloha Airlines, Cayman Airways, Delta Airlines, and a number of others. The Court notes, and Plaintiffs' counsel conceded at the hearing on this motion, that the members of the Alliance are separate juridical entities incorporated under the laws of various jurisdictions throughout the world.

United and other members of the Alliance promote the benefits of Star Alliance membership to their frequent flyers. For example, on its website, SIA notes that:

> As a member of the Star Alliance, United Airlines Mileage Plus members can apply qualifying miles earned on Singapore Airlines flights towards Premier Status, Premier Executive Status, and Premier Executive 1K Status.

At United's website, the airline touts the benefits of "simplified world travel through United's strategic alliances" and boasts:

> Over 500 destinations on six continents are available online to United Airlines customers. United, in cooperation with other leading airlines, extends the convenience of flying United to destinations beyond United routes. You'll still have simplified reservations, ticketing, one-stop check-in, reciprocal clubroom access, and coordinated baggage handling.

Regarding ticketing, United advises that:

> Flights operated within an alliance agreement are code share flights. Such flights are operated by one airline but listed as a flight of both. For example, for a flight to Cancun, Mexico, the flight may be operated by Mexicana Airlines but listed as both Mexicana and United. Through United's alliances, you have a greater choice of destinations, shorter travel times, and a greater choice of flight times.

Through the Star Alliance, the member airlines have sought to increase convenience to the airline passenger by arranging access to airport lounges worldwide to Star Alliance Gold members, establishing priority reservations and baggage handling, permitting frequent flyer miles to be combined in some circumstances, and by offering a "Round the World Fare" with a wide variety of itinerary options. United claims to have accomplished these objectives by creating "the largest airline network in the world."

D. THE STAR ALLIANCE AGREEMENT SIGNED BY SIA

Plaintiffs claim that United has created not just a "network" but a new "carrier." Such a determination could have profound consequences on Warsaw Convention litigation in that, as a "carrier," the Star Alliance could potentially be sued in the United States by passengers on any member airline for any airline accident throughout the world. Moreover, discovery obtained by Plaintiffs since the Court entered its first order on the present subject suggests otherwise.

In discovery proceedings involving SIA, Plaintiffs received a copy of the Star Alliance agreement. Plaintiffs contend that, through that agreement, the "Partner airlines" (a term coined by Plaintiffs that does not appear in the agreement), "are acting as de facto or ostensible agents thereof." (Plaintiff's Supp. Br. at 13). Along the same lines, Plaintiffs conclude:

> It is clear from the record ... that the Star Alliance exists; that it is a transportation enterprise; that it is a de facto or de jure partnership; that it is made up of individual airlines, who are partners and the[y] interchange functions and cooperate in the transportation enterprise.

(Id. at 16). While the Court agrees that the members of the alliance cooperate in air transportation matters, the Star Alliance's status as an independent legal entity—either as a de facto or de jure partnership—is undermined by the very agreement Plaintiffs rely on to make their case.

The Star Alliance Agreement expressly states the purpose of the airline network as follows:

> The Members intend that their respective customers will benefit from improved passenger transportation services, including the following: (a) improved interline services, (b) more efficient connections at the Members' principal hubs, (c) access to more destinations through Member networks and through measures to standardize, streamline and coordinate Member operations.

(Plaintiffs' Ex. C at 2). To accomplish this and other goals, the agreement states that its members intend to develop networks and services available to its members "while maintaining each Member's unique identity and culture." (Id.) In the paragraph describing the "Nature of the Alliance," the members agree:

> This Star Alliance Agreement does not create a partnership among the Members of the Star Alliance. Unless otherwise agreed, no Member is entitled to incur any obligations or make any commitments relating to the Star Alliance on behalf of any other Member.

Id.

Later in the document, in a section which permits the formation of so-called "special purpose entities," the parties to the agreement provide:

> The Members shall remain independent legal entities and shall not establish any incorporated or unincorporated legal entity on behalf of the Star Alliance or in the name of Star Alliance, except such special purpose entities as may be approved by the CEB....

Id. at 17.

Similarly, in a "code-share" agreement between United and SIA, the parties describe the nature of the relationship created by the agreement as follows:

> The relationship of [United] and [SIA] under this Agreement is that of independent contractors. Nothing in this Agreement is intended or shall be construed to create or establish any partnership or joint venture relationship between the Carriers.

(Plaintiffs' Ex. G).

Thus, while it is clear that the members of the Star Alliance have created an extensive network to further cooperation among the individual airlines, they have likewise taken care to indicate that the parties do not intend to create a new legal entity, nor to abandon their existing corporate structure and institutional cultures. The question is whether such an arrangement has created a "carrier" within the meaning of the Warsaw Convention.

III. DISCUSSION

Plaintiffs point out that the term "carrier" is not defined in the Warsaw Convention. Though true, careful study of the applicable provisions of the treaty and interpretive case law, and the employment of a modicum of reason and common sense, demonstrate that the term means what it appears to mean—the operator of the aircraft involved in an accident. See generally In re Air Crash Disaster Near Peggy's Cove, Nova Scotia on September 2, 1998, 2002 WL 334389 (E.D. Pa. Feb. 27, 2002). Because the operator may hire agents to perform duties for which it is responsible, those agents fall within the scope of Warsaw Convention liability limits with respect to any duties performed for the operator which bear some causal relationship to the injury or damage incurred between embarkation and disembarkation of a given flight. But such liability arises not because the agents engage in carriage but because they perform duties that are the ultimate responsibility of the carrier. Any other rule would permit the circumvention of Warsaw Convention liability limits by holding the carrier's agents liable under a different set of rules than apply to the carrier itself.

A. ARTICLE 17 OF THE WARSAW CONVENTION PERMITS SUIT AGAINST A SINGLE CARRIER

The Warsaw Convention governs international air crash litigation. Article 17 of the convention states:

> The carrier shall be liable for damage sustained in the event of the death or wounding of a passenger or any other bodily injury suffered by a passenger, if the accident which caused the damage so sustained took place on board the aircraft or in the course of embarking or disembarking.

These words are neither complex nor cryptic. Even a reader unfamiliar with this area of the law would understand that this provision holds the operator of an aircraft engaged in an accident causing injury or death liable for such damages. Likewise, the language does not speak of dual or multiple carriers, but rather "the carrier" suggest[s] that only one entity—the operator of the aircraft—bears liability for damages arising from injuries occurring on the aircraft. Efforts to read the term "carrier" expansively to include more than the operator of the aircraft have been rejected by the courts.

The leading case on this point is Kapar v. Kuwait Airways Corp., 845 F.2d 1100 (D.C. Cir. 1988). In that case, Kapar, an American citizen working for the Agency for International Development, bought an airline ticket in Yemen for travel from Yemen to Karachi, Pakistan through Kuwait City, Kuwait. He purchased the ticket, issued on Pan American World Airways ("Pan Am") ticket stock, through Marib Travel, an authorized Pan Am ticket agent. The flight from Yemen to Kuwait City was uneventful, but the Kuwait Airways flight to Karachi was hijacked by terrorists who had flown into Kuwait City on Middle East Airlines ("MEA"). The flight was diverted to Tehran, where Kapar was beaten and tortured. When he returned to the United States, Kapar sued Pan Am, MEA, and Kuwait Airways for his injuries. The trial court dismissed the case against Kuwait Airways and Pan Am for lack of treaty jurisdiction; MEA was dismissed for lack of personal jurisdiction.

On appeal, Kapar abandoned his argument that Pan Am acted as Kuwait Airway's agent in connection with the flight, and instead argued that Pan Am should be deemed a "carrier" thus making it subject to suit in the United States, its place of domicile. The court wrote:

> This contention is without merit. Although the term "carrier" is not defined in the Convention, the manner in which it is employed, particularly in the chapter titled "Liability of the Carrier," makes clear that the Convention's drafters were referring only to those airlines that actually transport passengers or baggage ("actual carriers"). See Air France v, Saks, 470 U.S. 392, 396–97, 105 S.Ct. 1338, 1340–41, 84 L.Ed.2d 286 (1985) ("The analysis must begin ... with the text of the treaty and the context in which the written words are used."). In Article 17, for example, the "carrier" is deemed liable for death or bodily injury "if the accident which caused the damage so sustained took place on board the aircraft or in the course of any of the operations of embarking or disembarking." Likewise, in Article 18(1), the "carrier" is deemed liable for damage to any checked baggage or other goods "if the occurrence which caused the damage so sustained took place during the transportation by air." In Article 30, moreover, the drafters even precluded the possibility that the actual carrier for one leg of a scheduled multi-leg trip could be held liable for injuries suffered on another airline during a different leg of the trip. When "successive carriers" provide transportation of this sort, a passenger "can take action only against the carrier who performed the transportation during which the accident ... occurred." In light of this provision, it cannot reasonably be concluded that the drafters intended an airline that merely issues a ticket to face potential liability as [the] "carrier." See Briscoe v. Compagnie Nationale Air France, 290 F. Supp. 863 (S.D.N.Y. 1968).

Id. at 1103 (footnotes omitted). Accord Stanford v. Kuwait Airlines Corp., 705 F. Supp. 142 (S.D.N.Y. 1989). Similarly, in Pflug, the Second Circuit, citing Kapar with favor, concurred that only the airline engaged in the actual transportation of an injured passenger can be held liable as "the carrier" within the meaning of Article 17. Pflug v.

Egyptair Corp., 961 F.2d 26, 31–32 (2nd Cir. 1992) (rejecting effort to bring Warsaw Convention action against subsidiary corporation operating in the United States).

Though their theories vary and are not always consistent, at least some of the Plaintiffs made the assertion in oral argument that the Star Alliance, of which SIA is a member, operated flight SQ006. Under that theory, the Star Alliance would be considered a general partnership which acted as the "carrier" in respect to that flight. The analysis set forth in the foregoing cases would permit a Warsaw Convention action against a "carrier" that operated as a partnership—that is, there is nothing in the treaty that would limit jurisdiction based in any way on the form of the business operating the aircraft involved in an accident. However, stating that conclusion does nothing to further the argument of Plaintiffs in this case.

The Star Alliance agreement, produced by SIA in discovery, expressly states the limited intentions of the parties to the agreement. The agreement expressly states the parties' intent not to create a general partnership, and ensures that the member airlines will remain independent legal entities. (Plaintiffs' Ex. C at 2, 17). As in any contract, the parties are free to create whatever relationship they wish, and Plaintiffs have presented no reason, compelling or otherwise, for disregarding the intent of the parties to the Star Alliance arrangement. That SIA chooses to ally itself with other airlines for a variety of purposes other than the operation of aircrafts is simply beside the point. See Kapar, 845 F.2d at 1103 (an airline that issues a ticket on behalf of another does not thereby become a "carrier.")

By reaching this conclusion, the Court does not ignore those cases, cited by Plaintiff, where Warsaw Convention liability limits were extended to certain agents of an airline. Those cases, however, address a different issue and are distinguishable from the circumstances presented in this case.

B. WARSAW CONVENTION LIABILITY—A CARRIER AND ITS AGENTS

The Court has thoroughly reviewed the authorities cited by both parties and concludes that none of the authorities cited would permit the exercise of jurisdiction over either United or SIA on any of Plaintiff's theories. In those instances where courts have permitted suit against an airline's agent, the agent's conduct allegedly bore some causal connection to the plaintiff's injury and the agent was providing a service for which the airline bore ultimate legal or contractual responsibility, such as maintenance of the downed aircraft. Moreover, in each of the cases Plaintiffs rely on, the courts included the agent within the scope of the term "carrier" under Article 17 to preserve the liability limits established in the Warsaw Convention. Here, Plaintiffs seek to use the principles established in those cases to create a sweeping expansion of Warsaw Convention jurisdiction, which is contrary to the purposes furthered by the holdings in those decisions. The Court will briefly survey those decisions.

The seminal case in the area appears to be Reed v. Wiser, 555 F.2d 1079 (2nd Cir. 1977). In Reed, the heirs of passengers killed on TWA Flight 841, which crashed into the eastern Mediterranean Sea near Greece when a suspected terrorist bomb detonated, sued employees of the airline instead of the airline itself. When the defendants sought to assert Warsaw Convention liability limits as a defense, the plaintiffs moved to strike the defense, and the trial judge granted the motion. The Second Circuit reversed, observing:

> Should employees not be covered by the provisions of the Convention, the entire character of international air disaster litigation involving planes owned and operated by American airlines would be radically changed. The liability limita-

> tions of the Convention could then be circumvented by the simple device of a suit against the pilot and/or other employees, which would force the American employer, if it had not already done so, to provide indemnity for higher recoveries as the price for service by employees who are essential to the continued operation of its airline. The increased cost would, of course, be passed on to passengers.

Id. at 1082. The Second Circuit found that providing such a means of circumventing convention liability limits would defeat that aspect of the treaty and "in the process the Convention's most fundamental objective of providing a uniform system of liability and litigation rules for international air disasters will be abandoned as well." Id. at 1092. Thus, the court held that the plaintiffs "may not recover from an air carrier's employees or from the carrier and its employees together a sum greater than that recoverable in a suit against the carrier itself as limited by the Warsaw Convention with its applicable agreements and protocols." Id. at 1093. Nothing in the analysis of this case broadens the definition of "carrier" beyond the entity that operated the downed aircraft.

The Ninth Circuit followed Reed in Dazo v. Globe Airport Security Servs., 268 F.3d 671 (9th Cir. 2001). In that case, the plaintiff lost her carry-on baggage, which allegedly contained over $100,000 in jewelry, during security screening on her way to the boarding gate. She sued for negligence and breach of an implied contract of bailment, and sought compensatory and punitive damages. Globe filed a motion to dismiss on the ground that the state law claims were preempted by the Warsaw Convention. The motion was granted and the plaintiff appealed.

On appeal, the Ninth Circuit stated the issue as follows: "We must first decide whether the Convention applies to claims brought against Globe, a company functioning as the Airlines' agent at the time of the theft." Id. at 675. The court noted that, while the issue was one of first impression in this circuit, other circuits had "consistently and almost uniformly extended the Convention's coverage to an airline's agents and employees." Id. (citing, inter alia, Reed, 555 F.2d at 1089–92). The court followed that line of authority, holding:

> Here, the theft of Dazo's bag occurred while Globe was conducting a security check that every airline or its agent must perform. See 49 U.S.C. §44901 ("The [security] screening must take place before boarding and be carried out by a weapon-detecting facility or procedure used or operated by an employee or agent of an air carrier, intrastate air carrier, or foreign air carrier."). In light of the compelling linguistic, textual, and historical evidence marshaled by the Second Circuit in Reed, and the strong policy rationales supporting the extension of the Convention to airlines' agents, we join those courts which have held that the Warsaw Convention applies to airlines' agents. In the instant case, the parties agree that Globe was acting as the Airlines' agent at the time of the theft. Therefore, Globe is a Warsaw Convention "carrier" and the Convention caps Globe's liability to Dazo.

Id. at 676–77. While the last sentence gives Plaintiffs something to argue about, this Court concludes that the Ninth Circuit did not mean to say that Globe was a separate carrier, but that, for the policy reasons discussed in Reed, Globe was to be treated in the same manner as the actual carrier because of its status as that carrier's agent.

These principles were most recently discussed in In re Air Crash Disaster Near Peggy's Cove, Nova Scotia on September 2, 1998, 2002 WL 334389 (E.D. Pa. Feb. 27, 2002), a case involving the crash of Swissair Flight 111 en route from New York to

Geneva, Switzerland. The plaintiffs claimed, among other things, that the in-flight entertainment system had been improperly installed and that its defective installation contributed to the crash. The question before the district court was whether the installer, SR Technics, could be sued for punitive damages under state law or whether the defendant could assert Warsaw Convention liability limits as a defense to such a claim. The court concluded that it must examine the term "carrier" under Article 17 to answer that question, noting that "[a]t a minimum, the term must include the air carrier that operates the flight itself, here Swissair and Delta, a point the plaintiffs concede. The question becomes whether the Convention contemplates and embraces a broader scope of 'carrier.'" Id. at *11. The Court then surveyed the law on the subject beginning with Reed. After discussing Reed, its rationale, and its progeny, the court concluded:

> [T]his court holds that the provisions of the Warsaw Convention extend beyond the carrier to include those independent agents which, pursuant to contracts or subcontracts with the carrier, perform services related to air travel and in furtherance of the carriage enterprise that the carrier would be bound to perform, either by law or in the interest of providing the best, safest, and most thorough carriage services, in furtherance of the performance of its contract with its customers. Such services necessarily would include, inter alia, inspection, service, maintenance, and repair of aircraft.

Id. at *16–*17. Because SR Technics performed maintenance and repair services, including oversight of the installation of the in-flight entertainment system, SR Technics was held to be the agent of the carrier on a matter relating to the accident in issue and therefore subject to Convention liability limits. Id. at *18–*19.

Dazo and Peggy's Cove are particularly noteworthy. These cases each involve efforts by plaintiffs to expand the defendant pool and circumvent the Warsaw Convention liability limits. The cases teach that, while suit may properly be brought against entities other than an airline, the Warsaw Convention's liability limits cannot be circumvented. Thus, these cases interpret "carrier" in a way to preserve, not expand, the scope of Warsaw Convention liability limits.

From the foregoing, the Court concludes that, in any given air crash case, suit may be brought against a single carrier—the operator of the aircraft involved in the accident—and any agent of the carrier whose conduct arguably bears some causal connection to the losses incurred in the accident. In this case, that means SIA, the carrier, and anyone acting on its behalf whose conduct allegedly resulted in the accident that occurred at the Taipei airport, may be sued under the Warsaw Convention, and may seek the protection of the Convention's liability limits.

United Airlines and the Star Alliance do not fall within that description. Even if the Star Alliance created a partnership for some purposes, the parties to that agreement manifested a clear and unequivocal intent not to create a general partnership for all purposes. Moreover, the purposes for which the purported partnership was created—customer service in the broadest sense of that term—had no bearing on the accident in this case. Because neither United nor the Star Alliance had any control over the operation of Flight SQ006, and performed no services that bore any possible causal relationship to the injuries suffered in the accident at the Taipei airport, controlling case law precludes suit against them under the Warsaw Convention.

IV. CONCLUSION

For the reasons set forth above, the motion for jurisdictional discovery is DENIED.

STETHEM v. ISLAMIC REPUBLIC OF IRAN

201 F. Supp. 2d 78 (D.D.C. 2002)

JACKSON, District Judge.

On the morning of Friday, June 14, 1985, Trans World Airlines ("TWA") Flight No. 847, a Boeing 727, took off from Athens, Greece, bound for Rome, Italy, with a full complement of 143 passengers and a crew of eight. On board were U.S. citizens Robert Stethem, Kurt Carlson, Stuart Dahl, Jeffery Ingalls, Clinton Suggs, Tony Watson, and Kenneth Bowen. All were U.S. military personnel, enroute back to the United States from various assignments abroad and coincidentally aboard the same plane traveling in civilian dress.

Shortly after takeoff the plane was commandeered at gunpoint by at least two hijackers, also armed with hand grenades, who forced the plane to divert first to a landing for fuel in Beirut, then on to Algiers, and back once more to Beirut, finally landing dramatically at night in Beirut about 16 hours after the flight had commenced. During the journey several of the servicemen were brutally beaten by their captors. One was executed by gunshot to the head and his body shoved from the plane onto the tarmac at the Beirut airport. Eventually debarked from the plane as prisoners of a local militia in Beirut, the surviving servicemen were held captive by confederates of the hijackers until June 30, 1985, when they were released to Syrian military personnel and ultimately flown home.

The airborne portion of their ordeal was characterized for some of them by excruciating pain from repeated beatings, and for all of them by stark terror in expectation of either an imminent violent death or prolonged captivity. While imprisoned in Beirut they were confined under execrable conditions, tormented with daily threats of torture and death, and vilified as citizens of a despised nation, all the while uncertain of their fate.

These two consolidated actions by the servicemen and their spouses, and by the personal representatives of the murder victim, seek to recover damages from the parties they hold ultimately responsible for these terrorist acts, the Islamic Republic of Iran and its Ministry of Information and Security, pursuant to the Foreign Sovereign Immunities Act ("FSIA"), 28 U.S.C. §§ 1602 et seq. Defaults were taken against defendants in both cases on December 1, 2000, and June 26, 2001, respectively, and upon the evidence adduced at an ex parte hearing before the Court on October 22–26, 2001, which the Court finds to be satisfactory for the purpose, the foregoing and following facts are found pursuant to Fed.R.Civ.P. 52(a). Judgments will consequently be entered for plaintiffs in accordance with the conclusions of law drawn therefrom....

III.

The hijackers—known only by the sobriquets "Crazy" (believed by the U.S. government to be one Izz Al-Din) and "Hitler" (true name Mohammed Ali Hamadi) by the TWA passengers at the time—have been reliably identified as belonging to Hizballah, a radical Shi'ite paramilitary organization recruited, trained and financially supported by the Ministry of Information and Security ("MOIS") of the Islamic Republic of Iran. Originally affiliated with Amal, the Lebanese militia supported by Syria during the Lebanese civil war, and a frequent collaborator with Amal even after shifting allegiance to Iran following the Israeli invasion of Lebanon in 1982, Hizballah has been implicated in numerous acts of terrorism for which this district court has held its patron state Iran liable under the FSIA.

The record in this case contains extensive documentary evidence from U.S. intelligence sources connecting Hizballah to Iran and its Ministry of Information and Security.

According to the testimony of U.S. Ambassador Robert Oakley who, as Director of Counterterrorism for the Department of State at the time, was directly involved in efforts to effect a military rescue or to induce the Lebanese or Algerian governments to secure the release of the passenger-hostages, the hijackers' initial demands—the release of prisoners in Israel and Kuwait—gave reason to believe they were agents of Amal. As later proved to be the case, however, Amal had employed Hizballah to undertake the actual hijacking, with support from Amal militia on the ground and in control of the Beirut airport. Further testimony from Robert McFarlane, U.S. National Security Advisor, established that his direct discussions with the leader of Amal (which had taken custody of all the hostages—save Ingalls—from the hijackers in Beirut) had been ineffectual in procuring their release. Not until approval had been given by Iranian President Rafsanjani from Tehran were they turned over to Syrian authorities in Damascus to be released.

IV.

While a foreign state is generally immune from the jurisdiction of the courts of the United States under the FSIA, see 28 U.S.C. § 1604, plaintiffs bring this action against defendants pursuant to section 1605(a)(7) of the Act. That section explicitly authorizes, as an exception to the general grant of sovereign immunity to foreign nations, suits against foreign states that sponsor terrorism for certain acts that cause personal injury or death if either the claimant or victim was a citizen of the United States at the time of the act. See 28 U.S.C. § 1605(a)(7). In numerous suits preceding this action, private claimants have successfully invoked this statutory exception to establish a basis by which federal district courts may exercise subject matter jurisdiction over claims similar to those brought by plaintiffs here against these same defendants. See, e.g., Weinstein v. Islamic Republic of Iran, 184 F.Supp.2d 13, 20 (D.D.C.2002); Wagner v. Islamic Republic of Iran, 172 F.Supp.2d 128, 133–134 (D.D.C.2001); Jenco v. Islamic Republic of Iran, 154 F.Supp.2d 27, 32–33 (D.D.C.2001). Plaintiffs' causes of action in this case are predicated on the unlawful detention and torture of plaintiffs, and, in the case of Robert Stethem, his summary execution—acts which unequivocally beget claims eligible for relief under section 1605(a)(7). See 28 U.S.C. § 1605(a)(7) and 28 U.S.C. § 1605 note; see also Jenco, 154 F.Supp.2d at 32 (claims arising out of the abduction and torture of a Catholic priest actionable under the FSIA); Wagner, 172 F.Supp.2d at 133–134 (terrorist bombing of the second U.S. Embassy in Beirut and resulting death of a U.S. servicemember constituted an extrajudicial killing for purposes of the FSIA).

The FSIA imposes two preconditions upon the exercise of subject matter jurisdiction by district courts over foreign states: the foreign state must have been designated a state sponsor of terrorism at the time the acts occurred, unless later so designated as a result of such act, and a plaintiff (either claimant or victim) must have been a United States citizen at the time of the incident. See 28 U.S.C. § 1605(a)(7)(A) and (B).

Both of these requirements are clearly satisfied here. Iran was designated as a state sponsor of terrorism pursuant to section 6(j) of the Export Administration Act of 1979 on January 19, 1984, and remains so designated today. The multiple plaintiffs bringing this action (except Chantal Gautier) have always been United States citizens. Accordingly, the Court finds that it has jurisdiction over the subject matter of this suit and the named defendants. And as the Court has previously found in so many similar cases before it, the evidence conclusively establishes that the Islamic Republic of Iran and its MOIS provided "material support or resources" to Hizballah, and Hizballah and its co-conspirator Amal were the perpetrators of these heinous acts of terrorism. Having concluded that defendants are liable for the tortious conduct alleged, the Court next considers the extent to which the plaintiffs should be compensated for the injuries they sustained as a result of their client organization's unconscionable behavior.

[After analyzing each plaintiff's loss, the court entered] judgment against the Islamic Republic of Iran and its Ministry of Information and Security, jointly and severally, for compensatory damages as follows:

Estate of Robert Stethem:	$2,404,665.00.
Richard Stethem:	$5,000,000.00.
Patricia Stethem:	$5,000,000.00.
Sheryl Sierralta:	$3,000,000.00.
Kenneth Stethem:	$3,000,000.00.
Patrick Stethem:	$3,000,000.00.
Kurt Carlson:	$1,500,000.00.
Cheryl Carlson:	$200,000.00.
Stuart Dahl:	$1,000,000.00.
Martha Dahl:	$ 200,000.00.
Jeffery Ingalls:	$1,000,000.00.
Clinton Suggs:	$1,500,000.00.
Chantal Gautier:	$ 200,000.00.
Tony Watson:	$1,000,000.00
Pamala Watson:	$ 200,000.00.
Kenneth Bowen:	$1,000,000.00.

Punitive Damages

Plaintiffs also request an award of punitive damages against defendant MOIS for its role in providing support and resources to Hizballah and Amal. (Punitive damages may not be assessed against the Islamic Republic of Iran, but may be awarded against an instrumentality of a foreign state. See Anderson v. Islamic Republic of Iran, 90 F.Supp.2d 107, 114 (D.D.C.2000); Alejandre v. Republic of Cuba, 996 F.Supp. 1239, 1253 (S.D.Fla. 1997).)

As in previous cases, the evidence clearly inculpates MOIS as the instigator and financier of terrorist acts by Hizballah and Amal in this case. The hostage taking, torture, and killing of innocent non-belligerents for political ends constitutes unconscionable conduct in any civilized society. Accordingly, the Court finds that not only are punitive damages authorized under the FSIA to punish the MOIS for its continued role in fomenting terrorist activity, and to the extent possible deter it from future criminal behavior, see 28 U.S.C. § 1606, but that the MOIS's role in sponsoring the agents responsible for the instant acts of terrorism warrants such an award. Consistent with this Court's prior experience and a calculation equivalent to approximately three times the estimated annual budget of MOIS for support of terrorism, the Court will assess punitive damages in the amount of $300,000,000 against the MOIS, to be awarded to all plaintiffs jointly and severally.

Notes

1. Most international carriers belong to the International Air Transport Association (www.iata.org), the prime vehicle for inter-airline cooperation on financial, legal, and technical matters. Founded in Havana, Cuba, in 1945 and now headquartered in Montreal, its membership (as of October 2005) consists of 270 airlines (representing more

than 140 countries), as well as numerous freight forwarders, industry suppliers, and travel agents.

2. Cases like *Robertson* arise because of the differences that exist between the liability regimes for domestic and international travel (recall that the Warsaw Convention gave her only two years to sue, whereas the law of the District of Columbia allowed three years). In light of this fact, should there be a single set of rules to govern all air passenger claims? Is such a system even possible?

3. As *Schopenhauer*, *Paradis*, and *Ehrlich* collectively explain, the Warsaw Convention (reproduced in Appendix 2) underwent numerous changes (in the form of agreements, amendments, and protocols) between its promulgation in 1929 and its demise in 1999 (*see* Appendices 8, 9, 11, 13, 15, and 23–25). As these cases also make clear, however, it will be some time before disputes are solely governed by the Montreal Convention (reprinted in Appendix 26; as of October 2005, it had been ratified by 66 countries). Even when they are, earlier precedents will still be of use because of the similarities between the old and new regimes. *See further* Sean D. Murphy, *Ratification of the 1999 Montreal Convention on Aviation Liability*, 98 Am. J. Int'l L. 177 (2004); Gregory C. Walker, *"Doing Business" in Montreal: The Effects of the Addition of "Fifth Forum" Jurisdiction Under the Montreal Convention*, 23 Penn St. Int'l L. Rev. 125 (2004); Jennifer McKay, Note, *The Refinement of the Warsaw System: Why the 1999 Montreal Convention Represents the Best Hope for Uniformity*, 34 Case W. Res. J. Int'l L. 73 (2002).

Warsaw Convention precedents will remain especially relevant in cases involving flight delays and lost or damaged baggage, because the Montreal Convention breaks little new ground in these areas. As a result, it has been suggested that passengers pack plenty of patience while leaving their valuables at home. *See further* Eloisa C. Rodriguez-Dod, *"Lucy in the Sky with Diamonds": Airline Liability for Checked-In Jewelry*, 69 J. Air L. & Com. 743 (2004). For those who fail to take such advice, chances are good that if their property is permanently lost—a fate suffered by one percent of all airline luggage—it eventually will end up at the Unclaimed Baggage Center in Scottsboro, Alabama (www.unclaimedbaggage.com). Founded in 1970, the block-long building now is one of the country's biggest tourist attractions, annually selling one million items to the public at steeply discounted prices. *See further* Sharon McDonnell, *Lost Luggage is Rare, But the Trauma Can Be Acute*, N.Y. Times, June 8, 2004, at C9 (noting that airlines are beginning to experiment with radio frequency ID tags, which they hope will lead to fewer lost bags).

4. In recent years, disputes like *Husain* have focused the public's attention on the medical risks of flying, including deep vein thrombosis (also known as "economy class syndrome"), which arises when a person sits for too long (a common occurrence on trans-oceanic flights), and disease transmission due to recirculating cabin air. To what extent should airlines be responsible for such incidents? *See further Prescod v. AMR, Inc.*, 383 F.3d 861 (9th Cir. 2004) (airline, which lost asthmatic passenger's carry-on bag that contained her nebulizer, held liable for her death); *Blansett v. Continental Airlines, Inc.*, 379 F.3d 177 (5th Cir.), *cert. denied*, 125 S. Ct. 672 (2004) (airline not liable for failing to warn about the dangers of deep vein thrombosis); Ruswantissa Abeyratne, *The Economy Class Syndrome and Air Carrier Liability*, 28 Transp. L.J. 251 (2001); Ruswantissa I.R. Abeyratne, *The Spread of Tuberculosis in the Aircraft Cabin—Issues of Air Carrier Liability*, 27 Transp. L.J. 41 (2000); Robert F. Ruckman, *ER in the Skies: In-Flight Medical Emergencies*, 65 J. Air L. & Com. 77 (1999); David Glynn, Comment, *Flying Hospitals: Coffee, Tea or Defibrillation?*, 27 Transp. L.J. 247 (2000).

5. In an example of art imitating life, in September 2005 the movie *Flightplan* opened as the country's No. 1 box office attraction. In it, Jodie Foster plays Kyle Pratt, a widow flying home from Berlin to New York. When her young daughter Julia (Marlene Lawston) goes missing, Pratt begs the flight attendants to help her look for the girl. They respond with rudeness and indifference (as in *Husain*), leaving Pratt to fend for herself. Upset by this depiction, real-life flight attendants denounced the film and urged the public to boycott it. *See further* Micheline Maynard, *'Flightplan' Irks Flights Attendants*, N.Y. Times, Sept. 28, 2005, at B2.

6. Did it strike you as strange, while reading *Peggy's Cove*, to have an airplane case being decided by reference to a maritime statute (i.e., the Death on the High Seas Act)? In fact, aviation tort suits often look to maritime law when crashes occur over water (or involve seaplanes), and there are numerous parallels between the two fields. *See further* James W. Huston & Bill O'Connor, *Admiralty Law and Jurisdiction in Air Crash Cases*, 69 J. Air L. & Com. 299 (2004); Ladd Sanger & Vickie S. Brandt, *Flying and Crashing on the Wings of Fortuosity: The Case for Applying Admiralty Jurisdiction to Aviation Accidents Over Navigable Waters*, 68 J. Air L. & Com. 283 (2003); Louisa S. Porter et al., *Maritime Law and Aviation Torts: Navigating Through Troubled Waters*, 49 Fed. Law. 24 (Nov./Dec. 2002).

7. As Chief Judge Giles explains, the destruction of Swissair Flight 111 was caused by a malfunction in its in-flight entertainment system. Another source of worry are the various devices that passengers bring on-board, such as cell phones, laptop computers, and headsets. Although the contention remains controversial and a definite link has not been shown, many people believe that such items could interfere with a plane's navigation system and cause a crash. *See further* Carolyn Ritchie, Comment, *Potential Liability from Electromagnetic Interference with Aircraft Systems Caused by Passengers' On-Board Use of Portable Electronic Devices*, 61 J. Air L. & Com. 683 (1996), and Matthew L. Wald, *Ready for Takeoff, With Emphasis on 'Off,'* N.Y. Times, Mar. 18, 2004, at E3. *But see* Ken Belson & Micheline Maynard, *Cellphones at 35,000 Feet? Changes in Technology and F.C.C. Rules May Be Coming*, N.Y. Times, Dec. 10, 2004, at C1.

8. The *Taipei* and *Stethem* cases are examples of plaintiffs attempting to find additional defendants to sue. In their search, many plaintiffs look to travel agents, although such suits generally are unsuccessful due to a lack of culpable activity. *See further* Tracy A. Bateman, Annotation, *Liability of Travel Publication, Travel Agent, or Similar Party for Personal Injury or Death of Traveler*, 2 A.L.R.5th 396 (1992 & 2005 Supp.).

9. The foregoing, of course, does not begin to exhaust the possible hazards faced by passengers and it is doubtful that a complete list of such dangers could be formulated. For a further look at potential complications, *see, e.g.*, Kathleen Bicek Bezdichek, Annotation, *Liability of Air Carrier for Injury to Passenger Caused by Fall of Object From Overhead Baggage Compartment*, 32 A.L.R.5th 1 (1995 & 2004 Supp.); Robert A. Brazener, Annotation, *Liability of Air Carrier for Damage or Injury Sustained by Passenger as Result of Hijacking*, 72 A.L.R.3d 1299 (1976 & 2005 Supp.); William G. Phelps, Annotation, *Validity, Construction, and Application of Provisions of Federal Aviation Act (49 U.S.C.A. §§ 1472 (I)(L), (N)) Punishing Air Piracy and Certain Acts Aboard Aircraft in Flight, or Boarding Aircraft*, 109 A.L.R. Fed. 488 (1992 & 2004 Supp.); David E. Rigney, Annotation, *Death or Injury to Occupant of Airplane From Collision or Near-Collision with Another Aircraft*, 64 A.L.R.5th 235 (1998 & 2004 Supp.); Thomas R. Trenker, Annotation, *Carrier's Liability Based on Serving Intoxicants to Passenger*, 76 A.L.R.3d 1218 (1977 & 2004 Supp.); Jay M. Zitter, Annotation, *Air Carrier's Liability for Injury From Condition of Airport Premises*, 14 A.L.R.5th 662 (1993 & 2005 Supp.); Blair J. Berkley, *Warsaw*

Convention Claims Arising From Airline-Passenger Violence, 6 UCLA J. Int'l & Foreign Affairs 499 (2001–02); Frank D. Cimino, Comment, *Air Turbulence Liability*, 64 J. Air L. & Com. 1163 (1999). *See also* Christopher Elliott, *A Necessity Airlines Shouldn't Take for Granted*, N.Y. Times, Dec. 6, 2005, at C10 (describing a 14-hour flight from Los Angeles to Sydney on a United Airlines 747 on which only two of the plane's 15 bathrooms were operational and pointing out that, subject to certain narrow exceptions, flying an aircraft "with nonworking lavatories is completely legal.").

As one would expect, popular culture also has weighed in on these matters. In addition to William Golding's classic novel *Lord of the Flies* (1954) and the hit ABC series *Lost* (2004–), both of which involve plane crashes on deserted islands, there have been numerous movies in which passengers have found themselves in varying types of trouble, including: *8 Heads in a Duffel Bag* (1997, starring Joe Pesci), *Air Force One* (1997, Harrison Ford), *Airplane!* (1980, Leslie Nielsen), *Alive* (1993, Ethan Hawke), *Con Air* (1997, Nicolas Cage), *Executive Decision* (1996, Kurt Russell), *Home Alone* (1990, Macaulay Culkin), *Passenger 57* (1992, Wesley Snipes), *Planes, Trains and Automobiles* (1987, John Candy), *Red Eye* (2005, Cillian Murphy), *Skyjacked* (1972, Charlton Heston), *The High and the Mighty* (1954, John Wayne), and *The Out-of-Towners* (1999, Steve Martin). Additionally, there is the film *Soul Plane* (2004, Kevin Hart), in which a passenger who has a bad flight sues an airline, collects $100 million, and uses the money to start his own carrier, complete with funky music, an onboard dance club, and a bathroom attendant.

Perhaps the most famous such story, however, is an episode of *The Twilight Zone* (CBS, 1959–65):

> Cited by many aficionados as the all-time best Twilight Zone episode, "Nightmare at 20,000 Feet" benefits immeasurably from a bravura performance by star William Shatner. While travelling through rough weather on a passenger plane, former mental patient Bob Wilson (Shatner) peers out of his window—and sees a hideous gremlin balanced on the plane's wing. Doubting his own sanity, Bob tries to convince himself that he is merely hallucinating ... and then the gremlin begins to tear the wing apart. [Grabbing a gun from a sleeping policeman, Bob shoots the gremlin, causing it to fall off the wing. But because no one else has seen the monster, and given his psychiatric history, Bob is placed in a straitjacket and taken back to the asylum. As the story ends, however, viewers learn that when the plane is next inspected, mechanics will find strange damage to its fuselage.]
>
> Adapted by Richard Matheson from his own short story, "Nightmare at 20,000 Feet" was originally telecast October 11, 1963. The story was later [included as one of the four segments of the] theatrical feature Twilight Zone: The Movie (1983) [with John Lithgow stepping into Shatner's role] and has since been mercilessly lampooned in TV comedy series ranging from The Simpsons to 3rd Rock from the Sun.

Hal Erickson, *The Twilight Zone: Nightmare at 20,000 Feet*, at www.allmovie.com.

10. In September 2005, in a scene straight out of a Hollywood script, passengers aboard JetBlue Airways's Flight 292 watched themselves on television as their crippled airplane made an emergency landing:

> Carrying 139 passengers and 6 crew, the Airbus A320-232 aircraft departed from Burbank at 3:17 p.m. to fly to [New York's] JFK airport.
>
> After takeoff, the pilots realized that they could not retract the landing gear of the airplane. They then flew low over Long Beach Municipal Airport to

> allow officials in the airport's control tower to take stock of the damage. [I]t was found that the tires on the nose gear were rotated ninety degrees to the left, perpendicular to the direction of flight.
>
> Rather than return to Long Beach Airport, it was decided that the airplane would land at Los Angeles International Airport in order to take advantage of its long, wide runways and modern safety equipment.
>
> Since JetBlue planes are equipped with DirecTV satellite television, passengers on flight 292 were able to watch live news coverage of their flight while the plane circled over the Pacific for hours. This flight, therefore, may have been the first in history where the passengers watched themselves during an emergency.

JetBlue Airways Flight 292, at en.wikipedia.org/wiki/JetBlue_Airways_Flight_292. *See further* Evan Henerson, *Travelers Tuned in to Own Crisis; In-Flight TV Riverting on Flight 292*, L.A. Daily News, Sept. 23, 2005, at N3 ("While the information from the captain and flight crew was consistent with what was being reported on the news, the tone and the sense of gravity from the two sources often diverged, passengers said. 'The captain apologized at first, saying there was a problem with the landing gear and it was no big deal; there was nothing really to worry about,' said Pia Varma, 23, of Encino. 'Then, on the news, they're saying this has never been attempted before and it's the scariest thing ever. It was a little nerve-racking.'").

Problem 16

While on a trans-Atlantic flight, a passenger was sexually assaulted by another passenger. If the victim sues the airline, will it be held liable? *See Wallace v. Korean Air*, 214 F.3d 293 (2d Cir. 2000), *cert. denied*, 531 U.S. 1144 (2001).

Chapter 5

Cargo

A. OVERVIEW

Air cargo normally is of high value and often is perishable. It moves under a contract of carriage, known as an air waybill (often shortened to "airbill"), that also serves as a delivery receipt. Along with their airbills, carriers also publish service guides and tariffs. Collectively, these documents spell out the conditions under which the carrier is willing to perform.

In addition to the carrier, shipper ("consignor"), and receiver ("consignee"), a number of other parties may be involved in the transaction, including banks, freight forwarders, consolidators, and warehouses. The presence of such parties often requires courts to go beyond the two primary bodies of law that govern air cargo: federal common law (for domestic shipments) and the Warsaw Convention of 1929 (which, as explained in Chapter 4, now is giving way to the Montreal Convention of 1999) (for international shipments).

B. SUITS AGAINST CARRIERS

1. FAIR OPPORTUNITY

WELLIVER v. FEDERAL EXPRESS

737 F. Supp. 205 (S.D.N.Y. 1990)

DUFFY, District Judge.

Plaintiffs Neil Welliver and Arlene Gostin bring this diversity action against defendant Federal Express Corporation ("Federal Express") for failure to deliver and loss of a package containing two original watercolor paintings. Federal Express moves pursuant to Fed. R. Civ. P. 56 for summary judgment dismissing certain causes of action and adjudging that the liability of Federal Express for all causes of action asserted by plaintiffs is limited to $500. Gostin cross-moves for summary judgment on the first cause of action alleging breach of contract of carriage.

The uncontradicted facts are as follows. In 1987, Welliver created two original watercolor paintings for publication in a limited edition luxury book, published by the Limited Editions Club. Gostin, a professor at the University of the Arts in Philadelphia and a professional printmaker, has been Welliver's printer since 1980. While Gostin was producing plates from the two paintings, she was authorized by Welliver to ship the paintings from Philadelphia to the Limited Editions Club in New York on his behalf.

On April 28, 1987, Gostin contacted Federal Express to arrange for shipment of the paintings. She also requested that the courier provide all necessary documentation and packaging materials. Gostin then prepared the watercolors for shipment by wrapping them in paper and masonite packaging material.

When the courier arrived, he informed Gostin that he was in a great hurry and did not have time to wait for her to fill out the necessary documents or to repackage the shipment into Federal Express' packaging materials. She agreed to have him fill out the airbill, number 1672350190. She gave him the necessary information on a piece of paper, which indicated the package was to be sent to Ben Schiff at the Limited Editions Club in New York. The courier assured her that he would take care of the rest, including completion of the necessary documentation. When she requested a receipt, the courier went out to his truck with the package and returned with a blank shipper's copy of the airbill on which he wrote the date and his employee number.

The face of the airbill expressly limits the potential liability of Federal Express to $100 for any loss or damage to cargo. The reverse side of the airbill, as well as the Service Guide that the airbill incorporates by reference, provides that the shipper can declare a higher value than $100 for the cargo, with the freight rate charge increased accordingly. It also provides that a shipper of items of "extraordinary" value, such as artwork, may declare up to $500.

The package containing the paintings was never received by Limited Editions and Federal Express admits that it was lost in transit. To date, it has not been located. Plaintiffs seek to recover the full value of Welliver's two original works of art. Four causes of action are alleged in the complaint: (1) breach of the contract of carriage; (2) negligence based on the loss of the package; (3) negligence based on the courier's alleged promise to fill out the airbill and his failure to do so; and (4) fraud based on the allegation that the courier knew his promise to fill out the airbill was false when he made it.

DISCUSSION

Federal Express is an all-cargo air carrier certified by the Civil Aeronautics Board and the Federal Aviation Administration to provide interstate cargo transportation services to the public. The liability of interstate common carriers for the loss, damage, or delay of goods in transit in general is controlled by federal law. North American Phillips Corp. v. Emery Air Freight Corp, 579 F.2d 229, 233–34 (2d Cir. 1978). Specifically, the declared value limitation of liability has survived deregulation of the airline industry as part of the federal common law of air carrier liability.

The declared value limitation in a contract of carriage applies whether the action sounds in tort or contract. Hopper Furs, Inc. v. Emery Air Freight Corp., 749 F.2d 1261, 1264 (8th Cir. 1984). Indeed, under federal common law the declared value limitation of liability provision in Federal Express' airbills has been held to be enforceable. See, e.g., United States Gold Corp. v. Federal Express Corp., 719 F. Supp. 1217, 1225 (S.D.N.Y. 1989) (collecting cases).

Although it is not contested that Gostin did not declare or pay for a higher value for the package, Gostin asserts that the declared value limitation in the airbill is unenforceable against her because she was not afforded "reasonable notice" of the provision. Federal Express argues that Gostin had such notice because she requested that the package be shipped pursuant to an airbill and received a copy of it, and she admits having previously shipped packages with Federal Express using airbills with language identical to the limitation of the liability provision at issue here.

While it is not necessary that Gostin actually read the terms on the airbill to be bound by the liability limitation, that provision is enforceable only if two requirements are met. The limitation of liability must have been the result of "a (1) 'fair, open, just and reasonable agreement' between carrier and shipper, entered into by the shipper 'for the purposes of obtaining the lower of two or more rates of charges proportioned to the amount of risk'... and (2) the shipper was given 'the option of higher recovery upon paying a higher rate.'"

In determining whether these requirements for enforceability have been met, courts have considered such factors as (1) whether the carrier has given adequate notice of the limitation of its liability to the shipper, (2) the economic stature and commercial sophistication of the parties, and (3) the availability of "spot" insurance to cover a shipper's exposure. United States Gold, 719 F. Supp. at 1225 (citations omitted). The reasonableness of notice is a question of law to be determined by the court. Deiro v. American Airlines, Inc., 816 F.2d 1360, 1364 (9th Cir. 1987).

That Gostin was afforded reasonable notice is not supported by the record before me. Gostin's version of the circumstances surrounding the pick-up of the package are not contradicted by Federal Express. Indeed, Federal Express' own telephone logs concerning the search for the missing package state that the courier verified Gostin's account of the incident. The courier was in a great hurry and never gave Gostin an opportunity to either fill out or review the airbill containing the limitation of liability provision prior to her turning over the package. Thus, it appears that she was not even given a copy of the airbill until after the courier had taken possession of the package, and therefore had no opportunity to read it until after the courier had departed with the package. Accordingly, Gostin was afforded neither reasonable notice of the limitation of liability provision nor a fair opportunity to declare a higher value for the shipment.

The cases relied on by Federal Express with regard to "reasonable notice" are unpersuasive because all involve either experienced, sophisticated shippers familiar with liability limitation provisions or shippers who actually declared a value for their shipments. See, e.g., United States Gold, 719 F. Supp. at 1225 (undisputed that both parties were sophisticated commercial entities and that shipper, from its extensive previous use of Federal Express, had more than adequate notice of the liability limitation, and even secured protection for its shipment from an outside insurer). Gostin does not have an account with Federal Express, having made no more than three shipments with Federal Express prior to April 1987. In addition, none of those shipments involved items that were irreplaceable or of significant value. Gostin thus had no reason to use the declared value option previously or to be familiar with the special limits for items of "extraordinary value." Moreover, Gostin avers that she had no knowledge of Federal Express' limitation of liability clause, and that if she had known of it, she would have made other arrangements for shipment of Welliver's paintings. In these circumstances, the fact that Gostin eventually received a copy of the airbill does not constitute "reasonable notice."

On the record before me, the liability limitation was not the result of a "fair, open, just and reasonable agreement" and Gostin was not given a fair opportunity to choose among different rates to obtain different coverage. The circumstances surrounding the pick-up of the package and the delivery of the airbill to Gostin outweigh the mere existence of the limitation provision. I find that the limitation of liability provision is therefore unenforceable and Federal Express is liable for the full value of the two lost paintings.

DOVER FARMS, INC. v. AMERICAN AIR LINES, INC.

268 A.2d 289 (N.J. Super. Ct. App. Div.),
certification denied, 270 A.2d 43 (N.J. 1970)

LEONARD, Judge.

Defendant, American Air Lines, Inc., appeals from a judgment entered by the trial court in favor of plaintiff Dover Farms, Inc. in the sum of $2240 plus interest and costs.

Dover Farms, Inc. (hereafter plaintiff), a baby chick hatchery, made arrangements with defendant, an interstate air freight carrier, to transport 8000 baby chicks to the buyer thereof, plaintiff Martin H. Bernstein, at Los Angeles, California, C.O.D.

Pursuant to those arrangements, boxes containing the chicks were delivered by plaintiff's truck to defendant's air terminal in Newark on April 16, 1968.

Plaintiff's truck driver testified as to the delivery of the boxes of chicks to defendant's receiving clerk. The driver secured an application—apparently the blank form of an air bill—from an inside clerk and delivered it to the "receiver." The latter, after weighing the chicks, partially filled out the air bill and returned it to plaintiff's driver. In turn, he gave the partially completed air bill to the inside clerk, who "filled the rest out."

The driver further testified that at the same time he also gave the inside clerk a copy of plaintiff's invoice to which there was attached, by a paper clip, an instruction sheet. The invoice showed the value of the chicks, $2240, defendant's flight number, and the departure and arrival times. The invoice was signed by defendant's clerk and returned to him. He also stated that the instruction sheet contained among other things, "how much it was supposed to be insured for."

Plaintiff's president testified that an instruction sheet was prepared and attached to the invoice which was given to the driver. It instructed defendant to insure the chicks for the "full value" as noted thereon. Nevertheless, the completed air bill, returned by defendant's clerk to plaintiff's driver, contained no "Declared Value." It merely disclosed 81 boxes at a total weight of 950 pounds, a weight rate shipping charge of $418.30, and a total charge of $439.96.

Defendant presented no witnesses and did not deny negligence in the transportation of the chicks. First, it argued that the air bill was clear on its face and that since no declared value was set forth thereon, defendant's filed tariff (Rule 52) limited plaintiff to a recovery of 50 cents per pound or a total of $475. Next, it contended that plaintiff's action was barred by Rule 60(c)(1) of its filed tariff until the freight charges have been paid.

The trial court found as follows:

> It is true that the Civil Aeronautics Board tariff (Rule 60(c)(1)) provides that "no claim for loss or damage to a shipment will be entertained until all transportation charges thereon have been paid." In this case the plaintiff was not charged with nor informed of the proper transportation charges because of the error of defendant's agent and the defendant [sic, plaintiff] has not yet been so informed. Therefore the Court holds that the aforementioned rule does not apply.
>
> Since the defendant failed to follow the instructions of the plaintiff's agent with regard to the manner in which the domestic airbill should have been completed and the same was therefore not properly prepared in one of its essentials, the provisions of the Civil Aeronautics Board tariffs do not apply.

The court thereupon concluded that there being no evidence to the contrary, plaintiff's shipment was lost due to defendant's negligence. Accordingly, judgment was entered in favor of plaintiff in the amount of $2240.

Defendant now contends that the trial court erred in not applying its filed tariff and limiting its liability to $475. It supports this contention with the same above-noted argument as it presented to the trial court.

Since defendant was an air carrier engaged in the interstate transportation of passengers and freight, the transportation of plaintiff's chicks to California was controlled by federal rather than state law. Thus, defendant was subject to the provisions of the Federal Aviation Act of 1958. Pursuant to §403(a) thereof (49 U.S.C.A. §1373(a)) it is required to file with the Civil Aeronautics Board tariffs containing its rules and regulations relating to its interstate transportation of passengers and cargo. It filed such tariffs. These tariffs are binding upon shipper and carrier alike.

The applicable tariff (Rule 52) provides, in effect, that defendant's liability was limited to 50 cents per pound unless the shipper declares a higher value to the carrier. The air bill given by defendant to plaintiff's agent provides that the goods are accepted subject to the filed tariffs, and that the declared value will "not be more than the value stated in the governing tariffs for each pound on which charges are assessed unless a higher value is declared and applicable charges paid thereon."

The air bill issued to the shipper and accepted by him constitutes the contract of carriage. Thus, generally, one is bound to the tariff value where no other value is specifically set forth. The shipper has an opportunity to declare any value he may choose on the shipment and thus apprise the carrier of the extent of its responsibility. If he does not do so, he cannot thereafter be heard to claim damages valued greatly in excess of the "value" of the shipment as determined by the contract. Having accepted the benefit of a lower rate dependent upon the specified valuation, the shipper is estopped from asserting a higher value.

However, the undisputed facts clearly establish that the shipper did declare a higher value. Plaintiff's agent gave defendant's agent instructions to insure the chicks for $2240. In spite of these instructions, the air bill, which was completely prepared by defendant's agents, contained no such "Declared Value." It was received by plaintiff's agent at a late hour during the night, and by the time defendant's omission could have been detected and rectified the chicks had already arrived dead or near dead in Los Angeles.

The undisputed evidence clearly leads to the conclusion that the full value was not placed on the air bill only as a result of the mutual mistake of the agents of the parties. Under these circumstances, we find that plaintiff is equitably entitled to be relieved from the result of this mutual mistake. The contract between the parties, the air bill, being the product of an honest mistake, will be reformed to meet the true intent of the parties. This may be done without violating any existing federal tariff or regulation.

However, plaintiff is not entitled to recover $2240 from defendant. Transportation charges consistent with this valuation must first be paid by plaintiff. See Tariff Rule 60(c)(1). Thus, this matter is remanded to the trial court so that these charges may be determined by agreement of the parties or by the court following a hearing. The amount thus ascertained shall be deducted from $2240 and a judgment shall be entered for the plaintiff in the reduced amount. No interest shall be payable thereon. In the light of this procedure, we find defendant's final point to be without merit. This is especially so since we have mandated that transportation charges be deducted from the judgment, not the reverse.

Affirmed as modified, and remanded in accordance herewith.

KESEL v. UNITED PARCEL SERVICE, INC.

339 F.3d 849 (9th Cir. 2003)

McKEOWN, Circuit Judge.

A package of paintings by prominent Ukrainian artists, en route from Odessa to California via United Parcel Service, arrived at a Kentucky warehouse, then vanished like the Ark of the Covenant. (We refer to the film, Raiders of the Lost Ark (Paramount Pictures 1981), in which the government, much to the chagrin of Indiana Jones, decided that placing the Ark inside a crate amid a giant warehouse filled with identical crates was the best way to ensure that it would never be found.) The shipper, Mark Kesel, contends that the paintings were worth far more than the $558 declared value listed on the waybill, and seeks to hold UPS liable for the full value of the paintings.

We must decide whether UPS violated the released valuation doctrine, which requires carriers to give interstate shippers reasonable notice of limited liability and a fair opportunity to buy more insurance. UPS provided notice of its limited liability ($100 per shipment) in the documents that constituted its shipping contract. Although Kesel, through his agent, was able to purchase insurance in excess of the limitation, UPS rebuffed the agent's attempt to insure the paintings for more than their value as stated on a Ukrainian customs form. The district court, on summary judgment, concluded that UPS complied with the released valuation doctrine, and limited its liability to $558. We agree and affirm.

BACKGROUND

Kesel is a corporate executive in the high technology arena and a sponsor of a foundation that distributes fine art from Russia and the Ukraine. During a trip to the Ukraine, Kesel and an Odessa-based artist, Sergei Belik, visited studios and selected seven paintings for an exhibition that the foundation planned to hold in San Francisco.

Before leaving Odessa, Kesel asked Belik to ship the paintings to California through UPS. He told Belik to declare the paintings at $13,500 for U.S. customs purposes and to insure them for $60,000, a figure based on Kesel's belief that the paintings could be sold in the United States for $8,000 to $10,000 apiece.

As required by Ukrainian law, Belik took the paintings to the customs commission in Odessa. According to Belik, if the commission decides that a work of art is not an antique, it does not estimate its artistic worth, but instead assigns a value based on the cost of materials. Belik paid the customs duties and the commission gave him a permit form that listed the value of the paintings as $558.

Belik took the customs form and the paintings to the UPS office in Odessa. He told the UPS clerk that he wanted to insure the paintings for $60,000. After consulting by phone with a central office, the UPS clerk "categorically refused" to insure the paintings for more than $558. Belik, without contacting Kesel, went ahead and shipped all seven paintings in a single package. On the waybill, the value "$558" appears in the box entitled "Declared Value for Insurance." Belik filled in the addresses on the waybill and signed it.

When the paintings did not arrive in California, Kesel called UPS, which traced the package to its international warehouse in Kentucky. Further efforts to locate the paintings failed, however, and they are presumed to be lost.

Kesel sued UPS in [a] California [state] court, alleging numerous federal and state claims, and seeking $60,000 in damages for the loss of the paintings. After UPS removed the case to federal court, Kesel amended his complaint to allege claims for negligence and breach of contract under federal common law, which governs contractual clauses limiting the liability of interstate carriers for damage to goods shipped by air.

The district court granted summary judgment for UPS, limiting its liability to $558. The court concluded that UPS had satisfied the released valuation doctrine. UPS's shipping contract provided reasonable notice of limited liability, the court reasoned, because the waybill and other documents informed the shipper that UPS would not be liable for more than the $100 per package "released value" unless the shipper declared a higher value on the waybill. Although these shipping documents imposed an upper limit of $50,000 on this additional insurance, the court concluded that UPS had given Kesel a fair opportunity to purchase greater liability because Belik insured the paintings for $558—more than the $100 released value that otherwise would have applied.

THE RELEASED VALUATION DOCTRINE

Whether Kesel can recover more than the $558 declared value for the lost paintings is an issue of federal common law that we review de novo. See King Jewelry, Inc. v. Fed. Express Corp., 316 F.3d 961, 965 (9th Cir.2003).

The essential facts regarding the shipment are not in dispute. "The released valuation doctrine, a federal common law creation, delineates what a carrier must do to limit its liability." Under this doctrine, in exchange for a low rate, the shipper "is deemed to have released the carrier from liability beyond a stated amount." Deiro v. American Airlines, 816 F.2d 1360, 1365 (9th Cir. 1987).

UPS can limit its liability to $558 only if it provided Kesel with "(1) reasonable notice of limited liability, and (2) a fair opportunity to purchase higher liability." Deiro, 816 F.2d at 1365 ("The shipper is bound only if he has reasonable notice of the rate structure and is given a fair opportunity to pay a higher rate in order to obtain greater protection.").

UPS's shipping agreement with Kesel comprised the air waybill that Belik signed, the Guide to UPS Services (the "Service Guide"), and UPS's General Tariff Containing Classifications, Rules and Practices for the Transportation of Property (the "Tariff"). See King Jewelry, 316 F.3d at 964 (noting that the airbill and Service Guide formed the contract between the shipper and FedEx). As we discuss below, because these documents gave Kesel reasonable notice of limited liability, and UPS gave Kesel a fair opportunity to purchase greater liability coverage, the district court properly limited UPS's liability to the amount stated on the waybill.

A. NOTICE OF LIMITED LIABILITY

UPS's waybill, Service Guide, and Tariff each contain "prominent notices of the liability limitation in plain language." For example, the front of the waybill instructs the reader in bold type to "See Instructions On Back." The reverse side of the waybill explains that "any liability of UPS shall be ... limited to proven damages up to a maximum per shipment of the local currency equivalent of USD 100 per shipment, unless a higher value has been declared...." UPS's Service Guide and Tariff both contain similar language.

Kesel does not dispute the presence of the limited liability language on the shipping documents. Rather, he argues that he lacked notice of UPS's liability limitation because the waybill and other materials are written in English—which Belik cannot read—and the back of the waybill was smudged. Also, according to Kesel, he and Belik misunderstood the purpose of the insurance they sought to buy from UPS, mistakenly believing that it would provide them with additional protection above and beyond UPS's liability for the full value of the paintings.

Despite an effort to suggest he was duped, Kesel cannot escape the broad reach of our precedent regarding notice of limited liability: "Federal common law has never required actual notice of a carrier's liability limitation." Deiro, 816 F.2d at 1366. Nor is "actual possession of the bill of lading with the [liability] limit ... required before a party with an economic interest in the shipped goods can be held to the limitation." Read-Rite Corp. v. Burlington Air Express, Ltd., 186 F.3d 1190, 1198 (9th Cir.1999). Kesel, who is fluent in English and had previously shipped expensive items through UPS—such as electronic equipment insured for up to a million dollars—knew how to find out the extent of UPS's liability. Whatever their alleged naivete in matters of international shipping, it would be "unfair to place the loss" on UPS merely because Belik or Kesel now claim to have "misunderstood the effect of the liability limitation commonly used by interstate carriers." Norton v. Jim Phillips Horse Transp., Inc., 901 F.2d 821, 830 (10th Cir.1989). Such a result would effectively spell the death knell for liability limitations in interstate shipping and dramatically alter the fairly settled landscape that defines the relationship between the shipper and the carrier.

B. FAIR OPPORTUNITY TO PURCHASE ADDITIONAL LIABILITY COVERAGE

The heart of Kesel's case is that UPS denied him a fair opportunity to purchase greater liability coverage because it refused to let Belik insure the paintings for more than $558—a fraction of the $50,000 maximum listed in UPS's waybill, Service Guide, and Tariff. Although this argument seemingly has appeal, it is inconsistent with King Jewelry, in which we held that "the released valuation doctrine only requires a fair opportunity to purchase a higher liability, not necessarily up to the full value of the item." 316 F.3d at 966. UPS in fact did allow Belik to buy insurance for more than the standard $100 per package limit that otherwise would have applied.

In King Jewelry, the plaintiff shipped marble candelabra through FedEx and attempted to insure them for their full $37,000 value. When the candelabra were damaged during shipment, FedEx sought to limit its liability to $500, which the waybill stated was the maximum liability for "items of extraordinary value." We held that FedEx was liable only for $500, and that it had complied with the released valuation doctrine by insuring the candelabra for that amount—less than their actual value, but higher than the $100 released value.

Kesel likens his situation to a case in which the carrier altogether refused to give shippers the opportunity to buy additional insurance. See Klicker v. Northwest Airlines, 563 F.2d 1310, 1312 (9th Cir.1977). In Klicker, the shippers informed the Northwest Airlines' ticket agent that their dog was worth $35,000, but the agent would not permit them to declare any value for the dog or buy any additional coverage. The dog died during the flight. We held that the airline was liable for the entire value of the dog, and that the airline could not rely on its tariff provision that limited recovery to $500 in the absence of a declared value. Kesel's case, however, presents a different scenario. In contrast to the airline in Klicker, UPS permitted Belik to declare a value for the paintings and to insure them for the declared value.

UPS does not have carte blanche to impose arbitrary limits, irrespective of its Tariff and waybill, on the insurance it offers to shippers. Nonetheless, in the context of its dual role as customs agent and carrier, UPS complied with its Tariff and shipping agreement in limiting available insurance to the value listed on the customs documents. The Service Guide explains that, for international shipments, the shipper must "provide required documentation for customs clearance.... By providing required documentation, the shipper certifies that all statements and information relating to exportation and importation are true and correct." According to the Guide, UPS requires the shipper to submit an invoice listing, among other things, the "total value of each item," and the shipper appoints UPS as "the agent for performance of customs clearance, where allowed by law."

Given these shipment guidelines and the circumstances of Kesel's shipment, UPS complied with the released valuation doctrine in limiting the insurance to the value listed on the form presented with the paintings. This procedure did not deprive Kesel of proper notice. Belik admits that the UPS agent clearly told him that it would not insure the paintings for more than the customs value, and Belik, without consulting Kesel, chose to ship through UPS fully aware of the limited liability. Nothing here supports a claim of coercion or misinformation.

The opportunity to purchase additional liability coverage from UPS was fair and it did not leave Belik in the lurch. Belik could have bought separate insurance elsewhere or shipped with a different carrier. Instead, Belik shipped the paintings through UPS, aware that he had only purchased $558 worth of liability, but hoping "in this particular case everything would be as normal." Through his agent, Kesel took the gamble that the paintings would not vanish. When they did, he was stuck with the bargain he struck—UPS's liability is limited to the $558 declared value stated on the waybill.

Affirmed.

FERGUSON, Circuit Judge, dissenting.

I respectfully dissent. The majority misconstrues our decision in King Jewelry, Inc. v. Fed. Express Corp., 316 F.3d 961 (9th Cir.2003), effectively permitting common carriers to manipulate their rate structures by adding unpublished terms to their tariffs at the time of shipment. Even more troubling, the majority holds that a shipper has presumptively been afforded a fair "opportunity to purchase additional coverage" anytime she "could have bought separate insurance elsewhere or shipped with a different carrier." In other words, after this decision, a carrier may comply with the requirements of the released valuation doctrine by posting a sign listing some (but not all) of their terms and doing business in a location where there are other carriers or third-party insurance providers. This evisceration of the protection afforded by the released valuation doctrine is unwarranted and unwise. Because I believe that, construing the facts in the light most favorable to Kesel, UPS did not provide a "fair opportunity" to purchase greater liability coverage, I must dissent.

Notes

1. The plaintiff in *Welliver* won because Gostin, who spoke English, proclaimed ignorance of FedEx's policies and was not given a copy of the airbill until after the package had been turned over to the courier. In contrast, the plaintiff in *Kesel* lost despite the fact that Belik did not speak English, was given a smudged airbill, and did not understand UPS's shipping conditions even after they were explained to him. Can these decisions be reconciled? If not, which one do you think is correctly decided?

2. The court in *Dover Farms*, after deciding that a mutual mistake had been made, reformed the contract to reflect "full value." Should it have done so? What if, instead of a mutual mistake, the carrier filled out the airbill as it did because it was rejecting the shipper's "offer" to have the chicks carried for full value? Moreover, if full value was critical to the shipper (as it apparently was), why did its driver not take the time to carefully examine the airbill before leaving the terminal? Does it seem to you that the court was simply substituting its view of what should have happened for what did happen? Is this proper? For an interesting critique, *see* Kenneth L. Schneyer, *The Culture of Risk: Deconstructing Mutual Mistake*, 34 Am. Bus. L.J. 429 (1997) (canvassing the arguments for and against the continued existence of the doctrine).

3. As *Kesel* explains, shippers have the option of purchasing additional insurance from third parties. In *Kemper Insurance Cos. v. Federal Express Corp.*, 252 F.3d 509 (1st Cir.), *cert. denied*, 534 U.S. 1020 (2001), various jewelry dealers purchased such insurance from Kemper. When their packages were lost, Kemper indemnified them and then brought a subrogation action against Federal Express for the full value of the goods. After finding that Kemper was entitled to only $100 per package because of Federal Express's liability limits, the court added this trenchant comment:

> Lastly, we must point out that Kemper is in no way harmed by this type of limitation clause; in fact, it is the very existence of such a limitation that allows Kemper to market third-party package insurance. If FedEx altered its contracts to offer the type of first-party insurance suggested by Kemper, a shipper would either choose to insure through FedEx and not purchase supplementary insurance from Kemper, or would choose the lower released value and purchase the same coverage from Kemper, which in that case admits it would have no cause of action under the released value doctrine. Even if the released value doctrine technically provides Kemper a cause of action as subrogee, we are not overly sympathetic to the insurer's plight on these facts.

Id. at 514.

It should be underscored here that most air cargo disputes actually are insurance disputes. With the real parties having long since been paid, the battle is not over the instant loss (which often is quite small dollar-wise) but instead how future losses will be allocated under the standardized language of the airbill. Depending on the answer, the premiums charged by a particular group of insurers may have to be adjusted substantially.

4. Notice the different hats that UPS wore in *Kesel*: customs agent, air carrier, warehouseman, and ground carrier. In an omitted footnote, the court explained the impact this had on the litigation:

> We agree with the district court that the Warsaw Convention, "an international treaty governing the liability of air carriers engaging in international air travel," does not apply to Kesel's claims. Wayne v. DHL Worldwide Express, 294 F.3d 1179, 1185 (9th Cir.2002) (internal quotation marks and citation omitted); see Convention for the Unification of Certain Rules Relating to International Transportation by Air, Oct. 12, 1929, 49 Stat. 3000, 3014, T.S. No. 876 (1934), reprinted in note following 49 U.S.C. § 40105 (the "Warsaw Convention"). Kesel alleges that the package disappeared, not during the flight from Odessa to the United States, but after it arrived at UPS's Kentucky warehouse. Federal common law governs liability limits on shipments by air within the United States. See Wayne, 294 F.3d at 1185.

339 F.3d at 852 n.2.

5. *Welliver*, *Dover Farms*, and *Kesel* are examples of air carriers trying to manage the risks that come with transporting unique, perishable, or high-value goods. Even greater challenges are presented when the goods involved are hazardous.

In 1996, a company called SabreTech illegally shipped 144 chemical oxygen generators on ValuJet Flight 592. Shortly after take-off from Miami, the cannisters ignited and the DC-9 crashed in the Florida Everglades, killing all 110 people aboard. In the aftermath of the tragedy, SabreTech was criminally prosecuted, ordered to pay $2 million in fines and $11 million in restitution, and went out of business; ValuJet, seeking to put the incident behind it and win back its customers, merged with the much smaller AirWays Corporation, another discount carrier, and adopted the name AirTran Airways (www.airtran.com); and a chastened FAA promised to do a better job overseeing start-up airlines. *See further United States v. SabreTech, Inc.*, 271 F.3d 1018 (11th Cir. 2001). A copy of the NTSB's accident report can be found at www.ntsb.gov/Publictn/1997/aar9706.pdf.

Long before the ValuJet disaster, however, the dangers posed by shipping hazardous materials was apparent. As a result, beginning in the 1950s the International Air Transport Association promulgated a set of dangerous goods regulations. These soon were made part of the national legislation of more than 80 countries and adopted as technical instructions by the International Civil Aviation Organization. In the United States, responsibility for these matters now rests with the Department of Transportation's Pipeline and Hazardous Materials Safety Administration (formerly the Research and Special Projects Administration), which promulgates appropriate regulations, and the FAA, which enforces them. *See further* 49 U.S.C. §§ 5101–5127; 49 C.F.R. parts 171–180; Lee Braem, *Hazardous Materials Transportation—Reviewing the Rules of the Road*, 17 Envtl. Compliance & Litig. Strategy 1 (July 2001).

6. September 11th was a watershed event for the air cargo industry. *See generally Air Line Pilots Ass'n v. Federal Express Corp.*, 402 F.3d 1245 (D.C. Cir. 2005) (operational consequences) and *Federal Express Corp. v. Mineta*, 373 F.3d 112 (D.C. Cir. 2004) (financial consequences). In the wake of the attacks, enormous pressure has been put on air cargo carriers to be more careful when accepting shipments. Worried that the cost of increased vigilance will be ruinous, the industry has steadfastly fought such proposals (although usually on the ground of technological inability). Nevertheless, in November 2004 the Transportation Security Administration released a long list of proposed air cargo handling rules. *See* 69 Fed. Reg. 65,258 (Nov. 10, 2004). Before the month was

out, however, this effort was under attack by critics who claimed the government had sold out to carriers; in response, Representative Edward J. Markey (D-Mass.) quickly introduced several bills calling for the inspection of all air cargo. *See further* Frances Fiorino, *Cargo Screening Redux*, Av. Wk. & Space Tech., May 9, 2005, at 14.

7. More information about the air cargo industry can be found at the web sites of the Air and Expedited Motor Carriers Association (www.aemca.org), Airforwarders Association (www.airforwarders.org), International Air Cargo Association (www.tiaca.org), and Regional Air Cargo Carriers Association (www.raccaonline.org), as well as those of the major air cargo carriers: DHL (www.dhl.com), Federal Express (www.fedex.com), and United Parcel Service (www.ups.com). Useful industry publications include *Air Cargo News* (www.aircargonews.com), *Air Cargo Week* (www.azfreight.com), and *Air Cargo World* (www.aircargoworld.com).

8. Lastly, a word must be said about the Berlin Airlift, one of the earliest clashes of the Cold War:

> On June 24, 1948, the Soviet Union blocked access to the three Western-held sectors of Berlin, [which were located] deep within the Soviet zone of Germany, by cutting off all rail and road routes. [In response, United States] General Lucius D. Clay suggested sending a large armoured column from West Germany to West Berlin. President Harry S. Truman [rejected this suggestion, however], believ[ing it] entailed an unacceptable risk of war. [Instead,] Clay was told to [speak with] General Curtis LeMay, [the] commander [of the United States Air Force in] Europe, to see if an airlift was possible.
>
> On June 25, Clay gave the order to launch a massive airlift, [one that] ultimately last[ed] 324 days. The first [American] airplane flew on the following day, and the first British airplane flew on the 28th. This aerial supplying of West Berlin became known as the Berlin Airlift. The U.S. action was given the name "Operation Vittles," while [the] British supply plan [became] known as "Operation Plainfare."
>
> Hundreds of aircraft, nicknamed Rosinenbomber ("raisin bombers") by the local population, were used to fly in a wide variety of cargo items, including more than 1.5 million tons of coal. At the height of the operation, on April 16, 1949, an allied aircraft landed in Berlin every minute, and [a total of] 12,840 tons of freight were delivered [that day].
>
> The [airlifted goods] ranged from large containers to small packets of candy for the children of Berlin. The aircraft were supplied and flown by the United States, United Kingdom and France, but crews also came from Australia, Canada, South Africa and New Zealand. [By the time the Soviets finally lifted the blockade on May 11, 1949], 278,228 flights [had been] made and 2,326,406 tons of food and supplies [had been] delivered.

Berlin Blockade, at en.wikipedia.org/wiki/Berlin_Airlift#The_Berlin_Airlift.

Problem 17

A shipper arranged to have a package flown overseas. On the airbill, it described the contents as "Dental Supplies—Gold Fillings" and listed the value as $25,000. The carrier accepted the package but demanded a substantially higher freight rate, which the shipper paid. When the package arrived at its destination, the contents were missing.

The shipper immediately demanded full restitution, whereupon the carrier pointed out that its tariff absolutely prohibited gold shipments. As a result, it has refused to do anything more than refund the freight payment. If the shipper sues, how should the court rule? *See Williams Dental Co. v. Air Express International*, 824 F. Supp. 435 (S.D.N.Y.), *aff'd mem.*, 17 F.3d 392 (2d Cir. 1993).

2. NOTICE

DALTON v. DELTA AIRLINES, INC.

570 F.2d 1244 (5th Cir. 1978)

BROWN, Chief Judge.

The Greyhounds Who Left The Driving To Delta

Patrick Dalton, a citizen of Ireland, charged Delta Airlines with negligence in the shipment of his five greyhound racing dogs from Ireland to Miami. On August 9, 1973, the dogs were shipped from Shannon, Ireland to Miami, Florida on a through air billing. They were carried by Irish Airlines from Shannon to Boston, and by Delta Airlines from Boston to Miami. The greyhounds arrived in good condition in Boston, were temporarily taken in charge by the shipper's agent and boarded at a kennel for the night. On the following day they were delivered in good condition to Delta for shipment to Miami. Upon arrival at Miami International Airport the dogs were dead. A local veterinarian performed an autopsy which revealed that the greyhounds had suffocated. The carcasses were subsequently destroyed.

Dalton sought $60,000 in compensatory and exemplary damages for the income and profits he would have received from racing the dogs had they arrived in good condition and for their value at the time of the loss.

The parties agreed that since the negligence complained of occurred on an international air shipment the claim is governed by the Warsaw Convention, 49 U.S.C. § 1502. Article 29 of the Convention contains a two-year statute of limitations on actions, providing that those not brought within the limitations period will be barred. Delta contended below that the action was governed by Article 26 and that since Dalton did not give timely written notice within 7 days as required by clause (2), he could not recover any damages, even though the suit was timely.

Article 29 [provides:]

> (1) The right to damages shall be extinguished if an action is not brought within 2 years, reckoned from the date of arrival at the destination, or from the date on which the aircraft ought to have arrived, or from the date on which the transportation stopped.
>
> (2) The method of calculating the period of limitation shall be determined by the law of the court to which the case is submitted.

Article 26 [provides:]

> (1) Receipt by the person entitled to the delivery of baggage or goods without complaint shall be prima facie evidence that the same have been delivered in good condition and in accordance with the document of transportation.

> (2) In case of damage, the person entitled to delivery must complain to the carrier forthwith after the discovery of the damage, and at the latest, within 3 days from the date of receipt in the case of baggage and 7 days from the date of receipt in the case of goods. In case of delay the complaint must be made at the latest within 14 days from the date on which the baggage or goods have been placed at his disposal.
>
> (3) Every complaint must be made in writing upon the document of transportation or by separate notice in writing dispatched within the times aforesaid.
>
> (4) Failing complaint within the times aforesaid, no action shall lie against the carrier, save in the case of fraud on his part.

The lower court agreed [with Delta] and granted [its] motion for summary judgment due to the undisputed fact that Dalton did not give written notice of his claim until the 20th day after the arrival of the dead greyhounds.

The Lost Chord In The Warsaw Concerto

Since the case primarily concerns an international convention and since courts seek so far as possible to obtain uniformity in interpretation, we asked the parties to file supplemental briefs on the holdings and interpretations of foreign courts and authorities concerning the applicable portions of the Warsaw Convention involved in this case. We also invited amicus briefs from carrier and shipper organizations but none was forthcoming.

Based on the supplemental briefs and the record before us we reverse the grant of summary judgment by the lower court.

As an international treaty accepted by the United States, the Warsaw Convention is absolutely binding. Our function is to construe the Convention, determine its meaning, and then apply it fairly. See Kelley v. Societe Anonyme Belge D'Exploitation, E.D.N.Y., 1965, 242 F.Supp. 129, 136. In Board of County Com'rs v. Aerolineas Peruanasa, S.A., 5 Cir., 1962, 307 F.2d 802, 806–07, this Court set forth other rules for construing treaties:

> (I)n construing (a) treaty, as other contracts, we give consideration to the intent of the parties so as to carry out their manifest purpose.... We proceed also under the admonition that where a treaty admits of two constructions, one restrictive of and the other favorable to the rights claimed under it, the latter is to be preferred.

Without addressing the merits of any other contentions raised on this appeal we reverse for the plaintiff due to what we perceive to be a serious gap in Article 26. The Article simply does not cover the fact situation here. By its own terms it is applicable only in cases of damage or delay. Our unfortunate greyhounds were neither damaged nor delayed; they were destroyed.

We find support for our holding in an article by a foreign authority, cited by Delta in its supplemental brief. Max Litvine, Droit Aerien Notions De Droit Belge Et De Droit International (Bruxelles, Establissements Emile Bruylant, 1970) at page 250 states (in translation):

> Article 26 presents a serious gap, as it indeed deals only with cases of damages and delays.
>
> What to decide in cases of loss or destruction?
>
> In Article 13, subparagraph 3 only will apply and the action of the one entitled to the right does not require a protest if it concerns a loss or a total destruction.

There are a number of reasons which support this reading of Article 26. At the very outset there is Article 13(3) which expressly covers the situation of goods which are lost. Article 13(3) provides:

> (3) If the carrier admits the loss of the goods, or if the goods have not arrived at the expiration of seven days after the date on which they ought to have arrived, the consignee shall be entitled to put into force against the carrier the rights which flow from the contract of transportation.

No notice of any kind is called for either in Article 13 or in Articles 12, 13, or 14, and there is no incorporation by reference of Article 26.

Likewise, Article 18(1) distinguishes between goods which are lost, those which are destroyed, and those which are damaged. Article 18 [provides:]

> (1) The carrier shall be liable for damage sustained in the event of the destruction or loss of, or of damage to, any checked baggage or any goods, if the occurrence which caused the damage so sustained took place during the transportation by air.

There is obviously a great similarity between the loss of goods and the destruction of goods. Lost, of course, means that the location, or even the existence of, the goods is not known or reasonably ascertainable. But the common factor of lost or destroyed goods is that, in either case, they are wholly without economic value or utility to the shipper/consignee beyond mere scrap value. Of course the situation of destruction of goods poses factual problems not present with lost goods, since, on our approach, there is for Article 26 purposes a decisive distinction between goods that are damaged—even severely—and those which are destroyed. But this is inherent in many cases of carrier liability.

A demijohn of rare brandy falling 15 feet off the conveyor belt to the airport's concrete apron is no longer that when the container is smashed and the contents run off in the view of covetous eyes. So it is with dogs, dogs bred, born and trained for kennel racing, not just for flesh, hide or hair. Recognizing, as we must, that live dogs are goods, when dead they are no longer just damaged goods. They are not at all the thing shipped. No one better than the carrier knows this fact. Notice is not needed since notice would serve no useful purpose to the carrier.

The facts of this case demonstrate the wisdom of the "no notice needed for destroyed goods" rule. The shipper's representative, presumably a trained dog handler, was at the Miami airport to pick up the dogs. Due to security restraints, he was unable to go directly to the plane. The dogs were to be brought by Delta to him at the designated pickup. When Delta's agent got there he brought, not dogs, but the sad news that the dogs were dead. Delta recognized this fact by arranging mutually with the shipper for an autopsy by a veterinarian used and selected by Delta.

This analysis and our result gains added strength from considering clause (1) of Article 26:

> (1) Receipt by the person entitled to the delivery of baggage or goods without complaint shall be prima facie evidence that the same have been delivered in good condition and in accordance with the document of transportation.

Unless notice or complaint of damage is given, the receipt of the goods is itself prima facie proof of good order. This clause places on the shipper the burden of proving that the goods were in fact damaged after receipt by the air carrier and prior to or upon delivery to the consignee. Oddly enough, apart from this burden of proof, no restriction (other than the two-year prescription period) is put on the right to sue the carrier. Whatever might be the case of damage discovered within 7 days, which might call for notice under the terms of clause (3), it would not be possible ever to comply with notice for damage discovered after 7 days. This presumably led commentators during the early days of the Warsaw Convention to point out that a conflict exists between clause (1) and clause (4) which terminates any right of action against the carrier, even those in which the shipper shoulders his considerable burden of overcoming the clause (1) presumption of delivery in good condition.

The Article 26(1) presumption is triggered, of course, only on receipt of the goods. The shipper here, who never in a realistic way ever received the goods shipped—five live racers—should not be in a worse position than had there been a receipt. Of course, at the time of any such supposed or theoretical receipt, the very facts then evident to everyone and utterly incapable of subsequently being altered demonstrated not that the goods "have been delivered in good condition and in accordance with the [contract] of transportation," but quite the contrary. In the very act of attempted delivery the presumption that the goods were in good condition was irrefutably not just overcome but demolished, thus triggering the application of the provisions relating to the carrier's liability and rights (see Articles 17, 18, 19, 20 and 21).

Thus where destruction of goods occurs on an international flight the shipper-consignee need not give Article 26(3) notice. We have been importuned by Delta to cut off the claim at the dollar limit prescribed by Article 22(2). That matter not having been dealt with below is to be determined anew on remand.

REVERSED and REMANDED.

STUD v. TRANS INTERNATIONAL AIRLINES

727 F.2d 880 (9th Cir. 1984)

GOODWIN, Circuit Judge.

Nevelle Stud, the owner and shipper of a horse named Super Clint, sued for damages sustained when the horse died ten days after shipment on a Transamerica flight. Stud appeals from a summary judgment for Transamerica.

In April 1980, Transamerica (successor to Trans International Airlines, the first named defendant in this action) transported Super Clint on a flight from Canada to New Zealand. Super Clint, for whom Stud had paid $300,000 the month before, seemed to be in good health upon arrival in New Zealand on April 4. Shortly afterward the horse became visibly ill; he died on April 14, 1980. A veterinarian who performed an autopsy on April 15 concluded that the cause of death was "pleuro pneumonia probably brought on by the stress of travel." A final autopsy report dated June 21, 1980, concluded that temperature fluctuations in the cabin of the airplane probably caused the illness that claimed Super Clint. On June 25, Stud's insurance agent submitted a written notice of claim to Transamerica's New Zealand ground handling agent.

After negotiations with Transamerica proved fruitless, Stud filed this action for damages, alleging breach of the carriage contract, negligence, and willful misconduct. The district court held that the Warsaw Convention barred Stud's claim because Stud had failed to give Transamerica timely written notice of his loss.

The Warsaw Convention, 49 Stat. 3000, T.S. 876, 137 L.N.T.S. 11, governs the international carriage of goods by air, and thus applies to the shipment of Super Clint.

Canada, New Zealand, and the United States are all parties to the Warsaw Convention in its original 1929 version. See Av.L.Rep. (CCH) ¶ 27,054. A protocol concluded at The Hague in 1955 amended portions of the Convention relevant to this case. 478 U.N.T.S. 371. Canada and New Zealand are parties to the Hague Protocol, 1964 Can.T.S. No. 29, 1967 N.Z.T.S. No. 11, but the earlier version of the Convention remains in force in this country because Congress has not ratified the Protocol.

Because our jurisdiction is based not simply on the existence of a federal question under the version of the Warsaw Convention in force in the United States, but on diversity of citizenship as well, we are not compelled to apply the United States version of the Convention. Instead, we use the choice of law rules of California, the state in which this action was filed, to determine the applicable law. California applies the law of the place where a contract is to be performed, or, if a contract does not specify a place of performance, the law of the place where it was made. Cal. Civ. Code § 1646. The contract of carriage was performed by shipping Super Clint between two Hague Protocol countries and the Air Waybill covering his shipment indicates that the contract of carriage was made in Canada, a Hague Protocol country. We therefore apply the Warsaw Convention as amended by the Hague Protocol.

Under the Convention, a carrier is prima facie liable for damage to goods shipped by air if the damage was caused during the transportation by air, Article 18, but can avoid this liability by proving that it and its agents took "all necessary measures" to avoid the damage. Article 20. To hold a carrier liable, the person entitled to delivery of the goods must comply with the notice of complaint requirement of Article 26(2). It states that "in case of damage, the person entitled to delivery must complain to the carrier forthwith after the discovery of the damage, and, at the latest, within ... fourteen days from the date of the receipt in the case of goods." (This is the Hague Protocol version of Article 26(2). See 478 U.N.T.S. at 385. The original version of Article 26(2), still in effect in the United States, requires notice of complaint within seven days of receipt of the goods. 49 Stat. at 3020.) If notice of complaint is not given within the prescribed time period, "no action shall lie against the carrier." Article 26(4). Because Stud did not complain to Transamerica within fourteen days after Super Clint's arrival in New Zealand, his action is barred.

Article 26(2) makes notice of complaint a prerequisite to recovery only "in case of damage." The Fifth Circuit has recently held that Article 26(2) does not require a notice of complaint to recover for lost or destroyed goods. Dalton v. Delta Airlines, 570 F.2d 1244 (5th Cir.1978). This position has merit in appropriate cases. Article 18 of the Convention, which creates liability, distinguishes among destruction, loss, and damage. Because the Convention's drafters made such a distinction in one Article, it is logical to construe Article 26(2), which speaks only of damage, as maintaining the distinction and not requiring notice of complaint when the goods have been lost or destroyed. Commentators from several foreign countries agree. M. Litvine, Droit Aerien 250 (1970) (Belgium); W. Guldimann, Internationales Lufttransportrecht 155 (1965) (Switzerland); H. Abraham, Das Recht der Luftfahrt 372 (1960) (West Germany).

Whether Article 26(2) requires notice of complaint thus depends on whether the shipped goods were destroyed or merely damaged. Applying this rule to the shipment of Super Clint is difficult because Super Clint presents a case of both damage and destruction. Following the analysis in Dalton v. Delta Airlines, Super Clint arguably was "destroyed" within the meaning of the Convention when he died. In Dalton, greyhounds that had been alive when handed over to the carrier died in transit. Because the dogs were dead on arrival, the court held that they had been destroyed, not merely damaged, observing that dead dogs were "not at all the thing shipped," and lost all economic value beyond scrap value. But unlike the dogs in Dalton, Super Clint arrived alive and in apparent good health. When he left Transamerica's hands, Super Clint had been neither lost nor destroyed. At most, according to the allegations of the complaint, the horse had been damaged.

The policy underlying Article 26(2) persuades us that the condition of the goods at the time they leave the carrier's hands should determine whether notice of complaint is a prerequisite to recovery. It is reasonable to interpret Article 26(2) not to require notice of complaint for destroyed goods because the very fact of destruction gives the carrier actual notice that a claim may be forthcoming. When the carrier opens the cargo bay at the end of a flight and discovers that an animal shipped live is now dead, the carrier knows that an injury has occurred for which it may be held liable. (One case [however has held] that Article 26(2) requires complaint even for destroyed goods if the destruction is not obvious enough to give notice to the carrier. [See] American Breeders Service v. KLM Royal Dutch Airlines, 17 Av.Cas. (CCH) 17,103 (N.Y.Sup.Ct.1982).) But the fact of destruction can be counted on to give the carrier actual notice only if the goods are still in its possession when the destruction occurs. Once the goods have left the carrier's possession, destruction can easily occur without the carrier's knowledge.

Post-delivery destruction resembles the situation presented by goods that are merely damaged. Mere damage to goods will often be hidden from view and fail to give the carrier actual notice of the loss. Rather than inquire in each case whether damage short of destruction was sufficiently obvious to give the carrier actual notice, Article 26(2) adopts a blanket rule making notice of complaint a prerequisite to recovery for any damage to goods. The same rule should apply to post-delivery destruction because the cause may also be hidden from the carrier. Article 26(2) required Stud to give notice of complaint within fourteen days of receipt of Super Clint as a precondition to recovery.

Stud gave Transamerica notice of complaint on June 25, 1980, four days after he received a final autopsy report on Super Clint, but more than two months after the horse's death. Stud claims that the complaint was timely because until he received the autopsy report, he did not know that he could hold Transamerica liable.

Stud's notice of complaint was not timely. Even if we assume for the sake of argument that the fourteen-day period may be enlarged when damage to or destruction of goods could not, in the exercise of due diligence, be discovered within that period, it should not be enlarged here. Within fourteen days of receipt, a diligent shipper would have known—and Stud in fact knew—of both the damage to and the destruction of Super Clint. The Convention did not require Stud to prove to a certainty at the time of giving notice that Transamerica had caused Super Clint's death. There was no need to wait for a final autopsy report before giving notice of complaint.

[As it happens,] Transamerica had actual knowledge of Super Clint's death shortly after it occurred. The horse was something of a celebrity and its death was reported in the local news media. Stud argues that this actual knowledge satisfies the notice requirement of Article 26(2). It does not. Article 26(3) requires that the notice of complaint be in writing. If written notice of a consignee's complaint is necessary to preserve the right of recovery, a carrier's actual knowledge of the loss, gleaned from a source other than a written notice of complaint, is necessarily insufficient. Shah Safari, Inc. v. Western Airlines, 17 Av.Cas. (CCH) 17,101 (W.D.Wash.1982); Amazon Coffee Co. v. Trans World Airlines, 18 Av.Cas. (CCH) 17,264 (N.Y.Sup.Ct.1983). One reason for the written notice requirement is to avoid endless speculation about who knew what and when they allegedly knew it.

Stud also claims that Transamerica waived its right to a notice of complaint by engaging in settlement negotiations for nearly two years before it raised in defense the lack of notice of complaint. Because Stud did not come forward with facts showing that Transamerica had intentionally relinquished a known right to notice of complaint, CBS, Inc. v. Merrick, 716 F.2d 1292, 1295 (9th Cir.1983), there was no waiver and the district court properly entered summary judgment against Stud on this point.

Affirmed.

G. D. SEARLE & CO. v. FEDERAL EXPRESS CORPORATION

248 F. Supp. 2d 905 (N.D. Cal. 2003)

ARMSTRONG, District Judge.

This action arises out of the international transportation of goods by air. Plaintiff alleges that on or about August 2, 1999, Knoll (now Abbot Laboratories) entrusted a shipment of Verapamil HCL Fine Powder, a powder used in heart medication, to Defendants Federal Express Corporation ("Federal Express") and Union Transportation GMBH ("Union Transport"). In exchange for agreed upon freight charges, Defendants were to transport the cargo, weighing in total 5,420 kg, from Germany to California, for delivery in two to three days. On August 2, 1999, Union Transport issued its own air waybill "as carrier" in Manheim, Germany, and issued an air waybill on behalf of Federal Express "as carrier." Federal Express received the cargo on August 3, 1999, in Frankfurt, Germany. The cargo arrived in San Francisco in two shipments on August 9, 1999 and August 10, 1999. According to Plaintiff, the cargo was damaged in transit, resulting in a total loss. Plaintiff claims damages in an amount up to or exceeding $850,000.

Notice of Claim to Union Transport

In its Reply brief, Union Transport argues that Plaintiff failed to provide timely written notice of the claim to Union Transport as required by the Warsaw Convention. Under the Warsaw Convention as amended by The Hague Protocol, the person entitled to delivery "must complain to the carrier forthwith after the discovery of the damage, and, at the latest, within fourteen days from the date of receipt in the case of cargo." The Hague Protocol, Art. XV. In the instant case, Plaintiff received the cargo on August 18, 1999. Although Plaintiff promptly informed Federal Express of its claim, Plaintiff did not send notice to Union Transport of a damage claim until September 23, 1999. Union Transport argues that notice to Federal Express is insufficient to fulfill the notice requirement with respect to Union Transport, since Federal Express and Union Transport each had separate airway bills with Plaintiff.

In support of its position, Union Transport cites Motorola, Inc. v. MSAS Cargo International, Inc., 42 F. Supp.2d 952 (N.D.Cal. 1998), where a district court held that timely notice to the first air carrier did not constitute timely notice to the second carrier where separate contracts existed between the parties. Although two separate airway bills were issued in the instant case, this case is distinguishable from Motorola, since here the airway bills specifically provide that a written complaint may be made "to the Carrier whose Air Waybill was used, or to the first Carrier or to the last Carrier or to the Carrier who performed the transportation during which the loss, damage or delay took place." The Ninth Circuit reviewed an air waybill with an identical provision and found that, in light of this provision, the Plaintiff could have fulfilled the notice requirement to one defendant by notifying another carrier. Hitachi Data Systems Corp. v. United Parcel Service, Inc., 76 F.3d 276 (9th Cir.1996). Accordingly, the Court finds that by providing timely notice to Federal Express, Plaintiff complied with its obligation to timely notify Union Transport.

[The remainder of the court's opinion is omitted.]

Notes

1. For another case examining the duty to give notice in the context of an animal shipment, *see Hughes-Gibb & Co. v. Flying Tiger Line, Inc.*, 504 F. Supp. 1239 (N.D. Ill. 1981) (although no notice had to be given for breeding swine that arrived dead, notice did have to be given for those that arrived alive but subsequently died due to mishandling during transport).

2. It is estimated that some two million animals fly commercially each year, many of whom are household pets. *See* Judith R. Karp, *Will That Be First Class, Business Class, or Pet Class? Changing Legal Trends for the Traveling Pet*, 4 San Diego Int'l L.J. 189 (2003), and Susan D. Semmel, Comment, *When Pigs Fly, They Go First Class: Service Animals in the Twenty-First Century*, 3 Barry L. Rev. 39 (2002). Of these animals, it is believed that approximately one percent, or about 20,000, are injured or killed. Not surprisingly, such incidents sometimes lead to litigation. In one particularly notable case, the plaintiff, relying on the Animal Welfare Act, filed suit for intentional infliction of emotional distress after his golden retriever died because the temperature inside the plane's cargo compartment was allowed to reach 140 degrees. In denying his claim, the court wrote:

> Gluckman's Fourth Cause of Action alleges that American has committed "the tort of outrage" in that the defendant acted "with reckless disregard of the extreme probability of its causing plaintiff severe emotional distress." Complaint at ¶ 53. In support of this claim, Gluckman indicates that American's acceptance of Floyd for transport violated the Animal Welfare Act, 7 U.S.C. § 2143, which prohibits any dog from being kept in temperatures higher than 85 degrees; violated a 1985 consent decree which required American to show a training videotape, entitled "Not Just Another Bag," to all its personnel responsible for handling animals; and violated its own internal policies which require it to refuse pets for transport if the temperature is above 85 degrees and the ground time exceeds 45 minutes.
>
> As deplorable as it may be for American to have caused the death of an innocent animal, the Court finds no allegation, and no evidence from the facts alleged, that American's conduct was directed intentionally at Gluckman. Accordingly, Gluckman's cause of action for intentional infliction of emotional distress is dismissed.

Gluckman v. American Airlines, Inc., 844 F. Supp. 151, 157–58 (S.D.N.Y. 1994).

In an effort to help pet owners, the Department of Transportation now requires airlines to report the number of pets killed, lost, or injured on their flights. This information can be viewed at airconsumer.ost.dot.gov/reports.

3. Assume that the airbills in *Searle* had not given the plaintiff the option of notifying either carrier. Assume further that the court, despite the *Motorola* precedent, still wanted to find that the plaintiff had met its notification obligation to Union Transport. Could it have done so?

4. While it probably goes without saying, it is not enough for a shipper to give timely notice to the carrier; it also must file suit prior to the bar date. *See further Seagate Technology LLC v. Dalian China Express International Corp.*, 169 F. Supp. 2d 1146 (N.D. Cal. 2001) (nine-month contractual requirement), and *Fireman's Fund Insurance Co. v. Panalpina, Inc.*, 2001 WL 59037 (N.D. Ill. 2001) (two-year statutory limit). *See also* Beverly L. Jacklin, Annotation, *Construction and Application of Warsaw Convention Provision (U.S.C.A. Conventions, Warsaw Convention Art. 29(1)) Establishing 2-Year Limitation Period for Damage Action*, 103 A.L.R. Fed. 286 (1991 & 2005 Supp.).

Problem 18

A shipper sent 50 packages to its overseas office. When its driver went to pick them up, eight were missing. She tried to note this fact on the airbill, but was told by the carrier's employees that such statements were not customary and, in any event, unnecessary because they already knew the shipment was short. One month later, when the packages still had not arrived, the shipper filed suit. If the carrier moves to dismiss for lack of timely written notice, how should the court rule? *See Highlands Insurance Co. v. Trinidad and Tobago (BWIA International) Airways Corp.*, 739 F.2d 536 (11th Cir. 1984).

3. DAMAGES

SOTHEBY'S v. FEDERAL EXPRESS CORPORATION

97 F. Supp. 2d 491 (S.D.N.Y. 2000)

CHIN, District Judge.

In this cargo case, Sotheby's, through an agent, hired Federal Express Corporation ("FedEx") to transport three pieces of artwork (the "Artwork") from London, England to Newark, New Jersey. The air waybill provided that the Artwork was to be flown on FedEx Flight 005 from London, England to Newark, New Jersey. FedEx in fact transported the Artwork to Newark on Flight 005, but then, due to its own weekend staffing needs, transported the Artwork on FedEx Flight 007 from Newark to Memphis, Tennessee and then from Memphis back to Newark the next day on FedEx Flight 3501. While in Memphis, one of the three pieces of Artwork, a painting, was damaged by a forklift.

Sotheby's moves for partial summary judgment holding FedEx liable for the full value of the damage to the painting and striking the limitation of liability affirmative defenses asserted by FedEx in its answer. FedEx cross-moves for partial summary judgment limiting its liability, if any, to twenty dollars per kilogram of the weight of the damaged painting, pursuant to Article 22 of the Convention for the Unification of Certain Rules Relating to International Transportation by Air, 49 Stat. 3000, T.S. 876 (1934), reprinted in 49 U.S.C. § 40105, commonly known as the Warsaw Convention. The issue before the Court is whether, under these circumstances, FedEx can take advantage of the limitation of liability provided by the Warsaw Convention. For the reasons that follow, Sotheby's motion is granted and FedEx's cross-motion is denied.

BACKGROUND

A. The Undisputed Facts

The undisputed facts, taken from the parties' Local Civil Rule 56.1 Statements and exhibits thereto, are as follow.

On October 10, 1997, Air Express International Limited ("AEI") booked transportation of Sotheby's Artwork for carriage by FedEx the following day from London, England to Newark, New Jersey. The Artwork had a total gross weight of 478 kilograms and a chargeable weight of 669 kilograms. AEI completed an air waybill, numbered 023-90756002, for the shipment. The air waybill specified London as the departure airport and Newark, New Jersey as the destination airport. It also included on its face both the date of the flight, October 11, and the flight number, 005. The designated spaces on the air waybill for listing stopping places between London and Newark were left blank and no other flight numbers appeared on the waybill. AEI did not make a special declaration of value or pay a supplementary sum for the shipment.

FedEx received the Artwork without taking exception to its condition or packaging, and stamped the air waybill as prepared by AEI. On October 11, 1997, FedEx Flight 005 carried the Artwork from London to Newark as scheduled. That same day, however, the Artwork was placed on FedEx Flight 007 and transported from Newark to Memphis, Tennessee where it was stored overnight. While in Memphis, one of the three pieces of Artwork, a painting by Sir Anthony Van Dyck entitled "Portrait of Prince Charles Louis, The Elector Palatine," was damaged. The following day, FedEx transported the Artwork, including the damaged painting, back from Memphis to Newark on FedEx Flight 3501. Upon the shipment's arrival in Newark, damage to the outer packaging of the painting was noted.

B. Additional Facts

Sotheby's contends that AEI specifically selected FedEx Flight 005 because it was a non-stop flight, that AEI advised FedEx that the Artwork had to be transported non-stop, and that FedEx contracted to carry the Artwork on Flight 005. (Pl. Local Civ. R. 56.1 St.). FedEx argues that it never agreed to ship the Artwork directly from Newark to London without stops, and asserts that it expressly reserved its right to route the shipment any way it saw fit. (Def. Opp. Local Civ. R. 56.1 St.). At oral argument, counsel for FedEx explained that the Artwork was taken from Newark to Memphis because weekend staffing shortages left FedEx without personnel to unload the cargo from the storage containers in Newark. (Tr. at 9).

According to FedEx, the terms and conditions of FedEx's International Express Freight Worldwide Service Guide ("Service Guide") applied to the transportation of the Artwork. (Def. Local Civ. R. 56.1 St.). Sotheby's disputes that these terms and conditions applied to the shipment but also contends, apparently in the alternative, that AEI did not make a special declaration of value or pay a supplementary fee because it was precluded from doing so by the Service Guide. (Pl. Opp. Local Civ. R. 56.1 St.). According to Sotheby's, the damaged painting is worth approximately $1,000,000. (Compl. ¶ 10).

DISCUSSION

A. Motion for Summary Judgment

The standards governing motions for summary judgment are well settled. A court may grant summary judgment only where there is no genuine issue of material fact and the moving party is therefore entitled to judgment as a matter of law. See Fed. R. Civ. P. 56(c); Matsushita Elec. Indus. Co. v. Zenith Radio Corp., 475 U.S. 574, 585–87, 106 S.Ct. 1348, 89 L.Ed.2d 538 (1986). Accordingly, the Court's task is not to "weigh the evidence and determine the truth of the matter but to determine whether there is a genuine issue for trial." Anderson v. Liberty Lobby, Inc., 477 U.S. 242, 249, 106 S.Ct. 2505, 91 L.Ed.2d 202 (1986). To create an issue for trial, there must be sufficient evidence in the record to support a jury verdict in the nonmoving party's favor. See id.

B. The Warsaw Convention

The parties agree that Sotheby's claim is governed by the provisions of the Warsaw Convention.

1. Liability

The first prong of Sotheby's motion seeks partial summary judgment holding FedEx liable for Sotheby's loss. Although FedEx argues that its liability, "if any," is limited in accordance with the Warsaw Convention, it does not otherwise contest this portion of Sotheby's motion, and counsel for FedEx admitted as much at oral argument. (Tr. at 2–3). Notably, FedEx does not raise the affirmative defenses, asserted in its answer, that Sotheby's (1) failed to provide timely notice of its claim, (2) breached the contract, (3) assumed the risk, or (4) failed to package the shipment adequately.

"In general, Article 18 of the Warsaw Convention presumes an air carrier liable for loss or damage to goods in transit." Tai Ping Ins. Co., Ltd. v. Northwest Airlines, Inc., 94 F.3d 29, 31 (2d Cir.1996). FedEx does not dispute that it received the Artwork without taking exception to its condition or packaging, and that the painting or its packaging was damaged in Memphis. (Pl. Local Civ. R. 56.1 St.; Def. Opp. Local Civ. R. 56.1 St.); see also Local Civ. R. 56.1(c) ("All material facts set forth in the statement required to be served by the moving party will be deemed admitted unless controverted by the statement required to be served by the opposing party.").

Moreover, the record contains uncontroverted evidence that the painting was damaged while in transit. For example, plaintiff has put forth: (1) a letter from FedEx to AEI stating that the shipment was "broken down in Memphis" and that "comments that were taken from the computer do state that the freight was damaged prior to build up at Memphis"; (2) a survey report from Crawford-THG International Loss Adjusters concluding that the blades of a forklift caused the damage to the painting; and (3) FedEx's answer admitting, upon information and belief, that the damage to the packaging was noted prior to delivery in Newark. (Affidavit of Matthew T. Loesberg, dated Nov. 24, 1999, at Exs. 2, 3, and 5). Accordingly, Sotheby's motion for summary judgment on the issue of liability is granted. I now turn to the second prong of Sotheby's motion and FedEx's cross-motion.

2. Limitation of Liability

Sotheby's and FedEx cross-move for partial summary judgment on the issue of whether FedEx is entitled to a limitation of liability for Sotheby's loss pursuant to Article 22 of the Warsaw Convention. Article 22(2) of the Warsaw Convention limits a carrier's liability to twenty dollars per kilogram, unless the shipper makes a special declaration of greater value and pays any required extra fees. See 49 U.S.C. §40105, Art. 22(2); Federal Ins. Co. v. Yusen Air & Sea Serv. Pte, Ltd., No. 97 Civ. 3830, 1998 WL 477987, at *2 (S.D.N.Y. Aug.14, 1998). Because AEI did not declare a greater value for the damaged painting, FedEx contends that its liability is limited to twenty dollars per kilogram.

Article 9 of the Warsaw Convention, however, provides that the Article 22 limitation of liability shall not apply "if the carrier accepts goods without an air waybill having been made out, or if the air waybill does not contain all the particulars set out in Article 8(a) to (i), inclusive, and (q)." 49 U.S.C. § 40105, Art. 9. Article 8(c), in turn, provides that the air waybill shall contain "[t]he agreed stopping places, provided that the carrier may reserve the right to alter the stopping places in case of necessity, and that if he exercises that right, the alteration shall not have the effect of depriving the transportation of its international character." 49 U.S.C. § 40105, Art. 8; see Intercargo Ins. Co. v. China Airlines, Ltd., 208 F.3d 64, 67 (2d Cir.2000). In other words, under the Warsaw Convention there is a limitation on a carrier's liability. The limitation does not apply, however, if the waybill does not list all the "agreed stopping places." The limitation is not lost, however, when the carrier makes an unlisted stop in a "case of necessity," and the carrier has reserved the right to do so.

In the Second Circuit, a carrier may include the required stopping place information on an air waybill either explicitly, or by incorporating its scheduled timetables reflecting those stops by reference. See Intercargo, 208 F.3d at 68; Tai Ping, 94 F.3d at 31. Sotheby's contends that FedEx may not limit its liability under Article 22(2) because the air waybill issued in connection with the shipment failed to include Memphis as an "agreed stopping place," either explicitly or by incorporation.

It is uncontested that the Artwork was transported to Memphis, and that the air waybill omits both the word "Memphis" and the transfer flight numbers 007 and 3501 that would have revealed the stop in Memphis by incorporation. Nevertheless, FedEx argues that its failure to include a reference to Memphis or the transfer flights on the air waybill does not deprive it of the protection of the liability limitation because Memphis was not an "agreed stopping place" within the meaning of Article 8(c). FedEx's argument is three-fold.

a. Article 8(c) Does Not Exclude Local Stops

First, FedEx argues at length that Article 8(c) refers only to countries in which the transportation stops, not local stops within those countries. In support of its argument, FedEx points to the purported purpose of Article 8(c)—providing notification to shippers of the international character of the transportation and the applicability of the Warsaw Convention—and its drafting history. This argument has been squarely rejected by the Second Circuit. As the Circuit Court recently explained,

> An air waybill that lists Johannesburg (or Los Angeles) as the place of departure and New York City (or Hong Kong) as the place of destination reveals the international character of the flight. In such cases, listing the stopping places can provide no further notice of this character (and the consequent applicability of the Warsaw Convention)—yet [Second Circuit precedent] clearly holds, as the Warsaw Convention facially requires, that the air waybill must nonetheless "contain ... the agreed stopping places" in order for the carrier to invoke the limited liability provisions.... We therefore disagree with those courts that have found ... that notification of the international character of the carriage was the purpose of the stopping place requirement.

Intercargo, 208 F.3d at 68.

Moreover, Second Circuit precedent demonstrates that local stops within a country are considered "stopping places" for purposes of Article 8(c). In Tai Ping, the court held that for transportation from Chicago, Illinois to Hong Kong, the carrier's "waybill did not effect a valid incorporation of regularly scheduled stops in Anchorage, Alaska and Narita, Japan by reference to its timetables." Tai Ping, 94 F.3d at 32. It is clear that although the stop in Alaska would not have involved a separate country, Article 8(c) required its inclusion on the waybill. See id.; see also Tai Ping Co. Ltd. v. Expeditors Int'l, E.I., 34 F.Supp.2d 169, 170–71 (S.D.N.Y.1998) (waybill for shipment from Cleveland, Ohio to Hong Kong failed to include stopping place of Fairbanks, Alaska). Accordingly, FedEx's first argument is rejected.

b. Plaintiff's Failure to "Agree" to Memphis

Second, FedEx argues that because Sotheby's did not agree to have its Artwork stop in Memphis, Memphis is not an "agreed" stopping place required by Article 8(c) to be included on the air waybill. Notwithstanding the fact that the Second Circuit has said that the meaning of "agreed stopping places" in Article 8(c) is clear and unambiguous, see Maritime Ins. Co. Ltd. v. Emery Air Freight Corp., 983 F.2d 437, 440 (2d Cir.1993), in this context, there is some ambiguity as to the meaning of "agreed." On the one hand, FedEx argues that "agreed stopping places" refers to places both the shipper and the carrier actually agreed would be stopping places when the waybill was issued. On the other hand, Sotheby's argues that FedEx's interpretation does not make sense.

I agree with Sotheby's. The term "agreed" cannot mean, as FedEx argues, that both the shipper and the carrier literally agreed to the stopping places before the waybill was issued. The Second Circuit has held that Article 8(c) is "a notice provision." Intercargo, 208 F.3d at 69. If "agreed" is interpreted to mean that both the shipper and carrier literally agreed to the stopping places, then notice to the shipper of those stopping places would be superfluous. Indeed, Intercargo implicitly acknowledges that shippers have not literally agreed to the stops in advance of the shipment; as the Second Circuit there held, "Article 8(c) is a notice provision. We decline to obscure still further the notice consignors receive by obliging them to deduce the stopping places from a factually incomplete or inaccurate listing of flights." Id. Had the shipper literally agreed to the stopping places in advance, there would be no reason for it to have to deduce stopping places at all.

Rather, a more logical interpretation of Article 8(c) is that it requires the carrier to include on the air waybill all stopping places contemplated by the carrier. The shipper then "agrees" to those stopping places, explicitly or implicitly, by accepting shipment under the waybill. Here, if FedEx contemplated shipping the Artwork to Memphis due to weekend staffing shortages, or otherwise, it should have included Memphis as a stopping place on the air waybill. Had FedEx included Memphis as a stop on the air waybill, Sotheby's would have had notice of the contemplated stop and it could have agreed to the stop or not. It would be illogical to reward FedEx for its failure to provide Sotheby's with notice of the stop in Memphis—and consequently the opportunity to agree or disagree to Memphis as a stopping place—by allowing FedEx to take advantage of the Warsaw Convention's limitation of liability. Indeed, Article 9's limitation of liability for failure to include agreed stopping places would be rendered meaningless by such a result.

FedEx's interpretation also makes no sense because it completely undermines the provision. Under FedEx's reading, a carrier could unilaterally decide to send cargo anywhere in the world but because the shipper had not "agreed" that these places were stopping places, the carrier would not be required to list them on the waybill and the carrier would not lose the limitation of liability. Such a result is nonsensical.

Moreover, the Convention provides that a carrier may at times, out of necessity, have to stop at places beyond its contemplation at the time of shipment. Article 8(c) expressly provides that "the carrier may reserve the right to alter the stopping places in case of necessity." This language would be superfluous under FedEx's interpretation, for no such language would be required if the carrier were obligated only to list the stopping places agreed to by the parties in advance. In other words, if a carrier did not lose the benefit of the limitation because it did not list a stop that had not been previously "agreed" to, there would be no need to provide that the limitation was not lost when the carrier made an unanticipated stop because of "necessity."

Finally, FedEx has not argued necessity as a defense; nor could it. FedEx surely should have anticipated the weekend staffing shortages, and it should have given Sotheby's notice that the goods would have to be flown to Memphis. At that point, Sotheby's could have "agreed" to Memphis as a stopping point, or it could have chosen another option. Accordingly, FedEx's second argument is rejected.

c. The Parties' Contract Does Not Preclude a Finding that Memphis Was an Agreed Stopping Place

Third, FedEx argues that the parties' contract precludes a finding that Memphis was an agreed stopping place required to be disclosed on the waybill by Article 8(c) because: (1) FedEx's Service Guide provides "there are no stopping places which are agreed at the time of tender of the shipment" and expressly reserves FedEx's right to route the shipment as it deemed appropriate; (2) paragraph 8.2 of the "Conditions of Contract" located on the reverse side of the air waybill provides that FedEx is authorized by the shipper "to select the routing and all intermediate stopping places that it deems appropriate or to change or deviate from the routing shown on the face hereof"; and (3) the face of the air waybill provides that the "shipper agrees that the shipment may be carried via intermediate stopping places which the carrier deems appropriate."

i. Routing Provisions

Whether located in the Service Guide or the air waybill, contractual language pertaining to routing, including language reserving FedEx's right to route plaintiff's shipment as it saw fit, does not absolve FedEx of its duty to include agreed stopping places on the air waybill. Under the Warsaw Convention, "routing" and "stopping place" are distinct concepts addressed in separate subsections. Article 8(p) of the Warsaw Convention explicitly addresses routing and is not included among the particulars required by Article 9. In contrast, Article 8(c) explicitly addresses stopping places and is a required particular under Article 9. See 49 U.S.C. §40105, Arts. 8(c), 8(p), [and] 9. The Warsaw Convention does not define either term.

Undefined terms in a statute are to be given their "ordinary or natural meaning[s]." National Broadcasting Co., Inc. v. Bear Stearns & Co., Inc., 165 F.3d 184, 188 (2d Cir.1999); cf. Kahn Lucas Lancaster, Inc. v. Lark Int'l Ltd., 186 F.3d 210, 215 (2d Cir.1999) ("Treaties are construed in much the same manner as statutes."). Moreover, "a statute should be construed so that all of its parts are given effect, and a construction ascribing to two separate statutory provisions the same meaning and scope is [therefore] disfavored." United States v. Stephenson, 183 F.3d 110, 121 (2d Cir.) (quotations and citations omitted), cert. denied, 528 U.S. 1013, 120 S.Ct. 517, 145 L.Ed.2d 400 (1999). Giving the terms their ordinary and natural meanings, and keeping in mind that the drafters of the Warsaw Convention chose to address the terms in separate statutory provisions, I hold that FedEx did not merely make a change in routing; it added Memphis as a stopping place. Indeed, two additional flights and an overnight stay were added to what was listed in the waybill as one flight. See Chubb & Son, Inc. v. Asiana Airlines, No. 96 Civ. 5082, 1997 WL 1040543, at *5 (S.D.N.Y. Jun.17, 1997) (Report and Recommendation of Magistrate Judge Peck) (finding carrier did not merely change routing but rather omitted stopping place).

FedEx argues that interpreting stopping place to mean any place where the transportation stops renders the term "route to be followed" meaningless. This argument is clearly incorrect. A carrier remains free to choose the route to be followed in going from point A to point B without disclosing a stopping place; for example, the carrier may choose to travel a longer distance in reaching its destination to avoid flying over water or certain countries' airspace. If a carrier chooses to stop at a particular location, however, and not just to pass over or through it, it must disclose that location as a stopping place on the air waybill in accordance with Article 8(c). Accordingly, FedEx may not use contractual language pertaining to routing as a shield against the consequences of its failure to include Memphis as a stopping place.

ii. Stopping Place Provisions

FedEx contends that the terms and conditions of its Service Guide, applicable to Sotheby's shipment via the air waybill, disclaimed agreement as to stopping places. The "Conditions of Contract" printed on the air waybill issued in connection with Sotheby's shipment do not expressly incorporate the terms and conditions of the Service Guide. I must therefore decide whether Paragraph 2.2.3 of the Conditions of Contract printed on the air waybill effectively incorporates the Service Guide by reference.

A contract must clearly and accurately identify a document to effectively incorporate it by reference. See New Moon Shipping Co., Ltd. v. MAN B & W Diesel AG, 121 F.3d 24, 30 (2d Cir.1997) ("Under general principles of contract law, a contract may incorporate another document by making clear reference to it and describing it in such terms that its identity may be ascertained beyond doubt."); see also Tai Ping, 94 F.3d at 32 (effective incorporation depends on accuracy of information in waybill). Paragraph 2.2.3 of the Conditions of Contract on Sotheby's air waybill incorporates the "applicable tariffs, rules, conditions of carriage, regulations and timetables" of the carrier into the contract of carriage. (Def. Local Civ. 56.1 St., Ex. A). This language does not make clear reference to the Service Guide, and as a result the air waybill does not effectively incorporate the Service Guide into the parties' contract of carriage. Thus, the terms and conditions of the Service Guide, including the disclaimer as to stopping places, are inapplicable to Sotheby's shipment and Sotheby's motion striking FedEx's affirmative defense based upon the Service Guide is granted.

FedEx's tariff, on the other hand, is incorporated into the provisions of the waybill. Although raised as a defense in its answer, FedEx has neither pressed the argument in its moving or opposition papers nor provided the Court with a copy of its tariff. The Court assumes FedEx does not contest that portion of Sotheby's motion. In any event, in reviewing a copy of the tariff Sotheby's submitted to the Court (FedEx does not contest its accuracy) it is clear that the tariff is of no assistance to FedEx. (See Certification of Gary James Piesley, dated November 22, 1999 at Ex. 4). The tariff merely defines stopping places as those places set forth on the face of the air waybill or incorporated by reference to timetables. Accordingly, Sotheby's motion striking FedEx's affirmative defense based upon the tariff is also granted.

Finally, FedEx argues that two provisions explicitly printed on the waybill—Sotheby's agreement that the Artwork could be carried "via intermediate stopping places which the carrier deems appropriate," and Sotheby's authorization that Fedex could "select ... intermediate stopping places,"—obviated its need to comply with Article 8(c). This argument fails for three reasons.

First, Memphis is not an "intermediate" stop on the planned route. The Artwork was not taken from London to Memphis to Newark; if that had happened, Memphis arguably would have qualified as an intermediate stop. Instead, FedEx took the Artwork from London to Newark as planned and then from Newark to Memphis and back. Memphis was not an "intermediate" stop; rather, it was an additional and, from Sotheby's point of view, superfluous stop.

Second, even assuming Memphis is considered an intermediate stop, the language on the waybill has the effect of relieving the carrier of the full liability that would ordinarily be imposed upon it by the Warsaw Convention. As a consequence, the contractual provision is rendered null and void by Article 23 of the Warsaw Convention. See 49 U.S.C. §40105, Art. 23 ("Any provision tending to relieve the carrier of liability or to fix a lower limit than that which is laid down in this convention shall be null and void, but the nullity of any such provision shall not involve the nullity of the whole contract, which shall remain subject to the provisions of this convention.").

Finally, Sotheby's agreement that the Artwork could be carried "via intermediate stopping places which the carrier deems appropriate" is expressly contingent upon Sotheby's not providing contrary instructions on the waybill. Here, the waybill does provide contrary instructions, that is, Sotheby's selection of Flight 005, a nonstop flight.

Although imposing liability on FedEx for the full value of the damaged painting may be harsh, FedEx could have complied with Article 8(c), and preserved its limitation of liability defense, simply by listing "Memphis" as a stopping place on the air waybill. Moreover, holding FedEx liable for its failure to include Memphis as a stopping place furthers Article 8(c)'s goal of providing accurate information to the shipper. See Intercargo, 208 F.3d at 69. Accordingly, I hold that Memphis was an agreed stopping place required to be disclosed on the air waybill by Article 8(c), the omission of which precludes FedEx from taking advantage of the Warsaw Convention's limitation of liability.

CONCLUSION

For the reasons set forth herein, Sotheby's motion for partial summary judgment is granted; FedEx's motion for partial summary judgment is denied.

CAPORICCI FOOTWEAR, LTD. v. FEDERAL EXPRESS CORPORATION

894 F. Supp. 258 (E.D. Va. 1995)

HILTON, District Judge.

This matter came before the Court on defendant's motion for summary judgment. Defendant Federal Express Corporation is a federally certificated all-cargo airline operating under authority granted to it by the Federal Aviation Administration. On or about

April 4, 1994, Plaintiff Caporicci Footwear, Inc. tendered twenty packages to Federal Express for shipment from Fairfax, Virginia to the International Shoe Company at 4995 N.W. 79th Ave. in Miami, Florida via Federal Express' Collect on Delivery (C.O.D.) Service. Upon delivery of the packages, Federal Express was to collect and return to Plaintiff cashier's checks totaling $97,800.

The address listed on the airbill was a self storage complex. The courier drove to a storage bay where an individual identifying himself as Bernie Felice, a representative of International Shoe Company, instructed him to deliver the packages in front of the door of the bay. The plaintiff had in fact previously dealt with an individual named Bernard Felice at the International Shoe Company. The courier unloaded the goods onto the ground in front of the bay and the person identifying himself as Felice handed him two facially valid cashier's checks in the amounts of $91,880.05 and $5,950.00. The plaintiff alleges that several unidentified individuals then loaded the packages onto a waiting U-Haul truck. Federal Express denies that there were any trucks present at the time of delivery. Federal Express subsequently returned the checks to the plaintiff who later discovered that the checks were drawn on a bank that does not exist.

The plaintiff brings this action alleging that Federal Express breached its contractual obligations by failing to go inside the office of the self storage complex to deliver the packages. The plaintiff argues that had the courier gone into the office of the complex he would have determined that there was no such company at that address. Plaintiff further asserts that delivering the packages outside of one of the storage bins constituted negligence and resulted in the conversion of its goods.

Under Fed. R. Civ. P. 56, a court should grant summary judgment if there is no genuine dispute of material facts and the moving party is entitled to judgment as a matter of law.

The liability of Federal Express and other federally certificated air carriers for loss attendant to goods in transit is governed exclusively by federal law. The airbills such as those used by Federal Express form the basic contract between the shipper and the carrier. The terms of the airbills, however, may be supplemented by incorporating the carrier's service guides by reference. Federal Express' July 1993 Service Guide was in effect on the date Plaintiff shipped its packages and Federal Express expressly incorporated the terms of this service guide into its Airbills. The language in the airbill states: "Use of this airbill constitutes your agreement to the service conditions in our current Service Guide, available upon request." Accordingly, the language found on the Airbills and in the July 1993 Service Guide constitute the contractual agreement between plaintiff and Federal Express.

Under the terms of the Airbills and Service Guides, the plaintiff assumed all risk of fraud. The reverse side of the Airbills provided that "all checks (including cashier's, certified, business and personal) and money orders are collected at your [the shipper's] risk, including risk of nonpayment and forgery." The plaintiff concedes that Federal Express is not responsible for accepting the fraudulent checks. The checks appeared to be valid cashier's checks and Federal Express discharged its contractual obligation by collecting, and then delivering, these apparently valid cashier's checks to the plaintiff.

The plaintiff argues, however, that Federal Express breached its contractual duties and was negligent by leaving the packages outside of the storage bays instead of delivering the goods to the office inside the building. The Airbills expressly state, however, that Federal Express may make an indirect delivery, which is a completed delivery to an address other than the address on the airbill if the recipient so instructs. Accordingly, even if it is assumed that Federal Express delivered the packages onto the recipient's truck rather than to the address indicated on the Airbills, a fact which Federal Express denies, this would not constitute a breach of the contracts. The courier was complying with the instructions of someone identifying himself as the recipient who possessed cashier's checks in the appropriate amount as payment for the goods. The courier complied with the instructions when delivery was made to the person who reasonably appeared to be a representative of the recipient and thereby discharged Federal Express' contractual obligations to make an indirect delivery.

Plaintiff argues that had Federal Express attempted delivery at United Shoe Distributors as required, it would have then ascertained that there was no such business at that address. Federal Express had no contractual obligation to verify that United Shoe Distributors or anyone else was actually doing business at the address located on Airbills. To impose such a requirement would make Federal Express plaintiff's agent for purpose of completing the transaction between it and the recipient. The Service Guide clearly states that no such agency relationship exists. The Guide states: "... Performance of the C.O.D. Service will not constitute use as the shippee's agent for any purpose...."

Plaintiff also seeks to recover under theories of negligence and conversion. The law is clear, however, that the contractual provisions found in the Airbills and Service Guide govern this action regardless of the theory under which the claim is made. Courts have consistently applied contract principles to enforce liability limits and other terms and conditions of performance of contracts of carriage offered by package express carriers. In fact, the contractual provisions govern even where it is alleged that the acts of an employee of the carrier resulted in the conversion of the goods. Because there is no evidence that the goods were converted for use by Federal Express, defendant's liability is governed by the terms of the contract.

Moreover, under Virginia law, a plaintiff cannot maintain an action in tort based on a breach of contract claim unless the tort amounts to an independent tort. An independent tort is one that is factually bound to the contractual breach but whose legal elements are distinct from it. Here, there is no independent duty on the defendant except that created by the contract, so the plaintiff cannot establish the basis for an independent tort of negligence.

Accordingly, the Court finds that there being no dispute as to any material fact, the defendant is entitled to judgment as a matter of law.

HAMPTON v. FEDERAL EXPRESS CORPORATION

917 F.2d 1119 (8th Cir. 1990)

RE, Chief Judge.

In this diversity action, Hampton, individually and on behalf of his deceased son, Carl, Missouri residents, sued defendant-appellee, Federal Express Corporation, a Delaware corporation, in the United States District Court for the Western District of Missouri, seeking a total of $3,081,000 for personal injury, wrongful death, and loss of services.

Hampton alleged that Federal Express, a common carrier, negligently failed to deliver blood samples of Carl Gerome Hampton, a cancer patient in need of a bone marrow transplant, that had to be matched with a potential bone marrow donor. Hampton appeals from judgment of the district court which granted the partial summary judgment motion of the carrier, Federal Express, limiting Hampton's recovery to $100 in damages.

The question presented is whether the district court erred in determining that the carrier, Federal Express, is entitled to partial summary judgment under the released value doctrine, limiting its liability to $100, the amount stated in the contract of carriage between it and the shipper.

Since, on the facts presented, the nature and extent of damages suffered by plaintiff Hampton were not reasonably foreseeable to the carrier, Federal Express, we affirm the judgment of the district court granting Federal Express' motion for partial summary judgment.

I. BACKGROUND

In March, 1988, Carl Gerome Hampton, a 13-year old cancer patient at Children's Memorial Hospital in Omaha, Nebraska, was awaiting a bone marrow transplant. A transplant operation was scheduled at the University of Iowa Hospital in Iowa City, Iowa, where five potential bone marrow donors had been found.

On March 21, 1988, in order to match Carl with the most suitable donor, five samples of Carl's blood were sent by the shipper, the Children's Memorial Hospital in Omaha, to Dr. Nancy Goeken at the Veterans Administration Medical Center in Iowa City. The shipper, the Children's Memorial Hospital, entered into a contract with the carrier, Federal Express, for the transport of the blood samples.

In a paragraph entitled "Damages or Loss," the contract of carriage, set forth in the airbill, stated:

> We are liable for no more than $100 per package in the event of physical loss or damage, unless you fill in a higher Declared Value to the left and document higher actual loss in the event of a claim. We charge 30 cents for each additional $100 of declared value up to the maximum shown in our Service Guide.

The reverse side of the airbill contains several paragraphs, entitled "Limitations On Our Liability," which state that:

> Our liability for loss or damage to your package is limited to your actual damages or $100, whichever is less, unless you pay for and declare a higher authorized value. We do not provide cargo liability insurance, but you may pay thirty cents for each additional $100 of declared value. If you declare a higher value and pay the additional charge, our liability will be the lesser of your declared value or the actual value of your package.

It is not disputed that the blood samples were never received by Dr. Goeken, that Carl Hampton, the infant cancer patient, never obtained a bone marrow transplant, and that he died on May 19, 1988.

Alleging causes of action for personal injury, wrongful death, and loss of services, Carl Jerry Hampton, individually and on behalf of his deceased son, Carl Gerome Hampton, filed suit in the United States District Court for the Western District of Missouri, seeking $3,081,000 in damages. On the basis of the released value doctrine, the district court granted Federal Express' motion for partial summary judgment, and entered judgment in favor of Hampton for $100.

II. DISCUSSION

A. The "Released Value Doctrine"

We have held that, under federal common law, "[a] common carrier may not exempt itself from liability for its negligence; however, a carrier may limit its liability." Hopper

Furs, Inc. v. Emery Air Freight Corp., 749 F.2d 1261, 1264 (8th Cir.1984). As stated by the Supreme Court in the leading case of Hart v. Pennsylvania R.R., 112 U.S. 331, 343, 5 S.Ct. 151, 157, 28 L.Ed. 717 (1884):

> where a contract * * * signed by the shipper, is fairly made, agreeing on the valuation of the property carried, with the rate of freight based on the condition that the carrier assumes liability only to the extent of the agreed valuation, even in case of loss or damage by the negligence of the carrier, the contract will be upheld as a proper and lawful mode of securing a due proportion between the amount for which the carrier may be responsible and the freight he receives, and of protecting himself against extravagant and fanciful valuations.

See generally First Pa. Bank, N.A. v. Eastern Airlines, Inc., 731 F.2d 1113, 1115–16 (3d Cir.1984). This body of law, which has come to be known as the "released value doctrine" of federal common law, requires that in order to limit its liability "the carrier must present the shipper with a reasonable opportunity to declare a value for the shipment above the maximum value set by the carrier, pay an additional fee, and thereby be insured at a higher rate should the shipment go awry." Husman Constr. Co. v. Purolator Courier Corp., 832 F.2d 459, 461 (8th Cir.1987).

In this case, the contract entered into by the shipper, the Children's Memorial Hospital, with the carrier, Federal Express, clearly limited the liability of the carrier to $100, and provided the shipper with an opportunity to declare a higher value. Furthermore, it is not disputed that the shipper never declared a higher value for the blood samples. Hence, should the released value doctrine apply, the liability of the carrier, Federal Express, would be limited to $100.

There is a question, however, as to whether the released value doctrine applies in a suit brought by a plaintiff not a party to the contract of carriage. Hampton contends that his damages should not be limited by the released value doctrine since he was not the shipper of the blood samples, and, therefore, was not a party to the contract with the carrier, Federal Express. In support of his contention, Hampton cites the decision of this court in Arkwright-Boston Mfrs. Mut. Ins. Co. v. Great Western Airlines, Inc., 767 F.2d 425 (8th Cir.1985). It is clear, however, that Arkwright is distinguishable from the present case.

In Arkwright, TRW purchased electronic goods from a dealer in Cedar Rapids, Iowa. Pursuant to TRW's specific instructions, the goods were shipped from the dealer to TRW in four packages by the carrier, Federal Express. Upon tender of the goods to Federal Express, title passed from the dealer to TRW. The airbills with Federal Express contained a clause limiting Federal Express' liability to $100 per package, in the absence of a greater declared value. As in this case, the airbills did not declare a value greater than $100 for each package. See id. at 426.

In Arkwright, Federal Express entered into a subcontract for the delivery of the packages with the defendant, Great Western. Subsequently, the goods were destroyed in transit in the crash of the defendant's airplane. See id. The plaintiff, Arkwright, TRW's insurer and the subrogee of TRW's rights against the defendant, then sued the defendant for $99,000, the amount the plaintiff paid to TRW for the goods destroyed in the crash. See id. at 425. Although the opinion does not indicate whether the plaintiff proceeded under a tort or contract theory, the district court granted summary judgment for the defendant and limited its liability for each package to $100, the limitation on liability contained in the airbills. See id. at 426.

On appeal, we reversed and remanded for a trial. Since the airbill did not expressly extend the liability limitation to a subcontractor of the carrier, such as the defendant, we held that, under federal common law, the defendant could not benefit from the limitation on liability contained in the airbill, which stated the contract between the parties. See id. at 428. In effect, the contract limitation did not inure to the benefit of the subcontractor, who also was not relieved of its liability in tort.

This case, however, differs from Arkwright since Hampton is suing the carrier, Federal Express, rather than a defendant who is not a party to the contract of carriage. In addition, in this case, unlike Arkwright, the contract between the shipper, the Children's Memorial Hospital, and the carrier, Federal Express, expressly limited the liability of the defendant, Federal Express, to $100. Hence, Arkwright does not support Hampton's assertion that the released value doctrine does not apply to this case.

In further support of his contention that the released value doctrine should not apply, Hampton cites two district court cases. In the first, a carrier was held liable to the consignee of the shipped goods, after the consignee brought an action for breach of contract. In the second, a carrier was held liable in tort to a plaintiff not a party to the contract of carriage. Neither case, however, is persuasive, since they are both factually distinguishable.

In the first case, New Dawn Natural Foods, Inc. v. Natural Nectar Corp., 655 F.Supp. 475 (E.D.Mo.1987), the plaintiff, the consignee of a shipment of ice cream, sued the defendants, including a carrier, on a breach of contract claim for damages caused by late delivery. The defendant carrier moved to dismiss for failure to state a claim for relief. The carrier contended that the plaintiff consignee was not a party to the contract between the carrier and its subcontractor and, hence, could not maintain an action on that contract. The court applied Missouri law, and concluded that "a consignee not in privity with a carrier has a cause of action against the carrier for damages arising out of the carrier's negligent performance of the contract to deliver." Id. at 476. Accordingly, the court denied the defendant carrier's motion to dismiss. In this case, however, unlike in New Dawn, the plaintiff is not the consignee of the shipment.

In the second case cited by Hampton, Reece v. Delta Air Lines, Inc., 686 F.Supp. 21 (D.Me.1988), the plaintiffs, the widow and two sisters of the decedent, sought damages for emotional distress caused by the defendant carrier's negligence in mishandling the remains of the plaintiffs' decedent, which were shipped in a coffin. The carrier moved for dismissal on the grounds that the waybill, which contained the contract entered into by the defendant carrier and the shipper, a funeral home, limited the total damages recoverable to fifty cents per pound. See id. at 22. The court concluded that "the contractual language cannot limit [the defendant carrier's] liability for any tort which is independent of the shipping contract." Id. From the nature of the shipment in Reece, however, it is clear that the carrier in that case knew the contents of the coffin and could foresee that the mishandling of the coffin would cause injuries of the type or nature suffered by the plaintiffs. Hence, in Reece, in contrast to this case, the damages suffered by the plaintiffs were reasonably foreseeable. Cf. Johnson v. State, 37 N.Y.2d 378, 383, 334 N.E.2d 590, 593, 372 N.Y.S.2d 638, 642 (1975) (A defendant is liable under "special circumstances," such as the negligent transmission of message of death and negligent mishandling of a corpse, because the injury suffered is "within the 'orbit of danger' and therefore within the 'orbit of the duty' for the breach of which a wrongdoer may be held liable." (citing Palsgraf v. Long Island R.R., 248 N.Y. 339, 343, 162 N.E. 99, 100 (1928)).

In a case factually similar to Reece, however, another district court granted a defendant carrier's motion to dismiss. In Neal v. Republic Airlines, Inc., 605 F.Supp. 1145 (N.D.Ill.1985), the plaintiffs, the children and heirs at law of the decedent, sued the defendant carrier for damages caused by the carrier's negligence in misdelivering the remains of the plaintiffs' decedent. In granting the defendant's motion, the court stated that "[w]here * * * it is clear plaintiffs seek damages for breach of the carriage contract with [the defendant carrier], they may not avoid that contract's liability limits by framing their complaint in terms of bailment and tort." Id. at 1148. Stating that the plaintiffs "must proceed, if at all, on a breach of contract theory," id., the court concluded that since the plaintiffs were not parties to the contract of carriage, they could not sue the carrier. See id. at 1150.

Apart from the district court cases discussed, Hampton has failed to cite any authority in support of his position that the released value doctrine does not apply. Even if the released value doctrine does not apply in this case, Hampton still cannot prevail under general principles of the common law.

B. Recovery in Contract

The arguments raised present important questions in contrasting a recovery based on contract or tort. English legal history shows that classifications and concepts that today seem absolutely distinct were once blended and spring from a common source. Tort and contract law is an example, since the law of contracts began with the common law action of assumpsit, which traces its origins to the law of tort. See 3 W. Holdsworth, A History of English Law 428–29 (3d ed.1923). Furthermore, in modern times, the difference between tort and contract liability "has become an increasingly difficult distinction to make." W. Keeton, Prosser and Keeton on the Law of Torts § 92 (5th ed.1984) (hereinafter Prosser). Although it may be true that "general propositions do not decide concrete cases," Lochner v. New York, 198 U.S. 45, 76, 25 S.Ct. 539, 547, 49 L.Ed. 937 (1905) (Holmes, J., dissenting), it is basic that, in contract law, the defendant's liability to a plaintiff arises from the contractual agreement between the parties. Tort liability, however, arises from "general obligations that are imposed by law—apart from and independent of promises made and therefore apart from the manifested intention of the parties—to avoid injury to others." Prosser at § 92.

In this case, even if it were to be assumed that Hampton may sue as a third party beneficiary of the contract between the shipper and the carrier, on the facts presented he still cannot recover in contract. See Osmond State Bank v. Uecker Grain, Inc., 227 Neb. 636, 639, 419 N.W.2d 518, 520 (1988) (under Nebraska law, the rights of a third party beneficiary depend on the liability of the promisor contained in the contract); Bridgman v. Curry, 398 N.W.2d 167, 170 (Iowa 1986) (under Iowa law, third party beneficiary must show that contract was formed for his express benefit). See also Restatement (Second) of Contracts § 302 (1981).

It is a fundamental principle of the law of damages that, in contract cases, a plaintiff can only recover for a loss which, in the ordinary course of events, would result from the defendant's breach or for a loss which was in the contemplation of the parties. In the words of the Restatement, "[d]amages are not recoverable for loss that the party in breach did not have reason to foresee as a probable result of the breach when the contract was made." Restatement (Second) of Contracts § 351(1) (1981). This rule of damages may be traced to Hadley v. Baxendale, 9 Ex. 341, 156 Eng. Rep. 145 (1854), in which:

> the plaintiffs, who were owners of a steam mill, delivered to defendant, a carrier, a broken shaft essential to the function of the mill. The defendant agreed

> to transport the shaft to an engineer who would make a new shaft using the former as a model. The defendant delayed and plaintiffs brought action for special damages equal to the loss of profits resulting from the idle steam mill. Since the defendant was not made aware that delay in carriage of the indispensable part would result in an idle mill and loss of profits, plaintiffs could not recover.

E. Re, Cases and Materials on Remedies 758 (2d ed.1987). See also Victoria Laundry (Windsor) Ltd. v. Newman Indus., 2 K.B. 528, 539 (1949) ("In cases of breach of contract the aggrieved party is only entitled to recover such part of the loss actually resulting as was at the time of the contract reasonably foreseeable as liable to result from the breach."). Hampton, in this case, cannot dispute that Federal Express had no knowledge of Hampton or of the contents of the package that it accepted for delivery. Hence, even apart from the limitation of liability provision, since the damages suffered by Hampton were not reasonably foreseeable, they would not be recoverable in a breach of contract action.

C. Recovery in Tort

The tort law of negligence, however, does not provide as clear a rule as to whether a defendant may be held liable for injuries or damages that are not reasonably foreseeable. Indeed, the wealth of literature on the subject is illustrative of the differences of opinion on the subject. Tort scholars state that, on the question of the recovery of damages that are not reasonably foreseeable, "there are two basic, fundamental, opposing and irreconcilable views, which have been in conflict for more than a century * * *." Prosser at §43. Under the first theory, a defendant is liable only for damages that are the natural and probable consequences of the negligent act. See, e.g., Milwaukee and St. P. Ry. v. Kellogg, 94 U.S. 469, 476, 24 L.Ed. 256 (1876). Under the second theory, the defendant may be liable to a plaintiff for all resulting damages, but only if the defendant owes a duty to the plaintiff. See Prosser at §43. The seminal case under this second theory is Palsgraf v. Long Island R.R., 248 N.Y. 339, 162 N.E. 99 (1928).

In Palsgraf, a passenger was running to board one of the defendant's trains. An employee of the defendant, in assisting the passenger to board the train, caused a package being held by the passenger to fall. The package, unknown to the employee, contained fireworks which exploded. The resulting concussion (or "stampede of frightened passengers") caused some scales on the platform, a considerable distance away, to fall on the plaintiff and injure her. See Palsgraf, 248 N.Y. at 340–41, 162 N.E. at 99; Prosser at §43 n.35.

In denying the plaintiff recovery, Justice Cardozo, then a judge of the Court of Appeals of the State of New York, stated that the package itself did not provide notice that, if it fell, it could cause injuries to persons at the other end of the platform. See id. at 341, 162 N.E. at 99. The court noted that "[t]he conduct of the defendant's guard, if a wrong in its relation to the holder of the package, was not a wrong in its relation to the plaintiff, standing far away[,]" and concluded that "[n]egligence is not actionable unless it involves the invasion of a legally protected interest, the violation of a right." Id. Hence, the court held that the defendant was not liable to the plaintiff since the defendant, under the circumstances, could not reasonably foresee any injury to the plaintiff.

Under Palsgraf, it is only when the defendant owes a duty to the plaintiff that the defendant is liable for all damages, whether or not reasonably foreseeable, caused by the defendant's negligent act. Notwithstanding the variety of views that have emerged from

Palsgraf and related cases, the Restatement has adopted the Palsgraf approach. See Restatement (Second) of Torts §281 comment c, illustration 1 (1965). See also Prosser at §43; Pizarro v. Hoteles Concorde Int'l, C.A., 907 F.2d 1256, 1259–60 (1st Cir.1990) ("'[T]he touchstone is foreseeability: [conduct results in] liability if, and to the extent that, a foreseeable risk of harm materializes.'" (quoting Peckham v. Continental Casualty Ins. Co., 895 F.2d 830, 836 (1st Cir.1990))).

Clearly, Federal Express had no knowledge of Hampton, and did not know that the package contained blood samples. It is equally clear that the shipper, Children's Memorial Hospital, did not declare a value higher than $100 for the package. Under these circumstances, Federal Express could not reasonably foresee any injury to Hampton, or the nature and extent of the injury. In accordance with the reasoning in Palsgraf, since there was no duty, there could be no recovery for negligence, and therefore the defendant, Federal Express, could not be held liable to the unforeseeable plaintiff, Hampton. Indeed, under any of the general principles and theories of the common law that have been considered and applied, it would seem clear that Hampton has no cause of action.

Finally, we note that the case at bar is analogous to a case decided in the United States District Court for the Middle District of Florida, Gibson v. Greyhound Bus Lines, Inc., 409 F.Supp. 321 (M.D.Fla.), aff'd mem., 539 F.2d 708 (5th Cir.1976). In Gibson, the plaintiff, a Florida wildlife officer, suffered injuries on duty when he was scratched by a racoon. In order to determine whether the plaintiff had been exposed to rabies, the racoon's head was shipped by the Hamilton County Department of Health to a Florida state laboratory in Jacksonville, Florida. The shipper, the Department of Health, entered into a contract of carriage with the defendant carrier. The defendant was given no special instructions on the handling of the package, which contained the racoon's head, and the shipper did not obtain insurance. See 409 F.Supp. at 322. The racoon's head was never delivered, and, as a result, the plaintiff received a precautionary series of rabies vaccinations. Because of an adverse reaction to the vaccinations the plaintiff suffered injuries and sued for damages. See id. at 323.

In moving for summary judgment, the defendant contended that, as a carrier, it was subject to Florida state regulations which, in the absence of a declaration of greater value, limited its liability to $50 for a shipment of less than 100 pounds. See id. at 323. It is noteworthy that the district court stated that "[t]he special importance of the shipment was not known to defendant." Id. at 324. As a consequence, the court concluded that the "[d]efendant assumed no special duty towards the goods[,] [and] * * * is, therefore, entitled to the limitation of liability." Id. Hence, the court granted the defendant's motion for summary judgment, and entered judgment for $50 in favor of the plaintiff.

Under the circumstances of this case, involving a contract of carriage, it would also seem unreasonable and unjust to hold Federal Express liable to Hampton. If Federal Express had known of the contents of the package, it might have charged a higher rate, exercised additional care, have obtained insurance, or might not have accepted the responsibility. Since Federal Express had no knowledge of the contents, and hence could not reasonably foresee the injury and damages that could be suffered, plaintiff Hampton cannot recover on its cause of action founded in tort.

III. CONCLUSION

Since we hold that there was no duty owed to Hampton, and that the injury and damages suffered were not reasonably foreseeable, Hampton is not entitled to recover.

Federal Express, however, does not appeal from the district court's award of $100 in damages to Hampton, on partial summary judgment. Hence, Federal Express' liability is limited to $100, the amount declared in the airbill. Accordingly, the order of the district court is affirmed.

Notes

1. As is obvious, all three of these opinions lack certain information that makes the propriety of their outcomes difficult to evaluate. In *Sotheby's*, for example, why did FedEx fail to have adequate personnel available in Newark to off-load the artwork? The court cryptically refers to "weekend staffing shortages," but a glance at the calendar reveals that October 11, 1997 (the day of the flight) was not only a Saturday but also Yom Kippur (the holiest day of the year for Jews) as well as the start of the Columbus Day weekend.

In *Caporicci*, the identities of Bernie Felice and International Shoe Company, and their previous dealings with the plaintiff, are left unclear. In fact, both were made up names being used by a group of mobsters in a carefully orchestrated plot that bears more than a passing resemblance to the HBO television show *The Sopranos.*

At the center of the caper was Stephen Xavier Cavano, an associate of Anthony "The Sheriff" Morelli, the boss of the Gambino crime family in Florida. Cavano, together with his bodyguard John Wayne Givens (a 6'4", 380-pound enforcer) and an accomplice named Richard Sabatino, had learned through a friend that Caporicci was an importer of expensive leather shoes. Thus, in addition to his other pursuits (which included drugs, kidnaping, racketeering, and robbery), Cavano decided to get into the shoe business:

> Frankie Bushemi, an associate of Cavano's, learned of a wholesale warehouse that had thousands of Caporicci shoes worth $1,300 a pair. Cavano devised a plan pursuant to which they would set up a purportedly legitimate shoe sales business, and then call the Caporicci company and request samples. They would pay for the samples to lull the company into believing they were a legitimate company and then order bulk amounts and pay with fraudulent cashier's checks created by [a dishonest printer named Michael] Cebelak. Michael contacted Morelli and obtained money for the initial samples.
>
> The plan worked. After the first samples were delivered and paid for, the group requested a second set of samples (worth $50,000) which they also paid for. Then they ordered 2000 pairs of shoes worth $250,000. When the shoes were delivered, the driver was given a fraudulent cashier's check. The group quickly moved the shoes to the house of Richie Sabatino.
>
> Once the checks were presented to a bank, Caporicci learned that they were fraudulent and the FBI was notified. Because of the police attention, the group could not sell the shoes in Florida and they were shipped to New York. Givens and Cavano went to New York to arrange for the shoe sales. They met Buddy LaForte, Cavano's cousin, a "made man" who was the Staten Island "boss." Buddy had his associates sell the shoes. Givens and Cavano kept several pairs for themselves[.]

1998 WL 34097211 (Brief of the United States in *United States v. Cavano*, 189 F.3d 483 (11th Cir.), *cert. denied*, 528 U.S. 989 (1999)). For a further discussion, *see Shoe Plot Suspects Arrested in Florida*, Wash. Times, Apr. 26, 1995, at C6.

Lastly, in *Hampton*, one wonders why, when the first shipment failed to arrive at the VA Medical Center in Iowa City, the Children's Memorial Hospital in Omaha did not simply send another sample. The authors have been advised by Carl's lawyer, Jerold L. Drake, that the answer is as follows: "At the time the blood was drawn, Carl's leukemia was in remission. Federal Express failed to notify anyone that it had lost the shipment, and due to a bureaucratic snafu, neither hospital discovered the error. By the time they finally realized what had happened, Carl's illness had returned and it was too late to do the operation."

2. As noted at the outset of this chapter, international air shipments are governed by the 1929 Warsaw Convention (*see* Appendix 2), although this instrument is slowly being phased out by the 1999 Montreal Convention (*see* Appendix 26). At the moment, however, a given cargo case may be controlled by Warsaw, Montreal, or one or more of the various amendments, agreements, or protocols that were concluded during the 70 years separating the two:

> In order to determine which liability regime to apply, one must assess whether the air transportation in question was international in character. If so, the international liability regime governing the origin and destination States will apply, provided the two States have ratified the same treaty. At this writing, there are numerous possibilities:
>
> • The original Warsaw Convention of 1929, unamended;
>
> • The Warsaw Convention as amended by the Hague Protocol of 1955;
>
> • The Warsaw Convention as amended by the Guadalajara Convention of 1961;
>
> • The Warsaw Convention as amended by Montreal Protocol No. 4 (MP4) of 1975;
>
> • The Montreal Convention of 1999, or
>
> • Domestic law, if it is deemed that the transportation falls outside the Warsaw regime or if the two relevant States have failed to ratify the same liability convention.
>
> For the United States, effective March 4, 1999, international aviation cargo liability law became governed by the original Warsaw Convention, as amended by the Hague Protocol, as amended by MP4. Then, on November 4, 2003, the United States became subject to the Montreal Convention of 1999, which entered into force on that date.
>
> Hopefully, the recent entry into force of the Montreal Convention of 1999 will re-establish the international legal uniformity the Warsaw Convention of 1929 sought to achieve, though for a transitional period at least, the courts of different nations will be applying different legal regimes.

Paul Stephen Dempsey, *International Air Cargo & Baggage Liability and the Tower of Babel*, 36 Geo. Wash. Int'l L. Rev. 239, 240–42 (2004). *See further Avero Belgium Insurance v. American Airlines, Inc.*, 423 F.3d 73 (2d Cir. 2005), and Warren L. Dean, Jr., *Aviation Liability Regimes in the New Millennium: Beyond the Wild Blue Yonder—Air Carrier Liability for International Air Cargo Shipments in the 21st Century*, 28 Transp. L.J. 239 (2001).

The effect of these changes can be seen most readily in *Sotheby's*. Because it was decided under the original Warsaw Convention, FedEx's failure to include Memphis in its airbill was fatal (an ironic fact, given that FedEx was founded in Memphis in 1971 and continues to be headquartered in that city). Now, however, this omission would not matter and the case would come out the other way:

> [U]nder the original Warsaw Convention, a carrier that failed to include required information in the air waybill lost the protection afforded by limitations of liability contained in the treaty. This provision was eliminated, however, by Montreal Protocol No. 4, and the treaty as currently in force in the United States provides that noncompliance with the provisions of the articles specifying what must be contained in the air waybill does not affect the existence or the validity of the contract of carriage, and that contract is nevertheless subject to the rules of the Convention, including those relating to limitation of liability.

22 *Williston on Contracts* §58:45, at 212–13 (Richard A. Lord ed., 4th ed. 2002).

3. When it was first promulgated, the Warsaw Convention directed that damages be measured according to the "Poincaré franc," a proposed (but never minted) French coin containing 65.5 milligrams of gold. The subsequent collapse of the gold standard made retention of the Poincaré franc impossible. As a result, in 1969 the International Monetary Fund created a new hypothetical currency—the Special Drawing Right, or SDR—which is a composite (or "basket") of numerous actual currencies (as of October 2005, one SDR was the equivalent of $1.42). In 1975, SDRs became the Warsaw Convention's new unit of measure by virtue of Montreal Protocol No. 4 (*see* Appendix 15). Although the United States had pushed for this change, it did not adopt it. As a result, in *Trans World Airlines, Inc. v. Franklin Mint Corp.*, 466 U.S. 243 (1984), the Supreme Court held that in international air cargo cases, American courts should continue to use the Poincaré franc. This decision became a nullity in 1999 when the United States finally became a party to Protocol No. 4.

Problem 19

A bank regularly shipped bonds on a particular airline using a "no declared value" airbill. After many months of uneventful transactions, a package containing $2.5 million of bearer bonds failed to arrive. When the airline investigated, it discovered that its chief airport agent, who regularly handled the bank's shipments, had not been to work since the disappearance; in addition, his co-workers reported that he had "acted weird" during the week before the incident. If the bonds are cashed and the bank sues the airline for its loss, how much will it be able to recover? *See Amerika Samoa Bank v. United Parcel Service*, 25 Am. Samoa 2d 159 (High Ct. 1994).

C. SUITS AGAINST THIRD PARTIES

FEDERAL EXPRESS CORPORATION v. UNITED STATES POSTAL SERVICE

55 F. Supp. 2d 813 (W.D. Tenn. 1999)

DONALD, District Judge.

Before the court is Plaintiff's, Federal Express Corporation, Rule 12(b)(6) motion to dismiss Defendant's, United States Postal Service, third counterclaim for failure to state a claim upon which relief can be granted. Defendant's third counterclaim alleges that Plaintiff violated the Tennessee Consumer Protection Act of 1977 ("TCPA"), Tenn.Code Ann. §47-18-101 et seq., by engaging in false and misleading comparative advertising. Plaintiff contends that Defendant's counterclaim under the TCPA is preempted by the Airline Deregulation Act ("ADA"), 49 U.S.C. §41713, and therefore should be dismissed.

For the following reasons, the court grants Plaintiff's motion to dismiss.

The motion currently before the court calls for the court to ascertain whether the ADA preempts claims of unfair and deceptive business practices brought under the TCPA. State law can be preempted by federal law either expressly, where the language of the statute explicitly forbids state law claims, or implicitly, where the structure and purpose of the statute suggests a prohibition against state law claims. See FMC Corp. v. Holliday, 498 U.S. 52, 56–57, 111 S.Ct. 403, 112 L.Ed.2d 356 (1990). Ultimately, a court's determination concerning the existence of preemption is a question of Congressional intent. Id. at 56, 111 S.Ct. 403. The court must begin its preemption analysis with a "presumption that Congress does not intend to supplant state law." Wellons v. Northwest Airlines, Inc., 165 F.3d 493, 494 (6th Cir.1999) (quoting New York State Conference of Blue Cross & Blue Shield Plans v. Travelers Ins. Co., 514 U.S. 645, 115 S.Ct. 1671, 131 L.Ed.2d 695 (1995)). In other words, the court will not construe a statute as being preemptive of state law unless Congress has expressed a "clear and manifest purpose" to preempt the state laws in question. Id. The court will assume that the ordinary meaning of the ADA's language "accurately expresses the legislative purpose." Id. at 57, 111 S.Ct. 403.

Plaintiff's invocation of preemption under the ADA is based upon the following language:

> Preemption.—(1) Except as provided in this subsection, a State, a political subdivision of a State, or political authority of at least 2 States may not enact or enforce a law, regulation, or other provision having the force and effect of law related to a price, route, or service of an air carrier that may provide air transportation under this subpart.

49 U.S.C. §41713(b)(1) (1996).

The United States Supreme Court has had two occasions to address the parameters of this preemption provision. [In] Morales v. Trans World Airlines, Inc., 504 U.S. 374, 112 S.Ct. 2031, 119 L.Ed.2d 157, [the Court considered] a State's enforcement of its own laws, [but] did not address what effect, if any, the ADA's preemption clause had on state law claims brought by individuals. That question was answered by American Airlines v. Wolens, 513 U.S. 219, 115 S.Ct. 817, 130 L.Ed.2d 715 (1995). In Wolens, the plaintiffs had brought a class action suit against American Airlines claiming that the airline had retroactively modified their accumulated benefits under the airline's frequent flyer program. The plaintiffs contended that these modifications constituted a breach of contract and a violation of the Illinois Consumer Fraud and Deceptive Business Practices Act ("Illinois Consumer Fraud Act"). On the other hand, American Airlines contended that these state law claims were preempted by the ADA. After rejecting the Illinois Supreme Court's distinction between matters essential and unessential, the Court proceeded to examine the Illinois Consumer Fraud Act.

The Court found the Illinois Consumer Act to be similar in effect to the [state advertising] guidelines that were preempted by the ADA in Morales. The Court identified intrusive regulation of airline business practices as the primary evil targeted by the ADA's preemption clause and then noted that the potential for this type of regulation was "inherent in state consumer protection legislation." Id. at 227–28, 115 S.Ct. 817. The Court construed the Act as "a means to guide and police the marketing practices of the airlines." Id. at 228, 115 S.Ct. 817. Since the purpose of the ADA was to "leave largely to the airlines themselves, and not at all to States, the selection and design of marketing mechanisms appropriate to the furnishing of air transportation services," the Court held that the ADA preempted the plaintiff's claims under the Illinois Consumer Fraud Act. Id.

The court finds the Wolens holding highly relevant to the case at hand. As an express delivery company owning and operating over 500 airplanes, Plaintiff is an air carrier under the ADA and immune from state law claims relating to its prices, routes, or services. Like the Illinois Consumer Fraud Act, the TCPA is prescriptive in nature and governs the conduct of those falling within its governance. Moreover, the TCPA's title and the nature of its provisions indicate that it is state consumer protection legislation, and as such, has "the potential for intrusive regulation of airline business practices." See Wolens at 227, 115 S.Ct. 817. Defendant's TCPA counterclaim alleges that Plaintiff knowingly made false representations about Defendant's mail delivery services in advertisements marketing Plaintiff's own express delivery services. As with any company, the content of Plaintiff's advertising is an integral part of its marketing efforts. In this context, allowing Defendant to pursue its TCPA counterclaim against Plaintiff would make the Act "a means to guide and police the marketing practices of the airlines," a result prohibited by the holding of Wolens. Id. at 228, 115 S.Ct. 817.

Defendant contends that the ADA's preemption clause is inapplicable because its TCPA claim does not relate to Plaintiffs prices, routes or services. Instead, Defendant argues that its TCPA claim affects Plaintiff in "too tenuous, remote, or peripheral a manner to have preemptive effect." Morales at 390, 112 S.Ct. 2031. To support this contention, Defendant notes that none of the advertisements about which it complains contained any references to Plaintiff's prices, rates, routes or services. Rather, Defendant alleges that Plaintiff made misleading statements about Defendant's products and services.

Defendant's argument might be well-taken if the court adopted a narrow construction of the ADA's preemption clause. However, the Supreme Court's jurisprudence on the scope of the ADA's preemption clause clearly indicates that it should be broadly construed. The Court in Wolens noted that the Morales opinion had defined the 'relating to' language in the ADA preemption clause as "having a connection with, or reference to, airline 'rates, routes, or services.'" Wolens at 223, 115 S.Ct. 817. Thus, the court cannot accept Defendant's contention unless it can be fairly said that its counterclaim has no connection with, or reference to airline rates, routes or services.

Plaintiff's allegedly misleading representations were not made in a vacuum. Rather, they were made in the context of comparative advertising that clearly suggested Plaintiff could offer services that Defendant was unable to provide its customers. Although the majority of the statements made in these advertisements were directed at Defendant's products and services, every single advertisement ended with a statement highlighting the superiority of Plaintiff's services to those of Defendant. See (Def.'s Ans., Ex. A-F). Moreover, contrary to Defendant's assertions, these advertisements did make representations as to Plaintiff's own services. Every advertisement ended with a suggestion that Plaintiff was superior because it offered services that Defendant could not offer.

For example, Plaintiff ran a radio advertisement on April 7, 1997 comparing Defendant's Global Priority Mail with its own global express delivery services. While most of the advertisement focused on Defendant's limited range of delivery, it ended with the statement, "[f]or true global service, no one makes your packages a priority like FedEx."

See (Def.'s Ans., Ex. F). This advertisement certainly represents that unlike Defendant, Plaintiff is able to deliver around the world.

In light of the nature of these allegedly false advertisements, the court cannot accept the contention that Defendant's TCPA claim has no connection with, or reference to airline rates, routes or services. The court concludes that Defendant's TCPA claim is preempted by § 41713 of the ADA.

This holding does not leave Defendant without a remedy for the alleged misrepresentations made by Plaintiff. As Plaintiff concedes, nothing in the ADA prohibits Defendant from pursuing these allegations under the Trademark Act of 1946 (Lanham Act), 15 U.S.C. § 1051 et seq. Moreover, the United States Department of Transportation has the authority to investigate any unfair and deceptive business practices of an airline and to issue cease and desist orders in the event that any such practices are found. See 49 U.S.C. § 41712; Morales at 390–91, 112 S.Ct. 2031; Wolens at 228, n.4, 115 S.Ct. 817. The court simply holds that Defendant cannot state a claim for relief under the TCPA where that claim is brought against an air carrier and relates to that carrier's prices, routes or services.

Based on the foregoing, Plaintiff's Rule 12(b)(6) motion to dismiss Defendant's TCPA claim is GRANTED.

ROYAL INSURANCE v. AMERFORD AIR CARGO

654 F. Supp. 679 (S.D.N.Y. 1987)

CANNELLA, District Judge.

Plaintiff's motion for summary judgment is denied. Defendant's motion for summary judgment is granted. Fed.R.Civ.P. 56(a), (b).

BACKGROUND

Defendant Amerford Air Cargo ["Amerford"] is an air freight forwarder. Its business consists of picking up goods from its customers, arranging air transport on a direct air carrier, consolidating the goods in preparation for transport, and delivering them to the air carrier. For this service, Amerford's customers pay a single fee, which includes the cost of the flight.

IBM World Trade Corporation and Semi-Alloys, Inc. ["IBM"] conducted business with Amerford on a regular basis. On November 2, 1984, IBM contracted with Amerford to deliver three cartons of goods to a Hong Kong consignee. An Amerford truck picked up the cartons from one of IBM's Westchester County facilities at 6:10 p.m. that evening. Amerford had already arranged for the goods to be shipped on a Japan Air Lines flight scheduled to depart the next morning. The goods, semi-alloy products having an actual value of $97,713.97, were stored overnight in Amerford's warehouse facility located near JFK International Airport. The next morning, Amerford employees preparing for the Japan Air Lines flight could not locate the cartons. Amerford contacted the New York City Police and the F.B.I., but their investigation yielded no direct evidence of theft.

In early December, IBM submitted to Amerford a claim for the full value of the goods. Amerford responded that its contractual liability was limited to $20.00 per kilo, or a total of $1,310.00, because IBM had not declared a higher value for the goods and paid the additional insurance fee. On January 8, 1985, IBM submitted an amended claim to Amerford for $1,310.00. On January 16, IBM's insurer, plaintiff Royal Insurance Co. ["Royal"] paid IBM's claim in full, and on January 22 it was subrogated to all of IBM's rights. On May 22, Royal commenced this action seeking the full value of the goods.

Amerford was not served with the summons and complaint until June 22. In the meantime, on June 7, Amerford sent IBM a check for $1,310.00 in settlement of its January 8 amended claim. On July 7, IBM returned the check to Amerford, stating that settlement of the claim was in subrogation. Both parties move for summary judgment.

DISCUSSION

The central issue in this case is whether Amerford is an "air carrier" within the meaning of the Warsaw Convention for the Unification of Certain Rules Relating to International Carriage By Air, 49 U.S.C. § 1502 note ["Convention"], thus entitling it to claim the limitation of liability protection found therein. If the Convention applies to Amerford, its liability will be limited to $1,310.00. If the Convention does not apply, Amerford may be liable for the full amount of Royal's claim.

Amerford's Status Under the Convention

Royal's first argument is that, because the loss took place while the goods were being stored in Amerford's JFK warehouse, Amerford should be deemed a warehouseman rather than an air carrier, and the extent of liability should be determined pursuant to the New York law relating to warehousemen.

Under New York law, a "warehouse unable to return bailed property either because it has lost the property as a result of its negligence or because it has converted the property will be liable for the full value of the goods at the time of the loss or conversion." I.C.C. Metals, Inc. v. Municipal Warehouse Co., 50 N.Y.2d 657, 662, 431 N.Y.S.2d 372, 376, 409 N.E.2d 849 (1980). A warehouseman may contractually limit his liability in the case of negligence, but in the case of conversion, "strong policy considerations bar enforcement of any such limitation." Id. at 663, 431 N.Y.S.2d at 376. In I.C.C. Metals, the New York Court of Appeals held that when a plaintiff offers uncontroverted proof of delivery to a warehouseman and subsequent proof that the goods were lost or not delivered upon demand, and the warehouse does "not come forward with adequate evidentiary proof in admissible form to support its suggested explanation" for the loss, conversion shall be presumed and the limitation of liability agreed upon shall not be enforceable. Id. at 668, 431 N.Y.S.2d at 379.

Amerford's proffered explanation is that the cartons must have been stolen by sophisticated thieves who knew exactly what they wanted, took nothing else and left no traces. However, mere speculation that theft must have been the cause of the loss, without more, is not sufficient to overcome the presumption. Id. at 664 n.3, 431 N.Y.S.2d at 377 n.3. In light of Amerford's warehousing of the goods and its suggested explanation for the loss, Royal seeks that the presumption of conversion be imputed to Amerford, making it liable for the full value of the goods.

The policy underlying the application of a presumption of conversion to a warehouseman who offers no explanation for the loss of goods placed with him is a sound one. However, the Court does not believe that Amerford can or should be viewed as a warehouseman solely because it stores goods temporarily in a warehouse facility prior to air transport. Without question, customers engage Amerford to ship goods by air, and any storage of such goods prior to flight is temporary and incidental to Amerford's main business purpose. In contrast, a warehouseman "is a person engaged in the business of storing goods for hire." N.Y.U.C.C. §7-102(1)(h) (McKinney 1964).

Amerford is and holds itself out to the public as an air freight forwarder or indirect air carrier. Federal regulations define an air freight forwarder to mean an indirect air carrier, itself defined as "any citizen of the United States, who undertakes indirectly to engage in air transportation of property only, and who (1) does not engage directly in the operation of aircraft in air transportation, and (2) does not engage in air transportation pursuant to any [Civil Aeronautics] Board order which has been issued for the purpose of authorizing air express service under a contract with a direct air carrier." 14 C.F.R. §296.1(e).

The difference between direct and indirect air carriers has been defined as follows:

> direct air carriers are those who operate aircraft, while indirect air carriers hold out a transportation service to the public under which they utilize the services of a direct carrier for the actual transportation by air; i.e. those persons who procure shipments from shippers, assemble them, and tender the consolidated lot gathered from the various shippers to a direct air carrier for transportation at a bulk rate which is lower than the rates collected by the forwarders from the shippers. Although they carry no merchandise themselves, the forwarders assume the responsibility of a carrier, but ship by air in direct carrier's planes. Upon arrival of the shipment at the airport of destination, the forwarder divides the bulk shipment and distributes the separate portions to the individual consignees. DHL Corp. v. Civil Aeronautics Board, 584 F.2d 914, 915 (9th Cir.1978).
>
> Factors to be considered "in determining whether a party acted only as a forwarder or as a forwarder-carrier include ... the way the party's obligation is expressed in documents pertaining to the agreement, ... [and] the history of dealings between the parties." Zima Corp. v. M.V. Roman Pazinski, 493 F.Supp. 268, 273 (S.D.N.Y.1980) (citations omitted). Another significant factor is how the party made its profit, in particular, ... whether the party "picked up the less-than-carload shipment at the shipper's place of business and engaged to deliver it safely at its ultimate destination ... [charging] a rate covering the entire transportation and [making] its profit by consolidating the shipment with others" ... [,] while the shipper "seldom if ever knew which carrier would be utilized in the carriage of his shipment...."

Id. (citations omitted).

All of these factors support the conclusion that Amerford is an indirect air carrier. First, when Amerford picked up the cartons, it issued an airway bill to IBM, which stated:

> Hereunder the sole responsibility of the Company is as indirect carrier, subject to its filed tariff or as agent for the direct carrier after issuance of direct carrier's airway bill.... "Carrier" includes the carrier or forwarder issuing this airway bill and all carriers that carry the goods hereunder or perform any other services related to such air carriage. For the purposes of the exemption from the limitation of liability provisions set forth as referred to herein, "Carrier" includes agents, servants, or representatives of any such air carrier.

Affidavit of Donald F. Greene, Amerford Claims Manager, Ex. B (filed S.D.N.Y. Feb. 25, 1986).

Second, Amerford and IBM had conducted business over an extended period of time and IBM was familiar with Amerford's business practices. IBM even maintained blank airway bills at its location.

Third, IBM always contracted with Amerford to handle the entire transaction, i.e., pick-up from its facility, temporary storage of the goods pending transport, and arrangement for their shipment via a direct air carrier. IBM paid one fee for these services, and it included the price of air transport on the direct carrier.

It is fairly well established in this Circuit that the agent of an air carrier may claim the limitation of liability provisions found in the Convention. See Baker v. Lansdell Protective Agency, Inc., 590 F.Supp. 165, 170–71 (S.D.N.Y.1984); Reed v. Wiser, 555 F.2d 1079, 1092 (2d Cir.), cert. denied, 434 U.S. 922, 98 S.Ct. 399, 54 L.Ed.2d 279 (1977) (Convention's limitation of liability applies to employees of air carrier); Julius Young Jewelry Mfg. Co. v. Delta Air Lines, 67 A.D.2d 148, 151, 414 N.Y.S.2d 528, 530 (1st Dep't 1979) ("To allow an agent ... which is performing services in furtherance of the contract of carriage, and in place of the carriers themselves, to be liable without limit would circumvent the Convention's purposes of providing uniform worldwide liability rules and definite limits to the carriers' obligations."). Thus, it seems clear that had IBM contracted with Japan Air Lines as a direct carrier and the latter had contracted with Amerford to act as its agent for the purpose of picking up the goods, storing them until a flight was available, and delivering them to the aircraft itself, Amerford would be entitled to claim the benefits of the Convention's limitation of liability provision. There is no logical reason to deny Amerford resort to the Convention solely because it does not undertake the functions of air carriage directly, especially as the Convention does not differentiate between direct and indirect carriers, or otherwise define air carrier. Accordingly, Amerford, as an indirect carrier, is entitled to claim the limitation of liability found in the Convention.

Limitation of Liability

The Warsaw Convention creates a presumption of liability. Trans World Airlines, Inc. v. Franklin Mint Corp., 466 U.S. 243, 247, 104 S.Ct. 1776, 1780, 80 L.Ed.2d 273 (1984). Article 18 of the Convention provides:

> (1) The carrier shall be liable for damage sustained in the event of the destruction or loss of, or of damage to, any checked baggage or any goods, if the occurrence which caused the damage so sustained took place during the transportation by air.
>
> (2) The transportation by air within the meaning of the preceding paragraph shall comprise the period during which the baggage or goods are in [the] charge of the carrier, whether in an airport or on board an aircraft, or, in the case of a landing outside an airport, in any place whatsoever.

49 U.S.C. § 1502 note. By its terms, the Convention applied to Amerford from the time it took possession of IBM's cartons.

Article 22 limits the liability of air carriers for lost goods to the equivalent of $20.00 per kilo, or $9.07 per pound, "unless the consignor [IBM] has made, at the time when the package was handed over to the carrier, a special declaration of the value at delivery and has paid a supplementary sum if the case so requires." 49 U.S.C. § 1502 note.

Royal's second argument is that, even if the Convention applies to Amerford as an indirect carrier, it is not entitled to a limitation of liability because of Article 25(1), which provides:

> The carrier shall not be entitled to avail himself of the provisions of this convention which exclude or limit his liability, if the damage is caused by his wilful

> misconduct or by such default on his part as, in accordance with the law of the court to which the case is submitted, is considered to be equivalent to wilful misconduct.

Royal argues that Amerford's failure to explain the loss of the goods while stored in its warehouse comes within the I.C.C. Metals holding and should, therefore, result in a presumption of conversion, or the "equivalent" of wilful misconduct. Royal cites the case of Colgate Palmolive Co. v. S/S Dart Canada, 724 F.2d 313 (2d Cir.1983), cert. denied, 466 U.S. 963, 104 S.Ct. 2181, 80 L.Ed.2d 562 (1984). In that case, plaintiff delivered goods to defendant shipping company, which provided for their storage at its New Jersey port facility prior to their being loaded aboard a vessel for transport. Part of the shipment never arrived, and the carrier had no explanation for the loss. Instead, it claimed that its liability was limited by the terms of the Carriage of Goods By Sea Act, 46 U.S.C. § 1304(5) ["COGSA"]. The limitation of liability had been contractually extended by the parties to cover that period of time when the goods were to be stored at the port facility prior to departure. The district court granted defendant's motion for summary judgment, thus limiting its liability to the amount agreed upon.

The Court of Appeals reversed, holding that, by its terms COGSA applied only to the time the goods were actually loaded on the vessel and until unloaded at the final destination. The Court further held that although parties could contractually extend COGSA's limitation of liability terms to the period prior to loading, state law governed such an agreement. Then the Court found that the defendant had acted as a warehouseman during the time the goods were being stored. Applying New Jersey law, which was similar to the New York rule espoused in I.C.C. Metals Corp., the Court imputed to defendant a presumption of conversion as it had offered no substantial explanation for the loss of the goods. Because the defendant had offered no evidence to rebut the presumption of conversion, the limitation of liability, although contractually agreed upon, was not available. The Court then granted judgment for the plaintiff in the full amount of the goods.

Colgate can be sufficiently distinguished from the instant case to warrant rejection of Royal's argument based on it. First, by its terms, COGSA applies only to the time when goods are actually on board a sea vessel. Thus, in Colgate state law had to be applied to the time period prior to loading when the goods were being stored at the port facility. In contrast here, the Convention's terms expressly apply from the time goods come under the charge and control of the air carrier. See Art. 18(2), 49 U.S.C. § 1502 note. Thus, the limitation of liability attaches from that point onward as a result of the Convention itself, not any contractually agreed limitation of liability, as was the case in Colgate. The limitation of liability prevails unless the shipper has declared a special value for his goods, or there has been wilful misconduct or its equivalent on the part of the air carrier.

The Court has already determined that Amerford is an air carrier whose entire range of operations from the time it takes charge of a shipper's goods falls within the scope of the Convention. Thus, whether Amerford is entitled to a limitation of liability, or not entitled to it because of wilful misconduct, is a matter of federal not state law. See Lerakoli, Inc. v. Pan American World Airways, Inc., 783 F.2d 33, 36–37 (2d Cir.1986). Using the I.C.C. Metals holding to determine whether Amerford's unexplained loss amounts to wilful misconduct is inappropriate because the case is premised on state law grounds and is nonetheless specifically limited to the potential liability of warehousemen for such unexplained losses.

For purposes of Article 25, wilful misconduct occurs "where an act or omission is taken with knowledge that the act probably will result in injury or damage or with reckless disregard of the probable consequences." Maschinenfabrik Kern v. Northwest Airlines, Inc., 562 F.Supp. 232, 240 (N.D.Ill.1983) (citing Berner v. British Commonwealth Pacific Airlines, Ltd., 346 F.2d 532, 536–37 (2d Cir.1965); Grey v. American Airlines, Ltd., 227 F.2d 282, 285 (2d Cir.1955), cert. denied, 350 U.S. 989, 76 S.Ct. 476, 100 L.Ed. 855 (1956)). Royal offers nothing to suggest that any actions taken by Amerford, or which Amerford failed to take, resulted in the loss of the goods. Indeed, the affidavits depict reasonable security measures taken by Amerford. Royal's argument must fail because it rests entirely upon the presumption of conversion found in I.C.C. Metals. But because the presumption cannot be imputed to Amerford, Royal is left with nothing to support its claim that Amerford's wilful misconduct negates Amerford's right to limit its liability.

The Court's holding is consistent with the purposes underlying the Warsaw Convention. These "fundamental purposes ... are to limit liability so as to fix costs to airlines [or air carriers] at a definite level and to establish a uniform body of world-wide liability rules to govern international aviation to aid recovery by users." Julius Young Jewelry, 414 N.Y.S.2d at 529. The Convention also provides expressly for "consignors to avoid the damage limitations applicable to baggage [and goods] by declaring an increased value at the time of delivery." Id. at 530 (discussing Art. 22(2) of the Convention). IBM did not avail itself of the opportunity to declare a higher value and thus cover the full value of the goods. Had it done so, it [or its insurer] would have been entitled to a full recovery from Amerford.

For all of the foregoing reasons, Royal's motion for summary judgment is denied and Amerford's motion for summary judgment is granted. Amerford's liability for the lost goods is limited to $1,310.00.

HIH MARINE INSURANCE SERVICES, INC. v. GATEWAY FREIGHT SERVICES

116 Cal. Rptr. 2d 893 (Ct. App. 2002)

SWAGER, Justice.

HIH Marine Insurance Services, Inc. (hereafter HIH Insurance) appeals a summary judgment dismissing its subrogation action against a cargo handler, Gateway Freight Services (hereafter Gateway). We affirm.

PROCEDURAL AND FACTUAL BACKGROUND

The litigation arises from the shipment of 20 packages of hard disk drives from Malaysia to San Francisco via China Airlines. The shipper was a Malaysian company, Perai Seagate Storage Products, and the ultimate consignee was its parent company, Seagate Technology (Seagate). The shipment was arranged by a freight forwarder with affiliates in Malaysia and the United States doing business as Dimerco Express (Malaysia) and Dimerco Express (USA).

The Dimerco companies had "an on-going business relationship" with China Airlines and had arranged for shipment of cargo on the airline "thousands of times over the course of a decade or more." China Airlines had provided Dimerco with a stock of its "air waybills," which the freight forwarder would fill out and execute for particular shipments. These air waybills consisted of a standard form, with spaces for handling instructions and declaration of value of the goods shipped. On the reverse side, the form had printed provisions limiting liability for damaged and lost cargo. The form had not changed for at least five years and represented the only documentation of the contract of carriage.

In the shipment of the hard disk drives in question, the air waybill lists Dimerco Express (Malaysia) as the shipper and Dimerco Express (USA) as the consignee. No handling instructions are set forth on the waybill other than to notify consignee upon arrival, and the notation "NVD," a customary trade expression indicating no value declared, appears in the space for "Declared Value for Carriage." To document the shipment, Dimerco Express (Malaysia) issued a cargo manifest attached to the waybill that identified Seagate as the consignee and its American affiliate as the break-bulk agent.

Gateway operated a cargo handling facility in South San Francisco outside the geographical limits of San Francisco International Airport and performed services for China Airlines under a ground handling agreement. Pursuant to this agreement, it took possession of cargo arriving at San Francisco International Airport on China Airlines and arranged for delivery to consignees. We can find no evidence in the record before us that Dimerco (USA) ever took possession of the shipment.

The shipment of hard disk drives left Malaysia on December 4, 1996, and arrived in San Francisco the next day. During shipment, Dimerco Express (USA) had arranged for the insurance of the cargo by HIH Insurance. Upon its arrival in San Francisco, Gateway received and transported the cargo to its storage warehouse in South San Francisco, where it was inventoried and placed on shelves to be held until the consignee, Seagate, could take possession. Gateway's warehouse records show that all 20 packages arrived at the warehouse, but before the cargo could be delivered to Seagate, four of the 20 packages were stolen.

Approximately six weeks later, a company contacted Seagate to complain about a defective hard disk drive, which turned out to be one of those stolen from the Gateway warehouse. A police investigation disclosed that two individuals, Lance Lo and Steve Toma, were active in marketing the stolen disk drives. Both were charged with possession of stolen property and pled guilty to the charges. Neither Lo nor Toma had any known relationship with Gateway, and the investigation did not reveal that any Gateway employee was involved in the theft.

HIH Insurance determined its insured, Dimerco Express (USA), was liable to Seagate for the loss of the four packages of stolen hard disk drives. On August 4, 1997, it paid Seagate the sum of $429,633.60 on behalf of its insured as compensation for the loss.

On June 2, 1998, HIH Insurance filed a subrogation action against Gateway, Lance Lo and Steve Toma to recover its payment of $429,633.60 for the loss. After answering the complaint, Gateway filed a motion for summary adjudication to determine that its liability could not exceed $20.00 per kilogram under both the Warsaw Convention, Oct. 12, 1929, 49 Stat. 3000, T.S. 876, and the federal common law governing the limitation of liability provisions of the air waybill. The gross weight of the stolen cargo was 1,561 kilograms. In an order filed September 10, 1999, the trial court granted the motion for summary adjudication but relied only on federal common law, ruling that the case was not governed by the Warsaw Convention.

Subsequently, Gateway filed a motion for summary judgment on the ground that a settlement between HIH Insurance and the two individual defendants eliminated any potential exposure it might have. Under the terms of the settlement, the individual defendants paid HIH Insurance the sum of $120,000 as compensation for the loss. In an order filed December 28, 1999, the trial court granted the motion. The order found that Gateway's maximum liability to HIH Insurance could not exceed $31,200; and since Gateway was entitled to offset the $120,000 settlement payment against this liability, its ultimate liability to HIH Insurance was reduced to zero. A judgment dismissing the complaint was entered on the order.

DISCUSSION

A. Legal Background

In the field of air carrier liability, the two alternative bodies of law limiting liability for lost goods—the Warsaw Convention and federal common law—are closely enough related that precedents and policies from one have possible relevance to the other. Therefore, we can best approach the federal common law issues raised in this appeal by first reviewing the trial court's adjudication of the Warsaw Convention issues.

The Warsaw Convention is a treaty with the force of federal law that offers a scheme of presumptive air carrier liability for damaged goods combined with strict monetary limitation on this liability. Jaycees Patou, Inc. v. Pier Air Intern., Ltd. (S.D.N.Y.1989) 714 F.Supp. 81, 82.) Article 22(2) of the Warsaw Convention limits the carrier's liability for lost or damaged cargo to a sum in francs equivalent to $20 per kilogram, "unless the consignor has made ... a special declaration of the value at delivery and has paid a supplementary sum if the case so requires." The scope of this limitation is governed by the provisions of Article 18(1) that imposes a liability for loss or damage "if the occurrence which caused the damage ... took place during the transportation by air." Article 18(2) defines transportation by air to "comprise the period during which the baggage or goods are in charge of the carrier, whether in an airport or on board an aircraft...."

In the present case, Gateway relied on the theory that transportation by air included the period during which the carrier held the goods in storage at the point of destination while awaiting delivery to the consignee. The theory found support in certain federal district court decisions (e.g., Royal Ins. v. Amerford Air Cargo (S.D.N.Y.1987) 654 F.Supp. 679, 681–683), and if the term "airport" was given a functional definition, it could be reconciled with language of Article 18(2) defining air transportation to include the period "during which the ... goods are in charge of the carrier ... in an airport." The theory, however, had been rejected by a divided panel in Victoria Sales Corp. v. Emery Air Freight, Inc. (2nd Cir.1990) 917 F.2d 705, 707, which held that the term "airport" should be given a simple geographical interpretation. Under this interpretation, the Warsaw Convention does not apply to loss or damage sustained outside the geographical borders of the airport. Whatever may be the merits of Victoria Sales Corp., the trial court properly regarded it as controlling federal authority, which precluded application of the Warsaw Convention. It is undisputed that the Gateway warehouse lies outside the boundaries of the San Francisco International Airport.

Article 18(3) of the Warsaw Convention provides a separate rule governing transportation with air transportation and land transportation segments. The subdivision provides that transportation by air does not extend to land transportation, but where a transportation contract calls for land transportation following air transportation, any damage is presumed to have occurred during the air transportation segment, "subject to proof to the contrary...." Gateway could not, however, rely on Article 18(3) without attempting to discredit its own records. Unless impeached, the warehouse records showing an initial inventory of 20 packages constituted "proof to the contrary," within the meaning of this provision.

B. Contractual Limitation of Liability

The alternative basis for limiting Gateway's liability is predicated on a provision on the reverse side of the China Airlines air waybill, which establishes the same monetary limitation of liability as the Warsaw Convention. The pertinent language in this provision is found in paragraphs 1, 4, 7 and 9.

Paragraph 1 implicitly defines "air carriage" to include "incidental" services: "As used in this contract 'Carrier' means all air carriers that carry or undertake to carry the goods hereunder or perform any other services incidental to such air carriage...." Paragraph 9 provides that "the Carrier shall be liable for the goods during the period they are in its charge or the charge of its agent." Paragraph 4 first addresses carriage governed by the Warsaw Convention or "Rules of Compensation" promulgated by the Republic of China and then provides: "in any carriage where neither the Warsaw Convention applies nor the said Rules of Compensation, ... Carrier's liability shall not exceed US$20.00 or the equivalent per kilogram of goods lost, damaged or delayed unless a higher value is declared by the shipper and a supplementary charge paid." Paragraph 7 extends this limitation of liability to the carrier's agents: "Any exclusion or limitation of liability applicable to Carrier shall apply to and be for the benefit of Carrier's agents, servants and representatives...."

HIH Insurance argues that this separate limitation of liability in the air waybill does not apply to the loss of the disks because the warehouse theft occurred after air transportation was concluded. In effect, it seeks an interpretation of the limitation of liability provision in the air waybill that would be roughly consistent with the narrow interpretation of the Warsaw Convention in Victoria Sales. Gateway argues that the air waybill provision extends to the present case because the theft occurred while it was performing a service incidental to air carriage, i.e., holding the cargo for delivery, as an agent of China Airlines. This interpretation would maintain the $20-per-kilogram limitation in cases involving losses outside the geographical boundaries of the airport, which are not covered by the Warsaw Convention as construed in Victoria Sales.

C. Federal Common Law

Both parties recognize that the air waybill provision was intended to come within the released value doctrine of federal common law. As explained in Deiro v. American Airlines, Inc. (9th Cir.1987) 816 F.2d 1360, 1365, "[U]nder the federal common law governing common carriers, carriers may partially limit their liability for injury, loss, or destruction of baggage on a 'released valuation' basis. [Citation.] ... [I]n exchange for a low carriage rate, the passenger-shipper is deemed to have released the carrier from liability beyond a stated amount." The federal courts have, however, restricted the application of this doctrine to cases where the carriers give "customers a fair opportunity to choose between higher or lower liability by paying a correspondingly greater or lesser charge. [Citation.] Therefore, the shipper is bound only if he has reasonable notice of the rate structure and is given a fair opportunity to pay the higher rate in order to obtain greater protection." (Ibid.; see also Klicker v. Northwest Airlines, Inc. (9th Cir.1977) 563 F.2d 1310, 1315.)

The principal importance of the released value doctrine is to uphold the enforceability of the limitation of liability provision in the air waybill, but the doctrine also contains a judicial limitation not found in contract language—the fair opportunity to choose requirement—and, in addition, HIH Insurance argues that the exceptional nature of federal common law calls for a narrow interpretation of the limitation of liability provision.

The record clearly discloses that China Airlines met the judicial requirement that the shipper be given a fair opportunity to avoid the limitation of liability by choosing a higher freight rate. The shipper, Dimerco Express, whether acting through Malaysian or American affiliates, was "a sophisticated business enterprise well familiar with released values and limitations of liability...." (Ruston Gas Turbines v. Pan American World Airlines (2d Cir.1985) 757 F.2d 29, 32.) It had made thousands of cargo shipments on China Airlines and actually possessed its own stock of original air waybills issued by the carrier. In filling out the air waybill, it was expressly given the right to declare a higher value and pay a supplemental charge. By instead marking "NVD" and omitting any special handling instructions, it pursued the commercially reasonable alternative of accepting a lower rate in exchange for limitation of liability, while securing insurance coverage through HIH Insurance to protect against loss in the shipment. We find no reason to doubt that, when it completed the air waybill "without taking the opportunity to declare a higher value, it implicitly agreed to the liability limitations" in the waybill. (Ibid.)

HIH Insurance is unable to cite persuasive authority in support of its argument that the released value doctrine is restricted by principles governing the scope of federal common law. The basis of the released value doctrine in federal common law received an exhaustive examination in Read-Rite Corp. v. Burlington Air Express, Ltd. (9th Cir.1999) 186 F.3d 1190, which does not suggest any restriction such as HIH Insurance urges. The Read-Rite court held that the released value doctrine, as articulated in the Deiro decision, meets the rule restricting federal common law "'to situations where there is a significant conflict between some federal policy or interest and the use of state law.' [Citation.]" (Read-Rite Corp. v. Burlington Air Express, Ltd., supra, at p. 1196.) "The scope and standard of limited liability of an air carrier for loss or damage to cargo are directly related to the carrier's rates and services, and go to the very heart of the ADA [Airline Deregulation Act of 1978]. Allowing states to decide individually when and how a common air carrier may limit its liability would 'significantly impact federal deregulation,' [citation].... Because the imposition of state standards to decide whether contractual limits on liability are enforceable is contrary to the language, intent, and purpose of the federal policy embodied in the ADA, we apply federal common law to this question." Id. at p. 1198.)

D. Application of Contract Provision

We turn now to the application of the contractual language to the facts of the present case. There can be no doubt that the limitation of liability extends to agents of the carrier. Paragraph 7 states that the "limitation of liability applicable to Carrier shall apply to ... Carrier's agents...." Similar provisions have been upheld under the parallel provisions of the Carriage of Goods by Sea Act, 46 U.S.C. § 1304(5) (Akiyama Corp. of America v. M.V. Hanjin Marseilles (9th Cir.1998) 162 F.3d 571, 573; Generali v. D'Amico (11th Cir.1985) 766 F.2d 485, 487–488), and have been implicitly sanctioned in decisions under the Warsaw Convention. (Railroad Salvage of Conn. v. Japan Freight (E.D.N.Y.1983) 556 F.Supp. 124, 126 [assumes that the limitation of liability would apply if goods had been lost at the defendant's storage facility but finds they were lost later after delivery to trucker]; Hartford Fire Ins. v. Empresa Ecuatoriana

(S.D.N.Y.1996) 945 F.Supp. 51, 56 [holds that provision does not apply to subcontractor which was not a party to air carriage contract or a beneficiary of the contract].)

It is undisputed that Gateway was acting as an agent for China Airlines when the hard disk drives were stolen. The more difficult question, however, is whether it was acting as its agent in a service "incidental to air carriage" within the meaning of paragraph 1 of the limitation of liability provisions. If paragraph 7 is read in the context of paragraph 1, it is clear that the limitation of liability extends only to "'those agents who perform services in furtherance of the contract of carriage,' (citation)...." (In re Air Disaster, Lockerbie, Scotland, Dec. 1988 (E.D.N.Y.1991) 776 F.Supp. 710, 714 [construing Warsaw Convention].)

Under this contract language, the agent's right to claim the benefit of the limitation of liability provision must be determined with reference to the scope of the air carrier's responsibilities. If the agent is engaging in a performance that the air carrier is obliged to offer as part of air carriage, then it should enjoy the same limitation of liability as the carrier would enjoy. As stated in Akiyama Corp. of America v. M.V. Hanjin Marseilles, supra, 162 F.3d at page 574, with reference to the Carriage of Goods by Sea Act, "the proper test is to consider 'the nature of the services performed compared to the carrier's responsibility under the carriage contract.' [Citation.]"

It is beyond question that a contract for air carriage embraces the responsibility to hold the goods at the destination for delivery to the consignee. The proper delivery of the goods is as essential as the transportation itself. In the case at bar, China Airlines was obliged not only to transport the 20 packages of hard disk drives but to deliver them to the consignee following the transportation. To discharge this obligation, it contracted with an agent, Gateway, engaged in the business of cargo handling. At the time the hard disk drives were stolen, Gateway was in fact holding the goods for delivery to the consignee pursuant to its contract with China Airlines. Under these facts, we conclude that Gateway was acting as an agent for China Airlines in a service incidental to "air carriage."

HIH Insurance cites authority to the effect that limitation of liability provisions should be strictly construed (Herd & Co. v. Krawill Machinery Corp. (1959) 359 U.S. 297, 305, 79 S.Ct. 766, 3 L.Ed.2d 820; Hartford Fire Ins. v. Empresa Ecuatoriana, supra, 945 F.Supp. at p. 56), but this principle should not operate to impose arbitrary and unexpected consequences. Like all contractual questions, the interpretation of the air waybill provision should be resolved in a manner consistent with the reasonable expectations of the parties. The parties had reason to expect that the terms of the air waybill would apply to all services that the air carrier was obliged to perform, including delivery to the consignee.

Though HIH Insurance vigorously contends that air transportation had been completed some time prior to the theft, it offers no test for determining when the air carriage in fact ended. We have no reason to adopt the rule of the Victoria Sales decision by finding that air transportation ends at the geographical boundaries of the airport. The Victoria Sales court predicated its decision solely on "the plain language" of the Warsaw Convention and conceded that another interpretation might have more sensible results. (Victoria Sales Corp. v. Emery Air Freight, Inc., supra, 917 F.2d 705, 707.) Indeed, it makes little sense to make the shipper's rights dependent on a factor, i.e., local geographical boundaries, that will vary from airport to airport and lies beyond the shipper's knowledge. Our interpretation of federal common law avoids the potentially irrational impact of the Victoria Sales decision by making the limitation of liability provision co-extensive with the air carrier's obligation of transportation and delivery.

The judgment is affirmed.

CONTINENTAL TIME CORP. v. MERCHANTS BANK OF NEW YORK

459 N.Y.S.2d 396 (Sup. Ct. 1983)

BLYN, Justice.

Motion by plaintiff for summary judgment.

The following undisputed facts appear from the papers submitted. On January 10, 1980 one Georges Bloch requested his Swiss bank, Credit Suisse (Credit), to issue an irrevocable letter of credit in favor of plaintiff Continental Time Corp. (Continental) in the principal sum of $236,961.90 in order to facilitate payment for a shipment of watches sold by Continental to Bloch. Said letter of credit was issued and, as amended, was valid until February 11, 1980 and payable upon presentation of certain documents. Defendant Merchants Bank of New York (Merchants) acted as the collecting bank on behalf of Continental in the presentation and negotiation of the documents called for by the letter of credit.

On January 23, 1980 Continental delivered to Merchants the various documents for presentation to Credit including a sight draft for the full amount. Merchants forwarded the documents on that date to Credit for payment.

By telex dated January 29, 1980 Credit advised Merchants it was refusing the documents because of an alleged discrepancy in one of them (airway bill) which telex further provided, "documents at your disposal * * * please authorize us to present documents on collection basis." By telex of the same date Merchants authorized Credit to present the documents on a collection basis. Bloch refused to pay alleging a setoff against Continental.

In this action Continental seeks to recover the principal amount of the letter of credit alleging in its complaint two causes of action. The first sounds in negligence and the second claims breach of contractual duties under sections 4-202, 4-501, 4-503 and 5-111 of the Uniform Commercial Code. Continental contends Merchants failed to (a) detect those material discrepancies claimed to exist by Credit in the documents delivered under the irrevocable letter of credit in the course of Merchants' review of the documents prior to delivery and presentment; (b) timely notify Continental of Credit's refusal to pay under the irrevocable letter of credit as well as the reasons therefor; (c) request instructions of Continental as to what to do following Credit's refusal to pay; (d) request the documents back for correction prior to the expiration date of the irrevocable letter of credit; and (e) receive authority from Continental to place the irrevocable letter of credit on a "collection basis." Simply stated Merchants takes the position it took all necessary and proper actions in presenting the documents for payment.

At the outset, since there appears to be some confusion in the parties' minds, it is necessary to identify the precise nature of the transaction at issue and the applicable legal standards. Article 4 of the Uniform Commercial Code is entitled "Bank Deposits and Collections." Part 2 of that article deals with the obligations in general of collecting banks and part 5 more specifically with the collection of documentary drafts, defined in subdivision (f) of section 4-104 of the Uniform Commercial Code as "any * * * draft with accompanying documents * * * to be delivered against honor of the draft." Article 5 of the Uniform Commercial Code deals with letters of credit. The Court of Appeals in United Bank v. Cambridge Sporting Goods Corp. (41 NY2d 254, 258–259) addressed the question of the law applicable to letters of credit and the relationship between them and documentary drafts as follows: "Article 5 of the Uniform Commercial Code, dealing with letters of credit, and the Uniform Customs and Practice for Documentary Credits promulgated by the International Chamber of Commerce, set forth the duties and obligations of the issuer of a letter of credit. A letter of credit is a commitment on the part of the issuing bank that it will pay a draft presented to it under the terms of the credit, and if it is a documentary draft, upon presentation of the required documents of title (see Uniform Commercial Code, § 5-103)."

In [a] footnote the court, citing subdivision (4) of section 5-102 of the Uniform Commercial Code, pointed out that the Uniform Customs and Practice for Documentary Credits controls, in lieu of article 5, when by its terms the letter of credit is made subject to the Uniform Customs and Practice. That is the case at bar. It is thus apparent that while it may be said that Merchants handled a single transaction for Continental, that transaction was duplex in nature, the documentary draft aspect being governed by article 4 of the Uniform Commercial Code and the letter of credit aspect being governed by the Uniform Customs and Practice rather than article 5 of the Uniform Commercial Code.

With that analytical preamble the court turns to the various grounds advanced by Continental for recovery as a matter of law.

Continental's first contention focuses on the letter of credit and the supporting airway bill. The letter of credit contains specific requirements regarding the language of the airway bill. The document presented to Credit was not filled in in the portion entitled "Airport of Departure" and "Airport of Destination." (This was the basis for the rejection by Credit.) The letter of credit is silent in that regard. The parties' reliance on sections of article 5 of the Uniform Commercial Code on this issue is misplaced. The Uniform Customs and Practice, however, provides that banks assume no responsibility or liability for the form and sufficiency of documents (art 9). Further, article 7 of the Uniform Customs and Practice provides, "Banks must examine all documents with reasonable care to ascertain that they appear on their face to be in accordance with [the letter of credit]." On the basis of the foregoing it may not be said as a matter of law that Merchants breached any duty in its review of the airway bill prior to presentation of the documents to Credit.

The next contention, although couched in terms of notice of refusal to pay under the letter of credit, in fact deals with Merchants' obligation to notify Continental of dishonor of the documentary draft. Section 4-501 of the Uniform Commercial Code, relied upon by Continental, imposes an obligation upon Merchants to do so "seasonably." Continental maintains no such notice was given. Merchants, pointing principally to the deposition of Continental's president in this action, argues otherwise. This court need not determine whether a bona fide issue of fact exists on the issue of notice of dishonor as such issue is a red herring in view of the additional obligations imposed upon Merchants which, as hereinafter set forth, this court finds it did not meet.

Beyond notice of dishonor of the documentary draft Merchants was obligated under subdivision (b) of section 4-503 of the Uniform Commercial Code to "use diligence and good faith to ascertain the reason for dishonor, must notify its transferor [Continental] of the dishonor and of the results of its effort to ascertain the reasons therefor and must request instructions." Continental contends Merchants failed to request instructions of it. The opposing affidavit of a Merchants' officer, who fails to indicate any source of his knowledge, opines: "Upon rejection by Credit Suisse of the documents, Merchants, as is its custom, telephoned its customer of the discrepancies and awaited their instructions.

After conferring with its customer, [as is its custom and practice] Merchants authorized Credit Suisse to re-present the documents on a collection basis as requested by Credit Suisse in order to have the documents paid." (Matter in brackets handwritten.) Such a conclusory statement of a custom of the bank totally devoid of evidentiary facts by an affiant with no personal knowledge is hardly laying bare one's proof to demonstrate the existence of a triable issue.

Rather than request instructions, the record is clear that Merchants unilaterally and without authorization from Continental placed the irrevocable letter of credit on a collection basis. Testimony by experts from both Merchants as well as Credit in a related federal action unequivocally establish that the steps taken by Merchants were contrary to banking custom and practice in failing to afford Continental an opportunity to cure the claimed deficiency in the airway bill and resubmit the letter of credit for payment, which it had a right to do, as well as destroying the irrevocability of the letter of credit (releasing Credit's obligation to pay). Moreover, such conduct is violative of article 3(c) of the Uniform Customs and Practice which provides that an irrevocable letter of credit cannot be canceled without the agreement of all the parties thereto, as well as contrary to decisions (1975–1979) of the International Chamber of Commerce Banking Commission under the Uniform Customs and Practice (references 13, 14).

For the foregoing reasons the motion is granted and the clerk is directed to enter judgment accordingly.

JOHN & JANE ROES, 1–100 v. FHP, INC.

985 P.2d 661 (Haw. 1999)

LEVINSON, Justice.

The plaintiffs-appellants John & Jane Roes 1–100 (hereinafter "plaintiffs") filed an action in the United States District Court for the District of Hawai'i, alleging, inter alia, (1) negligence and (2) intentional or negligent infliction of emotional distress. In December 1997, the plaintiffs and the defendant-appellee Continental Micronesia, Inc. (["CM"]) filed cross-motions for partial summary judgment, and the defendant-appellee FHP, Inc. ("FHP") filed a cross-motion for summary judgment. On February 23, 1998, the federal district court conducted a consolidated hearing on the motions. The court determined that, because the matter presented novel issues of state law, the following questions should be certified to this court:

> [1]. Whether the courts in the State of Hawai['] i recognize a cause of action based upon fear of developing AIDS, if an individual can prove exposure to HIV-positive blood?
>
> [2]. If such a cause of action exists, can damages be solely based upon emotional distress, or must the plaintiff demonstrate an underlying physical injury, separate and apart from the emotional distress?

We accepted certification. It appears that the pertinent claim for relief implicated by the facts of the present matter is negligent infliction of emotional distress (NIED). Accordingly, we answer the certified questions as follows:

> (1) Hawai'i law recognizes a cause of action for NIED arising out of a fear of developing AIDS following exposure to HIV-positive blood resulting in actual physical peril to the claimant; and

(2) damages may be based solely upon serious emotional distress, even absent proof of a predicate physical injury.

I. BACKGROUND

The plaintiffs were baggage handlers employed by Signature Support Flight Service, doing business at the Honolulu International Airport. On or about May 21, 1996, the plaintiffs were unloading baggage from CM Flight C0906, originating from Guam. Roe 1 moved a bag that, unbeknownst to him, contained a specimen of blood tainted with HIV. The blood was being transported for testing from FHP's facilities on Guam to a laboratory in Honolulu. The blood was allegedly placed in a glass vial, which had been inserted into a ziploc bag and then packaged in a polyethylene courier satchel.

When he moved the bag, Roe 1 noticed that his hands were wet with blood from the specimen. Two co-workers, Roes 2 and 3, assisted in the clean-up of the specimen and came into contact with the tainted blood. The plaintiffs assert that, at the time of the incident, they were suffering from open wounds on their hands. Each of the plaintiffs subsequently tested negative for HIV.

On March 3, 1997, the plaintiffs filed this action in the circuit court of the first circuit, State of Hawai'i. FHP filed a notice of removal to the United States District Court for the District of Hawai'i. On March 6, 1997, the plaintiffs filed an amended complaint in the federal district court, alleging, inter alia, (1) negligence, (2) negligence based upon respondeat superior, (3) failure to warn, (4) negligent failure to advise that the subject specimen was infectious and/or hazardous, (5) negligent failure to label the package containing the infectious specimen, (6) negligent entrustment of infectious material to a courier for packing and transportation, (7) negligent management, (8) "negligent/lack of proper training/education/supervision regarding the handling of infectious materials," (9) "negligent/lack of enforcement of IATA shipping guidelines/guidelines for diagnostic specimens/OSHA rules/laws/procedures," (10) negligent failure to provide protective gloves, (11) negligence by omission, (12) negligent shipping, (13) misrepresentation, (14) intentional/negligent infliction of emotional distress, and (15) loss of consortium. Essentially, the plaintiffs contended that they suffered from "AIDS phobia," inasmuch as they claimed damages arising out of the emotional distress that each of them experienced as a result of being negligently exposed to HIV.

II. STANDARD OF REVIEW

The issue presented by the certified question—whether, and to what extent, Hawai'i recognizes a claim for relief based on a fear of developing AIDS—is a question of law. "Questions of law are reviewable de novo under the right/wrong standard of review." Francis v. Lee Enters., Inc., 89 Hawai'i 234, 236, 971 P.2d 707, 709 (1999) (quoting Best Place, Inc. v. Penn America Ins. Co., 82 Hawai'i 120, 123, 920 P.2d 334, 337 (1996) (citation omitted)).

III. DISCUSSION

A. A Plaintiff May Assert A Claim For Relief For NIED In Hawai'i, By Virtue Of Negligent Exposure To HIV, Without Demonstrating A Predicate Harm.

This court first recognized the independent tort of negligent infliction of "mental" distress in Rodrigues v. State, 52 Haw. 156, 472 P.2d 509 (1970). In Rodrigues, the plaintiffs alleged emotional distress caused by the state having negligently caused extensive flood damage to their home. We acknowledged that, theretofore, the traditional rule had been "that there [was] no recovery for the negligent infliction of mental distress alone." 52 Haw. at 169, 472 P.2d at 518 (citations omitted). We then rejected the traditional rule, announcing that "the preferable approach is to adopt general standards to test the genuineness and seriousness of mental distress in any particular case" and holding that "serious mental distress may be found where a reasonable man, normally constituted, would be unable to adequately cope with the mental stress engendered by the circumstances of the case." Id. at 171, 173, 472 P.2d at 519–20. Thus, Hawai'i "became the first jurisdiction to allow recovery [for NIED] without a showing of physically manifested harm" to the plaintiff. Campbell v. Animal Quarantine Station, 63 Haw. 557, 560, 632 P.2d 1066, 1068 (1981).

A plaintiff asserting a claim of NIED based on a fear of developing AIDS will not necessarily experience a predicate physical injury. In the present case, for example, it appears that the plaintiffs have not contracted HIV, nor were they physically injured during their handling of the allegedly tainted blood sample. Thus, in order for an NIED claim to be available to the plaintiffs based solely upon their fear of AIDS, and in the absence of physical injury sustained by anyone as a result of the defendants' conduct, we would, of necessity, be obliged to carve out an exception to our general rule that recovery is permitted only when there is a predicate physical injury to someone.

Other jurisdictions have held that recovery for NIED may be allowable where a defendant's negligence places the plaintiff in actual physical peril. This principle comports with the reasonable person standard originally articulated in Rodrigues. In our view, a reasonable person would foreseeably be unable to cope with the mental stress engendered by an actual, direct, imminent, and potentially life-endangering threat to his or her physical safety. Cf. Bramer v. Dotson, 190 W.Va. 200, 437 S.E.2d 773, 775 (1993) (observing that "conventional wisdom mandates that fear of AIDS triggers genuine—not spurious—claims of emotional distress").

This concept is not, as CM suggests, a departure from "longstanding precedent in the areas of negligence theory and the independent cause of action for [NIED]," but merely entails a recognition that the reasonableness standard established in Rodrigues has broader application than has previously been employed. Accordingly, we hereby recognize an exception to the general rule that recovery for NIED is permitted only when there is some predicate injury to a person, and hold that a claim of NIED for which relief may be granted is stated, inter alia, where the negligent behavior of a defendant subjects an individual to an actual, direct, imminent, and potentially life-endangering threat to his or her physical safety by virtue of exposure to HIV.

B. Hawai'i Law Recognizes A Claim Of NIED Where An Individual Can Prove Exposure To HIV-Positive Blood.

A majority of the jurisdictions that have addressed the issue has determined, either expressly or by implication, that, where a plaintiff is actually "exposed" to HIV, he or she may state a claim for fear of contracting AIDS. We agree that "exposure" is aptly defined as "proof of both a scientifically accepted transmission of [HIV] ... and that the source of the allegedly transmitted blood or fluid was in fact HIV-positive[.]" Brown v. New York City Health and Hosps. Corp., 225 A.D.2d 36, 648 N.Y.S.2d 880, 886 (1996).

FHP attempts to rely on Transamerica Insurance Company v. Doe, 173 Ariz. 112, 840 P.2d 288 (Ct.App.1992), for the proposition that recovery should not be permitted for NIED based on fear of AIDS in the absence of physical injury resulting from exposure to HIV. In Transamerica, the Arizona Court of Appeals entertained this question in the context of an insurance policy that only provided coverage for "bodily injury." 840 P.2d at 289. Inasmuch as the Transamerica court was construing the language of an insurance policy and did not undertake to establish substantive tort law, the case is inapposite to the present matter.

Exposure to HIV-positive blood "makes the threat of infection much more of a real possibility to be feared and far more than a speculative worry." Brown, 648 N.Y.S.2d at 886 (citation omitted). As such, exposure to HIV-positive blood "involve[s] circumstances which guarantee the genuineness and seriousness of the claim." Rodrigues, 52 Haw. at 171, 472 P.2d at 519. Inasmuch as actual exposure to HIV-positive blood would in fact pose a direct, immediate, and serious threat to an individual's personal safety, such exposure would foreseeably engender serious mental distress in a reasonable person. Accordingly, we hold that a plaintiff states a claim of NIED for which relief may be granted where he or she alleges, inter alia, actual exposure to HIV-positive blood, whether or not there is a predicate physical harm.

We emphasize, assuming that a plaintiff has been exposed to HIV-positive blood, that liability will attach only to the extent that the resulting mental distress is within the range of that experienced by a reasonable person under the same circumstances. See Rodrigues, 52 Haw. at 173, 472 P.2d at 520. Moreover, any damages recoverable for NIED should be confined to the time between discovery of the actual exposure and the receipt of a reliable negative medical diagnosis.

IV. CONCLUSION

For the foregoing reasons, we answer the certified questions as [stated above] and return this case for further proceedings in the United States District Court for the District of Hawai'i.

Notes

1. The battle between Federal Express and the United States Postal Service was a fierce one, resulting in five different published opinions including the one reproduced above (the others can be found at 959 F. Supp. 832 (W.D. Tenn. 1997), 151 F.3d 536 (6th Cir. 1998), 40 F. Supp. 2d 943 (W.D. Tenn. 1999), and 75 F. Supp. 2d 807 (W.D. Tenn. 1999)). *See further* Hala Souman & Sean McMurrough, Note, *Federal Express Corporation v. United States Postal Service: You Can Sue the Post Office*, 11 Loy. Consumer L. Rep. 65 (1999).

Realizing that no one (except, of course, the lawyers) were profiting from the dispute, the two combatants finally agreed to bury the hatchet and then

> inked a seven year agreement calling for the post office to buy space on FedEx planes to transport Express Mail, Priority Mail and First Class Mail and for FedEx to locate 10,000 overnight collection boxes at post offices nationwide. [T]he deal was worth about $7 billion to FedEx—$6.3 billion in payments from the USPS for using its planes—and $900 million in additional revenue from those thousands of drop boxes.

FedEx To Buy Kinko's, E-Postal News, Jan. 12, 2004, at § 189.

No sooner had the fight between FedEx and USPS ended then a new carrier-versus-carrier war broke out. Hoping to keep it out of the marketplace, FedEx and UPS argued that because DHL Airways (DHL-A) was part of Brussels-based DHL Worldwide Express (DHL-WE), which in turned is owned by the German post office (Deutsche Post World Net), DHL-A could not fly any American route. To solve this problem, DHL-A severed itself from DHL-WE and changed its name to ASTAR Air Cargo (www.astaraircargo.us). Although FedEx and UPS insisted that nothing had changed substantively, in December 2003 Administrative Law Judge Burton S. Kolko found that Miami-based ASTAR was a United States citizen under 49 U.S.C. §40102(a)(15) and thus entitled to operate domestically. In May 2004, the United States Department of Transportation agreed with Judge Kolko. *See* Angela Greiling Keane, *DOT Sides With ASTAR, Striking UPS, FedEx Complaint*, Traffic World, May 13, 2004, at 1. Although FedEx and UPS could have pursued their allegation in front of a federal appeals court, they chose instead to meet the challenge head-on:

> DHL Friday made its second foray in as many weeks into UPS and FedEx territory with plans to invest $1.2 billion in its U.S. network.
>
> The third-place player claims 6–8 percent of the U.S. overnight and ground delivery business, which is dominated by the two competitors.
>
> In its quarterly call with analysts Wednesday, FedEx said it will invest $1.6 billion in improvements in 2005.
>
> DHL, the largest delivery company in Europe and a significant player in Asia and South America, started business in San Francisco in 1969. It began to ramp up [in the United States] last summer when it purchased Airborne's ground operations for $1.5 billion.
>
> DHL Airways, majority owned by Deutsche Post—the German postal monopoly—was sold to American investors who renamed it ASTAR. In a protracted fight, FedEx and UPS contested ASTAR's ownership, saying even though the investors are U.S. citizens, company direction would be coming from Deutsche Post. The Bush administration in mid-May said ASTAR was not controlled by foreign interests, allowing it to fly in the United States.
>
> "The only thing that's new here is the fact that DHL and Airborne are now backed by German postal monopoly funds as they try to buy their way into the U.S. market," said FedEx spokeswoman Kristin Krause. "We've been competing against Airborne and DHL for 30 years. We are confident in our ability to know what our customer wants and how to deliver it," she said.
>
> A.G. Edwards analyst Donald Broughton said, "FedEx has far bigger fish to fry than a small unionized company that lacks critical mass. DHL can't operate at a loss. If Deutsche Post keeps funding it, that threatens its assertion that DHL is an independent American company."

Jane Roberts, *New Centers Will Nudge DHL Further Into FedEx/UPS Turf*, Comm. Appeal (Memphis), June 26, 2004, at C1.

For a further look at the competition between private air cargo carriers, *see* Catherine B. Harrington, Comment, *Weather May Not Stop USPS, But Special Interests Will: The Bush Administration's GATS Offer Supports Private Express Delivery Services But Threatens to Stamp Out USPS*, 19 Am. U. Int'l L. Rev. 431 (2003).

2. As the court in *HIH Marine* observes, a divided panel of the Second Circuit in *Victoria Sales* rejected the interpretation of "airport" that the district court in *Royal Insurance* had used to determine the meaning of Article 18 of the Warsaw Convention. In his

dissent in *Victoria Sales*, Circuit Judge Van Graafeiland chided the majority for ignoring modern realities:

> The term "airport" is not defined in the Convention. Because of the tremendous growth in air cargo transportation and the virtual impossibility of crowding all the unloading and delivery facilities of every carrier into the geographical confines of busy airports, we ought to interpret the term "airport" in a manner that will carry out the general intent of the Convention's framers. See Reed v. Wiser, 555 F.2d 1079, 1090 (2d Cir.), cert. denied, 434 U.S. 922, 98 S.Ct. 399, 54 L.Ed.2d 279 (1977); Eck v. United Arab Airlines, 360 F.2d 804, 812–15 (2d Cir.1966). If, for example, a carrier's unloading facilities were partially within and partially without an airport's geographical boundaries, it would border on the absurd to determine Convention coverage by where in the carrier's building the goods were located, particularly if they were lying athwart the airport's geographical boundary line.

917 F.2d at 710–11.

3. When they are unable to rely on the Warsaw (or Montreal) Convention due to decisions like *Victoria Sales*, carriers fall back on the exculpatory clauses in their airbills. *See further Albingia Versicherungs A.G. v. Schenker Int'l Inc.*, 350 F.3d 916 (9th Cir. 2003), *cert. denied*, 541 U.S. 1041 (2004). As *HIH Marine* illustrates, these typically extend their protections to the carrier's "agents, servants, and employees." This produced a long-running battle, litigated primarily over ocean shipments, as to exactly which parties were covered by such clauses and the extent of their protection.

For many years, the seminal Supreme Court decision had been *Robert C. Herd & Co. v. Krawill Machinery Corp.*, 359 U.S. 297 (1959). *Herd* was problematic, however, because it said, in rather convoluted language, that while limitation clauses were valid they were to be strictly construed. To clear up the confusion caused by this pronouncement, the Supreme Court recently stepped back into the fray and held (as *HIH Marine* had predicted) that despite *Herd*, limitation clauses are to be interpreted like other contract provisions:

> This is a simple question of contract interpretation. It turns only on whether the Eleventh Circuit correctly applied this Court's decision in Robert C. Herd & Co. v. Krawill Machinery Corp., 359 U.S. 297, 79 S.Ct. 766, 3 L.Ed.2d 820 (1959). We conclude that it did not.
>
> In Herd, the bill of lading between a cargo owner and carrier said that, consistent with COGSA [the Carriage of Goods by Sea Act, 46 U.S.C. app. §§ 1301–1315], "'the Carrier's liability, if any, shall be determined on the basis of $500 per package.'" Id., at 302, 79 S.Ct. 766. The carrier then hired a stevedoring company to load the cargo onto the ship, and the stevedoring company damaged the goods. The Court held that the stevedoring company was not a beneficiary of the bill's liability limitation. Because it found no evidence in COGSA or its legislative history that Congress meant COGSA's liability limitation to extend automatically to a carrier's agents, like stevedores, the Court looked to the language of the bill of lading itself. It reasoned that a clause limiting "'the Carrier's liability'" did not "indicate that the contracting parties intended to limit the liability of stevedores or other agents.... If such had been a purpose of the contracting parties it must be presumed that they would in some way have expressed it in the contract." Ibid. The Court added that liability limitations must be "strictly construed and limited to intended beneficiaries." Id., at 305, 79 S.Ct. 766.

> The Eleventh Circuit, like respondents, made much of the Herd decision. Deriving a principle of narrow construction from Herd, the Court of Appeals concluded that the language of the ICC bill's [limitation] clause is too vague to clearly include Norfolk [the railroad which completed the last leg of the transportation journey for Hamburg Sud, the ocean carrier that had carrier the goods from Australia to the United States]. 300 F.3d, at 1308. Moreover, the lower court interpreted Herd to require privity between the carrier and the party seeking shelter under a [limitation] clause. Id., at 1308. But nothing in Herd requires the linguistic specificity or privity rules that the Eleventh Circuit attributes to it. The decision simply says that contracts for carriage of goods by sea must be construed like any other contracts: by their terms and consistent with the intent of the parties. If anything, Herd stands for the proposition that there is no special rule for [limitation] clauses.

Norfolk Southern Railway Co. v. Kirby, 125 S. Ct. 385, 397 (2004).

4. Although *Kirby* has cleared up the confusion surrounding limitation clauses, it does not get at the real problem: when it comes to the multimodal (also known as intermodal) transportation of goods, the world lacks a unified legal regime:

> By definition, intermodal movements involve the movement of passengers or freight from one mode of transportation to another. Freight can be lost or damaged in transit. The question then becomes, what are the legal rules under which liability is assessed? The problem is that the legal rules governing carrier liability for loss and damage in transit were developed historically on a mode-by-mode basis.
>
> For example, the Harter Act of 1906 governs domestic water transport; the Carriage of Goods by Sea Act (the domestic equivalent of the 1924 Hague Rules) governs international ocean transport to or from U.S. ports; the Warsaw Convention of 1929 governs international air transport; the Carmack Amendment of 1906 governs domestic rail and motor carriage. Though liability rules for the latter two modes were relatively harmonious until promulgation of the Motor Carrier Act of 1980, the Staggers Rail Act of 1980, and the Trucking Industry Regulatory Reform Act of 1994, now the Carmack rules apply differently between rail and motor carriers. Each of these statutes imposes different carrier obligations, has different bases of liability, burdens of proof, limitations of liability, exemptions, defenses, and amounts recoverable. Carriers' and shippers' attorneys vie for the modal regime that most benefits their clients. In circumstances where the identity of the carrier which caused the damage is at issue, one may find the maritime regime more favorable, while the other may argue in favor of the rail regime.
>
> The law can become more complicated still in international transportation. In Europe, international motor carriage is governed by the Convention on the Contract of International Carriage of Goods by Road; rail transport is governed by the Convention Concerning the Carriage of Goods by Rail. A number of countries have adopted updated versions of the Hague Rules (the Visby or Hamburg Rules); while others have adopted updated versions of the Warsaw Convention (the Hague Protocol, or Montreal Convention). The [United Nations'] Multimodal Liability Convention of 1980, which sought to harmonize

> many of these laws, has not been widely adopted. [In fact, only 10 countries have ratified the treaty.]
>
> The net result is a legal Tower of Babel, one which needlessly and wastefully taxes the free flow of commerce. Congress should promulgate one unified domestic liability regime for all modes of transport, while the Executive should attempt to reach a comprehensive unified body of law governing all modes internationally.

Paul Stephen Dempsey, *The Law of Intermodal Transportation: What It Was, What It Is, and What It Should Be*, 27 Transp. L.J. 367, 409–10 (2000). At the end of her opinion in *Kirby*, Justice O'Connor took note of the foregoing and scolded the transportation industry for failing to put its house in order:

> We hold that Norfolk is entitled to the protection of the liability limitations in the two bills of lading. Having undertaken this analysis, we recognize that our decision does no more than provide a legal backdrop against which future bills of lading will be negotiated. It is not, of course, this Court's task to structure the international shipping industry.

125 S. Ct. at 400. For the text of the United Nations' 1980 Multimodal Convention, *see* Appendix 18. For a further look at the legal problems that can arise during multimodal transportation, *see Commercial Union Ins. Co. v. Alitalia Airlines, S.p.A.*, 347 F.3d 448 (2d Cir. 2003) (pasta machine damaged while en route from manufacturer's plant in Italy to its warehouse in the United States).

5. In *Royal Insurance*, theft from Amerford's warehouse was suspected; in *HIH Marine*, theft from Gateway's warehouse was proved. Because they contain high value goods, air cargo warehouses often are targeted by thieves. *See further* Claire Mayhew, *The Detection and Prevention of Cargo Theft*, at www.aic.gov.au/publications/tandi/ti214.pdf (estimating that such thefts may total as much as $300 million annually). The most famous such incident, however, is still the December 1978 ransacking of the Lufthansa air cargo terminal in New York City, which netted $6 million and figured prominently in the 1990 movie *Goodfellas*:

> Jimmy Conway or Jimmy Burke (1931–1996) was an Irish-American gangster who is believed to have organized the Lufthansa Heist in 1978. His nickname was Jimmy The Gent, and he is familiar to most people via Robert De Niro's depiction of him in the movie Goodfellas.
>
> Burke was a mentor of Thomas DeSimone and Henry Hill, who were both teenagers in the 1960s. They carried out errands for Burke, such as selling stolen merchandise. When they were older, the pair helped Burke with the hijacking of delivery trucks. According to Hill, Burke would usually give $50 to the drivers of the trucks they stole, as if he were tipping them for the inconvenience, which led to his nickname Jimmy The Gent.
>
> The crime Burke is most famous for is the Lufthansa Heist, the theft of approximately $6,000,000 from the cargo terminal at JFK Airport, the largest robbery in American criminal history at the time. The robbery took place on December 11, 1978. Because it took place in the territory of the Gambino Mafia family, Burke had to get their permission (his contact in the Gambinos was John Gotti) and agree to pay them a portion of the loot.
>
> There were a number of murders and disappearances following the robbery as the criminals turned on each other. The get-away driver was shot dead

> within a few days because he did not dispose of the vehicle properly. Another robber was murdered along with his wife. A cocaine dealer named Theresa Ferrara, who had dated some of the Lufthansa Heist crew, was killed when it was found out she was an informant. Her dismembered body was eventually found dumped on a New Jersey beach.
>
> Martin Krugman, who provided some of the inside information for the heist, vanished not long afterwards and was never seen again. It is alleged he was killed on the orders of Burke, who did not want to pay Krugman the $500,000 share of the stolen money he was due.
>
> The year 1980 saw Henry Hill being arrested for drug-trafficking. He became an FBI informant in order to avoid prison. Also that year, one of the few criminals to have actually been prosecuted for the Lufthansa Heist, Louis Werner, became an informant after serving just twelve months of a fifteen-year prison sentence in the hopes of getting an early release.
>
> Partly thanks to the testimony of these informants, Jimmy Burke was taken into custody on April 1, 1980 on suspicion of a number of crimes. He was subsequently convicted at a trial in 1982 of fixing basketball games as part of a gambling scam in 1978 and was sentenced to twenty years' imprisonment. Authorities knew he had organized the Lufthansa Heist, but they did not have enough evidence to prove it.

Jimmy Conway, at en.wikipedia.org/wiki/Jimmy_Conway. For a further discussion, *see, e.g.*, Ernest Volkman & John Cummings, *The Heist: How a Gang Stole $8,000,000 at Kennedy Airport and Lived to Regret It* (1986).

6. Because of the earlier litigation between the parties, Justice Blyn provides only a thumbnail sketch of the facts in *Continental Time*. Accordingly, one must turn to Judge Lasker's opinion in *Continental Time Corporation v. Swiss Credit Bank*, 543 F. Supp. 408 (S.D.N.Y. 1982), to fully understand what is going on:

> Continental Time Corp. ("Continental") sues to recover damages allegedly arising out of Credit Suisse's ("Swiss Credit") wrongful refusal to honor its obligations under an irrevocable letter of credit. The letter of credit was issued on January 10, 1980, in favor of Continental. On January 21, 1980, Continental assigned its entire interest in the letter of credit to S. Frederick & Company ("Frederick") and to Arlington Distributing Co., Inc. ("Arlington"). On January 29, 1980, Swiss Credit advised Merchants Bank, where Frederick held his account, that the air waybill did not conform to the requirements of the letter of credit. The expiration date on the letter of credit subsequently passed with no payment made. On May 28, 1980, Frederick and Arlington separately instituted suit in Switzerland for recovery of their assigned portions of the letter of credit. The Swiss court consolidated the actions and granted Swiss Credit's application to join Georges Bloch, the person who had originally requested the issuance of the letter of credit, in the action. The suit in Switzerland is currently pending.
>
> It is true that this action includes other parties [among them Swiss Air, which transported the watches] and claims than those in the suit in Switzerland, relating to the purchase and sale of merchandise underlying the letter of credit transaction. However, this factor does not support Continental's contention that only this action can fully resolve the relevant issues, for it is settled that a letter of credit agreement constitutes an independent transaction be-

> tween the issuer and the beneficiary, to be resolved without reference to underlying contracts or transactions. Venizelos, S. A. v. Chase Manhattan Bank, 425 F.2d 461 (2d Cir. 1970).
>
> Swiss Credit's motion to dismiss the action as to it is granted on condition that it not oppose Continental's becoming a party to the Swiss litigation.

Id. at 409–11. Thus, Continental Time had three different causes of action: one against Bloch for failing to pay for the watches (with Bloch claiming he was entitled to various set-offs); another against Credit Suisse (the issuing bank) for failing to release the funds being held under the irrevocable letter of credit; and a third against Merchants Bank (the collecting bank) for telling Credit Suisse that it did not have to pay under the letter of credit.

Eventually, Continental Time settled with Merchants Bank for $150,000. Merchants Bank then sued Credit Suisse for indemnity. Although Credit Suisse moved to have the case dismissed for failure to state a claim, Judge Carter denied its motion on the ground that Credit Suisse knew Bloch (its long-time customer) would not make good on the letter of credit because he was experiencing financial problems. Presumably at Bloch's request, Credit Suisse failed to reveal this information to Merchants Bank. *See Merchants Bank of New York v. Credit Suisse Bank*, 585 F. Supp. 304 (S.D.N.Y. 1984).

7. Because it was answering certified questions put to it by the federal district court, the Hawaii Supreme Court in *FHP* also did not fully explain the underlying transaction.

FHP, Inc., a health maintenance organization, had hired Pan Oceania Air Express, a freight forwarder, to transport blood samples from Guam to Hawaii. Pan Oceania, in turn, arranged for TNT Skypack Inc. to handle the actual details. After the samples were packed by FHP, a TNT courier picked them up and boarded a flight operated by Continental Micronesia, Inc., a subsidiary of Continental Airlines. Following the mishap, FHP undertook to pay for two years of HIV testing for the three exposed baggage handlers. *See further* Lalaine Estella, *3 Airline Cargo Workers Sue Over Bloody Bag, Citing Risk of HIV Virus*, Pac. Daily News, Feb. 7, 1997, at 7.

Although the baggage handlers filed suit against CM, FHP, Pan Oceania, and TNT, liability clearly rested with FHP for insufficient packaging. Nevertheless, FHP sought to blame the other defendants for improperly caring for the samples. Should it also have looked to Signature Support Flight Service—the employer of the baggage handlers—perhaps on a theory of improper hiring or training (given that the plaintiffs first failed to spot the leaking contents and then cleaned it up in a manner that increased the number of people who were exposed)?

8. For a further look at air cargo transactions, *see* Stephen Dolan, *Reform of Air Cargo Transport Regulation Through the WTO and GATS*, 29 Transp. L.J. 189 (2002) (recent developments), and Joseph T. Sneed, *A Proposed Solution to the Documentary Problem of Airborne International Trade*, 65 Harv. L. Rev. 1392 (1952) (early history).

Problem 20

Because it did not have the necessary customs license, a freight forwarder arranged to have an accredited warehouseman run its storage facility. Under the parties' contract, the freight forwarder assumed responsibility for all cargo damage. A few months later, an expensive shipment of goods disappeared from the facility. After determining that the theft had occurred because the alarm system had malfunctioned, the warehouseman settled with the consignee's insurer. It then sought indemnification from the freight forwarder, who refused because: 1) the alarm had been installed and monitored by an independent contractor; 2) the warehouseman had unilaterally decided to settle the insurer's lawsuit; and, 3) under the contract, it was liable only for damaged (as opposed to lost) cargo. Are these contentions well-founded? *See Travelers Indem. Co. v. AMR Services Corp.*, 921 F. Supp. 176 (S.D.N.Y. 1996).

Chapter 6

Airports

A. OVERVIEW

The legal issues generated by airports can be divided into four categories: construction (who pays for it, where does it go, and must adjoining landowners be compensated?), use (by whom, when, and at what price?), security (are civil rights and air travel compatible after 9/11?), and air traffic control (how can collisions and other accidents be avoided or minimized?). After examining these subjects, we will close by taking a look at airport concessionaires.

B. CONSTRUCTION

GRIGGS v. COUNTY OF ALLEGHENY

369 U.S. 84,
rehearing denied, 369 U.S. 857 (1962)

Justice DOUGLAS delivered the opinion of the Court.

This case is here on a petition for a writ of certiorari to the Supreme Court of Pennsylvania which we granted because its decision seemed to be in conflict with United States v. Causby, 328 U.S. 256. The question is whether respondent has taken an air easement over petitioner's property for which it must pay just compensation as required by the Fourteenth Amendment. Chicago, B. & Q.R. Co. v. Chicago, 166 U.S. 226, 241. The Court of Common Pleas, pursuant to customary Pennsylvania procedure, appointed a Board of Viewers to determine whether there had been a "taking" and, if so, the amount of compensation due. The Board of Viewers met upon the property; it held a hearing, and in its report found that there had been a "taking" by respondent of an air easement over petitioner's property and that the compensation payable (damages suffered) was $12,690. The Court of Common Pleas dismissed the exceptions of each party to the Board's report. On appeal, the Supreme Court of Pennsylvania decided, by a divided vote, that if there were a "taking" in the constitutional sense, the respondent was not liable.

Respondent owns and maintains the Greater Pittsburgh Airport on land which it purchased to provide airport and air-transport facilities. The airport was designed for public use in conformity with the rules and regulations of the Civil Aeronautics Administration within the scope of the National Airport Plan provided for in 49 U.S.C. § 1101 et seq. By this Act the federal Administrator is authorized and directed to prepare and continually revise a "national plan for the development of public airports." § 1102(a). For this purpose he is authorized to make grants to "sponsors" for airport development. §§ 1103, 1104. Provision is made for apportionment of grants for this purpose among the States. § 1105. The applications for projects must follow the standards prescribed by the Administrator. § 1108.

It is provided in § 1108(d) that: "No project shall be approved by the Administrator with respect to any airport unless a public agency holds good title, satisfactory to the Administrator, to the landing area of such airport or the site therefor, or gives assurance satisfactory to the Administrator that such title will be acquired." The United States agrees to share from 50% to 75% of the "allowable project costs," depending, so far as material here, on the class and location of the airport. § 1109. Allowable costs payable by the Federal Government include "costs of acquiring land or interests therein or easements through or other interests in air space * * *." § 1112(a)(2).

Respondent executed three agreements with the Administrator of Civil Aeronautics in which it agreed, among other things, to abide by and adhere to the Rules and Regulations of C.A.A. and to "maintain a master plan of the airport," including "approach areas." It was provided that the "airport approach standards to be followed in this connection shall be those established by the Administrator"; and it was also agreed that respondent "will acquire such easements or other interests in lands and air space as may be necessary to perform the covenants of this paragraph." The "master plan" laid out and submitted by respondent included the required "approach areas"; and that "master plan" was approved. One "approach area" was to the northeast runway. As designed and approved, it passed over petitioner's home which is 3,250 feet from the end of that runway. The elevation at the end of that runway is 1,150.50 feet above sea level; the door sill at petitioner's residence, 1,183.64 feet; the top of petitioner's chimney, 1,219.64 feet. The slope gradient of the approach area is as 40 is to 3,250 feet or 81 feet, which leaves a clearance of 11.36 feet between the bottom of the glide angle and petitioner's chimney.

The airlines that use the airport are lessees of respondent; and the leases give them, among other things, the right "to land" and "take off." No flights were in violation of the regulations of C.A.A.; nor were any flights lower than necessary for a safe landing or take-off. The planes taking off from the northeast runway observed regular flight patterns ranging from 30 feet to 300 feet over petitioner's residence; and on let-down they were within 53 feet to 153 feet.

On take-off the noise of the planes is comparable "to the noise of a riveting machine or steam hammer." On the let-down the planes make a noise comparable "to that of a noisy factory." The Board of Viewers found that "The low altitude flights over plaintiff's property caused the plaintiff and occupants of his property to become nervous and distraught, eventually causing their removal therefrom as undesirable and unbearable for their residential use." Judge Bell, dissenting below, accurately summarized the uncontroverted facts as follows:

> Regular and almost continuous daily flights, often several minutes apart, have been made by a number of airlines directly over and very, very close to plaintiff's residence. During these flights it was often impossible for people in the house to converse or to talk on the telephone. The plaintiff and the members of his household (depending on the flight which in turn sometimes depended on the wind) were frequently unable to sleep even with ear plugs and sleeping pills; they would frequently be awakened by the flight and the noise of the planes; the windows of their home would frequently rattle and at times plaster fell down from the walls and ceilings; their health was affected and impaired, and they sometimes were compelled to sleep elsewhere. Moreover, their house was so close to the runways or path of glide that as the spokesman for the members of the Airlines Pilot Association admitted "If we had engine failure we would have no course but to plow into your house."

402 Pa. 411, 422, 168 A.2d 123, 128–129.

We start with United States v. Causby, supra, which held that the United States by low flights of its military planes over a chicken farm made the property unusable for that purpose and that therefore there had been a "taking," in the constitutional sense, of an air easement for which compensation must be made. At the time of the Causby case, Congress had placed the navigable airspace in the public domain, defining it as "airspace above the minimum safe altitudes of flight prescribed" by the C.A.A. 44 Stat. 574. We held that the path of the glide or flight for landing or taking off was not the downward reach of the "navigable airspace." 328 U.S. at 264. Following the decision in the Causby case, Congress redefined "navigable airspace" to mean "airspace above the minimum altitudes of flight prescribed by regulations issued under this chapter, and shall include airspace needed to insure safety in take-off and landing of aircraft." 72 Stat. 739, 49 U.S.C. § 1301(24), 49 U.S.C.A. § 1301(24). By the present regulations the "minimum safe altitudes" within the meaning of the statute are defined, so far as relevant here, as heights of 500 feet or 1,000 feet, "(e)xcept where necessary for takeoff or landing." But as we said in the Causby case, the use of land presupposes the use of some of the airspace above it. 328 U.S. at 264. Otherwise no home could be built, no tree planted, no fence constructed, no chimney erected. An invasion of the "superadjacent airspace" will often "affect the use of the surface of the land itself." 328 U.S. at 265.

It is argued that though there was a "taking," someone other than respondent was the taker—the airlines or the C.A.A. acting as an authorized representative of the United States. We think, however, that respondent, which was the promoter, owner, and lessor of the airport, was in these circumstances the one who took the air easement in the constitutional sense. Respondent decided, subject to the approval of the C.A.A., where the airport would be built, what runways it would need, their direction and length, and what land and navigation easements would be needed. The Federal Government takes nothing; it is the local authority which decides to build an airport vel non, and where it is to be located. We see no difference between its responsibility for the air easements necessary for operation of the airport and its responsibility for the land on which the runways were built. Nor did the Congress when it designed the legislation for a National Airport Plan. For, as we have already noted, Congress provided in 49 U.S.C.A. § 1109 for the payment to the owners of airports, whose plans were approved by the Administrator, of a share of "the allowable project costs" including the "costs of acquiring land or interests therein or easements through or other interests in air space." § 1112(a)(2). A county that designed and constructed a bridge would not have a usable facility unless it had at least an easement over the land necessary for the approaches to the bridge. Why should one who designs, constructs, and uses an airport be in a more favorable position so far as the Fourteenth Amendment is concerned? That the instant "taking" was "for public use" is not debatable. For respondent agreed with the C.A.A. that it would operate the airport "for the use and benefit of the public," that it would operate it "on fair and reasonable terms and without unjust discrimination," and that it would not allow any carrier to acquire "any exclusive right" to its use.

The glide path for the northeast runway is as necessary for the operation of the airport as is a surface right of way for operation of a bridge, or as is the land for the operation of a dam. See United States v. Virginia Electric Co., 365 U.S. 624, 630. As stated by the Supreme Court of Washington in Ackerman v. Port of Seattle, 55 Wash.2d 400, 401, 413, 348 P.2d 664, 671, "* * * an adequate approach way is as necessary a part of an airport as is the ground on which the airstrip, itself, is constructed * * *." Without the "approach areas," an airport is indeed not operable. Respondent in designing it had to acquire some private property. Our conclusion is that by constitutional standards it did not acquire enough.

Reversed.

Justice BLACK, with whom Justice FRANKFURTER concurs, dissenting.

In United States v. Causby, the Court held that by flying its military aircraft frequently on low landing and takeoff flights over Causby's chicken farm the United States had so disturbed the peace of the occupants and so frightened the chickens that it had "taken" a flight easement from Causby for which it was required to pay "just compensation" under the Fifth Amendment. Today the Court holds that similar low landing and take-off flights, making petitioner Griggs' property "undesirable and unbearable for * * * residential use," constitute a "taking" of airspace over Griggs' property—not, however, by the owner and operator of the planes as in Causby, but by Allegheny County, the owner and operator of the Greater Pittsburgh Airport to and from which the planes fly. Although I dissented in Causby because I did not believe that the individual aircraft flights "took" property in the constitutional sense merely by going over it and because I believed that the complexities of adjusting atmospheric property rights to the air age could best be handled by Congress, I agree with the Court that the noise, vibrations and fear caused by constant and extremely low overflights in this case have so interfered with the use and enjoyment of petitioner's property as to amount to a "taking" of it under the Causby holding. I cannot agree, however, that it was the County of Allegheny that did the "taking." I think that the United States, not the Greater Pittsburgh Airport, has "taken" the airspace over Griggs' property necessary for flight. While the County did design the plan for the airport, including the arrangement of its takeoff and approach areas, in order to comply with federal requirements it did so under the supervision of and subject to the approval of the Civil Aeronautics Administrator of the United States.

Congress has over the years adopted a comprehensive plan for national and international air commerce, regulating in minute detail virtually every aspect of air transit—from construction and planning of ground facilities to safety and methods of flight operations. As part of this overall scheme of development, Congress in 1938 declared that the United States has "complete and exclusive national sovereignty in the air space above the United States" and that every citizen has "a public right of freedom of transit in air commerce through the navigable air space of the United States." Although in Causby the Court held that under the then existing laws and regulations the airspace used in landing and take-off was not part of the "navigable airspace" as to which all have a right of free transit, Congress has since, in 1958, enacted a new law, as part of a regulatory scheme even more comprehensive than those before it, making it clear that the "airspace needed to insure safety in take-off and landing of aircraft" is "navigable airspace." Thus Congress has not only appropriated the airspace necessary for planes to fly at high altitudes throughout the country but has also provided the low altitude airspace essential for those same planes to approach and take off from airports. These airspaces are so much under the control of the Federal Government that every take-off from and every landing at airports such as the Greater Pittsburgh Airport is made under the direct signal and supervisory control of some federal agent.

In reaching its conclusion, however, the Court emphasizes the fact that highway bridges require approaches. Of course they do. But if the United States Highway Department purchases the approaches to a bridge, the bridge owner need not. The same is true where Congress has, as here, appropriated the airspace necessary to approach the Pittsburgh airport as well as all the other airports in the country. Despite this, however, the Court somehow finds a congressional intent to shift the burden of acquiring flight airspace to the local communities in 49 U.S.C.A. § 1112, which authorizes reimbursement to local communities for "necessary" acquisitions of "easements through or other interests in air space." But this is no different from the bridge-approach argument. Merely because local communities might eventually be reimbursed for the acquisition of necessary easements does not mean that local communities must acquire easements that the United States has already acquired. And where Congress has already declared airspace free to all—a fact not denied by the Court—pretty clearly it need not again be acquired by an airport. The "necessary" easements for which Congress authorized reimbursement in § 1112 were those "easements through or other interests in air space" necessary for the clearing and protecting of "aerial approaches" from physical "airport hazards"—a duty explicitly placed on the local communities by the statute (§ 1110) and by their contract with the Government. There is no such duty on the local community to acquire flight airspace. Having taken the airspace over Griggs' private property for a public use, it is the United States which owes just compensation.

The construction of the Greater Pittsburgh Airport was financed in large part by funds supplied by the United States as part of its plan to induce localities like Allegheny County to assist in setting up a national and international air transportation system. The Court's imposition of liability on Allegheny County, however, goes a long way toward defeating that plan because of the greatly increased financial burdens (how great one can only guess) which will hereafter fall on all the cities and counties which til now have given or may hereafter give support to the national program. I do not believe that Congress ever intended any such frustration of its own purpose.

Nor do I believe that Congress intended the wholly inequitable and unjust saddling of the entire financial burden of this part of the national program on the people of local communities like Allegheny County. The planes that take off and land at the Greater Pittsburgh Airport wind their rapid way through space not for the peculiar benefit of the citizens of Allegheny County but as part of a great, reliable transportation system of immense advantage to the whole Nation in time of peace and war. Just as it would be unfair to require petitioner and others who suffer serious and peculiar injuries by reason of these transportation flights to bear an unfair proportion of the burdens of air commerce, so it would be unfair to make Allegheny County bear expenses wholly out of proportion to the advantages it can receive from the national transportation system. I can see no justification at all for throwing this monkey wrench into Congress' finely tuned national transit mechanism. I would affirm the state court's judgment holding that the County of Allegheny has not "taken" petitioner's property.

NORTHWEST AIRLINES, INC. v. FEDERAL AVIATION ADMINISTRATION

14 F.3d 64 (D.C. Cir. 1994)

SENTELLE, Circuit Judge.

Petitioner, Northwest Airlines, Inc. ("Northwest"), seeks review of a decision of the Federal Aviation Administration ("FAA") approving [the] Memphis-Shelby County Airport Authority's application to impose a $3.00 Passenger Facility Charge ("PFC") on passengers enplaned at Memphis International Airport. Northwest argues the FAA's failure to consider the economic and competitive effects of its decision rendered its ruling arbitrary and capricious. See 5 U.S.C. § 706(2)(a). Northwest also claims that the FAA's approval of the PFC based on Memphis's proposed alternative project violated the PFC statute's requirements that PFC applications be tied to "specific projects," 49 U.S.C. app. § 1513(e)(2), and that the airlines be consulted about each of these projects before the application is submitted, id. § 1513(e)(11)(c). Finally, Northwest argues that the FAA violated the statute by allowing Memphis to impose PFCs on frequent flyer customers.

We do not reach Northwest's frequent flyer argument because the airline failed to exhaust its administrative remedies as required by 49 U.S.C. app. § 1486(e). On the merits of Northwest's remaining challenges, we defer to the FAA's reasonable construction of the PFC statute and reject the petition for review in large part. However, because we find that the FAA did violate the consultation provisions of the statute with respect to Memphis's proposed alternative project, we conclude that Memphis may not expend its PFC funds to finance this alternative project.

I. BACKGROUND

In 1990, Congress amended the Federal Aviation Act to allow local public airport authorities to petition the FAA for permission to impose PFCs on passengers using the airport. See Pub.L. No. 101-508, § 9110, 104 Stat. 1388-357 (codified as amended at 49 U.S.C. app. § 1513(e)). The statute authorizes the FAA to "grant a public agency which controls a commercial service airport authority to impose a fee of $1.00, $2.00, or $3.00 for each paying passenger of an air carrier enplaned at such airport to finance eligible airport-related projects to be carried out in connection with such airport or any other airport which such agency controls." 49 U.S.C. app. § 1513(e)(1). The FAA may only authorize an airport to collect PFCs in order to finance

> specific ... eligible airport-related project[s] which will—
>
> (i) preserve or enhance capacity, safety, or security of the national air transportation system,
>
> (ii) reduce noise resulting from an airport which is part of such system, or
>
> (iii) furnish opportunities for enhanced competition between or among air carriers.

Id. § 1513(e)(2)(B).

The statute further provides that "[b]efore submission of an application under [the PFC statute], a public agency shall provide reasonable notice to, and an opportunity for consultation with, air carriers operating at the airport." Id. § 1513(e)(11)(c). As part of this consultation process, the airport authority must provide air carriers with written notice of "individual projects being considered for funding through imposition" of PFCs. Id. § 1513(e)(11)(C)(i)(I).

On January 28, 1992, the Memphis-Shelby County Airport Authority ("Memphis") requested FAA permission to impose a $3.00 PFC on all passengers enplaned at Memphis International Airport. Memphis's application identified four primary projects that it hoped to finance with PFC revenue: 1) the acquisition of land and the relocation of roadways and utilities to allow future airport development; 2) construction of a new runway; 3) reconstruction and extension of an existing runway; and 4) construction of a new taxiway. In addition, Memphis's application identified a backup project for which the PFC revenue would be used in the event that the FAA failed to approve one or more of its primary projects. This alternative proposal was to use PFC revenues to purchase homes in high noise corridors to reduce the impact of noise on communities surrounding the airport. Memphis had not mentioned this alternative "noise compatibility project" when it consulted with Northwest and other airlines prior to submitting its PFC application.

On May 28, the FAA authorized Memphis to impose a $3.00 PFC and approved its runway and taxiway projects. Record of Decision, Memphis-Shelby County Airport Authority at 2–3 (May 28, 1992). However, because Memphis had yet to secure the required environmental clearance to proceed with its runway and taxiway projects, see 14 C.F.R. § 158.25(c)(1)(ii)(B), the FAA also approved the noise compatibility project as an "alternative use" for the PFC revenues "in the event that one or more of the primary projects [was] not implemented in a timely manner." Record of Decision at 4. Thus, the FAA's decision authorized Memphis only to "impose" the PFC but did not yet grant Memphis approval to "use" the PFC revenue on any particular project. Id.

Northwest now challenges the FAA's approval of the Memphis PFC.

II. DISCUSSION

A. Standard of Review

Each of Northwest's objections to the FAA's approval of the Memphis PFC ultimately attacks the FAA's interpretation of the PFC statute. We therefore evaluate these challenges under the framework set forth in Chevron U.S.A., Inc. v. Natural Resources Defense Council, Inc., 467 U.S. 837, 842–44 (1984). Chevron requires us first to ask

> whether Congress has directly spoken to the precise question at issue. If we can come to the unmistakable conclusion that Congress had an intention on the precise question at issue our inquiry ends there.... However, if the statute before us is silent or ambiguous with respect to the specific issue [ ] before us, we proceed to the second step. At this stage, we defer to the agency's interpretation of the statute if it is reasonable and consistent with the statute's purpose.

Nuclear Info. Resource Serv. v. Nuclear Regulatory Comm', 969 F.2d 1169, 1173 (D.C.Cir.1992) (en banc) (citations and internal quotations omitted). We evaluate Northwest's statutory challenges using this two-step analysis.

B. FAA's Failure to Consider the Economic and Competitive Effects of its Decision

In comments to the agency, Northwest objected that the imposition of a $3.00 PFC at its Memphis hub would place the airline at a competitive disadvantage with carriers whose hubs did not impose PFCs. Northwest argued that extreme competition in the airline industry would force Northwest to absorb the PFC itself rather than passing the charge along to its passengers. In hopes of escaping this "economic burden," Northwest urged the FAA to disapprove the Memphis PFC entirely, to lower the amount of the PFC to $1.00, or to exempt connecting passengers from the PFC charge. However, the agency did not weigh Northwest's potential economic losses as one of the factors bearing on its decision to approve the $3.00 Memphis PFC. Although the FAA's final order noted that the PFC, "as authorized by law, is expected to be paid by the passenger," the agency determined that "[a]ny decision by an air carrier to adjust its ticket prices to absorb the PFC is beyond the scope" of the PFC statute and the agency's responsibility. Record of Decision at 7. Thus, the FAA did not believe itself bound to consider the potential economic burden on Northwest as one of the factors relevant to its approval of the Memphis PFC.

Northwest now argues that the criteria for PFC approval set forth in the PFC statute, along with the general "public interest" criteria set forth in the Federal Aviation Act, made economic and competitive considerations "relevant factors" that the FAA was required to consider before approving a PFC at Memphis. Citing Citizens to Preserve Overton Park v. Volpe, 401 U.S. 402, 416 (1971), Northwest urges that the FAA's failure to consider these factors requires that the agency's decision be set aside. We disagree.

The PFC statute directs the FAA to approve PFCs only for eligible airport-related projects which will—

> (i) preserve or enhance capacity, safety, or security of the national air transportation system,
>
> (ii) reduce noise resulting from an airport which is part of such system, or
>
> (iii) furnish opportunities for enhanced competition between or among air carriers.

49 U.S.C. app. § 1513(e)(2)(B). Northwest argues that this language expressly directed the agency to consider the economic and competitive detriment Northwest would suffer as a result of the FAA's decision. According to Northwest, competition in the airline industry would force the airline to absorb any PFC imposed at Memphis, rather than passing the fee along to its customers. But, the argument continues, the cost of internalizing this fee would likely cause Northwest to decrease the number of flights it offers through Memphis, thereby diminishing the capacity and competitiveness of the national air transportation system. Because this result would directly contravene two goals of the PFC statute, Northwest argues that the FAA was required at least to consider this potential outcome in deciding to approve Memphis's request for a PFC.

The FAA denies that the PFC statute requires it to consider whether every PFC-funded project will enhance the capacity and competitiveness of the airline industry. Rather, as the FAA reads the statute, Congress's use of the disjunctive "or" to join the three PFC criteria means that the agency may approve any "eligible airport-related project" that meets any one of the three statutory criteria. In this case, the FAA determined that Memphis's proposed runway and taxiway projects would enhance the capacity and safety of the Memphis airport and that the alternative noise compatibility project would further the statutory goal of reducing airport noise. Having ensured that each possible use of the PFC funds satisfied one of the statutory goals, the agency claims that it was required to look no further. We defer to the FAA's interpretation of the statute.

As with all cases of statutory interpretation, "our starting point must be the language employed by Congress." Reiter v. Sonotone Corp., 442 U.S. 330, 337 (1979). In this case, Congress chose to join the three criteria for PFC approval with the word "or," which is "'[n]ormally ... to be accepted for its disjunctive connotation.'" Unification Church v. INS, 762 F.2d 1077, 1084 (D.C.Cir.1985) (quoting United States v. Moore, 613 F.2d 1029, 1040 (D.C.Cir.1979)). Thus, the most natural reading of the statute is the one proposed by the FAA—that is, by joining the criteria for PFC approval with an "or," Congress wanted only to ensure that all PFC-approved projects furthered one of the three statutory goals.

We acknowledge that it might be possible to read the statute as Northwest suggests—requiring that the agency consider each of the criteria set forth in § 1513(e)(2)(B) and approve only those projects that make some reasonable accommodation of the three competing factors. See Holyoke Water Power Co. v. FERC, 799 F.2d 755, 761 (D.C.Cir.1986) (MacKinnon, J., dissenting) (noting that the word "or" may sometimes be read to mean "and"). However, "[a]s we must defer to an agency's reasonable interpretation of an ambiguous statute that it must administer, we need not pass on whether there are valid alternative readings" of the PFC statute. International Union, UMW v. Federal Mine Safety and Health Admin., 920 F.2d 960, 963 (D.C.Cir.1990) (internal citation omitted). Rather, we need only ask whether the FAA's interpretation is reasonable; and we find it eminently reasonable for the agency to adopt the most natural reading of the statute. We therefore conclude that nothing in the PFC statute compelled the FAA to consider the potential economic harm Northwest might suffer as a result of the agency's decision to approve a PFC for Memphis.

Northwest next argues that general provisions of the Federal Aviation Act required the FAA to consider the competitive and economic consequences of its decision. Northwest cites two provisions in support of this argument. It first points to section 102 of the Act, which requires the FAA generally to consider economic and competitive factors when making decisions "in the public interest." 49 U.S.C. app. § 1302(a) (1988). Northwest also relies upon section 502(a)(5) of the Airport and Airways Improvement Act, which requires that "all airport and airway programs" be administered in accord with section 102 and "with due regard for the goals expressed therein [such as] fostering competition." 49 U.S.C. app. § 2201(a)(5). These general provisions add to the list of "relevant factors" in the PFC statute. According to Northwest, these provisions required the FAA to consider the potential economic and competitive burden its decision would place on Northwest and the airline industry.

We do not agree that the general language of these sections required the FAA to evaluate either the possibility that its decision would harm Northwest financially or the more remote chance that its decision would lead to a decline in airline competition. We begin by noting that the "public interest factors" set forth in § 102 of the Federal Aviation Act, 49 U.S.C. app. § 1302(a), do not apply of their own force to the FAA's administration of the PFC statute. Section 102 lists factors that the Civil Aeronautics Board ("CAB") was to consider when regulating for the "public convenience." Because the CAB's remaining regulatory functions were transferred to the Department of Transportation, 49 U.S.C. app. § 1551(b)(1)(E), and derivatively to the FAA, 49 C.F.R. § 1.47, after the CAB's abolition in 1985 the § 102 criteria bind the FAA when performing former CAB functions. But the PFC program, which was not established until 1990, was never administered by the CAB. Thus, § 102 has no direct bearing on the PFC program.

If the general criteria of § 102 have any bearing on the PFC program at all, it can only be through the provision of the Airport and Airways Improvement Act which requires that "all airport and airway programs ... be administered in a manner consistent with the provisions of section [ ] 102." 49 U.S.C. app. § 2201(a)(5). Nonetheless, we cannot conclude that a general congressional directive to give "due regard" to goals such as "fostering competition," id., required the FAA to factor into its PFC approval calculations the possibility that Northwest would make an independent business decision to internalize the cost of the PFC rather than passing it on to its customers, thereby causing the airline possibly to decrease the number of flights it offers through Memphis, thereby having some effect on competition in the airline industry.

In Horizon Air Industries v. DOT, 850 F.2d 775 (D.C.Cir.1988), we held that § 102 did not require the FAA expressly to consider the effect on competition that would result from its decision to award an exclusive commuter airline route to a particular carrier. Rather, we held that § 102 "merely stated as a general goal 'maximum reliance on competitive market forces,' 49 U.S.C. app. § 1302(a)(4); [and that] this generalization can hardly be read as a clear directive to focus on competitive effects in inherently non-market-oriented proceedings for award of international routes." Id. at 779. While the PFC approval process may not share the "inherently non-market-oriented" nature of the route allocations considered in Horizon, the result is the same. For Congress to set a goal that the FAA should in general rely on competitive market forces is not to say that it must engage in a calculation of the precise economic effects in every instance, especially where those effects are quite remote from the factual question posed by the relevant statute, here simply "capacity." We conclude, therefore, that the general "public interest" provisions of the Federal Aviation Act did not require the FAA to consider either the possibility that its decision would cause Northwest economic pain or the more remote prospect that its ruling would, in turn, adversely affect airline competition.

C. FAA's Approval of Alternative Projects

Northwest next raises two challenges related to the FAA's acceptance of Memphis's alternative "noise compatibility project" as a basis for approving the Memphis PFC. Northwest first argues that the FAA's policy of approving applications to impose PFCs for alternative uses violates the plain language of the PFC statute. Even if the "alternative use" policy is valid, however, Northwest argues that the FAA's decision must be set aside because Memphis disregarded its statutory obligation to consult with the airline regarding its alternative noise compatibility project before filing its application to impose a PFC. We consider these challenges in turn.

1. The FAA's "Alternative Use" Approval Policy

The PFC statute requires that the FAA only grant "authority to impose a fee under [the PFC statute] to finance specific projects." 49 U.S.C. § 1513(e)(2). Northwest contends that the FAA's policy of approving projects "in the alternative" violates this statutory command because it allows airport authorities to impose a PFC without first selecting a specific use for the funds. We disagree.

FAA regulations authorize airport agencies to "apply for the authority to impose PFCs in advance of ... an application to use PFC revenue," 14 C.F.R. § 158.25(a), provided that the airports' applications include a "description of alternative uses of the PFC revenue to ensure that such revenue will be used only on eligible projects in the event the proposed [primary] project is not [ultimately] approved," id. § 158.25(b)(14)(ii). The selection among these approved projects is made at a later date—when the airport authorities apply for FAA's permission to use the PFC revenues on one or more of these approved projects. See id. § 158.25(c)(2).

As Northwest points out, by requiring [the] FAA to approve requests "to impose" a PFC only "to finance specific projects," 49 U.S.C. app. § 1513(e)(2), Congress plainly intended to link the power to collect PFC revenues with the duty to spend these funds on particular projects. In this way, Congress ensured that PFCs would be imposed only to fund "eligible airport related projects." Id. § 1513(e)(2)(B). However, the statute does not speak to whether the FAA must identify a single "eligible airport related project" at the time it authorizes imposition of a PFC or whether it may approve a group of eligible projects and later decide which of these eligible projects will ultimately be funded.

In light of this statutory silence, we move on to the second step of the Chevron analysis and ask whether the FAA's adoption of a two-step approval process "is based on a permissible construction" of the PFC statute. Chevron, 467 U.S. at 837. We conclude that it is.

Northwest's objection to the FAA's "in the alternative" approval process is that the policy will lead to "all kinds of administrative artifice" because airport authorities will petition to impose PFCs for backup projects that clearly meet the criteria for PFC eligibility, but which the airports have no real intent to pursue. Northwest thus raises the specter of airports collecting PFC revenue now, only to spend it later on non-PFC eligible projects. Yet, we fail to see the danger.

FAA regulations require that airport authorities applying for permission to impose a PFC before seeking authority to use the PFC funds must provide the FAA with a description of alternative PFC-eligible uses for the funds in order "to ensure that [PFC] revenue will only be used on eligible projects." 14 C.F.R. § 158.25(b)(14)(ii). Once the airports are ready to spend the monies they have collected, they must again obtain the FAA's blessing of their proposed projects. See id. § 158.25(c)(2). The agency thus checks twice to ensure that PFC funds are spent only on "eligible airport related projects." These regulatory safeguards lead us to conclude that the FAA's two-step approval process is both "reasonable and consistent with the statute's purpose." Nuclear Info. Resource Serv., 969 F.2d at 1176. It is therefore entitled to deference.

2. Memphis's Failure to Consult With the Airlines Regarding its Proposed Backup Project

The PFC statute requires that "[b]efore submission of an application under this paragraph, a public agency shall provide reasonable notice to, and an opportunity for consultation with, air carriers operating at the airport." 49 U.S.C. app. § 1513(e)(11)(c). This consultation must "provide air carriers [with a] description of projects [and] justifications for projects" to be funded through the imposition of PFCs. Id. Northwest argues that Memphis's failure to consult with the airline regarding its alternative noise compatibility project before applying for permission to impose a PFC violated the express command of the PFC statute. We agree.

The FAA contends that Memphis's failure to consult Northwest about its alternative project was not unlawful because the airline will be consulted regarding the noise compatibility project before Memphis seeks the FAA's permission to spend its PFC funds. See 14 C.F.R. § 158.25(c)(2). But we cannot reconcile the agency's post-hoc consultation mechanism with the plain language of the statute, which requires consultation "before submission of [a PFC] application." 49 U.S.C. app. § 1513(e)(11)(c).

We therefore hold that the FAA's approval of the Memphis PFC violated the PFC statute insofar as it was based on a backup project for which no prior consultation with the airlines had occurred. Any attempt by Memphis to use its PFC funds to finance its noise compatibility project would therefore be unlawful. However, Memphis did consult with Northwest and the other airlines regarding its proposed primary projects before it applied to the FAA for permission to impose the PFC. Thus, with respect to the primary projects, no statutory violation occurred and Northwest can claim no harm. Memphis's use of its PFC revenues to finance these primary projects would thus be unproblematic.

III. CONCLUSION

The FAA's decision approving Memphis's primary projects and authorizing a $3.00 PFC at Memphis International Airport was based on a reasonable interpretation of the PFC statute. We therefore dismiss Northwest's petition in large part. However, because Memphis's failure to consult with Northwest and other airlines regarding its alternative noise compatibility project before applying for permission to impose the PFC violated the PFC statute, we hold that Memphis may not use its PFC revenues to finance this alternative project.

[The concurring opinion of Judge Williams is omitted.]

CITIZENS AGAINST BURLINGTON, INC. v. BUSEY

938 F.2d 190 (D.C. Cir.),
cert. denied, 502 U.S. 994 (1991)

THOMAS, Circuit Judge.

The city of Toledo decided to expand one of its airports and the Federal Aviation Administration decided to approve the city's plan. In this petition for review of the FAA's order, an alliance of people who live near the airport contends that the FAA has violated several environmental statutes and regulations. We hold that the FAA has complied with all of the statutes and all but one of the regulations.

I.

The Toledo Express Airport, object of the controversy in this case, lies about twenty-five miles to the west of downtown Toledo. Half a mile to the southwest of the airport, surrounded by four highways and intersected by three more, lies the Oak Openings Preserve Metropark, used by joggers, skiers, and birders, and site of one of the world's twelve communities of oak savannas. Within Oak Openings lies the Springbrook Group Camp, site of a primitive (tents only) campground, and used by hikers and campers, including Richard Van Landingham III, one of the petitioners in this lawsuit. Near the airport live Daniel Kasch, Carol Vaughan, and Professor William Reuter, three of the other petitioners. The Toledo-Lucas County Port Authority, one of the intervenors, wants to make the city of Toledo a cargo hub. Burlington Air Express, Inc., the other intervenor, wants to move its operations to Toledo. Kasch, Vaughan, Reuter, Van Landingham, and others have formed Citizens Against Burlington, Inc. to stop them.

Citizens Against Burlington first materialized about a year after the Port Authority first commissioned an "Airport Noise Compatibility Planning" study (known as a "Part 150 study," see generally 14 C.F.R. pt. 150 & apps. A & B) and began to consider the possibility of the airport's expansion. The Port Authority soon heard from Burlington

Air Express, which had been flying its planes out of an old World War II hangar at Baer Field, an Air National Guard airport in Fort Wayne. After looking at seventeen sites in four midwestern states, Burlington chose the Toledo Express Airport. Among Burlington's reasons were the quality of Toledo's work force and the airport's prior operating record, zoning advantages, and location (near major highways and close to Detroit and Chicago). For its part, the Port Authority expects the new hub to create one thousand new jobs in metropolitan Toledo and to contribute almost $68 million per year to the local economy after three years of the hub's operation. The Port Authority plans to pay for the new hub with both private and public funds. Much of the money, however, will come from user fees and lease agreements, and more than half will come from local bonds issued to private investors. Grants from the city of Toledo and the state of Ohio will make up another, much smaller portion of the costs. The Port Authority has applied for some federal funds as well, but the FAA has reacted coolly to the Port Authority's feelers.

The Port Authority agreed to let Burlington move to Toledo when Burlington's lease at Baer Field expired in October 1990. Burlington later extended its lease in Fort Wayne, and the Port Authority now expects Burlington to move to Toledo Express in January 1992. First, though, the Port Authority has to accommodate Burlington's operations. In the first stage of the airport's expansion, the Port Authority plans to build a concrete ramp for cargo planes, a warehouse for sorting freight, lighting for the warehouse and the area around it, a road to the warehouse, a fuel farm, a maintenance building, taxiway connections to one of the airport's runways and lighting for the new taxiways, an overrun area attached to one of the runways, new power outlets for parked airplanes, and storage areas for de-icing equipment. In the second stage of expansion, planned for the five years after Burlington's move, the Port Authority wants to extend one of the airport's primary runways, install a landing system nearby, and build a new taxiway parallel to the extended runway.

The Port Authority submitted its proposal to the FAA on February 2, 1989 and promptly hired Coffman Associates, Inc., a consulting firm, to prepare an environmental assessment, see 40 C.F.R. §§ 1501.3, 1508.9, and then to convert the environmental assessment into an environmental impact statement (EIS), see id. § 1501.4; 42 U.S.C. § 4332(2)(c). In December 1989, the FAA sent a draft of the EIS to the Environmental Protection Agency and several state and local agencies. See id. § 7609; 40 C.F.R. §§ 1503.1, 1503.2. Early the next month, the FAA made the draft public and held a public hearing. See id. § 1502.19. Over the following six weeks, Citizens Against Burlington sent the FAA twenty-five letters, commenting on virtually every aspect of the EIS. Individuals sent over three hundred more.

On May 11, 1990, the FAA published a final environmental impact statement. The first chapter of the statement explained that the Port Authority needed the FAA's approval for its plan to expand the Toledo Express Airport and described the role in that process that Congress meant for the agency to play. The second chapter of the EIS reviewed the particulars of the Port Authority's plan, listed the fourteen separate federal statutes and regulations that applied to the Port Authority's proposal, briefly described some alternatives to acting on the Port Authority's plan, and explained why the agency had decided not to discuss those possibilities more fully. The FAA then concluded that it had to consider in depth the environmental impacts of only two alternatives: the approval of the Port Authority's plan to expand the airport and no action. The third chapter of the EIS described the environment affected by the proposal, and the fourth chapter detailed the environmental consequences of the two alternatives. After summarizing the environmental impacts in the fifth chapter, the agency listed in the sixth chapter the statement's preparers. Appendices to the statement collected scientific data and relevant inter-agency correspondence. In the second volume of the statement, the FAA compiled copies of the hundreds of letters concerning the draft EIS, a transcript of the public hearing, and written comments submitted after the hearing had ended.

Having approved the final EIS, the agency faced a final choice: whether to endorse the Port Authority's plan, which the agency preferred, or not to endorse the plan. In a record of decision dated July 12, 1990, the FAA approved the plan to expand the Toledo Express Airport. See 49 U.S.C. app. §§ 1349(a), 2208(b). Five days later, Citizens petitioned this court for review of the FAA's order and for a stay of the order pending our decision. See id. app. § 1486(a), (d). On August 1, we denied the latter request.

Citizens continues to press for wide-ranging declaratory and injunctive relief, asking this court to vacate the FAA's decision, to force the agency to prepare a new EIS, to enjoin the agency from approving the Port Authority's current plan, and to enjoin any further construction at Toledo Express until the FAA complies with the applicable laws. Citizens contends that the FAA has violated the National Environmental Policy Act, regulations promulgated by the Council on Environmental Quality, the Department of Transportation Act, and the Airport and Airway Improvement Act. We consider these arguments in turn.

II.

A.

In the National Environmental Policy Act of 1969 (NEPA), Pub.L. No. 91-190, 83 Stat. 852 (1970) (codified as amended at 42 U.S.C. §§ 4321–4370b), Congress resolved "to create and maintain conditions under which man and nature can exist in productive harmony, and fulfill the social, economic, and other requirements of present and future generations of Americans." NEPA § 101(a), 42 U.S.C. § 4331(a). These sweeping policy goals have inspired some commentators to call NEPA an environmentalist Magna Carta. See, e.g., D. Mandelker, NEPA Law and Litigation § 1:01, at 1 (1990); cf. 40 C.F.R. § 1500.1(a) ("[NEPA] is our basic national charter for protection of the environment."). But instead of ordering, say, that deforested land be reforested, Congress chose to make NEPA procedural. NEPA commands agencies to imbue their decisionmaking, through the use of certain procedures, with our country's commitment to environmental salubrity. See Robertson v. Methow Valley Citizens Council, 490 U.S. 332, 348 (1989); see also 40 C.F.R. § 1502.1. NEPA does not mandate particular consequences.

Just as NEPA is not a green Magna Carta, federal judges are not the barons at Runnymede. Because the statute directs agencies only to look hard at the environmental effects of their decisions, and not to take one type of action or another, federal judges correspondingly enforce the statute by ensuring that agencies comply with NEPA's procedures, and not by trying to coax agency decisionmakers to reach certain results. See Baltimore Gas & Elec. Co. v. Natural Resources Defense Council, Inc., 462 U.S. 87, 97–98 (1983). As the Supreme Court has warned, "once an agency has made a decision subject to [NEPA]'s procedural requirements, the only role for a court is to insure that the agency has considered the environmental consequences; it cannot 'interject itself within the area of discretion of the executive as to the choice of the action to be taken.'" Strycker's Bay Neighborhood Council, Inc. v. Karlen, 444 U.S. 223, 227–28 (1980) (per curiam) (citation omitted); see Kleppe v. Sierra Club, 427 U.S. 390, 410 n. 21 (1976) ("Neither [NEPA] nor its legislative history contemplates that a court should substitute its judgment for that of the agency as to the environmental consequences of its actions.").

In short, the obligations that NEPA levies on agencies determine the role of the courts in the statute's enforcement. This case concerns the most important responsibility that NEPA demands—that an agency reviewing proposals for action prepare an environmental impact statement, and, more specifically, that the agency discuss in its statement alternatives to the action proposed. We consider here whether the FAA has complied with NEPA in publishing an environmental impact statement that discussed in depth two alternatives: approving the expansion of the Toledo Express Airport and not approving the expansion of the Toledo Express Airport.

(1)

Federal agencies must prepare environmental impact statements when they contemplate "major Federal actions significantly affecting the quality of the human environment." NEPA § 102(2)(c), 42 U.S.C. § 4332(2)(c). An EIS must discuss, among other things, "alternatives to the proposed action," NEPA § 102(2)(C)(iii), 42 U.S.C. § 4332(2)(C)(iii), and the discussion of alternatives forms "the heart of the environmental impact statement." 40 C.F.R. § 1502.14; see Alaska v. Andrus, 580 F.2d 465, 474 (D.C. Cir.), vacated in part as moot sub nom. Western Oil & Gas Ass'n v. Alaska, 439 U.S. 922 (1978).

The problem for agencies is that "the term 'alternatives' is not self-defining." Vermont Yankee Nuclear Power Corp. v. Natural Resources Defense Council, Inc., 435 U.S. 519, 551 (1978). Suppose, for example, that a utility applies for permission to build a nuclear reactor in Vernon, Vermont. Free-floating "alternatives" to the proposal for federal action might conceivably include everything from licensing a reactor in Pecos, Texas, to promoting imports of hydropower from Quebec. If the Nuclear Regulatory Commission had to discuss these and other imaginable courses of action, its statement would wither into "frivolous boilerplate," id., if indeed the agency were to prepare an EIS at all and not instead just deny the utility a permit. If, therefore, the consideration of alternatives is to inform both the public and the agency decisionmaker, the discussion must be moored to "some notion of feasibility." Vermont Yankee, 435 U.S. at 551; see id. ("Common sense also teaches us that the 'detailed statement of alternatives' cannot be found wanting simply because the agency failed to include every device and thought conceivable by the mind of man.").

Recognizing the harm that an unbounded understanding of alternatives might cause, see id. at 549–55, CEQ regulations oblige agencies to discuss only alternatives that are feasible, or (much the same thing) reasonable. 40 C.F.R. §§ 1502.14(a)–(c), 1508.25(b)(2); see Forty Most Asked Questions Concerning CEQ's NEPA Regulations, 46 Fed.Reg. 18,026, 18,026 (1981) [hereinafter Forty Questions]. But the adjective "reasonable" is no more self-defining than the noun that it modifies. Consider two possible alternatives to our nuclear reactor in Vernon. Funding research in cold fusion might be an unreasonable alternative by virtue of the theory's scientific implausibility. But licensing a reactor in Lake Placid, New York might also be unreasonable, even though it passes some objective test of scientific worth. In either case, the proposed alternative is reasonable only if it will bring about the ends of the federal action—only if it will do what the licensing of the reactor in Vernon is meant to do. See City of New York v. Department of Transp., 715 F.2d 732, 742–43 (2d Cir.1983) (construing NEPA § 102(2)(E), 42 U.S.C. § 4332(2)(E) (discussion of alternatives in environmental assessments)), cert. denied, 465 U.S. 1055 (1984); see also City of Angoon v. Hodel, 803 F.2d 1016, 1021 (9th Cir.1986) (per curiam) ("When the purpose is to accomplish one thing, it makes no sense to consider the alternative ways by which another thing might be achieved."), cert.

denied, 484 U.S. 870 (1987). If licensing the Vernon reactor is meant to help supply energy to New England, licensing a reactor in northern New York might make equal sense. If licensing the Vernon reactor is meant as well to stimulate the Vernon job market, licensing a reactor in Lake Placid would be far less effective. The goals of an action delimit the universe of the action's reasonable alternatives.

(2)

In the first chapter of its environmental impact statement, the FAA begins by noting that the Port Authority had requested the agency's approval of the plan to develop Toledo Express. The agency then explains that "[t]he purpose and need for this action lies in [the] FAA's responsibility to review the airport design and runway configuration with respect to its safety, efficiency and utility within the national airspace system and its environmental impact on the surrounding area." After surveying the engineering reasons that justify an extended runway and new facilities, the FAA concludes by stating that the agency "has a statutory mandate to facilitate the establishment of air cargo hubs under Section 502(a)(7) [of the Airport and Airway Improvement Act of 1982 (AAIA), 49 U.S.C. app. § 2201(a)(7)] and to undertake capacity enhancement projects under Section 502(a)(11) [of the AAIA, 49 U.S.C. app. § 2201(a)(11)]."

In the second chapter of the environmental impact statement, the FAA begins by stating:

> The scope of alternatives considered by the sponsoring Federal agency, where the Federal government acts as a proprietor, is wide ranging and comprehensive. Where the Federal government acts, not as a proprietor, but to approve and support a project being sponsored by a local government or private applicant, the Federal agency is necessarily more limited. In the latter instance, the Federal government's consideration of alternatives may accord substantial weight to the preferences of the applicant and/or sponsor in the siting and design of the project.

The agency goes on to explain:

> In the present system of federalism, the FAA does not determine where to build and develop civilian airports as an owner/operator. Rather, the FAA facilitates airport development by providing Federal financial assistance, and reviews and approves or disapproves revisions to Airport Layout Plans at Federally funded airports.... Similarly, under the Airline Deregulation Act of 1978, the FAA does not regulate rates, routes, and services of air carriers or cargo operators. Airline managements are free to decide which cities to serve based on market forces.

The EIS then describes five alternatives: approving the Port Authority's plan for expanding Toledo Express, approving other geometric configurations for expanding Toledo Express, approving other ways of channeling airplane traffic at Toledo Express, no action by the agency at all, and approving plans for other airports both in the Toledo metropolitan area and out of it, including Baer Field in Fort Wayne. Finally, the EIS briefly explains why the agency eliminated all the alternatives but the first and the fourth.

The FAA's reasoning fully supports its decision to evaluate only the preferred and do-nothing alternatives. The agency first examined Congress's views on how this country is to build its civilian airports. As the agency explained, Congress has told the FAA to nurture aspiring cargo hubs. See AAIA § 502(a)(7), (11), 49 U.S.C. app. § 2201(a)(7), (11).

At the same time, however, Congress has also said that the free market, not an ersatz Gosplan for aviation, should determine the siting of the nation's airports. See Airline Deregulation Act of 1978, Pub.L. No. 95-504, 92 Stat. 1705; see also 14 Weekly Comp. Pres. Doc. 1837, 1837–38 (Oct. 24, 1978) (remarks of Pres. Carter); Suburban O'Hare Comm'n v. Dole, 787 F.2d 186, 196 (7th Cir.) ("The decision to make O'Hare, or any other airport, a 'hub' airport belongs to the airlines and not to the government."), cert. denied, 479 U.S. 847 (1986). Congress has expressed its intent by statute, and the FAA took both of Congress's messages seriously.

The FAA also took into account the Port Authority's reasons for wanting a cargo hub in Toledo. In recent years, more than fifty major companies have left the Toledo metropolitan area, and with them, over seven thousand jobs. The Port Authority expects the cargo hub at Toledo Express to create immediately more than two hundred permanent and six hundred part-time jobs with a total payroll value of more than $10 million. After three years, according to the Port Authority, the hub should create directly more than one thousand permanent jobs at the airport and one hundred and fifty other, airport-related jobs. The University of Toledo estimates that the new Toledo Express will contribute at least $42 million to the local economy after one full year of operation and nearly $68 million per year after three. In addition, the Port Authority expects the expanded airport, and Burlington's presence there, to attract other companies to Toledo. All of those factors, the Port Authority hopes, will lead to a renaissance in the Toledo metropolitan region.

Having thought hard about these appropriate factors, the FAA defined the goal for its action as helping to launch a new cargo hub in Toledo and thereby helping to fuel the Toledo economy. The agency then eliminated from detailed discussion the alternatives that would not accomplish this goal. Each of the different geometric configurations would mean technological problems and extravagant costs. So would plans to route traffic differently at Toledo Express, or to build a hub at one of the other airports in the city of Toledo. None of the airports outside of the Toledo area would serve the purpose of the agency's action. The FAA thus evaluated the environmental impacts of the only proposal that might reasonably accomplish that goal—approving the construction and operation of a cargo hub at Toledo Express. It did so with the thoroughness required by law. See 40 C.F.R. § 1502.16.

We conclude that the FAA acted reasonably in defining the purpose of its action, in eliminating alternatives that would not achieve it, and in discussing (with the required do-nothing option) the proposal that would. The agency has therefore complied with NEPA.

B.

The regulations of the Council on Environmental Quality provide that an environmental impact statement "shall [contain] a full and fair discussion of significant environmental impacts" and that "[i]mpacts shall be discussed in proportion to their significance." 40 C.F.R. §§ 1502.1, 1502.2(b); see NEPA § 102(2)(C)(i), (ii), 42 U.S.C. § 4332(2)(C)(i), (ii). The EIS in this case discusses more than twenty impacts that the expanded Toledo Express would have on the environment, including the airport's effects on people's homes and neighborhoods; on the quality of the air, the water, and the earth; on architectural, archeological, and cultural resources; on sewage disposal; on traffic patterns; on swamps, marshes, bogs, and rivers; and on bats, butterflies, grass, flowers, and trees. The EIS also states flatly that "[a]ircraft sound emissions"—noise, in a word—are "often the most noticeable environmental effect[s] an airport will produce on the surrounding community." In all, the FAA devotes about half of its discussion on environmental consequences to the effects of an increase in noise. Although Citizens does not argue that the FAA failed to discuss the impacts of noise in rough proportion to the effects' importance, it does argue that the discussion is incomplete and unfair. We disagree.

The FAA begins its discussion in the EIS by describing how it assesses the effects of more noise. Using the same methods that the EPA and the Department of Housing and Urban Development use, the FAA measures in decibels the average day-night sound levels (Ldn) produced at particular sites during each twenty-four hour period, then corrects its measurement for variations in airplane speed and formation and the like, adds a ten-decibel penalty for planes that fly at night, and, under certain circumstances, modifies the result depending on the number of people affected. See 14 C.F.R. § 150.7; id. app. A § A150.205 (describing methodology). In response to the EPA's comments on the draft statement, the FAA applied a second method of study, analyzing the effects on noise levels of exposure at twenty-six places to a single event. The EIS thoroughly explains the social, psychological, physical, and structural impacts of noise from Toledo Express. The EIS also explains the resulting Ldn and the single-event analysis in both mathematical equations and readable English and illustrates the text and data in graphs, maps, charts, and tables.

Citizens concedes, if only implicitly, that the rule of reason guiding the FAA necessarily covers the agency's discussion of particular environmental impacts. Relying on Davison v. Department of Defense, 560 F.Supp. 1019 (S.D.Ohio 1982), however, Citizens contends that in discussing the impacts of noise, a reasonable agency would at least estimate the number of people whom an expanded airport would keep awake. Citizens points out, moreover, that the EPA criticized the FAA's original choice of methods, and that in response to the EPA's comments the FAA agreed to modify its analysis in future cases. For these reasons, Citizens argues, we should find that the FAA's discussion was inadequate.

We think that Davison provides only weak support for Citizens' argument. In Davison, the Air Force decided to sell part of an old base to a firm that planned to use it for a cargo hub. Reviewing the adequacy of the resulting EIS, the court held that the Air Force had unreasonably failed to quantify with some precision the people whom the hub activity would keep up at night, had unreasonably neglected to discuss whether local residents would become accustomed to the noise, and had unreasonably overlooked the physiological effects of long-term sleep disturbance. See 560 F.Supp. at 1036–37. Here, in contrast, the FAA did all but the first. On remand in Davison, moreover, the Air Force then stated in a supplement to the final EIS that "from one hundred to one thousand people may be awakened from sleep, possibly repeatedly, for up to four hours per night, approximately 250 nights per year." To the extent that the logic of Davison would impose a similar requirement on the FAA—and the Air Force's estimate in Davison was not quite the paradigm of precision that Citizens demands here—we think it inconsistent with circuit precedent.

In examining the impacts of noise on the environment, the FAA relies on wisdom and experience peculiar to the agency and alien to the judges on this court. We have thus held consistently that the rule of reason guides every aspect of the FAA's approach, including its choice of scientific method. See, e.g., Sierra Club v. Department of Transp., 753 F.2d 120, 128 (D.C.Cir.1985); see also Valley Citizens for a Safe Environment v. Aldridge, 886 F.2d 458, 469 (1st Cir.1989). Employing here a method that we have previously endorsed, see Sierra Club v. Department of Transp., 753 F.2d at 128, the FAA proceeded to mold a body of data, dissect it, and display it in comprehensible forms. The agency's choice of method was obviously not capricious. Nor were the factual conclusions that followed. See Marsh v. Oregon Natural Resources Council, 490 U.S. 360, 377 (1989) ("Because analysis of the relevant documents 'requires a high level of technical expertise,' we must defer to 'the informed discretion of the responsible federal agencies.'" (citations omitted)); Valley Citizens, 886 F.2d at 467–69.

The EPA's criticisms of the FAA, and the agencies' subsequent deal, do not change our view of the FAA's findings. Congress wants the EPA to participate when other agencies prepare environmental impact statements. See 42 U.S.C. § 7609(a). The EPA participated here. But the FAA, not the EPA, bore the ultimate statutory responsibility for actually preparing the environmental impact statement, and under the rule of reason, a lead agency does not have to follow the EPA's comments slavishly—it just has to take them seriously. The FAA considered the EPA's criticisms in this case and decided that enough had been done. That the FAA sensibly resolved to avoid any interagency disputes in the future does not make its decision in this case unreasonable. We uphold the FAA's discussion of the impacts of increased noise.

C.

The regulations of the Council on Environmental Quality require that an environmental impact statement "be prepared directly by or by a contractor selected by the lead agency." 40 C.F.R. § 1506.5(c). If the agency decides to contract out the work on the EIS, the agency must choose the contractor "to avoid a conflict of interest," and the contractor must "execute a disclosure statement prepared by the lead agency ... specifying that [it has] no financial or other interest in the outcome of the project." Id. Citizens argues that the FAA violated the regulations by publishing an EIS prepared for the most part by a contractor (Coffman Associates) that the agency did not itself select and that did not in any event fill out the necessary disclosure forms. The FAA maintains that it (the FAA), and not Coffman, prepared the EIS, that even if Coffman did prepare the EIS, it (the FAA), and not the Port Authority, selected Coffman, and that even though Coffman did not fill out the disclosure statement, its (Coffman's) failure to do so was harmless error.

We reject each of the FAA's contentions. Offered the choice of preparing the environmental impact statement in-house, the FAA chose the other permissible option and hired consultants, including Coffman. The FAA then wrote the consultants' names and qualifications, including Coffman's, in a chapter of the EIS entitled "List of Preparers," see id. § 1502.17, a gesture that undermines the agency's current litigating position—that Coffman did not prepare the EIS, but that the FAA did instead, mostly by commenting actively on Coffman's drafts. Ultimately, however, the agency's theory founders on the plain meaning of the regulations. Although the CEQ regulations do not define the word "prepare," the dictionary does; in context, it means here "to put into written form: draw up ... <directed the commission to prepare proposals.... >." Webster's Third New Int'l Dictionary 1790 (unabridged ed.1981); see Sierra Club v. Marsh, 714 F.Supp. 539, 550–51 (D.Me.1989). That is just what Coffman did, as the agency freely admits. We need not decide whether the FAA's active editing of Coffman's drafts—behavior consistent with the agency's obligation to "furnish guidance" to consultants and "participate in the preparation [of] and ... independently evaluate the statement prior to its approval," 40 C.F.R. § 1506.5(c)—made it, too, a preparer of the EIS. We are certain, however, that Coffman's initial drafts and responses to the FAA's comments made Coffman more than the agency's amanuensis.

Once the FAA decided not to prepare the environmental impact statement directly, it was obliged to pick a contractor itself, and not to delegate the responsibility. See id. The EIS states that the Port Authority, not the agency, chose Coffman to work on the environmental assessment, and later, on the environmental impact statement. The EIS also states that the agency "concurred" in Coffman's selection. The FAA argues that its concurrence in the Port Authority's choice satisfied its duty under the regulations. We need not page through the dictionary at length to decide that concurring in someone else's choice of consultant is not the same as choosing a consultant of one's own.

By failing to select the consultant that prepared the environmental impact statement, the FAA violated CEQ regulations. Citizens urges us to remedy this breach by invalidating the EIS. We see no reason to do so, however, at least not solely on the ground that the FAA neglected to search on its own for a competent contractor. This particular error did not compromise the "objectivity and integrity of the [NEPA] process." Forty Questions, 46 Fed.Reg. at 18,031; see Sierra Club v. Sigler, 695 F.2d 957, 963 n.3 (5th Cir.1983) (CEQ regulations are "'designed ... to minimize the conflict of interest inherent in the situation of those outside the government coming to the government for money, leases or permits while attempting impartially to analyze the environmental consequences of their getting it.'" (quoting 43 Fed.Reg. 55,987 (1978))); cf. 40 C.F.R. § 1500.3 ("[I]t is the [CEQ's] intention that any trivial violation of these regulations not give rise to any independent cause of action.").

The more serious infraction, in our view, was Coffman's failure to fill out the disclosure form exacted of consultants that prepare environmental impact statements. See id. § 1506.5(c). Citizens points out that Coffman (in addition to having prepared the EIS) has started to prepare the Port Authority's Part 150 study, and that the scope of the study will vary directly with the status of the airport (since the Port Authority is relying on the study to fine tune its mitigation plans). The FAA argues that Coffman had no reason to know while preparing the EIS that the agency would want it to expand the Part 150 study. The FAA may well be correct, but neither the petitioners nor this court can know for certain in the absence of a completed disclosure form. Moreover, the CEQ regulations prohibit broadly any "financial or other interest in the outcome of the project." Id.; see Forty Questions, 46 Fed.Reg. at 18,031 (interpreting "conflict of interest" to mean "any known benefits other than general enhancement of professional reputation"). The FAA promised the petitioners in a letter that "Coffman does not have an undisclosed stake in the project that would potentially disqualify it." That ipse dixit does not reassure us. We therefore order the FAA to have Coffman execute an appropriate disclosure statement, see 40 C.F.R. § 1506.5(c), and, should the agency find that a conflict exists, to decide—promptly—on the measures to take in response.

III.

Under section 4(f) of the Department of Transportation Act of 1966, the Secretary of Transportation may not approve a project requiring the use of a park unless he determines, first, that there is no "prudent and feasible alternative" to using the land, and second, that the project includes "all possible planning to minimize harm to the park ... resulting from the use." Transportation Act § 4(f), 49 U.S.C. § 303(c). The FAA (which is part of the Department of Transportation, see 49 U.S.C. § 106(a)) acknowledged that the proposed expansion of Toledo Express would constructively "use" the Springbrook campground since flights from the airport would subject the camp to nighttime noise of up to Ldn 75 decibels, about 10 to 15 decibels more than now. Cf. Allison v. Department of Transp., 908 F.2d 1024, 1030 (D.C.Cir.1990) (no section 4(f) use when a park is subjected to only minor increases in airplane noise). The agency nonetheless decided that while there might be a feasible alternative to using the campground, cf. Citizens to Preserve Overton Park, Inc. v. Volpe, 401 U.S. 402, 411 (1971) (alternative is "feasible" unless "as a matter of sound engineering" it should not be built), there existed no prudent one, and that the project would ease the harm to Springbrook by moving it elsewhere inside the park, but outside the reach of Ldn 65 decibels. Citizens argues that a feasible and prudent alternative to using the campground did exist: leaving the airport in Toledo alone and expanding the airport in Fort Wayne instead. Citizens also argues that the project does not adequately diminish the harm to Springbrook because the FAA did not consider, among other ideas, fining the owners of planes that are noisy, and because the FAA has not said where exactly in Oak Openings it plans to put the new campground.

Overton Park instructs courts to undertake "a thorough, probing, in-depth review" of decisions under section 4(f), 401 U.S. at 415, and to canvass the facts of section 4(f) cases "searching[ly] and careful[ly]," id. at 416. Our ultimate standard of review is nonetheless deferential. See id.; Eagle Found., Inc. v. Dole, 813 F.2d 798, 804 (7th Cir.1987). We are entrusted with ensuring that the agency looked hard at the pertinent facts and thought hard about the relevant factors. See id. at 803. We are required to repudiate agency caprice. Once we determine that the agency's decision was reasonable, however, we are not entitled to displace its decision with our own or with anyone else's. See Overton Park, 401 U.S. at 416.

Reasoning by analogy to NEPA, the FAA argues that an alternative must be imprudent under section 4(f)(1) if it fails to accomplish a proposal's objectives. According to the FAA, since a hub in Fort Wayne would do nothing for Toledo, and since the health of the Toledo economy was a primary reason for the Port Authority's application, Fort Wayne was an imprudent alternative and the FAA did not act arbitrarily in approving the use of Springbrook. In effect, the FAA's argument would mean that anytime an alternative is unreasonable under NEPA (and thus would not have to be discussed in detail in the environmental impact statement), the alternative would also be imprudent within the meaning of section 4(f)(1) of the Transportation Act (and thus would not block approval of a transportation project).

Although an agency's analysis under NEPA and the Transportation Act might proceed in similar tracks, the two statutes are not precisely the same. The Transportation Act differs from NEPA in at least two ways. First, the Transportation Act requires the agency to evaluate "prudent ... alternatives to using th[e] land"—alternatives to the project, that is—not alternatives to the federal action. Second, contrary to the FAA's argument, the case law uniformly holds that an alternative is imprudent under section 4(f)(1) if it does not meet the transportation needs of a project. See Hickory Neighborhood Defense League v. Skinner, 910 F.2d 159, 164 (4th Cir.1990); Druid Hills Civic Ass'n v. Federal Highway Admin., 772 F.2d 700, 715 (11th Cir.1985); Arizona Past & Future Found. v. Dole, 722 F.2d 1423, 1428–29 (9th Cir.1983). The Transportation Act is similar to NEPA in that the agency bears the responsibility for defining at the outset the transportation goals for a project and for determining which alternatives would reasonably fulfill those goals.

Having focused on the statutes' apparent similarities, and disregarded their differences, the FAA never quite specified with ideal coherence the transportation goals of the project at Toledo Express. In future cases, the agency should bear in mind the differences between NEPA and the Transportation Act, and the agency's section 4(f) documentation package should reflect the concerns specific to the latter statute. Still, in approving in this case the use of the park in Toledo, the FAA reasonably defined the transportation goals of the project as providing the Toledo area with a modern, effective cargo hub. Given this definition of the project's aims, the FAA need not have examined in detail the relative flaws of Baer Field, including its antiquated condition, its distance from Burlington's main markets (Detroit and Chicago), Fort Wayne's limited pool of labor, and the city's failure to come up with the necessary financing. It was enough for the agency to find that a hub in Baer Field would not fulfill the transportation goals of the project at Toledo Express and that Fort Wayne was therefore less than a prudent alternative to using Toledo. Because its conclusion was reasonable, the FAA did not violate section 4(f)(1).

Nor did the FAA violate section 4(f)(2), which requires that the "project include [ ] all possible planning to minimize harm to the park." Light from the expanded Toledo Express airport might temporarily blind amateur astrophotographers, and planes, in addition to stars, might appear in their pictures. More noise would make camping at Springbrook less enjoyable. The FAA thus plans to install shielded, low-pressure sodium lights in the airport's parking lots and to move the campground somewhere else in the park, out of the range of the Ldn 65 decibels. Citizens accepts the measures meant to save astrophotography, but it (and the EPA) would rather the FAA try other tactics to save the present campground, such as fining the owners of noisy planes or requiring the use of noise barriers. If Springbrook is to be moved, moreover, Citizens wants to know exactly where.

The deference we pay to decisions under section 4(f)(1), however, see Eagle Found., 813 F.2d at 803–08, applies as well to decisions under section 4(f)(2), see Coalition on Sensible Transp., Inc. v. Dole, 826 F.2d 60, 65–66 (D.C.Cir.1987). Congress wanted the agencies, not the courts, to evaluate plans to reduce environmental damage. The FAA thoroughly examined the impacts that the airport's expansion would have on protected parkland and proposed various tactics to mitigate them. The FAA then decided (with the support of the Department of the Interior) to move the campground to the half of Oak Openings that falls outside the range of Ldn 65 decibels. Citizens, dissatisfied, wants us to force the FAA to pinpoint the new campground's geographic coordinates. But federal courts are neither empowered nor competent to micromanage strategies for saving the nation's parklands. See id. at 66. Because the FAA's decision in this case does not reflect "a clear error of judgment," we are constrained to let it stand. Overton Park, 401 U.S. at 416.

IV.

Under section 509(b)(5) of the Airport and Airway Improvement Act of 1982 (AAIA), the FAA may not approve a project that harms the environment unless the agency first determines that there is no "feasible and prudent alternative" and that "all reasonable steps have been taken to minimize [the] adverse effect." AAIA § 509(b)(5), 49 U.S.C. app. § 2208(b)(5). Citizens argues that any time the FAA violates section 4(f)(1) of the Transportation Act, the agency automatically violates section 509(b)(5) of the AAIA as well. We recognize that some of section 509(b)(5) parrots some of section 4(f)(1). An agency that fails to choose a "prudent and feasible alternative," AAIA § 509(b)(5), 49 U.S.C. App. § 2208(b)(5), obviously fails at the same time to choose a "feasible and prudent alternative," Transportation Act § 4(f)(1), 49 U.S.C. § 303(c)(1). The agency can violate or observe two statutes synchronously. But we have already determined that the FAA did not violate section 4(f)(1): Fort Wayne was an imprudent, if feasible, alternative to Toledo. Therefore, although we agree in principle with this aspect of Citizens' theory, we have little trouble deciding under section 509(b)(5) that while Fort Wayne may have been a feasible alternative to Toledo, it was also an imprudent one.

We have also upheld in this case the informal finding required by section 4(f)(2) of the Transportation Act, that the Toledo Express project includes "all possible planning to minimize harm" to Oak Openings. Transportation Act §4(f)(2), 49 U.S.C. §303(c)(2). Section 509(b)(5) of the AAIA, though roughly congruous, commands agencies to find that "all reasonable steps have been taken to minimize such adverse effect." AAIA §509(b)(5), 49 U.S.C. App. §2208(b)(5). We do not decide whether and under what circumstances a mitigation plan that is unreasonable would still be possible—that is, whether the FAA might have to implement plans under section 4(f)(2) that it would not have to implement under section 509(b)(5). We do decide, however, that all plans that are impossible are necessarily unreasonable—that is, that when the FAA does not have to implement a particular plan under section 4(f)(2) of the Transportation Act, it is also spared from having to implement that plan under section 509(b)(5) of the AAIA. The FAA has done all that it could have for Oak Openings. It has therefore done all that it should have. With respect to Oak Openings, the FAA has not violated section 509(b)(5).

V.

We hold that the FAA has fulfilled the requirements of NEPA, the Transportation Act, the AAIA, and all the CEQ regulations but one. We therefore grant the petition for review and remand to the agency so that it may comply with 40 C.F.R. §1506.5(c). We affirm the FAA's decision in all other respects. Given the limited nature of what remains for the agency to do, we decline to enjoin the continuing development of Toledo Express or to grant any other of the equitable relief that the petitioners have asked for.

[The partial dissent of Judge Buckley is omitted.]

PINCZKOWSKI v. MILWAUKEE COUNTY

687 N.W.2d 791 (Wis. Ct. App. 2004),
aff'd, 706 N.W.2d 642 (Wis. 2005)

CURLEY, Judge.

Gloria Pinczkowski appeals the judgments of the trial court that determined: (1) the sale prices of adjacent properties sold to Milwaukee County were inadmissible at trial; (2) the letter of intent to purchase the Pinczkowski property from the Hertz Corporation was also inadmissible; and (3) Pinczkowski was not entitled to any housing replacement payment. Because clear precedent prohibits the introduction of the sale price of comparable properties when sold to a condemning authority engaged in negotiations to obtain property for a public project; a letter of intent submitted by a prospective buyer is not proper evidence of the condemnation property's fair market value; and, under the formula found in Wis. Stat. §32.19(4)(a) (2001–02), Pinczkowski was ineligible for any replacement housing payment, we affirm.

I. BACKGROUND

In 1987, Milwaukee County began planning to expand General Mitchell International Airport. These plans were detailed in an Airport Master Plan that was passed by the Milwaukee County Board of Supervisors in 1993 and included obtaining properties located near the airport for airport use. One such property was owned by Gloria Pinczkowski. The Pinczkowski property consisted of a large lot and a residence located on that lot. The area in which the Pinczkowski property was located had been zoned industrial, thus making their residential use a non-conforming use.

Soon after the completion of the Master Plan, the Milwaukee County Board of Supervisors approved the acquisition of the Pinczkowski property, along with the properties adjacent to that of Pinczkowski's, by either negotiated sale or condemnation. As a result, in 1997 and 1998, respectively, the County purchased the properties located to the north and south of Pinczkowski's after negotiating with the owners. Federal noise abatement funds were used for the purchase of one of the properties.

In connection with the airport expansion project, private businesses, such as the Hertz Corporation, were also asked to vacate their leaseholds and relocate to alternative sites. Consequently, in 1997, Hertz contacted Pinczkowski and sent a letter of intent expressing an interest in purchasing the property. However, Hertz subsequently abandoned its attempt to purchase the Pinczkowski property.

The reason why Hertz abandoned its attempt to purchase the Pinczkowski property is unclear. Pinczkowski argues that Hertz's assemblage plan was disrupted when the County purchased the adjacent properties. The County claims that Hertz stopped its pursuit after it realized that the County had plans to acquire the Pinczkowski property. In any event, representatives of Hertz were never deposed.

In 1999, the County offered to purchase the Pinczkowski property for $93,027. Because the Pinczkowski lot was larger than average in size, and because the property had a "higher and better use" if used for airport purposes, the County was required by WIS. ADMIN. CODE § COMM 202.68(7)(a)2 and (7)(c), respectively, to separate the amount attributable to the residence from the total amount—a calculation also referred to as the "carve-out" value. The County determined that the "carve-out" value of the residence was $53,748, or 57.8% of the total amount offered, and the remainder was thus attributed to the surrounding land. The County also determined that the reasonable cost of a replacement residence would be $77,926. Pursuant to Wis. Stat. § 32.19(4)(a)1, the County subtracted the "carve-out" value from the cost of a replacement residence, yielding $24,178. According to the letter sent to Pinczkowski, a housing replacement payment [of up to $25,000] was available to her, as long as she purchased a replacement home that cost at least $77,926. Pinczkowski, however, rejected the County's $93,027 offer and later purchased a new residence for $155,000.

Through an "Award of Damages," Milwaukee County acquired the Pinczkowski property by eminent domain on November 10, 2000. The County paid Pinczkowski a total of $350,000 in compensation, which was the calculated fair market value of the property. Dissatisfied with this award, Pinczkowski challenged it and, as a result, pursuant to Wis. Stat. § 32.06(10), a condemnation trial was held in March 2003.

At trial, Pinczkowski sought to introduce evidence to show that the fair market value of her property was higher than the County's calculation. To this end, Pinczkowski wanted to introduce evidence of the 1997 and 1998 purchase prices of the two adjacent properties, claiming that they were made voluntarily and, consequently, that these sales were an indication of the value of her property. (Neither property was a residence. One was an auto parts store and the other went by the name "Veterans Park," although structures existed on the property.)

Similarly, Pinczkowski also sought to introduce the Hertz letter, asserting that the letter showed that Hertz was willing to purchase her property for far more money than was offered by the County, had it also been able to acquire the additional properties previously purchased by the County. Hence, Pinczkowski sought to argue that the County ruined Hertz's "assemblage" plan and thereby reduced the value of her property.

In response to Pinczkowski's attempt to introduce the aforementioned evidence, the County filed a motion in limine to exclude the evidence, arguing that evidence of sales to a condemning authority as part of a condemnation project, and unaccepted offers to purchase such as Hertz's, are not admissible as evidence of value. The trial court granted the County's motion, thus barring Pinczkowski from introducing evidence of the sales of the adjacent properties and the Hertz letter. The trial court emphasized that it excluded evidence of the two sales because "the properties were purchased as part of Milwaukee County's airport expansion project and ... were not arms-length transactions as they were made by a condemning authority with the right to eminent domain." The trial court also specifically stated that the Hertz letter could not be used to establish value and that Pinczkowski's appraisers could not use it in arriving at an estimated fair market value for the Pinczkowski property. The jury, nonetheless, heard evidence indicating that Hertz had contacted Pinczkowski and that Hertz ended up purchasing a different property near the airport to which it subsequently moved its operation.

At the conclusion of the trial, the jury determined the fair market value of Pinczkowski's property was $300,000, reducing Pinczkowski's award by $50,000. Another $15,000 was deducted due to environmental factors, resulting in a final award of $285,000.

In addition to challenging the compensation [she] received, Pinczkowski also brought another action concerning the housing replacement payment. The cases were subsequently consolidated. After the County paid Pinczkowski $350,000 for the property, Pinczkowski sought to collect the $24,178 housing replacement payment mentioned in the earlier notice sent by the County. The County refused to pay Pinczkowski this amount, arguing that she was not entitled to any payment because the total amount she had already been paid was greater than the cost of the replacement residence. The County contended that the $24,178 replacement payment would have been applicable only if Pinczkowski had accepted the County's initial offer of $93,027. After the jury trial, the trial court granted the County's motion for summary judgment in regard to this issue.

Pinczkowski now appeals the trial court's exclusion of the evidence of the two adjacent properties' sales, as well as the Hertz letter. Pinczkowski also appeals the trial court's grant of summary judgment with respect to the housing replacement payment.

II. ANALYSIS

A. The trial court properly excluded evidence of the sale prices of adjacent properties.

Pinczkowski first argues that the trial court erred when, in response to the County's motion in limine, it barred Pinczkowski from introducing any evidence of the 1997 and 1998 sales of the adjacent properties as comparables to her property for use in their appraisers' calculations of fair market value. She claims this error requires a new trial.

Rulings on the admission of evidence "touching upon the value of property appropriated in condemnation cases" are largely a matter of the trial court's discretion. Calaway v. Brown County, 202 Wis.2d 736, 741, 553 N.W.2d 809 (Ct.App. 1996). In order for a discretionary act to withstand scrutiny, the appellate court must find "that the trial court examined the relevant facts, applied a proper standard of law, and, using a demonstrated rational process, reached a conclusion that a reasonable judge could reach." Loy v. Bunderson, 107 Wis.2d 400, 414–15, 320 N.W.2d 175 (1982). If the trial court bases its exercise of discretion upon an error of law, that constitutes a misuse of discretion. State v. Hutnik, 39 Wis.2d 754, 763, 159 N.W.2d 733 (1968).

Pinczkowski argues that, contrary to the trial court's findings, the sales of the adjacent properties were voluntary, arms-length transactions. She points out that the circumstances surrounding the sales had all the indicia of arms-length transactions—the County used standard real estate purchase contracts when purchasing the properties; the deeds did not contain the standard language found when acquired under threat of condemnation; there were no certificates of compensation following the closings, a statutory requirement for a negotiated purchase under condemnation pressure; and the sellers paid transfer taxes, which would be unnecessary if the properties had been taken by condemnation. Indeed, Pinczkowski indicates that the County's own expert described the sales as "voluntary."

Additionally, while acknowledging that Wisconsin case law prohibits the introduction of evidence of the amounts paid for land purchased in settlement or contemplation of condemnation, Pinczkowski attempts to distinguish these cases. Pinczkowski claims the sales were "voluntary sales of the immediately adjacent properties years before the acquisition of the property and not made under threat of condemnation or as part of an ongoing project," and thus she contends the properties' sale prices should have been admissible as evidence of market value. Finally, Pinczkowski cites foreign law for the proposition that the sale prices were admissible. We are unpersuaded by all of Pinczkowski's arguments.

First, we pause to examine Pinczkowski's characterization that these sales were not part of an ongoing project. We observe that, in the Airport Master Plan, compiled in April 1992, and, as noted, approved by the County Board on September 23, 1993, one of the adjacent properties, the sale price of which Pinczkowski was attempting to introduce, was listed in the appendix under the title "Properties to be Acquired—C1 Concept." Thus, it was public knowledge as early as April 1992 that the County intended to purchase the adjacent property for airport expansion. Moreover, a County inter-office memo dated August 29, 1996, entitled "Airport Parking Expansion Alternatives," sent to the then-County Board Chairperson, states the following with respect to the three properties:

> 5607 S. Sixth Street, Curtis Minten and Joan Otzelberger owners, also known as Veteran's Park, may be acquired under the HOPP Program and is currently in the appraisal stage. The owners have not firmly decided whether to sell the property.
>
> 5617 S. Sixth Street, [Gloria] Pinczkowski owner, is eligible for acquisition under the Homeowners' Protection Program (HOPP) and is being appraised. The owner has not firmly decided whether to sell the property.
>
> 5675 S. Sixth Street, Lake Auto Parts, Kenneth Zeck, owner. Mr. Zeck is interested in selling the property. This parcel is not part of the HOPP noise acquisition program.

Furthermore, the properties recommended for acquisition are programmed in the Master Plan for future cargo development. Consequently, the acquisition of these parcels is recommended as it would serve two purposes, auto parking and then cargo, and would, therefore, continue to be productive should a second parking structure be built.

Thus, the County's intentions to acquire these properties were well known in 1996. These facts defeat Pinczkowski's claim that the adjacent properties were not acquired "as a part of an on-going project."

Further, we note that the condemnation procedure set forth in Wis. Stat. § 32.05(2a) requires the condemning authority to first attempt to negotiate a purchase of the property. Thus, it would be expected that in furtherance of a large expansion project, such as what occurred here, some property owners, like those owning the adjacent properties, knowing that their properties eventually would be condemned, "voluntarily" agreed to a sale after they were approached by the County. Thus, the sales of the two properties adjacent to the Pinczkowski property can hardly be characterized as "not made under threat of condemnation."

With regard to the admissibility of the sale prices, evidence as to the price paid for property sold voluntarily to a condemning authority is generally inadmissible:

> In a majority of the cases in which the question has arisen, courts have held that evidence as to the price paid by the same or another condemning agency for other real property which, although subject to condemnation, was sold by the owner without the intervention of eminent domain proceedings, is rendered inadmissible to prove the value of the real property involved merely because the property was sold to a prospective condemnor.

J.H. Cooper, Annotation, Admissibility on Issue of Value of Real Property of Evidence of Sale Price of Other Real Property, 85 A.L.R.2d 110, § 10 (2004) (footnote omitted).

The obvious and well-founded reasons behind the rule are articulated in Kirkpatrick v. State, 53 Wis.2d 522, 192 N.W.2d 856 (1972):

> The problem with evidence of sales of other land to the condemning authority is that the price may very well not be the fair market value of land, no matter how comparable the land may be in its physical aspects. This is so merely because the price is not determined by an arms-length transaction, but rather by dealings between one who must buy and another who has no choice but to sell.

Id. at 526, 192 N.W.2d 856 (citation omitted).

Thus, we agree and adopt the trial court's conclusion that the purchases of the adjacent properties were inadmissible.

B. The trial court correctly excluded evidence of the Hertz letter.

Pinczkowski insists that the trial court erroneously excluded the Hertz letter on the ground that it may not be used to prove fair market value and contends that the trial court should have allowed the existence of the letter into evidence, excluding the amount stated. She maintains that barring the evidence affected her substantial rights and requires a new trial.

First, Pinczkowski contends that she wanted to introduce the Hertz letter, not as a representation of fair market value, but rather to show that there was a private market for the property. Specifically, she claims that even though it was undisputed that the "highest and best use" of the property was airport related, the excluded evidence was relevant to show that Hertz had plans to purchase both the Pinczkowski property and the adjacent properties. She thus argues that barring the evidence prevented discussion of "possible private party assemblage," and that the evidence would have shown that when the County purchased the adjacent properties, it ruined Hertz's assemblage plan.

Consequently, Pinczkowski argues that by ruining Hertz's plan, the County reduced the probable fair market value of the Pinczkowski property, which they contend was an unjust means for a government entity to reduce a condemnee's compensation.

Second, Pinczkowski argues that, because Hertz expressed an interest in the Pinczkowski property but later purchased a different property, the Hertz letter would also have "validated Pinczkowski's experts' approach to choice of comparables." She argues that the letter shows why Pinczkowski's appraisers, unlike the County's appraisers, relied on Hertz's eventual purchase of another property as a comparable sale in estimating the Pinczkowski property's value. She hence asserts that since Hertz showed an interest in two properties and ultimately purchased one of them, there is an indication that the two properties were comparable. Pinczkowski argues, therefore, that the Hertz letter would have made Pinczkowski's appraisers' estimates, which were higher than those of the County's experts, more credible, because it would have explained why the appraisers relied on Hertz's eventual purchase of the other property. Accordingly, Pinczkowski argues that allowing the Hertz letter into evidence would have resulted in a higher jury verdict.

"A [trial] court has broad discretion in determining the relevance and admissibility of proffered evidence." State v. Oberlander, 149 Wis.2d 132, 140, 438 N.W.2d 580 (1989) (citation omitted). We review the trial court's decision to exclude this evidence under the erroneous exercise of discretion standard. State v. Walters, 2004 WI 18, ¶ 13, 269 Wis.2d 142, 675 N.W.2d 778. "An appellate court will uphold an evidentiary ruling if it concludes that the [trial] court examined the relevant facts, applied a proper standard of law, used a demonstrated rational process, and reached a conclusion that a reasonable judge could reach." Id., ¶ 14, 675 N.W.2d 778. Therefore, this court will not find an erroneous exercise of discretion if a reasonable basis for the trial court's determination exists. State v. Pharr, 115 Wis.2d 334, 342, 340 N.W.2d 498 (1983).

A new trial shall not be granted unless the trial court made an erroneous ruling and the ruling affected the substantial rights of the parties. Martindale v. Ripp, 2001 WI 113, ¶ 31, 246 Wis.2d 67, 629 N.W.2d 698. The substantial rights of the parties are affected only if there is a reasonable possibility that the error contributed to the outcome of the case. Id., ¶ 32, 629 N.W.2d 698.

The general rule in Wisconsin is that unaccepted offers are impermissible as proof of fair market value in condemnation cases. Fox Wis. Theatres, Inc. v. City of Waukesha, 253 Wis. 452, 456–57, 34 N.W.2d 783 (1948). However, in certain situations, fair market value may be proved using offers to purchase, but only when they are "made with actual intent and pursuant to actual effort to purchase." Id. at 456, 34 N.W.2d 783 (quoted source omitted). Therefore, our supreme court has stated that, "[i]n order to qualify as probative evidence, there must be a preliminary foundation of 'the bona fides of the offer, the financial responsibility of the offeror, and his qualifications to know the value of the property.'" Bihlmire v. Hahn, 31 Wis.2d 537, 544–45, 143 N.W.2d 433 (1966) (quoting Fox Wis. Theatres, 253 Wis. at 458, 34 N.W.2d 783).

The trial court held that the Hertz letter was nothing more than a conditional letter of intent, and that any claim that the letter amounted to an actual offer is purely speculative. The trial court also concluded that even if Hertz did have the financial resources to complete the transaction, as well as the ability to know the proper value of the property, any possible transaction would, nonetheless, have been dependent on several conditions, including "necessary government approvals." No such approval was obtained and, given the history of the airport project, none would have been forthcoming. In addition, the trial court also noted that the letter of intent expired when Pinczkowski failed to sign it before its expiration date had passed and, thus, "cannot be considered 'bona fide.'" The trial court, therefore, concluded that the letter was merely an "unbinding letter of intent, which is one step removed from an offer," and that it "would not necessarily have lead [sic] to a formal offer, much less an actual sale."

These are reasonable findings. Because the Hertz letter was conditional and had expired, it does not appear to have been an offer, and its use as an indication of fair market value would, indeed, have been purely speculative. Therefore, the trial court did not erroneously exercise its discretion in concluding that this was not a bona fide offer and as such correctly excluded the Hertz letter. On appeal Pinczkowski, nonetheless, emphasizes that the Hertz letter has probative value that is unrelated to fair market value and that it should have been permitted. We are not persuaded.

Pinczkowski's first argument, according to which the Hertz letter should have been admitted to show that by purchasing the surrounding properties the County ruined Hertz's assemblage plan and reduced the value of the Pinczkowski property, is not convincing. Although Pinczkowski argues that she wanted to introduce the Hertz letter merely to show assemblage, she also argues that by allegedly spoiling Hertz's assemblage plan, the County reduced the probable fair market value of her property, which in turn reduced her compensation. It is thus apparent that Pinczkowski essentially was, indeed, trying to use the Hertz letter to show fair market value. As already established, the trial court acted reasonably in concluding that the Hertz letter was not an offer, and that even if it were, it may not be used to show fair market value because it was both expired and conditional and, therefore, entirely speculative for purposes of showing fair market value. See Fox Wisconsin Theatres, 253 Wis. at 456–58, 34 N.W.2d 783.

In addition, even if the letter were an offer, and even if it could be used to show fair market value, Pinczkowski's argument still lacks merit because it had been the County's stated public purpose for several years to acquire the Pinczkowski property, as well as the two adjacent properties, as part of the airport expansion project. It was, therefore, not possible for the County to ruin Hertz's plan, but it was, instead, entirely reasonable for the County to assume that Hertz was aware, or should have been aware, of the airport expansion plan.

Pinczkowski's next argument, that the Hertz letter shows why Pinczkowski's experts considered the property that Hertz eventually purchased as a comparable property, is equally unsuccessful. This argument was not raised below and we refuse to address it, see State v. Rogers, 196 Wis.2d 817, 827–29, 539 N.W.2d 897 (Ct.App.1995) (failure to raise specific challenges in the trial court waives the right to raise them on appeal).

We therefore agree with the trial court's assessment:

> As a matter of law, the Hertz letter of intent cannot be the basis of an expert's opinion. Though expert appraisers may typically rely upon offers, the Court finds that the "offer" here is only a highly speculative letter of intent. Here the letter of intent is not an offer and cannot be reasonably relied upon by the appraiser. As such, it is not admissible evidence despite the appraiser's reliance upon it.

In a related argument, Pinczkowski also contends that she was prejudiced because the jury did not hear that Hertz was interested enough in the Pinczkowski property to contact her. This argument is unconvincing. Even though the Hertz letter was excluded, the jury did hear testimony about Hertz's search for a new property and that Hertz had expressed an interest in the Pinczkowski property. The jury was also told about the property Hertz ultimately purchased, and became familiar with the assemblage theory via a hypothetical in which it was presumed that the County had not purchased the adjacent properties. Therefore, because the jury was, indeed, aware of Hertz's interest in the property, Pinczkowski was not prejudiced by the trial court's ruling regarding the Hertz letter.

C. Pinczkowski was not entitled to a housing replacement payment.

Pinczkowski's final argument is that the trial court erred when it determined that she was not entitled to a housing replacement payment pursuant to Wis. Stat. § 32.19(4)(a). Additionally, Pinczkowski submits that equitable estoppel prevents the County from reneging its offer to pay her the approximately $25,000 that was promised in a letter sent pursuant to the statute.

Wisconsin Stat. § 32.19(1) states that the legislature has declared "that it is in the public interest that persons displaced by any public project be fairly compensated for the property acquired and other losses ... suffered as the result of programs designed for the benefit of the public as a whole[.]" Section 32.19(4)(a) explains the formula for payment of up to $25,000 for replacement housing:

> (4) REPLACEMENT HOUSING. (a) Owner-occupants. In addition to amounts otherwise authorized by this subchapter, the condemnor shall make a payment, not to exceed $25,000, to any displaced person who is displaced from a dwelling actually owned and occupied, or from a mobile home site actually owned or occupied, by the displaced person for not less than 180 days prior to the initiation of negotiations for the acquisition of the property.... A displaced owner may elect to receive the payment under par. (b) 1. in lieu of the payment under this paragraph. Such payment includes only the following:
>
> 1. The amount, if any, which when added to the acquisition payment, equals the reasonable cost of a comparable replacement dwelling available on the private market, as determined by the condemnor.

During the process of acquiring Pinczkowski's property, the County, as required by WIS. ADMIN. CODE § COMM 202.06(6)(a), sent a notice to Pinczkowski in August 1999 setting forth the County's computation of the differential replacement payment. Section COMM 202.06(6)(a) directs:

> An agency shall provide a written notice to occupants indicating the differential replacement payment computation as specified under ss. Comm. 202.68–88 for residential occupants.... The notice shall be provided within 90 days of an expected date of vacation or at the request of a displaced person, whichever is sooner.

As noted, because Pinczkowski's lot was larger than a typical lot, and because the lot's highest and best use was not as a residence, the County was required to utilize the "carve out" method. The term "carve out" is defined in WIS. ADMIN. CODE § COMM 202.01(6) as: "a method for computing a replacement housing ... payment that is applied to separate the value of a portion of a property acquired[.]"

After applying the "carve out" formula, the County calculated that the Pinczkowski home, on a typical lot, represented 57.8% of the value of the total property. The County calculated that a comparable replacement dwelling would cost $79,900; it adjusted this amount by $1,973.53 to reflect market influences on the potential final sales price, which yielded a sum of $77,926.47. It subtracted the carve out amount—57.8% of the proposed sale price of $93,027 from the $77,926.47, and, had a sale occurred at that price, informed Pinczkowski she was entitled to a housing replacement payment of $24,178.47 if she bought a replacement dwelling that cost at least $77,926.47. After purchasing a new home for $155,000, Pinczkowski sought the housing replacement payment. The County refused to pay it, arguing that she was no longer eligible for this payment. The trial court agreed with the County. We agree with the trial court.

As noted, Pinczkowski did not accept the offer of $93,027 for the property, and sold it later for $350,000. Consequently, after applying the 57.8% carve out to the actual price, Pinczkowski is not entitled to any housing replacement payment because the acquisition payment was greater than the home purchased to replace the South Sixth Street property. Contrary to Pinczkowski's contention, the trial court considered the carve out amount in its decision and applied it properly.

Additionally, we also note that Pinczkowski, when applying for the housing replacement payment, signed an application that advised her that "any increase in the [b]asic [a]ward attributable to the residential portion shall be computed in the same percentage ratio established in the offering price of the [b]asic [a]ward." Thus, she knew, or should have known, that the carve out percentage, here 57.8%, would be used to decide whether she was eligible for a housing replacement payment, regardless of the purchase price. Thus, her contention that she believed the $53,748 or 57.8% of the $93,027 offer, stated in the letter explaining the housing replacement payment, would remain fixed is unsupported by the record.

Pinczkowski also asserts that she is entitled to the money because the County should be equitably estopped from withholding it. However, the elements of equitable estoppel have not been met here.

As set out in Milas v. Labor Association of Wisconsin, Inc., 214 Wis.2d 1, 11–12, 571 N.W.2d 656 (1997), equitable estoppel has four elements: (1) an action or non-action; (2) on the part of one against whom estoppel is asserted; (3) which induces reasonable reliance thereon by the other, either in action or non-action; and (4) which is to his or her detriment. Pinczkowski contends that the County's letter was a promise to pay her the near maximum housing replacement payment and she relied on it to her detriment. Assuming that equitable estoppel can bind a government agency, see Village of Hobart v. Brown County, 2004 WI App 66, 18 n.7, 271 Wis.2d 268, 678 N.W.2d 402 (noting "equitable estoppel 'is not applied as freely against governmental agencies as it is in the case of private persons'") (citation omitted), she is mistaken.

First, no promise was ever made to Pinczkowski that she would receive any housing replacement payment, regardless of the sale price of her home. The letter explaining the housing replacement payment formula contained the following information:

> A. Replacement Housing Payment
>
> This payment has been determined to be $24,178.47, based on a comparable housing study of houses presently for sale on the real estate market, provided you sell your house to Milwaukee County for the above stated appraisal amount, which included a carve-out amount of $53,748.00, and you purchase a replacement dwelling which costs at least $77,926.40.

Pinczkowski elected to hold out for a higher award. By doing so, she became ineligible for this housing replacement payment.

Secondly, Pinczkowski could not reasonably have relied on the amount of the payment as fixed, regardless of the sale price. The letter, and the formula set forth in the statute, clearly advised her otherwise. Accordingly, we affirm.

WEDEMEYER, Presiding Judge, dissenting.

[I]n my opinion, the trial court erred when it determined that the sales of the properties adjacent to the Pinczkowski property were not admissible into evidence. Because the sales were voluntary, arms-length transactions, this evidence should have been admitted. Accordingly, I would reverse on this basis.

Notes

1. There are 19,576 airfields in the United States, of which 5,280 are available for public use. Most commercial airports are owned and operated by counties or municipalities, although in some jurisdictions (such as Hawaii and Maryland), responsibility rests with the state. The federal government does not run such airports, although it does lease both Ronald Reagan Washington National and Washington Dulles International to the Metropolitan Washington Airports Authority (www.mwaa.com). A few commercial airports are privately owned—an example is Texas's Fort Worth Alliance Airport (www.allianceairport.com). Regardless of how they are owned, airports (other than military airports) must be certificated by the FAA if they are served by carriers utilizing aircraft with more than 30 seats or scheduled operators flying aircraft with more than nine seats.

While state and county airports generally are immune from suit, municipal airports generally are not. For a sampling of the case law, *see Japan Airlines Co. v. Port Authority of New York and New Jersey*, 178 F.3d 103 (2d Cir. 1999) (bi-state agency had no immunity in suit brought by airline for damage due to snow on runway); *Ludwig v. Learjet, Inc.*, 830 F. Supp. 995 (E.D. Mich. 1993) (City of Detroit was immune in action alleging that crash was caused by a too-short runway); *Anderson v. Alberto-Culver USA, Inc.*, 740 N.E.2d 819 (Ill. Ct. App. 2000), *appeal denied*, 747 N.E.2d 351 (Ill. 2001) (where airplane crashed after falling into ditch along runway, immunity of municipal defendants turned on whether their acts were ministerial or discretionary).

For a further look at airports, see the web sites of the Airports Council International (www.airports.org) and the American Association of Airport Executives (www.aaae.org). *See also Airport*, at en.wikipedia.org/wiki/Airport; Alastair Gordon, *Naked Airport: A Cultural History of the World's Most Revolutionary Structure* (2004); Hugh Pearman, *Airports: A Century of Architecture* (2004); Geza Szurovy, *The American Airport* (2003). In addition, Arthur Hailey's blockbuster novel *Airport* (1968) (made into a movie in 1970 starring Burt Lancaster but now better remembered for George Kennedy's performance as cigar-chomping mechanic Joe Patroni) remains an excellent read. Other popular culture offerings include the film *Die Hard 2* (1990, with Bruce Willis) as well as the short-lived television dramas *LAX* (NBC, 2004–05, with Heather Locklear) and *San Francisco International Airport* (NBC, 1970–71, with Lloyd Bridges).

2. Although the bulk of funding for airport construction and development is locally generated (commonly through the issuance of revenue bonds), federal support has been available since 1946 (when the Federal Airport Act was passed). In more recent times, Congress has enacted such legislation as the Airport and Airway Development Act of 1970 (which established the Airport Development Aid Program), the Airport and Airway Improvement Act of 1982 (the basis for the Airport Improvement Program (AIP)), and the Airport Noise and Capacity Act of 1990. In addition, pursuant to the Airport and Airway Revenue Act of 1970, the Airport and Airway Trust Fund, which is supported by assorted taxes on aviation cargo, fuel, mail, and passen-

ger tickets, has been used to pay for such things as the air traffic control system, navigation aids, a portion of the FAA's operating budget, and qualifying projects under the AIP.

To be eligible for AIP funds, an airport must be included in the National Plan of Integrated Airport Systems (NPIAS), a five-year document prepared by the Secretary of Transportation that identifies airports that are critical to the nation's air transportation needs. The current plan, covering the period 2005 to 2009, identifies more than 3,300 such airports and can be found at www.faa.gov/arp/planning/npias/index.cfm?nav=.

As *Griggs* and *Northwest* point out, however, federal money comes with strings attached. Thus, for example, AIP recipients must provide certain written assurances, including: (a) that their facilities will be available for use by the public on reasonable terms; (b) that they will not unjustly discriminate against any class or type of air service; (c) that they will not confer an exclusive right on any person or entity to conduct any aeronautical activity; (d) that they will charge substantially comparable rates, and impose substantially comparable conditions, on similarly situated entities; (e) that they will seek, to the extent possible, to restrict adjoining and nearby land to compatible uses; and, (f) that they will maintain a current airport layout plan and not make changes to it unless approved by the FAA following appropriate environmental and safety reviews. *See further* 49 U.S.C. §§47106–47107.

Moreover, courts are careful to limit airports to the amounts of money they actually need. *See, e.g., Village of Bensenville v. Federal Aviation Administration*, 376 F.3d 1114 (D.C. Cir. 2004) (no proof that environmental impact study of Chicago's O'Hare International Airport's planned modernization program would cost as much as $110 million). For a further discussion of airport funding, *see* David A. Basil, *Introduction Into the Legal Aspects of General Aviation Law*, 36 Urb. Law. 813 (2004); Anthony Ryan, *How Airline Security Fees in a Post September 11, 2001 Environment are Spiraling Out of Control*, 29 Transp. L.J. 253 (2002); Carolyn P. Meade, Note, *Aviation Taxes: Can We Leave FAA Funding on Auto-Pilot?*, 20 Va. Tax Rev. 191 (2000); Christopher R. Rowley, Comment, *Financing Airport Capital Development: The Aviation Industry's Greatest Challenge*, 63 J. Air L. & Com. 605 (1998).

3. The *Citizens* decision provides a useful overview of the various environmental statutes that govern the siting and building of airport projects, although at least two opinions have disagreed with its conclusion that a federal agency need only consider those alternatives that meet the sponsor's primary purpose. *See City of Bridgeton v. FAA*, 212 F.3d 448 (8th Cir. 2000) (Arnold, J., dissenting), *cert. denied*, 531 U.S. 1111 (2001), and *Simmons v. United States Army Corps of Engineers*, 120 F.3d 664 (7th Cir. 1997).

Some undertakings, such as the construction of a new runway, require the completion of a full "Environmental Impact Statement" (EIS). Others trigger the need for a less-demanding "Environmental Assessment" (EA), which leads to either an EIS or the issuing of a "Finding of No Significant Impact" (FONSI). Still other actions are "categorically excluded" because they "do not individually or cumulatively have a significant effect on the human environment." 40 C.F.R. §1508.4. Although the FAA publishes a list of categorical exclusions, if "extraordinary circumstances" are present an EA is required.

Following the release of either an EIS or a FONSI, the FAA normally prepares a "Record of Decision" (ROD), which is subject to judicial review. *See further Grand Canyon Trust v. Federal Aviation Administration*, 290 F.3d 339 (D.C. Cir. 2002), and *People of the State of California v. United States Department of Transportation*, 260 F.

Supp. 2d 969 (N.D. Cal. 2003). Challenging an airport's construction or expansion plans, however, often requires overcoming standing objections. *See, e.g.*, *Town of Stratford, Connecticut v. Federal Aviation Administration*, 285 F.3d 84 (D.C. Cir.), *rehearing denied*, 292 F.3d 251 (D.C. Cir. 2002) (environmental statutes did not provide a basis for claiming economic damages), and *City of Olmsted Falls, Ohio v. Federal Aviation Administration*, 292 F.3d 261 (D.C. Cir. 2002) (city could not assert the interests of its citizens, but could press for recovery of its own economic injuries).

For a further look at how environmental considerations can affect an airport's plans, *see, e.g.*, Annotation, *Necessity and Sufficiency of Environmental Impact Statements Under §102(2)(c) of National Environmental Policy Act of 1969 (42 U.S.C.A. §4332(2)(c)) in Cases Involving Transportation Projects*, 62 A.L.R. Fed. 664 (1983 & 2004 Supp.); Jeffrey A. Berger, *False Promises: NEPA's Role in Airport Expansions and the Streamlining of the Environmental Review Process*, 18 Envtl. L. & Lit. 279 (2003); Dan Kramer, *How Airport Noise and Airport Privatization Effect Economic Development in Communities Surrounding U.S. Airports*, 31 Transp. L.J. 213 (2004); Andrew C. Mergen, *The Changing Nature of Airport Environmental Litigation*, 18 Air & Space Law. 1 (Winter 2004).

4. As the *Pinczkowski* case explains, landowners whose property is "taken" for airport construction or expansion projects are entitled to "just compensation," which has been held to mean "fair market value." Three types of takings exist: a physical occupation of all or part of the land; a navigation easement to permit overflights; and a "de facto" taking (also known as inverse condemnation), which occurs when the owner retains possession but suffers a diminution in value due to a public act. *See further* Jay M. Zitter, Annotation, *Airport Operations or Flight of Aircraft as Constituting Taking or Damaging of Property*, 22 A.L.R.4th 863 (1983 & 2005 Supp.); Jay M. Zitter, Annotation, *Zoning Regulations Limiting Use of Property Near Airport as Taking of Property*, 18 A.L.R.4th 542 (1982 & 2005 Supp.); Paul Stephen Dempsey, *Local Airport Regulation: The Constitutional Tension Between Police Power, Preemption & Takings*, 11 Penn St. Envtl. L. Rev. 1 (2002); Jeffrey A. Berger, Comment, *Phoenix Grounded: The Impact of the Supreme Court's Changing Preemption Doctrine on State and Local Impediments to Airport Expansion*, 97 Nw. U. L. Rev. 941 (2003); Luis G. Zambrano, Comment, *Balancing the Rights of Landowners with the Needs of Airports: The Continuing Battle Over Noise*, 66 J. Air L. & Com. 445 (2000).

Rather than seek compensation through an inverse condemnation proceeding, some landowners attempt to pursue nuisance or trespass lawsuits against airport owners and users. *See further Vorhees v. Naper Aero Club, Inc.*, 272 F.3d 398 (7th Cir. 2001); *Casey v. Goulian*, 273 F. Supp. 2d 136 (D. Mass. 2003); Jack L. Litwin, Annotation, *Airport Operations or Flight of Aircraft as Nuisance*, 79 A.L.R.3d 253 (1977 & 2004 Supp.).

5. Congress has given the FAA authority to issue regulations governing objects affecting navigable airspace. *See* 49 U.S.C. §44718. As a result, the FAA must be notified of the construction or alteration of any structure that might obstruct aircraft or interfere with navigation equipment or facilities. Upon being informed, the FAA conducts an aeronautical study to determine whether the structure will have a "substantial adverse effect on air navigation." If the answer is "yes," the FAA issues a "hazard determination."

Because it is not meant to have legal consequences, a hazard determination is not considered a taking. *See Breneman v. United States*, 57 Fed. Cl. 571 (2003), *aff'd*, 97 Fed.

Appx. 329 (Fed. Cir.), *cert. denied*, 125 S. Ct. 670 (2004). Yet the practical consequences are serious: local governments will reject a permit application and insurance may be difficult, if not impossible, to obtain. Of course, once a permit is denied, the hazard determination can be challenged in court. *See further BFI Waste Systems of North America, Inc. v. Federal Aviation Administration*, 293 F.3d 527 (D.C. Cir. 2002); *D&F Afonso Realty Trust v. Garvey*, 216 F.3d 1191 (D.C. Cir. 2000); W.E. Shipley, Annotation, *Airport Operator's Rights and Remedies as to Uses of Adjoining Land Interfering With Aircraft Operation*, 25 A.L.R.2d 1454 (1952 & 2004 Supp.).

6. Given their size, cost, and civic importance (the NFL's New York Jets owe their moniker to the city's airfields and, in turn, inspired the naming of the NHL's Winnipeg Jets (now the Phoenix Coyotes)), it is not unusual for airport projects to become embroiled in local politics. *See, e.g.*, David M. Halbfinger, *Atlanta is Divided Over Renaming Airport for Former Mayor*, N.Y. Times, Aug. 13, 2003, at A22 (the proposal, intended to honor Maynard Jackson, the city's first African-American leader, eventually passed). On occasion, however, they gain even wider attention. *See, e.g.*, Michael S. Bennett, *Financing the Chek Lap Kok New Airport: A Case Study in Amending the Sino-British Joint Declaration on Hong Kong*, 9 J. Chinese L. 77 (1995).

7. Although most airport lawsuits occur before the project is built, some take place during or even after the job. Numerous mistakes, for example, delayed by two years the 1995 opening of Denver International Airport (the $4.9 billion successor to Stapleton International Airport), and engineers never managed to get its state-of-the-art baggage system to work (it eventually was removed). *See further* Paul Stephen Dempsey et al., *Denver International Airport: Lessons Learned* (1997), and Kirk Johnson, *Denver Airport Saw the Future. It Didn't Work.*, N.Y. Times, Aug. 27, 2005, at A1. As a result, the airport's early years were plagued by litigation involving, among others, bondholders, contractors, and the government. *See, e.g.*, *Sonnenfeld v. City and County of Denver*, 100 F.3d 744 (10th Cir. 1996), *cert. denied*, 520 U.S. 1228 (1997); *Bangert Brothers Construction Co. v. Americas Insurance Co.*, 888 F. Supp. 1069 (D. Colo.), *aff'd mem.*, 66 F.3d 338 (10th Cir. 1995); *City and County of Denver v. District Court in and for City and County of Denver*, 939 P.2d 1353 (Colo. 1997) (en banc).

Similarly, in May 2004, design and construction flaws caused the roof of Terminal 2E to collapse at Paris's Charles de Gaulle Airport, causing four deaths, just 11 months after the $1.2 billion structure was dedicated. *See further* Craig S. Smith, *Weakened Concrete is Cited in Collapse at Paris Airport*, N.Y. Times, July 7, 2004, at A1. The victims' relatives subsequently announced they would seek $800,000 in damages. *See further* Kristine Kwok, *Airport Tragedy Families to Sue French Government*, S. China Morning Post, Sept. 4, 2004, at 4.

Problem 21

After studying the matter, the FAA concluded that passenger demand at a particular airport was likely to double in the coming decade regardless of whether a second terminal was built. Accordingly, it approved federal funds for the project. In response, the surrounding city filed a lawsuit. As a matter of "common sense," it contends, a new terminal will attract additional users and cause increased congestion, noise, pollution, and traffic. The FAA disagrees, insisting that location, runway capacity, and ticket prices, but not terminal size or gate availability, determine how many people use an airport. Given these arguments, how should the court rule? *See City of Los Angeles v. Federal Aviation Administration*, 138 F.3d 806 (9th Cir. 1998).

C. USE

CITY OF BURBANK v. LOCKHEED AIR TERMINAL INC.

411 U.S. 624 (1973)

Justice DOUGLAS delivered the opinion of the Court.

The Court in Cooley v. Board of Wardens, 12 How. 299, first stated the rule of pre-emption which is the critical issue in the present case. Speaking through Mr. Justice Curtis, it said:

> Now the power to regulate commerce, embraces a vast field, containing not only many, but exceedingly various subjects, quite unlike in their nature; some imperatively demanding a single uniform rule, operating equally on the commerce of the United States in every port; and some, like the subject now in question, as imperatively demanding that diversity, which alone can meet the local necessities of navigation.... Whatever subjects of this power are in their nature national, or admit only of one uniform system, or plan or regulation, may justly be said to be of such a nature as to require exclusive legislation by Congress.

Id., at 319.

This suit brought by appellees asked for an injunction against the enforcement of an ordinance adopted by the City Council of Burbank, California, which made it unlawful for a so-called pure jet aircraft to take off from the Hollywood-Burbank Airport between 11 p.m. of one day and 7 a.m. the next day, and making it unlawful for the operator of that airport to allow any such aircraft to take off from that airport during such periods. The only regularly scheduled flight affected by the ordinance was an intrastate flight of Pacific Southwest Airlines originating in Oakland, California, and departing from Hollywood-Burbank Airport for San Diego every Sunday night at 11:30.

The District Court found the ordinance to be unconstitutional on both Supremacy Clause and Commerce Clause grounds. 318 F.Supp. 914. The Court of Appeals affirmed on the grounds of the Supremacy Clause both as respects pre-emption and as respects conflict. 457 F.2d 667. The case is here on appeal. 28 U.S.C. § 1254(2). We noted probable jurisdiction. 409 U.S. 840. We affirm the Court of Appeals.

The Federal Aviation Act of 1958, 72 Stat. 731, 49 U.S.C. § 1301 et seq., as amended by the Noise Control Act of 1972, 86 Stat. 1234, and the regulations under it, 14 CFR pts. 71, 73, 75, 77, 91, 93, 95, 97, are central to the question of pre-emption.

Section 1108(a) of the Federal Aviation Act, 49 U.S.C. § 1508(a), provides in part, "The United States of America is declared to possess and exercise complete and exclusive national sovereignty in the airspace of the United States...." By §§ 307(a), (c) of the Act, 49 U.S.C. §§ 1348(a), (c), the Administrator of the Federal Aviation Administration (FAA) has been given broad authority to regulate the use of the navigable airspace, "in order to insure the safety of aircraft and the efficient utilization of such airspace" and "for the protection of persons and property on the ground...."

The Solicitor General, though arguing against pre-emption, concedes that as respects "airspace management" there is pre-emption. That, however, is a fatal concession, for as the District Court found: "The imposition of curfew ordinances on a nationwide basis would result in a bunching of flights in those hours immediately preceding the curfew. This bunching of flights during these hours would have the twofold effect of increasing an already serious congestion problem and actually increasing, rather than relieving, the noise problem by increasing flights in the period of greatest annoyance to surrounding communities. Such a result is totally inconsistent with the objectives of the federal statutory and regulatory scheme." It also found "(t)he imposition of curfew ordinances on a nationwide basis would cause a serious loss of efficiency in the use of the navigable airspace."

Curfews such as Burbank has imposed would, according to the testimony at the trial and the District Court's findings, increase congestion, cause a loss of efficiency, and aggravate the noise problem. FAA has occasionally enforced curfews. See Virginians for Dulles v. Volpe, D.C., 344 F. Supp. 573. But the record shows that FAA has consistently opposed curfews, unless managed by it, in the interests of its management of the "navigable airspace."

As stated by Judge Dooling in American Airlines v. Hempstead, D.C., 272 F.Supp. 226, 230, aff'd, 2 Cir., 398 F.2d 369:

> The aircraft and its noise are indivisible; the noise of the aircraft extends outward from it with the same inseparability as its wings and tail assembly; to exclude the aircraft noise from the Town is to exclude the aircraft; to set a ground level decibel limit for the aircraft is directly to exclude it from the lower air that it cannot use without exceeding the decibel limit.

The Noise Control Act of 1972, which was approved October 27, 1972, provides that the Administrator "after consultation with appropriate Federal, State, and local agencies and interested persons" shall conduct a study of various facets of the aircraft noise problem and report to the Congress within nine months, i.e., by July 1973. The 1972 Act, by amending §611 of the Federal Aviation Act, also involves the Environmental Protection Agency (EPA) in the comprehensive scheme of federal control of the aircraft noise problem. Under the amended §611(b)(1), 86 Stat. 1239, 49 U.S.C. §1431(b)(1), FAA, after consulting with EPA, shall provide "for the control and abatement of aircraft noise and sonic boom, including the application of such standards and regulations in the issuance, amendment, modification, suspension, or revocation of any certificate authorized by this title." Section 611(b)(2), as amended, 86 Stat. 1239, 49 U.S.C. §1431(b)(2), provides that future certificates for aircraft operations shall not issue unless the new aircraft noise requirements are met. Section 611(c)(1), as amended, provides that not later than July 1973 EPA shall submit to FAA proposed regulations to provide such "control and abatement of aircraft noise and sonic boom" as EPA determines is "necessary to protect the public health and welfare." FAA is directed within 30 days to publish the proposed regulations in a notice of proposed rulemaking. Within 60 days after that publication, FAA is directed to commence a public hearing on the proposed rules. Section 611(c)(1). That subsection goes on to provide that within "a reasonable time after the conclusion of such hearing and after consultation with EPA," FAA is directed either to prescribe the regulations substantially as submitted by EPA, or prescribe them in modified form, or publish in the Federal Register a notice that it is not prescribing any regulation in response to EPA's submission together with its reasons therefor.

Section 611(c)(2), as amended, also provides that if EPA believes that FAA's action with respect to a regulation proposed by EPA "does not protect the public health and welfare from aircraft noise or sonic boom," EPA shall consult with FAA and may request FAA to review and report to EPA on the advisability of prescribing the regulation originally proposed by EPA. That request shall be published in the Federal Register; FAA shall complete the review requested and report to EPA in the time specified together with a detailed statement of FAA's findings and the reasons for its conclusion and shall identify any impact statement filed under § 102(2)(c) of the National Environmental Policy Act of 1969, 83 Stat. 853, 42 U.S.C. § 4332(2)(c), with respect to FAA's action. FAA's action, if adverse to EPA's proposal, shall be published in the Federal Register.

Congress did not leave FAA to act at large but provided in § 611(d), as amended, particularized standards:

> In prescribing and amending standards and regulations under this section, the FAA shall—
>
> (1) consider relevant available data relating to aircraft noise and sonic boom, including the results of research, development, testing, and evaluation activities conducted pursuant to this Act and the Department of Transportation Act;
>
> (2) consult with such Federal, State, and interstate agencies as [it] deems appropriate;
>
> (3) consider whether any proposed standard or regulation is consistent with the highest degree of safety in air commerce or air transportation in the public interest;
>
> (4) consider whether any proposed standard or regulation is economically reasonable, technologically practicable, and appropriate for the particular type of aircraft, aircraft engine, appliance, or certificate to which it will apply; and
>
> (5) consider the extent to which such standard or regulation will contribute to carrying out the purposes of this section.

The original complaint was filed on May 14, 1970; the District Court entered its judgment November 30, 1970; and the Court of Appeals announced its judgment and opinion March 22, 1972—all before the Noise Control Act of 1972 was approved by the President on October 27, 1972. That Act reaffirms and reinforces the conclusion that FAA, now in conjunction with EPA, has full control over aircraft noise, pre-empting state and local control.

There is, to be sure, no express provision of pre-emption in the 1972 Act. That, however, is not decisive. As we stated in Rice v. Santa Fe Elevator Corp., 331 U.S. 218, 230:

> Congress legislated here in a field which the States have traditionally occupied.... So we start with the assumption that the historic police powers of the States were not to be superseded by the Federal Act unless that was the clear and manifest purpose of Congress.... Such a purpose may be evidenced in several ways. The scheme of federal regulation may be so pervasive as to make reasonable the inference that Congress left no room for the States to supplement it.... Or the Act of Congress may touch a field in which the federal interest is so dominant that the federal system will be assumed to preclude enforcement of state laws on the same subject.... Likewise, the object sought to be obtained by the federal law and the character of obligations imposed by it may reveal the same purpose.... Or the state policy may produce a result inconsistent with the objective of the federal statute.

It is the pervasive nature of the scheme of federal regulation of aircraft noise that leads us to conclude that there is pre-emption. As Mr. Justice Jackson stated, concurring in Northwest Airlines, Inc. v. Minnesota, 322 U.S. 292, 303:

> Federal control is intensive and exclusive. Planes do not wander about in the sky like vagrant clouds. They move only by federal permission, subject to federal inspection, in the hands of federally certified personnel and under an intricate system of federal commands. The moment [an air] ship taxis onto a runway it is caught up in an elaborate and detailed system of controls.

Both the Senate and House Committees included in their Reports clear statements that the bills would not change the existing pre-emption rule. The House Report stated: "No provision of the bill is intended to alter in any way the relationship between the authority of the Federal Government and that of the State and local governments that existed with respect to matters covered by section 611 of the Federal Aviation Act of 1958 prior to the enactment of the bill." The Senate Report stated: "States and local governments are preempted from establishing or enforcing noise emission standards for aircraft unless such standards are identical to standards prescribed under this bill. This does not address responsibilities or powers of airport operators, and no provision of the bill is intended to alter in any way the relationship between the authority of the Federal government and that of State and local governments that existed with respect to matters covered by section 611 of the Federal Aviation Act of 1958 prior to the enactment of the bill."

These statements do not avail appellants. Prior to the 1972 Act, §611(a) provided that the [FAA] Administrator "shall prescribe and amend such rules and regulations as he may find necessary to provide for the control and abatement of aircraft noise and sonic boom." 82 Stat. 395. Under §611(b)(3) the Administrator was required to "consider whether any proposed standard, rule, or regulation is consistent with the highest degree of safety in air commerce or air transportation in the public interest." 82 Stat. 395. When the legislation which added this section to the Federal Aviation Act was considered at Senate hearings, Senator Monroney (the author of the 1958 Act) asked Secretary of Transportation Boyd whether the proposed legislation would "to any degree preempt State and local government regulation of aircraft noise and sonic boom." The Secretary requested leave to submit a written opinion, and in a letter dated June 22, 1968, he stated:

> The courts have held that the Federal Government presently preempts the field of noise regulation insofar as it involves controlling the flight of aircraft.... H.R. 3400 would merely expand the Federal Government's role in a field already preempted. It would not change this preemption. State and local governments will remain unable to use their police powers to control aircraft noise by regulating the flight of aircraft.

According to the Senate Report, it was "not the intent of the committee in recommending this legislation to effect any change in the existing apportionment of powers between the Federal and State and local governments," and the Report concurred in the views set forth by the Secretary in his letter.

The Senate version of the 1972 Act as it passed the Senate contained an express preemption section. But the Senate version never was presented to the House. Instead, the Senate passed, with amendments, the House version; the House, also with amendments, then concurred in the Senate amendments. The Act as passed combined provisions of both the House and Senate bills on the subject that each had earlier approved.

When the blended provisions of the present Act were before the House, Congressman Staggers, Chairman of the House Committee on Interstate and Foreign Commerce, in urging the House to accept the amended version, said:

> I cannot say what industry's intention may be, but I can say to the gentleman what my intention is in trying to get this bill passed. We have evidence that across America some cities and States are trying to pass noise regulations. Certainly we do not want that to happen. It would harass industry and progress in America. That is the reason why I want to get this bill passed during this session.

When the House approved the blended provisions of the bill, Senator Tunney moved that the Senate concur. He made clear that the regulations to be considered by EPA for recommendation to FAA would include:

> proposed means of reducing noise in airport environments through the application of emission controls on aircraft, the regulation of flight patterns and aircraft and airport operations, and modifications in the number, frequency, or scheduling of flights (as well as) ... the imposition of curfews on noisy airports, the imposition of flight path alternations in areas where noise was a problem, the imposition of noise emission standards on new and existing aircraft—with the expectation of a retrofit schedule to abate noise emissions from existing aircraft—the imposition of controls to increase the load factor on commercial flights, or other reductions in the joint use of airports, and such other procedures as may be determined useful and necessary to protect public health and welfare.

The statements by Congressman Staggers and Senator Tunney are weighty ones. For Congressman Staggers was Chairman of the House Committee on Interstate and Foreign Commerce which submitted the Noise Control Act and Report; and Senator Tunney was a member of the Senate Committee on Public Works, which submitted the Act and Report. When the President signed the bill he stated that "many of the most significant sources of noise move in interstate commerce and can be effectively regulated only at the federal level."

Our prior cases on pre-emption are not precise guidelines in the present controversy, for each case turns on the peculiarities and special features of the federal regulatory scheme in question. Cf. Hines v. Davidowitz, 312 U.S. 52; Huron Portland Cement Co. v. Detroit, 362 U.S. 440. Control of noise is of course deep-seated in the police power of the States. Yet the pervasive control vested in EPA and in FAA under the 1972 Act seems to us to leave no room for local curfews or other local controls. What the ultimate remedy may be for aircraft noise which plagues many communities and tens of thousands of people is not known. The procedures under the 1972 Act are under way. In addition the Administrator has imposed a variety of regulations relating to takeoff and landing procedures and runway preferences. The Federal Aviation Act requires a delicate balance between safety and efficiency, 49 U.S.C. § 1348(a), and the protection of persons on the ground. 49 U.S.C § 1348(c). Any regulations adopted by the Administrator to control noise pollution must be consistent with the "highest degree of safety." 49 U.S.C. § 1431(d)(3). The interdependence of these factors requires a uniform and exclusive system of federal regulation if the congressional objectives underlying the Federal Aviation Act are to be fulfilled.

If we were to uphold the Burbank ordinance and a significant number of municipalities followed suit, it is obvious that fractionalized control of the timing of takeoffs and landings would severely limit the flexibility of FAA in controlling air traffic flow. The difficulties of scheduling flights to avoid congestion and the concomitant decrease in safety would be compounded. In 1960 FAA rejected a proposed restriction on jet operations at the Los Angeles airport between 10 p.m. and 7 a.m. because such restrictions could "create critically serious problems to all air transportation patterns." 25 Fed.Reg. 1764–1765. The complete FAA statement said:

> The proposed restriction on the use of the airport by jet aircraft between the hours of 10 p.m. and 7 a.m. under certain surface wind conditions has also been reevaluated and this provision has been omitted from the rule. The practice of prohibiting the use of various airports during certain specific hours could create critically serious problems to all air transportation patterns. The network of airports throughout the United States and the constant availability of these airports are essential to the maintenance of a sound air transportation system. The continuing growth of public acceptance of aviation as a major force in passenger transportation and the increasingly significant role of commercial aviation in the nation's economy are accomplishments which cannot be inhibited if the best interest of the public is to be served. It was concluded therefore that the extent of relief from the noise problem which this provision might have achieved would not have compensated the degree of restriction it would have imposed on domestic and foreign air commerce.

This decision, announced in 1960, remains peculiarly within the competence of FAA, supplemented now by the input of EPA. We are not at liberty to diffuse the powers given by Congress to FAA and EPA by letting the States or municipalities in on the planning. If that change is to be made, Congress alone must do it.

Affirmed.

Justice REHNQUIST, with whom Justice STEWART, Justice WHITE, and Justice MARSHALL join, dissenting.

The Court concludes that congressional legislation dealing with aircraft noise has so "pervaded" that field that Congress has impliedly pre-empted it, and therefore the ordinance of the city of Burbank here challenged is invalid under the Supremacy Clause of the Constitution. The Court says that the 1972 "Act reaffirms and reinforces the conclusion that FAA, now in conjunction with EPA, has full control over aircraft noise, pre-empting state and local control." Yet the House and Senate committee reports explicitly state that the 1972 Act to which the Court refers was not intended to alter the balance between state and federal regulation which had been struck by earlier congressional legislation in this area. The House Report, H.R.Rep.No.92-842, in discussing the general pre-emptive effect of the entire bill, stated:

> The authority of State and local government to regulate use, operation, or movement of products is not affected at all by the bill. (The preemption provision discussed in this paragraph does not apply to aircraft. See discussion of aircraft noise below.)

Id., at 8. The report went on to state specifically:

> No provision of the bill is intended to alter in any way the relationship between the authority of the Federal Government and that of State and local governments that existed with respect to matters covered by section 611 of the Federal Aviation Act of 1958 prior to the enactment of the bill.

Id., at 10.

The report of the Senate Public Works Committee, S.Rep.No.92-1160, expressed the identical intent with respect to pre-emption:

> States and local governments are preempted from establishing or enforcing noise emission standards for aircraft (see American Airlines v. Hempstead, 272 F. Supp. 226 (EDNY 1967)), unless such standards are identical to standards prescribed under this bill. This does not address responsibilities or powers of airport operators, and no provision of the bill is intended to alter in any way the relationship between the authority of the Federal government and that of State and local governments that existed with respect to matters covered by section 611 of the Federal Aviation Act of 1958 prior to the enactment of the bill.

Id., at 10–11.

In the light of these specific congressional disclaimers of pre-emption in the 1972 Act, reference must necessarily be had to earlier congressional legislation on the subject. It was on the basis of these earlier enactments that the Court of Appeals concluded that Congress had pre-empted the field from state or local regulation of the type that the city of Burbank enacted.

The Burbank ordinance prohibited jet takeoffs from the Hollywood-Burbank Airport during the late evening and early morning hours. Its purpose was to afford local residents at least partial relief, during normal sleeping hours, from the noise associated with jet airplanes. The ordinance in no way dealt with flights over the city, cf. American Airlines, Inc. v. Town of Hempstead, 272 F. Supp. 226 (EDNY 1967), aff'd, 398 F.2d 369 (CA2 1968), cert. denied, 393 U.S. 1017 (1969), nor did it categorically prohibit all jet takeoffs during those hours.

Appellees do not contend that the noise produced by jet engines could not reasonably be deemed to affect adversely the health and welfare of persons constantly exposed to it; control of noise, sufficiently loud to be classified as a public nuisance at common law, would be a type of regulation well within the traditional scope of the police power possessed by States and local governing bodies. Because noise regulation has traditionally been an area of local, not national, concern, in determining whether congressional legislation has, by implication, foreclosed remedial local enactments "we start with the assumption that the historic police powers of the States were not to be superseded by the Federal Act unless that was the clear and manifest purpose of Congress." Rice v. Santa Fe Elevator Corp., 331 U.S. 218 (1947). This assumption derives from our basic constitutional division of legislative competence between the States and Congress; from "due regard for the presuppositions of our embracing federal system, including the principle of diffusion of power not as a matter of doctrinaire localism but as a promoter of democracy...." San Diego Building Trades Council v. Garmon, 359 U.S. 236 (1959). Unless the requisite pre-emptive intent is abundantly clear, we should hesitate to invalidate state and local legislation for the added reason that "the state is powerless to remove the ill effects of our decision, while the national government, which has the ultimate power, remains free to remove the burden." Penn Dairies, Inc. v. Milk Control Comm'n, 318 U.S. 261 (1943).

Since Congress' intent in enacting the 1972 Act was clearly to retain the status quo between the federal regulation and local regulation, a holding of implied pre-emption of the field depends upon whether two earlier congressional enactments, the Federal Aviation Act of 1958, 72 Stat. 731, 49 U.S.C. § 1301 et seq., and the 1968 noise abatement amendment to that Act, 49 U.S.C. § 1431, manifested the clear intent to preclude local regulations that our prior decisions require.

The 1958 Act was intended to consolidate in one agency in the Executive Branch the control over aviation that had previously been diffused within that branch. The paramount substantive concerns of Congress were to regulate federally all aspects of air safety, see, e.g., 49 U.S.C. § 1422 and, once aircraft were in "flight," airspace management, see, e.g., 49 U.S.C. §1348(a). See S.Rep.No.1811, 85th Cong., 2d Sess., 5–6, 13–15, U.S.Code Cong. & Admin. News 1958, p. 3741. While the Act might be broad enough to permit the Administrator to promulgate takeoff and landing rules to avoid excessive noise at certain hours of the day, see 49 U.S.C. § 1348(c), Congress was not concerned with the problem of noise created by aircraft and did not intend to preempt its regulation. Furthermore, while Congress clearly intended to pre-empt the States from regulating aircraft in flight, the author of the bill, Senator Monroney, specifically stated that FAA would not have control "over the ground space" of airports.

The development and increasing use of civilian jet aircraft resulted in congressional concern over the noise associated with those aircraft. Hearings were held over a period of several years, resulting in a report but no legislation. The report of the House Committee on Interstate and Foreign Commerce, H.R.Rep.No.36, 88th Cong., 1st Sess., shows clearly that the 1958 Act was thought by at least some in Congress neither to pre-empt local legislative action to alleviate the growing noise problem, nor to prohibit local curfews:

> Until Federal action is taken, the local governmental authorities must be deemed to possess the police power necessary to protect their citizens and property from the unreasonable invasion of aircraft noise. The wisdom of exercising such power or the manner of the exercise is a problem to be resolved on the local governmental level.
>
> Airports in the United States, as a general rule, are operated by a local governmental authority, either a municipality, a county, or some independent unit. These airport operators are closer, both geographically and politically, to the problem of the conflict of interests between those citizens who have been adversely affected by the aircraft noise and the needs of the community for air commerce. Some airport operators have exercised the proprietary right to restrict in a reasonable manner, the use of any runway by limiting either the hours during which it may be used or the types of civil transport aircraft that may use it.

H.R.Rep.No.36, 88th Cong., 1st Sess., 27.

Several years after the conclusion of these hearings, Congress enacted the 1968 noise abatement amendment, 82 Stat. 395, which added §611 to the 1958 Act, 49 U.S.C. § 1431, and which was the first congressional legislation dealing with the problem of aircraft noise. On its face, § 611 as added by the 1968 amendment neither pre-empted the general field of regulation of aircraft noise nor dealt specifically with the more limited question of curfews. The House Committee on Interstate and Foreign Commerce, after reciting the serious proportions of the problem, outlined the type of federal regulation that the Act sought to impose:

> The noise problem is basically a conflict between two groups or interests. On the one hand, there is a group who provide various air transportation services. On the other hand there is a group who live, work, and go to schools and churches in communities near airports. The latter group is frequently burdened to the point where they can neither enjoy nor reasonably use their land because of noise resulting from aircraft operations. Many of them derive no direct benefit from the aircraft operations which create the unwanted noise. Therefore, it is easy to understand why they complain, and complain most ve-

> hemently. The possible solutions to this demanding and vexing problem which appear to offer the most promise are (1) new or modified engine and airframe designs, (2) special flight operating techniques and procedures, and (3) planning for land use in areas adjacent to airports so that such land use will be most compatible with aircraft operations. This legislation is directed toward the primary problem; namely, reduction of noise at its source.

H.R.Rep.No.1463, 90th Cong., 2d Sess., 4.

Far from indicating any total pre-emptive intent, the House Committee observed:

> Rather, the committee expects manufacturers, air carriers, all other segments of the aviation community, and State and local civic and governmental entities to continue and increase their contributions toward the common goal of quiet.

Ibid.

The Senate Commerce Committee's view of the House bill followed a similar vein:

> This investment by the industry is representative of one of the avenues of approach to aircraft noise reduction, that is, the development of aircraft which generate less noise. Another approach to noise reduction is through the establishment of special flight operating techniques and procedures. The third principal control technique which merits serious consideration is the planning for land use in areas near airports so as to make such use compatible with aircraft operations. This is a matter largely within the province of State and local governments. While all of these techniques must be thoroughly studied and employed, the first order of business is to stop the escalation of aircraft noise by imposing standards which require the full application of noise reduction technology.
>
> A completely quiet airplane will not be developed within the foreseeable future. However, with the technological and regulatory means now at hand, it is possible to reduce both the level and the impact of aircraft noise. Within the limits of technology and economic feasibility, it is the view of the committee that the Federal Government must assure that the potential reductions are in fact realized.

S.Rep.No.1353, 90th Cong., 2d Sess., 2–3, U.S.Code Cong. & Admin. News 1968, p. 2690.

With specific emphasis on pre-emption, the Senate Committee observed:

> The bill is an amendment to a statute describing the powers and duties of the Federal Government with respect to air commerce. As indicated earlier in this report, certain actions by State and local public agencies, such as zoning to assure compatible land use, are a necessary part of the total attack on aircraft noise. In this connection, the question is raised whether this bill adds or subtracts anything from the powers of State or local governments. It is not the intent of the committee in recommending this legislation to effect any change in the existing apportionment of powers between the Federal and State and local governments.
>
> In this regard, we concur in the following views set forth by the Secretary in his letter to the committee of June 22, 1968:
>
> > The courts have held that the Federal Government presently preempts the field of noise regulation insofar as it involves controlling the flight of aircraft. Local noise control legislation limiting the permissible noise level of

> all overflying aircraft has recently been struck down because it conflicted with Federal regulation of air traffic. American Airlines v. Town of Hempstead, 272 F. Supp. 226 (U.S.D.C., E.D.N.Y., 1966). The court said, at 231, "The legislation operates in an area committed to Federal care, and noise limiting rules operating as do those of the ordinance must come from a Federal source." H.R. 3400 would merely expand the Federal Government's role in a field already preempted. It would not change this preemption. State and local governments will remain unable to use their police powers to control aircraft noise by regulating the flight of aircraft.
>
> However, the proposed legislation will not affect the rights of a State or local public agency, as the proprietor of an airport, from issuing regulations or establishing requirements as to the permissible level of noise which can be created by aircraft using the airport. Airport owners acting as proprietors can presently deny the use of their airports to aircraft on the basis of noise considerations so long as such exclusion is nondiscriminatory.
>
> Just as an airport owner is responsible for deciding how long the runways will be, so is the owner responsible for obtaining noise easements necessary to permit the landing and takeoff of the aircraft. The Federal Government is in no position to require an airport to accept service by larger aircraft and, for that purpose, to obtain longer runways. Likewise, the Federal Government is in no position to require an airport to accept service by noisier aircraft, and for that purpose to obtain additional noise easements. The issue is the service desired by the airport owner and the steps it is willing to take to obtain the service. In dealing with this issue, the Federal Government should not substitute its judgment for that of the States or elements of local government who, for the most part, own and operate our Nation's airports. The proposed legislation is not designed to do this and will not prevent airport proprietors from excluding any aircraft on the basis of noise considerations.
>
> Of course, the authority of units of local government to control the effects of aircraft noise through the exercise of land use planning and zoning powers is not diminished by the bill.
>
> Finally, since the flight of aircraft has been preempted by the Federal Government, State and local governments can presently exercise no control over sonic boom. The bill makes no change in this regard.

Id., at 6–7.

In terms of pre-emption analysis, the most reasonable reading of § 611 appears to be that it was enacted to enable the Federal Government to deal with the noise problem created by jet aircraft through study and regulation of the "source" of the problem—the mechanical and structural aspects of jet and turbine aircraft design. The authority to "prescribe and amend such rules and regulations as he may find necessary to provide for the control and abatement of aircraft noise and sonic boom," 49 U.S.C. § 1431(a), while a broad grant of authority to the Administrator, cannot fairly be read as prohibiting the States from enacting every type of measure, which might have the effect of reducing aircraft noise, in the absence of a regulation to that effect under this section. The statute established exclusive federal control of the technological methods for reducing the output of noise by jet aircraft, but that is a far cry from saying that it prohibited any local regulation of the times at which the local airport might be available for the use of jet aircraft.

The Court of Appeals found critical to its decision the distinction between the local government as an airport proprietor and the local government as a regulatory agency, which was reflected in the views of the Secretary of Transportation outlined in the Senate Report on the 1968 Amendment. Under its reasoning, a local government unit that owned and operated an airport would not be pre-empted by §611 from totally, or, as here, partially, excluding noisy aircraft from using its facilities, but a municipality having territorial jurisdiction over the airport would be pre-empted from enacting an ordinance having a similar effect. If the statute actually enacted drew this distinction, I would of course respect it. But since we are dealing with "legislative history," rather than the words actually written by Congress into law, I do not believe it is of the controlling significance attributed to it by the court below.

The pre-emption question to which the Secretary's letter was addressed related to "the field of noise regulation insofar as it involves controlling the flight of aircraft," and thus included types of regulation quite different from that enacted by the city of Burbank that would be clearly precluded. See American Airlines, Inc. v. Town of Hempstead, supra. But more important is the highly practical consideration that the Hollywood-Burbank Airport is probably the only non-federal airport in the country used by federally certified air carriers that is not owned and operated by a state or local government. There is no indication that this fact was brought to the attention of the Senate Committee, or that the Secretary of Transportation was aware of it in framing his letter. It simply strains credulity to believe that the Secretary, the Senate Committee, or Congress intended that all airports except the Hollywood-Burbank Airport could enact curfews.

Considering the language Congress enacted into law, the available legislative history, and the light shed by these on the congressional purpose, Congress did not intend either by the 1958 Act or the 1968 Amendment to oust local governments from the enactment of regulations such as that of the city of Burbank. The 1972 Act quite clearly intended to maintain the status quo between federal and local authorities. The legislative history of the 1972 Act, quite apart from its concern with avoiding additional pre-emption, discloses a primary focus on the alteration of procedures within the Federal Government for dealing with problems of aircraft noise already entrusted by Congress to federal competence. The 1972 Act set up procedures by which the Administrator of EPA would have a role to play in the formulation and review of standards promulgated by FAA dealing with noise emissions of jet aircraft. But because these agencies have exclusive authority to reduce noise by promulgating regulations and implementing standards directed at one or several of the causes of the level of noise, local governmental bodies are not thereby foreclosed from dealing with the noise problem by every other conceivable method.

A local governing body that owns and operates an airport is certainly not, by the Court's opinion, prohibited from permanently closing down its facilities. A local governing body could likewise use its traditional police power to prevent the establishment of a new airport or the expansion of an existing one within its territorial jurisdiction by declining to grant the necessary zoning for such a facility. Even though the local government's decision in each case were motivated entirely because of the noise associated with airports, I do not read the Court's opinion as indicating that such action would be prohibited by the Supremacy Clause merely because the Federal Government has undertaken the responsibility for some aspects of aircraft noise control. Yet if this may be done, the Court's opinion surely does not satisfactorily explain why a local governing body may not enact a far less "intrusive" ordinance such as that of the city of Burbank.

The history of congressional action in this field demonstrates, I believe, an affirmative congressional intent to allow local regulation. But even if it did not go that far, that history surely does not reflect "the clear and manifest purpose of Congress" to prohibit the exercise of "the historic police powers of the States" which our decisions require before a conclusion of implied preemption is reached. Clearly Congress could pre-empt the field to local regulation if it chose, and very likely the authority conferred on the Administrator of FAA by 49 U.S.C. § 1431 is sufficient to authorize him to promulgate regulations effectively pre-empting local action. But neither Congress nor the Administrator has chosen to go that route. Until one of them does, the ordinance of the city of Burbank is a valid exercise of its police power.

The District Court found that the Burbank ordinance would impose an undue burden on interstate commerce, and held it invalid under the Commerce Clause for that reason. Neither the Court of Appeals nor this Court's opinion, in view of their determination as to pre-emption, reached that question. The District Court's conclusion appears to be based, at least in part, on a consideration of the effect on interstate commerce that would result if all municipal airports in the country enacted ordinances such as that of Burbank. Since the proper determination of the question turns on an evaluation of the facts of each case, see, e.g., Bibb v. Navajo Freight Lines, Inc., 359 U.S. 520 (1959), and not on a predicted proliferation of possibilities, the District Court's conclusion is of doubtful validity. The Burbank ordinance did not affect emergency flights, and had the total effect of prohibiting one scheduled commercial flight each week and several additional private flights by corporate executives; such a result can hardly be held to be an unreasonable burden on commerce. Since the Court expresses no opinion on the question, however, I refrain from any further analysis of it.

CITY OF NAPLES AIRPORT AUTHORITY v. FEDERAL AVIATION ADMINISTRATION

409 F.3d 431 (D.C. Cir. 2005)

RANDOLPH, Circuit Judge.

This is a petition for judicial review of an order of the Associate Administrator of the Federal Aviation Administration—the FAA—disqualifying the City of Naples Airport Authority from receiving grants under the Airport and Airway Improvement Act of 1982, 49 U.S.C. § 47107 et seq. (the "Improvement Act"). In order to be eligible for grants, an airport must be "available for public use on reasonable conditions and without unjust discrimination." 49 U.S.C. § 47107(a)(1). The FAA determined that a noise restriction on certain aircraft imposed an unreasonable condition on public use of the Naples Municipal Airport.

The City of Naples is a southern Florida community, bounded on three sides by Collier County and on the west by the Gulf of Mexico. It has 23,000 permanent residents and 13,000 seasonal residents. The Naples airport is located within the city's boundaries. Portions of the airport abut the county line. The city leases the land to the Airport Authority, a five-member independent entity created by the Florida legislature for the purpose of operating and maintaining the Airport.

Neither the city nor the county provides funds to subsidize the airport, and no tax or other fiscal revenues are earmarked for the airport. The Airport Authority has no zoning power. The city is responsible for zoning in the areas surrounding the airport within its municipal boundary. The county is responsible for zoning all other property immediately adjacent to the airport.

In 1999, in response to complaints from residents, the Airport Authority commissioned a study to examine noise exposure from aircraft in the area surrounding the airport. The Airport Noise and Capacity Act of 1990, 49 U.S.C. §47521 et seq.—the Noise Act—governs the manner in which individual airports may adopt noise restrictions on aircraft. Aircraft are classified roughly according to the amount of noise they produce, from Stage 1 for the noisiest to Stage 3 for those that are relatively quieter. Section 47524(b) of the Noise Act sets forth certain procedural requirements with which an airport must comply in order to restrict Stage 2 aircraft. Section 47524(c) contains similar procedural requirements for restrictions on Stage 3 aircraft, but also requires FAA approval of any Stage 3 restriction.

The Airport Authority's study found that approximately 1,400 residents were exposed to noise levels in excess of [the Day-Night Average Sound Level] ("DNL") [of] 60 [decibels] ("dB") and that a restriction on all Stage 2 aircraft would affect only one percent of aircraft operations at the airport, while considerably reducing the number of people exposed to significant noise levels. Effective January 1, 2001, the Airport Authority adopted a ban against all Stage 2 aircraft.

Although the Airport Authority complied with the procedural requirements of §47524(b) of the Noise Act, the FAA ruled that the Stage 2 ban was "unreasonable" and, therefore, contrary to the Airport Authority's obligation under §47107(a)(1) of the Improvement Act. In the FAA's view, the Airport Authority failed to show that "noncompatible land uses exist in the DNL 60 dB contour."

The Airport Authority maintains §47524(b) of the Noise Act removed the FAA's power to withhold grants on the basis of an "unreasonable" Stage 2 ban. There is no dispute that before passage of the Noise Act in 1990, the FAA could withhold grants if an airport operator's noise restriction violated the grant assurances in §47107 of the Improvement Act. See City & County of San Francisco v. FAA, 942 F.2d 1391, 1394–95 (9th Cir.1991). Under §47533—the savings clause of the Noise Act—the law in effect before its enactment shall remain unaffected, "[e]xcept as provided by section 47524." 49 U.S.C. §47533(1).

Although §47524 of the Noise Act is silent about grant eligibility in the face of a Stage 2 restriction, the Airport Authority claims the provision removed the FAA's preexisting power to withhold grants when such a restriction proved unreasonable. One of the arguments is framed this way: If Congress had wanted to allow FAA review of such restrictions, Congress knew how to say as much. As cast, the "argument is weak." Doris Day Animal League v. Veneman, 315 F.3d 297, 299 (D.C.Cir.2003). It may "be made in any case in which there is a fair dispute about the meaning of a statute." Id. "Congress almost always could write a provision in a way more clearly favoring one side—or the other.... Its failure to speak with clarity signifies only that there is room for disagreement about the statute's meaning." Id.

If §47524(b) did not preclude FAA substantive review of Stage 2 noise restrictions, the Authority continues, there is no explaining §47524(c). Subsection (c) requires (with an exception) the FAA to find a Stage 3 restriction "reasonable" and not an undue burden on interstate commerce before it can become effective. If the FAA already could review Stage 3 restrictions for reasonableness when it doled out grants pursuant to the Improvement Act, §47524(c) would be "surplusage." Brief of Petitioner at 30. This would be a fair argument if the premise were accurate. But it is not. On its face,

§47524(c) gives the FAA considerably more power than it had when reviewing an airport operator's Stage 3 restriction at the grant stage. For one thing, the Stage 3 restriction cannot go into effect without the FAA's say-so. For another thing, subsection (c)'s requirement of FAA approval is not tied to grants; grants or not, no airport operator can impose a Stage 3 restriction unless the FAA gives its approval.

Still, the Authority has a point. Because in one subsection Congress explicitly required FAA approval of Stage 3 restrictions but in another subsection did not provide for substantive review of Stage 2 restrictions, this is some indication that Congress intended to allow airport operators to promulgate Stage 2 restrictions free from FAA review. See Russello v. United States, 464 U.S. 16, 23 (1983). But there is a contrary inference one may draw from another subsection of §47524 of the Noise Act. Section 47524(e) states that when an airport operator adopts an FAA-approved Stage 3 restriction in compliance with §47524(c), the operator becomes eligible for grants under the Improvement Act. In other words, the FAA may not withhold grants under the Improvement Act on the basis of a Stage 3 noise restriction imposed under §47524(c) of the Noise Act. No similar provision exists for Stage 2 restrictions. In the absence of such a provision, one may infer that Congress intended to continue allowing the FAA to withhold grants on the basis of a Stage 2 restriction even if the operator complies with the procedural requirements of §47524(b).

The Airport Authority also invokes some legislative history of the Noise Act. Congress considered but did not enact other versions of the Noise Act requiring FAA review of Stage 2 restrictions and conditioning grant eligibility on compliance with these requirements. 136 CONG. REC. 25,376–82 (1990) (Senate Bill 3094). The Authority also points to an exchange between Senators Lautenberg and Ford in committee to show that Congress understood an airport operator would be permitted to impose restrictions on Stage 2 aircraft without FAA approval and "without risking the loss of" grants under the Improvement Act. 136 CONG. REC. 36,252 (1990). These excerpts are not particularly telling. Both speak only to the FAA's power under §47524; neither deals with the FAA's pre-existing power to withhold grants under §47107(a)(1).

Because the Noise Act does not clearly reveal whether the FAA may withhold grants when an airport operator imposes an unreasonable Stage 2 noise restriction, we shall defer to the FAA's determination that it retains that power under the Improvement Act. The agency's interpretation is linguistically permissible, and it represents a reasonable resolution of statutory uncertainty, particularly in light of §47524(e) of the Noise Act and its savings clause in §47533. See Tax Analysts v. IRS, 117 F.3d 607, 613–16 (D.C.Cir.1997).

The question remains whether there is substantial evidence to support the FAA's ruling that the Authority's Stage 2 ban is unreasonable, or whether the FAA acted arbitrarily and capriciously, which amounts to the same thing in this context. Ass'n of Data Processing Serv. Orgs. v. Bd. of Governors of the Fed. Reserve Sys., 745 F.2d 677, 683 (D.C.Cir.1984). The ruling rested on the FAA's finding that noise levels between DNL 60 dB and DNL 65 dB were not incompatible with residential land use near the airport. The FAA promulgated non-binding guidelines regarding noise levels and land use in 1984. Those guidelines stated that levels below DNL 65 dB are generally compatible with all land use. Generally means not always. The guidelines thus acknowledged that "responsibility for determining the acceptable and permissible land uses and the relationship between specific properties and specific noise contours rests with the local authorities," to which the FAA added that its guidelines "are not intended to substitute federally determined land uses for those determined to be appropriate by local authorities in response to locally determined needs and values in achieving noise compatible land uses." 49 Fed.Reg. 49,260, 49,275 (Dec. 18, 1984).

The FAA cited two reasons why the Airport Authority's selection of DNL 60 dB as the maximum acceptable noise level was unreasonable: (1) local ordinances did not "unequivocally prohibit" development in areas subjected to noise levels of DNL 60 dB or higher; and (2) the area presently subjected to DNL 60 dB was not "uniquely quiet."

As to the first, the FAA found that the City of Naples did not really believe that DNL 60 dB exposed residents to a significant noise level because it had not completely banned development in the DNL 60 dB contour. (The evidence showed, however, that neither the city nor the county had approved any residential development in that area after the Airport Authority completed the study of sound levels. Amici Brief of City of Naples and Collier County at 14.) If the city did not believe that DNL 60 dB was a "significant noise threshold," the FAA reasoned, then the Airport Authority failed to demonstrate that "a land use compatibility problem exists in the DNL 60 dB" area. Without explaining how a local government could demonstrate the existence of a land use compatibility problem, the FAA stated that the City of Naples had merely adopted the DNL 60 dB level as a prophylactic against airport expansion and land use in the DNL 65 dB area. But there is no evidence—aside from speculation by an FAA employee—to support the FAA's conclusion about the city's motives. The record shows that during these proceedings the City of Naples did adopt an ordinance forbidding all noise in excess of DNL 60 dB, including music and construction equipment; that the area is a retirement community; that the area is one of outdoor living; and that aircraft noise is the leading cause of noise complaints. This evidence, much of which the FAA never addressed, all supports the conclusion that DNL 60 dB level is considered a significant noise threshold in the City of Naples.

There is also substantial evidence, including sound measurement data from the Airport Authority study, that Naples is a quiet community. The FAA concluded that the area is not "uniquely quiet," but it did not define what it meant by "uniquely." The FAA provided no data to contradict the study data. It did not perform any sound analysis. And it did not otherwise collect information on the subject. The FAA's Director of Airport Safety and Standards "inferred" from the fact that some residents lived in multi-family dwellings near multi-lane roads that the area was not "uniquely quiet," and the FAA's final decision simply stated that this "inference" was "reasonable." No mention of the sound measurement data was made.

The amici brief of the City of Naples and Collier County forcefully summarizes the state of the record. "Even if it had defined the term 'uniquely quiet,' the FAA did not cite any factual support for its finding that [Naples is] not a 'uniquely quiet' community. The FAA did not visit the area as part of its investigation, did not perform any analysis of the local soundscape, did not contact any residents or local officials to obtain any information on this subject, and did not cross-examine the principal author of the Part 161 Study on this subject. Instead, the FAA Associate Administrator relied on the anecdotal information that there was some noise in the area—largely the typical suburban noise associated with streets and shops—in an attempt to establish that ambient noise levels must have been high. Moreover, the Associate Administrator ignored the Airport Authority Executive Director's actual testimony, wherein he explained that the existence of multi-family housing, streets and shops did not negate the quiet nature of the community.

From this and other evidence, the Associate Administrator should have concluded that [the Naples] community revolves around this particular environment, that [its] economy is based almost entirely on the climate and amenities offered by [its] outdoor environment, and that [its] residents and visitors have an expectation of quiet throughout virtually the entire community. There was absolutely no basis for the Associate Administrator to conclude that the sound environment in this community does not support the Airport Authority's decision to ban Stage 2 aircraft." Amici Brief of City of Naples and Collier County at 19–20.

The Airport Authority and the City of Naples introduced ample evidence—much of which went unrebutted—demonstrating that the Stage 2 ban was justified. Because the FAA's conclusion to the contrary is not supported by substantial evidence, the petition for review is granted, the FAA's order is vacated, and the case is remanded to the FAA.

WESTERN AIR LINES, INC. v. PORT AUTHORITY OF NEW YORK AND NEW JERSEY

817 F.2d 222 (2d Cir. 1987),
cert. denied, 485 U.S. 1006 (1988)

FEINBERG, Chief Judge.

Western Air Lines, Inc. (Western) appeals from a judgment of the United States District Court for the Southern District of New York, after a bench trial before John M. Cannella, J., that dismissed its complaint seeking an injunction. 658 F.Supp. 952 (S.D.N.Y.1986). Western argues that a "perimeter rule," promulgated by the Port Authority of New York and New Jersey (the Authority), is preempted by a provision of the Airline Deregulation Act, 49 U.S.C. § 1305(a)(1), and violates the substantive provisions of two other aviation statutes, 49 U.S.C. §§ 1349(a) and 2210(a). Western also appeals from the dismissal of its claims for enforcement of the aviation statutes under 42 U.S.C. § 1983. Substantially for the reasons stated by the district court, we affirm the dismissal of the complaint.

Background

The Authority owns and operates LaGuardia, Kennedy International and Newark International Airports. In order to reduce ground congestion at LaGuardia, by far the smallest of the three airports, the Authority uses a perimeter rule. The current rule prohibits, with certain exceptions, non-stop flights to or from LaGuardia in excess of 1500 miles. The Authority believes that business travelers create considerably less airport congestion than vacationers and uses the perimeter rule to encourage the use of LaGuardia by business people, who often make relatively short trips, and the use of Newark and Kennedy for vacation flights.

The Federal Aviation Administration (the FAA) limits flights to and from LaGuardia through the use of "slots," each of which authorizes one landing or takeoff by the holder during a thirty-minute period. Western obtained several slots at LaGuardia as a result of a lottery conducted by the FAA. Western sought to use these slots for three daily non-stop flights in each direction between LaGuardia and Salt Lake City, where Western has a "hub." A hub is an airport used by an airline as the central point of its connecting flights. Airlines use hubs to connect two cities that cannot be served economically by non-stop flights. On the basis of its perimeter rule, however, the Authority refused

Western permission to conduct LaGuardia-Salt Lake City operations, since Salt Lake City is more than 1,500 miles from LaGuardia.

In the district court, Western's effort to enjoin the perimeter rule centered on three federal aviation statutes: 49 U.S.C. § 1305, which limits local authority to regulate airlines' "rates, routes or services"; 49 U.S.C. § 2210(a), which requires an airport proprietor receiving federal funds to make its facilities available on a reasonable and non-discriminatory basis; and 49 U.S.C. § 1349(a), which prohibits such proprietors from granting exclusive access to any airline. Western claimed that there is an implied private right of action under each statute; Western also relied on 42 U.S.C. § 1983. Western also claimed that under the Supremacy Clause, the perimeter rule was preempted by section 1305(a)(1).

The district court, relying on our holding in Montauk-Caribbean Airways, Inc. v. Hope, 784 F.2d 91 (2d Cir.), cert. denied, —U.S.—, 107 S.Ct. 248 (1986), ruled that the statutes relied on by Western do not provide a private right of action. In addition, the court dismissed Western's claims under section 1983 for lack of prosecution. The district court did find that Western could assert its preemption claim based on the Supremacy Clause. On the merits, however, it found that the Authority's perimeter rule was not preempted by section 1305.

Discussion

In Montauk-Caribbean, we held that there are no implied private rights of action to enforce sections 1349(a) and 1305(a). 784 F.2d at 97–98. We are, of course, bound by that decision, fairly construed. The district court correctly recognized that our analysis in Montauk-Caribbean applies equally to a suit claiming an implied right of action to enforce section 2210(a). See also Interface Group, Inc. v. Massachusetts Port Authority, 816 F.2d 9, 14–16 (1st Cir.1987); Arrow Airways, Inc. v. Dade County, 749 F.2d 1489, 1490–91 (11th Cir.1985). We also held in Montauk-Caribbean that sections 1305(a) and 1349(a) cannot be enforced through section 1983. 784 F.2d at 98. That holding would require dismissal of Western's section 1983 claims with respect to sections 1305(a) and 1349(a) in this case. We need not decide, however, whether there is a persuasive basis for reaching a different conclusion with respect to section 2210(a), see New York Airlines, Inc. v. Dukes County, 623 F.Supp. 1435 at 1443–48 (D.Mass.1985), because Judge Cannella did not abuse his discretion in holding that Western did not press its section 1983 claims in the district court.

Despite the lack of a private right of action to enforce the statutes, the district court held that Western could bring a Supremacy Clause challenge to the perimeter rule by claiming that the rule is preempted by section 1305(a)(1). The Authority argues that the absence of a private right to enforce section 1305(a)(1) requires dismissal of Western's Supremacy Clause claim. The Authority argues that Montauk-Caribbean settles the issue because the preemption claim based directly on section 1305(a)(1) that the Montauk-Caribbean court refused to recognize implicitly relied on the Supremacy Clause. The Authority also argues that as a general matter, the Supremacy Clause by itself cannot create a right of action. Although we recognize the potential anomaly of rejecting a private right of action to enforce a statute while allowing a claim under the Supremacy Clause that the statute preempts a local regulation, we find that Western properly brought its Supremacy Clause claim.

Turning to the merits, we affirm on the basis of Judge Cannella's well-reasoned opinion, to which we refer the reader, holding that the Authority's perimeter rule is not preempted by section 1305. Although, as Judge Cannella recognized, the perimeter rule may be a regulation "relating to ... routes" within the meaning of section 1305(a)(1), we agree with his conclusion that the rule, at least when enacted by a multi-airport proprietor such as the Authority, falls within the proprietary powers of airport operators exempted from preemption by section 1305(b)(1). Cf. City of Houston v. FAA, 679 F.2d 1184, 1196 (5th Cir.1982).

Western's other contentions require little discussion. In its reply brief on appeal Western argues, apparently for the first time, that the FAA, by granting slots, has preempted any regulation of those slots by the Authority. The statute, however, authorizes the Authority to regulate those slots in accordance with its proprietary powers. Since the district judge did not err in finding that the perimeter rule is within those proprietary powers, Western's contention fails. Western's remaining claims, that it was improperly denied an opportunity to cross-examine the Authority's witness at trial and that it is entitled to a new trial because the district court made inadequate findings of fact and conclusions of law, are without merit.

CITY OF LOS ANGELES v. UNITED STATES DEPARTMENT OF TRANSPORTATION

165 F.3d 972 (D.C. Cir.),
rehearing en banc denied,
179 F.3d 937 (D.C. 1999),
cert. denied, 528 U.S. 1074 (2000)

SILBERMAN, Circuit Judge.

The City of Los Angeles increased the landing fees at Los Angeles International Airport, and the airlines challenged those fees as unreasonable before the Department of Transportation. The DOT set aside the increased fees, reasoning that the City's attempt to recoup its "opportunity costs" through the fees was impermissible as a matter of statute. In City of Los Angeles v. DOT, 103 F.3d 1027 (D.C.Cir.1997), we rejected that statutory interpretation and remanded for the DOT to consider the opportunity cost issue as a matter of policy. The DOT did so, concluding that the City's claimed entitlement to recover its opportunity costs was unreasonable, and rejected the fees. The City petitions for review. We deny the petition.

I.

Until 1993, the City of Los Angeles, pursuant to a contractual agreement with the airlines, established landing fees at the Los Angeles International Airport (LAX) based on a residual methodology. Under that technique, the City estimated the revenue and cost attributable to non-aeronautical operations—such as parking contracts and concession franchising—for the coming fiscal year. Expected non-aeronautical surplus, if any, was then applied toward the anticipated cost of aeronautical operations. Landing fees were set (based on estimated landed weight) at a sufficient level to make up for the remaining aeronautical cost. In 1992, the last year in which the City used this methodology, the fee was $.51 per 1,000 pounds of landed weight. In 1993, the expiration of the City's contract with the airlines opened the door for the City to adopt the potentially more lucrative compensatory fee methodology. That approach treats aeronautical operations separately from non-aeronautical operations; the airport sets landing fees at a sufficient level to compensate it for the entirety of its aeronautical costs, and any surplus or deficit from non-aeronautical operations is irrelevant.

The City also decided in 1993, for the first time, to include in its estimated aeronautical costs a charge reflecting the current annual fair market rental value of the land on which the airfield rests. The City thought itself entitled to recover this "opportunity cost," for only then would the City be compensated fully for the cost of using the land as an airport instead of pursuing its alternative opportunity to earn profits by renting the land. The City appraised the current fair market value of the land at $150,000 per acre. (The City had purchased most of the 1,780.3 acres on which the airport is built over 50 years ago at an average price of $2,427 per acre.) Adjusting for the effects of federal grants and converting to an annual rental value, the City arrived at a figure of $8,348 per acre per year, or $14,861,900 per year for the entire 1,780.3 acres occupied by the airport. Putting this fair market rental value, among other costs, into its compensatory fee calculation, the City computed a landing fee of $1.56 per 1,000 pounds of landed weight (effective July 1, 1993), an increase of more than $1.00 over the 1992 fee. When contract negotiations looking to a compensatory fee agreement between the City and the airlines broke down, the City unilaterally imposed the $1.56 fee by ordinance, informing the airlines that they could not land at LAX unless they paid the increased fee.

The airlines challenged the fee increase pursuant to an expedited administrative procedure in which the Department of Transportation has authority to set aside unreasonable fees. The Department determined the fee unreasonable, reasoning that the Anti-Head Tax Act's "requirement of reasonable fees ... mandat[es] the use of historic cost for airfield land"—i.e., the original acquisition cost of the land on which the airport was built—and thereby forbids consideration of opportunity cost. Los Angeles Int'l Airport Rates Proceeding, Order No. 95-6-36, at 24 (June 30, 1995). In the meantime, the City had announced a new landing fee in 1995 of $2.06 per 1,000 pounds of landed weight (effective July 1, 1995), again including among its costs its claimed "opportunity cost," i.e., the forgone fair rental value of the airfield land. The airlines challenged this fee before the DOT, and the Department set the fee aside for the same reason given in rejecting the 1993 fee. Second Los Angeles Int'l Airport Rates Proceeding, Order No. 95-12-33 (December 22, 1995).

In City of Los Angeles v. DOT (LAX I), 103 F.3d 1027 (D.C.Cir.1997), we granted the City's petition for review of the Department's decision regarding the 1993 fee. (We had stayed proceedings relating to the 1995 fee pending our review of the Department's decision on the 1993 fee.) We concluded that the Department had no basis for its view that the Anti-Head Tax Act forbade the consideration of opportunity costs in determining the reasonableness of landing fees and permitted only the consideration of historic costs. Id. at 1032. Although we noted that "[h]istoric cost is ... one permissible measure of costs in cost-of-service rate-making," we rejected the "Secretary's view of historic cost as the apodictically indicated measure of 'actual cost.'" Id. Accordingly, we vacated the Secretary's decision and remanded "for his fuller consideration of the respective merits of the historic cost and [opportunity cost] methodologies here at issue." Id. We granted the Department's request for a remand of the 1995 fee proceeding to conduct a similar policy evaluation of the competing methodologies.

On remand, the DOT consolidated the 1993 and 1995 fee proceedings. As before, the Department held that the 1993 and 1995 fees should be set aside because it was unreasonable for the City to recover its claimed "opportunity cost." Los Angeles Int'l Airport Rates Proceeding and Second Los Angeles Int'l Airport Rates Proceeding (Remand Decision), Order 97-12-31 (December 23, 1997). But this time the Department rested its decision explicitly on policy grounds. It pointed to the airport's obligation as a federal airport grant recipient to keep the airport "available for public use," 49 U.S.C. §47107(a)(1), and to another provision that bars a grant recipient from making any alteration to the airport's layout unless the Secretary decides that the change will not "adversely affect the safety, utility, or efficiency of the airport," id. §47107(a)(16)(c). See Remand Decision at 13. These provisions forbid the City from converting the airfield land to rental property; the City at present has no lawful opportunity to use the land in any capacity other than as an airport. (Although the Department and the City seem to disagree on precisely when the City's grant assurance obligation will expire, it is undisputed that the grant assurance obligation is currently in force.) The Department therefore concluded that it would be unreasonable for the City to recover compensation through its landing fees for a "lost opportunity" that does not lawfully exist. See id. at 14.

Alternatively, the DOT held that even if the City were thought to incur opportunity costs, the fees should be set aside because the City's "benefits" from operating LAX already sufficed to cover the City's opportunity costs. The Department viewed the City, rather than the airport, as the relevant economic actor; pursuing the rental opportunity would require the City either to build a new airport (or expand an existing minor airport such as Long Beach or Orange County), or else simply to go without a major airport. The latter option, according to the Department, would entail an enormous loss to the City; a 1992 study quantified the benefits of LAX "in terms of jobs (402,000); direct, indirect, and induced economic impacts ($37 billion per year); and state and local taxes ($1.7 billion per year)." Id. at 17. And the City would sacrifice the current revenue the City earns from its airfield and non-airfield activities at LAX. In the Department's view, these losses far outweigh any reasonable forecast of rental revenue—the City's estimate of that revenue, recall, was a mere $14,861,900 per year. In short, the stream of benefits from using the land as rental property rather than as an airport would be smaller than the stream of benefits from operating the airport—i.e., the opportunity cost of using the land as an airport was already being covered. And the Department thought the calculus would not be much different if the City, rather than going without a major airport, attempted to build a new major airport or expand existing minor airports. Relying on the City's own appraisal firm's report that the "relocation of the Los Angeles International Airport (LAX) is practically impossible" given the paucity of alternative airport development sites and the prohibitive costs of acquiring such a site, the Department concluded that once these costs were taken into account, the net profit from renting the LAX land would again be outweighed by the benefits of using the LAX land as an airport. Id. at 18–19. In the end, the Department concluded that the City's analysis of its opportunity costs—which treated only the airport as the relevant economic actor and considered only the annual rental income of $14,861,900—was overly simplistic, and therefore rejected the City's attempt to include its self-described "opportunity costs" in calculating its landing fees.

II.

The City and the Department before us principally dispute the reasonableness of the City's methodology of fee calculation, not the reasonableness of the magnitude of the resulting fees.

A.

Reiterating its first reason for rejecting the City's fee methodology, the Department submits that it is unreasonable to attempt to include as an airfield cost the "opportunity cost" of employing the land as an airport rather than as rental property, for the proposed opportunity does not lawfully exist at present. As one of the members of the panel observed, in paraphrasing the DOT's argument, the City is like an owner of a hot dog stand who claims his opportunity cost is the revenue he would earn by selling cocaine rather than hot dogs. The City contends, however, that the Department has adopted an erroneous conception of opportunity cost; for an economist, we are told, the present impossibility of pursuing the opportunity to rent the airfield land does not mean that no opportunity cost has been incurred.

At bottom, the parties' dispute as to the concept of opportunity cost seems to rest on a single question: Should the legal barrier to pursuing the opportunity be treated as immutable? If opportunity costs are measured as of now and the grant assurance obligation is viewed as fixed, then the Department's view would seem inevitable. For then the City would have no opportunity to use the land in any non-airport capacity—the City at least would face enormous transition costs (the cost of violating the law or perhaps of buying a release from the obligation) in pursuing the opportunity, which alone could render the potential profit from that opportunity small or even negative. But if we ignore (i.e., treat as changeable at zero cost) the present legal hurdle to pursuing the opportunity, then the City's position is much stronger.

To be sure, an economist formulating an efficient plan for regulating the City's monopoly over landing space might well take the City's view, treating all regulatory tools—including existing grant assurance obligations—as easily changeable. Cf. WILLIAM J. BAUMOL & J. GREGORY SIDAK, TRANSMISSION PRICING AND STRANDED COSTS IN THE ELECTRIC POWER INDUSTRY 53 (1995). But the airlines' expert suggested otherwise when he testified that "[s]ometimes the opportunity is virtually nil, in which case there is no opportunity cost." In any event, that some or many economists would disapprove of the Department's approach does not answer the question presented to us. In reviewing the Department's order, we do not sit as a panel of referees on a professional economics journal, but as a panel of generalist judges obliged to defer to a reasonable judgment by an agency acting pursuant to congressionally delegated authority. See Air Canada v. DOT, 148 F.3d 1142, 1151 (D.C.Cir.1998); LAX I, 103 F.3d at 1031 (citing Northwest Airlines v. County of Kent, 510 U.S. 355, 366–68 (1994)).

The City argues that the Department's "no opportunity, hence no opportunity cost" rationale attempts an "end run" around our holding in LAX I that the Anti-Head Tax Act, 49 U.S.C. §40116(e)(2), does not itself proscribe consideration of opportunity costs in establishing reasonable landing fees. See LAX I, 103 F.3d at 1032. The City explains that under the Remand Decision, no airport that accepts federal grants (and thus gives grant assurances) could ever justify the recovery of opportunity costs—the result is a "per se rule" against using opportunity costs in calculating landing fees, which is another way for the Department to claim that it is legally mandated to reject the opportunity cost methodology. But the Department did not say that it was obliged to take into account the federal grants. Even if it were, in LAX I we addressed only the Anti-Head Tax Act and the expedited review provision, see LAX I, 103 F.3d at 1032 ("Nothing in the Anti-Head Tax Act or [the expedited review provision] ... prescribes an accounting rather than an economic conception of cost in airport ratemaking."), and did not analyze any argument based upon the federal airport grant provision.

Intervenor Airports Council International (ACI) points to a different alleged problem with the Department's "no opportunity, hence no opportunity costs" rationale: ACI submits that DOT has retroactively added new conditions to the City's grant assurances by relying on those grant assurances to deprive the City of the ability to recover its opportunity costs, which ACI claims conflicts with the "clear statement" requirement of Pennhurst State School & Hospital v. Halderman, 451 U.S. 1, 17 (1981). But we do not view the Department's reasoning as adding new conditions to the grant. Rather, the Department focused on a consequence of an unambiguously imposed condition—that the airport would be kept open for public use—that was present from the outset.

B.

Even were we to hold the Department's first rationale unlawful, we would uphold its order. We cannot say—and the City does not seriously argue—that the DOT's alternative rationale, that if the City is deemed to incur opportunity costs, those costs are already covered by the existing "benefits" enjoyed by the City, is an unreasonable one. See Air Canada, 148 F.3d at 1142; LAX I, 103 F.3d at 1031. The City does argue that the Department's "comprehensive opportunity cost analysis" rationale runs into a separate legal problem. By taking into account the current non-airfield revenue at LAX in deciding whether the City's opportunity costs are presently covered, it is claimed that the Department deprives the City of its right to use the compensatory fee methodology by forbidding the City from valuing its airfield assets without considering non-airfield revenues. The compensatory fee methodology, the City reminds us, was recognized by the Supreme Court in Northwest Airlines, 510 U.S. at 369, and codified by Congress, see 49 U.S.C. §47129(a)(2) ("A fee subject to a determination of reasonableness under this section may be calculated pursuant to either a compensatory or residual fee methodology or any combination thereof."). This is a clever argument, but not persuasive because the Department in no sense adopted a general requirement that airports must credit their non-airfield surpluses toward their airfield costs. The DOT is only taking into account non-airfield revenues, as well as all other economic benefits the City enjoys, in determining whether Los Angeles really has an uncovered opportunity cost. It is the City itself, by using the opportunity costs concept, that has invited the Department to think broadly about how such costs should be measured. And we cannot hold that it was unreasonable for the DOT, when faced with a demand for an economic analysis, to consider factors that an economist might take into account.

* * *

For the foregoing reasons, the petition for review is denied.

PARK SHUTTLE N FLY, INC. v. NORFOLK AIRPORT AUTHORITY

352 F. Supp. 2d 688 (E.D. Va. 2004)

JACKSON, District Judge.

The Court held a bench trial in the above-captioned matter on September 9, 2004. Having conducted a trial and thoroughly reviewed the evidence, arguments, and records in this case, the Court finds that this case is ripe for decision. For the reasons stated below, the Court awards judgment for the DEFENDANT.

I. PROCEDURAL HISTORY AND FACTUAL FINDINGS

A. Procedural History

The Plaintiff, Park Shuttle N Fly, Inc. ("Park Shuttle"), brought suit on June 30, 2003 alleging that the Defendant, Norfolk Airport Authority ("Authority"), had imposed an invalid privilege fee upon it for its use of the airport's facilities. The complaint alleged violations of the Due Process, Equal Protection, and Commerce clauses of the United States Constitution. The complaint stemmed from an Authority regulation imposed in May 2003 that required off-airport parking operators to pay a fee of 8% of the operators' gross monthly revenue for the privilege of accessing airport property to pick up or discharge customers. The Plaintiff alleged that this fee was different from the lump sum fee that other courtesy vehicle operators were required to pay, including hotels, taxis, and limousine services, among others. It also alleged that the amount of fee the Authority imposed was an "arbitrary, discriminatory, and artificial classification" that imposed an undue burden on interstate commerce and violated the due process and equal protection clauses of the Constitution. (Pl. Compl. at ¶ 11).

The Defendant filed a Motion to Dismiss on August 18, 2003 on the grounds that Plaintiff's complaint failed to state a claim upon which relief can be granted under Federal Rule of Civil Procedure 12(b)(6), and in the alternative for Summary Judgment on the Commerce Clause claim. On February 6, 2004 this Court granted Defendant's Motion to Dismiss Plaintiff's Equal Protection claim which alleged that Park Shuttle was treated differently than hotels, and the Due Process Claim. It denied Defendant's Motion to Dismiss the challenge to the amount of user fee charged and to the prohibition of Park Shuttle to pick up passengers wh[o] do not have prior arrangements with the company. It also denied the Motion to Dismiss and Summary Judgment on the Commerce Clause claim.

The Court also made several findings that are relevant to the analysis here. The Court found that the revenues Plaintiff paid to Defendant constitute a usage fee rather than a state-imposed tax. Park Shuttle N Fly, Inc. v. Norfolk Airport Auth., No. 2:03cv461, at *7 (February 6, 2004). In addition, the Court found that state law allows the Authority to impose usage fees of some kind, thus establishing a legitimate purpose for the regulation.

B. Factual Findings

1. Stipulated Facts

The Plaintiff, Park Shuttle, is a duly organized and existing Virginia corporation engaged in the business of operating a parking lot in close proximity to the Norfolk International Airport ("Airport"), which parking lot is used by persons traveling in interstate commerce by using the flight facilities at said Airport. (Final Pre-Trial Order at ¶ 1). The Norfolk Airport Authority ("Authority") is a political subdivision of the Commonwealth of Virginia and is an independent body that owns and operates the Airport pursuant to state law and the Code and Charter of the City of Norfolk. For purposes of this litigation, the Authority operates in its proprietary capacity and not in its governmental or regulatory capacity. (Final Pre-Trial Order at ¶ 2). The Authority is governed by a Board of Commissioners (the "Board"), which oversees the general operation and management of the Airport. At all relevant times, the Chairman of the Board is and has been Richard D. Roberts. As Chairman of the Board, Mr. Roberts is familiar with the overall operational, business, and financial aspects of the Airport and the Authority. Mr. Roberts presides at its meetings and activities. The other members of the Board are: Peter G. Decker, Jr., Esquire; Louis F. Ryan, Esquire; Thomas P. Host, III; Dr. Harold J. Cobb, Jr.; Robert D. Jack, Jr.; Gus J. James, II, Esquire; Robert T. Taylor; and Howard M. Webb, Sr. (Final Pre-Trial Order at ¶ 3). At all material times, the Executive Director of the Authority is and has been Kenneth R. Scott. As Executive Director, Mr. Scott is the highest-ranking employee and officer of the Authority. Mr. Scott reports to the Board. Mr. Scott is responsible for all day-to-day operations and management of the Airport, as well as strategic and financial planning. (Final Pre-Trial Order at ¶ 4).

The Airport is served by major airlines, including American, Continental, Delta, Northwest, Southwest, United, U.S. Airways, or their subsidiaries and affiliates. From 1998 through 2002, on average, approximately 3,079,470 passengers flew into and out of the Airport per year. This figure does not include people who come to the Airport to meet passengers or for other purposes. With the exception of 2001 (during which the September 11 terrorist attacks occurred), the number of passengers has increased every year. (Final Pre-Trial Order at ¶ 6). All passengers arriving at and departing from said Airport use automotive surface transportation for purposes of ingress and egress to and from the Airport facilities. (Final Pre-Trial Order at ¶ 7). Automotive surface transportation at the Airport, other than personal automobiles, consists of common carrier buses, limousines, taxi cabs, shuttles, and vehicles commonly denominated as "courtesy vehicles," which pick up and discharge customers of hotels, parking lots, motels, and car rental agencies. (Final Pre-Trial Order at ¶ 8).

A substantial portion of the traveling passengers using the facilities of the Airport reach the facilities by driving their automobiles or by taking limousines, taxi cabs, shuttles and courtesy vehicles. (Final Pre-Trial Order at ¶ 9). The Authority owns and operates the parking facilities located on Airport property. There are three parking lots and three parking garages on the Airport, containing a total of approximately 6,800 spaces. (Final Pre-Trial Order at ¶ 10).

At present, Park Shuttle operates the only known off-Airport parking facility. The Park Shuttle lot is located on Military Highway, approximately 1.5 miles from the main entrance to the Airport. (Final Pre-Trial Order at ¶ 11). The travelers who park their automobiles off the Airport on Park Shuttle's facility are then provided transportation to and from Park Shuttle's parking lot and the Airport by means of Park Shuttle's courtesy vehicles. Plaintiff's courtesy vehicles also transport its customers' luggage and drop off Park Shuttle's customers and luggage at the appropriate check-in and baggage check-in facility. The Authority's parking facility provides no such transportation of customers' luggage to the appropriate airline terminal. (Final Pre-Trial Order at ¶ 12). On an annual basis, more than 90% of Park Shuttle's revenues are generated from customers who are parking on Park Shuttle's property for the purpose of accessing the Airport and thereby traveling in interstate commerce. If the Airport did not exist, Plaintiff would have too few, if any, customers to operate its parking facility. (Final Pre-Trial Order at ¶ 13). Hotels located near the Airport provide courtesy vehicles to transport customers to the Airport. (Final Pre-Trial Order at ¶ 14).

On May 22, 2003, at its regularly scheduled meeting, the Board of Commissioners of the Authority adopted the Resolution Establishing Regulations and Fees for Off-Airport Public Parking Operators at Norfolk International Airport ("Resolution"). (Final Pre-Trial Order at ¶ 15). The Resolution provides, among other things, that all off-Airport parking operators shall pay a fee of 8% of the operator's gross monthly revenue derived from its customers who are transported to or from the Airport (the "Privilege Fee") for the privilege of accessing Airport property to pick up or discharge customers. The Resolution went into effect on July 1, 2003. (Final Pre-Trial Order at ¶ 16). At present, the Privilege Fee does not apply to vehicles operated by hotels, or to limos, taxi cabs or any other private or public vans transporting passengers to the Airport. Rather, such other businesses pay a different permit fee. (Final Pre-Trial Order at ¶ 17). The Authority has imposed a privilege fee of 8% of gross revenues for off-Airport rental car companies. At present, all rental car companies are located on the Airport and pay fees pursuant to concession agreements with the Authority. However, the Privilege Fee would apply to vehicles operated by an off-Airport rental car company in the event such a company were to open for business. (Final Pre-Trial Order at ¶ 18). The Authority does not require itself to pay a percentage of its gross revenue as required by the Authority of Park Shuttle. (Final Pre-Trial Order at ¶ 19).

In establishing the Privilege Fee, the Authority considered several factors, including, among others, the following: a) under federal law, and under mandates from the Federal Aviation Administration ("FAA") imposed pursuant to such law, the Airport is required to be self-sustaining. These requirements are also contained in the FAA Grant Assurances by which the Authority is bound. Thus, the Authority must maximize revenue in order to comply with these federal mandates; b) in order to attract airlines and maintain service, the Airport's rates and charges to airlines must be competitive; c) the Authority's expenses to operate the Airport have been increasing every year for the past five years. From fiscal year 1998–1999 through fiscal year 2002–2003, the Authority's expenses increased by approximately 7.6% annually. (The Authority fiscal year runs from July 1 through June 30.) The projected expenses for fiscal year 2003–2004 are expected to increase 42% over fiscal year 2002–2003; d) the predominant reasons for the increases in the Authority's expenses are the expansion of the Airport to accommodate the increasing volume of passengers and the additional security measures required as a result of the terrorist attacks of September 11, 2001. The Authority's only enterprise is the Airport; it does not have other businesses to offset such increased expenses; e) the Authority elected to impose the Privilege Fee in the form of a percentage of gross revenue because an increase in the receipts of an off-Airport parking operator corresponds to increased use of the Airport's facilities by the off-Airport parking operator; f) in selecting the 8% figure for the Privilege Fee, the Authority found that it was within the range charged by other airport operators, some of whom charge as much as 10%; g) the information on other airports was obtained from a survey entitled "2002 Ground Transportation Vehicle Fees Paid to Airports" compiled by the Airport Ground Transportation Association ("AGTA"), under the supervision of Ray Mundy, Ph.D., of the University of Missouri at St. Louis Center for Transportation Studies. The survey reveals that at least 16 airports across the United States charge percentage-based fees ranging from 4% to 10% to off-airport parking operators; h) the AGTA is a national organization comprised of major airport operators, ground transportation service providers, and manufacturers of ground transportation vehicles; i) also, in 2000, the Authority commissioned Leigh Fisher Associates, an airport management consulting firm, to study the types of fees charged to off-airport parking operators. The Leigh Fisher study also concluded that the range of fees charged by other airports was from 4% to 10%; j) in addition, the Authority considered that the vast majority, if not all, of Park Shuttle's customers are derived from the Airport; k) the Authority considered that Park Shuttle's marketing and advertising efforts, on their face, attempt to connect Park Shuttle with the Airport. For example, Park Shuttle's roadside billboard and the sign at its facility feature the phrase "Airport Valet Parking." Likewise, Park Shuttle's newspaper advertisements use the words "Airport Parking;" l) Park Shuttle has chosen to inextricably link itself to the Airport and has obtained its customers from the Airport; m) Park Shuttle not only uses the actual Airport roads, but Park Shuttle also benefits from the Airport as a whole in terms of its customer base and revenue source; n) other businesses such as hotels, limousines, and taxis, have other sources of revenue. For example, hotels exist primarily to provide lodging and conference services, and transportation between the hotels and the Airport is generally complimentary; o) the Authority does not provide the services offered by these other businesses, while the Authority does provide Airport parking; p) Park Shuttle's business is materially different from hotels, motels, taxicabs and limousine operators in that Park Shuttle's primary purpose is to provide parking, while the other businesses have primary purposes other than parking; q) other businesses such as hotels enhance the flow of passengers through the Airport by hosting conferences and by providing lodging for travelers. Off-airport parking operators such as Park Shuttle have the opposite effect: they compete directly with the Authority; r) at present, the Authority has excess parking capacity on average of at least 2000 spaces per day; s) in deciding to impose the Privilege Fee, the Authority also considered its need to retire debts incurred in connection with the operation and maintenance of the Airport; t) those who use the Airport for commercial purposes, such as off-Airport parking operators, cause the Authority to incur costs associated with maintaining and securing the terminals, gates, roadways, and other facilities used by such businesses. The Authority believes that such commercial users should pay for the privilege of using the Airport for commercial purposes and for the market generated by the Airport's existence and continuing operation. (Final Pre-Trial Order at ¶20).

Prior to adopting the Resolution imposing the Privilege Fee, the Authority provided written notice to those who would be affected, including Park Shuttle, and conducted a public hearing at a meeting of the Board's Ground Transportation Committee. In response to the notice, Park Shuttle's out-of-state counsel sent a letter to the Authority outlining various legal challenges and objections to the Privilege Fee. (Final Pre-Trial Order at ¶21). Mr. Ben Gordon and another Park Shuttle representative, Ms. Janet Ayers, were invited to and appeared at a meeting held on May 13, 2003 by the Board's Ground Transportation Committee. At this meeting, the Ground Transportation Committee, chaired by Mr. Peter G. Decker, Jr., received and considered the comments presented by Mr. Gordon and Ms. Ayers. (Final Pre-Trial Order at ¶22). The Ground Transportation Committee discussed the issue and voted unanimously to recommend the imposition of the Privilege Fee to the full Board. The Board adopted the Resolution upon the recommendation of the Ground Transportation Committee after due consideration of all the facts stated above. (Final Pre-Trial Order at ¶23).

Peter B. Mandle is an expert in the field of airport management. Mr. Mandle has more than 25 years of experience in traffic engineering and transportation planning, with emphasis on airport grounds transportation, parking, airport access and circulation, and other airport management-related areas. Mr. Mandle is employed by Leigh Fisher Associates. Mr. Mandle is generally familiar with operations of airports in the United States and the commercial grounds transportation management and business practices at such airports. (Final Pre-Trial Order at ¶24). Mr. Mandle evaluated the Privilege Fee imposed by the Authority and the circumstances under which it was enacted. Mr. Mandle also analyzed off-airport parking fees charged by other airports. Mr. Mandle's research and analysis of the foregoing is contained in a report title "Evaluation of Off-Airport Parking Lot Privilege Fees," dated June 10, 2004 (the "Mandle Report"). (Final Pre-Trial Order at ¶25).

The fees charged by airports to commercial ground transportation operators fall into four general categories: privilege fees; cost-recovery fees; monthly or annual fees; and other fees, such as those based on vehicle size or waiting time. (Final Pre-Trial Order at ¶26). Approximately 21 U.S. airports require that operators of off-airport parking facilities pay a privilege fee. As shown in Table 1 of the Mandle Report, these airports range in size from those serving fewer than 500,000 originating airline passengers to those which serve over 11 million originating airport passengers. (Final Pre-Trial Order at ¶27). As shown in Table 1 of the Mandle Report, the privilege fees range from 1% to 10% of gross receipts, with twelve airports charging 8% or higher. All of the 21 airports that charge off-airport parking operators privilege fees charge them as a percentage of gross receipts. (Final Pre-Trial Order at ¶ 28).

The factors typically considered by airport managers in assessing a privilege fee on off-airport parking operators are: the fees charged other companies, such as rental car companies, providing transportation services; the amount of off-airport parking lot privilege fees charged at other airports; and the amount of fees charged other airport concessionaires. (Final Pre-Trial Order at ¶ 29). As stated in Table 2 of the Mandle Report, eight of the airports similar in size to the Airport considered fees charged by other airports as a factor in establishing the off-airport parking privilege fee. (Final Pre-Trial Order at ¶ 30).

2. Additional Trial Factual Findings

The Defendant has a legitimate business interest to protect its sources of income. Park Shuttle is a direct competitor with the Authority. The Defendant decided to impose a privilege fee based on information from an AGTA study, the Leigh Fisher study regarding off-airport parking fees, and similar airport administrators. A privilege fee is a fee based upon the benefits a company receives from the entire existence of the airport. It differs from a permit fee or cost-recovery fee that is imposed for courtesy vehicles. The privilege fee is not based on any estimate of Plaintiff's actual use of the airport or any of the Authority's facilities, or on Defendant's lost revenue due to Plaintiff's business. It is greatly in excess of the fees imposed on hotel shuttle vans and taxicabs that provide transportation to or from the airport. The privilege fee is within the range of 4–10% that the Leigh Fisher study identified for establishing a privilege fee. The privilege fees imposed at other airports for off-airport parking companies also fall within this range. Instead of a privilege fee, many airports charge off-airport parking companies an annual permit fee or have standard fees unrelated to the companies' revenue. The particular characteristics of an airport have some bearing on the type and amount of fee imposed based on the relative benefits conferred by the airport and the parking operators. At the Norfolk International Airport, the Authority is currently able to meet the parking needs of its customers.

II. CONCLUSIONS OF LAW

A plaintiff alleging a violation of Equal Protection under the Fourteenth Amendment must first show that the government treated it differently than other individuals or groups. If the government action neither discriminates based on a suspect classification nor impinges a fundamental right, the Defendant must assert a legitimate purpose for treating the Plaintiff different from other similarly situated individuals or groups. Kimel v. Fla. Bd. of Regents, 528 U.S. 62, 84, 120 S.Ct. 631, 145 L.Ed.2d 522 (2000). For a mere economic regulation, the government need only show a rational basis for its action. Williamson v. Lee Optical, 348 U.S. 483, 489, 75 S.Ct. 461, 99 L.Ed. 563 (1955). The Plaintiff bears the ultimate burden of proving that the government's disparate treatment was so unrelated to the proffered purpose that it was irrational. Mass. Bd. of Ret. v. Murgia, 427 U.S. 307, 314, 96 S.Ct. 2562, 49 L.Ed.2d 520 (1976); Eldridge v. Bouchard, 645 F.Supp. 749, 755 (W.D.Va.1986).

The Commerce Clause prohibits a state from enacting any regulation that places an undue burden on interstate commerce. U.S. Const. Art. I, Sect. 8., Cl. 3. The actions of the state are treated as correct, unless they are proven to be unreasonable and arbitrary. Hendrick v. Maryland, 235 U.S. 610, 624, 35 S.Ct. 140, 59 L.Ed. 385 (1915). A government fee is reasonable if it (1) is based on some fair approximation of use of the facilities, (2) is not excessive in relation to the benefits conferred, and (3) does not discriminate against interstate commerce. Evansville-Vanderburgh Airport Auth. Dist. v. Delta Airlines, Inc., 405 U.S. 707, 716–17, 92 S.Ct. 1349, 31 L.Ed.2d 620 (1972).

III. ANALYSIS

A. Equal Protection

Plaintiff asserts varying equal protection violations. First, the Plaintiff alleges that the imposed privilege fee unconstitutionally discriminates against Park Shuttle because the type and amount of rate charged differs from the rate charged to every other type of courtesy vehicle company. The Defendant claims that it has legitimate reasons for imposing a type of privilege fee different from the fee imposed on other courtesy vehicle companies. The Court previously found that at least one legitimate basis for Defendant's classification did exist, protecting a source of its income. Park Shuttle's parking business does take away revenue that would otherwise go to the Authority, whereas hotels are in a completely different business. Park Shuttle N Fly, Inc. v. Norfolk Airport Auth., No. 03cv461 (E.D.Va. Feb. 6, 2004) (order partially granting Motion to Dismiss). Thus, the Authority can legitimately classify Park Shuttle differently because it is a revenue generating entity that can act to protect its source of revenue. The question currently before the Court is whether the amount of the privilege fee imposed on Park Shuttle is related to that legitimate government objective. See id.

The Plaintiff argues that the 8% privilege fee is arbitrary, not based on any determination of the revenue lost by the airport, and not based on Park Shuttle's actual use of the Authority's facilities. The Defendant contends that the 8% privilege fee was determined in several, non-arbitrary ways. First, the Authority, led by Mr. Scott, contacted directors at other airports, including the Raleigh-Durham airport and the Columbus, Ohio airport, to determine what type of payment structure they used. (Tr. at 60.) He was informed that the Raleigh-Durham airport imposes a 10% privilege fee, and the Columbus airport a 7–8% fee for off-Airport parking services. (Tr. at 62.)

Second, Mr. Scott relied on information provided by Leigh Fisher, an airport management consulting firm. In 2000, the Authority contacted the firm requesting information regarding the types of fees charged to off-airport parking operators. (Ex. 10). Leigh Fisher responded that there were three types of fees applicable to off-airport parking facilities: permit fees, cost-recovery fees, or privilege fees. (Tr. at 128.) Mr. Peter Mandle, an expert consultant from Leigh Fisher, testified that a permit fee usually applies to commercial vehicles such as taxis or limousines, and it is an annual or monthly fee based on obtaining a license. Each commercial operator is required to pay such a fee.

A cost-recovery fee applies to commercial vehicles and is a fee to reimburse the airport for the cost of building, operating, or maintaining facilities used by those vehicles. Cost-recovery fees can be assessed per vehicle, per operator, per vehicle trip, per passenger, or another measure of the actual use of the airport facilities.

A privilege fee is assessed for the privilege of doing business on airport property and from the benefits a company or vehicle operator derives from the presence of the entire airport. Leigh Fisher also reported that the privilege fees charged at other airports range from 4% to 10% for off-airport parking businesses. (Ex. 10).

Third, Mr. Scott testified that he determined the fee based on the 2002 Airport Ground Transportation Association ("AGTA") study regarding ground transportation vehicle fees paid to airports. (Tr. at 58.) The study surveyed various airports around the country, and tabulated the information regarding fees imposed for on and off airport rental car companies, on and off airport parking operators, as well as fees for other commercial vehicles such as taxis and limousines. (Ex. 33). Finally, in determining what type and amount of fee to impose, Mr. Scott also considered the fact that off-airport rental car companies were previously charged an 8% privilege fee for their use of the airport.

The Court finds that the privilege fee imposed on Park Shuttle is substantial in comparison to other commercial vehicle operators. For the months of July through December 2003, Park Shuttle paid an average of $2,269.09 per month as a privilege fee. Similarly, it paid an average of $2,137.84 for the first five months of 2004. Taxicabs, in comparison, are charged a fee of $15 per month to pick up passengers at the airport, and they must be registered in Norfolk. There is no charge to drop off passengers. (Ex. 19). The Authority also provides taxis with a holding area for operators to park and wait for customers. (Tr. at 16–17.) Limousines are not charged a fee to pick up passengers at the airport, but they must have a pre-arranged agreement with the customer. (Ex. 19). Hotels are charged an annual permit fee of $180 per year to pick up customers who call to be picked up at the airport. (Tr. at 21.)

To find that this type of governmental action violated the Equal Protection Clause, the Court must determine that officials reasonably could not have believed that the action was rationally related to a legitimate governmental interest. Front Royal County Indus. Park Corp. v. Town of Front Royal, 135 F.3d 275, 290 (4th Cir.1998); Star Scientific v. Beales, 278 F.3d 339, 351 (4th Cir.2002). Park Shuttle must therefore show that no reasonable official could have believed that the amount of the privilege was rationally related to the purpose of protecting the Authority's revenue. The Plaintiff has not met this burden. The Defendant, Norfolk Airport Authority, concedes that the fee imposed on Park Shuttle exceeds that imposed on other commercial vehicle operators, and concedes that it bears no relationship to either the cost of building or maintaining the airport or its roadway facilities. It is also irrelevant that the fee was not necessarily imposed due to lost revenue from parking, but instead due to increased security costs. The privilege fee is nevertheless rationally related to the legitimate purpose of protecting its revenue because the Authority has a right to charge commercial operators for the benefit and use of its facilities, and the amount of the fee is rational.

Park Shuttle generates more than 90% of its revenue from customers that access the airport. (Final Pre-Trial Order at ¶ 13). The vast majority of its business, therefore, is a direct result of the existence and operation of the airport. A benefit of this nature is specifically the type contemplated by the percentage based privilege fee. As Mr. Mandle testified, the privilege fee is designed to exact payment when a company benefits from the existence of the entire airport, as Plaintiff does here. Plaintiff concedes that without the airport, it would have too few customers to operate the parking facility. (Final Pre-Trial Order at ¶ 13).

Defendants conducted a reasonable inquiry into procedures used by other similar airports, and confirmed these results by the Leigh Fisher firm. (Tr. at 55.) It then established a fee squarely within the range suggested by Leigh Fisher, and comparable to other airports. (Ex. 33). The privilege fee structure is used in airports around the country for commercial businesses similar to Plaintiff's. Of the fifty-two airports surveyed in the 2002 AGTA study that charge off-airport parking fees, seventeen charged by percentage of gross revenue, and thirty-five either imposed no fee or charged using other methods. All of the airports using percentage-based fees had rates between the 4 and 10% indicated by Leigh Fisher.

The Defendant's rate also accounts for the relative benefits the Plaintiff and the Authority receive. Courts have upheld similar percentage-based fee structures based on an entity's comparison of the relative benefits it receives from various entities. See Alamo Rent-A-Car, Inc. v. Sarasota-Manatee Airport, 825 F.2d 367, 371–72 (11th Cir.1987) (finding privilege fee charged to off-airport rental car company constitutional). The AGTA did not include a consideration of the relative benefits of an off-airport parking facility, but such information is very relevant to decisions based on what fees to charge particular entities.

The Norfolk International Airport has approximately 6,800 parking spaces, and expects to be able to meet the parking demands of its customers for several years. (Tr. at 52.) It, therefore, does not currently have a particular need for off-airport parking services. Other airports that do have such a need based on limited parking facilities at the airport likely have a greater need for such companies. These airports derive a greater benefit from off-airport parking entities than does Defendant, and thus may vary the fees based on entirely different criteria. In addition, under the percentage based fee, increased revenue from Park Shuttle corresponds with increased usage of the airport, and thus Plaintiff pays more for the increased benefits it receives. The Authority does not have to show that the fee is the same as other airports, nor must it justify why some of Plaintiff's revenue is not exempted from the fee structure. It must merely show that the fee is rational based on the relative benefits and detriments it derives based on the operation of Plaintiff's business. See Alamo Rent-A-Car, 825 F.2d at 372.

Park Shuttle has presented no evidence on benefits it provides to the Authority, whereas the Authority shows that Park Shuttle derives enormous benefits from the airport. Almost all of its revenue is generated because of the airport, and the Authority can constitutionally impose a different fee as a result. See Williamson, 348 U.S. at 489, 75 S.Ct. 461; Allied Stores v. Bowers, 358 U.S. 522, 526–27, 79 S.Ct. 437, 3 L.Ed.2d 480 (1959) (finding states can vary the rates of taxes and fees based on legitimate classifications). Thus, even though Plaintiff is charged a much higher rate for essentially the same use of the airport, the Defendant's determination of relative benefits from Plaintiff as compared to similar commercial operators justifies the discrepancy, especially given the wide latitude governmental entities enjoy in determining the type and amount of fees charged for their services. See City of New Orleans v. Dukes, 427 U.S. 297, 303, 96 S.Ct. 2513, 49 L.Ed.2d 511 (1976). It is therefore rational for Defendant to charge a different, percentage-based fee to companies such as Park Shuttle that operate almost exclusively to supplement the airport's existing services.

B. Commerce Clause

The Plaintiff alleges that the Norfolk Airport Authority's privilege fee unconstitutionally interferes with interstate commerce by forcing airline passengers to pay additional fees. The Court has determined that the Authority's fee requirement is a user fee rather than a tax imposed upon Plaintiff. As such, the Court uses the analysis from Evansville-Vanderburgh Airport Auth. Dist. v. Delta Airlines, Inc., 405 U.S. 707, 92 S.Ct. 1349, 31 L.Ed.2d 620 (1972). A state may exact reasonable compensation for the use of those engaged in interstate commerce. Id. at 712, 92 S.Ct. 1349 (quoting Hendrick v. Maryland, 235 U.S. 610, 35 S.Ct. 140, 59 L.Ed. 385 (1915)). A fee is reasonable if it is based on some fair approximation of the use of the facilities, it is not excessive in relation to the benefits conferred, and it does not discriminate against interstate commerce. Northwest Airlines v. County of Kent, Michigan, 510 U.S. 355, 369, 114 S.Ct. 855, 127 L.Ed.2d 183 (1994); Evansville-Vanderburgh, 405 U.S. at 716, 92 S.Ct. 1349.

The Plaintiff claims that the Authority's fee is not based on any fair approximation of the use of the facilities involved. Park Shuttle argues that its use of the airport is limited to the access roads and driveways of the airport, and that it should not be charged based on its use of the entire airport. The Defendant responds that Plaintiff benefits from the entire existence of the airport and uses its passengers who by extension use the entire airport. Defendant's argument is consistent with arguments made in other federal courts considering the constitutionality of similar fees. See Alamo Rent-A-Car v. Sarasota-Manatee Airport Auth., 906 F.2d 516, 519 (11th Cir.1990) ("Alamo II").

The user fee is unquestionably inexact. Plaintiff is charged an 8% privilege fee regardless of how many customers park each month to access the airport. The fee also applies regardless of how many trips Plaintiff actually makes to the airport to pick up or drop off passengers. It also applies regardless of how many passengers use each parking spot at the facility, and how long each passenger parks the car. Thus, Defendant receives the same amount from Plaintiff whether one passenger parks one car for ten days and Park Shuttle makes a total of two trips to the airport, or whether ten passengers park ten cars for one day each and Park Shuttle makes twenty separate trips to the airport. At the same time, the hotels are charged the same, exponentially lower rate regardless of how many customers arrive via the airport, and how many trips their shuttle buses make to the airport. But, the user fee is not required to be exact, it just cannot be "manifestly disproportionate to the services rendered." Commonwealth Edison Co. v. Montana, 453 U.S. 609, 620–23 n.12, 101 S.Ct. 2946, 69 L.Ed.2d 884 (1981).

According to Park Shuttle's financial statements, it paid a total of $11,500.27 to the Defendant for the last six months of 2003. The Plaintiff has presented no information about the number of trips it made to the airport throughout those six months. The Plaintiff does, indicate, however, that over 90% of its revenue is generated by customers who seek access to the airport. The Plaintiff therefore gains enormous benefits from the existence of the airport and from passengers using its facilities. As long as a user fee is "based on some fair approximation of use or privilege for use, ... and is neither discriminatory against interstate commerce nor excessive in comparison with the governmental benefit conferred, it will pass constitutional muster, even though some other formula might reflect more exactly the relative use of the state facilities by individual users." Alamo II, 906 F.2d at 519 (quoting Evansville Vanderburgh, 405 U.S. at 716–17, 92 S.Ct. 1349). Although the user fee is not based upon an approximation of use, it is based on an approximation of Plaintiff's privilege for use of the facilities. In addition, though it may be deemed excessive in comparison with other commercial vehicle operators, the fee is not excessive when compared to the benefit the Authority confers. The Defendant allows Plaintiff access to its facility to directly compete with Defendant's own parking facilities, and earn revenue that would otherwise go to Defendant. Plaintiff may argue that some customers prefer the door-to-door service offered by Park Shuttle, but it cannot refute the enormous benefits it receives because of the Defendant, and because of the access Defendant allows to its facilities. The Court therefore finds that the privilege fee is not excessive in comparison with the government benefit conferred, and is based on a fair approximation of Plaintiff's privilege for use of the airport.

Finally, the regulation does not discriminate against interstate commerce. The regulation imposes a percentage fee without respect to the destination of airport customers. As such, it meets the requirements of Evansville-Vanderburgh, and does not unconstitutionally violate the Commerce Clause.

IV. CONCLUSION

The Court finds that Defendant's regulation is constitutionally valid as it satisfies the requirements of both the Equal Protection Clause and the Commerce Clause. For the reasons stated above, the Court awards judgment to the DEFENDANT.

Notes

1. In footnote 14 of his opinion in *City of Burbank*, Justice Douglas wrote:

> The letter from the Secretary of Transportation also expressed the view that "the proposed legislation will not affect the rights of a State or local public agency, as the proprietor of an airport, from issuing regulations or establishing requirements as to the permissible level of noise which can be created by aircraft using the airport. Airport owners acting as proprietors can presently deny the use of their airports to aircraft on the basis of noise considerations so long as such exclusion is nondiscriminatory." This portion as well was quoted with approval in the Senate Report.
>
> Appellants and the Solicitor General submit that this indicates that a municipality with jurisdiction over an airport has the power to impose a curfew on the airport, notwithstanding federal responsibility in the area. But, we are concerned here not with an ordinance imposed by the City of Burbank as "proprietor" of the airport, but with the exercise of police power. While the Hollywood-Burbank Airport may be the only major airport which is privately owned, many airports are owned by one municipality yet physically located in another. For example, the principal airport serving Cincinnati is located in Kentucky. Thus, authority that a municipality may have as a landlord is not necessarily congruent with its police power. We do not consider here what limits, if any, apply to a municipality as a proprietor.

411 U.S. at 635 n.14. Because of this footnote, airports regularly argue, and courts from time to time agree, that they have certain powers that are beyond the reach of the federal government:

> The legacy of Burbank is [the] proprietary powers distinction, introduced by the Secretary's letter and recognized in footnote 14 of the majority opinion. Because of footnote 14, Burbank came to stand for the so-called proprietor's exception, which holds that public or private airport owners retain certain powers that are not preempted by federal law. Proprietary powers, as distinct from police powers such as eminent domain, are those powers necessary to administer the airport, such as the power to build and maintain facilities, and the power to negotiate with air carriers. Footnote 14 is the first, and so far the only, recognition by the High Court that state and local governments may exert proprietary powers that would otherwise be preempted and unconstitutional.

Peter D. Irvine, Comment, *The Future of Stage 2 Airport Noise Restrictions: A Matter of Substantive Versus Procedural Review by the Federal Aviation Administration*, 11 Geo. Mason L. Rev. 179, 184–85 (2002).

As *City of Naples* makes clear, the Airport Noise and Capacity Act has cut back significantly on the proprietor's exception by expanding the review and approval powers of the FAA. For operational restrictions on Stage 2 aircraft, the FAA examines only the sufficiency of the airport's cost-benefit analysis. In contrast, limitations on less noisy

Stage 3 aircraft are subject to a thorough appraisal unless all of the affected operators agree to them. *See further* 49 U.S.C. §47524. Despite the enhanced role that Congress has given to the FAA, courts continue to assume jurisdiction over such dispues. *See, e.g.*, *National Business Aviation Association, Inc. v. City of Naples Airport Authority*, 162 F. Supp. 2d 1343 (M.D. Fla. 2001) (upholding ban on Stage 2 aircraft under 75,000 pounds).

2. The decision in *Western Air Lines* is an example of a local airport operating restriction being upheld because it was reasonable, non-arbitrary, non-discriminatory, and did not place an undue burden on interstate commerce.

In the 1970s, the Port Authority of New York and New Jersey resisted the introduction of the Concorde at John F. Kennedy International Airport, notwithstanding a Department of Transportation decision allowing the plane to operate under limited circumstances. The DOT initially ordered a 16-month test involving two flights a day at JFK and one at Washington Dulles International Airport, subject to a 10 p.m.–7 a.m. curfew. In response, the Port Authority issued a temporary ban to give itself time to study the noise impacts of supersonic operations. The Second Circuit upheld the ban, finding that the Port Authority was entitled to await the results of six months of operations at Dulles (which at the time was federally operated). *See British Airways Board v. Port Authority of New York and New Jersey*, 558 F.2d 75 (2d Cir. 1977).

At the end of the six months, President Jimmy Carter approved the operation of the Concorde at 13 airports, including JFK. The Port Authority then extended its ban indefinitely. This time, the Second Circuit ruled that the Port Authority's action was arbitrary and discriminatory because there was no sonic boom until the aircraft was well over water. *See British Airways Board v. Port Authority of New York and New Jersey,* 564 F.2d 1002 (2d Cir. 1977).

The restrictions at Love Field in Dallas also are instructive. A 1968 city ordinance declared that the operations of scheduled carriers would be transferred to Dallas-Fort Worth International Airport upon its opening in 1974. All of the carriers agreed to this change except Southwest Airlines, whose authority to continue operating at Love Field was upheld in court. *See Southwest Airlines Co. v. Texas International Airlines, Inc.*, 546 F.2d 84 (5th Cir.), *cert. denied*, 434 U.S. 832 (1977).

In 1980, Congress enacted the Wright Amendment, Pub. L. No. 96-192, 94 Stat. 35, which, with certain exceptions, banned all interstate operations from Love Field. In 1997, these exceptions were enlarged by the Shelby Amendment, Pub. L. No. 105-66, 111 Stat. 1425. A variety of state and federal suits were then filed, leading the DOT to rule that the 1968 ordinance was preempted to the extent it prohibited operations authorized by the Shelby and Wright Amendments. On appeal, this conclusion was upheld by the Fifth Circuit. *See American Airlines, Inc. v. Department of Transportation*, 202 F.3d 788 (5th Cir.), *cert. denied*, 530 U.S. 1274 (2000).

For a further look at local operating restrictions, *see, e.g.*, *National Helicopter Corp. of America v. City of New York*, 137 F.3d 81 (2d Cir. 1998) (approving limits on the number, but not the routes, of helicopter flights); *Alaska Airlines, Inc. v. City of Long Beach*, 951 F.2d 977 (9th Cir. 1991) (upholding a due process challenge to a rule limiting air carriers to 40 flights per day and requiring them to use quieter aircraft); *Global International Airways Corp. v. Port Authority of New York and New Jersey*, 727 F.2d 246 (2d Cir.), *rehearing denied*, 731 F.2d 127 (2d Cir. 1984) (allowing Authority to expedite phase-out of Stage 1 operations despite inconsistency with federal noise reduction schedule); *Santa Monica Airport Ass'n v. City of Santa Monica*, 659 F.2d 100 (9th Cir.

1981) (finding airport's exclusion of jets invalid under the dormant Commerce Clause because propeller aircraft were just as noisy).

3. *City of Los Angeles* and *Park Shuttle* are just two examples of the kinds of challenges that airports can run into when they try to charge for their facilities or services. But even when a particular levy is upheld, it can only be used for authorized purposes. In 2003, for example, the Sarasota-Manatee Airport Authority asked the FAA for permission to give subsidies to carriers that otherwise would not provide local service. The petition pointed out that whereas municipal airports are able to tap a variety of non-airport sources to fund such grants, independent airport authorities lack such alternatives. Despite the soundness of this argument, the FAA ruled that carrier subsidies do not qualify as a valid expenditure of airport funds. *See* 69 Fed. Reg. 61,544 (Oct. 19, 2004). In contrast, the FAA does allow airports to waive or discount landing fees to attract or retain carriers, reasoning that statutory assurances governing rates and charges "are much less prescriptive" than revenue diversion prohibitions.

4. At various points in its opinion in *City of Los Angeles*, the Ninth Circuit refers to the Anti-Head Tax Act, 49 U.S.C. § 40116. As has been explained elsewhere, this statute was enacted to ensure that air travelers did not pay both national user charges and local taxes:

> Airport "head taxes" came into vogue in the early 1970's. The typical airport head tax was a flat charge (of perhaps $1.00) imposed by a municipality upon a person enplaning at an airport. The municipalities typically required the airline to collect the tax together with the fare paid by the passenger. A head tax was also sometimes collected from deplaning passengers. The basic principle of head taxes was constitutionally approved by the United States Supreme Court in Evansville-Vanderburgh Airport Authority District v. Delta Airlines, 405 U.S. 707, 92 S.Ct. 1349, 31 L.Ed.2d 620 (1972).
>
> [To overturn Evansville, Congress passed the] Airport Development Acceleration Act of 1973. [This statute] was preceded by the Airport and Airway Development Act of 1970 and the Airport and Airway Revenue Act of 1970. In the 1970 Revenue Act, Congress imposed various taxes upon air users to finance certain airport improvements and development. The largest single component of this tax package in terms of revenues to be produced for the Airport and Airway Trust Fund was an eight percent tax on the price of domestic air passenger tickets.
>
> When Congress thus acted in 1970 to tax commercial aviation users to establish the Airport and Airways Trust Fund, it did so, according to the United States Supreme Court in Evansville-Vanderburgh Airport Authority District v. Delta Airlines, supra, with no evident purposes to preempt state and local taxes. Legislative discussion of the 1973 Act, however, indicates a conviction on the part of interested legislators that the Supreme Court in Evansville misread its earlier intent. Discussion in the Senate of Senate Bill 38, a part of which became 49 U.S.C. § 1513 [the former codification of 49 U.S.C. § 40116], as reported in Volume 119 of the Congressional Record, Part 3, pages 3349–3350, includes the following:
>
>> (MR. CANNON): Finally, Mr. President, S. 38 prohibits a new, inequitable, and potentially chaotic burden of taxation on the nearly 200 million persons who used air transportation each year. The bill prohibits the levying of State or local head taxes, fees, gross receipts taxes or other such charges either on passengers or on the carriage of such passengers in interstate commerce.

In 1970, Congress established a national, uniform system of user taxation on all users of the air transportation system and levied a tax of 8 percent on all airline tickets. That user tax was intended to finance aviation facilities development through a national program and Congress intended at the time that the Federal tax be the only tax on airline passengers.

Last year, however, the U.S. Supreme Court upheld the validity of several State and local passenger head taxes, overturning a precedent established more than a hundred years ago. By prohibiting State taxation on passengers or on air transportation, the committee has accepted greater responsibility for U.S. assistance. With the increased Federal assistance, we can see no valid reason for the continuance of local passenger taxation.

(MR. PEARSON): Finally, Mr. President, the committee bill prohibits State and local taxation of air fares. The Congress intended in 1970 to preempt the States and localities from levying such taxes, as taxation on air fares is one of the predominant sources of revenue for the trust fund. Recent Supreme Court decisions necessitate the clarification of this congressional policy determination.

If more than 500 localities or even a significant proportion of this number were unilaterally to levy taxes on airline passenger fares, there would result an unconscionable and unacceptable burden on interstate commerce. The national system of air service upon which 180 million airline passengers depend annually would become a hodgepodge of Balkanized assessments and levies against non-resident travelers whose business or leisure takes them across State lines. The committee bill prohibits State and local taxation of air fares, but this Federal preemption is carefully balanced by substantial increases in trust fund assistance for airport development and modernization.

State ex rel. Arizona Department of Revenue v. Cochise Airlines, 626 P.2d 596, 597–600 (Ariz. Ct. App. 1980). Of course, passenger facility charges, discussed earlier in this chapter in the *Northwest Airlines* case, are head taxes, but a specific statutory exception has been made for them. *See* 49 U.S.C. §40117.

5. For a further look at airport use issues, *see, e.g.*, M.O. Regensteiner, Annotation, *Validity, Construction, and Operation of Airport Operator's Grant of Exclusive or Discriminatory Privilege or Concession*, 40 A.L.R.2d 1060 (1955 & 2004 Supp.); John J. Corbett, *Small Communities Are Concerned About Congestion Pricing*, 17 Air & Space Law. 17 (Summer 2002); Mária Zulick Nucci, *Allocation of Economic Risk in Nonaeronautical Airport Revenue Contracts*, 16 Air & Space Law. 6 (Winter 2002); John Sabel, *Airline-Airport Facilities Agreements: An Overview*, 69 J. Air L. & Com. 769 (2004); Daniel R. Polsby, Comment, *Airport Pricing of Aircraft Takeoff and Landing Slots: An Economic Critique of Federal Regulatory Policy*, 89 Cal. L. Rev. 779 (2001). *See also* Soon-Kil Hong & Kwang Eui Yoo, *A Study in Airport Privatization in Korea: Policy and Legal Aspects of Corporatization and Localization Over Airport Management*, 66 J. Air L. & Com. 3 (2000).

Problem 22

In 1992, a helicopter company entered into a 20-year lease to operate a heliport in Washington, D.C. After the 9/11 attacks, however, the FAA banned all civilian flights within 25 nautical miles of the capital. As a result, the company went out of business. If it sues the United States, claiming that it is entitled to compensation for the loss of use, how should the court rule? *See Air Pegasus of D.C., Inc. v. United States*, 424 F.3d 1206 (Fed. Cir. 2005).

D. SECURITY

INTERNATIONAL SOCIETY FOR KRISHNA CONSCIOUSNESS, INC. v. LEE

505 U.S. 672 (1992)

Chief Justice REHNQUIST delivered the opinion of the Court.

In this case we consider whether an airport terminal operated by a public authority is a public forum and whether a regulation prohibiting solicitation in the interior of an airport terminal violates the First Amendment.

The relevant facts in this case are not in dispute. Petitioner International Society for Krishna Consciousness, Inc. (ISKCON) is a not-for-profit religious corporation whose members perform a ritual known as sankirtan. The ritual consists of "'going into public places, disseminating religious literature and soliciting funds to support the religion.'" 925 F.2d 576, 577 (CA2 1991). The primary purpose of this ritual is raising funds for the movement.

Respondent Walter Lee, now deceased, was the police superintendent of the Port Authority of New York and New Jersey and was charged with enforcing the regulation at issue. The Port Authority owns and operates three major airports in the greater New York City area: John F. Kennedy International Airport (Kennedy), La Guardia Airport (La Guardia), and Newark International Airport (Newark). The three airports collectively form one of the world's busiest metropolitan airport complexes. They serve approximately 8% of this country's domestic airline market and more than 50% of the trans-Atlantic market. By decade's end they are expected to serve at least 110 million passengers annually.

The airports are funded by user fees and operated to make a regulated profit. Most space at the three airports is leased to commercial airlines, which bear primary responsibility for the leasehold. The Port Authority retains control over unleased portions, including La Guardia's Central Terminal Building, portions of Kennedy's International Arrivals Building, and Newark's North Terminal Building (we refer to these areas collectively as the "terminals"). The terminals are generally accessible to the general public and contain various commercial establishments such as restaurants, snack stands, bars, newsstands, and stores of various types. Virtually all who visit the terminals do so for purposes related to air travel. These visitors principally include passengers, those meeting or seeing off passengers, flight crews, and terminal employees.

The Port Authority has adopted a regulation forbidding within the terminals the repetitive solicitation of money or distribution of literature. The regulation states:

> 1. The following conduct is prohibited within the interior areas of buildings or structures at an air terminal if conducted by a person to or with passers-by in a continuous or repetitive manner:
>
> (a) The sale or distribution of any merchandise, including but not limited to jewelry, food stuffs, candles, flowers, badges and clothing.

(b) The sale or distribution of flyers, brochures, pamphlets, books or any other printed or written material.

(c) The solicitation and receipt of funds.

Id., at 578–579.

The regulation governs only the terminals; the Port Authority permits solicitation and distribution on the sidewalks outside the terminal buildings. The regulation effectively prohibits ISKCON from performing sankirtan in the terminals. As a result, ISKCON brought suit seeking declaratory and injunctive relief under 42 U.S.C. § 1983, alleging that the regulation worked to deprive its members of rights guaranteed under the First Amendment. The District Court analyzed the claim under the "traditional public forum" doctrine. It concluded that the terminals were akin to public streets, 721 F.Supp. 572, 577 (SDNY 1989), the quintessential traditional public fora. This conclusion in turn meant that the Port Authority's terminal regulation could be sustained only if it was narrowly tailored to support a compelling state interest. Id., at 579. In the absence of any argument that the blanket prohibition constituted such narrow tailoring, the District Court granted ISKCON summary judgment.

The Court of Appeals affirmed in part and reversed in part. 925 F.2d 576 (1991). Relying on our recent decision in United States v. Kokinda, 497 U.S. 720 (1990), a divided panel concluded that the terminals are not public fora. As a result, the restrictions were required only to satisfy a standard of reasonableness. The Court of Appeals then concluded that, presented with the issue, this Court would find that the ban on solicitation was reasonable, but the ban on distribution was not. ISKCON and one of its members, also a petitioner here, sought certiorari respecting the Court of Appeals' decision that the terminals are not public fora and upholding the solicitation ban. Respondent cross-petitioned respecting the court's holding striking down the distribution ban. We granted both petitions to resolve whether airport terminals are public fora, a question on which the Circuits have split and on which we once before granted certiorari but ultimately failed to reach [a decision]. Board of Airport Comm'rs of Los Angeles v. Jews for Jesus, Inc., 482 U.S. 569 (1987). [We deal here only with petitioners' claim regarding the permissibility of solicitation. Respondent's cross-petition concerning the leafletting ban is disposed of in the companion case, Lee v. International Society for Krishna Consciousness, Inc., 505 U.S. 830 (1992).]

It is uncontested that the solicitation at issue in this case is a form of speech protected under the First Amendment. Heffron v. International Soc. for Krishna Consciousness, Inc., 452 U.S. 640 (1981); Kokinda, supra, 497 U.S., at 725 (citing Schaumburg v. Citizens for a Better Environment, 444 U.S. 620, 629 (1980)); Riley v. National Federation of Blind of N.C., Inc., 487 U.S. 781, 788–789 (1988). But it is also well settled that the government need not permit all forms of speech on property that it owns and controls. Postal Service v. Council of Greenburgh Civic Assns., 453 U.S. 114, 129, 101 (1981); Greer v. Spock, 424 U.S. 828 (1976). Where the government is acting as a proprietor, managing its internal operations, rather than acting as lawmaker with the power to regulate or license, its action will not be subjected to the heightened review to which its actions as a lawmaker may be subject. Kokinda, supra, 497 U.S., at 725 (plurality opinion) (citing Cafeteria & Restaurant Workers v. McElroy, 367 U.S. 886 (1961)). Thus, we have upheld a ban on political advertisements in city-operated transit vehicles, Lehman v. Shaker Heights, 418 U.S. 298 (1974), even though the city permitted other types of advertising on those vehicles. Similarly, we have permitted a school district to limit access to an internal mail system used to communicate with teachers employed by the district. Perry Ed. Assn. v. Perry Local Educators' Assn., 460 U.S. 37 (1983).

These cases reflect, either implicitly or explicitly, a "forum based" approach for assessing restrictions that the government seeks to place on the use of its property. Cornelius v. NAACP Legal Defense & Ed. Fund, Inc., 473 U.S. 788, 800 (1985). Under this approach, regulation of speech on government property that has traditionally been available for public expression is subject to the highest scrutiny. Such regulations survive only if they are narrowly drawn to achieve a compelling state interest. Perry, supra, 460 U.S., at 45. The second category of public property is the designated public forum, whether of a limited or unlimited character—property that the State has opened for expressive activity by part or all of the public. Ibid. Regulation of such property is subject to the same limitations as that governing a traditional public forum. Id., at 46. Finally, there is all remaining public property. Limitations on expressive activity conducted on this last category of property must survive only a much more limited review. The challenged regulation need only be reasonable, as long as the regulation is not an effort to suppress the speaker's activity due to disagreement with the speaker's view. Ibid.

The parties do not disagree that this is the proper framework. Rather, they disagree whether the airport terminals are public fora or non-public fora. They also disagree whether the regulation survives the "reasonableness" review governing non-public fora, should that prove the appropriate category. Like the Court of Appeals, we conclude that the terminals are non-public fora and that the regulation reasonably limits solicitation.

The suggestion that the government has a high burden in justifying speech restrictions relating to traditional public fora made its first appearance in Hague v. Committee for Industrial Organization, 307 U.S. 496, 515, 516 (1939). Justice Roberts, concluding that individuals have a right to use "streets and parks for communication of views," reasoned that such a right flowed from the fact that "streets and parks ... have immemorially been held in trust for the use of the public and, time out of mind, have been used for purposes of assembly, communicating thoughts between citizens, and discussing public questions." We confirmed this observation in Frisby v. Schultz, 487 U.S. 474, 481 (1988), where we held that a residential street was a public forum.

Our recent cases provide additional guidance on the characteristics of a public forum. In Cornelius we noted that a traditional public forum is property that has as "a principal purpose ... the free exchange of ideas." 473 U.S., at 800. Moreover, consistent with the notion that the government—like other property owners—"has power to preserve the property under its control for the use to which it is lawfully dedicated," Greer, 424 U.S., at 836, the government does not create a public forum by inaction. Nor is a public forum created "whenever members of the public are permitted freely to visit a place owned or operated by the Government." Ibid. The decision to create a public forum must instead be made "by intentionally opening a nontraditional forum for public discourse." Cornelius, supra, 473 U.S., at 802. Finally, we have recognized that the location of property also has bearing because separation from acknowledged public areas may serve to indicate that the separated property is a special enclave, subject to greater restriction. United States v. Grace, 461 U.S. 171, 179–180 (1983).

These precedents foreclose the conclusion that airport terminals are public fora. Reflecting the general growth of the air travel industry, airport terminals have only recently achieved their contemporary size and character. See H. Hubbard, M. McClintock & F. Williams, Airports: Their Location, Administration and Legal Basis 8 (1930) (noting that the United States had only 807 airports in 1930). [G]iven the lateness with which the modern air terminal has made its appearance, it hardly qualifies for the description of having "immemorially ... time out of mind" been held in the public trust and used for purposes of expressive activity. Hague, supra, 307 U.S., at 515. Moreover, even within the rather short history of air transport, it is only "[i]n recent years [that] it has become a common practice for various religious and non-profit organizations to use commercial airports as a forum for the distribution of literature, the solicitation of funds, the proselytizing of new members, and other similar activities." 45 Fed.Reg. 35314 (1980). Thus, the tradition of airport activity does not demonstrate that airports have historically been made available for speech activity. Nor can we say that these particular terminals, or airport terminals generally, have been intentionally opened by their operators to such activity; the frequent and continuing litigation evidencing the operators' objections belies any such claim.

Petitioners attempt to circumvent the history and practice governing airport activity by pointing our attention to the variety of speech activity that they claim historically occurred at various "transportation nodes" such as rail stations, bus stations, wharves, and Ellis Island. Even if we were inclined to accept petitioner's historical account describing speech activity at these locations, an account respondent contests, we think that such evidence is of little import for two reasons. First, much of the evidence is irrelevant to public fora analysis, because sites such as bus and rail terminals traditionally have had private ownership. See United Transportation Union v. Long Island R. Co., 455 U.S. 678, 687 (1982); H. Grant & C. Bohi, The Country Railroad Station in America 11–15 (1978); U.S. Dept. of Transportation, The Intercity Bus Terminal Study 31 (Dec. 1984). The development of privately owned parks that ban speech activity would not change the public fora status of publicly held parks. But the reverse is also true. The practices of privately held transportation centers do not bear on the government's regulatory authority over a publicly owned airport.

Second, the relevant unit for our inquiry is an airport, not "transportation nodes" generally. When new methods of transportation develop, new methods for accommodating that transportation are also likely to be needed. And with each new step, it therefore will be a new inquiry whether the transportation necessities are compatible with various kinds of expressive activity. To make a category of "transportation nodes," therefore, would unjustifiably elide what may prove to be critical differences of which we should rightfully take account. The "security magnet," for example, is an airport commonplace that lacks a counterpart in bus terminals and train stations. And public access to air terminals is also not infrequently restricted—just last year the Federal Aviation Administration required airports for a 4-month period to limit access to areas normally publicly accessible. See 14 CFR 107.11(f) (1991) and U.S. Dept. of Transportation News Release, Office of Assistant Secretary for Public Affairs, Jan. 18, 1991. To blithely equate airports with other transportation centers, therefore, would be a mistake.

The differences among such facilities are unsurprising since, as the Court of Appeals noted, airports are commercial establishments funded by users fees and designed to make a regulated profit, 925 F.2d, at 581, and where nearly all who visit do so for some travel related purpose, id., at 578. As commercial enterprises, airports must provide services attractive to the marketplace. In light of this, it cannot fairly be said that an airport terminal has as a principal purpose promoting "the free exchange of ideas." Cornelius v. NAACP Legal Defense & Ed. Fund, Inc., 473 U.S. 788, 800 (1985). To the contrary, the record demonstrates that Port Authority management considers the purpose of the terminals to be the facilitation of passenger air travel, not the promotion of expression. Even if we look beyond the intent of the Port Authority to the manner in which the terminals have been operated, the terminals have never been dedicated (except under the threat of court order) to expression in the form sought to be exercised here: i.e., the solicitation of contributions and the distribution of literature.

The terminals here are far from atypical. Airport builders and managers focus their efforts on providing terminals that will contribute to efficient air travel. See, e.g., R. Horonjeff & F. McKelvey, Planning and Design of Airports 326 (3d ed. 1983) ("The terminal is used to process passengers and baggage for the interface with aircraft and the ground transportation modes"). The Federal Government is in accord; the Secretary of Transportation has been directed to publish a plan for airport development necessary "to anticipate and meet the needs of civil aeronautics, to meet requirements in support of the national defense ... and to meet identified needs of the Postal Service." 49 U.S.C.App. §2203(a)(1); see also 45 Fed.Reg. 35317 (1980) ("The purpose for which the [Dulles and National airport] terminal[s] [were] built and maintained is to process and serve air travelers efficiently"). Although many airports have expanded their function beyond merely contributing to efficient air travel, few have included among their purposes the designation of a forum for solicitation and distribution activities. Thus, we think that neither by tradition nor purpose can the terminals be described as satisfying the standards we have previously set out for identifying a public forum.

The restrictions here challenged, therefore, need only satisfy a requirement of reasonableness. We reiterate what we stated in Kokinda: The restriction "'need only be reasonable; it need not be the most reasonable or the only reasonable limitation.'" 497 U.S., at 730 (plurality opinion) (quoting Cornelius, supra, 473 U.S., at 808). We have no doubt that under this standard the prohibition on solicitation passes muster.

We have on many prior occasions noted the disruptive effect that solicitation may have on business. "Solicitation requires action by those who would respond: The individual solicited must decide whether or not to contribute (which itself might involve reading the solicitor's literature or hearing his pitch), and then, having decided to do so, reach for a wallet, search it for money, write a check, or produce a credit card." Kokinda, supra, at 734; see Heffron, 452 U.S., at 663 (BLACKMUN, J., concurring in part and dissenting in part). Passengers who wish to avoid the solicitor may have to alter their paths, slowing both themselves and those around them. The result is that the normal flow of traffic is impeded. Id., at 653. This is especially so in an airport, where "[a]ir travelers, who are often weighted down by cumbersome baggage ... may be hurrying to catch a plane or to arrange ground transportation." 925 F.2d, at 582. Delays may be particularly costly in this setting, as a flight missed by only a few minutes can result in hours worth of subsequent inconvenience.

In addition, face-to-face solicitation presents risks of duress that are an appropriate target of regulation. The skillful, and unprincipled, solicitor can target the most vulnerable, including those accompanying children or those suffering physical impairment and who cannot easily avoid the solicitation. See, e.g., International Soc. for Krishna Consciousness, Inc. v. Barber, 506 F.Supp. 147, 159–163 (NDNY 1980), rev'd on other grounds, 650 F.2d 430 (CA2 1981). The unsavory solicitor can also commit fraud through concealment of his affiliation or through deliberate efforts to shortchange those who agree to purchase. 506 F.Supp. at 159–163. See 45 Fed.Reg. 35314–35315 (1980). Compounding this problem is the fact that, in an airport, the targets of such activity frequently are on tight schedules. This in turn makes such visitors unlikely to stop and formally complain to airport authorities. As a result, the airport faces considerable difficulty in achieving its legitimate interest in monitoring solicitation activity to assure that travelers are not interfered with unduly.

The Port Authority has concluded that its interest in monitoring the activities can best be accomplished by limiting solicitation and distribution to the sidewalk areas outside the terminals. Sloane Supp. Affidavit, ¶ 11, App. 514. This sidewalk area is frequented by an overwhelming percentage of airport users, see id., at ¶ 14, App. 515–516 (noting that no more than 3% of air travelers passing through the terminals are doing so on intraterminal flights, i.e., transferring planes). Thus the resulting access of those who would solicit the general public is quite complete. In turn we think it would be odd to conclude that the Port Authority's terminal regulation is unreasonable despite the Port Authority having otherwise assured access to an area universally traveled.

The inconveniences to passengers and the burdens on Port Authority officials flowing from solicitation activity may seem small, but viewed against the fact that "pedestrian congestion is one of the greatest problems facing the three terminals," 925 F.2d, at 582, the Port Authority could reasonably worry that even such incremental effects would prove quite disruptive. Moreover, "[t]he justification for the Rule should not be measured by the disorder that would result from granting an exemption solely to ISKCON." Heffron, supra, 452 U.S., at 652. For if ISKCON is given access, so too must other groups. "Obviously, there would be a much larger threat to the State's interest in crowd control if all other religious, nonreligious, and noncommercial organizations could likewise move freely." 452 U.S., at 653. As a result, we conclude that the solicitation ban is reasonable.

For the foregoing reasons, the judgment of the Court of Appeals sustaining the ban on solicitation in Port Authority terminals is affirmed.

[The concurring opinions of Justices Kennedy and O'Connor and the dissenting opinion of Justice Souter are omitted.]

UNITED STATES v. MARQUEZ

410 F.3d 612 (9th Cir. 2005)

TALLMAN, Circuit Judge.

Sergio Ramon Marquez was randomly selected for secondary security screening at Seattle-Tacoma International Airport and found to be in possession of two kilograms of cocaine lodged underneath his pants. He challenges the denial of his motion to suppress the evidence obtained during this administrative airport search. He questions whether an airport screening procedure subjecting passengers to a handheld magnetometer wand scan, in addition to the standard walkthrough magnetometer and x-ray luggage scan, is constitutionally reasonable where the passenger is randomly selected for more intrusive screening upon or before entering the Transportation Security Administration ("TSA") security checkpoint. We hold that this random, additional screening procedure is reasonable under the Fourth Amendment. Accordingly, we affirm the district court's denial of Marquez's motion to suppress.

I

On the afternoon of October 3, 2002, Marquez attempted to board a domestic flight to Anchorage from Seattle. After checking in for his flight, he proceeded to the TSA security checkpoint where he was diverted to Checkpoint B, the "selectee lane." A passenger chosen for the selectee lane is subjected to more thorough search procedures, regardless of whether or not the x-ray luggage scan reveals something suspicious or the walkthrough magnetometer sounds an alarm. The primary additional procedure involves a full-body wanding with a handheld magnetometer that uses technology similar to, but more sensitive than, the walkthrough magnetometer. According to testimony, a passenger is randomly selected for the selectee lane either by the airlines at the time of check-in or by TSA employees stationed at the security checkpoint entrance when the passenger presents his or her identification and boarding pass. It is not clear whether Marquez was selected by his airline or by the TSA employee who checked his identification and boarding pass before he entered the security line. For purposes of the constitutional analysis it is immaterial because there was no showing that the decision was supported by any articulable reason other than completely random selection.

Once in line, Marquez took off his coat and shoes and placed them on the x-ray scanner conveyor belt along with his carry-on luggage. He walked through the magnetometer and was instructed to sit down in the screening area. At this point, TSA screener Petersen, who was in charge of wanding the passengers in the selectee lane when Marquez passed through, retrieved Marquez's personal items from the x-ray belt. Petersen then approached Marquez and began to scan his person with the handheld magnetometer, screening Marquez's feet first, then having him stand up to screen the rest of his body.

Thus far, the wand had not indicated the presence of anything suspicious. However, the wand "alarmed" when it passed over Marquez's right hip. Petersen testified that he understood TSA policy to require him to determine the cause of the alarm. Thus, Petersen informed Marquez that he had to touch Marquez's hip in order to ascertain what had triggered the alarm. Marquez denied Petersen permission to touch his hip, and swatted Petersen's hand away when he tried to touch the area. Nonetheless, Petersen felt a "hard brick type of thing" and, on the basis of his experiences in the military and his TSA training, Petersen feared that the object might be C-4 explosives.

After swatting Petersen's hand away, Marquez continued to protest Petersen's subsequent attempts to determine the source of the alarm, telling Petersen that the wand must have been triggered by a metal rivet on his pants, and that there was no need to look any further. Petersen persisted as well, telling Marquez that he needed to determine what set off the wand, and Marquez continued to refuse, repeating that it was "[just] a rivet."

Petersen called for his supervisor. Marquez was becoming increasingly agitated, and, upon arrival, the supervisor recommended that he "[c]alm down a little bit" because they had "to get through this if [Marquez] wanted to fly." Both Petersen and his supervisor again attempted to obtain Marquez's permission to continue with the wanding and determine the source of the alarm, but Marquez refused. Ultimately, after entering a private screening room and in response to the supervisor's repeated requests to determine what caused the wand to alarm, Marquez quickly pulled down his pants, revealing "bricks of stuff in his crotch area ... with a pair of [spandex leggings] over the top." Port of Seattle Police were summoned, and an agent from the Drug Enforcement Agency ("DEA") also responded. The officers searched and questioned Marquez and then retrieved four wrapped bricks of cocaine from his person.

Marquez was charged with one count of possession with intent to distribute over 500 grams of cocaine, in violation of 21 U.S.C. § 841(a)(1). Marquez moved to suppress the evidence, arguing that the additional screening procedures were unreasonable because they were not based on individualized suspicion of wrongdoing. The district court denied the motion to suppress, concluding that the additional screening in the selectee lane was reasonable. Marquez entered into a conditional plea agreement with the Government and was sentenced to 60 months in prison. This appeal followed.

II

Motions to suppress are reviewed de novo. See United States v. Crawford, 372 F.3d 1048, 1053 (9th Cir.2004) (en banc). However, the trial court's factual findings are reviewed for clear error. See United States v. Bynum, 362 F.3d 574, 578 (9th Cir.2004).

This case presents a legally novel, yet practically ubiquitous, set of facts. The issue here is whether the random selection of Marquez to go to the selectee lane, where he would automatically be subjected to the wanding of his person with the handheld magnetometer in addition to the walkthrough magnetometer and the x-ray luggage scan, was reasonable. We conclude that it was.

A

Airport screenings of passengers and their baggage constitute administrative searches and are subject to the limitations of the Fourth Amendment. United States v. Davis, 482 F.2d 893, 908 (9th Cir.1973) (noting that airport screenings are considered to be administrative searches because they are "conducted as part of a general regulatory scheme" where the essential administrative purpose is "to prevent the carrying of weapons or explosives aboard aircraft"); see also id. at 895, 904. Thus, airport screenings must be reasonable. See Torbet v. United Airlines, Inc., 298 F.3d 1087, 1089 (9th Cir.2002). To judge reasonableness, it is necessary to balance the right to be free of intrusion with "society's interest in safe air travel." United States v. Pulido-Baquerizo, 800 F.2d 899, 901 (9th Cir.1986).

B

In Davis and its progeny, we have established a general reasonableness test for airport screenings. "An airport screening search is reasonable if: (1) it is no more extensive or intensive than necessary, in light of current technology, to detect weapons or explosives; (2) it is confined in good faith to that purpose; and (3) passengers may avoid the search by electing not to fly." Torbet, 298 F.3d at 1089 (citation omitted); see also Davis, 482 F.2d at 913; Pulido-Baquerizo, 800 F.2d at 901.

1

"Little can be done to balk the malefactor after [weapons or explosives are] successfully smuggled aboard, and as yet there is no foolproof method of confining the search to the few who are potential hijackers." Davis, 482 F.2d at 910. Thus, airport screenings of passengers and their carry-on luggage in order to detect weapons and explosives and deter potential passengers from carrying such items aboard is "reasonably necessary" and not overly intrusive in light of the interests at stake. Id.; see also Chandler v. Miller, 520 U.S. 305, 323, 117 S.Ct. 1295, 137 L.Ed.2d 513 (1997) (suggesting that "where the risk to public safety is substantial and real, blanket suspicionless searches calibrated to the risk may rank as 'reasonable'"). It is also necessary to provide for screening procedures designed to detect non-metallic threats to air safety. See Wayne R. Lafave, Search And Seizure: A Treatise On The Fourth Amendment § 10.6(d) (4th ed.2005). The intensity and extent of screening must take into account the fact that "[h]ijackers as well as airport officers know of the existence of plastic explosives or even ordinary dynamite." United States v. Albarado, 495 F.2d 799, 809 (2d Cir.1974); see also Pulido-Baquerizo, 800 F.2d at 901 (noting that weapons and explosives can be "small and easily concealed" and that "[t]heir detection is difficult").

We have previously found airport screenings which require passengers to walk through a magnetometer and submit carry-on luggage for x-ray screening to be reasonable. See, e.g., United States v. Doran, 482 F.2d 929, 932 (9th Cir.1973); Pulido-Baquerizo, 800 F.2d at 901–02; Torbet, 298 F.3d at 1089–90. Generally, such a search "is brief, is less intrusive than the typical search warrant execution, does not have a stigma attached to it, is not made by armed police, and is often made only with advance notice." LAFAVE, supra, § 10.6(c).

The added random screening procedure at issue in this case involving a handheld magnetometer scan of Marquez's person was no more extensive or intensive than necessary in order to detect weapons and explosives. It utilized the same technology and reported results based on the same type of information (e.g., the presence or absence of metal) as the walkthrough magnetometer. See United States v. $124,570 U.S. Currency, 873 F.2d 1240, 1245 (9th Cir.1989) (noting that, unlike this case, "the court cannot sustain a subsequent search that differs in material respects from the search initially approved"). While it arguably constituted a "slight privacy intrusion," Pulido-Baquerizo, 800 F.2d at 902, it was reasonably confined to procedures necessary to detect weapons and explosives, including those that may evade detection by the larger, less sensitive walkthrough magnetometer.

2

Airport screening procedures are conducted for two primary reasons: first, to prevent passengers from carrying weapons or explosives onto the aircraft; and second, to deter passengers from even attempting to do so. See Davis, 482 F.2d at 908.

In their briefs and at oral argument, neither party suggested that there was any purpose or goal in the instant search other than to detect weapons or explosives. TSA screener Petersen stated that he was trained to look for "anything that would bring a plane down" and that the search of Marquez was in accordance with this goal. He further testified repeatedly that he was not trained, nor told, to search for anything other than weapons or explosives, and he said explicitly that he was not trained to look for drugs: "Our job is to make the passengers in the airplanes safe, and we don't look for drugs." Moreover, nothing in the record indicates that he was looking for drugs or criminal evidence; rather, the record supports his assertion that he was trying to "ferret out firearms and explosive devices[.]" Pulido-Baquerizo, 800 F.2d at 902; see also $124,570 U.S. Currency, 873 F.2d at 1243 (noting that airport searches conducted as part of a general regulatory scheme rather than an attempt to secure evidence of a crime are valid).

Additionally, the randomness of the selection for the additional screening procedure arguably increases the deterrent effects of airport screening procedures because potential passengers may be influenced by their knowledge that they may be subject to random, more thorough screening procedures.

The mere fact that a screening procedure ultimately reveals contraband other than weapons or explosives does not render it unreasonable, post facto. "Of course, routine airport screening searches will lead to discovery of contraband and apprehension of law violators. This practical consequence does not alter the essentially administrative nature of the screening process, however, or render the searches unconstitutional." Davis, 482 F.2d at 908. The screening at issue here is not unreasonable simply because it revealed that Marquez was carrying cocaine rather than C-4 explosives.

3

Finally, "airport screening searches are valid only if they recognize the right of a person to avoid search by electing not to board the aircraft." Davis, 482 F.2d at 910–11; see also id. at 913. In this case, Marquez checked in, went to the security checkpoint, waited in line, placed his bag on the x-ray scanner, proceeded through the walkthrough magnetometer, and allowed Petersen to begin screening his person with the hand-held magnetometer; he had ample opportunity to choose to forego air travel in order to avoid the screening. There is no evidence before us that Marquez ever changed his mind about flying to Anchorage and that issue was neither briefed nor argued by the parties.

III

It is hard to overestimate the need to search air travelers for weapons and explosives before they are allowed to board the aircraft. As illustrated over the last three decades, the potential damage and destruction from air terrorism is horrifically enormous. See, e.g., Davis, 482 F.2d at 910; Pulido-Baquerizo, 800 F.2d at 901. However, even with the grave threat posed by airborne terrorist attacks, the vital and hallowed strictures of the Fourth Amendment still apply: these searches must be reasonable to comport with the Constitution.

The random, additional screening procedure in this case satisfies the Davis reasonableness test for airport searches. The procedure is geared towards detection and deterrence of airborne terrorism, and its very randomness furthers these goals. This was a limited search, confined in its intrusiveness (both in duration and scope) and in its attempt to discover weapons and explosives. Given the randomness, the limited nature of the intrusion, the myriad devices that can be used to bring planes down, and the absence of any indicia of improper motive, we hold that the random, more thorough screening involving scanning of Marquez's person with the handheld magnetometer was reasonable. The district court properly denied Marquez's motion to suppress the contraband found during TSA screening.

PEOPLE v. BARRON

808 N.E.2d 1051 (Ill. App. Ct. 2004)

BURKE, Justice.

Following a bench trial, defendant John Barron was found guilty of two counts of felony disorderly conduct (720 ILCS 5/26-1(a)(3) (West 2002)) for declaring to ticketing agents at Midway Airport that he had a bomb in his shoe. Defendant was sentenced to one year of conditional discharge and 185 days' imprisonment (time considered served). On appeal, defendant contends that the State failed to prove him guilty beyond a reasonable doubt because the evidence showed that his remarks were understood as a joke. Defendant argues that section 26-1(a)(3) of the Criminal Code of 1961 (Code) (720 ILCS 5/26-1(a)(3) (West 2002)) does not apply to remarks that are understood as jests. In the alternative, defendant contends that if section 26-1(a)(3) of the Code criminalizes a joking remark that is understood as such, the statute is unconstitutionally overbroad. For the reasons set forth below, we affirm.

At 1 p.m. on March 28, 2002, defendant approached the ticket counter of Frontier Airlines at Midway Airport in Chicago, Illinois to check in for a flight he was scheduled to take at 7 p.m. on that date. Because defendant was too early to check in for his scheduled flight, the ticket agent offered defendant the option of taking an earlier flight so that he could check his bag and enter through security. Defendant accepted the offer, and the ticket agent began to process defendant for his new flight.

During the check in process, defendant began to ask the ticket agent, "[A]re you going to check me?" The ticket agent informed defendant that he was not a random selectee, meaning that the computer had not chosen defendant and his baggage to be personally searched at that point, so he would not be searching defendant or his bag. Defendant then leaned in toward the ticket counter and began waiving his arms in the air while he stuck his right leg forward and said, "I only have one bomb in my shoe." The ticket agent responded that defendant could not "joke" about possessing a bomb and that he needed to "simmer down right now and not be saying those things." The ticket agent also detected the odor of alcohol coming from defendant at this time. Defendant quieted down for a short time before once again getting excited and repeatedly asking the ticket agent if he was going to check him.

Another ticket agent, who was working alongside the agent dealing with defendant, overheard defendant's statement that he had a bomb in his shoe. This agent also informed defendant not to make comments like that because they were taken seriously. Defendant responded by laughing at the agent. After defendant began to once again state that his bag should be checked because the agents did not know "what was in his bag," he was informed that if he made one more comment, he would be denied boarding. Defendant once again laughed at the agent, who then notified the police.

Defendant's person and baggage were subsequently searched by police officers and a bomb-sniffing dog. No bomb was found. Thereafter, defendant was taken to a police room where he admitted several times to the officers that he told the ticket agent he had a bomb in his shoe.

The State subsequently charged defendant with two counts of felony disorderly conduct. The statute under which defendant was charged, section 26-1 of the Code, provides, in pertinent part:

> (a) A person commits disorderly conduct when he knowingly:
>
> * * *
>
> (3) Transmits or causes to be transmitted in any manner to another a false alarm to the effect that a bomb or other explosive of any nature * * * is concealed in such place that its explosion or release would endanger human life, knowing at the time of such transmission that there is no reasonable ground for believing that such bomb * * * is concealed in such place * * *.

720 ILCS 5/26-1(a)(3) (West 2002).

Following a bench trial, defendant was found guilty of both counts of felony disorderly conduct. Defendant's subsequent motion for a new trial was denied and he was sentenced to one year of conditional discharge and 185 days' imprisonment (time considered served).

On appeal, defendant first contends that the State failed to prove him guilty beyond a reasonable doubt. Defendant argues that section 26-1(a)(3) of the Code distinguishes between comments which actually "alarm" an individual and those which are understood as joking remarks. According to defendant, section 26-1(a)(3) only criminalizes remarks which have the effect of frightening a reasonable person in the listener's position. Defendant claims that because the ticket agents perceived his comments as joking remarks, the State failed to prove all the material elements of the offense of felony disorderly conduct.

When a defendant challenges the sufficiency of the evidence, a reviewing court must view the evidence in the light most favorable to the prosecution and determine whether any rational trier of fact could have found the essential elements of the crime beyond a reasonable doubt. People v. Pollock, 202 Ill.2d 189, 217, 269 Ill.Dec. 197, 780 N.E.2d 669 (2002); see also People v. Cox, 195 Ill.2d 378, 387, 254 Ill.Dec. 720, 748 N.E.2d 166 (2001). In the instant case, defendant's first contention also involves construing section 26-1(a)(3) of the Code, which is an issue of law that we review de novo. People v. Harrell, 342 Ill.App.3d 904, 908, 277 Ill.Dec. 354, 795 N.E.2d 1022 (2003).

Defendant here attempts to place into section 26-1(a)(3) a requirement beyond that of the transmission of a false alarm. Specifically, defendant argues that section 26-1(a)(3) also requires that, once transmitted, the alarm must cause actual fear in the mind of the listener. As there have been no Illinois cases discussing this point, defendant cites to several cases from other jurisdictions in support of his contention, including Watts v. United States, 394 U.S. 705, 89 S.Ct. 1399, 22 L.Ed.2d 664 (1969), United States v. Cothran, 286 F.3d 173 (3rd Cir.2002), United States v. Malik, 16 F.3d 45 (2nd Cir.1994), and State ex rel. RT, 781 So.2d 1239 (La.2001). According to defendant, these cases stand for the proposition that, at least in certain circumstances, joking remarks cannot constitute criminal behavior. However, contrary to defendant's argument, these cases all share a similar fact which easily distinguishes them from the instant matter.

Defendant cites Watts, Cothran, Malik, and RT for the proposition that courts will utilize an objective test to determine whether a writing or comment constitutes a threat. While we agree with this contention, we also find it inapplicable to the matter at hand. In Watts, Cothran, Malik, and RT, the defendants were charged with violating various state or federal statutes that criminalized remarks which threatened or caused fear in a listener. In Watts, the defendant was charged with violating a statute which prohibits any threat to take the life of or to inflict bodily harm upon the President. Watts, 394 U.S. at 705, 89 S.Ct. 1399; see 18 U.S.C. §871(a). The defendant in Cothran was charged with violating a statute which prohibited an individual from making a comment that he possessed a weapon or explosive on an airplane which "reasonably may be believed." Cothran, 286 F.3d at 175. Because the matter was one of first impression, the Cothran court compared the statute which the defendant was charged under to the statutes at issue in Malik. Cothran, 286 F.3d at 175. In Malik, the defendant was charged with violating two federal statutes which prohibited mailing threatening communications and threatening to assault a United States judge. Malik, 16 F.3d at 47. Lastly, in RT, the defendant was charged with violating two state statutes, one of which prohibited terrorizing an individual so that he sustains a fear for his or another person's safety. RT, 781 So.2d at 1241.

Here, the statute at issue specifically defines the type of behavior that is threatening in such a manner that it is unnecessary to further examine the intent behind the remark or the effect on the listener. In other words, instead of simply prohibiting "threatening" behavior without defining precisely what that behavior consists of, section 26-1(a)(3) clearly states the nature of the prohibited behavior. The legislature has acted in this instance to remove the burden of determining when a defendant's behavior rises to the level of disorderly. Specifically, and as related to this case, the legislature has proclaimed that an individual cannot transmit to another person the false comment that an explosive device is concealed in such a place as to endanger human life, knowing that comment to be false. Unlike the statutes at issue in Watts, Cothran, Malik, and RT, section 26-1(a)(3) itself defines what is threatening, making the "objective test" defendant relies upon unnecessary.

An examination of the legislative intent behind section 26-1 further supports our interpretation. The principal rule of statutory construction requires this court to ascertain and give effect to the intention of the legislature. People ex rel. Sherman v. Cryns, 203 Ill.2d 264, 279, 271 Ill.Dec. 881, 786 N.E.2d 139 (2003). In affording the statute its plain, ordinary and popularly understood meaning, we must examine all the provisions of a statutory enactment as a whole. Cryns, 203 Ill.2d at 279, 271 Ill.Dec. 881, 786 N.E.2d 139. In so doing, "words and phrases must be interpreted in light of other relevant provisions of the statute and must not be construed in isolation." Cryns, 203 Ill.2d at 279–80, 271 Ill.Dec. 881, 786 N.E.2d 139.

Not only does the plain wording of subsection (a)(3) of section 26-1 make it clear that the crime of felony disorderly conduct is complete upon the transmission of a false alarm to another person, regardless of the effect the false alarm has upon the individual who receives it, but an examination of section 26-1 as a whole demonstrates the purpose behind subsection (a)(3). Section 26-1 begins by stating that an individual commits the offense of disorderly conduct when he knowingly behaves in any one of 12 enumerated ways. Subsection (a)(1) generally defines the behavior customarily designated as "disorderly" as, "any act [performed] in such unreasonable manner as to alarm or disturb another and to provoke a breach of the peace." 720 ILCS 5/26-1(a)(1) (West 2002). Compared to subsection (a)(1), the lack of the phrase "alarm or disturb another" from subsection (a)(3) evidences the legislative intent that the offense may be completed upon transmission of the words as described in subsection (a)(3) without regard to their effect on the person who receives them. 720 ILCS 5/26-1(a)(1), (a)(3). The Committee Comments to section 26-1 further lend support to this interpretation. The comments state that "the activity covered by [subsection (a)(3)] may be included in the general definition provided by [subsection (a)(1)]. However, to insure[ ] the prohibition of such conduct and remove all doubt, [subsection (a)(3) has] been specifically included." 720 ILCS Ann. 5/26-1, Committee Comments—1961, at 156 (Smith-Hurd 2003).

In line with our interpretation of section 26-1(a)(3), an individual may be found guilty of felony disorderly conduct upon transmission of a false alarm, regardless of the intention of the speaker or the effect the words have upon the person receiving them. Just as the false cry of "fire" in a crowded theater may cause panic and harm simply by its utterance, a false claim that a bomb or container holding a chemical, biological or radioactive agent is present in an airport may cause alarm and mass disruption. In light of our nation's recent history, this fact could not be more clear, nor the purpose behind section 26-1(a)(3) more necessary.

We therefore find that the evidence, when viewed in a light most favorable to the State, supports defendant's conviction. Clear and credible evidence was presented that defendant informed two ticket agents that he had a bomb in his shoe. Since defendant was not actually in possession of a concealed explosive device, and had no reasonable ground to believe that he was in possession of an explosive device, the State satisfied all the material elements of section 26-1(a)(3).

Lastly, we briefly note that defendant's alternative argument, that section 26-1(a)(3) is unconstitutionally overbroad, fails. Defendant argues that the comments he made would be understood by a reasonable person as a joke and, as such, their prohibition by section 26-1(a)(3) infringes on his first amendment right to free speech. Defendant has completely failed, however, to demonstrate how his remarks were or could be considered jovial. Subjectively, the record shows that the ticket agents did not perceive defendant's comments as being made in jest. Although one ticket agent may have told defendant that he could not "joke" about having a bomb, the agents contacted the police, who then employed bomb-searching dogs and arrested defendant. These actions do not equate with an understanding that defendant was joking. As one ticket agent testified at trial, agents are required to take all bomb threats seriously. Moreover, we fail to see how an individual in today's climate can be objectively perceived as a prankster when he excitedly and repeatedly announces in an airport that he is in possession of a bomb. Because the record does not support defendant's claim that his remarks were understood as a joke, and he has not shown that a reasonable person would have understood his comments as a joke, we need not further consider this argument.

For the reasons stated, we affirm the judgment of the circuit court of Cook County.

Notes

1. Despite deciding in ISKCON I (the opinion reprinted above) that airport terminals are not public fora and the Krishnas could not use them to solicit money, the Supreme Court struck down the Port Authority's leafleting ban in the companion case of *Lee v. International Society for Krishna Consciousness, Inc.*, 505 U.S. 830 (1992) (ISKCON II). In both instances, however, the Justices issued multiple opinions, so a clear rationale did not emerge. *See further Public Forum,* 106 Harv. L. Rev. 279 (1992) (explaining that ISKCON I was a 6–3 decision with a majority opinion by Chief Justice Rehnquist, concurrences by Justices Kennedy and O'Connor, and a dissent by Justice Souter, while ISKCON II was a 5–4 decision with no majority opinion, concurrences by Justices Kennedy, O'Connor, and Souter, and a dissent by Chief Justice Rehnquist).

Parsing its way through the various holdings, the Eleventh Circuit has concluded that airports can ban the sale of literature in and around their terminals and can limit (on reasonable terms) the areas in which non-fundraising activities take place. *See ISKCON Miami, Inc. v. Metropolitan Dade County*, 147 F.3d 1282 (11th Cir. 1998), *cert. denied*, 525 U.S. 1141 (1999). However, in *International Society for Krishna Consciousness of California, Inc. v. City of Los Angeles*, 59 Fed. Appx. 974 (9th Cir. 2003), the Ninth Circuit warned that airport regulations that pass muster under the federal constitution still may run afoul of a state's constitution.

Obviously, these issues have become magnified since 9/11, as airport officials look to "lock down" their facilities to improve security but, in doing so, make it more difficult for the Krishnas and others to spread their message. In your opinion, how should the line between airport safety and individual freedom of expression be drawn? In particular, how would you advise an airport manager faced with the following requests:

a) A group asks for space in the airport's main lobby, where it plans to distribute flyers calling George Bush a "war criminal" and demanding that the United States immediately stop its illegal military adventurism. The group does not plan to ask for donations, but will accept them if offered.

b) A second group asks for space on the airport's sidewalks, where it plans to set up a small booth to educate the public about animal cruelty and the need for stronger laws to stop such abuse. It will not ask for donations, and will tell those who wish to give that contributions should be made at their local ASPCA chapter. Informational pamphlets will be given to those who want them.

c) A third group asks for space in the airport's shopping concourse to display the works of disabled local artists. The group plans to sell the paintings and sculptures, which are moderately priced, and turn over the proceeds to their creators.

2. The notion of airports as places people sometimes use for purposes other than travel has not been lost on Hollywood. In the movie *The Terminal* (2004), for example,

Tom Hanks is Viktor Navorski, a man who ends up living in an airport terminal for a year when, for political reasons, he is unable to return to his country. *See further* Craig S. Smith, *16 Years on an Airport Bench, and 15 Minutes of Fame*, N.Y. Times, Aug. 21, 2004, at A3 (profiling Merhan Karimi Nasseri, the Iranian national whose life inside Terminal 1 of Paris's Charles de Gaulle International Airport inspired the film).

Likewise, in "The Diplomat's Club," a 1995 episode of the NBC sitcom *Seinfeld*, Kramer (played by Michael Richards) goes to the airport for no apparent reason and ends up becoming involved in a high-stakes betting match:

> Kramer: Hey, how you doin'?
>
> Earl: Pretty good.
>
> Kramer: Name's Kramer.
>
> Earl: Earl Haffler, nice to meet you. I'm headed to Houston, where you headed?
>
> Kramer: Oh, I'm happy right here.
>
> [Earl looks at Kramer in disbelief.]
>
> Kramer: Isn't this place amazing? Planes flying in from all corners of the world, and they know the minute they're arriving.
>
> Earl: Ah they don't know a darn thing. That's why my flight to Houston's been delayed. They're all morons. Matter of fact, I'll bet you that that flight to Pittsburgh takes off before my flight to Houston.
>
> Kramer: Bet? Um, not betting.
>
> Earl: Friendly wager.
>
> Kramer [a recovering gambler]: I haven't made a bet in three years, I—
>
> Earl: Ah c'mon. Keep things interesting, pass the time.
>
> Kramer: Okay, how much?
>
> Earl: How 'bout 200?
>
> Kramer: You're on, cowboy!

As the episode's title makes clear, Kramer met (and bet) Earl in an airline's VIP club. In real life, such clubs have existed since 1939, when American Airlines established the first one at recently opened LaGuardia Airport in New York City. *See Admirals Club History*, at www.aa.com/content/amrcorp/corporateinformation/facts/admiralshistory.jhtml. When the club proved successful, other airlines followed suit (today, for example, Continental has the President's Club, Delta offers the Crown Room Club, and United runs the Red Carpet Club). For an interesting case involving such facilities (which once were invitation-only but now are open to the public), *see Maslan v. American Airlines, Inc.*, 885 F. Supp. 90 (S.D.N.Y. 1995) (having paid $300 for a lifetime membership to defendant's Admirals' Club, plaintiff claimed he could not later be charged extra to use its conference rooms). For a further discussion, *see* Keith L. Alexander, *Is the Airline Terminal Club Still Viable?*, Wash Post., Apr. 5, 2005, at E1 (noting that many airlines are eliminating or sharply reducing their club programs because passengers do not have time to use them due to the lengthy security screenings that have become a fact of life since 9/11).

3. Both *Marquez* and *Barron* demonstrate how passenger screening has been stepped up since 9/11. At one time, responsibility for airport security was shared by airlines

(who inspected baggage, carry-on items, and passengers) and airports (which guarded operational areas). *See generally El Al Israel Airlines, Ltd. v. Tsui Yuan Tseng*, 525 U.S. 155 (1999) (denying recovery to a passenger who claimed that the airline's search caused her emotional distress). In the Aviation and Transportation Security Act of 2001 (ATSA), however, Congress transferred screening to the Transportation Security Administration (TSA). Although private screeners can still be used, they must meet TSA standards. *See further* Mara E. Rosales, *Opting In or Opting Out? One Airport's Choice*, 19 Air & Space Law. 1 (Spring/Summer 2004).

ATSA also requires airports to: (a) have a security program approved by the TSA; (b) conduct background checks on airport employees with access to secure areas (and deny entry to employees who have committed certain enumerated criminal offenses); (c) make their perimeters more secure; and, (d) install explosive detection systems (for which federal funds are available). For a further look at the TSA regulations and the changes they are causing, *see, e.g.*, *Green v. Transportation Security Administration*, 351 F. Supp. 2d 1119 (W.D. Wash. 2005) (unsuccessful constitutional challenge to TSA's "no-fly" list, pursuant to which certain members of the public are prohibited from flying or subjected to enhanced security checks); James L. Buchwalter, Annotation, *Validity of Airport Security Measures*, 125 A.L.R.5th 281 (2005); Paul Stephen Dempsey, *Aviation Security: The Role of Law in the War Against Terrorism*, 41 Colum. J. Transnat'l L. 649 (2003); Andrew Hessick, *The Federalization of Airport Security: Privacy Implications*, 24 Whittier L. Rev. 43 (2002); Kent C. Krause, *Putting the Transportation Security Administration in Historical Context*, 68 J. Air L. & Com. 233 (2003); Gregory Robert Schroer, *Doomed to Repeat the Past: How the TSA is Picking Up Where the FAA Left Off*, 32 Transp. L.J. 73 (2004); Charu A. Chandrasekhar, Comment, *Flying While Brown: Federal Civil Rights Remedies to Post-9/11 Airline Racial Profiling of South Asians*, 10 Asian L.J. 215 (2003); M. Reed Martz, Comment, *A Constitutional Analysis of Random Vehicle Searches at Airports*, 73 Miss. L.J. 263 (2003); Eric J. Miller, Comment, *The "Cost" of Securing Domestic Air Travel*, 21 J. Marshall J. Computer & Info. L. 405 (2003); Leslie Miller, *'Registered Traveler' Program in Works*, S. Fla. Sun-Sentinel, Nov. 4, 2005, at 12A (reporting on TSA's plan to let passengers avoid security delays by paying a fee and undergoing a background check); Eric Wilson, *Flight Suits*, N.Y. Times, June 23, 2005, at E1 (describing how travelers are simplifying their wardrobes to ease their way through airport security). *See also* Alex C. Hallett, Note, *An Argument for the Denial of Collective-Bargaining Rights of Federal Airport Security Screeners*, 72 Geo. Wash. L. Rev. 834 (2004), and Molly Selzer, Comment, *Federalization of Airport Security Workers: A Study of the Practical Impact of the Aviation and Transportation Security Act From A Labor Law Perspective*, 5 U. Pa. J. Lab. & Emp. L. 363 (2003).

4. In November 2005, the TSA announced it was revamping its passenger screening processes to keep would-be terrorists off-balance and, as part of the overhaul, would again allow small scissors and other sharp tools in carry-on luggage. *See* Eric Lipton, *Significant Changes in Air Passenger Screening Lie Ahead*, N.Y. Times, Dec. 1, 2005, at A24. This change did not sit well with Congress, despite agency assurances that other post-9/11 changes (such as arming pilots and strengthening cockpit doors) had made it unnecessary to continue the carry-on ban. *See* Matthew L. Wald, *Senators Criticize Decision to Allow Scissors on Planes*, N.Y. Times, Dec. 13, 2005, at A25.

In the middle of this debate, a man was shot and killed when he refused to obey a command to lie down. The order had been given by federal air marshals who were chasing Rigoberto Alpizar after he suddenly sprinted off American Airlines Flight 924 while the plane was beginning to push back from its gate at Miami International Airport. Alpizar, who may have said that he had a bomb in his backpack, was shot when he began to reach inside it. After the shooting, however, it was discovered that Alpizar was mentally disturbed (a fact his wife had been yelling as *she* chased the agents chasing her husband) and did not have a bomb; this information quickly caused widespread second-guessing (President Bush issued a statement supporting the agents) and the initiation of an official investigation. *See further* Abby Goodnough & Matthew L. Wald, *Air Marshals Shoot and Kill Man After Bomb Threat*, N.Y. Times, Dec. 8, 2005, at A1. In the meantime, commentators grimly noted that the killing was the first time since the Federal Air Marshal Service's creation in 1968 that an agent had used a weapon while on the job. *See further* Arian Campo-Flores & Mark Hosenball, *'Anxious to Get Home,'* Newsweek, Dec. 19, 2005, at 42 (observing that there now are several thousand air marshals, up from the pre-9/11 figure of 32, and questioning whether the agency, which has had several different overseers during its existence, is fit to do its job). For a further discussion, *see Federal Air Marshal Service*, at en.wikipedia.org/wiki/Federal_Air_Marshal_Service.

Problem 23

While getting out of their car, a husband and wife were blown up in an airport parking lot. An investigation revealed that a terrorist, who had been planning to set off the bomb when he reached the terminal, had pressed the detonator prematurely. Is the airport liable for the couple's deaths? *See In re World Trade Center Bombing Litigation*, 776 N.Y.S.2d 713 (Sup. Ct. 2004).

E. AIR TRAFFIC CONTROL

YAP v. SLATER

128 F. Supp. 2d 672 (D. Haw. 2000)

KAY, District Judge.

BACKGROUND

Denis C.F. Yap ("Plaintiff") worked as an air traffic controller ("ATC") and was forced to retire when he turned 56. In the instant lawsuit, he protests the Federal Aviation Administration ("FAA") requirement that he retire at age 56, while other ATCs are allowed to work past age 56. Plaintiff sues Rodney E. Slater ("Defendant" or "the Secretary") in his capacity as the Secretary of the United States Department of Transportation. Plaintiff's complaint alleges violations of the Age Discrimination in Employment Act, 29 U.S.C. §621 et seq. (1994) ("ADEA"), and his right to equal protection under the Fifth Amendment.

This motion was originally a motion for judgment on the pleadings. See Fed.R.Civ.P. 12(c); Mot., at 1. However, matters outside the pleadings have been presented for the Court's review and, therefore, the Court will treat the motion as one for partial summary judgment. See Fed.R.Civ.P. 12(c). The Court will set forth the mandatory retirement provisions in issue and then turn to the claims.

I. STATUTORY FRAMEWORK

Three different mandatory retirement schemes exist for ATCs employed by the FAA. The first group of ATCs are those hired before May 16, 1972. For these ATCs there is no mandatory retirement age so long as they remain members of the Civil Service Retirement System ("CSRS"), one of the retirement benefit plans administered by the Government. See 5 U.S.C. § 8335 note; Opp., Ex. D, at 2.

The second group of ATCs are those hired between May 16, 1972 and December 31, 1986 who are members of CSRS. In 1972, Congress enacted Public Law 92-297, codified at 5 U.S.C. § 8335 (1994). It states in relevant part:

> An air traffic controller shall be separated from the service on the last day of the month in which he becomes 56 years of age. The Secretary [of Transportation], under such regulations as he may prescribe, may exempt a controller having exceptional skills and experience as a controller from the automatic separation provisions of this subsection until that controller becomes 61 years of age.

5 U.S.C. § 8335(a). The stated purpose of the mandatory retirement age was

> to improve the conditions of employment for individuals employed as air traffic controllers in the Department of Transportation by offering preferential retirement benefits, job training and improved appeal procedures for controllers removed from control work, and the establishment of maximum recruitment and retention ages for controllers.

S.Rep. No. 92-774 (1972), reprinted in 1972 U.S.C.C.A.N. 2287, 2287. The report observed that,

> [A]ir traffic controllers are unique in that their work involves both physical and mental strain for the controller, and the safety of the public traveling by air. At large air terminals and en route centers in the United States, the role and importance of the controller is primary, a status to which airline pilots are the first to testify. Over a period of time the physical and mental efforts of monitoring radar screens to track all aircraft within the range of a regional facility or tower, or controlling tower traffic visually, or both, simply becomes too much for the average individual to sustain. Like skilled athletes, most controllers lose proficiency to some degree after age 40, and in the interest of the public's safety, should not be retained as controllers in busy facilities beyond the time they can perform satisfactorily.

Id. at 2288.

Besides implementing a mandatory retirement age, Public Law 92-297 recognized that the retirement benefit rules for other civil servants "are too strict when applied to air traffic controllers," many of whom burn out before meeting the requisite age and year in service requirements. See id. at 2289 ("Although there are some exceptions to the general rule, most controllers are not able to control traffic in busy facilities at any age near 55—the physical and emotional strength required to do the job, to work odd and continuously changing work shifts, and to insure air safety for the traveling public is simply too much for any man in that age bracket."). Accordingly, the new law eased the age and year in service requirements for air traffic controllers, giving them a "preferential system." See id. ("The committee recognizes that selecting air traffic controllers for preferential retirement treatment constitutes a significant change of policy for the civil service retirement system, but the unique employment of these employees justifies such a system. No other Government worker is so directly involved in the safety of millions of dollars of aviation equipment used to transport the public.").

The new law also recognized that retirement at 56 would be stressful as ATC job skills are not easily transferable to other jobs. The law therefore made job training available.

See id. at 2288 ("This training opportunity will remove much of the natural anxiety which controllers now feel when they are asked to step aside from active control work."). Finally, § 8 of Public Law 92-297 expressly provided that what is now codified as § 8335(a) "does not apply to a person appointed as an air traffic controller by the Department of Transportation before the date of enactment of this Act [May 16, 1972]." See 5 U.S.C. § 8335(a) note. Thus, while ATCs hired on or after May 16, 1972 face mandatory retirement at age 56, ATCs hired before May 16, 1972 are automatically exempted from the mandatory separation rules.

Finally, the third group of ATCs are those who are members of the Federal Employee Retirement System ("FERS"), a retirement system that became effective January 1, 1987. The purposes of establishing the FERS system are set forth at the beginning of Public Law 99-335, the FERS legislation:

> The purposes of this Act are—
>
> (1) to establish a Federal employees' retirement plan which is coordinated with title II of the Social Security Act;
>
> (2) to ensure a fully funded and financially sound retirement benefits plan for Federal employees;
>
> (3) to enhance portability of retirement assets earned as an employee of the Federal Government;
>
> (4) to provide options for Federal employees with respect to retirement planning;
>
> (5) to assist in building a quality career work force in the Federal Government;
>
> (6) to encourage Federal employees to increase personal savings for retirement; and,
>
> (7) to extend financial protection from disability to additional Federal employees and to increase such protection for eligible Federal employees.

Federal Employees' Retirement System Act of 1986, Pub.L. 99-335, § 100A, 100 Stat. 514. FERS was established as a new, distinct retirement benefit system for numerous federal employees, including ATCs. See, e.g., S.Rep. No. 166, at 10 (1986), reprinted in 1986 U.S.C.C.A.N. 1405 ("Although there are common elements between [FERS] and the existing [CSRS], the two will generally function as separate retirement programs.... [T]he two systems are quite different in regard to the employees covered, retirement eligibility requirements, benefits, and basic design."). Included within the new FERS scheme was a provision for the mandatory separation of ATCs covered by FERS. The provision, codified at 5 U.S.C. § 8425(a), states in relevant part:

> An air traffic controller who is otherwise eligible for immediate retirement under section 8412(e) shall be separated from the service on the last day of the month in which that air traffic controller becomes 56 years of age or completes 20 years of service if then over that age.

5 U.S.C. § 8425(a). Similarly to § 8335(a), § 8425(a) contains a waiver provision. FERS has a different way of calculating retirement eligibility and benefits. There were opportunities for ATCs to switch from CSRS to FERS. See Opp., Ex. D, at 2.

In addition to mandatory retirement, of course, an ATC may be removed from service for physical or mental reasons. See, e.g., 5 U.S.C. § 3381(a). The FAA annually tests ATCs to ensure they are healthy. See, e.g., Opp., Ex. J, at 5, 10 ("It is in the interest of the agency to develop and maintain the best possible Air Traffic Control Specialist

Workforce."); see generally Opp., Ex. I, at 1–2 (describing job of Aviation Medical Examiners, who are hired by the FAA to test, inter alia, ATCs to ensure that they meet Federal Aviation Regulations and are medically fit to perform safety-related duties).

II. BACKGROUND OF PLAINTIFF'S CASE

There do not appear to be any facts in dispute. See Reply, at 2 ("Plaintiff and [the Secretary] are in agreement concerning the relevant facts."). Plaintiff was born February 19, 1943. He began working as an ATC in June of 1973. Plaintiff is a member of CSRS, not FERS. See Reply, Ex. A, ¶2. He continually served in the position of ATC for over 25 years. Plaintiff presented the Court with evidence that he passed all Aviation Medical Examinations since 1985, see Opp., Ex. K, and claims that he has passed all examinations since his hire.

In August of 1981, many ATCs employed by the FAA engaged in an illegal strike under their former employee organization known as [the] Professional Air Traffic Controllers' Organization (PATCO). Plaintiff did not strike, which "required [him] to cross PATCO picket lines set up at the Honolulu FAA facility, at personal risk and ridicule by his co-workers." Opp., at 3. In and about October of 1981, President Reagan terminated the over 11,000 PATCO members who did engage in the strike. Following the strike, President Reagan issued a memorandum permitting the terminated ATCs to apply for federal employment with any federal agency except the FAA. See Opp., Ex. B ("these former federal employees should not be deemed suitable for employment with the [FAA]"). The bar on hiring by the FAA lasted until August of 1993, when it was lifted by President Clinton. See Opp., Ex. C ("I believe sanctions have been in effect long enough and that PATCO members should be eligible to apply, without preference, when there are openings with the FAA. It is time to put this chapter of labor-management relations behind us."). Eventually, some former PATCO strikers were rehired as ATCs, including some in Honolulu. See Compl., at 4. Some of these former strikers are now covered by FERS and may remain employed past age 56 if they have not accumulated twenty years of service. See 5 U.S.C. §8425(a). The current situation is therefore that some ATCs who did not strike are faced with mandatory retirement at age 56, while re-hired strikers face a more flexible/lenient mandatory retirement scheme under §8425.

In a supplement to his Opposition, Plaintiff submitted evidence of an additional group of ATCs who are exempt from the mandatory retirement age of 56. These ATCs are part of the FAA's Federal Contract Tower Program ("FCTP"). See Supp. Opp., at 2. These ATCs are not FAA employees, but do have FAA certification which allows them to be ATCs. Basically, through the FCTP, the FAA has out-sourced the ATC responsibilities at certain "Level I" (i.e., lowest level of take-off and landing) air traffic control towers across the United States. The FCTP lowered the cost of providing ATC service at these towers and also provided ATCs for towers that likely would not have been staffed at all because of expense. See Supp. Opp., Ex. A, at 1–3 of Executive Summary. "[A]ir traffic at Level I towers is less complex to control than air traffic at higher level towers." Id., at 1. Plaintiff included depositions of two ATCs employed by a company called Serco Management Services, who operates towers under the FCTP program. One of the deponents, Henry Hong, is 70 years old and currently an ATC on Molokai. The second deponent, Donald Waialae, is 66 years old and also works as an ATC at the airport on Molokai. Both men have passed Aviation Medical Examinations in the past year as a condition of their employment. See Supp. Opp., at 3.

In Defendant's reply to Plaintiff's supplement, he emphasizes that the FCTP has only been used at Level I, low activity airports and that there has been no attempt or Congressional approval to implement the use of similar programs at higher level facilities. Defendant attached a declaration by Mr. Eric Harrell, who is the FAA administrator who oversees the FCTP. See Harrell Decl. ¶ 1. (attached to Reply Supp. Opp.). Harrell explained that the FCTP is only currently in use at Level I facilities (less than 35 operations per hour) and is not in use, for example, at Level V facilities (which average 100 or more operations per hour). Harrell explained:

> In addition to having fewer operations, [ATCs] at Level I towers rely on visual methods to control aircraft, whereas controllers at higher level towers generally use radar equipment to control air traffic. Consequently, air traffic at Level I towers is less complex to control than air traffic at higher level towers.

Harrell Decl. ¶ 2. Expansion of the FCTP is still in the investigatory phase. See id. ¶ 8.

On December 16, 1998, approximately two months shy of his 56th birthday, Plaintiff wrote a letter directly to Defendant asking for a waiver under § 8335(a) which would allow him to work until age 61. See Compl., Ex. B. Plaintiff admitted that he was not going through the "bureaucratic channels" because time was of the essence. See id. As justification for the waiver, Plaintiff pointed out that fired strikers who had been rehired in 1995 were allowed to work past age 56 and some had even been hired after age 56. See id. In a response dated January 4, 1999, the FAA explained that the Secretary "may grant a waiver to mandatory separation at age 56 in cases of exceptional skills and experience of an air traffic controller. The waiver authority is intended only for extraordinary situations. The employee must document exceptional skills and experience over the skills and experience of other controllers." See Compl., Ex. C. The letter then explained the waiver request process (which Plaintiff had not followed) and how three different groups of ATCs exist. See id. The waiver was not granted.

Plaintiff turned 56 on February 19, 1999. Being covered by CSRS and having not received a waiver, Plaintiff was required to retire.

In the first count of his complaint, Plaintiff alleges that Defendant's actions violate the ADEA. In Count II, Plaintiff alleges that "the disparate enforcement of Public Law 92-927, by the FAA, on a basis not rationally related to air transportation safety violates Plaintiff's right to equal protection of the law in violation of the Fifth Amendment." Compl., at 6.

Defendant moved for judgment on the pleadings on the equal protection and the ADEA claims on December 30, 1999. After the Court granted a continuance to allow Plaintiff to do discovery, Plaintiff filed his opposition on July 27, 2000. Defendant filed a timely reply on August 21, 2000. On August 23, 2000, with leave of Court, Plaintiff filed a supplement to his opposition. Finally, on September 6, 2000, Defendant filed a reply to Plaintiff's supplement. The parties were notified that the motion would be treated as one for partial summary judgment, and agreed thereto. The matter came before the Court for hearing on September 18, 2000.

DISCUSSION

I. AGE DISCRIMINATION IN EMPLOYMENT ACT

Plaintiff's first cause of action is that the mandatory retirement provisions violate the ADEA. The ADEA prohibits federal agencies from engaging in age discrimination against employees over 40. "All personnel actions affecting employees or applicants for employment who are at least 40 years of age ... in executive agencies ... shall be made free from any discrimination based on age." 29 U.S.C. §633a(a); see also, e.g., Klein v. Secretary of Transp., 807 F.Supp. 1517, 1520, 1522 (E.D.Wash.1992) (rebuffed applicant for electronics technician position used §633a(a) as statutory basis for suit for age discrimination against FAA). The ADEA makes clear that federal employees are not protected by all sections of the ADEA, only what is codified at §§633a and 631(b). See 29 U.S.C. §633a(f) ("Any personnel action of any department, agency, or other entity referred to in subsection (a) of this section shall not be subject to, or affected by any provision of [the ADEA], other than the provisions of section 631(b) of this title and the provisions of this section."); see also Johnson v. Mayor and City of Baltimore, 472 U.S. 353, 356 n.1, 105 S.Ct. 2717, 86 L.Ed.2d 286 (1985) (noting that, "Federal employees are covered in a separate section of the [ADEA] and are treated differently from non-federal employees....").

Despite the ADEA's prohibition on age discrimination (which includes mandatory retirement ages), the Supreme Court has explained that when the ADEA was amended to prohibit age discrimination by the federal government, this did not render mandatory separation statutes such as §8335 illegal. See Johnson, 472 U.S. at 357, 105 S.Ct. 2717.

The 1978 Amendments eliminated substantially all federal age limits on employment, but they left untouched several mandatory retirement provisions of the federal civil service statute applicable to specific federal occupations, including firefighters, air traffic controllers, and law enforcement officers, as well as mandatory retirement provisions applicable to the Foreign Service and the Central Intelligence Agency. Id. (discussing mandatory retirement age for federal firefighters found in §8335(b)). The Court also noted that, "Congress, of course, may exempt federal employees from application of the ADEA and otherwise treat federal employees, whose employment relations it may directly supervise, differently from those of other employers ... indeed it has done so elsewhere in the ADEA." Id. at 366 n.10, 105 S.Ct. 2717.

This Court concludes that the specific mandatory separation statute at §8335 is an exception to the more general ADEA prohibitions on age discrimination. See Morton v. Mancari, 417 U.S. 535, 550–51, 94 S.Ct. 2474, 41 L.Ed.2d 290 (1974) ("Where there is no clear intention otherwise, a specific statute will not be controlled or nullified by a general one, regardless of the priority of enactment."). That the mandatory separation requirements for certain federal employees are properly treated as exceptions to the ADEA has been the holding of numerous federal courts. See, e.g., Strawberry v. Albright, 111 F.3d 943, 947 (D.C.Cir.1997) (holding that the specific statutes creating mandatory retirement ages for Foreign Service employees are an exception to the ADEA's general age discrimination prohibition); Palmer v. Ticcione, 576 F.2d 459, 465 & n.7 (2d Cir.1978) (noting that the ADEA's prohibitions have exceptions for certain federal employees, including air traffic controllers); Bowman v. United States Dep't of Justice, 510 F.Supp. 1183, 1186 (E.D.Va.1981), aff'd 679 F.2d 876 (4th Cir.1982) (finding claim by Bureau of Prisons correctional officer that the ADEA was superseded by §8335 meritless); cf. Riggin v. Office of Senate Fair Employment Practices, 61 F.3d 1563, 1566–69 (Fed.Cir.1995) (holding that "just as the ADEA does not conflict with or invalidate the mandatory retirement provisions applicable to other federal law enforcement officers," the more general Government Employee Rights Act of 1991 did not repeal the mandatory retirement requirements for Capitol Police officers found in the more specific §8335(d)).

The Court further finds that Plaintiff's citations to cases finding that employers who tried to enforce mandatory retirement ages had violated the ADEA are unavailing. See Opp., at 10 (citing, inter alia, EEOC v. Kentucky State Police Dep't, 860 F.2d 665, 667,

669 (6th Cir.1988) (ADEA violation found [regarding] mandatory retirement at age 55 for state police)). The ADEA is not applicable to air traffic controllers and therefore cases showing an action is illegal under the ADEA are inapposite.

The Court concludes that Plaintiff has not stated a cause of action under the ADEA because the mandatory retirement scheme he falls under is exempted from the ADEA's prohibitions. No questions of material fact exist that preclude judgment for Defendant and therefore, summary judgment is entered for Defendant on Plaintiff's ADEA claim.

II. EQUAL PROTECTION

Plaintiff also asserts a claim under the Equal Protection clause of the Fifth Amendment. He states in his complaint that, "the disparate enforcement of Public Law 92-927, by the FAA, on a basis not rationally related to air transportation safety violates Plaintiff's right to equal protection of the law in violation of the Fifth Amendment." Compl., at 6. Plaintiff argues that there are two classes of ATCs: 1) former PATCO strikers who were reinstated after 1993 and are covered by FERS and not subject to mandatory retirement at age 56, and 2) ATCs who did not strike in 1981 and who are forced to retire at age 56. See Opp., at 4. He argues that the "FAA is rewarding those very persons who put the air traveling public in jeopardy by engaging in an illegal strike." Id. He also argues that the creation of these two classes is not reasonably related to public aviation safety. Plaintiff argues that allowing FERS members to work long enough to become eligible for federal retirement benefits (even past age 56) undermines the FAA's argument that the mandatory retirement age of Public Law 92-297 is reasonably related to air public safety. See id. He also argues that the FAA's public safety argument is weakened by the fact that persons over age 56 can be employed as ATCs under the FCTP. See Supp. Opp., at 3–4.

Plaintiff challenges the existence of different mandatory retirement ages depending upon the retirement system of which an ATC is a member. The statutory classifications are between "grandfathered" CSRS members (who face no mandatory retirement), non-grandfathered CSRS members (such as Plaintiff, who must retire at 56), and FERS members (who must retire at 56 or at 20 years of service, whichever is later). The burden was on Plaintiff to attack every conceivable basis for the classifications. He has not met his burden. Defendant argues that the classifications are justified because it is Congress's right to treat employees hired at different times differently for retirement purposes. Instead of refuting this, Plaintiff argues it is unfair that some PATCO strikers are allowed to work past age 56.

Indeed, Plaintiff does not address (or negative) Congress's right to create different retirement ages for different employees hired at different times who are subject to different benefits calculations. The Supreme Court has upheld a system of different mandatory retirement ages based on a public employees's membership in one retirement plan versus another. See Vance v. Bradley, 440 U.S. 93, 99 S.Ct. 939, 59 L.Ed.2d 171 (1979). In Vance, foreign service officers challenged the fact that they were required to retire at age 60 because they were covered by the Foreign Service Retirement System ("FSRS"), while employees covered by CSRS did not face mandatory retirement until age 70. See id. at 94–96, 99 S.Ct. 939. The Court stated that the grouping of employees in one benefit plan versus another is acceptable as a function of legislative convenience.

The parties agree that an ATC's retirement and benefits plans differ significantly depending upon whether he is covered by CSRS or FERS. See Mot., at 4; Opp., at 6. In other words, the different retirement age classifications are not the only differences between the plans. In addition to concerns for the stressful nature of ATC work and the safety of the public, there are numerous considerations, such as, inter alia, varying employment and retirement benefits, encouraging prospective employees, keeping employees in the system until they are eligible for immediate retirement, as well as the expense of retirement plans. See, e.g., Pub.L. 99-335, § 100A (1986) (listing purposes of FERS statute including, inter alia, "to assist in building a quality career work force"). For Plaintiff to successfully challenge these classifications, he must meet his burden of showing that Congress had no rational reason to create different retirement schemes under CSRS and FERS. The Court finds that he has not done so and his claim must therefore fail. Moreover, for the reasons set forth above, the Court finds there is a rational basis for each of Public Laws 92-297 and 99-335.

Additionally, the Court finds Plaintiff's supplemental briefing on the FCTP to be a red herring. Plaintiff argues that the fact the FCTP hires ATCs over 56 undermines the FAA's safety rationale for the mandatory retirement scheme. The Court finds that the fact that the FCTP ATCs do not face an age limitation does not undermine the legislated mandatory retirement for FAA ATCs. First, the FCTP only operates at Level I towers, which experience a much lower volume of air traffic than the FAA operated and staffed towers. The same safety considerations do not apply to the Level I towers as apply to the Levels II–V towers staffed by FAA ATCs. Second, Defendant does not defend the classes of mandatory retirement based on safety. Instead, he defends the classification based on Congress's right to establish different retirement schemes for employees hired at different times. The FCTP ATCs are not affected by these classifications because they are not FAA employees. Their treatment is therefore irrelevant because, as non-employees, they are not subject to (nor recipients of the benefits of) the retirement benefit plans which create the different classes of mandatory retirement.

Furthermore, the Court notes that Plaintiff did not apply for a § 8335(a) waiver properly when he wrote directly to Defendant. Plaintiff admitted as much in his letter to Defendant. See Compl., Ex. B. He cannot complain now about not having received a waiver when he has only himself to blame for his failure to apply properly.

Finally, the Court notes that even if Plaintiff was a member of FERS (which of course, he could have become because there were opportunities to switch plans), he would still have been retired upon his 56th birthday. It is uncontested that at the time he retired, he had worked for the FAA for over 25 years. Accordingly, even if the mandatory retirement scheme in § 8425 applied to Plaintiff, he would be in the same position as he is now—retired.

CONCLUSION

For all of the above reasons, Defendant's motion for partial summary judgment is GRANTED.

ABRISCH v. UNITED STATES

359 F. Supp. 2d 1214 (M.D. Fla. 2004)

CORRIGAN, District Judge.

On the evening of December 12, 2001, flight N7701J, a Piper Cherokee single-engine aircraft, crashed about one mile from Runway 7 at Jacksonville International Airport ("JIA"), killing the pilot, Donald W. Weidner, and his three passengers, George Thomas Bowden and Adrienne and James Abrisch. Their next of kin and/or estate representatives each filed suit against the United States of America under the Federal Tort Claims

Act, 28 U.S.C. § 1346(b) and § 2671, claiming the Federal Aviation Administration ("FAA"), as an agent of the United States, breached its duty of care in providing air traffic control services to pilot Weidner, which negligence caused or contributed to the crash of the airplane. These suits were consolidated and tried for seven days in September and October of 2004 before the Court sitting without a jury. Following the submission of proposed findings of fact and conclusions of law by both sides, the Court heard closing arguments and, after careful consideration of the voluminous record and relevant law, these cases are now ready for decision.

All parties agree that the crash occurred because the pilot became spatially disoriented, causing him to lose the ability to control his airplane. I conclude that the plaintiffs have proven by a preponderance of the evidence that FAA air traffic controllers failed to give pilot Weidner the current weather information on that night which would have alerted him that weather conditions were rapidly deteriorating and that this failure contributed to the pilot's spatial disorientation. However, I further find that pilot Weidner himself also contributed to creating his spatial disorientation by forgoing the other options available to him and attempting instead to make his third instrument approach landing of the flight (after two missed approaches) when he was fatigued, ill, and on medication. Applying Florida comparative negligence principles, I hold that the FAA's negligence was the legal cause of 65% of the accident and that pilot Weidner's negligence was the legal cause of 35% of the accident. My full reasoning follows.

I. Findings of Fact

A. Background

On December 12, 2001, Donald W. Weidner, who was an attorney and a pilot, left his Jacksonville home at approximately 6:00 a.m. and drove to St. Augustine where he met his clients, Adrienne and James Abrisch. With Weidner piloting his single-engine plane, the three of them flew from St. Augustine to Fort Lauderdale to attend the deposition of Adrienne Abrisch, which began at 10:15 a.m. George Thomas Bowden, who practiced law with Mr. Weidner, met them in Fort Lauderdale and, following the deposition, which lasted until approximately 3:30 p.m., the four of them departed Fort Lauderdale, planning to fly first to St. Augustine to drop off the Abrisches and then to Craig Airport in Jacksonville.

Before departing from Fort Lauderdale, Weidner contacted an automated flight service to obtain the current weather conditions at St. Augustine and Craig. In the recording of that conversation, Weidner is heard deeply coughing and the preponderance of the evidence established that Weidner had ingested acetaminophen and pseudoephedrine, likely to relieve symptoms of a cold or upper respiratory infection. During this call, Weidner learned that an Airman's Meteorological Information (AIRMET) bulletin was in effect for Northeast Florida due to diminished visibility and that fog and low visibility conditions covered much of coastal Florida from Daytona northward. Weidner, who had been flying for over 20 years but had just been certified by the FAA in February 2001 to fly using instruments, then filed Instrument Flight Rules ("IFR") flight plans for both St. Augustine and Craig.

Unlike visual flight rules ("VFR") conditions in which pilots can fly by visual reference to the ground and horizon, under IFR conditions pilots fly by reference to instruments in the aircraft. Barbosa v. United States, 811 F.2d 1444, 1445 n.1 (11th Cir.1987). "[It] is presumed [during IFR conditions] that pilots cannot see other aircraft or the ground and are guided by air traffic controllers." Worthington v. United States, 807

F.Supp. 1545, 1549 (S.D.Ga.1992), rev'd on other grounds, 21 F.3d 399 (11th Cir.1994). When making an approach to an airport under IFR conditions, as Weidner anticipated by filing IFR flight plans for both St. Augustine and Craig, pilots use "instrument approach procedures." These are official published charts giving detailed instructions for descending and finding the runway using radio navigation aids to follow an increasingly narrow path until actually landing. At a certain point along this path, known as decision height, the pilot must have certain visual references in sight to legally continue with his approach. If none of those references are seen at decision height, the pilot must abort the landing, executing a "missed approach," where he flies a specific path upward and away from the airport runway area. See generally 14 C.F.R. § 91.175; testimony of radar flight track reconstruction expert Robert Cauble, Vol. II at Tr. 84-90, 108-09; and testimony of piloting techniques expert Lyle Schaefer, Vol. IV at Tr. 10-14, 20-21, 23-51.

The plane departed Fort Lauderdale Executive Airport at about 4:50 p.m. and at 6:09 p.m., while just south of Daytona Beach, Weidner contacted Miami Flight Watch to obtain a weather briefing for the conditions at his destination airports. Weidner reported to Miami Flight Watch that during his trip from Fort Lauderdale to his current location south of Daytona, he had enjoyed "smooth sailing all the way" with a "scattered layer below us ... periodically[,] but very smooth[,] a very nice flight." Joint Exhibit 2-B. Weidner's report is consistent with the testimony of the meteorology expert that Daytona was experiencing VFR conditions at that time. See testimony of Dr. Lee Ray Hoxit, Vol. VI at Tr. 168. Miami Flight Watch informed Weidner that St. Augustine was reporting two miles of visibility and 200 foot overcast with mist and Craig was reporting ½ mile visibility and 100 foot overcast with fog. Although Weidner had not requested the Jacksonville International Airport weather, he was also advised that JIA was reporting 1½ mile visibility with broken clouds at 200 feet and a 500 foot overcast in mist.

Due to weather, Weidner's attempt to land at St. Augustine was unsuccessful and he executed a missed approach. At 7:09 p.m., while en route to Craig Airport, the air traffic controller monitoring the Satellite Radar position asked Weidner whether he would attempt to land at JIA if he were unable to land at Craig. Weidner said he would and, at 7:16:51, Weidner advised the Satellite Radar controller that he had missed the approach at Craig and would like to be directed to JIA.

B. Air Traffic Control Operations at Jacksonville International Airport

On the night of the crash, JIA's permanent air traffic control tower, which is approximately 190 feet high, was closed for a four day period for renovations. During the closure, the radar room was still in operation but the Local and Ground air traffic controllers (who control flights on final approach, on the ground, and during take-off) operated out of a temporary control tower, located at ground level on JIA property between the taxiways near the approach ends of Runways 7 and 13. Not all of the equipment used in the permanent tower was available in the temporary tower. A written procedures manual outlined the plan for compensating for the lack of certain equipment during use of the temporary tower. For purposes of this decision, there were three significant differences in the operation of the temporary tower as compared to the permanent tower. See generally testimony of Steven Stump, Vol. I at Tr. 128–33; Michael Flanagan, Vol. I at Tr. 185–228, 250–56; Arnold Olinger, Vol. V at Tr. 281–84; Lawrence Haines, Vol. VI at Tr. 7–9, 17–18, 29; and Joint Exhibit 3 (Temporary Tower Operating/Briefing Guide).

First, under normal tower operations, weather data recorded by instruments at the airport and by the certified weather observer is updated on at least an hourly basis on an Automated Surface Observation System ("ASOS") machine. The controller in the tower can then supplement that information if warranted based on his own weather observations and he then enters that information into a machine called an IDS-4. IDS-4 monitors are available in the permanent tower and at every radar station in the windowless radar room and display the current weather at JIA and at other airports monitored by Jacksonville's radar operations. With each subsequent weather update to the IDS-4, a new sequential alphabetical code is assigned to the information, such as "Mike," "November," "Oscar," which permits air traffic controllers to refer to a weather sequence without recitation of the actual weather information contained therein. The temporary tower, however, did not have an ASOS machine or an IDS-4. Instead, weather information had to be relayed to the temporary tower controllers by Nextel walkie-talkie or by telephone from controllers in the radar room who would receive weather information from their IDS-4 monitors or from telephone calls from the on-duty certified weather observer. According to the temporary tower operating/briefing guide, the Data-1 controller in the radar room was given specific responsibility for passing current weather to the controllers in the temporary tower.

Second, while JIA's IDS-4 monitor updates and ATIS broadcasts [a continuous voice recording providing pilots with an airport's weather and other pertinent information] are usually handled by an air traffic controller in the permanent tower (who, again, has access to the weather information displayed on the ASOS monitor and can supplement that information by making his own observations from his location in the tower), during the temporary tower operations, a controller in the radar room was responsible for the ATIS broadcasts and for updating the IDS-4 display. According to the temporary tower operating/briefing guide, the Data-1 position was responsible for updating the IDS-4 and for alerting the Radar Supervisor-In-Charge of the need for an ATIS update.

Third, in contrast to communications between pilots and air traffic controllers on all other air traffic control frequencies, the communications over air traffic control frequencies originating in the temporary tower were not recorded. Thus, while the content of Weidner's communications with other air traffic controllers is a matter of stipulated fact based on the recordings, once the pilot was turned over to the Local controller for his final approach into JIA, no further recordings of any communications are available and the content of those communications is hotly disputed.

C. Weidner's flight toward Jacksonville

At 7:17 p.m., after Weidner notified the Satellite Radar controller that he wanted to be directed to JIA following his missed approach at Craig, the Satellite Radar controller directed Weidner to change frequencies to listen to the Information Mike ATIS broadcast for JIA, and to then contact the JIA approach frequency. The Information Mike ATIS broadcast had been recorded at 6:18 p.m. to reflect the weather as observed at JIA by a certified weather observer at 5:56 p.m., which included 1½ miles visibility in mist, ceiling broken at 200 feet, with an overcast layer at 500 feet and altimeter setting of 30.17. The Information Mike weather was the same JIA weather Weidner had heard at 6:09 p.m. from Miami Flight Watch.

However, apparently unbeknownst to the Satellite Radar controller who directed Weidner to pick up Information Mike, new and worse weather had more recently been observed by the certified weather observer at 6:56 p.m., who reported that the visibility had dropped to 1¼ mile in mist, and the ceiling was now broken at 100 feet, with an overcast layer at 500 feet. Instead of entering that 6:56 p.m. ASOS observation into the IDS-4 or recording a new ATIS broadcast, however, upon an inquiry from the Local controller in the temporary tower, the Radar Supervisor-In-Charge called the certified weather observer at 7:12:28 to question whether the visibility might be even worse than the new 1¼ mile observation. There is no evidence that the Radar Supervisor-In-Charge ever communicated his knowledge about the worsening weather to any other controllers in the radar room, including the Satellite Radar controller. The certified weather observer agreed that the visibility was further diminishing and at 7:16:51, he transmitted a new special ASOS observation for JIA of ½ mile visibility in fog, broken ceiling at 100 feet, and an overcast layer at 500 feet. The Data-1 controller in the radar room received the new ASOS and at 7:19:01, Data-1 relayed that weather information to the Ground controller in the temporary tower, advising Ground that the new 7:16:51 weather sequence would become Information November. The Data-1 controller then entered the new weather sequence into the IDS-4 system and gave the new weather to the Radar Supervisor-In-Charge who recorded a new ATIS broadcast, Information November, which became available to pilots at 7:24 p.m. At 7:26:22, Data-1 called the Ground controller in the temporary tower to advise him that the ATIS had been updated with Information November.

Meanwhile, at 7:19:50, after having picked up Information Mike from the ATIS as directed by the Satellite Radar controller, pilot Weidner reported onto the JIA approach frequency monitored by the East Radar controller who was also located in the radar room at JIA. At 7:20:01, the East Radar controller asked Weidner whether he had Information Mike and Weidner reported that he did. At 7:20:20 the East Radar controller instructed Weidner to switch to the North Radar frequency which instruction Weidner acknowledged on the East Radar frequency at 7:20:26.

Six seconds later, the North Radar controller made a blanket broadcast to alert pilots monitoring his frequency that updated weather had been received. He then recited the details of the Information November weather sequence including that the visibility was ½ mile in fog, ceiling 100 foot broken, 500 foot overcast, altimeter of 30.20 and [a] Runway Visual Range ("RVR") [the measure of visibility in the touchdown zone area] of 3500. The broadcast lasted approximately twelve seconds. During the next twenty to twenty-five seconds, the North Radar controller communicated with another pilot and there were short silences on the frequency. Then, at 7:21:08, pilot Weidner reported onto the North Radar frequency. The North Radar controller did not ask Weidner what weather information he had nor did he ask whether Weidner had heard the weather update the controller had recently announced. For the next ten minutes, Weidner remained on the North frequency, following the controller's directions toward his final approach. During that time (and after the new 7:24 p.m. ATIS), two other pilots checked on and announced that they had Information Mike. The North Radar controller did not tell them that Mike was no longer current, although he did tell both those pilots that the RVR was 3500. The Information November weather sequence was never repeated after Weidner checked onto the North Radar frequency at 7:21:08.

At 7:30 p.m., the certified weather observer transmitted yet another weather update to reflect further deteriorating conditions. At 7:30:04 the Data-1 controller alerted the temporary tower Ground controller that ¼ mile visibility with an indefinite ceiling of 100 feet had been observed. Data-1 did not advise other controllers in the radar room but that information became available to them shortly thereafter when it was posted on their IDS-4 monitors as Information Oscar.

At 7:31:26, without ever having confirmed the weather information Weidner had, the North Radar controller directed Weidner to turn to the tower frequency. At 7:31:31 Weidner acknowledged this direction and turned to the tower frequency then being monitored by the Local controller, William Lincoln, who would guide Weidner through the remainder of his flight.

D. The final approach

Weidner reported onto Lincoln's frequency at approximately 7:31 p.m. and remained there until radar lost contact with his plane at approximately 7:41 p.m. As noted above, recordings of the communications between Lincoln and Weidner are not available. There is no dispute that while on the Local controller's frequency, Weidner announced that he was executing a missed approach and he later stated that his instruments were malfunctioning. The radar flight track reveals that N7701J descended to approximately 500 feet and then deviated from the intended flight path to Runway 7, crossing the flight path while continuing to descend to an altitude of approximately 300 feet as the pilot apparently attempted without success to regain the proper course. The radar flight track shows the plane then began a straight climb to about 600 feet followed by a climbing left turn to an elevation of approximately 1000 feet, at which point the aircraft entered a spiraling downward turn, crashing to the ground seconds later. See Radar Data Study (Plaintiffs' Joint Exhibit 63) at Plot 3.

Wayne Bittner, who was operating the Ground control position in the temporary tower testified as to what he recalled about the air traffic control operations that evening. Bittner testified that he received the incoming telephone calls from Data-1 about the weather and wrote the information on a pad of paper which he and the Local controller Lincoln passed back and forth between them. Bittner also testified that he recalled that Lincoln may have been receiving separate phone calls to report RVR readings. Vol. VI at Tr. 5–7. Although Bittner recalled receiving the 7:19:01 weather sequence which would become Information November, he testified that he did not recall receiving the message at 7:26:22 to alert him that the ATIS had been updated with the Information November broadcast nor did he have any recollection of the 7:30:04 call advising him about the even newer weather observation, nor the call moments later advising him of the full new weather sequence which would become Information Oscar. See testimony of Wayne Bittner, Vol. VI at Tr. 42–55. Bittner was confident that, according to his standard operating procedures, he would have made notes about these calls on the pad he shared with Lincoln. Bittner further testified that he had no recollection of having overheard any of Lincoln's communications with planes on Lincoln's frequency. Id. at Tr. 63–64.

Additionally, four pilots testified as to what they overheard while monitoring the Local control frequency in preparation for take-off or landing at or near the time that Weidner was on that frequency. None of those pilots specifically recalled receiving weather information from the Local controller other than RVR and the two pilots who remembered overhearing Weidner on Lincoln's frequency could not recall hearing Lincoln give Weidner weather information. The pilot of one of the two single-engine flights that landed shortly before Weidner recalled that the Local controller did ask him to report his altitude upon seeing the runway environment. Those pilots who recalled any details of the weather they received that night recalled that the reported weather at the time was Information Mike.

The altimeter reading on Weidner's aircraft is some physical evidence which bears on the question of what weather information Weidner had been given at the time of the crash. To monitor the plane's altitude, a pilot sets a dial on his altimeter to match a barometric pressure reading announced by an air traffic facility. Each hundredth of an inch reflected on the altimeter's dial indicates approximately ten feet of altitude. See Aeronautical Information Manual, ¶7-2-3(b). A pilot's failure to correctly set his altimeter will affect his ability to properly follow approach procedures and land his aircraft. Id. at ¶7-2-3(d). On longer flights, pilots keep their altimeters adjusted to an airport's announced altimeter setting when within 100 miles of that airport and upon approaching an airport, pilots expect to hear regular altimeter readings from air traffic controllers. Altimeter settings are also included in ATIS broadcasts. See Aeronautical Information Manual, ¶4-1-13(b).

At the time Weidner was on his approach to Craig Airport, the proper altimeter setting for Craig was 30.19. The altimeter setting for JIA near the time of Weidner's approach, as announced in both Information November and Information Oscar, was 30.20. The previous altimeter setting for JIA, as announced in Information Mike, was 30.17. The NTSB Factual Report states, "Examination of the altimeter showed the [sic] it had received impact damage and all three hands had come loose on the face. The barometric was 30.20 in. Hg, the approximate altimeter setting at the time of the accident." See Plaintiffs' Joint Exhibit 1 at Bates # NTSB0567. However, the Jacksonville Sheriff's Office took photographs at the scene of the crash and one of those photographs shows the aircraft's altimeter on the ground near other wreckage. In that picture, the altimeter setting appears to be set at 30.18 or 30.17. The government's only evidence that the plane's altimeter was set at 30.20 is the NTSB statement quoted above. However, it is not clear whether this statement means that the airport's reported barometric reading was 30.20, which was the "approximate" setting of the plane's altimeter dial, or that the plane's altimeter dial was set at 30.20, which was the approximate altimeter reading at the airport. Based on the JSO picture, which even the government's own expert, Dr. Kenneth Orloff, conceded showed a setting of 30.17 or 30.18, I find that it is more likely than not that the altimeter's dial was set at 30.17 or 30.18 at the time of the crash (which is consistent with the proposition that pilot Weidner was still operating with Information Mike). Even without the JSO photograph (which was taken prior to the NTSB's arrival), there is enough ambiguity in the NTSB statement to discount it as "proof" that the plane's altimeter setting was 30.20, as the government contends.

Finally, there is the critical testimony of Mr. Lincoln, the Local controller. Again, in a departure from normal practice (apparently because the recording equipment in the temporary tower was inoperable), the FAA did not record the transmissions between Lincoln and Weidner that night. Because of the tragedy, none of the persons on board the plane can testify to these communications. Thus, we are left with the circumstantial and physical evidence described above and the testimony of Lincoln himself.

Lincoln provided personnel statements on December 12, 2001 (the night of the accident) and January 10, 2002 (see Plaintiffs' Joint Exhibit 22) and he was interviewed by the NTSB team investigating the crash on December 18, 2001. A summary of that interview is contained in the NTSB Group Chairman's report about the crash. See Plaintiffs' Joint Exhibit 1 at Bates # NTSB0575-0597. Lincoln also sat for a five hour deposition in this case in July of 2003 and provided a further declaration on April 14, 2004 filed in support of the government's motion for summary judgment. See Court Exhibit 5 and Plaintiffs' Joint Exhibit 20. Notwithstanding each of these opportunities, it was only at trial that Lincoln recalled having given Weidner full, timely and complete weather information including measurements for visibility, ceiling, wind, altimeter, temperature, dew point, RVR and PIREPS [reports from other pilots]. Upon questioning at trial, Lincoln testified that although he had reviewed some materials in advance of giving his earlier statements and deposition testimony, it was only when he heard tapes of conversations between the Ground controller and Data-1 shortly before testifying at trial that he recalled having given Weidner all of this information.

In addition to the inconsistencies between Lincoln's earlier statements and his trial testimony, Lincoln struggled even at trial to distinguish between what his usual practices were and what he actually recalled having done during a ten minute period one night nearly three years ago. Overall, while the Court has no reason to doubt Mr. Lincoln's good faith, in light of the inconsistencies in his prior statements and testimony, his sudden recall at trial and the other contradictory circumstantial and physical evidence, I find it more likely than not that Mr. Lincoln did not give full, updated weather to Mr. Weidner while Weidner was on the Local control frequency.

II. Conclusions of Law

A. Federal Tort Claims Act Liability

Under the Federal Tort Claims Act ("FTCA"), the United States may be held liable for "personal injury or death caused by the negligent or wrongful act or omission of any employee of the Government while acting within the scope of his office or employment, under circumstances where the United States, if a private person, would be liable to the claimant in accordance with the law of the place where the act or omission occurred." 28 U.S.C. § 1346(b)(1). Under the FTCA, the law of the state where the alleged negligent act or omission occurred governs the rights and liabilities of the parties. Richards v. United States, 369 U.S. 1, 11, 82 S.Ct. 585, 7 L.Ed.2d 492 (1962). Here, all the alleged acts or omissions took place in Florida and the parties agree that the Court must apply Florida substantive law in resolving issues of liability and damages.

B. Duty of care owed by Air Traffic Controllers

Applying Florida's traditional negligence principles, air traffic controllers owe pilots and their passengers the same duty of reasonable care that a reasonably careful person would use under like circumstances. Daley v. United States, 792 F.2d 1081, 1085 (11th Cir.1986). The duties of air traffic controllers are set forth in the Air Traffic Control Manual (FAA Order 7710.65), and, although those guidelines are evidence of the standard of care in the industry, an air traffic controller's duties are supplemented by the general duty of care owed under the circumstances. Id., Worthington, 807 F.Supp. at 1566. Thus, once they undertake to provide a service, even one not required by the Air Traffic Control Manual, under general negligence principles, air traffic controllers have a duty to provide such services with due care. Worthington, 807 F.Supp. at 1567. See also Pate v. Oakwood Mobile Homes, Inc., 374 F.3d 1081, 1087 n.5 (11th Cir.2004) (noting that, in contrast to the case before it in which OSHA employees' acts and omissions did not create liability for the plaintiff's injuries, "liability in air traffic controller cases stems from the public's reliance on such controllers").

In providing air traffic control services, air traffic controllers can presume that pilots know and will abide by the applicable Federal Aviation Regulations as well as information contained in the Air Traffic Control Manual and advisory circulars. Id. Among the duties assigned to pilots by law under the Federal Aviation Regulations is the final responsibility for the operation of an aircraft. 14 C.F.R. § 91.3(a). In carrying out this duty, a pilot "must be aware of those facts which are material to the proper operation of the aircraft and is charged with that which he should have known in the exercise of the highest degree of care." Worthington, 807 F.Supp. at 1567 (citations omitted).

Plaintiffs have advanced two theories of negligence in this case. First, plaintiffs claim that air traffic controllers breached their duty to provide the pilot of N7701J with accurate information about the current weather conditions at JIA. Second, plaintiffs claim that air traffic controllers failed in their duty to advise the pilot of the availability of alternate airports which the air traffic controllers knew were then reporting VFR conditions.

1. Claim regarding weather reports

Plaintiffs claim that air traffic controllers failed to provide Weidner with accurate, timely reports of the deteriorating weather conditions at JIA. Specifically, plaintiffs claim that Weidner had been advised that the visibility was 1 1/2 miles in mist with a 200 foot broken/500 foot overcast ceiling when in fact, by the time Weidner was making his final approach, air traffic controllers knew that conditions had deteriorated to 1/4 mile visibility with an indefinite ceiling of 100 feet. Weather observations made immediately after the crash reported visibility of 1/8 mile with vertical visibility of 100 feet. See Plaintiffs' Joint Exhibit 1 at Bates # NTSB0571. Information Mike suggested visibility substantially greater than what existed at the time of Weidner's final approach and a ceiling at least double that being observed. If controllers had transmitted the correct information, it would have reflected weather that was rapidly deteriorating and was below Weidner's permissible landing minimums.

As set forth in the Air Traffic Control Manual, the first priority duty of an air traffic controller is the separation of aircraft. Worthington, 807 F.Supp. at 1550. Weather service is an additional service to be provided as a second priority performed as an air traffic controller's other duties permit. Id. at 1567. Nonetheless, in this case, none of the air traffic controllers testified that they were too busy separating aircraft to provide weather information to pilots. To the contrary, the traffic was deemed to be moderate or light and pilots and air traffic controllers alike recognized the severity of the weather that evening. See, e.g., Plaintiffs' Joint Exhibit 1 at Bates # NTSB0575-0597 (NTSB Group Chairman's report containing statements of air traffic controllers describing traffic volume); testimony of air traffic support manager, Arnold Olinger, Vol. V at Tr. 281–84 (explaining that the temporary tower operations were selected for those days because of traffic volume); testimony of Data-1 controller Michael Flanagan, Vol. I at Tr. 257 (weather was changing rapidly); testimony of flight instructor Matthew Hiipakka, Court Exhibit 4 at Tr. 74 (weather could not have been more challenging); testimony of flight instructor Buz Russell, Court Exhibit 3 at Tr. 53 (pilot was caught off guard by thickness of fog, which was thicker than any he had ever flown in).

The government acknowledges that, based on the facts of this case, it cannot reasonably claim that air traffic controllers had no duty to disseminate weather information. See Doc. 112 (United States' Proposed Findings of Fact and Conclusions of Law) at 55. Rather, the government contends that the weather information provided by its air traffic controllers was sufficient to apprise the pilot of the relevant conditions that he would encounter at JIA. Id.

In factually similar circumstances involving a pilot flying through foggy conditions to make an approach to Runway 7 at JIA, the Eleventh Circuit held that "[t]he controllers deprived [the pilot] of accurate information" when they failed to advise him of current weather conditions thereby causing him to become confused when he reached decision height, expecting to have visual references sufficient to land and instead being enshrouded in fog. Worthington v. United States, 21 F.3d 399, 403 (11th Cir.1994). Under the reasoning of Worthington, the Court finds that in the circumstances of this case, air traffic controllers did in fact have a duty to provide Weidner with timely, accurate weather on the evening of December 12, 2001.

At 6:09 p.m., Weidner was advised of weather conditions at JIA which were consistent with the weather sequence reported as Information Mike. At 6:56 p.m., the certified weather observer reported conditions which were worse than reflected by the Information Mike broadcast. Controllers with access to an ASOS monitor were advised of this new observation right away. Rather than advising other radar room controllers, who work in a windowless room and are therefore entirely dependent on others to tell them weather conditions, no one disseminated the actual 6:56 p.m. observation or advised the other controllers that a change in the currently reported weather sequence was forthcoming. Instead, following communications between the Radar Supervisor-In-Charge and the certified weather observer at 7:12:28, new weather readings were made and a new observation was transmitted over the ASOS at 7:16:51. While the Data-1 controller conveyed this information to the Ground controller in the temporary tower, when Weidner announced his intentions to fly to JIA, the Satellite Radar controller advised him at 7:17:05 that Information Mike was current. At 7:24 p.m., the new weather sequence (Information November) was updated onto the ATIS; it became available to all radar room controllers on their IDS-4 monitors sometime before that, no later than 7:20:32. Weidner communicated with air traffic controllers at 7:19:50, 7:20:01, 7:20:20, 7:20:26, 7:21:08, 7:31:26 and 7:31:31 and none of them advised him of this new weather. Additionally, at 7:25:21 and 7:25:42 air traffic controllers were still not advising other pilots on Weidner's frequency about the new weather when those pilots checked in having Information Mike.

At 7:30 p.m., the certified weather observer transmitted even newer and worse weather (which would become Information Oscar). Weidner was not provided with this new weather in his communications with air traffic controllers at 7:31:26 and 7:31:31. Finally, as previously discussed, even when on the Local controller's frequency, the preponderance of the evidence establishes that Weidner did not receive the current weather. Thus, like the pilot in Worthington, "[b]ased on the information at [Weidner's] disposal, [Weidner] thought he would break through the fog at decision height and have visual references sufficient to complete a landing." Worthington, 21 F.3d at 403. Instead, because the controllers failed to give Weidner accurate weather information, Weidner unexpectedly failed to find any breaks in the clouds which would have allowed him to find visual references to the ground. Thus, air traffic controllers breached their duty of care by failing to provide Weidner with current weather information. See Worthington, 21 F.3d at 407 (the pilot did not have "the best possible weather information" because "of a series of imprecise communications combined with an absence of communication" by air traffic controllers).

2. Claim regarding alternate airports

Plaintiffs additionally claim that, given the unlikelihood that any aircraft would be able to land in the IFR conditions present at JIA, air traffic controllers had a duty to suggest alternate regional airports with better weather conditions, such as the nearby Gainesville Regional Airport, which was operating under VFR conditions on the evening of December 12, 2001. The government contends there is no support for this claim under the law. Plaintiffs cite to Insurance Company of State of Pennsylvania v. United States, 590 F.Supp. 435 (S.D.Miss.1984) as support. In that case, the pilot was low on fuel and, unable to land due to extreme weather at his destination airport, he specifically asked air traffic control about alternate airports at which he might attempt to land. Insurance Company of State of Pennsylvania, 590 F.Supp. at 439. Even though the air traffic controller had information about two very close airports operating with VFR conditions, he failed to provide this information to the pilot whose plane crashed when he ran out of fuel. Id. at 442–44. Here, by contrast, Weidner himself knew about the VFR conditions in Daytona, having recently flown by there. Moreover, there is no evidence that Weidner asked JIA controllers about alternate airports nor did Weidner give the controllers any reason to think he was "in trouble." Under these facts, the Court declines to find air traffic controllers breached any duty of reasonable care by their failure to suggest alternate airports.

C. Causation

Having proved that air traffic controllers acted negligently in failing to provide the pilot with current weather information, plaintiffs must additionally show by a preponderance of the evidence that such negligence was a legal cause of damage. Eleventh Circuit Pattern Jury Instructions (Civil Cases) State Claims Instructions 1.1 (1999). Negligence is a legal cause of damage if it directly and in natural and continuous sequence produces, or contributes substantially to producing such damage, so it can reasonably be said that, except for the negligence, the loss, injury or damage would not have occurred. Id. Negligence may be a legal cause of damage even though it operates in combination with the act of another, some natural cause, or some other cause if such other cause occurs at the same time as the negligence and if the negligence contributes substantially to producing such damage. Id. To prove causation under the facts of this case, plaintiffs must show that the air traffic controllers' failure to give the pilot Weidner timely and accurate weather was the legal and proximate cause of him becoming spatially disoriented.

According to the testimony of piloting techniques expert Lyle Schaefer, which the Court accepts for these purposes, operating on the mistaken assumption that Information Mike was current, Weidner would have reasonably begun to look for external reference points at an altitude of approximately 500 feet. See Vol. IV at Tr. 57–58. At that elevation, he could expect 1/8 to 3/8 of the cloud cover to be breaking, giving him obvious reference to the ground. As Weidner descended further to 300 feet or less, he likely continued searching for visual references outside which he could not see due to the deteriorating weather conditions that were known to air traffic controllers at the time. The medical and aeronautical experts agreed that by repeatedly turning his focus from his instruments to the outside environment and back, Weidner likely began to experience spatial disorientation. Then, in what was either an effort to attempt to combat those symptoms, or because he had reached decision height without visualizing any required reference on the runway environment, Weidner attempted to return his full attention to his instruments to execute a missed approach. Unfortunately, Weidner was unable to regain control of the aircraft and, as the parties have stipulated, N7701J crashed due to the pilot's becoming spatially disoriented. I find that the air traffic controllers' failure to provide Weidner with the current weather conditions was a legal and proximate cause of his becoming spatially disoriented. See Worthington, 21 F.3d at 406 ("Spatial disorientation and the failure to successfully execute a missed approach are precisely the harm that this defendant should have expected after depriving Mr. Worthington of accurate and timely information about weather conditions when he approached a landing strip shrouded with fog.").

D. Comparative Negligence

Under Florida's comparative negligence principles, I must determine whether the pilot's negligence also played a role in his becoming spatially disoriented and if so, to what extent. Hoffman v. Jones, 280 So.2d 431, 438 (Fla.1973) (announcing that under Florida law, where the finder of fact determines that both plaintiff and defendant were guilty of negligence which was, in some degree, a legal cause of the injury to the plaintiff, the negligence of the defendant and that of the plaintiff should be apportioned and the damages award be apportioned thereon). The Eleventh Circuit has specifically countenanced the use of comparative negligence principles in a Florida airplane crash case against the government. See Worthington, 21 F.3d at 407.

Experts for both the plaintiffs and the government essentially agreed that several risk factors can lead to creating an environment which is ripe for spatial disorientation to occur. Those factors include weather, turbulence, night, formation flying, aircraft maneuvers, VFR-IFR transition, head movement, anxiety, distraction, fatigue, illness, alcohol, instrument failure, inexperience and medication. Some of these factors admittedly overlap and any one or, more likely, some combination of these factors, can lead to spatial disorientation. Moreover, there is no precise formula as to which combination of these factors will cause spatial disorientation in a given situation. Nevertheless, in making my findings as to comparative negligence, I have attempted to determine which of these factors were present and whether the presence of a factor was due to a lack of reasonable care on the part of the pilot, air traffic controllers, both, or neither. Finally, I have considered whether the evidence supports a finding that any particular factor should be weighed more heavily than others in my analysis.

There was no evidence that turbulence, formation flying or alcohol played any role in the pilot's spatial disorientation and I have therefore not considered those factors. I further find that instrument failure did not play a role here—the pilot's own report of instrument failure was the only evidence of such failure and, given the testimony that pilots often erroneously report instrument failure during episodes of spatial disorientation, the preponderance of evidence does not support a finding that instrument failure occurred here. I also find that, while Weidner was not highly experienced in flying in IFR conditions, the testimony about his solid performance in executing the missed approaches at St. Augustine and Craig in IFR conditions, his certification in IFR flying by the FAA, and the evidence that even experienced instrument-rated pilots become spatially disoriented at times, leads me to find that inexperience was not a significant factor in Weidner becoming spatially disoriented. Additionally, that it was night is the fault of no one—it was simply a risk factor that was present.

The evidence does establish that the air traffic controllers' failure to provide the pilot with the correct weather led to the pilot being at a point in his final approach where the weather was worse than anticipated, thus preventing him from picking up any of the visual points on the ground that he would have expected to see. Additionally, because the weather was not what the pilot expected to find, he more likely than not engaged in early and frequent head movement by continuing to search for the ground, he more likely than not experienced anxiety as he failed to visually locate any ground contacts, he more likely than not experienced distraction when he diverted his focus from his instruments to the outside environment and he more likely than not engaged in additional aircraft maneuvers in attempting to maintain control of his aircraft. The negligence of the air traffic controllers in not providing accurate weather led to the presence of these factors.

However, having just missed two other approaches, Weidner's choice to fly to an airport with IFR conditions while fatigued, on medications and while ill (rather than, for example, flying to Daytona which he knew had been experiencing VFR conditions during his flight, or asking air traffic controllers for a VFR alternative), was also a failure of reasonable care which substantially contributed to his spatial disorientation. See Worthington, 21 F.3d at 407 (suggesting that the pilot's decision to attempt a landing at JIA in deteriorating weather conditions could be a failure to exercise reasonable care (though, if so, it would go "to apportion, not bar, liability")).

I therefore find that the air traffic controllers' negligence substantially contributed to the presence of the spatial disorientation risk factors of weather, head movement, aircraft maneuvers, anxiety and distraction and that the pilot's own negligence substantially contributed to the presence of VFR-IFR transition, fatigue, medication and illness. Although the weighing of these factors for the purposes of apportioning comparative negligence is not an exact science, after careful and even painstaking deliberation, I find the FAA's negligence was the legal cause of 65% of this accident and the negligence of the pilot, Mr. Weidner, was the legal cause of 35% of this accident.

III. Conclusion

I recognize (as the parties surely do) that we will never know for certain what actually occurred during the final moments of flight N7701J and what caused the plane to crash. Although I am required by the law to assess and quantify liability for this accident, the process of doing so is not reducible to a mathematical formula but, rather, reflects my best judgment based on the facts as I have found them proven by a preponderance of the evidence. I am certain that neither the air traffic controllers nor Mr. Weidner intentionally compromised the safety of this flight. Nonetheless, based on the evidence, it is more likely than not their combined failure to use reasonable care that led to this tragic accident.

Thus, I find the plaintiffs have proven by a preponderance of the evidence that the United States (through its agent, the FAA) is liable for this accident and that the government's negligence was 65% of the legal cause of the accident, the remaining 35% of the responsibility for the accident being due to the negligent actions of the pilot, Donald W. Weidner.

LAKOMY v. UNITED STATES

70 Fed. Appx. 199 (5th Cir. 2003)

PER CURIAM.

Plaintiffs-Appellees were flight attendants who sustained injuries when the pilots of their aircraft took evasive measures to avoid what the pilots perceived to be an imminent mid-air collision. After a bench trial, the district court entered judgment in favor of the flight attendants, concluding that air traffic controllers' negligence caused appellees' injuries and that the United States is liable for their negligence under the Federal Tort Claims Act ("FTCA"). See 28 U.S.C. §§ 1346(b), 2671–2680. Because we find that appellees presented insufficient evidence to conclude that the air traffic controllers' negligence was a proximate cause of the alleged injuries, we reverse.

I. FACTUAL AND PROCEDURAL BACKGROUND

A. The Incident

This appeal arises from an in-flight accident aboard Lufthansa Airlines Flight 436 ("Lufthansa 436") that occurred when the plane was en route from Dallas-Fort Worth Airport ("DFW") to Houston on June 21, 1996. Plaintiffs-Appellees are Irena Lakomy,

Peter Reil, Peter Lebens, Andreas Weber, and Ulrike Baumann, all German nationals and flight attendants aboard Lufthansa 436. Captain Rudiger Werner was the pilot in command of the aircraft, but he was designated the "pilot not flying" on this flight. His co-pilot was the "pilot flying." Lufthansa 436 is an Airbus A-340 equipped with a Traffic Collision Avoidance System ("TCAS"), a self-contained, on-board collision-avoidance system that is independent of ground-based radar and that derives its information from devices aboard other aircraft in flight. The use of the TCAS on Lufthansa 436 was mandated by law. Congress intended TCAS to be a "back-up" protective measure to the regular responsibilities of pilots and air traffic controllers to avoid collisions. See 49 U.S.C. §44716; 14 C.F.R. §121.356.

TCAS makes second-by-second calculations of the trajectories of aircraft in its vicinity. When the risk of a collision exceeds a certain threshold, TCAS issues a "traffic advisory." The size of the bubble of protection provided by TCAS is unknown to both the pilot and air traffic control. It issues the traffic advisory 40 seconds before the intruding aircraft's closest point of approach to the aircraft from which the TCAS is making its calculations. Pilots are instructed to respond to a TCAS traffic advisory by attempting to identify the other aircraft visually. If the threat of collision does not abate, TCAS issues a "resolution advisory" approximately 15 seconds later. This is 25 seconds before the intruding aircraft's closest point of approach to the aircraft from which the TCAS is making its calculations. Along with the resolution advisory, TCAS issues an aural command directing the pilots how to steer the aircraft to avoid the threat. Airlines in general, and Lufthansa in particular, instruct pilots that unless they have visually identified the aircraft posing the threat and have determined that no collision threat exists, they must follow the aural command issued by TCAS.

In addition to TCAS, pilots also rely on ground-based air traffic controllers ("ATCs") to provide certain air safety services. ATCs are employees of the Federal Aviation Administration. On the day of the incident, Lufthansa 436 was flying under Instrument Flight Rules ("IFR"), under which its flight pattern out of DFW was directed by air traffic control at the DFW Terminal Radar Control facility ("TRACON"). ATC Gregory Hood, acting under the supervision of ATC John Sullivan, was responsible for the airspace in which Lufthansa 436 operated. ATCs Hood and Sullivan were responsible for an area of air space totaling 1,000 square miles. Importantly, despite the assistance that they receive from ATCs and TCAS, pilots are ultimately in command of an aircraft and are directly responsible for the operation of that aircraft. See 14 C.F.R. §91.3.

As Lufthansa 436 departed DFW, the ATCs instructed it to ascend to a cruise altitude of 17,000 feet. Approximately five minutes into its flight, Lufthansa 436 reached an altitude of 10,000 feet. The flight attendants removed their safety belts and started to prepare beverage service in the rear of the aircraft. Meanwhile, a Cessna 421 entered Hood's and Sullivan's airspace. The Cessna 421 is a smaller airplane that flew under Visual Flight Rules ("VFR"), which it was permitted to do because of the clear skies. Pilots flying under VFR trust their eyesight to avoid mid-air collisions. They are not required to pre-clear a flight plan with air traffic control and are under no obligation to maintain a particular course. As it flew through the airspace manned by ATCs Hood and Sullivan, the Cessna maintained an altitude of 14,500 feet en route to Liberal, Kansas. It was equipped with a Mode C transponder, which, at 1200 code, caused the Cessna to appear on ATC Hood's radar screen as an "unidentified" aircraft about four minutes before the incident at issue took place. Several minutes after it first appeared on Hood's radar as an unidentified aircraft, and less than one minute before the incident, the Cessna contacted ATC to request traffic information. This occurred at 19:27:16 Universal Coordinated Time, or 2:27:16 p.m. Central Daylight Time. The Lufthansa 436 flight crew heard the exchange between the Cessna and the ATCs, but they did not correlate the Cessna's reported position with their own flight route. At 19:27:36, ATC Hood assigned the Cessna a transponder code, which rendered the Cessna a "radar identified" aircraft.

Shortly before 19:27:51, Lufthansa 436's TCAS issued a traffic advisory. At 19:27:51, Lufthansa 436 radioed to ATC that "we have a traffic ah...." The communication was cut off midsentence by a communication to ATC from an American Airlines flight. In response to the TCAS traffic advisory, the Lufthansa flight crew attempted without success to identify the intruding aircraft visually. TCAS then issued a resolution advisory and an aural command to "descend, descend." This occurred when the aircraft was at 13,744 feet (which is designated as Class E airspace), climbing at a rate of approximately 2,600 feet per minute. It was the first time this Lufthansa flight crew had ever received a TCAS resolution advisory. Believing that a mid-air collision was imminent, the Lufthansa flight crew performed a series of evasive maneuvers.

The Lufthansa training manual instructs pilots that a TCAS resolution advisory does not require abrupt or rapid pitch control inputs, as the advisory affords an ample 25 seconds to alter the aircraft's trajectory smoothly. The Lufthansa flight crew's inputs, however, were anything but smooth. The First Officer, who was the "pilot flying," moved his sidestick up full throttle. Under Lufthansa flight procedures, Captain Werner, as the "pilot not flying," should not have made any inputs to the aircraft's sidestick. He nonetheless moved his sidestick nose-down, then nose-up 1.3 seconds later. The pilots inputted a number of additional sidestick movements, including side-to-side movements not commanded by TCAS. The consecutive inputs sent the flight attendants in the rear of the aircraft hurtling against the aircraft's ceiling, and then against its sides, and then against its ceiling once more. By all accounts, the rear of the aircraft was a "war zone." The flight attendants suffered serious injuries.

After Lufthansa 436 began its evasive maneuvers, ATC Hood radioed Lufthansa 436 to say that there was traffic in its vicinity—the Cessna—at "one o'clock and a mile northbound fourteen thousand five hundred." This occurred at 19:27:59, eight seconds after Lufthansa 436 radioed ATC to report the TCAS traffic advisory. Several seconds later, ATC Hood informed the Cessna of the position of Lufthansa 436. The Cessna responded, "Yeah, we've been watchin' him."

The record makes clear that the two aircraft were never going to collide. Appellees' expert witness and the government's expert witness both testified that the Cessna crossed the projected flight path of Lufthansa 436 five miles ahead of Lufthansa 436. The government's expert added that when the Cessna crossed Lufthansa 436's flight path, the Cessna was 2,000 feet higher than Lufthansa 436. After the Cessna crossed Lufthansa 436's projected flight path, the two aircraft passed each other side by side. It was at this time, when the planes' flight paths were no longer merging and they were heading in opposite directions, that the TCAS issued its traffic advisory and then its resolution advisory. As the aircraft passed each other, they reached their closest point of approach. Experts determined, and the district court found, that when the aircraft were at their closest point vertically—approximately 700–800 feet—they were 2.76 miles apart horizontally. At their closest point horizontally—1.38 miles apart—they were 1100–1200 feet apart vertically. The only threat of a collision was that the Cessna's pilots might suicidally veer their aircraft into the Lufthansa.

The parties nevertheless contest whether the ATCs should have prevented the planes from coming this close to each other. The FAA Handbook 7110.65J sets forth the responsibilities of ATCs. The Handbook in effect on the day of the incident instructed ATCs that "the primary purpose of the ATC system is to prevent a collision between aircraft operating in the system and to organize and expedite the flow of traffic." U.S. DEP'T OF TRANSP., FED. AVIATION ADMIN., AIR TRAFFIC CONTROL HANDBOOK, 7110.65J (the "HANDBOOK"), § 2-1-1. The first priority duty of an ATC is to separate aircraft and issue "safety alerts":

> Issue a safety alert to an aircraft if you are aware the aircraft is in a position/altitude which, in your judgment, places it in unsafe proximity to terrain, obstructions, or other aircraft.... The issuance of a safety alert is a first priority once the controller observes and recognizes a situation of unsafe aircraft proximity to terrain, obstacles, or other aircraft. Conditions, such as workload, traffic volume, the quality/limitations of the radar system, and the available lead time to react are factors in determining whether it is reasonable for the controller to observe and recognize such situations.

HANDBOOK, § 2-1-6.

In addition to issuing safety alerts, ATCs apply "merging target procedures" as follows:

> a. Except while they are established in a holding pattern, apply merging target procedures to all radar identified:
>
> (1) Aircraft at 10,000 feet and above.
>
> (2) Turbojet aircraft regardless of altitude.
>
> (3) Presidential aircraft regardless of altitude.
>
> b. Issue traffic information to those aircraft listed in subpara a. whose targets appear likely to merge unless the aircraft are separated by more than the appropriate vertical separation minima.

HANDBOOK, § 5-1-8. When their workload permits, ATCs also issue traffic advisories:

> Where no separation minima applies, such as for VFR aircraft outside of Class B and Class C airspace, or a TRSA, issue traffic advisories to those aircraft on your frequency when in your judgment their proximity warrants it.

HANDBOOK, § 2-1-21.

ATCs are required to exercise their own judgment in determining whether aircraft come within an unsafe proximity. The Handbook does not oblige ATCs to prevent an on-board TCAS system from issuing its own traffic advisory or resolution advisory. Indeed, ATCs are not even aware of the bubble of protection provided by TCAS.

Here, the ATCs did not issue a safety alert and did not apply merging target procedures. They issued Lufthansa 436 a traffic advisory at 19:27:59, but this was too late to prevent appellees' injuries. By that time, the TCAS had already issued a resolution advisory, and the Lufthansa flight crew was already engaging in abrupt evasive maneuvers. At the time of the incident, the ATCs' workload level was "moderate." ATCs Hood and Sullivan testified that they could not recall any specific incident at the radar tower that prevented them from issuing a traffic advisory before the Lufthansa flight crew began their maneuvers.

B. Legal Proceedings

In federal district court, the flight attendants asserted claims of negligence against the United States, by and through its agency, the FAA. Plaintiffs-Appellees sought damages for personal injuries pursuant to the FTCA. The United States moved to dismiss for lack of subject matter jurisdiction, contending that the discretionary function exception to the FTCA applies to this lawsuit because the allegations give rise to impermissible judicial second-guessing of the FAA Administrator's decision to separate the layer of air safety protection provided by TCAS from the layer of protection provided by ground-based ATCs. The United States also asserted that ATCs Hood and Sullivan were not negligent, and that their negligence, if any, did not cause appellees' injuries.

After a two-day bench trial, the district court determined that the Lufthansa 436 flight crew's response to the TCAS resolution advisory was "excessive, unnecessary, and contrary to" their TCAS training, and that the flight crew's negligence was a proximate cause of the flight attendants' injuries. The district court also found that ATCs Hood and Sullivan were negligent for failing to provide a timely traffic advisory, to issue a safety alert, and to apply merging target procedures. The district court found that the ATCs' negligence was a proximate cause of the flight attendants' injuries. Further, the court found that the ATCs were more responsible than the Lufthansa flight crew and apportioned the fault at 55%–45%. The court also found it "unnecessary" to reach the United States' motion to dismiss for lack of jurisdiction because the lawsuit does not challenge an action of the Administrator of the FAA. The court reasoned that plaintiff's allegations challenge the actions of ATCs and not the Administrator of the FAA.

The United States timely appealed the trial court's findings on subject matter jurisdiction and proximate causation.

II. STANDARD OF REVIEW

The application of the discretionary function exception to the FTCA is a question of law that we review de novo. See Theriot v. United States, 245 F.3d 388, 394 (5th Cir.1998). To the extent that the district court made factual findings that underlie its decision, these factual findings are binding unless clearly erroneous. See id. The district court's finding as to proximate cause is also a factual finding that is reviewed for clear error. See Gavagan v. U.S., 955 F.2d 1016, 1019 (5th Cir.1992). A finding is "clearly erroneous" when, although there is evidence to support it, the reviewing court examines all of the evidence and "is left with the definite and firm conviction that a mistake has been committed." Theriot, 245 F.3d at 395 (citing United States v. United States Gypsum Co., 333 U.S. 364, 395, 68 S.Ct. 525, 542, 92 L.Ed. 746 (1948)). A trial court's decision to credit the testimony of one witness over that of another, unless internally inconsistent, is virtually never clear error. See id. Further, when the trial court is faced with testimony susceptible to multiple conclusions, its factual determinations stand so long as they are plausible, even if the evidence may have been weighed otherwise. See id.

III. DISCRETIONARY FUNCTION EXCEPTION

Appellant challenges the district court's determination that the United States is not immune from this lawsuit under the discretionary function exception to the FTCA. The FTCA provides that the United States shall be liable "in the same manner and to the same extent as a private individual under like circumstances." 28 U.S.C. § 2674. This broad waiver of sovereign immunity is subject to a number of exceptions, among them the discretionary function exception:

> Any claim based upon an act or omission of an employee of the Government, exercising due care, in the execution of a statute or regulation, whether or not such statute or regulation be valid, or based upon the exercise or performance

> or the failure to exercise or perform a discretionary function or duty on the part of a federal agency or an employee of the Government, whether or not the discretion involved be abused.

28 U.S.C. § 2680(a). The nature of the conduct, and not the status of the actor, governs whether the exception applies. United States v. Gaubert, 499 U.S. 315, 322, 111 S.Ct. 1267, 1272, 113 L.Ed.2d 335 (1991). The applicability of the discretionary function exception involves a two-step analysis.

First, because the exception covers only acts that are discretionary in nature, we must determine whether the challenged act involves an element of "judgment or choice." Gaubert, 499 U.S. at 322, 111 S.Ct. at 1272; Theriot, 245 F.3d at 397. This requirement is not satisfied if a federal statute, regulation or policy specifically prescribes the course of action that the government employee must follow, for in this situation the employee "'has no rightful option but to adhere to the directive.'" Gaubert, 499 U.S. at 322, 111 S.Ct. at 1272 (quoting Berkovitz v. United States, 486 U.S. 531, 536, 108 S.Ct. 1954, 1958–59, 100 L.Ed.2d 531 (1988)).

Second, we examine whether the judgment or decision is grounded on considerations of social, economic, or political public policy. Id. The exception applies to any judgment or choice that is "susceptible to policy analysis." Id. at 325, 111 S.Ct. at 1275. That is because the purpose of the discretionary function exception is to prevent judicial "second-guessing" of legislative and administrative decisions grounded in social, economic and political policy through tort actions. United States v. S.A. Empresa de Viacao Aerea Rio Grandense (Varig Airlines), 467 U.S. 797, 814, 104 S.Ct. 2755, 2765, 81 L.Ed.2d 660 (1984). If a regulation allows for employee discretion, the existence of the regulation in and of itself creates a presumption that the discretionary act involves consideration of the public policies that led to the promulgation of the regulation. Gaubert, 499 U.S. at 324, 111 S.Ct. at 1274.

An additional purpose of the discretionary function exception is to protect the government from liability that would "seriously handicap efficient government operations." Varig Airlines, 467 U.S. at 814, 104 S.Ct. at 2765.

Before it is possible to address whether a government action involved judgment or choice that is grounded in public policy, it is first necessary to identify the government action challenged. The United States argues that appellees challenge an action of the Administrator of the FAA. The Administrator of the FAA is authorized by statute "to reduce or eliminate the possibility or recurrence of accidents in air transportation." 49 U.S.C. § 44701(c). In so doing, the Administrator publishes the Handbook and employs ATCs to carry out its policies and procedures. The Administrator also promulgates regulations that require certain aircraft, including Lufthansa 436, to employ TCAS. See 49 U.S.C. § 44716; 14 C.F.R. § 121.356.

The United States asserts that the Administrator exercised her discretion by deciding that ATCs should perform certain services to ensure air traffic safety and by further deciding that the TCAS should perform an air safety service separate and distinct from that performed by ATCs. The United States notes that ATCs are not obliged to prevent TCAS from issuing a traffic advisory or a resolution advisory. Indeed, ATCs do not even know what circumstances give rise to such advisories. The United States argues that appellees' allegations in effect represent an impermissible attempt to second-guess an exercise of the Administrator's discretion by holding ATCs liable for failing to prevent a TCAS resolution advisory. Appellees argue, and the district court agreed, that their allegations do not challenge the Administrator's discretionary authority.

We agree with the district court that the nature of this lawsuit does not give rise to judicial second-guessing of the Administrator's discretion. Appellees assert that ATCs negligently permitted the two aircraft to come within an unsafe proximity. Appellees do not assert that ATCs negligently permitted the TCAS to issue a traffic advisory and resolution advisory. Nor do appellees question the judgment of the Administrator in establishing a system in which the TCAS issues warnings separate and independent from those issued by ATCs. They do not, for example, urge the Court to impose a new obligation upon ATCs to prevent TCAS resolution advisories. Therefore, although it is true that the Administrator of the FAA decided not to require ATCs to prevent TCAS resolution advisories, this lawsuit does not challenge that decision.

IV. PROXIMATE CAUSATION

The liability of the United States arises under the FTCA only when the law of the state where the act or omission occurred would impose it. 28 U.S.C. § 1346(b); Johnson v. Sawyer, 47 F.3d 716, 727 (5th Cir.1995). Here, that state is Texas, and under Texas law the ordinary rules of negligence apply to aircraft accidents. See, e.g., Hayes v. United States, 899 F.2d 438, 443 (5th Cir.1990). The common law doctrine of negligence in Texas consists of (1) a legal duty owed by one person to another; (2) a breach of that duty; and (3) damages proximately resulting from the breach. Greater Houston Transp. Co. v. Phillips, 801 S.W.2d 523, 525 (Tex.1990). Proximate cause comprises both "cause in fact" and foreseeability. Excel Corp. v. Apodaca, 81 S.W.3d 817, 820 (Tex.2002); Gutierrez v. Excel Corp., 106 F.3d 683, 687 (5th Cir.1997). A "cause in fact," which is also called a "but for" cause, is that which was a substantial factor in causing the injury and without which the harm would not have occurred. Apodaca, 81 S.W.3d at 820. Under Texas law, a finding of cause in fact must be established by probative evidence and cannot be supported by mere conjecture, guess, or speculation. See id. It may, however, be based on either direct or circumstantial evidence. See id.

The district court determined that "[h]ad the ATCs properly followed the [Handbook's] procedures, the harm to [appellees] would not have occurred." This, of course, is a factual finding reviewed for clear error. Gavagan, 955 F.2d at 1019. Whether it is supported by sufficient evidence is a question of federal law, see, e.g., Ayers v. United States, 750 F.2d 449, 452 (5th Cir.1985); Wardlaw v. Inland Container Corp., 76 F.3d 1372, 1375 n.1 (5th Cir.1996), but we refer to state law to determine the kind of evidence that must be produced. Patin v. Thoroughbred Power Boats, Inc., 294 F.3d 640, 647 n.12 (5th Cir.2002) (citing Tutor v. Ranger Ins. Co., 804 F.2d 1395, 1398 (5th Cir.1986)). Our inquiry requires a review of the entire record, including both direct and circumstantial evidence, to see whether we are left with the definite and firm conviction that a mistake has been committed. Theriot, 245 F.3d at 395.

The district court did not elaborate on the evidence on which it based its finding of proximate causation. It accepted appellees' argument that had the ATCs properly followed the Handbook, no evasive maneuvers would have been required. For this to be true, the ATCs' actions must have been sufficient to forestall a TCAS resolution advisory. This follows because the Lufthansa flight crew took evasive action in response to the TCAS resolution advisory, and they testified that they would have responded with similarly abrupt evasive maneuvers whenever it issued such a resolution advisory. Captain Werner testified that when the TCAS issues a resolution advisory, he has "only one thing in my mind," and that is "to carry out the prescribed maneuver." He "had to be quite clear about the fact that if I did not do anything at that moment, that the very next moment it would come to a mid-air collision." Captain Werner testified that it is "very difficult" for him to make a smooth adjustment "without any injuries." The inquiry, therefore, is whether the ATCs' negligence is a cause without which no TCAS resolution advisory would have issued. Apodaca, 81 S.W.3d at 820.

At trial, appellees produced only two pieces of evidence on point. First and foremost, appellees rely on Captain Werner's testimony that had the ATCs issued a timely traffic advisory, he would have "reduced the [Lufthansa's] climb rate." He did not testify to the extent of any such reduction or the impact that such a reduction would have had on the aircraft's altitude. Second, appellees fall back on the testimony of their expert witness, Andrew Hayes, who stated that the timely issuance of a traffic advisory "allows the flight crews to plan ahead and operate the aircraft in a manner so they don't have to make abrupt maneuver[s] when being surprised by an opposing aircraft." When asked whether the application of merging target procedures or the timely issuance of a traffic advisory would "have made an outcome different than it is in this case," Hayes responded "yes."

Captain Werner's testimony that he would have reduced the aircraft's climb rate does not support the flight attendant's case of proximate causation. TCAS does not warn pilots of only impending, imminent collisions. Rather, TCAS issues a resolution advisory when the risk that a collision might occur in 25 seconds exceeds a certain threshold. The record reflects, and the district court found, that the size of the bubble of protection provided by TCAS is unknown to both the pilot and air traffic control. The size of the bubble was also unknown to the district court. In this case, TCAS issued a resolution advisory even though the two aircraft were never on a collision course. It issued a resolution advisory after the Cessna had crossed the projected flight path of Lufthansa 436, when the two aircraft were passing each other, side by side, heading in opposite directions.

Because the size of the bubble of protection provided by TCAS is unknown, it is impossible to conclude that some kind of reduction in the climb rate would have steered the aircraft clear of this bubble. Perhaps evidence of a dramatic change in the aircraft's altitude would be sufficient, but appellees produced no such evidence. Captain Werner did not indicate the effect that his hypothetical reduction in the climb rate would have had on the aircraft's altitude. The record does not supply the facts and figures necessary to make an independent calculation. Although we can reasonably assume that a "reduction in the climb rate" would have had some impact on the aircraft's altitude, we cannot assume that such a reduction would have steered the aircraft clear of the TCAS's bubble of protection given that the size of this bubble is unknown.

Hayes's testimony does not support the flight attendants' case of proximate causation either. He offers conclusory testimony that a timely traffic advisory "allows the flight crews to plan ahead and operate the aircraft in a manner so they don't have to make abrupt maneuver[s] when being surprised by an opposing aircraft." He does not testify that the timely issuance of a traffic advisory prevents TCAS from issuing a resolution advisory. Nor does he testify that the Lufthansa flight crew would have reacted to a TCAS resolution advisory with anything but abrupt maneuvers. Indeed the evidence was quite to the contrary. As we have noted, Captain Werner testified that (1) he was required to respond to the TCAS resolution advisory unless he could identify the intruding aircraft visually, which he could not do; (2) he believed the TCAS resolution advisory meant that a collision was imminent unless he took immediate action; and (3) it would be "very difficult" for him to respond to a TCAS resolution advisory without causing injuries.

The record, when viewed in its entirety, makes clear that appellees failed to meet their burden of presenting sufficient evidence of proximate causation. We are therefore left with the definite and firm conviction that a mistake has been committed. Theriot, 245 F.3d at 395.

V. CONCLUSION

The district court's determination that the United States of America is liable for appellees' injuries is reversed.

Notes

1. As the *Yap* case explains, air traffic controllers suffer from enormous stress and tend to burn out at a young age. In the movie *Pushing Tin* (1999), which chronicles the professional and personal lives of two fictional controllers (played by John Cusack and Billy Bob Thornton), the frantic nature of their work is succinctly summed up by the quote that appears at the beginning of the movie (reportedly from a real-life controller): "You land a million planes safely, then you have one little mid-air and you never hear the end of it." For a further look at air traffic controllers, see the web sites of the International Federation of Air Traffic Controllers' Associations (www.ifatca.org) and the National Air Traffic Controllers Association (www.natca.org), as well as Milovan S. Brenlove, *Vectors to Spare: The Life of an Air Traffic Controller* (1993). The film *Ground Control* (1999) (with Kiefer Sutherland), although fictional, also is illuminating.

2. The PATCO strike, which is briefly described in *Yap*, marked a turning point in the history of the American labor movement and remains one of the enduring legacies of the Reagan Administration:

> On August 3, 1981, 12,176 air traffic controllers walked off the job. Led by their militant union, the Professional Air Traffic Controllers Organization (PATCO), the controllers believed that they had the power to paralyze the nation's air transport system and thereby put intense pressure on the Federal Aviation Administration (FAA) to accede to their bargaining demands. Contrary to the expectations of the controllers, the PATCO strike failed. In an unprecedented move, the federal government fired and replaced 11,301 of the strikers. Relying on non-striking controllers, supervisors, retirees, and, to a lesser extent, military controllers, the government was able to keep commercial air carrier traffic moving, though not without some delays and a reduction in volume.
>
> The story of PATCO's unsuccessful strike is also the story of the union's failure to prevail in the nation's courtrooms. Of course, PATCO also failed to get enough controllers out on strike to shut down the system and the union failed to obtain concrete support from other unions. The federal government, however, relied on the judicial system at every step in its struggles against PATCO, and it did so successfully. In addition to firing controllers, the federal government filed at least 104 civil actions in 85 federal district courts seeking injunctions ordering the controllers back to work. When the controllers violated court orders, the government sought and obtained civil and criminal contempt citations against many strikers. The Justice Department criminally prosecuted 71 controllers for violating the federal statute that makes it a felony to strike against the federal government. Furthermore, the FAA initiated proceedings to decertify PATCO as the exclusive bar-

gaining representative of the controllers. When the president fired the strikers, the courts upheld nearly all of the discharges. Finally, the commercial airlines sued PATCO for violating a 1970 injunction and consent decree not to strike, and the airlines obtained a judgment of $4.5 million in contempt fines and $29 million in compensatory damages against PATCO. Combined with millions of dollars in other strike-related debts, PATCO's debts were so high that the union filed for bankruptcy. In all, well over 150 legal actions arose out of the PATCO strike. In nearly every one of the significant court battles, PATCO and the controllers lost.

Neil Fox, *PATCO and the Courts: Public Sector Labor Law as Ideology*, 1985 U. Ill. L. Rev. 245, 245–46. For a further discussion, *see* Michael Round, *Grounded: Reagan and the PATCO Crash* (1999). Ironically, as this casebook was about to be printed, a new dispute between controllers and the federal government was brewing, leading some to predict that President Bush soon would face the same hard choices that confronted President Reagan. *See further Air Controllers, U.S. Clash on Pay*, S. Fla. Sun-Sentinel, Dec 20, 2005, at 2D.

3. Donald Weidner's death due to spatial disorientation, described in *Abrisch*, brings to mind the earlier death of John F. Kennedy, Jr.:

The cause of the plane crash that killed John F. Kennedy Jr., his wife and sister-in-law a year ago was probably that Mr. Kennedy, with hardly any experience flying his plane alone at night, became disoriented in haze, the National Transportation Safety Board said today in a staff report.

One of his flight instructors offered to fly with him that night, but Mr. Kennedy said "he wanted to do it alone," the instructor told the investigators who prepared the report.

Mr. Kennedy, who had not yet qualified for flying with instruments alone (as opposed to seeing visual cues through the windows), probably had less than one hour's experience flying his plane at night without an instructor, the report said. It noted that a common cause of crashes among pilots untrained in instrument flying was taking off when visibility was good (a situation known as Visual Flight Rules, or V.F.R.) but flying into conditions where it was not, making the piloting more difficult than they can handle.

In this case, the report said, the condition was haze that obscured the horizon. Pilots who cannot see the horizon must rely on instruments to tell if they are in level flight or if they are banking. But a disoriented pilot can bank a plane into a fatal spiral.

The report cited six kinds of illusion that can lead to disorientation, without stipulating which one came into play in this case. "Spatial disorientation as a result of continued V.F.R. flight into adverse weather conditions is regularly near the top of the cause/factor list in annual statistics on fatal aircraft accidents," the report said.

Using the autopilot would have helped, according to aviation experts, because it is not subject to disorientation, but Mr. Kennedy was flying his plane manually.

"Flying at night over featureless terrain or water, and particularly in haze or in overcast, is a prime setup for spatial disorientation, because you've lost the horizon," said Warren Morningstar, a spokesman for the Aircraft Owners and Pilots Association.

The crash killed Mr. Kennedy, 38, who was at the controls of his single-engine Piper Saratoga II; his wife, Carolyn Bessette Kennedy, 33; and her sister, Lauren G. Bessette, 34.

From the weather forecasts, Mr. Kennedy would have known that he would be out of sight of land on his trip, Mr. Morningstar said. "It becomes a question of pilot judgment: do you put yourself into that situation if you're not appropriately trained and rated," he said.

Exactly how much experience Mr. Kennedy had is not clear, because investigators did not recover his logbook. But they estimated that he had logged around 310 hours, including 55 at night. He had flown only about 72 hours without a flight instructor on board, an unusually low number, according to instructors. But he had been studying for his instrument rating, one reason for having few unsupervised hours.

Weather reports on the night of the crash—July 16, 1999—cited haze or mist and visibility as low as four miles. Pilots who flew over the Cape Cod-Martha's Vineyard area that night reported serious haze; one told investigators he had flown over Martha's Vineyard and thought there was a power failure on the island, because he could not see any lights.

The report said that investigators had interviewed one of Mr. Kennedy's flight instructors, who said he "would not have felt comfortable" with Mr. Kennedy "conducting night flight operations on a route similar to the one flown on, and in weather conditions similar to those that existed on, the night of the accident."

Another instructor told the investigators that he had made the flight to Martha's Vineyard with Mr. Kennedy six or seven times, often at night. "The instructor stated that the pilot was methodical about his flight planning and that he was very cautious about his aviation decision-making," the report said. The instructor also said that Mr. Kennedy "had the capability to conduct a night flight" to Martha's Vineyard, "as long as a visible horizon existed." The plane crashed about 7.5 miles southwest of Gay Head, at the island's western end.

Like most reports on the crashes of private planes, this one was issued by the board's staff, without a hearing or a meeting by the five board members to approve its contents, as is usually done for airline crashes. The report runs substantially longer than the average for general aviation accidents, however.

Matthew L. Wald, *Safety Board Blames Pilot Error in Crash of Kennedy Plane*, N.Y. Times, July 7, 2000, at B5.

4. Why did the flight attendants in *Lakomy* sue the United States rather than the pilots? What about the manufacturer of the Traffic Collision Avoidance System—should it have been named as a co-defendant? Likewise, what about the pilot of the Cessna?

5. In December 1995, American Airlines Flight 965 crashed into a mountain while attempting to land at Alfonso Bonilla Aragon Airport in Cali, Colombia. Of the 164 persons aboard, all but four were killed. In sorting out the liability issues, the Eleventh Circuit penned this rather frightening description of the region's air traffic control system:

> American [Airlines] provides special training to its pilots who fly into Central and South America in order to acquaint them with the unusual features of these regions. Among other things, pilots are instructed, in no uncertain terms, not to rely on local air traffic controllers ("ATCs") for information about their location or position in the sky. According to American's training materials, Latin American ATCs will assume when providing clearance that the pilot is on course, the plane is located where the pilot says it is, the pilot knows where the mountains are, and the pilot will refuse a clearance that will take the plane into a mountain. Because these assumptions may be incorrect, the ATCs will clear pilots to descend below minimum safe altitudes in mountainous areas.

Piamba Cortes v. American Airlines, Inc., 177 F.3d 1272, 1277 (11th Cir.), *rehearing and rehearing en banc denied*, 193 F.3d 525 (11th Cir. 1999), *cert. denied*, 528 U.S. 1136 (2000).

6. Prior to 9/11, the worst air disaster of all time—involving the loss of 583 lives—was the March 1977 runway collision between two 747s (KLM Flight 4805 and Pan Am Flight 1736) at Tenerife's Los Rodeos Airport in the Canary Islands. As would later be determined, the disaster was primarily caused by breakdowns between the controllers and the pilots:

> Tenerife ATC gave the KLM flight its ATC-clearance, [which is the] clearance to fly a certain route immediately after take-off (not a clearance to begin take-off), but the KLM captain apparently mistook this to be permission for the takeoff itself. Captain van Zanten released the brakes and the co-pilot responded with a heavy Dutch accent with words that could either be "We are at take off" or "We are taking off." The control tower was confused with the message and asked for the KLM plane to stand by. However, simultaneous communication from Pan Am caused a heterodyne, making the response inaudible. Ironically, Pan Am was reporting [that it] had not finished taxiing. Either message, if broadcast separately, might have given KLM time to abort its takeoff.
>
> Due to the fog, the KLM crew was not able to see the Pan Am 747 taxiing on the runway ahead of [it]. In addition, neither of the 747s could be seen from the control tower, and the airport was not equipped with runway radar.
>
> While the KLM [plane was starting] its take-off run, the tower told Pan Am to "report when runway clear." Pan Am radioed back: "OK, we'll report when we're clear." On hearing this, the KLM flight engineer expressed his concern about the Pan Am [plane] not being clear of the runway, but was overruled by the captain.
>
> Later investigation showed that there had been misinterpretations and false assumptions. Analysis of the cockpit voice recorder transcript show[ed] that the KLM pilot was convinced that he had been cleared for take-off, while the Tenerife control tower was certain that the KLM 747 was stationary at the end of the runway and awaiting takeoff clearance. [Other factors determined to have played a role were the] squelched radio messages (calls from both planes to the tower and vice versa canceled each other because they happened to be at precisely the same instant) [and] the use of non-standard phrases used by the KLM co-pilot ("We're at take off") and the Tenerife control tower ("O.K").

Tenerife Disaster, at en.wikipedia.org/wiki/Tenerife_Disaster#Investigation. Despite the passage of nearly three decades and numerous efforts aimed at preventing them, such mishaps continue to occur. *See further* Alan Levin, *Runway Safety Systems Failing to Stop Close Calls, NTSB Complains*, USA Today, Nov. 16, 2005, at 4A (reporting that 30 serious near-misses take place each year in the United States alone).

7. Just as not all controllers work at airports ("en route" controllers guide planes when they are between airports), not all airports have controllers. When approaching or leaving an "uncontrolled airport," also known as an "untowered airport," pilots use an open air radio frequency (CTAF or UNICOM) to advise other pilots of their presence and intentions. *See further Remo v. United States Federal Aviation Administration*, 852 F. Supp. 357 (E.D. Pa. 1994); *Emerald Development Co. v. McNeill*, 120 S.W.3d 605 (Ark. Ct. App. 2003); *Newman v. Thompson*, 497 S.E.2d 8 (Ga. Ct. App. 1998).

8. For additional examinations of the legal issues surrounding air traffic controllers, *see* James L. Rigelhaupt, Jr., Annotation, *Liability of United States for Negligence of Air Traffic Controller*, 46 A.L.R. Fed. 24 (1980 & 2005 Supp.); Kathleen McChesney Goodman & Scott Davis, *Free Flight and the Pilot-in-Command Concept—A Recipe for Disaster?*, 62 J. Air L. & Com. 653 (1997); Janie Lynn Treanor, Comment, *Privatization v. Corporatization of the Federal Aviation Administration: Revamping Air Traffic Control*, 63 J. Air L. & Com. 633 (1998).

Problem 24

While taking directions from a Level I tower, two small planes collided in mid-air, killing all those aboard. If the estates sue the United States for negligence and the government moves for dismissal because the air traffic controller was employed by a private contractor, how should the court rule? *See Alinsky v. United States*, 415 F.3d 639 (7th Cir. 2005).

F. CONCESSIONAIRES

JERRICO, INC. v. JERRY'S, INC.

376 F. Supp. 1079 (S.D. Fla. 1974)

FULTON, Chief Judge.

Plaintiff, Jerrico, Inc., has registered with the United States Patent Office the marks 'JERRY'S DRIVE-IN' [registration issued April 8, 1958] and 'JERRY'S RESTAURANT' [registration issued January 1, 1963] for restaurant services. Both registrations are in full force and effect and are retroactive to the dates of issuance. Plaintiff initiated this action against defendant, Jerry's, Inc., for infringement of these federally registered marks under the Lanham Act, 15 U.S.C. §1114(1) and for unfair competition. Defendant, Jerry's, Inc., denied infringement and raised several affirmative defenses. Defendant has also counterclaimed, seeking a declaratory judgment of its rights as between the parties to use the marks 'JERRY'S,' 'JERRY'S RESTAURANT' and 'JERRY'S CATERERS.'

HISTORY OF JERRICO, INC.

In 1946, Jerome M. Lederer opened his first restaurant in Lexington, Kentucky under the name 'JERRY'S.' Thereafter, from 1946 through 1956, Mr. Lederer opened a number of restaurants identified by the name 'JERRY'S DRIVE-IN' or 'JERRY'S RESTAURANT' in the Lexington and Louisville, Kentucky areas. In April, 1957, plaintiff opened its first restaurant outside the State of Kentucky in New Albany, Indiana. This restaurant was operated as a franchise under the name 'JERRY'S DRIVE-IN.' Subsequently, plaintiff opened restaurants in the States of Kentucky, Indiana, Florida, Ohio, Tennessee and Georgia, following the major highways in route from the midwest to Florida. The present action is concerned primarily with the plaintiff's Florida restaurant operations.

HISTORY OF JERRY'S, INC.

Defendant's business was founded by the late Gerard J. Pendergast, Sr. who was a pioneer in the airline catering business in Florida. In the early 1940s Mr. Pendergast began providing box lunches for National Airlines. This service was initially provided at St. Petersburg and then later at Tampa. Beginning in 1943 Mr. Pendergast moved the business to Jacksonville following National Airlines' change of headquarters. Mr. Pendergast conducted this business under the name 'JERRY'S CATERERS.'

In 1946 National Airlines moved its headquarters from Jacksonville to Miami and Mr. Pendergast likewise moved his food catering business to Miami at the request of the airline. [A short time later] a restaurant was opened at Miami International Airport under the names 'JERRY'S,' 'JERRY'S RESTAURANT' and 'JERRY'S CATERERS RESTAURANT.' At this time, Mr. Pendergast conducted an airline catering service from the restaurant under the names 'JERRY'S' and 'JERRY'S CATERERS.'

The defendant, 'JERRY'S INC.,' was incorporated in the State of Florida in 1964. Defendant presently conducts airline catering facilities under the name 'JERRY'S CATERERS' at various Florida airports, [including Cape Kennedy, Daytona Beach, Fort Lauderdale, Melbourne, Miami, Opa-Locka, Sarasota, Tallahassee, and West Palm Beach]. In addition to scheduled airline catering, defendant also provides catering services for unscheduled and charter flights.

Defendant also operates airport restaurants, coffee shops and cocktail lounges which are open to the general public at airports in [Daytona Beach, Fort Myers, Melbourne, Sarasota, Tallahassee, and West Palm Beach]. Some of these restaurants have been operating under the names 'JERRY'S,' 'JERRY'S RESTAURANT' and 'JERRY'S CATERERS,' with 'JERRY'S' being the lead name. In this regard, the name 'JERRY'S' has been prominently displayed by the defendant, particularly at the entrance of the above restaurants, in the use of billboards and in media advertising.

SPECIFIC FINDINGS OF FACT AND CONCLUSIONS OF LAW

1. This Court has jurisdiction under the trademark laws of the United States, 28 U.S.C. § 1338, and the Lanham Act, 15 U.S.C. § 1114(1).

2. The service marks registered to plaintiff are in full force and effect, retroactive to their dates of issuance and are incontestable. 15 U.S.C. § 1065.

3. Trademark infringement under 15 U.S.C. § 1114(1) is based solely on the likelihood for consumer confusion arising out of the infringer's use of a conflicting mark. American Foods, Inc. v. Golden Flake, Inc., 312 F.2d 619 (5th Cir. 1963).

4. In determining likelihood for confusion, the Court must consider: the degree of similarity between the marks in question; the distinctiveness of the marks involved; type of business in which the marks are used; extent of advertising and notoriety of the mark; type of consumers involved; and dates of adoption of the marks in controversy. Continental Motors Corp. v. Continental Aviation Corp., 357 F.2d 857 (5th Cir. 1967); Callman, The Law of Unfair Competition, Trademark and Monopolies § 980-80-4 (3d ed.).

5. An examination of the evidence adduced at the trial of this cause, in the light of the criteria discussed above, requires a finding that plaintiff's mark 'JERRY'S RESTAURANT' has been infringed. The evidence clearly establishes that the use by defendant and its subsidiaries of 'JERRY'S RESTAURANT' and 'JERRY'S CATERERS' for restaurant services open to the general public has caused confusion as to the source of defendant's services vis-a-vis the plaintiff's registered mark.

In making this finding, the Court has also taken into consideration the fact that defendant is essentially an airport food dispensing operator located almost solely at various Florida airports. The names of these airport restaurants are not essential to the successful operation of defendant's business because most of its patrons are so called 'captive customers.' No great financial burden would be imposed on defendant in requiring it to change the names of these restaurants to something other than 'JERRY'S.'

....

16. In connection with defendant's airline catering business, the Court finds that defendant was a pioneer in the industry in Florida. The use by the defendant of its tradename 'JERRY'S CATERERS' in connection with airline catering is also a right the defendant has acquired under the common law. This right may be maintained and exercised in the future and extends to the entire State of Florida. John R. Thompson Co. v. Holloway, 366 F.2d 108 (5th Cir. 1966); Turner v. HMH Pub., 380 F.2d 224 (5th Cir. 1967).

17. Plaintiff, Jerrico, Inc. presently does not, nor has it ever, engaged in the airline catering business. Plaintiff's marks are used in a completely different line of commerce and are not affected by defendant's airline catering activity.

[The remainder of the court's opinion is omitted.]

HASKINS v. TRANS WORLD AIRLINES, INC.

182 F.3d 925 (9th Cir. 1999)

PER CURIAM.

Plaintiffs, current and former black passenger service skycaps employed by defendant, Trans World Airlines, Inc. ("TWA"), appeal from the district court's dismissal as moot of their claims under Title VII of the Civil Rights Act of 1964, 42 U.S.C. § 2000e et seq., and denial of attorneys' fees. We affirm in part, reverse in part, and remand for further proceedings.

I.
Mootness

Plaintiffs filed this action in 1986, seeking to enjoin TWA from terminating all skycaps, the vast majority of whom are black. TWA, however, had decided prior to suit, over 12 years ago, not to eliminate the skycaps' jobs, but rather to replace individual skycaps with outside vendors through the course of natural attrition. The district court concluded the currently employed plaintiffs' claims are therefore moot. We agree.

Although plaintiffs alleged various other discrimination claims concerning wage, salary, and disciplinary practices, the district court found that these allegations were not "reasonably related" to the Equal Employment Opportunity Commission charge and therefore could not be pursued in federal court. Plaintiffs do not challenge the district court's holding, and we conclude that it is correct. See Green v. Los Angeles County Superintendent of Sch., 883 F.2d 1472, 1475–76 (9th Cir.1989).

As so limited, the currently employed plaintiffs' Title VII action concerned only the previously proposed, but never implemented, elimination of the skycaps' jobs. We conclude such claim is moot. A case is moot when "the issues presented are no longer 'live' or the parties lack a legally cognizable interest in the outcome." County of Los Angeles v. Davis, 440 U.S. 625, 631 (1979). Voluntary cessation of the complained of conduct can render a case moot if the alleged violation is not likely to recur and interim relief or events have eradicated the effects of the alleged violation. Id.

We believe TWA has, in this case, met the "heavy" burden of demonstrating mootness. The company decided in 1986, before this suit was initiated, not to proceed with the planned termination. In the intervening 12 years, TWA has adhered to that decision in the absence of any court order requiring it to do so. We find no evidence in the record that would suggest the company will alter its position if the district court's judgment is affirmed.

II.
Albuquerque Skycaps

Plaintiffs suggest that two of the formerly employed skycaps continue to have claims not mooted by TWA's decision not to eliminate the skycap positions. After TWA notified plaintiffs of the proposed terminations, it postponed the effective date of the planned furlough at all of the airports at issue, except Albuquerque and Tulsa. The furlough went into effect at the latter two airports in October 1983. Five of the seven skycaps at the Albuquerque airport formed a company with exclusive rights to provide skycap services for three airlines, including TWA. Their company did not fare well financially. Two of these five Albuquerque skycaps are plaintiffs in this action.

Plaintiffs contend that these two skycaps did not voluntarily terminate their employment at TWA and have claims for monetary damages that should be remanded to the district court for further proceedings. TWA responds that the Albuquerque skycaps never asked for a postponement of the furlough and voluntarily agreed to become independent contractors. In its memorandum decision, the district court specifically noted the different status of the Albuquerque skycaps, but apparently grouped them together with the other skycaps in determining that the Title VII claims were moot, and made no specific findings concerning their separate monetary claims.

Although we may ordinarily affirm "on the basis of any evidence in the record that supports the trial court's judgment," we conclude here that the district court's failure to make an express finding of fact requires remand because we cannot reach "a complete understanding of the issues ... without the aid of separate findings." South-Western Publ'g Co. v. Simons, 651 F.2d 653, 656 n.2 (9th Cir.1981). Thus, we reverse the judgment entered against the two Albuquerque skycaps and remand for further proceedings consistent with this Memorandum.

III.
Attorneys' Fees

Finally, plaintiffs contend that the district court abused its discretion in denying their request for attorneys' fees. To qualify as a "prevailing party" for purposes of 42 U.S.C. § 1988, plaintiffs must establish a "clear, causal relationship between the litigation brought and the practical outcome realized." American Constitutional Party v. Munro,

650 F.2d 184, 188 (9th Cir.1981). Plaintiffs have failed to establish a relationship between their lawsuit and TWA's decision not to eliminate the skycaps' jobs, which predated the filing of their action. Plaintiffs, however, might prevail on remand with respect to the claims of the two Albuquerque skycaps. We therefore affirm the denial of attorneys' fees as to all plaintiffs except the two Albuquerque skycaps, reverse the denial of attorneys' fees as to those two plaintiffs, and remand for further proceedings. Each party shall bear its own costs on appeal.

METROPOLITAN DADE COUNTY v. CBM INDUSTRIES OF MINNESOTA, INC.

776 So. 2d 937 (Fla. Dist. Ct. App. 2000), *review dismissed*, 797 So. 2d 585 (Fla. 2001)

LEVY, Judge.

Metropolitan Dade County ("the County") appeals from the denial of its Motion for Summary Judgment and the entry of Final Summary Judgment in favor of CBM Industries of Minnesota, Inc. ("CBM"), contending that an indemnity provision in the Management Agreement ("agreement") between the parties requires CBM to indemnify the County for attorney fees expended in defending a slip and fall claim. We agree with the County and reverse, concluding that the underlying Complaint raises alternative claims against the County sounding in negligence and vicarious liability for negligence stemming from CBM's negligent maintenance of the premises.

The County owns the Miami International Airport and contracted with CBM for janitorial and cleaning maintenance services at the airport. An airline employee slipped and fell at the airport and filed suit against the County for her injuries. The plaintiff later amended her Complaint to include CBM as a co-defendant. The County sought to invoke an indemnity provision contained in the agreement which provides:

> [CBM] shall indemnify and save the County harmless from any and all claims, liability, losses and causes of actions which may arise out of the willful, negligent, or unlawful acts or omissions of [CBM] in its operations under this Agreement and shall pay all claims and losses of any nature whatsoever in connection therewith, shall defend all suits, in the name of the County, when applicable, including appellate proceedings, and shall pay all costs, judgments, and attorneys fees, which may issue thereon; provided, however, that nothing herein shall be construed to require [CBM] to indemnify the County against liability resulting from the willful, negligent, or unlawful acts of omissions of the County, nor to be liable for loss or damage incurred or occasioned by [CBM] in the performance of operations under this Agreement. This provision shall survive the termination of this Agreement.

CBM denied any duty to defend and/or indemnify the County. After CBM settled the underlying suit on behalf of the County and itself, the County filed a cross-claim for indemnity of attorney fees against CBM, claiming that CBM had a duty to defend the County in the underlying suit pursuant to the indemnification clause contained in the maintenance agreement.

Thereafter, the County moved for Summary Judgment and CBM followed with a Motion for Judgment on the Pleadings. At a combined hearing on the County's Motion for Summary Judgment and CBM's Motion for Judgment on the Pleadings, the trial court entered Summary Judgment in favor of CBM after ruling that CBM's Motion for Judgment on the Pleadings could be treated as a Motion for Summary Judgment. The County appeals from the entry of Final Summary Judgment in favor of CBM. For the following reasons, we reverse.

In considering whether a party has a duty to defend an underlying lawsuit, the trial court is limited to reviewing the allegations raised in the underlying Complaint. See McCreary v. Florida Residential Property and Cas. Joint Underwriting Ass'n, 758 So.2d 692 (Fla. 4th DCA 1999); Westinghouse Elec. Corp. v. Dade County, 472 So.2d 866 (Fla. 3d DCA 1985). In the instant case, Count I of the Amended Complaint ("Complaint") alleges that the County, "by and through its agents and employees," negligently and carelessly maintained and controlled the premises. Count II of the Complaint, a negligence claim against CBM, states that CBM "was under contract with [the County] to maintain the hallway where the incident in question occurred." Read in its entirety, the Complaint states a cause of action for vicarious liability and negligence against the County.

The County relies heavily on Westinghouse Elec. Corp. v. Metropolitan Dade County, 592 So.2d 1134 (Fla. 3d DCA 1992) in support of its position that CBM had a duty to defend. CBM on the other hand argues that this case is more like SEFC Building Corp. v. McCloskey Window Cleaning Inc., 645 So.2d 1116 (Fla. 3d DCA 1994). Additionally, it was suggested at oral argument that the two opinions conflict. We find that the two opinions are wholly consistent with each other and that the instant case is controlled by Westinghouse.

In Westinghouse, the County contracted with Westinghouse for the installation and maintenance of escalators located at the County's Metrorail stations. The agreement contained an indemnification agreement similar to the one at issue here. Thereafter, the County and Westinghouse were sued for negligent maintenance and/or installation of the escalators. Additionally, other allegations were raised relating to the County's own negligence. On Summary Judgment, the trial court found that the claims raised against the County related to negligent maintenance and/or installation of the escalators. These were claims for which, indisputably, Westinghouse was responsible. Accordingly, the trial court held, and this Court agreed, that pursuant to the indemnity provision, Westinghouse had a duty to defend and indemnify the County for any allegations of negligent maintenance and/or installation. The trial court also held that since Westinghouse had a duty to defend the County on the vicarious liability claims, Westinghouse must defend the entire lawsuit. See Westinghouse, 592 So.2d at 1135 citing Metropolitan Dade Co. v. Florida Aviation Fueling Co., 578 So.2d 296 (Fla. 3d DCA 1991) (holding that Florida Aviation had a duty to defend the entire claim against the County where the Complaint raised alternative theories of liability, one a strict liability vicarious claim which was covered under the indemnification clause, [and] the other a negligence claim which was not covered).

In SEFC Building Corp. v. McCloskey Window Cleaning Inc., 645 So.2d 1116 (Fla. 3d DCA 1994), on the other hand, this Court declined to read an indemnity agreement to provide a duty to defend where the only claim raised against the party was a negligent claim for its own active negligence. In SEFC, a building owner ("Owner") contracted with a window service for exterior window cleaning. The agreement between the parties contained an indemnity provision which provided that the window service company agrees to indemnify the Owner for any suit arising out of or relating to the window service. See SEFC, 645 So.2d at 1117. An employee for the window cleaning company was injured while washing windows at the site and sued the Owner, alleging that his injuries were sustained as a result of the Owner's negligence. After being sued, the Owner asked that the window cleaning company assume the defense pursuant to the indemnity provision. The window cleaning company refused and the Owner filed a third-party claim for indemnification. On a Motion for Summary Judgment, the trial court concluded that the indemnity provision did not expressly provide an intent to defend and/or indemnify the Owner for its own wrongful acts. See SEFC, 645 So.2d at 1117.

The Court in Westinghouse, on the other hand, properly found a duty to defend because "when a complaint contains a covered claim, and a claim which is not covered by the indemnity agreement, then the duty to defend extends to the entire lawsuit." Westinghouse, 592 So.2d at 1135. The SEFC Court was also correct in refusing to find a duty to defend where the sole claim against the defendant was for its own negligence, a claim not covered within the indemnity clause.

In the instant case, the claim against the County provides that the County "by and through its agents and employees did negligently and carelessly own, design, operate, maintain and controlled the aforesaid premises...." We find that this allegation claims that the County is liable for its own negligence and vicariously liable for the negligence of its "agents." Since there is no dispute that CBM is the County's agent and that it had a duty to clean and maintain the area, CBM has a duty to defend and indemnify the County for any claims arising therefrom. Consequently, we find that the instant case is more like Westinghouse and Florida Aviation where the County was sued for the negligence of another and, alternatively, for its own negligence.

Accordingly, we reverse the Order granting Summary Final Judgment in favor of CBM and remand with directions to enter Final Summary Judgment in favor of the County.

Notes

1. As the court in *Jerrico* points out, airport restaurants enjoy a captive audience—travelers simply have no choice but to patronize them if they want to eat. The same, of course, is true of other airport retailers. Given this fact, airport prices tend to be quite high. Yet airport businesses insist that they must charge what they do if they are to overcome the following disadvantages: (a) high overhead (knowing that retail space is limited, airport authorities take advantage by charging above-market rents); (b) transient customers (which makes it impossible to build goodwill and repeat business); (c) unfavorable selling conditions (because passengers are time-pressed and focused on their itineraries, sales are often difficult to consummate); and, (d) fixed clientele (unlike other retailers, airport shops cannot increase the universe of potential customers simply by advertising more and running promotions—instead, they must hope that the airport can find additional ways to attract passengers).

Whatever the merits of these arguments and counter-arguments, one type of airport enterprise has long been viewed as a bargain by travelers and therefore eagerly sought out: duty free shops. Surprisingly, however, very few people understand how they work. In "The Airport," a 1992 episode of the NBC sitcom *Seinfeld*, for example, George (Jason Alexander) and Kramer (Michael Richards) have the following conversation while on their way to the airport:

> Kramer: If anything, we'll probably get there early. I'll have a chance to go to the duty free shop.

George: The duty free shop? Duty free is the biggest sucker deal in retail. Do you know how much duty is?

Kramer: Duty.

George: Yeah, "duty." Do you know how much duty is?

Kramer: No, I dunno how much duty is.

George: Duty is nothing. It's like sales tax.

Kramer: I still like to stop at the duty free shop.

George (repeating Kramer's words): I like to stop at the duty free shop.

[The pair begin to sing the words, growing more animated as they do.]

George and Kramer: I like to stop at the duty free shop! I like to stop at the duty free shop!

Although he did not know it, George actually was right to be skeptical about the bargains available at duty free shops:

A "duty" is the customs tax paid to import something into a country. Unfortunately, the merchandise in those duty-free shops you see at the airport isn't free of that tax for the buyer. It's the shops that don't have to pay a duty to import their merchandise. Because the goods are sold at an airport, seaport, or border, and are only sold to people leaving the country, the goods aren't completely imported into the country. Thus, the seller doesn't have to pay a customs tax. Presumably, the seller will pass this savings along to the buyer, but there's no guarantee this happens.

If you buy something at an airport duty-free store, your goods will be held until you are boarding the airplane. Near land borders, your purchases from a duty-free shop will be sealed and inspected when you cross the border. These measures ensure that you don't use or keep the item in the country where you bought it.

When you re-enter your home country, you may have to pay a duty on your purchases, regardless if you bought them at a duty-free store. The United States allows residents to return with up to $800 worth of goods purchased in other countries. This is called the personal exemption, and the specific amount can vary depending on which countries were visited. If you buy more than $800 of goods abroad, you'll have to pay a tax, even if you bought those things at duty-free shops.

Also, many countries limit the quantities of certain luxury goods you can bring into the country without being taxed. Liquor and cigarettes are often restricted, and you will be taxed if you bring more than the limit. The specifics of duty taxes and quantities vary between countries, so make sure to research the rules for your country and your destination.

Even if you don't pay a duty, you may not save money at duty-free shopping. An Australian article found that a camera selling for $129 at many New York stores cost $30 to $50 more at duty-free airport shops. One British study looked at a bottle of liquor that cost £14.49 in a regular store. Without duties, it should cost £4.74, but the duty-free shops charged £7.75 to £11.25. If you do plan to shop in a duty-free store, it pays to do some comparison shopping ahead of time.

Thrifty Traveler, at ask.yahoo.com/20031224.html. For a further discussion, *see, e.g.*, *Hostetter v. Idlewild Bon Voyage Liquor Corp.*, 377 U.S. 324 (1964) (explaining the constitutional underpinnings of duty free shopping); *Sakamoto v. Duty Free Shoppers*, 764 F.2d 1285 (9th Cir. 1985), *cert. denied*, 475 U.S. 1081 (1986) (examining the role such shopping plays in helping to finance airport operations); *Duty Free Air & Ship Supply, Inc. v. Atlanta Duty Free, LLC*, 620 S.E.2d 616 (Ga. Ct. App. 2005) (dispute between rival bidders for airport's duty free concession).

2. The *Haskins* case reflects a growing trend in the airline industry to outsource as many tasks as possible. Although customer service often suffers as a result, most commentators expect outsourcing to be even more popular in the future:

> Many believe that airlines will continue to move toward being "assetless" or toward the "virtual airline," where more and more functions are outsourced to more cost-efficient providers, making carriers more flexible. This has happened to a certain degree over the past ten years, as many peripheral employee functions have been outsourced, such as janitorial work, skycap services, and even ticket agent functions at smaller stations. Some carriers are [now even] outsourcing heavy-maintenance functions.

Raymond E. Neidl, *Can the Aviation Industry Shield Itself from Business Cycles?*, 13 Air & Space Law. 3, 30 (Spring 1999).

Of course, regardless of who employs them, and notwithstanding the advent of self-serve baggage carts, skycaps are likely to be a familiar sight at airports for many years to come. Which means that travelers will continue to face the difficult question of how much to tip them. In the previously mentioned *Seinfeld* episode "The Airport," viewers received the following sage advice:

> Skycap: Where you going?
>
> Jerry: Uh, JFK.
>
> Jerry (whispering to Elaine): I need some small bills for a tip. You got anything?
>
> Elaine: Yeah, you want five?
>
> Jerry: Gimme ten.
>
> Elaine: You're giving him ten dollars?
>
> Jerry: Well, we've got three bags.
>
> Elaine: That's a pretty big tip.
>
> Jerry: That's what they get!
>
> Elaine: They don't get that much.
>
> Jerry: Let's ask him.
>
> Elaine: We can't ask him.
>
> Jerry: Let's see what he says.
>
> Elaine: Jerry, we don't have time for this.
>
> Jerry: Two seconds.
>
> Jerry (to skycap): Excuse me, my friend and I here, we were having a discussion and we were wondering what you usually get for a tip.
>
> Skycap: Depends on the person, depends on the bag.

Jerry: Uh, how about a couple of people like us?

Skycap: People like you? I wouldn't expect much, you don't even look like you know what you're doing.

Jerry: C'mon, seriously.

Skycap: Well, since you asked, usually, I get five dollars a bag.

Elaine: What!?

Skycap: That's right.

Elaine: Five dollars a bag? I don't think so.

Skycap: Look, you asked, I told you.

Elaine: You got some nerve trying to take advantage of us.

Jerry: All right, look, we're late. Thank you very much.

Elaine: You're lucky I don't report you.

[As Jerry and Elaine walk away, the camera pans down to their luggage, where the skycap can be seen placing JFK tags on Jerry's two bags and a Honolulu tag on Elaine's bag.]

For a more serious look at skycaps, *see* Nick Anis, *Skycaps Can Be a Traveler's Best Friend*, at www.travel-watch.com/skycaps.htm.

3. What did you think of the decision in *CBM*? Is it correct? Assuming it is, what should CBM's attorneys have done when negotiating the contract to prevent the outcome?

4. While waiting for her flight, a woman had three or four drinks at the Chili's Too Restaurant at the Southwest International Airport in Fort Myers, Florida. Despite being intoxicated, she was allowed to go to her gate by the TSA screeners. There, she got into an altercation with Lisa Dazell, a Delta passenger service agent, after Dazell refused to let her board the plane.

Dazell subsequently brought suit against both the TSA and Chili's. In *Dazell v. Chertoff*, 2005 WL 2581017 (M.D. Fla. 2005), Judge Steele held that the TSA owed no duty to Dazell and therefore dismissed that portion of the complaint. How should he rule when he reaches the claim against Chili's? *See Fleuridor v. Surf Café*, 775 So. 2d 411 (Fla. Dist. Ct. App. 2001).

5. One of the country's largest airport concessionaires is Paradies Shops Inc. (www.theparadiesshops.com), which operates approximately 350 gift shops, newsstands, and speciality stores (such as The Sharper Image) in 60 airports and has annual gross revenues in excess of $200 million. The company was founded in 1960 by Daniel Paradies. In 1994, however, Paradies's unethical business practices landed him in jail:

> Defendant, Daniel M. Paradies ("Paradies"), was convicted by a jury on January 22, 1994 of eighty-three counts of mail fraud in violation of Title 18 U.S.C. §§ 1341 and 1346, and one count of conspiracy in violation of Title 18 U.S.C. § 371 by making corrupt payments to public officials in violation of Title 18 U.S.C. § 666. The charges arose out of Defendant's participation in fraudulent schemes involving the concessions at the Atlanta Hartsfield International Airport ("Atlanta Airport"). On April 19, 1994, the Court sentenced Paradies to thirty-three months in prison, which was at the low end of the range determined by the application of the Federal Sentencing Guidelines.

> Paradies then embarked on a lengthy appellate process. [See] United States v. Paradies, 98 F.3d 1266 (11th Cir.1996), [cert. denied,] 522 U.S. 1014 (1997). Currently before the Court are Defendant's Motion for Re-sentencing pursuant to 28 U.S.C. § 2255.
>
> Prior to his conviction, Paradies was the President, Chief Executive Officer, and principal shareholder of The Paradies Shops, Incorporated ("Paradies Shops"), a chain of gift shops located in major airports throughout the United States. Paradies also was the President of Paradies Midfield Corporation ("Midfield"), a company that operated gift shops exclusively in the Atlanta Airport. Paradies Shops owned sixty-five percent of Midfield's stock. The remaining thirty-five percent of Midfield's stock was owned by minority-controlled businesses. In 1979, when Midfield first contracted to operate gift shops in the Atlanta Airport, its other stockholders included three corporations, each wholly-owned by African-Americans. Mack Wilbourn ("Wilbourn") held 18.3 percent of Midfield stock, Nathaniel Goldston ("Goldston") held 13.7 percent, and Joanne McClinton ("McClinton") held three percent of the stock. The ownership of Midfield complied with a minority participation requirement.
>
> The alleged wrongdoing began in 1985, when Ira Jackson ("Jackson"), a member of the Atlanta City Council, made a "loan" to Goldston of fifty thousand dollars through Jackson's wife. The Government produced evidence at trial that the purported loan actually was the purchase of Goldston's interest in Midfield. After Jackson made the "loan," he requested an opinion from the City's Board of Ethics whether it would be permissible for his wife to purchase Goldston's interest in Midfield. The Board concluded that the purchase would violate Jackson's fiduciary duty to the city. Despite the Board's opinion, Jackson not only retained Goldston's interest, but also acquired the interests of Wilbourn and McClinton.
>
> Paradies denied any knowledge of Jackson's interest in Midfield. The Government, however, proved at trial that Paradies and Jackson conspired to use Jackson's influence, first as an Atlanta City Council member, and later as the Commissioner of Aviation in Atlanta, to reduce rents for Paradies' concessions at the Atlanta Airport. In exchange for Jackson's assistance, Paradies paid Jackson in the form of management fees and dividends.
>
> Paradies also was involved in a separate fraudulent scheme. Paradies had an agreement with Harold Echols ("Echols"), another concessionaire at the Atlanta airport, concerning direct payoffs to Atlanta City Council members. Echols made routine payments to Jackson and other City Council members for favorable votes in matters before the Council, and Paradies reimbursed him for the payments.

United States v. Paradies, 14 F. Supp. 2d 1315, 1316–18 (N.D. Ga. 1998). Despite his crimes, Judge Alaimo agreed to reduce Paradies's sentence to 18 months because of his advanced age (76), health problems (angina, depression, enlarged prostate, and osteoarthritis), philanthropy, and patriotism, which included serving as "an officer in the Air Force during World War II." *Id.* at 1322.

6. For a further look at the people who work in and around airports, *see Overview of Airport Careers*, at www3.ccps.virginia.edu/career_prospects/briefs/P-S/SummaryAirport.shtml.

Problem 25

An airport authority has announced that starting immediately, newspaper publishers will have to pay a monthly fee of $20 per vending machine (currently the publishers pay nothing, although they are responsible for installing, maintaining, and repairing their machines). In addition, the authority has decided that except for a single identifying strip, the publishers will not be allowed to place any advertising on their machines. Instead, all machines will carry a large sign for a local soft drink company, which is paying the authority separately for this privilege. If the publishers object to the plan, claiming that it violates their First Amendment rights (i.e., freedom of speech and freedom from forced association), how should the court rule? *See Atlanta Journal and Constitution v. City of Atlanta Dep't of Aviation*, 322 F.3d 1298 (11th Cir. 2003).

Appendices

Appendix 1

Convention Relating to the Regulation of Aerial Navigation

Done at Paris—October 13, 1919
Entered into force—Date varied by country
Did not go into effect in the United States
11 L.N.T.S. 173

THE UNITED STATES OF AMERICA, BELGIUM, BOLIVIA, BRAZIL, THE BRITISH EMPIRE, CHINA, CUBA, ECUADOR, FRANCE, GREECE, GUATEMALA, HAITI, THE HEDJAZ, HONDURAS, ITALY, JAPAN, LIBERIA, NICARAGUA, PANAMA, PERU, POLAND, PORTUGAL, ROUMANIA, THE SERB-CROAT-SLOVENE STATE, SIAM, CZECHOSLOVAKIA AND URUGUAY,

Recognising the progress of aerial navigation, and that the establishment of regulations of universal application will be to the interest of all;

Appreciating the necessity of an early agreement upon certain principles and rules calculated to prevent controversy;

Desiring to encourage the peaceful intercourse of nations by means of aerial communications;

Have determined for these purposes to conclude a convention, and have appointed as their Plenipotentiaries the following, reserving the right of substituting others to sign the same convention:

. . .

Who have agreed as follows:

CHAPTER I.
GENERAL PRINCIPLES.

Article 1.

The High Contracting Parties recognise that every Power has complete and exclusive sovereignty over the air space above its territory. For the purpose of the present Convention, the territory of a State shall be understood as including the national territory, both that of the mother country and of the colonies, and the territorial waters adjacent thereto.

Article 2.

Each contracting State undertakes in time of peace to accord freedom of innocent passage above its territory to the aircraft of the other contracting States, provided that the conditions laid down in the present Convention are observed. Regulations made by a contracting State as to the admission over its territory of the aircraft of the other contracting States shall be applied without distinction of nationality.

Article 3.

Each contracting State is entitled for military reasons or in the interest of public safety to prohibit the aircraft of the other contracting States, under the penalties provided by its legislation and subject to no distinction being made in this respect between its private aircraft and those of the other contracting States, from flying over certain areas of its territory. In that case the locality and the extent of the prohibited areas shall be published and notified beforehand to the other contracting States.

Article 4.

Every aircraft which finds itself above a prohibited area shall, as soon as aware of the fact, give the signal of distress provided in paragraph 17 of Annex D and land as soon as possible outside the prohibited area at one of the nearest aerodromes of the State unlawfully flown over.

CHAPTER II.
NATIONALITY OF AIRCRAFT.

Article 5.

No contracting State shall, except by a special and temporary authorisation, permit the flight above its territory of an aircraft which does not possess the nationality of a contracting State.

Article 6.

Aircraft possess the nationality of the State on the register of which they are entered, in accordance with the provisions of Section I (c) of Annex A.

Article 7.

No aircraft shall be entered on the register of one of the contracting States unless it belongs wholly to nationals of such State. No incorporated company can be registered as the owner of an aircraft unless it possess the nationality of the State in which the aircraft is registered, unless the president or chairman of the company and at least two-thirds of the directors possess such nationality, and unless the company fulfills all other conditions which may be prescribed by the laws of the said State.

Article 8.

An aircraft cannot be validly registered in more than one State.

Article 9.

The contracting States shall exchange every month among themselves and transmit to the International Commission for Air Navigation referred to in Article 34 copies of registrations and of cancellations of registration which shall have been entered on their official registers during the preceding month.

Article 10.

All aircraft engaged in international navigation shall bear their nationality and registration marks as well as the name and residence of the owner in accordance with Annex A.

CHAPTER III.
CERTIFICATES OF AIRWORTHINESS AND COMPETENCY.

Article 11.

Every aircraft engaged in international navigation shall, in accordance with the conditions laid down in Annex B, be provided with a certificate of airworthiness issued or rendered valid by the State whose nationality it possesses.

Article 12.

The commanding officer, pilots, engineers and other members of the operating crew of every aircraft shall, in accordance with the conditions laid down in Annex E, be provided with certificates of competency and licences issued or rendered valid by the State whose nationality the aircraft possesses.

Article 13.

Certificates of airworthiness and of competency and licences issued or rendered valid by the State whose nationality the aircraft possesses, in accordance with the regulations established by Annex B and Annex E and hereafter by the International Commission for Air Navigation, shall be recognised as valid by the other States. Each State has the right to refuse to recognise for the purpose of flights within the limits of and above its own territory certificates of competency and licences granted to one of its nationals by another contracting State.

Article 14.

No wireless apparatus shall be carried without a special licence issued by the State whose nationality the aircraft possesses. Such apparatus shall not be used except by members of the crew provided with a special licence for the purpose. Every aircraft used in public transport and capable of carrying ten or more persons shall be equipped with sending and receiving wireless apparatus when the methods of employing such apparatus shall have been determined by the International Commission for Air Navigation. The Commission may later extend the obligation of carrying wireless apparatus to all other classes of aircraft in the conditions and according to the methods which it may determine.

CHAPTER IV.
ADMISSION TO AIR NAVIGATION ABOVE FOREIGN TERRITORY.

Article 15.

Every aircraft of a contracting State has the right to cross the air space of another State without landing. In this case it shall follow the route fixed by the State over which the flight takes place. However, for reasons of general security, it will be obliged to land if ordered to do so by means of the signals provided in Annex D. Every aircraft which passes from one State into another shall, if the regulations of the latter State require it, land in one of the aerodromes fixed by the latter. Notification of these aerodromes shall be given by the contracting States to the International Commission for Air Navigation and by it transmitted to all the contracting States. The establishment of international airways shall be subject to the consent of the States flown over.

Article 16.

Each contracting State shall have the right to establish reservations and restrictions in favour of its national aircraft in connection with the carriage of persons and goods for hire between two points on its territory. Such reservations and restrictions shall be immediately published, and shall be communicated to the International Commission for Air Navigation, which shall notify them to the other contracting States.

Article 17.

The aircraft of a contracting State which establishes reservations and restrictions in accordance with Article 16, may be subjected to the same reservations and restrictions in any other contracting State, even if the latter State does not itself impose the reservations and restrictions on other foreign aircraft.

Article 18.

Every aircraft passing through the territory of a contracting State including landing and stoppages reasonably necessary for the purpose of such transit, shall be exempt from any seizure on the ground of infringement of patent, design or model, subject to the deposit of security the amount of which in default of amicable agreement shall be fixed with the least possible delay by the competent authority of the place of seizure.

CHAPTER V.
RULES TO BE OBSERVED ON DEPARTURE[,] WHEN UNDER WAY AND ON LANDING.

Article 19.

Every aircraft engaged in international navigation shall be provided with:

(a) A certificate of registration in accordance with Annex A;

(b) A certificate of airworthiness in accordance with Annex B;

(c) Certificates and licences of the commanding officer, pilots and crew in accordance with Annex E;

(d) If it carries passengers, a list of their names;

(e) if it carries freight, bills of lading and manifest;

(f) Log books in accordance with Annex C;

(g) If equipped with wireless, the special licences prescribed by Article 14.

Article 20.

The log books shall be kept for two years after the last entry.

Article 21.

Upon the departure or landing of an aircraft, the authorities of the country shall have, in all cases, the right to visit the aircraft and to verify all the documents with which it must be provided.

Article 22.

Aircraft of the contracting States shall be entitled to the same measures of assistance for landing, particularly in case of distress, as national aircraft.

Article 23.

With regard to the salvage of aircraft wrecked at sea the principles of maritime law will apply, in the absence of any agreement to the contrary.

Article 24.

Every aerodrome in a contracting State, which upon payment of charges is open to public use by its national aircraft, shall likewise be open to the aircraft of all the other contracting States. In every such aerodrome there shall be a single tariff or charges for landing and length of stay applicable alike to national and foreign aircraft.

Article 25.

Each contracting State undertakes to adopt measures to ensure that every aircraft flying above the limits of its territory and that every aircraft wherever it may be, carrying its nationality mark, shall comply with the regulations contained in Annex D. Each of the contracting States undertakes to ensure the prosecution and punishment of all persons contravening these regulations.

CHAPTER VI.
PROHIBITED TRANSPORT.

Article 26.

The carriage by aircraft of explosives and of arms and munitions of war is forbidden in international navigation. No foreign aircraft shall be permitted to carry such articles between any two points in the same contracting State.

Article 27.

Each State may, in aerial navigation, prohibit or regulate the carriage or use of photographic apparatus. Any such regulations shall be at once notified to the International Commission for Air Navigation, which shall communicate this information to the other contracting States.

Article 28.

As a measure of public safety, the carriage of objects other than those mentioned in Articles 26 and 27 may be subjected to restrictions by any contracting State. Any such regulations shall be at once notified to the International Commission for Air Navigation, which shall communicate this information to the other contracting States.

Article 29.

All restrictions mentioned in Article 28 shall be applied equally to national and foreign aircraft.

CHAPTER VII.
STATE AIRCRAFT.

Article 30.

The following shall be deemed to be State aircraft:

(a) Military aircraft.

(b) Aircraft exclusively employed in State service, such as Posts, Customs, Police.

Every other aircraft shall be deemed to be private aircraft. All State aircraft other than military, customs and police aircraft shall be treated as private aircraft and as such shall be subject to all the provisions of the present Convention.

Article 31.

Every aircraft commanded by a person in military service detailed for the purpose shall be deemed to be a military aircraft.

Article 32.

No military aircraft of a contracting State shall fly over the territory of another contracting State nor land thereon without special authorisation. In case of such authorisation the military aircraft shall enjoy, in principle, in the absence of special stipulation, the privileges which are customarily accorded to foreign ships of war. A military aircraft which is forced to land or which is requested or summoned to land shall by reason thereof acquire no right to the privileges referred to in the above paragraph.

Article 33.

Special arrangements between the States concerned will determine in what cases police and customs aircraft may be authorised to cross the frontier. They shall in no case be entitled to the privileges referred to in Article 32.

CHAPTER VIII.
INTERNATIONAL COMMISSION FOR AIR NAVIGATION.

Article 34.

There shall be instituted, under the name of the International Commission for Air Navigation, a permanent Commission placed under the direction of the League of Nations and composed of:

Two Representatives of each of the following States:

The United States of America, France, Italy and Japan;

One Representative of Great Britain and one of each of the British Dominions and of India;

One Representative of each of the other contracting States.

Each of the five States first-named (Great Britain, the British Dominions and India counting for this purpose as one State) shall have the least whole number of votes which, exceeding by at least one vote the total number when multiplied by five, will give a product of the votes of all the other contracting States.

All the States other than the five first-named shall each have one vote.

The International Commission for Air Navigation shall determine the rules of its own procedure and the place of its permanent seat, but it shall be free to meet in such places as it may deem convenient. Its first meeting shall take place at Paris. This meeting shall be convened by the French Government as soon as a majority of the signatory States shall have notified to it their ratification of the present Convention.

The duties of this Commission shall be:

(a) To receive proposals from or to make proposals to any of the contracting States for the modification or amendment of the provisions of the present Convention, and to notify changes adopted;

(b) To carry out the duties imposed upon it by the present Article and by Articles 9, 13, 14, 15, 17, 27, 28, 36 and 37 of the present Convention;

(c) To amend the provisions of the Annexes A-G;

(d) To collect and communicate to the contracting States information of every kind concerning international air navigation;

(e) To collect and communicate to the contracting States all information relating to wireless telegraphy, meteorology and medical science which may be of interest to air navigation;

(f) To ensure the publication of maps for air navigation in accordance with the provisions of Annex F;

(g) To give its opinion on questions which the States may submit for examination.

Any modification of the provisions of any one of the Annexes may be made by the International Commission for Air Navigation when such modification shall have been approved by three-fourths of the total possible votes which could be cast if all the States were represented and shall become effective from the time when it shall have been notified by the International Commission for Air Navigation to all the contracting States.

Any proposed modification of the Articles of the present Convention shall be examined by the International Commission for Air Navigation, whether it originates with one of the contracting States or with the Commission itself. No such modification shall be proposed for adoption by the contracting States, unless it shall have been approved by at least two-thirds of the total possible votes.

All such modifications of the Articles of the Convention (but not of the provisions of the Annexes) must be formally adopted by the contracting States before they become effective.

The expenses of organisation and operation of the International Commission for Air Navigation shall be borne by the contracting States in proportion to the number of votes at their disposal.

The expenses occasioned by the sending of technical delegations will be borne by their respective States.

CHAPTER IX.
FINAL PROVISIONS.

Article 35.

The High Contracting Parties undertake as far as they are respectively concerned to cooperate as far as possible in international measures concerning:

(a) The collection and dissemination of statistical, current, and special meteorological information, in accordance with the provisions of Annex G;

(b) The publication of standard aeronautical maps, and the establishment of a uniform system of ground marks for flying, in accordance with the provisions of Annex F;

(c) The use of wireless telegraphy in air navigation, the establishment of the necessary wireless stations, and the observance of international wireless regulations.

Article 36.

General provisions relative to customs in connection with international air navigation are the subject of a special agreement contained in Annex H to the present Convention.

Nothing in the present Convention shall be construed as preventing the contracting States from concluding, in conformity with its principles, special protocols as between State and State in respect of customs, police, posts and other matters of common interest in connection with air navigation. Any such protocols shall be at once notified to the International Commission for Air Navigation, which shall communicate this information to the other contracting States.

Article 37.

In the case of a disagreement between two or more States relating to the interpretation of the present Convention, the question in dispute shall be determined by the Permanent Court of International Justice to be established by the League of Nations, and, until its establishment, by arbitration. If the parties do not agree on the choice of the arbitrators, they shall proceed as follows:

Each of the parties shall name an arbitrator, and the arbitrators shall meet to name an umpire. If the arbitrators cannot agree, the parties shall each name a third State, and the third State so named shall proceed to designate the umpire, by agreement or by each proposing a name and then determining the choice by lot.

Disagreement relating to the technical regulations annexed to the present Convention shall be settled by the decision of the International Commission for Air Navigation by a majority of votes. In case the difference involves the question whether the interpretation of the Convention or that of a regulation is concerned[,] final decision shall be made by arbitration as provided in the first paragraph of this Article.

Article 38.

In case of war, the provisions of the present Convention shall not affect the freedom of action of the contracting States either as belligerents or as neutrals.

Article 39.

The provisions of the present Convention are completed by the Annexs A to H, which, subject to Article 34 (c), shall have the same effect and shall come into force at the same time as the Convention itself.

Article 40.

The British Dominions and India shall be deemed to be States for the purposes of the present Convention. The territories and nationals of Protectorates or of territories administered in the name of the League of Nations shall, for the purposes of the present Convention, be assimilated to the territory and nationals of the Protecting or Mandatory States.

Article 41.

States which have not taken part in the war of 1914-1919 shall be permitted to adhere to the present Convention. This adhesion shall be notified through the diplomatic channel to the Government of the French Republic, and by it to all the signatory or adhering States.

Article 42.

A State which took part in the war of 1914 to 1919 but which is not a signatory of the present Convention, may adhere only if it is a member of the League of Nations or, until January 1, 1923, if its adhesion is approved by the Allied and Associated Powers signatories of the Treaty of Peace concluded with the said State. After January 1, 1923, this adhesion may be admitted if it is agreed to by at least three-fourths of the signatory and adhering States voting under the conditions provided by Article 34 of the present Convention. Applications for adhesion shall be addressed to the Government of the French Republic, which will communicate them to the other contracting Powers. Unless the State applying is admitted ipso facto as a Member of the League of Nations, the French Government will receive the votes of the said Powers and will announce to them the result of the voting.

Article 43.

The present Convention may not be denounced before January 1, 1922. In case of denunciation, notification thereof shall be made to the Government of the French Republic, which shall communicate it to the other contracting Parties. Such denunciation shall not take effect until at least one year after the giving of notice, and shall take effect only with respect to the Power which has given notice.

[The annexes are omitted.]

Appendix 2

Convention for the Unification of Certain Rules Relating to International Transportation by Air

Done at Warsaw—October 12, 1929
Entered into force—February 13, 1933
Effective in the United States—October 29, 1934
49 Stat. 3000, T.S. No. 876,
2 Bevans 983, 137 L.N.T.S. 11

THE PRESIDENT OF THE GERMAN REICH, THE FEDERAL PRESIDENT OF THE REPUBLIC OF AUSTRIA, HIS MAJESTY THE KING OF THE BELGIANS, THE PRESIDENT OF THE UNITED STATES OF BRAZIL, HIS MAJESTY THE KING OF THE BULGARIANS, THE PRESIDENT OF THE NATIONALIST GOVERNMENT OF CHINA, HIS MAJESTY THE KING OF DENMARK AND ICELAND, HIS MAJESTY THE KING OF EGYPT, HIS MAJESTY THE KING OF SPAIN, THE CHIEF OF STATE OF THE REPUBLIC OF ESTONIA, THE PRESIDENT OF THE REPUBLIC OF FINLAND, THE PRESIDENT OF THE FRENCH REPUBLIC, HIS MAJESTY THE KING OF GREAT BRITAIN, IRELAND, AND THE BRITISH DOMINIONS BEYOND THE SEAS, EMPEROR OF INDIA, THE PRESIDENT OF THE HELLENIC REPUBLIC, HIS MOST SERENE HIGHNESS THE REGENT OF THE KINGDOM OF HUNGARY, HIS MAJESTY THE KING OF ITALY, HIS MAJESTY THE EMPEROR OF JAPAN, THE PRESIDENT OF THE REPUBLIC OF LATVIA, HER ROYAL HIGHNESS THE GRAND DUCHESS OF LUXEMBURG, THE PRESIDENT OF THE UNITED MEXICAN STATES, HIS MAJESTY THE KING OF NORWAY, HER MAJESTY THE QUEEN OF THE NETHERLANDS, THE PRESIDENT OF THE REPUBLIC OF POLAND, HIS MAJESTY THE KING OF RUMANIA, HIS MAJESTY THE KING OF SWEDEN, THE SWISS FEDERAL COUNCIL, THE PRESIDENT OF THE CZECHOSLOVAK REPUBLIC, THE CENTRAL EXECUTIVE COMMITTEE OF THE UNION OF SOVIET SOCIALIST REPUBLICS, THE PRESIDENT OF THE UNITED STATES OF VENEZUELA, HIS MAJESTY THE KING OF YUGOSLAVIA:

Having recognized the advantage of regulating in a uniform manner the conditions of international transportation by air in respect of the documents used for such transportation and of the liability of the carrier,

Have nominated to this end their respective Plenipotentiaries, who, being thereto duly authorized, have concluded and signed the following convention:

CHAPTER I. SCOPE-DEFINITIONS

Article 1

(1) This convention shall apply to all international transportation of persons, baggage, or goods performed by aircraft for hire. It shall apply equally to gratuitous transportation by aircraft performed by an air transportation enterprise.

(2) For the purposes of this convention the expression "international transportation" shall mean any transportation in which, according to the contract made by the parties, the place of departure and the place of destination, whether or not there be a break in the transportation or a transshipment, are situated either within the territories of two High Contracting Parties, or within the territory of a single High Contracting Party, if

there is an agreed stopping place within a territory subject to the sovereignty, suzerainty, mandate or authority of another power, even though that power is not a party to this convention. Transportation without such an agreed stopping place between territories subject to the sovereignty, suzerainty, mandate, or authority of the same High Contracting Party shall not be deemed to be international for the purposes of this convention.

(3) Transportation to be performed by several successive air carriers shall be deemed, for the purposes of this convention, to be one undivided transportation, if it has been regarded by the parties as a single operation, whether it has been agreed upon under the form of a single contract or of a series of contracts, and it shall not lose its international character merely because one contract or a series of contracts is to be performed entirely within a territory subject to the sovereignty, suzerainty, mandate, or authority of the same High Contracting Party.

Article 2

(1) This convention shall apply to transportation performed by the state or by legal entities constituted under public law provided it falls within the conditions laid down in article 1.

(2) This convention shall not apply to transportation performed under the terms of any international postal convention.

CHAPTER II. TRANSPORTATION DOCUMENTS

SECTION I.-PASSENGER TICKET

Article 3

(1) For the transportation of passengers the carrier must deliver a passenger ticket which shall contain the following particulars:

(a) The place and date of issue;

(b) The place of departure and of destination;

(c) The agreed stopping places, provided that the carrier may reserve the right to alter the stopping places in case of necessity, and that if he exercises that right, the alteration shall not have the effect of depriving the transportation of its international character;

(d) The name and address of the carrier or carriers;

(e) A statement that the transportation is subject to the rules relating to liability established by this convention.

(2) The absence, irregularity, or loss of the passenger ticket shall not affect the existence or the validity of the contract of transportation, which shall none the less be subject to the rules of this convention. Nevertheless, if the carrier accepts a passenger without a passenger ticket having been delivered he shall not be entitled to avail himself of those provisions of this convention which exclude or limit his liability.

SECTION II.-BAGGAGE CHECK

Article 4

(1) For the transportation of baggage, other than small personal objects of which the passenger takes charge himself, the carrier must deliver a baggage check.

(2) The baggage check shall be made out in duplicate, one part for the passenger and the other part for the carrier.

(3) The baggage check shall contain the following particulars:

(a) The place and date of issue;

(b) The place of departure and of destination;

(c) The name and address of the carrier or carriers;

(d) The number of the passenger ticket;

(e) A statement that delivery of the baggage will be made to the bearer of the baggage check;

(f) The number and weight of the packages;

(g) The amount of the value declared in accordance with article 22(2);

(h) A statement that the transportation is subject to the rules relating to liability established by this convention.

(4) The absence, irregularity, or loss of the baggage check shall not affect the existence or the validity of the contract of transportation which shall none the less be subject to the rules of this convention. Nevertheless, if the carrier accepts baggage without a baggage check having been delivered, or if the baggage check does not contain the particulars set out at (d), (f), and (h) above, the carrier shall not be entitled to avail himself of those provisions of the convention which exclude or limit his liability.

SECTION III.-AIR WAYBILL

Article 5

(1) Every carrier of goods has the right to require the consignor to make out and hand over to him a document called an "air waybill": every consignor has the right to require the carrier to accept this document.

(2) The absence, irregularity, or loss of this document shall not affect the existence or the validity of the contract of transportation which shall, subject to the provisions of article 9, be none the less governed by the rules of this convention.

Article 6

(1) The air waybill shall be made out by the consignor in three original parts and be handed over with the goods.

(2) The first part shall be marked "for the carrier", and shall be signed by the consignor. The second part shall be marked "for the consignee"; it shall be signed by the consignor and by the carrier and shall accompany the goods. The third part shall be signed by the carrier and handed by him to the consignor after the goods have been accepted.

(3) The carrier shall sign on acceptance of the goods.

(4) The signature of the carrier may be stamped; that of the consignor may be printed or stamped.

(5) If, at the request of the consignor, the carrier makes out the air waybill, he shall be deemed, subject to proof to the contrary, to have done so on behalf of the consignor.

Article 7

The carrier of goods has the right to require the consignor to make out separate waybills when there is more than one package.

Article 8

The air waybill shall contain the following particulars:

(a) The place and date of its execution;

(b) The place of departure and of destination;

(c) The agreed stopping places, provided that the carrier may reserve the right to alter the stopping places in case of necessity, and that if he exercises that right the alteration shall not have the effect of depriving the transportation of its international character;

(d) The name and address of the consignor;

(e) The name and address of the first carrier;

(f) The name and address of the consignee, if the case so requires;

(g) The nature of the goods;

(h) The number of packages, the method of packing, and the particular marks or numbers upon them;

(i) The weight, the quantity, the volume, or dimensions of the goods;

(j) The apparent condition of the goods and of the packing;

(k) The freight, if it has been agreed upon, the date and place of payment, and the person who is to pay it;

(l) If the goods are sent for payment on delivery, the price of the goods, and, if the case so requires, the amount of the expenses incurred;

(m) The amount of the value declared in accordance with article 22(2);

(n) The number of parts of the air waybill;

(o) The documents handed to the carrier to accompany the air waybill;

(p) The time fixed for the completion of the transportation and a brief note of the route to be followed, if these matters have been agreed upon;

(q) A statement that the transportation is subject to the rules relating to liability established by this convention.

Article 9

If the carrier accepts goods without an air waybill having been made out, or if the air waybill does not contain all the particulars set out in article 8(a) to (i), inclusive, and (q), the carrier shall not be entitled to avail himself of the provisions of this convention which exclude or limit his liability.

Article 10

(1) The consignor shall be responsible for the correctness of the particulars and statements relating to the goods which he inserts in the air waybill.

(2) The consignor shall be liable for all damages suffered by the carrier or any other person by reason of the irregularity, incorrectness or incompleteness of the said particulars and statements.

Article 11

(1) The air waybill shall be prima facie evidence of the conclusion of the contract, of the receipt of the goods and of the conditions of transportation.

(2) The statements in the air waybill relating to the weight, dimensions, and packing of the goods, as well as those relating to the number of packages, shall be prima facie evidence of the facts stated; those relating to the quantity, volume, and condition of the goods shall not constitute evidence against the carrier except so far as they both have been, and are stated in the air waybill to have been, checked by him in the presence of the consignor, or relate to the apparent condition of the goods.

Article 12

(1) Subject to his liability to carry out all his obligations under the contract of transportation, the consignor shall have the right to dispose of the goods by withdrawing them at the airport of departure or destination, or by stopping them in the course of the journey on any landing, or by calling for them to be delivered at the place of destination, or in the course of the journey to a person other than the consignee named in the air waybill, or by requiring them to be returned to the airport of departure. He must not exercise this right of disposition in such a way as to prejudice the carrier or other consignors, and he must repay any expenses occasioned by the exercise of this right.

(2) If it is impossible to carry out the orders of the consignor the carrier must so inform him forthwith.

(3) If the carrier obeys the orders of the consignor for the disposition of the goods without requiring the production of the part of the air waybill delivered to the latter, he will be liable, without prejudice to his right of recovery from the consignor, for any damage which may be caused thereby to any person who is lawfully in possession of that part of the air waybill.

(4) The right conferred on the consignor shall cease at the moment when that of the consignee begins in accordance with article 13, below. Nevertheless, if the consignee declines to accept the waybill or the goods, or if he cannot be communicated with, the consignor shall resume his right of disposition.

Article 13

(1) Except in the circumstances set out in the preceding article, the consignee shall be entitled, on arrival of the goods at the place of destination, to require the carrier to hand over to him the air waybill and to deliver the goods to him, on payment of the charges due and on complying with the conditions of transportation set out in the air waybill.

(2) Unless it is otherwise agreed, it shall be the duty of the carrier to give notice to the consignee as soon as the goods arrive.

(3) If the carrier admits the loss of the goods, or if the goods have not arrived at the expiration of seven days after the date on which they ought to have arrived, the consignee shall be entitled to put into force against the carrier the rights which flow from the contract of transportation.

Article 14

The consignor and the consignee can respectively enforce all the rights given them by articles 12 and 13, each in his own name, whether he is acting in his own interest or in the interest of another, provided that he carries out the obligations imposed by the contract.

Article 15

(1) Articles 12, 13, and 14 shall not affect either the relations of the consignor and the consignee with each other or the relations of third parties whose rights are derived either from the consignor or from the consignee.

(2) The provisions of articles 12, 13, and 14 can only be varied by express provision in the air waybill.

Article 16

(1) The consignor must furnish such information and attach to the air waybill such documents as are necessary to meet the formalities of customs, octroi, or police before the goods can be delivered to the consignee. The consignor shall be liable to the carrier for any damage occasioned by the absence, insufficiency, or irregularity of any such information or documents, unless the damage is due to the fault of the carrier or his agents.

(2) The carrier is under no obligation to enquire into the correctness or sufficiency of such information or documents.

CHAPTER III. LIABILITY OF THE CARRIER

Article 17

The carrier shall be liable for damage sustained in the event of the death or wounding of a passenger or any other bodily injury suffered by a passenger, if the accident which caused the damage so sustained took place on board the aircraft or in the course of any of the operations of embarking or disembarking.

Article 18

(1) The carrier shall be liable for damage sustained in the event of the destruction or loss of, or of damage to, any checked baggage or any goods, if the occurrence which caused the damage so sustained took place during the transportation by air.

(2) The transportation by air within the meaning of the preceding paragraph shall comprise the period during which the baggage or goods are in charge of the carrier, whether in an airport or on board an aircraft, or, in the case of a landing outside an airport, in any place whatsoever.

(3) The period of the transportation by air shall not extend to any transportation by land, by sea, or by river performed outside an airport. If, however, such transportation takes place in the performance of a contract for transportation by air, for the purpose of loading, delivery or transshipment, any damage is presumed, subject to proof to the contrary, to have been the result of an event which took place during the transportation by air.

Article 19

The carrier shall be liable for damage occasioned by delay in the transportation by air of passengers, baggage, or goods.

Article 20

(1) The carrier shall not be liable if he proves that he and his agents have taken all necessary measures to avoid the damage or that it was impossible for him or them to take such measures.

(2) In the transportation of goods and baggage the carrier shall not be liable if he proves that the damage was occasioned by an error in piloting, in the handling of the

aircraft, or in navigation and that, in all other respects, he and his agents have taken all necessary measures to avoid the damage.

Article 21

If the carrier proves that the damage was caused by or contributed to by the negligence of the injured person the court may, in accordance with the provisions of its own law, exonerate the carrier wholly or partly from his liability.

Article 22

(1) In the transportation of passengers the liability of the carrier for each passenger shall be limited to the sum of 125,000 francs. Where, in accordance with the law of the court to which the case is submitted, damages may be awarded in the form of periodical payments, the equivalent capital value of the said payments shall not exceed 125,000 francs. Nevertheless, by special contract, the carrier and the passenger may agree to a higher limit of liability.

(2) In the transportation of checked baggage and of goods, the liability of the carrier shall be limited to a sum of 250 francs per kilogram, unless the consignor has made, at the time when the package was handed over to the carrier, a special declaration of the value at delivery and has paid a supplementary sum if the case so requires. In that case the carrier will be liable to pay a sum not exceeding the declared sum, unless he proves that that sum is greater than the actual value to the consignor at delivery.

(3) As regards objects of which the passenger takes charge himself the liability of the carrier shall be limited to 5,000 francs per passenger.

(4) The sums mentioned above shall be deemed to refer to the French franc consisting of 65 1/2 milligrams of gold at the standard of fineness of nine hundred thousandths. These sums may be converted into any national currency in round figures.

Article 23

Any provision tending to relieve the carrier of liability or to fix a lower limit than that which is laid down in this convention shall be null and void, but the nullity of any such provision shall not involve the nullity of the whole contract, which shall remain subject to the provisions of this convention.

Article 24

(1) In the cases covered by articles 18 and 19 any action for damages, however founded, can only be brought subject to the conditions and limits set out in this convention.

(2) In the cases covered by article 17 the provisions of the preceding paragraph shall also apply, without prejudice to the questions as to who are the persons who have the right to bring suit and what are their respective rights.

Article 25

(1) The carrier shall not be entitled to avail himself of the provisions of this convention which exclude or limit his liability, if the damage is caused by his wilful misconduct or by such default on his part as, in accordance with the law of the court to which the case is submitted, is considered to be equivalent to wilful misconduct.

(2) Similarly the carrier shall not be entitled to avail himself of the said provisions, if the damage is caused under the same circumstances by any agent of the carrier acting within the scope of his employment.

Article 26

(1) Receipt by the person entitled to the delivery of baggage or goods without complaint shall be prima facie evidence that the same have been delivered in good condition and in accordance with the document of transportation.

(2) In case of damage, the person entitled to delivery must complain to the carrier forthwith after the discovery of the damage, and, at the latest, within 3 days from the date of receipt in the case of baggage and 7 days from the date of receipt in the case of goods. In case of delay the complaint must be made at the latest within 14 days from the date on which the baggage or goods have been placed at his disposal.

(3) Every complaint must be made in writing upon the document of transportation or by separate notice in writing dispatched within the times aforesaid.

(4) Failing complaint within the times aforesaid, no action shall lie against the carrier, save in the case of fraud on his part.

Article 27

In the case of the death of the person liable, an action for damages lies in accordance with the terms of this convention against those legally representing his estate.

Article 28

(1) An action for damages must be brought, at the option of the plaintiff, in the territory of one of the High Contracting Parties, either before the court of the domicile of the carrier or of his principal place of business, or where he has a place of business through which the contract has been made, or before the court at the place of destination.

(2) Questions of procedure shall be governed by the law of the court to which the case is submitted.

Article 29

(1) The right to damages shall be extinguished if an action is not brought within 2 years, reckoned from the date of arrival at the destination, or from the date on which the aircraft ought to have arrived, or from the date on which the transportation stopped.

(2) The method of calculating the period of limitation shall be determined by the law of the court to which the case is submitted.

Article 30

(1) In the case of transportation to be performed by various successive carriers and falling within the definition set out in the third paragraph of article 1, each carrier who accepts passengers, baggage or goods shall be subject to the rules set out in this convention, and shall be deemed to be one of the contracting parties to the contract of transportation insofar as the contract deals with that part of the transportation which is performed under his supervision.

(2) In the case of transportation of this nature, the passenger or his representative can take action only against the carrier who performed the transportation during which the accident or the delay occurred, save in the case where, by express agreement, the first carrier has assumed liability for the whole journey.

(3) As regards baggage or goods, the passenger or consignor shall have a right of action against the first carrier, and the passenger or consignee who is entitled to delivery shall have a right of action against the last carrier, and further, each may take action against the carrier who performed the transportation during which the destruction, loss, damage, or delay took place. These carriers shall be jointly and severally liable to the passenger or to the consignor or consignee.

CHAPTER IV. PROVISIONS RELATING TO COMBINED TRANSPORTATION

Article 31

(1) In the case of combined transportation performed partly by air and partly by any other mode of transportation, the provisions of this convention shall apply only to the transportation by air, provided that the transportation by air falls within the terms of article 1.

(2) Nothing in this convention shall prevent the parties in the case of combined transportation from inserting in the document of air transportation conditions relating to other modes of transportation, provided that the provisions of this convention are observed as regards the transportation by air.

CHAPTER V. GENERAL AND FINAL PROVISIONS

Article 32

Any clause contained in the contract and all special agreements entered into before the damage occurred by which the parties purport to infringe the rules laid down by this convention, whether by deciding the law to be applied, or by altering the rules as to jurisdiction, shall be null and void. Nevertheless for the transportation of goods arbitration clauses shall be allowed, subject to this convention, if the arbitration is to take place within one of the jurisdictions referred to in the first paragraph of article 28.

Article 33

Nothing contained in this convention shall prevent the carrier either from refusing to enter into any contract of transportation or from making regulations which do not conflict with the provisions of this convention.

Article 34

This convention shall not apply to international transportation by air performed by way of experimental trial by air navigation enterprises with the view to the establishment of regular lines of air navigation, nor shall it apply to transportation performed in extraordinary circumstances outside the normal scope of an air carrier's business.

Article 35

The expression "days" when used in this convention means current days, not working days.

Article 36

This convention is drawn up in French in a single copy which shall remain deposited in the archives of the Ministry for Foreign Affairs of Poland and of which one duly certified copy shall be sent by the Polish Government to the Government of each of the High Contracting Parties.

Article 37

(1) This convention shall be ratified. The instruments of ratification shall be deposited in the archives of the Ministry for Foreign Affairs of Poland, which shall give notice of the deposit to the Government of each of the High Contracting Parties.

(2) As soon as this convention shall have been ratified by five of the High Contracting Parties it shall come into force as between them on the ninetieth day after the deposit of the fifth ratification. Thereafter it shall come into force between the High Contracting Parties which shall have ratified and the High Contracting Party which deposits its instrument of ratification on the ninetieth day after the deposit.

(3) It shall be the duty of the Government of the Republic of Poland to notify the Government of each of the High Contracting Parties of the date on which this convention comes into force as well as the date of the deposit of each ratification.

Article 38

(1) This convention shall, after it has come into force, remain open for adherence by any state.

(2) The adherence shall be effected by a notification addressed to the Government of the Republic of Poland, which shall inform the Government of each of the High Contracting Parties thereof.

(3) The adherence shall take effect as from the ninetieth day after the notification made to the Government of the Republic of Poland.

Article 39

(1) Any one of the High Contracting Parties may denounce this convention by a notification addressed to the Government of the Republic of Poland, which shall at once inform the Government of each of the High Contracting Parties.

(2) Denunciation shall take effect six months after the notification of denunciation, and shall operate only as regards the party which shall have proceeded to denunciation.

Article 40

(1) Any High Contracting Party may, at the time of signature or of deposit of ratification or of adherence, declare that the acceptance which it gives to this convention does not apply to all or any of its colonies, protectorates, territories under mandate, or any other territory subject to its sovereignty or its authority, or any other territory under its suzerainty.

(2) Accordingly any High Contracting Party may subsequently adhere separately in the name of all or any of its colonies, protectorates, territories under mandate, or any other territory subject to its sovereignty or to its authority or any other territory under its suzerainty which have been thus excluded by its original declaration.

(3) Any High Contracting Party may denounce this convention, in accordance with its provisions, separately or for all or any of its colonies, protectorates, territories under

mandate, or any other territory subject to its sovereignty or to its authority, or any other territory under its suzerainty.

Article 41

Any High Contracting Party shall be entitled not earlier than two years after the coming into force of this convention to call for the assembling of a new international conference in order to consider any improvements which may be made in this convention. To this end it will communicate with the Government of the French Republic which will take the necessary measures to make preparations for such conference.

This convention, done at Warsaw on October 12, 1929, shall remain open for signature until January 31, 1930.

Additional Protocol With Reference to Article 2

The High Contracting Parties reserve to themselves the right to declare at the time of ratification or of adherence that the first paragraph of article 2 of this convention shall not apply to international transportation by air performed directly by the state, its colonies, protectorates, or mandated territories, or by any other territory under its sovereignty, suzerainty, or authority.

Appendix 3

Convention on International Civil Aviation

Done at Chicago—December 7, 1944
Entered into force—April 4, 1947
Effective in the United States—April 4, 1947
61 Stat. 1180, T.I.A.S. No. 1591,
3 Bevans 944, 15 U.N.T.S. 295, ICAO Doc. 7300

Preamble

WHEREAS the future development of international civil aviation can greatly help to create and preserve friendship and understanding among the nations and peoples of the world, yet its abuse can become a threat to the general security; and

WHEREAS it is desirable to avoid friction and to promote that cooperation between nations and peoples upon which the peace of the world depends;

THEREFORE, the undersigned governments having agreed on certain principles and arrangements in order that international civil aviation may be developed in a safe and orderly manner and that international air transport services may be established on the basis of equality of opportunity and operated soundly and economically;

Have accordingly concluded this Convention to that end.

PART I
AIR NAVIGATION

CHAPTER I
GENERAL PRINCIPLES AND APPLICATION OF THE CONVENTION

Article 1
Sovereignty

The contracting States recognize that every State has complete and exclusive sovereignty over the airspace above its territory.

Article 2
Territory

For the purposes of this Convention the territory of a State shall be deemed to be the land areas and territorial waters adjacent thereto under the sovereignty, suzerainty, protection or mandate of such State.

Article 3
Civil and state aircraft

(a) This Convention shall be applicable only to civil aircraft, and shall not be applicable to state aircraft.

(b) Aircraft used in military, customs and police services shall be deemed to be state aircraft.

(c) No state aircraft of a contracting State shall fly over the territory of another State or land thereon without authorization by special agreement or otherwise, and in accordance with the terms thereof.

(d) The contracting States undertake, when issuing regulations for their state aircraft, that they will have due regard for the safety of navigation of civil aircraft.

Article 4
Misuse of civil aviation

Each contracting State agrees not to use civil aviation for any purpose inconsistent with the aims of this Convention.

CHAPTER II
FLIGHT OVER TERRITORY OF CONTRACTING STATES

Article 5
Right of non-scheduled flight

Each contracting State agrees that all aircraft of the other contracting States, being aircraft not engaged in scheduled international air services shall have the right, subject to the observance of the terms of this Convention, to make flights into or in transit non-stop across its territory and to make stops for non-traffic purposes without the necessity of obtaining prior permission, and subject to the right of the State flown over to require landing. Each contracting State nevertheless reserves the right, for reasons of safety of flight, to require aircraft desiring to proceed over regions which are inaccessible or without adequate air navigation facilities to follow prescribed routes, or to obtain special permission for such flights. Such aircraft, if engaged in the carriage of passengers, cargo, or mail for remuneration or hire on other than scheduled international air services, shall also, subject to the provisions of Article 7, have the privilege of taking on or discharging passengers, cargo, or mail, subject to the right of any State where such embarkation or discharge takes place to impose such regulations, conditions or limitations as it may consider desirable.

Article 6
Scheduled air services

No scheduled international air service may be operated over or into the territory of a contracting State, except with the special permission or other authorization of that State, and in accordance with the terms of such permission or authorization.

Article 7
Cabotage

Each contracting State shall have the right to refuse permission to the aircraft of other contracting States to take on in its territory passengers, mail and cargo carried for remuneration or hire and destined for another point within its territory. Each contracting State undertakes not to enter into any arrangements which specifically grant any such privilege on an exclusive basis to any other State or an airline of any other State, and not to obtain any such exclusive privilege from any other State.

Article 8
Pilotless aircraft

No aircraft capable of being flown without a pilot shall be flown without a pilot over the territory of a contracting State without special authorization by that State and in accordance with the terms of such authorization. Each contracting State undertakes to insure that the flight of such aircraft without a pilot in regions open to civil aircraft shall be so controlled as to obviate danger to civil aircraft.

Article 9
Prohibited areas

(a) Each contracting State may, for reasons of military necessity or public safety, restrict or prohibit uniformly the aircraft of other States from flying over certain areas of its territory, provided that no distinction in this respect is made between the aircraft of the State whose territory is involved, engaged in international scheduled airline services, and the aircraft of the other contracting States likewise engaged. Such prohibited areas shall be of reasonable extent and location so as not to interfere unnecessarily with air navigation. Descriptions of such prohibited areas in the territory of a contracting State, as well as any subsequent alterations therein, shall be communicated as soon as possible to the other contracting States and to the International Civil Aviation Organization.

(b) Each contracting State reserves also the right, in exceptional circumstances or during a period of emergency, or in the interest of public safety, and with immediate effect, temporarily to restrict or prohibit flying over the whole or any part of its territory, on condition that such restriction or prohibition shall be applicable without distinction of nationality to aircraft of all other States.

(c) Each contracting State, under such regulations as it may prescribe, may require any aircraft entering the areas contemplated in subparagraphs (a) or (b) above to effect a landing as soon as practicable thereafter at some designated airport within its territory.

Article 10
Landing at customs airport

Except in a case where, under the terms of this Convention or a special authorization, aircraft are permitted to cross the territory of a contracting State without landing, every aircraft which enters the territory of a contracting State shall, if the regulations of that State so require, land at an airport designated by that State for the purpose of customs and other examination. On departure from the territory of a contracting State, such aircraft shall depart from a similarly designated customs airport. Particulars of all designated customs airports shall be published by the State and transmitted to the International Civil Aviation Organization established under Part II of this Convention for communication to all other contracting States.

Article 11
Applicability of air regulations

Subject to the provisions of this Convention, the laws and regulations of a contracting State relating to the admission to or departure from its territory of aircraft engaged in international air navigation, or to the operation and navigation of such aircraft while within its territory, shall be applied to the aircraft of all contracting States without distinction as to nationality, and shall be complied with by such aircraft upon entering or departing from or while within the territory of that State.

Article 12
Rules of the air

Each contracting State undertakes to adopt measures to insure that every aircraft flying over or maneuvering within its territory and that every aircraft carrying its nationality mark, wherever such aircraft may be, shall comply with the rules and regulations relating to the flight and maneuver of aircraft there in force. Each contracting State undertakes to keep its own regulations in these respects uniform, to the greatest possible extent, with those established from time to time under this Convention. Over the high seas, the rules in force shall be those established under this Convention. Each contracting State undertakes to insure the prosecution of all persons violating the regulations applicable.

Article 13
Entry and clearance regulations

The laws and regulations of a contracting State as to the admission to or departure from its territory of passengers, crew or cargo of aircraft, such as regulations relating to entry, clearance, immigration, passports, customs, and quarantine shall be complied with by or on behalf of such passengers, crew or cargo upon entrance into or departure from, or while within the territory of that State.

Article 14
Prevention of spread of disease

Each contracting State agrees to take effective measures to prevent the spread by means of air navigation of cholera, typhus (epidemic), smallpox, yellow fever, plague, and such other communicable diseases as the contracting States shall from time to time decide to designate, and to that end contracting States will keep in close consultation with the agencies concerned with international regulations relating to sanitary measures applicable to aircraft. Such consultation shall be without prejudice to the application of any existing international convention on this subject to which the contracting States may be parties.

Article 15
Airport and similar charges

Every airport in a contracting State which is open to public use by its national aircraft shall likewise, subject to the provisions of Article 68, be open under uniform conditions to the aircraft of all the other contracting States. The like uniform conditions shall apply to the use, by aircraft of every contracting State, of all air navigation facilities, including radio and meteorological services, which may be provided for public use for the safety and expedition of air navigation. Any charges that may be imposed or permitted to be imposed by a contracting State for the use of such airports and air navigation facilities by the aircraft of any other contracting State shall not be higher,

(a) As to aircraft not engaged in scheduled international air services, than those that would be paid by its national aircraft of the same class engaged in similar operations, and

(b) As to aircraft engaged in scheduled international air services, than those that would be paid by its national aircraft engaged in similar international air services.

All such charges shall be published and communicated to the International Civil Aviation Organization: provided that, upon representation by an interested contracting State, the charges imposed for the use of airports and other facilities shall be subject to review by the Council, which shall report and make recommendations thereon for the consideration of the State or States concerned. No fees, dues or other charges shall be imposed by any contracting State in respect solely of the right of transit over or entry into or exit from its territory of any aircraft of a contracting State or persons or property thereon.

Article 16
Search of aircraft

The appropriate authorities of each of the contracting States shall have the right, without unreasonable delay, to search aircraft of the other contracting States on landing or departure, and to inspect the certificates and other documents prescribed by this Convention.

CHAPTER III
NATIONALITY OF AIRCRAFT

Article 17
Nationality of aircraft

Aircraft have the nationality of the State in which they are registered.

Article 18
Dual registration

An aircraft cannot be validly registered in more than one State, but its registration may be changed from one State to another.

Article 19
National laws governing registration

The registration or transfer of registration of aircraft in any contracting State shall be made in accordance with its law and regulations.

Article 20
Display of marks

Every aircraft engaged in international air navigation shall bear its appropriate nationality and registration marks.

Article 21
Report of registrations

Each contracting State undertakes to supply to any other contracting State or to the International Civil Aviation Organization, on demand, information concerning the registration and ownership of any particular aircraft registered in that State. In addition, each contracting State shall furnish reports to the International Civil Aviation Organization, under such regulations as the latter may prescribe, giving such pertinent data as can be made available concerning the ownership and control of aircraft registered in that State and habitually engaged in international air navigation. The data thus obtained by the International Civil Aviation Organization shall be made available by it on request to the other contracting States.

CHAPTER IV
MEASURES TO FACILITATE AIR NAVIGATION

Article 22
Facilitation of formalities

Each contracting State agrees to adopt all practicable measures, through the issuance of special regulations or otherwise, to facilitate and expedite navigation by aircraft between the territories of contracting States, and to prevent unnecessary delays to aircraft, crews, passengers and cargo, especially in the administration of the laws relating to immigration, quarantine, customs and clearance.

Article 23
Customs and immigration procedures

Each contracting State undertakes, so far as it may find practicable, to establish customs and immigration procedures affecting international air navigation in accordance with the practices which may be established or recommended from time to time, pursuant to this Convention. Nothing in this Convention shall be construed as preventing the establishment of customs-free airports.

Article 24
Customs duty

(a) Aircraft on a flight to, from, or across the territory of another contracting State shall be admitted temporarily free of duty, subject to the customs regulations of the State. Fuel, lubricating oils, spare parts, regular equipment and aircraft stores on board an aircraft of a contracting State, on arrival in the territory of another contracting State and retained on board on leaving the territory of that State shall be exempt from customs duty, inspection fees or similar national or local duties and charges. This exemption shall not apply to any quantities or articles unloaded, except in accordance with the customs regulations of the State, which may require that they shall be kept under customs supervision.

(b) Spare parts and equipment imported into the territory of a contracting State for incorporation in or use on an aircraft of another contracting State engaged in international air navigation shall be admitted free of customs duty, subject to compliance with the regulations of the State concerned, which may provide that the articles shall be kept under customs supervision and control.

Article 25
Aircraft in distress

Each contracting State undertakes to provide such measures of assistance to aircraft in distress in its territory as it may find practicable, and to permit, subject to control by its own authorities, the owners of the aircraft or authorities of the State in which the aircraft is registered to provide such measures of assistance as may be necessitated by the circumstances. Each contracting State, when undertaking search for missing aircraft, will collaborate in coordinated measures which may be recommended from time to time pursuant to this Convention.

Article 26
Investigation of accidents

In the event of an accident to an aircraft of a contracting State occurring in the territory of another contracting State, and involving death or serious injury, or indicating serious technical defect in the aircraft or air navigation facilities, the State in which the accident occurs will institute an inquiry into the circumstances of the accident, in accordance, so far as its laws permit, with the procedure which may be recommended by the International Civil Aviation Organization. The State in which the aircraft is registered shall be given the opportunity to appoint observers to be present at the inquiry and the State holding the inquiry shall communicate the report and findings in the matter to that State.

Article 27
Exemption from seizure on patent claims

(a) While engaged in international air navigation, any authorized entry of aircraft of a contracting State into the territory of another contracting State or authorized transit across the territory of such State with or without landings shall not entail any seizure or detention of the aircraft or any claim against the owner or operator thereof or any other interference therewith by or on behalf of such State or any person therein, on the ground that the construction, mechanism, parts, accessories or operation of the aircraft is an infringement of any patent, design, or model duly granted or registered in the State whose territory is entered by the aircraft, it being agreed that no deposit of security in connection with the foregoing exemption from seizure or detention of the aircraft shall in any case be required in the State entered by such aircraft.

(b) The provisions of paragraph (a) of this Article shall also be applicable to the storage of spare parts and spare equipment for the aircraft and the right to use and install the same in the repair of an aircraft of a contracting State in the territory of any other contracting State, provided that any patented part or equipment so stored shall not be sold or distributed internally in or exported commercially from the contracting State entered by the aircraft.

(c) The benefits of this Article shall apply only to such States, parties to this Convention, as either (1) are parties to the International Convention for the Protection of Industrial Property and to any amendments thereof; or (2) have enacted patent laws which recognize and give adequate protection to inventions made by the nationals of the other States parties to this Convention.

Article 28
Air navigation facilities and standard systems

Each contracting State undertakes, so far as it may find practicable, to:

(a) Provide, in its territory, airports, radio services, meteorological services and other air navigation facilities to facilitate international air navigation, in accordance with the standards and practices recommended or established from time to time, pursuant to this Convention;

(b) Adopt and put into operation the appropriate standard systems of communications procedure, codes, markings, signals, lighting and other operational practices and rules which may be recommended or established from time to time, pursuant to this Convention;

(c) Collaborate in international measures to secure the publication of aeronautical maps and charts in accordance with standards which may be recommended or established from time to time, pursuant to this Convention.

CHAPTER V
CONDITIONS TO BE FULFILLED WITH RESPECT TO AIRCRAFT

Article 29
Documents carried in aircraft

Every aircraft of a contracting State, engaged in international navigation, shall carry the following documents in conformity with the conditions prescribed in this Convention:

(a) Its certificate of registration;

(b) Its certificate of airworthiness;

(c) The appropriate licenses for each member of the crew;

(d) Its journey log book;

(e) If it is equipped with radio apparatus, the aircraft radio station license;

(f) If it carries passengers, a list of their names and places of embarkation and destination;

(g) If it carries cargo, a manifest and detailed declarations of the cargo.

Article 30
Aircraft radio equipment

(a) Aircraft of each contracting State may, in or over the territory of other contracting States, carry radio transmitting apparatus only if a license to install and operate such apparatus has been issued by the appropriate authorities of the State in which the aircraft is registered. The use of radio transmitting apparatus in the territory of the contracting State whose territory is flown over shall be in accordance with the regulations prescribed by that State.

(b) Radio transmitting apparatus may be used only by members of the flight crew who are provided with a special license for the purpose, issued by the appropriate authorities of the State in which the aircraft is registered.

Article 31
Certificates of airworthiness

Every aircraft engaged in international navigation shall be provided with a certificate of airworthiness issued or rendered valid by the State in which it is registered.

Article 32
Licenses of personnel

(a) The pilot of every aircraft and the other members of the operating crew of every aircraft engaged in international navigation shall be provided with certificates of competency and licenses issued or rendered valid by the State in which the aircraft is registered.

(b) Each contracting State reserves the right to refuse to recognize, for the purpose of flight above its own territory, certificates of competency and licenses granted to any of its nationals by another contracting State.

Article 33
Recognition of certificates and licenses

Certificates of airworthiness and certificates of competency and licenses issued or rendered valid by the contracting State in which the aircraft is registered, shall be recognized as valid by the other contracting States, provided that the requirements under which such certificates or licenses were issued or rendered valid are equal to or above the minimum standards which may be established from time to time pursuant to this Convention.

Article 34
Journey log books

There shall be maintained in respect of every aircraft engaged in international navigation a journey log book in which shall be entered particulars of the aircraft, its crew and of each journey, in such form as may be prescribed from time to time pursuant to this Convention.

Article 35
Cargo restrictions

(a) No munitions of war or implements of war may be carried in or above the territory of a State in aircraft engaged in international navigation, except by permission of such State. Each State shall determine by regulations what constitutes munitions of war or implements of war for the purposes of this Article, giving due consideration, for the purposes of uniformity, to such recommendations as the International Civil Aviation Organization may from time to time make.

(b) Each contracting State reserves the right, for reasons of public order and safety, to regulate or prohibit the carriage in or above its territory of articles other than those enumerated in paragraph (a): provided that no distinction is made in this respect between its national aircraft engaged in international navigation and the aircraft of the other States so engaged; and provided further that no restriction shall be imposed which may interfere with the carriage and use on aircraft of apparatus necessary for the operation or navigation of the aircraft or the safety of the personnel or passengers.

Article 36
Photographic apparatus

Each contracting State may prohibit or regulate the use of photographic apparatus in aircraft over its territory.

CHAPTER VI
INTERNATIONAL STANDARDS AND RECOMMENDED PRACTICES

Article 37
Adoption of international standards and procedures

Each contracting State undertakes to collaborate in securing the highest practicable degree of uniformity in regulations, standards, procedures, and organization in relation to aircraft, personnel, airways and auxiliary services in all matters in which such uniformity will facilitate and improve air navigation. To this end the International Civil Aviation Organization shall adopt and amend from time to time, as may be necessary, international standards and recommended practices and procedures dealing with:

(a) Communications systems and air navigation aids, including ground marking;

(b) Characteristics of airports and landing areas;

(c) Rules of the air and air traffic control practices;

(d) Licensing of operating and mechanical personnel;

(e) Airworthiness of aircraft;

(f) Registration and identification of aircraft;

(g) Collection and exchange of meteorological information;

(h) Log books;

(i) Aeronautical maps and charts;

(j) Customs and immigration procedures;

(k) Aircraft in distress and investigation of accidents;

and such other matters concerned with the safety, regularity, and efficiency of air navigation as may from time to time appear appropriate.

Article 38
Departures from international standards and procedures

Any State which finds it impracticable to comply in all respects with any such international standard or procedure, or to bring its own regulations or practices into full accord with any international standard or procedure after amendment of the latter, or which deems it necessary to adopt regulations or practices differing in any particular respect from those established by an international standard, shall give immediate notification to the International Civil Aviation Organization of the differences between its own practice and that established by the international standard. In the case of amendments to international standards, any State which does not make the appropriate amendments to its own regulations or practices shall give notice to the Council within sixty days of the adoption of the amendment to the international standard, or indicate the action which it proposes to take. In any such case, the Council shall make immediate notification to all other states of the difference which exists between one or more features of an international standard and the corresponding national practice of that State.

Article 39
Endorsement of certificates and licenses

(a) Any aircraft or part thereof with respect to which there exists an international standard of airworthiness or performance, and which failed in any respect to satisfy that standard at the time of its certification, shall have endorsed on or attached to its airworthiness certificate a complete enumeration of the details in respect of which it so failed.

(b) Any person holding a license who does not satisfy in full the conditions laid down in the international standard relating to the class of license or certificate which he holds shall have endorsed on or attached to his license a complete enumeration of the particulars in which he does not satisfy such conditions.

Article 40
Validity of endorsed certificates and licenses

No aircraft or personnel having certificates or licenses so endorsed shall participate in international navigation, except with the permission of the State or States whose territory is entered. The registration or use of any such aircraft, or of any certificated aircraft part, in any State other than that in which it was originally certificated shall be at the discretion of the State into which the aircraft or part is imported.

Article 41
Recognition of existing standards of airworthiness

The provisions of this Chapter shall not apply to aircraft and aircraft equipment of types of which the prototype is submitted to the appropriate national authorities for certification prior to a date three years after the date of adoption of an international standard of airworthiness for such equipment.

Article 42
Recognition of existing standards of competency of personnel

The provisions of this Chapter shall not apply to personnel whose licences are originally issued prior to a date one year after initial adoption of an international standard of qualification for such personnel; but they shall in any case apply to all personnel whose licenses remain valid five years after the date of adoption of such standard.

PART II
THE INTERNATIONAL CIVIL AVIATION ORGANIZATION

CHAPTER VII
THE ORGANIZATION

Article 43
Name and composition

An organization to be named the International Civil Aviation Organization is formed by the Convention. It is made up of an Assembly, a Council, and such other bodies as may be necessary.

Article 44
Objectives

The aims and objectives of the Organization are to develop the principles and techniques of international air navigation and to foster the planning and development of international air transport so as to:

(a) Insure the safe and orderly growth of international civil aviation throughout the world;

(b) Encourage the arts of aircraft design and operation for peaceful purposes;

(c) Encourage the development of airways, airports, and air navigation facilities for international civil aviation;

(d) Meet the needs of the peoples of the world for safe, regular, efficient and economical air transport;

(e) Prevent economic waste caused by unreasonable competition;

(f) Insure that the rights of contracting States are fully respected and that every contracting State has a fair opportunity to operate international airlines;

(g) Avoid discrimination between contracting States;

(h) Promote safety of flight in international air navigation;

(i) Promote generally the development of all aspects of international civil aeronautics.

Article 45
Permanent seat

The permanent seat of the Organization shall be at such place as shall be determined at the final meeting of the Interim Assembly of the Provisional International Civil Aviation Organization set up by the Interim Agreement on International Civil Aviation signed at Chicago on December 7, 1944. The seat may be temporarily transferred elsewhere by decision of the Council, and otherwise than temporarily by decision of the Assembly, such decision to be taken by the number of votes specified by the Assembly. The number of votes so specified will not be less than three-fifths of the total number of contracting States.

Article 46
First meeting of Assembly

The first meeting of the Assembly shall be summoned by the Interim Council of the above-mentioned Provisional Organization as soon as the Convention has come into force, to meet at a time and place to be decided by the Interim Council.

Article 47
Legal capacity

The Organization shall enjoy in the territory of each contracting State such legal capacity as may be necessary for the performance of its functions. Full juridical personality shall be granted wherever compatible with the constitution and laws of the State concerned.

CHAPTER VIII
THE ASSEMBLY

Article 48
Meetings of the Assembly and voting

(a) The Assembly shall meet not less than once in three years and shall be convened by the Council at a suitable time and place. An extraordinary meeting of the Assembly may be held at any time upon the call of the Council or at the request of not less than one-fifth of the total number of contracting States addressed to the Secretary General.

(b) All contracting States shall have an equal right to be represented at the meetings of the Assembly and each contracting State shall be entitled to one vote. Delegates representing contracting States may be assisted by technical advisers who may participate in the meetings but shall have no vote.

(c) A majority of the contracting States is required to constitute a quorum for the meetings of the Assembly. Unless otherwise provided in this Convention, decisions of the Assembly shall be taken by a majority of the votes cast.

Article 49
Powers and duties of the Assembly

The powers and duties of the Assembly shall be to:

(a) Elect at each meeting its President and other officers;

(b) Elect the contracting States to be represented on the Council, in accordance with the provisions of Chapter IX;

(c) Examine and take appropriate action on the reports of the Council and decide on any matter referred to it by the Council;

(d) Determine its own rules of procedure and establish such subsidiary commissions as it may consider to be necessary or desirable;

(e) Vote annual budgets and determine the financial arrangements of the Organization, in accordance with the provisions of Chapter XII;

(f) Review expenditures and approve the accounts of the Organization;

(g) Refer, at its discretion, to the Council, to subsidiary commissions, or to any other body any matter within its sphere of action;

(h) Delegate to the Council the powers and authority necessary or desirable for the discharge of the duties of the Organization and revoke or modify the delegations of authority at any time;

(i) Carry out the appropriate provisions of Chapter XIII;

(j) Consider proposals for the modification or amendment of the provisions of this Convention and, if it approves of the proposals, recommend them to the contracting States in accordance with the provisions of Chapter XXI;

(k) Deal with any matter within the sphere of action of the Organization not specifically assigned to the Council.

CHAPTER IX
THE COUNCIL

Article 50
Composition and election of Council

(a) The Council shall be a permanent body responsible to the Assembly. It shall be composed of thirty-three contracting States elected by the Assembly. An election shall be held at the first meeting of the Assembly and thereafter every three years, and the members of the Council so elected shall hold office until the next following election.

(b) In electing the members of the Council, the Assembly shall give adequate representation to (1) the States of chief importance in air transport; (2) the States not otherwise included which make the largest contribution to the provision of facilities for international civil air navigation; and (3) the States not otherwise included whose designation will insure that all the major geographic areas of the world are represented on the Council. Any vacancy on the Council shall be filled by the Assembly as soon as possible; any contracting State so elected to the Council shall hold office for the unexpired portion of its predecessor's term of office.

(c) No representative of a contracting State on the Council shall be actively associated with the operation of an international air service or financially interested in such a service.

Article 51
President of Council

The Council shall elect its President for a term of three years. He may be reelected. He shall have no vote. The Council shall elect from among its members one or more Vice Presidents who shall retain their right to vote when serving as acting President. The President need not be selected from among the representatives of the members of the Council but, if a representative is elected, his seat shall be deemed vacant and it shall be filled by the State which he represented. The duties of the President shall be to:

(a) Convene meetings of the Council, the Air Transport Committee, and the Air Navigation Commission;

(b) Serve as representative of the Council; and

(c) Carry out on behalf of the Council the functions which the Council assigns to him.

Article 52
Voting in Council

Decisions by the Council shall require approval by a majority of its members. The Council may delegate authority with respect to any particular matter to a committee of its members. Decisions of any committee of the Council may be appealed to the Council by any interested contracting State.

Article 53
Participation without a vote

Any contracting State may participate, without a vote, in the consideration by the Council and by its committees and commissions of any question which especially affects its interests. No member of the Council shall vote in the consideration by the Council of a dispute to which it is a party.

Article 54
Mandatory functions of Council

The Council shall:

(a) Submit annual reports to the Assembly;

(b) Carry out the directions of the Assembly and discharge the duties and obligations which are laid on it by this Convention;

(c) Determine its organization and rules of procedure;

(d) Appoint and define the duties of an Air Transport Committee, which shall be chosen from among the representatives of the members of the Council, and which shall be responsible to it;

(e) Establish an Air Navigation Commission, in accordance with the provisions of Chapter X;

(f) Administer the finances of the Organization in accordance with the provisions of Chapters XII and XV;

(g) Determine the emoluments of the President of the Council;

(h) Appoint a chief executive officer who shall be called the Secretary General, and make provision for the appointment of such other personnel as may be necessary, in accordance with the provisions of Chapter XI;

(i) Request, collect, examine and publish information relating to the advancement of air navigation and the operation of international air services, including information about the costs of operation and particulars of subsidies paid to airlines from public funds;

(j) Report to contracting States any infraction of this Convention, as well as any failure to carry out recommendations or determinations of the Council;

(k) Report to the Assembly any infraction of this Convention where a contracting State has failed to take appropriate action within a reasonable time after notice of the infraction;

(l) Adopt, in accordance with the provisions of Chapter VI of this Convention, international standards and recommended practices; for convenience, designate them as Annexes to this Convention; and notify all contracting States of the action taken;

(m) Consider recommendations of the Air Navigation Commission for amendment of the Annexes and take action in accordance with the provisions of Chapter XX;

(n) Consider any matter relating to the Convention which any contracting State refers to it.

Article 55
Permissive functions of Council

The Council may:

(a) Where appropriate and as experience may show to be desirable, create subordinate air transport commissions on a regional or other basis and define groups of states or airlines with or through which it may deal to facilitate the carrying out of the aims of this Convention;

(b) Delegate to the Air Navigation Commission duties additional to those set forth in the Convention and revoke or modify such delegations of authority at any time;

(c) Conduct research into all aspects of air transport and air navigation which are of international importance, communicate the results of its research to the contracting States, and facilitate the exchange of information between contracting States on air transport and air navigation matters;

(d) Study any matters affecting the organization and operation of international air transport, including the international ownership and operation of international air services on trunk routes, and submit to the Assembly plans in relation thereto;

(e) Investigate, at the request of any contracting State, any situation which may appear to present avoidable obstacles to the development of international air navigation; and, after such investigation, issue such reports as may appear to it desirable.

CHAPTER X
THE AIR NAVIGATION COMMISSION

Article 56
Nomination and appointment of Commission

The Air Navigation Commission shall be composed of fifteen members appointed by the Council from among persons nominated by contracting States. These persons shall have suitable qualifications and experience in the science and practice of aeronautics. The Council shall request all contracting States to submit nominations. The President of the Air Navigation Commission shall be appointed by the Council.

Article 57
Duties of Commission

The Air Navigation Commission shall:

(a) Consider, and recommend to the Council for adoption, modifications of the Annexes to this Convention;

(b) Establish technical subcommissions on which any contracting State may be represented, if it so desires;

(c) Advise the Council concerning the collection and communication to the contracting States of all information which it considers necessary and useful for the advancement of air navigation.

CHAPTER XI
PERSONNEL

Article 58
Appointment of personnel

Subject to any rules laid down by the Assembly and to the provisions of this Convention, the Council shall determine the method of appointment and of termination of appointment, the training, and the salaries, allowances, and conditions of service of the Secretary General and other personnel of the Organization, and may employ or make use of the services of nationals of any contracting State.

Article 59
International character of personnel

The President of the Council, the Secretary General, and other personnel shall not seek or receive instructions in regard to the discharge of their responsibilities from any authority external to the Organization. Each contracting State undertakes fully to respect the international character of the responsibilities of the personnel and not to seek to influence any of its nationals in the discharge of their responsibilities.

Article 60
Immunities and privileges of personnel

Each contracting State undertakes, so far as possible under its constitutional procedure, to accord to the President of the Council, the Secretary General, and the other personnel of the Organization, the immunities and privileges which are accorded to corresponding personnel of other public international organizations. If a general international agreement on the immunities and privileges of international civil servants is arrived at, the immunities and privileges accorded to the President, the Secretary General, and the other personnel of the Organization shall be the immunities and privileges accorded under that general international agreement.

CHAPTER XII
FINANCE

Article 61
Budget and apportionment of expenses

The Council shall submit to the Assembly annual budgets, annual statements of accounts and estimates of all receipts and expenditures. The Assembly shall vote the budgets with whatever modification it sees fit to prescribe, and, with the exception of assessments under Chapter XV to States consenting thereto, shall apportion the expenses of the Organization among the contracting States on the basis which it shall from time to time determine.

Article 62
Suspension of voting power

The Assembly may suspend the voting power in the Assembly and in the Council of any contracting State that fails to discharge within a reasonable period its financial obligations to the Organization.

Article 63
Expenses of delegations and other representatives

Each contracting State shall bear the expenses of its own delegation to the Assembly and the remuneration, travel, and other expenses of any person whom it appoints to serve on the Council, and of its nominees or representatives on any subsidiary committees or commissions of the Organization.

CHAPTER XIII
OTHER INTERNATIONAL ARRANGEMENTS

Article 64
Security arrangements

The Organization may, with respect to air matters within its competence directly affecting world security, by vote of the Assembly enter into appropriate arrangements with any general organization set up by the nations of the world to preserve peace.

Article 65
Arrangements with other international bodies

The Council, on behalf of the Organization, may enter into agreements with other international bodies for the maintenance of common services and for common arrangements concerning personnel and, with the approval of the Assembly, may enter into such other arrangements as may facilitate the work of the Organization.

Article 66
Functions relating to other agreements

(a) The Organization shall also carry out the functions placed upon it by the International Air Services Transit Agreement and by the International Air Transport Agreement drawn up at Chicago on December 7, 1944, in accordance with the terms and conditions therein set forth.

(b) Members of the Assembly and the Council who have not accepted the International Air Services Transit Agreement or the International Air Transport Agreement drawn up at Chicago on December 7, 1944 shall not have the right to vote on any questions referred to the Assembly or Council under the provisions of the relevant Agreement.

PART III
INTERNATIONAL AIR TRANSPORT

CHAPTER XIV
INFORMATION AND REPORTS

Article 67
File reports with Council

Each contracting State undertakes that its international airlines shall, in accordance with requirements laid down by the Council, file with the Council traffic reports, cost statistics and financial statements showing among other things all receipts and the sources thereof.

CHAPTER XV
AIRPORTS AND OTHER AIR NAVIGATION FACILITIES

Article 68
Designation of routes and airports

Each contracting State may, subject to the provisions of this Convention, designate the route to be followed within its territory by any international air service and the airports which any such service may use.

Article 69
Improvement of air navigation facilities

If the Council is of the opinion that the airports or other air navigation facilities, including radio and meteorological services, of a contracting State are not reasonably adequate for the safe, regular, efficient, and economical operation of international air services, present or contemplated, the Council shall consult with the State directly concerned, and other States affected, with a view to finding means by which the situation may be remedied, and may make recommendations for that purpose. No contracting State shall be guilty of an infraction of this Convention if it fails to carry out these recommendations.

Article 70
Financing of air navigation facilities

A contracting State, in the circumstances arising under the provisions of Article 69, may conclude an arrangement with the Council for giving effect to such recommendations. The State may elect to bear all of the costs involved in any such arrangement. If the State does not so elect, the Council may agree, at the request of the State, to provide for all or a portion of the costs.

Article 71
Provision and maintenance of facilities by Council

If a contracting State so requests, the Council may agree to provide, man, maintain, and administer any or all of the airports and other air navigation facilities including radio and meteorological services, required in its territory for the safe, regular, efficient and economical operation of the international air services of the other contracting States, and may specify just and reasonable charges for the use of the facilities provided.

Article 72
Acquisition or use of land

Where land is needed for facilities financed in whole or in part by the Council at the request of a contracting State, that State shall either provide the land itself, retaining title if it wishes, or facilitate the use of the land by the Council on just and reasonable terms and in accordance with the laws of the State concerned.

Article 73
Expenditure and assessment of funds

Within the limit of the funds which may be made available to it by the Assembly under Chapter XII, the Council may make current expenditures for the purposes of this Chapter from the general funds of the Organization. The Council shall assess the capital funds required for the purposes of this Chapter in previously agreed proportions over a reasonable period of time to the contracting States consenting thereto whose airlines use the facilities. The Council may also assess to States that consent any working funds that are required.

Article 74
Technical assistance and utilization of revenues

When the Council, at the request of a contracting State, advances funds or provides airports or other facilities in whole or in part, the arrangement may provide, with the consent of that State, for technical assistance in the supervision and operation of the airports and other facilities, and for the payment, from the revenues derived from the operation of the airports and other facilities, of the operating expenses of the airports and the other facilities, and of interest and amortization charges.

Article 75
Taking over of facilities from Council

A contracting State may at any time discharge any obligation into which it has entered under Article 70, and take over airports and other facilities which the Council has provided in its territory pursuant to the provisions of Articles 71 and 72, by paying to the Council an amount which in the opinion of the Council is reasonable in the circumstances. If the State considers that the amount fixed by the Council is unreasonable it may appeal to the Assembly against the decision of the Council and the Assembly may confirm or amend the decision of the Council.

Article 76
Return of funds

Funds obtained by the Council through reimbursement under Article 75 and from receipts of interest and amortization payments under Article 74 shall, in the case of advances originally financed by States under Article 73, be returned to the States which were originally assessed in the proportion of their assessments, as determined by the Council.

CHAPTER XVI
JOINT OPERATING ORGANIZATIONS AND POOLED SERVICES

Article 77
Joint operating organizations permitted

Nothing in this Convention shall prevent two or more contracting States from constituting joint air transport operating organizations or international operating agencies and from pooling their air services on any routes or in any regions, but such organizations or agencies and such pooled services shall be subject to all the provisions of this Convention, including those relating to the registration of agreements with the Council. The Council shall determine in what manner the provisions of this Convention relating to nationality of aircraft shall apply to aircraft operated by international operating agencies.

Article 78
Function of Council

The Council may suggest to contracting States concerned that they form joint organizations to operate air services on any routes or in any regions.

Article 79
Participation in operating organizations

A State may participate in joint operating organizations or in pooling arrangements, either through its government or through an airline company or companies designated by its government. The companies may, at the sole discretion of the State concerned, be state-owned or partly state-owned or privately owned.

PART IV
FINAL PROVISIONS

CHAPTER XVII
OTHER AERONAUTICAL AGREEMENTS AND ARRANGEMENTS

Article 80
Paris and Habana Conventions

Each contracting State undertakes, immediately upon the coming into force of this Convention, to give notice of denunciation of the Convention relating to the Regulation of Aerial Navigation signed at Paris on October 13, 1919 or the Convention on Commercial Aviation signed at Habana on February 20, 1928, if it is a party to either. As between contracting States, this Convention supersedes the Conventions of Paris and Habana previously referred to.

Article 81
Registration of existing agreements

All aeronautical agreements which are in existence on the coming into force of this Convention, and which are between a contracting State and any other State or between an airline of a contracting State and any other State or the airline of any other State, shall be forthwith registered with the Council.

Article 82
Abrogation of inconsistent arrangements

The contracting States accept this Convention as abrogating all obligations and understandings between them which are inconsistent with its terms, and undertake not to enter into any such obligations and understandings. A contracting State which, before becoming a member of the Organization has undertaken any obligations toward a non-contracting State or a national of a contracting State or of a non-contracting State inconsistent with the terms of this Convention, shall take immediate steps to procure its release from the obligations. If an airline of any contracting State has entered into any such inconsistent obligations, the State of which it is a national shall use its best efforts to secure their termination forthwith and shall in any event cause them to be terminated as soon as such action can lawfully be taken after the coming into force of this Convention.

Article 83
Registration of new arrangements

Subject to the provisions of the preceding Article, any contracting State may make arrangements not inconsistent with the provisions of this Convention. Any such arrangement shall be forthwith registered with the Council, which shall make it public as soon as possible.

CHAPTER XVIII
DISPUTES AND DEFAULT

Article 84
Settlement of disputes

If any disagreement between two or more contracting States relating to the interpretation or application of this Convention and its Annexes cannot be settled by negotiation, it shall, on the application of any State concerned in the disagreement, be decided by the Council. No member of the Council shall vote in the consideration by the Council of any dispute to which it is a party. Any contracting State may, subject to Article 85, appeal from the decision of the Council to an ad hoc arbitral tribunal agreed upon with the other parties to the dispute or to the Permanent Court of International Justice. Any such appeal shall be notified to the Council within sixty days of receipt of notification of the decision of the Council.

Article 85
Arbitration procedure

If any contracting State party to a dispute in which the decision of the Council is under appeal has not accepted the Statute of the Permanent Court of International Justice and the contracting States parties to the dispute cannot agree on the choice of the arbitral tribunal, each of the contracting States parties to the dispute shall name a single arbitrator who shall name an umpire. If either contracting State party to the dispute fails to name an arbitrator within a period of three months from the date of the appeal, an arbitrator shall be named on behalf of that State by the President of the Council from a list of qualified and available persons maintained by the Council. If, within thirty days, the arbitrators cannot agree on an umpire, the President of the Council shall designate an umpire from the list previously referred to. The arbitrators and the umpire shall then jointly constitute an arbitral tribunal. Any arbitral tribunal established under this or the preceding Article shall settle its own procedure and give its decisions by majority vote, provided that the Council may determine procedural questions in the event of any delay which in the opinion of the Council is excessive.

Article 86
Appeals

Unless the Council decides otherwise any decision by the Council on whether an international airline is operating in conformity with the provisions of this Convention shall remain in effect unless reversed on appeal. On any other matter, decisions of the Council shall, if appealed from, be suspended until the appeal is decided. The decisions of the Permanent Court of International Justice and of an arbitral tribunal shall be final and binding.

Article 87
Penalty for non-conformity of airline

Each contracting State undertakes not to allow the operation of an airline of a contracting State through the airspace above its territory if the Council has decided that the airline concerned is not conforming to a final decision rendered in accordance with the previous Article.

Article 88
Penalty for non-conformity by State

The Assembly shall suspend the voting power in the Assembly and in the Council of any contracting State that is found in default under the provisions of this Chapter.

CHAPTER XIX
WAR

Article 89
War and emergency conditions

In case of war, the provisions of this Convention shall not affect the freedom of action of any of the contracting States affected, whether as belligerents or as neutrals. The same principle shall apply in the case of any contracting State which declares a state of national emergency and notifies the fact to the Council.

CHAPTER XX
ANNEXES

Article 90
Adoption and amendment of Annexes

(a) The adoption by the Council of the Annexes described in Article 54, subparagraph (l), shall require the vote of two-thirds of the Council at a meeting called for that purpose and shall then be submitted by the Council to each contracting State. Any such Annex or any amendment of an Annex shall become effective within three months after its submission to the contracting States or at the end of such longer period of time as the Council may prescribe, unless in the meantime a majority of the contracting States register their disapproval with the Council.

(b) The Council shall immediately notify all contracting States of the coming into force of any Annex or amendment thereto.

CHAPTER XXI
RATIFICATIONS, ADHERENCES, AMENDMENTS, AND DENUNCIATIONS

Article 91
Ratification of Convention

(a) This Convention shall be subject to ratification by the signatory States. The instruments of ratification shall be deposited in the archives of the Government of the United States of America, which shall give notice of the date of the deposit to each of the signatory and adhering States.

(b) As soon as this Convention has been ratified or adhered to by twenty-six States it shall come into force between them on the thirtieth day after deposit of the twenty-sixth instrument. It shall come into force for each State ratifying thereafter on the thirtieth day after the deposit of its instrument of ratification.

(c) It shall be the duty of the Government of the United States of America to notify the government of each of the signatory and adhering States of the date on which this Convention comes into force.

Article 92
Adherence to Convention

(a) This Convention shall be open for adherence by members of the United Nations and States associated with them, and States which remained neutral during the present world conflict.

(b) Adherence shall be effected by a notification addressed to the Government of the United States of America and shall take effect as from the thirtieth day from the receipt of the notification by the Government of the United States of America, which shall notify all the contracting States.

Article 93
Admission of other States

States other than those provided for in Articles 91 and 92 (a) may, subject to approval by any general international organization set up by the nations of the world to preserve peace, be admitted to participation in this Convention by means of a four-fifths vote of the Assembly and on such conditions as the Assembly may prescribe: provided that in each case the assent of any State invaded or attacked during the present war by the State seeking admission shall be necessary.

Article 93 bis

(a) Notwithstanding the provisions of Articles 91, 92 and 93 above:

(1) A State whose government the General Assembly of the United Nations has recommended be debarred from membership in international agencies established by or brought into relationship with the United Nations shall automatically cease to be a member of the International Civil Aviation Organization;

(2) A State which has been expelled from membership in the United Nations shall automatically cease to be a member of the International Civil Aviation Organization unless the General Assembly of the United Nations attaches to its act of expulsion a recommendation to the contrary.

(b) A State which ceases to be a member of the International Civil Aviation Organization as a result of the provisions of paragraph (a) above may, after approval by the General Assembly of the United Nations, be readmitted to the International Civil Aviation Organization upon application and upon approval by a majority of the Council.

(c) Members of the Organization which are suspended from the exercise of the rights and privileges of membership in the United Nations shall, upon the request of the latter, be suspended from the rights and privileges of membership in this Organization.

Article 94
Amendment of Convention

(a) Any proposed amendment to this Convention must be approved by a two-thirds vote of the Assembly and shall then come into force in respect of States which have ratified such amendment when ratified by the number of contracting States specified by the Assembly. The number so specified shall not be less than two-thirds of the total number of contracting States.

(b) If in its opinion the amendment is of such a nature as to justify this course, the Assembly in its resolution recommending adoption may provide that any State which has not ratified within a specified period after the amendment has come into force shall thereupon cease to be a member of the Organization and a party to the Convention.

Article 95
Denunciation of Convention

(a) Any contracting State may give notice of denunciation of this Convention three years after its coming into effect by notification addressed to the Government of the United States of America, which shall at once inform each of the contracting States.

(b) Denunciation shall take effect one year from the date of the receipt of the notification and shall operate only as regards the State effecting the denunciation.

CHAPTER XXII
DEFINITIONS

Article 96

For the purpose of this Convention the expression:

(a) "Air service" means any scheduled air service performed by aircraft for the public transport of passengers, mail or cargo.

(b) "International air service" means an air service which passes through the air space over the territory of more than one State.

(c) "Airline" means any air transport enterprise offering or operating an international air service.

(d) "Stop for non-traffic purposes" means a landing for any purpose other than taking on or discharging passengers, cargo or mail.

SIGNATURE OF CONVENTION

IN WITNESS WHEREOF, the undersigned plenipotentiaries, having been duly authorized, sign this Convention on behalf of their respective governments on the dates appearing opposite their signatures.

DONE at Chicago the seventh day of December 1944, in the English language. A text drawn up in the English, French and Spanish languages, each of which shall be of equal authenticity, shall be open for signature at Washington, D.C. Both texts shall be deposited in the archives of the Government of the United States of America, and certified copies shall be transmitted by that Government to the governments of all the States which may sign or adhere to this Convention.

Appendix 4

International Air Services Transit Agreement

Done at Chicago—December 7, 1944
Entered into force—January 30, 1945
Effective in the United States—February 8, 1945
59 Stat. 1693, T.I.A.S. No. 487,
3 Bevans 916, 84 U.N.T.S. 389, ICAO Doc. 7500

The States which sign and accept this International Air Services Transit Agreement, being members of the International Civil Aviation Organization, declare as follows:

Article I

Section 1

Each contracting State grants to the other contracting States the following freedoms of the air in respect of scheduled international air services:

1. The privilege to fly across its territory without landing;

2. The privilege to land for non-traffic purposes.

The privileges of this section shall not be applicable with respect to airports utilized for military purposes to the exclusion of any scheduled international air services. In areas of active hostilities or of military occupation, and in time of war along the supply routes leading to such areas, the exercise of such privileges shall be subject to the approval of the competent military authorities.

Section 2

The exercise of the foregoing privileges shall be in accordance with the provisions of the Interim Agreement on International Civil Aviation and, when it comes into force, with the provisions of the Convention on International Civil Aviation, both drawn up at Chicago on December 7, 1944.

Section 3

A contracting State granting to the airlines of another contracting State the privilege to stop for non-traffic purposes may require such airlines to offer reasonable commercial service at the points at which such stops are made.

Such requirement shall not involve any discrimination between airlines operating on the same route, shall take into account the capacity of the aircraft, and shall be exercised in such a manner as not to prejudice the normal operations of the international air services concerned or the rights and obligations of a contracting State.

Section 4

Each contracting State may, subject to the provisions of this Agreement,

1. Designate the route to be followed within its territory by any international air service and the airports which any such service may use;

2. Impose or permit to be imposed on any such service just and reasonable charges for the use of such airports and other facilities; these charges shall not be higher than

would be paid for the use of such airports and facilities by its national aircraft engaged in similar international services: provided that, upon representation by an interested contracting State, the charges imposed for the use of airports and other facilities shall be subject to review by the Council of the International Civil Aviation Organization established under the above-mentioned Convention, which shall report and make recommendations thereon for the consideration of the State or States concerned.

Section 5

Each contracting State reserves the right to withhold or revoke a certificate or permit to an air transport enterprise of another State in any case where it is not satisfied that substantial ownership and effective control are vested in nationals of a contracting State, or in case of failure of such air transport enterprise to comply with the laws of the State over which it operates, or to perform its obligations under this Agreement.

Article II

Section 1

A contracting State which deems that action by another contracting State under this Agreement is causing injustice or hardship to it, may request the Council to examine the situation. The Council shall thereupon inquire into the matter, and shall call the States concerned into consultation. Should such consultation fail to resolve the difficulty, the Council may make appropriate findings and recommendations to the contracting States concerned. If thereafter a contracting State concerned shall in the opinion of the Council unreasonably fail to take suitable corrective action, the Council may recommend to the Assembly of the above-mentioned Organization that such contracting State be suspended from its rights and privileges under this Agreement until such action has been taken. The Assembly by a two-thirds vote may so suspend such contracting State for such period of time as it may deem proper or until the Council shall find that corrective action has been taken by such State.

Section 2

If any disagreement between two or more contracting States relating to the interpretation or application of this Agreement cannot be settled by negotiation, the provisions of Chapter XVIII of the above-mentioned Convention shall be applicable in the same manner as provided therein with reference to any disagreement relating to the interpretation or application of the above-mentioned Convention.

Article III

This Agreement shall remain in force as long as the above-mentioned Convention; provided, however, that any contracting State, a party to the present Agreement, may denounce it on one year's notice given by it to the Government of the United States of America, which shall at once inform all other contracting States of such notice and withdrawal.

Article IV

Pending the coming into force of the above-mentioned Convention, all references to it herein, other than those contained in Article II, Section 2, and Article V, shall be deemed to be references to the Interim Agreement on International Civil Aviation drawn up at Chicago on December 7, 1944; and references to the International Civil Aviation Organization, the Assembly, and the Council shall be deemed to be references to the Provisional International Civil Aviation Organization, the Interim Assembly, and Interim Council respectively.

Article V

For the purposes of this Agreement, "territory" shall be defined as in Article 2 of the above-mentioned Convention.

Article VI

Signatures and Acceptances of Agreement

The undersigned delegates to the International Civil Aviation Conference, convened in Chicago on November 1, 1944, have affixed their signatures to this Agreement with the understanding that the Government of the United States of America shall be informed at the earliest possible date by each of the governments on whose behalf the Agreement has been signed whether signature on its behalf shall constitute an acceptance of the Agreement by that government and an obligation binding upon it.

Any State a member of the International Civil Aviation Organization may accept the present Agreement as an obligation binding upon it by notification of its acceptance to the Government of the United States, and such acceptance shall become effective upon the date of the receipt of such notification by that Government.

This Agreement shall come into force as between contracting States upon its acceptance by each of them. Thereafter it shall become binding as to each other State indicating its acceptance to the Government of the United States on the date of the receipt of the acceptance by that Government. The Government of the United States shall inform all signatory and accepting States of the date of all acceptances of the Agreement, and of the date on which it comes into force for each accepting State.

IN WITNESS WHEREOF, the undersigned, having been duly authorized, sign this Agreement on behalf of their respective governments on the dates appearing opposite their respective signatures.

DONE at Chicago the seventh day of December, 1944, in the English language. A text drawn up in the English, French, and Spanish languages, each of which shall be of equal authenticity, shall be opened for signature at Washington, D.C. Both texts shall be deposited in the archives of the Government of the United States of America, and certified copies shall be transmitted by that Government to the governments of all the States which may sign or accept this Agreement.

Appendix 5

International Air Transport Agreement

Done at Chicago—December 7, 1944
Entered into force—February 8, 1945
Not in effect in the United States
59 Stat. 1701, T.I.A.S. No. 488, 171 U.N.T.S. 387

The States which sign and accept this International Air Transport Agreement being members of the International Civil Aviation Organization declare as follows:

Article I

Section 1

Each contracting State grants to the other contracting States the following freedoms of the air in respect of scheduled international air services:

1. The privilege to fly across its territory without landing;

2. The privilege to land for non-traffic purposes;

3. The privilege to put down passengers, mail and cargo taken on in the territory of the State whose nationality the aircraft possesses;

4. The privilege to take on passengers, mail and cargo destined for the territory of the State whose nationality the aircraft possesses;

5. The privilege to take on passengers, mail and cargo destined for the territory of any other contracting State and the privilege to put down passengers, mail and cargo coming from any such territory.

With respect to the privileges specified under paragraphs 3, 4 and 5 of this section, the undertaking of each contracting State relates only to through services on a route constituting a reasonably direct line out from and back to the homeland of the State whose nationality the aircraft possesses.

The privileges of this section shall not be applicable with respect to airports utilized for military purposes to the exclusion of any scheduled international air services. In areas of active hostilities or of military occupation, and in time of war along the supply routes leading to such areas, the exercise of such privileges shall be subject to the approval of the competent military authorities.

Section 2

The exercise of the foregoing privileges shall be in accordance with the provisions of the Interim Agreement on International Civil Aviation and, when it comes into force, with the provisions of the Convention on International Civil Aviation, both drawn up at Chicago on December 7, 1944.

Section 3

A contracting State granting to the airlines of another contracting State the privilege to stop for non-traffic purposes may require such airlines to offer reasonable commercial service at the points at which such stops are made.

Such requirement shall not involve any discrimination between airlines operating on the same route, shall take into account the capacity of the aircraft, and shall be exercised in such a manner as not to prejudice the normal operations of the international air services concerned or the rights and obligations of any contracting State.

Section 4

Each contracting State shall have the right to refuse permission to the aircraft of other contracting States to take on in its territory passengers, mail and cargo carried for remuneration or hire and destined for another point within its territory. Each contracting State undertakes not to enter into any arrangements which specifically grant any such privilege on an exclusive basis to any other State or an airline of any other State, and not to obtain any such exclusive privilege from any other State.

Section 5

Each contracting State may, subject to the provisions of this Agreement,

1. Designate the route to be followed within its territory by any international air service and the airports which any such service may use;

2. Impose or permit to be imposed on any such service just and reasonable charges for the use of such airports and other facilities; these charges shall not be higher than would be paid for the use of such airports and facilities by its national aircraft engaged in similar international services: provided that, upon representation by an interested contracting State, the charges imposed for the use of airports and other facilities shall be subject to review by the Council of the International Civil Aviation Organization established under the above-mentioned Convention, which shall report and make recommendations thereon for the consideration of the State or States concerned.

Section 6

Each contracting State reserves the right to withhold or revoke a certificate or permit to an air transport enterprise of another State in any case where it is not satisfied that substantial ownership and effective control are vested in nationals of a contracting State, or in case of failure of such air transport enterprise to comply with the laws of the State over which it operates, or to perform its obligations under this Agreement.

Article II

Section 1

The contracting States accept this Agreement as abrogating all obligations and understandings between them which are inconsistent with its terms, and undertake not to enter into any such obligations and understandings. A contracting State which has undertaken any other obligations inconsistent with this Agreement shall take immediate steps to procure its release from the obligations. If an airline of any contracting State has entered into any such inconsistent obligations, the State of which it is a national shall use its best efforts to secure their termination forthwith and shall in any event cause them to be terminated as soon as such action can lawfully be taken after the coming into force of this Agreement.

Section 2

Subject to the provisions of the preceding section, any contracting State may make arrangements concerning international air services not inconsistent with this Agreement. Any such arrangement shall be forthwith registered with the Council, which shall make it public as soon as possible.

Article III

Each contracting State undertakes that in the establishment and operation of through services due consideration shall be given to the interests of the other contracting States so as not to interfere unduly with their regional services or to hamper the development of their through services.

Article IV

Section 1

Any contracting State may by reservation attached to this Agreement at the time of signature or acceptance elect not to grant and receive the rights and obligations of Article I, Section 1, paragraph 5, and may at any time after acceptance, on six months' notice, given by it to the Council, withdraw itself from such rights and obligations. Such contracting State may on six months' notice to the Council assume or resume, as the case may be, such rights and obligations. No contracting State shall be obliged to grant any rights under the said paragraph to any contracting State not bound thereby.

Section 2

A contracting State which deems that action by another contracting State under this Agreement is causing injustice or hardship to it, may request the Council to examine the situation. The Council shall thereupon inquire into the matter, and shall call the States concerned into consultation.

Should such consultation fail to resolve the difficulty, the Council may make appropriate findings and recommendations to the contracting States concerned. If thereafter a contracting State concerned shall in the opinion of the Council unreasonably fail to take suitable corrective action, the Council may recommend to the Assembly of the above-mentioned Organization that such contracting State be suspended from its rights and privileges under this Agreement until such action has been taken. The Assembly by a two-thirds vote may so suspend such contracting State for such period of time as it may deem proper or until the Council shall find that corrective action has been taken by such State.

Section 3

If any disagreement between two or more contracting States relating to the interpretation or application of this Agreement cannot be settled by negotiation, the provisions of Chapter XVIII of the above-mentioned Convention shall be applicable in the same manner as provided therein with reference to any disagreement relating to the interpretation or application of the above-mentioned Convention.

Article V

This agreement shall remain in force as long as the above-mentioned Convention; provided, however, that any contracting State, a party to the present Agreement, may denounce it on one year's notice given by it to the Government of the United States of America, which shall at once inform all other contracting States of such notice and withdrawal.

Article VI

Pending the coming into force of the above-mentioned Convention, all references to it herein other than those contained in Article IV, Section 3, and Article VII shall be deemed to be references to the Interim Agreement on International Civil Aviation drawn up at Chicago on December 7, 1944; and references to the International Civil Aviation Organization, the Assembly, and the Council shall be deemed to be references to the Provisional International Civil Aviation Organization, the Interim Assembly, and the Interim Council, respectively.

Article VII

For the purposes of this Agreement, "territory" shall be defined as in Article 2 of the above-mentioned Convention.

Article VIII

Signatures and Acceptances of Agreement

The undersigned delegates to the International Civil Aviation Conference, convened in Chicago on November 1, 1944, have affixed their signatures to this Agreement with the understanding that the Government of the United States of America shall be informed at the earliest possible date by each of the governments on whose behalf the Agreement has been signed whether signature on its behalf shall constitute an acceptance of the Agreement by that government and an obligation binding upon it.

Any State a member of the International Civil Aviation Organization may accept the present Agreement as an obligation binding upon it by notification of its acceptance to the Government of the United States, and such acceptance shall become effective upon the date of the receipt of such notification by that Government.

This Agreement shall come into force as between contracting States upon its acceptance by each of them. Thereafter it shall become binding as to each other State indicating its acceptance to the Government of the United States on the date of the receipt of the acceptance by that Government. The Government of the United States shall inform all signatory and accepting States of the date of all acceptances of the Agreement, and of the date on which it comes into force for each accepting State.

IN WITNESS WHEREOF, the undersigned, having been duly authorized, sign this Agreement on behalf of their respective governments on the date appearing opposite their respective signatures.

DONE at Chicago the seventh day of December 1944 in the English language. A text drawn up in the English, French, and Spanish languages, each of which shall be of equal authenticity, shall be opened for signature at Washington, D.C. Both texts shall be deposited in the archives of the Government of the United States of America, and certified copies shall be transmitted by that Government to the governments of all the States which may sign or accept this Agreement.

Appendix 6

Convention on the International Recognition of Rights in Aircraft

Done at Geneva—June 19, 1948
Entered into force—September 17, 1953
Effective in the United States—September 17, 1953
4 U.S.T. 1830, T.I.A.S. No. 2847, 310 U.N.T.S. 151, ICAO Doc. 7620

WHEREAS the International Civil Aviation Conference, held at Chicago in November-December 1944, recommended the early adoption of a Convention dealing with the transfer of title to aircraft,

WHEREAS it is highly desirable in the interest of the future expansion of international civil aviation that rights in aircraft be recognised internationally,

THE UNDERSIGNED, duly authorized,

HAVE AGREED, on behalf of their respective Governments,

AS FOLLOWS:

Article I

1. The Contracting States undertake to recognise:

(a) rights of property in aircraft;

(b) rights to acquire aircraft by purchase coupled with possession of the aircraft;

(c) rights to possession of aircraft under leases of six months or more;

(d) mortgages, hypotheques and similar rights in aircraft which are contractually created as security for payment of an indebtedness;

provided that such rights

(i) have been constituted in accordance with the law of the Contracting State in which the aircraft was registered as to nationality at the time of their constitution, and

(ii) are regularly recorded in a public record of the Contracting State in which the aircraft is registered as to nationality.

The regularity of successive recordings in different Contracting States shall be determined in accordance with the law of the State where the aircraft was registered as to nationality at the time of each recording.

2. Nothing in this Convention shall prevent the recognition of any rights in aircraft under the law of any Contracting State; but Contracting States shall not admit or recognise any right as taking priority over the rights mentioned in paragraph 1 of this Article.

Article II

1. All recordings relating to a given aircraft must appear in the same record.

2. Except as otherwise provided in this Convention, the effects of the recording of any right mentioned in Article I, paragraph 1, with regard to third parties shall be determined according to the law of the Contracting State where it is recorded.

3. A Contracting State may prohibit the recording of any right which cannot validly be constituted according to its national law.

Article III

1. The address of the authority responsible for maintaining the record must be shown on every aircraft's certificate of registration as to nationality.

2. Any person shall be entitled to receive from the authority duly certified copies or extracts of the particulars recorded. Such copies or extracts shall constitute prima facie evidence of the contents of the record.

3. If the law of a Contracting State provides that the filing of a document for recording shall have the same effect as the recording, it shall have the same effect for the purposes of this Convention. In that case, adequate provision shall be made to ensure that such document is open to the public.

4. Reasonable charges may be made for services performed by the authority maintaining the record.

Article IV

1. In the event that any claims in respect of:

(a) compensation due for salvage of the aircraft, or

(b) extraordinary expenses indispensable for the preservation of the aircraft give rise, under the law of the Contracting State where the operations of salvage or preservation were terminated, to a right conferring a charge against the aircraft, such right shall be recognised by Contracting States and shall take priority over all other rights in the aircraft.

2. The rights enumerated in paragraph 1 shall be satisfied in the inverse order of the dates of the incidents in connexion with which they have arisen.

3. Any of the said rights may, within three months from the date of the termination of the salvage or preservation operations, be noted on the record.

4. The said rights shall not be recognised in other Contracting States after expiration of the three months mentioned in paragraph 3 unless, within this period,

(a) the right has been noted on the record in conformity with paragraph 3, and

(b) the amount has been agreed upon or judicial action on the right has been commenced.

As far as judicial action is concerned, the law of the forum shall determine the contingencies upon which the three months period may be interrupted or suspended.

5. This Article shall apply notwithstanding the provisions of Article I, paragraph 2.

Article V

The priority of a right mentioned in Article I, paragraph 1 (d), extends to all sums thereby secured. However, the amount of interest included shall not exceed that accrued during the three years prior to the execution proceedings together with that accrued during the execution proceedings.

Article VI

In case of attachment or sale of an aircraft in execution, or of any right therein, the Contracting States shall not be obliged to recognise, as against the attaching or executing creditor or against the purchaser, any right mentioned in Article I, paragraph 1, or the transfer of any such right, if constituted or effected with knowledge of the sale or execution proceedings by the person against whom the proceedings are directed.

Article VII

1. The proceedings of a sale of an aircraft in execution shall be determined by the law of the Contracting State where the sale takes place.

2. The following provisions shall however be observed:

(a) The date and place of the sale shall be fixed at least six weeks in advance.

(b) The executing creditor shall supply to the Court or other competent authority a certified extract of the recordings concerning the aircraft. He shall give public notice of the sale at the place where the aircraft is registered as to nationality, in accordance with the law there applicable, at least one month before the day fixed, and shall concurrently notify by registered letter, if possible by air mail, the recorded owner and the holders of recorded rights in the aircraft and of rights noted on the record under Article IV, paragraph 3, according to their addresses as shown on the record.

3. The consequences of failure to observe the requirements of paragraph 2 shall be as provided by the law of the Contracting State where the sale takes place. However, any sale taking place in contravention of the requirements of that paragraph may be annulled upon demand made within six months from the date of the sale by any person suffering damage as the result of such contravention.

4. No sale in execution can be effected unless all rights having priority over the claim of the executing creditor in accordance with this Convention which are established before the competent authority, are covered by the proceeds of sale or assumed by the purchaser.

5. When injury or damage is caused to persons or property on the surface of the Contracting State where the execution sale takes place, by any aircraft subject to any right referred to in Article I held as security for an indebtedness, unless adequate and effective insurance by a State or an insurance undertaking in any State has been provided by or on behalf of the operator to cover such injury or damage, the national law of such Contracting State may provide in case of the seizure of such aircraft or any other aircraft owned by the same person and encumbered with any similar right held by the same creditor:

(a) that the provisions of paragraph 4 above shall have no effect with regard to the person suffering such injury or damage or his representative if he is an executing creditor;

(b) that any right referred to in Article I held as security for an indebtedness encumbering the aircraft may not be set up against any person suffering such injury or damage or his representative in excess of an amount equal to 80% of the sale price.

In the absence of other limit established by the law of the Contracting State where the execution sale takes place, the insurance shall be considered adequate within the meaning of the present paragraph if the amount of the insurance corresponds to the value when new of the aircraft seized in execution.

6. Costs legally chargeable under the law of the Contracting State where the sale takes place, which are incurred in the common interest of creditors in the course of execution proceedings leading to sale, shall be paid out of the proceeds of sale before any claims, including those given preference by Article IV.

Article VIII

Sale of an aircraft in execution in conformity with the provisions of Article VII shall effect the transfer of the property in such aircraft free from all rights which are not assumed by the purchaser.

Article IX

Except in the case of a sale in execution in conformity with the provisions of Article VII, no transfer of an aircraft from the nationality register or the record of a Contracting State to that of another Contracting State shall be made, unless all holders of recorded rights have been satisfied or consent to the transfer.

Article X

1. If a recorded right in an aircraft of the nature specified in Article I, and held as security for the payment of an indebtedness, extends, in conformity with the law of the Contracting State where the aircraft is registered, to spare parts stored in a specified place or places, such right shall be recognised by all Contracting States, as long as the spare parts remain in the place or places specified, provided that an appropriate public notice, specifying the description of the right, the name and address of the holder of this right and the record in which such right is recorded, is exhibited at the place where the spare parts are located, so as to give due notification to third parties that such spare parts are encumbered.

2. A statement indicating the character and the approximate number of such spare parts shall be annexed to or included in the recorded document. Such parts may be replaced by similar parts without affecting the right of the creditor.

3. The provisions of Article VII, paragraphs 1 and 4, and of Article VIII shall apply to a sale of spare parts in execution. However, where the executing creditor is an unsecured creditor, paragraph 4 of Article VII in its application to such a sale shall be construed so as to permit the sale to take place if a bid is received in an amount not less than two-thirds of the value of the spare parts as determined by experts appointed by the authority responsible for the sale. Further, in the distribution of the proceeds of sale, the competent authority may, in order to provide for the claim of the executing creditor, limit the amount payable to holders of prior rights to two-thirds of such proceeds of sale after payment of the costs referred to in Article VII, paragraph 6.

4. For the purpose of this Article the term "spare parts" means parts of aircraft, engines, propellers, radio apparatus, instruments, appliances, furnishings, parts of any of the foregoing, and generally any other articles of whatever description maintained for installation in aircraft in substitution for parts or articles removed.

Article XI

1. The provisions of this Convention shall in each Contracting State apply to all aircraft registered as to nationality in another Contracting State.

2. Each Contracting State shall also apply to aircraft there registered as to nationality:

(a) The provisions of Articles II, III, IX, and

(b) The provisions of Article IV, unless the salvage or preservation operations have been terminated within its own territory.

Article XII

Nothing in this Convention shall prejudice the right of any Contracting State to enforce against an aircraft its national laws relating to immigration, customs or air navigation.

Article XIII

This Convention shall not apply to aircraft used in military, customs or police services.

Article XIV

For the purpose of this Convention, the competent judicial and administrative authorities of the Contracting States may, subject to any contrary provision in their national law, correspond directly with each other.

Article XV

The Contracting States shall take such measures as are necessary for the fulfilment of the provisions of this Convention and shall forthwith inform the Secretary General of the International Civil Aviation Organization of these measures.

Article XVI

For the purposes of this Convention the term "aircraft" shall include the airframe, engines, propellers, radio apparatus, and all other articles intended for use in the aircraft whether installed therein or temporarily separated therefrom.

Article XVII

If a separate register of aircraft for purposes of nationality is maintained in any territory for whose foreign relations a Contracting State is responsible, references in this Convention to the law of the Contracting State shall be construed as references to the law of that territory.

Article XVIII

This Convention shall remain open for signature until it comes into force in accordance with the provisions of Article XX.

Article XIX

1. This Convention shall be subject to ratification by the signatory States.

2. The instruments of ratification shall be deposited in the archives of the International Civil Aviation Organization, which shall give notice of the date of deposit to each of the signatory and adhering States.

Article XX

1. As soon as two of the signatory States have deposited their instruments of ratification of this Convention, it shall come into force between them on the ninetieth day after the date of the deposit of the second instrument of ratification. It shall come into force, for each State which deposits its instrument of ratification after that date, on the ninetieth day after the deposit of its instrument of ratification.

2. The International Civil Aviation Organization shall give notice to each signatory State of the date on which this Convention comes into force.

3. As soon as this Convention comes into force, it shall be registered with the United Nations by the Secretary General of the International Civil Aviation Organization.

Article XXI

1. This Convention shall, after it has come into force, be open for adherence by non-signatory States.

2. Adherence shall be effected by the deposit of an instrument of adherence in the archives of the International Civil Aviation Organization, which shall give notice of the date of the deposit to each signatory and adhering State.

3. Adherence shall take effect as from the ninetieth day after the date of the deposit of the instrument of adherence in the archives of the International Civil Aviation Organization.

Article XXII

1. Any Contracting State may denounce this Convention by notification of denunciation to the International Civil Aviation Organization, which shall give notice of the date of receipt of such notification to each signatory and adhering State.

2. Denunciation shall take effect six months after the date of receipt by the International Civil Aviation Organization of the notification of denunciation.

Article XXIII

1. Any State may at the time of deposit of its instrument of ratification or adherence, declare that its acceptance of this Convention does not apply to any one or more of the territories for the foreign relations of which such State is responsible.

2. The International Civil Aviation Organization shall give notice of any such declaration to each signatory and adhering State.

3. With the exception of territories in respect of which a declaration has been made in accordance with paragraph 1 of this Article, this Convention shall apply to all territories for the foreign relations of which a Contracting State is responsible.

4. Any State may adhere to this Convention separately on behalf of all or any of the territories regarding which it has made a declaration in accordance with paragraph 1 of this Article and the provisions of paragraphs 2 and 3 of Article XXI shall apply to such adherence.

5. Any Contracting State may denounce this Convention, in accordance with the provisions of Article XXII, separately for all or any of the territories for the foreign relations of which such State is responsible.

IN WITNESS WHEREOF the undersigned Plenipotentiaries, having been duly authorized, have signed this Convention.

DONE at Geneva, on the nineteenth day of the month of June of the year one thousand nine hundred and forty-eight in the English, French and Spanish languages, each text being of equal authenticity. This Convention shall be deposited in the archives of the International Civil Aviation Organization where, in accordance with Article XVIII, it shall remain open for signature.

Appendix 7

Convention on Damage Caused by Foreign Aircraft to Third Parties on the Surface

Done at Rome—October 7, 1952
Entered into force—February 4, 1958
Not in effect in the United States
310 U.N.T.S. 181, ICAO Doc. 7364, 19 J. Air L. & Com. 447

THE STATES SIGNATORY to this Convention,

MOVED by a desire to ensure adequate compensation for persons who suffer damage caused on the surface by foreign aircraft, while limiting in a reasonable manner the extent of the liabilities incurred for such damage in order not to hinder the development of international civil air transport, and also,

CONVINCED of the need for unifying to the greatest extent possible, through an international convention, the rules applying in the various countries of the world to the liabilities incurred for such damage,

HAVE APPOINTED to such effect the undersigned Plenipotentiaries who, duly authorised,

HAVE AGREED AS FOLLOWS:

CHAPTER I
PRINCIPLES OF LIABILITY

Article 1

1. Any person who suffers damage on the surface shall, upon proof only that the damage was caused by an aircraft in flight or by any person or thing falling therefrom, be entitled to compensation as provided by this Convention. Nevertheless there shall be no right to compensation if the damage is not a direct consequence of the incident giving rise thereto, or if the damage results from the mere fact of passage of the aircraft through the airspace in conformity with existing air traffic regulations.

2. For the purpose of this Convention, an aircraft is considered to be in flight from the moment when power is applied for the purpose of actual take-off until the moment when the landing run ends. In the case of an aircraft lighter than air, the expression "in flight" relates to the period from the moment when it becomes detached from the surface until it becomes again attached thereto.

Article 2

1. The liability for compensation contemplated by Article 1 of this Convention shall attach to the operator of the aircraft.

2. (a) For the purposes of this Convention the term "operator" shall mean the person who was making use of the aircraft at the time the damage was caused, provided that if control of the navigation of the aircraft was retained by the person from whom the right to make use of the aircraft was derived, whether directly or indirectly, that person shall be considered the operator.

(b) A person shall be considered to be making use of an aircraft when he is using it personally or when his servants or agents are using the aircraft in the course of their employment, whether or not within the scope of their authority.

3. The registered owner of the aircraft shall be presumed to be the operator and shall be liable as such unless, in the proceedings for the determination of his liability, he proves that some other person was the operator and, in so far as legal procedures permit, takes appropriate measures to make that other person a party in the proceedings.

Article 3

If the person who was the operator at the time the damage was caused had not the exclusive right to use the aircraft for a period of more than fourteen days, dating from the moment when the right to use commenced, the person from whom such right was derived shall be liable jointly and severally with the operator, each of them being bound under the provisions and within the limits of liability of this Convention.

Article 4

If a person makes use of an aircraft without the consent of the person entitled to its navigational control, the latter, unless he proves that he has exercised due care to prevent such use, shall be jointly and severally liable with the unlawful user for damage giving a right to compensation under Article 1, each of them being bound under the provisions and within the limits of liability of this Convention.

Article 5

Any person who would otherwise be liable under the provisions of this Convention shall not be liable if the damage is the direct consequence of armed conflict or civil disturbance, or if such person has been deprived of the use of the aircraft by act of public authority.

Article 6

1. Any person who would otherwise be liable under the provisions of this Convention shall not be liable for damage if he proves that the damage was caused solely through the negligence or other wrongful act or omission of the person who suffers the damage or of the latter's servants or agents. If the person liable proves that the damage was contributed to by the negligence or other wrongful act or omission of the person who suffers the damage, or of his servants or agents, the compensation shall be reduced to the extent to which such negligence or wrongful act or omission contributed to the damage. Nevertheless there shall be no such exoneration or reduction if, in the case of the negligence or other wrongful act or omission of a servant or agent, the person who suffers the damage proves that his servant or agent was acting outside the scope of his authority.

2. When an action is brought by one person to recover damages arising from the death or injury of another person, the negligence or other wrongful act or omission of such other person, or of his servants or agents, shall also have the effect provided in the preceding paragraph.

Article 7

When two or more aircraft have collided or interfered with each other in flight and damage for which a right to compensation as contemplated in Article 1 results, or when two or more aircraft have jointly caused such damage, each of the aircraft concerned shall be considered to have caused the damage and the operator of each aircraft shall be liable, each of them being bound under the provisions and within the limits of liability of this Convention.

Article 8

The persons referred to in paragraph 3 of Article 2 and in Articles 3 and 4 shall be entitled to all defences which are available to an operator under the provisions of this Convention.

Article 9

Neither the operator, the owner, any person liable under Article 3 or Article 4, nor their respective servants or agents, shall be liable for damage on the surface caused by an aircraft in flight or any person or thing falling therefrom otherwise than as expressly provided in this Convention. This rule shall not apply to any such person who is guilty of a deliberate act or omission done with intent to cause damage.

Article 10

Nothing in this Convention shall prejudice the question whether a person liable for damage in accordance with its provisions has a right of recourse against any other person.

CHAPTER II
EXTENT OF LIABILITY

Article 11

1. Subject to the provisions of Article 12, the liability for damage giving a right to compensation under Article 1, for each aircraft and incident, in respect of all persons liable under this Convention, shall not exceed:

(a) 500,000 francs for aircraft weighing 1,000 kilogrammes or less;

(b) 500,000 francs plus 400 francs per kilogramme over 1,000 kilogrammes for aircraft weighing more than 1,000 but not exceeding 6,000 kilogrammes;

(c) 2,500,000 francs plus 250 francs per kilogramme over 6,000 kilogrammes for aircraft weighing more than 6,000 but not exceeding 20,000 kilogrammes;

(d) 6,000,000 francs plus 150 francs per kilogramme over 20,000 kilogrammes for aircraft weighing more than 20,000 but not exceeding 50,000 kilogrammes;

(e) 10,500,000 francs plus 100 francs per kilogramme over 50,000 kilogrammes for aircraft weighing more than 50,000 kilogrammes.

2. The liability in respect of loss of life or personal injury shall not exceed 500,000 francs per person killed or injured.

3. "Weight" means the maximum weight of the aircraft authorised by the certificate of airworthiness for take-off, excluding the effect of lifting gas when used.

4. The sums mentioned in francs in this Article refer to a currency unit consisting of 65.5 milligrammes of gold of millesimal fineness 900.

These sums may be converted into national currencies in round figures. Conversion of the sums into national currencies other than gold shall, in case of judicial proceedings, be made according to the gold value of such currencies at the date of the judgment, or, in cases covered by Article 14, at the date of the allocation.

Article 12

1. If the person who suffers damage proves that it was caused by a deliberate act or omission of the operator, his servants or agents, done with intent to cause damage, the liability of the operator shall be unlimited; provided that in the case of such act or omission of such servant or agent, it is also proved that he was acting in the course of his employment and within the scope of his authority.

2. If a person wrongfully takes and makes use of an aircraft without the consent of the person entitled to use it, his liability shall be unlimited.

Article 13

1. Whenever, under the provisions of Article 3 or Article 4, two or more persons are liable for damage, or a registered owner who was not the operator is made liable as such as provided in paragraph 3 of Article 2, the persons who suffer damage shall not be entitled to total compensation greater than the highest indemnity which may be awarded under the provisions of this Convention against any one of the persons liable.

2. When the provisions of Article 7 are applicable, the person who suffers the damage shall be entitled to be compensated up to the aggregate of the limits applicable with respect to each of the aircraft involved, but no operator shall be liable for a sum in excess of the limit applicable to his aircraft unless his liability is unlimited under the terms of Article 12.

Article 14

If the total amount of the claims established exceeds the limit of liability applicable under the provisions of this Convention, the following rules shall apply, taking into account the provisions of paragraph 2 of Article 11:

(a) If the claims are exclusively in respect of loss of life or personal injury or exclusively in respect of damage to property, such claims shall be reduced in proportion to their respective amounts.

(b) If the claims are both in respect of loss of life or personal injury and in respect of damage to property, one half of the total sum distributable shall be appropriated preferentially to meet claims in respect of loss of life and personal injury and, if insufficient, shall be distributed proportionately between the claims concerned. The remainder of the total sum distributable shall be distributed proportionately among the claims in respect of damage to property and the portion not already covered of the claims in respect of loss of life and personal injury.

CHAPTER III
SECURITY FOR OPERATOR'S LIABILITY

Article 15

1. Any Contracting State may require that the operator of an aircraft registered in another Contracting State shall be insured in respect of his liability for damage sustained in its territory for which a right to compensation exists under Article 1 by means of insurance up to the limits applicable according to the provisions of Article 11.

2. (a) The insurance shall be accepted as satisfactory if it conforms to the provisions of this Convention and has been effected by an insurer authorised to effect such insurance under the laws of the State where the aircraft is registered or of the State where the insurer has his residence or principal place of business, and whose financial responsibility has been verified by either of those States.

(b) If insurance has been required by any State under paragraph 1 of this Article, and a final judgment in that State is not satisfied by payment in the currency of that State, any Contracting State may refuse to accept the insurer as financially responsible until such payment, if demanded, has been made.

3. Notwithstanding the last preceding paragraph the State overflown may refuse to accept as satisfactory insurance effected by an insurer who is not authorised for that purpose in a contracting State.

4. Instead of insurance, any of the following securities shall be deemed satisfactory if the security conforms to Article 17:

(a) a cash deposit in a depository maintained by the Contracting State where the aircraft is registered or with a bank authorised to act as a depository by that State;

(b) a guarantee given by a bank authorised to do so by the Contracting State where the aircraft is registered, and whose financial responsibility has been verified by that State;

(c) a guarantee given by the contracting State where the aircraft is registered, if that State undertakes that it will not claim immunity from suit in respect of that guarantee.

5. Subject to paragraph 6 of this Article, the State overflown may also require that the aircraft shall carry a certificate issued by the insurer certifying that insurance has been effected in accordance with the provisions of this Convention, and specifying the person or persons whose liability is secured thereby, together with a certificate or endorsement issued by the appropriate authority in the State where the aircraft is registered or in the State where the insurer has his residence or principal place of business certifying the financial responsibility of the insurer. If other security is furnished in accordance with the provisions of paragraph 4 of this Article, a certificate to that effect shall be issued by the appropriate authority in the State where the aircraft is registered.

6. The certificate referred to in paragraph 5 of this Article need not be carried in the aircraft if a certified copy has been filed with the appropriate authority designated by the State overflown or, if the International Civil Aviation Organization agrees, with that Organization, which shall furnish a copy of the certificate to each contracting State.

7. (a) Where the State overflown has reasonable grounds for doubting the financial responsibility of the insurer, or of the bank which issues a guarantee under paragraph 4 of this Article, that State may request additional evidence of financial responsibility, and if any question arises as to the adequacy of that evidence the dispute affecting the States concerned shall, at the request of one of those States, be submitted to an arbitral tribunal which shall be either the Council of the International Civil Aviation Organization or a person or body mutually agreed by the parties.

(b) Until this tribunal has given its decision the insurance or guarantee shall be considered provisionally valid by the State overflown.

8. Any requirements imposed in accordance with this Article shall be notified to the Secretary General of the International Civil Aviation Organization who shall inform each contracting State thereof.

9. For the purpose of this Article, the term "insurer" includes a group of insurers, and for the purpose of paragraph 5 of this Article, the phrase "appropriate authority in a State" includes the appropriate authority in the highest political subdivision thereof which regulates the conduct of business by the insurer.

Article 16

1. The insurer or other person providing security required under Article 15 for the liability of the operator may, in addition to the defences available to the operator, and the defence of forgery, set up only the following defences against claims based on the application of this Convention:

(a) that the damage occurred after the security ceased to be effective. However, if the security expires during a flight, it shall be continued in force until the next landing specified in the flight plan, but no longer than twenty-four hours; and if the security ceases to be effective for any reason other than the expiration of its term, or a change of operator, it shall be continued until fifteen days after notification to the appropriate authority of the State which certifies the financial responsibility of the insurer or the guarantor that the security has ceased to be effective, or until effective withdrawal of the certificate of the insurer or the certificate of guarantee if such a certificate has been required under paragraph 5 of Article 15, whichever is the earlier;

(b) that the damage occurred outside the territorial limits provided for by the security, unless flight outside of such limits was caused by force majeure, assistance justified by the circumstances, or an error in piloting, operation or navigation.

2. The State which has issued or endorsed a certificate pursuant to paragraph 5 of Article 15 shall notify the termination or cessation, otherwise than by the expiration of its term, of the insurance or other security to the interested contracting States as soon as possible.

3. Where a certificate of insurance or other security is required under paragraph 5 of Article 15 and the operator is changed during the period of the validity of the security, the security shall apply to the liability under this Convention of the new operator, unless he is an unlawful user, but not beyond fifteen days from the time when the insurer or guarantor notifies the appropriate authority of the State where the certificate was issued that the security has become ineffective or until the effective withdrawal of the certificate of the insurer if such a certificate has been required under paragraph 5 of Article 15, whichever is the shorter period.

4. The continuation in force of the security under the provisions of paragraph 1 of this Article shall apply only for the benefit of the person suffering damage.

5. Without prejudice to any right of direct action which he may have under the law governing the contract of insurance or guarantee, the person suffering damage may bring a direct action against the insurer or guarantor only in the following cases:

(a) where the security is continued in force under the provisions of paragraph 1(a) and (b) of this Article;

(b) the bankruptcy of the operator.

6. Excepting the defences specified in paragraph 1 of this Article, the insurer or other person providing security may not, with respect to direct actions brought by the person suffering damage based upon application of this Convention, avail himself of any grounds of nullity or any right of retroactive cancellation.

7. The provisions of this Article shall not prejudice the question whether the insurer guarantor has a right of recourse against any other person.

Article 17

1. If security is furnished in accordance with paragraph 4 of Article 15, it shall be specifically and preferentially assigned to payment of claims under the provisions of this Convention.

2. The security shall be deemed sufficient if, in the case of an operator of one aircraft, it is for an amount equal to the limit applicable according to the provisions of Article 11, and in the case of an operator of several aircraft, if it is for an amount not less than the aggregate of the limits of liability applicable to the two aircraft subject to the highest limits.

3. As soon as notice of a claim has been given to the operator, the amount of the security shall be increased up to a total sum equivalent to the aggregate of:

(a) the amount of the security then required by paragraph of this Article, and

(b) the amount of the claim not exceeding the applicable limit of liability.

This increased security shall be maintained until every claim has been disposed of.

Article 18

Any sums due to an operator from an insurer shall be exempt from seizure and execution by creditors of the operator until claims of third parties under this Convention have been satisfied.

CHAPTER IV
RULES OF PROCEDURE AND LIMITATION OF ACTIONS

Article 19

If a claimant has not brought an action to enforce his claim or if notification of such claim has not been given to the operator within a period of six months from the date of the incident which gave rise to the damage, the claimant shall only be entitled to compensation out of the amount for which the operator remains liable after all claims made within that period have been met in full.

Article 20

1. Actions under the provisions of this Convention may be brought only before the courts of the Contracting State where the damage occurred. Nevertheless, by agreement between any one or more claimants and any one or more defendants, such claimants may take action before the courts of any other Contracting State, but no such proceedings shall have the effect of prejudicing in any way the rights of persons who bring actions in the State where the damage occurred. The parties may also agree to submit disputes to arbitration in any Contracting State.

2. Each Contracting State shall take all necessary measures to ensure that the defendant and all other parties interested are notified of any proceedings concerning them and have a fair and adequate opportunity to defend their interests.

3. Each Contracting State shall so far as possible ensure that all actions arising from a single incident and brought in accordance with paragraph 1 of this Article are consolidated for disposal in a single proceeding before the same court.

4. Where any final judgment, including a judgment by default, is pronounced by a court competent in conformity with this Convention, on which execution can be issued according to the procedural law of that court, the judgment shall be enforceable upon compliance with the formalities prescribed by the laws of the Contracting State, or of any territory, State or province thereof, where execution is applied for:

(a) in the Contracting State where the judgment debtor has his residence or principal place of business or,

(b) if the assets available in that State and in the State where the judgment was pronounced are insufficient to satisfy the judgment, in any other Contracting State where the judgment debtor has assets.

5. Notwithstanding the provisions of paragraph 4 of this Article, the court to which application is made for execution may refuse to issue execution if it is proved that any of the following circumstances exist:

(a) the judgment was given by default and the defendant did not acquire knowledge of the proceedings in sufficient time to act upon it;

(b) the defendant was not given a fair and adequate opportunity to defend his interests;

(c) the judgment is in respect of a cause of action which had already, as between the same parties, formed the subject of a judgment or an arbitral award which, under the law of the State where execution is sought, is recognized as final and conclusive;

(d) the judgment has been obtained by fraud of any of the parties;

(e) the right to enforce the judgment is not vested in the person by whom the application for execution is made.

6. The merits of the case may not be reopened in proceedings for execution under paragraph 4 of this Article.

7. The court to which application for execution is made may also refuse to issue execution if the judgment concerned is contrary to the public policy of the State in which execution is requested.

8. If, in proceedings brought according to paragraph 4 of this Article, execution of any judgment is refused on any of the grounds referred to in subparagraphs (a), (b) or (d) of paragraph 5 or paragraph 7 of this Article, the claimant shall be entitled to bring a new action before the courts of the State where execution has been refused. The judgment rendered in such new action may not result in the total compensation awarded exceeding the limits applicable under the provisions of this Convention. In such new action the previous judgment shall be a defence only to the extent to which it has been satisfied. The previous judgment shall cease to be enforceable as soon as the new action has been started. The right to bring a new action under this paragraph shall, notwithstanding the provisions of Article 21, be subject to a period of limitation of one year from the date on which the claimant has received notification of the refusal to execute the judgment.

9. Notwithstanding the provisions of paragraph 4 of this Article, the court to which application for execution is made shall refuse execution of any judgment rendered by a court of a State other than that in which the damage occurred until all the judgments rendered in that State have been satisfied. The court applied to shall also refuse to issue execution until final judgment has been given on all actions filed in the State where the damage occurred by those persons who have complied with the time limit referred to in Article 19, if the judgment debtor proves that the total amount of compensation which might be awarded by such judgments might exceed the applicable limit of liability under the provisions of this Convention. Similarly such court shall not grant execution

when, in the case of actions brought in the State where the damage occurred by those persons who have complied with the time limit referred to in Article 19, the aggregate of the judgments exceeds the applicable limit of liability, until such judgments have been reduced in accordance with Article 14.

10. Where a judgment is rendered enforceable under this Article, payment of costs recoverable under the judgment shall also be enforceable. Nevertheless the court applied to for execution may, on the application of the judgment debtor, limit the amount of such costs to a sum equal to ten per centum of the amount for which the judgment is rendered enforceable. The limits of liability prescribed by this Convention shall be exclusive of costs.

11. Interest not exceeding four per centum per annum may be allowed on the judgment debt from the date of the judgment in respect of which execution is granted.

12. An application for execution of a judgment to which paragraph 4 of this Article applies must be made within five years from the date when such judgment became final.

Article 21

1. Actions under this Convention shall be subject to a period of limitation of two years from the date of the incident which caused the damage.

2. The grounds for suspension or interruption of the period referred to in paragraph 1 of this Article shall be determined by the law of the court trying the action; but in any case the right to institute an action shall be extinguished on the expiration of three years from the date of the incident which caused the damage.

Article 22

In the event of the death of the person liable, an action in respect of liability under the provisions of this Convention shall lie against those legally responsible for his obligations.

CHAPTER V
APPLICATION OF THE CONVENTION AND GENERAL PROVISIONS

Article 23

1. This Convention applies to damage contemplated in Article 1 caused in the territory of a Contracting State by an aircraft registered in the territory of another Contracting State.

2. For the purpose of this Convention a ship or aircraft on the high seas shall be regarded as part of the territory of the State in which it is registered.

Article 24

This Convention shall not apply to damage caused to an aircraft in flight, or to persons or goods on board such aircraft.

Article 25

This Convention shall not apply to damage on the surface if liability for such damage is regulated either by a contract between the person who suffers such damage and the operator or the person entitled to use the aircraft at the time the damage occurred, or by the law relating to workmen's compensation applicable to a contract of employment between such persons.

Article 26

This Convention shall not apply to damage caused by military, customs or police aircraft.

Article 27

Contracting States will, as far as possible, facilitate payment of compensation under the provisions of this Convention in the currency of the State where the damage occurred.

Article 28

If legislative measures are necessary in any Contracting State to give effect to this Convention, the Secretary General of the International Civil Aviation Organization shall be informed forthwith of the measures so taken.

Article 29

As between Contracting States which have also ratified the International Convention for the Unification of Certain Rules relating to Damage caused by Aircraft to Third Parties on the Surface opened for signature at Rome on the 29 May 1933, the present Convention upon its entry into force shall supersede the said Convention of Rome.

Article 30

For the purposes of this Convention:

"Person" means any natural or legal person, including a State.

"Contracting State" means any State which has ratified or adhered to this Convention and whose denunciation thereof has not become effective.

"Territory of a State" means the metropolitan territory of a State and all territories for the foreign relations of which that State is responsible, subject to the provisions of Article 36.

CHAPTER VI
FINAL PROVISIONS

Article 31

This Convention shall remain open for signature on behalf of any State until it comes into force in accordance with the provisions of Article 33.

Article 32

1. This Convention shall be subject to ratification by the signatory States.

2. The instruments of ratification shall be deposited with the International Civil Aviation Organization.

Article 33

1. As soon as five of the signatory States have deposited their instruments of ratification of this Convention, it shall come into force between them on the ninetieth day after

the date of the deposit of the fifth instrument of ratification. It shall come into force, for each State which deposits its instrument of ratification after that date, on the ninetieth day after the deposit of its instrument of ratification.

2. As soon as this Convention comes into force, it shall be registered with the United Nations by the Secretary General of the International Civil Aviation Organization.

Article 34

1. This Convention shall, after it has come into force, be open for adherence by any non-signatory State.

2. The adherence of a State shall be effected by the deposit of an instrument of adherence with the International Civil Aviation Organization and shall take effect as from the ninetieth day after the date of the deposit.

Article 35

1. Any Contracting State may denounce this Convention by notification of denunciation to the International Civil Aviation Organization.

2. Denunciation shall take effect six months after the date of receipt by the International Civil Aviation Organization of the notification of denunciation; nevertheless, in respect of damage contemplated in Article 1 arising from an incident which occurred before the expiration of the six months period, the Convention shall continue to apply as if the denunciation had not been made.

Article 36

1. This Convention shall apply to all territories for the foreign relations of which a Contracting State is responsible, with the exception of territories in respect of which a declaration has been made in accordance with paragraph 2 of this Article or paragraph 3 of Article 37.

2. Any State may at the time of deposit of its instrument of ratification or adherence, declare that its acceptance of this Convention does not apply to any one or more of the territories for the foreign relations of which such State is responsible.

3. Any Contracting State may subsequently, by notification to the International Civil Aviation Organization, extend the application of this Convention to any or all of the territories regarding which it has made a declaration in accordance with paragraph 2 of this Article or paragraph 3 of Article 37. The notification shall take effect as from the ninetieth day after its receipt by the Organization.

4. Any Contracting State may denounce this Convention, in accordance with the provisions of Article 35, separately for any or all of the territories for the foreign relations of which such State is responsible.

Article 37

1. When the whole or part of the territory of a Contracting State is transferred to a non-contracting State, this Convention shall cease to apply to the territory so transferred, as from the date of the transfer.

2. When part of the territory of a Contracting State becomes an independent State responsible for its own foreign relations, this Convention shall cease to apply to the territory which becomes an independent State, as from the date on which it becomes independent.

3. When the whole or part of the territory of another State is transferred to a Contracting State, the Convention shall apply to the territory so transferred as from the date of the transfer; provided that, if the territory transferred does not become part of the metropolitan territory of the Contracting State concerned, that Contracting State may, before or at the time of the transfer, declare by notification to the International Civil Aviation Organization that the Convention shall not apply to the territory transferred unless a notification is made under paragraph 3 of Article 36.

Article 38

The Secretary General of the International Civil Aviation Organization shall give notice to all signatory and adhering States and to all States members of the Organization or of the United Nations:

(a) of the deposit of any instrument of ratification or adherence and the date thereof, within thirty days from the date of the deposit, and

(b) of the receipt of any denunciation or of any declaration or notification made under Article 36 or 37 and the date thereof, within thirty days from the date of the receipt.

The Secretary General of the Organization shall also notify these States of the date on which the Convention comes into force in accordance with paragraph 1 of Article 33.

Article 39

No reservations may be made to this Convention.

IN WITNESS WHEREOF the undersigned Plenipotentiaries, having been duly authorised, have signed this Convention.

DONE at Rome on the seventh day of the month of October of the year One Thousand Nine Hundred and Fifty Two in the English, French and Spanish languages, each text being of equal authenticity. This Convention shall be deposited with the International Civil Aviation Organization where, in accordance with Article 31, it shall remain open for signature, and the Secretary General of the Organization shall send certified copies thereof to all signatory and adhering States and to all States members of the Organization or the United Nations.

Appendix 8

Protocol to Amend the Convention for the Unification of Certain Rules Relating to International Carriage by Air, Signed at Warsaw on 12 October 1929

Done at The Hague—September 28, 1955
Entered into force—August 1, 1963
Effective in the United States—December 14, 2003
478 U.N.T.S. 371, ICAO Doc. 7632, 22 J. Air L. & Com. 422

The GOVERNMENTS UNDERSIGNED,

CONSIDERING that it is desirable to amend the Convention for the Unification of Certain Rules Relating to International Carriage by Air signed at Warsaw on 12 October 1929,

HAVE AGREED as follows:

CHAPTER I
AMENDMENTS TO THE CONVENTION

Article I

In Article 1 of the Convention—

a) paragraph 2 shall be deleted and replaced by the following:

"2. For the purposes of this Convention, the expression international carriage means any carriage in which, according to the agreement between the parties, the place of departure and the place of destination, whether or not there be a break in the carriage or a transhipment, are situated either within the territories of two High Contracting Parties or within the territory of a single High Contracting Party if there is an agreed stopping place within the territory of another State, even if that State is not a High Contracting Party. Carriage between two points within the territory of a single High Contracting Party without an agreed stopping place within the territory of another State is not international carriage for the purposes of this Convention."

b) paragraph 3 shall be deleted and replaced by the following:

"3. Carriage to be performed by several successive air carriers is deemed, for the purposes of this Convention, to be one undivided carriage if it has been regarded by the parties as a single operation, whether it had been agreed upon under the form of a single contract or of a series of contracts, and it does not lose its international character merely because one contract or a series of contracts is to be performed entirely within the territory of the same State."

Article II

In Article 2 of the Convention—

paragraph 2 shall be deleted and replaced by the following:

"2. This Convention shall not apply to carriage of mail and postal packages."

Article III

In Article 3 of the Convention—

a) paragraph 1 shall be deleted and replaced by the following:

"1. In respect of the carriage of passengers a ticket shall be delivered containing:

a) an indication of the places of departure and destination;

b) if the places of departure and destination are within the territory of a single High Contracting Party, one or more agreed stopping places being within the territory of another State, an indication of at least one such stopping place;

c) a notice to the effect that, if the passenger's journey involves an ultimate destination or stop in a country other than the country of departure, the Warsaw Convention may be applicable and that the Convention governs and in most cases limits the liability of carriers for death or personal injury and in respect of loss of or damage to baggage."

b) paragraph 2 shall be deleted and replaced by the following:

"2. The passenger ticket shall constitute prima facie evidence of the conclusion and conditions of the contract of carriage. The absence, irregularity or loss of the passenger ticket does not affect the existence or the validity of the contract of carriage which shall, none the less, be subject to the rules of this Convention. Nevertheless, if, with the consent of the carrier, the passenger embarks without a passenger ticket having been delivered, or if the ticket does not include the notice required by paragraph 1 c) of this Article, the carrier shall not be entitled to avail himself of the provisions of Article 22."

Article IV

In Article 4 of the Convention—

a) paragraphs 1, 2 and 3 shall be deleted and replaced by the following:

"1. In respect of the carriage of registered baggage, a baggage check shall be delivered, which, unless combined with or incorporated in a passenger ticket which complies with the provisions of Article 3, paragraph 1, shall contain:

a) an indication of the places of departure and destination;

b) if the places of departure and destination are within the territory of a single High Contracting Party, one or more agreed stopping places being within the territory of another State, an indication of at least one such stopping place;

c) a notice to the effect that; if the carriage involves an ultimate destination or stop in a country other than the country of departure, the Warsaw Convention may be applicable and that the Convention governs and in most cases limits the liability of carriers in respect of loss of or damage to baggage."

b) paragraph 4 shall be deleted and replaced by the following:

"2. The baggage check shall constitute prima facie evidence of the registration of the baggage and of the conditions of the contract of carriage. The absence, irregularity or loss of the baggage check does not affect the existence or the validity of the contract of carriage which shall, none the less, be subject to the rules of this Convention. Nevertheless, if the carrier takes charge of the baggage without a baggage check having been delivered or if the baggage check (unless combined with or incorporated in the passenger ticket which complies with the provisions of Article 3, paragraph 1c)) does not include the notice required by paragraph 1c) of this Article, he shall not be entitled to avail himself of the provisions of Article 22, paragraph 2."

Article V

In Article 6 of the Convention—

paragraph 3 shall be deleted and replaced by the following:

"3. The carrier shall sign prior to the loading of the cargo on board the aircraft."

Article VI

Article 8 of the Convention shall be deleted and replaced by the following:

"The air waybill shall contain:

a) an indication of the places of departure and destination;

b) if the places of departure and destination are within the territory of a single High Contracting Party, one or more agreed stopping places being within the territory of another State, an indication of at least one such stopping place;

c) a notice to the consignor to the effect that, if the carriage involves an ultimate destination or stop in a country other than the country of departure, the Warsaw Convention may be applicable and that the convention governs and in most cases limits the liability of carriers in respect of loss of or damage to cargo.

Article VII

Article 9 of the Convention shall be deleted and replaced by the following:

"If, with the consent of the carrier, cargo is loaded on board the aircraft without an air waybill having been made out, or if the air waybill does not include the notice required by Article 8, paragraph c), the carrier shall not be entitled to avail himself of the provisions of Article 22, paragraph 2."

Article VIII

In Article 10 of the Convention—

paragraph 2 shall be deleted and replaced by the following:

"2. The consignor shall indemnify the carrier against all damage suffered by him, or by any other person to whom the carrier is liable, by reason of the irregularity, incorrectness or incompleteness of the particulars and statements furnished by the consignor."

Article IX

To Article 15 of the Convention—

The following paragraph shall be added:

"3. Nothing in this Convention prevents the issue of a negotiable air waybill."

Article X

Paragraph 2 of Article 20 of the Convention shall be deleted.

Article XI

Article 22 of the Convention shall be deleted and replaced by the following:

"Article 22

1. In the carriage of persons the liability of the carrier for each passenger is limited to the sum of two hundred and fifty thousand francs. Where, in accordance with the law of the court seised of the case, damages may be awarded in the form of periodical payments, the equivalent capital value of the said payments shall not exceed two hundred

and fifty thousand francs. Nevertheless, by special contract, the carrier and the passenger may agree to a higher limit of liability.

2. a) In the carriage of registered baggage and of cargo, the liability of the carrier is limited to a sum of two hundred and fifty francs per kilogramme, unless the passenger or consignor has made, at the time when the package was handed over to the carrier, a special declaration of interest in delivery at destination and has paid a supplementary sum if the case so requires. In that case the carrier will be liable to pay a sum not exceeding the declared sum, unless he proves that that sum is greater than the passenger's or consignor's actual interest in delivery at destination.

b) In the case of loss, damage or delay of part of registered baggage or cargo, or of any object contained therein, the weight to be taken into consideration in determining the amount to which the carrier's liability is limited shall be only the total weight of the package or packages concerned. Nevertheless, when the loss, damage or delay of a part of the registered baggage or cargo, or of an object contained therein, affects the value of other packages covered by the same baggage check or the same air waybill, the total weight of such package or packages shall also be taken into consideration in determining the limit of liability.

3. As regards objects of which the passenger takes charge himself the liability of the carrier is limited to five thousand francs per passenger.

4. The limits prescribed in this article shall not prevent the court from awarding, in accordance with its own law, in addition, the whole or part of the court costs and of the other expenses of the litigation incurred by the plaintiff. The foregoing provision shall not apply if the amount of the damages awarded, excluding court costs and other expenses of the litigation, does not exceed the sum which the carrier has offered in writing to the plaintiff within a period of six months from the date of the occurrence causing the damage, or before the commencement of the action, if that is later.

5. The sums mentioned in francs in this Article shall be deemed to refer to a currency unit consisting of sixty-five and a half milligrammes of gold of millesimal fineness nine hundred. These sums may be converted into national currencies in round figures. Conversion of the sums into national currencies other than gold shall, in case of judicial proceedings, be made according to the gold value of such currencies at the date of the judgment."

Article XII

In Article 23 of the Convention, the existing provision shall be renumbered as paragraph 1 and another paragraph shall be added as follows:

"2. Paragraph 1 of this Article shall not apply to provisions governing loss or damage resulting from the inherent defect, quality or vice of the cargo carried."

Article XIII

In Article 25 of the Convention—

paragraphs 1 and 2 shall be deleted and replaced by the following:

"The limits of liability specified in Article 22 shall not apply if it is proved that the damage resulted from an act or omission of the carrier, his servants or agents, done with intent to cause damage or recklessly and with knowledge that damage would probably result; provided that, in the case of such act or omission of a servant or agent, it is also proved that he was acting within the scope of his employment."

Article XIV

After Article 25 of the Convention, the following article shall be inserted:

"Article 25A

1. If an action is brought against a servant or agent of the carrier arising out of damage to which this Convention relates, such servant or agent, if he proves that he acted within the scope of his employment, shall be entitled to avail himself of the limits of liability which that carrier himself is entitled to invoke under Article 22.

2. The aggregate of the amounts recoverable from the carrier, his servants and agents, in that case, shall not exceed the said limits.

3. The provisions of paragraphs 1 and 2 of this article shall not apply if it is proved that the damage resulted from an act or omission of servant or agent done with intent to cause damage or recklessly and with knowledge that damage would probably result."

Article XV

In Article 26 of the Convention—

paragraph 2 shall be deleted and replaced by the following:

"2. In the case of damage, the person entitled to delivery must complain to the carrier forthwith after the discovery of the damage, and, at the latest, within seven days from the date of receipt in the case of baggage and fourteen days from the date of receipt in the case of cargo. In the case of delay the complaint must be made at the latest within twenty-one days from the date on which the baggage or cargo have been placed at this disposal."

Article XVI

Article 34 of the Convention shall be deleted and replaced by the following:

"The provisions of Articles 3 to 9 inclusive relating to documents of carriage shall not apply in the case of carriage performed in extraordinary circumstances outside the normal scope of an air carrier's business."

Article XVII

After article 40 of the Convention, the following Article shall be inserted:

"Article 40A

1. In Article 37, paragraph 2 and Article 40, paragraph 1, the expression High Contracting Party shall mean State. In all other cases, the expression High Contracting Party shall mean a State whose ratification of or adherence to the Convention has become effective and whose denunciation thereof has not become effective.

2. For the purposes of the Convention the word territory means not only the metropolitan territory of a State but also all other territories for the foreign relations of which that State is responsible."

CHAPTER II
SCOPE OF APPLICATION OF THE CONVENTION AS AMENDED

Article XVIII

The Convention as amended by this Protocol shall apply to international carriage as defined in Article 1 of the Convention, provided that the places of departure and destination referred to in that Article are situated either in the territories of two parties to this Protocol or within the territory of a single party to this Protocol with an agreed stopping place within the territory of another State.

CHAPTER III
FINAL CLAUSES

Article XIX

As between the Parties to this Protocol, the Convention and the Protocol shall be read and interpreted together as one single instrument and shall be known as the Warsaw Convention as amended at The Hague, 1955.

Article XX

Until the date on which this Protocol comes into force in accordance with the provisions of Article XXII, paragraph 1, it shall remain open for signature on behalf of any State which up to that dare has ratified or adhered to the Convention or which has participated in the Conference at which this Protocol was adopted.

Article XXI

1. This Protocol shall be subject to ratification by the signatory States.

2. Ratification of this Protocol by any State which is not a Party to the Convention shall have the effect of adherence to the Convention as amended by this Protocol.

3. The instruments of ratification shall be deposited with the Government of the People's Republic of Poland.

Article XXII

1. As soon as thirty signatory States have deposited their instruments of ratification of this Protocol, it shall come into force between them on the ninetieth day after the deposit of the thirtieth instrument of ratification. It shall come into force for each State ratifying thereafter on the ninetieth day after the deposit of its instrument of ratification.

2. As soon as this Protocol comes into force it shall be registered with the United Nations by the Government of the People's Republic of Poland.

Article XXIII

1. This Protocol shall, after it has come into force, be open for adherence by any non-signatory State.

2. Adherence to this Protocol by any State which is not a Party to the Convention shall have the effect of adherence to the Convention as amended by this Protocol.

3. Adherence shall be effected by the deposit of an instrument of adherence with the Government of the People's Republic of Poland and shall take effect on the ninetieth day after the deposit.

Article XXIV

1. Any Party to this Protocol may denounce the Protocol by notification addressed to the Government of the People's Republic of Poland.

2. Denunciation shall take effect six months after the date of receipt by the Government of the People's Republic of Poland of the notification of denunciation.

3. As between the Parties to this Protocol, denunciation by any of them of the Convention in accordance with Article 39 thereof shall not be construed in any way as a denunciation of the Convention as amended by this Protocol.

Article XXV

1. This Protocol shall apply to all territories for the foreign relations of which a State Party to this Protocol is responsible, with the exception of territories in respect of which a declaration has been made in accordance with paragraph 2 of this Article.

2. Any State may, at the time of deposit of its instrument of ratification or adherence, declare that its acceptance of this Protocol does not apply to any one or more of the territories for the foreign relations of which such State is responsible.

3. Any State may subsequently, by notification to the Government of the People's Republic of Poland, extend the application of this Protocol to any or all of the territories regarding which it has made a declaration in accordance with paragraph 2 of this Article. The notification shall take effect on the ninetieth day after its receipt by that Government.

4. Any State Party to this Protocol may denounce it, in accordance with the provisions of Article XXIV, paragraph 1, separately for any or all of the territories for the foreign relations of which such State is responsible.

Article XXVI

No reservation may be made to this Protocol except that a State may at any time declare by a notification addressed to the Government of the People's Republic of Poland that the Convention as amended by this Protocol shall not apply to the carriage of persons, cargo and baggage for its military authorities on aircraft, registered in that State, the whole capacity of which has been reserved by or on behalf of such authorities.

Article XXVII

The Government of the People's Republic of Poland shall give immediate notice to the Governments of all States signatories to the Convention or this Protocol, all States Parties to the Convention or this Protocol, and all States Members of the International Civil Aviation Organization or of the United Nations and to the International Civil Aviation Organization:

a) of any signature of this Protocol and the date thereof;

b) of the deposit of any instrument of ratification or adherence in respect of this Protocol and the date thereof;

c) of the date on which this Protocol comes into force in accordance with Article XXII, paragraph 1;

d) of the receipt of any notification of denunciation and the date thereof;

e) of the receipt of any declaration or notification made under Article XXV and the date thereof; and

f) of the receipt of any notification made under Article XXVI and the date thereof.

IN WITNESS WHEREOF the undersigned Plenipotentiaries, having been duly authorized, have signed this Protocol.

DONE AT The Hague on the twenty-eighth day of the month of September of the year One Thousand Nine Hundred and Fifty-five, in three authentic texts in the English, French and Spanish languages. In the case of any inconsistency, the text in the French language, in which language the Convention was drawn up, shall prevail. This Protocol shall be deposited with the Government of the People's Republic of Poland with which, in accordance with Article XX, it shall remain open for signature, and that Government shall send certified copies thereof to the Governments of all States signatories to the Convention or this Protocol, all States Parties to the Convention on this Protocol, and all States Members of the International Civil Aviation Organization or of the United Nations, and to the International Civil Aviation Organization.

Appendix 9

Convention Supplementary to the Warsaw Convention for the Unification of Certain Rules Relating to International Carriage by Air Performed by a Person Other than the Contracting Carrier

Done at Guadalajara—September 18, 1961
Entered into force—May 1, 1964
Not in effect in the United States
500 U.N.T.S. 31, ICAO Doc. 8181

The States Signatory to the Present Convention,

Noting that the Warsaw Convention does not contain particular rules relating to international carriage by air performed by a person who is not a party to the agreement for carriage,

Considering that it is therefore desirable to formulate rules to apply in such circumstances,

Have Agreed As Follows:

Article I

In this Convention:

(a) "Warsaw Convention" means the Convention for the Unification of Certain Rules Relating to International Carriage by Air signed at Warsaw on 12 October 1929, or the Warsaw Convention as amended at The Hague, 1955, according to whether the carriage under the agreement referred to in paragraph (b) is governed by the one or by the other;

(b) "contracting carrier" means a person who as a principal makes an agreement for carriage governed by the Warsaw Convention with a passenger or consignor or with a person acting on behalf of the passenger or consignor;

(c) "actual carrier" means a person other than the contracting carrier, who, by virtue of authority from the contracting carrier, performs the whole or part of the carriage contemplated in paragraph (b) but who is not with respect to such part a successive carrier within the meaning of the Warsaw Convention. Such authority is presumed in the absence of proof to the contrary.

Article II

If an actual carrier performs the whole or part of carriage which, according to the agreement referred to in Article I, paragraph (b), is governed by the Warsaw Convention, both the contracting carrier and the actual carrier shall, except as otherwise provided in this Convention, be subject to the rules of the Warsaw Convention, the former for the whole of the carriage contemplated in the agreement, the latter solely for the carriage which he performs.

Article III

1. The acts and omissions of the actual carrier and of his servants and agents acting within the scope of their employment shall, in relation to the carriage performed by the actual carrier, be deemed to be also those of the contracting carrier.

2. The acts and omissions of the contracting carrier and of his servants and agents acting within the scope of their employment shall, in relation to the carriage performed by the actual carrier, be deemed to be also those of the actual carrier. Nevertheless, no such act or omission shall subject the actual carrier to liability exceeding the limits specified in Article 22 of the Warsaw Convention. Any special agreement under which the contracting carrier assumes obligations not imposed by the Warsaw Convention or any waiver of rights conferred by that Convention or any special declaration of interest in delivery at destination contemplated in Article 22 of the said Convention, shall not affect the actual carrier unless agreed to by him.

Article IV

Any complaint to be made or order to be given under the Warsaw Convention to the carrier shall have the same effect whether addressed to the contracting carrier or to the actual carrier. Nevertheless, orders referred to in Article 12 of the Warsaw Convention shall only be effective if addressed to the contracting carrier.

Article V

In relation to the carriage performed by the actual carrier, any servant or agent of that carrier or of the contracting carrier shall, if he proves that he acted within the scope of his employment, be entitled to avail himself of the limits of liability which are applicable under this Convention to the carrier whose servant or agent he is unless it is proved that he acted in a manner which, under the Warsaw Convention, prevents the limits of liability from being invoked.

Article VI

In relation to the carriage performed by the actual carrier, the aggregate of the amounts recoverable from that carrier and the contracting carrier, and from their servants and agents acting within the scope of their employment, shall not exceed the highest amount which could be awarded against either the contracting carrier or the actual carrier under this Convention, but none of the persons mentioned shall be liable for a sum in excess of the limit applicable to him.

Article VII

In relation to the carriage performed by the actual carrier, an action for damages may be brought, at the option of the plaintiff, against that carrier or the contracting carrier, or against both together or separately. If the action is brought against only one of those carriers, that carrier shall have the right to require the other carrier to be joined in the proceedings, the procedure and effects being governed by the law of the court seised of the case.

Article VIII

Any action for damages contemplated in Article VII of this Convention must be brought, at the option of the plaintiff, either before a court in which an action may be brought against the contracting carrier, as provided in Article 28 of the Warsaw Convention, or before the court having jurisdiction at the place where the actual carrier is ordinarily resident or has his principal place of business.

Article IX

1. Any contractual provision tending to relieve the contracting carrier or the actual carrier of liability under this Convention or to fix a lower limit than that which is ap-

plicable according to this Convention shall be null and void, but the nullity of any such provision does not involve the nullity of the whole agreement, which shall remain subject to the provisions of this Convention.

2. In respect of the carriage performed by the actual carrier, the preceding paragraph shall not apply to contractual provisions governing loss or damage resulting from the inherent defect, quality or vice of the cargo carried.

3. Any clause contained in an agreement for carriage and all special agreements entered into before the damage occurred by which the parties purport to infringe the rules laid down by this Convention, whether by deciding the law to be applied, or by altering the rules as to jurisdiction, shall be null and void. Nevertheless, for the carriage of cargo arbitration clauses are allowed, subject to this Convention, if the arbitration is to take place in one of the jurisdictions referred to in Article VIII.

Article X

Except as provided in Article VII, nothing in this Convention shall affect the rights and obligations of the two carriers between themselves.

Article XI

Until the date on which the Convention comes into force in accordance with the provisions of Article XIII, it shall remain open for signature on behalf of any State which at that date is a Member of the United Nations or of any of the Specialized Agencies.

Article XII

1. This Convention shall be subject to ratification by the signatory States.

2. The instruments of ratification shall be deposited with the Government of the United States of Mexico.

Article XIII

1. As soon as five of the signatory States have deposited their instruments of ratification of this Convention, it shall come into force between them on the ninetieth day after the date of the deposit of the fifth instrument of ratification. It shall come into force for each State ratifying thereafter on the ninetieth day after the deposit of its instrument of ratification.

2. As soon as this Convention comes into force, it shall be registered with the United Nations and the International Civil Aviation Organization by the Government of the United States of Mexico.

Article XIV

1. This Convention shall, after it has come into force, be open for accession by any State Member of the United Nations or of any of the Specialized Agencies.

2. The accession of a State shall be effected by the deposit of an instrument of accession with the Government of the United States of Mexico and shall take effect as from the ninetieth day after the date of such deposit.

Article XV

1. Any Contracting State may denounce this Convention by notification addressed to the Government of the United States of Mexico.

2. Denunciation shall take effect six months after the date of receipt by the Government of the United States of Mexico of the notification of denunciation.

Article XVI

1. Any Contracting State may at the time of its ratification of or accession to this Convention or at any time thereafter declare by notification to the Government of the United States of Mexico that the Convention shall extend to any of the territories for whose international relations it is responsible.

2. The Convention shall, ninety days after the date of the receipt of such notification by the Government of the United States of Mexico, extend to the territories named therein.

3. Any Contracting State may denounce this Convention, in accordance with the provisions of Article XV, separately for any or all of the territories for the international relations of which such State is responsible.

Article XVII

No reservation may be made to this Convention.

Article XVIII

The Government of the United States of Mexico shall give notice to the International Civil Aviation Organization and to all States Members of the United Nations or of any of the Specialized Agencies:

(a) of any signature of this Convention and the date thereof;

(b) of the deposit of any instrument of ratification or accession and the date thereof;

(c) of the date on which this Convention comes into force in accordance with Article XIII, paragraph 1;

(d) of the receipt of any notification of denunciation and the date thereof;

(e) of the receipt of any declaration or notification made under Article XVI and the date thereof.

IN WITNESS WHEREOF the undersigned Plenipotentiaries, having been duly authorized, have signed this Convention.

DONE at Guadalajara on the eighteenth day of September One Thousand Nine Hundred and Sixty-one in three authentic texts drawn up in the English, French and Spanish languages. In case of any inconsistency, the text in the French language, in which language the Warsaw Convention of 12 October 1929 was drawn up, shall prevail. The Government of the United States of Mexico will establish an official translation of the text of the Convention in the Russian language.

This Convention shall be deposited with the Government of the United States of Mexico with which in accordance with Article XI, it shall remain open for signature, and that Government shall send certified copies thereof to the International Civil Aviation Organization and to all States Members of the United Nations or of any Specialized Agency.

Appendix 10

Convention on Offences and Certain Other Acts Committed on Board Aircraft

Done at Tokyo—September 14, 1963
Entered into force—December 4, 1969
Effective in the United States—December 4, 1969
20 U.S.T. 2941, T.I.A.S. No. 6768,
704 U.N.T.S. 219, ICAO Doc. 8364,
2 I.L.M. 1042, 58 Am. J. Int'l L. 566

THE STATES Parties to this Convention,

HAVE AGREED as follows:

CHAPTER I
SCOPE OF THE CONVENTION

Article 1

1. This Convention shall apply in respect of:

(a) offences against penal law;

(b) acts which, whether or not they are offences, may or do jeopardize the safety of the aircraft or of persons or property therein or which jeopardize good order and discipline on board.

2. Except as provided in Chapter III, this Convention shall apply in respect of offences committed or acts done by a person on board any aircraft registered in a Contracting State, while that aircraft is in flight or on the surface of the high seas or of any other area outside the territory of any State.

3. For the purposes of this Convention, an aircraft is considered to be in flight from the moment when power is applied for the purpose of takeoff until the moment when the landing run ends.

4. This Convention shall not apply to aircraft used in military, customs or police services.

Article 2

Without prejudice to the provisions of Article 4 and except when the safety of the aircraft or of persons or property on board so requires, no provision of this Convention shall be interpreted as authorizing or requiring any action in respect of offences against penal laws of a political nature or those based on racial or religious discrimination.

CHAPTER II
JURISDICTION

Article 3

1. The State of registration of the aircraft is competent to exercise jurisdiction over offences and acts committed on board.

2. Each Contracting State shall take such measures as may be necessary to establish its jurisdiction as the State of registration over offences committed on board aircraft registered in such State.

3. This Convention does not exclude any criminal jurisdiction exercised in accordance with national law.

Article 4

A Contracting State which is not the State of registration may not interfere with an aircraft in flight in order to exercise its criminal jurisdiction over an offence committed on board except in the following cases:

(a) the offence has effect on the territory of such State;

(b) the offence has been committed by or against a national or permanent resident of such State;

(c) the offence is against the security of such State;

(d) the offence consists of a breach of any rules or regulations relating to the flight or manoeuvre of aircraft in force in such State;

(e) the exercise of jurisdiction is necessary to ensure the observance of any obligation of such State under a multilateral international agreement.

CHAPTER III
POWERS OF THE AIRCRAFT COMMANDER

Article 5

1. The provisions of this Chapter shall not apply to offences and acts committed or about to be committed by a person on board an aircraft in flight in the airspace of the State of registration or over the high seas or any other area outside the territory of any State unless the last point of takeoff or the next point of intended landing is situated in a State other than that of registration, or the aircraft subsequently flies in the airspace of a State other than that of registration with such person still on board.

2. Notwithstanding the provisions of Article 1, paragraph 3, an aircraft shall for the purposes of this Chapter, be considered to be in flight at any time from the moment when all its external doors are closed following embarkation until the moment when any such door is opened for disembarkation. In the case of a forced landing, the provisions of this Chapter shall continue to apply with respect to offences and acts committed on board until competent authorities of a State take over the responsibility for the aircraft and for the persons and property on board.

Article 6

1. The aircraft commander may, when he has reasonable grounds to believe that a person has committed, or is about to commit, on board the aircraft, an offence or act contemplated in Article 1, paragraph 1, impose upon such person reasonable measures including restraint which are necessary:

(a) to protect the safety of the aircraft, or of persons or property therein; or

(b) to maintain good order and discipline on board; or

(c) to enable him to deliver such person to competent authorities or to disembark him in accordance with the provisions of this Chapter.

2. The aircraft commander may require or authorize the assistance of other crew members and may request or authorize, but not require, the assistance of passengers to restrain any person whom he is entitled to restrain. Any crew member or passenger may also take reasonable preventive measures without such authorization when he has reasonable grounds to believe that such action is immediately necessary to protect the safety of the aircraft, or of persons or property therein.

Article 7

1. Measures of restraint imposed upon a person in accordance with Article 6 shall not be continued beyond any point at which the aircraft lands unless:

(a) such point is in the territory of a non-Contracting State and its authorities refuse to permit disembarkation of that person or those measures have been imposed in accordance with Article 6, paragraph 1(c) in order to enable his delivery to competent authorities;

(b) the aircraft makes a forced landing and the aircraft commander is unable to deliver that person to competent authorities; or

(c) that person agrees to onward carriage under restraint.

2. The aircraft commander shall as soon as practicable, and if possible before landing in the territory of a State with a person on board who has been placed under restraint in accordance with the provisions of Article 6, notify the authorities of such State of the fact that a person on board is under restraint and of the reasons for such restraint.

Article 8

1. The aircraft commander may, in so far as it is necessary for the purpose of subparagraph (a) or (b) or paragraph 1 of Article 6, disembark in the territory of any State in which the aircraft lands any person who he has reasonable grounds to believe has committed, or is about to commit, on board the aircraft an act contemplated in Article 1, paragraph 1(b).

2. The aircraft commander shall report to the authorities of the State in which he disembarks any person pursuant to this Article, the fact of, and the reasons for, such disembarkation.

Article 9

1. The aircraft commander may deliver to the competent authorities of any Contracting State in the territory of which the aircraft lands any person who he has reasonable grounds to believe has committed on board the aircraft an act which, in his opinion, is a serious offence according to the penal law of the State of registration of the aircraft.

2. The aircraft commander shall as soon as practicable and if possible before landing in the territory of a Contracting State with a person on board whom the aircraft commander intends to deliver in accordance with the preceding paragraph, notify the authorities of such State of his intention to deliver such person and the reasons therefor.

3. The aircraft commander shall furnish the authorities to whom any suspected offender is delivered in accordance with the provisions of this Article with evidence and information which, under the law of the State of registration of the aircraft, are lawfully in his possession.

Article 10

For actions taken in accordance with this Convention, neither the aircraft commander, any other member of the crew, any passenger, the owner or operator of the aircraft, nor the person on whose behalf the flight was performed shall be held responsible in any proceeding on account of the treatment undergone by the person against whom the actions were taken.

CHAPTER IV
UNLAWFUL SEIZURE OF AIRCRAFT

Article 11

1. When a person on board has unlawfully committed by force or threat thereof an act of interference, seizure, or other wrongful exercise of control of an aircraft in flight or when such an act is about to be committed, Contracting States shall take all appropriate measures to restore control of the aircraft to its lawful commander or to preserve his control of the aircraft.

2. In the cases contemplated in the preceding paragraph, the Contracting State in which the aircraft lands shall permit its passengers and crew to continue their journey as soon as practicable, and shall return the aircraft and its cargo to the persons lawfully entitled to possession.

CHAPTER V
POWERS AND DUTIES OF STATES

Article 12

Any Contracting State shall allow the commander of an aircraft registered in another Contracting State to disembark any person pursuant to Article 8, paragraph 1.

Article 13

1. Any Contracting State shall take delivery of any person whom the aircraft commander delivers pursuant to Article 9, paragraph 1.

2. Upon being satisfied that the circumstances so warrant, any Contracting State shall take custody or other measures to ensure the presence of any person suspected of an act contemplated in Article 11, paragraph 1 and of any person of whom it has taken delivery. The custody and other measures shall be as provided in the law of that State but may only be continued for such time as is reasonably necessary to enable any criminal or extradition proceedings to be instituted.

3. Any person in custody pursuant to the previous paragraph shall be assisted in communicating immediately with the nearest appropriate representative of the State of which he is a national.

4. Any Contracting State, to which a person is delivered pursuant to Article 9, paragraph 1, or in whose territory an aircraft lands following the commission of an act contemplated in Article 11, paragraph 1, shall immediately make a preliminary enquiry into the facts.

5. When a State, pursuant to this Article, has taken a person into custody, it shall immediately notify the State of registration of the aircraft and the State of nationality of the detained person and, if it considers it advisable, any other interested State of the fact

that such person is in custody and of the circumstances which warrant his detention. The State which makes the preliminary enquiry contemplated in paragraph 4 of this Article shall promptly report its findings to the said States and shall indicate whether it intends to exercise jurisdiction.

Article 14

1. When any person has been disembarked in accordance with Article 8, paragraph 1, or delivered in accordance with Article 9, paragraph 1, or has disembarked after committing an act contemplated in Article 11, paragraph 1, and when such person cannot or does not desire to continue his journey and the State of landing refuses to admit him, that State may, if the person in question is not a national or permanent resident of that State, return him to the territory of the State of which he is a national or permanent resident or to the territory of the State in which he began his journey by air.

2. Neither disembarkation, nor delivery, not the taking of custody or other measures contemplated in Article 13, paragraph 2, nor return of the person concerned, shall be considered as admission to the territory of the Contracting State concerned for the purpose of its law relating to entry or admission of persons and nothing in this Convention shall affect the law of a Contracting State relating to the expulsion of persons from its territory.

Article 15

1. Without prejudice to Article 14, any person who has been disembarked in accordance with Article 8, paragraph 1, or delivered in accordance with Article 9, paragraph 1, or has disembarked after committing an act contemplated in Article 11, paragraph 1, and who desires to continue his journey shall be at liberty as soon as practicable to proceed to any destination of his choice unless his presence is required by the law of the State of landing for the purpose of extradition or criminal proceedings.

2. Without prejudice to its law as to entry and admission to, and extradition and expulsion from its territory, a Contracting State in whose territory a person has been disembarked in accordance with Article 8, paragraph 1, or delivered in accordance with Article 9, paragraph 1 or has disembarked and is suspected of having committed an act contemplated in Article 11, paragraph 1, shall accord to such person treatment which is no less favourable for his protection and security than that accorded to nationals of such Contracting State in like circumstances.

CHAPTER VI
OTHER PROVISIONS

Article 16

1. Offences committed on aircraft registered in a Contracting State shall be treated, for the purpose of extradition, as if they had been committed not only in the place in which they have occurred but also in the territory of the State of registration of the aircraft.

2. Without prejudice to the provisions of the preceding paragraph, nothing in this Convention shall be deemed to create an obligation to grant extradition.

Article 17

In taking any measures for investigation or arrest or otherwise exercising jurisdiction in connection with any offence committed on board an aircraft the Contracting States shall pay due regard to the safety and other interests of air navigation and shall so act as to avoid unnecessary delay of the aircraft, passengers, crew or cargo.

Article 18

If Contracting States establish joint air transport operating organizations or international operating agencies, which operate aircraft not registered in any one State those States shall, according to the circumstances of the case, designate the State among them which, for the purposes of this Convention, shall be considered as the State of registration and shall give notice thereof to the International Civil Aviation Organization which shall communicate the notice to all States Parties to this Convention.

CHAPTER VII
FINAL CLAUSES

Article 19

Until the date on which this Convention comes into force in accordance with the provisions of Article 21, it shall remain open for signature on behalf of any State which at that date is a Member of the United Nations or of any of the Specialized Agencies.

Article 20

1. This Convention shall be subject to ratification by the signatory States in accordance with their constitutional procedures.

2. The instruments of ratification shall be deposited with the International Civil Aviation Organization.

Article 21

1. As soon as twelve of the signatory States have deposited their instruments of ratification of this Convention, it shall come into force between them on the ninetieth day after the date of the deposit of the twelfth instrument of ratification. It shall come into force for each State ratifying thereafter on the ninetieth day after the deposit of its instrument of ratification.

2. As soon as this Convention comes into force, it shall be registered with the Secretary-General of the United Nations by the International Civil Aviation Organization.

Article 22

1. This Convention shall, after it has come into force, be open for accession by any State Member of the United Nations or of any of the Specialized Agencies.

2. The accession of a State shall be effected by the deposit of an instrument of accession with the International Civil Aviation Organization and shall take effect on the ninetieth day after the date of such deposit.

Article 23

1. Any Contracting State may denounce this Convention by notification addressed to the International Civil Aviation Organization.

2. Denunciation shall take effect six months after the date of receipt by the International Civil Aviation Organization of the notification of denunciation.

Article 24

1. Any dispute between two or more Contracting States concerning the interpretation or application of this Convention which cannot be settled through negotiation, shall, at the request of one of them, be submitted to arbitration. If within six months from the date of the request for arbitration the Parties are unable to agree on the organization of the arbitration, any one of those Parties may refer the dispute to the International Court of Justice by request in conformity with the Statute of the Court.

2. Each State may at the time of signature or ratification of this Convention or accession thereto, declare that it does not consider itself bound by the preceding paragraph. The other Contracting States shall not be bound by the preceding paragraph with respect to any Contracting State having made such a reservation.

3. Any Contracting State having made a reservation in accordance with the preceding paragraph may at any time withdraw this reservation by notification to the International Civil Aviation Organization.

Article 25

Except as provided in Article 24 no reservation may be made to this Convention.

Article 26

The International Civil Aviation Organization shall give notice to all States Members of the United Nations or of any of the Specialized Agencies:

(a) of any signature of this Convention and the date thereof;

(b) of the deposit of any instrument of ratification or accession and the date thereof;

(c) of the date on which this Convention comes into force in accordance with Article 21, paragraph 1;

(d) of the receipt of any notification of denunciation and the date thereof; and

(e) of the receipt of any declaration or notification made under Article 24 and the date thereof.

IN WITNESS WHEREOF the undersigned Plenipotentiaries, having been duly authorized, have signed this Convention.

DONE at Tokyo on the fourteenth day of September One Thousand Nine Hundred and Sixty-three in three authentic texts drawn up in the English, French and Spanish languages. This Convention shall be deposited with the International Civil Aviation Organization with which, in accordance with Article 19, it shall remain open for signature and the said Organization shall send certified copies thereof to all States Members of the United Nations or of any Specialized Agency.

Appendix 11

Montreal Intercarrier Agreement Relating to Liability Limitations of the Warsaw Convention and the Hague Protocol

Civil Aeronautics Board Agreement No. 18990, Executive Order No. 23680 (May 13, 1966), 31 Fed. Reg. 7302 (May 19, 1966)

The undersigned carriers (hereinafter referred to as "the Carriers") hereby agree as follows:

1. Each of the Carriers shall, effective 16th May 1966, include the following in its conditions of carriage, including tariffs embodying conditions of carriage filed by it with any government:

"The carrier shall avail itself of the limitation of liability provided in the Convention for the Unification of Certain Rules Relating to International Carriage by Air signed at Warsaw 12th October 1929, or provided in the said Convention as amended by the Protocol signed at The Hague 28th September 1955. However in accordance with Article 22(1) of said Convention, or said Convention as amended by said Protocol, the Carrier agrees that, as to all international transportation by the Carrier as defined in the said Convention, or said Convention as amended by said Protocol, which, according to the Contract of Carriage, includes a point in the United States of America as a point of origin, point of destination, or agreed stopping place

(i) The limit for each passenger for death, wounding, or other bodily injury shall be the sum of US $75,000 inclusive of legal fees and costs, except that, in case of a claim brought in a State where provision is made for separate award of legal fees and costs, the limit shall be the sum of US $58,000 exclusive of legal fees and costs.

(ii) The Carrier shall not, with respect to any claim arising out of the death, wounding, or other bodily injury of a passenger, avail itself of any defense under Article 20(1) of said Convention or said Convention as amended by said Protocol.

Nothing herein shall be deemed to affect the rights and liabilities of the Carrier with regard to any claim brought by, on behalf of, or in respect of any person who has wilfully caused damage which resulted in death, wounding, or other bodily injury of a passenger."

2. Each carrier shall, at the time of delivery of the ticket, furnish to each passenger whose transportation is governed by the Convention, or the Convention as amended by the Hague Protocol, and by the special contract described in paragraph 1, the following notice, which shall be printed in type at least as large as 10 point modern type and in ink contrasting with the stock in (i) each ticket; (ii) a piece of paper either placed in the ticket envelope with the ticket or attached to the ticket; or (iii) on the ticket envelope:

"ADVICE TO INTERNATIONAL PASSENGERS ON LIMITATION OF LIABILITY

Passengers on a journey involving an ultimate destination or a stop in a country other than the country of origin are advised that the provisions of the treaty known as the Warsaw Convention may be applicable to the entire journey, including any portion entirely within the country of origin or destination. For such passengers on a journey to, from, or with an agreed stopping place in the United States of America, the Convention and special contracts of carriage embodied in applicable tariffs provide that the liability of [(name of carrier) and certain other] carriers parties to such special contracts for death of or personal injury to passengers is limited in most cases to proven damages not to exceed US $75,000 per passenger , and that this liability up to such limit shall not depend on negligence on the part of the carrier. For such passengers travelling by a carrier not a party to such special contracts or on a journey not to, from, or having an agreed stopping place in the United States of America, liability of the carrier for death or personal injury to passengers is limited in most cases to approximately US $10,000 or US $20,000.

The names of Carriers parties to such special contracts are available at all ticket offices of such carriers and may be examined on request. Additional protection can usually be obtained by purchasing insurance from a private company. Such insurance is not affected by any limitation of the carrier's liability under the Warsaw Convention or such special contracts of carriage.

For further information please consult your airline or insurance company representative."

3. This Agreement shall be filed with the Civil Aeronautics Board of the United States for approval pursuant to Section 412 of the Federal Aviation Act of 1958, as amended and filed with other governments as required. The Agreement shall become effective upon approval by said Board pursuant to said Section 412.

4. This Agreement may be signed in any number of counterparts, all of which shall constitute one Agreement. Any carrier may become a party to this Agreement by signing a counterpart hereof and depositing it with Civil Aeronautics Board.

5. Any carrier party hereto may withdraw from this Agreement by giving twelve (12) months' written notice of withdrawal to said Civil Aeronautics Board and the other Carriers parties to the Agreement.

Appendix 12

Convention for the Suppression of Unlawful Seizure of Aircraft

Done at The Hague—December 16, 1970
Entered into force—October 14, 1971
Effective in the United States—October 14, 1971
22 U.S.T. 1641, T.I.A.S. No. 7192,
860 U.N.T.S. 105, ICAO Doc. 8920, 10 I.L.M. 133

Preamble

THE STATES PARTIES TO THIS CONVENTION

CONSIDERING that unlawful acts of seizure or exercise of control of aircraft in flight jeopardize the safety of persons and property, seriously affect the operation of air services, and undermine the confidence of the peoples of the world in the safety of civil aviation;

CONSIDERING that the occurrence of such acts is a matter of grave concern;

CONSIDERING that, for the purpose of deterring such acts, there is an urgent need to provide appropriate measures for punishment of offenders;

HAVE AGREED AS FOLLOWS:

Article 1

Any person who on board an aircraft in flight:

(a) unlawfully, by force or threat thereof, or by any other form of intimidation, seizes, or exercises control of, that aircraft, or attempts to perform any such act, or

(b) is an accomplice of a person who performs or attempts to perform any such act commits an offence (hereinafter referred to as "the offence").

Article 2

Each Contracting State undertakes to make the offence punishable by severe penalties.

Article 3

1. For the purposes of this Convention, an aircraft is considered to be in flight at any time from the moment when all its external doors are closed following embarkation until the moment when any such door is opened for disembarkation. In the case of a forced landing, the flight shall be deemed to continue until the competent authorities take over the responsibility for the aircraft and for persons and property on board.

2. This Convention shall not apply to aircraft used in military, customs or police services.

3. This Convention shall apply only if the place of take-off or the place of actual landing of the aircraft on board which the offence is committed is situated outside the territory of the State of registration of that aircraft; it shall be immaterial whether the aircraft is engaged in an international or domestic flight.

4. In the cases mentioned in Article 5, this Convention shall not apply if the place of take-off and the place of actual landing of the aircraft on board which the offence is

committed are situated within the territory of the same State where that State is one of those referred to in that Article.

5. Notwithstanding paragraphs 3 and 4 of this Article, Articles 6, 7, 8, and 10 shall apply whatever the place of take-off or the place of actual landing of the aircraft, if the offender or the alleged offender is found in the territory of a State other than the State of registration of that aircraft.

Article 4

1. Each Contracting State shall take such measures as may be necessary to establish its jurisdiction over the offence and any other act of violence against passengers or crew committed by the alleged offender in connection with the offence, in the following cases:

(a) when the offence is committed on board an aircraft registered in that State;

(b) when the aircraft on board which the offence is committed lands in its territory with the alleged offender still on board;

(c) when the offence is committed on board an aircraft leased without crew to a lessee who has his principal place of business or, if the lessee has no such place of business, his permanent residence, in that State.

2. Each Contracting State shall likewise take such measures as may be necessary to establish its jurisdiction over the offence in the case where the alleged offender is present in its territory and it does not extradite him pursuant to Article 8 to any of the States mentioned in paragraph 1 of this Article.

3. This Convention does not exclude any criminal jurisdiction exercised in accordance with national law.

Article 5

The Contracting States which establish joint air transport operating organizations or international operating agencies, which operate aircraft which are subject to joint or international registration shall, by appropriate means, designate for each aircraft the State among them which shall exercise the jurisdiction and have the attributes of the State of registration for the purpose of this Convention and shall give notice thereof to the International Civil Aviation Organization which shall communicate the notice to all States Parties to this Convention.

Article 6

1. Upon being satisfied that the circumstances so warrant, any Contracting State in the territory of which the offender or the alleged offender is present, shall take him into custody or take other measures to ensure his presence. The custody and other measures shall be as provided in the law of that State but may only be continued for such time as is necessary to enable any criminal or extradition proceedings to be instituted.

2. Such State shall immediately make a preliminary enquiry into the facts.

3. Any person in custody pursuant to paragraph 1 of this Article shall be assisted in communicating immediately with the nearest appropriate representative of the State of which he is a national.

4. When a State, pursuant to this Article, has taken a person into custody, it shall immediately notify the State of registration of the aircraft, the State mentioned in Article

4, paragraph 1(c), the State of nationality of the detained person and, if it considers it advisable, any other interested States of the fact that such person is in custody and of the circumstances which warrant his detention. The State which makes the preliminary enquiry contemplated in paragraph 2 of this Article shall promptly report its findings to the said States and shall indicate whether it intends to exercise jurisdiction.

Article 7

The Contracting State in the territory of which the alleged offender is found shall, if it does not extradite him, be obliged, without exception whatsoever and whether or not the offence was committed in its territory, to submit the case to its competent authorities for the purpose of prosecution. Those authorities shall take their decision in the same manner as in the case of any ordinary offence of a serious nature under the law of that State.

Article 8

1. The offence shall be deemed to be included as an extraditable offence in any extradition treaty existing between Contracting States. Contracting States undertake to include the offence as an extraditable offence in every extradition treaty to be concluded between them.

2. If a Contracting State which makes extradition conditional on the existence of a treaty receives a request for extradition from another Contracting State with which it has no extradition treaty, it may at its option consider this Convention as the legal basis for extradition in respect of the offence. Extradition shall be subject to the other conditions provided by the law of the requested State.

3. Contracting States which do not make extradition conditional on the existence of a treaty shall recognize the offence as an extraditable offence between themselves subject to the conditions provided by the law of the requested State.

4. The offence shall be treated, for the purpose of extradition between Contracting States, as if it had been committed not only in the place in which it occurred but also in the territories of the States required to establish their jurisdiction in accordance with Article 4, paragraph 1.

Article 9

1. When any of the acts mentioned in Article 1(a) has occurred or is about to occur, Contracting States shall take all appropriate measures to restore control of the aircraft to its lawful commander or to preserve his control of the aircraft.

2. In the cases contemplated by the preceding paragraph, any Contracting State in which the aircraft or its passengers or crew are present shall facilitate the continuation of the journey of the passengers and crew as soon as practicable, and shall without delay return the aircraft and its cargo to the persons lawfully entitled to possession.

Article 10

1. Contracting States shall afford one another the greatest measure of assistance in connection with criminal proceedings brought in respect of the offence and other acts mentioned in Article 4. The law of the State requested shall apply in all cases.

2. The provisions of paragraph 1 of this Article shall not affect obligations under any other treaty, bilateral or multilateral, which governs or will govern, in whole or in part, mutual assistance in criminal matters.

Article 11

Each Contracting State shall in accordance with its national law report to the Council of the International Civil Aviation Organization as promptly as possible any relevant information in its possession concerning:

(a) the circumstances of the offence;

(b) the action taken pursuant to Article 9;

(c) the measures taken in relation to the offender or the alleged offender, and, in particular, the results of any extradition proceedings or other legal proceedings.

Article 12

1. Any dispute between two or more Contracting States concerning the interpretation or application of this Convention which cannot be settled through negotiation, shall, at the request of one of them, be submitted to arbitration. If within six months from the date of the request for arbitration the Parties are unable to agree on the organization of the arbitration, any one of those Parties may refer the dispute to the International Court of Justice by request in conformity with the Statute of the Court.

2. Each State may at the time of signature or ratification of this Convention or accession thereto, declare that it does not consider itself bound by the preceding paragraph. The other Contracting States shall not be bound by the preceding paragraph with respect to any Contracting State having made such a reservation.

3. Any Contracting State having made a reservation in accordance with the preceding paragraph may at any time withdraw this reservation by notification to the Depositary Governments.

Article 13

1. This Convention shall be open for signature at The Hague on 16 December 1970, by States participating in the International Conference on Air Law held at The Hague from 1 to 16 December 1970 (hereinafter referred to as The Hague Conference). After 31 December 1970, the Convention shall be open to all States for signature in Moscow, London and Washington. Any State which does not sign this Convention before its entry into force in accordance with paragraph 3 of this Article may accede to it at any time.

2. This Convention shall be subject to ratification by the signatory States. Instruments of ratification and instruments of accession shall be deposited with the Governments of the Union of Soviet Socialist Republics, the United Kingdom of Great Britain and Northern Ireland, and the United States of America, which are hereby designated the Depositary Governments.

3. This Convention shall enter into force thirty days following the date of the deposit of instruments of ratification by ten States signatory to this Convention which participated in The Hague Conference.

4. For other States, this Convention shall enter into force on the date of entry into force of this Convention in accordance with paragraph 3 of this Article, or thirty days following the date of deposit of their instruments of ratification or accession, whichever is later.

5. The Depositary Governments shall promptly inform all signatory and acceding States of the date of each signature, the date of deposit of each instrument of ratification or accession, the date of entry into force of this Convention, and other notices.

6. As soon as this Convention comes into force, it shall be registered by the Depositary Governments pursuant to Article 102 of the Charter of the United Nations and pursuant to Article 83 of the Convention on International Civil Aviation (Chicago, 1944).

Article 14

1. Any Contracting State may denounce this Convention by written notification to the Depositary Governments.

2. Denunciation shall take effect six months following the date on which notification is received by the Depositary Governments.

IN WITNESS WHEREOF the undersigned Plenipotentiaries, being duly authorised thereto by their Governments, have signed this Convention.

DONE at The Hague, this sixteenth day of December, one thousand nine hundred and seventy, in three originals, each being drawn up in four authentic texts in the English, French, Russian and Spanish languages.

Appendix 13

Protocol to Amend the Convention for the Unification of Certain Rules Relating to International Carriage by Air, Signed at Warsaw on 12 October 1929, as Amended by the Protocol Done at the Hague on 28 September 1955

Done at Guatemala City—March 8, 1971
Not in force
ICAO Doc. 8932, 10 I.L.M. 613

The Governments Undersigned,

Considering that it is desirable to amend the Convention for the Unification of Certain Rules Relating to International Carriage by Air signed at Warsaw on 12 October 1929 as amended by the Protocol done at The Hague on 28 September 1955,

Have Agreed as follows:

Chapter I
Amendments to the Convention

Article I

The Convention which the provisions of the present Chapter modify is the Warsaw Convention as amended at The Hague in 1955.

Article II

Article 3 of the Convention shall be deleted and replaced by the following:

"Article 3

1. In respect of the carriage of passengers an individual or collective document of carriage shall be delivered containing:

(a) an indication of the places of departure and destination;

(b) if the places of departure and destination are within the territory of a single High Contracting Party, one or more agreed stopping places being within the territory of another State, an indication of at least one such stopping place.

2. Any other means which would preserve a record of the information indicated in (a) and (b) of the foregoing paragraph may be substituted for the delivery of the document referred to in that paragraph.

3. Non-compliance with the provisions of the foregoing paragraphs shall not affect the existence or the validity of the contract of carriage, which shall, nonetheless, be subject to the rules of this Convention including those relating to limitation of liability."

Article III

Article 4 of the Convention shall be deleted and replaced by the following:

"Article 4

1. In respect of the carriage of checked baggage, a baggage check shall be delivered, which, unless combined with or incorporated in a document of carriage which complies with the provisions of Article 3, paragraph 1, shall contain:

(a) an indication of the places of departure and destination;

(b) if the places of departure and destination are within the territory of a single High Contracting Party, one or more agreed stopping places being within the territory of another State, an indication of at least one such stopping place.

2. Any other means which would preserve a record of the information indicated in (a) and (b) of the foregoing paragraph may be substituted for the delivery of the baggage check referred to in that paragraph.

3. Non-compliance with the provisions of the foregoing paragraphs shall not affect the existence or the validity of the contract of carriage, which shall, none the less, be subject to the rules of this Convention including those relating to limitation of liability."

Article IV

Article 17 of the Convention shall be deleted and replaced by the following:

"Article 17

1. The carrier is liable for damage sustained in case of death or personal injury of a passenger upon condition only that the event which caused the death or injury took place on board the aircraft or in the course of any of the operations of embarking or disembarking. However, the carrier is not liable if the death or injury resulted solely from the state of health of the passenger.

2. The carrier is liable for damage sustained in case of destruction or loss of, or of damage to, baggage upon condition only that the event which caused the destruction, loss or damage took place on board the aircraft or in the course of any of the operations of embarking or disembarking or during any period within which the baggage was in charge of the carrier. However, the carrier is not liable if the damage resulted solely from the inherent defect, quality or vice of the baggage.

3. Unless otherwise specified, in this Convention the term 'baggage' means both checked baggage and objects carried by the passenger."

Article V

In Article 18 of the Convention, paragraphs 1 and 2 shall be deleted and replaced by the following:

"1. The carrier is liable for damage sustained in the event of the destruction or loss of, or of damage to, any cargo, if the occurrence which caused the damage so sustained took place during the carriage by air.

2. The carriage by air within the meaning of the preceding paragraph comprises the period during which the cargo is in charge of the carrier, whether in an airport or on board an aircraft, or, in the case of a landing outside an airport, in any place whatsoever."

Article VI

Article 20 of the Convention shall be deleted and replaced by the following:

"Article 20

1. In the carriage of passengers and baggage the carrier shall not be liable for damage occasioned by delay if he proves that he and his servants and agents have taken all necessary measures to avoid the damage or that it was impossible for them to take such measures.

2. In the carriage of cargo the carrier shall not be liable for damage resulting from destruction, loss, damage or delay if he proves that he and his servants and agents have taken all necessary measures to avoid the damage or that it was impossible for them to take such measures."

Article VII

Article 21 of the Convention shall be deleted and replaced by the following:

"Article 21

If the carrier proves that the damage was caused or contributed to by the negligence or other wrongful act or omission of the person claiming compensation, the carrier shall be wholly or partly exonerated from his liability to such person to the extent that such negligence or wrongful act or omission caused or contributed to the damage. When by reason of the death or injury of a passenger compensation is claimed by a person other than the passenger, the carrier shall likewise be wholly or partly exonerated from his liability to the extent that he proves that the damage was caused or contributed to by the negligence or other wrongful act or omission of that passenger."

Article VIII

Article 22 of the Convention shall be deleted and replaced by the following:

"Article 22

1. (a) In the carriage of persons the liability of the carrier is limited to the sum of one million five hundred thousand francs for the aggregate of the claims, however founded, in respect of damage suffered as a result of the death or personal injury of each passenger. Where, in accordance with the law of the court seised of the case, damages may be awarded in the form of periodic payments, the equivalent capital value of the said payments shall not exceed one million five hundred thousand francs.

(b) In the case of delay in the carriage of persons the liability of the carrier for each passenger is limited to sixty-two thousand five hundred francs.

(c) In the carriage of baggage the liability of the carrier in the case of destruction, loss, damage or delay is limited to fifteen thousand francs for each passenger.

2. (a) In the carriage of cargo, the liability of the carrier is limited to a sum of two hundred and fifty francs per kilogramme, unless the consignor has made, at the time when the package was handed over to the carrier, a special declaration of interest in delivery at destination and has paid a supplementary sum if the case so requires. In that case the carrier will be liable to pay a sum not exceeding the declared sum, unless he proves that that sum is greater than the consignor's actual interest in delivery at destination.

(b) In the case of loss, damage or delay of part of the cargo, or of any object contained therein, the weight to be taken into consideration in determining the amount to which the carrier's liability is limited shall be only the total weight of the package or packages concerned. Nevertheless, when the loss, damage or delay of a part of the cargo, or of an object contained therein, affects the value of other packages covered by the same air waybill, the total weight of such package or packages shall also be taken into consideration in determining the limit of liability.

3. (a) The courts of the High Contracting Parties which are not authorized under their law to award the costs of the action, including lawyers' fees, shall, in actions to which this Convention applies, have the power to award, in their discretion, to the claimant the whole or part of the costs of the action, including lawyers' fees which the court considers reasonable.

(b) The costs of the action including lawyers' fees shall be awarded in accordance with subparagraph (a) only if the claimant gives a written notice to the carrier of the amount claimed including the particulars of the calculation of that amount and the carrier does not make, within a period of six months after his receipt of such notice, a written offer of settlement in an amount at least equal to the compensation awarded within the applicable limit. This period will be extended until the time of commencement of the action if that is later.

(c) The costs of the action including lawyers' fees shall not be taken into account in applying the limits under this Article.

4. The sums mentioned in francs in this Article and Article 42 shall be deemed to refer to a currency unit consisting of sixty-five and a half milligrammes of gold of millesimal fineness nine hundred. These sums may be converted into national currencies in round figures. Conversion of the sums into national currencies other than gold shall, in case of judicial proceedings, be made according to the gold value of such currencies at the date of the judgment."

Article IX

Article 24 of the Convention shall be deleted and replaced by the following:

"Article 24

1. In the carriage of cargo, any action for damages, however founded, can only be brought subject to the conditions and limits set out in this Convention.

2. In the carriage of passengers and baggage any action for damages, however founded, whether under this Convention or in contract or in tort or otherwise, can only be brought subject to the conditions and limits of liability set out in this Convention without prejudice to the question as to who are the persons who have the right to bring suit and what are their respective rights. Such limits of liability constitute maximum limits and may not be exceeded whatever the circumstances which gave rise to the liability."

Article X

Article 25 of the Convention shall be deleted and replaced by the following:

"Article 25

The limit of liability specified in paragraph 2 of Article 22 shall not apply if it is proved that the damage resulted from an act or omission of the carrier, his servants or agents, done with intent to cause damage or recklessly and with knowledge that damage would probably result; provided that, in the case of such act or omission of a servant or agent, it is also proved that he was acting within the scope of his employment."

Article XI

In Article 25A of the Convention, paragraphs 1 and 3 shall be deleted and replaced by the following:

"1. If an action is brought against a servant or agent of the carrier arising out of damage to which the Convention relates, such servant or agent, if he proves that he acted within the scope of his employment, shall be entitled to avail himself of the limits of liability which that carrier himself is entitled to invoke under this Convention.

3. The provisions of paragraphs 1 and 2 of this Article shall not apply to the carriage of cargo if it is proved that the damage resulted from an act or omission of the servant or agent done with intent to cause damage or recklessly and with knowledge that damage would probably result."

Article XII

In Article 28 of the Convention, the present paragraph 2 shall be renumbered as paragraph 3 and a new paragraph 2 shall be inserted as follows:

"2. In respect of damage resulting from the death, injury or delay of a passenger or the destruction, loss, damage or delay of baggage, the action may be brought before one of the Courts mentioned in paragraph 1 of this Article, or in the territory of one of the High Contracting Parties, before the Court within the jurisdiction of which the carrier has an establishment if the passenger has his domicile or permanent residence in the territory of the same High Contracting Party."

Article XIII

After Article 30 of the Convention, the following Article shall be inserted:

"Article 30A

Nothing in this Convention shall prejudice the question whether a person liable for damage in accordance with its provisions has a right of recourse against any other person."

Article XIV

After Article 35 of the Convention, the following Article shall be inserted:

"Article 35A

No provision contained in this Convention shall prevent a State from establishing and operating within its territory a system to supplement the compensation payable to claimants under the Convention in respect of death, or personal injury, of passengers. Such a system shall fulfil the following conditions:

(a) it shall not in any circumstances impose upon the carrier, his servants or agents, any liability in addition to that provided under this Convention;

(b) it shall not impose upon the carrier any financial or administrative burden other than collecting in that State contributions from passengers if required so to do;

(c) it shall not give rise to any discrimination between carriers with regard to the passengers concerned and the benefits available to the said passengers under the system shall be extended to them regardless of the carrier whose services they have used;

(d) if a passenger has contributed to the system, any person suffering damage as a consequence of death or personal injury of such passenger shall be entitled to the benefits of the system."

Article XV

After Article 41 of the Convention, the following Article shall be inserted:

"Article 42

1. Without prejudice to the provisions of Article 41, Conferences of the Parties to the Protocol done at Guatemala City on the eighth March 1971 shall be convened during the fifth and tenth years respectively after the date of entry into force of the said Protocol for the purpose of reviewing the limit established in Article 22, paragraph 1(a) of the Convention as amended by that Protocol.

2. At each of the Conferences mentioned in paragraph 1 of this Article the limit of liability in Article 22, paragraph 1(a) in force at the respective dates of these Conferences shall not be increased by an amount exceeding one hundred and eighty-seven thousand five hundred francs.

3. Subject to paragraph 2 of this Article, unless before the thirty-first December of the fifth and tenth years after the date of entry into force of the Protocol referred to in paragraph 1 of this Article the aforesaid Conferences decide otherwise by a two-thirds majority vote of the Parties present and voting, the limit of liability in Article 22, paragraph 1(a) in force at the respective dates of these Conferences shall on those dates be increased by one hundred and eighty-seven thousand five hundred francs.

4. The applicable limit shall be that which, in accordance with the preceding paragraphs, is in effect on the date of the event which caused the death or personal injury of the passenger."

Chapter II
Scope of Application of the Convention As Amended

Article XVI

The Warsaw Convention as amended at The Hague in 1955 and by this Protocol shall apply to international carriage as defined in Article 1 of the Convention, provided that the places of departure and destination referred to in that Article are situated either in the territories of two Parties to this Protocol or within the territory of a single Party to this Protocol with an agreed stopping place in the territory of another State.

Chapter III
Final Clauses

Article XVII

As between the Parties to this Protocol, the Warsaw Convention as amended at The Hague in 1955 and this Protocol shall be read and interpreted together as one single instrument and shall be known as the Warsaw Convention as amended at The Hague, 1955, and at Guatemala City, 1971.

Article XVIII

Until the date on which this Protocol enters into force in accordance with the provisions of Article XX, it shall remain open for signature by all States Members of the United Nations or of any of the Specialized Agencies or of the International Atomic Energy Agency or Parties to the Statute of the International Court of Justice, and by any other State invited by the General Assembly of the United Nations to become a Party to this Protocol.

Article XIX

1. This Protocol shall be subject to ratification by the signatory States.

2. Ratification of this Protocol by any State which is not a Party to the Warsaw Convention or by any State which is not a Party to the Warsaw Convention as amended at The Hague, 1955, shall have the effect of accession to the Warsaw Convention as amended at the Hague, 1955, and at Guatemala City, 1971.

3. The instruments of ratification shall be deposited with the International Civil Aviation Organization.

Article XX

1. This Protocol shall enter into force on the ninetieth day after the deposit of the thirtieth instrument of ratification on the condition, however, that the total international scheduled air traffic, expressed in passenger-kilometers, according to the statistics for the year 1970 published by the International Civil Aviation Organization, of the airlines of five States which have ratified this Protocol, represents at least 40% of the total international scheduled air traffic of the airlines of the member States of the International Civil Aviation Organization in that year. If, at the time of deposit of the thirtieth instrument of ratification, this condition has not been fulfilled, the Protocol shall not come into force until the ninetieth day after this condition shall have been satisfied. This Protocol shall come into force for each State ratifying after the deposit of the last instrument of ratification necessary for entry into force of this Protocol on the ninetieth day after the deposit of its instrument of ratification.

2. As soon as this Protocol comes into force it shall be registered with the United Nations by the International Civil Aviation Organization.

Article XXI

1. After the entry into force of this Protocol it shall be open for accession by any State referred to in Article XVIII.

2. Accession to this Protocol by any State which is not a Party to the Warsaw Convention or by any State which is not a Party to the Warsaw Convention as amended at The Hague, 1955, shall have the effect of accession to the Warsaw Convention as amended at The Hague, 1955, and at Guatemala City, 1971.

3. Accession shall be effected by the deposit of an instrument of accession with the International Civil Aviation Organization and shall take effect on the ninetieth day after the deposit.

Article XXII

1. Any Party to this Protocol may denounce the Protocol by notification addressed to the International Civil Aviation Organization.

2. Denunciation shall take effect six months after the date of receipt by the International Civil Aviation Organization of the notification of denunciation.

3. As between the Parties to this Protocol, denunciation by any of them of the Warsaw Convention in accordance with Article 39 thereof or of the Hague Protocol in accordance with Article XXIV thereof shall not be construed in any way as a denunciation of the Warsaw Convention as amended at The Hague, 1955, and at Guatemala City, 1971.

Article XXIII

1. Only the following reservations may be made to this Protocol:

(a) a State whose courts are not authorized under its law to award the costs of the action including lawyers' fees may at any time by a notification addressed to the International Civil Aviation Organization declare that Article 22, paragraph 3(a) shall not apply to its courts; and

(b) a State may at any time declare by a notification addressed to the International Civil Aviation Organization that the Warsaw Convention as amended at The Hague 1955, and at Guatemala City, 1971 shall not apply to the carriage of persons, baggage and cargo for its military authorities on aircraft, registered in that State, the whole capacity of which has been reserved by or on behalf of such authorities.

2. Any State having made a reservation in accordance with the preceding paragraph may at any time withdraw such reservation by notification to the International Civil Aviation Organization.

Article XXIV

The International Civil Aviation Organization shall promptly inform all signatory or acceding States of the date of each signature, the date of deposit of each instrument of ratification or accession, the date of entry into force of this Protocol, and other relevant information.

Article XXV

As between the Parties to this Protocol which are also Parties to the Convention, Supplementary to the Warsaw Convention, for the Unification of Certain Rules Relating to International Carriage by Air Performed by a Person Other than the Contracting Carrier, signed at Guadalajara on 18 September 1961 (hereinafter referred to as the "Guadalajara Convention") any reference to the "Warsaw Convention" contained in the Guadalajara Convention shall include reference to the Warsaw Convention as amended at The Hague, 1955, and at Guatemala City, 1971, in cases where the carriage under the agreement referred to in Article 1, paragraph (b) of the Guadalajara Convention is governed by this Protocol.

Article XXVI

This Protocol shall remain open, until 30 September 1971, for signature by any State referred to in Article XVIII, at the Ministry of External Relations of the Republic of Guatemala and thereafter, until it enters into force in accordance with Article XX, at the International Civil Aviation Organization. The Government of the Republic of Guatemala shall promptly inform the International Civil Aviation Organization of any signature and the date thereof during the time that the Protocol shall be open for signature in Guatemala.

IN WITNESS WHEREOF the undersigned Plenipotentiaries, having been duly authorized, have signed this Protocol.

DONE at Guatemala City on the eighth day of the month of March of the year One Thousand Nine Hundred and Seventy-one in three authentic texts in the English, French and Spanish languages. The International Civil Aviation Organization shall establish an authentic text of this Protocol in the Russian language. In the case of any inconsistency, the text in the French language, in which language the Warsaw Convention of 12 October 1929 was drawn up, shall prevail.

Appendix 14

Convention for the Suppression of Unlawful Acts Against the Safety of Civil Aviation

Done at Montreal—September 23, 1971
Entered into force—January 26, 1973
Effective in the United States—January 26, 1973
24 U.S.T. 564, T.I.A.S. No. 7570,
974 U.N.T.S. 177, ICAO Doc. 8966, 10 I.L.M. 1151

THE STATES PARTIES TO THIS CONVENTION,

CONSIDERING that unlawful acts against the safety of civil aviation jeopardize the safety of persons and property, seriously affect the operation of air services, and undermine the confidence of the peoples of the world in the safety of civil aviation;

CONSIDERING that the occurrence of such acts is a matter of grave concern;

CONSIDERING that, for the purpose of deterring such acts, there is an urgent need to provide appropriate measures for punishment of offenders;

HAVE AGREED AS FOLLOWS:

Article 1

1. Any person commits an offence if he unlawfully and intentionally:

(a) performs an act of violence against a person on board an aircraft in flight if that act is likely to endanger the safety of that aircraft; or

(b) destroys an aircraft in service or causes damage to such an aircraft which renders it incapable of flight or which is likely to endanger its safety in flight; or

(c) places or causes to be placed on an aircraft in service, by any means whatsoever, a device or substance which is likely to destroy that aircraft, or to cause damage to it which renders it incapable of flight, or to cause damage to it which is likely to endanger its safety in flight; or

(d) destroys or damages air navigation facilities or interferes with their operation, if any such act is likely to endanger the safety of aircraft in flight; or

(e) communicates information which he knows to be false, thereby endangering the safety of an aircraft in flight.

2. Any person also commits an offence if he:

(a) attempts to commit any of the offences mentioned in paragraph 1 of this Article; or

(b) is an accomplice of a person who commits or attempts to commit any such offence.

Article 2

For the purposes of this Convention:

(a) an aircraft is considered to be in flight at any time from the moment when all its external doors are closed following embarkation until the moment when any such door is opened for disembarkation; in the case of a forced landing, the flight shall be deemed to continue until the competent authorities take over the responsibility for the aircraft and for persons and property on board;

(b) an aircraft is considered to be in service from the beginning of the preflight preparation of the aircraft by ground personnel or by the crew for a specific flight until twenty-four hours after any landing; the period of service shall, in any event, extend for the entire period during which the aircraft is in flight as defined in paragraph (a) of this Article.

Article 3

Each Contracting State undertakes to make the offences mentioned in Article 1 punishable by severe penalties.

Article 4

1. This Convention shall not apply to aircraft used in military, customs or police services.

2. In the cases contemplated in subparagraphs (a), (b), (c) and (e) of paragraph 1 of Article 1, this Convention shall apply, irrespective of whether the aircraft is engaged in an international or domestic flight, only if:

(a) the place of take-off or landing, actual or intended, of the aircraft is situated outside the territory of the State of registration of that aircraft; or

(b) the offence is committed in the territory of a State other than the State of registration of the aircraft.

3. Notwithstanding paragraph 2 of this Article, in the cases contemplated in subparagraphs (a), (b), (c) and (e) of paragraph 1 of Article 1, this Convention shall also apply if the offender or the alleged offender is found in the territory of a State other than the State of registration of the aircraft.

4. With respect to the States mentioned in Article 9 and in the cases mentioned in subparagraphs (a), (b), (c) and (e) of paragraph 1 of Article 1, this Convention shall not apply if the places referred to in subparagraph (a) of paragraph 2 of this Article are situated within the territory of the same State where that State is one of those referred to in Article 9, unless the offence is committed or the offender or alleged offender is found in the territory of a State other than that State.

5. In the cases contemplated in subparagraph (d) of paragraph 1 of Article 1, this Convention shall apply only if the air navigation facilities are used in international air navigation.

6. The provisions of paragraphs 2, 3, 4 and 5 of this Article shall also apply in the cases contemplated in paragraph 2 of Article 1.

Article 5

1. Each Contracting State shall take such measures as may be necessary to establish its jurisdiction over the offences in the following cases:

(a) when the offence is committed in the territory of that State;

(b) when the offence is committed against or on board an aircraft registered in that State;

(c) when the aircraft on board which the offence is committed lands in its territory with the alleged offender still on board;

(d) when the offence is committed against or on board an aircraft leased without crew to a lessee who has his principal place of business or, if the lessee has no such place of business, his permanent residence, in that State.

2. Each Contracting State shall likewise take such measures as may be necessary to establish its jurisdiction over the offences mentioned in Article 1, paragraph 1 (a), (b) and (c), and in Article 1, paragraph 2, in so far as that paragraph relates to those offences, in the case where the alleged offender is present in its territory and it does not extradite him pursuant to Article 8 to any of the States mentioned in paragraph 1 of this Article.

3. This Convention does not exclude any criminal jurisdiction exercised in accordance with national law.

Article 6

1. Upon being satisfied that the circumstances so warrant, any Contracting State in the territory of which the offender or the alleged offender is present, shall take him into custody or take other measures to ensure his presence. The custody and other measures shall be as provided in the law of that State but may only be continued for such time as is necessary to enable any criminal or extradition proceedings to be instituted.

2. Such State shall immediately make a preliminary enquiry into the facts.

3. Any person in custody pursuant to paragraph 1 of this Article shall be assisted in communicating immediately with the nearest appropriate representative of the State of which he is a national.

4. When a State, pursuant to this Article, has taken a person into custody, it shall immediately notify the States mentioned in Article 5, paragraph 1, the State of nationality of the detained person and, if it considers it advisable, any other interested States of the fact that such person is in custody and of the circumstances which warrant his detention. The State which makes the preliminary enquiry contemplated in paragraph 2 of this Article shall promptly report its findings to the said States and shall indicate whether it intends to exercise jurisdiction.

Article 7

The Contracting State in the territory of which the alleged offender is found shall, if it does not extradite him, be obliged, without exception whatsoever and whether or not the offence was committed in its territory, to submit the case to its competent authorities for the purpose of prosecution. Those authorities shall take their decision in the same manner as in the case of any ordinary offence of a serious nature under the law of that State.

Article 8

1. The offences shall be deemed to be included as extraditable offences in any extradition treaty existing between Contracting States. Contracting States undertake to include the offences as extraditable offences in every extradition treaty to be concluded between them.

2. If a Contracting State which makes extradition conditional on the existence of a treaty receives a request for extradition from another Contracting State with which it has no extradition treaty, it may at its option consider this Convention as the legal basis for extradition in respect of the offences. Extradition shall be subject to the other conditions provided by the law of the requested State.

3. Contracting States which do not make extradition conditional on the existence of a treaty shall recognize the offences as extraditable offences between themselves subject to the conditions provided by the law of the requested State.

4. Each of the offences shall be treated, for the purpose of extradition between Contracting States, as if it had been committed not only in the place in which it occurred but also in the territories of the States required to establish their jurisdiction in accordance with Article 5, paragraph 1 (b), (c) and (d).

Article 9

The Contracting States which establish joint air transport operating organizations or international operating agencies, which operate aircraft which are subject to joint or international registration shall, by appropriate means, designate for each aircraft the State among them which shall exercise the jurisdiction and have the attributes of the State of registration for the purpose of this Convention and shall give notice thereof to the International Civil Aviation Organization which shall communicate the notice to all States Parties to this Convention.

Article 10

1. Contracting States shall, in accordance with international and national law, endeavour to take all practicable measures for the purpose of preventing the offences mentioned in Article 1.

2. When, due to the commission of one of the offences mentioned in Article 1, a flight has been delayed or interrupted, any Contracting State in whose territory the aircraft or passengers or crew are present shall facilitate the continuation of the journey of the passengers and crew as soon as practicable, and shall without delay return the aircraft and its cargo to the persons lawfully entitled to possession.

Article 11

1. Contracting States shall afford one another the greatest measure of assistance in connection with criminal proceedings brought in respect of the offences. The law of the State requested shall apply in all cases.

2. The provisions of paragraph 1 of this Article shall not affect obligations under any other treaty, bilateral or multilateral, which governs or will govern, in whole or in part, mutual assistance in criminal matters.

Article 12

Any Contracting State having reason to believe that one of the offences mentioned in Article 1 will be committed shall, in accordance with its national law, furnish any relevant information in its possession to those States which it believes would be the States mentioned in Article 5, paragraph 1.

Article 13

Each Contracting State shall in accordance with its national law report to the Council of the International Civil Aviation Organization as promptly as possible any relevant information in its possession concerning:

(a) the circumstances of the offence;

(b) the action taken pursuant to Article 10, paragraph 2;

(c) the measures taken in relation to the offender or the alleged offender and, in particular, the results of any extradition proceedings or other legal proceedings.

Article 14

1. Any dispute between two or more Contracting States concerning the interpretation or application of this Convention which cannot be settled through negotiation, shall, at the request of one of them, be submitted to arbitration. If within six months from the date of the request for arbitration the Parties are unable to agree on the organization of the arbitration, any one of those Parties may refer the dispute to the International Court of Justice by request in conformity with the Statute of the Court.

2. Each State may at the time of signature or ratification of this Convention or accession thereto, declare that it does not consider itself bound by the preceding paragraph. The other Contracting States shall not be bound by the preceding paragraph with respect to any Contracting State having made such a reservation.

3. Any Contracting State having made a reservation in accordance with the preceding paragraph may at any time withdraw this reservation by notification to the Depositary Governments.

Article 15

1. This Convention shall be open for signature at Montreal on 23 September 1971, by States participating in the International Conference on Air Law held at Montreal from 8 to 23 September 1971 (hereinafter referred to as the Montreal Conference). After 10 October 1971, the Convention shall be open to all States for signature in Moscow, London and Washington. Any State which does not sign this Convention before its entry into force in accordance with paragraph 3 of this Article may accede to it at any time.

2. This Convention shall be subject to ratification by the signatory States. Instruments of ratification and instruments of accession shall be deposited with the Governments of the Union of Soviet Socialist Republics, the United Kingdom of Great Britain and Northern Ireland, and the United States of America, which are hereby designated the Depositary Governments.

3. This Convention shall enter into force thirty days following the date of the deposit of instruments of ratification by ten States signatory to this Convention which participated in the Montreal Conference.

4. For other States, this Convention shall enter into force on the date of entry into force of this Convention in accordance with paragraph 3 of this Article, or thirty days following the date of deposit of their instruments of ratification or accession, whichever is later.

5. The Depositary Governments shall promptly inform all signatory and acceding States of the date of each signature, the date of deposit of each instrument of ratification or accession, the date of entry into force of this Convention, and other notices.

6. As soon as this Convention comes into force, it shall be registered by the Depositary Governments pursuant to Article 102 of the Charter of the United Nations and pursuant to Article 83 of the Convention on International Civil Aviation (Chicago, 1944).

Article 16

1. Any Contracting State may denounce this Convention by written notification to the Depositary Governments.

2. Denunciation shall take effect six months following the date on which notification is received by the Depositary Governments.

IN WITNESS WHEREOF the undersigned Plenipotentiaries, being duly authorized thereto by their Governments, have signed this Convention.

DONE at Montreal, this twenty-third day of September, one thousand nine hundred and seventy-one, in three originals, each being drawn up in four authentic texts in the English, French, Russian and Spanish languages.

Appendix 15

Additional Protocol No. 4 to the Convention for the Unification of Certain Rules Relating to International Carriage by Air Signed at Warsaw on October 12, 1929, as Amended by the Protocol Done at the Hague on September 28, 1955

Done at Montreal—September 25, 1975
Entered into force—June 14, 1998
Effective in the United States—March 4, 1999
2145 U.N.T.S. 31, ICAO Doc. 9148

The Governments Undersigned considering that it is desirable to amend the Convention for the Unification of Certain Rules Relating to International Carriage by Air signed at Warsaw on 12 October 1929 as amended by the Protocol done at The Hague on 28 September 1955,

Have agreed as follows:

CHAPTER I
AMENDMENTS TO THE CONVENTION

Article I

The Convention which the provisions of the present Chapter modify is the Warsaw Convention as amended at The Hague in 1955.

Article II

In Article 2 of the Convention—

paragraph 2 shall be deleted and replaced by the following:

"2. In the carriage or postal items the carrier shall be liable only to the relevant postal administration in accordance with the rules applicable to the relationship between the carriers and the postal administrations.

3. Except as provided in paragraph 2 of this Article, the provisions of this Convention shall not apply to the carriage of postal items."

Article III

In Chapter II of the Convention—

Section III (Articles 5 to 16) shall be deleted and replaced by the following:

"Section III.—Documentation relating to cargo

Article 5

1. In respect of the carriage of cargo an air waybill shall be delivered.

2. Any other means which would preserve a record of the carriage to be performed may, with the consent of the consignor, be substituted for the delivery of an air waybill. If such other means are used, the carrier shall, if so requested by the consignor, deliver

to the consignor a receipt for the cargo permitting identification of the consignment and access to the information contained in the record preserved by such other means.

3. The impossibility of using, at points of transit and destination, the other means which would preserve the record of the carriage referred to in paragraph 2 of this Article does not entitle the carrier to refuse to accept the cargo for carriage.

Article 6

1. The air waybill shall be made out by the consignor in three original parts.

2. The first part shall be marked "for the carrier"; it shall be signed by the consignor. The second part shall be marked "for the consignee"; it shall be signed by the consignor and by the carrier. The third part shall be signed by the carrier and handed by him to the consignor after the cargo has been accepted.

3. The signature of the carrier and that of the consignor may be printed or stamped.

4. If, at the request of the consignor, the carrier makes out the air waybill, he shall be deemed, subject to proof to the contrary, to have done so on behalf of the consignor.

Article 7

When there is more than one package:

a. the carrier of cargo has the right to require the consignor to make out separate air waybills;

b. the consignor has the right to require the carrier to deliver separate receipts when the other means referred to in paragraph 2 of Article 5 are used.

Article 8

The air waybill and the receipt for the cargo shall contain:

a. an indication of the places of departure and destination;

b. if the places of departure and destination are within the territory of a single High Contracting Party, one or more agreed stopping places being within the territory of another State, an indication of at least one such stopping place; and

c. an indication of the weight of the consignment.

Article 9

Non-compliance with the provisions of Articles 5 to 8 shall not affect the existence or the validity of the contract of carriage, which shall, nonetheless, be subject to the rules of this Convention including those relating to limitation of liability.

Article 10

1. The consignor is responsible for the correctness of the particulars and statements relating to the cargo inserted by him or on his behalf in the air waybill or furnished by him or on his behalf to the carrier for insertion in the receipt for the cargo or for insertion in the record preserved by the other means referred to in paragraph 2 of Article 5.

2. The consignor shall indemnify the carrier against all damage suffered by him, or by any other person to whom the carrier is liable, by reason of the irregularity, incorrectness or incompleteness of the particulars and statements furnished by the consignor or on his behalf.

3. Subject to the provisions of paragraphs 1 and 2 of this Article, the carrier shall indemnify the consignor against all damage suffered by him, or by any other person to whom the consignor is liable, by reason of the irregularity, incorrectness or incomplete-

ness of the particulars and statements inserted by the carrier or on his behalf in the receipt for the cargo or in the record preserved by the other means referred to in paragraph 2 of Article 5.

Article 11

1. The air waybill or the receipt for the cargo is prima facie evidence of the conclusion of the contract, of the acceptance of the cargo and of the conditions of carriage mentioned therein.

2. Any statements in the air waybill or the receipt for the cargo relating to the weight, dimensions and packing of the cargo, as well as those relating to the number of packages, are prima facie evidence of the facts stated; those relating to the quantity, volume and condition of the cargo do not constitute evidence against the carrier except so far as they both have been, and are stated in the air waybill to have been, checked by him in the presence of the consignor, or relate to the apparent condition of the cargo.

Article 12

1. Subject to his liability to carry out all his obligations under the contract of carriage, the consignor has the right to dispose of the cargo by withdrawing it at the airport of departure or destination, or by stopping it in the course of the journey on any landing, or by calling for it to be delivered at the place of destination or in the course of the journey to a person other than the consignee originally designated, or by requiring it to be returned to the airport of departure. He must not exercise this right of disposition in such a way as to prejudice the carrier or other consignors and he must repay any expenses occasioned by the exercise of this right.

2. If it is impossible to carry out the orders of the consignor the carrier must so inform him forthwith.

3. If the carrier obeys the orders of the consignor for the disposition of the cargo without requiring the production of the part of the air waybill or the receipt for the cargo delivered to the latter, he will be liable, without prejudice to his right of recovery from the consignor, for any damage which may be caused thereby to any person who is lawfully in possession of that part of the air waybill or the receipt for the cargo.

4. The right conferred on the consignor ceases at the moment when that of the consignee begins in accordance with Article 13. Nevertheless, if the consignee declines to accept the cargo, or if he cannot be communicated with, the consignor resumes his right of disposition.

Article 13

1. Except when the consignor has exercised his right under Article 12, the consignee is entitled, on arrival of the cargo at the place of destination, to require the carrier to deliver the cargo to him, on payment of the charges due and on complying with the conditions of carriage.

2. Unless it is otherwise agreed, it is the duty of the carrier to give notice to the consignee as soon as the cargo arrives.

3. If the carrier admits the loss of the cargo, or if the cargo has not arrived at the expiration of seven days after the date on which it ought to have arrived, the consignee is entitled to enforce against the carrier the rights which flow from the contract of carriage.

Article 14

The consignor and the consignee can respectively enforce all the rights given them by Articles 12 and 13, each in his own name, whether he is acting in his own interest or in the interest of another, provided that he carries out the obligations imposed by the contract of carriage.

Article 15

1. Articles 12, 13 and 14 do not affect either the relations of the consignor and the consignee with each other or the mutual relations of third parties whose rights are derived either from the consignor or from the consignee.

2. The provisions of Articles 12, 13 and 14 can only be varied by express provision in the air waybill or the receipt for the cargo.

Article 16

1. The consignor must furnish such information and such documents as are necessary to meet the formalities of customs, octroi or police before the cargo can be delivered to the consignee. The consignor is liable to the carrier for any damage occasioned by the absence, insufficiency or irregularity of any such information or documents, unless the damage is due to the fault of the carrier, his servants or agents.

2. The carrier is under no obligation to enquire into the correctness or sufficiency of such information or documents."

Article IV

Article 18 of the Convention shall be deleted and replaced by the following:

"Article 18

1. The carrier is liable for damage sustained in the event of the destruction or loss of, or damage to, any registered baggage, if the occurrence which caused the damage so sustained took place during the carriage by air.

2. The carrier is liable for damage sustained in the event of the destruction or loss of, or damage to, cargo upon condition only that the occurrence which caused the damage so sustained took place during the carriage by air.

3. However, the carrier is not liable if he proves that the destruction, loss of, or damage to, the cargo resulted solely from one or more of the following:

a. inherent defect, quality or vice of that cargo;

b. defective packing of that cargo performed by a person other than the carrier or his servants or agents;

c. an act of war or an armed conflict;

d. an act of public authority carried out in connexion with the entry, exit or transit of the cargo.

4. The carriage by air within the meaning of the preceding paragraphs of this Article comprises the period during which the baggage or cargo is in the charge of the carrier, whether in an airport or on board an aircraft, or, in the case of a landing outside an airport, in any place whatsoever.

5. The period of the carriage by air does not extend to any carriage by land, by sea or by river performed outside an airport. If, however, such carriage takes place in the performance of a contract for carriage by air, for the purpose of loading, delivery or transhipment, any damage is presumed, subject to proof to the contrary, to have been the result of an event which took place during the carriage by air."

Article V

Article 20 of the Convention shall be deleted and replaced by the following:

"Article 20

In the carriage of passengers and baggage, and in the case of damage occasioned by delay in the carriage of cargo, the carrier shall not be liable if he proves that he and his servants and agents have taken all necessary measures to avoid the damage or that it was impossible for them to take such measures."

Article VI

Article 21 of the Convention shall be deleted and replaced by the following:

"Article 21

1. In the carriage of passengers and baggage, if the carrier proves that the damage was caused by or contributed to by the negligence of the person suffering the damage the Court may, in accordance with the provisions of its own law, exonerate the carrier wholly or partly from his liability.

2. In the carriage of cargo, if the carrier proves that the damage was caused by or contributed to by the negligence or other wrongful act or omission of the person claiming compensation, or the person from whom he derives his rights, the carrier shall be wholly or partly exonerated from his liability to the claimant to the extent that such negligence or wrongful act or omission caused or contributed to the damage."

Article VII

In Article 22 of the Convention—

a. in paragraph 2(a) the words "and of cargo" shall be deleted.

b. after paragraph 2(a) the following paragraph shall be inserted:

"(b) In the carriage of cargo, the liability of the carrier is limited to a sum of 17 Special Drawing Rights per kilogramme, unless the consignor has made, at the time when the package was handed over to the carrier, a special declaration of interest in delivery at destination and has paid a supplementary sum if the case so requires. In that case the carrier will be liable to pay a sum not exceeding the declared sum, unless he proves that the sum is greater than the consignor's actual interest in delivery at destination."

c. paragraph 2(b) shall be designated as paragraph 2(c).

d. after paragraph 5 the following paragraph shall be inserted:

"6. The sums mentioned in terms of the Special Drawing Right in this Article shall be deemed to refer to the Special Drawing Right as defined by the International Monetary Fund. Conversion of the sums into national currencies shall, in case of judicial proceedings, be made according to the value of such currencies in terms of the Special Drawing Right at the date of the judgment. The value of a national currency, in terms of the Special Drawing Right, of a High Contracting Party which is a Member of the International Monetary Fund, shall be calculated in accordance with the method of valuation applied by the International Monetary Fund, in effect at the date of the judgment, for its operations and transactions. The value of a national currency, in terms of the Special Drawing Right, of a High Contracting Party which is not a Member of the International Monetary Fund, shall be calculated in a manner determined by that High Contracting Party.

Nevertheless, those States which are not Members of the International Monetary Fund and whose law does not permit the application of the provisions of paragraph 2(b) of Article 22 may, at the time of ratification or accession or at any time thereafter, declare that the limit of liability of the carrier in judicial proceedings in their territories is fixed at a sum of two hundred and fifty monetary units per kilogramme. This monetary unit corresponds to sixty-five and a half milligrammes of gold of millesimal fineness nine hundred. This sum may be converted into the national currency concerned in round figures. The conversion of this sum into the national currency shall be made according to the law of the State concerned."

Article VIII

Article 24 of the Convention shall be deleted and replaced by the following:

"Article 24

1. In the carriage of passengers and baggage, any action for damages, however founded, can only be brought subject to the conditions and limits set out in this Convention, without prejudice to the question as to who are the persons who have the right to bring suit and what are their respective rights.

2. In the carriage of cargo, any action for damages, however, founded whether under this Convention or in contract or in tort or otherwise, can only be brought subject to the conditions and limits of liability set out in this Convention without prejudice to the question as to who are the persons who have the right to bring suit and what are their respective rights. Such limits of liability constitute maximum limits and may not be exceeded whatever the circumstances which gave rise to the liability."

Article IX

Article 25 of the Convention shall be deleted and replaced by the following:

"Article 25

In the carriage of passengers and baggage, the limits of liability specified in Article 22 shall not apply if it is proved that the damage resulted from an act or omission of the carrier, his servants or agents, done with intent to cause damage or recklessly and with knowledge that damage would probably result; provided that, in the case of such act or omission of a servant or agent, it is also proved that he was acting within the scope of his employment."

Article X

In Article 25 A of the Convention—

paragraph 3 shall be deleted and replaced by the following:

"3. In the carriage of passengers and baggage, the provisions of paragraphs 1 and 2 of this Article shall not apply if it is proved that the damage resulted from an act or omission of the servant or agent done with intent to cause damage or recklessly and with knowledge that damage would probably result."

Article XI

After Article 30 of the Convention, the following Article shall be inserted:

"Article 30A

Nothing in this Convention shall prejudice the question whether a person liable for damage in accordance with its provisions has a right of recourse against any other person."

Article XII

Article 33 of the Convention shall be deleted and replaced by the following:

"Article 33

Except as provided in paragraph 3 of Article 5, nothing in this Convention shall prevent the carrier either from refusing to enter into any contract of carriage or from making regulations which do not conflict with the provisions of this Convention."

Article XIII

Article 34 of the Convention shall be deleted and replaced by the following:

"Article 34

The provisions of Articles 3 to 8 inclusive relating to documents of carriage shall not apply in the case of carriage performed in extraordinary circumstances outside the normal scope of an air carrier's business."

CHAPTER II
SCOPE OF APPLICATION OF THE CONVENTION AS AMENDED

Article XIV

The Warsaw Convention as amended at The Hague in 1955 and by this Protocol shall apply to international carriage as defined in Article 1 of the Convention, provided that the places of departure and destination referred to in that Article are situated either in the territories of two Parties to this Protocol or within the territory of a single Party to this Protocol with an agreed stopping place in the territory of another State.

CHAPTER III
FINAL CLAUSES

Article XV

As between the Parties to this Protocol, the Warsaw Convention as amended at The Hague in 1955 and this Protocol shall be read and interpreted together as one single instrument and shall be known as the Warsaw Convention as amended at The Hague, 1955, and by Protocol No. 4 of Montreal, 1975.

Article XVI

Until the date on which this Protocol comes into force in accordance with the provisions of Article XVIII, it shall remain open for signature by any State.

Article XVII

1. This Protocol shall be subject to ratification by the signatory States.

2. Ratification of this Protocol by any State which is not a Party to the Warsaw Convention or by any State which is not a Party to the Warsaw Convention as amended at The Hague, 1955, shall have the effect of accession to the Warsaw Convention as amended at The Hague, 1955, and by Protocol No. 4 of Montreal, 1975.

3. The instruments of ratification shall be deposited with the Government of the Polish People's Republic.

Article XVIII

1. As soon as thirty signatory States have deposited their instruments of ratification of this Protocol, it shall come into force between them on the ninetieth day after the deposit of the thirtieth instrument of ratification. It shall come into force for each State ratifying thereafter on the ninetieth day after the deposit of its instrument of ratification.

2. As soon as this Protocol comes into force it shall be registered with the United Nations by the Government of the Polish People's Republic.

Article XIX

1. This Protocol, after it has come into force, shall be open for accession by any non-signatory State.

2. Accession to this Protocol by any State which is not a Party to the Warsaw Convention or by any State which is not a Party to the Warsaw Convention is amended at The Hague, 1955, shall have the effect of accession to the Warsaw Convention as amended at The Hague, 1955, and by Protocol No. 4 of Montreal, 1975.

3. Accession shall be effected by the deposit of an instrument of accession with the Government of the Polish People's Republic and shall take effect on the ninetieth day after the deposit.

Article XX

1. Any Party to this Protocol may denounce the Protocol by notification addressed to the Government of the Polish People's Republic.

2. Denunciation shall take effect six months after the date of receipt by the Government of the Polish People's Republic of the notification of denunciation.

3. As between the Parties to this Protocol, denunciation by any of them of the Warsaw Convention in accordance with Article 39 thereof or of The Hague Protocol in accordance with Article XXIV thereof shall not be construed in any way as a denunciation of the Warsaw Convention as amended at The Hague, 1955, and by Protocol No. 4 of Montreal, 1975.

Article XXI

1. Only the following reservations may be made to this Protocol:

a. a State may at any time declare by a notification addressed to the Government of the Polish People's Republic that the Warsaw Convention as amended at The Hague, 1955, and by Protocol No. 4 of Montreal, 1975, shall not apply to the carriage of persons, baggage and cargo for its military authorities on aircraft, registered in that State, the whole capacity of which has been reserved by or on behalf of such authorities; and

b. any State may declare at the time of ratification of or accession to the Additional Protocol No. 3 of Montreal, 1975, or at any time thereafter, that it is not bound by the provisions of the Warsaw Convention as amended at The Hague, 1955, and by Protocol No. 4 of Montreal, 1975, in so far as they relate to the carriage of passengers and baggage. Such declaration shall have effect ninety days after the date of receipt of the declaration by the Government of the Polish People's Republic.

2. Any State having made a reservation in accordance with the preceding paragraph may at any time withdraw such reservation by notification to the Government of the Polish People's Republic.

Article XXII

The Government of the Polish People's Republic shall promptly inform all States Parties to the Warsaw Convention or to that Convention as amended, all signatory or acceding States to the present Protocol, as well as the International Civil Aviation Organization, of the date of each signature, the date of deposit of each instrument of ratification or accession, the date of coming into force of this Protocol, and other relevant information.

Article XXIII

As between the Parties to this Protocol which are also Parties to the Convention, Supplementary to the Warsaw Convention, for the Unification of Certain Rules Relating to International Carriage by Air Performed by a Person Other than the Contracting Carrier, signed at Guadalajara on 18 September 1961 (hereinafter referred to as the "Guadalajara Convention") any reference to the "Warsaw Convention" contained in the Guadalajara Convention shall include reference to the Warsaw Convention as amended at The Hague, 1955, and by Protocol No. 4 of Montreal, 1975, in cases where the carriage under the agreement referred to in Article 1, paragraph (b) of the Guadalajara Convention is governed by this Protocol.

Article XXIV

If two or more States are Parties both to this Protocol and to the Guatemala City Protocol, 1971, or to the Additional Protocol No. 3 of Montreal, 1975, the following rules shall apply between them:

a. the provisions resulting from the system established by this Protocol, concerning cargo and postal items, shall prevail over the provisions resulting from the system established by the Guatemala City Protocol, 1971, or by the Additional Protocol No. 3 of Montreal, 1975;

b. the provisions resulting from the system established by the Guatemala City Protocol, 1971, or by the Additional Protocol No. 3 of Montreal, 1975, concerning passengers and baggage, shall prevail over the provisions resulting from the system established by this Protocol.

Article XXV

This Protocol shall remain open for signature until 1 January 1976 at the Headquarters of the International Civil Aviation Organization and thereafter until it comes into force in accordance with Article XVIII at the Ministry for Foreign Affairs of the Polish People's Republic. The International Civil Aviation Organization shall promptly inform the Government of the Polish People's Republic of any signature and the date thereof during the time that the Protocol shall be open for signature at the Headquarters of the International Civil Aviation Organization.

In witness whereof the undersigned Plenipotentiaries, having been duly authorized, have signed this Protocol.

Done at Montreal on the twenty-fifth day of September of the year One Thousand Nine Hundred and Seventy-five in four authentic texts in the English, French, Russian and Spanish languages. In the case of any inconsistency, the text in the French language, in which language the Warsaw Convention of 12 October 1929 was drawn up, shall prevail.

Appendix 16

Agreement Between the Government of the United States of America and the Government of the United Kingdom of Great Britain and Northern Ireland Concerning Air Services

Done at Bermuda—July 23, 1977
Entered into force—July 23, 1977
Effective in the United States—July 23, 1977
28 U.S.T. 5367, T.I.A.S. No. 8641

The Government of the United States of America and the Government of the United Kingdom of Great Britain and Northern Ireland;

Resolved to provide safe, adequate and efficient international air transportation responsive to the present and future needs of the public and to the continued development of international commerce;

Desiring the continuing growth of adequate, economical and efficient air transportation by airlines at reasonable charges, without unjust discrimination or unfair or destructive competitive practices;

Resolved to provide a fair and equal opportunity for their designated airlines to compete in the provision of international air services;

Desiring to ensure the highest degree of safety and security in international air transportation;

Seeking to encourage the efficient use of available resources, including petroleum, and to minimize the impact of air services on the environment;

Believing that both scheduled and charter air transportation are important to the consumer interest and are essential elements of a healthy international air transport system;

Reaffirming their adherence to the Convention on International Civil Aviation opened for signature at Chicago on 7 December 1944; and

Desiring to conclude a new agreement complementary to that Convention for the purpose of replacing the Final Act of the Civil Aviation Conference held at Bermuda, from 15 January to 11 February 1946, and the annexed Agreement between the Government of the United States of America and the Government of the United Kingdom relating to Air Services between their Respective Territories, as subsequently amended ("the 1946 Bermuda Agreement");

Have agreed as follows:

ARTICLE 1
Definitions

For the purposes of this Agreement unless otherwise stated, the term:

(a) "Aeronautical authorities" means, in the case of the United States, the Department of Transportation, the Civil Aeronautics Board, or their successor agencies; and in the case of the United Kingdom, the Secretary of State for Trade, the Civil Aviation Authority, or their successors;

(b) "Agreement" means this Agreement, its Annexes, and any amendments thereto;

(c) "Air service" means scheduled air service or charter air service or both, as the context requires, performed by aircraft for the public transport of passengers, cargo or mail, separately or in combination, for compensation;

(d) "Airport" means a landing area, terminals and related facilities used by aircraft;

(e) "All-cargo air service" means air service performed by aircraft on which cargo or mail (with ancillary attendants) is carried, separately or in combination but on which revenue passengers are not carried;

(f) "Combination air service" means air service performed by aircraft on which passengers are carried and on which cargo or mail may also be carried if authorized by the relevant national license or certificate;

(g) "Convention" means the Convention on International Civil Aviation, opened for signature at Chicago on 7 December 1944, and includes: (i) any amendment thereto which has entered into force under Article 94(a) thereof and has been ratified by both Contracting Parties; and (ii) any Annex or any amendment thereto adopted under Article 90 of that Convention, insofar as such amendment or Annex is at any given time effective for both Contracting Parties;

(h) "Designated airline" means an airline designated and authorized in accordance with Article 3 of this Agreement;

(i) "Gateway route segment" means that part of a route described in Annex 1 which lies between the point of last departure or first arrival served by a designated airline in its homeland and the point or points served by that airline in the territory of the other Contracting Party;

(j) "International air service" means an air service which passes through the air space over the territory of more than one State;

(k) "Revenue passenger" means a passenger paying 25 percent or more of the normal applicable fare;

(l) "Stop for non-traffic purposes" means a landing for any purpose other than taking on or discharging passengers, cargo or mail carried for compensation;

(m) "Tariff" means the price to be charged for the public transport of passengers, baggage and cargo (excluding mail) on scheduled air services including the conditions governing the availability or applicability of such price and the charges and conditions for services ancillary to such transport but excluding the commissions to be paid to air transportation intermediaries;

(n) "Territory" means the land areas under the sovereignty, jurisdiction, protection, or trusteeship of a Contracting Party, and the territorial waters adjacent thereto; and

(o) "User charge" means a charge made to airlines for the provision for aircraft, their crews and passengers of airport or air navigation property or facilities, including related services and facilities.

ARTICLE 2
Grant of Rights

(1) Each Contracting Party grants to the other Contracting Party the following rights for the conduct of international air services by its airlines:

(a) the right to fly across its territory without landing; and

(b) the right to make stops in its territory for non-traffic purposes.

(2) Each Contracting Party grants to the other Contracting Party the rights specified in this Agreement for the purposes of operating scheduled international air services on the routes specified in Annex 1. Such services and routes are hereafter called "the agreed services" and "the specified routes" respectively. The airlines designated by each Contracting Party may make stops in the territory of the other Contracting Party at the points specified and to the extent specified for each route in Annex 1 for the purpose of taking on board and discharging passengers, cargo or mail, separately or in combination, in scheduled international air service.

(3) Each Contracting Party grants to the other Contracting Party the rights specified in Annex 4 for the purposes of operating charter international air services.

(4) Nothing in paragraphs (2) or (3) of this Article shall be deemed to confer on the airline or airlines of one Contracting Party the rights to take on board, in the territory of the other Contracting Party, passengers, cargo or mail carried for compensation and destined for another point in the territory of that other Contracting Party except to the extent such rights are authorized in Annex 1 or Annex 4.

(5) If because of armed conflict, political disturbances or developments, or special and unusual circumstances, a designated airline of one Contracting Party is unable to operate a service on its normal routing, the other Contracting Party shall use its best efforts to facilitate the continued operation of such service through appropriate rearrangements of such routes, including the grant of rights for such time as may be necessary to facilitate viable operations.

ARTICLE 3
Designation and Authorization of Airlines

(1)(a) Each Contracting Party shall have the right to designate an airline or airlines for the purpose of operating the agreed services on each of the routes specified in Annex 1 and to withdraw or alter such designations. Such designations shall be made in writing and shall be transmitted to the other Contracting Party through diplomatic channels.

(b) A Contracting Party may request consultations with regard to the designation of an airline or airlines under subparagraph (a) of this paragraph. If, however, agreement is not reached within 60 days from the date of the designation, the designation shall be regarded as a proper designation under this Article.

(2) Notwithstanding paragraph (1) of this Article, for the purpose of operating the agreed combination air services on US Routes 1 and 2, and UK Routes 1, 2, 3, 4 and 5, each Contracting Party shall have the right to designate not more than:

(a) two airlines on each of two gateway route segments of its own choosing;

(b) one airline on each gateway route segment other than those selected under subparagraph (a) of this paragraph, except that each Contacting Party may designate not more than:

(i) two airlines on any gateway route segment other than those selected under subparagraph (a) of this paragraph, provided: (A) the total on-board passenger traffic carried by the designated airlines of both Contracting Parties in scheduled air service on a gateway route segment exceeds 600,000 one-way revenue passengers in each of two consecutive twelve month periods; or (B) the total on-board passenger traffic carried by its designated airline in scheduled air service on the gateway route segment exceeds

450,000 one-way revenue passengers in each of two consecutive twelve month periods. For the purpose of this subparagraph, the revenue passenger levels specified must be reached for the first time after the entry into force of this Agreement; and

(ii) two airlines on any gateway route segment other than those selected under subparagraph (a) or permitted under subparagraph (b)(i) of this paragraph, where either the other Contracting Party has not made a designation three years after the right to operate that gateway route segment becomes effective or the airline designated by it does not by then operate (either nonstop or in combination with another gateway route segment) or operates fewer than 100 round trip combination flights within a twelve month period. An additional designation under this subparagraph shall continue in force notwithstanding subsequent regular operation by an airline of the other Contracting Party.

If coincident gateway route segments appear on more than one route, the limitations set forth in this paragraph apply to the coincident segments taken together. A Contracting Party making designations under this paragraph shall specify which subparagraph applies.

(3) Notwithstanding paragraph (1) of this Article, for the purpose of operating the agreed all-cargo air services on US Route 7 and on UK Routes 10, 11 and 12 (taken together), each Contracting Party shall have the right to designate not more than a total of three airlines, except that, if the airline or airlines designated by one Contracting Party are licensed or certificated by their own aeronautical authorities and authorized by the other Contracting Party to offer all-cargo air services on a gateway route segment on which the airline or airlines designated by the other Contracting Party are not licensed or certificated by their own aeronautical authorities to offer such services, that other Contracting Party may designate an additional airline on the relevant route or routes to operate all-cargo air services only on that gateway route segment, notwithstanding the fact that such designation will result in the designation of more than three airlines on the relevant route or routes.

(4) Notwithstanding paragraph (1) of this Article, a Contracting Party receiving a designation of an airline which is authorized by that airline's own aeronautical authorities only to operate aircraft having a maximum passenger capacity of 30 seats or less and a maximum payload capacity of 7,500 pounds or less and which was not designated under the 1946 Bermuda Agreement may refuse to regard such designation as a proper designation under this Article if it would result in more than three such airlines or more than the number designated under the 1946 Bermuda Agreement (whichever is greater), operating at any point in the territory of the Contracting Party receiving the designation.

(5) If either Contracting Party wishes to designate an airline or airlines for the routes set forth in paragraphs (2) or (3) of this Article, in addition to the designations specifically permitted by those paragraphs, it shall notify the other Contracting Party. The second Contracting Party may either: (i) accept such further designation; or (ii) request consultations. After consultations the second Contracting Party may decline to accept the designation.

(6) On receipt of a designation made by one Contracting Party under the terms of paragraphs (1), (2) or (3) of this Article, or accepted under the terms of paragraph (5) of this Article, and on receipt of an application or applications from the airline so designated for operating authorizations and technical permissions in the form and manner prescribed for such applications, the other Contracting Party shall grant the appropriate operating authorizations and technical permissions, provided:

(a) substantial ownership and effective control of that airline are vested in the Contracting Party designating the airline or in its nationals;

(b) the designated airline is qualified to meet the conditions prescribed under the laws and regulations normally applied to the operation of international air services by the Contracting Party considering the application or applications; and

(c) the other Contracting Party is maintaining and administering the standards set forth in Article 6 (Airworthiness).

If the aeronautical authorities of the Contracting Party considering the application or applications are not satisfied that these conditions are met at the end of a 90-day period from receipt of the application or applications from the designated airlines, either Contracting Party may request consultations, which shall be held within 30 days of the request.

(7) When an airline has been designated and authorized in accordance with the terms of this Article, it may operate the relevant agreed services on the specified routes in Annex 1, provided, however, that the airline complies with the applicable provisions of this Agreement.

ARTICLE 4
Application of Laws

(1) The laws and regulations of one Contracting Party relating to the admission to or departure from its territory of aircraft engaged in international air navigation, or to the operation and navigation of such aircraft while within its territory, shall be applied to the aircraft of the airline or airlines designated by the other Contracting Party and shall be complied with by such aircraft upon entrance into or departure from and while within the territory of the first Contracting Party.

(2) The laws and regulations of one Contracting Party relating to the admission to or departure from its territory of passengers, crew, cargo or mail of aircraft, including regulations relating to entry, clearance, immigration, passports, customs and quarantine, shall be complied with by or on behalf of such passengers, crew, cargo or mail of the airlines of the other Contracting Party upon entrance into or departure from and while within the territory of the first Contracting Party.

ARTICLE 5
Revocation or Suspension of Operating Authorization

(1) Each Contracting Party shall have the right to revoke, suspend, limit or impose conditions on the operating authorizations or technical permissions of an airline designated by the other Contracting Party where:

(a) substantial ownership and effective control of that airline are not vested in the Contracting Party designating the airline or in nationals of such Contracting Party; or

(b) that airline has failed to comply with the laws or regulations of the first Contracting Party; or

(c) the other Contracting Party is not maintaining and administering safety standards as set forth in Article 6 (Airworthiness).

(2) Unless immediate revocation, suspension or imposition of the conditions mentioned in paragraph (1) of this Article is essential to prevent further noncompliance with subparagraphs (b) or (c) of paragraph (1) of this Article, such rights shall be exercised only after consultation with the other Contracting Party.

ARTICLE 6
Airworthiness

(1) Certificates of airworthiness, certificates of competency, and licenses issued or rendered valid by one Contracting Party, and still in force, shall be recognized as valid by the other Contracting Party for the purpose of operating the air services provided for in this Agreement, provided that the requirements under which such certificates or licenses were issued or rendered valid are equal to or above the minimum standards which may be established pursuant to the Convention. Each Contracting Party reserves the right, however, to refuse to recognize as valid for the purpose of flights above its own territory, certificates of competency and licenses granted to its own nationals by the other Contracting Party.

(2) The competent aeronautical authorities of each Contracting Party may request consultations concerning the safety and security standards and requirements maintained and administered by the other Contracting Party relating to aeronautical facilities, aircrew, aircraft, and the operation of the designated airlines. If, following such consultations, the competent aeronautical authorities of either Contracting Party find that the other Contracting Party does not effectively maintain and administer safety and security standards and requirements in these areas that are equal to or above the minimum standards which may be established pursuant to the Convention, they will notify the other Contracting Party of such findings and the steps considered necessary to bring the safety and security standards and requirements of the other Contracting Party to standards at least equal to the minimum standards which may be established pursuant to the Convention, and the other Contracting Party shall take appropriate corrective action. Each Contracting Party reserves the right to withhold, revoke or limit, pursuant to Articles 2 (Grant of Rights), 3 (Designation and Authorization of Airlines), and 5 (Revocation or Suspension of Operating Authorization), the operating authorization or technical permission of an airline or airlines designated by the other Contracting Party, in the event the other Contracting Party does not take such appropriate action within a reasonable time.

ARTICLE 7
Aviation Security

The Contracting Parties reaffirm their grave concern about acts or threats against the security of aircraft, which jeopardize the safety of persons or property, adversely affect the operation of air services and undermine public confidence in the safety of civil aviation. The Contracting Parties agree to provide maximum aid to each other with a view to preventing hijackings and sabotage to aircraft, airports and air navigation facilities and threats to aviation security. They reaffirm their commitments under and shall have regard to the provisions of the Convention on Offences and certain other Acts Committed on Board Aircraft, signed at Tokyo on 14 September 1963, the Convention for the Suppression of Unlawful Seizure of Aircraft, signed at the Hague on 16 December 1970, and the Convention for the Suppression of Unlawful Acts against the Safety of Civil Aviation, signed at Montreal on 23 September 1971. The Contracting Parties shall also have regard to applicable aviation security provisions established by the International Civil Aviation Organization. When incidents or threats of hijacking or sabotage against aircraft, airports or air navigation facilities occur, the Contracting Parties shall assist each other by facilitating communications intended to terminate such incidents rapidly and safely. Each Contracting Party shall give sympathetic consideration to any request from the other for special security measures for its aircraft or passengers to meet a particular threat.

ARTICLE 8
Commercial Operations

(1) The designated airline or airlines of one Contracting Party shall be entitled, in accordance with the laws and regulations relating to entry, residence and employment of the other Contracting Party, to bring in and maintain in the territory of the other Contracting Party those of their own managerial, technical, operational and other specialist staff who are required for the provision of air services.

(2) Each Contracting Party agrees to use its best efforts to ensure that the designated airlines of the other Contracting Party are offered the choice, subject to reasonable limitations which may be imposed by airport authorities, of providing their own services for ground handling operations; of having such operations performed entirely or in part by another airline, an organization controlled by another airline, or a servicing agent, as authorized by the airport authority; or of having such operations performed by the airport authority.

(3) Each Contracting Party grants to each designated airline of the other Contracting Party the right to engage in the sale of air transportation in its territory directly and, at the airline's discretion, through its agents. Each airline shall have the right to sell such transportation, and any person shall be free to purchase such transportation, in the currency of that territory or in freely convertible currencies of other countries.

(4) Each designated airline shall have the right to convert and remit to its country on demand local revenues in excess of sums locally disbursed. Conversion and remittance shall be permitted without restrictions at the rate of exchange applicable to current transactions which is in effect at the time such revenues are presented for conversion and remittance. Both Contracting Parties have accepted the obligations set out in Article VIII of the Articles of Agreement of the International Monetary Fund.

(5) Each Contracting Party shall use its best efforts to secure for the designated airlines of the other Contracting Party on a reciprocal basis an exemption from taxes, charges and fees imposed by State, regional and local authorities on the items listed in paragraphs (1) and (2) of Article 9 (Customs Duties), as well as from fuel through-put charges, in the circumstances described under those paragraphs, except to the extent that the charges are based on the actual cost of providing the service.

ARTICLE 9
Customs Duties

(1) Aircraft operated in international air services by the designated airlines of either Contracting Party, their regular equipment, fuel, lubricants, consumable technical supplies, spare parts including engines, and aircraft stores including but not limited to such items as food, beverages and tobacco, which are on board such aircraft, shall be relieved on the basis of reciprocity from all customs duties, national excise taxes, and similar national fees and charges not based on the cost of services provided, on arriving in the territory of the other Contracting Party, provided such equipment and supplies remain on board the aircraft.

(2) There shall also be relieved from the duties, fees and charges referred to in paragraph (1) of this Article, with the exception of charges based on the cost of the service provided:

(a) aircraft stores, introduced into or supplied in the territory of a Contracting Party, and taken on board, within reasonable limits, for use on outbound aircraft engaged in an international air service of a designated airline of the other Contracting Party;

(b) spare parts including engines introduced into the territory of a Contracting Party for the maintenance or repair of aircraft used in an international air service of a designated airline of the other Contracting Party; and

(c) fuel, lubricants and consumable technical supplies introduced into or supplied in the territory of a Contracting Party for use in an aircraft engaged in an international air service of a designated airline of the other Contracting Party, even when these supplies are to be used on a part of the journey performed over the territory of the Contracting Party in which they are taken on board.

(3) Equipment and supplies referred to in paragraphs (1) and (2) of this Article may be required to be kept under the supervision or control of the appropriate authorities.

(4) The reliefs provided for by this Article shall also be available in situations where the designated airlines of one Contracting Party have entered into arrangements with another airline or airlines for the loan or transfer in the territory of the other Contracting Party of the items specified in paragraphs (1) and (2) of this Article provided such other airline or airlines similarly enjoy such reliefs from such other Contracting Party.

ARTICLE 10
User Charges

(1) Each Contracting Party shall use its best efforts to ensure that user charges imposed or permitted to be imposed by its competent charging authorities on the designated airlines of the other Contracting Party are just and reasonable. Such charges shall be considered just and reasonable if they are determined and imposed in accordance with the principles set forth in paragraphs (2) and (3) of this Article, and if they are equitably apportioned among categories of users.

(2) Neither Contracting Party shall impose or permit to be imposed on the designated airlines of the other Contracting Party user charges higher than those imposed on its own designated airlines operating similar international air services.

(3) User charges may reflect, but shall not exceed, the full cost to the competent charging authorities of providing appropriate airport and air navigation facilities and services, and may provide for a reasonable rate of return on assets, after depreciation. In the provision of facilities and services, the competent authorities shall have regard to such factors as efficiency, economy, environmental impact and safety of operation. User charges shall be based on sound economic principles and on the generally accepted accounting practices within the territory of the appropriate Contracting Party.

(4) Each Contracting Party shall encourage consultations between its competent charging authorities and airlines using the services and facilities, where practicable through the airlines' representative organizations. Reasonable notice should be given to users of any proposals for changes in user charges to enable them to express their views before changes are made.

(5) For the purposes of paragraph (4) of this Article, each Contracting Party shall use its best efforts to encourage the competent charging authorities and the airlines to exchange such information as may be necessary to permit an accurate review of the reasonableness of the charges in accordance with the principles set out in this Article.

(6) In the event that agreement is reached between the Contracting Parties that an existing user charge should be revised, the appropriate Contracting Party shall use its best efforts to put the revision into effect promptly.

ARTICLE 11
Fair Competition

(1) The designated airline or airlines of one Contracting Party shall have a fair and equal opportunity to compete with the designated airline or airlines of the other Contracting Party.

(2) The designated airline or airlines of one Contracting Party shall take into consideration the interests of the designated airline or airlines of the other Contracting Party so as not to affect unduly that airline's or those airlines' services on all or part of the same routes. In particular, when a designated airline of one Contracting Party proposes to inaugurate services on a gateway route segment already served by a designated airline or airlines of the other Contracting Party, the incumbent airline or airlines shall each refrain from increasing the frequency of their services to the extent and for the time necessary to ensure that the airline inaugurating service may fairly exercise its rights under paragraph (1) of this Article. Such obligation to refrain from increasing frequency shall not last longer than two years or beyond the point when the inaugurating airline matches the frequencies of any incumbent airline, whichever occurs first, and shall not apply if the services to be inaugurated are limited as to their capacity by the license or certificate granted by the designating Contracting Party.

(3) Services provided by a designated airline under this Agreement shall retain as their primary objective the provision of capacity adequate to the traffic demands between the country of which such airline is a national and the country of ultimate destination of the traffic. The right to embark or disembark on such services international traffic destined for and coming from third countries at a point or points on the routes specified in this Agreement shall be exercised in accordance with the general principles of orderly development of international air transport to which both Contracting Parties subscribe and shall be subject to the general principle that capacity should be related to:

(a) the traffic requirements between the country of origin and the countries of ultimate destination of the traffic;

(b) the requirements of through airline operations; and

(c) the traffic requirements of the area through which the airline passes, after taking account of local and regional services.

(4) The frequency and capacity of services to be provided by the designated airlines of the Contracting Parties shall be closely related to the requirements of all categories of public demand for the carriage of passengers and cargo including mail in such a way as to provide adequate service to the public and to permit the reasonable development of routes and viable airline operations. Due regard shall be paid to efficiency of operation so that frequency and capacity are provided at levels appropriate to accommodate the traffic at load factors consistent with tariffs based on the criteria set forth in paragraph (2) of Article 12 (Tariffs).

(5) The Contracting Parties recognize that airline actions leading to excess capacity or to the underprovision of capacity can both run counter to the interests of the travelling public. Accordingly, in the particular case of combination air services on the North Atlantic routes specified in paragraph (1) of Annex 2, they have agreed to establish the procedures set forth in Annex 2. With respect to other routes and services, if one Contracting Party believes that the operations of a designated airline or airlines of the other Contracting Party have been inconsistent with the principles set forth in this Article, it may request consultations pursuant to Article 16 (Consultations) for the purpose of reviewing the operations in question to determine whether

they are in conformity with these principles. In such consultations there shall be taken into consideration the operations of all airlines serving the market in question and designated by the Contracting Party whose airline or airlines are under review. If the Contracting Parties conclude that the operations under review are not in conformity with the principles set forth in this Article, they may decide upon appropriate corrective or remedial measures, except that, where frequency or capacity limitations are already provided for a route specified in Annex 1, the Contracting Parties may not vary those limitations or impose additional limitations except by amendment of this Agreement.

(6) Neither Contracting Party shall unilaterally restrict the operations of the designated airlines of the other except according to the terms of this Agreement or by such uniform conditions as may be contemplated by the Convention.

ARTICLE 12
Tariffs

(1) Tariffs of the designated airlines of the Contracting Parties for carriage between their territories shall be established in accordance with the procedures set out in this Article.

(2) The tariffs charged by the designated airlines of one Contracting Party for public transport to or from the territory of the other Contracting Party shall be established at the lowest level consistent with a high standard of safety and an adequate return to efficient airlines operating on the agreed routes. Each tariff shall, to the extent feasible, be based on the costs of providing such service assuming reasonable load factors. Additional relevant factors shall include among others the need of the airline to meet competition from scheduled or charter air services, taking into account differences in cost and quality of service, and the prevention of unjust discrimination and undue preferences or advantages. To further the reasonable interests of users of air transport services, and to encourage the further development of civil aviation, individual airlines should be encouraged to initiate innovative, cost-based tariffs.

(3) The tariffs charged by the designated airlines of one Contracting Party for public transport between the territory of the other Contracting Party and the territory of a third State shall be subject to the approval of the other Contracting Party and such third State; provided, however, that a Contracting Party shall not require a different tariff from the tariff of its own airlines for comparable service between the same points. The designated airlines of each Contracting Party shall file such tariffs with the other Contracting Party, in accordance with its requirements.

(4) Any tariff agreements with respect to public transport between the territories of the Contracting Parties concluded as a result of inter-carrier discussions, including those held under the traffic conference procedures of the International Air Transport Association, or any other association of international airlines, and involving the airlines of the Contracting Parties will be subject to the approval of the aeronautical authorities of those Contracting Parties, and may be disapproved at any time whether or not previously approved. The submission of such agreements is not the filing of a tariff for the purposes of the provisions of paragraph (5) of this Article. Such agreements shall be submitted to the aeronautical authorities of both Contracting Parties for approval at least 105 days before the proposed date of effectiveness, accompanied by such justification as each Contracting Party may require of its own designated airlines. The period of 105 days may be reduced with the consent of the aeronautical au-

thorities of the Contracting Party with whom a filing is made. The aeronautical authorities of each Contracting Party shall use their best efforts to approve or disapprove (in whole or in part) each agreement submitted in accordance with this paragraph on or before the 60th day after its submission. Each Contracting Party may require that tariffs reflecting agreements approved by it be filed and published in accordance with its laws.

(5) Any tariff of a designated airline of one Contracting Party for public transport between the territories of the Contracting Parties shall, if so required, be filed with the aeronautical authorities of the other Contracting Party at least 75 days prior to the proposed effective date unless the aeronautical authorities of that Contracting Party permit the filing to be made on shorter notice. Such tariff shall become effective unless action is taken to continue in force the existing tariff as provided in paragraph (7) of this Article.

(6) If the aeronautical authorities of one Contracting Party, on receipt of any filing referred to in paragraph (5) of this Article, are dissatisfied with the tariff proposed or desire to discuss the tariff with the other Contracting Party, the first Contracting Party shall so notify the other Contracting Party through diplomatic channels within 30 days of the filing of such tariff, but in no event less than 15 days prior to the proposed effective date of such tariff. The Contracting Party receiving the notification may request consultations and, if so requested, such consultations shall be held at the earliest possible date for the purpose of attempting to reach agreement on the appropriate tariff. If notification of dissatisfaction is not given as provided in this paragraph, the tariff shall be deemed to be approved by the aeronautical authorities of the Contracting Party receiving the filing and shall become effective on the proposed date.

(7) If agreement is reached on the appropriate tariff under paragraph (6) of this Article, each Contracting Party shall exercise its best efforts to put such tariff into effect. If an agreement is not reached prior to the proposed effective date of the tariff, or if consultations are not requested, the aeronautical authorities of the Contracting Party expressing dissatisfaction with that tariff may take action to continue in force the existing tariffs beyond the date on which they would otherwise have expired at the levels and under the conditions (including seasonal variations) set forth therein. In this event the other Contracting Party shall similarly take any action necessary to continue the existing tariffs in effect. In no circumstances, however, shall a Contracting Party require a different tariff from the tariff of its own designated airlines for comparable service between the same points.

(8) The aeronautical authorities of each Contracting Party shall exercise their best efforts to ensure that the designated airlines conform to the agreed tariffs filed with the aeronautical authorities of the Contracting Parties, and that no airline rebates any portion of such tariffs by any means, directly or indirectly.

(9) In order to avoid tariff disputes to the greatest extent possible:

(a) a continuing Tariff Working Group shall be established to make recommendations on tariff-making standards, as provided in Annex 3;

(b) the aeronautical authorities will keep one another informed of such guidance as they may give to their own airlines in advance of or during traffic conferences of the International Air Transport Association; and

(c) during the period that the aeronautical authorities of either Contracting Party have agreements under consideration pursuant to paragraph (4) of this Article, the Contracting Parties may exchange views and recommendations, orally or in writing.

Such views and recommendations shall, if requested by either Contracting Party, be presented to the aeronautical authorities of the other Contracting Party, who will take them into account in reaching their decision.

ARTICLE 13
Commissions

(1) The airlines of each Contracting Party may be required to file with the aeronautical authorities of both Contracting Parties the level or levels of commissions and all other forms of compensation to be paid or provided by such airline in any manner or by any device, directly or indirectly, to or for the benefit of any person (other than its own bona fide employees) for the sale of air transportation between the territories of the Contracting Parties. The aeronautical authorities of each Contracting Party shall exercise their best efforts to ensure that the commissions and compensation paid by the airlines of each Contracting Party conform to the level or levels of commissions and compensation filed with the aeronautical authorities.

(2) The level of commissions and other forms of compensation paid with respect to the sale, within the territory of a Contracting Party, of air transportation, shall be subject to the laws and regulations of such Contracting Party, which shall be applied in a nondiscriminatory fashion.

ARTICLE 14
Charter Air Service

(1) The Contracting Parties recognize the need to further the maintenance and development, where a substantial demand exists or may be expected, of a viable network of scheduled air services, consistently and readily available, which caters for all segments of demand and particularly for those needing a wide and flexible range of air services.

(2) The Contracting Parties also recognize the substantial and growing demand from that section of the travelling public which is price rather than time sensitive, for air services at the lowest possible level of fares. The Contracting Parties, therefore, taking into account the relationship of scheduled and charter air services and the need for a total air service system, shall further the maintenance and development of efficient and economic charter air services so as to meet that demand.

(3) The Contracting Parties shall therefore apply the provisions of Annex 4 to charter air services between their territories.

ARTICLE 15
Transitional Provisions

(1) Designation. On the entry into force of this Agreement, and until 1 November 1977, all designations and authorizations in effect pursuant to the 1946 Bermuda Agreement shall remain in effect. Additional designations shall be subject to the provisions of Article 3 (Designation and Authorization of Airlines) of this Agreement. By 1 November 1977, each Contracting Party shall indicate to the other all the initial designations applicable under this Agreement. Notwithstanding the provisions of Article 3, until 1 November 1977:

(a) the United States shall be entitled to retain two designated airlines to operate combination air services on each of three gateway route segments on US Routes 1 and 2, taken together; and

(b) the United Kingdom shall be entitled to retain three designated airlines to operate combination air services on one gateway route segment on UK Routes 1, 2, 3, 4 and 5, taken together.

(2) Capacity. Notwithstanding the provisions of Annex 2, as regards the winter traffic season of 1977/78 the following procedures shall apply:

Paragraph (3): Airlines shall file schedules not later than 120 days prior to the winter traffic season, instead of 180 days.

Paragraph (3): Airlines shall refile amendments not later than 105 days prior to the winter traffic season, instead of 165 days.

Paragraph (4): A Contracting Party's notice of inconsistency shall be given within 90 days, instead of 150 days.

Paragraph (5): If requested, consultations shall begin not later than 75 days prior to the winter traffic season, instead of 90 days.

Paragraph (6): If agreement on capacity to be operated is not achieved, paragraph (6) procedures shall apply within 60 days prior to the winter traffic season, instead of 75 days.

(3) Tariffs. All tariffs filed to become effective on or after 1 November 1977, and all agreements filed to become effective on or after 1 January 1978 shall be subject to the provisions of Article 12 (Tariffs). Agreements filed to become effective prior to 1 January 1978 shall be subject to the provisions of Article 12 to the greatest extent feasible. Tariffs filed to become effective prior to 1 November 1977 shall be subject to the provisions of the 1946 Bermuda Agreement, and all tariffs in effect under the 1946 Bermuda Agreement shall continue in force, but either Contracting Party may notify the other Contracting Party of its dissatisfaction with any such tariffs, and the procedures set forth in this Agreement shall then apply.

ARTICLE 16
Consultations

Either Contracting Party may at any time request consultations on the implementation, interpretation, application or amendment of this Agreement or compliance with this Agreement. Such consultations shall begin within a period of 60 days from the date the other Contracting Party receives the request, unless otherwise agreed by the Contracting Parties.

ARTICLE 17
Settlement of Disputes

(1) Any dispute arising under this Agreement, other than disputes where self-executing mechanisms are provided in Article 12 (Tariffs) and Annex 2, which is not resolved by a first round of formal consultations, may be referred by agreement of the Contracting Parties for decision to some person or body. If the Contracting Parties do not so agree, the dispute shall at the request of either Contracting Party be submitted to arbitration in accordance with the procedures set forth below.

(2) Arbitration shall be by a tribunal of three arbitrators to be constituted as follows:

(a) within 30 days after the receipt of a request for arbitration, each Contracting Party shall name one arbitrator. Within 60 days after these two arbitrators have been nominated, they shall by agreement appoint a third arbitrator, who shall act as President of the arbitral tribunal;

(b) if either Contracting Party fails to name an arbitrator, or if the third arbitrator is not appointed in accordance with subparagraph (a) of this paragraph, either Contracting Party may request the President of the International Court of Justice to appoint the necessary arbitrator or arbitrators within 30 days. If the President is of the same nationality as one of the Parties, the most senior Vice-President who is not disqualified on that ground shall make the appointment.

(3) Except as otherwise agreed by the Contracting Parties, the arbitral tribunal shall determine the limits of its jurisdiction in accordance with this Agreement, and shall establish its own procedure. At the direction of the tribunal or at the request of either of the Contracting Parties, a conference to determine the precise issues to be arbitrated and the specific procedures to be followed shall be held no later than 15 days after the tribunal is fully constituted.

(4) Except as otherwise agreed by the Contracting Parties or prescribed by the tribunal, each Party shall submit a memorandum within 45 days of the time the tribunal is fully constituted. Replies shall be due 60 days later. The tribunal shall hold a hearing at the request of either Party or at its discretion within 15 days after replies are due.

(5) The tribunal shall attempt to render a written decision within 30 days after completion of the hearing or, if no hearing is held, after the date both replies are submitted, whichever is sooner. The decision of the majority of the tribunal shall prevail.

(6) The Contracting Parties may submit requests for clarification of the decision within 15 days after it is rendered and any clarification given shall be issued within 15 days of such request.

(7) Each Contracting Party shall, consistent with its national law, give full effect to any decision or award of the arbitral tribunal. In the event that one Contracting Party does not give effect to any decision or award, the other Contracting Party may take such proportionate steps as may be appropriate.

(8) The expenses of the arbitral tribunal, including the fees and expenses of the arbitrators, shall be shared equally by the Contracting Parties. Any expenses incurred by the President of the International Court of Justice in connection with the procedures of paragraph (2)(b) of this Article shall be considered to be part of the expenses of the arbitral tribunal.

ARTICLE 18
Amendment

Any amendments or modifications of this Agreement agreed by the Contracting Parties shall come into effect when confirmed by an Exchange of Notes.

ARTICLE 19
Termination

Either Contracting Party may at any time give notice in writing to the other Contracting Party of its decision to terminate this Agreement. Such notice shall be sent simultaneously to the International Civil Aviation Organization. This Agreement shall terminate at midnight (at the place of receipt of the notice) immediately before the first anniversary of the date of receipt of the notice by the other Contracting Party, unless the notice is withdrawn by agreement before the end of this period.

ARTICLE 20
Registration with ICAO

This Agreement and all amendments thereto shall be registered with the International Civil Aviation Organization.

ARTICLE 21
Entry into Force

This Agreement shall enter into force on the date of signature.

IN WITNESS WHEREOF the undersigned, being duly authorized thereto by their respective Governments, have signed the present Agreement.

DONE in duplicate at Bermuda this 23rd day of July, Nineteen Hundred and Seventy-Seven.

[The annexes are omitted.]

Appendix 17

Protocol to Amend the Convention on Damage Caused by Foreign Aircraft to Third Parties on the Surface Signed at Rome on 7 October 1952

Done at Montreal—September 23, 1978
Entered into force—July 25, 2002
Not in effect in the United States
ICAO Doc. 9257

THE GOVERNMENTS UNDERSIGNED,

CONSIDERING that it is desirable to amend the Convention on Damage Caused by Foreign Aircraft to Third Parties on the Surface signed at Rome on 7 October 1952,

HAVE AGREED as follows:

CHAPTER I
AMENDMENTS TO THE CONVENTION

Article I

The Convention which the provisions of the present Chapter modify is the Convention on Damage Caused by Foreign Aircraft to Third Parties on the Surface signed at Rome on 7 October 1952.

Article II

In Article 2 of the Convention the following shall be added as new paragraph 4:

"4. If the aircraft is registered as the property of a State, the liability devolves upon the person to whom, in accordance with the law of the State concerned, the aircraft has been entrusted for operation."

Article III

Article 11 of the Convention shall be deleted and replaced by the following:

"Article 11

1. Subject to the provisions of Article 12, the liability for damage giving a right to compensation under Article 1, for each aircraft and incident, in respect of all persons liable under this Convention shall not exceed:

(a) 300,000 Special Drawing Rights for aircraft weighing 2,000 kilogrammes or less;

(b) 300,000 Special Drawing Rights plus 175 Special Drawing Rights per kilogramme over 2,000 kilogrammes for aircraft weighing more than 2,000 but not exceeding 6,000 kilogrammes;

(c) 1,000,000 Special Drawing Rights plus 62.5 Special Drawing Rights per kilogramme over 6,000 kilogram for aircraft weighing more than 6,000 but not exceeding 30,000 kilogram;

(d) 2,500,000 Special Drawing Rights plus 65 Special Drawing Rights per kilogramme over 30,000 kilogram for aircraft weighing more than 30,000 kilogram.

2. The liability in respect of loss of life or personal injury shall not exceed 125,000 Special Drawing Rights per person killed or injured.

3. "Weight" means the maximum weight of the aircraft authorized by the certificate of airworthiness for take-off, excluding the effect of lifting gas when used.

4. The sums mentioned in terms of the Special Drawing Right in paragraphs 1 and 2 of this Article shall be deemed to refer to the Special Drawing Right as defined by the International Monetary Fund. Conversion of the sums into national currencies shall, in case of judicial proceedings, be made according to the value of such currencies in terms of the Special Drawing Right at the date of the judgment. The value of a national currency, in terms of the Special Drawing Right, of a Contracting State which is a Member of the International Monetary Fund, shall be calculated in accordance with the method of valuation applied by the International Monetary Fund, in effect at the date of the judgment, for its operations and transactions. The value of a national currency, in terms of the Special Drawing Right, of a Contracting State which is not a Member of the International Monetary Fund, shall be calculated in a manner determined by that Contracting State.

Nevertheless, those States which are not Members of the International Monetary Fund and whose law does not permit the application of the provisions of paragraphs 1 and 2 of this Article and of this paragraph may, at the time of ratification or accession or at any time thereafter, declare that the limit of liability provided for in this Convention shall, in judicial proceedings in their territories, be fixed as follows:

(a) 4,500,000 monetary units for aircraft referred to in subparagraph (a) of paragraph 1 of this Article;

(b) 4,500,000 monetary units plus 2,625 monetary units per kilogramme for aircraft referred to in subparagraph (b) of paragraph 1 of this Article;

(c) 15,000,000 monetary units plus 937.5 monetary units per kilogramme for aircraft referred to in subparagraph (c) of paragraph 1 of this Article;

(d) 37,500,000 monetary units plus 975 monetary units per kilogramme for aircraft referred to in subparagraph (d) of paragraph 1 of this Article;

(e) 1,875,000 monetary units in respect of loss of life or personal injury referred to in paragraph 2 of this Article.

The monetary unit referred to in this paragraph corresponds to sixty-five and a half milligrammes of gold of millesimal fineness nine hundred. This sum may be converted into the national currency concerned in round figures. The conversion of this sum into the national currency shall be made according to the law of the State concerned.

Article IV

Article 14 of the Convention shall be deleted and replaced by the following:

"Article 14

If the total amount of the claims established exceeds the limit of liability applicable under the provisions of this Convention, the following rules shall apply, taking into account the provisions of paragraph 2 of Article 11:

(a) If the claims are exclusively in respect of loss of life or personal injury or exclusively in respect of damage to property, such claims shall be reduced in proportion to their respective amounts;

(b) If the claims are both in respect of loss of life or personal injury and in respect of damage to property, the total sum distributable shall be appropriated preferentially to meet proportionately the claims in respect of loss of life and personal injury. The remainder, if any, of the total sum distributable shall be distributed proportionately among the claims in respect of damage to property."

Article V

In the title of Chapter III the word "SECURITY" shall be deleted and replaced by "GUARANTEE."

Article VI

In Article 15 of the Convention:

(a) paragraph 1 shall be deleted and replaced by the following:

"1. Any Contracting State may require that the operator of an aircraft referred to in paragraph 1 of Article 23 shall be covered by insurance or guaranteed by other security in respect of his liability for damage sustained in its territory for which a right of compensation exists under Article 1 up to the limits applicable according to the provisions of Article 11. The operator shall provide evidence of such guarantee if the State overflown so requests."

(b) paragraphs 2, 3, 4, 5 and 6 shall be deleted;

(c) paragraph 7 shall be renumbered as paragraph 2 and shall read as follows:

"2. A Contracting State overflown may at any time require consultation with the State of the aircraft's registry, with the State of the operator or with any other Contracting State where the guarantees are provided, if it believes that the insurer or other person providing the guarantee is not financially capable of meeting the obligations imposed by this Convention."

(d) paragraph 8 shall be renumbered as paragraph 3;

(e) paragraph 9 shall be deleted.

Article VII

In Article 16 of the Convention:

(a) the word "security" in paragraph 1 shall be deleted and replaced by "guarantee";

(b) subparagraph (a) of paragraph 1 shall be deleted and replaced by the following:

"(a) that the damage occurred after the guarantee ceased to be effective. However, if the guarantee expires during a flight, it should be continued in force until the next landing specified in the flight plan, but no longer than twenty-four hours;"

(c) subparagraph (b) of paragraph 1 shall be deleted and replaced by the following:

"(b) that the damage occurred outside the territorial limits provided by the guarantee, unless flight outside of such limits was caused by force majeure, assistance justified by the circumstances or an error in piloting, operation or navigation."

(d) paragraphs 2 and 3 shall be deleted;

(e) paragraph 4 shall be renumbered as paragraph 2 and the word "security" shall be deleted and replaced by "guarantee";

(f) paragraph 5 shall be renumbered as paragraph 3 and the words "governing the contract of insurance or guarantee" shall be deleted and replaced by "applicable to the guarantee"; in subparagraph (a) of that paragraph the word "security" shall be deleted and replaced by "guarantee";

(g) paragraphs 6 and 7 shall be renumbered as paragraphs 4 and 5, respectively, and in the new paragraph 4 the word "security" shall be replaced by "guarantee."

Article VIII

In Article 17 of the Convention:

(a) paragraph 1 shall be deleted and replaced by the following:

"1. If a guarantee is furnished in accordance with Article 15, it shall be specifically and preferentially assigned to payment of claims under the provisions of this Convention."

(b) in paragraph 2 the word "security" shall be deleted and replaced by "guarantee";

(c) paragraph 3 shall be deleted and replaced by the following:

"3. As soon as notice of a claim has been given to the operator, he shall ensure that the guarantee is maintained up to a sum equivalent to the aggregate of:

(a) the amount of the guarantee then required by paragraph 2 of this Article, and

(b) the amount of the claim not exceeding the applicable limit of liability.

The above-mentioned sum shall be maintained until every claim has been disposed of."

Article IX

In Article 19 of the Convention no amendment has been made in the English text.

Article X

In Article 20 of the Convention:

(a) in paragraph 4 delete the words "or of any territory, State or province thereof" and replace by "or of any of its constituent subdivisions, such as States, Republics, territories or provinces";

(b) in paragraph 9 the subparagraphs shall be designated as (a), (b) and (c), respectively;

(c) paragraph 11 shall be deleted and replaced by the following:

"11. Interest may be allowed on the judgment debt according to the law of the Court seized of the case."

(d) in paragraph 12 delete the word "five" and replace by "two."

Article XI

In Article 21 of the Convention no amendment has been made in the English text.

Article XII

In Article 23 of the Convention paragraph 1 shall be deleted and replaced by the following:

"1. This Convention applies to damage contemplated in Article 1 caused in the territory of a Contracting State by an aircraft registered in another Contracting State or by an aircraft, whatever its registration may be, the operator of which has his principal place of business or, if he has no such place of business, his permanent residence in another Contracting State."

Article XIII

Article 26 of the Convention shall be deleted and replaced by the following:

"Article 26

This Convention shall not apply to damage caused by aircraft used in military, customs and police services."

Article XIV

In the Convention after Article 26 insert Article 27 as follows:

"Article 27

This Convention shall not apply to nuclear damage."

Article XV

Articles 27 and 28 of the Convention shall be renumbered as Articles 28 and 29, respectively.

Article XVI

Article 29 of the Convention shall be deleted.

Article XVII

In Article 30 of the Convention the last two paragraphs shall be deleted and replaced by the following:

"Contracting State" means a State for which this Convention is in force."

"State of the Operator" means any Contracting State other than the State of registry on whose territory the operator has his principal place of business or, if he has no such place of business, his permanent residence."

Article XVIII

Articles 36 and 37 of the Convention shall be deleted and in Article 38, which shall be renumbered as Article 36, the words "or of any declaration of notification made under Articles 36 and 37" shall be deleted. [In addition,] Article 39 shall be renumbered as Article 37.

CHAPTER II
FINAL PROVISIONS

Article XIX

As between the Parties to this Protocol, the Convention and the Protocol shall be read and interpreted together as one single instrument and shall be known as the Rome Convention of 1952 as amended at Montreal in 1978.

Article XX

Until the date on which this Protocol comes into force in accordance with Article XXII, it shall remain open for signature by any State.

Article XXI

1. This Protocol shall be subject to ratification by the signatory States.

2. Ratification of this Protocol by any State which is not a Party to the Convention shall have the effect of accession to the Convention as amended by this Protocol.

3. The instruments of ratification shall be deposited with the International Civil Aviation Organization.

Article XXII

1. As soon as five of the signatory States have deposited their instruments of ratification of this Protocol, it shall come into force between them on the ninetieth day after the date of the deposit of the fifth instrument of ratification. It shall come into force, for each State which deposits its instrument of ratification after that date, on the ninetieth day after its deposit of its instrument of ratification.

2. As soon as this Protocol comes into force, it shall be registered with the United Nations by the Secretary General of the International Civil Aviation Organization.

Article XXIII

1. This Protocol shall, after it has come into force, be open for accession by any non-signatory State.

2. Accession to this Protocol by any State which is not a Party to the Convention shall have the effect of accession to the Convention as amended by this Protocol.

3. Accession shall be effected by the deposit of an instrument of accession with the International Civil Aviation Organization and shall take effect on the ninetieth day after the deposit.

Article XXIV

1. Any Party to this Protocol may denounce the Protocol by notification addressed to the International Civil Aviation Organization.

2. Denunciation shall take effect six months after the date of receipt by the International Civil Aviation Organization of the notification of denunciation; nevertheless, in respect of damage contemplated in Article 1 of the Convention arising from an incident which occurred before the expiration of the six months period, the Convention shall continue to apply as if the denunciation had not been made.

3. As between the Parties to this Protocol, denunciation by any of them of the Rome Convention of 1952 in accordance with Article 35 thereof shall not be construed in any way as a denunciation of the Rome Convention of 1952 as amended at Montreal in 1978.

Article XXV

No reservations may be made to this Protocol.

Article XXVI

1. The Secretary General of the International Civil Aviation Organization shall give notice to all States Parties to the Rome Convention or to that Convention as amended by this Protocol, all signatory and adhering States and to all States members of the Organization or of the United Nations:

(a) of the deposit of any instrument of ratification of, or adherence to, this Protocol and the date of, thereof, within thirty days from the date of the deposit, and

(b) of the receipt of any denunciation of this Protocol and the date thereof, within thirty days from the date of the receipt.

2. The Secretary General of the Organization shall also notify these States of the date on which this Protocol comes into force in accordance with Article XXII.

Article XXVII

This Protocol shall remain open for signature at the Headquarters of the International Civil Aviation Organization until it comes into force in accordance with Article XXII.

DONE at Montreal on the twenty-third day of September of the year One Thousand Nine Hundred and Seventy-eight in four authentic texts in the English, French, Russian and Spanish languages.

IN WITNESS WHEREOF the undersigned Plenipotentiaries, having been duly authorized, have signed this Protocol in the name of....

Appendix 18

United Nations Convention on International Multimodal Transport of Goods

Done at Geneva—May 24, 1980
Not in force
U.N. Doc. TD/MT/CONF/16

THE STATES PARTIES TO THIS CONVENTION,

RECOGNIZING

(a) that international multimodal transport is one means of facilitating the orderly expansion of world trade;

(b) the need to stimulate the development of smooth, economic and efficient multimodal transport services adequate to the requirements of the trade concerned;

(c) the desirability of ensuring the orderly development of international multimodal transport in the interest of all countries and the need to consider the special problems of transit countries;

(d) the desirability of determining certain rules relating to the carriage of goods by international multimodal transport contracts, including equitable provisions concerning the liability of multimodal transport operators;

(e) the need that this Convention should not affect the application of any international convention or national law relating to the regulation and control of transport operations;

(f) the right of each State to regulate and control at the national level multimodal transport operators and operations;

(g) the need to have regard to the special interest and problems of developing countries, for example, as regards introduction of new technologies, participation in multimodal services of their national carriers and operators, cost efficiency thereof and maximum use of local labour and insurance;

(h) the need to ensure a balance of interests between suppliers and users of multimodal transport services;

(i) the need to facilitate customs procedures with due consideration to the problems of transit countries;

AGREEING to the following basic principles;

(a) that a fair balance of interests between developed and developing countries should be established and an equitable distribution of activities between these groups of countries should be attained in international multimodal transport;

(b) that consultation should take place on terms and conditions of service, both before and after the introduction of any new technology in the multimodal transport of goods, between the multimodal transport operator, shippers, shippers' organizations and appropriate national authorities;

(c) the freedom for shippers to choose between multimodal and segmented transport services;

(d) that the liability of the multimodal transport operator under this Convention should be based on the principle of presumed fault or neglect,

HAVE DECIDED to conclude a Convention for this purpose and have thereto agreed as follows:

PART I. GENERAL PROVISIONS

Article 1
Definitions

For the purposes of this Convention:

1. "International multimodal transport" means the carriage of goods by at least two different modes of transport on the basis of a multimodal transport contract from a place in one country at which the goods are taken in charge by the multimodal transport operator to a place designated for delivery situated in a different country. The operations of pick-up and delivery of goods carried out in the performance of a unimodal transport contract, as defined in such contract, shall not be considered as international multimodal transport.

2. "Multimodal transport operator" means any person who on his own behalf or through another person acting on his behalf concludes a multimodal transport contract and who acts as a principal, not as an agent or on behalf of the consignor or of the carriers participating in the multimodal transport operations, and who assumes responsibility for the performance of the contract.

3. "Multimodal transport contract" means a contract whereby a multimodal transport operator undertakes, against payment of freight, to perform or to procure the performance of international multimodal transport.

4. "Multimodal transport document" means a document which evidences a multimodal transport contract, the taking in charge of the goods by the multimodal transport operator, and an undertaking by him to deliver the goods in accordance with the terms of that contract.

5. "Consignor" means any person by whom or in whose name or on whose behalf a multimodal transport contract has been concluded with the multimodal transport operator, or any person by whom or in whose name or on whose behalf the goods are actually delivered to the multimodal transport operator in relation to the multimodal transport contract.

6. "Consignee" means the person entitled to take delivery of the goods.

7. "Goods" includes any container, pallet or similar article of transport or packaging, if supplied by the consignor.

8. "International convention" means an international agreement concluded among States in written form and governed by international law.

9. "Mandatory national law" means any statutory law concerning carriage of goods the provisions of which cannot be departed from by contractual stipulation to the detriment of the consignor.

10. "Writing" means, inter alia, telegram or telex.

Article 2
Scope of application

The provisions of this Convention shall apply to all contracts of multimodal transport between places in two States, if:

(a) the place for the taking in charge of the goods by the multimodal transport operator as provided for in the multimodal transport contract is located in a Contracting State, or

(b) the place for delivery of the goods by the multimodal transport operator as provided for in the multimodal transport contract is located in a Contracting State.

Article 3
Mandatory application

1. When a multimodal transport contract has been concluded which according to article 2 shall be governed by this Convention, the provisions of this Convention shall be mandatorily applicable to such contract.

2. Nothing in this Convention shall affect the right of the consignor to choose between multimodal transport and segmented transport.

Article 4
Regulation and control of multimodal transport

1. This Convention shall not affect, or be incompatible with, the application of any international convention or national law relating to the regulation and control of transport operations.

2. This Convention shall not affect the right of each State to regulate and control at the national level multimodal transport operations and multimodal transport operators, including the right to take measures relating to consultations, especially before the introduction of new technologies and services, between multimodal transport operators, shippers, shippers' organizations and appropriate national authorities on terms and conditions of service; licensing of multimodal transport operators; participation in transport; and all other steps in the national economic and commercial interest.

3. The multimodal transport operator shall comply with the applicable law of the country in which he operates and with the provisions of this Convention.

PART II. DOCUMENTATION

Article 5
Issue of multimodal transport document

1. When the goods are taken in charge by the multimodal transport operator, he shall issue a multimodal transport document which, at the option of the consignor, shall be in either negotiable or non-negotiable form.

2. The multimodal transport document shall be signed by the multimodal transport operator or by a person having authority from him.

3. The signature on the multimodal transport document may be in handwriting, printed in facsimile, perforated, stamped, in symbols, or made by any other mechanical or electronic means, if not inconsistent with the law of the country where the multimodal transport document is issued.

4. If the consignor so agrees, a non-negotiable multimodal transport document may be issued by making use of any mechanical or other means preserving a record of the particulars stated in article 8 to be contained in the multimodal transport document. In such a case the multimodal transport operator, after having taken the goods in charge, shall deliver to the consignor a readable document containing all the particulars so

recorded, and such document shall for the purposes of the provisions of this Convention be deemed to be a multimodal transport document.

Article 6
Negotiable multimodal transport document

1. Where a multimodal transport document is issued in negotiable form:

(a) it shall be made out to order or to bearer;

(b) if made out to order it shall be transferable by endorsement;

(c) if made out to bearer it shall be transferable without endorsement;

(d) if issued in a set of more than one original it shall indicate the number of originals in the set;

(e) if any copies are issued each copy shall be marked "non-negotiable copy."

2. Delivery of the goods may be demanded from the multimodal transport operator or a person acting on his behalf only against surrender of the negotiable multimodal transport document duly endorsed where necessary.

3. The multimodal transport operator shall be discharged from his obligation to deliver the goods if, where a negotiable multimodal transport document has been issued in a set of more than one original, he or a person acting on his behalf has in good faith delivered the goods against surrender of one of such originals.

Article 7
Non-negotiable multimodal transport document

1. Where a multimodal transport document is issued in non-negotiable form it shall indicate a named consignee.

2. The multimodal transport operator shall be discharged from his obligation to deliver the goods if he makes delivery thereof to the consignee named in such non-negotiable multimodal transport document or to such other person as he may be duly instructed, as a rule, in writing.

Article 8
Contents of the multimodal transport document

1. The multimodal transport document shall contain the following particulars:

(a) the general nature of the goods, the leading marks necessary for identification of the goods, an express statement, if applicable, as to the dangerous character of the goods, the number of packages or pieces, and the gross weight of the goods or their quantity otherwise expressed, all such particulars as furnished by the consignor;

(b) the apparent condition of the goods;

(c) the name and principal place of business of the multimodal transport operator;

(d) the name of the consignor;

(e) the consignee, if named by the consignor;

(f) the place and date of taking in charge of the goods by the multimodal transport operator;

(g) the place of delivery of the goods;

(h) the date or the period of delivery of the goods at the place of delivery, if expressly agreed upon between the parties;

(i) a statement indicating whether the multimodal transport document is negotiable or non-negotiable;

(j) the place and date of issue of the multimodal transport document;

(k) the signature of the multimodal transport operator or of a person having authority from him;

(l) the freight for each mode of transport, if expressly agreed between the parties, or the freight, including its currency, to the extent payable by the consignee or other indication that freight is payable by him.

(m) the intended journey route, modes of transport and places of transhipment, if known at the time of issuance of the multimodal transport document;

(n) the statement referred to in paragraph 3 of article 28;

(o) any other particulars which the parties may agree to insert in the multimodal transport document, if not inconsistent with the law of the country where the multimodal transport document is issued.

2. The absence from the multimodal document of one or more of the particulars referred to in paragraph 1 of this article shall not affect the legal character of the document as a multimodal transport document provided that it nevertheless meets the requirements set out in paragraph 4 of article 1.

Article 9
Reservations in the multimodal transport document

1. If the multimodal transport document contains particulars concerning the general nature, leading marks, number of packages or pieces, weight or quantity of the goods which the multimodal transport operator or a person acting on his behalf knows, or has reasonable grounds to suspect, do not accurately represent the goods actually taken in charge, or if he has no reasonable means of checking such particulars, the multimodal transport operator or a person acting on his behalf shall insert in the multimodal transport document a reservation specifying these inaccuracies, grounds of suspicion or the absence of reasonable means of checking.

2. If the multimodal transport operator or a person acting on his behalf fails to note on the multimodal transport document the apparent condition of the goods, he is deemed to have noted on the multimodal transport document that the goods were in apparent good condition.

Article 10
Evidentiary effect of the multimodal transport document

Except for particulars in respect of which and to the extent to which a reservation permitted under article 9 has been entered:

(a) the multimodal transport document shall be prima facie evidence of the taking in charge by the multimodal transport operator of the goods as described therein; and

(b) proof to the contrary by the multimodal transport operator shall not be admissible if the multimodal transport document is issued in negotiable form and has been transferred to a third party, including a consignee, who has acted in good faith in reliance on the description of the goods therein.

Article 11
Liability for intentional misstatements or omissions

When the multimodal transport operator, with intent to defraud, gives in the multimodal transport document false information concerning the goods or omits any information required to be included under paragraph 1(a) or (b) of article 8 or under article 9, he shall be liable, without the benefit of the limitation of liability provided for in this Convention, for any loss, damage or expenses incurred by a third party, including a consignee, who acted in reliance on the description of the goods in the multimodal transport document issued.

Article 12
Guarantee by the consignor

1. The consignor shall be deemed to have guaranteed to the multimodal transport operator the accuracy, at the time the goods were taken in charge by the multimodal transport operator, or particulars relating to the general nature of the goods, their marks, number, weight and quantity and, if applicable, to the dangerous character of the goods, as furnished by him for insertion in the multimodal transport document.

2. The consignor shall indemnify the multimodal transport operator against loss resulting from inaccuracies in or inadequacies of the particulars referred to in paragraph 1 of this article. The consignor shall remain liable even if the multimodal transport document has been transferred by him. The right of the multimodal transport operator to such indemnity shall in no way limit his liability under the multimodal transport contract to any person other than the consignor.

Article 13
Other documents

The issue of the multimodal transport document does not preclude the issue, if necessary, of other documents relating to transport or other services involved in international multimodal transport, in accordance with applicable international conventions or national law. However, the issue of such other documents shall not affect the legal character of the multimodal transport document.

PART III. LIABILITY OF THE MULTIMODAL TRANSPORT OPERATOR

Article 14
Period of responsibility

1. The responsibility of the multimodal transport operator for the goods under this Convention covers the period from the time he takes the goods in his charge to the time of their delivery.

2. For the purpose of this article, the multimodal transport operator is deemed to be in charge of the goods:

(a) from the time he has taken over the goods from:

(i) the consignor or a person acting on his behalf; or

(ii) an authority or other third party to whom, pursuant to law or regulations applicable at the place of taking in charge, the goods must be handed over for transport;

(b) until the time he has delivered the goods:

(i) by handing over the goods to the consignee; or

(ii) in cases where the consignee does not receive the goods from the multimodal transport operator, by placing them at the disposal of the consignee in accordance with the multimodal transport contract or with the law or with the usage of the particular trade applicable at the place of delivery; or

(iii) by handing over the goods to an authority or other third party to whom, pursuant to law or regulations applicable at the place of delivery, the goods must be handed over.

3. In paragraphs 1 and 2 of this article, reference to the multimodal transport operator shall include his servants or agents or any other person of whose services he makes use for the performance of the multimodal transport contract, and reference to the consignor or consignee shall include their servants or agents.

Article 15
The liability of the multimodal transport operator for his servants, agents and other persons

Subject to article 21, the multimodal transport operator shall be liable for the acts and omissions of his servants or agents, when any such servant or agent is acting within the scope of his employment, or of any other person of whose services he makes use for the performance of the multimodal transport contract, when such person is acting in the performance of the contract, as if such acts and omissions were his own.

Article 16
Basis of liability

1. The multimodal transport operator shall be liable for loss resulting from loss of or damage to the goods, as well as from delay in delivery, if the occurrence which caused the loss, damage or delay in delivery took place while the goods were in his charge as defined in article 14, unless the multimodal transport operator proves that he, his servants or agents or any other person referred to in article 15 took all measures that could reasonably be required to avoid the occurrence and its consequences.

2. Delay in delivery occurs when the goods have not been delivered within the time expressly agreed upon or, in the absence of such agreement, within the time which it would be reasonable to require of a diligent multimodal transport operator, having regard to the circumstances of the case.

3. If the goods have not been delivered within 90 consecutive days following the date of delivery determined according to paragraph 2 of this article, the claimant may treat the goods as lost.

Article 17
Concurrent causes

Where fault or neglect on the part of the multimodal transport operator, his servants or agents or any person referred to in article 15 combines with another cause to produce loss, damage or delay in delivery, the multimodal transport operator shall be liable only to the extent that the loss, damage or delay in delivery is attributable to such fault or neglect, provided that the multimodal transport operator proves the part of the loss, damage or delay in delivery not attributable thereto.

Article 18
Limitation of liability

1. When the multimodal transport operator is liable for loss resulting from loss of or damage to the goods according to article 16, his liability shall be limited to an amount not exceeding 920 units of account per package or other shipping unit or 2.75 units of account per kilogramme of gross weight of the goods lost or damaged, whichever is the higher.

2. For the purpose of calculating which amount is the higher in accordance with paragraph 1 of this article, the following rules apply:

(a) where a container, pallet or similar article of transport is used to consolidate goods, the packages or other shipping units enumerated in the multimodal transport document as packed in such article of transport are deemed packages or shipping units. Except as aforesaid the goods in such article of transport are deemed one shipping unit.

(b) in cases where the article of transport itself has been lost or damaged, that article of transport, if not owned or otherwise supplied by the multimodal transport operator, is considered one separate shipping unit.

3. Notwithstanding the provisions of paragraphs 1 and 2 of this article, if the international multimodal transport does not, according to the contract, include carriage of goods by sea or by inland waterways, the liability of the multimodal transport operator shall be limited to an amount not exceeding 8.33 units of account per kilogramme of gross weight of the goods lost or damaged.

4. The liability of the multimodal transport operator for loss resulting from delay in delivery according to the provisions of article 16 shall be limited to an amount equivalent to two and a half times the freight payable for the goods delayed, but not exceeding the total freight payable under the multimodal transport contract.

5. The aggregate liability of the multimodal transport operator, under paragraphs 1 and 4 or paragraphs 3 and 4 of this article, shall not exceed the limit of liability for total loss of the goods as determined by paragraph 1 or 3 of this article.

6. By agreement between the multimodal transport operator and the consignor, limits of liability exceeding those provided for in paragraphs 1, 3 and 4 of this article may be fixed in the multimodal transport document.

7. "Unit of account" means the unit of account mentioned in article 31.

Article 19
Localized damage

When the loss of or damage to the goods occurred during one particular stage of the multimodal transport, in respect of which an applicable international convention or mandatory national law provides a higher limit of liability than the limit that would follow from application of paragraphs 1 to 3 of article 18, then the limit of the multimodal transport operator's liability for such loss or damage shall be determined by reference to the provisions of such convention or mandatory national law.

Article 20
Non-contractual liability

1. The defences and limits of liability provided for in this Convention shall apply in any action against the multimodal transport operator in respect of loss resulting from

loss of or damage to the goods, as well as from delay in delivery, whether the action be founded in contract, in tort or otherwise.

2. If an action in respect of loss resulting from loss of or damage to the goods or from delay in delivery is brought against the servant or agent of the multimodal transport operator, if such servant or agent proves that he acted within the scope of his employment, or against any other person of whose services he makes use for the performance of the multimodal transport contract, if such other person proves that he acted within the performance of the contract, the servant or agent or such other person shall be entitled to avail himself of the defences and limits of liability which the multimodal transport operator is entitled to invoke under this Convention.

3. Except as provided in article 21, the aggregate of the amounts recoverable from the multimodal transport operator and from a servant or agent or any other person of whose services he makes use for the performance of the multimodal transport contract shall not exceed the limits of liability provided for in this Convention.

Article 21
Loss of the right to limit liability

1. The multimodal transport operator is not entitled to the benefit of the limitation of liability provided for in this Convention if it is proved that the loss, damage or delay in delivery resulted from an act or omission of the multimodal transport operator done with the intent to cause such loss, damage or delay or recklessly and with knowledge that such loss, damage or delay would probably result.

2. Notwithstanding paragraph 2 of article 20, a servant or agent of the multimodal transport operator or other person of whose services he makes use for the performance of the multimodal transport contract is not entitled to the benefit of the limitation of liability provided for in this Convention if it is proved that the loss, damage or delay in delivery resulted from an act or omission of such servant, agent or other person, done with the intent to cause such loss, damage or delay or recklessly and with knowledge that such loss, damage or delay would probably result.

PART IV. LIABILITY OF THE CONSIGNOR

Article 22
General rule

The consignor shall be liable for loss sustained by the multimodal transport operator if such loss is caused by the fault or neglect of the consignor, or his servants or agents when such servants or agents are acting within the scope of their employment. Any servant or agent of the consignor shall be liable for such loss if the loss is caused by fault or neglect on his part.

Article 23
Special rules on dangerous goods

1. The consignor shall mark or label in a suitable manner dangerous goods as dangerous.

2. When the consignor hands over dangerous goods to the multimodal transport operator or any person acting on his behalf, the consignor shall inform him of the dangerous character of the goods and, if necessary, the precautions to be taken. If the con-

signor fails to do so and the multimodal transport operator does not otherwise have knowledge of their dangerous character:

(a) the consignor shall be liable to the multimodal transport operator for all loss resulting from the shipment of such goods; and

(b) the goods may at any time be unloaded, destroyed or rendered innocuous, as the circumstances may require, without payment of compensation.

3. The provisions of paragraph 2 of this article may not be invoked by any person if during the multimodal transport he has taken the goods in his charge with knowledge of their dangerous character.

4. If, in cases where the provisions of paragraph 2(b) of this article do not apply or may not be invoked, dangerous goods become an actual danger to life or property, they may be unloaded, destroyed or rendered innocuous, as the circumstances may require, without payment of compensation except where there is an obligation to contribute in general average or where the multimodal transport operator is liable in accordance with the provisions of article 16.

PART V. CLAIMS AND ACTIONS

Article 24
Notice of loss, damage or delay

1. Unless notice of loss or damage, specifying the general nature of such loss or damage, is given in writing by the consignee to the multimodal transport operator not later than the working day after the day when the goods were handed over to the consignee, such handing over is prima facie evidence of the delivery by the multimodal transport operator of the goods as described in the multimodal transport document.

2. Where the loss or damage is not apparent, the provisions of paragraph 1 of this article apply correspondingly if notice in writing is not given within six consecutive days after the day when the goods were handed over to the consignee.

3. If the state of the goods at the time they were handed over to the consignee has been the subject of a joint survey or inspection by the parties or their authorized representatives at the place of delivery, notice in writing need not be given of loss or damage ascertained during such survey or inspection.

4. In the case of any actual or apprehended loss or damage the multimodal transport operator and the consignee shall give all reasonable facilities to each other for inspecting and tallying the goods.

5. No compensation shall be payable for loss resulting from delay in delivery unless notice has been given in writing to the multimodal transport operator within 60 consecutive days after the day when the goods were delivered by handing over to the consignee or when the consignee has been notified that the goods have been delivered in accordance with paragraph 2(b)(ii) or (iii) of article 14.

6. Unless notice of loss or damage, specifying the general nature of the loss or damage, is given in writing by the multimodal transport operator to the consignor not later than 90 consecutive days after the occurrence of such loss or damage or after the delivery of the goods in accordance with paragraph 2(b) of article 14, whichever is later, the failure to give such notice is prima facie evidence that the multimodal transport operator has sustained no loss or damage due to the fault or neglect of the consignor, his servants or agents.

7. If any of the notice periods provided for in paragraphs 2, 5 and 6 of this article terminates on a day which is not a working day at the place of delivery, such period shall be extended until the next working day.

8. For the purpose of this article, notice given to a person acting on the multimodal transport operator's behalf, including any person of whose services he makes use at the place of delivery, or to a person acting on the consignor's behalf, shall be deemed to have been given to the multimodal transport operator, or to the consignor, respectively.

Article 25
Limitation of actions

1. Any action relating to international multimodal transport under this Convention shall be time-barred if judicial or arbitral proceedings have not been instituted within a period of two years. However, if notification in writing, stating the nature and main particulars of the claim, has not been given within six months after the day when the goods were delivered or, where the goods have not been delivered, after the day on which they should have been delivered, the action shall be time-barred at the expiry of this period.

2. The limitation period commences on the day after the day on which the multimodal transport operator has delivered the goods or part thereof or, where the goods have not been delivered, on the day after the last day on which the goods should have been delivered.

3. The person against whom a claim is made may at any time during the running of the limitation period extend that period by a declaration in writing to the claimant. This period may be further extended by another declaration or declarations.

4. Provided that the provisions of another applicable international convention are not to the contrary, a recourse action for indemnity by a person held liable under this Convention may be instituted even after the expiration of the limitation period provided for in the preceding paragraphs if instituted within the time allowed by the law of the State where proceedings are instituted; however, the time allowed shall not be less than 90 days commencing from the day when the person instituting such action for indemnity has settled the claim or has been served with process in the action against himself.

Article 26
Jurisdiction

1. In judicial proceedings relating to international multimodal transport under this Convention, the plaintiff, at his option, may institute an action in a court which, according to the law of the State where the court is situated, is competent and within the jurisdiction of which is situated one of the following places:

(a) the principal place of business or, in the absence thereof, the habitual residence of the defendant; or

(b) the place where the multimodal transport contract was made, provided that the defendant has there a place of business, branch or agency through which the contract was made; or

(c) the place of taking the goods in charge for international multimodal transport or the place of delivery; or

(d) any other place designated for that purpose in the multimodal transport contract and evidenced in the multimodal transport document.

2. No judicial proceedings relating to international multimodal transport under this Convention may be instituted in a place not specified in paragraph 1 of this article. The provisions of this article do not constitute an obstacle to the jurisdiction of the Contracting States for provisional or protective measures.

3. Notwithstanding the preceding provisions of this article, an agreement made by the parties after a claim has arisen, which designates the place where the plaintiff may institute an action, shall be effective.

4. (a) Where an action has been instituted in accordance with the provisions of this article or where judgement in such an action has been delivered, no new action shall be instituted between the same parties on the same grounds unless the judgement in the first action is not enforceable in the country in which the new proceedings are instituted.

(b) For the purposes of this article neither the institution of measures to obtain enforcement of a judgement nor the removal of an action to a different court within the same country shall be considered as the starting of a new action.

Article 27
Arbitration

1. Subject to the provisions of this article, parties may provide by agreement evidenced in writing that any dispute that may arise relating to international multimodal transport under this Convention shall be referred to arbitration.

2. The arbitration proceedings shall, at the option of the claimant, be instituted at one of the following places:

(a) a place in a State within whose territory is situated:

(i) the principal place of business of the defendant or, in the absence thereof, the habitual residence of the defendant; or

(ii) the place where the multimodal transport contract was made, provided that the defendant has there a place of business, branch or agency through which the contract was made; or

(iii) the place of taking the goods in charge for international multimodal transport or the place of delivery; or

(b) any other place designated for the purpose in the arbitration clause or agreement.

3. The arbitrator or arbitration tribunal shall apply the provisions of this Convention.

4. The provisions of paragraphs 2 and 3 of this article shall be deemed to be part of every arbitration clause or agreement and any term of such clause or agreement which is inconsistent therewith shall be null and void.

5. Nothing in this article shall affect the validity of an agreement on arbitration made by the parties after the claim relating to the international multimodal transport has arisen.

PART VI. SUPPLEMENTARY PROVISIONS

Article 28
Contractual stipulations

1. Any stipulation in a multimodal transport contract or multimodal transport document shall be null and void to the extent that it derogates, directly or indirectly, from

the provisions of this Convention. The nullity of such a stipulation shall not affect the validity of other provisions of the contract or document of which it forms a part. A clause assigning benefit of insurance of the goods in favour of the multimodal transport operator or any similar clause shall be null and void.

2. Notwithstanding the provisions of paragraph 1 of this article, the multimodal transport operator may, with the agreement of the consignor, increase his responsibilities and obligations under this Convention.

3. The multimodal transport document shall contain a statement that the international multimodal transport is subject to the provisions of this Convention which nullify any stipulation derogating therefrom to the detriment of the consignor or the consignee.

4. Where the claimant in respect of the goods has incurred loss as a result of a stipulation which is null and void by virtue of the present article, or as a result of the omission of the statement referred to in paragraph 3 of this article, the multimodal transport operator must pay compensation to the extent required in order to give the claimant compensation in accordance with the provisions of this Convention for any loss of or damage to the goods as well as for delay in delivery. The multimodal transport operator must, in addition, pay compensation for costs incurred by the claimant for the purpose of exercising his right, provided that costs incurred in the action where the foregoing provision is invoked are to be determined in accordance with the law of the State where proceedings are instituted.

Article 29
General average

1. Nothing in this Convention shall prevent the application of provisions in the multimodal transport contract or national law regarding the adjustment of general average, if and to the extent applicable.

2. With the exception of article 25, the provisions of this Convention relating to the liability of the multimodal transport operator for loss of or damage to the goods shall also determine whether the consignee may refuse contribution in general average and the liability of the multimodal transport operator to indemnify the consignee in respect of any such contribution made or any salvage paid.

Article 30
Other conventions

1. This Convention does not modify the rights or duties provided for in the Brussels International Convention for the unification of certain rules relating to the limitation of owners of sea-going vessels of 25 August 1924; in the Brussels International Convention relating to the limitation of the liability of owners of sea-going ships of 10 October 1957; in the London Convention on limitation of liability for maritime claims of 19 November 1976; and in the Geneva Convention relating to the limitation of the liability of owners of inland navigation vessels (CLN) of 1 March 1973, including amendments to these Conventions, or national law relating to the limitation of liability of owners of sea-going ships and inland navigation vessels.

2. The provisions of articles 26 and 27 of this Convention do not prevent the application of the mandatory provisions of any other international convention relating to matters dealt with in the said articles, provided that the dispute arises exclusively between parties having their principal place of business in States parties to such other

convention. However, this paragraph does not affect the application of paragraph 3 of article 27 of this Convention.

3. No liability shall arise under the provisions of this Convention for damage caused by a nuclear incident if the operator of a nuclear installation is liable for such damage:

(a) under either the Paris Convention of 29 July 1960 on Third Party Liability in the Field of Nuclear Energy as amended by the Additional Protocol of 28 January 1964 or the Vienna Convention of 21 May 1963 on Civil Liability for Nuclear Damage, or amendments thereto; or

(b) by virtue of national law governing the liability for such damage, provided that such law is in all respects as favourable to persons who may suffer damage as either the Paris or Vienna Conventions.

4. Carriage of goods such as carriage of goods in accordance with the Geneva Convention of 19 May 1956 on the Contract for the International Carriage of Goods by Road in article 2, or the Berne Convention of 7 February 1970 concerning the Carriage of Goods by Rail, article 2, shall not for the States Parties to Conventions governing such carriage be considered as international multimodal transport within the meaning of article 1, paragraph 1, of this Convention, in so far as such States are bound to apply the provisions of such Conventions to such carriage of goods.

Article 31
Unit of account or monetary unit and conversion

1. The unit of account referred to in article 18 of this Convention is the Special Drawing Right as defined by the International Monetary Fund. The amounts referred to in article 18 shall be converted into the national currency of a State according to the value of such currency on the date of the judgement or award or the date agreed upon by the parties. The value of a national currency, in terms of the Special Drawing Right, of a Contracting State which is a member of the International Monetary Fund, shall be calculated in accordance with the method of valuation applied by the International Monetary Fund, in effect on the date in question, for its operations and transactions. The value of a national currency in terms of the Special Drawing Right of a Contracting State which is not a member of the International Monetary Fund, shall be calculated in a manner determined by that State.

2. Nevertheless, a State which is not a member of the International Monetary Fund and whose law does not permit the application of the provisions of paragraph 1 of this article may, at the time of signature, ratification, acceptance, approval or accession or at any time thereafter, declare that the limits of liability provided for in this Convention to be applied in its territory shall be fixed as follows: with regard to the limits provided for in paragraph 1 of article 18 to 13,750 monetary units per package or other shipping unit or 41.25 monetary units per kilogramme of gross weight of the goods, and with regard to the limit provided for in paragraph 3 of article 18 to 124 monetary units.

3. The monetary unit referred to in paragraph 2 of this article corresponds to sixty-five and a half milligrammes of gold of millesimal fineness nine hundred. The conversion of the amount referred to in paragraph 2 of this article into national currency shall be made according to the law of the State concerned.

4. The calculation mentioned in the last sentence of paragraph 1 of this article and the conversion referred to in paragraph 3 of this article shall be made in such a manner as to express in the national currency of the Contracting State as far as possible the same real value for the amounts in article 18 as is expressed there in units of account.

5. Contracting States shall communicate to the depositary the manner of calculation pursuant to the last sentence of paragraph 1 of this article, or the result of the conversion pursuant to paragraph 3 of this article, as the case may be, at the time of signature or when depositing their instruments of ratification, acceptance, approval or accession, or when availing themselves of the option provided for in paragraph 2 of this article and whenever there is a change in the manner of such calculation or in the result of such conversion.

PART VII. CUSTOMS MATTERS

Article 32
Customs transit

1. Contracting States shall authorize the use of the procedure of customs transit for international multimodal transport.

2. Subject to provisions of national law or regulations and intergovernmental agreements, the customs transit of goods in international multimodal transport shall be in accordance with the rules and principles contained in articles I to VI of the Annex to this Convention.

3. When introducing laws or regulations in respect of customs transit procedures relating to multimodal transport of goods, Contracting States should take into consideration articles I to VI of the Annex to this Convention.

PART VIII. FINAL CLAUSES

Article 33
Depositary

The Secretary-General of the United Nations is hereby designated as the depositary of this Convention.

Article 34
Signature, ratification, acceptance, approval and accession

1. All States are entitled to become Parties to this Convention by:

(a) signature not subject to ratification, acceptance or approval; or

(b) signature subject to and followed by ratification, acceptance or approval; or

(c) accession.

2. This Convention shall be open for signature as from 1 September 1980 until and including 31 August 1981 at the Headquarters of the United Nations in New York.

3. After 31 August 1981, this Convention shall be open for accession by all States which are not signatory States.

4. Instruments of ratification, acceptance, approval and accession are to be deposited with the depositary.

5. Organizations for regional economic integration, constituted by sovereign States members of UNCTAD, and which have competence to negotiate, conclude and apply international agreements in specific fields covered by this Convention shall be similarly entitled to become Parties to this Convention in accordance with the provisions of paragraphs 1 to 4 of this article, thereby assuming in relation to other Parties to this

Convention the rights and duties under this Convention in the specific fields referred to above.

Article 35
Reservations

No reservation may be made to this Convention.

Article 36
Entry into force

1. This Convention shall enter into force 12 months after the Governments of 30 States have either signed it not subject to ratification, acceptance or approval or have deposited instruments of ratification, acceptance, approval or accession with the depositary.

2. For each State which ratifies, accepts, approves or accedes to this Convention after the requirements for entry into force given in paragraph 1 of this article have been met, the Convention shall enter into force 12 months after the deposit by such State of the appropriate instrument.

Article 37
Date of application

Each Contracting State shall apply the provisions of this Convention to multimodal transport contracts concluded on or after the date of entry into force of this Convention in respect of that State.

Article 38
Rights and obligations under existing conventions

If, according to articles 26 or 27, judicial or arbitral proceedings are brought in a Contracting State in a case relating to international multimodal transport subject to this Convention which takes place between two States of which only one is a Contracting State, and if both these States are at the time of entry into force of this Convention equally bound by another international convention, the court or arbitral tribunal may, in accordance with the obligations under such convention, give effect to the provisions thereof.

Article 39
Revision and amendments

1. At the request of not less than one third of the Contracting States, the Secretary-General of the United Nations shall, after the entry into force of this Convention, convene a conference of the Contracting States for revising or amending it. The Secretary-General of the United Nations shall circulate to all Contracting States the texts of any proposals for amendments at least three months before the opening date of the conference.

2. Any decision by the revision conference, including amendments, shall be taken by a two thirds majority of the States present and voting. Amendments adopted by the conference shall be communicated by the depositary to all the Contracting States for acceptance and to all the States signatories of the Convention for information.

3. Subject to paragraph 4 below, any amendment adopted by the conference shall enter into force only for those Contracting States which have accepted it, on the first day of the month following one year after its acceptance by two thirds of the Contract-

ing States. For any State accepting an amendment after it has been accepted by two-thirds of the Contracting States, the amendment shall enter into force on the first day of the month following one year after its acceptance by that State.

4. Any amendment adopted by the conference altering the amounts specified in article 18 and paragraph 2 of article 31 or substituting either or both the units defined in paragraphs 1 and 3 of article 31 by other units shall enter into force on the first day of the month following one year after its acceptance by two-thirds of the Contracting States. Contracting States which have accepted the altered amounts or the substituted units shall apply them in their relationship with all Contracting States.

5. Acceptance of amendments shall be effected by the deposit of a formal instrument to that effect with the depositary.

6. Any instrument of ratification, acceptance, approval or accession deposited after the entry into force of any amendment adopted by the conference shall be deemed to apply to the Convention as amended.

Article 40
Denunciation

1. Each Contracting State may denounce this Convention at any time after the expiration of a period of two years from the date on which this Convention has entered into force by means of a notification in writing addressed to the depositary.

2. Such denunciation shall take effect on the first day of the month following the expiration of one year after the notification is received by the depositary. Where a longer period is specified in the notification, the denunciation shall take effect upon the expiration of such longer period after the notification is received by the depositary.

IN WITNESS WHEREOF the undersigned, being duly authorized thereto, have affixed their signatures hereunder on the dates indicated.

DONE at Geneva on 24 May 1980 in one original in the Arabic, Chinese, English, French, Russian and Spanish languages, all texts being equally authentic.

[The annex is omitted.]

Appendix 19

Protocol Relating to an Amendment to the Convention on International Civil Aviation

Done at Montreal—May 10, 1984
Entered into force—October 1, 1998
Not in effect in the United States
23 I.L.M. 705, ICAO Doc. 9436

THE ASSEMBLY OF THE INTERNATIONAL CIVIL AVIATION ORGANIZATION,

HAVING MET in its Twenty-fifth Session (Extraordinary) at Montreal on 10 May 1984,

HAVING NOTED that international civil aviation can greatly help to create and preserve friendship and understanding among the nations and peoples of the world, yet its abuse can become a threat to general security,

HAVING NOTED that it is desirable to avoid friction and to promote that co-operation between nations and peoples upon which the peace of the world depends,

HAVING NOTED that it is necessary that international civil aviation may be developed in a safe and orderly manner,

HAVING NOTED that in keeping with elementary considerations of humanity the safety and the lives of persons on board civil aircraft must be assured,

HAVING NOTED that in the Convention on International Civil Aviation done at Chicago on 7 December 1944 the contracting States

- recognize that every State has complete and exclusive sovereignty over the airspace above its territory,

- undertake, when issuing regulations for their state aircraft, that they will have due regard for the safety of navigation of civil aircraft, and

- agree not to use civil aviation for any purpose inconsistent with the aims of the Convention,

HAVING NOTED the resolve of the contracting States to take appropriate measures designed to prevent the violation of other States' airspace and the use of civil aviation for purposes inconsistent with the aims of the Convention and to enhance further the safety of international civil aviation,

HAVING NOTED the general desire of contracting States to reaffirm the principle of non-use of weapons against civil aircraft in flight,

1. DECIDES that it is desirable therefore to amend the Convention on International Civil Aviation done at Chicago on 7 December 1944,

2. APPROVES, in accordance with the provision of Article 94(a) of the Convention aforesaid, the following proposed amendment to the said Convention:

Insert, after Article 3, a new Article 3bis:

"Article 3bis

(a) The contracting States recognize that every State must refrain from resorting to the use of weapons against civil aircraft in flight and that, in case of interception, the lives of persons on board and the safety of aircraft must not be endangered. This provision shall not be interpreted as modifying in any way the rights and obligations of States set forth in the Charter of the United Nations.

(b) The contracting States recognize that every State, in the exercise of its sovereignty, is entitled to require the landing at some designated airport of a civil aircraft flying above its territory without authority or if there are reasonable grounds to conclude that it is being used for any purpose inconsistent with the aims of this Convention; it may also give such aircraft any other instructions to put an end to such violations. For this purpose, the contracting States may resort to any appropriate means consistent with relevant rules of international law, including the relevant provisions of this Convention, specifically paragraph (a) of this Article. Each contracting State agrees to publish its regulations in force regarding the interception of civil aircraft.

(c) Every civil aircraft shall comply with an order given in conformity with paragraph (b) of this Article. To this end each contracting State shall establish all necessary provisions in its national laws or regulations to make such compliance mandatory for any civil aircraft registered in that State or operated by an operator who has his principal place of business or permanent residence in that State. Each contracting State shall make any violation of such applicable laws or regulations punishable by severe penalties and shall submit the case to its competent authorities in accordance with its laws or regulations.

(d) Each contracting State shall take appropriate measures to prohibit the deliberate use of any civil aircraft registered in that State or operated by an operator who has his principal place of business or permanent residence in that State for any purpose inconsistent with the aims of this Convention. This provision shall not affect paragraph (a) or derogate from paragraphs (b) and (c) of this Article."

3. SPECIFIES, pursuant to the provision of the said Article 94(a) of the said Convention, one hundred and two as the number of contracting States upon whose ratification the proposed amendment aforesaid shall come into force, and

4. RESOLVES that the Secretary General of the International Civil Aviation Organization draw up a Protocol, in the English, French, Russian and Spanish languages, each of which shall be of equal authenticity, embodying the proposed amendment abovementioned and the matter hereinafter appearing:

(a) The Protocol shall be signed by the President of the Assembly and its Secretary General.

(b) The Protocol shall be open to ratification by any State which has ratified or adhered to the said Convention on International Civil Aviation.

(c) The instruments of ratification shall be deposited with the International Civil Aviation Organization.

(d) The Protocol shall come into force in respect of the States which have ratified it on the date on which the one hundred and second instrument of ratification is so deposited.

(e) The Secretary General shall immediately notify all contracting States of the date of deposit of each ratification of the Protocol.

(f) The Secretary General shall notify all States parties to the said Convention of the date on which the Protocol comes into force.

(g) With respect to any contracting State ratifying the Protocol after the date aforesaid, the Protocol shall come into force upon deposit of its instrument of ratification with the International Civil Aviation Organization.

CONSEQUENTLY, pursuant to the aforesaid action of the Assembly,

This Protocol has been drawn up by the Secretary General of the Organization.

IN WITNESS WHEREOF, the President and the Secretary General of the aforesaid Twenty-fifth Session (Extraordinary) of the Assembly of the International Civil Aviation Organization, being authorized thereto by the Assembly, sign this Protocol.

DONE at Montreal on the 10th day of May of the year one thousand nine hundred and eighty-four, in a single document in the English, French, Russian and Spanish languages, each text being equally authentic. This Protocol shall remain deposited in the archives of the International Civil Aviation Organization, and certified copies thereof shall be transmitted by the Secretary General of the Organization to all States parties to the Convention on International Civil Aviation done at Chicago on the seventh day of December 1944.

Appendix 20

Protocol for the Suppression of Unlawful Acts of Violence at Airports Serving International Civil Aviation, Supplementary to the Convention for the Suppression of Unlawful Acts Against the Safety of Civil Aviation, Done at Montreal, on 23 September 1971

Done at Montreal—February 24, 1988
Entered into force—August 6, 1989
Effective in the United States—November 18, 1994
1589 U.N.T.S. 474, ICAO Doc. 9518, 27 I.L.M. 627

THE STATES PARTIES TO THIS PROTOCOL,

CONSIDERING that unlawful acts of violence which endanger or are likely to endanger the safety of persons at airports serving international civil aviation or which jeopardize the safe operation of such airports undermine the confidence of the peoples of the world in safety at such airports and disturb the safe and orderly conduct of civil aviation for all States;

CONSIDERING that the occurrence of such acts is a matter of grave concern to the international community and that, for the purpose of deterring such acts, there is an urgent need to provide appropriate measures for punishment of offenders;

CONSIDERING that it is necessary to adopt provisions supplementary to those of the Convention for the Suppression of Unlawful Acts against the Safety of Civil Aviation, done at Montreal on 23 September 1971, to deal with such unlawful acts of violence at airports serving international civil aviation;

HAVE AGREED AS FOLLOWS:

Article I

This Protocol supplements the Convention for the Suppression of Unlawful Acts against the Safety of Civil Aviation, done at Montreal on 23 September 1971 (hereinafter referred to as "the Convention"), and, as between the Parties to this Protocol, the Convention and the Protocol shall be read and interpreted together as one single instrument.

Article II

1. In Article 1 of the Convention, the following shall be added as new paragraph 1 bis: "1 bis. Any person commits an offence if he unlawfully and intentionally, using any device, substance or weapon: (a) performs an act of violence against a person at an airport serving international civil aviation which causes or is likely to cause serious injury or death; or (b) destroys or seriously damages the facilities of an airport serving international civil aviation or aircraft not in service located thereon or disrupts the services of the airport, if such an act endangers or is likely to endanger safety at that airport."

2. In paragraph 2(a) of Article 1 of the Convention, the following words shall be inserted after the words "paragraph 1": "or paragraph 1 bis."

Article III

In Article 5 of the Convention, the following shall be added as paragraph 2 bis: "2 bis. Each Contracting State shall likewise take such measures as may be necessary to establish its jurisdiction over the offences mentioned in Article 1, paragraph 1 bis, and in Article 1, paragraph 2, in so far as that paragraph relates to those offences, in the case where the alleged offender is present in its territory and it does not extradite him pursuant to Article 8 to the State mentioned in paragraph 1 (a) of this Article."

Article IV

This Protocol shall be open for signature at Montreal on 24 February 1988 by States participating in the International Conference on Air Law held at Montreal from 9 to 24 February 1988. After 1 March 1988, the Protocol shall be open for signature to all States in London, Moscow, Washington and Montreal, until it enters into force in accordance with Article VI.

Article V

1. This Protocol shall be subject to ratification by the signatory States.

2. Any State which is not a Contracting State to the Convention may ratify this Protocol if at the same time it ratifies or accedes to the Convention in accordance with Article 15 thereof.

3. Instruments of ratification shall be deposited with the Governments of the Union of Soviet Socialist Republics, the United Kingdom of Great Britain and Northern Ireland and the United States of America or with the International Civil Aviation Organization, which are hereby designated the Depositaries.

Article VI

1. As soon as ten of the signatory States have deposited their instruments of ratification of this Protocol, it shall enter into force between them on the thirtieth day after the date of the deposit of the tenth instrument of ratification. It shall enter into force for each State which deposits its instrument of ratification after that date on the thirtieth day after deposit of its instrument of ratification.

2. As soon as this Protocol enters into force, it shall be registered by the Depositaries pursuant to Article 102 of the Charter of the United Nations and pursuant to Article 83 of the Convention on International Civil Aviation (Chicago, 1944).

Article VII

1. This Protocol shall, after it has entered into force, be open for accession by any non-signatory State.

2. Any State which is not a Contracting State to the Convention may accede to this Protocol if at the same time it ratifies or accedes to the Convention in accordance with Article 15 thereof.

3. Instruments of accession shall be deposited with the Depositaries and accession shall take effect on the thirtieth day after the deposit.

Article VIII

1. Any Party to this Protocol may denounce it by written notification addressed to the Depositaries.

2. Denunciation shall take effect six months following the date on which notification is received by the Depositaries.

3. Denunciation of this Protocol shall not of itself have the effect of denunciation of the Convention.

4. Denunciation of the Convention by a Contracting State to the Convention as supplemented by this Protocol shall also have the effect of denunciation of this Protocol.

Article IX

1. The Depositaries shall promptly inform all signatory and acceding States to this Protocol and all signatory and acceding States to the Convention:

(a) of the date of each signature and the date of deposit of each instrument of ratification of, or accession to, this Protocol, and

(b) of the receipt of any notification of denunciation of this Protocol and the date thereof.

2. The Depositaries shall also notify the States referred to in paragraph 1 of the date on which this Protocol enters into force in accordance with Article VI.

IN WITNESS WHEREOF the undersigned Plenipotentiaries, being duly authorized thereto by their Governments, have signed this Protocol.

DONE at Montreal on the twenty-fourth day of February of the year One Thousand Nine Hundred and Eighty-eight, in four originals, each being drawn up in four authentic texts in the English, French, Russian and Spanish languages.

Appendix 21

Convention on the Marking of Plastic Explosives for the Purpose of Detection

Done at Montreal—March 1, 1991
Entered into force—June 21, 1998
Effective in the United States—June 21, 1998
ICAO Doc. 9571, 30 I.L.M. 721

THE STATES PARTIES TO THIS CONVENTION,

CONSCIOUS of the implications of acts of terrorism for international security;

EXPRESSING deep concern regarding terrorist acts aimed at destruction of aircraft, other means of transportation and other targets;

CONCERNED that plastic explosives have been used for such terrorist acts;

CONSIDERING that the marking of such explosives for the purpose of detection would contribute significantly to the prevention of such unlawful acts;

RECOGNIZING that for the purpose of deterring such unlawful acts there is an urgent need for an international instrument obliging States to adopt appropriate measures to ensure that plastic explosives are duly marked;

CONSIDERING United Nations Security Council Resolution 635 of 14 June 1989, and United Nations General Assembly Resolution 44/29 of 4 December 1989 urging the International Civil Aviation Organization to intensify its work on devising an international regime for the marking of plastic or sheet explosives for the purpose of detection;

BEARING IN MIND Resolution A27-8 adopted unanimously by the 27th Session of the Assembly of the International Civil Aviation Organization which endorsed with the highest and overriding priority the preparation of a new international instrument regarding the marking of plastic or sheet explosives for detection;

NOTING with satisfaction the role played by the Council of the International Civil Aviation Organization in the preparation of the Convention as well as its willingness to assume functions related to its implementation;

HAVE AGREED AS FOLLOWS:

Article I

For the purposes of this Convention:

1. "Explosives" mean explosive products, commonly known as "plastic explosives," including explosives in flexible or elastic sheet form, as described in the Technical Annex to this Convention.

2. "Detection agent" means a substance as described in the Technical Annex to this Convention which is introduced into an explosive to render it detectable.

3. "Marking" means introducing into an explosive a detection agent in accordance with the Technical Annex to this Convention.

4. "Manufacture" means any process, including reprocessing, that produces explosives.

5. "Duly authorized military devices" include, but are not restricted to, shells, bombs, projectiles, mines, missiles, rockets, shaped charges, grenades and perforators

manufactured exclusively for military or police purposes according to the laws and regulations of the State Party concerned.

6. "Producer State" means any State in whose territory explosives are manufactured.

Article II

Each State Party shall take the necessary and effective measures to prohibit and prevent the manufacture in its territory of unmarked explosives.

Article III

1. Each State Party shall take the necessary and effective measures to prohibit and prevent the movement into or out of its territory of unmarked explosives.

2. The preceding paragraph shall not apply in respect of movements for purposes not inconsistent with the objectives of this Convention, by authorities of a State Party performing military or police functions, of unmarked explosives under the control of that State Party in accordance with paragraph 1 of Article IV.

Article IV

1. Each State Party shall take the necessary measures to exercise strict and effective control over the possession and transfer of possession of unmarked explosives which have been manufactured in or brought into its territory prior to the entry into force of this Convention in respect of that State, so as to prevent their diversion or use for purposes inconsistent with the objectives of this Convention.

2. Each State Party shall take the necessary measures to ensure that all stocks of those explosives referred to in paragraph 1 of this Article not held by its authorities performing military or police functions are destroyed or consumed for purposes not inconsistent with the objectives of this Convention, marked or rendered permanently ineffective, within a period of three years from the entry into force of this Convention in respect of that State.

3. Each State Party shall take the necessary measures to ensure that all stocks of those explosives referred to in paragraph 1 of this Article held by its authorities performing military or police functions and that are not incorporated as an integral part of duly authorized military devices are destroyed or consumed for purposes not inconsistent with the objectives of this Convention, marked or rendered permanently ineffective, within a period of fifteen years from the entry into force of this Convention in respect of that State.

4. Each State Party shall take the necessary measures to ensure the destruction, as soon as possible, in its territory of unmarked explosives which may be discovered therein and which are not referred to in the preceding paragraphs of this Article, other than stocks of unmarked explosives held by its authorities performing military or police functions and incorporated as an integral part of duly authorized military devices at the date of the entry into force of this Convention in respect of that State.

5. Each State Party shall take the necessary measures to exercise strict and effective control over the possession and transfer of possession of the explosives referred to in paragraph II of Part 1 of the Technical Annex to this Convention so as to prevent their diversion or use for purposes inconsistent with the objectives of this Convention.

6. Each State Party shall take the necessary measures to ensure the destruction, as soon as possible, in its territory of unmarked explosives manufactured since the coming into force of this Convention in respect of that State that are not incorporated as specified in paragraph II (d) of Part 1 of the Technical Annex to this Convention and of un-

marked explosives which no longer fall within the scope of any other sub-paragraphs of the said paragraph II.

Article V

1. There is established by this Convention an International Explosives Technical Commission (hereinafter referred to as "the Commission") consisting of not less than fifteen nor more than nineteen members appointed by the Council of the International Civil Aviation Organization (hereinafter referred to as "the Council") from among persons nominated by States Parties to this Convention.

2. The members of the Commission shall be experts having direct and substantial experience in matters relating to the manufacture or detection of, or research in, explosives.

3. Members of the Commission shall serve for a period of three years and shall be eligible for re-appointment.

4. Sessions of the Commission shall be convened, at least once a year at the Headquarters of the International Civil Aviation Organization, or at such places and times as may be directed or approved by the Council.

5. The Commission shall adopt its rules of procedure, subject to the approval of the Council.

Article VI

1. The Commission shall evaluate technical developments relating to the manufacture, marking and detection of explosives.

2. The Commission, through the Council, shall report its findings to the States Parties and international organizations concerned.

3. Whenever necessary, the Commission shall make recommendations to the Council for amendments to the Technical Annex to this Convention. The Commission shall endeavour to take its decisions on such recommendations by consensus. In the absence of consensus the Commission shall take such decisions by a two-thirds majority vote of its members.

4. The Council may, on the recommendation of the Commission, propose to States Parties amendments to the Technical Annex to this Convention.

Article VII

1. Any State Party may, within ninety days from the date of notification of a proposed amendment to the Technical Annex to this Convention, transmit to the Council its comments. The Council shall communicate these comments to the Commission as soon as possible for its consideration. The Council shall invite any State Party which comments on or objects to the proposed amendment to consult the Commission.

2. The Commission shall consider the views of States Parties made pursuant to the preceding paragraph and report to the Council. The Council, after consideration of the Commission's report, and taking into account the nature of the amendment and the comments of States Parties, including producer States, may propose the amendment to all States Parties for adoption.

3. If a proposed amendment has not been objected to by five or more States Parties by means of written notification to the Council within ninety days from the date of notification of the amendment by the Council, it shall be deemed to have been adopted,

and shall enter into force one hundred and eighty days thereafter or after such other period as specified in the proposed amendment for States Parties not having expressly objected thereto.

4. States Parties having expressly objected to the proposed amendment may, subsequently, by means of the deposit of an instrument of acceptance or approval, express their consent to be bound by the provisions of the amendment.

5. If five or more States Parties have objected to the proposed amendment, the Council shall refer it to the Commission for further consideration.

6. If the proposed amendment has not been adopted in accordance with paragraph 3 of this Article, the Council may also convene a conference of all States Parties.

Article VIII

1. States Parties shall, if possible, transmit to the Council information that would assist the Commission in the discharge of its functions under paragraph 1 of Article VI.

2. States Parties shall keep the Council informed of measures they have taken to implement the provisions of this Convention. The Council shall communicate such information to all States Parties and international organizations concerned.

Article IX

The Council shall, in co-operation with States Parties and international organizations concerned, take appropriate measures to facilitate the implementation of this Convention, including the provision of technical assistance and measures for the exchange of information relating to technical developments in the marking and detection of explosives.

Article X

The Technical Annex to this Convention shall form an integral part of this Convention.

Article XI

1. Any dispute between two or more States Parties concerning the interpretation or application of this Convention which cannot be settled through negotiation shall, at the request of one of them, be submitted to arbitration. If within six months from the date of the request for arbitration the Parties are unable to agree on the organization of the arbitration, any one of those Parties may refer the dispute to the International Court of Justice by request in conformity with the Statute of the Court.

2. Each State Party may, at the time of signature, ratification, acceptance or approval of this Convention or accession thereto, declare that it does not consider itself bound by the preceding paragraph. The other States Parties shall not be bound by the preceding paragraph with respect to any State Party having made such a reservation.

3. Any State Party having made a reservation in accordance with the preceding paragraph may at any time withdraw this reservation by notification to the Depositary.

Article XII

Except as provided in Article XI no reservation may be made to this Convention.

Article XIII

1. This Convention shall be open for signature in Montreal on 1 March 1991 by States participating in the International Conference on Air Law held at Montreal from

12 February to 1 March 1991. After 1 March 1991 the Convention shall be open to all States for signature at the Headquarters of the International Civil Aviation Organization in Montreal until it enters into force in accordance with paragraph 3 of this Article. Any State which does not sign this Convention may accede to it at any time.

2. This Convention shall be subject to ratification, acceptance, approval or accession by States. Instruments of ratification, acceptance, approval or accession shall be deposited with the International Civil Aviation Organization, which is hereby designated the Depositary. When depositing its instrument of ratification, acceptance, approval or accession, each State shall declare whether or not it is a producer State.

3. This Convention shall enter into force on the sixtieth day following the date of deposit of the thirty-fifth instrument of ratification, acceptance, approval or accession with the Depositary, provided that no fewer than five such States have declared pursuant to paragraph 2 of this Article that they are producer States. Should thirty-five such instruments be deposited prior to the deposit of their instruments by five producer States, this Convention shall enter into force on the sixtieth day following the date of deposit of the instrument of ratification, acceptance, approval or accession of the fifth producer State.

4. For other States, this Convention shall enter into force sixty days following the date of deposit of their instruments of ratification, acceptance, approval or accession.

5. As soon as this Convention comes into force, it shall be registered by the Depositary pursuant to Article 102 of the Charter of the United Nations and pursuant to Article 83 of the Convention on International Civil Aviation (Chicago, 1944).

Article XIV

The Depositary shall promptly notify all signatories and States Parties of:

1. each signature of this Convention and date thereof;

2. each deposit of an instrument of ratification, acceptance, approval or accession and date thereof, giving special reference to whether the State has identified itself as a producer State;

3. the date of entry into force of this Convention;

4. the date of entry into force of any amendment to this Convention or its Technical Annex;

5. any denunciation made under Article XV; and

6. any declaration made under paragraph 2 of Article XI.

Article XV

1. Any State Party may denounce this Convention by written notification to the Depositary.

2. Denunciation shall take effect one hundred and eighty days following the date on which notification is received by the Depositary.

IN WITNESS WHEREOF the undersigned Plenipotentiaries, being duly authorized thereto by their Governments, have signed this Convention.

DONE at Montreal, this first day of March, one thousand nine hundred and ninety-one, in one original, drawn up in five authentic texts in the English, French, Russian, Spanish and Arabic languages.

[The annex is omitted.]

Appendix 22

Agreement to Ban Smoking on International Passenger Flights

Done at Chicago—November 1, 1994
Entered into force—March 1, 1995
Effective in the United States—March 1, 1995
T.I.A.S. No. 12578

THE PARTIES TO THIS AGREEMENT,

RECOGNIZING that eliminating smoking on board aircraft reduces the health hazards to passengers and crew and enhances aviation safety; and

RECOGNIZING that Resolution A29-15 adopted by the International Civil Aviation Organization on October 8, 1992 called on all Contracting States "to take necessary measures as soon as possible to restrict smoking progressively on all international passenger flights";

HAVE AGREED AS FOLLOWS:

Article 1

Each Party shall prohibit smoking on all passenger flights operated by its airlines between points in the territory of one Party and points in the territory of another Party, except for flights operated via an intermediate point in the territory of a State which is not a party to this Agreement. No Party shall be obliged to prohibit smoking on flights chartered by a single person, company or organization and in respect of which no charge or other financial obligation is imposed on any passenger in connection with the flight.

Article 2

This prohibition shall apply to all locations within the aircraft and shall be in effect from the time an aircraft commences enplanement of passengers to the time deplanement of passengers is completed.

Article 3

Each Party shall take all measures that it considers reasonable to secure compliance by its airlines and by their passengers and crew with the prohibition of smoking contained in this Agreement, including the imposition of appropriate penalties for non-compliance.

Article 4

1. This Agreement shall be open for signature by the Governments of Australia, Canada, and the United States of America.

2. Accession to this Agreement shall be accomplished by the deposit of an instrument of accession with the Government of Canada and the Agreement shall enter into force with respect to that acceding Party on the 60th day following the deposit of such instrument.

Article 5

Any Party may denounce this Agreement at any time by depositing a written notice with the Government of Canada. The denunciation shall be effective 12 months following such notification.

Article 6

The original of this Agreement shall be deposited with the Government of Canada which shall transmit certified copies thereof to all Parties which may sign or accede to this Agreement, and which shall register this Agreement and any amendments thereto with the United Nations in accordance with Article 102 of the United Nations Charter and with the International Civil Aviation Organization. The Government of Canada shall notify signatory and acceding Parties and the International Civil Aviation Organization of all signatures, accessions or denunciations thereto, and of the entry into force of this Agreement.

Article 7

This Agreement shall enter into force on the 120th day following signature by the Governments of Australia, Canada, and the United States of America.

IN WITNESS WHEREOF, the undersigned, being duly authorized by their respective Governments, have signed this Agreement.

DONE at Chicago, this 1st day of November, 1994, in the English and French languages, each text being equally authentic.

Appendix 23

IATA Intercarrier Agreement on Passenger Liability

Done at Kuala Lumpur (October 31, 1995),
Adopted by United States Department of Transportation
Order No. 96-11-6 (November 12, 1996),
Modified by DOT Order No. 97-1-2 (January 10, 1997)

WHEREAS the Warsaw Convention system is of great benefit to international air transportation; and

NOTING that the Convention's limits of liability, which have not been amended since 1955, are now grossly inadequate in most countries and that international airlines have previously acted together to increase them to the benefit of passengers;

The undersigned carriers agree:

1. To take action to waive the limitation of liability on recoverable compensatory damages in Article 22 paragraph 1 of the Warsaw Convention as to claims for death, wounding or other bodily injury of a passenger within the meaning of Article 17 of the Convention, so that recoverable compensatory damages may be determined and awarded by reference to the law of the domicile of the passenger.

2. To reserve all available defences pursuant to the provisions of the Convention; nevertheless, any carrier may waive any defence up to a specified monetary amount of recoverable compensatory damages as circumstances may warrant.

3. To reserve their rights of recourse against any other person, including rights of contribution or indemnity, with respect to any sums paid by the carrier.

4. To encourage other airlines involved in the international carriage of passengers to apply the terms of this Agreement to such carriage.

5. To implement the provisions of this Agreement no later than 1 November 1996 or upon receipt of requisite government approvals, whichever is later.

6. That nothing in this Agreement shall affect the rights of the passenger or the claimant otherwise available under the Convention.

7. That this Agreement may be signed in any number of counterparts, all of which shall constitute one Agreement. Any carrier may become a party to this Agreement by signing a counterpart hereof and depositing it with the Director General of the International Air Transport Association (IATA).

8. That any carrier party hereto may withdraw from this Agreement by giving twelve (12) months' written notice of withdrawal to the Director General of IATA and to the other carriers parties to the Agreement.

Appendix 24

Agreement on Measures to Implement the IATA Intercarrier Agreement

Done at Miami (February 1, 1996),
Adopted by United States Department of Transportation
Order No. 96-11-6 (November 12, 1996),
Modified by DOT Order No. 97-1-2 (January 10, 1997)

I.

Pursuant to the IATA Intercarrier Agreement of 31 October 1995, the undersigned carriers agree to implement said Agreement by incorporating in their conditions of carriage and tariffs, where necessary, the following:

1. [CARRIER] shall not invoke the limitation of liability in Article 22(1) of the Convention as to any claim for recoverable compensatory damages arising under Article 17 of the Convention.

2. [CARRIER] shall not avail itself of any defence under Article 20(1) of the Convention with respect to that portion of such claim which does not exceed 100,000 SDRs [unless option II(2) is used].

3. Except as otherwise provided in paragraphs 1 and 2 hereof, [CARRIER] reserves all defences available under the Convention to any such claim. With respect to third parties, the carrier also reserves all rights of recourse against any other person, including without limitation, rights of contribution and indemnity.

II.

At the option of the carrier, its conditions of carriage and tariffs also may include the following provisions:

1. [CARRIER] agrees that subject to applicable law, recoverable compensatory damages for such claims may be determined by reference to the law of the domicile or permanent residence of the passenger.

2. [CARRIER] shall not avail itself of any defence under Article 20(1) of the Convention with respect to that portion of such claims which does not exceed 100,000 SDRs, except that such waiver is limited to the amounts shown below for the routes indicated, as may be authorised by governments concerned with the transportation involved.

[Amounts and routes to be inserted]

3. Neither the waiver of limits nor the waiver of defences shall be applicable in respect of claims made by public social insurance or similar bodies however asserted. Such claims shall be subject to the limit in Article 22(1) and to the defences under Article 20(1) of the Convention. The carrier will compensate the passenger or his dependents for recoverable compensatory damages in excess of payments received from any public social insurance or similar body.

III.

Furthermore, at the option of a carrier, additional provisions may be included in its conditions of carriage and tariffs, provided they are not inconsistent with this Agreement and are in accordance with applicable law.

IV.

Should any provision of this Agreement or a provision incorporated in a condition of carriage or tariff pursuant to this Agreement be determined to be invalid, illegal or unenforceable by a court of competent jurisdiction, all other provisions shall nevertheless remain valid, binding and effective.

V.

1. This Agreement may be signed in any number of counterparts, all of which shall constitute one Agreement. Any carrier may become Party to this Agreement by signing a counterpart hereof and depositing it with the Director General of the International Air Transport Association (IATA).

2. Any carrier Party hereto may withdraw from this Agreement by giving twelve (12) months written notice of withdrawal to the Director General of IATA and to the other carriers Parties to the Agreement.

3. The Director General of IATA shall declare this Agreement effective on November 1st, 1996 or such later date as all requisite government approvals have been obtained for this Agreement and the IATA Intercarrier Agreement of 31 October 1995.

Appendix 25

ATA Provisions Implementing the IATA Intercarrier Agreement to Be Included in Conditions of Carriage and Tariffs

Done at Washington, D.C. (May 16, 1996),
Adopted by United States Department of Transportation
Order No. 96-11-6 (November 12, 1996),
Modified by DOT Order No. 97-1-2 (January 10, 1997)

I.

Pursuant to the IATA Intercarrier Agreement of 31 October 1995 (IIA), and the Agreement of Measures to Implement the IATA Intercarrier Agreement (MIA), each of the undersigned carriers ("the Carrier") shall, on or before November 1, 1996, include the following in its conditions of carriage, including tariffs embodying conditions of carriage filed by it with any government:

"The Carrier agrees in accordance with Article 22(1) of the Convention for the Unification of Certain Rules Relating to International Transportation by Air signed at Warsaw October 12, 1929 or, where applicable, that Convention as amended by the Protocol signed at The Hague on 28 September 1955 ("The Convention") that, as to all international carriage or transportation hereunder as defined in the Convention:

1. The Carrier shall not invoke the limitation of liability in Article 22(1) of the Convention as to any claim for recoverable compensatory damages arising under Article 17 of the Convention.

2. The Carrier shall not avail itself of any defense under Article 20(1) of the Convention with respect to that portion of such claim which does not exceed 100,000 SDRs.

3. Except as otherwise provided in paragraphs 1 and 2 hereof, the Carrier reserves all defenses available under the Convention to such claims. With respect to third parties, the Carrier reserves all rights of recourse against any other person, including without limitation, rights of contribution and indemnity.

4. The Carrier agrees that subject to applicable law recoverable compensatory damages for such claims may be determined by reference to the law of the domicile or permanent residence of the passenger."

II.

The Carrier shall, at the time of delivery of the ticket, furnish to each passenger whose transportation is governed by the Convention, the following notice:

"ADVICE TO INTERNATIONAL PASSENGERS ON CARRIER LIABILITY

Passengers on a journey involving an ultimate destination or a stop in a country other than the country of departure are advised that a treaty known as the Warsaw Convention may apply to the entire journey, including any portion thereof entirely within a country. For such passengers, the Warsaw Convention, including special contracts of carriage embodied in applicable tariffs, governs the liability of the Carrier for death of or injury to passengers. The names of carriers party to such special contracts are available at all ticket offices of such carriers and may be examined upon request."

III.

The implementation of this Agreement shall constitute a withdrawal by the Carrier from the intercarrier agreement, approved by CAB Order E-23680 and dated May 13, 1966, relating to the liability limits of the Convention for the Unification of Certain Rules Relating to International Transportation by Air signed at Warsaw October 12, 1929, and said withdrawal shall be effective on the date the provisions in the Carrier's conditions of carriage adopted pursuant to Paragraph 1 of this Agreement become effective.

IV.

Nothing in this Agreement shall be deemed to affect the rights of the passenger, the claimant and/or the Carrier under the Convention, other than as set forth in Paragraph 1 herein. If any provision of this Agreement is determined by a court of competent authority to be prohibited or unenforceable, it shall as to that jurisdiction be ineffective only to the extent of such prohibition or unenforceability without invalidating the remaining provisions of this Agreement. Any such prohibition or unenforceability in one jurisdiction shall not invalidate or render unenforceable that provision in any other jurisdiction.

V.

The Carrier may encourage other carriers engaged in international carriage or transportation as defined in the Convention to become party to the IIA and the MIA, and to this Agreement or any other satisfactory implementation of the IIA and the MIA.

VI.

This Agreement shall be filed with the US Department of Transportation for approval pursuant to 49 U.S.C. sections 41308 and 41309 and filed with other governments as required. This Agreement shall become effective upon approval by that Department under 49 U.S.C. section 41309, and action by that Department to provide that the adherence to, and the implementation of, this Agreement by the Carrier shall constitute compliance with all regulations of that Department that incorporate the intercarrier agreement referred to in paragraph III of this Agreement.

VII.

This Agreement may be signed in any number of counterparts, all of which shall constitute one agreement. Any carrier may become a party to this Agreement by signing a counterpart hereof and depositing it with the U.S. Department of Transportation.

Appendix 26

Convention for the Unification of Certain Rules for International Carriage by Air

Done at Montreal—May 28, 1999
Entered into force—November 4, 2003
Effective in the United States—November 4, 2003
ICAO Doc. 9740

THE STATES PARTIES TO THIS CONVENTION,

RECOGNIZING the significant contribution of the Convention for the Unification of Certain Rules Relating to International Carriage by Air signed in Warsaw on 12 October 1929, hereinafter referred to as the "Warsaw Convention," and other related instruments to the harmonization of private international air law;

RECOGNIZING the need to modernize and consolidate the Warsaw Convention and related instruments;

RECOGNIZING the importance of ensuring protection of the interests of consumers in international carriage by air and the need for equitable compensation based on the principle of restitution;

REAFFIRMING the desirability of an orderly development of international air transport operations and the smooth flow of passengers, baggage and cargo in accordance with the principles and objectives of the Convention on International Civil Aviation, done at Chicago on 7 December 1944;

CONVINCED that collective State action for further harmonization and codification of certain rules governing international carriage by air through a new Convention is the most adequate means of achieving an equitable balance of interests;

HAVE AGREED AS FOLLOWS:

Chapter I
General Provisions

Article 1—Scope of Application

1. This Convention applies to all international carriage of persons, baggage or cargo performed by aircraft for reward. It applies equally to gratuitous carriage by aircraft performed by an air transport undertaking.

2. For the purposes of this Convention, the expression international carriage means any carriage in which, according to the agreement between the parties, the place of departure and the place of destination, whether or not there be a break in the carriage or a transhipment, are situated either within the territories of two States Parties, or within the territory of a single State Party if there is an agreed stopping place within the territory of another State, even if that State is not a State Party. Carriage between two points within the territory of a single State Party without an agreed stopping place within the territory of another State is not international carriage for the purposes of this Convention.

3. Carriage to be performed by several successive carriers is deemed, for the purposes of this Convention, to be one undivided carriage if it has been regarded by the parties as a single operation, whether it had been agreed upon under the form of a single contract

or of a series of contracts, and it does not lose its international character merely because one contract or a series of contracts is to be performed entirely within the territory of the same State.

4. This Convention applies also to carriage as set out in Chapter V, subject to the terms contained therein.

Article 2—Carriage Performed by State and Carriage of Postal Items

1. This Convention applies to carriage performed by the State or by legally constituted public bodies provided it falls within the conditions laid down in Article 1.

2. In the carriage of postal items, the carrier shall be liable only to the relevant postal administration in accordance with the rules applicable to the relationship between the carriers and the postal administrations.

3. Except as provided in paragraph 2 of this Article, the provisions of this Convention shall not apply to the carriage of postal items.

Chapter II
Documentation and Duties of the Parties Relating to the Carriage of Passengers, Baggage and Cargo

Article 3—Passengers and Baggage

1. In respect of carriage of passengers, an individual or collective document of carriage shall be delivered containing:

(a) an indication of the places of departure and destination;

(b) if the places of departure and destination are within the territory of a single State Party, one or more agreed stopping places being within the territory of another State, an indication of at least one such stopping place.

2. Any other means which preserves the information indicated in paragraph 1 may be substituted for the delivery of the document referred to in that paragraph. If any such other means is used, the carrier shall offer to deliver to the passenger a written statement of the information so preserved.

3. The carrier shall deliver to the passenger a baggage identification tag for each piece of checked baggage.

4. The passenger shall be given written notice to the effect that where this Convention is applicable it governs and may limit the liability of carriers in respect of death or injury and for destruction or loss of, or damage to, baggage, and for delay.

5. Non-compliance with the provisions of the foregoing paragraphs shall not affect the existence or the validity of the contract of carriage, which shall, nonetheless, be subject to the rules of this Convention including those relating to limitation of liability.

Article 4—Cargo

1. In respect of the carriage of cargo, an air waybill shall be delivered.

2. Any other means which preserves a record of the carriage to be performed may be substituted for the delivery of an air waybill. If such other means are used, the carrier shall, if so requested by the consignor, deliver to the consignor a cargo receipt permitting identification of the consignment and access to the information contained in the record preserved by such other means.

Article 5—Contents of Air Waybill or Cargo Receipt

The air waybill or the cargo receipt shall include:

(a) an indication of the places of departure and destination;

(b) if the places of departure and destination are within the territory of a single State Party, one or more agreed stopping places being within the territory of another State, an indication of at least one such stopping place; and

(c) an indication of the weight of the consignment.

Article 6—Document Relating to the Nature of the Cargo

The consignor may be required, if necessary to meet the formalities of customs, police and similar public authorities, to deliver a document indicating the nature of the cargo. This provision creates for the carrier no duty, obligation or liability resulting therefrom.

Article 7—Description of Air Waybill

1. The air waybill shall be made out by the consignor in three original parts.

2. The first part shall be marked "for the carrier"; it shall be signed by the consignor. The second part shall be marked "for the consignee"; it shall be signed by the consignor and by the carrier. The third part shall be signed by the carrier who shall hand it to the consignor after the cargo has been accepted.

3. The signature of the carrier and that of the consignor may be printed or stamped.

4. If, at the request of the consignor, the carrier makes out the air waybill, the carrier shall be deemed, subject to proof to the contrary, to have done so on behalf of the consignor.

Article 8—Documentation for Multiple Packages

When there is more than one package:

(a) the carrier of cargo has the right to require the consignor to make out separate air waybills;

(b) the consignor has the right to require the carrier to deliver separate cargo receipts when the other means referred to in paragraph 2 of Article 4 are used.

Article 9—Non-compliance with Documentary Requirements

Non-compliance with the provisions of Articles 4 to 8 shall not affect the existence or the validity of the contract of carriage, which shall, nonetheless, be subject to the rules of this Convention including those relating to limitation of liability.

Article 10—Responsibility for Particulars of Documentation

1. The consignor is responsible for the correctness of the particulars and statements relating to the cargo inserted by it or on its behalf in the air waybill or furnished by it or on its behalf to the carrier for insertion in the cargo receipt or for insertion in the record preserved by the other means referred to in paragraph 2 of Article 4. The foregoing shall also apply where the person acting on behalf of the consignor is also the agent of the carrier.

2. The consignor shall indemnify the carrier against all damage suffered by it, or by any other person to whom the carrier is liable, by reason of the irregularity, incorrect-

ness or incompleteness of the particulars and statements furnished by the consignor or on its behalf.

3. Subject to the provisions of paragraphs 1 and 2 of this Article, the carrier shall indemnify the consignor against all damage suffered by it, or by any other person to whom the consignor is liable, by reason of the irregularity, incorrectness or incompleteness of the particulars and statements inserted by the carrier or on its behalf in the cargo receipt or in the record preserved by the other means referred to in paragraph 2 of Article 4.

Article 11—Evidentiary Value of Documentation

1. The air waybill or the cargo receipt is prima facie evidence of the conclusion of the contract, of the acceptance of the cargo and of the conditions of carriage mentioned therein.

2. Any statements in the air waybill or the cargo receipt relating to the weight, dimensions and packing of the cargo, as well as those relating to the number of packages, are prima facie evidence of the facts stated; those relating to the quantity, volume and condition of the cargo do not constitute evidence against the carrier except so far as they both have been, and are stated in the air waybill or the cargo receipt to have been, checked by it in the presence of the consignor, or relate to the apparent condition of the cargo.

Article 12—Right of Disposition of Cargo

1. Subject to its liability to carry out all its obligations under the contract of carriage, the consignor has the right to dispose of the cargo by withdrawing it at the airport of departure or destination, or by stopping it in the course of the journey on any landing, or by calling for it to be delivered at the place of destination or in the course of the journey to a person other than the consignee originally designated, or by requiring it to be returned to the airport of departure. The consignor must not exercise this right of disposition in such a way as to prejudice the carrier or other consignors and must reimburse any expenses occasioned by the exercise of this right.

2. If it is impossible to carry out the instructions of the consignor, the carrier must so inform the consignor forthwith.

3. If the carrier carries out the instructions of the consignor for the disposition of the cargo without requiring the production of the part of the air waybill or the cargo receipt delivered to the latter, the carrier will be liable, without prejudice to its right of recovery from the consignor, for any damage which may be caused thereby to any person who is lawfully in possession of that part of the air waybill or the cargo receipt.

4. The right conferred on the consignor ceases at the moment when that of the consignee begins in accordance with Article 13. Nevertheless, if the consignee declines to accept the cargo, or cannot be communicated with, the consignor resumes its right of disposition.

Article 13—Delivery of the Cargo

1. Except when the consignor has exercised its right under Article 12, the consignee is entitled, on arrival of the cargo at the place of destination, to require the carrier to deliver the cargo to it, on payment of the charges due and on complying with the conditions of carriage.

2. Unless it is otherwise agreed, it is the duty of the carrier to give notice to the consignee as soon as the cargo arrives.

3. If the carrier admits the loss of the cargo, or if the cargo has not arrived at the expiration of seven days after the date on which it ought to have arrived, the consignee is entitled to enforce against the carrier the rights which flow from the contract of carriage.

Article 14—Enforcement of the Rights of Consignor and Consignee

The consignor and the consignee can respectively enforce all the rights given to them by Articles 12 and 13, each in its own name, whether it is acting in its own interest or in the interest of another, provided that it carries out the obligations imposed by the contract of carriage.

Article 15—Relations of Consignor and Consignee or Mutual Relations of Third Parties

1. Articles 12, 13 and 14 do not affect either the relations of the consignor and the consignee with each other or the mutual relations of third parties whose rights are derived either from the consignor or from the consignee.

2. The provisions of Articles 12, 13 and 14 can only be varied by express provision in the air waybill or the cargo receipt.

Article 16—Formalities of Customs, Police or Other Public Authorities

1. The consignor must furnish such information and such documents as are necessary to meet the formalities of customs, police and any other public authorities before the cargo can be delivered to the consignee. The consignor is liable to the carrier for any damage occasioned by the absence, insufficiency or irregularity of any such information or documents, unless the damage is due to the fault of the carrier, its servants or agents.

2. The carrier is under no obligation to enquire into the correctness or sufficiency of such information or documents.

Chapter III
Liability of the Carrier and Extent of Compensation for Damage

Article 17—Death and Injury of Passengers—Damage to Baggage

1. The carrier is liable for damage sustained in case of death or bodily injury of a passenger upon condition only that the accident which caused the death or injury took place on board the aircraft or in the course of any of the operations of embarking or disembarking.

2. The carrier is liable for damage sustained in case of destruction or loss of, or of damage to, checked baggage upon condition only that the event which caused the destruction, loss or damage took place on board the aircraft or during any period within which the checked baggage was in the charge of the carrier. However, the carrier is not liable if and to the extent that the damage resulted from the inherent defect, quality or vice of the baggage. In the case of unchecked baggage, including personal items, the carrier is liable if the damage resulted from its fault or that of its servants or agents.

3. If the carrier admits the loss of the checked baggage, or if the checked baggage has not arrived at the expiration of twenty-one days after the date on which it ought to have arrived, the passenger is entitled to enforce against the carrier the rights which flow from the contract of carriage.

4. Unless otherwise specified, in this Convention the term "baggage" means both checked baggage and unchecked baggage.

Article 18—Damage to Cargo

1. The carrier is liable for damage sustained in the event of the destruction or loss of, or damage to, cargo upon condition only that the event which caused the damage so sustained took place during the carriage by air.

2. However, the carrier is not liable if and to the extent it proves that the destruction, or loss of, or damage to, the cargo resulted from one or more of the following:

(a) inherent defect, quality or vice of that cargo;

(b) defective packing of that cargo performed by a person other than the carrier or its servants or agents;

(c) an act of war or an armed conflict;

(d) an act of public authority carried out in connection with the entry, exit or transit of the cargo.

3. The carriage by air within the meaning of paragraph 1 of this Article comprises the period during which the cargo is in the charge of the carrier.

4. The period of the carriage by air does not extend to any carriage by land, by sea or by inland waterway performed outside an airport. If, however, such carriage takes place in the performance of a contract for carriage by air, for the purpose of loading, delivery or transhipment, any damage is presumed, subject to proof to the contrary, to have been the result of an event which took place during the carriage by air. If a carrier, without the consent of the consignor, substitutes carriage by another mode of transport for the whole or part of a carriage intended by the agreement between the parties to be carriage by air, such carriage by another mode of transport is deemed to be within the period of carriage by air.

Article 19—Delay

The carrier is liable for damage occasioned by delay in the carriage by air of passengers, baggage or cargo. Nevertheless, the carrier shall not be liable for damage occasioned by delay if it proves that it and its servants and agents took all measures that could reasonably be required to avoid the damage or that it was impossible for it or them to take such measures.

Article 20—Exoneration

If the carrier proves that the damage was caused or contributed to by the negligence or other wrongful act or omission of the person claiming compensation, or the person from whom he or she derives his or her rights, the carrier shall be wholly or partly exonerated from its liability to the claimant to the extent that such negligence or wrongful act or omission caused or contributed to the damage. When by reason of death or injury of a passenger compensation is claimed by a person other than the passenger, the carrier shall likewise be wholly or partly exonerated from its liability to the extent that it proves that the damage was caused or contributed to by the negligence or other wrongful act or omission of that passenger. This Article applies to all the liability provisions in this Convention, including paragraph 1 of Article 21.

Article 21—Compensation in Case of Death or Injury of Passengers

1. For damages arising under paragraph 1 of Article 17 not exceeding 100,000 Special Drawing Rights for each passenger, the carrier shall not be able to exclude or limit its liability.

2. The carrier shall not be liable for damages arising under paragraph 1 of Article 17 to the extent that they exceed for each passenger 100,000 Special Drawing Rights if the carrier proves that:

(a) such damage was not due to the negligence or other wrongful act or omission of the carrier or its servants or agents; or

(b) such damage was solely due to the negligence or other wrongful act or omission of a third party.

Article 22—Limits of Liability in Relation to Delay, Baggage and Cargo

1. In the case of damage caused by delay as specified in Article 19 in the carriage of persons, the liability of the carrier for each passenger is limited to 4,150 Special Drawing Rights.

2. In the carriage of baggage, the liability of the carrier in the case of destruction, loss, damage or delay is limited to 1,000 Special Drawing Rights for each passenger unless the passenger has made, at the time when the checked baggage was handed over to the carrier, a special declaration of interest in delivery at destination and has paid a supplementary sum if the case so requires. In that case the carrier will be liable to pay a sum not exceeding the declared sum, unless it proves that the sum is greater than the passenger's actual interest in delivery at destination.

3. In the carriage of cargo, the liability of the carrier in the case of destruction, loss, damage or delay is limited to a sum of 17 Special Drawing Rights per kilogramme, unless the consignor has made, at the time when the package was handed over to the carrier, a special declaration of interest in delivery at destination and has paid a supplementary sum if the case so requires. In that case the carrier will be liable to pay a sum not exceeding the declared sum, unless it proves that the sum is greater than the consignor's actual interest in delivery at destination.

4. In the case of destruction, loss, damage or delay of part of the cargo, or of any object contained therein, the weight to be taken into consideration in determining the amount to which the carrier's liability is limited shall be only the total weight of the package or packages concerned. Nevertheless, when the destruction, loss, damage or delay of a part of the cargo, or of an object contained therein, affects the value of other packages covered by the same air waybill, or the same receipt or, if they were not issued, by the same record preserved by the other means referred to in paragraph 2 of Article 4, the total weight of such package or packages shall also be taken into consideration in determining the limit of liability.

5. The foregoing provisions of paragraphs 1 and 2 of this Article shall not apply if it is proved that the damage resulted from an act or omission of the carrier, its servants or agents, done with intent to cause damage or recklessly and with knowledge that damage would probably result; provided that, in the case of such act or omission of a servant or agent, it is also proved that such servant or agent was acting within the scope of its employment.

6. The limits prescribed in Article 21 and in this Article shall not prevent the court from awarding, in accordance with its own law, in addition, the whole or part of the

court costs and of the other expenses of the litigation incurred by the plaintiff, including interest. The foregoing provision shall not apply if the amount of the damages awarded, excluding court costs and other expenses of the litigation, does not exceed the sum which the carrier has offered in writing to the plaintiff within a period of six months from the date of the occurrence causing the damage, or before the commencement of the action, if that is later.

Article 23—Conversion of Monetary Units

1. The sums mentioned in terms of Special Drawing Right in this Convention shall be deemed to refer to the Special Drawing Right as defined by the International Monetary Fund. Conversion of the sums into national currencies shall, in case of judicial proceedings, be made according to the value of such currencies in terms of the Special Drawing Right at the date of the judgement. The value of a national currency, in terms of the Special Drawing Right, of a State Party which is a Member of the International Monetary Fund, shall be calculated in accordance with the method of valuation applied by the International Monetary Fund, in effect at the date of the judgement, for its operations and transactions. The value of a national currency, in terms of the Special Drawing Right, of a State Party which is not a Member of the International Monetary Fund, shall be calculated in a manner determined by that State.

2. Nevertheless, those States which are not Members of the International Monetary Fund and whose law does not permit the application of the provisions of paragraph 1 of this Article may, at the time of ratification or accession or at any time thereafter, declare that the limit of liability of the carrier prescribed in Article 21 is fixed at a sum of 1,500,000 monetary units per passenger in judicial proceedings in their territories; 62,500 monetary units per passenger with respect to paragraph 1 of Article 22; 15,000 monetary units per passenger with respect to paragraph 2 of Article 22; and 250 monetary units per kilogramme with respect to paragraph 3 of Article 22. This monetary unit corresponds to sixty-five and a half milligrammes of gold of millesimal fineness nine hundred. These sums may be converted into the national currency concerned in round figures. The conversion of these sums into national currency shall be made according to the law of the State concerned.

3. The calculation mentioned in the last sentence of paragraph 1 of this Article and the conversion method mentioned in paragraph 2 of this Article shall be made in such manner as to express in the national currency of the State Party as far as possible the same real value for the amounts in Articles 21 and 22 as would result from the application of the first three sentences of paragraph 1 of this Article. States Parties shall communicate to the depositary the manner of calculation pursuant to paragraph 1 of this Article, or the result of the conversion in paragraph 2 of this Article as the case may be, when depositing an instrument of ratification, acceptance, approval of or accession to this Convention and whenever there is a change in either.

Article 24—Review of Limits

1. Without prejudice to the provisions of Article 25 of this Convention and subject to paragraph 2 below, the limits of liability prescribed in Articles 21, 22 and 23 shall be reviewed by the Depositary at five-year intervals, the first such review to take place at the end of the fifth year following the date of entry into force of this Convention, or if the Convention does not enter into force within five years of the date it is first open for signature, within the first year of its entry into force, by reference to an inflation factor which corresponds to the accumulated rate of inflation since the previous revision or in

the first instance since the date of entry into force of the Convention. The measure of the rate of inflation to be used in determining the inflation factor shall be the weighted average of the annual rates of increase or decrease in the Consumer Price Indices of the States whose currencies comprise the Special Drawing Right mentioned in paragraph 1 of Article 23.

2. If the review referred to in the preceding paragraph concludes that the inflation factor has exceeded 10 per cent, the Depositary shall notify States Parties of a revision of the limits of liability. Any such revision shall become effective six months after its notification to the States Parties. If within three months after its notification to the States Parties a majority of the States Parties register their disapproval, the revision shall not become effective and the Depositary shall refer the matter to a meeting of the States Parties. The Depositary shall immediately notify all States Parties of the coming into force of any revision.

3. Notwithstanding paragraph 1 of this Article, the procedure referred to in paragraph 2 of this Article shall be applied at any time provided that one-third of the States Parties express a desire to that effect and upon condition that the inflation factor referred to in paragraph 1 has exceeded 30 percent since the previous revision or since the date of entry into force of this Convention if there has been no previous revision. Subsequent reviews using the procedure described in paragraph 1 of this Article will take place at five-year intervals starting at the end of the fifth year following the date of the reviews under the present paragraph.

Article 25—Stipulation on Limits

A carrier may stipulate that the contract of carriage shall be subject to higher limits of liability than those provided for in this Convention or to no limits of liability whatsoever.

Article 26—Invalidity of Contractual Provisions

Any provision tending to relieve the carrier of liability or to fix a lower limit than that which is laid down in this Convention shall be null and void, but the nullity of any such provision does not involve the nullity of the whole contract, which shall remain subject to the provisions of this Convention.

Article 27—Freedom to Contract

Nothing contained in this Convention shall prevent the carrier from refusing to enter into any contract of carriage, from waiving any defences available under the Convention, or from laying down conditions which do not conflict with the provisions of this Convention.

Article 28—Advance Payments

In the case of aircraft accidents resulting in death or injury of passengers, the carrier shall, if required by its national law, make advance payments without delay to a natural person or persons who are entitled to claim compensation in order to meet the immediate economic needs of such persons. Such advance payments shall not constitute a recognition of liability and may be offset against any amounts subsequently paid as damages by the carrier.

Article 29—Basis of Claims

In the carriage of passengers, baggage and cargo, any action for damages, however founded, whether under this Convention or in contract or in tort or otherwise, can only be brought subject to the conditions and such limits of liability as are set out in this Convention without prejudice to the question as to who are the persons who have the right to bring suit and what are their respective rights. In any such action, punitive, exemplary or any other non-compensatory damages shall not be recoverable.

Article 30—Servants, Agents—Aggregation of Claims

1. If an action is brought against a servant or agent of the carrier arising out of damage to which the Convention relates, such servant or agent, if they prove that they acted within the scope of their employment, shall be entitled to avail themselves of the conditions and limits of liability which the carrier itself is entitled to invoke under this Convention.

2. The aggregate of the amounts recoverable from the carrier, its servants and agents, in that case, shall not exceed the said limits.

3. Save in respect of the carriage of cargo, the provisions of paragraphs 1 and 2 of this Article shall not apply if it is proved that the damage resulted from an act or omission of the servant or agent done with intent to cause damage or recklessly and with knowledge that damage would probably result.

Article 31—Timely Notice of Complaints

1. Receipt by the person entitled to delivery of checked baggage or cargo without complaint is prima facie evidence that the same has been delivered in good condition and in accordance with the document of carriage or with the record preserved by the other means referred to in paragraph 2 of Article 3 and paragraph 2 of Article 4.

2. In the case of damage, the person entitled to delivery must complain to the carrier forthwith after the discovery of the damage, and, at the latest, within seven days from the date of receipt in the case of checked baggage and fourteen days from the date of receipt in the case of cargo. In the case of delay, the complaint must be made at the latest within twenty-one days from the date on which the baggage or cargo have been placed at his or her disposal.

3. Every complaint must be made in writing and given or dispatched within the times aforesaid.

4. If no complaint is made within the times aforesaid, no action shall lie against the carrier, save in the case of fraud on its part.

Article 32—Death of Person Liable

In the case of the death of the person liable, an action for damages lies in accordance with the terms of this Convention against those legally representing his or her estate.

Article 33—Jurisdiction

1. An action for damages must be brought, at the option of the plaintiff, in the territory of one of the States Parties, either before the court of the domicile of the carrier or of its principal place of business, or where it has a place of business through which the contract has been made or before the court at the place of destination.

2. In respect of damage resulting from the death or injury of a passenger, an action may be brought before one of the courts mentioned in paragraph 1 of this Article, or in the territory of a State Party in which at the time of the accident the passenger has his or her principal and permanent residence and to or from which the carrier operates ser-

vices for the carriage of passengers by air, either on its own aircraft, or on another carrier's aircraft pursuant to a commercial agreement, and in which that carrier conducts its business of carriage of passengers by air from premises leased or owned by the carrier itself or by another carrier with which it has a commercial agreement.

3. For the purposes of paragraph 2,

(a) "commercial agreement" means an agreement, other than an agency agreement, made between carriers and relating to the provision of their joint services for carriage of passengers by air;

(b) "principal and permanent residence" means the one fixed and permanent abode of the passenger at the time of the accident. The nationality of the passenger shall not be the determining factor in this regard.

4. Questions of procedure shall be governed by the law of the court seised of the case.

Article 34—Arbitration

1. Subject to the provisions of this Article, the parties to the contract of carriage for cargo may stipulate that any dispute relating to the liability of the carrier under this Convention shall be settled by arbitration. Such agreement shall be in writing.

2. The arbitration proceedings shall, at the option of the claimant, take place within one of the jurisdictions referred to in Article 33.

3. The arbitrator or arbitration tribunal shall apply the provisions of this Convention.

4. The provisions of paragraphs 2 and 3 of this Article shall be deemed to be part of every arbitration clause or agreement, and any term of such clause or agreement which is inconsistent therewith shall be null and void.

Article 35—Limitation of Actions

1. The right to damages shall be extinguished if an action is not brought within a period of two years, reckoned from the date of arrival at the destination, or from the date on which the aircraft ought to have arrived, or from the date on which the carriage stopped.

2. The method of calculating that period shall be determined by the law of the court seised of the case.

Article 36—Successive Carriage

1. In the case of carriage to be performed by various successive carriers and falling within the definition set out in paragraph 3 of Article 1, each carrier which accepts passengers, baggage or cargo is subject to the rules set out in this Convention and is deemed to be one of the parties to the contract of carriage in so far as the contract deals with that part of the carriage which is performed under its supervision.

2. In the case of carriage of this nature, the passenger or any person entitled to compensation in respect of him or her can take action only against the carrier which performed the carriage during which the accident or the delay occurred, save in the case where, by express agreement, the first carrier has assumed liability for the whole journey.

3. As regards baggage or cargo, the passenger or consignor will have a right of action against the first carrier, and the passenger or consignee who is entitled to delivery will have a right of action against the last carrier, and further, each may take action against the carrier which performed the carriage during which the destruction, loss, damage or

delay took place. These carriers will be jointly and severally liable to the passenger or to the consignor or consignee.

Article 37—Right of Recourse against Third Parties

Nothing in this Convention shall prejudice the question whether a person liable for damage in accordance with its provisions has a right of recourse against any other person.

Chapter IV
Combined Carriage

Article 38—Combined Carriage

1. In the case of combined carriage performed partly by air and partly by any other mode of carriage, the provisions of this Convention shall, subject to paragraph 4 of Article 18, apply only to the carriage by air, provided that the carriage by air falls within the terms of Article 1.

2. Nothing in this Convention shall prevent the parties in the case of combined carriage from inserting in the document of air carriage conditions relating to other modes of carriage, provided that the provisions of this Convention are observed as regards the carriage by air.

Chapter V
Carriage by Air Performed by a Person other than the Contracting Carrier

Article 39—Contracting Carrier—Actual Carrier

The provisions of this Chapter apply when a person (hereinafter referred to as "the contracting carrier") as a principal makes a contract of carriage governed by this Convention with a passenger or consignor or with a person acting on behalf of the passenger or consignor, and another person (hereinafter referred to as "the actual carrier") performs, by virtue of authority from the contracting carrier, the whole or part of the carriage, but is not with respect to such part a successive carrier within the meaning of this Convention. Such authority shall be presumed in the absence of proof to the contrary.

Article 40—Respective Liability of Contracting and Actual Carriers

If an actual carrier performs the whole or part of carriage which, according to the contract referred to in Article 39, is governed by this Convention, both the contracting carrier and the actual carrier shall, except as otherwise provided in this Chapter, be subject to the rules of this Convention, the former for the whole of the carriage contemplated in the contract, the latter solely for the carriage which it performs.

Article 41—Mutual Liability

1. The acts and omissions of the actual carrier and of its servants and agents acting within the scope of their employment shall, in relation to the carriage performed by the actual carrier, be deemed to be also those of the contracting carrier.

2. The acts and omissions of the contracting carrier and of its servants and agents acting within the scope of their employment shall, in relation to the carriage performed by the actual carrier, be deemed to be also those of the actual carrier. Nevertheless, no such act or omission shall subject the actual carrier to liability exceeding the amounts referred to in Articles 21, 22, 23 and 24. Any special agreement under which the contract-

ing carrier assumes obligations not imposed by this Convention or any waiver of rights or defences conferred by this Convention or any special declaration of interest in delivery at destination contemplated in Article 22 shall not affect the actual carrier unless agreed to by it.

Article 42—Addressee of Complaints and Instructions

Any complaint to be made or instruction to be given under this Convention to the carrier shall have the same effect whether addressed to the contracting carrier or to the actual carrier. Nevertheless, instructions referred to in Article 12 shall only be effective if addressed to the contracting carrier.

Article 43—Servants and Agents

In relation to the carriage performed by the actual carrier, any servant or agent of that carrier or of the contracting carrier shall, if they prove that they acted within the scope of their employment, be entitled to avail themselves of the conditions and limits of liability which are applicable under this Convention to the carrier whose servant or agent they are, unless it is proved that they acted in a manner that prevents the limits of liability from being invoked in accordance with this Convention.

Article 44—Aggregation of Damages

In relation to the carriage performed by the actual carrier, the aggregate of the amounts recoverable from that carrier and the contracting carrier, and from their servants and agents acting within the scope of their employment, shall not exceed the highest amount which could be awarded against either the contracting carrier or the actual carrier under this Convention, but none of the persons mentioned shall be liable for a sum in excess of the limit applicable to that person.

Article 45—Addressee of Claims

In relation to the carriage performed by the actual carrier, an action for damages may be brought, at the option of the plaintiff, against that carrier or the contracting carrier, or against both together or separately. If the action is brought against only one of those carriers, that carrier shall have the right to require the other carrier to be joined in the proceedings, the procedure and effects being governed by the law of the court seised of the case.

Article 46—Additional Jurisdiction

Any action for damages contemplated in Article 45 must be brought, at the option of the plaintiff, in the territory of one of the States Parties, either before a court in which an action may be brought against the contracting carrier, as provided in Article 33, or before the court having jurisdiction at the place where the actual carrier has its domicile or its principal place of business.

Article 47—Invalidity of Contractual Provisions

Any contractual provision tending to relieve the contracting carrier or the actual carrier of liability under this Chapter or to fix a lower limit than that which is applicable according to this Chapter shall be null and void, but the nullity of any such provision does not involve the nullity of the whole contract, which shall remain subject to the provisions of this Chapter.

Article 48—Mutual Relations of Contracting and Actual Carriers

Except as provided in Article 45, nothing in this Chapter shall affect the rights and obligations of the carriers between themselves, including any right of recourse or indemnification.

Chapter VI
Other Provisions

Article 49—Mandatory Application

Any clause contained in the contract of carriage and all special agreements entered into before the damage occurred by which the parties purport to infringe the rules laid down by this Convention, whether by deciding the law to be applied, or by altering the rules as to jurisdiction, shall be null and void.

Article 50—Insurance

States Parties shall require their carriers to maintain adequate insurance covering their liability under this Convention. A carrier may be required by the State Party into which it operates to furnish evidence that it maintains adequate insurance covering its liability under this Convention.

Article 51—Carriage Performed in Extraordinary Circumstances

The provisions of Articles 3 to 5, 7 and 8 relating to the documentation of carriage shall not apply in the case of carriage performed in extraordinary circumstances outside the normal scope of a carrier's business.

Article 52—Definition of Days

The expression "days" when used in this Convention means calendar days, not working days.

Chapter VII
Final Clauses

Article 53—Signature, Ratification and Entry into Force

1. This Convention shall be open for signature in Montreal on 28 May 1999 by States participating in the International Conference on Air Law held at Montreal from 10 to 28 May 1999. After 28 May 1999, the Convention shall be open to all States for signature at the Headquarters of the International Civil Aviation Organization in Montreal until it enters into force in accordance with paragraph 6 of this Article.

2. This Convention shall similarly be open for signature by Regional Economic Integration Organisations. For the purpose of this Convention, a "Regional Economic Integration Organisation" means any organisation which is constituted by sovereign States of a given region which has competence in respect of certain matters governed by this Convention and has been duly authorized to sign and to ratify, accept, approve or accede to this Convention. A reference to a "State Party" or "States Parties" in this Convention, otherwise than in paragraph 2 of Article 1, paragraph 1(b) of Article 3, paragraph (b) of Article 5, Articles 23, 33, 46 and paragraph (b) of Article 57, applies equally to a Regional Economic Integration Organisation. For the purpose of Article 24,

the references to "a majority of the States Parties" and "one-third of the States Parties" shall not apply to a Regional Economic Integration Organisation.

3. This Convention shall be subject to ratification by States and by Regional Economic Integration Organisations which have signed it.

4. Any State or Regional Economic Integration Organisation which does not sign this Convention may accept, approve or accede to it at any time.

5. Instruments of ratification, acceptance, approval or accession shall be deposited with the International Civil Aviation Organization, which is hereby designated the Depositary.

6. This Convention shall enter into force on the sixtieth day following the date of deposit of the thirtieth instrument of ratification, acceptance, approval or accession with the Depositary between the States which have deposited such instrument. An instrument deposited by a Regional Economic Integration Organisation shall not be counted for the purpose of this paragraph.

7. For other States and for other Regional Economic Integration Organisations, this Convention shall take effect sixty days following the date of deposit of the instrument of ratification, acceptance, approval or accession.

8. The Depositary shall promptly notify all signatories and States Parties of:

(a) each signature of this Convention and date thereof;

(b) each deposit of an instrument of ratification, acceptance, approval or accession and date thereof;

(c) the date of entry into force of this Convention;

(d) the date of the coming into force of any revision of the limits of liability established under this Convention;

(e) any denunciation under Article 54.

Article 54—Denunciation

1. Any State Party may denounce this Convention by written notification to the Depositary.

2. Denunciation shall take effect one hundred and eighty days following the date on which notification is received by the Depositary.

Article 55—Relationship with other Warsaw Convention Instruments

This Convention shall prevail over any rules which apply to international carriage by air:

1. between States Parties to this Convention by virtue of those States commonly being Party to

(a) the Convention for the Unification of Certain Rules Relating to International Carriage by Air Signed at Warsaw on 12 October 1929 (hereinafter called the Warsaw Convention);

(b) the Protocol to Amend the Convention for the Unification of Certain Rules Relating to International Carriage by Air Signed at Warsaw on 12 October 1929, Done at The Hague on 28 September 1955 (hereinafter called The Hague Protocol);

(c) the Convention, Supplementary to the Warsaw Convention, for the Unification of Certain Rules Relating to International Carriage by Air Performed by a Person Other than the Contracting Carrier, signed at Guadalajara on 18 September 1961 (hereinafter called the Guadalajara Convention);

(d) the Protocol to Amend the Convention for the Unification of Certain Rules Relating to International Carriage by Air Signed at Warsaw on 12 October 1929 as Amended by the Protocol Done at The Hague on 28 September 1955 Signed at Guatemala City on 8 March 1971 (hereinafter called the Guatemala City Protocol);

(e) Additional Protocol Nos. 1 to 3 and Montreal Protocol No. 4 to amend the Warsaw Convention as amended by The Hague Protocol or the Warsaw Convention as amended by both The Hague Protocol and the Guatemala City Protocol Signed at Montreal on 25 September 1975 (hereinafter called the Montreal Protocols); or

2. within the territory of any single State Party to this Convention by virtue of that State being Party to one or more of the instruments referred to in sub-paragraphs (a) to (e) above.

Article 56—States with more than one System of Law

1. If a State has two or more territorial units in which different systems of law are applicable in relation to matters dealt with in this Convention, it may at the time of signature, ratification, acceptance, approval or accession declare that this Convention shall extend to all its territorial units or only to one or more of them and may modify this declaration by submitting another declaration at any time.

2. Any such declaration shall be notified to the Depositary and shall state expressly the territorial units to which the Convention applies.

3. In relation to a State Party which has made such a declaration:

(a) references in Article 23 to "national currency" shall be construed as referring to the currency of the relevant territorial unit of that State; and

(b) the reference in Article 28 to "national law" shall be construed as referring to the law of the relevant territorial unit of that State.

Article 57—Reservations

No reservation may be made to this Convention except that a State Party may at any time declare by a notification addressed to the Depositary that this Convention shall not apply to:

(a) international carriage by air performed and operated directly by that State Party for non-commercial purposes in respect to its functions and duties as a sovereign State; and/or

(b) the carriage of persons, cargo and baggage for its military authorities on aircraft registered in or leased by that State Party, the whole capacity of which has been reserved by or on behalf of such authorities.

IN WITNESS WHEREOF the undersigned Plenipotentiaries, having been duly authorized, have signed this Convention.

DONE at Montreal on the 28th day of May of the year one thousand nine hundred and ninety-nine in the English, Arabic, Chinese, French, Russian and Spanish languages, all texts being equally authentic. This Convention shall remain deposited in the archives of the International Civil Aviation Organization, and certified copies thereof shall be transmitted by the Depositary to all States Parties to this Convention, as well as to all States Parties to the Warsaw Convention, The Hague Protocol, the Guadalajara Convention, the Guatemala City Protocol, and the Montreal Protocols.

Appendix 27

Multilateral Agreement on the Liberalization of International Air Transportation

Done at Washington, D.C.—May 1, 2001
Entered into force—December 21, 2001
Effective in the United States—December 21, 2001

The Parties to this Agreement (hereinafter, "the Parties");

Desiring to promote an international aviation system based on competition among airlines in the marketplace with minimum interference and regulation;

Desiring to facilitate the expansion of international air transport opportunities;

Recognizing that efficient and competitive international air services enhance trade, benefit consumers, and promote economic growth;

Recognizing the contribution made by the Asia-Pacific Economic Cooperation forum in facilitating discussions on the liberalization of air services;

Desiring to make it possible for airlines to offer the traveling and shipping public a variety of service options and wishing to encourage individual airlines to develop and implement innovative and competitive prices;

Desiring to ensure the highest degree of safety and security in international air transport and reaffirming their grave concern about acts or threats against the security of aircraft, which jeopardize the safety of persons or property, adversely affect the operation of air transportation, and undermine public confidence in the safety of civil aviation; and

Noting the Convention on International Civil Aviation, opened for signature at Chicago on December 7, 1944;

Have agreed as follows:

Article 1
Definitions

For the purposes of this Agreement, unless otherwise stated, the term:

1. "Agreement" means this Agreement, its Annex and Appendix, and any amendments thereto;

2. "Air transportation" means the public carriage by aircraft of passengers, baggage, cargo, and mail, separately or in combination, for remuneration or hire;

3. "Convention" means the Convention on International Civil Aviation, opened for signature at Chicago on December 7, 1944, and includes:

a. any amendment that has entered into force under Article 94(a) of the Convention and has been ratified by all Parties to this Agreement; and

b. any Annex or any amendment thereto adopted under Article 90 of the Convention, insofar as such Annex or amendment is at any given time effective for all Parties to this Agreement;

4. "Designated airline" means an airline designated and authorized in accordance with Article 3 of this Agreement;

5. "Full cost" means the cost of providing service, including a reasonable amount for administrative overhead;

6. "International air transportation" means air transportation that passes through the airspace over the territory of more than one State or APEC member economy as identified in the Appendix to the Annex;

7. "Price" means any fare, rate or charge for the carriage of passengers, baggage and/or cargo (excluding mail) in air transportation, including surface transportation in connection with international air transportation, if applicable, charged by airlines, including their agents, and the conditions governing the availability of such fare, rate or charge;

8. "Stop for non-traffic purposes" means a landing for any purpose other than taking on or discharging passengers, baggage, cargo and/or mail in air transportation;

9. "Territory" means the land areas under the sovereignty, jurisdiction, authority, administration, protection, or trusteeship of a Party, and the territorial waters adjacent thereto; and

10. "User charge" means a charge imposed on airlines for the provision of airport, air navigation, or aviation security facilities or services including related services and facilities.

Article 2
Grant of Rights

1. Each Party grants to the other Parties the following rights for the conduct of international air transportation by the airlines of the other Parties:

a. the right to fly across its territory without landing;

b. the right to make stops in its territory for non-traffic purposes;

c. the right, in accordance with the terms of their designations, to perform scheduled and charter international air transportation between points on the following route:

i. from points behind the territory of the Party designating the airline via the territory of that Party and intermediate points to any point or points in the territory of the Party granting the right and beyond;

ii. for all-cargo service or services, between the territory of the Party granting the right and any point or points; and

d. the rights otherwise specified in this Agreement.

2. Each designated airline may on any or all flights and at its option:

a. operate flights in either or both directions;

b. combine different flight numbers within one aircraft operation;

c. serve behind, intermediate, and beyond points and points in the territories of the Parties on the routes in any combination and in any order;

d. omit stops at any point or points;

e. transfer traffic from any of its aircraft to any of its other aircraft at any point on the routes;

f. serve points behind any point in its territory with or without change of aircraft or flight number and hold out and advertise such services to the public as through services;

g. make stopovers at any points whether within or outside the territory of any Party;

h. carry transit traffic through any other Party's territory; and

i. combine traffic on the same aircraft regardless of where such traffic originates;

without directional or geographic limitation and without loss of any right to carry traffic otherwise permissible under this Agreement.

3. The provisions of paragraph 2 of this Article shall apply subject to the requirement that, with the exception of all-cargo services, the service serves a point in the territory of the Party designating the airline.

4. On any segment or segments of the routes above, any designated airline may perform international air transportation without any limitation as to change, at any point on the route, in type or number of aircraft operated; provided that, with the exception of all cargo services, in the outbound direction, the transportation beyond such point is a continuation of the transportation from the territory of the Party that has designated the airline and, in the inbound direction, the transportation to the territory of the Party that has designated the airline is a continuation of the transportation from beyond such point.

5. Nothing in this Agreement shall be deemed to confer on the airline or airlines of one Party the right to take on board, in the territory of another Party, passengers, baggage, cargo, or mail carried for compensation and destined for another point in the territory of that other Party.

Article 3
Designation and Authorization

1. Each Party shall have the right to designate as many airlines as it wishes to conduct international air transportation in accordance with this Agreement and to withdraw or alter such designations. Such designations shall be transmitted to the concerned Parties in writing through diplomatic or other appropriate channels and to the Depositary.

2. On receipt of such a designation, and of applications from the designated airline, in the form and manner prescribed for operating authorizations and technical permissions, each Party shall grant appropriate authorizations and permissions with minimum procedural delay, provided that:

a. effective control of that airline is vested in the designating Party, its nationals, or both;

b. the airline is incorporated in and has its principal place of business in the territory of the Party designating the airline;

c. the airline is qualified to meet the conditions prescribed under the laws, regulations, and rules normally applied to the operation of international air transportation by the Party considering the application or applications; and

d. the Party designating the airline is in compliance with the provisions set forth in Article 6 (Safety) and Article 7 (Aviation Security).

3. Notwithstanding paragraph 2, a Party need not grant authorizations and permissions to an airline designated by another Party if the Party receiving the designation determines that substantial ownership is vested in its nationals.

4. Parties granting operating authorizations in accordance with paragraph 2 of this Article shall notify such action to the Depositary.

5. Nothing in this Agreement shall be deemed to affect a Party's laws and regulations concerning the ownership and control of airlines that it designates. Acceptance of such designations by the other Parties shall be subject to paragraphs 2 and 3 of this Article.

Article 4
Revocation of Authorization

1. Each Party may withhold, revoke, suspend, limit or impose conditions on the operating authorizations or technical permissions of an airline designated by another Party where:

a. effective control of that airline is not vested in the designating Party, its nationals, or both;

b. the first Party determines that substantial ownership is vested in its nationals;

c. the airline is not incorporated or does not have its principal place of business in the territory of the party designating the airline;

d. the airline has failed to comply with the laws, regulations, and rules referred to in Article 5 (Application of Laws) of this Agreement; or

e. the other Party is not maintaining and administering the standards as set forth in Article 6 (Safety).

2. Unless immediate action is essential to prevent further non-compliance with subparagraphs 1(d) or 1(e) of this Article, the rights established by this Article shall be exercised only after consultation with the Party designating the airline.

3. A Party that has exercised its right to withhold, revoke, suspend, limit or impose conditions on the operating authorizations of an airline or airlines in accordance with paragraph 1 of this Article shall notify its action to the Depositary.

4. This Article does not limit the rights of any Party to withhold, revoke, suspend, limit or impose conditions on the operating authorization or technical permission of an airline or airlines of other Parties in accordance with the provisions of Article 7 (Aviation Security).

Article 5
Application of Laws

1. While entering, within, or leaving the territory of one Party, its laws, regulations and rules relating to the operation and navigation of aircraft shall be complied with by the airlines designated by any other Party.

2. While entering, within, or leaving the territory of one Party, its laws, regulations and rules relating to the admission to or departure from its territory of passengers, crew or cargo on aircraft (including regulations relating to entry, clearance, aviation security, immigration, passports, customs and quarantine or, in the case of mail, postal regulations) shall be complied with by, or on behalf of, such passengers, crew or cargo of the airlines of any other Party.

3. No Party shall give preference to its own or any other airline over a designated airline of the other Parties engaged in similar international air transport in the application of its customs, immigration and quarantine regulations.

4. Passengers, baggage and cargo in direct transit through the territory of any Party and not leaving the area of the airport reserved for such purpose shall not undergo any examination except for reasons of aviation security, narcotics control, prevention of illegal entry or in special circumstances.

Article 6
Safety

1. Each Party shall recognize as valid, for the purpose of operating the air transportation provided for in this Agreement, certificates of airworthiness, certificates of competency, and licenses issued or validated by the other Parties and still in force, provided that the requirements for such certificates or licenses at least equal the minimum standards that may be established pursuant to the Convention. Each Party may, however, refuse to recognize as valid for the purpose of flight above its own territory, certificates of competency and licenses for its own nationals granted or validated by another Party.

2. Each Party may request consultations with another Party concerning the safety standards maintained by that other Party relating to aeronautical facilities, aircrews, aircraft, and operation of the designated airlines. If, following such consultations, the first Party finds that the other Party does not effectively maintain and administer safety standards and requirements in these areas that at least equal the minimum standards that may be established pursuant to the Convention, the other Party shall be notified of such findings and the steps considered necessary to conform with these minimum standards, and the other Party shall take appropriate corrective action. Each Party reserves the right to withhold, revoke, suspend, or limit or impose conditions on the operating authorization or technical permission of an airline or airlines designated by the other Party in the event the other Party does not take such appropriate corrective action within a reasonable time.

Article 7
Aviation Security

1. In accordance with their rights and obligations under international law, the Parties reaffirm that their obligation to each other to protect the security of civil aviation against acts of unlawful interference forms an integral part of this Agreement. Without limiting the generality of their rights and obligations under international law, the Parties shall in particular act in conformity with the provisions of the Convention on Offenses and Certain Other Acts Committed on Board Aircraft, done at Tokyo on September 14, 1963, the Convention for the Suppression of Unlawful Seizure of Aircraft, done at The Hague on December 16, 1970, the Convention for the Suppression of Unlawful Acts against the Safety of Civil Aviation, done at Montreal on September 23, 1971, and the Protocol for the Suppression of Unlawful Acts of Violence at Airports Serving International Civil Aviation, done at Montreal on February 24, 1988.

2. Each Party shall provide upon request of another Party all necessary assistance to that other Party to prevent acts of unlawful seizure of civil aircraft and other unlawful acts against the safety of such aircraft, of their passengers and crew, and of airports and air navigation facilities, and to address any other threat to the security of civil air navigation.

3. Each Party shall, in its relations with the other Parties, act in conformity with the aviation security standards and appropriate recommended practices established by the International Civil Aviation Organization and designated as Annexes to the Convention; it shall require that operators of aircraft of its registry, operators of aircraft who have their principal place of business or permanent residence in its territory, and the operators of airports in its territory act in conformity with such aviation security provisions.

4. Each Party shall observe the security provisions required by the other Parties for entry into, for departure from, and while within their respective territories and each Party shall ensure that adequate measures are effectively applied within its territory to

protect aircraft and to inspect passengers, crew, and their baggage and carry-on items, as well as cargo and aircraft stores, prior to and during boarding or loading. Each Party shall also give positive consideration to any request from another Party for special security measures to meet a particular threat.

5. When an incident or threat of an incident of unlawful seizure of aircraft or other unlawful acts against the safety of passengers, crew, aircraft, airports or air navigation facilities occurs, the Parties shall assist each other by facilitating communications and other appropriate measures intended to terminate rapidly and safely such incident or threat.

6. When a Party has reasonable grounds to believe that another Party has departed from the aviation security provisions of this Article, the aeronautical authorities of that Party may request immediate consultations with the aeronautical authorities of the other Party. Failure to reach a satisfactory agreement within 15 days from the date of such request shall constitute grounds to withhold, revoke, suspend, limit, or impose conditions on the operating authorization and technical permissions of an airline or airlines of the other Party. When required by an emergency, a Party may take interim action prior to the expiry of 15 days.

7. Any Party that has exercised its right to withhold, revoke, suspend, or limit or impose conditions on the operating authorization of an airline or airlines in accordance with paragraph 6 of this Article shall notify such action to the Depositary.

Article 8
Commercial Opportunities

1. The airlines of each Party shall have the right to:

a. establish offices in the territory of the other Parties for the promotion and sale of air transportation;

b. engage in the sale of air transportation in the territory of the other Parties directly and, at the airlines' discretion, through their agents. The airlines shall have the right to sell such transportation, and any person shall be free to purchase such transportation, in local currency or in freely convertible currencies;

c. convert and remit to the territory of its incorporation, on demand, local revenues in excess of sums locally disbursed. Conversion and remittance shall be permitted promptly without restrictions or taxation in respect thereof at the rate of exchange applicable to current transactions and remittance on the date the carrier makes the initial application for remittance; and

d. pay for local expenses, including purchases of fuel, in the territories of the other Parties in local currency. At their discretion, the airlines of each Party may pay for such expenses in the territory of the other Parties in freely convertible currencies according to local currency regulation.

2. The designated airlines of each Party shall have the right:

a. in accordance with the laws, regulations and rules of the other Parties relating to entry, residence, and employment, to bring in and maintain in the territories of the other Parties managerial, sales, technical, operational, and other specialist staff required for the provision of air transportation;

b. to perform their own ground-handling in the territory of the other Parties ("self-handling") or, at their option, select among competing agents for such services in whole or in part. The rights shall be subject only to physical constraints resulting from considerations of airport safety. Where such considerations preclude self-handling, ground services shall be available on an equal basis to all airlines; charges shall be based on the costs of services provided; and such services shall be comparable to the kind and quality of services as if self-handling were possible; and

c. in operating or holding out the authorized services on the agreed routes, to enter into cooperative marketing arrangements such as blocked-space, code-sharing or leasing arrangements, with:

i. an airline or airlines of any Party;

ii. an airline or airlines of any State or APEC member economy as identified in the Appendix to the Annex that is not party to this Agreement; and

iii. a surface transportation provider of any State or APEC member economy as identified in the Appendix to the Annex;

provided that all participants in such arrangements hold the appropriate authority and meet the requirements applied to such arrangements.

3. Notwithstanding any other provision of this Agreement, airlines and indirect providers of cargo transportation of the Parties shall be permitted without restriction to employ in connection with international air transportation any surface transportation for cargo to or from any points within or outside the territories of the Parties, including transport to and from all airports with customs facilities, and including, where applicable, the right to transport cargo in bond under applicable laws and regulations. Such cargo, whether moving by surface or by air, shall have access to airport customs processing and facilities. Airlines may elect to perform their own surface transportation or to provide it through arrangements with other surface carriers, including surface transportation operated by other airlines and indirect providers of cargo air transportation. Such intermodal cargo services may be offered at a single, through price for the air and surface transportation combined, provided that shippers are not misled as to the facts concerning such transportation.

Article 9
Customs Duties and Charges

1. On arriving in the territory of one Party, aircraft operated in international air transportation by the designated airline or airlines of any other Party, their regular equipment, ground equipment, fuel, lubricants, consumable technical supplies, spare parts (including engines), aircraft stores (including but not limited to such items of food, beverages and liquor, tobacco and other products destined for sale to or use by passengers in limited quantities during flight), and other items intended for or used solely in connection with the operation or servicing of aircraft engaged in international air transportation shall be exempt, on the basis of reciprocity, from all import restrictions, property taxes and capital levies, customs duties, excise taxes, and similar fees and charges that are (i) imposed by the national or central authorities, and (ii) not based on the cost of services provided, provided that such equipment and supplies remain on board the aircraft.

2. There shall also be exempt, on the basis of reciprocity, from the taxes, levies, duties, fees and charges referred to in paragraph 1 of this Article, with the exception of charges based on the cost of the service provided:

a. aircraft stores introduced into or supplied in the territory of a Party and taken on board, within reasonable limits, for use on outbound aircraft of airlines of the other

Parties engaged in international air transportation, even when these stores are to be used on a part of the journey performed over the territory of the Party in which they are taken on board;

b. ground equipment and spare parts (including engines) introduced into the territory of a Party for the servicing, maintenance, or repair of aircraft of airlines of the other Parties used in international air transportation;

c. fuel, lubricants and consumable technical supplies introduced into or supplied in the territory of a Party for use in an aircraft of airlines of the other Parties engaged in international air transportation, even when these supplies are to be used on a part of the journey performed over the territory of the Party in which they are taken on board; and

d. promotional and advertising materials introduced into or supplied in the territory of one Party and taken on board, within reasonable limits, for use on outbound aircraft of an airline of the other Parties engaged in international air transportation, even when these stores are to be used on a part of the journey performed over the territory of the Party in which they are taken on board.

3. Equipment and supplies referred to in paragraphs 1 and 2 of this Article may be required to be kept under the supervision or control of the appropriate authorities.

4. The exemptions provided by this Article shall also be available where the designated airlines of one Party have contracted with another airline, which similarly enjoys such exemptions from another Party or Parties, for the loan or transfer in the territory of the other Party or Parties of the items specified in paragraphs 1 and 2 of this Article.

Article 10
User Charges

1. User charges that may be imposed by the competent charging authorities or bodies of each Party on the airlines of the other Parties shall be just, reasonable, not unjustly discriminatory, and equitably apportioned among categories of users. In any event, any such user charges shall be assessed on the airlines of the other Parties on terms not less favorable than the most favorable terms available to any other airline at the time the charges are assessed.

2. User charges imposed on the airlines of the other Parties may reflect, but shall not exceed, the full cost to the competent charging authorities or bodies of providing the appropriate airport, airport environmental, air navigation, and aviation security facilities and services at the airport or within the airport system. Such charges may include a reasonable return on assets, after depreciation. Facilities and services for which charges are made shall be provided on an efficient and economic basis.

3. Each Party shall encourage consultations between the competent charging authorities or bodies in its territory and the airlines using the services and facilities, and shall encourage the competent charging authorities or bodies and the airlines to exchange such information as may be necessary to permit an accurate review of the reasonableness of the charges in accordance with the principles of paragraphs 1 and 2 of this Article. Each Party shall encourage the competent charging authorities to provide users with reasonable notice of any proposal for changes in user charges to enable users to express their views before changes are made.

4. No Party shall be held, in dispute resolution procedures pursuant to Article 14, to be in breach of a provision of this Article, unless (i) it fails to undertake a review of the

charge or practice that is the subject of complaint by another Party within a reasonable amount of time; or (ii) following such a review it fails to take all steps within its power to remedy any charge or practice that is inconsistent with this Article.

Article 11
Fair Competition

1. Each Party shall allow a fair and equal opportunity for the designated airlines of all Parties to compete in providing the international air transportation governed by this Agreement.

2. Each Party shall allow each designated airline to determine the frequency and capacity of the international air transportation it offers based upon commercial considerations in the marketplace. Consistent with this right, no Party shall act to limit the volume of traffic, frequency or regularity of service, or the aircraft type or types operated by the designated airlines of the other Parties, except as may be required for customs, technical, operational, or environmental reasons under uniform conditions consistent with Article 15 of the Convention.

3. No Party shall impose on another Party's designated airlines a first-refusal requirement, uplift ratio, no-objection fee, or any other requirement with respect to capacity, frequency or traffic.

4. No Party shall require the filing of schedules, programs for charter flights, or operational plans by airlines of the other Parties for approval, except as may be required on a non-discriminatory basis to enforce the uniform conditions foreseen by paragraph 2 of this Article. If a Party requires filings to enforce the uniform conditions as foreseen by paragraph 2 of this Article or requires filings for informational purposes, it shall minimize the administrative burdens of filing requirements and procedures on air transportation intermediaries and on designated airlines of the other Parties.

5. Subject to the provisions of this Agreement, no Party may apply its laws, regulations, and rules to restrict the operation or sale of the charter international air transportation provided for in this Agreement, except that the Parties may require compliance with their own requirements relating to the protection of charter passenger funds and charter passenger cancellation and refund rights.

6. Pursuant to paragraph 1 of this Article, the airlines of each Party shall be entitled to market their services on a fair and nondiscriminatory basis through computer reservations systems (CRSs) used by travel agencies or travel companies in the territories of the Parties. In addition, CRS vendors of each Party that are not in violation of the CRS rules, if any, that apply in the territories of the Parties in which they are operating shall be entitled to non-discriminatory, effective, and unimpaired access to market, maintain, operate and freely make available their CRSs to travel agencies or travel companies in the territories of the Parties. In particular, if any airline of any Party chooses to participate in a CRS offered to travel agents or travel companies in the territory of another Party, that airline shall participate in CRSs of that other Party operated in the territory of its incorporation as fully as it does in any CRS in the territory of that other Party, unless it can show that the fees charged by that CRS for participation in the territory of its incorporation are not commercially reasonable (fees are presumed to be commercially reasonable if the fees charged the airline for participation in the territory of its incorporation by any other CRS that is used by travel agents or travel companies equal or exceed those charged by the CRS of the other Party for such participation). Airlines and

CRS vendors of one Party shall not discriminate against travel agencies or travel companies in that Party's territory because of their use of a CRS of another Party.

Article 12
Pricing

Prices for international air transportation operated pursuant to this Agreement shall not be subject to the approval of any Party, nor may they be required to be filed with any Party, provided that a Party may require that they be filed for informational purposes for so long as the laws of that Party continue to so require.

Article 13
Consultations

Each Party shall have the right to request consultations with one or more other Parties relating to the implementation or application of this Agreement. Unless otherwise agreed, such consultations shall begin at the earliest possible date, but not later than 60 days from the date the other Party or Parties receive, through diplomatic or other appropriate channels, a written request, including an explanation of the issues to be raised. When the date for consultations has been agreed, the requesting Party shall also notify all other Parties of the consultations and the issues to be raised. Any Party may attend, subject to the consent of the Parties involved in the consultations. Once the consultations have been concluded, all Parties shall be notified of the results.

Article 14
Settlement of Disputes

1. Any dispute arising under this Agreement that is not resolved by a first round of consultations may be referred by agreement of the Parties involved for decision to some person or body. If the Parties involved do not so agree, the dispute shall at the request of one Party be submitted to arbitration with respect to another Party in accordance with the procedures set forth below. The Party submitting the dispute to arbitration shall notify all other Parties of the dispute at the same time that it submits its arbitration request.

2. Arbitration shall be by a panel of three arbitrators to be constituted as follows:

a. within 30 days after the receipt of a request for arbitration, each Party to the dispute shall name one arbitrator. Within 60 days after these two arbitrators have been named, the Parties to the dispute shall by agreement appoint a third arbitrator, who shall act as President of the arbitral panel;

b. if either Party to the dispute fails to name an arbitrator, or if the third arbitrator is not appointed in accordance with subparagraph (a) of this paragraph, either Party may request the President of the Council of the International Civil Aviation Organization to appoint the necessary arbitrator or arbitrators within 30 days. If the President of the Council is of the same nationality as one of the Parties to the dispute, the most senior Vice President who is not disqualified on that ground shall make the appointment.

3. Except as otherwise agreed by the Parties to the dispute, the arbitral panel shall determine the limits of its jurisdiction in accordance with this Agreement and shall establish its own procedural rules. The arbitral panel, once formed, may recommend interim measures pending its final determination. At the direction of the arbitral panel or at the request of either of the Parties to the dispute, a conference concerning the precise issues to be arbitrated and the specific procedures to be followed shall be held on a date determined by the arbitral panel, in no event later than 15 days after the third arbitrator has

been appointed. If the Parties to the dispute are unable to reach agreement on these issues, the arbitral panel shall determine the precise issues to be arbitrated and the specific procedures to be followed.

4. Except as otherwise agreed by the Parties to the dispute or as directed by the panel, the complaining Party shall submit a memorandum within 45 days of the time the third arbitrator is appointed, and the reply of the responding Party shall be due 60 days after the complaining Party submits its memorandum. The complaining Party may submit a pleading in response to such reply within 30 days after the submission of the responding Party's reply and the responding Party may submit a pleading in response to the complaining Party's pleading within 30 days after the submission of such pleading. The arbitral panel shall hold a hearing at the request of either Party or on its own initiative within 15 days after the last pleading is due.

5. The arbitral panel shall attempt to render a written decision within 30 days after completion of the hearing or, if no hearing is held, after the date the last pleading is submitted. The decision of the majority of the arbitral panel shall prevail.

6. The Parties to the dispute may submit requests for clarification of the decision within 15 days after it is rendered, and any clarification given shall be issued within 15 days of such request.

7. In the case of a dispute involving more than two Parties, multiple Parties may participate on either or both sides of a proceeding described in this Article. The procedures set out in this Article shall be applied with the following exceptions:

a. with respect to paragraph 2(a), the Parties on each side of a dispute shall together name one arbitrator;

b. with respect to paragraph 2(b), if the Parties on one side of a dispute fail to name an arbitrator within the permitted time, the Party or Parties on the other side of the dispute may utilize the procedures in paragraph 2(b) to secure the appointment of an arbitrator; and

c. with respect to paragraphs 3, 4, and 6, each of the Parties on either side of the dispute has the right to take the action provided to a Party.

8. Any other Party that is directly affected by the dispute has the right to intervene in the proceedings, under the following conditions:

a. a Party desiring to intervene shall file a declaration to that effect with the arbitral panel no later than 10 days after the third arbitrator has been named;

b. the arbitral panel shall notify the Parties to the dispute of any such declaration, and the Parties to the dispute shall each have 30 days from the date such notification is sent to submit to the arbitral panel any objection to an intervention under this paragraph. The arbitral panel shall decide whether to allow any intervention within 15 days after the date such objections are due;

c. if the arbitral panel decides to allow an intervention, the intervening Party shall notify all other Parties to the Agreement of the intervention, and the arbitral panel shall take the necessary steps to make the documents of the case available to the intervening Party, who may file pleadings of a type and within a time limit to be set by the arbitral panel, within the timetable set out in paragraph 4 of this Article to the extent practical, and may participate in any subsequent proceedings; and

d. the decision of the arbitral panel will be equally binding upon the intervening Party.

9. All Parties to the dispute, including intervening Parties, shall, to the degree consistent with their law, give full effect to any decision or award of the arbitral panel.

10. The arbitral panel shall transmit copies of its decision or award to the Parties to the dispute, including any intervening Parties. The arbitral panel shall provide to the Depositary a copy of the decision or award, provided that appropriate treatment shall be accorded to confidential business information.

11. The expenses of the arbitral panel, including the fees and expenses of the arbitrators, shall be shared equally by all of the Parties to the dispute, including intervening Parties. Any expenses incurred by the President of the Council of the International Civil Aviation Organization in connection with the procedures of paragraph 2(b) of this Article shall be considered to be part of the expenses of the arbitral panel.

Article 15
Relationship to Other Agreements

Upon entry into force of this Agreement between one Party and any other Party, any bilateral air transport agreement existing between them at the time of such entry into force shall be suspended and shall remain suspended for so long as this Agreement shall remain in force between them.

Article 16
Relationship to Annex

The Annex is an integral part of this Agreement and, unless expressly provided otherwise, a reference to this Agreement includes a reference to the Annex relating thereto.

Article 17
Amendment

1. Any Party may propose amendments to this Agreement by forwarding a proposed amendment to the Depositary. Upon receiving such a proposal, the Depositary shall forward the proposal to the other Parties through diplomatic or other appropriate channels.

2. The Agreement may be amended in accordance with the following procedures:

a. if agreed by at least a simple majority of all Parties as of the date of proposal of the amendment, negotiations shall be held to consider the proposal;

b. unless otherwise agreed, the Party proposing the amendment shall host the negotiations, which shall begin not more than 90 days after agreement is reached to hold such negotiations. All Parties shall have a right to participate in the negotiations;

c. if adopted by at least a simple majority of the Parties attending such negotiations, the Depositary shall then prepare and transmit a certified copy of the amendment to the Parties for their acceptance;

d. any amendment shall enter into force, as between the Parties which have accepted it, 30 days following the date on which the Depositary has received written notification of acceptance from a simple majority of the Parties; and

e. following entry into force of such an amendment, it shall enter into force for any other Party 30 days following the date the Depositary receives written notification of acceptance from that Party;

3. In lieu of the procedures set forth in paragraph 2, the Agreement may be amended in accordance with the following procedures:

a. if all Parties as of the time of proposal of the amendment give written notice through diplomatic or other appropriate channels to the Party proposing the amendment of their consent to its adoption, the Party proposing the amendment shall so notify the Depositary, which shall then prepare and transmit a certified copy of such amendment to all of the Parties for their acceptance; and

b. an amendment so adopted shall enter into force for all Parties 30 days following the date on which the Depositary has received written notification of acceptance from all of the Parties.

Article 18
Withdrawal

A Party may withdraw from this agreement by giving written notice of withdrawal to the Depositary. The withdrawal shall be effective 12 months after receipt of the notice by the Depositary, unless the Party withdraws its notice by written communication to the Depositary prior to the end of the 12-month period.

Article 19
Responsibilities of the Depositary

1. The original of this Agreement shall be deposited with the Government of New Zealand, which is hereby designated as the Depositary of the Agreement.

2. The Depositary shall transmit certified copies of this Agreement and any amendments or protocols to all signatory and acceding States and all APEC member economies which have agreed to be bound by this Agreement in accordance with the Annex.

3. The Depositary shall notify all signatory and acceding States and all APEC member economies which have agreed to be bound by this Agreement in accordance with the Annex of:

a. expressions of consent to be bound by this Agreement and any amendments in accordance with Articles 20 and 17, and instruments of APEC member economies indicating their agreement to be bound by this Agreement in accordance with the Annex or their acceptance of any amendments in accordance with Article 17;

b. the respective dates on which the Agreement enters into force in accordance with Article 20, paragraphs 2, 3, and 6, and the respective dates on which the rights and obligations described in paragraph 2 of the Annex become effective following the deposit of a written instrument by APEC member economies pursuant to paragraph 1 of the Annex;

c. notifications regarding non-application of the Agreement received in accordance with Article 20, paragraph 5;

d. any notification of withdrawal received in accordance with Article 18;

e. the convening of negotiations to consider amendments in accordance with Article 17, paragraph 2(a);

f. the respective dates on which an amendment enters into force in accordance with Article 17, paragraphs 2(d), 2(e) and 3(b); and

g. notifications received pursuant to Article 4, paragraph 3 and Article 7, paragraph 7.

4. Following entry into force of this Agreement, the Depositary shall transmit a certified true copy of this Agreement to the Secretary General of the United Nations for registration and publication in accordance with Article 102 of the Charter of the United Nations and to the Secretary General of the International Civil Aviation Organization in

accordance with Article 83 of the Convention. The Depositary shall likewise transmit certified true copies of any amendments which enter into force.

5. The Depositary shall maintain a centralized register of airline designations and operating authorizations in accordance with Article 3, paragraphs 1 and 4 of this Agreement.

6. The Depositary shall make available to the Parties copies of any arbitral decision or award issued under Article 14 of this Agreement.

Article 20
Entry into Force

1. This Agreement shall be open for signature by Brunei Darussalam, Chile, New Zealand, Singapore, and the United States of America.

2. This Agreement shall enter into force on the date four of the States identified in paragraph 1 of this Article have signed not subject to ratification, acceptance or approval, or have deposited with the Depositary an instrument of ratification, acceptance or approval. The signatories to this Agreement may permit services consistent with the terms of the Agreement upon signature pending entry into force of the Agreement with respect to all of the States identified in paragraph 1 of this Article.

3. After this Agreement has entered into force in accordance with paragraph 2 of this Article, it shall enter into force for a remaining signatory on the date the Depositary receives the instrument of ratification, acceptance or approval of that signatory.

4. After this Agreement has entered into force in accordance with paragraph 2 of this Article, any State which is a party to the aviation security conventions listed in Article 7, paragraph 1 may accede to this Agreement by deposit of an instrument of accession with the Depositary.

5. This Agreement shall not apply between an acceding State or an APEC member economy which agrees to be bound by this Agreement in accordance with the Annex and any Party to this Agreement or APEC member economy which, within 90 days of the date of the Depositary's notification to the Parties of the deposit of the instrument of accession or written instrument indicating agreement to be bound, notifies the Depositary in writing that it shall not apply between that Party or such APEC member economy and such acceding State or APEC member economy. Any signatory that expresses its consent to be bound after the Agreement has entered into force pursuant to paragraph 2 of this Article, upon expressing its consent to be bound, may notify the Depositary in writing that the Agreement shall not apply between that signatory and any State that acceded to the Agreement, or any APEC member economy that agreed to be bound by the Agreement in accordance with the Annex, before the Agreement entered into force for that signatory.

6. This Agreement shall enter into force as between the acceding State and all Parties other than those which, pursuant to paragraph 5 of this Article, have notified the Depositary of the non-application of the Agreement, on the 30th day after the expiry of the 90-day period referred to in paragraph 5 of this Article.

IN WITNESS WHEREOF, the undersigned, being duly authorized by their respective Governments, have signed this Agreement.

DONE at Washington, this 1st day of May, 2001, in the English, Spanish and Malay languages, each text being authentic. In case of divergence between the three language texts, the English language text shall prevail.

ANNEX

1. After the entry into force of this Agreement, any member economy of the Asia Pacific Economic Cooperation forum ("APEC member economy") as listed in the Appendix to this Annex may, by a written instrument delivered to the Depositary, agree to be bound by this Agreement if it meets the following criteria:

a. it is unable to accede under the terms of Article 20 of the Agreement; and

b. it agrees to be bound by the aviation security conventions listed in Article 7, paragraph 1 of this Agreement or such conventions otherwise apply to it.

2. Any APEC member economy which agrees to be bound by the Agreement as provided for in paragraph 1 shall, in its relations with all Parties (other than those with which the Agreement shall not apply pursuant to a notification of non-application of the Agreement under Article 20, paragraph 5), have all of the rights and obligations provided for Parties under this Agreement. A Party (other than those with which the Agreement shall not apply pursuant to a notification of non-application of the Agreement under Article 20, paragraph 5) shall, in its relations with such APEC member economy, have all of the rights and obligations provided for Parties under this Agreement. The rights and obligations described in this paragraph shall be effective on the 30th day after the expiry of the 90-day period referred to in paragraph 5 of Article 20.

APPENDIX

Australia; Brunei Darussalam; Canada; Chile; People's Republic of China; Hong Kong Special Administrative Region; Indonesia; Japan; Korea; Malaysia; Mexico; New Zealand; Papua New Guinea; Peru; Philippines; Russia; Singapore; Chinese Taipei; Thailand; United States; Vietnam.

Appendix 28

Convention on International Interests in Mobile Equipment

Done at Cape Town—November 16, 2001
Entered into force—March 1, 2006
Effective in the United States—March 1, 2006
ICAO Doc. 9793

THE STATES PARTIES TO THIS CONVENTION,

AWARE of the need to acquire and use mobile equipment of high value or particular economic significance and to facilitate the financing of the acquisition and use of such equipment in an efficient manner,

RECOGNISING the advantages of asset-based financing and leasing for this purpose and desiring to facilitate these types of transaction by establishing clear rules to govern them,

MINDFUL of the need to ensure that interests in such equipment are recognised and protected universally,

DESIRING to provide broad and mutual economic benefits for all interested parties,

BELIEVING that such rules must reflect the principles underlying asset-based financing and leasing and promote the autonomy of the parties necessary in these transactions,

CONSCIOUS of the need to establish a legal framework for international interests in such equipment and for that purpose to create an international registration system for their protection,

TAKING INTO CONSIDERATION the objectives and principles enunciated in existing Conventions relating to such equipment,

HAVE AGREED upon the following provisions:

Chapter I
Sphere of application and general provisions

Article 1—Definitions

In this Convention, except where the context otherwise requires, the following terms are employed with the meanings set out below:

(a) "agreement" means a security agreement, a title reservation agreement or a leasing agreement;

(b) "assignment" means a contract which, whether by way of security or otherwise, confers on the assignee associated rights with or without a transfer of the related international interest;

(c) "associated rights" means all rights to payment or other performance by a debtor under an agreement which are secured by or associated with the object;

(d) "commencement of the insolvency proceedings" means the time at which the insolvency proceedings are deemed to commence under the applicable insolvency law;

(e) "conditional buyer" means a buyer under a title reservation agreement;

(f) "conditional seller" means a seller under a title reservation agreement;

(g) "contract of sale" means a contract for the sale of an object by a seller to a buyer which is not an agreement as defined in (a) above;

(h) "court" means a court of law or an administrative or arbitral tribunal established by a Contracting State;

(i) "creditor" means a chargee under a security agreement, a conditional seller under a title reservation agreement or a lessor under a leasing agreement;

(j) "debtor" means a chargor under a security agreement, a conditional buyer under a title reservation agreement, a lessee under a leasing agreement or a person whose interest in an object is burdened by a registrable non-consensual right or interest;

(k) "insolvency administrator" means a person authorised to administer the reorganisation or liquidation, including one authorised on an interim basis, and includes a debtor in possession if permitted by the applicable insolvency law;

(l) "insolvency proceedings" means bankruptcy, liquidation or other collective judicial or administrative proceedings, including interim proceedings, in which the assets and affairs of the debtor are subject to control or supervision by a court for the purposes of reorganisation or liquidation;

(m) "interested persons" means:

(i) the debtor;

(ii) any person who, for the purpose of assuring performance of any of the obligations in favour of the creditor, gives or issues a suretyship or demand guarantee or a standby letter of credit or any other form of credit insurance;

(iii) any other person having rights in or over the object;

(n) "internal transaction" means a transaction of a type listed in Article 2(2)(a) to (c) where the centre of the main interests of all parties to such transaction is situated, and the relevant object located (as specified in the Protocol), in the same Contracting State at the time of the conclusion of the contract and where the interest created by the transaction has been registered in a national registry in that Contracting State which has made a declaration under Article 50(1);

(o) "international interest" means an interest held by a creditor to which Article 2 applies;

(p) "International Registry" means the international registration facilities established for the purposes of this Convention or the Protocol;

(q) "leasing agreement" means an agreement by which one person (the lessor) grants a right to possession or control of an object (with or without an option to purchase) to another person (the lessee) in return for a rental or other payment;

(r) "national interest" means an interest held by a creditor in an object and created by an internal transaction covered by a declaration under Article 50(1);

(s) "non-consensual right or interest" means a right or interest conferred under the law of a Contracting State which has made a declaration under Article 39 to secure the performance of an obligation, including an obligation to a State, State entity or an intergovernmental or private organisation;

(t) "notice of a national interest" means notice registered or to be registered in the International Registry that a national interest has been created;

(u) "object" means an object of a category to which Article 2 applies;

(v) "pre-existing right or interest" means a right or interest of any kind in or over an object created or arising before the effective date of this Convention as defined by Article 60(2)(a);

(w) "proceeds" means money or non-money proceeds of an object arising from the total or partial loss or physical destruction of the object or its total or partial confiscation, condemnation or requisition;

(x) "prospective assignment" means an assignment that is intended to be made in the future, upon the occurrence of a stated event, whether or not the occurrence of the event is certain;

(y) "prospective international interest" means an interest that is intended to be created or provided for in an object as an international interest in the future, upon the occurrence of a stated event (which may include the debtor's acquisition of an interest in the object), whether or not the occurrence of the event is certain;

(z) "prospective sale" means a sale which is intended to be made in the future, upon the occurrence of a stated event, whether or not the occurrence of the event is certain;

(aa) "Protocol" means, in respect of any category of object and associated rights to which this Convention applies, the Protocol in respect of that category of object and associated rights;

(bb) "registered" means registered in the International Registry pursuant to Chapter V;

(cc) "registered interest" means an international interest, a registrable non-consensual right or interest or a national interest specified in a notice of a national interest registered pursuant to Chapter V;

(dd) "registrable non-consensual right or interest" means a non-consensual right or interest registrable pursuant to a declaration deposited under Article 40;

(ee) "Registrar" means, in respect of the Protocol, the person or body designated by that Protocol or appointed under Article 17(2)(b);

(ff) "regulations" means regulations made or approved by the Supervisory Authority pursuant to the Protocol;

(gg) "sale" means a transfer of ownership of an object pursuant to a contract of sale;

(hh) "secured obligation" means an obligation secured by a security interest;

(ii) "security agreement" means an agreement by which a chargor grants or agrees to grant to a chargee an interest (including an ownership interest) in or over an object to secure the performance of any existing or future obligation of the chargor or a third person;

(jj) "security interest" means an interest created by a security agreement;

(kk) "Supervisory Authority" means, in respect of the Protocol, the Supervisory Authority referred to in Article 17(1);

(ll) "title reservation agreement" means an agreement for the sale of an object on terms that ownership does not pass until fulfilment of the condition or conditions stated in the agreement;

(mm) "unregistered interest" means a consensual interest or non-consensual right or interest (other than an interest to which Article 39 applies) which has not been registered, whether or not it is registrable under this Convention; and (nn) "writing" means a record of information (including information communicated by teletransmission) which is in tangible or other form and is capable of being reproduced in tangible form on a subsequent occasion and which indicates by reasonable means a person's approval of the record.

Article 2—The international interest

1. This Convention provides for the constitution and effects of an international interest in certain categories of mobile equipment and associated rights.

2. For the purposes of this Convention, an international interest in mobile equipment is an interest, constituted under Article 7, in a uniquely identifiable object of a category of such objects listed in paragraph 3 and designated in the Protocol:

(a) granted by the chargor under a security agreement;

(b) vested in a person who is the conditional seller under a title reservation agreement; or

(c) vested in a person who is the lessor under a leasing agreement.

An interest falling within sub-paragraph (a) does not also fall within sub-paragraph (b) or (c).

3. The categories referred to in the preceding paragraphs are:

(a) airframes, aircraft engines and helicopters;

(b) railway rolling stock; and

(c) space assets.

4. The applicable law determines whether an interest to which paragraph 2 applies falls within subparagraph (a), (b) or (c) of that paragraph.

5. An international interest in an object extends to proceeds of that object.

Article 3—Sphere of application

1. This Convention applies when, at the time of the conclusion of the agreement creating or providing for the international interest, the debtor is situated in a Contracting State.

2. The fact that the creditor is situated in a non-Contracting State does not affect the applicability of this Convention.

Article 4—Where debtor is situated

1. For the purposes of Article 3(1), the debtor is situated in any Contracting State:

(a) under the law of which it is incorporated or formed;

(b) where it has its registered office or statutory seat;

(c) where it has its centre of administration; or

(d) where it has its place of business.

2. A reference in sub-paragraph (d) of the preceding paragraph to the debtor's place of business shall, if it has more than one place of business, mean its principal place of business or, if it has no place of business, its habitual residence.

Article 5—Interpretation and applicable law

1. In the interpretation of this Convention, regard is to be had to its purposes as set forth in the preamble, to its international character and to the need to promote uniformity and predictability in its application.

2. Questions concerning matters governed by this Convention which are not expressly settled in it are to be settled in conformity with the general principles on which it is based or, in the absence of such principles, in conformity with the applicable law.

3. References to the applicable law are to the domestic rules of the law applicable by virtue of the rules of private international law of the forum State.

4. Where a State comprises several territorial units, each of which has its own rules of law in respect of the matter to be decided, and where there is no indication of the relevant territorial unit, the law of that State decides which is the territorial unit whose rules shall govern. In the absence of any such rule, the law of the territorial unit with which the case is most closely connected shall apply.

Article 6—Relationship between the Convention and the Protocol

1. This Convention and the Protocol shall be read and interpreted together as a single instrument.

2. To the extent of any inconsistency between this Convention and the Protocol, the Protocol shall prevail.

Chapter II
Constitution of an international interest

Article 7—Formal requirements

An interest is constituted as an international interest under this Convention where the agreement creating or providing for the interest:

(a) is in writing;

(b) relates to an object of which the chargor, conditional seller or lessor has power to dispose;

(c) enables the object to be identified in conformity with the Protocol; and

(d) in the case of a security agreement, enables the secured obligations to be determined, but without the need to state a sum or maximum sum secured.

Chapter III
Default remedies

Article 8—Remedies of chargee

1. In the event of default as provided in Article 11, the chargee may, to the extent that the chargor has at any time so agreed and subject to any declaration that may be made by a Contracting State under Article 54, exercise any one or more of the following remedies:

(a) take possession or control of any object charged to it;

(b) sell or grant a lease of any such object;

(c) collect or receive any income or profits arising from the management or use of any such object.

2. The chargee may alternatively apply for a court order authorising or directing any of the acts referred to in the preceding paragraph.

3. Any remedy set out in sub-paragraph (a), (b) or (c) of paragraph 1 or by Article 13 shall be exercised in a commercially reasonable manner. A remedy shall be deemed

to be exercised in a commercially reasonable manner where it is exercised in conformity with a provision of the security agreement except where such a provision is manifestly unreasonable.

4. A chargee proposing to sell or grant a lease of an object under paragraph 1 shall give reasonable prior notice in writing of the proposed sale or lease to:

(a) interested persons specified in Article 1(m)(i) and (ii); and

(b) interested persons specified in Article 1(m)(iii) who have given notice of their rights to the chargee within a reasonable time prior to the sale or lease.

5. Any sum collected or received by the chargee as a result of exercise of any of the remedies set out in paragraph 1 or 2 shall be applied towards discharge of the amount of the secured obligations.

6. Where the sums collected or received by the chargee as a result of the exercise of any remedy set out in paragraph 1 or 2 exceed the amount secured by the security interest and any reasonable costs incurred in the exercise of any such remedy, then unless otherwise ordered by the court the chargee shall distribute the surplus among holders of subsequently ranking interests which have been registered or of which the chargee has been given notice, in order of priority, and pay any remaining balance to the chargor.

Article 9—Vesting of object in satisfaction; redemption

1. At any time after default as provided in Article 11, the chargee and all the interested persons may agree that ownership of (or any other interest of the chargor in) any object covered by the security interest shall vest in the chargee in or towards satisfaction of the secured obligations.

2. The court may on the application of the chargee order that ownership of (or any other interest of the chargor in) any object covered by the security interest shall vest in the chargee in or towards satisfaction of the secured obligations.

3. The court shall grant an application under the preceding paragraph only if the amount of the secured obligations to be satisfied by such vesting is commensurate with the value of the object after taking account of any payment to be made by the chargee to any of the interested persons.

4. At any time after default as provided in Article 11 and before sale of the charged object or the making of an order under paragraph 2, the chargor or any interested person may discharge the security interest by paying in full the amount secured, subject to any lease granted by the chargee under Article 8(1)(b) or ordered under Article 8(2). Where, after such default, the payment of the amount secured is made in full by an interested person other than the debtor, that person is subrogated to the rights of the chargee.

5. Ownership or any other interest of the chargor passing on a sale under Article 8(1)(b) or passing under paragraph 1 or 2 of this Article is free from any other interest over which the chargee's security interest has priority under the provisions of Article 29.

Article 10—Remedies of conditional seller or lessor

In the event of default under a title reservation agreement or under a leasing agreement as provided in Article 11, the conditional seller or the lessor, as the case may be, may:

(a) subject to any declaration that may be made by a Contracting State under Article 54, terminate the agreement and take possession or control of any object to which the agreement relates; or

(b) apply for a court order authorising or directing either of these acts.

Article 11—Meaning of default

1. The debtor and the creditor may at any time agree in writing as to the events that constitute a default or otherwise give rise to the rights and remedies specified in Articles 8 to 10 and 13.

2. Where the debtor and the creditor have not so agreed, "default" for the purposes of Articles 8 to 10 and 13 means a default which substantially deprives the creditor of what it is entitled to expect under the agreement.

Article 12—Additional remedies

Any additional remedies permitted by the applicable law, including any remedies agreed upon by the parties, may be exercised to the extent that they are not inconsistent with the mandatory provisions of this Chapter as set out in Article 15.

Article 13—Relief pending final determination

1. Subject to any declaration that it may make under Article 55, a Contracting State shall ensure that a creditor who adduces evidence of default by the debtor may, pending final determination of its claim and to the extent that the debtor has at any time so agreed, obtain from a court speedy relief in the form of such one or more of the following orders as the creditor requests:

(a) preservation of the object and its value;

(b) possession, control or custody of the object;

(c) immobilisation of the object; and

(d) lease or, except where covered by sub-paragraphs (a) to (c), management of the object and the income therefrom.

2. In making any order under the preceding paragraph, the court may impose such terms as it considers necessary to protect the interested persons in the event that the creditor:

(a) in implementing any order granting such relief, fails to perform any of its obligations to the debtor under this Convention or the Protocol; or

(b) fails to establish its claim, wholly or in part, on the final determination of that claim.

3. Before making any order under paragraph 1, the court may require notice of the request to be given to any of the interested persons.

4. Nothing in this Article affects the application of Article 8(3) or limits the availability of forms of interim relief other than those set out in paragraph 1.

Article 14—Procedural requirements

Subject to Article 54(2), any remedy provided by this Chapter shall be exercised in conformity with the procedure prescribed by the law of the place where the remedy is to be exercised.

Article 15—Derogation

In their relations with each other, any two or more of the parties referred to in this Chapter may at any time, by agreement in writing, derogate from or vary the effect of any of the preceding provisions of this Chapter except Articles 8(3) to (6), 9(3) and (4), 13(2) and 14.

Chapter IV
The international registration system

Article 16—The International Registry

1. An International Registry shall be established for registrations of:

(a) international interests, prospective international interests and registrable non-consensual rights and interests;

(b) assignments and prospective assignments of international interests;

(c) acquisitions of international interests by legal or contractual subrogations under the applicable law;

(d) notices of national interests; and

(e) subordinations of interests referred to in any of the preceding sub-paragraphs.

2. Different international registries may be established for different categories of object and associated rights.

3. For the purposes of this Chapter and Chapter V, the term "registration" includes, where appropriate, an amendment, extension or discharge of a registration.

Article 17—The Supervisory Authority and the Registrar

1. There shall be a Supervisory Authority as provided by the Protocol.

2. The Supervisory Authority shall:

(a) establish or provide for the establishment of the International Registry;

(b) except as otherwise provided by the Protocol, appoint and dismiss the Registrar;

(c) ensure that any rights required for the continued effective operation of the International Registry in the event of a change of Registrar will vest in or be assignable to the new Registrar;

(d) after consultation with the Contracting States, make or approve and ensure the publication of regulations pursuant to the Protocol dealing with the operation of the International Registry;

(e) establish administrative procedures through which complaints concerning the operation of the International Registry can be made to the Supervisory Authority;

(f) supervise the Registrar and the operation of the International Registry;

(g) at the request of the Registrar, provide such guidance to the Registrar as the Supervisory Authority thinks fit;

(h) set and periodically review the structure of fees to be charged for the services and facilities of the International Registry;

(i) do all things necessary to ensure that an efficient notice-based electronic registration system exists to implement the objectives of this Convention and the Protocol; and

(j) report periodically to Contracting States concerning the discharge of its obligations under this Convention and the Protocol.

3. The Supervisory Authority may enter into any agreement requisite for the performance of its functions, including any agreement referred to in Article 27(3).

4. The Supervisory Authority shall own all proprietary rights in the data bases and archives of the International Registry.

5. The Registrar shall ensure the efficient operation of the International Registry and perform the functions assigned to it by this Convention, the Protocol and the regulations.

Chapter V
Other matters relating to registration

Article 18—Registration requirements

1. The Protocol and regulations shall specify the requirements, including the criteria for the identification of the object:

(a) for effecting a registration (which shall include provision for prior electronic transmission of any consent from any person whose consent is required under Article 20);

(b) for making searches and issuing search certificates, and, subject thereto;

(c) for ensuring the confidentiality of information and documents of the International Registry other than information and documents relating to a registration.

2. The Registrar shall not be under a duty to enquire whether a consent to registration under Article 20 has in fact been given or is valid.

3. Where an interest registered as a prospective international interest becomes an international interest, no further registration shall be required provided that the registration information is sufficient for a registration of an international interest.

4. The Registrar shall arrange for registrations to be entered into the International Registry data base and made searchable in chronological order of receipt, and the file shall record the date and time of receipt.

5. The Protocol may provide that a Contracting State may designate an entity or entities in its territory as the entry point or entry points through which the information required for registration shall or may be transmitted to the International Registry. A Contracting State making such a designation may specify the requirements, if any, to be satisfied before such information is transmitted to the International Registry.

Article 19—Validity and time of registration

1. A registration shall be valid only if made in conformity with Article 20.

2. A registration, if valid, shall be complete upon entry of the required information into the International Registry data base so as to be searchable.

3. A registration shall be searchable for the purposes of the preceding paragraph at the time when:

(a) the International Registry has assigned to it a sequentially ordered file number; and

(b) the registration information, including the file number, is stored in durable form and may be accessed at the International Registry.

4. If an interest first registered as a prospective international interest becomes an international interest, that international interest shall be treated as registered from the time of registration of the prospective international interest provided that the registra-

tion was still current immediately before the international interest was constituted as provided by Article 7.

5. The preceding paragraph applies with necessary modifications to the registration of a prospective assignment of an international interest.

6. A registration shall be searchable in the International Registry data base according to the criteria prescribed by the Protocol.

Article 20—Consent to registration

1. An international interest, a prospective international interest or an assignment or prospective assignment of an international interest may be registered, and any such registration amended or extended prior to its expiry, by either party with the consent in writing of the other.

2. The subordination of an international interest to another international interest may be registered by or with the consent in writing at any time of the person whose interest has been subordinated.

3. A registration may be discharged by or with the consent in writing of the party in whose favour it was made.

4. The acquisition of an international interest by legal or contractual subrogation may be registered by the subrogee.

5. A registrable non-consensual right or interest may be registered by the holder thereof.

6. A notice of a national interest may be registered by the holder thereof.

Article 21—Duration of registration

Registration of an international interest remains effective until discharged or until expiry of the period specified in the registration.

Article 22—Searches

1. Any person may, in the manner prescribed by the Protocol and regulations, make or request a search of the International Registry by electronic means concerning interests or prospective international interests registered therein.

2. Upon receipt of a request therefor, the Registrar, in the manner prescribed by the Protocol and regulations, shall issue a registry search certificate by electronic means with respect to any object:

(a) stating all registered information relating thereto, together with a statement indicating the date and time of registration of such information; or

(b) stating that there is no information in the International Registry relating thereto.

3. A search certificate issued under the preceding paragraph shall indicate that the creditor named in the registration information has acquired or intends to acquire an international interest in the object but shall not indicate whether what is registered is an international interest or a prospective international interest, even if this is ascertainable from the relevant registration information.

Article 23—List of declarations and declared non-consensual rights or interests

The Registrar shall maintain a list of declarations, withdrawals of declaration and of the categories of nonconsensual right or interest communicated to the Registrar by the

Depositary as having been declared by Contracting States in conformity with Articles 39 and 40 and the date of each such declaration or withdrawal of declaration. Such list shall be recorded and searchable in the name of the declaring State and shall be made available as provided in the Protocol and regulations to any person requesting it.

Article 24—Evidentiary value of certificates

A document in the form prescribed by the regulations which purports to be a certificate issued by the International Registry is prima facie proof:

(a) that it has been so issued; and

(b) of the facts recited in it, including the date and time of a registration.

Article 25—Discharge of registration

1. Where the obligations secured by a registered security interest or the obligations giving rise to a registered non-consensual right or interest have been discharged, or where the conditions of transfer of title under a registered title reservation agreement have been fulfilled, the holder of such interest shall, without undue delay, procure the discharge of the registration after written demand by the debtor delivered to or received at its address stated in the registration.

2. Where a prospective international interest or a prospective assignment of an international interest has been registered, the intending creditor or intending assignee shall, without undue delay, procure the discharge of the registration after written demand by the intending debtor or assignor which is delivered to or received at its address stated in the registration before the intending creditor or assignee has given value or incurred a commitment to give value.

3. Where the obligations secured by a national interest specified in a registered notice of a national interest have been discharged, the holder of such interest shall, without undue delay, procure the discharge of the registration after written demand by the debtor delivered to or received at its address stated in the registration.

4. Where a registration ought not to have been made or is incorrect, the person in whose favour the registration was made shall, without undue delay, procure its discharge or amendment after written demand by the debtor delivered to or received at its address stated in the registration.

Article 26—Access to the international registration facilities

No person shall be denied access to the registration and search facilities of the International Registry on any ground other than its failure to comply with the procedures prescribed by this Chapter.

Chapter VI
Privileges and immunities of the Supervisory Authority and the Registrar

Article 27—Legal personality; immunity

1. The Supervisory Authority shall have international legal personality where not already possessing such personality.

2. The Supervisory Authority and its officers and employees shall enjoy such immunity from legal or administrative process as is specified in the Protocol.

3. (a) The Supervisory Authority shall enjoy exemption from taxes and such other privileges as may be provided by agreement with the host State.

(b) For the purposes of this paragraph, "host State" means the State in which the Supervisory Authority is situated.

4. The assets, documents, data bases and archives of the International Registry shall be inviolable and immune from seizure or other legal or administrative process.

5. For the purposes of any claim against the Registrar under Article 28(1) or Article 44, the claimant shall be entitled to access to such information and documents as are necessary to enable the claimant to pursue its claim.

6. The Supervisory Authority may waive the inviolability and immunity conferred by paragraph 4.

Chapter VII
Liability of the Registrar

Article 28—Liability and financial assurances

1. The Registrar shall be liable for compensatory damages for loss suffered by a person directly resulting from an error or omission of the Registrar and its officers and employees or from a malfunction of the international registration system except where the malfunction is caused by an event of an inevitable and irresistible nature, which could not be prevented by using the best practices in current use in the field of electronic registry design and operation, including those related to back-up and systems security and networking.

2. The Registrar shall not be liable under the preceding paragraph for factual inaccuracy of registration information received by the Registrar or transmitted by the Registrar in the form in which it received that information nor for acts or circumstances for which the Registrar and its officers and employees are not responsible and arising prior to receipt of registration information at the International Registry.

3. Compensation under paragraph 1 may be reduced to the extent that the person who suffered the damage caused or contributed to that damage.

4. The Registrar shall procure insurance or a financial guarantee covering the liability referred to in this Article to the extent determined by the Supervisory Authority, in accordance with the Protocol.

Chapter VIII
Effects of an international interest as against third parties

Article 29—Priority of competing interests

1. A registered interest has priority over any other interest subsequently registered and over an unregistered interest.

2. The priority of the first-mentioned interest under the preceding paragraph applies:

(a) even if the first-mentioned interest was acquired or registered with actual knowledge of the other interest; and

(b) even as regards value given by the holder of the first-mentioned interest with such knowledge.

3. The buyer of an object acquires its interest in it:

(a) subject to an interest registered at the time of its acquisition of that interest; and

(b) free from an unregistered interest even if it has actual knowledge of such an interest.

4. The conditional buyer or lessee acquires its interest in or right over that object:

(a) subject to an interest registered prior to the registration of the international interest held by its conditional seller or lessor; and

(b) free from an interest not so registered at that time even if it has actual knowledge of that interest.

5. The priority of competing interests or rights under this Article may be varied by agreement between the holders of those interests, but an assignee of a subordinated interest is not bound by an agreement to subordinate that interest unless at the time of the assignment a subordination had been registered relating to that agreement.

6. Any priority given by this Article to an interest in an object extends to proceeds.

7. This Convention:

(a) does not affect the rights of a person in an item, other than an object, held prior to its installation on an object if under the applicable law those rights continue to exist after the installation; and

(b) does not prevent the creation of rights in an item, other than an object, which has previously been installed on an object where under the applicable law those rights are created.

Article 30—Effects of insolvency

1. In insolvency proceedings against the debtor an international interest is effective if prior to the commencement of the insolvency proceedings that interest was registered in conformity with this Convention.

2. Nothing in this Article impairs the effectiveness of an international interest in the insolvency proceedings where that interest is effective under the applicable law.

3. Nothing in this Article affects:

(a) any rules of law applicable in insolvency proceedings relating to the avoidance of a transaction as a preference or a transfer in fraud of creditors; or

(b) any rules of procedure relating to the enforcement of rights to property which is under the control or supervision of the insolvency administrator.

Chapter IX
Assignments of associated rights and international interests; rights of subrogation

Article 31—Effects of assignment

1. Except as otherwise agreed by the parties, an assignment of associated rights made in conformity with Article 32 also transfers to the assignee:

(a) the related international interest; and

(b) all the interests and priorities of the assignor under this Convention.

2. Nothing in this Convention prevents a partial assignment of the assignor's associated rights. In the case of such a partial assignment the assignor and assignee may agree as to their respective rights concerning the related international interest assigned under the preceding paragraph but not so as adversely to affect the debtor without its consent.

3. Subject to paragraph 4, the applicable law shall determine the defences and rights of set-off available to the debtor against the assignee.

4. The debtor may at any time by agreement in writing waive all or any of the defences and rights of set-off referred to in the preceding paragraph other than defences arising from fraudulent acts on the part of the assignee.

5. In the case of an assignment by way of security, the assigned associated rights revest in the assignor, to the extent that they are still subsisting, when the obligations secured by the assignment have been discharged.

Article 32—Formal requirements of assignment

1. An assignment of associated rights transfers the related international interest only if it:

(a) is in writing;

(b) enables the associated rights to be identified under the contract from which they arise; and

(c) in the case of an assignment by way of security, enables the obligations secured by the assignment to be determined in accordance with the Protocol but without the need to state a sum or maximum sum secured.

2. An assignment of an international interest created or provided for by a security agreement is not valid unless some or all related associated rights also are assigned.

3. This Convention does not apply to an assignment of associated rights which is not effective to transfer the related international interest.

Article 33—Debtor's duty to assignee

1. To the extent that associated rights and the related international interest have been transferred in accordance with Articles 31 and 32, the debtor in relation to those rights and that interest is bound by the assignment and has a duty to make payment or give other performance to the assignee, if but only if:

(a) the debtor has been given notice of the assignment in writing by or with the authority of the assignor; and

(b) the notice identifies the associated rights.

2. Irrespective of any other ground on which payment or performance by the debtor discharges the latter from liability, payment or performance shall be effective for this purpose if made in accordance with the preceding paragraph.

3. Nothing in this Article shall affect the priority of competing assignments.

Article 34—Default remedies in respect of assignment by way of security

In the event of default by the assignor under the assignment of associated rights and the related international interest made by way of security, Articles 8, 9 and 11 to 14 apply in the relations between the assignor and the assignee (and, in relation to associated rights, apply in so far as those provisions are capable of application to intangible property) as if references:

(a) to the secured obligation and the security interest were references to the obligation secured by the assignment of the associated rights and the related international interest and the security interest created by that assignment;

(b) to the chargee or creditor and chargor or debtor were references to the assignee and assignor;

(c) to the holder of the international interest were references to the assignee; and

(d) to the object were references to the assigned associated rights and the related international interest.

Article 35—Priority of competing assignments

1. Where there are competing assignments of associated rights and at least one of the assignments includes the related international interest and is registered, the provisions of Article 29 apply as if the references to a registered interest were references to an assignment of the associated rights and the related registered interest and as if references to a registered or unregistered interest were references to a registered or unregistered assignment.

2. Article 30 applies to an assignment of associated rights as if the references to an international interest were references to an assignment of the associated rights and the related international interest.

Article 36—Assignee's priority with respect to associated rights

1. The assignee of associated rights and the related international interest whose assignment has been registered only has priority under Article 35(1) over another assignee of the associated rights:

(a) if the contract under which the associated rights arise states that they are secured by or associated with the object; and

(b) to the extent that the associated rights are related to an object.

2. For the purposes of sub-paragraph (b) of the preceding paragraph, associated rights are related to an object only to the extent that they consist of rights to payment or performance that relate to:

(a) a sum advanced and utilised for the purchase of the object;

(b) a sum advanced and utilised for the purchase of another object in which the assignor held another international interest if the assignor transferred that interest to the assignee and the assignment has been registered;

(c) the price payable for the object;

(d) the rentals payable in respect of the object; or

(e) other obligations arising from a transaction referred to in any of the preceding subparagraphs.

3. In all other cases, the priority of the competing assignments of the associated rights shall be determined by the applicable law.

Article 37—Effects of assignor's insolvency

The provisions of Article 30 apply to insolvency proceedings against the assignor as if references to the debtor were references to the assignor.

Article 38—Subrogation

1. Subject to paragraph 2, nothing in this Convention affects the acquisition of associated rights and the related international interest by legal or contractual subrogation under the applicable law.

2. The priority between any interest within the preceding paragraph and a competing interest may be varied by agreement in writing between the holders of the respective interests but an assignee of a subordinated interest is not bound by an agreement to subordinate that interest unless at the time of the assignment a subordination had been registered relating to that agreement.

Chapter X
Rights or interests subject to declarations by Contracting States

Article 39—Rights having priority without registration

1. A Contracting State may at any time, in a declaration deposited with the Depositary of the Protocol declare, generally or specifically:

(a) those categories of non-consensual right or interest (other than a right or interest to which Article 40 applies) which under that State's law have priority over an interest in an object equivalent to that of the holder of a registered international interest and which shall have priority over a registered international interest, whether in or outside insolvency proceedings; and

(b) that nothing in this Convention shall affect the right of a State or State entity, intergovernmental organisation or other private provider of public services to arrest or detain an object under the laws of that State for payment of amounts owed to such entity, organisation or provider directly relating to those services in respect of that object or another object.

2. A declaration made under the preceding paragraph may be expressed to cover categories that are created after the deposit of that declaration.

3. A non-consensual right or interest has priority over an international interest if and only if the former is of a category covered by a declaration deposited prior to the registration of the international interest.

4. Notwithstanding the preceding paragraph, a Contracting State may, at the time of ratification, acceptance, approval of, or accession to the Protocol, declare that a right or interest of a category covered by a declaration made under sub-paragraph (a) of paragraph 1 shall have priority over an international interest registered prior to the date of such ratification, acceptance, approval or accession.

Article 40—Registrable non-consensual rights or interests

A Contracting State may at any time in a declaration deposited with the Depositary of the Protocol list the categories of non-consensual right or interest which shall be registrable under this Convention as regards any category of object as if the right or interest were an international interest and shall be regulated accordingly. Such a declaration may be modified from time to time.

Chapter XI
Application of the Convention to sales

Article 41—Sale and prospective sale

This Convention shall apply to the sale or prospective sale of an object as provided for in the Protocol with any modifications therein.

Chapter XII
Jurisdiction

Article 42—Choice of forum

1. Subject to Articles 43 and 44, the courts of a Contracting State chosen by the parties to a transaction have jurisdiction in respect of any claim brought under this Convention, whether or not the chosen forum has a connection with the parties or the transaction. Such jurisdiction shall be exclusive unless otherwise agreed between the parties.

2. Any such agreement shall be in writing or otherwise concluded in accordance with the formal requirements of the law of the chosen forum.

Article 43—Jurisdiction under Article 13

1. The courts of a Contracting State chosen by the parties and the courts of the Contracting State on the territory of which the object is situated have jurisdiction to grant relief under Article 13(1)(a), (b), (c) and Article 13(4) in respect of that object.

2. Jurisdiction to grant relief under Article 13(1)(d) or other interim relief by virtue of Article 13(4) may be exercised either:

(a) by the courts chosen by the parties; or

(b) by the courts of a Contracting State on the territory of which the debtor is situated, being relief which, by the terms of the order granting it, is enforceable only in the territory of that Contracting State.

3. A court has jurisdiction under the preceding paragraphs even if the final determination of the claim referred to in Article 13(1) will or may take place in a court of another Contracting State or by arbitration.

Article 44—Jurisdiction to make orders against the Registrar

1. The courts of the place in which the Registrar has its centre of administration shall have exclusive jurisdiction to award damages or make orders against the Registrar.

2. Where a person fails to respond to a demand made under Article 25 and that person has ceased to exist or cannot be found for the purpose of enabling an order to be made against it requiring it to procure discharge of the registration, the courts referred to in the preceding paragraph shall have exclusive jurisdiction, on the application of the debtor or intending debtor, to make an order directed to the Registrar requiring the Registrar to discharge the registration.

3. Where a person fails to comply with an order of a court having jurisdiction under this Convention or, in the case of a national interest, an order of a court of competent jurisdiction requiring that person to procure the amendment or discharge of a registration, the courts referred to in paragraph 1 may direct the Registrar to take such steps as will give effect to that order.

4. Except as otherwise provided by the preceding paragraphs, no court may make orders or give judgments or rulings against or purporting to bind the Registrar.

Article 45—Jurisdiction in respect of insolvency proceedings

The provisions of this Chapter are not applicable to insolvency proceedings.

Chapter XIII
Relationship with other Conventions

Article 45 bis—Relationship with the United Nations Convention on the Assignment of Receivables in International Trade

This Convention shall prevail over the United Nations Convention on the Assignment of Receivables in International Trade, opened for signature in New York on 12 December 2001, as it relates to the assignment of receivables which are associated rights related to international interests in aircraft objects, railway rolling stock and space assets.

Article 46—Relationship with the UNIDROIT Convention on International Financial Leasing

The Protocol may determine the relationship between this Convention and the UNIDROIT Convention on International Financial Leasing, signed at Ottawa on 28 May 1988.

Chapter XIV
Final provisions

Article 47—Signature, ratification, acceptance, approval or accession

1. This Convention shall be open for signature in Cape Town on 16 November 2001 by States participating in the Diplomatic Conference to Adopt a Mobile Equipment Convention and an Aircraft Protocol held at Cape Town from 29 October to 16 November 2001. After 16 November 2001, the Convention shall be open to all States for signature at the Headquarters of the International Institute for the Unification of Private Law (UNIDROIT) in Rome until it enters into force in accordance with Article 49.

2. This Convention shall be subject to ratification, acceptance or approval by States which have signed it.

3. Any State which does not sign this Convention may accede to it at any time.

4. Ratification, acceptance, approval or accession is effected by the deposit of a formal instrument to that effect with the Depositary.

Article 48—Regional Economic Integration Organisations

1. A Regional Economic Integration Organisation which is constituted by sovereign States and has competence over certain matters governed by this Convention may similarly sign, accept, approve or accede to this Convention. The Regional Economic Integration Organisation shall in that case have the rights and obligations of a Contracting State, to the extent that that Organisation has competence over matters governed by this Convention. Where the number of Contracting States is relevant in this Convention, the Regional Economic Integration Organisation shall not count as a Contracting State in addition to its Member States which are Contracting States.

2. The Regional Economic Integration Organisation shall, at the time of signature, acceptance, approval or accession, make a declaration to the Depositary specifying the matters governed by this Convention in respect of which competence has been transferred to that Organisation by its Member States. The Regional Economic Integration Organisation shall promptly notify the Depositary of any changes to the distribution of competence, including new transfers of competence, specified in the declaration under this paragraph.

3. Any reference to a "Contracting State" or "Contracting States" or "State Party" or "States Parties" in this Convention applies equally to a Regional Economic Integration Organisation where the context so requires.

Article 49—Entry into force

1. This Convention enters into force on the first day of the month following the expiration of three months after the date of the deposit of the third instrument of ratification, acceptance, approval or accession but only as regards a category of objects to which a Protocol applies:

(a) as from the time of entry into force of that Protocol;

(b) subject to the terms of that Protocol; and

(c) as between States Parties to this Convention and that Protocol.

2. For other States this Convention enters into force on the first day of the month following the expiration of three months after the date of the deposit of their instrument of ratification, acceptance, approval or accession but only as regards a category of objects to which a Protocol applies and subject, in relation to such Protocol, to the requirements of sub-paragraphs (a), (b) and (c) of the preceding paragraph.

Article 50—Internal transactions

1. A Contracting State may, at the time of ratification, acceptance, approval of, or accession to the Protocol, declare that this Convention shall not apply to a transaction which is an internal transaction in relation to that State with regard to all types of objects or some of them.

2. Notwithstanding the preceding paragraph, the provisions of Articles 8(4), 9(1), 16, Chapter V, Article 29, and any provisions of this Convention relating to registered interests shall apply to an internal transaction.

3. Where notice of a national interest has been registered in the International Registry, the priority of the holder of that interest under Article 29 shall not be affected by the fact that such interest has become vested in another person by assignment or subrogation under the applicable law.

Article 51—Future Protocols

1. The Depositary may create working groups, in co-operation with such relevant non-governmental organisations as the Depositary considers appropriate, to assess the feasibility of extending the application of this Convention, through one or more Protocols, to objects of any category of high-value mobile equipment, other than a category referred to in Article 2(3), each member of which is uniquely identifiable, and associated rights relating to such objects.

2. The Depositary shall communicate the text of any preliminary draft Protocol relating to a category of objects prepared by such a working group to all States Parties to this Convention, all member States of the Depositary, member States of the United Nations which are not members of the Depositary and the relevant intergovernmental organisations, and shall invite such States and organisations to participate in intergovernmental negotiations for the completion of a draft Protocol on the basis of such a preliminary draft Protocol.

3. The Depositary shall also communicate the text of any preliminary draft Protocol prepared by such a working group to such relevant non-governmental organisa-

tions as the Depositary considers appropriate. Such non-governmental organisations shall be invited promptly to submit comments on the text of the preliminary draft Protocol to the Depositary and to participate as observers in the preparation of a draft Protocol.

4. When the competent bodies of the Depositary adjudge such a draft Protocol ripe for adoption, the Depositary shall convene a diplomatic conference for its adoption.

5. Once such a Protocol has been adopted, subject to paragraph 6, this Convention shall apply to the category of objects covered thereby.

6. Article 45 bis of this Convention applies to such a Protocol only if specifically provided for in that Protocol.

Article 52—Territorial units

1. If a Contracting State has territorial units in which different systems of law are applicable in relation to the matters dealt with in this Convention, it may, at the time of ratification, acceptance, approval or accession, declare that this Convention is to extend to all its territorial units or only to one or more of them and may modify its declaration by submitting another declaration at any time.

2. Any such declaration shall state expressly the territorial units to which this Convention applies.

3. If a Contracting State has not made any declaration under paragraph 1, this Convention shall apply to all territorial units of that State.

4. Where a Contracting State extends this Convention to one or more of its territorial units, declarations permitted under this Convention may be made in respect of each such territorial unit, and the declarations made in respect of one territorial unit may be different from those made in respect of another territorial unit.

5. If by virtue of a declaration under paragraph 1, this Convention extends to one or more territorial units of a Contracting State:

(a) the debtor is considered to be situated in a Contracting State only if it is incorporated or formed under a law in force in a territorial unit to which this Convention applies or if it has its registered office or statutory seat, centre of administration, place of business or habitual residence in a territorial unit to which this Convention applies;

(b) any reference to the location of the object in a Contracting State refers to the location of the object in a territorial unit to which this Convention applies; and

(c) any reference to the administrative authorities in that Contracting State shall be construed as referring to the administrative authorities having jurisdiction in a territorial unit to which this Convention applies.

Article 53—Determination of courts

A Contracting State may, at the time of ratification, acceptance, approval of, or accession to the Protocol, declare the relevant "court" or "courts" for the purposes of Article 1 and Chapter XII of this Convention.

Article 54—Declarations regarding remedies

1. A Contracting State may, at the time of ratification, acceptance, approval of, or accession to the Protocol, declare that while the charged object is situated within, or controlled from its territory the chargee shall not grant a lease of the object in that territory.

2. A Contracting State shall, at the time of ratification, acceptance, approval of, or accession to the Protocol, declare whether or not any remedy available to the creditor under any provision of this Convention which is not there expressed to require application to the court may be exercised only with leave of the court.

Article 55—Declarations regarding relief pending final determination

A Contracting State may, at the time of ratification, acceptance, approval of, or accession to the Protocol, declare that it will not apply the provisions of Article 13 or Article 43, or both, wholly or in part. The declaration shall specify under which conditions the relevant Article will be applied, in case it will be applied partly, or otherwise which other forms of interim relief will be applied.

Article 56—Reservations and declarations

1. No reservations may be made to this Convention but declarations authorised by Articles 39, 40, 50, 52, 53, 54, 55, 57, 58 and 60 may be made in accordance with these provisions.

2. Any declaration or subsequent declaration or any withdrawal of a declaration made under this Convention shall be notified in writing to the Depositary.

Article 57—Subsequent declarations

1. A State Party may make a subsequent declaration, other than a declaration authorised under Article 60, at any time after the date on which this Convention has entered into force for it, by notifying the Depositary to that effect.

2. Any such subsequent declaration shall take effect on the first day of the month following the expiration of six months after the date of receipt of the notification by the Depositary. Where a longer period for that declaration to take effect is specified in the notification, it shall take effect upon the expiration of such longer period after receipt of the notification by the Depositary.

3. Notwithstanding the previous paragraphs, this Convention shall continue to apply, as if no such subsequent declarations had been made, in respect of all rights and interests arising prior to the effective date of any such subsequent declaration.

Article 58—Withdrawal of declarations

1. Any State Party having made a declaration under this Convention, other than a declaration authorised under Article 60, may withdraw it at any time by notifying the Depositary. Such withdrawal is to take effect on the first day of the month following the expiration of six months after the date of receipt of the notification by the Depositary.

2. Notwithstanding the previous paragraph, this Convention shall continue to apply, as if no such withdrawal of declaration had been made, in respect of all rights and interests arising prior to the effective date of any such withdrawal.

Article 59—Denunciations

1. Any State Party may denounce this Convention by notification in writing to the Depositary.

2. Any such denunciation shall take effect on the first day of the month following the expiration of twelve months after the date on which notification is received by the Depositary.

3. Notwithstanding the previous paragraphs, this Convention shall continue to apply, as if no such denunciation had been made, in respect of all rights and interests arising prior to the effective date of any such denunciation.

Article 60—Transitional provisions

1. Unless otherwise declared by a Contracting State at any time, the Convention does not apply to a pre-existing right or interest, which retains the priority it enjoyed under the applicable law before the effective date of this Convention.

2. For the purposes of Article 1(v) and of determining priority under this Convention:

(a) "effective date of this Convention" means in relation to a debtor the time when this Convention enters into force or the time when the State in which the debtor is situated becomes a Contracting State, whichever is the later; and

(b) the debtor is situated in a State where it has its centre of administration or, if it has no centre of administration, its place of business or, if it has more than one place of business, its principal place of business or, if it has no place of business, its habitual residence.

3. A Contracting State may in its declaration under paragraph 1 specify a date, not earlier than three years after the date on which the declaration becomes effective, when this Convention and the Protocol will become applicable, for the purpose of determining priority, including the protection of any existing priority, to pre-existing rights or interests arising under an agreement made at a time when the debtor was situated in a State referred to in sub-paragraph (b) of the preceding paragraph but only to the extent and in the manner specified in its declaration.

Article 61—Review Conferences, amendments and related matters

1. The Depositary shall prepare reports yearly or at such other time as the circumstances may require for the States Parties as to the manner in which the international regimen established in this Convention has operated in practice. In preparing such reports, the Depositary shall take into account the reports of the Supervisory Authority concerning the functioning of the international registration system.

2. At the request of not less than twenty-five percent of the States Parties, Review Conferences of States Parties shall be convened from time to time by the Depositary, in consultation with the Supervisory Authority, to consider:

(a) the practical operation of this Convention and its effectiveness in facilitating the asset-based financing and leasing of the objects covered by its terms;

(b) the judicial interpretation given to, and the application made of the terms of this Convention and the regulations;

(c) the functioning of the international registration system, the performance of the Registrar and its oversight by the Supervisory Authority, taking into account the reports of the Supervisory Authority; and

(d) whether any modifications to this Convention or the arrangements relating to the International Registry are desirable.

3. Subject to paragraph 4, any amendment to this Convention shall be approved by at least a two-thirds majority of States Parties participating in the Conference referred to in the preceding paragraph and shall then enter into force in respect of States which have ratified, accepted or approved such amendment when ratified, accepted, or ap-

proved by three States in accordance with the provisions of Article 49 relating to its entry into force.

4. Where the proposed amendment to this Convention is intended to apply to more than one category of equipment, such amendment shall also be approved by at least a two-thirds majority of States Parties to each Protocol that are participating in the Conference referred to in paragraph 2.

Article 62—Depositary and its functions

1. Instruments of ratification, acceptance, approval or accession shall be deposited with the International Institute for the Unification of Private Law (UNIDROIT), which is hereby designated the Depositary.

2. The Depositary shall:

(a) inform all Contracting States of:

(i) each new signature or deposit of an instrument of ratification, acceptance, approval or accession, together with the date thereof;

(ii) the date of entry into force of this Convention;

(iii) each declaration made in accordance with this Convention, together with the date thereof;

(iv) the withdrawal or amendment of any declaration, together with the date thereof; and

(v) the notification of any denunciation of this Convention together with the date thereof and the date on which it takes effect;

(b) transmit certified true copies of this Convention to all Contracting States;

(c) provide the Supervisory Authority and the Registrar with a copy of each instrument of ratification, acceptance, approval or accession, together with the date of deposit thereof, of each declaration or withdrawal or amendment of a declaration and of each notification of denunciation, together with the date of notification thereof, so that the information contained therein is easily and fully available; and

(d) perform such other functions customary for depositaries.

IN WITNESS WHEREOF the undersigned Plenipotentiaries, having been duly authorised, have signed this Convention.

DONE at Cape Town, this sixteenth day of November, two thousand and one, in a single original in the English, Arabic, Chinese, French, Russian and Spanish languages, all texts being equally authentic, such authenticity to take effect upon verification by the Joint Secretariat of the Conference under the authority of the President of the Conference within ninety days hereof as to the conformity of the texts with one another.

Appendix 29

Protocol to the Convention on International Interests in Mobile Equipment on Matters Specific to Aircraft Equipment

Done at Cape Town—November 16, 2001
Entered into force—March 1, 2006
Effective in the United States—March 1, 2006
ICAO Doc. 9794

THE STATES PARTIES TO THIS PROTOCOL,

CONSIDERING it necessary to implement the Convention on International Interests in Mobile Equipment (hereinafter referred to as "the Convention") as it relates to aircraft equipment, in the light of the purposes set out in the preamble to the Convention,

MINDFUL of the need to adapt the Convention to meet the particular requirements of aircraft finance and to extend the sphere of application of the Convention to include contracts of sale of aircraft equipment,

MINDFUL of the principles and objectives of the Convention on International Civil Aviation, signed at Chicago on 7 December 1944,

HAVE AGREED upon the following provisions relating to aircraft equipment:

Chapter I
Sphere of application and general provisions

Article I—Defined terms

1. In this Protocol, except where the context otherwise requires, terms used in it have the meanings set out in the Convention.

2. In this Protocol the following terms are employed with the meanings set out below:

(a) "aircraft" means aircraft as defined for the purposes of the Chicago Convention which are either airframes with aircraft engines installed thereon or helicopters;

(b) "aircraft engines" means aircraft engines (other than those used in military, customs or police services) powered by jet propulsion or turbine or piston technology and:

(i) in the case of jet propulsion aircraft engines, have at least 1750 lb of thrust or its equivalent; and

(ii) in the case of turbine-powered or piston-powered aircraft engines, have at least 550 rated take-off shaft horsepower or its equivalent,

together with all modules and other installed, incorporated or attached accessories, parts and equipment and all data, manuals and records relating thereto;

(c) "aircraft objects" means airframes, aircraft engines and helicopters;

(d) "aircraft register" means a register maintained by a State or a common mark registering authority for the purposes of the Chicago Convention;

(e) "airframes" means airframes (other than those used in military, customs or police services) that, when appropriate aircraft engines are installed thereon, are type certified by the competent aviation authority to transport:

(i) at least eight (8) persons including crew; or

(ii) goods in excess of 2750 kilograms,

together with all installed, incorporated or attached accessories, parts and equipment (other than aircraft engines), and all data, manuals and records relating thereto;

(f) "authorised party" means the party referred to in Article XIII(3);

(g) "Chicago Convention" means the Convention on International Civil Aviation, signed at Chicago on 7 December 1944, as amended, and its Annexes;

(h) "common mark registering authority" means the authority maintaining a register in accordance with Article 77 of the Chicago Convention as implemented by the Resolution adopted on 14 December 1967 by the Council of the International Civil Aviation Organization on nationality and registration of aircraft operated by international operating agencies;

(i) "de-registration of the aircraft" means deletion or removal of the registration of the aircraft from its aircraft register in accordance with the Chicago Convention;

(j) "guarantee contract" means a contract entered into by a person as guarantor;

(k) "guarantor" means a person who, for the purpose of assuring performance of any obligations in favour of a creditor secured by a security agreement or under an agreement, gives or issues a suretyship or demand guarantee or a standby letter of credit or any other form of credit insurance;

(l) "helicopters" means heavier-than-air machines (other than those used in military, customs or police services) supported in flight chiefly by the reactions of the air on one or more power-driven rotors on substantially vertical axes and which are type certified by the competent aviation authority to transport:

(i) at least five (5) persons including crew; or

(ii) goods in excess of 450 kilograms,

together with all installed, incorporated or attached accessories, parts and equipment (including rotors), and all data, manuals and records relating thereto;

(m) "insolvency-related event" means:

(i) the commencement of the insolvency proceedings; or

(ii) the declared intention to suspend or actual suspension of payments by the debtor where the creditor's right to institute insolvency proceedings against the debtor or to exercise remedies under the Convention is prevented or suspended by law or State action;

(n) "primary insolvency jurisdiction" means the Contracting State in which the centre of the debtor's main interests is situated, which for this purpose shall be deemed to be the place of the debtor's statutory seat or, if there is none, the place where the debtor is incorporated or formed, unless proved otherwise;

(o) "registry authority" means the national authority or the common mark registering authority, maintaining an aircraft register in a Contracting State and responsible for the registration and de-registration of an aircraft in accordance with the Chicago Convention; and

(p) "State of registry" means, in respect of an aircraft, the State on the national register of which an aircraft is entered or the State of location of the common mark registering authority maintaining the aircraft register.

Article II—Application of Convention as regards aircraft objects

1. The Convention shall apply in relation to aircraft objects as provided by the terms of this Protocol.

2. The Convention and this Protocol shall be known as the Convention on International Interests in Mobile Equipment as applied to aircraft objects.

Article III—Application of Convention to sales

The following provisions of the Convention apply as if references to an agreement creating or providing for an international interest were references to a contract of sale and as if references to an international interest, a prospective international interest, the debtor and the creditor were references to a sale, a prospective sale, the seller and the buyer respectively: Articles 3 and 4; Article 16(1)(a); Article 19(4); Article 20(1) (as regards registration of a contract of sale or a prospective sale); Article 25(2) (as regards a prospective sale); and Article 30.

In addition, the general provisions of Article 1, Article 5, Chapters IV to VII, Article 29 (other than Article 29(3) which is replaced by Article XIV(1) and (2)), Chapter X, Chapter XII (other than Article 43), Chapter XIII and Chapter XIV (other than Article 60) shall apply to contracts of sale and prospective sales.

Article IV—Sphere of application

1. Without prejudice to Article 3(1) of the Convention, the Convention shall also apply in relation to a helicopter, or to an airframe pertaining to an aircraft, registered in an aircraft register of a Contracting State which is the State of registry, and where such registration is made pursuant to an agreement for registration of the aircraft it is deemed to have been effected at the time of the agreement.

2. For the purposes of the definition of "internal transaction" in Article 1 of the Convention:

(a) an airframe is located in the State of registry of the aircraft of which it is a part;

(b) an aircraft engine is located in the State of registry of the aircraft on which it is installed or, if it is not installed on an aircraft, where it is physically located; and

(c) a helicopter is located in its State of registry, at the time of the conclusion of the agreement creating or providing for the interest.

3. The parties may, by agreement in writing, exclude the application of Article XI and, in their relations with each other, derogate from or vary the effect of any of the provisions of this Protocol except Article IX (2)-(4).

Article V—Formalities, effects and registration of contracts of sale

1. For the purposes of this Protocol, a contract of sale is one which:

(a) is in writing;

(b) relates to an aircraft object of which the seller has power to dispose; and

(c) enables the aircraft object to be identified in conformity with this Protocol.

2. A contract of sale transfers the interest of the seller in the aircraft object to the buyer according to its terms.

3. Registration of a contract of sale remains effective indefinitely. Registration of a prospective sale remains effective unless discharged or until expiry of the period, if any, specified in the registration.

Article VI—Representative capacities

A person may enter into an agreement or a sale, and register an international interest in, or a sale of, an aircraft object, in an agency, trust or other representative capacity. In such case, that person is entitled to assert rights and interests under the Convention.

Article VII—Description of aircraft objects

A description of an aircraft object that contains its manufacturer's serial number, the name of the manufacturer and its model designation is necessary and sufficient to identify the object for the purposes of Article 7(c) of the Convention and Article V(1)(c) of this Protocol.

Article VIII—Choice of law

1. This Article applies only where a Contracting State has made a declaration pursuant to Article XXX(1).

2. The parties to an agreement, or a contract of sale, or a related guarantee contract or subordination agreement may agree on the law which is to govern their contractual rights and obligations, wholly or in part.

3. Unless otherwise agreed, the reference in the preceding paragraph to the law chosen by the parties is to the domestic rules of law of the designated State or, where that State comprises several territorial units, to the domestic law of the designated territorial unit.

Chapter II
Default remedies, priorities and assignments

Article IX—Modification of default remedies provisions

1. In addition to the remedies specified in Chapter III of the Convention, the creditor may, to the extent that the debtor has at any time so agreed and in the circumstances specified in that Chapter:

(a) procure the de-registration of the aircraft; and

(b) procure the export and physical transfer of the aircraft object from the territory in which it is situated.

2. The creditor shall not exercise the remedies specified in the preceding paragraph without the prior consent in writing of the holder of any registered interest ranking in priority to that of the creditor.

3. Article 8(3) of the Convention shall not apply to aircraft objects. Any remedy given by the Convention in relation to an aircraft object shall be exercised in a commercially reasonable manner. A remedy shall be deemed to be exercised in a commercially reasonable manner where it is exercised in conformity with a provision of the agreement except where such a provision is manifestly unreasonable.

4. A chargee giving ten or more working days' prior written notice of a proposed sale or lease to interested persons shall be deemed to satisfy the requirement of providing "reasonable prior notice" specified in Article 8(4) of the Convention. The foregoing shall not prevent a chargee and a chargor or a guarantor from agreeing to a longer period of prior notice.

5. The registry authority in a Contracting State shall, subject to any applicable safety laws and regulations, honour a request for de-registration and export if:

(a) the request is properly submitted by the authorised party under a recorded irrevocable deregistration and export request authorisation; and

(b) the authorised party certifies to the registry authority, if required by that authority, that all registered interests ranking in priority to that of the creditor in whose favour the authorisation has been issued have been discharged or that the holders of such interests have consented to the de-registration and export.

6. A chargee proposing to procure the de-registration and export of an aircraft under paragraph 1 otherwise than pursuant to a court order shall give reasonable prior notice in writing of the proposed deregistration and export to:

(a) interested persons specified in Article 1(m)(i) and (ii) of the Convention; and

(b) interested persons specified in Article 1(m)(iii) of the Convention who have given notice of their rights to the chargee within a reasonable time prior to the de-registration and export.

Article X—Modification of provisions regarding relief pending final determination

1. This Article applies only where a Contracting State has made a declaration under Article XXX(2) and to the extent stated in such declaration.

2. For the purposes of Article 13(1) of the Convention, "speedy" in the context of obtaining relief means within such number of working days from the date of filing of the application for relief as is specified in a declaration made by the Contracting State in which the application is made.

3. Article 13(1) of the Convention applies with the following being added immediately after sub-paragraph (d): "(e) if at any time the debtor and the creditor specifically agree, sale and application of proceeds therefrom", and Article 43(2) applies with the insertion after the words "Article 13(1)(d)" of the words "and (e)".

4. Ownership or any other interest of the debtor passing on a sale under the preceding paragraph is free from any other interest over which the creditor's international interest has priority under the provisions of Article 29 of the Convention.

5. The creditor and the debtor or any other interested person may agree in writing to exclude the application of Article 13(2) of the Convention.

6. With regard to the remedies in Article IX(1):

(a) they shall be made available by the registry authority and other administrative authorities, as applicable, in a Contracting State no later than five working days after the creditor notifies such authorities that the relief specified in Article IX(1) is granted or, in the case of relief granted by a foreign court, recognised by a court of that Contracting State, and that the creditor is entitled to procure those remedies in accordance with the Convention; and

(b) the applicable authorities shall expeditiously co-operate with and assist the creditor in the exercise of such remedies in conformity with the applicable aviation safety laws and regulations.

7. Paragraphs 2 and 6 shall not affect any applicable aviation safety laws and regulations.

Article XI—Remedies on insolvency

1. This Article applies only where a Contracting State that is the primary insolvency jurisdiction has made a declaration pursuant to Article XXX(3).

Alternative A

2. Upon the occurrence of an insolvency-related event, the insolvency administrator or the debtor, as applicable, shall, subject to paragraph 7, give possession of the aircraft object to the creditor no later than the earlier of:

(a) the end of the waiting period; and

(b) the date on which the creditor would be entitled to possession of the aircraft object if this Article did not apply.

3. For the purposes of this Article, the "waiting period" shall be the period specified in a declaration of the Contracting State which is the primary insolvency jurisdiction.

4. References in this Article to the "insolvency administrator" shall be to that person in its official, not in its personal, capacity.

5. Unless and until the creditor is given the opportunity to take possession under paragraph 2:

(a) the insolvency administrator or the debtor, as applicable, shall preserve the aircraft object and maintain it and its value in accordance with the agreement; and

(b) the creditor shall be entitled to apply for any other forms of interim relief available under the applicable law.

6. Sub-paragraph (a) of the preceding paragraph shall not preclude the use of the aircraft object under arrangements designed to preserve the aircraft object and maintain it and its value.

7. The insolvency administrator or the debtor, as applicable, may retain possession of the aircraft object where, by the time specified in paragraph 2, it has cured all defaults other than a default constituted by the opening of insolvency proceedings and has agreed to perform all future obligations under the agreement. A second waiting period shall not apply in respect of a default in the performance of such future obligations.

8. With regard to the remedies in Article IX(1):

(a) they shall be made available by the registry authority and the administrative authorities in a Contracting State, as applicable, no later than five working days after the date on which the creditor notifies such authorities that it is entitled to procure those remedies in accordance with the Convention; and

(b) the applicable authorities shall expeditiously co-operate with and assist the creditor in the exercise of such remedies in conformity with the applicable aviation safety laws and regulations.

9. No exercise of remedies permitted by the Convention or this Protocol may be prevented or delayed after the date specified in paragraph 2.

10. No obligations of the debtor under the agreement may be modified without the consent of the creditor.

11. Nothing in the preceding paragraph shall be construed to affect the authority, if any, of the insolvency administrator under the applicable law to terminate the agreement.

12. No rights or interests, except for non-consensual rights or interests of a category covered by a declaration pursuant to Article 39(1), shall have priority in insolvency proceedings over registered interests.

13. The Convention as modified by Article IX of this Protocol shall apply to the exercise of any remedies under this Article.

Alternative B

2. Upon the occurrence of an insolvency-related event, the insolvency administrator or the debtor, as applicable, upon the request of the creditor, shall give notice to the creditor within the time specified in a declaration of a Contracting State pursuant to Article XXX(3) whether it will:

(a) cure all defaults other than a default constituted by the opening of insolvency proceedings and agree to perform all future obligations, under the agreement and related transaction documents; or

(b) give the creditor the opportunity to take possession of the aircraft object, in accordance with the applicable law.

3. The applicable law referred to in sub-paragraph (b) of the preceding paragraph may permit the court to require the taking of any additional step or the provision of any additional guarantee.

4. The creditor shall provide evidence of its claims and proof that its international interest has been registered.

5. If the insolvency administrator or the debtor, as applicable, does not give notice in conformity with paragraph 2, or when the insolvency administrator or the debtor has declared that it will give the creditor the opportunity to take possession of the aircraft object but fails to do so, the court may permit the creditor to take possession of the aircraft object upon such terms as the court may order and may require the taking of any additional step or the provision of any additional guarantee.

6. The aircraft object shall not be sold pending a decision by a court regarding the claim and the international interest.

Article XII—Insolvency assistance

1. This Article applies only where a Contracting State has made a declaration pursuant to Article XXX(1).

2. The courts of a Contracting State in which an aircraft object is situated shall, in accordance with the law of the Contracting State, co-operate to the maximum extent possible with foreign courts and foreign insolvency administrators in carrying out the provisions of Article XI.

Article XIII—De-registration and export request authorisation

1. This Article applies only where a Contracting State has made a declaration pursuant to Article XXX(1).

2. Where the debtor has issued an irrevocable de-registration and export request authorisation substantially in the form annexed to this Protocol and has submitted such authorisation for recordation to the registry authority, that authorisation shall be so recorded.

3. The person in whose favour the authorisation has been issued (the "authorised party") or its certified designee shall be the sole person entitled to exercise the remedies specified in Article IX(1) and may do so only in accordance with the authorisation and applicable aviation safety laws and regulations. Such authorisation may not be revoked by the debtor without the consent in writing of the authorised party. The registry authority shall remove an authorisation from the registry at the request of the authorised party.

4. The registry authority and other administrative authorities in Contracting States shall expeditiously co-operate with and assist the authorised party in the exercise of the remedies specified in Article IX.

Article XIV—Modification of priority provisions

1. A buyer of an aircraft object under a registered sale acquires its interest in that object free from an interest subsequently registered and from an unregistered interest, even if the buyer has actual knowledge of the unregistered interest.

2. A buyer of an aircraft object acquires its interest in that object subject to an interest registered at the time of its acquisition.

3. Ownership of or another right or interest in an aircraft engine shall not be affected by its installation on or removal from an aircraft.

4. Article 29(7) of the Convention applies to an item, other than an object, installed on an airframe, aircraft engine or helicopter.

Article XV—Modification of assignment provisions

Article 33(1) of the Convention applies as if the following were added immediately after sub-paragraph (b): "and (c) the debtor has consented in writing, whether or not the consent is given in advance of the assignment or identifies the assignee."

Article XVI—Debtor provisions

1. In the absence of a default within the meaning of Article 11 of the Convention, the debtor shall be entitled to the quiet possession and use of the object in accordance with the agreement as against:

(a) its creditor and the holder of any interest from which the debtor takes free pursuant to Article 29(4) of the Convention or, in the capacity of buyer, Article XIV(1) of this Protocol, unless and to the extent that the debtor has otherwise agreed; and

(b) the holder of any interest to which the debtor's right or interest is subject pursuant to Article 29(4) of the Convention or, in the capacity of buyer, Article XIV(2) of this Protocol, but only to the extent, if any, that such holder has agreed.

2. Nothing in the Convention or this Protocol affects the liability of a creditor for any breach of the agreement under the applicable law in so far as that agreement relates to an aircraft object.

Chapter III
Registry provisions relating to international interests in aircraft objects

Article XVII—The Supervisory Authority and the Registrar

1. The Supervisory Authority shall be the international entity designated by a Resolution adopted by the Diplomatic Conference to Adopt a Mobile Equipment Convention and an Aircraft Protocol.

2. Where the international entity referred to in the preceding paragraph is not able and willing to act as Supervisory Authority, a Conference of Signatory and Contracting States shall be convened to designate another Supervisory Authority.

3. The Supervisory Authority and its officers and employees shall enjoy such immunity from legal and administrative process as is provided under the rules applicable to them as an international entity or otherwise.

4. The Supervisory Authority may establish a commission of experts, from among persons nominated by Signatory and Contracting States and having the necessary qualifications and experience, and entrust it with the task of assisting the Supervisory Authority in the discharge of its functions.

5. The first Registrar shall operate the International Registry for a period of five years from the date of entry into force of this Protocol. Thereafter, the Registrar shall be appointed or reappointed at regular five-yearly intervals by the Supervisory Authority.

Article XVIII—First regulations

The first regulations shall be made by the Supervisory Authority so as to take effect upon the entry into force of this Protocol.

Article XIX—Designated entry points

1. Subject to paragraph 2, a Contracting State may at any time designate an entity or entities in its territory as the entry point or entry points through which there shall or may be transmitted to the International Registry information required for registration other than registration of a notice of a national interest or a right or interest under Article 40 in either case arising under the laws of another State.

2. A designation made under the preceding paragraph may permit, but not compel, use of a designated entry point or entry points for information required for registrations in respect of aircraft engines.

Article XX—Additional modifications to Registry provisions

1. For the purposes of Article 19(6) of the Convention, the search criteria for an aircraft object shall be the name of its manufacturer, its manufacturer's serial number and its model designation, supplemented as necessary to ensure uniqueness. Such supplementary information shall be specified in the regulations.

2. For the purposes of Article 25(2) of the Convention and in the circumstances there described, the holder of a registered prospective international interest or a registered prospective assignment of an international interest or the person in whose favour a prospective sale has been registered shall take such steps as are within its power to procure the discharge of the registration no later than five working days after the receipt of the demand described in such paragraph.

3. The fees referred to in Article 17(2)(h) of the Convention shall be determined so as to recover the reasonable costs of establishing, operating and regulating the International Registry and the reasonable costs of the Supervisory Authority associated with the performance of the functions, exercise of the powers, and discharge of the duties contemplated by Article 17(2) of the Convention.

4. The centralised functions of the International Registry shall be operated and administered by the Registrar on a twenty-four hour basis. The various entry points shall be operated at least during working hours in their respective territories.

5. The amount of the insurance or financial guarantee referred to in Article 28(4) of the Convention shall, in respect of each event, not be less than the maximum value of an aircraft object as determined by the Supervisory Authority.

6. Nothing in the Convention shall preclude the Registrar from procuring insurance or a financial guarantee covering events for which the Registrar is not liable under Article 28 of the Convention.

Chapter IV
Jurisdiction

Article XXI—Modification of jurisdiction provisions

For the purposes of Article 43 of the Convention and subject to Article 42 of the Convention, a court of a Contracting State also has jurisdiction where the object is a helicopter, or an airframe pertaining to an aircraft, for which that State is the State of registry.

Article XXII—Waivers of sovereign immunity

1. Subject to paragraph 2, a waiver of sovereign immunity from jurisdiction of the courts specified in Article 42 or Article 43 of the Convention or relating to enforcement of rights and interests relating to an aircraft object under the Convention shall be binding and, if the other conditions to such jurisdiction or enforcement have been satisfied, shall be effective to confer jurisdiction and permit enforcement, as the case may be.

2. A waiver under the preceding paragraph must be in writing and contain a description of the aircraft object.

Chapter V
Relationship with other conventions

Article XXIII—Relationship with the Convention on the International Recognition of Rights in Aircraft

The Convention shall, for a Contracting State that is a party to the Convention on the International Recognition of Rights in Aircraft, signed at Geneva on 19 June 1948, supersede that Convention as it relates to aircraft, as defined in this Protocol, and to aircraft objects. However, with respect to rights or interests not covered or affected by the present Convention, the Geneva Convention shall not be superseded.

Article XXIV—Relationship with the Convention for the Unification of Certain Rules Relating to the Precautionary Attachment of Aircraft

1. The Convention shall, for a Contracting State that is a Party to the Convention for the Unification of Certain Rules Relating to the Precautionary Attachment of Aircraft, signed at Rome on 29 May 1933, supersede that Convention as it relates to aircraft, as defined in this Protocol.

2. A Contracting State Party to the above Convention may declare, at the time of ratification, acceptance, approval of, or accession to this Protocol, that it will not apply this Article.

Article XXV—Relationship with the UNIDROIT Convention on International Financial Leasing

The Convention shall supersede the UNIDROIT Convention on International Financial Leasing, signed at Ottawa on 28 May 1988, as it relates to aircraft objects.

Chapter VI
Final provisions

Article XXVI—Signature, ratification, acceptance, approval or accession

1. This Protocol shall be open for signature in Cape Town on 16 November 2001 by States participating in the Diplomatic Conference to Adopt a Mobile Equipment

Convention and an Aircraft Protocol held at Cape Town from 29 October to 16 November 2001. After 16 November 2001, this Protocol shall be open to all States for signature at the Headquarters of the International Institute for the Unification of Private Law (UNIDROIT) in Rome until it enters into force in accordance with Article XXVIII.

2. This Protocol shall be subject to ratification, acceptance or approval by States which have signed it.

3. Any State which does not sign this Protocol may accede to it at any time.

4. Ratification, acceptance, approval or accession is effected by the deposit of a formal instrument to that effect with the Depositary.

5. A State may not become a Party to this Protocol unless it is or becomes also a Party to the Convention.

Article XXVII—Regional Economic Integration Organisations

1. A Regional Economic Integration Organisation which is constituted by sovereign States and has competence over certain matters governed by this Protocol may similarly sign, accept, approve or accede to this Protocol. The Regional Economic Integration Organisation shall in that case have the rights and obligations of a Contracting State, to the extent that that Organisation has competence over matters governed by this Protocol. Where the number of Contracting States is relevant in this Protocol, the Regional Economic Integration Organisation shall not count as a Contracting State in addition to its Member States which are Contracting States.

2. The Regional Economic Integration Organisation shall, at the time of signature, acceptance, approval or accession, make a declaration to the Depositary specifying the matters governed by this Protocol in respect of which competence has been transferred to that Organisation by its Member States. The Regional Economic Integration Organisation shall promptly notify the Depositary of any changes to the distribution of competence, including new transfers of competence, specified in the declaration under this paragraph.

3. Any reference to a "Contracting State" or "Contracting States" or "State Party" or "States Parties" in this Protocol applies equally to a Regional Economic Integration Organisation where the context so requires.

Article XXVIII—Entry into force

1. This Protocol enters into force on the first day of the month following the expiration of three months after the date of the deposit of the eighth instrument of ratification, acceptance, approval or accession, between the States which have deposited such instruments.

2. For other States this Protocol enters into force on the first day of the month following the expiration of three months after the date of the deposit of its instrument of ratification, acceptance, approval or accession.

Article XXIX—Territorial units

1. If a Contracting State has territorial units in which different systems of law are applicable in relation to the matters dealt with in this Protocol, it may, at the time of ratification, acceptance, approval or accession, declare that this Protocol is to extend to all its territorial units or only to one or more of them and may modify its declaration by submitting another declaration at any time.

2. Any such declaration shall state expressly the territorial units to which this Protocol applies.

3. If a Contracting State has not made any declaration under paragraph 1, this Protocol shall apply to all territorial units of that State.

4. Where a Contracting State extends this Protocol to one or more of its territorial units, declarations permitted under this Protocol may be made in respect of each such territorial unit, and the declarations made in respect of one territorial unit may be different from those made in respect of another territorial unit.

5. If by virtue of a declaration under paragraph 1, this Protocol extends to one or more territorial units of a Contracting State:

(a) the debtor is considered to be situated in a Contracting State only if it is incorporated or formed under a law in force in a territorial unit to which the Convention and this Protocol apply or if it has its registered office or statutory seat, centre of administration, place of business or habitual residence in a territorial unit to which the Convention and this Protocol apply;

(b) any reference to the location of the object in a Contracting State refers to the location of the object in a territorial unit to which the Convention and this Protocol apply; and

(c) any reference to the administrative authorities in that Contracting State shall be construed as referring to the administrative authorities having jurisdiction in a territorial unit to which the Convention and this Protocol apply and any reference to the national register or to the registry authority in that Contracting State shall be construed as referring to the aircraft register in force or to the registry authority having jurisdiction in the territorial unit or units to which the Convention and this Protocol apply.

Article XXX—Declarations relating to certain provisions

1. A Contracting State may, at the time of ratification, acceptance, approval of, or accession to this Protocol, declare that it will apply any one or more of Articles VIII, XII and XIII of this Protocol.

2. A Contracting State may, at the time of ratification, acceptance, approval of, or accession to this Protocol, declare that it will apply Article X of this Protocol, wholly or in part. If it so declares with respect to Article X(2), it shall specify the time-period required thereby.

3. A Contracting State may, at the time of ratification, acceptance, approval of, or accession to this Protocol, declare that it will apply the entirety of Alternative A, or the entirety of Alternative B of Article XI and, if so, shall specify the types of insolvency proceeding, if any, to which it will apply Alternative A and the types of insolvency proceeding, if any, to which it will apply Alternative B.

A Contracting State making a declaration pursuant to this paragraph shall specify the time-period required by Article XI.

4. The courts of Contracting States shall apply Article XI in conformity with the declaration made by the Contracting State which is the primary insolvency jurisdiction.

5. A Contracting State may, at the time of ratification, acceptance, approval of, or accession to this Protocol, declare that it will not apply the provisions of Article XXI, wholly or in part. The declaration shall specify under which conditions the relevant Ar-

ticle will be applied, in case it will be applied partly, or otherwise which other forms of interim relief will be applied.

Article XXXI—Declarations under the Convention

Declarations made under the Convention, including those made under Articles 39, 40, 50, 53, 54, 55, 57, 58 and 60 of the Convention, shall be deemed to have also been made under this Protocol unless stated otherwise.

Article XXXII—Reservations and declarations

1. No reservations may be made to this Protocol but declarations authorised by Articles XXIV, XXIX, XXX, XXXI, XXXIII and XXXIV may be made in accordance with these provisions.

2. Any declaration or subsequent declaration or any withdrawal of a declaration made under this Protocol shall be notified in writing to the Depositary.

Article XXXIII—Subsequent declarations

1. A State Party may make a subsequent declaration, other than a declaration made in accordance with Article XXXI under Article 60 of the Convention, at any time after the date on which this Protocol has entered into force for it, by notifying the Depositary to that effect.

2. Any such subsequent declaration shall take effect on the first day of the month following the expiration of six months after the date of receipt of the notification by the Depositary. Where a longer period for that declaration to take effect is specified in the notification, it shall take effect upon the expiration of such longer period after receipt of the notification by the Depositary.

3. Notwithstanding the previous paragraphs, this Protocol shall continue to apply, as if no such subsequent declarations had been made, in respect of all rights and interests arising prior to the effective date of any such subsequent declaration.

Article XXXIV—Withdrawal of declarations

1. Any State Party having made a declaration under this Protocol, other than a declaration made in accordance with Article XXXI under Article 60 of the Convention, may withdraw it at any time by notifying the Depositary. Such withdrawal is to take effect on the first day of the month following the expiration of six months after the date of receipt of the notification by the Depositary.

2. Notwithstanding the previous paragraph, this Protocol shall continue to apply, as if no such withdrawal of declaration had been made, in respect of all rights and interests arising prior to the effective date of any such withdrawal.

Article XXXV—Denunciations

1. Any State Party may denounce this Protocol by notification in writing to the Depositary.

2. Any such denunciation shall take effect on the first day of the month following the expiration of twelve months after the date of receipt of the notification by the Depositary.

3. Notwithstanding the previous paragraphs, this Protocol shall continue to apply, as if no such denunciation had been made, in respect of all rights and interests arising prior to the effective date of any such denunciation.

Article XXXVI—Review Conferences, amendments and related matters

1. The Depositary, in consultation with the Supervisory Authority, shall prepare reports yearly, or at such other time as the circumstances may require, for the States Parties as to the manner in which the international regime established in the Convention as amended by this Protocol has operated in practice.

In preparing such reports, the Depositary shall take into account the reports of the Supervisory Authority concerning the functioning of the international registration system.

2. At the request of not less than twenty-five percent of the States Parties, Review Conferences of the States Parties shall be convened from time to time by the Depositary, in consultation with the Supervisory Authority, to consider:

(a) the practical operation of the Convention as amended by this Protocol and its effectiveness in facilitating the asset-based financing and leasing of the objects covered by its terms;

(b) the judicial interpretation given to, and the application made of the terms of this Protocol and the regulations;

(c) the functioning of the international registration system, the performance of the Registrar and its oversight by the Supervisory Authority, taking into account the reports of the Supervisory Authority; and

(d) whether any modifications to this Protocol or the arrangements relating to the International Registry are desirable.

3. Any amendment to this Protocol shall be approved by at least a two-thirds majority of States Parties participating in the Conference referred to in the preceding paragraph and shall then enter into force in respect of States which have ratified, accepted or approved such amendment when it has been ratified, accepted or approved by eight States in accordance with the provisions of Article XXVIII relating to its entry into force.

Article XXXVII—Depositary and its functions

1. Instruments of ratification, acceptance, approval or accession shall be deposited with the International Institute for the Unification of Private Law (UNIDROIT), which is hereby designated the Depositary.

2. The Depositary shall:

(a) inform all Contracting States of:

(i) each new signature or deposit of an instrument of ratification, acceptance, approval or accession, together with the date thereof;

(ii) the date of entry into force of this Protocol;

(iii) each declaration made in accordance with this Protocol, together with the date thereof;

(iv) the withdrawal or amendment of any declaration, together with the date thereof; and

(v) the notification of any denunciation of this Protocol together with the date thereof and the date on which it takes effect;

(b) transmit certified true copies of this Protocol to all Contracting States;

(c) provide the Supervisory Authority and the Registrar with a copy of each instrument of ratification, acceptance, approval or accession, together with the date of deposit thereof, of each declaration or withdrawal or amendment of a declaration and of each notification of denunciation, together with the date of notification thereof, so that the information contained therein is easily and fully available; and

(d) perform such other functions customary for depositaries.

IN WITNESS WHEREOF the undersigned Plenipotentiaries, having been duly authorised, have signed this Protocol.

DONE at Cape Town, this sixteenth day of November, two thousand and one, in a single original in the English, Arabic, Chinese, French, Russian and Spanish languages, all texts being equally authentic, such authenticity to take effect upon verification by the Joint Secretariat of the Conference under the authority of the President of the Conference within ninety days hereof as to the conformity of the texts with one another.

Annex

FORM OF IRREVOCABLE DE-REGISTRATION AND EXPORT REQUEST AUTHORISATION

Annex referred to in Article XIII

[Insert Date]

To: [Insert Name of Registry Authority]

Re: Irrevocable De-Registration and Export Request Authorisation

The undersigned is the registered [operator] [owner] [select the term that reflects the relevant nationality registration criterion] of the [insert the airframe/helicopter manufacturer name and model number] bearing manufacturers serial number [insert manufacturer's serial number] and registration [number] [mark] [insert registration number/mark] (together with all installed, incorporated or attached accessories, parts and equipment, the "aircraft").

This instrument is an irrevocable de-registration and export request authorisation issued by the undersigned in favour of [insert name of creditor] ("the authorised party") under the authority of Article XIII of the Protocol to the Convention on International Interests in Mobile Equipment on Matters specific to Aircraft Equipment.

In accordance with that Article, the undersigned hereby requests:

(i) recognition that the authorised party or the person it certifies as its designee is the sole person entitled to:

(a) procure the de-registration of the aircraft from the [insert name of aircraft register] maintained by the [insert name of registry authority] for the purposes of Chapter III of the Convention on International Civil Aviation, signed at Chicago, on 7 December 1944, and

(b) procure the export and physical transfer of the aircraft from [insert name of country]; and

(ii) confirmation that the authorised party or the person it certifies as its designee may take the action specified in clause (i) above on written demand without the consent of the undersigned and that, upon such demand, the authorities in [insert name of country] shall co-operate with the authorised party with a view to the speedy completion of such action.

The rights in favour of the authorised party established by this instrument may not be revoked by the undersigned without the written consent of the authorised party.

Please acknowledge your agreement to this request and its terms by appropriate notation in the space provided below and lodging this instrument in [insert name of registry authority].

[insert name of operator/owner]

____

Agreed to and lodged this [insert date]

By: [insert name of signatory]

Its: [insert title of signatory]

____

[insert relevant notational details]

Appendix 30

United States Model Open Skies Agreement

Promulgated in United States Department of Transportation
Order No. 92-8-13 (August 5, 1992);
Last revised April 13, 2004

The Government of the United States of America and the Government of [country] (hereinafter, "the Parties");

Desiring to promote an international aviation system based on competition among airlines in the marketplace with minimum government interference and regulation;

Desiring to facilitate the expansion of international air transport opportunities;

Desiring to make it possible for airlines to offer the traveling and shipping public a variety of service options at the lowest prices that are not discriminatory and do not represent abuse of a dominant position, and wishing to encourage individual airlines to develop and implement innovative and competitive prices;

Desiring to ensure the highest degree of safety and security in international air transport and reaffirming their grave concern about acts or threats against the security of aircraft, which jeopardize the safety of persons or property, adversely affect the operation of air transportation, and undermine public confidence in the safety of civil aviation; and

Being Parties to the Convention on International Civil Aviation, opened for signature at Chicago on December 7, 1944;

Have agreed as follows:

Article 1
Definitions

For the purposes of this Agreement, unless otherwise stated, the term:

1. "Aeronautical authorities" means, in the case of the United States, the Department of Transportation, or its successor, and in the case of [country], the [appropriate officials], and any person or agency authorized to perform functions exercised by the said [appropriate officials];

2. "Agreement" means this Agreement, its Annexes, and any amendments thereto;

3. "Air transportation" means the public carriage by aircraft of passengers, baggage, cargo, and mail, separately or in combination, for remuneration or hire;

4. "Convention" means the Convention on International Civil Aviation, opened for signature at Chicago on December 7, 1944, and includes:

a) any amendment that has entered into force under Article 94(a) of the Convention and has been ratified by both Parties, and

b) any Annex or any amendment thereto adopted under Article 90 of the Convention, insofar as such Annex or amendment is at any given time effective for both Parties;

5. "Designated airline" means an airline designated and authorized in accordance with Article 3 of this Agreement;

6. "Full cost" means the cost of providing service plus a reasonable charge for administrative overhead;

7. "International air transportation" means air transportation that passes through the airspace over the territory of more than one State;

8. "Price" means any fare, rate or charge for the carriage of passengers (and their baggage) and/or cargo (excluding mail) in air transportation charged by airlines, including their agents, and the conditions governing the availability of such fare, rate or charge;

9. "Stop for non-traffic purposes" means a landing for any purpose other than taking on or discharging passengers, baggage, cargo and/or mail in air transportation;

10. "Territory" means the land areas under the sovereignty, jurisdiction, protection, or trusteeship of a Party, and the territorial waters adjacent thereto; and

11. "User charge" means a charge imposed on airlines for the provision of airport, air navigation, or aviation security facilities or services including related services and facilities.

Article 2
Grant of Rights

1. Each Party grants to the other Party the following rights for the conduct of international air transportation by the airlines of the other Party:

a) the right to fly across its territory without landing;

b) the right to make stops in its territory for non-traffic purposes; and

c) the rights otherwise specified in this Agreement.

2. Nothing in this Article shall be deemed to confer on the airline or airlines of one Party the rights to take on board, in the territory of the other Party, passengers, their baggage, cargo, or mail carried for compensation and destined for another point in the territory of that other Party.

Article 3
Designation and Authorization

1. Each Party shall have the right to designate as many airlines as it wishes to conduct international air transportation in accordance with this Agreement and to withdraw or alter such designations. Such designations shall be transmitted to the other Party in writing through diplomatic channels, and shall identify whether the airline is authorized to conduct the type of air transportation specified in Annex I or in Annex II or both.

2. On receipt of such a designation, and of applications from the designated airline, in the form and manner prescribed for operating authorizations and technical permissions, the other Party shall grant appropriate authorizations and permissions with minimum procedural delay, provided:

a) substantial ownership and effective control of that airline are vested in the Party designating the airline, nationals of that Party, or both;

b) the designated airline is qualified to meet the conditions prescribed under the laws and regulations normally applied to the operation of international air transportation by the Party considering the application or applications; and

c) the Party designating the airline is maintaining and administering the standards set forth in Article 6 (Safety) and Article 7 (Aviation Security).

Article 4
Revocation of Authorization

1. Either Party may revoke, suspend or limit the operating authorizations or technical permissions of an airline designated by the other Party where:

a) substantial ownership and effective control of that airline are not vested in the other Party, the Party's nationals, or both;

b) that airline has failed to comply with the laws and regulations referred to in Article 5 (Application of Laws) of this Agreement; or

c) the other Party is not maintaining and administering the standards as set forth in Article 6 (Safety).

2. Unless immediate action is essential to prevent further noncompliance with subparagraphs 1b or 1c of this Article, the rights established by this Article shall be exercised only after consultation with the other Party.

3. This Article does not limit the rights of either Party to withhold, revoke, limit or impose conditions on the operating authorization or technical permission of an airline or airlines of the other Party in accordance with the provisions of Article 7 (Aviation Security).

Article 5
Application of Laws

1. While entering, within, or leaving the territory of one Party, its laws and regulations relating to the operation and navigation of aircraft shall be complied with by the other Party's airlines.

2. While entering, within, or leaving the territory of one Party, its laws and regulations relating to the admission to or departure from its territory of passengers, crew or cargo on aircraft (including regulations relating to entry, clearance, aviation security, immigration, passports, customs and quarantine or, in the case of mail, postal regulations) shall be complied with by, or on behalf of, such passengers, crew or cargo of the other Party's airlines.

Article 6
Safety

1. Each Party shall recognize as valid, for the purpose of operating the air transportation provided for in this Agreement, certificates of airworthiness, certificates of competency, and licenses issued or validated by the other Party and still in force, provided that the requirements for such certificates or licenses at least equal the minimum standards that may be established pursuant to the Convention. Each Party may, however, refuse to recognize as valid for the purpose of flight above its own territory, certificates of competency and licenses granted to or validated for its own nationals by the other Party.

2. Either Party may request consultations concerning the safety standards maintained by the other Party relating to aeronautical facilities, aircrews, aircraft, and operation of the designated airlines. If, following such consultations, one Party finds that the other Party does not effectively maintain and administer safety standards and requirements in these areas that at least equal the minimum standards that may be established pursuant to the Convention, the other Party shall be notified of such findings and the steps considered necessary to conform with these minimum standards, and the other

Party shall take appropriate corrective action. Each Party reserves the right to withhold, revoke, or limit the operating authorization or technical permission of an airline or airlines designated by the other Party in the event the other Party does not take such appropriate corrective action within a reasonable time.

Article 7
Aviation Security

1. In accordance with their rights and obligations under international law, the Parties reaffirm that their obligation to each other to protect the security of civil aviation against acts of unlawful interference forms an integral part of this Agreement. Without limiting the generality of their rights and obligations under international law, the Parties shall in particular act in conformity with the provisions of the Convention on Offenses and Certain Other Acts Committed on Board Aircraft, done at Tokyo September 14, 1963, the Convention for the Suppression of Unlawful Seizure of Aircraft, done at The Hague December 16, 1970, the Convention for the Suppression of Unlawful Acts against the Safety of Civil Aviation, done at Montreal September 23, 1971, and the Protocol for the Suppression of Unlawful Acts of Violence at Airports Serving International Civil Aviation, done at Montreal February 24, 1988.

2. The Parties shall provide upon request all necessary assistance to each other to prevent acts of unlawful seizure of civil aircraft and other unlawful acts against the safety of such aircraft, of their passengers and crew, and of airports and air navigation facilities, and to address any other threat to the security of civil air navigation.

3. The Parties shall, in their mutual relations, act in conformity with the aviation security standards and appropriate recommended practices established by the International Civil Aviation Organization and designated as Annexes to the Convention; they shall require that operators of aircraft of their registry, operators of aircraft who have their principal place of business or permanent residence in their territory, and the operators of airports in their territory act in conformity with such aviation security provisions.

4. Each Party agrees to observe the security provisions required by the other Party for entry into, for departure from, and while within the territory of that other Party and to take adequate measures to protect aircraft and to inspect passengers, crew, and their baggage and carry-on items, as well as cargo and aircraft stores, prior to and during boarding or loading. Each Party shall also give positive consideration to any request from the other Party for special security measures to meet a particular threat.

5. When an incident or threat of an incident of unlawful seizure of aircraft or other unlawful acts against the safety of passengers, crew, aircraft, airports or air navigation facilities occurs, the Parties shall assist each other by facilitating communications and other appropriate measures intended to terminate rapidly and safely such incident or threat.

6. When a Party has reasonable grounds to believe that the other Party has departed from the aviation security provisions of this Article, the aeronautical authorities of that Party may request immediate consultations with the aeronautical authorities of the other Party. Failure to reach a satisfactory agreement within 15 days from the date of such request shall constitute grounds to withhold, revoke, limit, or impose conditions on the operating authorization and technical permissions of an airline or airlines of that Party. When required by an emergency, a Party may take interim action prior to the expiry of 15 days.

Article 8
Commercial Opportunities

1. The airlines of each Party shall have the right to establish offices in the territory of the other Party for the promotion and sale of air transportation.

2. The designated airlines of each Party shall be entitled, in accordance with the laws and regulations of the other Party relating to entry, residence, and employment, to bring in and maintain in the territory of the other Party managerial, sales, technical, operational, and other specialist staff required for the provision of air transportation.

3. Each designated airline shall have the right to perform its own ground-handling in the territory of the other Party ("self-handling") or, at its option, select among competing agents for such services in whole or in part. The rights shall be subject only to physical constraints resulting from considerations of airport safety. Where such considerations preclude self-handling, ground services shall be available on an equal basis to all airlines; charges shall be based on the costs of services provided; and such services shall be comparable to the kind and quality of services as if self-handling were possible.

4. Any airline of each Party may engage in the sale of air transportation in the territory of the other Party directly and, at the airline's discretion, through its agents, except as may be specifically provided by the charter regulations of the country in which the charter originates that relate to the protection of passenger funds, and passenger cancellation and refund rights. Each airline shall have the right to sell such transportation, and any person shall be free to purchase such transportation, in the currency of that territory or in freely convertible currencies.

5. Each airline shall have the right to convert and remit to its country, on demand, local revenues in excess of sums locally disbursed. Conversion and remittance shall be permitted promptly without restrictions or taxation in respect thereof at the rate of exchange applicable to current transactions and remittance on the date the carrier makes the initial application for remittance.

6. The airlines of each Party shall be permitted to pay for local expenses, including purchases of fuel, in the territory of the other Party in local currency. At their discretion, the airlines of each Party may pay for such expenses in the territory of the other Party in freely convertible currencies according to local currency regulation.

7. In operating or holding out the authorized services on the agreed routes, any designated airline of one Party may enter into cooperative marketing arrangements such as blocked-space, code-sharing or leasing arrangements, with

a) an airline or airlines of either Party;

b) an airline or airlines of a third country; [and

c) a surface transportation provider of any country;]

provided that all participants in such arrangements (i) hold the appropriate authority and (ii) meet the requirements normally applied to such arrangements.

8. Notwithstanding any other provision of this Agreement, airlines and indirect providers of cargo transportation of both Parties shall be permitted, without restriction, to employ in connection with international air transportation any surface transportation for cargo to or from any points in the territories of the Parties or in third countries, including transport to and from all airports with customs facilities, and including, where applicable, the right to transport cargo in bond under applicable laws and regulations. Such cargo, whether moving by surface or by air, shall have access to

airport customs processing and facilities. Airlines may elect to perform their own surface transportation or to provide it through arrangements with other surface carriers, including surface transportation operated by other airlines and indirect providers of cargo air transportation. Such intermodal cargo services may be offered at a single, through price for the air and surface transportation combined, provided that shippers are not misled as to the facts concerning such transportation.

Article 9
Customs Duties and Charges

1. On arriving in the territory of one Party, aircraft operated in international air transportation by the designated airlines of the other Party, their regular equipment, ground equipment, fuel, lubricants, consumable technical supplies, spare parts (including engines), aircraft stores (including but not limited to such items of food, beverages and liquor, tobacco and other products destined for sale to or use by passengers in limited quantities during flight), and other items intended for or used solely in connection with the operation or servicing of aircraft engaged in international air transportation shall be exempt, on the basis of reciprocity, from all import restrictions, property taxes and capital levies, customs duties, excise taxes, and similar fees and charges that are (a) imposed by the national authorities, and (b) not based on the cost of services provided, provided that such equipment and supplies remain on board the aircraft.

2. There shall also be exempt, on the basis of reciprocity, from the taxes, levies, duties, fees and charges referred to in paragraph 1 of this Article, with the exception of charges based on the cost of the service provided:

a) aircraft stores introduced into or supplied in the territory of a Party and taken on board, within reasonable limits, for use on outbound aircraft of an airline of the other Party engaged in international air transportation, even when these stores are to be used on a part of the journey performed over the territory of the Party in which they are taken on board;

b) ground equipment and spare parts (including engines) introduced into the territory of a Party for the servicing, maintenance, or repair of aircraft of an airline of the other Party used in international air transportation;

c) fuel, lubricants and consumable technical supplies introduced into or supplied in the territory of a Party for use in an aircraft of an airline of the other Party engaged in international air transportation, even when these supplies are to be used on a part of the journey performed over the territory of the Party in which they are taken on board; and

d) promotional and advertising materials introduced into or supplied in the territory of one Party and taken on board, within reasonable limits, for use on outbound aircraft of an airline of the other Party engaged in international air transportation, even when these stores are to be used on a part of the journey performed over the territory of the Party in which they are taken on board.

3. Equipment and supplies referred to in paragraphs 1 and 2 of this Article may be required to be kept under the supervision or control of the appropriate authorities.

4. The exemptions provided by this Article shall also be available where the designated airlines of one Party have contracted with another airline, which similarly enjoys such exemptions from the other Party, for the loan or transfer in the territory of the other Party of the items specified in paragraphs 1 and 2 of this Article.

Article 10
User Charges

1. User charges that may be imposed by the competent charging authorities or bodies of each Party on the airlines of the other Party shall be just, reasonable, not unjustly discriminatory, and equitably apportioned among categories of users. In any event, any such user charges shall be assessed on the airlines of the other Party on terms not less favorable than the most favorable terms available to any other airline at the time the charges are assessed.

2. User charges imposed on the airlines of the other Party may reflect, but shall not exceed, the full cost to the competent charging authorities or bodies of providing the appropriate airport, airport environmental, air navigation, and aviation security facilities and services at the airport or within the airport system. Such charges may include a reasonable return on assets, after depreciation. Facilities and services for which charges are made shall be provided on an efficient and economic basis.

3. Each Party shall encourage consultations between the competent charging authorities or bodies in its territory and the airlines using the services and facilities, and shall encourage the competent charging authorities or bodies and the airlines to exchange such information as may be necessary to permit an accurate review of the reasonableness of the charges in accordance with the principles of paragraphs 1 and 2 of this Article. Each Party shall encourage the competent charging authorities to provide users with reasonable notice of any proposal for changes in user charges to enable users to express their views before changes are made.

4. Neither Party shall be held, in dispute resolution procedures pursuant to Article 14, to be in breach of a provision of this Article, unless (a) it fails to undertake a review of the charge or practice that is the subject of complaint by the other Party within a reasonable amount of time; or (b) following such a review it fails to take all steps within its power to remedy any charge or practice that is inconsistent with this Article.

Article 11
Fair Competition

1. Each Party shall allow a fair and equal opportunity for the designated airlines of both Parties to compete in providing the international air transportation governed by this Agreement.

2. Each Party shall allow each designated airline to determine the frequency and capacity of the international air transportation it offers based upon commercial considerations in the marketplace. Consistent with this right, neither Party shall unilaterally limit the volume of traffic, frequency or regularity of service, or the aircraft type or types operated by the designated airlines of the other Party, except as may be required for customs, technical, operational, or environmental reasons under uniform conditions consistent with Article 15 of the Convention.

3. Neither Party shall impose on the other Party's designated airlines a first-refusal requirement, uplift ratio, no-objection fee, or any other requirement with respect to capacity, frequency or traffic that would be inconsistent with the purposes of this Agreement.

4. Neither Party shall require the filing of schedules, programs for charter flights, or operational plans by airlines of the other Party for approval, except as may be required on a non-discriminatory basis to enforce the uniform conditions foreseen by paragraph

2 of this Article or as may be specifically authorized in an Annex to this Agreement. If a Party requires filings for information purposes, it shall minimize the administrative burdens of filing requirements and procedures on air transportation intermediaries and on designated airlines of the other Party.

Article 12
Pricing

1. Each Party shall allow prices for air transportation to be established by each designated airline based upon commercial considerations in the marketplace. Intervention by the Parties shall be limited to:

a) prevention of unreasonably discriminatory prices or practices;

b) protection of consumers from prices that are unreasonably high or restrictive due to the abuse of a dominant position; and

c) protection of airlines from prices that are artificially low due to direct or indirect governmental subsidy or support.

2. Prices for international air transportation between the territories of the Parties shall not be required to be filed. Notwithstanding the foregoing, the designated airlines of the Parties shall continue to provide immediate access, on request, to information on historical, existing, and proposed prices to the aeronautical authorities of the Parties in a manner and format acceptable to those aeronautical authorities.

3. Neither Party shall take unilateral action to prevent the inauguration or continuation of a price proposed to be charged or charged by (i) an airline of either Party for international air transportation between the territories of the Parties, or (ii) an airline of one Party for international air transportation between the territory of the other Party and any other country, including in both cases transportation on an interline or intraline basis. If either Party believes that any such price is inconsistent with the considerations set forth in paragraph 1 of this Article, it shall request consultations and notify the other Party of the reasons for its dissatisfaction as soon as possible. These consultations shall be held not later than 30 days after receipt of the request, and the Parties shall cooperate in securing information necessary for reasoned resolution of the issue. If the Parties reach agreement with respect to a price for which a notice of dissatisfaction has been given, each Party shall use its best efforts to put that agreement into effect. Without such mutual agreement, the price shall go into effect or continue in effect.

Article 13
Consultations

Either Party may, at any time, request consultations relating to this Agreement. Such consultations shall begin at the earliest possible date, but not later than 60 days from the date the other Party receives the request unless otherwise agreed.

Article 14
Settlement of Disputes

1. Any dispute arising under this Agreement, except those that may arise under paragraph 3 of Article 12 (Pricing), that is not resolved by a first round of formal consultations may be referred by agreement of the Parties for decision to some person or body. If the Parties do not so agree, the dispute shall, at the request of either Party, be submitted to arbitration in accordance with the procedures set forth below.

2. Arbitration shall be by a tribunal of three arbitrators to be constituted as follows:

a) Within 30 days after the receipt of a request for arbitration, each Party shall name one arbitrator. Within 60 days after these two arbitrators have been named, they shall by agreement appoint a third arbitrator, who shall act as President of the arbitral tribunal;

b) If either Party fails to name an arbitrator, or if the third arbitrator is not appointed in accordance with subparagraph a of this paragraph, either Party may request the President of the Council of the International Civil Aviation Organization to appoint the necessary arbitrator or arbitrators within 30 days. If the President of the Council is of the same nationality as one of the Parties, the most senior Vice President who is not disqualified on that ground shall make the appointment.

3. Except as otherwise agreed, the arbitral tribunal shall determine the limits of its jurisdiction in accordance with this Agreement and shall establish its own procedural rules. The tribunal, once formed, may recommend interim relief measures pending its final determination. At the direction of the tribunal or at the request of either of the Parties, a conference to determine the precise issues to be arbitrated and the specific procedures to be followed shall be held not later than 15 days after the tribunal is fully constituted.

4. Except as otherwise agreed or as directed by the tribunal, each Party shall submit a memorandum within 45 days of the time the tribunal is fully constituted. Replies shall be due 60 days later. The tribunal shall hold a hearing at the request of either Party or on its own initiative within 15 days after replies are due.

5. The tribunal shall attempt to render a written decision within 30 days after completion of the hearing or, if no hearing is held, after the date both replies are submitted. The decision of the majority of the tribunal shall prevail.

6. The Parties may submit requests for clarification of the decision within 15 days after it is rendered and any clarification given shall be issued within 15 days of such request.

7. Each Party shall, to the degree consistent with its national law, give full effect to any decision or award of the arbitral tribunal.

8. The expenses of the arbitral tribunal, including the fees and expenses of the arbitrators, shall be shared equally by the Parties. Any expenses incurred by the President of the Council of the International Civil Aviation Organization in connection with the procedures of paragraph 2b of this Article shall be considered to be part of the expenses of the arbitral tribunal.

Article 15
Termination

Either Party may, at any time, give notice in writing to the other Party of its decision to terminate this Agreement. Such notice shall be sent simultaneously to the International Civil Aviation Organization. This Agreement shall terminate at midnight (at the place of receipt of the notice to the other Party) immediately before the first anniversary of the date of receipt of the notice by the other Party, unless the notice is withdrawn by agreement of the Parties before the end of this period.

Article 16
Registration with ICAO

This Agreement and all amendments thereto shall be registered with the International Civil Aviation Organization.

Article 17
Entry into Force

This Agreement and its Annexes shall enter into force on the date of signature.

IN WITNESS WHEREOF the undersigned, being duly authorized by their respective Governments, have signed this Agreement.

DONE at _____________, this _______day of ________, 20__, in duplicate, in the English and ___________ languages, each text being equally authentic.

FOR THE GOVERNMENT OF [country]:

FOR THE GOVERNMENT OF THE UNITED STATES OF AMERICA:

ANNEX I
Scheduled Air Transportation

Section 1
Routes

Airlines of each Party designated under this Annex shall, in accordance with the terms of their designation, be entitled to perform scheduled international air transportation between points on the following routes:

A. Routes for the airline or airlines designated by the Government of the United States:

1. From points behind the United States via the United States and intermediate points to a point or points in [country] and beyond.

2. [For all-cargo service or services, between [country] and any point or points.]

B. Routes for the airline or airlines designated by the Government of [country]:

1. From points behind [country] via [country] and intermediate points to a point or points in the United States and beyond.

2. [For all-cargo service or services, between the United States and any point or points.]

Section 2
Operational Flexibility

Each designated airline may, on any or all flights and at its option:

1. operate flights in either or both directions;

2. combine different flight numbers within one aircraft operation;

3. serve behind, intermediate, and beyond points and points in the territories of the Parties on the routes in any combination and in any order;

4. omit stops at any point or points;

5. transfer traffic from any of its aircraft to any of its other aircraft at any point on the routes; and

6. serve points behind any point in its territory with or without change of aircraft or flight number and may hold out and advertise such services to the public as through services;

without directional or geographic limitation and without loss of any right to carry traffic otherwise permissible under this Agreement;

provided that, [with the exception of all-cargo services,] the service serves a point in the territory of the Party designating the airline.

Section 3
Change of Gauge

On any segment or segments of the routes above, any designated airline may perform international air transportation without any limitation as to change, at any point on the route, in type or number of aircraft operated; provided that, [with the exception of all-cargo services,] in the outbound direction, the transportation beyond such point is a continuation of the transportation from the territory of the Party that has designated the airline and, in the inbound direction, the transportation to the territory of the Party that has designated the airline is a continuation of the transportation from beyond such point.

ANNEX II
Charter Air Transportation

Section 1

A. Airlines of each Party designated under this Annex shall, in accordance with the terms of their designation, have the right to carry international charter traffic of passengers (and their accompanying baggage) and/or cargo (including, but not limited to, freight forwarder, split, and combination (passenger/cargo) charters):

1. Between any point or points in the territory of the Party that has designated the airline and any point or points in the territory of the other Party; and

2. Between any point or points in the territory of the other Party and any point or points in a third country or countries, provided that, [except with respect to cargo charters,] such service constitutes part of a continuous operation, with or without a change of aircraft, that includes service to the homeland for the purpose of carrying local traffic between the homeland and the territory of the other Party.

B. In the performance of services covered by this Annex, airlines of each Party designated under this Annex shall also have the right: (1) to make stopovers at any points whether within or outside of the territory of either Party; (2) to carry transit traffic through the other Party' territory; (3) to combine on the same aircraft traffic originating in one Party's territory, traffic originating in the other Party's territory, and traffic originating in third countries; and (4) to perform international air transportation without any limitation as to change, at any point on the route, in type or number of aircraft operated; provided that, [except with respect to cargo charters,] in the outbound direction, the transportation beyond such point is a continuation of the transportation from the territory of the Party that has designated the airline and in the inbound direction, the transportation to the territory of the Party that has designated the airline is a continuation of the transportation from beyond such point.

C. Each Party shall extend favorable consideration to applications by airlines of the other Party to carry traffic not covered by this Annex on the basis of comity and reciprocity.

Section 2

A. Any airline designated by either Party performing international charter air transportation originating in the territory of either Party, whether on a one-way or round-trip basis, shall have the option of complying with the charter laws, regulations, and rules either of its homeland or of the other Party. If a Party applies different rules, regulations, terms, conditions, or limitations to one or more of its airlines, or to airlines of different countries, each designated airline shall be subject to the least restrictive of such criteria.

B. However, nothing contained in the above paragraph shall limit the rights of either Party to require airlines designated under this Annex by either Party to adhere to requirements relating to the protection of passenger funds and passenger cancellation and refund rights.

Section 3

Except with respect to the consumer protection rules referred to in the preceding paragraph, neither Party shall require an airline designated under this Annex by the other Party, in respect of the carriage of traffic from the territory of that other Party or of a third country on a one-way or round-trip basis, to submit more than a declaration of conformity with the applicable laws, regulations and rules referred to under section 2 of this Annex or of a waiver of these laws, regulations, or rules granted by the applicable aeronautical authorities.

Index